L. F.

D1277467

Biology Data Book

Second Edition

VOLUME III

Biology Data Book
Second Edition
VOLUME III

COMPILED AND EDITED BY

Philip L. Altman and Dorothy S. Dittmer

Federation of American Societies for Experimental Biology

BETHESDA, MARYLAND

ALBRIGHT COLLEGE LIBRARY

©1974, by Federation of American Societies for Experimental Biology

All rights reserved. This book is protected by copyright. No part of it may

be produced in any manner without written permission from the publisher.

PRINTED IN THE UNITED STATES OF AMERICA

Library of Congress Catalog Card Number: 72-87738

International Standard Book Number: 0-913822-08-6

574.083
A469b2
v. 3

145775

FOREWORD

This volume of the *Biology Data Book* completes the second edition of a three-volume compilation of evaluated reference data in the life sciences. The preparation of the 281 groups of tables, graphs, and diagrams—constituting some 2100 pages—required four years, and the cooperative efforts of 712 eminent scientists. These experts from all over the world contributed and reviewed the data, and in addition provided more than 18,000 literature citations from which the information was derived.

Volume I of the *Biology Data Book* was published in 1972, and consists of five sections covering GENETICS AND CYTOLOGY; REPRODUCTION; DEVELOPMENT AND GROWTH; MATERIALS AND METHODS; and PROPERTIES OF BIOLOGICAL SUBSTANCES. Also included are nine appendixes of useful general information. Volume II, published in 1973, contains many new tables in its sections on BIOLOGICAL REGULATORS AND TOXINS; ENVIRONMENT AND SURVIVAL; and PARASITISM. The section on SENSORY AND NEURO- BIOLOGY is entirely new to the Biological Handbooks Series; its 35 tables cover neurophysiology, neurochemistry, neuroelectric properties, electroencephalograms, and the special senses. Each of the three volumes is indexed independently, and can be purchased separately by those interested only in data limited to particular fields.

This 2100-page "library" of biological reference data concludes a publication program begun a quarter of a century ago in the National Academy of Sciences–National Research Council (NAS–NRC). Ten handbooks, five in biology and five in toxicology, were produced by the time the project was transferred to the Federation of American Societies for Experimental Biology (FASEB) in 1959. Under FASEB auspices, six biological handbooks have been completed, in addition to the present three-volume *Biology Data Book*. Except for Volumes II and III of this last publication, all of the books were financed by agencies of the federal government. Two of these agencies must be acknowledged for their long-term generous support: the U.S. Air Force for 22 years of assistance, and the National Institutes of Health/National Library of Medicine for 15 years.

Gratitude must also be expressed to the biologists who served on the NAS–NRC and FASEB Handbooks Committees, and on the advisory committees for each book in the series. The former selected the fields to be covered, and the latter selected the tables to be included in each volume and recommended the scientists most eminently qualified to compile the data. Since 1959, more than 3000 prominent scientists have participated in the evaluation, contribution, and review of over 6000 pages of quantitative and descriptive data, including nearly 54,000 source

references. Without their expertise in providing the "best values" available, the Biological Handbooks Series could never have achieved its reputation for scientific excellence and accuracy. The unremunerated intellectual contributions of these dedicated authorities is sincerely appreciated.

Among those associated with the Handbooks Project since its inception are three distinguished biologists, who deserve special mention. One is Dr. J. W. Heim, who conceived the project, persuaded the NAS–NRC to assume responsibility for its establishment and operation, and provided Air Force funds to keep it solvent. Another is Dr. T. C. Byerly who was Chairman of the NAS–NRC Committee for the first 10 years of the project, and helped nurture it through its early days to maturity and eventual transfer to FASEB. The third member of this triumvirate is Dr. R. L. Zwemer, the only one of the original NAS–NRC Committee to serve the entire 25 years of the project's existence, including the last 15 years as Chairman of the FASEB Handbooks Committee. His efforts in enlisting the financial assistance of new sponsors through the years assured continuity of the undertaking; his unqualified support of, and interest in, the project merit a special salute. Drs. Zwemer, Byerly, and Heim were decisively instrumental in fostering, expediting, and maintaining the Biological Handbooks.

As a precaution against the introduction of errors in the volumes, all compilation, editing, indexing, and composition of copy have been performed within the confines of the Office of Biological Handbooks by a veteran staff. The product of their labors—the data books themselves—attest to the efficiency and devotion of this exceptional group of professionals. And no one better exemplifies the high standards of accuracy and meticulousness in the preparation of publication copy than the co-editor of the series for the past 20 years, Dorothy S. Dittmer.

With Volume III of the *Biology Data Book,* the publication program supervised by the Committee on Biological Handbooks and supported exclusively by government funds comes to an end, and a new series of data books begins. As in the past, the project will continue to be nonprofit. Future responsibility for policy and guidance has been assumed by the FASEB Publications Committee, and an Editorial Board has been formed to provide advice and recommendations in the preparation of new fascicles. Production time for future volumes will be cut in half, as a result of a new approach whereby the essential data for a discrete subject will be covered in approximately 300 pages. However, there will be no compromise in retrieving and disseminating the most useful, reliable, reference data available in the life sciences.

1 July 1974
Bethesda, Maryland

Philip L. Altman, *Director*
Office of Biological Handbooks

FASEB PUBLICATIONS COMMITTEE

FRANK G. STANDAERT, *Chairman*
AMERICAN SOCIETY FOR PHARMACOLOGY AND EXPERIMENTAL THERAPEUTICS
Georgetown University School of Medicine and Dentistry
Washington, D.C. 20007

ELIJAH ADAMS
AMERICAN SOCIETY OF BIOLOGICAL CHEMISTS
University of Maryland School
of Medicine
Baltimore, Maryland 21201

EUGENE L. HESS*
Federation of American Societies
for Experimental Biology
9650 Rockville Pike
Bethesda, Maryland 20014

EDWIN M. LERNER, II
AMERICAN ASSOCIATION OF IMMUNOLOGISTS
Leonard Wood
Memorial
Washington, D.C. 20037

DONALD B. HACKEL
AMERICAN SOCIETY FOR EXPERIMENTAL
PATHOLOGY
Duke University Medical Center
Durham, North Carolina 27706

WILLIAM G. HOEKSTRA
AMERICAN INSTITUTE OF NUTRITION
University of Wisconsin
Madison, Wisconsin 53706

CHARLES S. TIDBALL
AMERICAN PHYSIOLOGICAL SOCIETY
George Washington University
Medical Center
Washington, D.C. 20005

BIOLOGY DATA BOOK ADVISORY COMMITTEE

RAYMUND L. ZWEMER, *Chairman*
Federation of American Societies for Experimental Biology
Bethesda, Maryland 20014

ROBERT H. BURRIS
University of Wisconsin
Madison, Wisconsin 53706

RAY G. DAGGS
American Physiological Society
Bethesda, Maryland 20014

NOBLE O. FOWLER
University of Cincinnati College
of Medicine
Cincinnati, Ohio 45229

KARL F. HEUMANN*
Federation of American Societies
for Experimental Biology
Bethesda, Maryland 20014

ROSS A. McFARLAND
Harvard University School of
Public Health
Boston, Massachusetts 02115

ARTHUR B. OTIS
University of Florida College
of Medicine
Gainesville, Florida 32601

NATHAN W. SHOCK
Baltimore City Hospitals
Baltimore, Maryland 21224

WALTER SHROPSHIRE, JR.
Radiation Biology Laboratory of the
Smithsonian Institution
Rockville, Maryland 20852

THURLO B. THOMAS†
Carleton College
Northfield, Minnesota 55057

BETTY M. TWAROG
Tufts University
Medford, Massachusetts 02155

HAROLD L. WILCKE
Ralston Purina Company
St. Louis, Missouri 63199

HANDBOOK STAFF

PHILIP L. ALTMAN, *Director*

DOROTHY S. DITTMER, *Editor*

ELSIE COMSTOCK
CLAIRE L. DOYLE

JEAN M. GIEGOLD
SAKI HIMEL

GERALDINE M. JOHNSON
ETHEL E. KETCHUM

* *ex officio*
† deceased

CONTRIBUTORS AND REVIEWERS

ABRAMSON, D. I.
University of Illinois College of
Medicine
Chicago, Illinois 60680

ALMQUIST, H. J.
Route 1, Box 90
Kelseyville, California 95451

ALTLAND, PAUL D.
NIH, National Institute of Arthritis,
Metabolism, and Digestive Diseases
Bethesda, Maryland 20014

ANDREW, WARREN
Indiana University School of Medicine
Indianapolis, Indiana 46202

ARNOLD, JOHN W.
Canada Department of Agriculture
Ottawa, Ontario K1A 0C6, Canada

ATTEBERY, B. A.
University of Kansas Medical Center
Kansas City, Kansas 66103

BADEER, HENRY S.
Creighton University School of
Medicine
Omaha, Nebraska 68131

BALIS, M. EARL
Sloan-Kettering Institute for Cancer
Research
New York, New York 10021

BALLARD, W. W.
Dartmouth College
Hanover, New Hampshire 03755

BARTELS, HEINZ
Medizinische Hochschule Hannover
3 Hannover, Germany

BASS, DAVID E.
U.S. Army Research Institute of En-
vironmental Medicine
Natick, Massachusetts 01760

BASSHAM, JAMES A.
University of California
Berkeley, California 94720

BEERSTECHER, ERNEST, JR.
University of Texas
Houston, Texas 77023

BELL, J. M.
University of Saskatchewan
Saskatoon, Saskatchewan, S7N 0W0,
Canada

BENNETT, ALBERT F.
University of California
Berkeley, California 94720

BIRD, HERBERT R.
University of Wisconsin
Madison, Wisconsin 53706

BISHOP, DAVID W.
Medical College of Ohio
Toledo, Ohio 43614

BLANCHARD, GWYNN D.
University of West Florida
Pensacola, Florida 32504

BLOMQVIST, GUNNAR
University of Texas Medical School
Dallas, Texas 75235

BOWIE, E. J. W.
Mayo Clinic
Rochester, Minnesota 55901

BOWMAN, RUSSEL O.
3551 Flair Drive
Dallas, Texas 75229

BRAUNWALD, EUGENE
Harvard Medical School
Boston, Massachusetts 02115

BRECHER, GEORGE
University of California School of
Medicine
San Francisco, California 94143

BRETT, J. R.
Fisheries Research Board of Canada
Nanaimo, British Colombia, Canada

BREUER, L. H.
Ralston Purina Company
St. Louis, Missouri 63188

BRINKHOUS, K. M.
University of North Carolina School
of Medicine
Chapel Hill, North Carolina 27514

BROUN, GORONWY O., JR.
Saint Louis University School of
Medicine
St. Louis, Missouri 63104

BROUN, GORONWY O., SR.
Saint Louis University School of
Medicine
St. Louis, Missouri 63104

BROWER, JAMES E.
Northern Illinois University
DeKalb, Illinois 60115

BROWN, E. B., JR.
University of Kansas Medical Center
Kansas City, Kansas 66103

BROWN, ELLEN
University of California Medical
Center
San Francisco, California 94122

BUCK, JOHN B.
NIH, National Institute of Arthritis,
Metabolism, and Digestive Diseases
Bethesda, Maryland 20014

CALCAGNO, PHILIP L.
Georgetown University Hospital
Washington, D.C. 20007

CARTWRIGHT, GEORGE E.
University of Utah College of Medicine
Salt Lake City, Utah 84112

CHRISTISON, G. I.
University of Saskatchewan
Saskatoon, Saskatchewan, S7N 0W0,
Canada

COCHRANE, VINCENT W.
Wesleyan University
Middletown, Connecticut 06457

COLE, D. F.
University of London
London, WC1H 9QS, England

CONRAD, MARGARET C.
East Virginia Medical School
Norfolk, Virginia 23507

CONTI, S. F.
University of Kentucky
Lexington, Kentucky 40506

COON, WILLIAM W.
University of Michigan Medical School
Ann Arbor, Michigan 48104

COPENHAVER, W. M.
University of Miami School of
Medicine
Miami, Florida 33152

CORBIN, JAMES E.
University of Illinois
Urbana, Illinois 61801

COURTICE, F. C.
John Curtin School of Medical
Research
Canberra City, A.C.T. 2601, Australia

COX, ROBERT H.
University of Pennsylvania
Philadelphia, Pennsylvania 19146

CUMINGS, J. N.
National Hospital
London, WC1N 3AY, England

CUNHA, T. J.
University of Florida
Gainesville, Florida 32611

DABROWSKI, Z.
  Jagiellonian University
  Krakow, Poland
DAVIS, WALTER E.
  University of North Carolina School
    of Medicine
  Chapel Hill, North Carolina 27514
DAWE, ALBERT R.
  Office of Naval Research
  Chicago, Illinois 60605
DAWSON, WILLIAM R.
  University of Michigan
  Ann Arbor, Michigan 48104
DESSAUER, HERBERT C.
  Louisiana State University Medical
    Center
  New Orleans, Louisiana 70112
DIGGS, LEMUEL W.
  University of Tennessee College of
    Medicine
  Memphis, Tennessee 38103
DILL, DAVID B.
  Desert Research Institute
  Boulder City, Nevada 89005
*DuBOIS, EUGENE F.
DUNLAP, J. S.
  Washington State University
  Pullman, Washington 99163
DUSTAN, HARRIET P.
  Cleveland Clinic Foundation
  Cleveland, Ohio 44106

EDELMANN, CHESTER M., JR.
  Albert Einstein College of Medicine
  Bronx, New York 10461
ELLEFSON, R. D.
  Mayo Clinic
  Rochester, Minnesota 55901
ELWYN, DAVID H.
  Mount Sinai School of Medicine
  New York, New York 10029
ENGELMANN, FRANZ
  University of California
  Los Angeles, California 90024
EVELEIGH, DOUGLAS E.
  Rutgers University
  New Brunswick, New Jersey 08903

FOGG, G. E.
  University College of North Wales
  Anglesey, Wales
FORWARD, DOROTHY F.
  University of Toronto
  Toronto, Ontario, M5S 1A1, Canada
FRIEDMAN, M. H. F.
  Jefferson Medical College
  Philadelphia, Pennsylvania 19107

FRY, F. E. J.
  University of Toronto
  Toronto, Ontario, M5G 1G6, Canada

GERGELY, J.
  Boston Biomedical Research Institute
  Boston, Massachusetts 02114
GILBERT, DANIEL L.
  NIH, National Institute of Neuro-
    logical Diseases and Stroke
  Bethesda, Maryland 20014
GLAZER, A. N.
  University of California
  Los Angeles, California 90024
GLEYSTEEN, JOHN J.
  NIH, National Heart and Lung
    Institute
  Bethesda, Maryland 20014
GRACE, T. D. C.
  CSIRO, Division of Entomology
  Canberra City, A.C.T. 2601, Australia
GRAY, GARY M.
  Stanford University Medical Center
  Stanford, California 94305
GRIFFITH, J. Q., JR.
  6 North Fredericksburg Avenue
  Margate, New Jersey 08402
GRODZINSKI, Z.
  ul. Krupnicza 50
  30-060 Krakow, Poland
GROSSMAN, MORTON I.
  Veterans Administration Center
  Los Angeles, California 90073

HAMILTON, PAUL B.
  Alfred I. duPont Institute
  Wilmington, Delaware 19899
HANSARD, SAM L.
  University of Tennessee
  Knoxville, Tennessee 37901
HARRIS, JOHN E.
  University of Minnesota Medical
    School
  Minneapolis, Minnesota 55455
HARTROFT, W. STANLEY
  University of Hawaii School of
    Medicine
  Honolulu, Hawaii 96816
HATHAWAY, WILLIAM E.
  University of Colorado Medical Center
  Denver, Colorado 80220
HEATH, TREVOR J.
  University of New South Wales
  Kensington, N.S.W. 2003, Australia
HEINEMANN, HENRY O.
  New York Hospital-Cornell Medical
    Center
  New York, New York 10021

HENSCHEL, AUSTIN
  National Institute for Occupational
    Safety and Health
  Cincinnati, Ohio 45202
HERBIG, FRANCIS
  Saint Louis University School of
    Medicine
  St. Louis, Missouri 63104
HOLLERMAN, CHARLES E.
  Georgetown University Hospital
  Washington, D.C. 20007
HOUSE, H. L.
  Canadian Department of Agriculture
  Belleville, Ontario, Canada
HOVERSLAND, ARTHUR S.
  California State University
  Fresno, California
HUDSON, JACK W.
  Cornell University
  Ithaca, New York 14850
HUNSAKER, WALTER G.
  Animal Research Institute
  Ottawa, Ontario, K1A 0C6, Canada
HURTADO, ALBERTO
  Universidad Peruana Cayetano Heredia
  Lima, Peru
HUTCHISON, VICTOR H.
  University of Oklahoma
  Norman, Oklahoma 73069

IBER, FRANK L.
  Veterans Administration Hospital
  Baltimore, Maryland 21218
INTAGLIETTA, M.
  University of California
  San Diego, California 92037

JACOBSON, N. L.
  Iowa State University
  Ames, Iowa 50010
JENKINS, DAVID E.
  Milton S. Hershey Medical Center
  Hershey, Pennsylvania 17033
JOHNSON, CLARENCE L.
  USDI, Western Fish Nutrition
    Laboratory
  Nordland, Washington 98358
JOHNSON, HERMAN L.
  U.S. Army Medical Research and
    Nutrition Laboratory
  Denver, Colorado 80240
JOHNSON, PAUL E.
  National Research Council
  Washington, D.C. 20418
JONES, JACK COLVARD
  University of Maryland
  College Park, Maryland 20740

---

* Deceased

JOSE, PEDRO A.
Georgetown University Hospital
Washington, D.C. 20007

KARLANDER, EDWARD P.
University of Maryland
College Park, Maryland 20742
KLEIBER, MAX
University of California
Davis, California 95616
KNIGHT, ALLEN W.
University of California
Davis, California 95616
KOFT, BERNARD W.
Rutgers University
New Brunswick, New Jersey 08903
KRATZER, F. H.
University of California
Davis, California 95616
KRITCHEVSKY, DAVID
Wistar Institute of Anatomy and
Biology
Philadelphia, Pennsylvania 19104
KRUTA, VLADISLAV
Tvrdého 13
60200 Brno, Czechoslovakia

LANGHAM, MAURICE E.
Johns Hopkins University School of
Medicine
Baltimore, Maryland 21205
LANSFORD, EDWIN M., JR.
Southwestern University
Georgetown, Texas 78626
LASCELLES, PETER T.
National Hospital
London, WC1N 3AY, England
*LASIEWSKI, ROBERT C.
LASSEN, N. A.
Bispebjerg Hospital
2400 Copenhagen, Denmark
LEBDA, NANCY J. A.
University of Rochester School of
Medicine and Dentistry
Rochester, New York 14642
LEITCH, ISABELLA
30 Ashgrove Road West
Aberdeen, AB2 5DY, Scotland
LEOPOLD, IRVING H.
Mount Sinai School of Medicine
New York, New York 10029
LINDSAY, HUGH A.
Fairmont Clinic
Fairmont, West Virginia 26554
LINK, Roger P.
University of Illinois
Urbana, Illinois 61801

LOFTFIELD, ROBERT B.
University of New Mexico School of
Medicine
Albuquerque, New Mexico 87106
LOONEY, JOSEPH M.
75 Park Street
West Roxbury, Massachusetts 02132
LUFT, ULRICH C.
Lovelace Foundation for Medical
Education and Research
Albuquerque, New Mexico 87108

McCHESNEY, E. W.
Albany Medical College of Union
University
Albany, New York 12208
McCUTCHEON, F. HAROLD
Scallop Isle Estuarine Laboratory
Beaufort, North Carolina 28516

MADDRELL, S. H. P.
University of Cambridge
Cambridge, England
MASTER, ARTHUR M.
Mount Sinai School of Medicine
New York, New York 10029
MEISTER, ALTON
Cornell University Medical College
New York, New York 10021
MENDLOWITZ, MILTON
Mount Sinai School of Medicine
New York, New York 10029
MERRILL, EDWARD W.
Massachusetts Institute of Technology
Cambridge, Massachusetts 02139
MICHAELSON, S. M.
University of Rochester School of
Medicine and Dentistry
Rochester, New York 14642
MITCHELL, JERE H.
University of Texas Medical School
Dallas, Texas 75235
MONAGLE, J. E.
Department of National Health and
Welfare
Ottawa 3, Ontario, Canada
MONIE, I. W.
University of California School of
Medicine
San Francisco, California 94143
MOSHIRI, GERALD A.
University of West Florida
Pensacola, Florida 32504

NACE, PAUL F.
Staten Island Community College
Staten Island, New York 10301

NAFTCHI, N. ERIC
New York University Medical Center
New York, New York 10016
NASH, MARTIN A.
Albert Einstein College of Medicine
Bronx, New York 10461
NAUMANN, HANS N.
University of Tennessee College of
Medicine
Memphis, Tennessee 38103
NIRENBERG, MARSHALL W.
NIH, National Heart and Lung
Institute
Bethesda, Maryland 20014

ODELL, T. T.
Oak Ridge National Laboratory
Oak Ridge, Tennessee 37830
OSBALDISTON, G. W.
Yale University School of Medicine
New Haven, Connecticut 06510
OWEN, CHARLES A.
Mayo Clinic
Rochester, Minnesota 55901

PALMER, MAUREEN F.
Queen Elizabeth College
London, W.8, England
PASSMORE, R.
University Medical School
Edinburgh, EH8 9AG, Scotland
PATTON, ROBERT L.
Cornell University
Ithaca, New York 14850
PENNER, JOHN A.
University of Michigan Medical School
Ann Arbor, Michigan 48104
PERLMAN, D.
University of Wisconsin
Madison, Wisconsin 53706
PERLOFF, JOSEPH K.
Hospital of the University of Pennsyl-
vania
Philadelphia, Pennsylvania 19104
PERRY, T. W.
Purdue University
West Lafayette, Indiana 47907
PLATNER, W. S.
University of Missouri School of
Medicine
Columbia, Missouri 65201
POOL, PETER E.
North County Cardiovascular Medical
Group
Solana Beach, California 92075
POPE, A. L.
University of Wisconsin
Madison, Wisconsin 53706

---

* Deceased

POPOVIC, VOJIN
  Emory University Medical School
  Atlanta, Georgia 30322

RADFORD, EDWARD P.
  Johns Hopkins University
  Baltimore, Maryland 21205
RANDALL, WALTER C.
  Loyola University Stritch School of
    Medicine
  Maywood, Illinois 60153
RAPER, A. JARRELL
  Medical College of Virginia
  Richmond, Virginia 23298
REBUCK, JOHN W.
  Henry Ford Hospital
  Detroit, Michigan 48202
REKERS, PAUL E.
  11600 Wilshire Boulevard
  Los Angeles, California 90025
REYNOLDS, JOHN D.
  University of New South Wales
  Kensington, N.S.W. 2003, Australia
REYNOLDS, MONICA
  University of Pennsylvania
  Kennett Square, Pennsylvania 19348
RICHARDSON, DAVID W.
  Medical College of Virginia
  Richmond, Virginia 23298
RIGDON, R. H.
  University of Texas Medical Branch
  Galveston, Texas 77550
ROBERTS, JOHN L.
  University of Massachusetts
  Amherst, Massachusetts 01002
*ROOT, WALTER S.

SALLACH, H. J.
  University of Wisconsin
  Madison, Wisconsin 53706
SALTIN, BENGT
  Gymnastikoch Idrottshögsklan
  Stockholm, Sweden
SCHEER, BRADLEY T.
  University of Oregon
  Eugene, Oregon 97403
SCHLANT, ROBERT C.
  Emory University School of Medicine
  Atlanta, Georgia 30303
SCHOFFENIELS, E.
  University of Liège
  Liège, Belgium
SELIGER, VACLAV
  Charles University
  Prague 1, Czechoslovakia
SELKURT, EWALD E.
  Indiana University School of Medicine
  Indianapolis, Indiana 46202
SEVERINGHAUS, JOHN W.
  University of California Medical Center
  San Francisco, California 94143
SHOCK, NATHAN W.
  NIH, Gerontology Research Center
  Baltimore, Maryland 21224

SIGGAARD-ANDERSEN, OLE
  Rigshospitalet
  DK-2200 Copenhagen N, Denmark
SINGER, RICHARD B.
  New England Mutual Life Insurance
    Co.
  Boston, Massachusetts 02117
SLEIGHT, PETER
  Radcliffe Infirmary
  Oxford, OX2 6HE, England
SMILEY, K. L.
  USDA, Northern Regional Research
    Laboratory
  Peoria, Illinois 61604
SMILEY, M. J.
  USDA, Northern Regional Research
    Laboratory
  Peoria, Illinois 61604
SMITH, CARL C.
  University of Cincinnati Medical
    Center
  Cincinnati, Ohio 45219
SMITH, FRANK A.
  University of Rochester School of
    Medicine and Dentistry
  Rochester, New York 14642
SMITH, KENNETH A.
  Massachusetts Institute of Technology
  Cambridge, Massachusetts 02139
SMITH, S. E.
  Cornell University
  Ithaca, New York 14850
STROUD, ROBERT C.
  NIH, National Heart and Lung
    Institute
  Bethesda, Maryland 20014
SULLIVAN, J. BOLLING
  Duke University Marine Laboratory
  Beaufort, North Carolina 28516

THIMANN, KENNETH V.
  University of California
  Santa Cruz, California 95060
TRAUTWEIN, WOLFGANG
  Universität des Saarlandes
  665 Homburg, Germany
TYZNIK, W. J.
  Ohio State University
  Columbus, Ohio 43210

UMBREIT, W. W.
  Rutgers University
  New Brunswick, New Jersey 08903

VAN PILSUM, JOHN F.
  University of Minnesota
  Minneapolis, Minnesota 55455
VESTAL, J. ROBIE
  University of Cincinnati
  Cincinnati, Ohio 45221

WAINIO, WALTER
  Rutgers University
  New Brunswick, New Jersey 08903

WARD, JAMES W.
  University of South Florida College of
    Medicine
  Tampa, Florida 33620
WATERHOUSE, D. F.
  CSIRO, Division of Entomology
  Canberra City, A.C.T. 2601, Australia
WEBER, KENNETH C.
  West Virginia University Medical
    Center
  Morgantown, West Virginia 26506
WEDGWOOD, RALPH J.
  University of Washington School of
    Medicine
  Seattle, Washington 98105
WEIBEL, EWALD R.
  University of Bern
  3000 Bern, Switzerland
WEIDMANN, SILVIO
  University of Bern
  3000 Bern, Switzerland
WHITING, NICHOLAS H.
  University of West Florida
  Pensacola, Florida 32504
WIDDICOMBE, JOHN G.
  St. George's Hospital Medical School
  London, SW17 0QT, England
WINTROBE, M. M.
  University of Utah Medical Center
  Salt Lake City, Utah 84112
WIXOM, ROBERT L.
  University of Missouri Medical Center
  Columbia, Missouri 65201
WOHLRAB, HARTMUT
  Boston Biomedical Research Institute
  Boston, Massachusetts 02114
WOLFE, GERALDINE F.
  University of Cincinnati Medical Center
  Cincinnati, Ohio 45219
WOODBURY, ROBERT A.
  University of Tennessee Medical Units
  Memphis, Tennessee 38103

XANTHOU, MARIETA
  9, Maiandrou Street
  Athens 612, Greece

YOUNG, JACK E.
  Jackson Memorial Hospital
  Miami, Florida 33152
YOUNG, JOEL E.
  Texas Instruments Health Services, Inc.
  Dallas, Texas 75234

ZBARSKY, S. H.
  University of British Columbia
  Vancouver 8, British Columbia,
    Canada
ZIPKIN, I.
  University of California
  San Francisco, California 94122
ZUSI, RICHARD L.
  National Musuem of Natural History
  Washington, D.C. 20560

---

*Deceased

CONTENTS

X. NUTRITION, DIGESTION, AND EXCRETION

XI. METABOLISM

XIII. BLOOD AND OTHER BODY FLUIDS

APPENDIXES

INTRODUCTION

The first edition of the *Biology Data Book,* published in 1964, was a 630-page compendium of "broad scope and limited coverage designed to serve as a basic reference in the field of biology." The scope of the second edition of the *Biology Data Book* is broader, and the coverage is not so limited. This newer edition should therefore be even more useful, than was the original publication, in providing information in subject areas outside the user's own field of competence.

Since it was impractical, as well as impossible, to include data for all species, contributors were instructed to restrict coverage to man and the more important laboratory, domestic, commercial, and field organisms. Despite this restriction, data for many more species—than the 400 covered in the 1964 volume—can now be found in the second edition.

As a result of the broadened scope and coverage, and the inclusion of data for additional species, the revised *Biology Data Book* appears as three volumes totaling more than 2100 pages. A brief description of the contents of Volumes I and II are given in the Foreword to this volume.

Contents and Review

Volume III of the *Biology Data Book* is arranged in four sections, with the data organized in the form of 114 tables (quantitative and descriptive), graphs, and diagrams. In addition, two appendixes of animal and plant names are included. Contents of this volume were verified by 207 outstanding authorities in the fields of biology and medicine. The review process to which the data were subjected was designed to eliminate, insofar as possible, material of questionable validity and errors of transcription.

Headnote

An explanatory headnote, serving as an introduction to the subject matter, may precede a table. More frequently, tables are prefaced by a short headnote containing such important information as units of measurement, abbreviations, definitions, and estimate of the range of variation. To interpret the data, it is essential to read the related headnote.

Exceptions

Occasionally, differences in values for the same specifications, certain inconsistencies in nomenclature, and some overlapping of coverage may occur among tables. These result, not from oversight or failure to choose between alternatives, but from a deliberate intent to respect the judgment and preferences of the individual contributors.

Conventions and Terminology

The main conventions used throughout this volume were adapted from the third edition of the *CBE Style Manual,* published in 1972 for the Council of Biology Editors by the American Institute of Biological Sciences. Terminology was checked against *Webster's Third New International Dictionary,* published in 1961 by G. & C. Merriam Company.

Contributors and References

Appended to the tables are the names of the contributors, and a list of the literature citations arranged in alphabetical sequence. The reference abbreviations conform to those in *ACCESS: Key to the Source Literature of the Chemical Sciences,* published by the American Chemical Society in 1969.

Animal and Plant Classification

Animal and plant taxa are arranged according to the classification outlines designated Appendixes III and IV at the back of Volume I of this *Biology Data Book.* The outlines were compiled from information provided by specialists at the Smithsonian Institution's National Museum of Natural History, the U.S. Department of Agriculture, and the Americal Type Culture Collection. The classifications reflect some of the recent agreements reached by the International Commissions on Nomenclature in the biological sciences.

Scientific Names

In the tables, a synonym following the scientific name of an organism indicates that the synonym, although cited in the reference, is no longer the preferred name. No other attempt was made to provide taxonomic synonymy. All scientific names were either verified in standard taxonomic checklists and classification lists, or submitted for authentication to the appropriate authorities at the institutions listed above.

Upon the advice of these experts, some subspecies of plants appearing in Volume I have been changed to varieties in Volumes II and III.

To aid the user in identifying an organism, the index includes the taxonomic orders for animals, and the families for plants. Two appendixes provide cross-reference to scientific and equivalent common names occurring in this volume.

Range of Variation

Values are generally presented as either the mean, plus and

continued

minus the standard deviation, or the mean and the lower and upper limit of the range of individual values about the mean. The several methods used to estimate the range—depending on the information available—are designated by the letters "a, b, c, or d" to identify the type of range in descending order of accuracy.

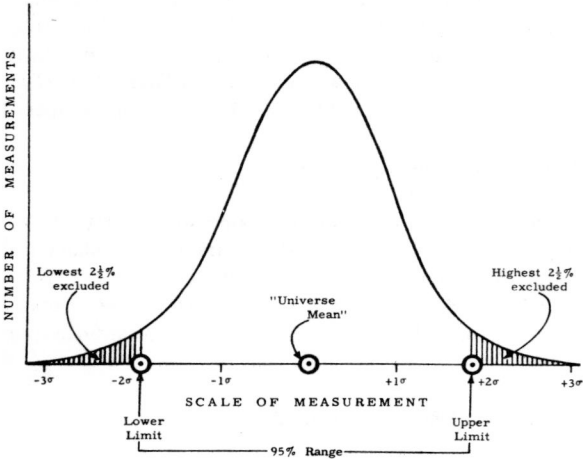

"a"—When the group of values is relatively large, a 95% range is derived by curve fitting. A recognized type of normal frequency curve is fitted to a group of measured values, and the extreme 2.5% of the area under the curve at each end is excluded (*see* illustration).

"b"—When the group of values is too small for curve fitting, as is usually the case, a 95% range is estimated by a simple statistical calculation. Assuming a normal symmetrical distribution, the standard deviation is multiplied by a factor of 2, then subtracted from and added to the mean to give the lower and upper range limits.

"c"—A less dependable, but commonly applied, procedure takes as range limits the lowest value and the highest value of the reported sample group of measurements. It underestimates the 95% range for small samples and overestimates for larger sample sizes, but where there is marked asymmetry in the position of the mean within the sample range, this method may be used in preference to the preceding one.

"d"—Another estimate of the lower and upper limits of the range of variation is based on the judgment of an individual experienced in measuring the quantity in question. The trustworthiness of such limits should not be underestimated.

ABBREVIATIONS AND SYMBOLS

Only those abbreviations and symbols not generally defined in the headnote, body, or footnotes of a table are included in this list.

Measurements

yr	=	year
mo	=	month
wk	=	week
da	=	day
hr	=	hour
min	=	minute; minimum
s	=	second
ms	=	millisecond
m	=	meter
km	=	kilometer
cm	=	centimeter
mm	=	millimeter
μ	=	micron
mμ	=	millimicron
nm	=	nanometer
Å	=	Angstrom
ft	=	foot
wt	=	weight
g	=	gram
kg	=	kilogram
mg	=	milligram
μg	=	microgram
ng	=	nanogram
pg	=	picogram
mmole	=	millimole
μmole	=	micromole
$\mu\mu$mole	=	micromicromole
nmole	=	nanomole
matom	=	milliatom
μatom	=	microatom
meq	=	milliequivalent
μeq	=	microequivalent
neq	=	nanoequivalent
mgEq	=	milligram equivalent
lb	=	pound
oz	=	ounce
vol	=	volume
ml	=	milliliter
μl	=	microliter
%	=	parts per hundred
‰	=	parts per thousand
temp	=	temperature
T	=	temperature
°C	=	degrees Celsius
°K	=	degrees Kelvin
cal	=	calorie
kcal	=	kilocalorie
Mcal	=	megacalorie

Q_{10}	=	logarithmic relation of increasing rate of reactions per 10°C increase in temperature
atm	=	atmosphere
mm Hg	=	millimeters of mercury
mosmole	=	milliosmole
μosmole	=	microosmole
P_{O_2}	=	oxygen pressure
P_{CO_2}	=	carbon dioxide pressure
BTPS	=	body temperature & ambient pressure, saturated with water vapor
STPD	=	standard temperature & pressure, dry
V	=	volt
mV	=	millivolt
μF	=	microfarad
no.	=	number
avg	=	average
max	=	maximum
±	=	plus or minus
SD	=	standard deviation
SE	=	standard error
log	=	logarithm
Δ	=	change or difference
d	=	derivative of
<	=	less than
>	=	more than
≮	=	not less than
≯	=	not more than
→	=	yields
°	=	degree (angular)
×	=	times; by; crossed with
~	=	proportional to; high-energy bond
∿	=	approximately
approx.	=	approximately

Biological and Chemical Specifications

♂	=	male
♀	=	female
♂♀	=	male & female
sp.	=	species (singular)
spp.	=	species (plural)
Hb	=	hemoglobin
RBC	=	red blood cells
WBC	=	white blood cells
DNA	=	deoxyribonucleic acid
RNA	=	ribonucleic acid
tRNA	=	transfer ribonucleic acid
CMP	=	cytidine 5′-monophosphate
FSH	=	follicle-stimulating hormone

IU	=	international unit
munits	=	milliunits
μunits	=	microunits
i.p.	=	intraperitoneal
i.v.	=	intravenous
pH	=	hydrogen ion concentration (negative log)
D	=	dextro (configuration)
L	=	levo (configuration)
m	=	meta
o	=	ortho
p	=	para
n	=	normal
N	=	normal; *nitro*
M	=	molar
mM	=	millimolar
μM	=	micromolar
H	=	*hydro;* hydrogen bond
O	=	*oxy*
S	=	*sulf; sulfo*
mol	=	molecular
Ala	=	alanine
Arg	=	arginine
Asn	=	asparagine
Asp	=	aspartic acid
Cys	=	cysteine
CyS	=	cystine
Gln	=	glutamine
Glu	=	glutamic acid
Gly	=	glycine
His	=	histidine
Ile	=	isoleucine
Leu	=	leucine
Lys	=	lysine
Met	=	methionine
Orn	=	ornithine
Phe	=	phenylalanine
Pro	=	proline
Ser	=	serine
Thr	=	threonine
Trp	=	tryptophan
Tyr	=	tyrosine
Val	=	valine

Miscellaneous

Fn	=	footnote
ad lib	=	*ad libitum* (as desired)
cf.	=	*confer* (compare)
e.g.	=	*exempli gratia* (for example)
i.e.	=	*id est* (that is)

Biology Data Book
Second Edition

VOLUME III

X. NUTRITION, DIGESTION, AND EXCRETION

168. NUTRIENTS: CHEMICAL ELEMENTS

All organisms require carbon, hydrogen, nitrogen, oxygen, phosphorus, and sulfur. These elements are universal constituents of protoplasm. *Abbreviations and Symbols:* Capital letters indicate data are pertinent to all organisms studied; lower case letters and symbols indicate data apply to one or more species or strains, but not to all forms studied. R and r = required (accumulation in the tissues of an organism is not alone sufficient evidence that an element is required); ℝ = not required; uF = utilized as effectively as, replaces wholly, or is interchangeable with, another element; U< and u< = can partially replace, or spare the use of, another element; s = stimulates growth or other processes; a = accumulates in the tissues; c = commonly present at similar concentrations in the food and tissues, but requirement is uncertain.

	Nutrient	Vertebrates	Invertebrates [1]	Insects	Protozoans [2]	Prokaryotes [3]	Algae	Fungi	Spermatophytes
1	Aluminum	ℝ	....	ℝ	ℝ	ℝ	ℝ	ℝ, c	r, s, a
2	Arsenic	ℝ	a	ℝ	ℝ	ℝ	ℝ	ℝ	ℝ
3	Boron	ℝ	ℝ	ℝ	ℝ	r	r	r?	ℝ
4	Bromine	U<	r?, a?[4]	ℝ	ℝ	ℝ	ℝ, a	r[5]	ℝ
5	Calcium	R	r	r, c	R	R	R	R[6]	ℝ
6	Chlorine	R	r	r, c	ℝ	r, s	R	R	R
7	Chromium	r, a	....	ℝ	ℝ	uF	ℝ	c	r, s
8	Cobalt	R	....	r?, s?	ℝ	r	ℝ	r	ℝ
9	Copper	R	r	r, c	r	r	R	R	r
10	Fluorine	ℝ, s	a	ℝ	ℝ	ℝ	ℝ	r[5]	ℝ, a
11	Gallium	ℝ	ℝ	ℝ	ℝ	ℝ	ℝ	ℝ, s	r
12	Iodine	R	r?, a	ℝ	ℝ	R, s	R, a	ℝ	r
13	Iron	R	r	r	R	R, u<	R	R[7]	ℝ, s
14	Magnesium	R	R	r	R	r	R	R[7]	R
15	Manganese	R	r[8]	r, a, c	r	R, uF	R	R, u<[9]	R
16	Molybdenum	r[10]	....	ℝ	ℝ	r[11], u<, s	R	r[12,13]	R
17	Potassium	R	R	R, a, c	R	r	R, a	R	R, a
18	Rubidium	ℝ	....	ℝ	ℝ	uF, u<[14]	ℝ	R	R
19	Selenium	R	....	ℝ	ℝ	ℝ	ℝ	ℝ	ℝ, a
20	Silicon	ℝ, c	r	ℝ	r	ℝ	r	c	r
21	Sodium	R	....	r?, c	r	r	r, a	R	r?, s, a
22	Strontium	U<	....	ℝ	ℝ	uF	ℝ, uF	ℝ, s	ℝ
23	Tungsten	ℝ	....	ℝ	ℝ	ℝ	ℝ	s	ℝ
24	Vanadium	ℝ	r[15]	ℝ	ℝ, s?	ℝ	r	r	ℝ
25	Zinc	R	r?, a	r	r	r	r	R[8]	R
	Reference	4,15-17,22, 27,28,38,40, 43,44,46-51, 53,54,56-59, 64,69,70	5,8,10,13,20, 25,26	13,19, 30,31, 65,67	12,13,23,24, 32-34,42	6,9,21,29,36, 37,60,62,63	13,23,24, 38,39, 52	1,2,9,11, 14,18,21, 40,55,62, 63,66,68	3,7,13,26,35, 41,45,61,63

1/ Other than insects and protozoans. 2/ Includes the colorless phytoflagellates. 3/ Includes Schizomycetes, Rickettsiales, and Cyanophyta. 4/ Occurs as dibromotyrosine in scleroprotein of certain corals. 5/ Necessary in secondary fermentations. 6/ Has a special role in sterol deficiency in oomycetes. 7/ Several trace elements at relatively high concentrations are necessary for secondary metabolism. 8/ In blood respiratory pigment of *Pinna nobilis* (*P. squamosa*). 9/ Can replace magnesium in reactions involving adenosine triphosphate. Increases the longevity of *Torulopsis*. [22] 10/ Xanthine oxidase factor. 11/ Required for assimilatory nitrate reduction and nitrogen fixation by some bacteria and blue-green algae. 12/ Required by *Pilobolus* as the growth factor coprogen. 13/ Required by all fungi exhibiting nitrate reduction. 14/ Replaces potassium in some organisms, and spares potassium in others. 15/ In blood pigment of certain tunicates.

continued

Contributors: Eveleigh, Douglas E.; Fogg, G. E.; Hansard, Sam L.; House, H. L.; Kratzer, F. H.; Vestal, J. Robie; Zipkin, I.

References

[1] Ainsworth, G. C., and A. S. Sussman, ed. 1965. The Fungi. Academic Press, New York. v. 1.

[2] Allen, P. J. 1965. Annu. Rev. Phytopathol. 3:313.

[3] Arnon, D. I. 1951. Mineral Nutrition of Plants. Univ. Wisconsin Press, Madison.

[4] Assali, N. S. 1968. Biology of Gestation. Academic Press, London. v. 2.

[5] Baldwin, E., ed. 1964. An Introduction to Comparative Biochemistry. Ed. 4. Univ. Press, Cambridge, England.

[6] Bartha, R., and E. J. Ordal. 1965. J. Bacteriol. 89: 1015.

[7] Bonner, J., and J. E. Varner, ed. 1965. Plant Biochemistry. Ed. 2. Academic Press, New York.

[8] Bourne, G. H., and G. W. Kidder, ed. 1953. Biochemistry and Physiology of Nutrition. Academic Press, New York.

[9] Brock, T. D. 1970. Biology of Microorganisms. Prentice-Hall, Englewood Cliffs, N.J.

[10] Buchsbaum, R. 1948. Animals Without Backbones. Rev. ed. Univ. Chicago Press, Chicago.

[11] Burnett, J. H. 1968. Fundamentals of Mycology. St. Martin, New York.

[12] Calkins, G., and F. M. Summers, ed. 1964. Protozoa in Biological Research. S. Hafner, New York.

[13] Chilean Nitrate Educational Bureau, Inc. 1948. Bibliography of the Literature on the Minor Elements. New York.

[14] Cochrane, V. W. 1958. Physiology of Fungi. J. Wiley, New York.

[15] Comar, C. L., and F. Bronner, ed. 1960-64. Miner. Metab. 1-2B.

[16] Crampton, E. W., and L. E. Harris. 1969. Applied Animal Nutrition. W. H. Freeman, San Francisco.

[17] Cuthbertson, D. 1969. The Science of Nutrition of Farm Livestock. Pergamon Press, London.

[18] Foster, J. W. 1949. Chemical Activities of Fungi. J. Wiley, New York.

[19] Gilmour, D. 1961. Biochemistry of Insects. Academic Press, New York.

[20] Gortner, R. A., and W. A. Gortner, ed. 1949. Outlines of Biochemistry. Ed. 3. J. Wiley, New York.

[21] Guirard, B. M., and E. E. Snell. 1962. Bacteria 4:33.

[22] Guyton, A. C. 1966. Textbook of Medical Physiology. Ed. 3. W. B. Saunders, Philadelphia.

[23] Hall, R. P. 1953. Protozoology. Prentice-Hall, New York.

[24] Hall, R. P. 1965. Protozoan Nutrition. Blaisdell, New York.

[25] Heilbrunn, L. V. 1952. An Outline of General Physiology. Ed. 3. W. B. Saunders, Philadelphia.

[26] Hoagland, D. R. 1948. Mineral Nutrition of Plants. Chronica Botanica, Waltham, Mass.

[27] Hodge, H. C. 1964. In Mineral Metabolism. Academic Press, New York. v. 2., part B, p. 573.

[28] Hodge, H. C., and F. A. Smith. 1965. In J. H. Simons, ed. Fluorine Chemistry. Academic Press, New York. v. 4.

[29] Holm-Hansen, O. 1968. Annu. Rev. Microbiol. 22: 47.

[30] House, H. L. 1965. In M. Rockstein, ed. The Physiology of Insecta. Academic Press, New York. v. 2, pp. 769-813.

[31] House, H. L. 1972. In N. T-W-Fiennes, ed. International Encyclopaedia of Food and Nutrition, Biology of Nutrition. Pergamon Press, Oxford. v. 18, pp. 513-573.

[32] Hutner, S. H., ed. 1964. Biochemistry and Physiology of Protozoa. Academic Press, New York. v. 3.

[33] Hutner, S. H., and A. Lwoff, ed. 1955. Ibid. v. 2.

[34] Hutner, S. H., et al. 1950. Proc. Amer. Phil. Soc. 94:152.

[35] International Union of Biological Sciences. 1950. Trace Elements in Plant Physiology. Chronica Botanica, Waltham, Mass.

[36] Knight, S. G. 1951. In C. H. Werkman and P. W. Wilson, ed. Bacterial Physiology. Academic Press, New York. pp. 500-516.

[37] Kolodziej, B. J., and R. A. Slepecky. 1964. J. Bacteriol. 88:821.

[38] Leninhan, J. M. A., and S. S. Thompson. 1965. Activation Analysis. Academic Press, New York.

[39] Lewin, R. A., ed. 1962. Physiology and Biochemistry of Algae. Academic Press, New York.

[40] Lewis, D. 1961. Digestion Physiology and Nutrition of the Ruminant. Butterworth, London.

[41] Loosli, J. K. 1950-51. In D. E. H. Frear, ed. Agricultural Chemistry. Van Nostrand, New York. v. 1, pp. 615-647.

[42] Lwoff, A., ed. 1951. Biochemistry and Physiology of Protozoa. Academic Press, New York. v. 1.

[43] Maynard, L. A., and J. K. Loosli. 1969. Animal Nutrition. Ed. 6. McGraw-Hill, New York.

[44] Mertz, W. 1967. Fed. Proc. Fed. Amer. Soc. Exp. Biol. 26:186.

[45] Miller, E. C. 1938. Plant Physiology. Ed. 2. McGraw-Hill, New York.

[46] Mills, C. F. 1970. Trace Elements Metabolism in Animals. E. and S. Livingstone, Edinburgh.

[47] Mitchell, H. H. 1962-64. Comparative Nutrition of Man and Domestic Animals. Academic Press, New York. v. 1 & 2.

[48] Morgan, J. T., and D. Lewis. 1962. Nutrition of Pigs and Poultry. Butterworth, London.

[49] Muth, O. H. 1967. Selenium Biomed. Int. Symp., 1st, 1966.

[50] Muth, O. H., and J. E. Oldfield, ed. 1970. Symp. Sulfur Nutr., 1969.

[51] National Research Council, Committee on Animal Nutrition. 1962-71. Recommended Nutrient Allowances. Washington, D.C. no. 1-10.

[52] O'Kelley, J. C. 1968. Annu. Rev. Plant Physiol. 19: 89.

[53] Peisach, J., et al., ed. 1966. Biochem. Copper Proc. Symp., 1965.

[54] Prasad, A. S. 1966. Zinc Metabolism. C. C. Thomas, Springfield, Ill.

continued

[55] Rainbow, C., and A. H. Rose. 1963. Biochemistry of Industrial Microbiology. Academic Press, New York.

[56] Rosenfeld, I., and O. A. Beath. 1964. Selenium. Ed. 2. Academic Press, New York.

[57] Schutto, K. H. 1964. The Biology of the Trace Elements. J. B. Lippincott, Philadelphia.

[58] Scott, M. L., et al. 1969. Nutrition of the Chicken. M. L. Scott, Ithaca, N.Y.

[59] Smith, F. A., ed. 1966. Pharmacology of Fluorides. J. Springer, New York.

[60] Snell, E. E. 1957. Trace Anal. Pap. Symp., p. 547.

[61] Sprague, H. B., ed. 1964. Hunger Signs in Crops. Ed. 3. D. McKay, New York.

[62] Stanier, R. Y., et al. 1970. The Microbial World. Ed. 3. Prentice-Hall, Englewood Cliffs, N.J. pp. 67-78.

[63] Steward, F. C., ed. 1963. Plant Physiology. McGraw-Hill, New York. v. 3.

[64] Underwood, E. J. 1971. Trace Elements in Human and Animal Nutrition. Ed. 3. Academic Press, New York.

[65] Vanderzant, E. S. 1965. J. Insect Physiol. 11:659.

[66] Weinberg, E. D. 1970. Advan. Microbial Physiol. 4:1.

[67] Wigglesworth, V. B. 1965. The Principles of Insect Physiology. Ed. 6. Methuen, London.

[68] Williams, R. J. P. 1967. Endeavour 26:96.

[69] World Health Organization. 1970. World Health Organ. Monogr. Ser. 59.

[70] Zipkin, I. 1966. In A. E. Nizel, ed. The Science of Nutrition and Its Application in Clinical Dentistry. Ed. 2. W. B. Saunders, Philadelphia. pp. 111-124.

169. NUTRIENTS: LIPIDS

Abbreviations and Symbols: Capital letters indicate data are pertinent to all organisms studied; lower case letters and symbols indicate data apply to one or more species or strains, but not to all forms studied. R and r = required; R̶ = not required; rm = required by one or more mutants; U and u = utilized; u̶ = utilized as effectively as a related substance; U< = utilized less effectively than a related substance; U> = utilized more effectively than a related substance; s = stimulates growth or other processes; i = inhibits growth or other processes.

	Nutrient	Vertebrates	Insects	Protozoans[1]	Prokaryotes[2]	Algae	Fungi	Spermatophytes
				Sterols				
1	Cholesterol	R̶	r[3]	r[4]	r[5,6], s[7], i[8]	R̶	r[9,10]	R̶
2	7-Dehydrocholesterol	U	u̶	R̶, u̶[11]	r[5,6]	R̶	r[9,10]	R̶
3	Ergostanol acetate	R̶	...	R̶, u̶[11]	r[5,6]	R̶	R̶	R̶
4	Ergosterol	U	u̶	R̶, u̶[11]	r[5,6], i	R̶	s[10,12]	R̶
5	Stigmasterol	R̶, s	u̶	r[13]	r[5,6]	R̶	s[10]	R̶
			Long-Chain Fatty Acids & Their Derivatives					
6	Arachidonic acid	R̶[14], U>	s	....	....	R̶	R̶	R̶
7	Linoleic acid	R	r	u̶	r[6]	R̶	R̶, rm	R̶
8	Linolenic acid	R̶[14], U<	u̶	....	r[6]	R̶	r	R̶
9	Oleic acid	R̶	r	r, s, i	r[6]	R̶	r[12], rm	R̶
10	Palmitic acid	R̶	u	r[15]	r	...	r, s	...
11	Myrj G 2144[16]	R̶	R̶	R̶, s	R̶	R̶	R̶	R̶
12	Tween 80, 85[17]	R̶	R̶	R̶, s	r[6]	R̶	R̶	R̶

[1] Includes the colorless phytoflagellates. [2] Includes Schizomycetes, Rickettsiales, and Cyanophyta. [3] Apparently all insects need an exogenous sterol source and all insects devoid of symbionts need sterols in their diets, but several species utilize various other sterols as effectively as cholesterol; cholesterol (a Δ^5-sterol) is apparently ineffective in *Drosophila pachea* which utilizes only a Δ^7-sterol, and in *Xyleborus ferrugineus* which uses only ergosterol ($\Delta^{5,7,22}$-sterol) & 7-dehydrocholesterol ($\Delta^{5,7}$-sterol); since their symbionts possibly may furnish sterols, *Oncopeltus fasciatus* and *Myzus persicae* may need none in food. [4] Required by various *Trichomonas* species. [5] Can be used by certain soil bacteria as the sole source of carbon and energy. [6] Required for growth of some *Mycoplasma* species. [7] Enhanced growth of some gram-negative bacteria at 0.1% in nutrient broth. [8] Inhibited growth of some gram-negative bacteria at 0.1% in nutrient broth. [9] Required only by *Labyrinthula vitellina* var. *pacifica,* which also requires fucosterol, campesterol, β-sitosterol, γ-sitosterol, brassicasterol, and poriferasterol. [10] Induces oospore and oogonium formation in Pythiaceae. [11] Utilized in place of cholesterol by *Trichomonas.* [12] Required for anaerobic growth of yeasts. [13] Required by *Paramecium aurelia* which also requires sitosterol. [14] Required by monogastric animals, in addition to linoleic acid. [15] Required by *Trichomonas gallinae.* [16] A synthetic detergent (polyoxalkaline derivative of oleic acid). [17] Synthetic detergents (sorbitan esters of fatty acids, e.g., oleic).

continued

Nutrient	Vertebrates	Insects	Protozoans[1]	Prokaryotes[2]	Algae	Fungi	Spermatophytes
	Phospholipids						
13 Lecithin[15]	R	UF, s	s	r[6]	R	R	R
Reference	1,4,12,15, 16,18,29, 33,36,42	6,7,11, 19,20, 40,44	5,13,14,21, 23,27,28, 32,37,43	2,22,35	3,26, 34, 39	8-10,17, 22,24, 25	30,31,38,41

[1] Includes the colorless phytoflagellates. [2] Includes Schizomycetes, Rickettsiales, and Cyanophyta. [6] Required for growth of some *Mycoplasma* species. [15] A poorly defined, complex mixture of diesters of α-glycerophosphoryl choline, with many unsaturated fatty acids and other substances (especially amino acids).

Contributors: Eveleigh, Douglas E.; Hansard, Sam L.; House, H. L.; Kratzer, F. H.; Vestal, J. Robie

References

[1] Aaes-Jorgensen, E. 1961. Physiol. Rev. 41:1.
[2] Buetow, D. E., and B. H. Levedahl. 1964. Annu. Rev. Microbiol. 18:167.
[3] Burlew, J. S. 1953. Carnegie Inst. Wash. Publ. 600.
[4] Burton, B. T., ed. 1965. The Heinz Handbook of Nutrition. Ed. 2. McGraw-Hill, Blakiston Division, New York.
[5] Calkins, G., and F. M. Summers, ed. 1964. Protozoa in Biological Research. S. Hafner, New York.
[6] Chu, H.-M., et al. 1970. J. Insect Physiol. 16:1379.
[7] Clayton, R. E. 1970. In E. Sondheimer and J. B. Simeone, ed. Chemical Ecology. Academic Press, New York. pp. 235-280.
[8] Cochrane, V. W. 1958. Physiology of Fungi. J. Wiley, New York.
[9] Crocken, B. J., and J. F. Nyc. 1964. J. Biol. Chem. 239:1727.
[10] Foster, J. W. 1949. Chemical Activities of Fungi. Academic Press, New York.
[11] Gilmour, D. 1961. Biochemistry of Insects. Academic Press, New York.
[12] Greenberg, D. M., ed. 1968. Metabolic Pathways. Academic Press, New York. v. 2.
[13] Hall, R. P. 1953. Protozoology. Prentice-Hall, New York.
[14] Hall, R. P. 1965. Protozoan Nutrition. Blaisdell, New York.
[15] Harris, R. S., et al., ed. 1968. Vitam. Horm. (New York) 26.
[16] Hassinen, J. B., et al. 1950. Arch. Biochem. 25:91.
[17] Hendrix, J. W. 1970. Annu. Rev. Phytopathol. 8:111.
[18] Holman, R. T., ed. 1966-70. Progr. Chem. Fats Other Lipids 9(1-5).
[19] House, H. L. 1965. In M. Rockstein, ed. The Physiology of Insecta. Academic Press, New York. v. 2, pp. 769-813.
[20] House, H. L. 1972. In N. T-W-Fiennes, ed. International Encyclopaedia of Food and Nutrition, Biology of Nutrition. Pergamon Press, Oxford. v. 18, pp. 513-573.
[21] Hutner, S. H., ed. 1964. Biochemistry and Physiology of Protozoa. Academic Press, New York. v. 3.

[22] Hutner, S. H., and G. G. Holz, Jr. 1962. Annu. Rev. Microbiol. 16:189.
[23] Hutner, S. H., and A. Lwoff, ed. 1955. Biochemistry and Physiology of Protozoa. Academic Press, New York. v. 2.
[24] Keith, A. D., et al. 1969. J. Bacteriol. 98:415.
[25] Lechevalier, H. A., and D. Pramer. 1970. The Microbes. J. B. Lippincott, Philadelphia.
[26] Lewin, R. A., ed. 1962. Physiology and Biochemistry of Algae. Academic Press, New York.
[27] Lund, P. G., and M. S. Shorb. 1962. J. Protozool. 9:151.
[28] Lwoff, A., ed. 1951. Biochemistry and Physiology of Protozoa. Academic Press, New York. v. 1.
[29] Maynard, L. A., and J. K. Loosli. 1969. Animal Nutrition. Ed. 6. McGraw-Hill, New York.
[30] Meyer, B. S., and D. B. Anderson. 1952. Plant Physiology. Ed. 2. Van Nostrand-Reinhold, New York.
[31] Miller, E. C. 1938. Plant Physiology. Ed. 2. McGraw-Hill, New York.
[32] Miner, R. W. 1953. Ann. N.Y. Acad. Sci. 56:815.
[33] Morton, H. A., ed. 1970. Fat-Soluble Vitamins. Pergamon Press, Oxford.
[34] Myers, J. 1951. Annu. Rev. Microbiol. 5:157.
[35] Panos, C. 1967. A Microbial Enigma: Mycoplasma and Bacterial L-Forms. World, Cleveland.
[36] Rosenberg, H. R. 1945. Chemistry and Physiology of the Vitamins. Rev. ed. Interscience, New York.
[37] Shorb, M. S., and P. G. Lund. 1959. J. Protozool. 6:122.
[38] Skoog, F., ed. 1951. Plant Growth Substances. Univ. Wisconsin Press, Madison.
[39] Smith, G. M., ed. 1951. Manual of Phycology. Ronald Press, New York.
[40] Srivastava, P. N., and J. L. Auclair. 1970. Entomol. Exp. Appl. 13:208.
[41] Steward, F. C. 1965. Plant Physiology. Academic Press, New York. v. 4A.
[42] Wagner, A. F., and K. Folkers. 1964. Vitamins and Coenzymes. Interscience, New York.
[43] Werkman, C. H., and P. W. Wilson, ed. 1951. Bacterial Physiology. Academic Press, New York.
[44] Wigglesworth, V. B. 1965. The Principles of Insect Physiology. Ed. 6. Methuen, London.

Amino acids not known to be required from the environment have been omitted (e.g., hydroxyproline, 3,5-diidotyrosine, norleucine, ornithine, thyroxine). No distinction has been made between dextro- and levo-isomers, although the levo-isomers are usually nutritionally superior. In most studies with multicellular animals, microorganisms were present and in some instances supplied one or more amino acids. When requirement and utilization are noted together, at least one member of the group of organisms requires the amino acid specifically for energy or synthesis of other compounds, and other members, although not requiring it, utilize it as a general nitrogen source. *Abbreviations and Symbols:* Capital letters indicate data are pertinent to all organisms studied; lower case letters and symbols indicate data apply to one or more species or strains, but not to all forms studied. R and r = required; rm = required by one or more mutants; Ɍ = not required; U and u = utilized as a source of nitrogen and/or carbon although not a specific requirement; ᴜꜰ = replaces effectively one or more of the other amino acids, one of the interchangeable series being required in the diet; ɰ = not utilized; s = stimulates growth or other processes; n = serves as a complete nitrogen source; nn = serves as the simplest complete nitrogen source.

	Nutrient	Vertebrates	Insects	Protozoans[1]	Prokaryotes[2]	Algae	Fungi	Spermatophytes
1	Organic nitrogen	R, U, n	R, U, n	r, U, n	r, rm, u, n	Ɍ, u, n	r, rm, u, n[3]	Ɍ, u, n
2	Proteins	Ɍ[4], U	Ɍ[4], U, s, n	r[5], u, n	Ɍ, u	Ɍ	Ɍ, u, n[6]	Ɍ
3	Polypeptides[7], peptones	Ɍ, U	Ɍ	r, u, n	Ɍ, u	Ɍ, u, n	r[8], u, n	Ɍ, u, n
4	Amino acids	R, U	R, U, nn	r[9], u, n	r, rm, u, s, nn	Ɍ, u, n[10]	r, rm, u, n[11]	Ɍ, u, n[12]
5	Alanine	Ɍ, U	r, ᴜꜰ	u	r, rm, u, s, nn	Ɍ, u, n	u, ᴜꜰ[13], s, n	Ɍ, u, n
6	Arginine	r[14], U	R[15]	r, u, s	r, rm, u, s, nn	Ɍ, u, n	r, rm, u, n	Ɍ, u, n
7	Aspartic acid	Ɍ, U	r[16], ᴜꜰ	u, s	r, rm, u, s, nn	Ɍ, u, n	rm, u, ᴜꜰ[13], n	Ɍ, u, n
8	Citrulline	Ɍ, U, ᴜꜰ	u, ᴜꜰ[15]	u	r, rm, u	Ɍ	rm, u, n	Ɍ
9	Cysteine	Ɍ, U	r, u	u	r, rm, u, s, nn	Ɍ, u, n	r[17], rm, u, n	Ɍ, u, n
10	Cystine	Ɍ, U[18]	r[19], ᴜꜰ	u	r, rm, u, s, nn	Ɍ	rm, u, n	Ɍ, u, n
11	Glutamic acid	Ɍ, U, s	r[16]	u, s	r, rm, u, s, nn	Ɍ, u, n	r, rm, u, ᴜꜰ[13], n	Ɍ, u, n
12	Glycine	r[20], U	r	r, u	r, rm, u, s, nn	Ɍ, u, n	rm, u, n	Ɍ, u, n
13	Histidine	R[21]	R	r, u, s	r, rm, u, s, nn	Ɍ, u, n	r, rm, u, s, n	Ɍ, u, n
14	Isoleucine	R	R	r, u	r, rm, u, s	Ɍ, u, n	rm, u, n	Ɍ, u, n
15	Leucine	R	R, ᴜꜰ	r, u	r, rm, u, s, nn	Ɍ, ɰ	r, rm, u, n	Ɍ, u, n
16	Lysine	R	R	r, u	r, rm, u, s, nn	Ɍ, u, n	rm, u, s, n	Ɍ, u, n
17	Methionine	R[22]	R[19]	r, u	r, rm, u, s, nn	Ɍ, ɰ	r[17], rm, u, n	Ɍ, u, n

[1] Includes the colorless phytoflagellates. [2] Includes Schizomycetes, Rickettsiales, and Cyanophyta. [3] Most species grow better on organic than on inorganic nitrogen. [4] Suitable amino acid combinations are assumed to be able to replace complete proteins. [5] Many species require living prey. [6] Nemin promotes trap formation in nematode-trapping fungi. [7] *See* strepogenin, Table 45. [8] Necessary for growth of certain *Mucor rouxii* strains under high carbon dioxide tensions. *Saccharomycopsis guttulata* grows only with amino nitrogen compounds in a gas phase of 15% carbon dioxide and 2% oxygen. [9] *Glaucoma scintillans, Herpetomonas culicidarum, Tetrahymena geleii,* and *Tritrichomonas foetus* require arginine, histidine, isoleucine, leucine, lysine, methionine, phenylalanine, tryptophan, and valine; in addition, *G. scintillans* and *T. foetus* require glycine, proline, serine, and threonine, and *H. culicidarum* requires tyrosine. *Paramecium aurelia* requires arginine, histidine, isoleucine, leucine, lysine, methionine, phenylalanine, serine, threonine, tryptophan, and tyrosine. *Trichomonas gallinae* requires proline. *Tetrahymena geleii* needs no other carbon source. [10] Data are based mainly on *Chlorella pyrenoidosa.* [11] Amino acid mixtures are superior to ammonium as a nitrogen source for most fungi.

[12] Several intact plants (clover, orchid embryo, young orchid, pea, tobacco, tomato) grew on single amino acids as the sole nitrogen source. Growth attained on some amino acids is superior to that achieved with ammonium or nitrate as the nitrogen source; on other amino acids the effect is inferior. Some plants grow less well on amino acids than on inorganic nitrogen. Species differ markedly in amino acid utilization. [13] Alanine, aspartic acid, and glutamic acid are interchangeable for a *Neurospora* mutant. [14] Required by rat and chicken. [15] Arginine and citrulline are interchangeable for some insects; citrulline can partly replace arginine in *Drosophila melanogaster.* [16] *Phormia regina* requires aspartic acid or glutamic acid, but not both. [17] Many aquatic phycomycetes require cysteine or methionine as a form of reduced sulfur. [18] Cystine can partly replace methionine, which is required. [19] Some species apparently require either cystine or methionine, but not both, and proline. *Blattella germanica* requires neither cystine nor methionine in the presence of inorganic sulfates; threonine and tryptophan may not be required. [20] Required by chick for rapid growth. [21] Not required for maintaining nitrogen balance in man. [22] Amount required by man depends on the amount of cystine in the diet.

continued

	Nutrient	Vertebrates	Insects	Protozoans[1]	Prokaryotes[2]	Algae	Fungi	Spermato-phytes
18	Phenylalanine	R[23]	R, ʟꜰ	r, u	r, rm, u, s	R, ʟ	rm, u, s, n	R, u, n
19	Proline	r, U	r[19]	r, u	r, rm, u, s, nn	R, ʟ	rm, u, s[24], n	R, u, n
20	Serine	r, U	r	r, u, s	r, rm, u, s, nn	R, ʟ	rm, u, n	R, u, n
21	Threonine	R	R[19], ʟꜰ	r, u	r, rm, u, s	R, u, n	rm, u, n	R, u, n
22	Tryptophan[25]	R	R[19], ʟꜰ, s	r, u	r, rm, u, s, nn	R, u, n	r, rm, u, s, n	R, u, n
23	Tyrosine	R, U[26]	ʟꜰ[27]	r, u	r, rm, u, s, nn	....	rm, u, s, n	R, u, n
24	Valine	R	R, ʟꜰ	r, u, s	r, rm, u, s	R, u, n	rm, u, n	R, u, n
	Reference	20,26,40, 41,46,49, 53,55,66, 68	19,28-30, 67	9,14,15,22-25, 34,35,37,38, 43,50,51,54, 64	21,39,57	16,27,32, 33,36-38, 43-45,48, 52	1,2,4,5,7,8,10- 12,17,59,63	3,6,13,18, 31,42,47, 56,58,60- 62,65

[1] Includes the colorless phytoflagellates. [2] Includes Schizomycetes, Rickettsiales, and Cyanophyta. [19] Some species apparently require either cystine or methionine, but not both, and proline. *Blattella germanica* requires neither cystine nor methionine in the presence of inorganic sulfates; threonine and tryptophan may not be required. [23] Amount required by man depends on the amount of tyrosine in the diet. [24] Stimulates spore germination in *Rhizopus*. [25] Precursor of niacin; spares niacin for some organisms. [26] Tyrosine can partly replace phenylalanine, which is required. [27] May replace phenylalanine in certain insects but not in others.

Contributors: Eveleigh, Douglas E.; Fogg, G. E.; Hansard, Sam L.; House, H. L.; Kratzer, F. H.; Vestal, J. Robie

References

[1] Adler, H. I., ed. 1969. Microbial Genet. Bull. 31.

[2] Ainsworth, G. C., and A. S. Sussman, ed. 1965. The Fungi. Academic Press, New York. v. 1.

[3] Audus, L. J., and J. H. Quastel. 1947. Nature (London) 160:222.

[4] Bachmann, B. J., ed. 1970. Neurospora Newslett. 16.

[5] Barratt, R. W., et al. 1965. Genetics 52:233.

[6] Brigham, R. O. 1917. Soil Sci. 3:155.

[7] Brock, T. D. 1970. Biology of Microorganisms. Prentice-Hall, Englewood Cliffs, N.J.

[8] Burnett, J. H. 1968. Fundamentals of Mycology. St. Martin, New York.

[9] Calkins, G., and F. M. Summers, ed. 1964. Protozoa in Biological Research. S. Hafner, New York.

[10] Cantino, E. C., and G. Turian. 1959. Annu. Rev. Microbiol. 13:97.

[11] Clutterbuck, A. J. 1969. Aspergillus Newslett. 10:30.

[12] Cochrane, V. W. 1958. Physiology of Fungi. J. Wiley, New York.

[13] Crowther, E. M. 1925. J. Agr. Sci. 15:300.

[14] Doyle, W. L. 1943. Biol. Rev. Cambridge Phil. Soc. 18:119.

[15] Elliott, A. M. 1949. Physiol. Zool. 22:337.

[16] Fogg, G. E. 1953. The Metabolism of Algae. Methuen, London.

[17] Foster, J. W. 1949. Chemical Activities of Fungi. Academic Press, New York.

[18] Ghosh, B. P., and R. H. Burris. 1950. Soil Sci. 70(3):187.

[19] Gilmour, D. 1961. Biochemistry of Insects. Academic Press, New York.

[20] Greenberg, D. M., ed. 1967-68. Metabolic Pathways. Academic Press, New York. v. 1-3.

[21] Guirard, B. M., and E. E. Snell. 1962. Bacteria 4:33.

[22] Hall, R. P. 1943. Vitam. Horm. (New York) 1:249.

[23] Hall, R. P. 1953. Protozoology. Prentice-Hall, New York.

[24] Hall, R. P. 1965. Protozoan Nutrition. Blaisdell, New York.

[25] Hall, R. P., and H. W. Schoendorn. 1939. Physiol. Zool. 12:201.

[26] Harrow, B. 1962. Textbook of Biochemistry. Ed. 8. W. B. Saunders, Philadelphia.

[27] Hayward, J. 1965. Physiol. Plant. 18:201.

[28] House, H. L. 1965. In M. Rockstein, ed. The Physiology of Insecta. Academic Press, New York. v. 2, pp. 769-813.

[29] House, H. L. 1969. Entomol. Exp. Appl. 12:651.

[30] House, H. L. 1972. In N. T-W-Fiennes, ed. International Encyclopaedia of Food and Nutrition, Biology of Nutrition. Pergamon Press, Oxford. v. 18, pp. 513-573.

[31] Hutchinson, H. B., and N. H. J. Miller. 1911. Centralbl. Bakteriol. Parasitenk., II, 30:513.

[32] Hutner, S. H., ed. 1964. Biochemistry and Physiology of Protozoa. Academic Press, New York. v. 3.

[33] Hutner, S. H., and A. Lwoff, ed. 1955. Ibid. v. 2.

[34] Kidder, G. W. 1951. Annu. Rev. Microbiol. 5:139.

[35] Kidder, G. W., and V. C. Dewey. 1945. Arch. Biochem. 6:425.

[36] Lewin, R. A., ed. 1962. Physiology and Biochemistry of Algae. Academic Press, New York.

[37] Lwoff, A. 1943. L'évolution physiologique. Hermann, Paris.

[38] Lwoff, A., ed. 1951. Biochemistry and Physiology of Protozoa. Academic Press, New York. v. 1.

[39] Mahler, H. R., and E. H. Cordes. 1966. Biological Chemistry. Harper and Row, New York.

continued

[40] Maynard, L. A., and J. K. Loosli. 1969. Animal Nutrition. Ed. 6. McGraw-Hill, New York.

[41] Meister, A. 1965. Biochemistry of the Amino Acids. Academic Press, New York.

[42] Miller, E. C. 1938. Plant Physiology. Ed. 2. McGraw-Hill, New York.

[43] Miner, R. W. 1953. Ann. N.Y. Acad. Sci. 56:815.

[44] Myers, J. 1944. Plant Physiol. 19:579.

[45] Myers, J. 1951. Annu. Rev. Microbiol. 5:157.

[46] Neurath, H., ed. 1963-70. The Proteins. Ed. 2. Academic Press, New York. v. 1-5.

[47] Nightingale, G. T. 1947. Bot. Rev. 3:85.

[48] Oppenheimer, C. H., ed. 1963. Symp. Mar. Microbiol., 1961.

[49] Oser, B. L., ed. 1965. Hawk's Physiological Chemistry. Ed. 14. McGraw-Hill, Blakiston Division, New York.

[50] Pringsheim, E. G. 1937. Nature (London) 139:196.

[51] Pringsheim, E. G. 1937. Planta 27:61.

[52] Pringsheim, E. G. 1946. Pure Cultures of Algae. Univ. Press, Cambridge, England.

[53] Prosser, C. L., and F. A. Brown, Jr. 1961. Comparative Animal Physiology. Ed. 2. W. B. Saunders, Philadelphia.

[54] Scheer, B. T. 1948. Comparative Physiology. J. Wiley, New York.

[55] Scott, M. L., et al. 1969. Nutrition of the Chicken. M. L. Scott, Ithaca, N.Y.

[56] Skoog, F., ed. 1951. Plant Growth Substances. Univ. Wisconsin Press, Madison.

[57] Sober, H. A., ed. 1970. Handbook of Biochemistry: Selected Data for Molecular Biology. Ed. 2. Chemical Rubber, Cleveland.

[58] Spoerl, E. 1948. Amer. J. Bot. 35:88.

[59] Stanier, R. Y., et al. 1970. The Microbial World. Ed. 3. Prentice-Hall, Englewood Cliffs, N.J.

[60] Steinberg, R. A. 1947. J. Agr. Res. 75:81.

[61] Steward, F. C. 1965. Plant Physiology. Academic Press, New York. v. 4A.

[62] Tanaka, I. 1931. Jap. J. Bot. 5:323.

[63] Tatum, E. L. 1944. Annu. Rev. Biochem. 13:667.

[64] Trager, W. 1941. Physiol. Rev. 21:1.

[65] Virtanen, A. I., and H. Linkola. 1946. Nature (London) 158:515.

[66] West, E. S., et al. 1966. Textbook of Biochemistry. Ed. 4. Macmillan, New York.

[67] Wigglesworth, V. B. 1965. The Principles of Insect Physiology. Ed. 6. Methuen, London.

[68] Williams, V. A., and H. B. Williams. 1967. Basic Physical Chemistry for the Life Sciences. W. H. Freeman, San Francisco.

171. NUTRIENTS: PURINES AND PYRIMIDINES

Purine and pyrimidine compounds are essential components of the nucleic acids. Inability to synthesize these compounds makes it necessary for many organisms to obtain them from the environment or diet. For some organisms the requirement is for a specific compound, or compounds; for others, any one of an interchangeable series of compounds satisfies the need. *Abbreviations and Symbols:* Capital letters indicate data are pertinent to all organisms studied; lower case letters and symbols indicate data apply to one or more species or strains, but not to all forms studied. R and r = required; Ř = not required; rm = required by one or more mutants; u = utilized; ɰ = not utilized; ᴜꜰ = utilized as effectively as, or is interchangeable with, one or more related compounds, the presence of at least one of the series being required; u< = can partially replace, or spare the use of, one or more required, or interchangeably required, compounds; s = stimulates growth or other processes; i = inhibits growth or other processes.

	Nutrient	Vertebrates	Insects[1]	Protozoans[2]	Prokaryotes[3]	Algae	Fungi	Spermatophytes
1	Purine compounds	Ř	r	r, s	r, u, s	Ř	rm, u, s	Ř
2	Adenine	Ř	r, s	r?[4], u<[5]	r	Ř	r[6], rm, u, s	Ř
3	Adenosine	Ř	ᴜꜰ, s	Ř, u<[5]	r	Ř	rm, u	Ř
4	Adenosine triphosphate	Ř	ᴜꜰ	Ř, s	r	Ř	Ř, ᴜꜰ	Ř

[1] Diptera and Coleoptera apparently respond beneficially to nucleic acids and their components in food. In *Drosophila melanogaster,* requirement and utilization of ribonucleic acid and its components vary with genetic strain and the presence of other substances (including pteroylmonoglutamic acid and certain amino acids) in the diet. *D. melanogaster,* but not *Pseudosarcophaga* sp. *(Agria affinis)* can utilize component nucleosides. [2] Includes the colorless phytoflagellates. [3] Includes Schizomycetes, Rickettsiales, and Cyanophyta. [4] In vitro studies indicate possible requirement by *Plasmodium.* [5] Spares, but cannot replace, guanine, guanosine, and guanylic acid in *Tetrahymena.* [6] Required by *Saccharomyces octosporus* on certain media.

continued

	Nutrient	Vertebrates	Insects[1]	Protozoans[2]	Prokaryotes[3]	Algae	Fungi	Spermatophytes
5	Adenylic acid	R	ᴜꜰ, s	r, u<[5]	r	R	R, u	R
6	Guanine	R	r	r[7]	r	R	r, rm, s	R
7	Guanosine	R	ᴜꜰ, s	r?[4], ᴜꜰ, u<[8], i	r	R	R, u	R
8	Guanylic acid	R	ᴜꜰ, s	ᴜꜰ, s	r	R	R, u	R
9	Hypoxanthine	R	u	ᴜꜰ, u<[5]	r, u<	R	rm, u, s	R
10	Xanthine	R	s	r?[4], u̸	r	R	R, u	R
11	Others	...	.....	s[9]	r	....	u	R
12	Pyrimidine compounds	R	r	r, s	r, u, s	r	r, rm, s	R
13	Cytidine	R	u	ᴜꜰ, i	r	R	R, rm, s	R
14	Cytidylic acid	R	u	ᴜꜰ, s	r	R	R, rm, s[10]	R
15	Cytosine	R	u	r?[4], u̸, i	r	R	R, rm, u	R
16	Orotic acid	R	R	R, u̸	r	R	R, rm, u, s[10]	R
17	Pyrimidine	R	R	r?[4], u[11]	r	r[11]	r, rm, u, s[11]	R
18	Thymidine	R	ᴜꜰ	u<[12]	r	R	R	R
19	Thymine	R	u̸	r?, u<[12]	r	R	R, u	R
20	Uracil	R	u̸	r?[4], ᴜꜰ[13]	r, u<	R	R, rm, s[10]	R
21	Uridine	R	R	ᴜꜰ	r	R	R, rm, s	R
22	Uridylic acid	R	u	ᴜꜰ	r	R	R, rm, s[10]	R
Reference		31,34,35, 38,43,50, 51	13,17-19,23	7,15,16,20,21, 24-26,29,30, 32,46	14,45,49	23,28,33,40	1-4,6,8-10, 12,14,36, 39,41,47	5,11,22, 27,37, 42,44, 48,49

[1] Diptera and Coleoptera apparently respond beneficially to nucleic acids and their components in food. In *Drosophila melanogaster,* requirement and utilization of ribonucleic acid and its components vary with genetic strain and the presence of other substances (including pteroylmonoglutamic acid and certain amino acids) in the diet. *D. melanogaster,* but not *Pseudosarcophaga* sp. *(Agria affinis)* can utilize component nucleosides. [2] Includes the colorless phytoflagellates. [3] Includes Schizomycetes, Rickettsiales, and Cyanophyta. [4] In vitro studies indicate possible requirement by *Plasmodium.* [5] Spares, but cannot replace, guanine, guanosine, and guanylic acid in *Tetrahymena.* [7] Required by *Tetrahymena,* but replaceable by guanosine or guanylic acid. [8] Spares pteroylglutamic acid in *Herpetomonas culicidarum.* [9] Methyl purines (theobromine, theophylline, caffeine) stimulate some Ciliatea, including Suctoria. [10] Stimulates mutants of *Neurospora.* [11] Pyrimidine moiety of thiamine. [12] Spares pteroylglutamic acid in *Tetrahymena.* [13] Replaces, or is interchangeable with, cytidine, cytidylic acid, uridine, or uridylic acid, in *Tetrahymena.*

Contributors: Eveleigh, Douglas E.; Fogg, G. E.; Hansard, Sam L.; House, H. L.; Kratzer, F. H.; Vestal, J. Robie

References

[1] Adler, H. I., ed. 1969. Microbial Genet. Bull. 31.
[2] Ainsworth, G. C., and A. S. Sussman, ed. 1965. The Fungi. Academic Press, New York. v. 1.
[3] Bachmann, B. J., ed. 1970. Neurospora Newslett. 16.
[4] Barratt, R. W., et al. 1965. Genetics 52:233.
[5] Bonner, D. M., and J. Bonner. 1940. Amer. J. Bot. 27:38.
[6] Burnett, J. H. 1968. Fundamentals of Mycology. St. Martin, New York.
[7] Calkins, G., and F. M. Summers, ed. 1964. Protozoa in Biological Research. S. Hafner, New York.
[8] Clutterbuck, A. J. 1969. Aspergillus Newslett. 10: 30.
[9] Cochrane, V. W. 1958. Physiology of Fungi. J. Wiley, New York.
[10] Davidson, J. N., and W. E. Cohn, ed. 1969. Progr. Nucleic Acid Res. Mol. Biol. 9.

[11] Deysson, M. 1953. Bull. Soc. Bot. Fr. 100:14.
[12] Foster, J. W. 1949. Chemical Activities of Fungi. Academic Press, New York.
[13] Gilmour, D. 1961. Biochemistry of Insects. Academic Press, New York.
[14] Guirard, B. M., and E. E. Snell. 1962. Bacteria 4:33.
[15] Hall, R. P. 1953. Protozoology. Prentice-Hall, New York.
[16] Hall, R. P. 1965. Protozoan Nutrition. Blaisdell, New York.
[17] House, H. L. 1965. In M. Rockstein, ed. The Physiology of Insecta. Academic Press, New York. v. 2, pp. 769-813.
[18] House, H. L. 1969. Entomol. Exp. Appl. 12:651.
[19] House, H. L. 1972. In N. T-W-Fiennes, ed. International Encyclopaedia of Food and Nutrition, Biology of Nutrition. Pergamon Press, Oxford. v. 18, pp. 513-573.

continued

[20] Hutner, S. H., ed. 1964. Biochemistry and Physiology of Protozoa. Academic Press, New York. v. 3.

[21] Hutner, S. H., and A. Lwoff, ed. 1955. Ibid. v. 2.

[22] Jones, R. F., and H. G. Baker. 1943. Ann. Bot. (London) 7:379.

[23] Kalckar, H. M. 1947. Symp. Soc. Exp. Biol. 1:38.

[24] Kidder, G. W. 1947. Ann. N.Y. Acad. Sci. 49:99.

[25] Kidder, G. W. 1951. Annu. Rev. Microbiol. 5:139.

[26] Kidder, G. W., and V. C. Dewey. 1948. Proc. Nat. Acad. Sci. U.S. 34:566.

[27] Kotsovsky, D. 1942. Biologe (Munich) 11:276.

[28] Lewin, R. A., ed. 1962. Physiology and Biochemistry of Algae. Academic Press, New York.

[29] Lilly, D. M., et al. 1953. Proc. Soc. Exp. Biol. Med. 83:434.

[30] Lwoff, A., ed. 1951. Biochemistry and Physiology of Protozoa. Academic Press, New York. v. 1.

[31] Maynard, L. A., and J. K. Loosli. 1969. Animal Nutrition. Ed. 6. McGraw-Hill, New York.

[32] Miner, R. W. 1953. Ann. N.Y. Acad. Sci. 56:815.

[33] Myers, J. 1951. Annu. Rev. Microbiol. 5:157.

[34] Nicholson, D. E. 1965. Metabolic Pathways. Ed. 4. Chorley and Pickergill, London.

[35] Oser, B. L., ed. 1965. Hawk's Physiological Chemistry. Ed. 14. McGraw-Hill, Blakiston Division, New York.

[36] Pastan, I., and R. Perlman. 1970. Science 169:339.

[37] Porutskii, G. V. 1949. Dokl. Akad. Nauk SSSR 64:103.

[38] Prosser, C. L., and F. A. Brown, Jr. 1961. Comparative Animal Physiology. Ed. 2. W. B. Saunders, Philadelphia.

[39] Robbins, W. J., and V. Kavanagh. 1942. Bot. Rev. 8:411.

[40] Sager, R., and S. Granick. 1953. Ann. N.Y. Acad. Sci. 56:831.

[41] Schopfer, W. H. 1943. Plants and Vitamins. Chronica Botanica, Waltham, Mass.

[42] Schreiner, O., and J. Skinner. 1917. U.S. Dep. Agr. Bur. Soils Bull. 87.

[43] Sebrell, W. H., Jr., and R. S. Harris. 1954. The Vitamins. Academic Press, New York. v. 1 & 2.

[44] Skoog, F., ed. 1951. Plant Growth Substances. Univ. Wisconsin Press, Madison.

[45] Sober, H. A., ed. 1970. Handbook of Biochemistry: Selected Data for Molecular Biology. Ed. 2. Chemical Rubber, Cleveland.

[46] Sprince, H., et al. 1953. Ann. N.Y. Acad. Sci. 56:1016.

[47] Stanier, R. Y., et al. 1970. The Microbial World. Ed. 3. Prentice-Hall, Englewood Cliffs, N.J.

[48] Steinberg, R. A. 1947. J. Agr. Res. 75:81.

[49] Steward, F. C. 1965. Plant Physiology. Academic Press, New York. v. 4A.

[50] Wagner, A. F., and K. Folkers. 1964. Vitamins and Coenzymes. Interscience, New York.

[51] White, A., et al. 1968. Principles of Biochemistry. Ed. 4. McGraw-Hill, New York.

172. NUTRIENTS: VITAMINS AND RELATED COMPOUNDS

Many vitamins and related compounds are probably indispensable participants in the metabolic activities of all living substances, and are in this sense universally "required." Data, however, have been limited to the presently known requirement, or nonrequirement, for compounds obtained from the external environment or in the diet, and do not include metabolically essential compounds provided to an organism by associated microorganisms (e.g., by the intestinal flora of mammals). *Abbreviations and Symbols:* Capital letters indicate data are pertinent to all organisms studied; lower case letters and symbols indicate data apply to one or more species or strains, but not to all forms studied. R and r = required; R̸ = not required; rm = required by one or more mutants; u = utilized; u⸱ᶠ = utilized as effectively as a related vitamin or compound; u> = utilized more effectively than a related vitamin or compound; u< = utilized less effectively than a related vitamin; ψ = not utilized in place of the related vitamin; s = stimulates growth or other processes; i = inhibits growth or other processes; * = supplied by microorganisms in ruminant animals.

Nutrient (Synonym)	Vertebrates	Insects	Protozoans [1]	Prokaryotes [2]	Algae	Fungi	Spermato-phytes
Vitamins							
1 Thiamine	R*	r	r	r	r	r[3,4], rm, s, i[5]	R̸, s
2 Riboflavin	R*	r	r	r	R̸	r[6], rm	R̸
3 Niacin	r	r	r	r	R̸	r[7], rm, s	R̸, s?
4 Niacinamide	u⸱ᶠ	u⸱ᶠ	u⸱ᶠ	r	R̸	r, rm, u⸱ᶠ, s	R̸, s?

[1] Includes the colorless phytoflagellates. [2] Includes Schizomycetes, Rickettsiales, and Cyanophyta. [3] Required by the yeast phase of *Histoplasma capsulatum*. [4] Required by most Pythiaceae. [5] Inhibits growth of *Saccharomyces cerevisiae* strains and *Rhizopus nigricans*. [7] Required with thiamine for anaerobic growth of *Mucor rouxii*.

continued

Nutrient (Synonym)	Vertebrates	Insects	Protozoans[1]	Prokaryotes[2]	Algae	Fungi	Spermatophytes
5 B₆ (Pyridoxine)	R*	r	r	r	Ɍ, s	r, rm, s	Ɍ, s
6 Pyridoxal	uF	uF	uF	r	Ɍ	r, uF, s	Ɍ
7 Pyridoxamine	uF	uF	uF	r	Ɍ	r, uF, s	Ɍ
8 Biotin	R*	r	r, s	r	r	r[3], rm, s	Ɍ
9 Pantothenic acid	R*	r	r	r	r	r[6], rm, s	Ɍ, s
10 Folic acid (Pteroylglutamic acid)	R*	r	r	r	Ɍ	Ɍ, s	Ɍ
11 p-Aminobenzoic acid	Ɍ, s	Ɍ	r	r	Ɍ	r, rm, s	Ɍ
12 Inositol	r	r	Ɍ	r	Ɍ	r, rm, s	Ɍ, s
13 B₁₂ (Cobalamin; cyanocobalamin)	R*	r?, s	r	r, uF[8]	r	r, rm	Ɍ, s
14 Choline group[9]	r	r	Ɍ	r	Ɍ	r, rm, s	Ɍ, s
15 Ascorbic acid	r	r[10]	r, s	Ɍ, s	r?, s	Ɍ, s	Ɍ, s
16 A	R	Ɍ	r?	Ɍ	Ɍ	r	Ɍ, s
17 D	R[11]	Ɍ	Ɍ	Ɍ	Ɍ	Ɍ, s	Ɍ
18 E	R	r, s	r[12]	Ɍ	Ɍ	Ɍ	Ɍ
19 K	R*	Ɍ	Ɍ	r	Ɍ	Ɍ	Ɍ
Compounds Chemically Related to Vitamins							
20 β-Alanine	Ɍ	Ɍ	Ɍ, ψ	r, uF	Ɍ	Ɍ, rm, uF	Ɍ
21 Biocytin	Ɍ	Ɍ	Ɍ	u, ψ[13]	Ɍ	Ɍ, uF	Ɍ
22 β-Carotene[14]	Ɍ, u<	r[15]	Ɍ	Ɍ	Ɍ	Ɍ	Ɍ
23 Coenzyme A	Ɍ, u<	Ɍ, uF	Ɍ	r, u>	Ɍ	Ɍ, s	Ɍ
24 Desthiobiotin	Ɍ	Ɍ	Ɍ	Ɍ	Ɍ	Ɍ, uF, i	Ɍ
25 5,6-Dimethylbenzimidazole	Ɍ	Ɍ	Ɍ	Ɍ	Ɍ	Ɍ	Ɍ
26 Diphosphothiamine	Ɍ, uF	Ɍ, uF	Ɍ, uF	r, u>	Ɍ	Ɍ, uF, u<	Ɍ
27 Folic acid conjugates[16]	Ɍ, uF	Ɍ, uF	Ɍ, uF	r	Ɍ	Ɍ	Ɍ
28 Folinic acid[17]	Ɍ, u<	Ɍ, uF	Ɍ, uF	r[18]	Ɍ	Ɍ	Ɍ
29 Hesperidin[19]	Ɍ	Ɍ	Ɍ	Ɍ	Ɍ	Ɍ	Ɍ, s
30 Lactobacillus bulgaricus factor[20]	Ɍ	Ɍ	Ɍ	r, u>	Ɍ	Ɍ	Ɍ
31 Lipothiamide	Ɍ, uF	Ɍ	Ɍ	Ɍ	Ɍ	Ɍ	Ɍ
32 Lyxoflavine	Ɍ	Ɍ	Ɍ	uF, i	Ɍ	Ɍ	Ɍ
33 Nicotinamide adenine dinucleotide (Diphosphopyridine nucleotide)	Ɍ, uF	Ɍ, uF?	Ɍ	r, uF	Ɍ	r	Ɍ
34 Nicotinamide adenine dinucleotide phosphate (Triphosphopyridine nucleotide)	Ɍ, uF	Ɍ	Ɍ	r	Ɍ	r, uF, s	Ɍ
35 Oxybiotin (o-Heterobiotin)	Ɍ	Ɍ	Ɍ	Ɍ	Ɍ	Ɍ, u<, s	Ɍ
36 Pantoic acid	Ɍ	Ɍ	Ɍ	r, uF	Ɍ	Ɍ, u	Ɍ
37 Pantothenic acid conjugate	Ɍ	Ɍ	Ɍ	r	Ɍ	Ɍ	Ɍ
38 Pimelic acid	Ɍ	Ɍ	Ɍ, u<	r	Ɍ	Ɍ, s	Ɍ

[1] Includes the colorless phytoflagellates. [2] Includes Schizomycetes, Rickettsiales, and Cyanophyta. [3] Required by the yeast phase of *Histoplasma capsulatum*. [6] Rarely a natural requirement. [8] Replaces cobalt requirement in some blue-green algae. [9] Includes choline, betaine, and other methyl donors. [10] Required in food by phytophagous species only. [11] D₂ active for mammals only; D₃ active for all, and required by chicken. [12] Required by a variant of *Trichomonas gallinae*. [13] Not utilized as a source of biotin in some *Lactobacillus* species. [14] And other carotenoid precursors of vitamin A. [15] Required by some species for normal sensitivity to light. [16] Di-, tri-, and hepta-glutamates of folic acid. [17] The citrovorum factor; required by *Leuconostoc citrovorum*. [18] Required as a cofactor for the utilization of nucleic acid bases by *Mycoplasma laidlawii*. [19] Hesperidin, rutin, and citrin = vitamin P series. [20] Pantetheine (thiol form) and pantethine (disulfide form).

continued

Nutrient (Synonym)	Vertebrates	Insects	Protozoans[1]	Prokaryotes[2]	Algae	Fungi	Spermato-phytes
39 Pseudovitamin B_{12}	R	R	R	r	R	R	R
40 Pteroic acid	R	R	R, uF, u	r	R	R	R
41 Pyridoxal phosphate	R, uF	R, uF	R, uF	r	R	R, u, uF	R
42 Pyridoxamine phosphate	R, uF	R, uF	R, uF	r	R	R, u, uF	R
43 Pyrimidine	R	R	r, u[21,22]	r[21,22]	r[21,22]	r, rm, u[21,22], s[21,22]	R
44 Rhizopterin	R	R	R	R, s[23]	R	R	R
45 α-Ribazole	R	R	R	R	R	R	R
46 Rutin[19]	R	R	R	R	R	R, u[24]	R
47 Thiazole	R	R	r, u[22,25]	r[22,25]	r[22,25]	r, rm, u[22,25], s[22,25]	R
48 Xanthopterin	r[26]	R	R	R	R	R	R
Reference	3,7,17,18, 21,23,24, 35,39,40, 42,43,45-47,49,53-55,58,62, 63	8, 12, 13,20, 30,31, 52,61, 64,65	8,11,16,25-27,32-34, 37,41,52, 65	22,29,50,57, 60	8, 28, 36, 41, 44, 48	1,2,4,5,9,10,14,15, 19,22,38,51,59	6,8,56

[1] Includes the colorless phytoflagellates. [2] Includes Schizomycetes, Rickettsiales, and Cyanophyta. [19] Hesperidin, rutin, and citrin = vitamin P series. [21] Thiamine or pyrimidine moiety (thiazole moiety is synthesized). [22] Thiamine, or pyrimidine + thiamine moieties (pyrimidine and thiazole moieties combine to give thiamine). [23] Stimulates growth of *Streptococcus faecalis,* R. [24] Utilized by *Aspergillus flavus* and *Polyporus versicolor.* [25] Thiamine or thiazole moiety (pyrimidine moiety is synthesized). [26] More active than folic acid in relieving anemia of Chinook salmon.

Contributors: Eveleigh, Douglas E.; Fogg, G. E.; Hansard, Sam L.; House, H. L.; Kratzer, F. H.; Vestal. J. Robie

References
[1] Adler, H. I., ed. 1969. Microbial Genet. Bull. 31.
[2] Ainsworth, G. C., and A.,S. Sussman, ed. 1965. The Fungi. Academic Press, New York. v. 1.
[3] Albanese, A. A. 1970. Newer Methods of Nutritional Biochemistry. Academic Press, New York. v. 1-4.
[4] Bachmann, B. J., ed. 1970. Neurospora Newslett. 16.
[5] Barratt, R. W., et al. 1965. Genetics 52:233.
[6] Bessey, O. A., et al. 1953. Annu. Rev. Biochem. 22: 545.
[7] Bourne, G. H., and G. W. Kidder, ed. 1953. Biochemistry and Physiology of Nutrition. Academic Press, New York.
[8] Briggs, G. M. Unpublished. National Institutes of Health, Bethesda, Md., 1953.
[9] Brock, T. D. 1970. Biology of Microorganisms. Prentice-Hall, Englewood Cliffs, N.J.
[10] Burnett, J. H. 1968. Fundamentals of Mycology. St. Martin, New York.
[11] Calkins, G., and F. M. Summers, ed. 1964. Protozoa in Biological Research. S. Hafner, New York.
[12] Chauvin, R. W. 1949. Physiologie de l'insecte. W. Junk, Haag.
[13] Clayton, R. E. 1970. In E. Sondheimer and J. B. Simeone, ed. Chemical Ecology. Academic Press, New York. pp. 235-280.
[14] Clutterbuck, A. J. 1969. Aspergillus Newslett. 10: 30.
[15] Cochrane, V. W. 1958. Physiology of Fungi. J. Wiley, New York.
[16] Cooperman, J. M., et al. 1952. J. Nutr. 46:467.
[17] Crampton, E. W., and L. E. Harris. 1969. Applied Animal Nutrition. W. H. Freeman, San Francisco.
[18] Cuthbertson, E., ed. 1969. Nutrition of Animals of Agricultural Importance. Pergamon Press, London.
[19] Foster, J. W. 1949. Chemical Activities of Fungi. Academic Press, New York.
[20] Gilmour, D. 1961. Biochemistry of Insects. Academic Press, New York.
[21] Greenberg, D. M., ed. 1968. Metabolic Pathways. Academic Press, New York. v. 2.
[22] Guirard, B. M., and E. E. Snell. 1962. Bacteria 4:33.
[23] Guyton, A. C. 1966. Textbook of Medical Physiology. Ed. 3. W. B. Saunders, Philadelphia.
[24] Halfez, E. S. E., and I. A. Dyer. 1969. Animal Growth and Nutrition. Lea and Febiger, Philadelphia.
[25] Hall, R. P. 1943. Vitam. Horm. (New York) 1:249.
[26] Hall, R. P. 1953. Protozoology. Prentice-Hall, New York.
[27] Hall, R. P. 1965. Protozoan Nutrition. Blaisdell, New York.

continued

[28] Hill, M. N. 1963. The Sea. Interscience, New York. v. 2.

[29] Holm-Hansen, O. 1968. Annu. Rev. Microbiol. 22: 47.

[30] House, H. L. 1966. J. Insect Physiol. 12:409.

[31] House, H. L. 1969. Entomol. Exp. Appl. 12:651.

[32] Hutner, S. H., ed. 1964. Biochemistry and Physiology of Protozoa. Academic Press, New York. v. 3.

[33] Hutner, S. H., and A. Lwoff, ed. 1955. Ibid. v. 2.

[34] Kidder, G. W. 1951. Annu. Rev. Microbiol. 5: 139.

[35] Kujawsky, W. F. 1965-67. Bibliography of Vitamin E. Distillation Products Industries, Rochester, N.Y.

[36] Lewin, R. A., ed. 1962. Physiology and Biochemistry of Algae. Academic Press, New York.

[37] Lwoff, A., ed. 1951. Biochemistry and Physiology of Protozoa. Academic Press, New York. v. 1.

[38] Mandelstam, J., and K. McQuillen. 1968. Biochemistry of Bacterial Growth. J. Wiley, New York.

[39] Maynard, L. A., and J. K. Loosli. 1969. Animal Nutrition. Ed. 6. McGraw-Hill, New York.

[40] McCormick, D. B., and L. D. Wright, ed. 1970. Vitamins and Coenzymes. Academic Press, New York. v. 18.

[41] Miner, R. W. 1953. Ann. N.Y. Acad. Sci. 56:815.

[42] Mitchell, H. H. 1962-64. Comparative Nutrition of Man and Domestic Animals. Academic Press, New York. v. 1 & 2.

[43] Morton, H. A., ed. 1970. Fat-Soluble Vitamins. Pergamon Press, Oxford.

[44] Myers, J. 1951. Annu. Rev. Microbiol. 5:157.

[45] National Research Council, Committee on Animal Nutrition. 1964. Nat. Acad. Sci. Nat. Res. Counc. Publ. 1137.

[46] Nicholson, D. E. 1965. Metabolic Pathways. Ed. 4. Chorley and Pickergill, London.

[47] Nutrition Foundation. 1967. Present Knowledge of Nutrition. Ed. 3. New York.

[48] Oppenheimer, C. H., ed. 1968. Mar. Biol. Proc. 4th Int. Interdisciplinary Conf., 1966.

[49] Oser, B. L., ed. 1965. Hawk's Physiological Chemistry. Ed. 14. McGraw-Hill, Blakiston Division, New York.

[50] Razin, S. 1969. Annu. Rev. Microbiol. 23:317.

[51] Robbins, W. J., and V. Kavanagh. 1942. Bot. Rev. 8:411.

[52] Robinson, F. A. 1951. The Vitamin B Complex. J. Wiley, New York.

[53] Scott, M. L., et al. 1969. Nutrition of the Chicken. M. L. Scott, Ithaca, N.Y.

[54] Sebrell, W. H., Jr., and R. S. Harris. 1954. The Vitamins. Academic Press, New York. v. 1 & 2.

[55] Sebrell, W. H., Jr., and R. S. Harris. 1967-70. Ibid. Ed. 2. v. 1-3.

[56] Skoog, F., ed. 1951. Plant Growth Substances. Univ. Wisconsin Press, Madison.

[57] Snell, E. E. 1950. In P. György, ed. Vitamin Methods. Academic Press, New York. v. 1, pp. 327-505.

[58] Somogyi, J. C. 1966. Antivitamins. S. Karger, Basel.

[59] Stanier, R. Y., et al. 1970. The Microbial World. Ed. 3. Prentice-Hall, Englewood Cliffs, N.J.

[60] Stecher, P. G., et al., ed. 1968. The Merck Index. Ed. 8. Merck, Rahway, N.J.

[61] Trager, W. 1947. Biol. Rev. Cambridge Phil. Soc. 22:148.

[62] Wagner, A. F., and K. Folkers. 1964. Vitamins and Coenzymes. Interscience, New York.

[63] White, A., et al. 1968. Principles of Biochemistry. Ed. 4. McGraw-Hill, New York.

[64] Wigglesworth, V. B. 1965. The Principles of Insect Physiology. Ed. 6. Methuen, London.

[65] Williams, R. J., et al. 1950. The Biochemistry of B Vitamins. Reinhold, New York.

173. NUTRIENTS: MISCELLANEOUS GROWTH FACTORS

Many of the compounds listed are utilized by some organisms only for their carbon, nitrogen, and/or hydrogen content (e.g., carbon dioxide, glutamine, and asparagine). *Abbreviations and Symbols:* Capital letters indicate data are pertinent to all organisms studied; lower case letters and symbols indicate data apply to one or more species or strains, but not to all forms studied. R and r = required; ℞ = not required; rm = required by one or more mutants; ⊫ = replaces effectively, or is utilized interchangeably with, one or more substances, but one of the interchangeable substances must be present; s = stimulates growth or other processes; i = inhibits growth or other processes.

Nutrient	Vertebrates	Insects	Protozoans[1]	Prokaryotes[2]	Algae	Fungi	Spermatophytes
1 Adenylthiomethylpentose	℞	℞	℞	℞	R	℞	℞
2 o-Aminobenzoic acid[3]	℞	℞	℞	r, ⊫	℞	r, rm, ⊫[4]	℞
3 Antibiotics[5]	℞, s	℞	℞, s	℞, rm, i	℞	℞, s	℞, s
4 Asparagine	℞	℞	℞	r	℞	℞, s, i	℞

[1] Includes the colorless phytoflagellates. [2] Includes Schizomycetes, Rickettsiales, and Cyanophyta. [3] Synonym: anthranilic acid; precursor of niacin. [4] Substitutes for tryptophan and/or indole. [5] Aureomycin, penicillin, streptomycin, bacitracin, neomycin, and other anti-infective substances (e.g., arsenicals and sulfonamides, small amounts of which may stimulate growth).

continued

173. NUTRIENTS: MISCELLANEOUS GROWTH FACTORS

Nutrient	Vertebrates	Insects	Protozoans [1]	Prokaryotes [2]	Algae	Fungi	Spermatophytes
5 Bifidus factor	R	R	R	r	R	R	R
6 Carbon dioxide	R	R	r [6]	r	R	r [7], s, i	R
7 Carnitine	R	r [8]	R	R	R	R	R
8 Coprogen	R	R	R	R	R	R	R
9 N-d-Glucosylglycine ester	R	R	R	r	R	r	R
10 Glutamine	R	R	R	r, s	R	R, s, i	R
11 Glutathione	R	s [9]	R	r	R	R	R
12 Guanidine	R	R	r? [10]	R	R	R	R
13 Hematin [11]	R	r	r	r	R	r	R
14 p-Hydroxybenzoic acid	R	R	R	rm	R	rm	R
15 Indoleacetic acid [12]	R	R	R, s [13], i	R, s	R, s	r?, s	R, s
16 Mucin	R	R	R	r	R	R	R
17 Mycobactin [14]	R	R	R	r	R	R	R
18 Putrescine	R	R	R	r	R	rm	R
19 Quinic acid [15]	R	⊫ [16]	R	rm	R	rm	R
20 Shikimic acid [15]	R	⊫ [16]	R	rm	R	rm	R
21 Spermidine [17]	R	R	R	r	R	R	R
22 Strepogenin [18]	R	R	R	r [19], rm, s	R	R, s?	R
23 Thioctic acid [20]	R	R	r [21]	r, ⊫	R	R	R
24 Tricarboxylic acid cycle intermediates [22]	R	R	R, s [23]	r, rm	R	r	R
25 Unidentified factors [24]	r	r	r	r	.....	r	...
Reference	20,31,32, 38,39,45-47	17,18, 23, 37	6,10,12,14, 21,22,24-27, 30,34	19,41,42	16,24,25, 29,30, 35,36	1-5,8,9,11, 13,15,19, 43	7,28,33,40,44

[1] Includes the colorless phytoflagellates. [2] Includes Schizomycetes, Rickettsiales, and Cyanophyta. [6] Required by some colorless phytoflagellates. [7] Required in higher-than-atmospheric concentrations by some species, and essential in anaerobic growth of *Mucor rouxii*. [8] Required by *Tenebrio molitor;* interchangeable with 4-amino-3-hydroxybutyric acid. [9] Stimulates larval growth of *Aedes aegypti* and *Drosophila*. [10] May be required in vitro by *Plasmodium;* not required by *Tetrahymena*. [11] Also hemin, protohemin, protoporphyrin, and several other porphyrins. [12] And related auxins. [13] Stimulates growth of *Euglena gracilis*. [14] $C_{47}H_{75}ON_5$. [15] Probable precursor of aromatic amino acids. [16] Spares or replaces phenylalanine or tyrosine in *Blattella germanica*. [17] Also agmatine and spermine. [18] Also d-alanylhistidine, amino-*n*-butyryl-l-histidine, car-

nosine, and various tyrosine peptides. [19] The "streptogenin" requirement of *Lactobacillus casei* can be overcome by glutamic acid, cysteine, and serine. [20] Exists in tissues as lipothiamide, which catalyzes the oxidation of pyruvate and α-ketoglutarate. [21] Required by *Tetrahymena geleii* (8 strains) and *T. vorax* (2 strains); spared but not replaced by acetate; may be required by *Peranema trichophorum*. [22] Acetate, citrate, fumarate, α-ketoglutarate, oxalacetate, succinate, *cis*-aconitate, isocitrate, malate, and oxalosuccinate. [23] Several intermediates are utilized for growth by the "acetate" flagellates; acetate is used by most species. Utilization or availability of individual intermediates and related compounds (such as pyruvate) varies widely among species. [24] Tissue extracts and unknown substances or complexes in living tissue or protoplasm.

Contributors: Eveleigh, Douglas E.; Fogg, G. E.; Hansard, Sam L.; House, H. L.; Kratzer, F. H.; Vestal, J. Robie

References

[1] Adler, H. I., ed. 1969. Microbial Genet. Bull. 31.
[2] Ainsworth, G. C., and A. S. Sussman, ed. 1965. The Fungi. Academic Press, New York. v. 1.
[3] Archibald, R. M., and F. Reiss. 1950. Ann. N.Y. Acad. Sci. 50:1388.
[4] Bachmann, B. J., ed. 1970. Neurospora Newslett. 16.
[5] Barratt, R. W., et al. 1965. Genetics 52:233.
[6] Bessey, O. A., et al. 1953. Annu. Rev. Biochem. 22: 545.
[7] Bonner, J., and A. W. Galston. 1952. Principles of Plant Physiology. W. H. Freeman, San Francisco.
[8] Brock, T. D. 1970. Biology of Microorganisms. Prentice-Hall, Englewood Cliffs, N.J.
[9] Burnett, J. H. 1968. Fundamentals of Mycology. St. Martin, New York.
[10] Calkins, G., and F. M. Summers, ed. 1964. Protozoa in Biological Research. S. Hafner, New York.
[11] Cockrane, V. W. 1958. Physiology of Fungi. J. Wiley, New York.

continued

[12] Cowperthwaite, J., et al. 1953. Ann. N.Y. Acad. Sci. 56:972.

[13] Davis, B. D. 1950. Nature (London) 166:1120.

[14] Doyle, W. L. 1943. Biol. Rev. Cambridge Phil. Soc. 18:119.

[15] Foster, J. W. 1949. Chemical Activities of Fungi. Academic Press, New York.

[16] Ghosh, B. P., and R. H. Burris. 1950. Soil Sci. 70(3): 187.

[17] Gilmour, D. 1961. Biochemistry of Insects. Academic Press, New York.

[18] Gordon, H. T. Unpublished. Univ. California Dep. Entomology, Berkeley, 1953.

[19] Guirard, B. M., and E. E. Snell. 1962. Bacteria 4: 33.

[20] Guyton, A. C. 1966. Textbook of Medical Physiology. Ed. 3. W. B. Saunders, Philadelphia.

[21] Hall, R. P. 1953. Protozoology. Prentice-Hall, New York.

[22] Hall, R. P. 1965. Protozoan Nutrition. Blaisdell, New York.

[23] House, H. L. 1962. Annu. Rev. Biochem. 31:653.

[24] Hutner, S. H., ed. 1964. Biochemistry and Physiology of Protozoa. Academic Press, New York. v. 3.

[25] Hutner, S. H., and A. Lwoff, ed. 1955. Ibid. v. 2.

[26] Kidder, G. W. 1947. Ann. N.Y. Acad. Sci. 49:99.

[27] Kidder, G. W. 1951. Annu. Rev. Microbiol. 5:139.

[28] Klosa, J. 1952. Naturwissenschaften 39:405.

[29] Lewin, R. A., ed. 1962. Physiology and Biochemistry of Algae. Academic Press, New York.

[30] Lwoff, A., ed. 1951. Biochemistry and Physiology of Protozoa. Academic Press, New York. v. 1.

[31] Maynard, L. A., and J. K. Loosli. 1969. Animal Nutrition. Ed. 6. McGraw-Hill, New York.

[32] Meister, A. 1965. Biochemistry of the Amino Acids. Academic Press, New York.

[33] Miller, E. C. 1938. Plant Physiology. Ed. 2. McGraw-Hill, New York.

[34] Miner, R. W. 1953. Ann. N.Y. Acad. Sci. 56:815.

[35] Myers, J. 1951. Annu. Rev. Microbiol. 5:157.

[36] Sager, R., and S. Granick. 1953. Ann. N.Y. Acad. Sci. 56:831.

[37] Schultz, J., et al. 1946. Anat. Rec. 96:540.

[38] Scott, M. L., et al. 1969. Nutrition of the Chicken. M. L. Scott, Ithaca, N.Y.

[39] Sebrell, W. H., Jr., and R. S. Harris. 1954. The Vitamins. Academic Press, New York. v. 1 & 2.

[40] Skoog, F., ed. 1951. Plant Growth Substances. Univ. Wisconsin Press, Madison.

[41] Snell, E. E. 1949. Annu. Rev. Microbiol. 3:97.

[42] Snell, E. E. 1951. In C. H. Werkman and P. W. Wilson, ed. Bacterial Physiology. Academic Press, New York. pp. 215-256.

[43] Stanier, R. Y., et al. 1970. The Microbial World. Ed. 3. Prentice-Hall, Englewood Cliffs, N.J.

[44] Steward, F. C., ed. 1965. Plant Physiology. McGraw-Hill, New York. v. 4A.

[45] Vallee, B. L., and W. E. C. Wacker. 1970. In H. Neurath, ed. The Proteins. Ed. 2. Academic Press, New York. v. 5.

[46] West, E. S., et al. 1966. Textbook of Biochemistry. Ed. 4. Macmillan, New York.

[47] White, A., et al. 1968. Principles of Biochemistry. Ed. 4. McGraw-Hill, New York.

174. NUTRITIONAL STANDARDS: MAN

Part I. United States: Children and Adults

Daily allowances are those recommended by the Food and Nutrition Board, National Research Council (1968 revision) for the maintenance of good nutrition in nearly all normal, healthy people in the United States, under usual environmental stresses. These allowances can be obtained from a variety of common foods that also provide other nutrients for which human requirements are less well defined. For a detailed discussion of dietary allowances, formulas for adjusting calorie allowances at various body weights and ages, and information on nutrients not tabulated, consult the reference. **Age:** Values are for midpoint of range, unless otherwise indicated. **Niacin** equivalents include dietary sources of the vitamin itself, plus 1 mgEq for each 60 mg of dietary tryptophan. **Folic Acid** allowances refer to dietary sources as determined by the *Lactobacillus casei* assay. Pure forms of folic acid may be effective in doses less than one-fourth the recommended daily allowance.

Subjects						Water-soluble Vitamins							Fat-soluble Vitamins			Minerals				
Sex	Age yr[1]	Wt kg	Ht cm	Calories	Protein g	Thiamine mg	Riboflavin mg	Niacin mgEq	B6 mg	Folic Acid mg	B12 µg	Ascorbic Acid mg	A IU	D IU	E IU	Ca g	I µg	Fe mg	Mg mg	P g
1 ♂♀	0-2 mo	4	55	kg × 120	kg × 2.2[2]	0.2	0.4	5	0.2	0.05	1.0	35	1500	400	5	0.4	25	6	40	0.2

[1] Unless otherwise specified. [2] Assumes protein equivalent to human milk; for proteins not 100% utilized, factors should be increased proportionately.

continued

174. NUTRITIONAL STANDARDS: MAN

Part I. United States: Children and Adults

						Water-soluble Vitamins							Fat-soluble Vitamins			Minerals				
	Sex	Age yr[1]	Wt kg	Ht cm	Calories	Protein g	Thiamine mg	Riboflavin mg	Niacin mgEq	B6 mg	Folic Acid mg	B12 µg	Ascorbic Acid mg	A IU	D IU	E IU	Ca g	I µg	Fe mg	Mg mg	P g
2		2-6 mo	7	63	kg×110	kg×2.0[2]	0.4	0.5	7	0.3	0.05	1.5	35	1500	400	5	0.5	40	10	60	0.4
3		0.5-1	9	72	kg×100	kg×1.8[2]	0.5	0.6	8	0.4	0.1	2.0	35	1500	400	5	0.6	45	15	70	0.5
4		1-2	12	81	1100	25	0.6	0.6	8	0.5	0.1	2.0	40	2000	400	10	0.7	55	15	100	0.7
5		2-3	14	91	1250	25	0.6	0.7	8	0.6	0.2	2.5	40	2000	400	10	0.8	60	15	150	0.8
6		3-4	16	100	1400	30	0.7	0.8	9	0.7	0.2	3	40	2500	400	10	0.8	70	10	200	0.8
7		4-6	19	110	1600	30	0.8	0.9	11	0.9	0.2	4	40	2500	400	10	0.8	80	10	200	0.8
8		6-8	23	121	2000	35	1.0	1.1	13	1.0	0.2	4	40	3500	400	15	0.9	100	10	250	0.9
9		8-10	28	131	2200	40	1.1	1.2	15	1.2	0.3	5	40	3500	400	15	1.0	110	10	250	1.0
10	♂	10-12	35	140	2500	45	1.3	1.3	17	1.4	0.4	5	40	4500	400	20	1.2	125	10	300	1.2
11		12-14	43	151	2700	50	1.4	1.4	18	1.6	0.4	5	45	5000	400	20	1.4	135	18	350	1.4
12		14-18	59	170	3000	60	1.5	1.5	20	1.8	0.4	5	55	5000	400	25	1.4	150	18	400	1.4
13		18-22	67	175	2800	60	1.4	1.6	18	2.0	0.4	5	60	5000	400	30	0.8	140	10	400	0.8
14		22-35[3]	70	175	2800	65	1.4	1.7	18	2.0	0.4	5	60	5000	....	30	0.8	140	10	350	0.8
15		35-55	70	173	2600	65	1.3	1.7	17	2.0	0.4	5	60	5000	....	30	0.8	125	10	350	0.8
16		55 to 75+	70	171	2400	65	1.2	1.7	14	2.0	0.4	6	60	5000	....	30	0.8	110	10	350	0.8
17	♀	10-12	35	142	2250	50	1.1	1.3	15	1.4	0.4	5	40	4500	400	20	1.2	110	18	300	1.2
18		12-14	44	154	2300	50	1.2	1.4	15	1.6	0.4	5	45	5000	400	20	1.3	115	18	350	1.3
19		14-16	52	157	2400	55	1.2	1.4	16	1.8	0.4	5	50	5000	400	25	1.3	120	18	350	1.3
20		16-18	54	160	2300	55	1.2	1.5	15	2.0	0.4	5	50	5000	400	25	1.3	115	18	350	1.3
21		18-22	58	163	2000	55	1.0	1.5	13	2.0	0.4	5	55	5000	400	25	0.8	100	18	350	0.8
22		22-35[3]	58	163	2000	55	1.0	1.5	13	2.0	0.4	5	55	5000	....	25	0.8	100	18	300	0.8
23		35-55	58	160	1850	55	1.0	1.5	13	2.0	0.4	5	55	5000	....	25	0.8	90	18	300	0.8
24		55 to 75+	58	157	1700	55	1.0	1.5	13	2.0	0.4	6	55	5000	....	25	0.8	80	10	300	0.8
25	Pregnant				+200[4]	65	+0.1[4]	1.8	15	2.5	0.8	8	60	6000	400	30	+0.4[4]	125	18	450	+0.4[4]
26	Lactating				+1000[4]	75	+0.5[4]	2.0	20	2.5	0.5	6	60	8000	400	30	+0.5[4]	150	18	450	+0.5[4]

[1] Unless otherwise specified. [2] Assumes protein equivalent to human milk; for proteins not 100% utilized, factors should be increased proportionately. [3] Values are for reference subjects at age 22. [4] Allowance is in addition to that given for the nonpregnant and nonlactating woman of similar age.

Contributor: Johnson, Paul E.

Reference: National Research Council, Food and Nutrition Board. 1968. Nat. Acad. Sci. Publ. 1694.

Part II. Canada and United Kingdom: Children and Adults

Individuals vary in their needs for energy and nutrients beyond the requirements imposed by body size, sex, and occupation. The quantity of a nutrient required may also depend on the quality of the diet, since the efficiency with which nutrients are absorbed and utilized by the body is influenced by the composition and nature of the diet as a whole. The dietary standard for Canada recommends daily intake of nutrients adequate for the maintenance of health among the majority of Canadians; allowances are in excess of known minimal requirements. For the United Kingdom, recommended intakes are the amounts sufficient, or more than sufficient, for the nutritional needs of practically all

continued

Part II. Canada and United Kingdom: Children and Adults

healthy persons in a population. **Weight:** United Kingdom values for children and adolescents are 1965 averages in London [3]; values for adults are those recommended for the 1957 FAO (Food and Agriculture Organization) reference man and woman, with a nominal reduction for the elderly. **Protein:** Canadian values are based on the Canadian dietary net protein utilization value of 70, when protein is fed at the 10% level; United Kingdom values are recommended intakes calculated to provide 10% of the daily energy requirements. **Thiamine:** Values for the United Kingdom were calculated from energy requirements and the recommended in-

take of 0.4 mg/1000 calories. **Vitamin A:** Canadian values are based on a mixed diet containing equal parts of vitamin A and carotene; the suggested intake of preformed vitamin A is approximately two-thirds the indicated recommendation. For a discussion of United Kingdom values for vitamin A, consult reference 2. **Vitamin D:** No dietary source may be necessary for subjects adequately exposed to sunlight; requirement for the housebound may be greater than the amounts recommended. Data in brackets refer to the column heading in brackets.

	Subjects					Water-soluble Vitamins				Fat-soluble Vitamins		Minerals [1]	
Sex	Age yr	Wt kg	Calories	Protein g	Thiamine mg	Riboflavin mg	Niacin mg [mgEq [2]]	Ascorbic Acid mg	A IU [retinol equivalent [3]]	D IU [μg chole- calciferol]	Ca [4] g	Fe mg
							Canada [1]						
1	♂♀ 0-1	3.2-9.1	360-900	7-13	0.3	0.5	3	20	1000	400	0.5	5
2	1-2	9.1-11.8	900-1200	12-16	0.4	0.6	4	20	1000	400	0.7	5
3	2-3	14.1	1400	17	0.4	0.7	4	20	1000	400	0.7	5
4	4-6	18.1	1700	20	0.5	0.9	5	20	1000	400	0.7	5
5	7-9	25.9	2100	24	0.7	1.1	7	30	1500	400	1.0	5
6	10-12	34.9	2500	30	0.8	1.3	8	30	2000	400	1.2	12
7	♂ 13-15	49.0	3100	40	0.9	1.6	9	30	2700	400	1.2	12
8	16-17	61.7	3700	45	1.1	1.9	11	30	3200	400	1.2	12
9	18-19	65.3	3800	47	1.1	1.9	11	30	3200	400	0.9	6
10	25-29	71.7	2850[5]	48	0.9	1.4	9	30	3700	....	0.5	6
11	♀ 13-15	49.0	2600	39	0.8	1.3	8	30	2700	400	1.2	12
12	16-17	54.4	2400	41	0.7	1.2	7	30	3200	400	1.2	12
13	18-19	56.2	2450	41	0.7	1.2	7	30	3200	400	0.9	10
14	25-29	56.2	2400[5]	39	0.7	1.2	7	30	3700	....	0.5	10
15	Pregnant [6]	56.2	Up to 2900	39 [7]; 48 [8]	0.85	1.45	8.5	40	4200	400	1.2	13
16	Lactating [9]	56.2	2900-3400	62	1.0	1.7	10	50	5200	400	1.2	13
						United Kingdom [10] [2]							
17	♂♀ 0-1	7.3	800	20	0.3	0.4	[5]	15	[450]	[10]	0.6 [11]	6 [11]
18	1-2	11.4	1200	30	0.5	0.6	[7]	20	[300]	[10]	0.5	7
19	2-3	13.5	1400	35	0.6	0.7	[8]	20	[300]	[10]	0.5	7
20	3-5	16.5	1600	40	0.6	0.8	[9]	20	[300]	[10]	0.5	8
21	5-7	20.5	1800	45	0.7	0.9	[10]	20	[300]	[2.5]	0.5	8
22	7-9	25.1	2100	53	0.8	1.0	[11]	20	[400]	[2.5]	0.5	10
23	♂ 9-12	31.9	2500	63	1.0	1.2	[14]	25	[575]	[2.5]	0.7	13
24	12-15	45.5	2800	70	1.1	1.4	[16]	25	[725]	[2.5]	0.7	14
25	15-18	61.0	3000	75	1.2	1.7	[19]	30	[750]	[2.5]	0.6	15

[1] Iodine in table salt in proportions of 1:10,000, as prevails in Canada, meets Canadian requirements. The British Medical Association (1950) recommended daily intakes of 100 μg iodine for adults and 150 μg for children, adolescents, and pregnant and lactating women. [2] 1 niacin equivalent = 1 mg available niacin or 60 mg tryptophan. [3] 1 retinol equivalent = 1 μg retinol or 6 μg β-carotene or 12 μg other biologically active carotenoids. [4] For Canadians, phosphorus intake should equal calcium intake. [5] For subjects in the lightest work category (regarded as typical). [6] Except for protein, increases are for the third

trimester only. [7] For the first trimester (from Protein Revision to reference 1, 23 Dec. 1968). [8] For the second and third trimesters. [9] Average daily secretion during lactation was 850 ml. [10] Ages of subjects in the United Kingdom were measured from one birthday to the next. Unless otherwise indicated, other values are midpoints of ranges. [11] Infants were not breast-fed. Infants entirely breast-fed receive smaller quantities of calcium and iron; these smaller quantities are adequate, since absorption from breast milk is higher.

continued

Part II. Canada and United Kingdom: Children and Adults

	Subjects					Water-soluble Vitamins				Fat-soluble Vitamins		Minerals 1/	
	Sex	Age yr	Wt kg	Calories	Protein g	Thiamine mg	Riboflavin mg	Niacin mg [mgEq 2/]	Ascorbic Acid mg	A IU [retinol equivalent 3/]	D IU [μg cholecalciferol]	Ca 4/ g	Fe mg
26		18-35 12,13/	65	2700	68	1.1	1.7	[18]	30	[750]	[2.5]	0.5	10
27		18-35 12,14/	65	3000	75	1.2	1.7	[18]	30	[750]	[2.5]	0.5	10
28		18-35 12,15/	65	3600	90	1.4	1.7	[18]	30	[750]	[2.5]	0.5	10
29		35-65 13/	65	2600	65	1.0	1.7	[18]	30	[750]	[2.5]	0.5	10
30		35-65 14/	65	2900	73	1.2	1.7	[18]	30	[750]	[2.5]	0.5	10
31		35-65 15/	65	3600	90	1.4	1.7	[18]	30	[750]	[2.5]	0.5	10
32		65-75 13/	63	2350	59	0.9	1.7	[18]	30	[750]	[2.5]	0.5	10
33		75 & over 13/	63	2100	53	0.8	1.7	[18]	30	[750]	[2.5]	0.5	10
34	♀	9-12	33	2300	58	0.9	1.2	[13]	25	[575]	[2.5]	0.7	13
35		12-15	48.6	2300	58	0.9	1.4	[16]	25	[725]	[2.5]	0.7	14
36		15-18	56.1	2300	58	0.9	1.4	[16]	30	[750]	[2.5]	0.6	15
37		18-55 16,17/	55	2200	55	0.9	1.3	[15]	30	[750]	[2.5]	0.5	12
38		18-55 15,16/	55	2500	63	1.0	1.3	[15]	30	[750]	[2.5]	0.5	12
39		55-75 13/	53	2050	51	0.8	1.3	[15]	30	[750]	[2.5]	0.5	10
40		75 & over 13/	53	1900	48	0.7	1.3	[15]	30	[750]	[2.5]	0.5	10
41	Pregnant 8/	....		2400	60	1.0	1.6	[18]	60	[750]	[10] 18/	1.2 19/	15
42	Lactating	....		2700	68	1.1	1.8	[21]	60	[1200]	[10]	1.2	15

1/ Iodine in table salt in proportions of 1:10,000, as prevails in Canada, meets Canadian requirements. The British Medical Association (1950) recommended daily intakes of 100 μg iodine for adults and 150 μg for children, adolescents, and pregnant and lactating women. 2/ 1 niacin equivalent = 1 mg available niacin or 60 mg tryptophan. 3/ 1 retinol equivalent = 1 μg retinol or 6 μg β-carotene or 12 μg other biologically active carotenoids. 4/ For Canadians, phosphorus intake should equal calcium intake. 8/ For the second and third trimesters. 12/ Values are for 25-year-olds. 13/ Sedentary. 14/ Moderately active. 15/ Very active. 16/ Values are for 35-year-olds. 17/ In most occupations. 18/ For all three trimesters. 19/ For the third trimester only.

Contributors: Monagle, J. E.; Leitch, Isabella

References
[1] Canadian Council on Nutrition. 1964. Can. Bull. Nutr. 6(1).
[2] Department of Health and Social Security, London. 1969. Rep. Publ. Health Med. Subj. 120.
[3] Tanner, J. M., et al. 1965. Arch. Dis. Childhood 41:613.

Part III. Other Countries and United Nations Agency: Adults

Different criteria were used in each country to determine dietary standards for the reference man and woman; therefore no uniform agreement exists among countries as to the nutrient allowances considered desirable. For a discussion of the criteria used in each country, consult the reference.

	Country or Agency	Subjects					Water-soluble Vitamins					Minerals	
		Sex	Age yr	Wt kg	Calories	Protein g	Thiamine mg	Riboflavin mg	Niacin Equivalent mg	Ascorbic Acid mg	Vitamin A IU	Ca g	Fe mg
1	Australia	♂	25	70	2900	70 1/	1.2	1.5	18 2/	30	2500 3/	0.4-0.8	10
2		♀	25	58	2100	58 1/	0.8	1.1	14 2/	30	2500 3/	0.4-0.8	10
3	Central America	♂	25	55	2700	65 4/	1.1	1.6	17.8	60	Fn 5/	0.45	10
4	& Panama	♀	25	50	2000	60 4/	0.8	1.2	13.2	50	Fn 5/	0.45	10

1/ A practical protein allowance may be calculated on the basis of 10-12% of the calories being derived from protein. 2/ Preformed niacin + (grams protein × 0.16). 3/ 3 IU carotene is equivalent to 1 IU vitamin A activity. 4/ 30% as protein of high biological value. 5/ 1.3 mg vitamin A alcohol is recommended; one-fifth of the ingested total is assumed to be preformed vitamin A, and four-fifths to be β-carotene. 1 IU = 0.3 μg vitamin A alcohol.

continued

Part III. Other Countries and United Nations Agency: Adults

| Country or Agency | Subjects | | | Calories | Protein g | Water-soluble Vitamins | | | | Vitamin A IU | Minerals | |
	Sex	Age yr	Wt kg			Thiamine mg	Riboflavin mg	Niacin Equivalent mg	Ascorbic Acid mg		Ca g	Fe mg
5 Colombia	♂	20-29	65	2850	68	1.1	1.7	18.8	50	5000	0.5	10
6	♀	20-29	55	1900	60	0.8	1.1	12.5	50	5000	0.5	15
7 France	♂	....	65	3000[6]	90[7]	......	...	.....	......	....	....	...
8	♀	....	55	2400[6]	75[7]	......	...	.....	......	....	....	...
9 Germany, East	♂	18-35	....	2700	85[8]	1.6	1.5	18	70	5000	0.8	10
10	♀	18-35	....	2300	75[8]	1.4	1.3	15	70	5000	0.8	15
11 West	♂	25	72	2550	72	1.7	1.8	18	75	5000[9]	0.8	10
12	♀	25	60	2200	60	1.5	1.8	14	75	5000[9]	0.8	12
13 India	♂	25.4	55	2800	55[10]	....	...	.....	......	....	....	...
14	♀	21.5	45	2300	45[10]	....	...	.....	......	....	....	...
15 Japan	♂	26-29	56[11]	3000	70	1.5	1.5	15	65	2000[12]	0.6	10
16	♀	26-29	49[11]	2400	60	1.2	1.2	12	60	2000[12]	0.6	10
17 Netherlands	♂	20-29	70	3000	70[13]	1.2	1.8	12	50	5500[14]	1.0	10
18	♀	20-29	60	2400	60[13]	1.0	1.5	10	50	5500[14]	1.0	12
19 Norway	♂	25	70	3400	70	1.7	1.8	17	30	2500[15]	0.8	12
20	♀	25	60	2500	60	1.3	1.5	13	30	2500[15]	0.8	12
21 Philippines	♂	....	53	2400	53	1.2	1.2	.....	70	5000[16]	0.5	...
22	♀	....	46	1800	46	0.9	0.9	.....	70	5000[16]	0.5	...
23 South Africa	♂	....	73	3000	65	1.0	1.6	15	40	4000[17]	0.7	9
24	♀	....	60	2300	55	0.8	1.4	12	40	4000[17]	0.6	12
25 Union of Soviet	♂	....	....	....	......	2.0[18]	2.5	15	70[18]	5000[19]	....	...
26 Socialist Republics	♀	....	....	....	......	2.0[18]	2.5	15	70[18]	5000[19]	....	...
27 FAO[20]	♂	25	65	3200	46[21]	1.3	1.8	21.1	......	Fn[22]	0.4-0.5	...
28	♀	25	65	2300	39[21]	0.9	1.3	15.2	......	Fn[22]	0.4-0.5	...

6/ Includes up to 10% alcohol. 7/ More than 25% as animal protein. 8/ Protein allowance is 12% of calories. 9/ Four-fifths of the vitamin A allowance is assumed to be contributed by carotene. 10/ Allowance is 1 g vegetable protein per kilogram body weight in properly balanced diets. 11/ 1961 average. 12/ Or 6000 IU carotene. 13/ One-third of the protein allowance is assumed to be from animal sources. 14/ 1500 IU is assumed to be preformed vitamin A, and 4000 IU is assumed to be carotene. 15/ In animal foods.

16/ 90% vitamin A allowance is assumed to be contributed by carotene. 17/ Two-thirds vitamin A allowance is assumed to be contributed by carotene. 18/ Increased up to 50% in the far north. 19/ IU is equivalent to 0.3 μg natural vitamin. 20/ Food and Agriculture Organization of the United Nations. 21/ Based on 0.71 g protein per kilogram body weight; value is 20% above the requirements for reference protein. 22/ 750 μg retinol; 1 μg β-carotene is equivalent to 0.167 μg retinol.

Contributor: Johnson, Paul E.

Reference: National Research Council, Food and Nutrition Board. 1968. Nat. Acad. Sci. Publ. 1694:68.

175. NUTRITIONAL STANDARDS: DOMESTIC ANIMALS

Part I. General Requirements

Values are given in terms of requirements per animal per day, unless otherwise indicated. **Avg Daily Gain:** Values enclosed in ⟨brackets⟩ refer to the specification similarly enclosed. **DE** = apparent digestible energy. **ME** = metabolizable energy; calculations for sheep and dairy cattle are based on the assumption that ME = 0.82 DE, for rabbits on ME = 0.95 DE, and for swine on ME = 0.96 DE. **TDN** = total digestible nutrient; calculations for beef cattle are based on 3.6155 kcal ME/g TDN; and for dairy cattle, horse, sheep, and swine on 4.4 kcal DE/g TDN. Data in [brackets] refer to the column heading in [brackets].

continued

Part I. General Requirements

	Subjects	Specification	Body Weight kg	Avg Daily Gain [1] g	Daily Feed g	Protein Total g	Protein Digestible g	DE [1], kcal [ME, Mcal]	TDN kg	Reference
	Bos taurus, beef [2]									3
1	Steer	Growth	150	0	2700	210	110	[5.6]	1.5	
2				250	3100	340	220	[7.1]	2.0	
3				500	3200	390	260	[8.4]	2.3	
4				750	3200	430	290	[9.0]	2.5	
5			200	0	3300	260	140	[6.8]	1.9	
6				250	4500	450	270	[9.3]	2.6	
7				500	4900	540	350	[11.2]	3.1	
8				750	5000	560	360	[12.5]	3.5	
9			300	0	4500	350	190	[9.3]	2.6	
10				250	6100	540	320	[12.6]	3.5	
11				500	7700	770	470	[15.9]	4.4	
12				750	8000	890	570	[18.2]	5.0	
13			400	0	5600	440	240	[11.5]	3.2	
14				250	7700	640	350	[15.9]	4.4	
15				500	9700	860	500	[20.0]	5.5	
16				750	9900	880	510	[22.6]	6.3	
17	Calf	Finishing	150	900	3500	450	300	[9.9]	2.7	
18			200	1000	5000	610	410	[13.4]	3.7	
19			300	1100	7100	870	580	[19.0]	5.3	
20			400	1100	8800	980	620	[23.5]	6.5	
21			450	1050	9400	1040	670	[25.1]	6.9	
22	Yearling	Finishing	250	1300	7200	800	510	[18.8]	5.2	
23			300	1300	8300	920	920	[21.7]	6.0	
24			400	1300	10,300	1140	730	[26.9]	7.4	
25			500	1200	11,500	1280	820	[30.0]	8.3	
26	2-yr old	Finishing	350	1400	10,300	1140	730	[26.4]	7.3	
27			400	1400	11,300	1250	800	[28.9]	8.0	
28			500	1400	13,400	1490	950	[34.3]	9.5	
29			550	1300	13,700	1520	970	[35.1]	9.7	
30	Bull, moderately	Growth &	300	1000	8700	1210	840	[20.4]	5.6	
31	active	mainte-	400	900	10,000	1330	900	[23.5]	6.5	
32		nance	500	700	12,000	1600	1080	[25.8]	7.1	
33			600	500	11,600	1420	940	[24.9]	6.9	
34			700	300	12,700	1410	900	[26.2]	7.2	
35			800	0	9900	990	600	[20.4]	5.6	
36			900	0	10,700	1070	650	[22.0]	6.1	
37	Heifer	Growth	150	0	2700	210	110	[5.6]	1.5	
38				250	3200	360	230	[7.3]	2.0	
39				500	3200	390	260	[8.4]	2.3	
40				750	3300	440	300	[9.3]	2.6	
41			200	0	3300	260	140	[6.8]	1.9	
42				250	4600	460	280	[9.5]	2.6	
43				500	5000	560	360	[11.4]	3.2	
44				750	5400	600	380	[13.5]	3.7	
45			300	0	4500	350	190	[9.3]	2.6	
46				250	6200	550	320	[12.8]	3.5	
47				500	8200	820	500	[16.9]	4.7	
48				750	8600	950	610	[19.6]	5.4	

[1] Unless otherwise indicated. [2] Requirements are based on dry feed containing 100% dry matter.

continued

Part I. General Requirements

	Subjects	Specification	Body Weight kg	Avg Daily Gain g	Daily Feed g	Protein Total g	Protein Digestible g	DE, kcal [ME, Mcal]	TDN kg	Reference
49			400	0	5600	440	240	[11.5]	3.2	
50				250	7700	640	350	[15.9]	4.4	
51				500	10,200	910	530	[21.0]	5.8	
52				750	10,600	940	550	[24.2]	6.7	
53	Calf	Finishing	150	800	3500	450	300	[9.9]	2.7	
54			200	900	5000	610	410	[13.4]	3.7	
55			300	1000	7300	890	590	[19.5]	5.4	
56			400	950	8700	970	620	[23.2]	6.4	
57	Yearling	Finishing	250	1200	7600	840	540	[19.8]	5.5	
58			300	1200	8600	950	610	[22.4]	6.2	
59			400	1200	10,700	1190	760	[27.9]	7.7	
60			450	1100	11,000	1220	780	[28.7]	7.9	
61	Cow, dry	Pregnancy	350	....	5800	340	160	[10.3]	2.8	
62			400	....	6400	380	180	[11.5]	3.2	
63			450	....	6800	400	190	[12.4]	3.4	
64			500	....	7600	440	210	[13.6]	3.8	
65			550	....	8000	470	220	[14.4]	4.0	
66			600	....	8600	500	240	[15.5]	4.3	
67	nursing calf	First 3-4 mo	350	....	8600	790	460	[17.7]	4.9	
68		postpartum	400	....	9300	860	500	[19.2]	5.3	
69			450	....	9900	910	530	[20.4]	5.6	
70			500	....	10,500	970	570	[21.6]	6.0	
	B. taurus, dairy [3]									5
71	Veal calf	Growth &	35	500	700	155	130	3100	0.7	
72		finishing	40	800	1100	240	205	4800	1.1	
73			75	1000	1400	310	260	6200	1.4	
74			100	1150	1700	375	320	7500	1.7	
75			150	1300	2400	485	410	10,600	2.4	
	Bull									
76	Young (large	Growth	40	200	500	110	100	2200	0.5	
77	breeds)		45	300	600	135	120	2600	0.6	
78	5 wk	Growth	55	400	1200	180	145	4000	0.9	
79	9 wk	Growth	75	800	2100	345	255	6600	1.5	
80	13 wk	Growth	100	1000	3200	455	320	9700	2.2	
81	20 wk	Growth	150	1000	4500	520	355	13,200	3.0	
82	27 wk	Growth	200	1000	5900	595	390	16,700	3.8	
83	34 wk	Growth	250	1000	7300	670	430	19,800	4.5	
84	41 wk	Growth	300	1000	8700	745	465	22,900	5.2	
85	49 wk	Growth	350	1000	10,200	830	500	26,000	5.9	
86	56 wk	Growth	400	1000	11,800	930	540	29,100	6.6	
87	63 wk	Growth	450	1000	12,500	1055	590	30,800	7.0	
88	70 wk	Growth	500	900	13,000	1110	610	32,200	7.3	
89	79 wk	Growth	550	800	13,800	1160	625	33,900	7.7	
90	88 wk	Growth	600	700	13,800	1190	630	33,900	7.7	
91	99 wk	Growth	650	600	13,600	1220	635	33,500	7.6	
92	112 wk	Growth	700	500	13,400	1235	630	33,100	7.5	
93	128 wk	Growth	750	400	13,200	1240	620	32,600	7.4	
94	>128 wk	Growth	800	250	12,700	1165	570	31,300	7.1	
95			850	100	12,100	1060	510	30,000	6.8	
96	Mature	Maintenance	500	....	8300	640	300	20,300	4.6	
97		& breeding	600	....	9600	735	345	23,800	5.4	

[3] All feed data for dairy cattle on dry matter basis.

continued

Part I. General Requirements

	Subjects	Specification	Body Weight kg	Avg Daily Gain g	Daily Feed g	Protein Total g	Protein Digestible g	DE, kcal [ME, Mcal]	TDN kg	Reference
98			700	....	10,900	830	390	26,900	6.1	
99			800	....	12,000	915	430	29,500	6.7	
100			900	....	13,100	1000	470	32,200	7.3	
101			1000	....	14,100	1075	505	34,800	7.9	
102			1100	....	15,100	1160	545	37,000	8.4	
103			1200	....	16,100	1235	580	39,700	9.0	
104			1300	....	17,100	1310	615	42,300	9.6	
105			1400	....	18,100	1380	650	44,500	10.1	
106	Heifer (large	Growth	40	200	500[4]	110	100	2200	0.5	
107	breeds)		45	300	600[4]	135	120	2600	0.6	
108	5 wk	Growth	55	400	1200	180	145	4000	0.9	
109	10 wk	Growth	75	750	2100	330	245	6600	1.5	
110	15 wk	Growth	100	750	2900	370	260	8800	2.0	
111	24 wk	Growth	150	750	4100	435	295	11,900	2.7	
112	34 wk	Growth	200	750	5300	500	330	15,000	3.4	
113	43 wk	Growth	250	750	6500	570	365	17,600	4.0	
114	53 wk	Growth	300	750	7500	640	395	19,800	4.5	
115	62 wk	Growth	350	750	8400	715	430	21,600	4.9	
116	72 wk	Growth	400	750	9300	800	465	22,900	5.2	
117	82 wk	Growth	450	700	9500	885	495	23,400	5.3	
118	93 wk	Growth	500	600	9500	935	505	23,400	5.3	
119	107 wk	Growth	550	400	8900	915	475	22,000	5.0	
120	133 wk	Growth	600	150	8600	810	405	19,000	4.3	
121	Cow, mature	Mainte-	350	....	5000	468	220	12,300	2.8	
122		nance[4]	400	....	5500	521	245	13,600	3.1	
123			450	....	6000	585	275	15,000	3.4	
124			500	....	6500	638	300	16,300	3.7	
125			550	....	7000	691	325	17,600	4.0	
126			600	....	7500	734	345	18,900	4.2	
127			650	....	8000	776	365	19,800	4.5	
128			700	....	8500	830	390	21,100	4.8	
129			750	....	9000	872	410	22,000	5.0	
130			800	....	9500	915	430	23,300	5.3	
131		Maintenance	350	....	6400	570	315	15,800	3.6	
132		& pregnan-	400	....	7200	650	355	i7,200	4.0	
133		cy, last 2	450	....	7900	730	400	19,400	4.4	
134		mo	500	....	8600	780	430	21,100	4.8	
135			550	....	9300	850	465	22,900	5.2	
136			600	....	10,000	910	500	24,600	5.6	
137			650	....	10,600	960	530	26,400	6.0	
138			700	....	11,300	1000	555	27,700	6.3	
139			750	....	12,000	1080	595	29,500	6.7	
140			800	....	12,600	1150	630	31,200	7.1	
141	*Canis familaris*	Lactation	....	....	....	140-160[5]	105-123[5]	2700-3100[5]	0.6-0.7[2]	7
142	Young	Growth	2.3	....	180[6]	20	16	500	....	
143			4.5	....	300[6]	40	32	900	....	

[4] To allow for growth, add 20% to maintenance allowance during first lactation and 10% during second. [5] Per kg dry feed; amount needed varies with rate of milk production. [6] Young pups from 7-9 wk of age consume daily the equivalent of ∿7.5% of their body weight as air-dry food; this drops to the equivalent of ∿3.5% of their body weight at 18 wk of age. Values given are based on maximum requirements.

continued

Part I. General Requirements

	Subjects	Specification	Body Weight kg	Avg Daily Gain g	Daily Feed g	Protein Total g	Protein Digestible g	DE, kcal [ME, Mcal]	TDN kg	Reference
144			6.8	....	380[6]	60	48	1150	....	
145			9.1	....	490[6]	80	64	1450	....	
146			13.6	....	680[6]	120	96	2000	....	
147			22.7	....	1130[6]	200	160	3000	....	
148	Adult	Maintenance	2.3	0	90	10	8	250	....	
149			4.5	0	150	20	16	450	....	
150			6.8	0	190	30	24	550	....	
151			9.1	0	250	40	32	725	....	
152			13.6	0	340	60	48	1000	....	
153			22.7	0	570	100	80	1700	....	
154			50.0	0	1200	210	168	3500	....	
155	*Cavia porcellus*	Growth	....	....	8/100 g body wt	2/100 g body wt[7]	....	....	....	6
	Equus caballus[8,9]									2
156	270 kg at maturity	Growth	90	410	2770	360	240	7600	1.72	
157			185	180	2680	270	200	7400	1.68	
158			270	0	3400	270	190	9400	2.13	
159	365 kg at maturity	Growth	90	640	3040	500	340	8400	1.91	
160			185	410	4260	410	280	11,800	2.68	
161			270	230	4720	360	270	13,000	2.95	
162			365	0	4220	320	230	11,600	2.63	
163	455 kg at maturity	Growth	90	730	3040	540	380	8400	1.91	
164			185	540	4490	500	340	12,400	2.81	
165			270	360	5170	450	300	14,200	3.22	
166			365	230	5580	410	290	15,400	3.49	
167			455	0	4940	410	270	13,600	3.08	
168	545 kg at maturity	Growth	90	1000	3400	820	500	9400	2.13	
169			185	820	5080	640	450	14,000	3.18	
170			270	590	5940	540	390	16,400	3.72	
171			365	360	6080	500	340	16,800	3.81	
172			455	180	6080	450	320	18,800	3.81	
173			545	0	5670	450	310	15,600	3.54	
174	635 kg at maturity	Growth	90	1220	3630	860	600	10,000	2.27	
175			185	1000	5310	770	540	14,600	3.31	
176			270	820	6530	680	490	18,000	4.08	
177			365	590	6990	640	430	19,200	4.35	
178			455	360	6990	540	380	19,200	4.35	
179			545	180	6800	500	360	18,800	4.26	
180			635	0	6350	500	350	17,600	3.99	
181	Mature	Light work	185	0	3760	200	140	10,400	2.36	
182			270	0	5080	260	190	14,000	3.18	
183			365	0	6260	330	230	17,200	3.90	
184			455	0	7390	390	270	20,400	4.63	
185			545	0	8480	450	310	23,400	5.31	
186			635	0	9530	500	350	26,200	5.94	
187		Medium work	185	0	4350	200	140	12,000	2.72	
188			270	0	5900	260	190	16,200	3.67	

[6] Young pups from 7-9 wk of age consume daily the equivalent of ∼7.5% of their body weight as air-dry food; this drops to the equivalent of ∼3.5% of their body weight at 18 wk of age. Values given are based on maximum requirements. [7] Total protein required is 25-30 g/100 g diet.

[8] Requirements are based on air-dry feed containing 90% dry matter. [9] Little specific information exists on nutrient requirements of horses; data were derived in many instances from experimental results obtained with cattle.

continued

Part I. General Requirements

	Subjects	Specification	Body Weight kg	Avg Daily Gain [1] g	Daily Feed g	Protein Total g	Protein Digestible g	DE[1], kcal [ME, Mcal]	TDN kg	Reference
189			365	0	7350	330	230	20,200	4.58	
190			455	0	8620	390	270	23,800	5.40	
191			545	0	9930	450	310	27,400	6.21	
192			635	0	11,110	500	350	30,600	6.94	
193	♀	Pregnancy, last quarter	185	....	2630	260	180	7200	1.63	
194			270	....	3630	360	250	10,000	2.27	
195			365	....	4450	440	300	12,200	2.77	
196			455	....	5310	510	360	14,600	3.31	
197			545	....	6080	590	420	16,800	3.81	
198			635	....	6800	670	470	18,800	4.26	
199		Lactation, peak	185	....	6990	790	550	19,200	4.35	
200			270	....	7980	890	630	22,000	4.99	
201			365	....	9430	1060	740	26,000	5.90	
202			455	....	10,430	1160	810	28,800	6.53	
203			545	....	11,520	1300	910	31,800	7.21	
204			635	....	13,150	1410	980	36,200	8.21	
	Felis catus[8]									6
205	Young	Growth	....	....	....	>30/100 g diet	....	250/kg body wt [10,11]	....	
206	Adult	Maintenance	....	....	....	21/100 g diet	....	90/kg body wt [10]	....	
207	*Macaca mulatta*[8]	Growth	<0.5 [12]	1000/6 mo	....	8/kg body wt	....	250/kg body wt [10]	....	6
208			3	....	140 [13]	17/100 g diet	....	100/kg body wt [10]	....	
	Mesocricetus auratus[8,14]									6
209	Young	Growth	0.03	2.1	....	....	....	....	....	
210			0.06	1.1	6.0	0.96	....	....	....	
211			0.09	0.6	5.8	....	....	....	....	
212	Adult	Maintenance	0.06-0.10	....	....	....	....	24 [10]	....	
	Mus musculus[8]									6
213	21-da weanling, ♂	Growth	0.009-0.010	5-13/14 da	....	....	....	....	....	
214	CF No. 1 weanling, ♂	Growth	....	13-14/ 14 da	3.5 [15]	0.56 [15]	....	[14.5]	....	
215					3.9-4.0/ g of gain [15]	....	12/100 g diet	16-18/g of gain [15]	....	
216	Adult, ♀	Pregnancy & lactation	....	....	....	....	....	400/100 g diet	....	
	Oryctolagus cuniculus[16]									1
217	♂♀	Growth	3.0(1.81-4.08)	....	145.1	22.7	13.6	....	0.086	
218		Growth & fattening	1.81	31.75	113.4	18.1	13.6	....	0.073	
219			2.27	31.75	136.1	22.7	18.1	....	0.086	
220			2.72	31.75	154.2	22.7	18.1	....	0.100	
221			3.18	31.75	172.4	27.2	22.7	....	0.113	
222		Maintenance	2.27	0	90.7	13.6	9.1	....	0.050	
223			4.54	0	149.7	18.1	13.6	....	0.082	
224			6.80	0	204.1	22.7	18.1	....	0.113	

[1] Unless otherwise indicated. [8] Requirements are based on air-dry feed containing 90% dry matter. [10] Gross energy. [11] But decreased rapidly to ∿134 kcal gross energy/ kg body weight at 30 wk of age. [12] Average birth weight. [13] Calculated from 170-g intake in a 3.5- to 4.0-kg monkey and 80-g intake in a 2-kg monkey, which produced the same growth. [14] Synonym: *Cricetus auratus*. [15] Based on average daily feed requirements during 2-wk period following weaning. [16] Values based on air-dry weights.

continued

ALBRIGHT COLLEGE LIBRARY

145775

Part I. General Requirements

	Subjects	Specification	Body Weight kg	Avg Daily Gain g	Daily Feed g	Protein Total g	Digestible g	DE, kcal [ME, Mcal]	TDN kg	Reference
225	♀	Pregnancy	2.27	....	113.4	18.1	13.6	....	0.068	
226			4.54	....	186.0	27.2	22.7	....	0.109	
227			6.80	....	254.0	36.3	27.2	....	0.150	8
	Ovis aries [17]									
228	Lambs, ♂♀	Early-weaned [18]	10	250	600	96	69	1920	0.44	
229			20	275	1000	160	115	3210	0.74	
230			30	300	1400	196	133	4490	1.02	
231		Fattening [19]	30	200	1300	143	87	3650	0.83	
232			35	220	1400	154	94	4140	0.94	
233			40	250	1600	176	107	4920	1.12	
234			45	250	1700	187	114	5240	1.19	
235			50	220	1800	198	121	5540	1.26	
236			55	200	1900	209	127	5850	1.33	
	Lambs & yearlings [20]									
237	♂	Replacement	40	250	1800	184	108	5150	1.17	
238			60	200	2300	219	122	6070	1.38	
239			80	150	2800	249	134	6780	1.54	
240			100	100	2800	249	134	6780	1.54	
241			120	50	2600	231	125	6290	1.43	
242	♀	Replacement	30	180	1300	130	75	3560	0.81	
243			40	120	1400	133	74	3600	0.82	
244			50	80	1500	133	73	3650	0.83	
245			60	40	1500	133	72	3650	0.83	
246			70	10	1400	129	70	3430	0.78	
247	Ewes [21]	Nonpregnant	50	10	1000	89	48	2420	0.55	
248			60	10	1100	98	53	2680	0.61	
249			70	10	1200	107	58	2900	0.66	
250			80	10	1300	116	63	3170	0.72	
251		Nonlactating; pregnancy, first 15 wk	50	30	1100	99	54	2640	0.60	
252			60	30	1300	117	64	3170	0.72	
253			70	30	1400	126	69	3390	0.77	
254			80	30	1500	135	74	3610	0.82	
255		Pregnancy, last 6 wk; or ⟨lactation, last 8 wk suckling single lamb⟩	50	175 ⟨45⟩	1700	158	88	4360	0.99	
256			60	175 ⟨45⟩	1900	177	99	4840	1.10	
257			70	175 ⟨45⟩	2100	195	109	5370	1.22	
258			80	175 ⟨45⟩	2200	205	114	5630	1.28	
259			90	175 ⟨45⟩	2300	214	120	5850	1.33	
260		Lactation, first 8 wk suckling singles, or ⟨last 8 wk suckling twins⟩	50	−25 ⟨+80⟩	2100	218	130	5980	1.36	
261			60	−25 ⟨+80⟩	2300	239	143	6600	1.50	
262			70	−25 ⟨+80⟩	2500	260	155	7170	1.63	
263			80	−25 ⟨+80⟩	2600	270	161	7440	1.69	

[17] Requirements are based on feed containing 100% dry matter; to convert to an as-fed feed basis, divide values given here by percentage of dry matter in feed used. [18] 40-kg early-weaned lamb is fed same as finishing lamb of equal weight. [19] For maximum weight gains. If lambs are held for later market, they should be fed similarly to replacement ewe lambs. Lambs capable of gaining faster than indicated need to be fed at higher level; self-feeding permits lambs to finish most rapidly. [20] Requirements for replacement lambs start at time they are weaned. [21] Values are for ewes in moderate condition, not excessively fat or thin. For fat ewes, feed at values for next lower weight; for thin ewes, feed at values for next higher weight.

continued

Part I. General Requirements

	Subjects	Specification	Body Weight kg	Avg Daily Gain g	Daily Feed g	Protein Total g	Protein Digestible g	DE[1], kcal [ME, Mcal]	TDN kg	Reference
264		Lactation,	50	−60	2400	276	173	6860	1.56	
265		first 8 wk	60	−60	2600	299	187	7440	1.69	
266		suckling	70	−60	2800	322	202	8010	1.82	
267		twins	80	−60	3000	345	216	8580	1.95	
	Rattus norvegicus, laboratory									6
268	♂, 23 da [22]	Growth	0.055	5.0 [23]	9	1.8 [24,25]	1.1 [26,27]	36 [10]	....	
269	33 da [28]	Growth	0.110	5.4 [23]	15	3.0 [24,25]	1.8 [26,27]	60 [10]	....	
270	42 da [29]	Growth	0.165	5.7 [23]	18	3.6 [24,25]	2.2 [26,27]	72 [10]	....	
271	53 da [30]	Growth	0.220	5.5 [23]	21	4.2 [24,25]	2.5 [26,27]	84 [10]	....	
272	108 da [31]	Growth	0.385	3.9 [23]	20	4.0 [24,25]	2.4 [26,27]	80 [10]	....	
273	350 da, adult	Maintenance	0.550	....	19	1.33 [24,32]	0.76 [26,33]	76 [10]	....	
274	♀, 26 da [28]	Growth	0.065	4.2 [23]	10	2.0 [24,25]	1.2 [26,27]	40 [10]	....	
275	35 da [29]	Growth	0.098	3.9 [23]	14	2.8 [24,25]	1.7 [26,27]	56 [10]	....	
276	44 da [30]	Growth	0.130	3.7 [23]	15	3.0 [24,25]	1.8 [26,27]	60 [10]	....	
277	96 da [31]	Growth	0.228	2.5 [23]	16	3.2 [24,25]	1.9 [26,27]	64 [10]	....	
278	350 da, adult	Maintenance	0.325	....	13	0.91 [24,32]	0.52 [26,33]	52 [10]	....	
279	adult	Pregnancy [34]	....	4	19	3.8 [24,25]	2.3 [26,27]	76 [10]	....	
280		Lactation [35]	....	0	33	6.6 [24,25]	4.0 [26,27]	131 [10]	....	
281	*Sus scrofa*	Growth	5-10	300	600	132	....	2100	....	9
282			10-20	500	1250	225	....	4370	....	
283			20-35	600	1700	272	....	5610	....	
284		Finishing,	35-60	750	2500	350	....	8250	....	
285		full-fed	60-100	900	3500	455	....	11,550	....	
286	Boar, young	Maintenance	110-180	250	2500	350	....	8250	....	
287	mature	Maintenance	180-250	450	2000	280	....	6600	....	
288	Gilt	Pregnancy	110-160	350	2000	280	....	6600	....	
289		Lactation	140-200	150	5000	750	....	16,500	....	
290	Sow	Pregnancy	160-250	450	2000	280	....	6600	....	
291		Lactation	200-250	300	5500	825	....	18,150	....	
	Gallus gallus									4
292	Single-comb	Growth	0.250	....	27	5.4	....	....	....	
293	White Leg-		0.500	....	45	9	....	....	....	
294	horn or simi-		0.750	....	57	9.1	....	....	....	
295	lar breeds		1.000	....	65	10.4	....	....	....	
296			1.250	....	79	12.6	....	....	....	
297			1.500	....	84	10.1	....	....	....	
298	Adult	60% egg production	1.800	....	110	16.5	....	....	....	
299		Breeding	1.800	....	110	16.5	....	....	....	
300	Heavy breeds	Growth	0.250	....	35	8	....	....	....	
301			0.500	....	57	13	....	....	....	
302			0.750	....	73	17	....	....	....	
303			1.000	....	84	19	....	....	....	
304			1.500	....	100	20	....	....	....	

[1] Unless otherwise indicated. [10] Gross energy. [22] 10% of mature weight. [23] Expected daily gain from 21 da of age to age specified. [24] Dietary N × 6.25. [25] Total protein required is 20 g/100 g diet. [26] Dietary N × 6.25, with a true digestibility and biological value of 100%. [27] Digestible protein required is 12 g/100 g diet, calculated as in footnote 26. [28] 20% of mature weight. [29] 30% of mature weight. [30] 40% of mature weight. [31] 70% of mature weight. [32] Total protein required is 7 g/100 g diet. [33] Digestible protein required is 4 g/100 g diet, calculated as in footnote 26. [34] Female carrying litter of 8 or 9 pups. [35] Female suckling litter of 6 or 7 pups.

continued

Part I. General Requirements

	Subjects	Specification	Body Weight kg	Avg Daily Gain g	Daily Feed g	Protein Total g	Protein Digestible g	DE, kcal [ME, Mcal]	TDN kg	Reference
305	Adult	60% egg production	2.500	....	125	18.7	....	....	....	
306		Breeding	2.500	....	125	18.7	....	....	....	

Contributors: Bird, Herbert R.; Christison, G. I., and Bell, J. M.; Corbin, James E.; Cunha, T. J.; Jacobson, N. L.; Perry, T. W.; Pope, A. L.; Smith, S. E.; Tyznik, W. J.

References
[1] National Research Council, Agricultural Board. 1966. Nat. Acad. Sci. Nat. Res. Counc. Publ. 1194.
[2] Ibid. 2045, 1973.
[3] Ibid. 1754, 1970.
[4] Ibid. 1861, 1971.
[5] Ibid. 1916, 1971.
[6] Ibid. 2028, 1972.
[7] Ibid. 2043, 1972.
[8] Ibid. Nutrient Requirements of Sheep. Ed. 5. 1974.
[9] Ibid. Nutrient Requirements of Swine. Ed. 7. 1973.

Part II. Minerals

Values are given in terms of requirements per animal per day, unless otherwise indicated. *Abbreviation:* R = required. **Avg Daily Gain:** Values enclosed in (parentheses) or ⟨brackets⟩ refer to the specification similarly enclosed.

	Subjects	Specification	Body Weight kg	Avg Daily Gain g	Calcium g[1]	Iodine mg[1]	Magnesium g[1]	Phosphorus g[1]	Sodium + Chlorine[1] g[1]	Reference
	Bos taurus, beef									5
1	Steer	Growth	150	0	5	R	R	5	....	
2				250	8	R	R	7	....	
3				500	12	R	R	10	....	
4				750	17	R	R	13	....	
5			200	0	6	R	R	6	....	
6				250	8	R	R	8	....	
7				500	13	R	R	10	....	
8				750	18	R	R	14	....	
9			300	0	8	R	R	8	....	
10				250	11	R	R	11	....	
11				500	14	R	R	14	....	
12				750	17	R	R	15	....	
13			400	0	10	R	R	10	....	
14				250	14	R	R	14	....	
15				500	17	R	R	17	....	
16				750	18	R	R	18	....	
17		Growth & finishing[2]	....	....	0.18-0.60%	R	0.4-1.0[3] dry feed	0.18-0.43%	0.1%[4]	
18	Calf	Finishing	150	900	21	R	R	15	....	
19			200	1000	23	R	R	17	....	
20			300	1100	26	R	R	19	....	
21			400	1100	25	R	R	20	....	
22			450	1050	21	R	R	21	....	

[1] Unless otherwise indicated. [2] Also required: potassium, 0.6-0.8%; sulfur, 0.1%; and the following minerals, per kilogram dry feed—cobalt, 0.05-0.10 mg; copper, 4 mg; iron, 10 mg; manganese, 1.0-10.0 mg; selenium, 0.05-0.10 mg; and zinc, 10-30 mg. [3] Per kg dry feed. [4] Sodium only.

continued

Part II. Minerals

	Subjects	Specification	Body Weight kg	Avg Daily Gain g	Calcium g[1]	Iodine mg[1]	Magnesium g	Phosphorus g[1]	Sodium + Chlorine[1] g[1]	Reference
23	Yearling	Finishing	250	1300	29	R	R	20	....	
24			300	1300	29	R	R	21	....	
25			400	1300	28	R	R	23	....	
26			500	1200	26	R	R	26	....	
27	2-yr old	Finishing	350	1400	30	R	R	24	....	
28			400	1400	30	R	R	25	....	
29			500	1400	30	R	R	30	....	
30			550	1300	30	R	R	30	....	
31	Bull[5]	Breeding	....	....	0.18-0.29%	50-100 μg[3]	R	0.18-0.23%	0.1%[4]	
32	Bull, moderate-	Growth &	300	1000	23	R	R	18	....	
33	ly active	mainte-	400	900	19	R	R	18	....	
34		nance	500	700	21	R	R	21	....	
35			600	500	21	R	R	21	....	
36			700	300	23	R	R	23	....	
37			800	0	18	R	R	18	....	
38			900	0	19	R	R	19	....	
39	Heifer	Growth	150	0	5	R	R	5	....	
40				250	8	R	R	7	....	
41				500	12	R	R	10	....	
42				750	17	R	R	13	....	
43			200	0	6	R	R	6	....	
44				250	8	R	R	8	....	
45				500	13	R	R	10	....	
46				750	18	R	R	14	....	
47			300	0	8	R	R	8	....	
48				250	11	R	R	11	....	
49				500	15	R	R	15	....	
50				750	17	R	R	15	....	
51			400	0	10	R	R	10	....	
52				250	14	R	R	14	....	
53				500	18	R	R	18	....	
54				750	19	R	R	19	....	
55		Growth & finishing[2]	....	....	0.18-0.60%	R	0.4-1.0[3]	0.18-0.43%	0.1%[4]	
56	Calf	Finishing	150	800	18	R	R	13	....	
57			200	900	21	R	R	15	....	
58			300	1000	23	R	R	18	....	
59			400	950	23	R	R	19	....	
60	Yearling	Finishing	250	1200	27	R	R	20	....	
61			300	1200	27	R	R	20	....	
62			400	1200	30	R	R	24	....	
63			450	1100	24	R	R	24	....	
64	Cow[5]	Pregnancy;	....	....	0.18%	50-100 μg[3]	R	0.18%	0.1%[4]	
65		nonlactat-	350	....	9	R	R	9	....	
66		ing	400	....	10	R	R	10	....	
67			450	....	12	R	R	12	....	

[1] Unless otherwise indicated. [2] Also required: potassium, 0.6-0.8%; sulfur, 0.1%; and the following minerals, per kilogram dry feed—cobalt, 0.05-0.10 mg; copper, 4 mg; iron, 10 mg; manganese, 1.0-10.0 mg; selenium, 0.05-0.10 mg; and zinc, 10-30 mg. [3] Per kg dry feed. [4] Sodium only. [5] Also required, per kilogram dry feed: cobalt, 0.05-0.10 mg; and selenium, 0.05-0.10 mg.

continued

Part II. Minerals

	Subjects	Specification	Body Weight kg	Avg Daily Gain g	Calcium g [1]	Iodine mg [1]	Magnesium g	Phosphorus g [1]	Sodium + Chlorine [1] g [1]	Reference
68			500	....	12	R	R	12	....	
69			550	....	12	R	R	12	....	
70			600	....	13	R	R	13	....	
71		Lactation	....	....	0.18-0.29%	50-100 μg [3]	R	0.18-0.23%	0.1% [4]	
72		First 3-4	350	....	25	R	R	20	....	
73		mo post-	400	....	26	R	R	21	....	
74		partum	450	....	28	R	R	22	....	
75		with nursing calf	500	....	28	R	R	23	....	
	B. taurus, dairy [6]									7
76	Veal calf	Growth &	....	....	5.5 [3]	0.1 [3]	0.6 [3]	4.2 [3]	2.5 [3]	
77		finishing	35	500	3.0	R	R	2.3	R	
78			40	800	4.8	R	R	3.7	R	
79			75	1000	7.9	R	R	5.9	R	
80			100	1150	11.1	R	R	8.0	R	
81			150	1300	16.0	R	R	11.0	R	
	Bulls									
82	Young (large	Growth	40	200	2.2	R	R	1.7	R	
83	breeds)		45	300	3.2	R	R	2.5	R	
84	5 wk	Growth	55	400	4.5	R	R	3.5	R	
85	9 wk	Growth	75	800	9.7	R	R	7.5	R	
86	13 wk	Growth	100	1000	13	R	R	10	R	
87	20 wk	Growth	150	1000	18	R	R	14	R	
88	27 wk	Growth	200	1000	21	R	R	16	R	
89	34 wk	Growth	250	1000	24	R	R	18	R	
90	41 wk	Growth	300	1000	27	R	R	20	R	
91	49 wk	Growth	350	1000	29	R	R	22	R	
92	56 wk	Growth	400	1000	30	R	R	23	R	
93	63 wk	Growth	450	1000	30	R	R	23	R	
94	70 wk	Growth	500	900	30	R	R	23	R	
95	79 wk	Growth	550	800	30	R	R	23	R	
96	88 wk	Growth	600	700	30	R	R	23	R	
97	99 wk	Growth	650	600	30	R	R	23	R	
98	112 wk	Growth	700	500	30	R	R	23	R	
99	128 wk	Growth	750	400	30	R	R	23	R	
100	>128 wk	Growth	800	250	30	R	R	23	R	
101			850	100	30	R	R	23	R	
102	Mature	Maintenance	....	....	2.4 [3]	0.1 [3]	0.8 [3]	1.8 [3]	2.5 [3]	
103		& breeding	500	....	20	R	R	15	R	
104			600	....	22	R	R	17	R	
105			700	....	25	R	R	19	R	
106			800	....	27	R	R	21	R	
107			900	....	30	R	R	23	R	
108			1000	....	32	R	R	25	R	

[1] Unless otherwise indicated. [3] Per kg dry feed. [4] Sodium only. [6] Also required: cobalt, copper, iron, manganese, potassium, selenium, sulfur, and zinc. In excess, fluorine and molybdenum are toxic.

continued

Part II. Minerals

Subjects	Specification	Body Weight kg	Avg Daily Gain g	Calcium g	Iodine mg	Magnesium g	Phosphorus g	Sodium + Chlorine g	Reference
109		1100	....	35	R	R	27	R	
110		1200	....	38	R	R	29	R	
111		1300	....	40	R	R	31	R	
112		1400	....	43	R	R	33	R	
113 Heifer (large breeds)	Growth	....	....	3.4[3]	0.1[3]	0.8[3]	2.6[3]	2.5[3]	
114		40	200	2.2	R	R	1.7	R	
115		45	300	3.2	R	R	2.5	R	
116 5 wk	Growth	55	400	4.5	R	R	3.5	R	
117 10 wk	Growth	75	750	9.1	R	R	7.0	R	
118 15 wk	Growth	100	750	10.9	R	R	8.4	R	
119 24 wk	Growth	150	750	15	R	R	12	R	
120 34 wk	Growth	200	750	18	R	R	14	R	
121 43 wk	Growth	250	750	21	R	R	16	R	
122 53 wk	Growth	300	750	24	R	R	18	R	
123 62 wk	Growth	350	750	25	R	R	19	R	
124 72 wk	Growth	400	750	26	R	R	20	R	
125 82 wk	Growth	450	700	27	R	R	21	R	
126 93 wk	Growth	500	600	27	R	R	21	R	
127 107 wk	Growth	550	400	26	R	R	20	R	
128 133 wk	Growth	600	150	24	R	R	18	R	
129 Cow	Dry, maintenance	....	....	3.4[3]	0.6[3]	0.8[3]	2.6[3]	2.5[3]	
130	Maintenance	350	....	14	R	R	11	R	
131		400	....	17	R	R	13	R	
132		450	....	18	R	R	14	R	
133		500	....	20	R	R	15	R	
134		550	....	21	R	R	16	R	
135		600	....	22	R	R	17	R	
136		650	....	23	R	R	18	R	
137		700	....	25	R	R	19	R	
138		750	....	26	R	R	20	R	
139		800	....	27	R	R	21	R	
140	Maintenance & pregnancy, last 2 mo	350	....	21	R	R	16	R	
141		400	....	23	R	R	18	R	
142		450	....	26	R	R	20	R	
143		500	....	29	R	R	22	R	
144		550	....	31	R	R	24	R	
145		600	....	34	R	R	26	R	
146		650	....	36	R	R	28	R	
147		700	....	39	R	R	30	R	
148		750	....	42	R	R	32	R	
149		800	....	44	R	R	34	R	
150	Lactation	....	....	4.3-5.3[3,7]	0.6[3]	1.0[3]	3.3-3.9[3,7]	4.5[3]	
Canis familiaris[8]									
151 Young	Growth	2.3	....	1.8	0.25	0.090	1.4	1.8	9
152		4.5	....	3.0	0.45	0.150	2.4	3.0	

[3] Per kg dry feed. [7] Amount needed varies with rate of milk production. [8] Also required: copper, iron, manganese, potassium, zinc, and probably cobalt. In excess, iodine is toxic.

continued

Part II. Minerals

	Subjects	Specification	Body Weight kg	Avg Daily Gain g	Calcium g	Iodine mg	Magnesium g	Phosphorus g	Sodium + Chlorine g	Reference
153			6.8	....	3.8	0.55	0.190	3.0	3.8	
154			9.1	....	4.9	0.70	0.250	4.0	4.9	
155			13.6	....	6.8	1.00	0.340	5.4	6.8	
156			22.7	....	11.3	1.60	0.550	9.0	11.3	
157	Adult	Maintenance	2.3	....	0.9	0.12	0.045	0.7	0.9	
158			4.5	....	1.5	0.22	0.075	1.2	1.5	
159			6.8	....	1.9	0.27	0.095	1.5	1.9	
160			9.1	....	2.4	0.35	0.125	1.9	2.4	
161			13.6	....	3.4	0.50	0.170	2.7	3.4	
162			22.7	....	5.6	0.80	0.225	5.0	5.6	
163			50.0	....	10.0	1.50	0.425	8.0	10.0	
164	*Cavia porcellus* 9/	Growth	....	....	0.1/100 g body wt	R	0.028/100 g body wt	0.05/100 g body wt	R	8
165					1.20/100 g diet	....	0.35/100 g diet	0.60/100 g diet	....	
	Equus caballus 10/									4
166	270 kg at maturity	Growth	90	410	11	0.10	R	10	R	
167			185	180	11	0.10	R	11	R	
168			270	0	6	0.10	R	6	50-60	
169	365 kg at maturity	Growth	90	640	14	0.10	R	11	R	
170			185	410	17	0.10	R	13	R	
171			270	230	13	0.10	R	13	R	
172			365	0	9	0.10	R	9	50-60	
173	455 kg at maturity	Growth	90	730	16	0.10	R	11	R	
174			185	540	15	0.10	R	12	R	
175			270	360	14	0.10	R	12	R	
176			365	230	13	0.10	R	12	R	
177			455	0	11	0.10	R	11	50-60	
178	545 kg at maturity	Growth	90	1000	19	0.10	R	16	R	
179			185	820	18	0.10	R	17	R	
180			270	590	18	0.10	R	17	R	
181			365	360	18	0.10	R	17	R	
182			455	180	12	0.10	R	12	R	
183			545	0	12	0.10	R	12	50-60	
184	635 kg at maturity	Growth	90	1220	24	0.10	R	17	R	
185			185	1000	21	0.10	R	17	R	
186			270	820	19	0.10	R	17	R	
187			365	590	18	0.10	R	17	R	
188			455	360	14	0.10	R	14	R	
189			545	180	13	0.10	R	13	R	
190			635	0	13	0.10	R	13	50-60	
191	Mature	Light work	185	0	6	0.10	R	6	50-60	
192			270	0	9	0.10	R	9	50-60	
193			365	0	10	0.10	R	10	50-60	
194			455	0	12	0.10	R	12	50-60	
195			545	0	14	0.10	R	14	50-60	
196			635	0	16	0.10	R	16	50-60	
197		Medium work	185	0	8	0.10	R	8	50-60	
198			270	0	10	0.10	R	10	50-60	

9/ Also required: cobalt, copper, iron, manganese, potassium, and zinc. 10/ Also required: cobalt, copper, fluorine, iron, and potassium. In excess, fluorine is toxic. Molybdenum, selenium, and sulfur were not demonstrated to be essential.

continued

Part II. Minerals

	Subjects	Specification	Body Weight kg	Avg Daily Gain g	Calcium g[1]	Iodine mg	Magnesium g[1]	Phosphorus g[1]	Sodium + Chlorine[1] g[1]	Reference
199			365	0	12	0.10	R	12	50-60	
200			455	0	14	0.10	R	14	50-60	
201			545	0	16	0.10	R	16	50-60	
202			635	0	18	0.10	R	18	50-60	
203	♀	Pregnancy, last quarter	185	....	9	0.10[11]	R	8	R	
204			270	....	12	0.10[11]	R	11	R	
205			365	....	14	0.10[11]	R	13	R	
206			455	....	16	0.10[11]	R	15	R	
207			545	....	18	0.10[11]	R	17	R	
208			635	....	20	0.10[11]	R	19	R	
209		Lactation, peak	185	....	18	0.10	R	13	R	
210			270	....	23	0.10	R	18	R	
211			365	....	27	0.10	R	22	R	
212			455	....	30	0.10	R	24	R	
213			545	....	34	0.10	R	27	R	
214			635	....	37	0.10	R	30	R	
215	*Felis catus*	Growth	....	....	R	R	....	....	....	8
216	*Macaca mulatta*[12]	Growth	3	....	0.86/100 g diet	....	0.23/100 g diet	....	....	8
217	*Mesocricetus auratus*[13]	Growth	....	....	0.6/100 g diet	....	....	0.35/100 g diet	....	8
218	*Mus musculus*[14]	Growth[15]	....	....	0.021	....	....	0.018	0.018	8
219					0.6/100 g diet			0.5/100 g diet	0.5/100 g diet	
220	*Oryctolagus cuniculus*[16]	Maintenance	....	0	0.4%	....	R	0.22%	....	1-3
221	*Ovis aries*[17]	Maintenance	....	....	0.21-0.52%	0.10-0.80[3]	0.04-0.08%	0.16-0.37%	0.04%[4]	10
222	Lamb, ♂♀	Early-weaned	10	250	2.8	....	....	1.7	....	
223			20	275	5.0	....	....	3.0	....	
224			30	300	7.2	....	....	4.3	....	
225		Fattening	30	200	4.8	....	....	3.0	....	
226			35	220	4.8	....	....	3.0	....	
227			40	250	5.0	....	....	3.1	....	
228			45	250	5.0	....	....	3.1	....	
229			50	220	5.0	....	....	3.1	....	
230			55	200	5.0	....	....	3.1	....	
	Lamb & yearling[18]									
231	♂	Replacement	40	250	6.3	....	....	3.5	....	
232			60	200	7.2	....	....	4.0	....	
233			80	150	7.9	....	....	4.4	....	
234			100	100	8.3	....	....	4.6	....	
235			120	50	8.5	....	....	4.7	....	

[1] Unless otherwise indicated. [3] Per kg dry feed. [4] Sodium only. [11] Supplemental iodine is required in the goiter belt. [12] Presumably also required: copper, fluorine, iodine, iron, manganese, phosphorus, potassium, sodium chloride, sulfur, and zinc. [13] Synonym: *Cricetus auratus.* [14] Also required: iron, manganese, potassium, and zinc. [15] Based on average daily feed requirements during 2-wk period following weaning. [16] Also required: copper, iron, manganese, and potassium. [17] Also required: cobalt, 0.1 ppm; copper, 5 ppm; iodine, 0.1-0.8 ppm; iron, 30-50 ppm; magnesium 0.04-0.08%; manganese, 20-40 ppm; molybdenum, >0.5 ppm; potassium, 0.50%; selenium, 0.1 ppm; sodium, 0.04-0.08%; sulfur, 0.14-0.26%; and zinc, 35-50 ppm. [18] Replacement lambs' requirements start at time they are weaned.

continued

Part II. Minerals

	Subjects	Specification	Body Weight kg	Avg Daily Gain g	Calcium g	Iodine mg [1]	Magnesium g [1]	Phosphorus g	Sodium + Chlorine [1] g	Reference
236	♀	Replacement	30	180	5.9	....	....	3.3	....	
237			40	120	6.1	....	....	3.4	....	
238			50	80	6.3	....	....	3.5	....	
239			60	40	6.5	....	....	3.6	....	
240			70	10	6.5	....	....	3.6	....	
241	Ewe	Nonpregnant, or ⟨nonlactating; pregnancy, first 15 wk⟩	50	10 ⟨30⟩	3.0	....	....	2.8	....	
242			60	10 ⟨30⟩	3.1	....	....	2.9	....	
243			70	10 ⟨30⟩	3.2	....	....	3.0	....	
244			80	10 ⟨30⟩	3.3	....	....	3.1	....	
245		Pregnancy, last 6 wk; or ⟨lactation, last 8 wk suckling single lamb⟩	50	175 ⟨45⟩	4.1	....	....	3.9	....	
246			60	175 ⟨45⟩	4.4	....	....	4.1	....	
247			70	175 ⟨45⟩	4.5	....	....	4.3	....	
248			80	175 ⟨45⟩	4.8	....	....	4.5	....	
249			90	175 ⟨45⟩	5.0	....	....	4.7	....	
250		Lactation, first 8 wk suckling singles or ⟨twins⟩; or ⟨last 8 wk suckling twins⟩ suckling singles	50	−25(−60) ⟨+80⟩	10.9	....	....	7.8		
251			60	−25(−60) ⟨+80⟩	11.5	....	....	8.2	....	
252			70	−25(−60) ⟨+80⟩	12.0	....	....	8.6	....	
253			80	−25(−60) ⟨+80⟩	12.6	....	....	9.0	....	
254	Rattus norvegicus, laboratory [19]	Growth	....	....	0.05 [20,21]	1.5 μg [21]	4 mg [21]	0.04 [21]	0.010 [21]	8
255					0.5/100 g diet	15 μg/100 g diet	40 μg/100 g diet	0.4/100 g diet	0.10/100 g diet	
256		Gestation	....	....	0.12 [21]	3 μg [21]	10 mg [21]	0.10 [21]	0.015 [21]	
257					0.6/100 g diet	15 μg/100 g diet	50 μg/100 g diet	0.5/100 g diet	0.075/100 g diet	
258		Lactation	....	....	0.18 [21]	4.5 μg [21]	15 mg [21]	0.15 [21]	0.020 [21]	
259					0.6/100 g diet	15 μg/100 g diet	50 μg/100 g diet	0.5/100 g diet	0.068/100 g diet	
260	Sus scrofa	Growth	5-10	....	4.8	0.2/kg feed	0.4/kg feed	3.6	3.0	11
261			10-20	....	8.1	0.2/kg feed	0.4/kg feed	6.3	6.25	
262			20-35	....	10.2	0.2/kg feed	0.4/kg feed	8.5	8.50	
263		Finishing, full-fed	35-60	....	12.5	0.2/kg feed	0.4/kg feed	10.0	12.5	
264			60-100	....	17.5	0.2/kg feed	0.4/kg feed	14.0	17.5	
265	Boar, young mature	Maintenance	110-180	....	18.8	0.2/kg feed	0.4/kg feed	12.5	12.5	
266		Maintenance	180-250	....	15.0	0.2/kg feed	0.4/kg feed	10.0	10.0	
267	Gilt	Pregnancy	110-160	....	15.0	0.2/kg feed	0.4/kg feed	10.0	10.0	
268		Lactation	140-200	....	37.5	0.2/kg feed	0.4/kg feed	25.0	25.0	
269	Sow	Pregnancy	160-250	....	15.0	0.2/kg feed	0.4/kg feed	10.0	10.0	
270		Lactation	200-250	....	41.2	0.2/kg feed	0.4/kg feed	27.5	27.5	

[1] Unless otherwise indicated. [19] Also required: manganese, potassium, and sulfur. For growth, copper, iron, selenium, and zinc are required, but the need for these minerals during gestation and lactation is in question. [20] For maintenance, 10-15 mg/da are required after a period of 40-50 mg/da. [21] Calculated from values obtained experimentally, assuming a daily feed intake of 10 g for growth, 20 g for pregnancy, and 30 g for lactation. [22] Also required: manganese, potassium, and zinc.

continued

Part II.   Minerals

	Subjects	Specification	Body Weight kg	Avg Daily Gain g	Calcium g	Iodine mg	Magnesium g	Phosphorus g	Sodium + Chlorine[1] g	Reference
	Gallus gallus [22]									6
271	Single-comb	Growth	0.250	....	0.27	0.009	0.013	0.19	0.040[4]	
272	White Leg-		0.500	....	0.45	0.015	0.022	0.31	0.067[4]	
273	horn or sim-		0.750	....	0.57	0.020	0.028	0.40	0.085[4]	
274	ilar breeds		1.000	....	0.52	0.023	....	0.26	0.097[4]	
275			1.250	....	0.63	0.028	....	0.32	0.119[4]	
276			1.500	....	0.67	0.029	....	0.34	0.126[4]	
277	Adult	60% egg production	1.800	....	3.0	0.033	....	0.66	0.165[4]	
278		Breeding	1.800	....	3.0	0.033	....	0.66	0.165[4]	
279	Heavy breeds	Growth	0.250	....	0.35	0.011	0.017	0.24	0.052[4]	
280			0.500	....	0.57	0.020	0.028	0.40	0.085[4]	
281			0.750	....	0.73	0.025	0.036	0.51	0.10[4]	
282			1.000	....	0.84	0.029	0.042	0.59	0.12[4]	
283			1.500	....	1.0	0.035	0.050	0.70	0.15[4]	
284	Adult	60% egg production	2.500	....	3.44	0.037	....	0.75	0.19[4]	
285		Breeding	2.500	....	3.44	0.037	....	0.75	0.19[4]	

[1] Unless otherwise indicated.   [4] Sodium only.

Contributors: Bird, Herbert R.;   Christison, G. I., and Bell, J. M.;   Corbin, James E.;   Cunha, T. J.;   Jacobson, N. L.; Perry, T. W.; Pope, A. L.; Smith, S. E.; Tyznik, W. J.

References
[1] Chapin, R. E., and S. E. Smith. 1967. J. Anim. Sci. 26:67.
[2] Mathiew, L. G., and S. E. Smith. 1961. Ibid. 20:510.
[3] National Research Council, Agricultural Board. 1966. Nat. Acad. Sci. Nat. Res. Counc. Publ. 1194.
[4] Ibid. 2045, 1973.
[5] Ibid. 1754, 1970.
[6] Ibid. 1861, 1971.
[7] Ibid. 1916, 1971.
[8] Ibid. 2028, 1972.
[9] Ibid. 2043, 1972.
[10] Ibid. Nutrient Requirements of Sheep. Ed. 5. 1974.
[11] Ibid. Nutrient Requirements of Swine. Ed. 7. 1973.

Part III.   Vitamins

Values are given in terms of requirements per animal per day, unless otherwise indicated. **Avg Daily Gain:** Values enclosed in (parentheses) or ⟨brackets⟩ refer to the specification similarly enclosed. *Abbreviation:* R = required.

	Subjects	Specification	Body Weight kg	Avg Daily Gain g	Riboflavin mg	Niacin mg	B_6 mg	Pantothenic Acid[1] mg	B_{12} μg	A[1] IU	D IU	Reference
	Bos taurus, beef [2]											3
1	Steer	Growth	150	0	....	....	....	....	....	6000	......	
2				250	....	....	....	....	....	6800	......	
3				500	....	....	....	....	....	7000	......	
4				750	....	....	....	....	....	7000	......	
5			200	0	....	....	....	....	....	7400	......	
6				250	....	....	....	....	....	10,000	......	
7				500	....	....	....	....	....	10,800	......	
8				750	....	....	....	....	....	11,200	......	

[1] Unless otherwise indicated.   [2] Supplemental B vitamins are required up to the time that a functional rumen develops, which usually has occurred by weaning time.

continued

Part III. Vitamins

	Subjects	Specification	Body Weight kg	Avg Daily Gain g	Riboflavin mg	Niacin mg	B$_6$ mg	Pantothenic Acid mg	B$_{12}$ μg	A [1] IU	D IU	Reference
9			300	0	....	....	....	....	....	10,000	......	
10				250	....	....	....	....	....	13,600	......	
11				500	....	....	....	....	....	17,400	......	
12				750	....	....	....	....	....	17,800	......	
13			400	0	....	....	....	....	....	12,400	......	
14				250	....	....	....	....	....	17,200	......	
15				500	....	....	....	....	....	21,600	......	
16				750	....	....	....	....	....	22,000	......	
17		Growth & finishing[3]	......	....	....	....	....	....	....	2200[4,5]	275[4]	
18	Calf	Finishing	150	900	....	....	....	....	....	7800	......	
19			200	1000	....	....	....	....	....	11,000	......	
20			300	1100	....	....	....	....	....	15,800	......	
21			400	1100	....	....	....	....	....	19,600	......	
22			450	1050	....	....	....	....	....	20,800	......	
23	Yearling	Finishing	250	1300	....	....	....	....	....	16,000	......	
24			300	1300	....	....	....	....	....	18,400	......	
25			400	1300	....	....	....	....	....	22,800	......	
26			500	1200	....	....	....	....	....	25,600	......	
27	2 yr old	Finishing	350	1400	....	....	....	....	....	22,800	......	
28			400	1400	....	....	....	....	....	25,200	......	
29			500	1400	....	....	....	....	....	29,800	......	
30			550	1300	....	....	....	....	....	30,400	......	
31	Bull	Growth & mainte-nance, with moderate activity	300	1000	....	....	....	....	....	34,000	......	
32			400	900	....	....	....	....	....	38,800	......	
33			500	700	....	....	....	....	....	46,600	......	
34			600	500	....	....	....	....	....	45,200	......	
35			700	300	....	....	....	....	....	49,400	......	
36			800	0	....	....	....	....	....	38,500	......	
37			900	0	....	....	....	....	....	41,600	......	
38		Breeding[3]	......	....	....	....	....	....	....	3900[4,5]	275[4]	
39	Heifer	Growth	150	0	....	....	....	....	....	6000	......	
40				250	....	....	....	....	....	7000	......	
41				500	....	....	....	....	....	7200	......	
42				750	....	....	....	....	....	7400	......	
43			200	0	....	....	....	....	....	7400	......	
44				250	....	....	....	....	....	10,200	......	
45				500	....	....	....	....	....	11,200	......	
46				750	....	....	....	....	....	12,000	......	
47			300	0	....	....	....	....	....	10,000	......	
48				250	....	....	....	....	....	13,800	......	
49				500	....	....	....	....	....	18,200	......	
50				750	....	....	....	....	....	19,000	......	
51			400	0	....	....	....	....	....	12,400	......	
52				250	....	....	....	....	....	17,200	......	
53				500	....	....	....	....	....	22,600	......	
54				750	....	....	....	....	....	23,600	......	
55		Growth & finishing[3]	......	....	....	....	....	....	....	2200[4,5]	275[4]	

[1] Unless otherwise indicated. [3] Also required: vitamin E, 15-60 IU. [4] Per kg dry feed. [5] May be vitamin A or provita-min A.

continued

Part III. Vitamins

	Subjects	Specification	Body Weight kg	Avg Daily Gain g	Riboflavin mg	Niacin mg	B_6 mg	Pantothenic Acid mg	B_{12} µg	A [1] IU	D IU	Reference
56	Calf	Finishing	150	800	....	....	....	....	....	7800	......	
57			200	900	....	....	....	....	....	11,000	......	
58			300	1000	....	....	....	....	....	16,200	......	
59			400	950	....	....	....	....	....	19,400	......	
60	Yearling	Finishing	250	1200	....	....	....	....	....	16,800	......	
61			300	1200	....	....	....	....	....	19,200	......	
62			400	1200	....	....	....	....	....	23,800	......	
63			450	1100	....	....	....	....	....	24,400	......	
64	Cow	Pregnancy; nonlactating	......	....	....	....	....	....	....	2800[4,5]	275[4]	
65			350	....	....	....	....	....	....	14,000	......	
66			400	....	....	....	....	....	....	15,500	......	
67			450	....	....	....	....	....	....	16,800	......	
68			500	....	....	....	....	....	....	18,200	......	
69			550	....	....	....	....	....	....	19,500	......	
70			600	....	....	....	....	....	....	20,800	......	
71		Lactation[3]	......	....	....	....	....	....	....	3900[4,5]	275[4]	
72		First 3-4 mo post- partum, with nursing calf	350	....	....	....	....	....	....	33,200	......	
73			400	....	....	....	....	....	....	36,000	......	
74			450	....	....	....	....	....	....	38,500	......	
75			500	....	....	....	....	....	....	41,000	......	
	B. taurus, dairy											5
76	Calf	Fed milk replacer[6,7]	......	....	6.5[4]	2.6[4]	6.5[4]	13[4]	70[4]	3800[4]	600[4]	
77	Veal calf	Growth & finishing	......	....	....	....	....	....	....	1600[4]	250[4]	
78			35	500	....	....	....	....	....	1500	230	
79			40	800	....	....	....	....	....	2100	330	
80			75	1000	....	....	....	....	....	3200	495	
81			100	1150	....	....	....	....	....	4000	660	
82			150	1300	....	....	....	....	....	6000	990	
	Bull											
83	Young	Growth	40	200	....	....	....	....	....	1700	265	
84	(large breeds)		45	300	....	....	....	....	....	1900	300	
85	5 wk	Growth	55	400	....	....	....	....	....	2300	360	
86	9 wk	Growth	75	800	....	....	....	....	....	3200	495	
87	13 wk	Growth	100	1000	....	....	....	....	....	4000	660	
88	20 wk	Growth	150	1000	....	....	....	....	....	6000	990	
89	27 wk	Growth	200	1000	....	....	....	....	....	8000	1320	
90	34 wk	Growth	250	1000	....	....	....	....	....	10,000	......	
91	41 wk	Growth	300	1000	....	....	....	....	....	13,000	......	
92	49 wk	Growth	350	1000	....	....	....	....	....	15,000	......	
93	56 wk	Growth	400	1000	....	....	....	....	....	17,000	......	
94	63 wk	Growth	450	1000	....	....	....	....	....	19,000	......	
95	70 wk	Growth	500	900	....	....	....	....	....	21,000	......	
96	79 wk	Growth	550	800	....	....	....	....	....	23,000	......	

[1] Unless otherwise indicated. [3] Also required: vitamin E, 15-60 IU. [4] Per kg dry feed. [5] May be vitamin A or pro-vitamin A. [6] Also suggested for milk replacer, per kg dry feed: thiamine, 6.5 mg; biotin, 0.1 mg; folic acid, 0.5 mg; and choline, 2.6 mg. It appears that when calves have functional rumens—usually by 6 wk of age—adequate amounts of B-complex vitamins are furnished by a combination of rumen synthesis and natural feedstuffs. [7] Also required: vitamin E, 300 mg/kg dry feed.

continued

Part III. Vitamins

	Subjects	Specification	Body Weight kg	Avg Daily Gain g	Riboflavin mg	Niacin mg	B$_6$ mg	Pantothen- ic Acid mg	B$_{12}$ µg	A IU	D IU	Ref- er- ence
97	88 wk	Growth	600	700	....	....	....	....	....	26,000	......	
98	99 wk	Growth	650	600	....	....	....	....	....	28,000	......	
99	112 wk	Growth	700	500	....	....	....	....	....	30,000	......	
100	128 wk	Growth	750	400	....	....	....	....	....	32,000	......	
101	>128	Growth	800	250	....	....	....	....	....	34,000	......	
102	wk		850	100	....	....	....	....	....	36,000	......	
103	Mature	Maintenance	......	....	....	....	....	....	....	3200[4]	300[4]	
104		Maintenance	500	....	....	....	....	....	....	21,000	......	
105		& breeding	600	....	....	....	....	....	....	26,000	......	
106			700	....	....	....	....	....	....	30,000	......	
107			800	....	....	....	....	....	....	34,000	......	
108			900	....	....	....	....	....	....	38,000	......	
109			1000	....	....	....	....	....	....	42,000	......	
110			1100	....	....	....	....	....	....	47,000	......	
111			1200	....	....	....	....	....	....	51,000	......	
112			1300	....	....	....	....	....	....	55,000	......	
113			1400	....	....	....	....	....	....	59,000	......	
114	Heifer	Growth	......	....	....	....	....	....	....	1500[4]	250[4]	
115	(large		40	200	....	....	....	....	....	1700	265	
116	breeds)		45	300	....	....	....	....	....	1900	300	
117	5 wk	Growth	55	400	....	....	....	....	....	2300	360	
118	10 wk	Growth	75	750	....	....	....	....	....	3200	495	
119	15 wk	Growth	100	750	....	....	....	....	....	4000	660	
120	24 wk	Growth	150	750	....	....	....	....	....	6000	990	
121	34 wk	Growth	200	750	....	....	....	....	....	8000	1320	
122	43 wk	Growth	250	750	....	....	....	....	....	10,000	......	
123	53 wk	Growth	300	750	....	....	....	....	....	13,000	......	
124	62 wk	Growth	350	750	....	....	....	....	....	15,000	......	
125	72 wk	Growth	400	750	....	....	....	....	....	17,000	......	
126	82 wk	Growth	450	700	....	....	....	....	....	19,000	......	
127	93 wk	Growth	500	600	....	....	....	....	....	21,000	......	
128	107 wk	Growth	550	400	....	....	....	....	....	23,000	......	
129	133 wk	Growth	600	150	....	....	....	....	....	26,000	......	
130	Cow	Mainte- nance, dry	......	....	....	....	....	....	....	3200[4]	300[4]	
131		Maintenance	350	....	....	....	....	....	....	15,000	......	
132			400	....	....	....	....	....	....	17,000	......	
133			450	....	....	....	....	....	....	19,000	......	
134			500	....	....	....	....	....	....	21,000	......	
135			550	....	....	....	....	....	....	23,000	......	
136			600	....	....	....	....	....	....	26,000	......	
137			650	....	....	....	....	....	....	28,000	......	
138			700	....	....	....	....	....	....	30,000	......	
139			750	....	....	....	....	....	....	32,000	......	
140			800	....	....	....	....	....	....	34,000	......	
141		Maintenance	350	....	....	....	....	....	....	27,000	......	
142		& pregnan-	400	....	....	....	....	....	....	30,000	......	
143		cy, last 2	450	....	....	....	....	....	....	34,000	......	
144		mo	500	....	....	....	....	....	....	38,000	......	

[4] Per kg dry feed.

continued

Part III. Vitamins

	Subjects	Specification	Body Weight kg	Avg Daily Gain g	Riboflavin mg	Niacin mg	B_6 mg	Pantothenic Acid mg	B_{12} µg	A IU	D IU	Reference
145			550	....	....	....	....	....	....	42,000	......	
146			600	....	....	....	....	....	....	46,000	......	
147			650	....	....	....	....	....	....	50,000	......	
148			700	....	....	....	....	....	....	53,000	......	
149			750	....	....	....	....	....	....	57,000	......	
150			800	....	....	....	....	....	....	61,000	......	
151		Lactation	......	....	....	....	....	....	....	3200[4]	300[4]	7
	Canis familiaris											
152	Young	Growth	2.3	....	0.34	1.8	0.15	0.34	3	900	48	
153			4.5	....	0.57	3.0	0.27	0.57	6	1500	80	
154			6.8	....	0.72	3.8	0.34	0.72	8	1900	100	
155			9.1	....	0.93	4.9	0.44	0.93	10	2450	130	
156			13.6	....	1.30	6.8	0.61	1.30	14	3400	180	
157			22.7	....	2.15	11.3	1.00	2.15	23	5650	300	
158	Adult	Maintenance	2.3	....	0.17	0.9	0.08	0.17	2	450	24	
159			4.5	....	0.28	1.5	0.13	0.28	3	750	40	
160			6.8	....	0.35	1.9	0.17	0.35	4	950	50	
161			9.1	....	0.46	2.5	0.22	0.46	5	1225	65	
162			13.6	....	0.65	3.4	0.30	0.65	7	1700	90	
163			22.7	....	1.08	5.6	0.50	1.08	11	2825	150	
164			50.0	....	2.30	12.0	1.20	2.30	24	6000	315	
165	*Cavia por-cellus*[8,9]	Growth	......	....	0.13/100 g body wt	0.4/100 g body wt	0.13/100 g body wt	0.16/100 g body wt	....	150/100 g body wt	......	6
166					1.6[10]	5[10]	1.6[10]	2.0[10]	....	1800[10]	......	
	Equus caballus[11]											2
167	270 kg at	Growth	90	410	....	R	....	....	....	1700	R	
168	maturity		185	180	....	R	....	....	....	3300	R	
169			270	0	....	R	....	....	....	5000	R	
170	365 kg at	Growth	90	640	....	R	....	....	....	1700	R	
171	maturity		185	410	....	R	....	....	....	3300	R	
172			270	230	....	R	....	....	....	5000	R	
173			365	0	....	R	....	....	....	6700	R	
174	455 kg at	Growth	90	730	....	R	....	....	....	1700	R	
175	maturity		185	540	....	R	....	....	....	3300	R	
176			270	360	....	R	....	....	....	5000	R	
177			365	230	....	R	....	....	....	6700	R	
178			455	0	....	R	....	....	....	8300	R	
179	545 kg at	Growth	90	1000	....	R	....	....	....	1700	R	
180	maturity		185	820	....	R	....	....	....	3300	R	
181			270	590	....	R	....	....	....	5000	R	
182			365	360	....	R	....	....	....	6700	R	
183			455	180	....	R	....	....	....	8300	R	
184			545	0	....	R	....	....	....	10,000	R	
185	635 kg at	Growth	90	1220	....	R	....	....	....	1700	R	
186	maturity		185	1000	....	R	....	....	....	3300	R	
187			270	820	....	R	....	....	....	5000	R	
188			365	590	....	R	....	....	....	6700	R	
189			455	360	....	R	....	....	....	8300	R	

[8] Also required: thiamine, folic acid, choline, ascorbic acid, and α-tocopherol. [9] Vitamin K is required for reproduction but not for growth. [10] Per 100 g diet. [11] Also required: thiamine. Requirement unknown: ascorbic acid and vitamin E.

continued

Part III. Vitamins

	Subjects	Specification	Body Weight kg	Avg Daily Gain g	Riboflavin mg	Niacin mg	B_6 mg	Pantothenic Acid mg	B_{12} µg	A IU	D IU	Reference
190			545	180	....	R	....	....	....	10,000	R	
191			635	0	....	R	....	....	....	11,700	R	
192	Mature	Light work	185	0	....	R	....	....	....	3300	R	
193			270	0	....	R	....	....	....	5000	R	
194			365	0	....	R	....	....	....	6700	R	
195			455	0	....	R	....	....	....	8300	R	
196			545	0	....	R	....	....	....	10,000	R	
197			635	0	....	R	....	....	....	11,700	R	
198		Medium work	185	0	....	R	....	....	....	3300	R	
199			270	0	....	R	....	....	....	5000	R	
200			365	0	....	R	....	....	....	6700	R	
201			455	0	....	R	....	....	....	8300	R	
202			545	0	....	R	....	....	....	10,000	R	
203			635	0	....	R	....	....	....	11,700	R	
204	♀	Pregnancy, last quarter	185	....	....	R	....	....	....	9300	R	
205			270	....	....	R	....	....	....	14,000	R	
206			365	....	....	R	....	....	....	18,700	R	
207			455	....	....	R	....	....	....	23,300	R	
208			545	....	....	R	....	....	....	28,000	R	
209			635	....	....	R	....	....	....	32,700	R	
210		Lactation, peak	185	....	....	R	....	....	....	9300	R	
211			270	....	....	R	....	....	....	14,000	R	
212			365	....	....	R	....	....	....	18,700	R	
213			455	....	....	R	....	....	....	23,300	R	
214			545	....	....	R	....	....	....	28,000	R	
215			635	....	....	R	....	....	....	32,700	R	
216	Felis catus [12]	Growth	......	....	0.4 [10]	4 [10]	0.2 [10]	0.5 [10]	....	2500 [10]	100 [10]	6
217	Macaca mulatta [13]	Growth	3	....	0.17 [10]	11.4 [10]	(0.29-2.9) [10]	R	2.5 [10]	2300 [10]	143 [10]	6
218	Mesocricetus auratus [14,15]	Growth	......	....	0.6 [10]	....	0.6 [10]	1 [10]	1 [10]	1800 [10]	......	6
219	Mus musculus [16]	Growth [17]	......	....	>0.4 [10]	1.0 [10]	0.1 [10]	>0.85 [10]	>0.5 [10]	>50 [10]	15 [10]	6
220		Pregnancy & lactation	......	....	0.7 [10]	....	....	1.02 [10]	0.05 [10]	>50 [10]	......	
221	Oryctolagus cuniculus [18]	Maintenance	......	0	R	<11/kg body wt	0.039	R	R	R	R	1
222	Ovis aries Lamb, ♂♀	Early-weaned	10	250	....	....	....	....	....	850	67	8
223			20	275	....	....	....	....	....	1700	133	
224			30	300	....	....	....	....	....	2550	200	

[10] Per 100 g diet. [12] Also required: thiamine, inositol, choline, and α-tocopherol. Not required: folic acid and ascorbic acid. Requirement unknown: biotin and vitamin K. [13] Also required: thiamine, biotin, folic acid, ascorbic acid, and vitamin K. Requirement unknown: inositol, choline, and α-tocopherol. [14] Synonym: *Cricetus auratus.* [15] Also required: thiamine and α-tocopherol. Not required: folic acid and ascorbic acid. Requirement unknown: biotin, inositol, choline, and vitamin K. [16] Also required: thiamine, biotin, folic acid, choline, and α-tocopherol. Requirement unknown: inositol and vitamin K. [17] Based on average daily feed requirements during 2-wk period following weaning. [18] Also required: biotin, folic acid, choline, and α-tocopherol; for reproduction, vitamin K required. Not required: ascorbic acid.

continued

Part III. Vitamins

	Subjects	Specification	Body Weight kg	Avg Daily Gain g	Riboflavin mg	Niacin mg	B_6 mg	Pantothenic Acid [1] mg	B_{12} µg	A IU	D IU	Reference
225		Fattening	30	200	....	....	....	....	....	765	166	
226			35	220	....	....	....	....	....	892	194	
227			40	250	....	....	....	....	....	1020	222	
228			45	250	....	....	....	....	....	1148	250	
229			50	220	....	....	....	....	....	1275	278	
230			55	200	....	....	....	....	....	1402	305	
	Lamb & yearling [19]											
231	♂	Replacement	40	250	....	....	....	....	....	1700	222	
232			60	200	....	....	....	....	....	2550	333	
233			80	150	....	....	....	....	....	3400	444	
234			100	100	....	....	....	....	....	4250	555	
235			120	50	....	....	....	....	....	5100	666	
236	♀	Replacement	30	180	....	....	....	....	....	1275	166	
237			40	120	....	....	....	....	....	1700	222	
238			50	80	....	....	....	....	....	2125	278	
239			60	40	....	....	....	....	....	2550	333	
240			70	10	....	....	....	....	....	2970	388	
241	Ewe	Nonpreg- nant	50	10	....	....	....	....	....	850	278	
242			60	10	....	....	....	....	....	1020	333	
243			70	10	....	....	....	....	....	1190	388	
244			80	10	....	....	....	....	....	1360	444	
245		Nonlactat- ing; preg- nancy, first 15 wk	50	30	....	....	....	....	....	1275	278	
246			60	30	....	....	....	....	....	1530	333	
247			70	30	....	....	....	....	....	1785	388	
248			80	30	....	....	....	....	....	2040	444	
249		Pregnancy, last 6 wk; or ⟨lacta- tion, last 8 wk suckling single lamb⟩	50	175 ⟨45⟩	....	....	....	....	....	4250	278	
250			60	175 ⟨45⟩	....	....	....	....	....	5100	333	
251			70	175 ⟨45⟩	....	....	....	....	....	5950	388	
252			80	175 ⟨45⟩	....	....	....	....	....	6800	444	
253			90	175 ⟨45⟩	....	....	....	....	....	7650	500	
254		Lactation, first 8 wk suckling singles or (twins); or ⟨last 8 wk suckling twins⟩	50	−25(−60) ⟨+80⟩	..	....	....	....	....	4250	278	
255			60	−25(−60) ⟨+80⟩	..	....	....	....	....	5100	333	
256			70	−25(−60) ⟨+80⟩	..	....	....	....	....	5950	388	
257			80	−25(−60) ⟨+80⟩	..	....	....	....	....	6800	444	
258	*Rattus nor- vegi- cus* [20]	Growth	......	....	0.025[21]	0.15[21,22]	0.07[21]	0.08[21,23]	0.05[21]	20[21]	10[21]	6
259					0.25[10]	1.5[10]	0.7[10]	0.8[10]	0.5[10]	200[10]	100[10]	
260		Pregnancy	......	....	0.08[21]	....	0.012[21]	0.16[21,23]	0.1[21]	240[21]	0.6[21]	
261					0.4[10]	....	0.06[10]	0.8[10]	0.5[10]	1200[10]	3[10]	
262		Lactation	......	....	0.12[21]	....	0.012[21]	0.3[21]	0.15[21]	360[21]	0.6[21]	
263					0.4[10]	....	0.04[10]	1.0[10]	0.5[10]	1200[10]	2[10]	
264	*Sus scrofa*	Growth	5-10	....	1.8	13.2	0.9	7.8	13.2	1300	132	9
265			10-20	....	3.8	22.5	1.9	13.8	18.8	2200	250	
266			20-35	....	4.4	23.8	1.9	18.7	18.7	2200	340	

[1] Unless otherwise indicated. [10] Per 100 g diet. [19] Replacement lambs' requirements start at time they are weaned. [20] Also required: thiamine, choline, α-tocopherol, and vitamin K. Not required: ascorbic acid. [21] Calculated from values obtained experimentally, assuming a daily feed intake of 10 g for growth, 20 g for pregnancy, and 30 g for lactation. [22] Assuming there is no more than 0.15% tryptophan in the diet. [23] As calcium pantothenate, 0.8 mg calcium pantothenate per 100 g diet was sufficient to permit tissue acetylation reactions in the adult animal.

continued

Part III. Vitamins

	Subjects	Specification	Body Weight kg	Avg Daily Gain g	Riboflavin mg	Niacin mg	B$_6$ mg	Pantothenic Acid mg	B$_{12}$ µg	A IU	D IU	Reference
267		Finishing, full-fed	35-60	....	5.5	25.0	....	27.5	27.7	3250	412	
268			60-100	....	7.7	35.0	....	38.5	38.5	4550	437	
	Boar											
269	Young	Maintenance	110-180	....	10.0	55.0	....	41.3	35.0	10,250	690	
270	Mature	Maintenance	180-250	....	8.0	44.0	....	33.0	28.0	8200	550	
271	Gilt	Pregnancy	110-160	....	8.0	44.0	....	33.0	28.0	8200	550	
272		Lactation	140-200	....	17.5	87.5	....	65.0	55.0	16,500	1100	
273	Sow	Pregnancy	160-250	....	8.0	44.0	....	33.0	28.0	8200	550	
274		Lactation	200-250	....	19.3	96.3	....	71.5	60.5	18,150	1210	
	Gallus gallus [24/]											4
275	Single-	Growth	0.250	....	0.096	0.73	0.081	0.27	0.24	40	5.4	
276	comb		0.500	....	0.162	1.21	0.13	0.45	0.40	68	9.0	
277	White		0.750	....	0.206	1.54	0.17	0.57	0.51	86	11.4	
278	Leghorn		1.000	....	0.117	0.71	....	0.65	....	98	13.0	
279	or similar		1.250	....	0.142	0.87	....	0.79	....	118	15.8	
280	breeds		1.500	....	0.151	0.92	....	0.84	....	126	16.8	
281	Adult	60% egg-production	1.800	....	0.242	....	0.33	0.242	....	440	55	
282		Breeding	1.800	....	0.420	....	0.49	1.10	0.33	440	55	
283	Heavy	Growth	0.250	....	0.12	0.95	0.10	0.35	0.32	52	7.0	
284	breeds		0.500	....	0.20	1.53	0.17	0.57	0.51	86	11.4	
285			0.750	....	0.26	1.97	0.22	0.73	0.66	110	14.6	
286			1.000	....	0.30	2.3	0.25	0.84	0.76	126	16.8	
287			1.500	....	0.36	2.7	0.30	1.0	0.90	150	20.0	
288	Adult	60% egg-production	2.500	....	0.27	....	0.37	0.27	....	500	62	
289		Breeding	2.500	....	0.48	....	0.56	1.25	0.37	500	62	

24/ Also required: thiamine, biotin, folic acid, vitamin E, and vitamin K; for growth, choline required.

Contributors: Bird, Herbert R.; Christison, G. I., and Bell, J. M.; Corbin, James E.; Cunha, T. J.; Jacobson, N. L.; Perry, T. W.; Pope, A. L.; Smith, S. E.; Tyznik, W. J.

References

[1] National Research Council, Agricultural Board. 1966. Nat. Acad. Sci. Nat. Res. Counc. Publ. 1194.
[2] Ibid. 2045, 1973.
[3] Ibid. 1754, 1970.
[4] Ibid. 1861, 1971.
[5] Ibid. 1916, 1971.
[6] Ibid. 2028, 1972.
[7] Ibid. 2043, 1972.
[8] Ibid. Nutrient Requirements of Sheep. Ed. 5. 1974.
[9] Ibid. Nutrient Requirements of Swine. Ed. 7. 1973.

Essential amino acids are not synthesized by the body, and therefore must be supplied by the diet in proper proportions and amounts to meet the requirements for normal growth in the young and for maintenance of nitrogen balance in the adult. Nonessential amino acids, if not supplied in the diet, can be synthesized in adequate amounts from other nitrogen sources, and can be utilized by man and probably by most other vertebrates. **Amino Acid: DAAN =** dispensable amino acid nitrogen.

	Subjects	Requirement for	Amino Acid	Value[1]	Unit of Measurement	Reference
	Homo sapiens					
1	<1 yr old	Growth	L-His	34	mg·kg body wt⁻¹·da⁻¹	1
2			L-Ile	126		
3			L-Leu	150		
4			L-Lys	103		
5			L-Met	45[2]		
6			L-Phe	90[3]		
7			L-Thr	87		
8			L-Trp	22		
9			L-Val	105		
10	>1 yr old	Growth	L-Ile	1000	mg/da	3-6
11			L-Leu	1500		
12			L-Lys	1600		
13			L-Met	800[2]		
14			L-Phe	800[3]		
15			L-Thr	1000		
16			L-Trp	250		
17			L-Val	900		
18	Adult ♂	Maintenance	L-Cys + L-Met	1100[4]	mg/da	12
19			L-Ile	700		
20			L-Leu	1100		
21			L-Lys	800		
22			L-Phe + L-Tyr	1100[5]		
23			L-Thr	500		
24			L-Trp	250		
25			L-Val	800		
26	Adult ♀	Maintenance	L-Cys + L-Met	550[4]	mg/da	12
27			L-Ile	450		
28			L-Leu	620		
29			L-Lys	500		
30			L-Phe + L-Tyr	1120[5]		
31			L-Thr	305		
32			L-Trp	157		
33			L-Val	650		
	Canis familiaris					
34	Immature	Growth	L-Arg	270	mg·kg body wt⁻¹·da⁻¹	2
35			L-Cys + L-Met	210[4]		
36			L-His	60		
37			L-Ile	330		

	Subjects	Requirement for	Amino Acid	Value	Unit of Measurement	Reference
38			L-Leu	370		
39			L-Lys	220		
40			L-Phe + L-Tyr	190[5]		
41			L-Thr	140		
42			L-Trp	60		
43			L-Val	300		
44	Adult	Nitrogen balance	L-Arg	48	mg·kg body wt⁻¹·da⁻¹	11
45			L-Cys + L-Met	53[4]		
46			L-His	22		
47			L-Ile	70		
48			L-Leu	106		
49			L-Lys	68		
50			L-Phe + L-Tyr	86[5]		
51			L-Thr	44		
52			L-Trp	13		
53			L-Val	66		
	Rattus norvegicus					
54	Immature	Growth	L-Arg	0.60	% of diet	10
55			L-Asn	0.40		
56			L-Cys + L-Met	0.60[4]		
57			L-Glu	4.00		
58			L-His	0.30		
59			L-Ile	0.55		
60			L-Leu	0.75		
61			L-Lys	0.90		
62			L-Phe + L-Tyr	0.80[5]		
63			L-Pro	0.40		
64			L-Thr	0.50		
65			L-Trp	0.15		
66			L-Val	0.60		
67			DAAN	0.55		
68	Adult	Maintenance	L-Cys + L-Met	0.23[4]	% of diet	10
69			L-His	0.07		
70			L-Ile	0.43		
71			L-Leu	0.25		
72			L-Lys	0.14		
73			L-Phe + L-Tyr	0.19[5]		

[1] Unless otherwise indicated. [2] In presence of adequate L-cystine. [3] In presence of adequate L-tyrosine. [4] 30-50% of total requirement may be furnished by L-cystine. [5] 30-50% of total requirement may be furnished by L-tyrosine.

continued

	Subjects	Require-ment for	Amino Acid	Value[1]	Unit of Measure-ment	Ref-er-ence		Subjects	Require-ment for	Amino Acid	Value	Unit of Measure-ment	Ref-er-ence
74			L-Thr	0.17			117			L-Trp	0.13		
75			L-Trp	0.07			118			L-Val	0.50		
76			L-Val	0.31			119	Adult	Gesta-tion	L-Cys + L-Met	0.35[4]	% of diet	9
77			DAAN	0.42			120			L-His	0.20		
78		Gesta-tion	L-Arg	0.75	% of diet	10	121			L-Ile	0.43		
79			L-Cys + L-Met	0.60[4]			122			L-Leu	0.66		
80			L-His	0.54			123			L-Lys	0.49		
81			L-Ile	0.55			124			L-Phe + L-Tyr	0.52[5]		
82			L-Leu	0.75			125			L-Thr	0.42		
83			L-Lys	1.24			126			L-Trp	0.08		
84			L-Phe + L-Tyr	0.80[5]			127			L-Val	0.46		
85			L-Thr	0.50				*Gallus gallus*					
86			L-Trp	0.20			128	Meat-	Growth	L-Arg	1.40	% of diet	8
87			L-Val	0.60			129	type, 0-		L-Cys + L-Met	0.86[4]		
88			DAAN	0.87				6 wk					
89		Lacta-tion	L-Arg	0.75	% of diet	10	130	old		Gly and/or L-Ser	1.15		
90			L-Cys + L-Met	1.00[4]			131			L-His	0.46		
91			L-His	0.54			132			L-Ile	0.86		
92			L-Ile	0.55			133			L-Leu	1.60		
93			L-Leu	0.75			134			L-Lys	1.25		
94			L-Lys	1.24			135			L-Phe + L-Tyr	1.50[5]		
95			L-Phe + L-Tyr	0.80[5]			136			L-Thr	0.80		
96			L-Thr	0.50			137			L-Trp	0.23		
97			L-Trp	0.20			138			L-Val	1.0		
98			DAAN	0.84				Replacement ♀					
	Sus scrofa						139	0-6 wk	Growth	L-Arg	1.20	% of diet	8
99	5-10 kg	Growth	L-Arg	Fn[6]	% of diet	9	140	old		L-Cys + L-Met	0.75[4]		
100			L-Cys + L-Met	0.80[4]			141			Gly and/or L-Ser	1.00		
101			L-His	0.27			142			L-His	0.40		
102			L-Ile	0.76			143			L-Ile	0.75		
103			L-Leu	0.90			144			L-Leu	1.40		
104			L-Lys	1.20			145			L-Lys	1.10		
105			L-Phe	Fn[6]			146			L-Phe + L-Tyr	1.30[5]		
106			L-Thr	0.70			147			L-Thr	0.70		
107			L-Trp	0.18			148			L-Trp	0.20		
108			L-Val	0.65			149			L-Val	0.85		
109	20-35 kg	Growth	L-Arg	0.20	% of diet	9	150	14-20	Growth	L-Arg	0.95	% of diet	8
110			L-Cys + L-Met	0.50[4]			151	wk old		L-Cys + L-Met	0.60[4]		
111			L-His	0.18			152			Gly and/or L-Ser	0.80		
112			L-Ile	0.50			153			L-His	0.32		
113			L-Leu	0.60			154			L-Ile	0.60		
114			L-Lys	0.70			155			L-Leu	1.10		
115			L-Phe + L-Tyr	0.50[5]									
116			L-Thr	0.45									

[1] Unless otherwise indicated. [4] 30-50% of total require-ment may be furnished by L-cystine. [5] 30-50% of total requirement may be furnished by L-tyrosine. [6] Required, but level has not been established.

continued

	Subjects	Requirement for	Amino Acid	Value	Unit of Measurement	Reference
156			L-Lys	0.90		
157			L-Phe + L-Tyr	1.05 5/		
158			L-Thr	0.55		
159			L-Trp	0.16		
160			L-Val	0.70		
161	Breeding ♀; adult	Egg production	L-Arg	0.80	% of diet	8
162			L-Cys + L-Met	0.53 4/		
163			L-Ile	0.50		
164			L-Leu	1.20		
165			L-Lys	0.50		
166			L-Thr	0.40		
167			L-Trp	0.11		
168			L-Arg	0.8	% of diet	7
169			L-Ile	0.5		
170			L-Leu	1.2		
171			L-Lys	0.5		
172			L-Met	0.28 7/		
173			L-Trp	0.15		
174			L-His	0.3	% of diet	13
175			L-Phe	0.7 8/		
176			L-Thr	0.55		
177			L-Val	0.8		
178	*Meleagris gallopavo* 0-4 wk old	Growth	L-Arg	1.6	% of diet	8
179			L-Cys + L-Met	0.87 4/		
180			Gly and/or L-Ser	1.0		
181			L-His	0.55		
182			L-Ile	1.1		
183			L-Leu	1.9		
184			L-Lys	1.5		

	Subjects	Requirement for	Amino Acid	Value	Unit of Measurement	Reference
185			L-Phe + L-Tyr	1.80 5/		
186			L-Thr	1.00		
187			L-Trp	0.26		
188			L-Val	1.2		
189	♂, 8-12 wk old; ♀, 8-11 wk old	Growth	L-Arg	1.3	% of diet	8
190			L-Cys + L-Met	0.74 4/		
191			Gly and/or L-Ser	0.8		
192			L-His	0.45		
193			L-Ile	0.85		
194			L-Leu	1.5		
195			L-Lys	1.2		
196			L-Phe + L-Tyr	1.4 5/		
197			L-Thr	0.8		
198			L-Trp	0.2		
199			L-Val	0.95		
200	♂, 20-24 wk old; ♀, 17-20 wk old	Growth	L-Arg	0.8	% of diet	8
201			L-Cys + L-Met	0.43 4/		
202			Gly and/or L-Ser	0.5		
203			L-His	0.25		
204			L-Ile	0.55		
205			L-Leu	0.95		
206			L-Lys	0.75		
207			L-Phe + L-Tyr	0.90 5/		
208			L-Thr	0.50		
209			L-Trp	0.13		
210			L-Val	0.60		

4/ 30-50% of total requirement may be furnished by L-cystine. 5/ 30-50% of total requirement may be furnished by L-tyrosine. 7/ Requirement for methionine plus cystine may be met by 0.53% methionine. 8/ Requirement for phenylalanine plus tyrosine may be met by 1.0% phenylalanine.

Contributors: Breuer, L. H.; Almquist, H. J.

References

[1] Holt, L. E., Jr., et al. 1960. Protein and Amino Acid Requirements in Early Life. New York Univ. Press, New York.

[2] Mabee, P. M., and A. F. Morgan. 1951. J. Nutr. 43: 261.

[3] Nakagawa, I., et al. 1960. Ibid. 71:176.

[4] Nakagawa, I., et al. 1961. Ibid. 73:186.

[5] Nakagawa, I., et al. 1961. Ibid. 74:401.

[6] Nakagawa, I., et al. 1962. Ibid. 77:61.

[7] National Research Council, Agricultural Board. 1966. Nat. Acad. Sci. Nat. Res. Counc. Publ. 1345:6.

[8] Ibid. 1861, 1970.

[9] Ibid. 1923, 1971.

[10] Ibid. 2028, 1972.

[11] Ibid. 2043, 1972.

[12] National Research Council, Food and Nutrition Board. 1959. Ibid. 711.

[13] Scott, M. L., et al. 1969. Nutrition of the Chicken. M. L. Scott, Ithaca, New York. p. 86.

Enzyme Commission No. = number assigned by the International Union of Biochemistry on the Nomenclature and Classification of Enzymes (*see* reference 20 in Part I). For a detailed discussion of the methods of preparation and of the physical and kinetic properties of proteolytic enzymes, consult reference 38 in Part I.

Part I. Physical Properties

$s_{20,w}$ (sedimentation coefficient) and $D_{20,w}$ (diffusion coefficient): Values are for data normalized to standard conditions of water at 20°C and extrapolated to zero protein concentration. **Isoelectric Point:** Values given are apparent pH values determined from electrophoretic mobility measurements. $E_{1\,cm}^{1\%}$ = extinction coefficient of a 1% protein solution of 1-cm thickness at the wavelength (λ) specified. Data in brackets refer to the column heading in brackets.

	Enzyme [Commission No.]	Source	$s_{20,w}$ s·10^{13}	$D_{20,w}$ cm²·s⁻¹ × 10⁷	Molecular Weight	Iso-electric Point pH	$E_{1\,cm}^{1\%}$ λ, nm	$E_{1\,cm}^{1\%}$ Value	Reference
				Enzymes					
1	Leucine aminopeptidase [3.4.1.1]	*Bos taurus* lens	12.56	3.75	326,000	4.9	281	8.6	18,29
2	Carboxypeptidase A [3.4.2.1]	*Bos taurus* pancreas	3.06	8.82	34,300	5.60[1]	278	19.4	2,27,39, 41,46, 49
3	Carboxypeptidase B [3.4.2.2]	*Sus scrofa* pancreas	3.23	8.16	34,300	....	278	21.4	11
4	Pepsin [3.4.4.1]	*Sus scrofa* stomach mucosa	2.88	8.71	32,700	<1.0	280	14.3	4,8,37, 40,52
5	Trypsin [3.4.4.4]	*Bos taurus* pancreas	2.50	9.40	23,800	10.5	280	15.4	5,6,30,31
6	Chymotrypsin A[2] [3.4.4.5]	*Bos taurus* pancreas	2.56	10.2	25,000	8.1- 8.6[3]	280	20.4	1,30,43, 45,53
7	Papain [3.4.4.10]	*Carica papaya*[4] latex	2.42	10.27	23,400	8.75	278	25.0	12,13,28
8	Ficin [3.4.4.12]	*Ficus glabrata* latex	.....	.....	25,500	....	280	21.0	10
9	Subtilopeptidase A[5] [3.4.4.16] Type BPN′	*Bacillus subtilis* N′	2.76	9.04	27,600	7.8	278	11.7	17,34
10	Type Carlsberg	*Bacillus subtilis* Carlsberg	2.85	.....	27,600	9.4	280	8.6; 9.8	15,16,22, 47
11	*Streptococcus* peptidase A[6] [3.4.4.18]	*Streptococcus* sp. 5797[7]	.....	.....	32,000	....	280	16.4	9,32,33
12	Bromelain [3.4.4.24]	*Ananas comosus*	2.73	7.77	33,000	9.55	280	19.0	35
13	AL-1 protease [3.4.4.x]	Myxobacter, AL-1	2.40	14.0	14,300	....	280	15.8	21
14	α-Lytic protease [3.4.4.x]	*Sorangium* sp. 495	2.2	.....	20,100	....	280	9.65	23-25
				Enzyme Precursors					
15	Chymotrypsinogen A	*Bos taurus* pancreas	2.54	9.5	25,100	9.1	282	20.0	7,36,42, 50,51
16	Pepsinogen	*Sus scrofa* stomach mucosa	3.24	.....	40,400; 38,944	3.7	278	12.5	3,19,36, 40,52
17	Streptococcal proteinase zymogen	*Streptococcus* sp. 5797[7]	.....	.....	44,000	....	280	13.7	9,32,33
18	Trypsinogen	*Bos taurus* pancreas	2.7	9.7	24,500	9.3	280	15.2	14,26,36, 44,48

[1] Determined at 0.3 ionic strength. [2] Synonym: α-chymotrypsin. [3] Depends on the ionic strength of the buffer. [4] Synonym: *Papaya carica*. [5] Synonym: subtilisin. [6] Synonym: streptococcal proteinase. [7] Group A; American Type Culture Collection No. 12112.

Contributor: Glazer, A. N.

continued

177. PROPERTIES OF PROTEOLYTIC ENZYMES AND THEIR PRECURSORS

Part I. Physical Properties

References

[1] Anderson, E. A., and R. A. Alberty. 1948. J. Phys. Colloid Chem. 52:1345.

[2] Anson, M. L. 1937. J. Gen. Physiol. 20:663.

[3] Arnon, R., and G. E. Perlmann. 1963. J. Biol. Chem. 238:653.

[4] Blumenfeld, O. O., et al. 1960. Ibid. 235:379.

[5] Cunningham, L. W., Jr. 1954. Ibid. 211:13.

[6] Cunningham, L. W., Jr., et al. 1953. Discuss. Faraday Soc. 13:58.

[7] Desnuelle, P., and M. Rovery. 1961. Advan. Protein Chem. 16:139.

[8] Edelhoch, H. 1957. J. Amer. Chem. Soc. 79:6100.

[9] Elliott, S. D. 1950. J. Exp. Med. 92:201.

[10] Englund, P. T., et al. 1968. Biochemistry 7:163.

[11] Folk, J. E., et al. 1960. J. Biol. Chem. 235:2272.

[12] Glazer, A. N., and E. L. Smith. 1961. Ibid. 236:2948.

[13] Glazer, A. N., and E. L. Smith. 1971. In P. D. Boyer, ed. The Enzymes. Academic Press, New York. v. 3, pp. 501-546.

[14] Green, N. M., and H. Neurath. 1954. In H. Neurath and K. Bailey, ed. The Proteins. Academic Press, New York. v. 2(B), pp. 1057-1198.

[15] Güntelberg, A. V. 1954. C. R. Trav. Lab. Carlsberg 29:27.

[16] Güntelberg, A. V., and M. Ottesen. 1954. Ibid. 29:36.

[17] Hagihara, B., et al. 1958. J. Biochem. (Tokyo) 45:185.

[18] Hanson, H., et al. 1965. Hoppe Seylers Z. Physiol. Chem. 340:107.

[19] Herriott, R. M. 1938. J. Gen. Physiol. 21:501.

[20] International Union of Biochemistry. 1965. Enzyme Nomenclature. Elsevier, New York.

[21] Jackson, R. L., and R. S. Wolfe. 1968. J. Biol. Chem. 243:879.

[22] Johansen, J. T. 1970. C. R. Trav. Lab. Carlsberg 37:145.

[23] Jurasek, L., and D. R. Whitaker. 1965. Can. J. Biochem. 43:1955.

[24] Jurasek, L., and D. R. Whitaker. 1965. Ibid. 45:917.

[25] Kaplan, H., and D. R. Whitaker. 1969. Ibid. 47:305.

[26] Kay, C. M., et al. 1961. J. Biol. Chem. 236:118.

[27] Keller, P. J., et al. 1956. Ibid. 223:457.

[28] Kimmel, J. R., and E. L. Smith. 1954. Ibid. 207:515.

[29] Kretschmer, K., and H. Hanson. 1965. Hoppe Seylers Z. Physiol. Chem. 340:126.

[30] Kunitz, M., and J. H. Northrop. 1936. J. Gen. Physiol. 19:991.

[31] Laskowski, M. 1961. In C. Long, ed. Biochemists' Handbook. Van Nostrand, New York, pp. 301-302.

[32] Liu, T.-Y., and S. D. Elliott. 1965. J. Biol. Chem. 240:1138.

[33] Liu, T.-Y., et al. 1963. Ibid. 238:251.

[34] Matsubara, H., et al. 1965. Ibid. 240:1125.

[35] Murachi, T., et al. 1964. Biochemistry 3:48.

[36] Northrop, J. H., et al. 1948. Crystalline Enzymes. Ed. 2. Columbia Univ. Press, New York.

[37] Perlmann, G. E. 1955. Advan. Protein Chem. 10:23.

[38] Perlmann, G. E., and L. Lorand, ed. 1970. Methods Enzymol. 19.

[39] Putnam, F. W., and H. Neurath. 1946. J. Biol. Chem. 166:603.

[40] Rajagopalan, T. G., et al. 1966. Ibid. 241:4940.

[41] Rupley, J. A., and H. Neurath. 1960. Ibid. 235:609.

[42] Schwert, G. W. 1951. Ibid. 190:799.

[43] Schwert, G. W., and S. Kaufman. 1951. Ibid. 190:807.

[44] Smillie, L. B., and C. M. Kay. 1961. Ibid. 236:112.

[45] Smith, E. L., and D. M. Brown. 1952. Ibid. 195:525.

[46] Smith, E. L., et al. 1949. Ibid. 180:33.

[47] Smith, E. L., et al. 1966. Ibid. 241:5974.

[48] Tietze, F. 1953. Ibid. 204:1.

[49] Vallee, B. L., et al. 1960. Ibid. 235:64.

[50] Wilcox, P. E., et al. 1957. Biochim. Biophys. Acta 24:72.

[51] Wilcox, P. E., et al. 1957. J. Biol. Chem. 228:999.

[52] Williams, R. C., and T. G. Rajagopalan. 1966. Ibid. 241:4951.

[53] Worthington Biochemical Corporation. 1967. Enzymes and Enzyme Reagents. Freehold, N.J.

Part II. Kinetic Properties

K_m (Michaelis constant) = $(k_{-1} + k_{+2})/k_{+1}$, where k_{-1} = velocity constant for dissociation of the enzyme-substrate complex into substrate and enzyme, k_{+2} = velocity constant for the breakdown of the enzyme-substrate complex into

continued

Part II. Kinetic Properties

products, and k_{+1} = velocity constant for formation of the enzyme-substrate complex. k_{cat} (catalytic coefficient) = V_{max}/E_0, where E_0 = total enzyme concentration, in moles·liter^{-1}, and V_{max} (maximal velocity, in moles·liter^{-1}·s^{-1}) =

$v(1 + K_m/S)$, where v is the measured velocity, in moles·liter^{-1}·s^{-1}, at a substrate concentration S, in moles·liter^{-1} Data in brackets refer to the column heading in brackets.

Enzyme [Commission No.]	Source	Optimum pH	Substrate	Temp °C	pH	K_m moles·liter^{-1}	k_{cat} s^{-1}	Reference
1 Leucine aminopeptidase [3.4.1.1]	*Bos taurus* lens	9-10	L-Leucinamide [L]	40	9.0	3.13×10^{-2}	2.76×10^4	12
2 Carboxypeptidase A [3.4.2.1]	*Bos taurus* pancreas	7.4	Benzyloxycarbonylglycyl-L-phenylalanine	25	7.5	5.83×10^{-3}	106	1,24, 27
3 Carboxypeptidase B [3.4.2.2]	*Sus scrofa* pancreas	7.9- 8.0	Hippuryl-L-arginic acid	23	8.0	0.4×10^{-4}	238	5,28
4			Hippuryl-L-arginine	23	8.0	2.1×10^{-4}	105	5,28
5 Pepsin [3.4.4.1]	*Sus scrofa* stomach mucosa	1.8-4	N-acetyl-L-phenylalanyl-L-tyrosine	37	2.0	2.2×10^{-3}	0.085	15,16, 22, 23
6			Benzyloxycarbonyl-L-histidinyl-L-phenylalanyl-L-tryptophan ethyl ester	37	4.0	2.3×10^{-4}	0.51	15,16, 22, 23
7 Trypsin [3.4.4.4]	*Bos taurus* pancreas	7.6-8	Benzoyl-L-arginine ethyl ester	25	8.0	8×10^{-5}	14.3	8,14, 19, 20
8 Chymotrypsin A [2] [3.4.4.5]	*Bos taurus* pancreas	7-9	Acetyl-L-tyrosine ethyl ester	25	8.0	0.7×10^{-3}	193	3,10, 19
9 Papain [3.4.4.10]	*Carica papaya* [3] latex	5-8	Benzoyl-L-arginine ethyl ester	25	6.0	1.33×10^{-2}	28.5	2,18, 26
10 Ficin [3.4.4.12]	*Ficus glabrata* latex	5-8	Benzoyl-L-arginine ethyl ester	35	6.0	4.17×10^{-2}	9.4	25
Subtilopeptidase A [4] [3.4.4.16]								
11 Type BPN'	*Bacillus subtilis* N'	8-10	Benzoyl-L-arginine ethyl ester	37	8.0	1×10^{-2}	4.6	7,11
12 Type Carlsberg	*Bacillus subtilis* Carlsberg	8-10	Benzoyl-L-arginine ethyl ester	37	8.0	7×10^{-3}	16.1	7,9
13 *Streptococcus* peptidase A [5] [3.4.4.18]	*Streptococcus* sp. 5797 [6]	7.4- 7.7	Benzyloxycarbonyl-L-phenylalanyl-L-leucine	37	7.6	1.2×10^{-3}	1.02	4,6
14 Bromelain [3.4.4.24]	*Ananas comosus*	5-8	Benzoyl-L-argininamide	25	6.0	1.2×10^{-3}	0.0035	13,21
15			Benzoyl-L-arginine ethyl ester	25	6.0	0.17	0.50	13,21
16 α-Lytic protease [3.4.4.x]	*Sorangium* sp. 495	7-8	Acetyl-L-valine methyl ester	25	7.0	7.2×10^{-2}	0.94	17

[L] The enzyme was preincubated for 20 min with 0.0025 *M* Mn^{2+} at pH 9.0 and 40°C; the assay was performed in the presence of 0.002 *M* Mn^{2+}. [2] Synonym: α-chymotrypsin.

[3] Synonym: *Papaya carica*. [4] Synonym: subtilisin. [5] Synonym: streptococcal proteinase. [6] Group A; American Type Culture Collection No. 12112.

Contributor: Glazer, A. N.

References

[1] Anson, M. L. 1937. J. Gen. Physiol. 20:663.
[2] Blumberg, S., et al. 1970. Eur. J. Biochem. 15:97.
[3] Cunningham, L. W., Jr., and C. S. Brown. 1956. J. Biol. Chem. 221:287.

[4] Elliott, S. D. 1950. J. Exp. Med. 92:201.
[5] Folk, J. E., et al. 1960. J. Biol. Chem. 235:2272.
[6] Gerwin, B. I., et al. 1966. Ibid. 241:3331.
[7] Glazer, A. N. 1967. Ibid. 242:433.

continued

Part II.   Kinetic Properties

[8] Green, N. M., and H. Neurath. 1953. Ibid. 204:379.

[9] Güntelberg, A. V. 1954. C. R. Trav. Lab. Carlsberg 29:27.

[10] Gutfreund, H., and J. M. Sturtevant. 1956. Biochem. J. 63:655.

[11] Hagihara, B., et al. 1958. J. Biochem. (Tokyo) 45:185.

[12] Hanson, H., et al. 1965. Hoppe Seylers Z. Physiol. Chem. 340:107.

[13] Inagami, T., and T. Murachi. 1963. Biochemistry 2:1439.

[14] Inagami, T., and J. M. Sturtevant. 1960. Biochim. Biophys. Acta 38:64.

[15] Inouye, K., et al. 1966. Biochemistry 5:2473.

[16] Jackson, W. T., et al. 1966. Ibid. 5:4105.

[17] Kaplan, H., and D. R. Whitaker. 1969. Can. J. Biochem. 47:305.

[18] Kimmel, J. R., and E. L. Smith. 1954. J. Biol. Chem. 207:515.

[19] Kunitz, M., and J. H. Northrop. 1936. J. Gen. Physiol. 19:991.

[20] Laskowski, M. 1961. In C. Long, ed. Biochemists' Handbook. Van Nostrand, New York. pp. 301-302.

[21] Murachi, T., et al. 1964. Biochemistry 3:48.

[22] Northrop, J. H. 1922. J. Gen. Physiol. 5:263.

[23] Rajagopalan, T. G., et al. 1966. J. Biol. Chem. 241:4940.

[24] Smith, E. L., and H. T. Hanson. 1949. Ibid. 176:997.

[25] Whitaker, J. R. 1969. Biochemistry 8:1896.

[26] Whitaker, J. R., and M. L. Bender. 1965. J. Amer. Chem. Soc. 87:2728.

[27] Whitaker, J. R., et al. 1966. Biochemistry 5:386.

[28] Wolff, E. C., et al. 1962. J. Biol. Chem. 237:3095.

178.   CATALYTIC ACTION OF DIGESTIVE ENZYMES

Enzyme Commission No. = number assigned by the International Union of Biochemistry on the Nomenclature and Classification of Enzymes [4]. **Method:** Mano = manometric; Col = colorimetric; Chem = chemical; Titr = titrimetric; Phys = physical; Pol = polariscopic; Enz = enzymatic. **Conditions Suitable for Enzyme Action** vary with the method used and with the source of the enzyme. Data in brackets refer to the column heading in brackets.

	Enzyme (Synonym) [Commission No.]	Reaction Catalyzed	Occurrence	Method	Conditions Suitable for Enzyme Action		
					Temp °C	pH	Substrate Concentration [Cofactor]
1	Xanthine oxidase [1.2.3.2]	Xanthine or aldehyde→uric or other acids	Intestinal mucosa	Mano	20	7.5	3 mM
2	Lipoxygenase (Lipoxidase) [1.13.1.13]	Unsaturated fat→peroxide of unsaturated fat	Intestinal mucosa	Col	25	6.5	0.02%
3	Hypoxanthine phosphoribosyltransferase (Nucleoside phosphorylase) [2.4.2.8]	Inosinic acid→hypoxanthine + ribose 1-phosphate	Intestinal mucosa	Col	30	7.5	1 mM
4	Phosphoglucomutase [2.7.5.1]	Glucose 1-phosphate→glucose 6-phosphate	Pancreas	Chem	30	7.5-9.2	1 μM [Co^{2+}, Mg^{2+}, Mn^{2+}]
5	Phosphoglyceromutase [2.7.5.3]	3-Phosphoglycerate→2-phosphoglycerate	Pancreas	Chem	24	7	10 μM
6	Ribonuclease [2.7.7.16]	Ribonucleic acid→ribonucleotides	Pancreas	Chem	25	4-5	0.25 mg P/ml
7	Carboxylesterase (Esterase) [3.1.1.1]	Ethyl butyrate→ethanol + butyrate	Gastric & intestinal mucosa, pancreas	Titr	20	8.0	Saturated
8	Lipase [3.1.1.3]	Fats→glycerol + fatty acids	Pancreas	Titr	30	9.0	2.5 g/15 ml [$CaCl_2$]
9	Phospholipase A (Lecithinase A) [3.1.1.4]	Lecithin→lysolecithin + fatty acid	Pancreas	Chem	38	7.0	Egg yolk [Ca^{2+}]
10	Lysophospholipase (Lecithinase B) [3.1.1.5]	Lysolecithin→glycerylphosphorylcholine + fatty acid	Pancreas	Chem	41	4.0	....

continued

Enzyme (Synonym) [Commission No.]	Reaction Catalyzed	Occurrence	Method	Conditions Suitable for Enzyme Action		
				Temp °C	pH	Substrate Concentration [Cofactor]
11 Acetylcholinesterase [3.1.1.7]	Acetylcholine→acetate + choline	Pancreas	Mano	37	7.4	3 mg/ml
12 Cholesterol esterase [3.1.1.13]	Cholesterol esters→cholesterol + acids	Intestinal mucosa, pancreas	.....	....	5.3 or 7.0	....
13 Alkaline phosphatase [3.1.3.1]	Phosphomonoester→alcohol + phosphate	Intestinal mucosa	Chem, Col	37	9.8	100 μM
14 Phytase [3.1.3.8]	Phytate→inositol + phosphate	Intestinal mucosa	Chem	37	5.5-7.8	0.1% [Mg^{2+}]
15 Phosphodiesterase [3.1.4.1]	Cyclic glucose 1,2-phosphate→glucose 1-phosphate	Pancreas	Chem	37	8.0	0.15 M
16 Deoxyribonuclease [3.1.4.5]	Thymonucleic acid→nucleotides	Intestinal mucosa, pancreas	Phys	37	6-7	0.5% [Mg^{2+}, Mn^{2+}]
17 α-Amylase [3.2.1.1]	Starch or glycogen→dextrins + maltose	Saliva, intestinal mucosa, pancreas	Chem, Pol	37	7.0	1% [NaCl]
18 Oligo-1,6-glucosidase (α-1,6-Glucosidase) [3.2.1.10]	Isomaltose→glucose	Pancreas	Chem, Enz	37	6.0	28 mM
19 α-Glucosidase (α-1,4-Glucosidase, maltase) [3.2.1.20]	Maltose→glucose	Intestinal mucosa, pancreas	Pol, Enz	30	7.2	50 mg/ml
20 β-Glucosidase [3.2.1.21]	β-Glucosides→D-glucose + an alcohol	Intestinal mucosa	Pol	30	4.4-5.0	1 mg/ml
21 β-Galactosidase (Lactase) [3.2.1.23]	Lactose→glucose + galactose	Intestinal mucosa, pancreas	Chem, Enz	38	5.6	2.5%
22 β-Fructofuranosidase (Invertase) [3.2.1.26]	Sucrose→glucose + fructose	Intestinal mucosa	Pol	20	4.5	16%
23 Leucine aminopeptidase (Leucylpeptidase) [3.4.1.1]	Leucyl peptides→leucine + other amino acids	Intestinal mucosa	.....	40	8-9	50 mM [Mg^{2+}, Mn^{2+}]
24 Carboxypeptidase A [3.4.2.1]	Peptide with free —COOH→amino acid + peptide	Pancreas	Titr	25	8.5	6% edestin
25 Pepsin [3.4.4.1]	Proteins→peptones, peptides, amino acids	Gastric mucosa	Col	20	1.5-2.0	2%
26 Rennin [3.4.4.3]	Casein→paracasein	Young ruminant stomach	Phys	40	5.8	Raw milk
27 Trypsin [3.4.4.4]	Proteins→polypeptides + amino acids	Pancreas	Col	25	8-9	2.2%
28 Chymotrypsin A [3.4.4.5]	Proteins→polypeptides + amino acids	Pancreas	Chem	38	7.6	5% casein
29 Pancreatopeptidase E (Elastase) [3.4.4.7]	Elastin→polypeptides	Pancreas	Chem	25	8.8	0.25%
30 Enteropeptidase (Enteropeptidase E, enterokinase) [3.4.4.8]	Trypsinogen→trypsin	Intestinal mucosa	Chem	5	5.8	0.065%
31 Salivain [1/] [3.4.4.x]	Proteins→peptides	Saliva	Col	50	9.2	1% hemoglobin
32 Urease [3.5.1.5]	Urea→CO_2 + NH_3	Gastric mucosa	Chem, Col	20	7.0	1.5%
33 Arginase [3.5.3.1]	L-Arginine→L-ornithine + urea	Intestinal mucosa, pancreas	Mano	38	9.5	0.66% [Cu^{2+}, Mn^{2+}]
34 Guanine deaminase (Guanase) [3.5.4.3]	Guanine→xanthine + NH_3	Pancreas	Chem	40	8.7	Saturated

[1/] Enzyme with trypsin-like action; no number yet assigned.

continued

Enzyme (Synonym) [Commission No.]	Reaction Catalyzed	Occurrence	Method	Conditions Suitable for Enzyme Action		
				Temp °C	pH	Substrate Concentration [Cofactor]
35 Adenosine deaminase [3.5.4.4]	Adenosine→inosine + NH_3	Intestinal mucosa	Col	25	7.4	20 μM
36 ATPase (Adenosine triphosphatase) [3.6.1.3]	Adenosine 5'-triphosphate→adenosine 5'-diphosphate + phosphate	Intestinal mucosa, pancreas	Chem	37	7.5	1 mg P/ml [Ca^{2+}]
37 Amino acid decarboxylase (Amino acid carboxylase) [4.1.1.—]	Amino acid→amine + CO_2	Pancreas	Mano	30	4.5-5.0	1 mM [Pyridoxal 5-phosphate]
38 Carbonate dehydratase (Carbonic anhydrase) [4.2.1.1]	H_2CO_3→CO_2 + H_2O	Gastric mucosa	Mano	15	5-9	80 mM
39 Conjugase	Folate 2/→pterin + glutamic acid	Pancreas	.....	37	7-8	[Ca^{2+}]

2/ Pteroylglutamate.

Contributors: Smiley, K. L., and Smiley, M. J.; Perlman, D.

References

[1] Barman, T. E. 1969. Enzyme Handbook. Springer-Verlag, New York. v. 1-2.

[2] Boyer, P. D., ed. 1970-73. The Enzymes. Ed. 3. Academic Press, New York. v. 1-8.

[3] Dixon, M., and E. C. Webb. 1964. Enzymes. Ed. 2. Academic Press, New York.

[4] International Union of Biochemistry. 1965. Enzyme Nomenclature. Elsevier, New York.

[5] Sumner, J. B., and G. F. Somers. 1953. Chemistry and Methods of Enzymes. Ed. 3. Academic Press, New York.

179. DIGESTIVE ENZYMES: VERTEBRATE TISSUES AND SECRETIONS

Enzyme Commission No. = number assigned by the International Union of Biochemistry on the Nomenclature and Classification of Enzymes [32]. **Occurrence: T** = in tissue (presence identified in organ extracts or by histology); **S** = in secretion, either in the active state or as a precursor. *Symbols:* + = present; — = absent; ± = doubtful.

Enzyme (Synonym) [Commission No.]	Organ	Source	Occurrence		Reference		Enzyme (Synonym) [Commission No.]	Organ	Source	Occurrence		Reference	
			T	S	T	S				T	S	T	S
1 Ribonuclease [2.7.7.16; 2.7.7.17]	Salivary gland	*Homo sapiens*	+		18		13		*Ovis aries*	+		2	
2		*Mus* sp.	+		19		14		*Rattus* sp.	+		46	
3		*Oryctolagus cuniculus*	+		50		15		*Sus scrofa*	+		43	
4	Pancreas	*Homo sapiens*	—		50		16 Carboxylic ester hydrolases [3.1.1]	Pancreas	*Rattus* sp.		+	20	
5		*Bos* sp.	+		8								
6		*Canis familiaris*	—		50								
7		*Capra* sp.	+		50								
8		*Cavia porcellus*	+		50		17 Lipase [3.1.1.3]; esterases [3.1]	Salivary gland	*Homo sapiens*	+	+	8	34
9		*Equus caballus*	+		50		18		*Bos* sp.	+	+	12	
10		*Felis catus*	+		50		19		*Canis familiaris*	+	+	12	34
11		*Mus* sp.	+		46		20		*Equus caballus*		+	44	
12		*Oryctolagus cuniculus*	—		50		21		*Oryctolagus cuniculus*	+		12	

continued

#	Enzyme (Synonym) [Commission No.]	Organ	Source	Occurrence T	Occurrence S	Reference T	Reference S
22			*Ovis aries*	+	+	12	34
23			*Rattus* sp.	+		12	
24			*Sus scrofa*	+		12	
25		Esoph-agus	*Homo sapiens*	+		8	
26		Stom-ach	*Homo sapiens*	+	+	8	42
27			*Bos* sp.	+		34	
28			*Canis familiaris*	+	+	42	
29			*Cavia porcellus*	+		34	
30			*Equus caballus*	+		34	
31			*Felis catus*	+		34	
32			*Oryctolagus cuniculus*	+	+	34	42
33			*Ovis aries*	+		34	
34			*Rattus* sp.	+		34	
35			*Sus scrofa*	±		21	
36			*Gallus gallus* L/	+		34	
37		Pan-creas	*Homo sapiens*	+	+	42	
38			*Bos* sp.	+		34	
39			*Canis familiaris*	+	+	4	
40			*Cavia porcellus*		+	42	
41			*Felis catus*	+		4	
42			*Oryctolagus cuniculus*		+	4	
43			*Ovis aries*	+		34	
44			*Rattus* sp.	+	+	4	20
45			*Sus scrofa*	+		28	
46		Small intes-tine	*Homo sapiens*	+	±	15	52
47			*Canis familiaris*	+	±	42	52
48			*Capra* sp.		±	52	
49			*Equus caballus*		−	1	
50			*Felis catus*	−	+	44	39
51			*Oryctolagus cuniculus*		±	52	
52			*Sus scrofa*	+	±	34	52
53		Cecum & co-lon	*Homo sapiens*	+		15	
54			*Canis familiaris*		+	42	
55			*Felis catus*	+		39	
56			*Ovis aries*	−		42	
57	Phospho-monoes-terases (Phospha-tases) [3.1.3]	Sali-vary gland	*Homo sapiens*		+	34	
58			*Bos* sp.	+		12	
59			*Canis familiaris*	+		12	
60			*Felis catus*	+		44	
61			*Oryctolagus cuniculus*	+		12	
62			*Ovis aries*	+		12	
63			*Rattus* sp.	+		12	
64			*Sus scrofa*	+		12	
65		Stom-ach	*Homo sapiens*	+		34	
66			*Felis catus*	+		44	
67			*Oryctolagus cuniculus*	+		44	

#	Enzyme (Synonym) [Commission No.]	Organ	Source	Occurrence T	Occurrence S	Reference T	Reference S
68		Pan-creas	*Bos* sp.	+		16	
69			*Felis catus*	+		44	
70			*Mus* sp.	+		41	
71			*Sus scrofa*	+		36	
72		Small intes-tine	*Homo sapiens*	+		44	
73			*Bos* sp., steer	+		29	
74			*Canis familiaris*	+		44	
75			*Cavia porcellus*	+		41	
76			*Felis catus*	+		44	
77			*Oryctolagus cuniculus*	+		44	
78			*Rattus* sp.	+		41	
79			*Sus scrofa*	+		44	
80			*Gallus gallus* L/	+		41	
81		Cecum & co-lon	*Homo sapiens*	+		44	
82	Amylase [3.2.1.1]	Sali-vary gland	*Homo sapiens*		+	34	
83			*Bos* sp.		+	12	
84			*Canis familiaris*		+	12	
85			*Capra* sp.		−	42	
86			*Cavia porcellus*	+	+	33	34
87			*Equus caballus*		±	42	
88			*Felis catus*		−	34	
89			*Macaca mulatta*		+	34	
90			*Mus* sp.	+		31	
91			*Oryctolagus cuniculus*		+	12	
92			*Ovis aries*		−	34	
93			*Rattus* sp.	+	+	33	48
94			*Sus scrofa*		+	34	
95			*Gallus gallus* L/		+	34	
96			*Rana* sp.		+	34	
97		Stom-ach	*Bos* sp.	+		44	
98			*Canis familiaris*		±	42	
99			*Rattus* sp.	+		40	
100			*Sus scrofa*		−	17	
101		Pan-creas	*Homo sapiens*		+	28	
102			*Bos* sp.	+	+	42	
103			*Canis familiaris*	+	+	4	
104			*Felis catus*		+	4	
105			*Oryctolagus cuniculus*		+	45	
106			*Ovis aries*	+	+	34	
107			*Rattus* sp.	+	+	4	
108			*Sus scrofa*	+	+	34	30
109			*Columba* sp.	+		47	
110			*Gallus gallus* L/	+		34	
111		Small intes-tine	*Homo sapiens*	+	±	34	42
112			*Canis familiaris*		+	52	
113			*Capra* sp.		±	52	

L/ Synonym: *G. domesticus.*

continued

No.	Enzyme (Synonym) [Commission No.]	Organ	Source	Occurrence T	Occurrence S	Reference T	Reference S
114			Equus caballus		+	1	
115			Felis catus		+	52	
116			Oryctolagus cuniculus		+	52	
117			Rattus sp.	+		27	
118			Sus scrofa		+	52	
119			Gallus gallus 1/	+		34	
120		Cecum & colon	Canis familiaris		+	42	
121			Equus caballus	+		51	
122			Rattus sp.	+		40	
123	α-Glucosidase (Maltase) [3.2.1.20]	Pancreas	Homo sapiens		+	4	
124			Canis familiaris		+	4	
125			Felis catus	+		4	
126			Rana sp.	+		44	
127		Small intestine	Equus caballus		+	1	
128			Rattus sp.	+		27	
129			Rana sp.	-		44	
130	β-Galactosidase (Lactase) [3.2.1.23]	Salivary gland	Bos sp.	+		12	
131			Canis familiaris	+		12	
132			Oryctolagus cuniculus	+		12	
133			Ovis aries	+		12	
134			Rattus sp.	+		12	
135			Sus scrofa	+		12	
136		Small intestine	Equus caballus		+	1	
137	β-Fructofuranosidase (Invertase) [3.2.1.26]	Small intestine	Homo sapiens		+	52	
138			Canis familiaris		+	52	
139			Capra sp.		±	52	
140			Equus caballus		+	1	
141			Felis catus		±	52	
142			Sus scrofa		±	52	
143	Peptidases (Erepsin) [3.4]	Salivary gland	Homo sapiens		+	34	
144			Macaca mulatta		+	3	
145		Stomach	Homo sapiens	-		10	
146			Rattus sp.	-		10	
147			Sus scrofa	+		34	
148		Pancreas	Homo sapiens	+	+	42	
149			Bos sp.	+		6	
150			Canis familiaris	+	+	4	
151			Cavia porcellus	+		34	
152			Felis catus	+		34	
153			Oryctolagus cuniculus	+		34	
154			Rattus sp.	+		46	
155			Sus scrofa	+		34	
156			Rana sp.	+		34	
157		Small intestine	Homo sapiens	+	+	42	
158			Canis familiaris	+	+	42	4
159			Capra sp.	-		52	
160			Cavia porcellus	+		34	

No.	Enzyme (Synonym) [Commission No.]	Organ	Source	Occurrence T	Occurrence S	Reference T	Reference S
161			Felis catus	±	±	34	52
162			Oryctolagus cuniculus	+	-	42	52
163			Rattus sp.	+		27	
164			Sus scrofa	-		52	
165			Rana sp.	+		34	
166		Cecum & colon	Canis familiaris		±	37	
167	Carboxypeptidase [3.4.2.1; 3.4.2.2]	Salivary gland	Gallus gallus 1/		+	35	
168		Pancreas	Rattus sp.	+		46	
169	Pepsin 2/ [3.4.4.1]	Esophagus	Bos sp.	-		42	
170			Canis familiaris	-		42	
171			Ovis aries	-		42	
172			Sus scrofa	-		42	
173			Rana sp.	+	+	42	
174		Stomach	Homo sapiens	+	+	34	
175			Bos sp.		+	4	
176			Canis familiaris		+	3	
177			Felis catus		+	25	
178			Macaca mulatta		+	49	
179			Marmota monax 3/	+	±	26	
180			Oryctolagus cuniculus	+		42	
181			Ovis aries	+		44	
182			Rattus rattus	+	+	44	20
183			Sus scrofa	+	+	34	17
184			Columba sp.		+	23	
185			Gallus gallus 1/	+		23	
186			Testudo graeca	+	+	53	
187			Tiliqua rugosus 4/; T. nigrolutea	+	+	53	
188			Necturus maculosus 5/	+	+	24	
189			Rana sp.	+	+	34	22
190			Raja erinacea; R. laevis 6/; R. ocellata 7/	+		5	
191			Squalus sp. 8/	+		7	
192		Small intestine	Bos sp.	-		42	
193			Equus caballus	-		42	
194			Oryctolagus cuniculus	-		42	
195			Sus scrofa	±		42	
196		Cecum & colon	Oryctolagus cuniculus	+		44	
197	Trypsin 9/ [3.4.4.4]	Salivary gland	Cavia porcellus	+		33	
198			Rattus sp.	+		33	
199		Pancreas	Homo sapiens		+	4	
200			Bos sp.	+	+	8	42

1/ Synonym: *G. domesticus*. 2/ Acid protease. 3/ Very small amount of pepsin found in hibernating animal. 4/ Synonym: *Trachysaurus rugosus*. 5/ Synonym: *N. maculatus*. 6/ Synonym: *R. stabuliforis*. 7/ Synonym: *R. diaphanes*. 8/ Synonym: *Acanthias* sp. 9/ Nonacid protease.

continued

No.	Enzyme (Synonym) [Commission No.]	Organ	Source	Occur. T	S	Ref. T	S
201			*Canis familiaris*	+	+	4	
202			*Oryctolagus cuniculus*		+	4	
203			*Ovis aries*	+	+	44	
204			*Rattus* sp.	+		4	
205			*Sus scrofa*	+	+	34|42	
206			*Columba* sp.	+		47	
207			*Rana* sp.	+		44	
208		Small intestine	*Canis familiaris*		±	52	
209			*Capra* sp.		−	52	
210			*Equus caballus*		+	1	
211			*Oryctolagus cuniculus*		−	52	
212			*Sus scrofa*		−	52	
213	Chymotrypsin [3.4.4.5; 3.4.4.6]	Pancreas	*Columba* sp.	+		47	
214			*Gallus gallus* 1/	+	+	6 |35	
215	Pancreatopeptidase E [3.4.4.7]	Pancreas	*Canis familiaris*	+		11	
216			*Cavia porcellus*	+		13	
217			*Rattus* sp.	+		13	
218			*Sus scrofa*	+	+	38	
219	Enteropeptidase (Enterokinase) [3.4.4.8]	Small intestine	*Homo sapiens*		+	52	
220			*Bos* sp.		+	34	
221			*Canis familiaris*	+	+	4	
222			*Capra* sp.		+	34	
223			*Equus caballus*		+	34	
224			*Felis catus*	+	+	34	
225			*Macaca mulatta*	+		34	
226			*Oryctolagus cuniculus*		+	34	
227			*Ovis aries*		+	34	
228			*Rattus* sp.	+		41	
229			*Sus scrofa*	+	+	43|34	
230		Cecum & colon	*Canis familiaris*		−	37	
231	Rennin 10/ [3.4.4.3]	Stomach	*Homo sapiens*		+	35	
232			*Bos* sp.	+	+	8 |34	

No.	Enzyme (Synonym) [Commission No.]	Organ	Source	Occur. T	S	Ref. T	S
233			*Canis familiaris*		±	3	
234			*Capra* sp.		±	44	
235			*Ovis aries*	+		8	
236			*Sus scrofa*		+	34	
237		Small intestine	*Homo sapiens*	+		15	
238	Urease [3.5.1.5]	Stomach	*Homo sapiens*	+		14	
239			*Bos* sp.	+		44	
240			*Canis familiaris*	+		14	
241			*Felis catus*	+		14	
242			*Oryctolagus cuniculus*	+		14	
243			*Ovis aries*	+		44	
244			*Rattus* sp.	+		14	
245			*Sus scrofa*	+		14	
246			*Rana* sp.	+		14	
247		Small intestine	*Capra* sp.		−	44	
248			*Felis catus*	+	−	34|52	
249	Carbonate dehydratase (Carbonic anhydrase) [4.2.1.1]	Salivary gland	*Canis familiaris*	+		9	
250		Stomach	*Cavia porcellus*	+		36	
251			*Felis catus*	+		4	
252			*Mus* sp.	+		36	
253			*Oryctolagus cuniculus*	+		4	
254			*Rattus* sp.	+		4	
255		Pancreas	*Cavia porcellus*	+		36	
256			*Felis catus*	+		4	
257			*Mus* sp.	+		36	
258			*Oryctolagus cuniculus*	+		4	
259			*Rattus* sp.	+		4	
260		Small intestine	*Oryctolagus cuniculus*	+		4	
261			*Rattus* sp.	+		4	

1/ Synonym: *G. domesticus*.   10/ Present only in young animals.

Contributor: Friedman, M. H. F.

References

[1] Alexander, F., and A. K. Chowdhury. 1958. Nature (London) 181:190.

[2] Aqvist, S. E. G., and C. B. Anfinsen. 1959. J. Biol. Chem. 234:1112.

[3] Babkin, B. P. 1929. Die äussere Sekretion der Verdauungsdrüsen. Ed. 2. Springer-Verlag, Berlin.

[4] Babkin, B. P. 1950. Secretory Mechanism of the Digestive Glands. Ed. 2. P. B. Hoeber, New York.

[5] Babkin, B. P., et al. 1935. J. Biol. Bd. Can. 1:251.

[6] Barman, T. E. 1969. Enzyme Handbook. Springer-Verlag, New York.

[7] Beauvalet, H. 1933. C. R. Soc. Biol. 12:640.

[8] Boyer, P. D., ed. 1970-73. The Enzymes. Ed. 3. Academic Press, New York.

[9] Brusilow, S. W., and C. L. Diaz. 1962. Amer. J. Physiol. 202:158.

continued

[10] Burnstone, M. S., and J. E. Folk. 1956. J. Histochem. Cytochem. 4:217.

[11] Carter, A. E. 1956. Science 123:669.

[12] Chauncey, H. H., and G. Quintarelli. 1961. Amer. J. Anat. 108:263.

[13] Cohen, H., et al. 1958. Proc. Soc. Exp. Biol. Med. 97:8.

[14] Conway, E. J. 1953. The Biochemistry of Gastric Acid Secretion. C. C. Thomas, Springfield, Ill.

[15] Dawson, I., and J. Pryse-Davis. 1963. Gastroenterology 44:745.

[16] Dotti, L. B., and I. S. Kleiner. 1942. Amer. J. Physiol. 138:557.

[17] Dukes, H. H. 1955. The Physiology of Domestic Animals. Ed. 2. Comstock, Ithaca.

[18] Eichel, H. J., et al. 1964. Arch. Biochem. Biophys. 107:197.

[19] Ellem, K. A. O., and J. S. Colter. 1961. J. Cell. Comp. Physiol. 58:267.

[20] Erlanson, C., and B. Borgstrom. 1968. Biochim. Biophys. Acta 167:629.

[21] Evans, R. A., and D. A. Stansfield. 1961. Nature (London) 190:1110.

[22] Friedman, M. H. F. 1937. J. Cell. Comp. Physiol. 10:37.

[23] Friedman, M. H. F. 1939. Ibid. 13:219.

[24] Friedman, M. H. F. 1942. Ibid. 20:379.

[25] Friedman, M. H. F. 1950. Amer. J. Physiol. 163:712.

[26] Friedman, M. H. F., and J. Armour. 1936. J. Cell. Comp. Physiol. 8:201.

[27] Genderen, H. van, and C. Engel. 1938. Enzymologia 5:71.

[28] Gjessing, E., and J. C. Hartnett. 1960. Fed. Proc. Fed. Amer. Soc. Exp. Biol. 19:49.

[29] Harris, E. S., et al. 1952. Proc. Soc. Exp. Biol. Med. 81:593.

[30] Hickson, J. C. D. 1970. J. Physiol. (London) 266:299.

[31] Hilton, F. 1967. Proc. Soc. Exp. Biol. Med. 126:263.

[32] International Union of Biochemistry. 1965. Enzyme Nomenclature. Elsevier, New York.

[33] Junqueira, L. C. U. 1967. Secretory Mech. Salivary Glands Proc. Int. Conf., p. 286.

[34] Koningsberger, V. J., et al., ed. 1946. Tabulae Biol. 21(1).

[35] Kulka, R. G., et al. 1967. Secretory Mech. Salivary Glands Proc. Int. Conf., p. 254.

[36] Kurata, Y. 1953. Stain Technol. 28:231.

[37] Kuvaeva, I. B. 1957. Fiziol. Zh. SSSR 43:311.

[38] Lewis, U. J., et al. 1956. J. Biol. Chem. 222:705.

[39] Martin, B. F. 1959. Nature (London) 183:1464.

[40] McGeachin, R. L., and K. F. Norwood, Jr. 1959. Amer. J. Physiol. 196:972.

[41] Moog, F. 1962. Fed. Proc. Fed. Amer. Soc. Exp. Biol. 21:51.

[42] Oppenheimer, C. 1925-26. Die Fermente und ihre Wirkungen. Ed. 5. G. Thieme, Leipzig. Bd. 1-2.

[43] Oppenheimer, C. 1929. Ibid. Bd. 3-4.

[44] Oppenheimer, C. 1936-39. Ibid. Suppl. Bd. 1-2.

[45] Ridderstop, A. S., and S. L. Bonting. 1969. Pfluegers Arch. 313:53.

[46] Rutter, W. J., et al. 1967. Secretory Mech. Salivary Glands Proc. Int. Conf., p. 238.

[47] Salmon, A. J. 1967. Proc. Soc. Exp. Biol. Med. 126:694.

[48] Schneyer, L. H., and C. A. Schneyer. 1956. Fed. Proc. Fed. Amer. Soc. Exp. Biol. 15:164.

[49] Smith, G. P., and F. P. Brooks. 1959. Ibid. 18:147.

[50] Sreebny, L. M., and D. A. Johnson. 1967. Secretory Mech. Salivary Glands Proc. Int. Conf., p. 275.

[51] Sym, E. A., et al. 1939. Enzymologia 6:113.

[52] Wright, R. D., et al. 1940. Quart. J. Exp. Physiol. Cog. Med. Sci. 30:73.

[53] Wright, R. D., et al. 1957. Ibid. 42:1.

180. PATHWAYS OF CARBOHYDRATE DIGESTION: MAN AND LABORATORY MAMMALS

In the intestine, oligosaccharides and disaccharides are hydrolyzed by microvillar membrane enzymes located on the luminal surface of the intestinal cell. These small saccharides are split to monosaccharides on the outer surface of the intestinal cell. The only form in which sugar enters the intestinal cell in significant amounts is as monosaccharide (hexose). Apart from the small fraction of hexose metabolized (oxidized) during passage through the intestinal mucosal cell, phosphorylation of hexoses does not occur as a mechanism for absorption of hexoses into the cell or for

continued

delivery from the cell into the portal blood. A number of so-called structural polysaccharides occurring in foods are not digestible in the alimentary tract of vertebrates and so pass into the feces essentially unaltered. These include cellulose, lignin, mannan, xylan, pectic acids, alginic acid, and chitin.

ENZYME KEY

A = α-amylase, salivary and pancreatic
B = maltase
C = α-limit dextrinase (isomaltase)

D = lactase
E = sucrase
F = glucosephosphate isomerase

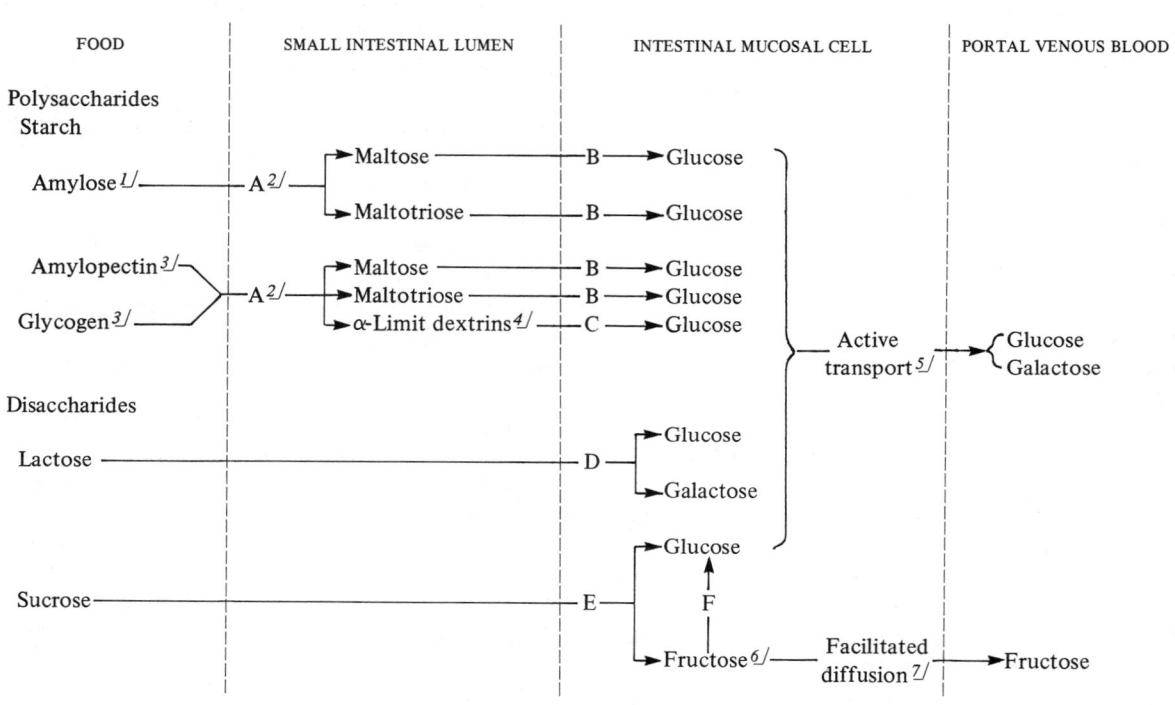

[1/] Amylose is a straight-chain polymer of glucose with α-1, 4-glucosidic linkages. [2/] α-Amylase hydrolyzes 1,4-glucosidic linkages in chains of glucose containing 4 or more residues; it does not split maltotriose or maltose. α-Amylase does not split the 1,6-linkages in amylopectin, and acts only weakly on the 1,4-linkages adjacent to the 1,6-branching points so that oligosaccharides with 5-8 residues, the α-limit dextrins, are also formed as luminal end products. [3/] Amylopectin and glycogen are branched-chain polymers of glucose with α-1,4-linkages in the straight-chain portions and α-1,6-linkages at the points of branching. [4/] The α-limit dextrins consist of moderate-sized (mol wt, 1500), branched saccharides having both 1,4- and 1,6-linkages. [5/] Active transport indicates uphill movement against a cell-to-lumen concentration gradient by a process that requires stereospecificity, energy, and Na^+. [6/] Some fructose is transformed to glucose in the intestinal mucosal cell and some passes through unchanged. [7/] Facilitated diffusion is a process requiring a specific entry mechanism, but in which the saccharide moves down its concentration gradient; energy and Na^+ are not required.

continued

180. PATHWAYS OF CARBOHYDRATE DIGESTION: MAN AND LABORATORY MAMMALS

Contributor: Grossman, Morton I.

Reference: Gray, G. 1967. Fed. Proc. Fed. Amer. Soc. Exp. Biol. 26:1415.

181. PATHWAYS OF PROTEIN DIGESTION: MAN AND LABORATORY MAMMALS

Pepsin, trypsin, and chymotrypsin are endopeptidases, i.e., they hydrolyze peptide bonds in the interior of the peptide chains as well as terminal bonds. The carboxypeptidases and leucine aminopeptidase are exopeptidases, and can act only on terminal peptide bonds.

ENZYME KEY (SPECIFICITY)

A = pepsin (hydrolyzes peptide bonds in which an aromatic amino acid is present)

B = trypsin (hydrolyzes peptide bonds to which L-arginine or L-lysine contributes the carbonyl group)

C = chymotrypsin (hydrolyzes peptide bonds in which an aromatic amino acid contributes the carbonyl group); elastase (hydrolyzes peptide bonds in which an aliphatic amino acid contributes the carbonyl group)

D = carboxypeptidase A (acts on those linkages in which a nonbasic amino acid, particularly a neutral aromatic amino acid, is C-terminal and has a free carboxyl group)

E = carboxypeptidase B (acts on those linkages in which a basic amino acid is C-terminal and has a free carboxyl group)

F = various peptidases (only a few intestinal mucosal peptidases characterized; best known is leucine aminopeptidase); brush border peptide hydrolases (most active against peptides containing bulky—aliphatic or aromatic—amino acids such a leucine, methionine, phenylalanine)

G = peptides containing mainly proline, hydroxyproline, or glycine units (may be preferentially absorbed intact to be hydrolyzed within the cell sap by soluble peptidases different from the brush border enzymes)

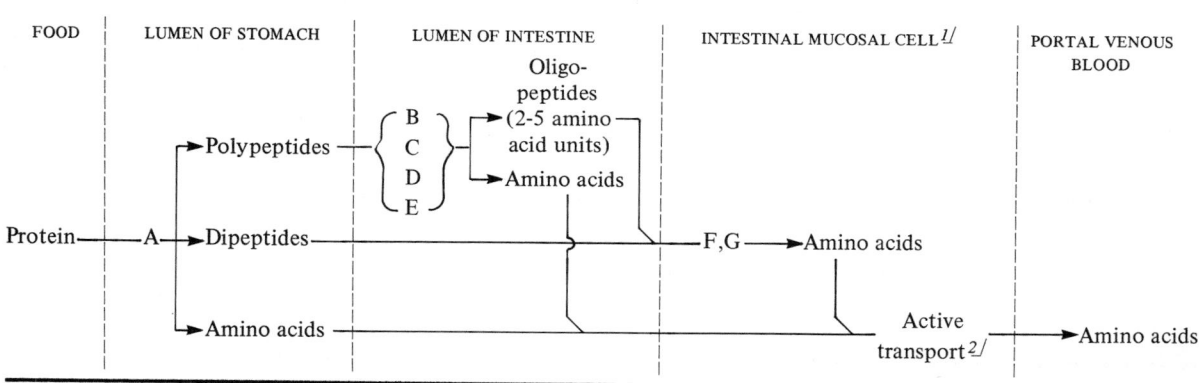

L/ Amino acids and dipeptides enter onto or into the intestinal mucosal cells. Amino acids pass through unaltered (with a few exceptions, such as transamination of glutamic acid), and dipeptides are split to amino acids in the micro-villi or the interior of the cell where the peptidases are localized. 2/ There are at least 3 active transport systems for amino acids: (i) for neutral amino acids; (ii) for basic amino acids; and (iii) for proline and related amino acids.

Contributor: Grossman, Morton I.

General References

[1] Gardner, J. D., et al. 1970. N. Engl. J. Med. 283: 1317.

[2] Gray, G. M., and H. L. Cooper. 1971. Gastroenterology 61:535.

182. PATHWAYS OF LIPID DIGESTION: MAN AND LABORATORY MAMMALS

Abbreviations: ATP = adenosine 5′-triphosphate; CoA = coenzyme A.

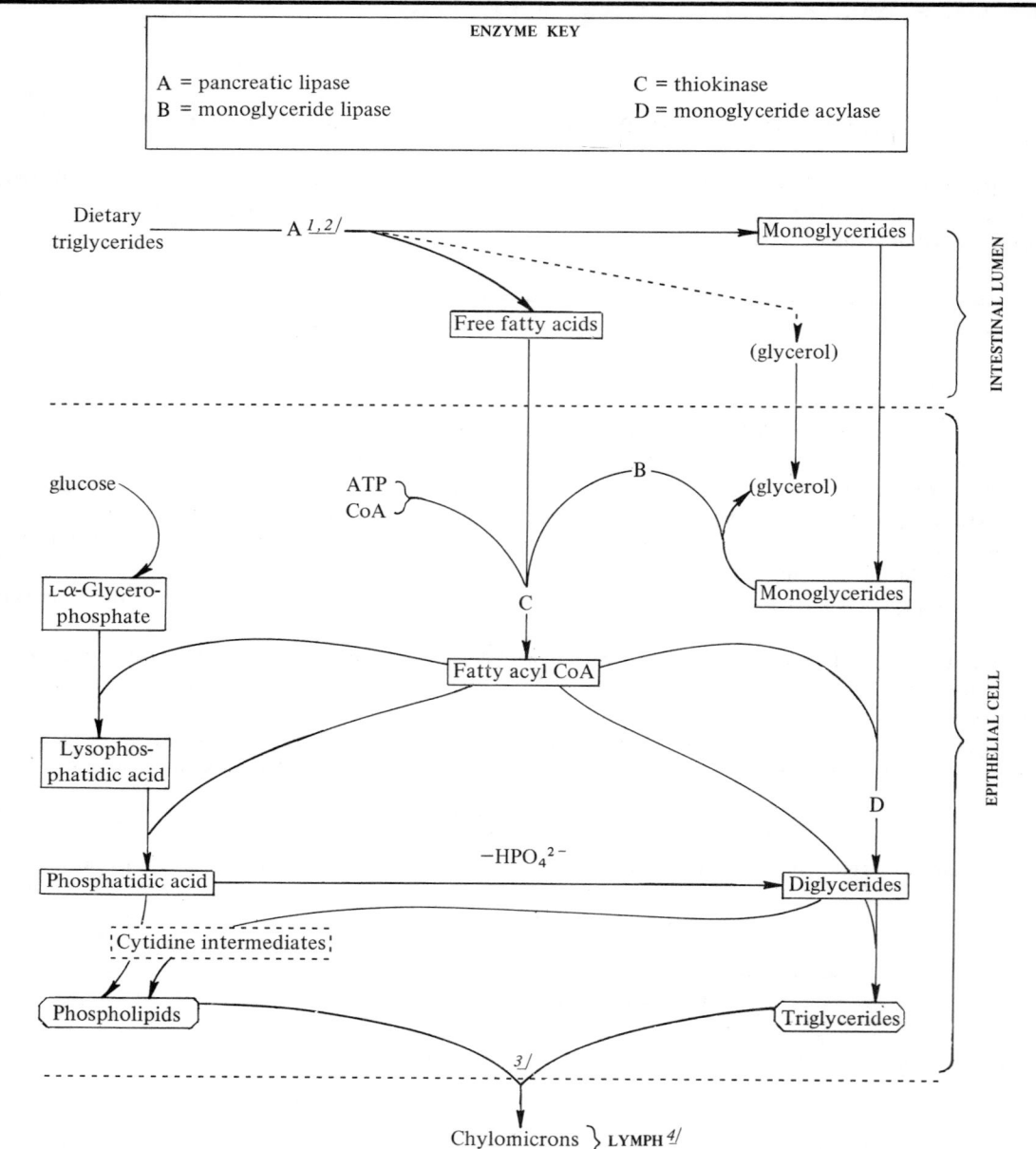

ENZYME KEY

A = pancreatic lipase   C = thiokinase
B = monoglyceride lipase   D = monoglyceride acylase

[1/] Pancreatic lipase acts preferentially on ester linkages at the terminal or 1 position of glycerol. Thus the major products of digestion are fatty acids and monoglycerides. [2/] Bile salts in their conjugated form participate in at least three reactions during fat digestion and absorption: (i) as a cofactor for pancreatic lipase; (ii) to form micelles containing monoglyceride and fatty acid, as well as other lipids (these micelles are probably the form in which lipid is presented to the mucosal cell for absorption); (iii) as a cofactor for thiokinase in the intestinal mucosal cell. [3/] Absorbed fatty acids go mainly into the triglycerides of chylomicrons, but small amounts are synthesized into cholesterol esters and phospholipids which also are constituents of chylomicrons. [4/] Fatty acids with chain lengths shorter than 10 carbon atoms are absorbed mainly into the portal blood, those with longer chain lengths mainly into the lymph.

Contributor: Grossman, Morton I.

Reference: Isselbacher, K. J. 1967. Fed. Proc. Fed. Amer. Soc. Exp. Biol. 26:1420.

Values are based on a "normal" dietary intake, including ∼10g nitrogen/day, and a body weight of 70 kg, unless specific weight was recorded. Where the value is unspecified, the chemical was identified qualitatively only. Values in parentheses are ranges, estimate "c" (*see* Introduction).

Part I. Compounds Other Than Steroids

Values in brackets refer to the column heading in brackets.

	Constituent (Synonym)	Amount Excreted mg·kg body wt^{-1}·da^{-1} [1/] [μg·kg body wt^{-1}·da^{-1}]	Reference		Constituent (Synonym)	Amount Excreted mg·kg body wt^{-1}·da^{-1} [1/] [μg·kg body wt^{-1}·da^{-1}]	Reference
	General Chemical Constituents			33	Xanthophyll + carotene	[(20-600)]	42
1	Wet weight	1765(615-2915)	30		Lipids & Miscellaneous Organic Acids		
2	Solids	394(140-560)	47		Fats		
3	Water	(910-1820)	40	34	Total	64(26-160)	12,15,47
	Electrolytes			35	Neutral	(10-45)	14
4	Aluminum	600[2/]	23	36	Unsaponifiable	33(22-38)[3/]	46
5	Arsenic	[33(1-116)]	36		Free fatty acids		
6	Calcium	(5-10)	6,9,16	37	Total	(41-92)	4,12,18,22
7	Chlorine	[(210-500)]	5	38	Myristic + linoleic	3.5	32
8	Cobalt	(2-20)[2/]	19	39	Palmitic	(13-30)	18,32
9	Copper	[27(23-37)]	23	40	Stearic	(14-33)	18,32
10	Iron	[120(65-208)]	10	41	Oleic	(5-20)	18,32
11	Lead	[4.2]	23	42	Linolenic	(1.6-3.6)	18,32
12	Magnesium	2.5(1.510-3.185)	26		Soaps		
13	Manganese	[(18-120)]	23,24	43	Total	53(40-66)[3/]	46
14	Mercury	140[2/]	39	44	Lauric acid (*n*-Do-decanoic)	0.3[4/]	34
15	Nickel	[(1.2-2.5)]	24	45	Myristic acid (*n*-Tetradecanoic)	1.9[4/]	34
16	Phosphorus	[9.9(7.1-20.0)]	10	46	*n*-Pentadecanoic acid	0.4[4/]	34
17	Potassium	6.7	8	47	Palmitic acid (*n*-Hexadecanoic)	38.8[4/]	34
18	Silver	800[2/]	23	48	Margaric acid (*n*-Heptadecanoic)	1.3[4/]	34
19	Sodium	1.7	8	49	Stearic acid (*n*-Octadecanoic)	49.2[4/]	34
20	Sulfur, total	2.0	8	50	Palmitoleic acid (Δ^{9,10}-Hexadecenoic)	1.1[4/]	34
21	Tin	[(170-450)]	8,23	51	Oleic acid (Δ^{9,10}-Octadecenoic)	7.0[4/]	34
22	Zinc	[100(58-144)]	41		Other organic anions		
	Vitamins & Related Compounds			52	Formate	Unspecified	33
23	Thiamine	[7.80(0.67-18.00)]	11	53	Acetate	Unspecified	33
24	Riboflavin	[14.7(8.0-23.0)]	11	54	Propionate	Unspecified	33
25	Niacin	[52(12-124)]	11	55	Butyrate (*n*-Butyrate)	Unspecified	33
26	Biotin	[1.90(0.63-6.64)]	11				
27	Pantothenic acid	[31.40(3.85-63.40)]	11	56	Isobutyrate	Unspecified	33
28	Folic acid (Pteroyl-glutamic acid)	[4.3(1.8-7.7)]	11	57	Valerate (*n*-Valerate)	Unspecified	33
29	*p*-Aminobenzoic acid	[3.50(1.01-8.20)]	11				
30	Ascorbic acid	[(60-70)]	7				
31	Vitamin E (α-Tocopherol)	[308(226-391)]	25				
32	Xanthophyll	[(8-100)]	42				

[1/] Unless otherwise indicated. [2/] ng·kg body wt^{-1}·da^{-1}. [3/] For 8- to 10-yr-olds. [4/] Expressed as percent of total fatty acids.

continued

Part I. Compounds Other Than Steroids

	Constituent (Synonym)	Amount Excreted mg·kg body wt^{-1}·da^{-1} [μg·kg body wt^{-1}·da^{-1}]	Reference		Constituent (Synonym)	Amount Excreted mg·kg body wt^{-1}·da^{-1} [μg·kg body wt^{-1}·da^{-1}]	Reference
58	Isovalerate	Unspecified	33	75	Lysine, total	5.7(4.5-6.9)	37
59	Lactate	Unspecified	33	76	Threonine, total	4.0(3.3-5.2)	37
60	Succinate	Unspecified	33	77	Valine, total	4.6(3.6-6.2)	37
61	Fumarate	Unspecified	33	78	Histamine, free	[0.045]	38
62	Long-chain alcohols	1.9(0.7-2.6)	3	79	conjugated	[1.044]	38
63	Long-chain esters	1.9(0.7-2.6)	3	80	Imidazole derivatives	[(0-200)]	27
64	Mono- & di-glycerides	1.2(0.4-1.7)	3	81	Purine bases	(2-3)	28
65	Triglycerides	5.71(0.86-23.14)	3,12		Porphyrins		
66	Phospholipids	4.00(1.86-6.29)	3,12	82	Bilirubin	[140]	44
67	Hydrocarbons	3.9(1.4-5.6)	3	83	Coproporphyrin	[(5-14)]	35,45
68	Phenol (Carbolic acid)	(0-3)	13	84	Protoporphyrin	[14]	17,45
	Nitrogenous Substances			85	Stercobilinogen + urobilinogen	2	43
69	Nitrogen, total	(11.4-36.0)	20	86	Uroporphyrin	[(0.14-1.60)]	36,45
70	ammonia	(0.36-1.20)	31		Enzymes[5]		
	Amino acids			87	Trypsin [3.4.4.4]	Consult references	1,2,29
71	Arginine, total	3.8(2.9-5.0)	37	88	Chymotrypsin [3.4.4.5; 3.4.4.6]	Consult references	1,2,29
72	Histidine, total	1.7(1.4-2.1)	37				
73	Isoleucine, total	4.3(3.3-5.5)	37				
74	Leucine, total	5.6(4.3-6.9)	37				

[5] Enzyme Commission Number, in brackets, was assigned by the International Union of Biochemistry on the Nomenclature and Classification of Enzymes [21].

Contributor: Van Pilsum, John

References

[1] Ammann, R., et al. 1964. Klin. Wochenschr. 42: 5333.

[2] Ammann, R. W., et al. 1968. Amer. J. Dig. Dis. 13(2):123.

[3] Aylward, F., and P. A. Wills. 1962. Brit. J. Nutr. 16:339.

[4] Aylward, F., and P. D. S. Wood. 1962. Ibid. 16:345.

[5] Cammidge, P. J. 1914. The Faeces of Children and Adults. W. Wood, New York.

[6] Chen, T., and L. B. Dotti. 1967. Clin. Chim. Acta 18:453.

[7] Chinn, H., and C. J. Farmer. 1939. Proc. Soc. Exp. Biol. Med. 41:561.

[8] Clark, G. W. 1926. Univ. Calif. Berkeley Publ. Physiol. 5(17):195.

[9] Comar, C. L., and F. Bronner, ed. 1960. Miner. Metab. 1(A):264.

[10] Daum, K., et al. 1951. J. Amer. Diet. Ass. 27:475.

[11] Denko, C. W., et al. 1946. Arch. Biochem. 10:33.

[12] Erb, W., and E. Böhle. 1968. Z. Klin. Chem. Klin. Biochem. 6(5):379.

[13] Folin, O., and W. Denis. 1916. J. Biol. Chem. 26:507.

[14] Fowweather, F. S. 1926. Brit. J. Exp. Pathol. 7:15.

[15] Friedner, S., and S. Moberg. 1967. Clin. Chim. Acta 18:345.

[16] Goiffon, R., et al. 1961. Gastroenterology 96:312.

[17] Goldberg, J. S. 1966. Calif. Med. 104:488.

[18] Gompertz, S. M., and H. G. Sammons. 1963. Clin. Chim. Acta 8:591.

[19] Harp, M. J., and F. I. Scoular. 1952. J. Nutr. 47:67.

[20] Haverback, B. J., et al. 1963. Gastroenterology 44: 588.

[21] International Union of Biochemistry. 1965. Enzyme Nomenclature. Elsevier, New York.

[22] Jover, A., and R. S. Gordon, Jr. 1962. J. Lab. Clin. Med. 59:878.

[23] Kehoe, R. A., et al. 1940. J. Nutr. 19:579.

[24] Kent, N. L., and R. A. McCance. 1941. Biochem. J. 35:877.

[25] Klatskin, G., and D. W. Molander. 1952. J. Lab. Clin. Med. 39:802.

[26] Leichsenring, J. M., et al. 1951. J. Nutr. 45:477.

[27] Loeper, M., et al. 1934. Bull. Soc. Chim. Biol. 16: 385.

[28] Mendel, L. B., and J. F. Lyman. 1910. J. Biol. Chem. 8:115.

[29] Oser, B. L., ed. 1965. Hawk's Physiological Chemistry. Ed. 14. Blakiston, New York.

[30] Rendtorff, R. C., and M. Kashgarian. 1967. Dis. Colon Rectum 10:222.

continued

Part I. Compounds Other Than Steroids

[31] Robinson, C. S. 1922. J. Biol. Chem. 52:445.

[32] Rogers, A. I., et al. 1967. Amer. J. Dig. Dis. 12:664.

[33] Rubenstein, R., et al. 1969. Clin. Sci. 37(2):549.

[34] Sammons, H. G., and S. M. Wiggs. 1960. Clin. Chim. Acta 5:141.

[35] Schwartz, S., et al. 1960. Methods Biochem. Anal. 8:221.

[36] Schwarz, L., and W. Deckert. 1931. Arch. Hyg. Bakteriol. 106:346.

[37] Sheffner, A. L., et al. 1948. J. Biol. Chem. 175:107.

[38] Sjaastad, O. 1966. Scand. J. Gastroenterol. 1:1.

[39] Stock, A. 1940. Biochem. Z. 304:73.

[40] Sunderman, F. W., and F. Boerner. 1949. Normal Values in Clinical Medicine. W. B. Saunders, Philadelphia.

[41] Tribble, H. M., and F. I. Scoular. 1954. J. Nutr. 52: 210.

[42] Wald, G., et al. 1941. Science 94:95.

[43] Watson, C. J. 1937. Arch. Intern. Med. 59:196.

[44] Watson, C. J. 1963. J. Clin. Pathol. 16:1.

[45] Watson, C. J., et al. 1968. Arch. dermatol. 98(5):451.

[46] Williams, H. H., et al. 1943. J. Nutr. 25:379.

[47] Wollaeger, E. E., et al. 1947. Gastroenterology 9:272.

Part II. Steroids

	Constituent (Synonym)	Amount Excreted mg·kg body wt^{-1}·da^{-1}	Reference
1	Steroids, total	(14.29-21.43)	18
2	neutral	(9-14)	1,7
3	free	27.00(10.43-54.86)	11
4	esters	6.00(0.71-22.14)	11
5	unsaponifiable	(7.14-10.00)	18
	Bile Acids		
6	Bile acids, total	(1-10)	2,10,12,13,18
	Hydroxycholanic acids		
7	Lithocholic acid (3α-Hydroxy-5β-cholanoic acid)	(0.157-1.143)	10
8	3β-Hydroxy-5β-cholanic acid (3β-Hydroxy-5β-cholanoic acid)	(0.034-0.619)	10
	Dihydroxycholanic acids		
9	Chenodeoxycholic acid (3α,7α-Dihydroxy-5β-cholanoic acid)	Unspecified	3,4,8,9,14-16,19
10	3α,7β-Dihydroxy-5β-cholanic acid (3α,7β-Dihydroxy-5β-cholanoic acid)	Unspecified	3,4,8,9,14-16,19
11	3β,7α-Dihydroxy-5β-cholanic acid (3β,7α-Dihydroxy-5β-cholanoic acid)	Unspecified	3,4,8,9,14-16,19
12	Deoxycholic acid (3α,12α-Dihydroxy-5β-cholanoic acid)	(0.071-2.729)	10
13	3α,12β-Dihydroxy-5β-cholanic acid (3α,12β-Dihydroxy-5β-cholanoic acid)	Unspecified	3,4,8,9,14-16,19
14	3β,12α-Dihydroxy-5β-cholanic acid (3β,12α-Dihydroxy-5β-cholanoic acid)	(0.01-0.77)	10
15	3β,12β-Dihydroxy-5β-cholanic acid (3β,12β-Dihydroxy-5β-cholanoic acid)	Unspecified	3,4,8,9,14-16,19
	Trihydroxycholanic acids		
16	Cholic acid (3α,7α,12α-Trihydroxy-5β-cholanic acid)	Unspecified	3,4,8,9,14-16,19
17	3α,7α,12α-Trihydroxy-5α-cholanic acid (3α,7α,12α-Trihydroxy-5α-cholanoic acid)	Unspecified	3,4,8,9,14-16,19
18	3α,7β,12α-Trihydroxy-5β-cholanic acid (3α,7β,12α-Trihydroxy-5β-cholanoic acid)	Unspecified	3,4,8,9,14-16,19
19	3β,7α,12α-Trihydroxy-5α-cholanic acid (3β,7α,12α-Trihydroxy-5α-cholanoic acid)	Unspecified	3,4,8,9,14-16,19
20	3β,7β,12α-Trihydroxy-5α-cholanic acid (3β,7β,12α-Trihydroxy-5α-cholanoic acid)	Unspecified	3,4,8,9,14-16,19
	Hydroxyketocholanic acids		
21	3α-Hydroxy-7-keto-5β-cholanic acid (3α-Hydroxy-7-keto-5β-cholanoic acid)	Unspecified	3,4,8,9,14-16,19
22	3α-Hydroxy-12-keto-5β-cholanic acid (3α-Hydroxy-12-keto-5β-cholanoic acid)	(0.023-0.243)	10
23	3β-Hydroxy-12-keto-5β-cholanic acid (3β-Hydroxy-12-keto-5β-cholanoic acid)	(0.004-0.714)	10

continued

Part II. Steroids

	Constituent (Synonym)	Amount Excreted mg·kg body wt^{-1}·da^{-1}	Reference
24	3-Keto-7α-hydroxy-5β-cholanic acid (3-Keto-7α-hydroxy-5β-cholanoic acid)	Unspecified	3,4,8,9,14-16,19
25	3-Keto-12α-hydroxy-5β-cholanic acid (3-Keto-12α-hydroxy-5β-cholanoic acid)	Unspecified	3,4,8,9,14-16,19
	Dihydroxyketocholanic acids		
26	3α,7α-Dihydroxy-12-keto-5β-cholanic acid (3α,7α-Dihydroxy-12-keto-5β-cholanoic acid)	Unspecified	3,4,8,9,14-16,19
27	3α,12α-Dihydroxy-7-keto-5β-cholanic acid (3α,12α-Dihydroxy-7-keto-5β-cholanoic acid)	Unspecified	3,4,8,9,14-16,19
	Ketocholanic acids		
28	3-Keto-5β-cholanic acid (3-Keto-5β-cholanoic acid)	Unspecified	3,4,8,9,14-16,19
29	3,12-Diketo-5β-cholanic acid (3,12-Diketo-5β-cholanoic acid)	Unspecified	3,4,8,9,14-16,19
	Androgens		
	Androstanediols		
30	Androstane-3α,17α-diol (5α-Androstane-3α,17α-diol)	Unspecified	17
31	Androstane-3α,17β-diol (5α-Androstane-3α,17β-diol)	Unspecified	17
32	Androstane-3β,17α-diol (5α-Androstane-3β,17α-diol)	Unspecified	17
33	Androstane-3β,17β-diol (5α-Androstane-3β,17β-diol)	Unspecified	17
34	Etiocholane-3α,17β-diol (5β-Androstane-3α,17β-diol)	Unspecified	17
	Androstenediols		
35	Androstenediol (5-Androstene-3β,17β-diol)	Unspecified	17
36	5-Androstene-3α,17β-diol	Unspecified	17
37	5-Androstene-3β,17α-diol	Unspecified	17
38	Dehydroepiandrosterone (5-Androsten-3β-ol-17-one)	Unspecified	17
	"Pregnanes"		
	Pregnanediols		
39	Allopregnane-3α,20α-diol (5α-Pregnane-3α,20α-diol)	Unspecified	17
40	Allopregnane-3β,20α-diol (5α-Pregnane-3β,20α-diol)	Unspecified	17
41	5β-Pregnane-3α,20α-diol	Unspecified	17
42	5β-Pregnane-3β,20α-diol	Unspecified	17
	Pregnenediols		
43	5-Pregnene-3α,20α-diol	Unspecified	17
44	5-Pregnene-3β,20α-diol	Unspecified	17
45	Pregnenolone (3β-Hydroxy-5-pregnene-20-one)	Unspecified	17
	Other Steroids or Sterols		
46	Brassicasterol (24α-Methylcholest-5,22-dien-3β-ol)	Unspecified	6
47	Campestanol (24α-Methyl-5α-cholestan-3β-ol)	Unspecified	6
48	Campesterol (24α-Methylcholest-5-en-3β-ol)	0.6	5
49	Cholestanol (Cholestan-3β-ol)	Unspecified	6
50	Cholesterol (Cholest-5-en-3β-ol)	1.4	5
51	Cholesteryl sulfate	(0.20-1.21)	5
52	Coprostanone (5β-Cholestan-3-one)	0.6	8
53	Coprosterol (Coprostanol; 5β-cholestan-3β-ol)	6	5,8
54	Fucosterol (24-Ethylidene-cholest-5-en-3β-ol)	Unspecified	6
55	Lathosterol (5α-Cholest-7-en-3β-ol)	Unspecified	6
56	β-Sitosterol (24β-Ethylcholest-5-en-3β-ol)	0.6	8
57	Stigmastanol (β-Sitostanol; 24β-ethylcholestan-3β-ol)	Unspecified	6
58	Stigmasterol (24β-Ethylcholest-5,22-dien-3β-ol)	2	8

continued

183. EXCRETION PRODUCTS IN FECES: MAN

Part II. Steroids

Contributor: Van Pilsum, John

References

[1] Aylward, F., and P. A. Wills. 1962. Brit. J. Nutr. 16:339.

[2] Aylward, F., and P. D. S. Wood. 1962. Ibid. 16:345.

[3] Carey, J. B., and C. J. Watson. 1963. J. Biol. Chem. 216:847.

[4] Danielsson, H., et al. 1963. Ibid. 238:2299.

[5] Eneroth, P., and E. Nyström. 1968. Steroids 11:187.

[6] Eneroth, P., and E. Nyström. 1968. Ibid. 11:417.

[7] Eneroth, P., et al. 1964. J. Lipid Res. 5:245.

[8] Eneroth, P., et al. 1966. Ibid. 7:511.

[9] Eneroth, P., et al. 1966. Ibid. 7:524.

[10] Eneroth, P., et al. 1968. Acta Chem. Scand. 22:1729.

[11] Erb, W., and E. Böhle. 1968. Z. Klin. Chem. Klin. Biochem. 6(5):379.

[12] Evrard, E., and G. Janssen. 1968. J. Lipid Res. 9(2):226.

[13] Forman, D. T., et al. 1969. Clin. Chem. 14(4):348.

[14] Hamilton, J. G. 1963. Arch. Biochem. Biophys. 101:7.

[15] Heftmann, E., et al. 1959. Ibid. 84:324.

[16] Jenke, M., and F. Bandow. 1937. Hoppe Seylers Z. Physiol. Chem. 249:16.

[17] Laatikainen, T., and R. Vihko. 1970. Eur. J. Biochem. 13:534.

[18] Moore, R. B., et al. 1968. J. Clin. Invest. 47:1517.

[19] Norman, A., and R. H. Palmer. 1964. J. Lab. Clin. Med. 63:986.

184. EXCRETION PRODUCTS IN SWEAT: MAN

Eccrine sweat, a clear aqueous solution, is generally 99.0-99.5% water and 0.5-1.0% solids (approximately half organic and half inorganic solids) [37]. Although much is known about the chemical composition of sweat secreted onto the skin surface, the concentrations of solutes in sweat as it is formed in the coil of the gland has until very recently remained essentially unknown [71]. Sweat in the secretory part of the gland is isotonic or slightly hypertonic to plasma, and variable reabsorption occurs in the duct [26, 65, 72]. Thus, the osmolality of sweat removed from the secretory coil averages 323, while the osmolality of plasma averages 296, giving a sweat:plasma ratio of 1.1 [12, 65]. Secretion of many substances is directly related to plasma concentration. However, for many other inorganic and organic constituents, concentration gradients between plasma and sweat reveal striking differences in both directions. Inorganic ingredients, except potassium, are generally in lower concentrations in sweat than in plasma, whereas organic materials, except such substances as glucose and uric acid, are in higher concentrations in sweat than in plasma. While glucose may have a concentration of 100 mg/100 ml in blood,

it rarely exceeds 2 or 3 mg/100 ml in sweat, but lactic acid may be 200 mg/100 ml in sweat, while only 20 mg/100 ml in plasma [28]. Relationships between the excretion of electrolytes in simultaneously collected sweat and urine are inconsistent, and alterations of acid-base balance do not appear to modify remarkably the composition of sweat as compared to the modifications occurring in urine [5]. Thus, the secretion of sweat does not play a significant role in maintaining homeostasis of the body except in terms of heat exchange. The presence of high concentrations of pyruvate and lactate in sweat indicates anaerobic metabolism underlying sweat gland function, and it is calculated that sufficient energy could be obtained from the anaerobic breakdown of glycogen to account for the osmotic work of formation of the most dilute sweat. However, the glands consume oxygen and contain cytochrome oxidase, succinic dehydrogenase, and plentiful mitochondria, which indicates that the glands are not totally anaerobic [33]. For additional information, consult references 2, 9, 23, 25, 27, 28, 31, 45, 46, 52, 55, 57, 60, 61, and 65-67. Values in parentheses are ranges, estimate "c" (*see* Introduction).

Property or Constituent	Value	Reference
Physical Properties & General Chemical Constituents		
1 pH	(3.8-8.2)	26,62
2 Specific gravity	(1.001-1.006)	62
3 Freezing point	(−0.60 to −0.09)°C	36
4 Production rate, maximum	(17.7-38.2) ml/hr	47

Property or Constituent	Value	Reference
5 Water	(99.0-99.5)%	62
6 Solids, total	(1.174-1.597)%	54
Electrolytes		
7 Calcium	(1.0-24) mg/100 ml	7,21,61
8 Chloride	(36-468) mg/100 ml	20,48,77, 78

continued

	Property or Constituent	Value	Reference		Property or Constituent	Value	Reference
9	Copper	6 µg/100 ml	51	41	Uric acid N	(0-27) mg/100 ml	36,49
10	Iodine	0.9(0.5-1.2) µg/100 ml	73		Amino acids		
11	Iron	27(22-45) µg/100 ml	18,21,22, 43	42	Alanine	3.21 ± 0.72 mg/100 ml	19
				43	Arginine	13.6(6.05-17.00) mg/ 100 ml	32
12	Magnesium	(4-286) µg/100 ml	7,51				
13	Manganese	6(3-7) µg/100 ml	51	44	Aspartic acid	4.58 ± 0.76 mg/100 ml	19
14	Phosphorus	(9-43) µg/100 ml	21,51	45	Citrulline	6.99 ± 0.91 mg/100 ml	19
15	Potassium	(21-126) mg/100 ml	3,8,30,35	46	Glutamic acid	5.43 ± 0.69 mg/100 ml	19
16	Sodium	(24-312) mg/100 ml	13,15,20, 31,68	47	Glycine	2.95 ± 0.74 mg/100 ml	19
				48	Histidine	8(4.25-14.00) mg/100 ml	32
17	Sulfur	(0.7-7.4) mg/100 ml	75				
18	Zinc	93 ± 26 µg/100 ml	59	49	Isoleucine	2.27(1.63-3.73) mg/ 100 ml	32
19	Bicarbonate	(1.6-18.6) vol %	36				
20	Sulfate	(4.0-6) mg/100 ml	36	50	Leucine	2.69(1.98-3.75) mg/ 100 ml	32
	Vitamins & Related Compounds			51	Lysine	2.26(1.96-3.38) mg/ 100 ml	32
21	Thiamine	0.15(0-0.6) µg/100 ml	46,50	52	Ornithine	2.03 ± 1.01 mg/100 ml	19
22	Riboflavin	(0-0.5) µg/100 ml	46,50	53	Phenylalanine	2.19(1.70-3.47) mg/ 100 ml	32
23	Niacin	(1.7-8.7) µg/100 ml	40				
24	Vitamin B_6	(0.04-0.17) µg/100 ml	38	54	Threonine	5.38(2.13-8.18) mg/ 100 ml	32
25	Pantothenic acid	(1.5-7.7) µg/100 ml	74				
26	Folic acid	(0.53-0.88) µg/100 ml	41	55	Tryptophan	1.12(0.75-1.85) mg/ 100 ml	32
27	p-Aminobenzoic acid	0.24(0.08-1.70) µg/ 100 ml	42	56	Tyrosine	3.15(1.32-5.45) mg/ 100 ml	32
28	Inositol	21(15-36) µg/100 ml	42	57	Valine	2.96(2.40-4.35) mg/ 100 ml	32
29	Choline	7.1 µg/100 ml	39				
30	Ascorbic acid	(0-600) µg/100 ml	46		Miscellaneous compounds		
31	Dehydroascorbic acid	70.5 µg/100 ml	70	58	Creatine	(0.2-1.55) mg/100 ml	4
	Carbohydrates & Organic Acids			59	Creatinine	(0.1-1.3) mg/100 ml	1,49,61
				60	Histamine (base)	(10-20) µg/liter	29
32	Sugar, as glucose	(0-3) mg/100 ml	31,49,61	61	Urea	(12-57) mg/100 ml	11,13,61, 69
33	Lactic acid	(285-336) mg/100 ml	6,16,33, 76,77				
				62	Uric acid	0.16(0.07-0.25) mg/ 100 ml	63
34	Pyruvic acid	(0.9-6.9) mg/100 ml	36				
35	Phenol	(2-8) mg/100 ml	64		Hormones, Enzymes [1], Miscellaneous Organic Compounds		
	Nitrogenous Substances						
	Nitrogen			63	Corticoids	(4-8) µg/100 ml	17,56
36	Total	(21-50) mg/100 ml	24	64	Alkaline phosphatase [3.1.3.1]	(0.1-5.3) King-Armstrong units	49
37	Nonprotein N	(66-108) mg/100 ml	58				
38	Amino acid N	(1.1-10.2) mg/100 ml	37	65	Ketone bodies, total	(0.4-0.6) mmole/liter	1
39	Ammonia N	(2.0-35) mg/100 ml	12,37,46, 53				
40	Urea N	(5-36) mg/100 ml	10,14,44, 50,79				

[1] Enzyme Commission Number, in brackets, was assigned by the International Union of Biochemistry on the Nomenclature and Classification of Enzymes [34].

Contributor: Randall, Walter C.

References
[1] Adams, R., et al. 1958. Quart. J. Exp. Physiol. 43: 241.

[2] Adolph, E. F. 1947. Physiology of Man in the Desert. Interscience, New York.

[3] Ahlman, K. L., et al. 1952. J. Appl. Physiol. 4: 911.

[4] Ahlman, K. L., et al. 1953. Acta Endocrinol. (Copenhagen) 13:773.

continued

[5] Armatruda, T. T., and L. G. Welt. 1953. J. Appl. Physiol. 5:759.

[6] Astrand, I. 1963. Acta Physiol. Scand. 58:359.

[7] Bara, B. 1963. Pol. Arch. Med. Wewn. 33:1125.

[8] Borchardt, W. 1926. Pfluegers Arch. Gesamte Physiol. Menschen Tiere 214:169.

[9] Brown, G., and R. L. Dobson. 1967. J. Appl. Physiol. 23:97.

[10] Brusilow, S. W., and E. H. Gordes. 1964. J. Clin. Invest. 43:477.

[11] Brusilow, S. W., and E. H. Gordes. 1965. Amer. J. Physiol. 209:1213.

[12] Brusilow, S. W., and E. H. Gordes. 1969. Ibid. 214:513.

[13] Bulmer, M. G. 1957. J. Physiol. (London) 137:261.

[14] Bulmer, M. G., and G. D. Forwell. 1956. Ibid. 132:115.

[15] Cage, G. W., and R. L. Dobson. 1965. J. Clin. Invest. 44:1270.

[16] Collins, K. J. 1962. J. Appl. Physiol. 17:99.

[17] Collins, K. J., et al. 1969. J. Physiol. (London) 202:645.

[18] Coltman, C. A., and N. J. Rowe. 1966. Amer. J. Clin. Nutr. 18:270.

[19] Coltman, C. A., et al. 1966. Ibid. 18:373.

[20] Conn, J. W. 1949. Arch. Intern. Med. 83:416.

[21] Consolazio, F. C., et al. 1962. J. Nutr. 78:78.

[22] Consolazio, F. C., et al. 1962. Ibid. 79:407.

[23] Dill, D. B. 1938. Life, Heat, and Altitude. Harvard Univ. Press, Cambridge.

[24] Dill, D. B., et al. 1938. Amer. J. Physiol. 123:412.

[25] Dill, D. B., et al. 1967. J. Appl. Physiol. 23:746.

[26] Dobson, R. L. 1962. Advan. Biol. Skin 3:54.

[27] Dobson, R. L. 1965. Arch. Environ. Health 11:423.

[28] Fiedler, H. P. 1968. Der Schweiss, Entstehung, Zusammensetzung und Bekäpfung mit einem Beitrag über die Desodorierung. Cantor, Württemberg.

[29] Garden, J. W. 1966. J. Appl. Physiol. 21:631.

[30] Gordon, R. S., and H. L. Andrews. 1966. Fed. Proc. Fed. Amer. Soc. Exp. Biol. 25:1372.

[31] Gordon, R. S., and G. W. Cage. 1966. Lancet 1:1246.

[32] Hier, S. W., et al. 1946. J. Biol. Chem. 166:327.

[33] Hubbard, J. L., and J. S. Weiner. 1969. J. Appl. Physiol. 27:715.

[34] International Union of Biochemistry. 1965. Enzyme Nomenclature. Elsevier, New York.

[35] Isaksson, B., and B. Sjogren. 1963. Scand. J. Clin. Lab. Invest., Suppl. 69:108.

[36] Itoh, S. 1960. In H. Yoshimura, et al., ed. Essential Problems in Climatic Physiology. Nankodo, Kyoto. pp. 3-25.

[37] Itoh, S., and T. Nakayama. 1952. Jap. J. Physiol. 2:248.

[38] Johnson, B. C., et al. 1945. J. Biol. Chem. 158:619.

[39] Johnson, B. C., et al. 1945. Ibid. 159:5.

[40] Johnson, B. C., et al. 1945. Ibid. 159:231.

[41] Johnson, B. C., et al. 1945. Ibid. 159:425.

[42] Johnson, B. C., et al. 1945. Ibid. 161:357.

[43] Johnson, F. A., et al. 1950. J. Nutr. 42:285.

[44] Komives, G. K., et al. 1966. J. Appl. Physiol. 21:1681.

[45] Kuno, Y. 1934. Physiology of Human Perspiration. J. and A. Churchill, London.

[46] Kuno, Y. 1956. Human Perspiration. C. C. Thomas, Springfield, Ill.

[47] Ladell, W. S. S. 1949. J. Physiol. (London) 108:440.

[48] Lieberman, J., and F. Kellogg. 1963. Amer. J. Med. Sci. 246:261.

[49] Lowenthal, L. J. A., and W. M. Politzer. 1963. Nord. Med. 69:3.

[50] Mickelson, O., and A. Keys. 1943. J. Biol. Chem. 149:479.

[51] Mitchell, H. H., and T. S. Hamilton. 1949. Ibid. 178:345.

[52] Montagna, W. 1962. The Structure and Function of the Skin. Academic Press, New York.

[53] Morimoto, T., and R. E. Johnson. 1967. Nature (London) 216:813.

[54] Mosher, H. H. 1932. J. Biol. Chem. 99:78.

[55] Newburgh, L. H. 1949. Physiology of Heat Regulation. W. B. Saunders, Philadelphia.

[56] Nichols, J., and A. T. Miller. 1948. Proc. Soc. Exp. Biol. Med. 69:448.

[57] O'Hara, K. 1966. Jap. J. Physiol. 16:274.

[58] Peters, J. P., and D. D. Van Slyke. 1946. Quantitative Clinical Chemistry. Williams and Wilkins, Baltimore, v. 1.

[59] Prasas, A. S., et al. 1963. J. Lab. Clin. Med. 62:84.

[60] Robinson, S., and A. H. Robinson. 1954. Methods Med. Res. 6:100.

[61] Robinson, S., and A. H. Robinson. 1954. Physiol. Rev. 34:221.

[62] Rothman, S. 1954. Physiology and Biochemistry of the Skin. Univ. Chicago Press, Chicago.

[63] Saiki, A. K., et al. 1932. Amer. J. Physiol. 100:328.

[64] Schultz, W. 1940. Arch. Dermatol. Syph. 181:471.

[65] Schulz, I., et al. 1965. Pfluegers Arch. Gesamte Physiol. Menschen Tiere 284:360.

[66] Schulz, I., et al. 1966. Proc. Int. Res. Conf. Pathogenesis Cystic Fibrosis, 3rd, Bethesda, 1964, p. 136.

[67] Schulz, I. J. 1969. J. Clin. Invest. 48:1470.

[68] Schwartz, I. L., and J. H. Thaysen. 1956. Ibid. 35:114.

[69] Schwartz, I. L., et al. 1953. J. Exp. Med. 97:429.

[70] Shields, J. B., et al. 1945. J. Biol. Chem. 161:351.

[71] Slegers, J. F. G. 1963. Dermatologica 127:242.

[72] Slegers, J. F. G. 1964. Pfluegers Arch. Gesamte Physiol. Menschen Tiere 279:269.

[73] Spector, H., et al. 1945. J. Biol. Chem. 161:137.

[74] Spector, H., et al. 1945. Ibid. 161:145.

[75] Talbert, G. A., et al. 1933. Amer. J. Physiol. 106:488.

[76] Thurmon, F. M., and B. Ottenstein. 1952. J. Invest. Dermatol. 18:333.

[77] Van Heyningen, R., and J. S. Weiner. 1952. J. Physiol. (London) 116:395.

[78] Warwick, W. J., and L. Hansen. 1965. Pediatrics 36:261.

[79] Weiner, J. S., and R. E. Van Heyningen. 1952. J. Appl. Physiol. 4:734.

Values are based on a "normal" dietary intake, including ~10 g nitrogen/day, and a body weight of 70 kg unless the specific weight was recorded. Data in brackets refer to the column heading in brackets. Values in parentheses are ranges, estimate "c" (*see* Introduction).

Part I. Compounds Other Than Steroids

Although multiple listings of several compounds are possible with the classification systems used, all compounds are listed singly. Consult the index for alphabetical listing of all compounds.

	Constituent (Synonym)	Amount Excreted mg·kg body wt^{-1}·da^{-1} [1/] [μg·kg body wt^{-1}·da^{-1}]	Reference
	General Chemical Constituents		
1	Solids	860(780-1000)	37,148, 182,240
2	Solids, total nondialyzable	(1-10)	32,36
3	Water	20,000(7,000-42,000)	140
	Electrolytes		
4	Aluminum	[1.1(0.7-1.6)]	48,130
5	Arsenic	[0.33(0-1.30)]	273
6	Beryllium	Trace	81
7	Bismuth	0.36[2/]	67
8	Bromine	[(12-110)]	52
9	Cadmium	46(0-126)[2/]	48,117, 146
10	Calcium	(0.05-11.43)	45,48,182
11	Chlorine	100(40-180)	182
12	Cobalt	(20-140)[2/]	48,106, 115
13	Copper	500(300-700)[2/]	62,193, 196,204
14	Fluorine	[22(7-100[3/])]	160,182
15	Iodine	[(0.1-7.0)]	39
16	Iron	[(1.4-4.3)]	48,77
17	Lead	[0.7(0.1-2.4)]	48,95, 117,130, 141
18	Magnesium	1.35(0.42-2.40)	48,76,102
19	Manganese	[(0.02-1.40)]	5,48,130, 131
20	Mercury	[(0.48-5.40)]	48,203, 238
21	Molybdenum	(140-430)[2/]	48
22	Nickel	(2-66)[2/]	131,165, 176
23	Phosphorus, inorganic	12(10-15)	267
24	organic	[131(89-187)]	202
25	Potassium	34(16-56)	182
26	Selenium	[0.5(0-2.0)]	92,237
27	Silicon	[130(60-200)]	31

	Constituent (Synonym)	Amount Excreted mg·kg body wt^{-1}·da^{-1} [1/] [μg·kg body wt^{-1}·da^{-1}]	Reference
28	Sodium	60(25-94)	48,182
29	Strontium	[5.7]	48
30	Sulfur, total	16.0(5.1-20.6)	80
31	ethereal	0.95(0.56-1.40)	80
32	inorganic	11.1(3.5-17.5)	80
33	neutral	1.90(1.05-2.60)	80
34	Tin	(130-250)[2/]	49,130
35	Zinc	[8.4(3.7-11.7)]	48,61, 117,256
36	Bicarbonate	2.0(0.5-12.0)	86
37	Pyrophosphate	[57]	101
	Vitamins & Related Compounds		
38	Thiamine	[3.0(0.6-6.0)]	65
39	Riboflavin	[12.4(2.0-24.0)]	65,180
40	Niacin	[3.4(2.0-20.0)]	65,121
41	Niacinamide	[20(10-50)]	65,121
42	N-Methylnicotinamide	[(40-600)]	65,121
43	Trigonelline	[(30-300)]	188
44	Vitamin B$_6$ (Pyridoxine)	[(0.08-2.70)]	119
45	(Pyridoxal)	[1.029]	51
46		[1.0(0.7-5.3)]	51,119, 201
47	Pyridoxal phosphate	[0.571]	51
48	Pyridoxamine	[1.6(0.4-3.0)]	51,201
49	4-Pyridoxic acid	[(9-160)]	51,119, 201
50	Biotin	[0.5(0.2-1.0)]	65
51	Pantothenic acid	[45(16-100)]	65
52	Folic acid	[(0.006-0.174)]	54,65,205
53	p-Aminobenzoic acid	[(2-3)]	65
54	Inositol	[200]	122
55	Vitamin B$_{12}$ (Cyanocobalamin)	[0.00234]	4,205
56	Choline	[79(68-130)]	120
57	Ascorbic acid	[(100-400)]	44
58	Dehydroascorbic acid	[(190-290)]	44
59	Diketogulonic acid	[(140-190)]	44
60	Neopterin	Trace	219
61	Vitamins A, D, & K	(0-Trace)	240

[1/] Unless otherwise indicated. [2/] ng·kg body wt^{-1}·da^{-1}. [3/] Upper limit of range obtained in area of Texas where dental fluorosis is endemic.

continued

Part I. Compounds Other Than Steroids

	Constituent (Synonym)	Amount Excreted mg·kg body wt^{-1}·da^{-1} [μg·kg body wt^{-1}·da^{-1}]	Reference		Constituent (Synonym)	Amount Excreted mg·kg body wt^{-1}·da^{-1} [1/] [μg·kg body wt^{-1}·da^{-1}]	Reference
	Lipids				**Amino Sugars & Mucopolysaccharides**		
62	Lipids, nondialyzable	[223(0-455)]	32,135	93	Amino sugars, bound, nondialyzable	[(200-700)]	32
63	Phospholipid	Trace	285	94	Sialic acids, bound, non-dialyzable	[581(367-795)]	32,135
64	Sphingomyelins, C$_{18}$ & C$_{24}$	Trace	167	95	Oligosaccharides as Hexosamine	(1.03-2.57)	154
65	Cholesterol	[(0-70)]	158,262, 263	96	3^2-α-N-Acetylneur-aminyllactose	Trace	116
	Carbohydrates & Derivatives			97	N-Acetylneur-aminyl-3-galactosyl-N-acetylgalactos-amine	Trace	116
	Pentoses			98	N-Acetylneur-aminyl-3^2-α-N-ace-tylneuraminyl-3-β-galactosyl-N-acetyl-galactosamine	Trace	116
66	Arabinose	Trace	40,255				
67	Ribose	Trace	255				
68	Ribulose	Trace	85				
69	Xylose	Trace	40,85				
70	Xylulose	Trace	254	99	6^2-α-N-Acetylneur-aminyllactose	Trace	116
71	D-2-Deoxyribose (Deoxyribose)	Trace	255	100	6^2-α-N-Acetylneur-aminyl-N-acetyllac-tosamine	Trace	116
72	Hexoses, bound, nondia-lyzable	(0.3-1.6)	32				
	Hexoses			101	Acid mucopolysaccha-rides	[(30-140)]	136,248
73	Fructose	Trace	40	102	Glycosaminoglycans, acidic	[69]	129,172, 280
74	Galactose	Trace	40,255				
75	Glucose	(0-1.4)	26,40,192	103	Chondroitin sulfate A	[21]	42,260
76	Psicose (Allulose)	Trace	40	104	Chondroitin sulfate B	[0.7]	260
77	Sorbose	Trace	40	105	Chondroitin sulfate C	[23]	260
78	Fucose, free	Trace	40	106	Heparitin sulfate	[55]	260
79	bound, nondia-lyzable	0.089	32,35,105	107	Hyaluronic acid	[0.7]	260
	Disaccharides			108	Keratosulfate	[0.7]	260
80	Lactose	Trace	40		**Amino Acids & Derivatives**		
81	Sucrose	Trace	40				
82	Oligosaccharides, as fu-cose	(0.60-2.40)	154	109	Amino acids, total	(20-40)	41
	Sugar alcohols			110	free	(13-20)	41
83	Adonitol (Ribitol)	Trace	195,234	111	α-	0.340(0.179-0.543)[4/]	278
84	Arabitol	(0-4)	195,234				
85	Erythritol	(0.2-2.0)	195,234	112	Amino acid nitrogen	(3-6)	107
86	Glycerol	[(40-160)]	195,234	113	Alanine, total	1.028(0.529-1.500)	41,53
87	Mannitol	(0-8)	195,234				
88	Sorbitol	(0-8)	195	114	β-Alanine	(0.2-0.3)	58
89	Threitol	Trace	195,234	115	Arginine, total	0.45(0.34-0.50)	259
90	Xylitol	Trace	195	116	free	0.16(0.07-0.30)	41
	Sugar acids						
91	D-Glucaric acid	[122(42-202)]	171				
92	Glucuronic acid	Trace	255				

1/ Unless otherwise indicated. 4/ meq·kg body wt^{-1}·da^{-1}.

continued

Part I. Compounds Other Than Steroids

	Constituent (Synonym)	Amount Excreted mg·kg body wt^{-1}·da^{-1} [μg·kg body wt^{-1}·da^{-1}]	Reference		Constituent (Synonym)	Amount Excreted mg·kg body wt^{-1}·da^{-1} [μg·kg body wt^{-1}·da^{-1}]	Reference
117	Asparagine	2.4(1.1-3.8)	210,236	150	Tryptophan, total	0.40(0.23-0.70)	90,268, 284
118	Aspartic acid, total	1.7(1.2-2.7)	284				
119	free	0.04(0.01-0.07)	284	151	free	0.20(0.11-0.36)	90,268, 284
120	Citrulline	0.09(0-2.80)	286				
121	Cystine, total	1.7(1.0-2.6)	252	152	Tyrosine, total	0.70(0.44-0.82)	252,268, 284
122	free	1.3(0.6-1.9)	108,228				
123	Glutamic acid, total	(3.7-5.0)	41,111	153	free	0.20(0.15-0.30)	252,268, 284
124	free	0.8(0-1.5)	41,111				
125	Glutamine	(0.3-6.4)	210,230	154	Valine, total	0.30(0.25-0.42)	73,228, 268
126	Glycine, total	6.5	73				
127	free	2.2	41	155	free	0.09(0.04-0.18)	73,228, 268
128	Histidine, total	2.7(1.0-5.0)	41,252, 284				
				156	β-Aminoisobutyric acid	[(0.7-4.0)]	88
129	free	2.0(1.2-2.7)	41,284	157	δ-Aminolevulinic acid	[(10-60)]	87,224
130	Hydroxyproline Total	0.51(0.43-0.60)	41,74, 103,134		Arginine derivatives		
				158	Creatine	0.8(0-2.0)	133,259
				159	Creatinine	23(15-30)	250,259
131	Nondialyzable	0.05(0.04-0.05)	103	160	Guanidinoacetic acid	(0.2-0.5)	259
132	Isoleucine, total	0.2(0.1-0.3)	73,228, 284	161	Guanidino-N,N-dimethylarginine	Trace	126
133	free	0.08(0.04-0.20)	73,228, 284	162	Guanidino-N,N'-dimethylarginine	Trace	126
134	Leucine, total	0.30(0.22-0.45)	73,228, 284		Cysteine derivatives		
				163	S-Methylcysteine	[21]	251
135	free	0.13(0.05-0.17)	73,228, 284	164	S-(1,2-Dicarboxyethyl)-cysteine	Trace	145
136	Lysine, total	0.80(0.48-1.70)	73,228, 284	165	S-(1-Methyl-2-carboxyethyl)cysteine	Trace	138
137	free	0.40(0.17-0.67)	73,111, 228	166	S-(1,2-Dimethyl-2-carboxyethyl)cysteine	Trace	138
138	Methionine, total	0.14(0.10-0.17)	73,228, 284	167	S-(Carboxymethylthio)-cysteine	Trace	257
139	free	0.05(0.03-0.10)	73,228, 284	168	S-(2-Hydroxy-2-carboxyethylthio)cysteine	Trace	257
140	Ornithine	0.15	41	169	3-(S-Cysteinyl)glutaric acid	Trace	138
141	Phenylalanine, total	0.30(0.21-0.54)	41,73,284		Glycine derivatives		
142	free	0.17(0.09-0.23)	41,73,284	170	Ethanolamine	[(70-700)]	152
143	Proline, total	0.61(0.30-0.90)	284	171	Glyoxylic acid (Glyoxalic acid)	[50]	112
144	free	0.12(0.03-0.20)	284				
145	Serine, total	0.6(0.5-0.7)	41,268	172	Oxalic acid	[(125-780)]	43,91, 112,137, 182
146	free	0.3(0.2-0.5)	41,268				
147	Taurine	(0.11-0.20)	286				
148	Threonine, total	0.50(0.36-2.60)	41,73, 228,268, 284	173	Formic acid	0.8(0.4-2.0)	20
				174	Hippuric acid	(7.0-18.0)	282
149	free	0.25(0.11-0.35)	41,73, 228,268, 284	175	o-Aminohippuric acid	[60]	38

continued

Part I. Compounds Other Than Steroids

	Constituent (Synonym)	Amount Excreted mg·kg body wt^{-1}·da^{-1} [μg·kg body wt^{-1}·da^{-1}]	Reference		Constituent (Synonym)	Amount Excreted mg·kg body wt^{-1}·da^{-1} [μg·kg body wt^{-1}·da^{-1}]	Reference
176	m-Hydroxyhippuric acid	Trace	57,239	207	m-Hydroxyphenylacetic acid	Trace	57,239
177	p-Hydroxyhippuric acid	Trace	57,239	208	p-Hydroxyphenylacetic acid	[(200-1200)]	282,288
	Histidine derivatives			209	3-Methoxy-4-hydroxyphenylacetic acid	Trace	57,239
178	1-Methylhistidine	Trace	243		Proline derivative		
179	3-Methylhistidine	Trace	243	210	Pyrrole-2-carboxylic acid	[(2.2-5.5)]	89
180	Histamine, free	[0.18(0.03-0.44)]	209,232				
181	conjugated	[0.43(0.01-1.41)]	209,232		Serine derivatives		
182	1,4-Dimethylhistamine (1,4-Methylhistamine)	[(2-7)]	249	211	Pyruvic acid	[(104-333)]	287
				212	Lactic acid	[(100-150)]	287
183	Urocanic acid	Trace	226		Tryptophan derivatives		
184	Imidazole derivatives	(2-3)	139	213	Tryptamine	[(1.3-2.8)]	189,226
185	Imidazoleacetic acid	[92(0-208)]	170	214	Kynurenine	[(23-78)]	2
186	1-Methylimidazole-4-acetic acid	[(11-64)]	249	215	Acetylkynurenine	[30]	38
				216	3-Hydroxykynurenine	[75]	38
187	5-Methylimidazole-4-acetic acid	[(0-163)]	249	217	Kynurenic acid	[30]	38
188	Imidazolelactic acid	[240(0-508)]	170,233	218	Xanthurenic acid	[(2-182)]	14,38,265
189	4-Aminoimidazole-5-carboxamide	[15]	56	219	o-Aminobenzoic acid (Anthranilic acid)	[(2-9)]	2
190	Formiminoglutamic acid	(0.7-1.5)	53,123	220	3-Hydroxy-o-aminobenzoic acid (3-Hydroxyanthranilic acid)	[(0-48)]	2,223
191	Ergothioneine (Ergothionine)	(1.7-4.0)	179	221	Quinolinic acid	[(86-186)]	253
	Leucine derivative				Indole derivatives		
192	Isovaleric acid	[(0-5.5)]	190	222	Indican, metabolic (Indoxylsulfate)	[1111(509-1731)]	59,216, 227
	Lysine derivatives			223	Indole-3-carboxylic acid	Trace	63
193	ε-N-Methyllysine	[90]	12,126				
194	ε-N,ε-N-Dimethyllysine	Trace	126	224	Indoleacetic acid	[(20-60)]	282
195	ε-N,ε-N,ε-N-Trimethyllysine	Trace	126	225	5-Hydroxyindoleacetic acid	[(20-80)]	143,144, 282
196	1,5-Pentanediamine (Cadaverine)	Trace	113	226	Indoleacetylglutamine	Trace	63
	Methionine derivatives			227	Indole-3-aceturic acid (Indoleaceturic acid)	Trace	63
197	Methionine sulfoxide	[(0-310)]	41,286	228	5-Hydroxyskatole, sulfate ester	[(0-34)]	157
198	Spermine	Trace	113				
199	Spermidine	Trace	113	229	6-Hydroxyskatole, sulfate ester	[(1-60)]	157
	Ornithine derivative			230	7-Hydroxyskatole, sulfate ester	[(0-4)]	157
200	Putrescine	Trace	113				
	Phenylalanine & tyrosine derivatives				Valine derivatives		
201	m-Tyramine	[(1.0-2.5)]	127	231	Isobutylamine	Trace	16
202	p-Tyramine	[(0.5-2.5)]	127	232	Isobutyric acid	[(0-6.5)]	190
203	3-Methoxytyramine	[(0-0.5)]	127	233	Methylmalonic acid	[(14-114)]	64,72,96
204	Tyrosine-O-sulfate	[(300-500)]	187		Carbohydrate derivatives		
205	Phenylacetic acid	Trace	70	234	O-Xylosylserine	[14]	251
206	o-Hydroxyphenylacetic acid	[(0-30)]	57,239, 288				

continued

Part I. Compounds Other Than Steroids

	Constituent (Synonym)	Amount Excreted mg·kg body wt^{-1}·da^{-1} [1] [μg·kg body wt^{-1}·da^{-1}]	Reference
235	Galactosyl-δ-hydroxy-lysine	Trace	126
236	Glucosylgalactosyllysine	Trace	126
237	2-Acetamido-1-(β'-L-aspartamido)-1,2-dideoxy-β-D-glucose	Trace	184
	Peptides & Nonenzymatic Proteins		
	Peptides		
238	36 individual	Traces	8
239	Hydroxyproline-containing glyco-	23	34
240	Fuco-	Trace	35
	Dipeptides		
241	Anserine + carnosine	[(45-140)]	58
242	β-Aspartylglycine	[(143-286)]	194
243	Prolylhydroxyproline	[260]	134
244	Protein, total	(0.5-2.0)	21,32, 100,110, 124,207, 217
245	nitrogen	[(80-320)[5]]	
	α-Globulins		
246	α$_1$-Globulin	Trace	22,25,99, 185,269
247	α$_1$-Lipoprotein	Trace	22,25,99, 185,269
248	α$_1$-Seromucoid	Trace	22,25,99, 185,269
249	α$_2$-Proteins	Trace	22,25,99, 185,269
250	α$_2$-Macroglobulin	Trace	22,25,99, 185,269
251	Barium α$_2$-glycoprotein	Trace	22,25,99, 185,269
252	Zinc α$_2$-glycoprotein	Trace	22,25,99, 185,269
	β-Globulins		
253	β-Protein	Trace	22,25,99, 185,269
254	β-Microglobulin	Trace	22,25,99, 185,269
255	β$_1$A Globulin	Trace	22,25,99, 185,269
256	β$_2$A Globulin	Trace	22,25,99, 185,269

	Constituent (Synonym)	Amount Excreted mg·kg body wt^{-1}·da^{-1} [μg·kg body wt^{-1}·da^{-1}]	Reference
	γ-Globulins		
257	γ-Globulin	Trace	22,25,99, 185,269
258	γ-L-Globulin	Trace	22,25,99, 185,269
259	Post-γ-protein	Trace	22,25,99, 185,269
	Immunoglobulins		
260	IgA(C)[b]	[40(20-70)]	24
261	IgA(P)[a]	[20(10-40)]	24
262	IgG	[50(20-90)]	19,24
263	γA	[20]	28
264	3Sγ,G	[3(2-5)]	198
265	7Sγ,G	[40]	28
266	Light chains	[50(20-100)]	24
267	F$_c$ fragment	[3(1-6)]	23,24
268	Poliomyelitis antibodies	Trace	163,242
269	Tetanus antibodies	Trace	163,242
	Other proteins		
270	Glycoproteins (Tamm-Horsfall, etc.)	[(250-500)]	3,32,98, 245
271	α$_2$HS Glycoprotein	[16(10-20)]	199
272	B-1E Globulin	Trace	22,25,99, 185,269
273	Fucoproteins	Trace	35
274	Haptoglobin	Trace	22,25,99, 185,269
275	Prealbumin	Trace	22,25,99, 185,269
276	Ceruloplasmin	Trace	22,25,99, 185,269
277	Fibrinogen	Trace	22,25,99, 185,269
278	Hemopexin	Trace	22,25,99, 185,269
279	Transferrin	Trace	22,25,99, 185,269
	Purine Bases; Purine & Pyrimidine Derivatives		
280	Purine bases, total	[(200-1000)]	182
281	Adenine	[20(16-24)]	277
	Derivatives		
282	3',5'-Cyclic adenosine monophosphate (3', 5'-Adenosine monophosphate, cyclic)	[(10-30)]	1,13,186, 247
283	Hypoxanthine	[140(80-190)]	277

[1] Unless otherwise indicated. [5] Calculated from total protein content.

continued

Part I. Compounds Other Than Steroids

	Constituent (Synonym)	Amount Excreted mg·kg body wt^{-1}·da^{-1} [1/] [μg·kg body wt^{-1}·da^{-1}]	Reference		Constituent (Synonym)	Amount Excreted mg·kg body wt^{-1}·da^{-1} [μg·kg body wt^{-1}·da^{-1}]	Reference
284	1-Methylhypoxanthine	[6(3-10)]	277		Porphyrin derivatives		
				312	Bilirubin	Trace	166,174
285	Uric acid	2.0(0.8-3.0)	182	313	Coproporphyrins I & III	[(0.24-4.00)]	208,225, 272
286	1,3-Dimethyluric acid	Trace	69				
287	Allantoin	[170(140-210)]	281	314	Porphobilinogen	[(10-30)]	168,224
288	1-Methylinosine	Trace	47	315	Urobilin + urobilinogen	[12(1-42)]	132,147, 271
289	Guanine	[6(3-9)]	277				
	Derivatives			316	Uroporphyrin	[(0.1-0.4)]	225
290	N^2-Methylguanine	[7(6-9)]	277	317	Urea	(200-500)	182
291	7-Methylguanine	[90(80-110)]	277		Nonsteroid Hormones & Derivatives		
292	8-Hydroxy-7-methylguanine	[20(16-30)]	277				
				318	Adrenocorticotropin (ACTH)	Consult reference	213
293	N^2-Methylguanosine	Trace	47		Catecholamines & derivatives		
294	N^2-Dimethylguanosine	Trace	47		Epinephrine		
295	3',5'-Cyclic guanosine monophosphate (3', 5'-Guanosine monophosphate, cyclic)	Trace	94	319	Total	[0.63(0.20-1.06)]	125
				320	Free	[(0.02-0.13)]	125
				321	Conjugated	[(0.19-0.61)]	125
					Norepinephrine		
296	Xanthine	[90(70-120)]	277	322	Total	[1.9(0.5-3.2)]	50,125, 155,159, 264,275
297	Theophylline (1,3-Dimethylxanthine)	Trace	69				
	Other purine derivatives			323	Free	[(0.3-1.1)]	125
298	6-Succinopurine	[14]	276	324	Conjugated	[(1.0-2.9)]	125
299	N-[(9-β-D-Ribofuranosyl-9H-purin-6-yl)carbamoyl]threonine	Trace	46	325	Dopamine	[(1-6)]	18,30,50, 178
				326	Metanephrine	[(0.4-6.0)]	27,29, 127,159
	Pyrimidine derivatives			327	Normetanephrine (Normethanephrine)	[(0.1-4.4)]	27,29, 127,159
300	Deoxycytidine	(4-57)[2/]	229				
301	Pseudouridine	(0.7-1.3)	75	328	p-Octopamine	Trace	57,239
	Other Nitrogenous Substances			329	Synephrine (p-Sympatol)	Trace	57,239
302	Nitrogen, total	(130-300)	182	330	p-Hydroxymandelic acid	Trace	57,239
303	ammonia	(3-13)	270	331	3,4-Dihydroxymandelic acid	[(0.5-2.5)]	66,221, 274
304	nondialyzable	(0.2-0.8)	32				
	Amines				4-Hydroxy-3-methoxymandelic acid		
305	Aminoacetone	[(2-20)]	224	332	(3-Methoxy-4-hydroxymandelic acid)	[62(47-75)]	57,175 239,264
306	n-Butylamine	Trace	16				
307	n-Hexylamine	Trace	16	333	(Vanillylmandelic acid)	[66(44-90)]	66,283
308	p-Hydroxybenzylamine	[2]	127				
309	Propane-1,3-diamine (1,3-Diaminopropane)	Trace	113	334	4-Hydroxy-3-methoxyphenylglycol (3-Methoxy-4-hydroxyphenylglycol)	[27(12-52)]	175
310	N-Methyl-2-pyridone-5-carboxamide	[240]	38				
311	4-Methylthiazole-5-acetic acid	Trace	11				

1/ Unless otherwise indicated. 2/ ng·kg body wt^{-1}·da^{-1}.

continued

Part I. Compounds Other Than Steroids

	Constituent (Synonym)	Amount Excreted mg·kg body wt^{-1}·da^{-1} [μg·kg body wt^{-1}·da^{-1}]	Reference
335	Erythropoietin	Consult references	78,150, 258
336	Follicle-stimulating hormone (FSH)	Consult references	7,17,169
337	Gonadotropin[6] (Chorionic gonadotropin)	Consult reference	244
338	Growth hormone	Consult reference	82
339	Insulin	Consult references	151,211, 261
340	Luteinizing hormone (ICSH)	Consult references	7,17
341	Proinsulin	Consult reference	212
342	Melanocyte-stimulating hormone (Melanotropin)	Consult reference	231
343	Parathyroid hormone	Consult reference	60
	Serotonin (5-Hydroxytryptamine)		
344	Total	[(0.25-1.71)]	127,142
345	Glucose conjugate	[(0.26-0.93)]	143
346	Sulfate conjugate	[(0.47-1.42)]	143
347	Vasopressin (Antidiuretic hormone)	Consult references	83,214
	Enzymes [7] & Related Compounds		
348	L-Lactate dehydrogenase (Lactic acid dehydrogenase) [1.1.1.27]	Consult references	110,279
349	Diamine oxidase (Histaminase) [1.4.3.6]	Consult reference	128
350	Aspartate aminotransferase (Glutamate-oxalacetate transaminase) [2.6.1.1]	Consult reference	200
351	Alanine aminotransferase (Glutamate-pyruvate transaminase) [2.6.1.2]	Consult reference	200
352	Ribonuclease [2.7.7.16]	Consult reference	149
353	Esterases [3.1._._]	Consult reference	218
354	Lipase [3.1.1.3]	Consult references	6,177
355	Cholinesterase [3.1.1.8]	Consult reference	200
356	Alkaline phosphatase [3.1.3.1]	Consult references	68,279

	Constituent (Synonym)	Amount Excreted mg·kg body wt^{-1}·da^{-1} [1] [μg·kg body wt^{-1}·da^{-1}]	Reference
357	Acid phosphatase [3.1.3.2]	Consult references	10,68,279
358	Deoxyribonuclease [3.1.4.5]	Consult reference	200
359	Arylsulfatase [3.1.6.1]	Consult reference	279
360	α-Amylase, salivary & pancreatic [3.2.1.1]	Consult references	6,15,156
361	α-Glucosidase (Maltase) [3.2.1.20]	Consult references	79,84
362	Trehalase [3.2.1.28]	Consult reference	55
363	β-Glucuronidase [3.2.1.31]	Consult references	161,197, 222,279
364	Hyaluronidase (Hyaluronate lyase) [4.2.99.1]	Consult reference	200
365	Leucine aminopeptidase [3.4.1.1]	Consult reference	279
366	Alanine aminopeptidase [3.4.1.x]	Consult reference	191
367	Glycine aminopeptidase [3.4.1.x]	Consult reference	200
368	Trypsin [3.4.4.4]	Consult reference	200
369	Cathepsin [3.4.4.9; 3.4.4.23]	Consult reference	164
370	Renin [3.4.4.15]	Consult reference	153
371	Kallikreins [3.4.4.21]	Consult reference	200
372	Inorganic pyrophosphatase (Pyrophosphatase) [3.6.1.1]	Consult reference	266
373	Cadaverinase	Consult reference	128
374	Dihydroxyphenylalanine oxidase	Consult reference	206
375	γ-Glutamyl transpeptidase	Consult references	181,241
376	Pepsinogens	Consult reference	220
377	Urokinase	Consult reference	33
378	Uropepsinogen	Consult reference	114
	Miscellaneous Organic Compounds		
379	Ketone bodies, total	[600]	97,235
	Organic acids		
380	Total	0.787(0.253-1.321)[4]	93
	Citric acid cycle components		
381	Citric acid	(3-20)	246,287
382	Aconitic acid	Trace	104

[1] Unless otherwise indicated. [4] meq·kg body wt^{-1}·da^{-1}. [6] A gonadotropin-inhibiting substance is also present in urine [183]. [7] Enzyme Commission Number, in brackets, was assigned by the International Union of Biochemistry on the Nomenclature and Classification of Enzymes [118].

continued

Part I. Compounds Other Than Steroids

Constituent (Synonym)	Amount Excreted mg·kg body wt^{-1}·da^{-1} [1/] [µg·kg body wt^{-1}·da^{-1}]	Reference		Constituent (Synonym)	Amount Excreted mg·kg body wt^{-1}·da^{-1} [1/] [µg·kg body wt^{-1}·da^{-1}]	Reference
383 α-Ketoglutaric acid	(0.218-1.458)	287	396	Pyrocatechol (Catechol)	[71(17-125)]	109
384 Succinic acid	[(54-202)]	287	397	Ferulic acid (3-Methoxy-4-hydroxycinnamic acid)	Trace	57,70,239
385 Fumaric acid	[(0-70)]	287				
386 Malic acid	[(40-300)]	287	398	p-Hydroxybenzoic acid	Trace	57,226, 239
Other acids						
387 Acetic acid	[(12.5-195.0)]	190	399	m-Hydroxyphenyl-β-hydroxypropionic acid	Trace	57,239
388 Acetoacetic acid	[40(30-60)]	235				
389 Caproic acid	[(0-4.5)]	190	400	Vanillic acid (3-Methoxy-4-hydroxybenzoic acid)	Trace	57,239
390 Carbonic acid	2.7(2.1-3.3)	86				
391 Glycolic acid	[600]	112				
392 Mevalonic acid	Trace	71				
393 Propionic acid	[(0-6.3)]	190	401	Homovanillic acid	(0.05-1.60)	162,215, 282
394 Organic bases, total	0.395(0.193-0.597)4/	93				
			402	Procoagulant	Trace	9
Phenolic compounds			403	Reducing substances	(7-21)	37
395 Phenol, free	3.2(1.6-4.6)	173				

1/ Unless otherwise indicated. 4/ meq·kg body wt^{-1}·da^{-1}.

Contributor: Van Pilsum, John

References

[1] Abdulla, Y. H., and K. Hamadah. 1970. Lancet 1(7643):378.

[2] Abul-Fadl, M. A. M., and A. S. Khalafallah. 1961. Brit. J. Cancer 15:479.

[3] Ada, G. L., and A. Gottschalk. 1952. Aust. J. Sci. 14:160.

[4] Adams, J. F. 1970. Brit. Med. J. 1(5689):138.

[5] Ajemian, R. S., and N. E. Whitman. 1969. Amer. Ind. Hyg. Ass. J. 30(1):52.

[6] Ambromovage, A. M., et al. 1968. Ann. Surg. 167:539.

[7] Anderson, R. N., and A. Albert. 1968. Mayo Clin. Proc. 43:354.

[8] Ansorge, S., and H. Hanson. 1967. Hoppe Seylers Z. Physiol. Chem. 348:334.

[9] Aoki, N., and K. N. von Kaulla. 1966. Thromb. Diath. Haemorrh. 16:586.

[10] Aoyama, S. 1961. Acta Sch. Med. Univ. Kioto 37:203.

[11] Ariaey-Nejad, et al. 1970. Amer. J. Clin. Nutr. 23:764.

[12] Asatoor, A. M. 1969. Clin. Chim. Acta 26(1):147.

[13] Aurbach, G. D., and B. A. Houston. 1968. J. Biol. Chem. 243(22):5935.

[14] Austin, W. H., and S. C. Littlefield. 1966. J. Lab. Clin. Med. 67:516.

[15] Aw, S. E. 1966. Nature (London) 209:298.

[16] Baba, S. 1969. Yakugaku Zasshi 89(12):1712.

[17] Baghdassarian, A., et al. 1971. Clin. Chim. Acta 31:428.

[18] Barbeau, A., and T. L. Sourkes. 1961. Rev. Can. Biol. 20:197.

[19] Bell, L. E., and H. Chaplin. 1970. J. Lab. Clin. Invest. 75:636.

[20] Benedict, E. M., and G. A. Harrop. 1922. J. Biol. Chem. 54:443.

[21] Berggård, I. 1961. Ark. Kemi 18:291.

[22] Berggård, I. 1961. Clin. Chim. Acta 6:413.

[23] Berggård, I., and H. Bennich. 1967. Nature (London) 214:697.

[24] Berggård, I., and P. Peterson. 1967. Gamma Globulins Proc. Nobel Symp., 3rd, p. 71.

[25] Berggård, I., et al. 1964. Clin. Chim. Acta 10:1.

[26] Bernard, A. G., and J. Ginsburg. 1965. Brit. Med. J. 2(5477):1437.

[27] Bertani, L. M., et al. 1970. Clin. Chim. Acta 30:227.

[28] Bienenstock, J., and T. B. Tomasi. 1968. J. Clin. Invest. 47:1162.

[29] Bigelow, L. B., and H. Weil-Malherbe. 1968. Anal. Biochem. 26(1):92.

[30] Bishoff, F., and A. Torres. 1962. Clin. Chem. 8:370.

[31] Bloomfield, I. J., et al. 1932. Pub. Health Rep. 50:421.

[32] Boas, N. F. 1965. Amino Sugars 2A:95.

[33] Boomgaard, J. B., et al. 1966. Clin. Chim. Acta 13:484.

[34] Bourrillon, R., and J. L. Vernay. 1966. Biochim. Biophys. Acta 117(2):319.

[35] Bourrillon, R., et al. 1965. Bull. Soc. Chim. Biol. 47:1795.

[36] Boyce, W. H., et al. 1961. J. Clin. Invest. 40:1453.

[37] Bradley, S. E. 1945. Med. Clin. N. Amer. 29:1314.

[38] Brown, R. R., et al. 1961. J. Clin. Invest. 40:617.

continued

Part I. Compounds Other Than Steroids

[39] Bruger, M., et al. 1941. J. Lab. Clin. Med. 26:1942.

[40] Butts, W. C., and R. L. Jolley. 1970. Clin. Chem. 16:722.

[41] Carsten, M. E. 1952. J. Amer. Chem. Soc. 74:5954.

[42] Chakrapani, B., and B. K. Vachawat. 1969. Indian J. Biochem. 6(4):166.

[43] Charransol, G., and P. Desgrez. 1970. J. Chromatogr. 48(3):530.

[44] Chen, S. D., and C. Shuck. 1951. J. Nutr. 23:111.

[45] Chen, T., and L. B. Dotti. 1967. Clin. Chim. Acta 18:453.

[46] Chheda, G. B. 1969. Life Sci. 8:979.

[47] Chheda, G. B., et al. 1969. J. Pharm. Sci. 58(1):75.

[48] Christian, G. D. 1969. Anal. Chem. 41(1):24A.

[49] Clark, G. W. 1926. Univ. Calif. Berkeley Publ. Physiol. 5(17):195.

[50] Comoy, E., and C. Bohuon. 1970. Clin. Chim. Acta 30:191.

[51] Contractor, S. F., and B. Shane. 1968. Ibid. 21:71.

[52] Conway, E. J., and J. C. Flood. 1936. Biochem. J. 30:716,

[53] Cooperman, J. M., et al. 1969. Proc. Soc. Exp. Biol. Med. 131(2):434.

[54] Cooperman, J. M., et al. 1970. Clin. Chem. 16(5):375.

[55] Courtois, J. E., and J. F. Demelier. 1966. Bull. Soc. Chim. Biol. 48:277.

[56] Coward, R. F., and P. Smith. 1965. Clin. Chim. Acta 12:206.

[57] Coward, R. F., et al. 1964. Ibid. 9:381.

[58] Crokaert, R. 1953. Ann. Soc. Roy. Sci. Med. Natur. Bruxelles 6:157.

[59] Curzon, G., and J. Walsh. 1962. Clin. Chim. Acta 7:657.

[60] Davies, B. M. A. 1958. J. Endocrinol. 16:369.

[61] Dawson, J. B., and B. E. Walker. 1969. Clin. Chim. Acta 26:465.

[62] Dawson, J. B., et al. 1968. Ibid. 21:33.

[63] Decker, P., and H. Gerdemann. 1959. Deut. Tieraerztl. Wochenschr. 66:305.

[64] Degrazia, J. A., et al. 1969. Clin. Chim. Acta 23:279.

[65] Denko, C. W., et al. 1946. Arch. Biochem. 10:33.

[66] Dequattro, V., et al. 1964. J. Lab. Clin. Med. 63:864.

[67] Devoto, G. 1968. Boll. Soc. Ital. Biol. Sper. 44(15):1253.

[68] Dietz, A. A., and L. K. Hodges. 1967. Clin. Chim. Acta 15:393.

[69] Dikstein, S., et al. 1958. J. Biol. Chem. 230:203.

[70] Dirscherl, W., and U. Pelzer. 1970. Hoppe Seylers Z. Physiol. Chem. 351(9):1151.

[71] Dmitrieva, N. A., et al. 1968. Vop. Med. Khim. 14(1):106.

[72] Dreyfus, P. M., and V. E. Dubé. 1967. Clin. Chim. Acta 15:525.

[73] Dunn, M. S., et al. 1947. Arch. Biochem. 13:207.

[74] Dupont, A. 1967. Clin. Chim. Acta 18:59.

[75] Eisen, A. Z., et al. 1962. J. Lab. Clin. Med. 59:620.

[76] Evans, R. A., and L. Watson. 1966. Lancet 1(7436):522.

[77] Figueroa, W. G., et al. 1955. J. Lab. Clin. Med. 46:534.

[78] Finn, P. H. 1965. Brit. Med. J. 1:697.

[79] Fleury, P. F., et al. 1951. Bull. Soc. Chim. Biol. 33:1762.

[80] Folin, O. 1905. Amer. J. Physiol. 13:45.

[81] Foreman, J. K., et al. 1970. Analyst (London) 95(1134):797.

[82] Franchemont, P. 1965. Ann. Endocrinol. 26:627.

[83] Frandsen, P. 1969. Acta Endocrinol. (Copenhagen) 62:31.

[84] Franzini, C., and P. A. Bonini. 1967. Clin. Chim. Acta 17:505.

[85] Futterman, S., and J. H. Foe. 1955. J. Biol. Chem. 215:257.

[86] Gamble, J. L. 1954. Chemical Anatomy, Physiology, and Pathology of Extracellular Fluid. Ed. 6. Harvard Univ. Press, Cambridge.

[87] Gentz, J., et al. 1969. Clin. Chim. Acta 23:257.

[88] Gerber, G. B., and G. Gerber. 1960. Ibid. 5:607.

[89] Gerber, G. B., et al. 1964. Ibid. 9:185.

[90] Gibbs, C. C. J., et al. 1967. Ibid. 17:317.

[91] Giterson, A. L., et al. 1970. Ibid. 29:342.

[92] Glover, J. R. 1967. Ann. Occup. Hyg. 10:3.

[93] Goldberg, G., et al. 1966. Clin. Chem. 12:830.

[94] Goldberg, N. D., et al. 1969. J. Biol. Chem. 244(16):4458.

[95] Goldwater, L. J. 1967. World Health Organ. Chron. 21:191.

[96] Gompertz, D., et al. 1967. Clin. Chim. Acta 18:197.

[97] Göschke, H. 1970. Ibid. 28:359.

[98] Gottschalk, A. 1966. Glycoproteins. Elsevier, Amsterdam.

[99] Grant, G. H. 1957. J. Clin. Pathol. 10:360.

[100] Grasslin, D., et al. 1970. Z. Klin. Chem. Klin. Biochem. 8(3):288.

[101] Gundlach, G., et al. 1968. Urologe (Berlin) 7:56.

[102] Gwens, M. H. 1918. J. Biol. Chem. 34:119.

[103] Haddad, J. G., et al. 1970. Clin. Chim. Acta 30:282.

[104] Halpern, M. N. 1960. Ibid. 5:264.

[105] Hamerman, D., and F. T. Hatch. 1955. Proc. Soc. Exp. Biol. Med. 89:279.

[106] Harp, M. J., and F. I. Scoular. 1952. J. Nutr. 47:67.

continued

Part I. Compounds Other Than Steroids

[107] Harrow, B., and A. Mazur. 1962. Textbook of Biochemistry. Ed. 8. W. B. Saunders, Philadelphia.

[108] Haux, P., and S. Natelson. 1970. Clin. Chem. 16(5): 366.

[109] Heistand, R. N. 1969. Amer. Ind. Hyg. Ass. J. 30(1):66.

[110] Hemmingsen, L., and F. Skov. 1968. Clin. Chim. Acta 19:81.

[111] Hier, S. W. 1948. Trans. N. Y. Acad. Sci. 10:200.

[112] Hockaday, T. D. R., et al. 1965. J. Lab. Clin. Med. 65:667.

[113] Holder, S., and H. J. Bremer. 1966. J. Chromatogr. 25:48.

[114] Hostrup, H., and P. Bastrup-Madsen. 1967. Acta Med. Scand. 158:193.

[115] Hubbard, D. M., et al. 1966. Arch. Environ. Health 13:191.

[116] Huttunen, J. K. 1967. Ann. Med. Exp. Biol. Fenn. 44(Suppl.12):5.

[117] Iguchi, T. 1968. Gifu Daigaku Igakubu Kiyo 15(3): 840.

[118] International Union of Biochemistry. 1965. Enzyme Nomenclature. Elsevier, New York.

[119] Johnson, B. C., et al. 1945. J. Biol. Chem. 158:619.

[120] Johnson, B. C., et al. 1945. Ibid. 159:5.

[121] Johnson, B. C., et al. 1945. Ibid. 159:231.

[122] Johnson, B. C., et al. 1945. Ibid. 161:357.

[123] Johnson, J. M., et al. 1965. Clin. Chim. Acta 12: 440.

[124] Jorgensen, M. B. 1967. Acta Med. Scand. 181:153.

[125] Kahane, Z., et al. 1967. J. Lab. Clin. Med. 69:1042.

[126] Kakimoto, Y., and S. Akayawa. 1970. J. Biol. Chem. 245:5751.

[127] Kakimoto, Y., and M. D. Armstrong. 1962. Ibid. 237:208.

[128] Kapeller-Adler, R., and R. Renwick. 1956. Clin. Chim. Acta 1:197.

[129] Kaplan, D., et al. 1968. J. Lab. Clin. Med. 71:48.

[130] Kehoe, R. A., et al. 1940. J. Nutr. 19:579.

[131] Kent, N. L., and R. A. McCance. 1941. Biochem. J. 35:877.

[132] Kerkhoff, J. F., and H. J. Peters. 1968. Clin. Chim. Acta 21:133.

[133] Kibrick, A. C. 1965. Ibid. 11:408.

[134] Kibrick, A. C., et al. 1964. Ibid. 10:344.

[135] King, J. S., et al. 1958. J. Clin. Invest. 37:315.

[136] King, J. S., Jr., et al. 1962. Clin. Chim. Acta 7:316.

[137] Koch, G. H. 1969. Anal. Biochem. 27(1):162.

[138] Kodama, H. 1968. Biochim. Biophys. Acta 165(3): 432.

[139] Koessler, K. K., and M. T. Hanke. 1924. J. Biol. Chem. 59:803.

[140] Kolmer, J. A., et al. 1951. Approved Laboratory Technique. Ed. 5. Appleton-Century-Crofts, New York.

[141] Kopito, L., and H. Schwachman. 1967. J. Lab. Clin. Med. 70:326.

[142] Korf, J. 1969. Clin. Chim. Acta 23(3):483.

[143] Korf, J., and J. B. Sebens. 1970. Ibid. 27:149.

[144] Korf, J., and T. V. Sikkema. 1969. Ibid. 26:301.

[145] Kuwaki, T., and S. Mizuhara. 1966. Biochim. Biophys. Acta 115:491.

[146] Lehnert, G., et al. 1968. Z. Klin. Chem. Klin. Biochem. 6(3):174.

[147] Lemberg, R., and J. W. Legge. 1949. Hematin Compounds and Bile Pigments. Interscience, New York.

[148] Levinson, S. A., and R. P. MacFate. 1961. Clinical Laboratory Diagnosis. Ed. 6. Lea and Febiger, Philadelphia.

[149] Levy, A. L., and A. Rottino. 1960. Clin. Chem. 6: 43.

[150] Lewis, J. P., et al. 1964. Proc. Soc. Exp. Biol. Med. 116:742.

[151] Lieberman, L. L. 1968. Lancet 1(7534):148.

[152] Luck, J. M., and A. Wilcox. 1953. J. Biol. Chem. 205:859.

[153] Lumbers, E. R., and S. L. Skinner. 1969. Aust. J. Exp. Biol. Med. Sci. 47(2):251.

[154] Lundblad, A. 1966. Biochim. Biophys. Acta 130: 130.

[155] Mabry, C. C., and P. W. Warth. 1969. Amer. J. Clin. Pathol. 52(1):57.

[156] MacFate, R. P. 1961. Ass. Clin. Sci. Proc. 2nd Appl. Seminar 2:14.

[157] Mahon, M. E., and G. L. Mattok. 1967. Can. J. Biochem. 45:1317.

[158] Mattice, M. R. 1936. Chemical Procedures for Clinical Laboratories. Lea and Febiger, Philadelphia.

[159] Mattok, G. L., et al. 1966. Clin. Chim. Acta 14:99.

[160] McClure, F. J. 1944. Pub. Health Rep. 59:1575.

[161] Melicow, M. M. et al. 1961. J. Urol. 86:89.

[162] Mellinger, T. J. 1958. Amer. J. Clin. Pathol. 49:200.

[163] Merler, E., et al. 1963. J. Clin. Invest. 42:1340.

[164] Merten, R., and H. Woyta. 1954. Z. Gesamte Exp. Med. 123:315.

[165] Mertz, D. P., et al. 1970. Z. Klin. Chem. Klin. Biochem. 8:30.

[166] Michaelsson, M. 1961. Scand. J. Clin. Lab. Invest. Suppl. 13.

[167] Michalec, C., and Z. Kolman. 1967. J. Chromatogr. 31:636.

[168] Moore, D. J., and R. F. Labbe. 1964. Clin. Chem. 10:1105.

[169] Mori, K. F. 1968. J. Endocrinol. 42(1):55.

[170] Mosebach, K. O., et al. 1967. Hoppe Seylers Z. Physiol. Chem. 348:620.

[171] Mowat, A. P. 1968. J. Endocrinol. 42(4):585.

[172] Murata, K., et al. 1970. Clin. Chim. Acta 28:213.

[173] Müting, D., et al. 1970. 27:177.

[174] Naumann, H. N. 1936. Biochem. J. 30:762.

continued

185. EXCRETION PRODUCTS IN URINE: MAN

Part I. Compounds Other Than Steroids

[175] Nicholas, N. L., et al. 1969. Clin. Chem. 15(9): 884.

[176] Nomoto, S., and F. W. Sunderman, Jr. 1970. Ibid. 16(6):477.

[177] Nothmann, M. M., et al. 1955. Arch. Intern. Med. 96:188.

[178] Oberman, Z., et al. 1970. Clin. Chim. Acta 29:391.

[179] Ohara, M., et al. 1952. Jap. J. Med. Sci. Biol. 5:259.

[180] Oldham, H., et al. 1950. J. Nutr. 41:231.

[181] Orlowski, M., and A. Szewczyuk. 1962. Clin. Chim. Acta 7:755.

[182] Oser, B. L., ed. 1965. Hawk's Physiological Chemistry. Ed. 14. McGraw-Hill, New York.

[183] Ota, M., et al. 1968. Fert. Steril. 19:100.

[184] Palo, J., and K. Mattsson. 1970. J. Chromatogr. 50(3):534.

[185] Patte, J. C., et al. 1958. Rev. Fr. Etud. Clin. Biol. 3:960.

[186] Paul, M. I., et al. 1970. Amer. J. Psychiat. 126(10): 1493.

[187] Percy, A. K., et al. 1968. Biochem. Med. 2(3):198.

[188] Perlzweig, W. A., et al. 1942. J. Amer. Med. Ass. 118:28.

[189] Perry, T. L. 1962. Science 136:879.

[190] Perry, T. L., et al. 1970. Clin. Chim. Acta 29:369.

[191] Peters, J. E., and N. Rehfeld. 1969. Ibid. 24:314.

[192] Peterson, J. I., and D. S. Young. 1968. Anal. Biochem. 23:301.

[193] Pirke, K. M., and D. Stam. 1970. Z. Klin. Chem. Klin. Biochem. 8:61.

[194] Pisano, J. J., et al. 1966. Arch. Biochem. Biophys. 117:394.

[195] Pitkänen, E., and A. Pitkänen. 1964. Ann. Med. Exp. Biol. 42:113.

[196] Plooij, M., et al. 1959. Ned. Tijdschr. Geneesk. 103:1528.

[197] Plum, C. M. 1967. Enzymol. Biol. Clin. 8:97.

[198] Poortmans, J. R., and R. W. Jeanloz. 1967. Biochim. Biophys. Acta 133:363.

[199] Poortmans, J. R., et al. 1967. Clin. Chim. Acta 17: 305.

[200] Raab, W. 1967. Enzymes Urine Kidney Proc. Int. Conf., p. 17.

[201] Rabinowitz, J. C., and E. E. Snell. 1949. Proc. Soc. Exp. Biol. Med. 70:235.

[202] Rae, J. J. 1937. Biochem. J. 31:1622.

[203] Rathje, A. O. 1969. Amer. Ind. Hyg. Ass. J. 30(2): 126.

[204] Ravesteyn, A. H. van. 1944. Acta Med. Scand. 118: 163.

[205] Register, V. D., and H. P. Sarett. 1951. Proc. Soc. Exp. Biol. Med. 77:837.

[206] Richterich, R., et al. 1970. Clin. Chim. Acta 29: 299.

[207] Rigas, D. A., and C. G. Heller. 1951. J. Clin. Invest. 30:853.

[208] Rogers, C. J. 1964. Clin. Chem. 10:678.

[209] Rose, B., et al. 1951. Proc. Clin. ACTH Conf., 2nd, 1:519.

[210] Rosenblum, R., and M. Wolfman. 1968. Biochem. Med. 2(2):93.

[211] Rubenstein, A. H., et al. 1967. Metab. Clin. Exp. 16:234.

[212] Rubenstein, A. H., et al. 1968. Lancet 7556:1353.

[213] Rubin, B. L., et al. 1954. J. Clin. Endocrinol. Metab. 14:154.

[214] Ruch, W. 1967. Acta Endocrinol. (Copenhagen) 54:113.

[215] Ruthven, C. R. J., and M. Sandler. 1966. Clin. Chim. Acta 14:511.

[216] Rylance, H. J. 1969. Ibid. 26(1):99.

[217] Saifer, A., and S. Gerstenfeld, 1964. Clin. Chem. 10:321.

[218] Saint-Cyr, C. de V., et al. 1963. Rev. Fr. Etud. Clin. Biol. 8:241.

[219] Sakurai, A., and M. Goto. 1967. J. Biochem. (Tokyo) 61:142.

[220] Samloff, I. M., and P. L. Townes. 1970. Gastroenterology 58(4):462.

[221] Sato, T., and V. DeQuattro. 1969. J. Lab. Clin. Med. 74(4):672.

[222] Schapiro, A., et al. 1967. Enzymol. Biol. Clin. 8: 135.

[223] Schievelbein, H., and E. Buchfink. 1967. Clin. Chim. Acta 18:291.

[224] Schlenker, F. S., et al. 1964. Amer. J. Clin. Pathol. 42:349.

[225] Schwartz, S., et al. 1960. Methods Biochem. Anal. 8:221.

[226] Scott, C. D., et al. 1967. Proc. Soc. Exp. Biol. Med. 125:181.

[227] Sharlit, H. 1938. Arch. Pediat. 55:277.

[228] Sheffner, A. L., et al. 1948. J. Biol. Chem. 175:107.

[229] Shejbal, J., et al. 1967. Clin. Chim. Acta 16:324.

[230] Sherrard, D. J., and D. P. Simpson. 1969. J. Lab. Clin. Med. 73(5):877.

[231] Shizume, K., et al. 1962. Gen. Comp. Endocrinol. (Suppl. 1):110.

[232] Sjaastad, O. 1966. Scand. J. Clin. Lab. Invest. 18: 617.

[233] Smith, I., and L. J. Rider. 1967. Proc. Soc. Exp. Biol. Med. 124:233.

[234] Spencer, N. 1967. J. Chromatogr. 30:566.

[235] Stark, I. E., and M. Somogyi. 1943. J. Biol. Chem. 147:319.

[236] Stein, W. H. 1953. 201:45.

[237] Sterner, J. H., and V. Lidfeldt. 1941. J. Pharmacol. Exp. Ther. 73:205.

continued

Part I. Compounds Other Than Steroids

[238] Stock, A. 1940. Biochem. Z. 304:73.

[239] Studnitz, W. von, et al. 1964. Clin. Chim. Acta 9: 224.

[240] Sunderman, F. W., and F. Boerner. 1949. Normal Values in Clinical Medicine. W. B. Saunders, Philadelphia.

[241] Szasz, G. 1970. Z. Klin. Chem. Klin. Biochem. 8:1.

[242] Takatsuki, K., and E. F. Osserman. 1964. J. Immunol. 92:100.

[243] Tallan, H. H., et al. 1954. J. Biol. Chem. 206:825.

[244] Tamada, T., et al. 1966. Amer. J. Obstet. Gynecol. 95(2):249.

[245] Tamm, I., and F. L. Horsfall, Jr. 1952. J. Exp. Med. 95:71.

[246] Taussky, H. H. 1949. J. Biol. Chem. 181:195.

[247] Taylor, A. L., et al. 1970. J. Clin. Endocrinol. 30: 316.

[248] Teller, W. M., et al. 1962. J. Lab. Clin. Med. 59:95.

[249] Tham, R. 1966. J. Chromatogr. 23:207.

[250] Thrasher, K., et al. 1969. Steroids 14(5):455.

[251] Tominaga, F., et al. 1965. J. Biochem. (Tokyo) 57(6):717.

[252] Tompsett, S. L., and J. Fitzpatrick. 1950. Brit. J. Exp. Pathol. 31:70.

[253] Toseland, P. A. 1969. Clin. Chim. Acta 25:185.

[254] Touster, O., et al. 1954. J. Amer. Chem. Soc. 76: 5005.

[255] Tower, D. B., et al. 1956. Neurology 6:37.

[256] Tribble, H. M., and F. I. Scoular. 1954. J. Nutr. 52:210.

[257] Ubuka, T., et al. 1968. Biochim. Biophys. Acta 158(3):493.

[258] Van Dyke, D. D., et al. 1966. Blood 28:535.

[259] Van Pilsum, J. F., et al. 1956. J. Biol. Chem. 222: 225.

[260] Varadi, D. P., et al. 1967. Biochim. Biophys. Acta 141:103.

[261] Varandani, P. T., et al. 1970. Diabetes 19:98.

[262] Vela, B. A., and H. F. Acevedo. 1969. Steroids 14(5):499.

[263] Vela, B. A., and H. F. Acevedo. 1970. Clin. Chim. Acta 29:1251.

[264] Voorhess, M. L., and L. I. Gardner. 1962. J. Clin. Endocrinol. Metab. 22:126.

[265] Wachsmuth, H., and R. Denissen. 1967. Clin. Chim. Acta 15:529.

[266] Wakid, N. W., et al. 1970. Ibid. 30:527.

[267] Walker, B. S. 1931. J. Lab. Clin. Med. 17:347.

[268] Wallraff, E. B., et al. 1950. J. Clin. Invest. 29: 1542.

[269] Walravens, P., et al. 1967. Clin. Chim. Acta 18:335.

[270] Wang, C. C., et al. 1930. J. Nutr. 3:79.

[271] Watson, C. J. 1937. Arch. Intern. Med. 59:196.

[272] Watson, C. J., et al. 1949. J. Clin. Invest. 28:447.

[273] Webster, S. H. 1941. Pub. Health Rep. 56:1953.

[274] Weil-Malherbe, H. 1967. J. Clin. Invest. 69:1025.

[275] Weil-Malherbe, H. 1968. Methods Biochem. Anal. 16:293.

[276] Weissmann, B., and A. B. Gutman. 1957. J. Biol. Chem. 229:239.

[277] Weissmann, B., et al. 1957. Ibid. 224:423.

[278] Wells, M. G. 1969. Clin. Chim. Acta 25(1):27.

[279] Werner, M., et al. 1970. Ibid. 29:437.

[280] Wessler, E. 1967. Ibid. 16:235.

[281] Wiechouski, W. 1909. Biochem. Z. 19:368.

[282] Williams, C. M., and C. C. Sweeley. 1961. J. Clin. Endocrinol. Metab. 21:1500.

[283] Wisser, H., and D. Stamm. 1970. Z. Klin. Chem. Klin. Biochem. 8(1):21.

[284] Woodson, H. W., et al. 1948. J. Biol. Chem. 172:613.

[285] Wybenga, D., and V. J. Pileggi. 1967. Clin. Chim. Acta 16:147.

[286] Young, M. K., et al. 1951. Tex. Univ. Publ. 5109: 189.

[287] Zaura, D. S., and J. Metcoff. 1969. Anal. Chem. 41(13):1781.

[288] Zelnicek, E., et al. 1968. Scr. Med. 40(3/4):65.

Part II. Steroids

For information on additional urinary steroids consult reference 9.

Constituent (Synonym)	Specification	Amount Excreted μg·kg body wt^{-1}·da^{-1} [ng·kg body wt^{-1}·da^{-1}]	Reference		Constituent (Synonym)	Specification	Amount Excreted μg·kg body wt^{-1}·da^{-1} [ng·kg body wt^{-1}·da^{-1}]	Reference
		Androgens		3		60+ yr old	70(30-130)	8
1	Androgens	♂, 3-5 yr old	210	8	4		♀, 3-5 yr old	50	8
2		20-40 yr old	260(200-330)	8	5		20-40 yr old	200(180-210)	8

continued

Part II. Steroids

#	Constituent (Synonym)	Specification	Amount Excreted μg·kg body wt^{-1}·da^{-1} [ng·kg body wt^{-1}·da^{-1}]	Reference
6		60+ yr old	40(15-130)	8
7	C$_{19}$-Alcohols 16-Androsten-3α-ol (3α-Hydroxy-5α-androst-16-ene)	♂	15.03(0.24-23.70)	3
8		♀	[5(3-6)]	3
9	16-Etiocholen-3α-ol (3α-Hydroxy-5β-androst-16-ene)	♂	0.147	3
10		♀	25.71(8.57-31.43)	3
11	5,16-Androstadien-3β-ol (3β-Hydroxy-androsta-5,16-diene)	♂	1.09	3
12	C$_{19}$-17-Hydroxy steroids	♂	80(40-170)	27,28
13		♀	60(20-140)	27,28
14	Androstane-3α,17α-diol (5α-Androstane-3α,17α-diol)	♀, 4-9 mo pregnant	(0.27-1.49)	17
15	Etiocholane-3α,17α-diol (5β-Androstane-3α,17α-diol)	....	Trace	24
16	Androstenediol (Androst-5-ene-3β,17β-diol)	♂	4.30(3.50-5.10)	17
17		♀, 4-9 mo pregnant	(0.31-2.30)	17
18	5-Androstene-3β,17α-diol (Androst-5-ene-3β,17α-diol)	♂	9.12(8.12-10.12)	17
19		♀, 4-9 mo pregnant	(5.29-13.36)	17
20	Epitestosterone	♂, 16-29 yr old	0.97(0.29-2.29)	10,35
21		32-43 yr old	0.67(0.21-1.57)	10,35
22		♀, 19-67 yr old	[(340(140-790)]	35
23		20-42 yr old	[(150(30-320)]	10,34
24	Testosterone	♂, 21-30 yr old	(0.43-1.91)	10,13,35,43
25		31-40 yr old	(0.49-1.29)	10,13,35,43
26		41-50 yr old	0.73	10,13,43
27		♀, 20-42 yr old	(0.04-0.20)	10,13,34,43
28	C$_{19}$-16- & 17-Ketosteroids Total	♂	180(110-220)	42
29		♀	110(70-200)	42
30	Conjugates Glucuronide fraction, total	....	(20-45)	32
31	Sulfate fraction, total	....	(8-21)	32
32	Androstane-3α,11β-diol-17-one (3α,11β-Dihydroxy-5α-androstane-17-one)	♂♀	(20-23)	11
33	Etiocholane-3α,11β-diol-17-one (3α,11β-Dihydroxy-5β-androstane-17-one)	♂♀	8	11
34	5-Androstene-3α,16α-diol-17-one (3α,16α-Dihydroxy-androst-5-en-17-one)	♂	[130(<70-230)]	16
35		♀	[170(110-210)]	16
36	5-Androstene-3β,17β-diol-16-one (3β,17β-Dihydroxy-androst-5-en-16-one)	♂	3.44(1.97-5.14)	16
37		♀	1.94(0.85-2.60)	16
38	4-Androstene-3,17-dione (Δ^4-Androsten-3,17-dione)	♂	0.571(0.143-1.714)	35
39		♀	0.557(0.071-1.143)	34,35
40	Androsterone	♂	(35.7-58.6)	30,40
41		♀	(18.6-41.4)	3,30,40
42	Conjugates Glucuronide fraction	....	(6.2-22.0)	32
43	Sulfate fraction	....	(1.4-6.0)	32
44	Dehydroepiandrosterone	♂	21.4(2.9-60.0)	6
45		♀	8.0(2.9-15.7)	3

continued

Part II. Steroids

	Constituent (Synonym)	Specification	Amount Excreted $\mu g \cdot kg$ body $wt^{-1} \cdot da^{-1}$ [$ng \cdot kg$ body $wt^{-1} \cdot da^{-1}$]	Reference
	Conjugates			
46	Glucuronide fraction	....	(0.4-1.1)	32
47	Sulfate fraction	....	(6-17)	32
48	Etiocholan-3α-ol-11,17-dione (3α-Hydroxy-5β-androstane-11,17-dione)	♂♀	(8-10)	11
	Etiocholanolone conjugates			
49	Glucuronide fraction	....	(12-32)	32
50	Sulfate fraction	....	(0.6-6.0)	32
51	16α-Hydroxyandrosterone	♂	1.14(0.40-2.13)	16
52		♀	1.77(0.39-3.14)	16
53	18-Hydroxyandrosterone	♀, 4-9 mo pregnant	(0.23-1.47)	17
54	16α-Hydroxydehydroepiandrosterone	♂	8.19(6.00-15.14)	16
55		♀	7.93(3.01-10.43)	16
56	16β-Hydroxydehydroepiandrosterone	♂	1.04(0.54-1.65)	16
57		♀	0.74(0.27-1.23)	16
58	16α-Hydroxyepiandrosterone	♂	[510(210-930)]	16
59		♀	[540(70-800)]	16
60	16α-Hydroxyetiocholanolone	♂	[170(<70-570)]	16
61		♀	[90(<70-100)]	16
62	7-Ketodehydroepiandrosterone	♂	[260(70-570)]	35
63		♀	[210(70-430)]	35
	Estrogens			
64	Estrogens, total	♂	[207(120-329)]	4
65		♀, follicular phase	[286(171-514)]	4,26
66		luteal phase	[771(386-1571)]	4,26
67		post-menopause	[96(23-224)]	4
68	Estradiol	♂, 12-14 yr old	[17(4-30)]	37
69		18-45 yr old	[27(10-49)]	37
70		45-63 yr old	[66(39-107)]	37
71		♀, follicular phase	[30(0-50)]	26,29,37
72		luteal phase	[100(70-170)]	26,29,37
73		post-menopause	[10(0-90)]	22,37,44
74	Estriol	♂, 12-14 yr old	[31(21-63)]	37
75		18-45 yr old	[116(43-207)]	37
76		45-63 yr old	[89(29-180)]	37
77		♀, follicular phase	[100(0-300)]	26,29,37
78		luteal phase	[400(130-1300)]	26,29,37
79		post-menopause	[50(0-180)]	22,37
80	Estrone	♂, 12-14 yr old	[16(0-36)]	37
81		18-45 yr old	[73(50-86)]	37
82		45-63 yr old	[151(103-171)]	37
83		♀, follicular phase	[80(60-120)]	26,29,37
84		luteal phase	[200(170-400)]	26,29,37
85		post-menopause	[30(0-120)]	22,37
	"Pregnanes"			
	C_{21}-CH_3-Alcohols			
86	Pregnanediols	♂	13(5-20)	18,19

continued

Part II. Steroids

	Constituent (Synonym)	Specification	Amount Excreted μg·kg body wt^{-1}·da^{-1} [ng·kg body wt^{-1}·da^{-1}]	Reference		Constituent (Synonym)	Specification	Amount Excreted μg·kg body wt^{-1}·da^{-1} [ng·kg body wt^{-1}·da^{-1}]	Reference
87		♀, follicular phase	18(13-25)	18	101	Allopregnane-3β,21-diol-20-one (3β,21-Dihydroxy-5α-pregnan-20-one)	♀, 4-9 mo pregnant	(2.86-5.57)	17
88		luteal phase	55(30-70)	18	102	Allopregnane-3α,21-diol-20-one (3α, 21-Dihydroxy-5α-pregnan-20-one) + pregnane-3α,21-diol-20-one (3α,21-Dihydroxy-5β-pregnan-20-one)	♀, 4-9 mo pregnant	(0.77-6.33)	17
89		post-menopause	10(5-14)	18					
90	Allopregnane-3β,20α-diol (5α-Pregnane-3β,20α-diol)	♀, 4-9 mo pregnant	(9.00-75.43)	17	103	16α-Hydroxypregnenolone	♀,4-9 mo pregnant	(<0.14-0.19)	17
91	5β-Pregnane-3α,20α-diol	♀, 4-9 mo pregnant	(0.50-5.91)	17	104	21-Hydroxypregnenolone	♂	(1.52-2.48)	17
92	Allopregnane-3α,20α-diol (5α-Pregnane-3α,20α-diol) + 5β-pregnane-3β,20α-diol	♀, 4-9 mo pregnant	(3.57-23.36)	17	105		♀, 4-9 mo pregnant	(1.19-3.07)	17
93	Pregnanetriol	♀, follicular phase	25	38	106	Progesterone	♂	[4.0(0.6-7.4)]	36
94		luteal phase	32	38	107		♀	[5.9(1.6-14.0)]	36
95		post-menopause	11	38	108	14α-Hydroxyprogesterone	♀, late in pregnancy	[7]	2
96	5-Pregnene-3β,20α-diol (Pregn-5-ene-3β,20α-diol)	♂	8.54(7.26-9.82)	17			Other Adrenal Corticoids		
97		♀, 4-9 mo pregnant	(2.26-12.31)	17	109	Aldosterone	♂♀	(0.01-3.21)	1,5,15, 23,31, 41
98	5-Pregnene-3β,17α,20α-triol (Pregn-5-ene-3β,17α,20α-triol)	♂	1.48(1.04-1.92)	17	110	C_{21}-17-Hydroxycorticosteroids Total	♂, 15-69 yr old	109(40-236)	39
99	5-Pregnen-3β-ol-20α-yl 2'-acetamido-2'-deoxy-D-glucopyranoside (3β-Hydroxy-Δ^5-pregnen-20α-yl 2'-acetamido-2'-deoxy-D-glucopyranoside)	....	Trace	21	111		♀, 15-68 yr old	53(26-79)	39
					112	Hydrocortisone (Cortisol)	....	(0.27-1.47)	20,23, 33
100	C_{21}-Ketosteroids Allopregnane-3β,16α-diol-20-one (3β, 16α-Dihydroxy-5α-pregnan-20-one)	♀,4-9 mo pregnant	(0.20-0.76)	17	113	11-Deoxycortisol (11-Desoxycortisol)	....	6.43	23
					114	6-Hydroxycortisol	♂	5.00(1.43-11.43)	39
					115		♀	3.71(1.43-6.00)	12,39
					116	Tetrahydrocortisol	....	(8-80)	14,25, 29
					117	Tetrahydro-11-deoxycortisol (Tetrahydro-11-desoxycortisol)	....	(0-39)	25

continued

Part II. Steroids

Constituent (Synonym)	Specification	Amount Excreted $\mu g \cdot kg$ body $wt^{-1} \cdot da^{-1}$ [$ng \cdot kg$ body $wt^{-1} \cdot da^{-1}$]	Reference
118 C_{21}-17-Ketogenicadrenocorticoids	♂	210(150-310)	7
119	♀	180(120-300)	7
120 Corticosterone	....	0.043(0-0.229)	20,23

Constituent (Synonym)	Specification	Amount Excreted $\mu g \cdot kg$ body $wt^{-1} \cdot da^{-1}$ [$ng \cdot kg$ body $wt^{-1} \cdot da^{-1}$]	Reference
121 Deoxycorticosterone (11-Desoxycorticosterone)	....	1.36	23
122 Tetrahydrocortisone	....	(7.14-78.57)	14,25, 29

Contributor: Van Pilsum, John

References

[1] Bayard, F., et al. 1970. J. Clin. Endocrinol. 31:507.

[2] Bhavnanai, B., et al. 1969. Biochemistry 8(5):2105.

[3] Brooksbank, B. W. L., and D. B. Gower. 1970. Acta Endocrinol. (Copenhagen) 63(1):70.

[4] Brown, J. B., et al. 1968. J. Endocrinol. 42(1):5.

[5] Buchner, M., and B. Schulke. 1969. Endokrinologie 55(1-2):6.

[6] Chambers, R., et al. 1967. Clin. Chim. Acta 17:135.

[7] Diszfalusy, E., et al. 1955. Acta Endocrinol. (Copenhagen) 18:356.

[8] Dorfman, R. I., and R. A. Shipley. 1956. The Androgens. J. Wiley, New York.

[9] Dorfman, R. I., and F. Ungar. 1965. Metabolism of Steroid Hormones. Academic Press, New York.

[10] Drosdowsy, M. A., et al. 1968. Bull. Soc. Chim. Biol. 50(10):1723.

[11] Feher, T. 1966. Clin. Chim. Acta 14:91.

[12] Ghosh, P. C., and G. W. Pennington. 1969. Steroids 13(2):247.

[13] Graef, V., et al. 1968. Z. Klin. Chem. Klin. Biochem. 6(3):159.

[14] Green, A. G., et al. 1968. Clin. Chim. Acta 20:189.

[15] Holzel, W., and M. Buchner. 1967. Acta Biol. Med. Ger. 19(1):189.

[16] Jänne, O., and R. Vihko. 1969. Steroids 14(3):235.

[17] Jänne, O., and R. Vihko. 1970. Acta Endocrinol. (Copenhagen) 65(1):50.

[18] Klopper, A., et al. 1955. J. Endocrinol. 12:209.

[19] Levell, M. J., and T. K. Cottam. 1969. Clin. Chim. Acta 23(1):231.

[20] Martin, M. M., and A. L. A. Martin. 1970. Ibid. 27(3):379.

[21] Matsui, M., and D. K. Fukushima. 1969. Biochemistry 8(7):2997.

[22] McBride, J. M. 1957. J. Clin. Endocrinol. Metab. 17:1440.

[23] New, M. I., and M. P. Seaman. 1970. Clin. Chim. Acta 30:361.

[24] Peng, T. C., and P. L. Munson. 1968. Steroids 11:105.

[25] Pieterse, E. W. M. G., et al. 1969. Clin. Chim. Acta 25(2):243.

[26] Pieterse, E. W. M. G., et al. 1969. Ibid. 26(1):111.

[27] Reddy, W. J., et al. 1952. Metab. Clin. Exp. 1:511.

[28] Reddy, W. J., et al. 1956. J. Clin. Endocrinol. Metab. 16:380.

[29] Romanoff, L. P., et al. 1957. Ibid. 17:777.

[30] Rubin, B. L., et al. 1954. Recent Progr. Hormone Res. 9:213.

[31] Salokangas, A., and H. Adlercreutz. 1968. Ann. Med. Exp. Biol. Fenn. 46(2):158.

[32] Sarfaty, G. A., and M. B. Summers. 1964. Clin. Chim. Acta 10:505.

[33] Schachinger, V., and L. Zicha. 1968. Endokrinologie 53(3-4):153.

[34] Schollberg, K., and W. Hubl. 1968. Ibid. 53(3-4):222.

[35] Schubert, K., and G. Frankenberg. 1968. Ibid. 53(5-6):322.

[36] Schubert, K., et al. 1969. Ibid. 54(5-6):354.

[37] Steczek, K., et al. 1968. Ibid. 53(1-2):72.

[38] Stern, M. I. 1957. J. Endocrinol. 16:180.

[39] Thrasher, K., et al. 1969. Steroids 14(5):455.

[40] Treiber, L., and G. W. Oertel. 1967. Clin. Chim. Acta 17:81.

[41] Venning, E. H., et al. 1956. J. Clin. Endocrinol. Metab. 16:1326.

continued

Part II. Steroids

[42] Vestergaard, P., and J. F. Sayegh. 1966. Clin. Chim. Acta 14:247.

[43] Vestergaard, P., et al. 1966. Ibid. 14:540.

[44] Wrenn, T. R., et al. 1968. J. Reprod. Fert. 16(2): 301.

186. PROPERTIES OF AND EXCRETION PRODUCTS IN URINE: MAMMALS OTHER THAN MAN

For calculation of values based on body weight, the following weights, in kilograms, were assumed unless a specific weight was recorded: cat, 2.5; cattle, 500; dog, 12; goat, 50; guinea pig, 0.5; horse, 630; monkey, 12; mouse, 0.04; rabbit, 2.0; rat, 0.33; sheep, 60; swine, 200. **Value:** Unspecified indicates chemical was identified qualitatively only. Values in parentheses are ranges, estimate "c" (*see* Introduction).

	Property or Constituent (Synonym)	Value mg·kg body wt^{-1}·da^{-1} [1]	Reference
	Cat		
	Property		
1	Volume	(10-30)[2]	76,221
2	Specific gravity	1.030(1.020-1.040)[3]	53
3	Freezing point depression	5.0°C	53
	Electrolytes		
4	Calcium	(200-450)[4]	59
5	Chloride	109	221
6	Phosphorus, inorganic	49	221
7	Sulfate, inorganic	106	221
	Vitamin		
8	Riboflavin	(6-40)[4]	198
9	N'-Methylnicotinamide	(30-200)[4]	54
	Nitrogenous substances		
10	Nitrogen, total	(500-1100)	76,221
11	ammonia	60	60,76
	Amino acids		
12	Alanine	Unspecified	40
13	Felinine	Unspecified	23,40,72
14	Glycine	Unspecified	40,72
15	Methylhistidine	Unspecified	40,72
16	Taurine	Unspecified	40,72
17	Purine derivative: Uric acid	(0.2-13.0)	76
	Indole derivatives		
18	Indican, metabolic (Indoxylsulfuric acid)	Unspecified	44
19	Indoleacetic acid	Unspecified	44
	Miscellaneous		
20	Allantoin	80	107
21	Creatine	10	221

	Property or Constituent (Synonym)	Value mg·kg body wt^{-1}·da^{-1} [1]	Reference
22	Creatinine	(12-30)	76
23	Histamine	(6-300)[4]	4
24	Imidazole derivatives	(3-4)	93
25	Urea	(800-4000)	76,221
26	Hormones: 17-Hydroxy-corticosteroids	0.832(0.272-1.392)	184
	Enzymes[5]		
27	Lactate dehydrogenase (Lactic dehydrogenase) [1.1.1.27]	Consult reference	100
28	Aspartate aminotransferase (Glutamic-oxaloacetic transaminase) [2.6.1.1]	Consult reference	100
29	Alanine aminotransferase (Glutamic-pyruvic transaminase) [2.6.1.2]	Consult reference	100
30	Fructosediphosphate aldolase [4.1.2.13] (Aldolase)	Consult reference	100
31	Urokinase	Consult reference	138
32	Organic acid: Phenol (Carbolic acid)	(8-25)	61
	Cattle		
	Property		
33	Volume	28(17-45)[2]	17,196
34	Specific gravity	(1.023-1.045)[3]	17,118
	Electrolytes		
35	Calcium	(0.10-3.60)	64,77,78,85,118

[1] Unless otherwise specified. [2] ml·kg body wt^{-1}·da^{-1}. [3] Relative value. [4] μg·kg body wt^{-1}·da^{-1}. [5] Enzyme Commission Number, in brackets, was assigned by the International Union of Biochemistry on the Nomenclature and Classification of Enzymes [95].

continued

	Property or Constituent (Synonym)	Value mg·kg body wt^{-1}·da^{-1} [1]	Reference
36	Chlorine	(10-140)	17,99
37	Magnesium	(2-7)	21,64,85
38	Phosphorus	(0.008-6.195)	21,64,118, 122
39	Potassium	(240-320)	85
40	Sodium	(2-40)	85
41	Sulfur, inorganic	(0.2-5.0)[6]	29
42	ethereal	(1.6-7.0)[6]	29
43	neutral	(0.8-3.0)[6]	29
44	Sulfate, total	(3-15)[6]	29
	Vitamins		
45	Thiamine	10[4]	200
46	Riboflavin	20[4]	200
47	Niacin	(40-50)[4]	200
48	Pantothenic acid	170[4]	200
49	Ascorbic acid	(40-140)[4]	207
	Nitrogenous substances		
50	Nitrogen, total	(40-450)	29,91,141, 143
51	ammonia	(1-17)	91,141
52	amino	(2.52-7.56)	132
	Amino acids		
53	Alanine	Unspecified	38
54	β-Alanine	Unspecified	38
55	γ-Aminobutyric acid (γ-Amino-n-butyric acid)	Unspecified	38
56	β-Aminoisobutyric acid	Unspecified	38
57	Arginine	Unspecified	38
58	Aspartic acid	Unspecified	38
59	Cysteic acid	Unspecified	38
60	Glutamic acid	Unspecified	38
61	Glycine	Unspecified	38
62	Histidine	Unspecified	38
63	Hydroxyproline	Unspecified	38
64	Isoleucine	Unspecified	38
65	Leucine	Unspecified	38
66	Lysine	Unspecified	38
67	Methionine sulfone	Unspecified	38
68	Methionine sulfoxide	Unspecified	38
69	Phenylalanine	Unspecified	38
70	Proline	Unspecified	38
71	Threonine	Unspecified	38
72	Tyrosine	Unspecified	38
73	Protein	19.60(8.96-33.60)	188
74	Purine bases	(0.2-3.0)	91,141
75	Derivative: Uric acid	(1-4)	91,141

	Property or Constituent (Synonym)	Value mg·kg body wt^{-1}·da^{-1} [1]	Reference
	Indole derivatives		
76	Indican, metabolic (Indoxylsulfuric acid)	Unspecified	44
77	Indoleacetic acid (3-Indoleacetic acid)	Unspecified	44,194, 195
78	5-Hydroxyindoleacetic acid	(140-784)[4]	169
79	Indoleaceturic acid	Unspecified	44
80	Indoleacetylglutamine	Unspecified	44
81	β-3-Indole-3-propionic acid (β-3-Indolepropionic acid)	Unspecified	194,195
82	Skatoxylsulfuric acid	Unspecified	44
	Miscellaneous		
83	Allantoin	(20-60)	91,107, 141
84	o-Aminobenzoic acid (Anthranilic acid)	33.6[4]	148
85	Creatine	(1-2)	141
86	Creatinine	(15-30)	27,29,118, 141
87	Hippuric acid	(50-200)	27,29,194, 195,213
88	3-Hydroxyanthranilic acid	20[4]	148
89	3-Hydroxykynurenine	(140-600)[4]	147
90	Kynurenine	(140-380)[4]	147
91	Phenacetylglycine	Unspecified	194,195
92	Urea	(50-60)	141
93	Xanthurenic acid	61[4]	119
	Hormones & derivatives, ♀		
	Nonsteroids		
94	Epinephrine (Adrenaline)	60[7]	3
95	Norepinephrine (Noradrenaline)	140[7]	3
96	Luteotropin (Prolactin)	Unspecified	28
97	Androgens	7[4]	88,104
98	Androstane-3β,17α-diol (5α-Androstane-3β,17α-diol)	Unspecified	83,102
99	Etiocholane-3α,17α-diol (5β-Androstane-3α,17α-diol)	6[4]	83,102
	17-Ketosteroids		
100	Total	(6-12)[4]	87
101	5α-Androstanedione	Unspecified	83
102	5β-Androstanedione	Unspecified	83
103	Androsterone	Unspecified	82,83

[1] Unless otherwise specified.   [4] μg·kg body wt^{-1}·da^{-1}.   [6] After fasting.   [7] ng·kg body wt^{-1}·da^{-1}.

continued

	Property or Constituent (Synonym)	Value mg·kg body wt^{-1}·da^{-1} [1]	Reference		Property or Constituent (Synonym)	Value mg·kg body wt^{-1}·da^{-1} [1]	Reference
104	Epiandrosterone	Unspecified	82,83	132	4-Hydroxy-β-3-methoxyphenylpropionic acid (β-3-Methoxy-4-hydroxyphenylpropionic acid)	Unspecified	194,195
105	Dehydroepiandrosterone	Unspecified	87				
106	Etiocholanolone	Unspecified	82,87	133	o-Hydroxyphenylacetic acid	Unspecified	194,195
107	11-Ketoetiocholanolone (11-Ketoetiocholanone)	Unspecified	87	134	p-Hydroxyphenylacetic acid	Unspecified	194,195
	Estrogens			135	o-Hydroxyphenylpropionic acid	Unspecified	194,195
108	Total	(30-42) [4]	92	136	p-Hydroxyphenylpropionic acid	Unspecified	194,195
109	Estradiol, total	(22-32) [4]	92	137	o-Methoxybenzoic acid	Unspecified	194,195
110	(Estradiol-17β)	(0.14-1.40) [4]	92,222, 223	138	m-Methoxybenzoic acid	Unspecified	194,195
111	α-Estradiol (Estradiol-17α)	(22-30) [4]	92,102	139	o-Methoxyphenylacetic acid	Unspecified	194,195
112	Estrone	8 [4]	92,102	140	p-Methoxyphenylacetic acid	Unspecified	194, 195
	Progesterone & related compounds			141	o-Methoxyphenylpropionic acid	Unspecified	194,195
113	Progesterone	(14-20) [4]	92	142	p-Methoxyphenylpropionic acid	Unspecified	194,195
114	Pregnanediols	(0.6-77.4) [4]	57,58	143	Phenol	Unspecified	194,195
115	Allopregnane-3α,20α-diol (5α-Pregnane-3α,20α-diol)	Unspecified	57	144	Phenylacetic acid	Unspecified	194,195
116	5β-Pregnane-3α,20α-diol	Unspecified	57	145	Salicylic acid (o-Hydroxybenzoic acid)	Unspecified	194,195
117	Allopregnane-3β,20β-diol (5α-Pregnane-3β,20β-diol)	Unspecified	57	146	Veratric acid (3,4-Dimethoxybenzoic acid)	Unspecified	194,195
118	5β-Pregnane-3α,20β-diol	Unspecified	57	147	Organic acid: Citric acid	(1.0-3.8)	21,106
119	Pregnan-3α-ol-20-one (3α-Hydroxy-5β-pregnan-20-one)	Unspecified	83		Miscellaneous		
				148	Gonadotropin inhibitor	Consult reference	7
120	5β-Pregnanedione	Unspecified	83	149	Ketone bodies (Acetone bodies)	(0.5-5.0)	29,103
	Aromatic compounds						
121	p-Anisic acid (p-Methoxybenzoic acid)	Unspecified	194,195		Dog		
122	Benzoic acid	Unspecified	194,195		Properties		
123	p-Cresol	Unspecified	194,195	150	Volume	(20-167) [2]	17,196
124	3,4-Dimethoxyphenylacetic acid	Unspecified	194,195	151	Specific gravity	1.025(1.015-1.060) [3]	17,53
125	3,4-Dimethoxyphenylpropionic acid	Unspecified	194,195	152	Freezing point depression	(1.573-3.638)°C	53
126	p-Ethylphenol	Unspecified	194,195		Electrolytes		
127	Guaiacol	Unspecified	194,195	153	Calcium	(1-3)	17,192, 215
128	Hydrocinnamic acid (β-Phenylpropionic acid)	Unspecified	194,195	154	Chlorine	9	96
129	m-Hydroxybenzoic acid	Unspecified	194,195	155	Magnesium	(1.7-3.0)	70,73,192, 215
130	p-Hydroxybenzoic acid	Unspecified	194,195	156	Phosphorus	(20-50)	70,73,219
131	4-Hydroxy-3-methoxyphenylacetic acid (3-Methoxy-4-hydroxyphenylacetic acid)	Unspecified	194,195	157	Potassium	(40-100)	192,215
				158	Sodium	66	96
				159	Sulfur, total	(25-40)	26,211
				160	ethereal	(1.3-3.5)	211

[1] Unless otherwise specified. [2] ml·kg body wt^{-1}·da^{-1}. [3] Relative value. [4] μg·kg body wt^{-1}·da^{-1}.

continued

	Property or Constituent (Synonym)	Value mg·kg body wt^{-1}·da^{-1} [1]	Reference		Property or Constituent (Synonym)	Value mg·kg body wt^{-1}·da^{-1} [1]	Reference
161	neutral	(5-10)	211	195	Creatinine	(15-80)	27,79,80, 211
162	Sulfate, total	(30-50)	211				
	Vitamins			196	Hippuric acid	34	47
163	Thiamine	(10-20)[4]	219	197	Histamine	(10-300)[4]	4,136
164	Riboflavin	(10-234)[4]	66,173 219	198	1-Methylimidazole-4-acetic acid	Unspecified	202
165	Niacinimide (Nicotinamide)	(300-400)[4]	54	199	1-Methylimidazole-5-acetic acid	Unspecified	202
166	N'-Methylnicotinamide	(90-800)[4]	54	200	Urea	(300-500)	110,164, 219
167	Pantothenic acid	130[4]	185				
168	Choline	(200-500)[4]	114		Steroid hormones		
169	Vitamin A (Retinol)	(1.192-19.583)[8]	220	201	Formaldehydrogenic steroids	10[4]	36
170	Carbohydrate derivatives: Acid mucopolysaccharides	Unspecified	30	202	17-Hydroxycorticosteroids	72(50-93)[4]	218
	Nitrogenous substances			203	17-Ketosteroids	(40-100)[4]	149
171	Nitrogen, total	(250-800)	11,26,70, 73,79, 110	204	Androgens	(10-30)[4]	149
				205	Aldosterone	Unspecified	42
				206	Cortisone	Unspecified	16
172	ammonia	(15-60)	11,79,80	207	Hydrocortisone	Unspecified	16
173	amino	21	80		Organic acids		
	Amino acids			208	Citric acid	(2-20)	22,106, 139
174	Alanine	Unspecified	40				
175	Arginine	(0.2-1.9)	205	209	Phenol (Carbolic acid)	5	61
176	Glutamic acid	Unspecified	40	210	Miscellaneous: Ketone bodies (Acetone bodies)	(5-6)	116
177	Glycine	Unspecified	40				
178	Lysine	3.5	205				
179	Methylhistidine	Unspecified	40				
180	Ornithine	0.1	205		Goat		
181	Taurine	3.629(2.002-6.257)[6]	40,153		Properties		
				211	Volume	(7-40)[2]	10,17,196
182	Tryptophan	Unspecified	44	212	Specific gravity	(1.015-1.062)[3]	10,53
	Purine & pyrimidine derivatives			213	Solids	(700-2000)	10
183	Deoxycytidine	(0.40-1.40)	183		Electrolytes		
184	Uric acid	4.5	134	214	Calcium	(1.0-3.4)	10,141
	Indole derivatives			215	Chlorides	(186-376)	10
185	Indican, metabolic (Indoxylsulfuric acid)	Unspecified	44	216	Phosphorus	1	141
				217	Bicarbonates	(112-358)	10
186	Indoleacetic acid	Unspecified	44	218	Carbonates	(50-200)	10
187	Indoleaceturic acid	Unspecified	44	219	Phosphates, total	(13.2-42.0)	10
188	Indoleacetylglutamine	Unspecified	44		Vitamins		
189	5-Oxyindoleacetic acid	Unspecified	44	220	Thiamine	6[4]	120
190	Serotonin	(5-32)[4]	206	221	Riboflavin	20[4]	120
191	Skatoxylsulfuric acid	Unspecified	44	222	Niacin	(50-200)[4]	151
	Miscellaneous			223	N'-Methylnicotinamide	(60-90)[4]	151
192	Allantoin	(35-108)	2,15,68, 80,109	224	Pantothenic acid	160[4]	120
					Nitrogenous substances		
193	4-Amino-5-imidazole-carboxamide	73[4]	125	225	Nitrogen, total	(89-400)	10,91,141
				226	ammonia	(1.6-6.0)	10,141
194	Creatine	(10-50)	79,141, 211	227	Purine bases	(2-8)	91,141
				228	Derivative: Uric acid	(0.4-6.8)	10,91,141

[1] Unless otherwise specified. [2] ml·kg body wt^{-1}·da^{-1}. [3] Relative value. [4] µg·kg body wt^{-1}·da^{-1}. [6] After fasting. [8] International units.

continued

	Property or Constituent (Synonym)	Value mg·kg body wt^{-1}·da^{-1} [1]	Reference		Property or Constituent (Synonym)	Value mg·kg body wt^{-1}·da^{-1} [1]	Reference
	Indole derivatives				Nitrogenous substances		
229	Indican, metabolic (Indoxylsulfuric acid)	Unspecified	44	260	Nitrogen, total	(100-160)	91,144
					Amino acids		
230	Indoleacetic acid	Unspecified	44	261	Glycine	Unspecified	40
231	Indoleaceturic acid	Unspecified	44	262	Taurine	Unspecified	40
232	Indoleacetylglutamine	Unspecified	44	263	Purine bases	40[4]	91
233	Indole-3-carboxylic acid	Unspecified	44	264	Derivative: Uric acid	(1-2)	91
					Indole derivatives		
234	Skatoxylsulfuric acid	Unspecified	44	265	Indican, metabolic (Indoxylsulfuric acid)	Unspecified	44
	Miscellaneous						
235	Allantoin	(10-70)	10,91,141	266	Indoleacetic acid	Unspecified	44
236	Creatine	(3.0-19.6)	10,141	267	Indoleaceturic acid	Unspecified	44
237	Creatinine	(10-22)	10,141	268	Indole-3-carboxylic acid	Unspecified	44
238	Hippuric acid	(200-300)	141	269	5-Oxyindoleacetic acid	Unspecified	44
239	Urea	(144-466)	10,141	270	Skatoxylsulfuric acid	Unspecified	44
240	Hormones: Gonado-tropins	Unspecified	94		Miscellaneous		
241	Organic acid: Phenol (Carbolic acid)	15	61	271	Allantoin	(5-15)	91
				272	Hippuric acid	100	81
242	17-Ketosteroids	0.166	175	273	Histamine	(0.1-3.0)[4]	4
				274	o-Hydroxyhippuric acid	Unspecified	31
	Guinea Pig						
243	Electrolytes: Sulfur, neutral	(5-8)	27	275	4-Hydroxy-3-me-thoxymandelic acid	Unspecified	31
	Nitrogenous substances				Steroid hormones & derivatives		
244	Nitrogen, total	180	187	276	17-Ketosteroids, ♂	22.1(20.1-24.2)[4]	155
	Amino acids			277	Estrogens, total, ♂	(20-1000)[4]	51,113
245	Alanine	Unspecified	40	278	♀	(200-400)[4]	51,113
246	Glutamine	Unspecified	40	279	Estradiol (Estradiol-17β), ♂	14.0[4]	156
247	Glycine	Unspecified	40				
	Miscellaneous			280	α-Estradiol (Estra-diol-17α), ♂	14.0[4]	156
248	Allantoin	50	137				
249	Creatinine	30	27,187	281	Estrone, ♂	144.9[4]	156
250	Homovanillic acid	0.281	129		Aromatic acids		
251	Organic acid: Phenol (Carbolic acid)	24	4	282	Ferulic acid (4-Hy-droxy-3-methoxycin-namic acid)	Unspecified	31
	Horse			283	m-Hydroxybenzoic acid	Unspecified	31
	Properties			284	p-Hydroxybenzoic acid	Unspecified	31
252	Volume	7(3-18)[2]	17,196	285	m-Hydroxycinnamic acid	Unspecified	31
253	Specific gravity	(1.020-1.060)[3]	17,196				
254	Freezing point depres-sion	(1.77-2.00)°C	53	286	p-Hydroxycinnamic acid	Unspecified	31
	Vitamins			287	4-Hydroxy-3-methoxy-phenylacetic acid	Unspecified	31
255	Riboflavin	2[4]	166				
256	Niacin	(2-7)[4]	180,200	288	4-Hydroxy-3-methoxy-phenylpropionic acid	Unspecified	31
257	N'-Methylnicotinamide	(3-20)[4]	189				
258	Vitamin B$_{12}$ (Cobal-amin)	11(3-20)[7]	1	289	o-Hydroxyphenylacetic acid	Unspecified	31
259	Ascorbic acid	90[4]	207	290	m-Hydroxyphenylace-tic acid	Unspecified	31

[1] Unless otherwise specified. [2] ml·kg body wt^{-1}·da^{-1}. [3] Relative value. [4] μg·kg body wt^{-1}·da^{-1}. [7] ng·kg body wt^{-1}·da^{-1}.

continued

Property or Constituent (Synonym)	Value mg·kg body wt^{-1}·da^{-1} [1]	Reference		Property or Constituent (Synonym)	Value mg·kg body wt^{-1}·da^{-1} [1]	Reference
291	p-Hydroxyphenylacetic acid	Unspecified	31	323	Creatinine	(20-60)	49,97,163
				324	Hippuric acid	(4-5)	90
292	o-Hydroxyphenylpropionic acid	Unspecified	31	325	Urea	(200-700)	90,163
					Hormones & derivatives		
293	m-Hydroxyphenylpropionic acid	Unspecified	31	326	17-Ketosteroids	(0.21-1.35)	145
				327	Androgens	10[4]	210
294	β-Resorcylic acid (2,4-Dihydroxybenzoic acid)	Unspecified	31	328	Androsterone glucuronide	(0.58-8.52)[4]	145,209
				329	Dehydroepiandrosterone glucuronide	(Trace-2.65)[4]	145,209
295	Salicylic acid (o-Hydroxybenzoic acid)	Unspecified	31	330	Dehydroepiandrosterone sulfate	(0.52-2.25)[4]	209
296	Vanillic acid (4-Hydroxy-3-methoxybenzoic acid)	Unspecified	31	331	Etiocholanolone glucuronide	(0.81-2.50)[4]	145,209
				332	11-Deoxy-17-ketosteroids, total	(1.97-13.98)[4]	145
297	Organic acid: Citric acid	1.673	106	333	Estrogens, total, ♀	(8-167)[7]	32
	Monkey			334	Estradiol	Unspecified	32
				335	Estriol	Unspecified	32
298	Property: Volume	(70-80)[2]	13	336	Estrone	Unspecified	32
	Electrolytes			337	17-Hydroxycorticoids	(0.65-1.50)	145
299	Calcium	15	13		Miscellaneous		
300	Chlorine	100	13	338	FSH inhibitor	Consult reference	171
301	Magnesium	5.2	13	339	Gonadotropin inhibitor	Consult reference	171
302	Phosphorus	15	13		Mouse		
303	Potassium	200	13				
304	Sulfur, inorganic	12	13		Nitrogenous substances		
305	ethereal	(3-4)	13	340	Amino acid: Taurine	11.89(9.39-14.64)[6]	40,153
306	neutral	(4-5)	13				
307	Sulfate, total	(20-30)	13	341	Pyrimidine derivative: Deoxycytidine	(125-625)[4]	183
	Vitamins				Miscellaneous		
308	Vitamin B$_6$	3.8(1.6-7.8)[4]	18	342	4-Amino-5-imidazole-carboxamide	260[4]	125
309	4-Pyridoxic acid	23(17-27)[4]	18				
	Nitrogenous substances			343	Homovanillic acid	40[4]	129
310	Nitrogen, total	(140-400)	13,90,163		Rabbit		
311	ammonia	(2-10)	13,90,163				
	Amino acids			344	Property: Volume	(50-75)[2]	140
312	Alanine	Unspecified	40		Electrolytes		
313	Glutamic acid	Unspecified	40	345	Calcium	(3-7)	208
314	Taurine	Unspecified	40	346	Chlorine	(190-300)	140
315	Purine bases	(5-6)	90,163	347	Phosphorus	(10-60)	25,130,208
316	Derivative: Uric acid	(1-2)	49,163				
	Indole derivatives			348	Sulfur, neutral	(4-10)	27
317	Indican, metabolic (Indoxylsulfuric acid)	Unspecified	44		Vitamins		
				349	Niacin	(250-700)[4]	54
318	Indoleacetic acid	Unspecified	44	350	B$_{12}$ (Cobalamin)	500(400-600)[7]	1,168
319	5-Oxyindoleacetic acid	Unspecified	44		Nitrogenous substances		
320	Skatoxylsulfuric acid	Unspecified	44	351	Nitrogen, total	(120-300)	130,187,208
	Miscellaneous						
321	Allantoin	(5-10)	49,109				
322	Creatine	(0-14)	97,163	352	ammonia	(3-5)	20

[1] Unless otherwise specified. [2] ml·kg body wt^{-1}·da^{-1}. [4] μg·kg body wt^{-1}·da^{-1}. [6] After fasting. [7] ng·kg body wt^{-1}·da^{-1}.

continued

	Property or Constituent (Synonym)	Value mg·kg body wt^{-1}·da^{-1} [1]	Reference		Property or Constituent (Synonym)	Value mg·kg body wt^{-1}·da^{-1} [1]	Reference
353	Amino acid: Taurine	4.130-(2.628-5.256)	153	378	Fructosediphosphate aldolase [4.1.2.13] (Aldolase)	Consult reference	100
354	Purine derivatives: Uric acid	(4-6)	68,69	379	Urokinase	Consult reference	75
	Indole derivatives			380	Organic acid: Phenol (Carbolic acid)	30	61
355	Indican, metabolic (Indoxylsulfuric acid)	Unspecified	5,44	381	Miscellaneous: Ketone bodies (Acetone bodies)	(0.4-1.0)	9
356	Indoleaceturic acid	Unspecified	44				
357	Indole-3-carboxylic acid	Unspecified	44		Rat		
	Miscellaneous			382	Property: Volume	(150-300)[2]	74
358	Allantoin	(60-80)	49,107, 109,137		Electrolytes		
359	4-Amino-5-imidazole-carboxamide	97[4]	125	383	Beryllium	Unspecified	65
360	Coproporphyrins I & III	(3-12)[4]	178,179	384	Calcium	(3-9)	56,135
				385	Chlorine	(50-75)	101,115, 203
361	Creatine	(13-20)	140	386	Phosphorus	30	164
362	Creatinine	(20-50)	20,27,33, 140,168, 187	387	Potassium	(50-60)	101,135, 203
				388	Sodium	110	101,203
363	Hippuric acid	100	55	389	Sulfur, neutral	(7-20)	27
364	Histamine	20-200[4]	4	390	Bicarbonate	6	101,203
365	3-Hydroxyanthranilic acid	39[4]	190		Vitamins		
366	8-Hydroxyquinaldic acid	Unspecified	170	391	Thiamine	(3-13)[4]	172,214
				392	Riboflavin	(40-80)[4]	66,166, 173
367	Kynurenic acid	Unspecified	170	393	Niacin	(90-120)[4]	89
368	Quinaldic acid	(1.088-2.082)	170	394	Trigonelline	(300-700)[4]	89
369	Quinaldylglycine	Unspecified	170	395	Niacinamide	(200-700)[4]	54
370	Urea	(1200-1500)	86	396	N'-Methylnicotinamide	(900-5000)[4]	54
371	Xanthurenic acid	Unspecified	170	397	6-Hydroxynicotinic acid	Unspecified	112
	Steroid hormones & derivatives			398	6-Hydroxynicotinamide	Unspecified	112
372	Androgens	(3-20)[4]	41	399	Pantothenic acid	(300-600)[4]	126
373	17-Ketosteroids	(30-1000)[4]	39,41,46	400	Vitamin B$_{12}$ (Cobalamin)	203(63-342)[7]	167
374	α-Estradiol-17β-D-gluco-pyranoside (17α-Estradiol-17β-D-glucopyranoside)	Unspecified	217	401	Ascorbic acid	(1000-6000)[2]	108,142
	Enzymes[5]				Carbohydrate derivatives		
375	Lactate dehydrogenase (Lactic dehydrogenase) [1.1.1.27]	Consult reference	100	402	Hexosamine	(2.4-7.2)	131
					Mucopolysaccharides		
376	Aspartate aminotransferase (Glutamic oxaloacetic transaminase) [2.6.1.1]	Consult reference	100	403	Total	135(93-177)[9]	105
				404	Nonsulfated	80(27-132)[9]	105
				405	Sulfated	55(24-87)[9]	105
				406	Sialic acid	(3.6-9.6)	131
					Nitrogenous substances		
377	Alanine aminotransferase (Glutamic pyruvic transaminase) [2.6.1.2]	Consult reference	100	407	Nitrogen, total	(200-1000)	24,71,187
				408	ammonia	(10-30)	63,74

[1] Unless otherwise specified. [2] ml·kg body wt^{-1}·da^{-1}. [4] µg·kg body wt^{-1}·da^{-1}. [5] Enzyme Commission Number, in brackets, was assigned by the International Union of Biochemistry on the Nomenclature and Classification of Enzymes [95]. [7] ng·kg body wt^{-1}·da^{-1}. [9] Expressed as µg uronic acid·kg body wt^{-1}·da^{-1}.

continued

Property or Constituent (Synonym)	Value mg·kg body wt^{-1}·da^{-1} [1]	Reference		Property or Constituent (Synonym)	Value mg·kg body wt^{-1}·da^{-1} [1]	Reference
	Amino acids				Indole derivatives		
409	Alanine	Unspecified	40	446	Indican, metabolic (Indoxylsulfuric acid)	Unspecified	44
410	Arginine, total	2.7	8	447	Indoleacetic acid	Unspecified	44
411	free	1.3	8	448	Indoleaceturic acid	Unspecified	44
412	Aspartic acid, free	290[4]	8	449	Indole-3-carboxylic acid	Unspecified	44
413	Citrulline	(0.54-2.50)	162				
414	Cystine, total	500[4]	8	450	5-Oxyindoleacetic acid	Unspecified	44
415	Glutamic acid, total	7.1	8,40	451	Skatoxylsulfuric acid	Unspecified	44
416	Glycine, total	6.9	8,40		Miscellaneous		
417	Histidine, total	1.5	8	452	Allantoin	(100-600)	12,67,109, 153
418	free	430[4]	8				
419	Hydroxyproline	61[4]	191	453	4-Amino-5-imidazole-carboxamide	72[4]	125
420	Isoleucine, total	2.2	8				
421	free	430[4]	8	454	Ammonia	80	101,203
422	Leucine, free	2.4	8	455	Creatine	(0-13)	35,204
423	Lysine, total	4.6	8	456	Creatinine	(24-40)	12,27,63, 204
424	free	1.0	8				
425	Methionine, free	400[4]	8	457	Hippuric acid	16.06(6.67-23.33)	201
426	Methylhistidine	Unspecified	40				
427	Phenylalanine, free	800[4]	8	458	Histamine	(20-200)[4]	4
428	Taurine	(5-31)	40,153, 162	459	Homovanillic acid	31[4]	129
				460	Urea	(1000-1600)	63,154
429	Threonine, total	2.9	8	461	Steroid hormones: Androgens	18[4]	50
430	free	630[4]	8				
431	Tryptophan, free	470[4]	8		Enzymes [5]		
432	Tyrosine, free	470[4]	8	462	Lactate dehydrogenase [1.1.1.27]	Consult reference	111
433	Valine, free	930[4]	8				
	Purines, pyrimidines, & derivatives			463	Isocitrate dehydrogenase (Isocitric acid dehydrogenase) [1.1.1.42]	Consult reference	160
434	Adenosine-3′,5′-monophosphate (Cyclic adenosine monophosphate)	(20-70)[4]	6,159				
				464	Glutamate dehydrogenase [1.4.1.2]	Consult reference	111
				465	Cholinesterase [3.1.1.8]	Consult reference	161
435	Guanine	Unspecified	117	466	Alkaline phosphatase [3.1.3.1]	Consult reference	111
436	1-Methylguanine	Unspecified	117				
437	7-Methylguanine	Unspecified	117	467	Acid phosphatase [3.1.3.2]	Consult reference	111
438	N^2-Dimethylguanine	Unspecified	117				
439	Cyclic guanosine monophosphate (Guanosine-3′,5′-monophosphate)	0.04	159	468	β-Glucosidase [3.2.1.21]	Consult reference	165
				469	β-Galactosidase [3.2.1.23]	Consult reference	165
440	Xanthine	Unspecified	117	470	Chitobiase (N-Acetyl-β-glucosaminidase) [3.2.1.29]	Consult reference	165
441	Hypoxanthine	Unspecified	117				
442	1-Methylhypoxanthine	Unspecified	117	471	β-Glucuronidase [3.2.1.31]	Consult reference	128,165
443	Uric acid	(8-12)	12,62,67				
444	Deoxycytidine	(0.091-1.818)	183	472	Oxytocic esterase	Consult reference	19
445	2-Methyl-4-amino-5-hydroxymethylpyrimidine	Unspecified	216				

[1] Unless otherwise specified. [4] μg·kg body wt^{-1}·da^{-1}.
[5] Enzyme Commission Number, in brackets, was assigned by the International Union of Biochemistry on the Nomenclature and Classification of Enzymes [95].

continued

	Property or Constituent (Synonym)	Value mg·kg body wt^{-1}·da^{-1} [1]	Reference
	Organic acids		
473	Acetic acid	30	101
474	cis-Aconitic acid	5	101
475	Citric & isocitric acids	25	101
476	Fumaric acid	6	101
477	α-Ketoglutaric acid	7	101
478	Lactic acid	3	101
479	Phenol (Carbolic acid)	(6-60)	45
480	Succinic acid	4	101

Sheep

	Property or Constituent (Synonym)	Value mg·kg body wt^{-1}·da^{-1} [1]	Reference
	Properties		
481	Volume	(10-40)[2]	17,127, 196
482	Specific gravity	1.030(1.015-1.045)[3]	53
	Electrolytes		
483	Calcium	2	141
484	Phosphorus	0.2	141
485	Potassium	(300-420)	48,181
486	Sodium	1.4	48
487	Sulfur, total	10	212
488	inorganic	5	212
489	ethereal	4	212
490	neutral	5	212
491	Phosphate	4	181
	Vitamins		
492	Niacin	(80-130)[4]	151
493	N'-Methylnicotinamide	(18-60)[4]	151
494	Vitamin B$_{12}$ (Cobalamin)	(0.0038-0.1700)[10]	43
495	Choline	60[4]	114
496	Ascorbic acid	50[4]	152
497	Carbohydrates: Sugars, reducing	40	212
	Nitrogenous substances		
498	Nitrogen, total	(120-350)	81,91,141
499	ammonia	(0-8)	81,141
500	urea	(108-170)	127
501	Amino acids, total	3	212
502	Protein, total	8	146
503	muco-	4	37,146
504	Purine bases	(2-5)	91,141
505	Derivative: Uric acid	(2-4)	91,141
	Indole derivatives		
506	Indican, metabolic (Indoxylsulfuric acid)	Unspecified	44
507	Indoleacetic acid	Unspecified	44
508	Indoleaceturic acid	Unspecified	44

	Property or Constituent (Synonym)	Value mg·kg body wt^{-1}·da^{-1} [1]	Reference
509	Indoleacetylglutamine	Unspecified	44
510	Skatoxylsulfuric acid	Unspecified	44
	Miscellaneous		
511	Allantoin	(20-50)	91,137, 141
512	Creatine	(0-6)	141
513	Creatinine	10	141
514	Hippuric acid	(20-40)	141,150
515	Histamine, conjugated	0.25[4]	186
516	free	0.16[4]	186
517	Urea	210	141
	Hormones		
518	Estrogens, total, ♀	(0.05-3.00)[4]	14
519	Estradiol	(0.28-8.33)[4]	157
520	Estrone	(0.3-8.0)[4]	157
521	Gonadotropins	Unspecified	197
522	Vasopressin	Unspecified	224
	Aromatic acids		
523	Benzoic acid & phenylacetic acid	Unspecified	121

Swine

	Property or Constituent (Synonym)	Value mg·kg body wt^{-1}·da^{-1} [1]	Reference
	Properties		
524	Volume	(5-30)[2]	17,196
525	Specific gravity	1.012(1.010-1.050)	17,53
526	Electrolyte: Sulfur, neutral	(1-3)	27
527	Vitamin: Ascorbic acid	160[4]	207
	Nitrogenous substances		
528	Nitrogen, total	(40-240)	123,133, 187
529	α-amino	(2-10)	84
530	Purine bases	(3-4)	91
531	Derivative: Uric acid	(1-2)	91
	Indole derivatives		
532	Indican, metabolic (Indoxylsulfuric acid)	Unspecified	44
533	Indoleacetic acid	Unspecified	44
534	Indoleaceturic acid	Unspecified	44
535	Indole-3-carboxylic acid	Unspecified	44
536	Skatoxylsulfuric acid	Unspecified	44
	Miscellaneous		
537	Acetylkynurenine	(480-600)[4]	182
538	Allantoin	(20-80)	91,107, 137
539	o-Aminohippuric acid	(510-780)[4]	182

[1] Unless otherwise specified. [2] ml·kg body wt^{-1}·da^{-1}. [3] Relative value. [4] μg·kg body wt^{-1}·da^{-1}. [10] pg·kg body wt^{-1}·da^{-1}.

continued

Property or Constituent (Synonym)	Value mg·kg body wt^{-1}·da^{-1} [1]	Reference	Property or Constituent (Synonym)	Value mg·kg body wt^{-1}·da^{-1} [1]	Reference
540	o-Aminobenzoyl glucuronide (Anthranilic acid glucuronide)	78[4]	182	556	11-Ketoetiocholanolone	Unspecified	34
541	Creatine	(15-25)	123,124		Estrogens, ♀		
542	Creatinine	(20-90)	27,123, 124,182, 187	557	Estradiol	Unspecified	52
				558	Estrone	(6-60)[4]	52
					Progesterones, ♀		
543	Heterocyclic amines	(5-140)[4]	158	559	5β-Pregnane-3α,20α-diol (3α,20α-Dihydroxy-5β-pregnane)	Unspecified	52
544	Hydroxykynurenine	(60-160)[4]	182				
545	Kynurenic acid	(84-107)[4]	170,182	560	Allopregnan-3β-ol-20-one (3β-Hydroxy-5α-pregnan-20-one; 5α-pregnan-3β-ol-20-one)	Unspecified	52,174
546	Kynurenine	(143-202)[4]	182				
547	N-Methyl-2-pyridone-5-carboxamide	7[4]	182				
548	Urea	430	193	561	5β-Pregnane-3α-ol-20-one (3α-Hydroxy-5β-pregnan-20-one)	(16-40)[4]	52,174
549	Xanthurenic acid	(169-227)[4]	170,182				
	Steroid hormones			562	Pregnane-3α,6α-diol-20-one	(2-10)[4]	52,98,174
	Androgens, 17-ketosteroids						
550	Androsterone	Unspecified	34		Adrenal corticoids		
551	Epiandrosterone (Isoandrosterone)	Unspecified	34	563	Aldosterone	(0.20-0.40)[4]	176,199
				564	Cortisone	Unspecified	199
552	Dehydroepiandrosterone (Dehydroisoandrosterone)	Unspecified	34	565	Hydrocortisone (Cortisol)	170(62-263)[4]	177,199
				566	Tetrahydrocortisone	Unspecified	199
553	11β-Hydroxyandrosterone	Unspecified	34	567	Tetrahydrocortisol	Unspecified	199
					Organic acids		
554	Etiocholanolone	Unspecified	34	568	Citric acid	1.935	106
555	11β-Hydroxyetiocholanolone	Unspecified	34	569	Phenol (Carbolic acid)	(1-3)	61

[1] Unless otherwise specified. [4] μg·kg body wt^{-1}·da^{-1}.

Contributor: Van Pilsum, John

References
[1] Alexander, F., and M. E. Davis. 1969. Brit. Vet. J. 125:169.

[2] Allan, F. W., and L. R. Carecedo. 1931. J. Biol. Chem. 93:293.

[3] Alvarez, M. B., et al. 1970. J. Dairy Sci. 53(71):928.

[4] Anrep, G. V., et al. 1944. J. Physiol. (London) 103:155.

[5] Asayama, C. 1916. J. Amer. Med. Ass. 67:475.

[6] Aurbach, G. D., and B. A. Houston. 1968. J. Biol. Chem. 243(22):5935.

[7] Ayalon, N., et al. 1970. Int. J. Fert. 15:40.

[8] Bakerman, H. A., et al. 1951. J. Biol. Chem. 188:117.

[9] Banerjee, S., and G. Bhattacharya. 1949. Ibid. 178:145.

[10] Barakat, M. Z., and M. M. El-Guindi. 1968. Zentralbl. Veterinaermed. A15:60.

[11] Bartlett, P. D., et al. 1949. J. Biol. Chem. 180:1021.

[12] Bass, A. D., et al. 1950. Proc. Soc. Exp. Biol. Med. 73:687.

[13] Baumann, L., and E. Oviatt. 1915. J. Biol. Chem. 22:43.

[14] Beck, A. B. 1950. Aust. J. Agr. Res. 1:322.

[15] Beher, W. T., and O. H. Gaebler. 1950. J. Nutr. 41:447.

[16] Bekaert, J., et al. 1954. Ann. Endocrinol. 15:946.

[17] Benjamin, M. M. 1961. Outline of Veterinary Clinical Pathology. Iowa State Univ. Press, Ames.

[18] Benson, E. M., et al. 1968. J. Nutr. 96(1):83.

[19] Beraldo, W. T., et al. 1966. Amer. J. Physiol. 211:975.

[20] Bernheim, F., et al. 1945. Ibid. 145:115.

[21] Blosser, T. H., and V. R. Smith. 1950. J. Dairy Sci. 33:329.

[22] Boothby, W. M., and M. Adams. 1934. Amer. J. Physiol. 107:471.

continued

[23] Borchers, J., et al. 1967. Deut. Tieraerztl. Wochenschr. 74:532.

[24] Bothwell, J. W., and J. N. Williams, Jr. 1951. J. Nutr. 45:245.

[25] Brain, R. T., et al. 1928. Biochem. J. 22:628.

[26] Bressami, R., et al. 1965. J. Nutr. 87:77.

[27] Brody, S., et al. 1934. Mo. Agr. Exp. Sta. Res. Bull. 214:34.

[28] Calaprice, A. 1966. Acta Med. Vet. 12:147.

[29] Carpenter, T. A. 1927. Amer. J. Physiol. 81:519.

[30] Castor, C. W., et al. 1965. J. Clin. Invest. 44:1034.

[31] Chapman, D. I. 1969. Comp. Biochem. Physiol. 30: 339.

[32] Chatterjee, S., and B. K. Anand. 1967. Indian J. Med. Res. 44(9):973.

[33] Cheetham, R. W. S., and H. Zwarenstein. 1938. Biochem. J. 32:871.

[34] Clark, A. F., et al. 1965. Endocrinology 76:427.

[35] Coffman, J. R., and F. C. Kock. 1939. Proc. Soc. Exp. Biol. Med. 42:779.

[36] Corcoran, A. C., and I. H. Page. 1948. J. Lab. Clin. Med. 33:1326.

[37] Correlius, C. E., and J. A. Bishop. 1967. Amer. J. Vet. Res. 28:883.

[38] Coulson, C. B., et al. 1960. J. Comp. Pathol. 70: 199.

[39] Danford, P. A., and H. G. Danford. 1950. Endocrinology 47:139.

[40] Datta, S. P., and H. Harris. 1953. Ann. Eugen. 18: 107.

[41] Davis, C. T., et al. 1949. Endocrinology 44:83.

[42] Davis, J. O. 1956. Amer. J. Physiol. 187:45.

[43] Dawbarn, M. C., and D. C. Hein. 1957. Aust. J. Exp. Biol. Med. Sci. 35:273.

[44] Decker, P., and H. Gerdemann. 1959. Deut. Tieraerztl. Wochenschr. 66:305.

[45] Deichmann, W., and L. J. Schafer. 1942. Amer. J. Clin. Pathol. 12:129.

[46] DeKoning, K. B., and S. J. Glass. 1948. Proc. Soc. Exp. Biol. Med. 68:320.

[47] Delprat, G. D., and G. H. Whipple. 1921. J. Biol. Chem. 49:229.

[48] Dewhurst, J. K., et al. 1968. J. Physiol. (London) 195:609.

[49] Dinning, J. S., and P. L. Day. 1949. J. Biol. Chem. 181:897.

[50] Dorfman, R. I. 1938. Ibid. 123:xxx.

[51] Dow, D. S., and C. E. Allen. 1949. Sci. Agr. 29:330.

[52] Edgerton, L. A., and R. E. Erb. 1969. J. Anim. Sci. 29:188.

[53] Ellenberger, W., and A. Scheunert. 1925. Lehrbuch der vergleichenden Physiologie der Haussaugetiere. Ed. 3. P. Parey, Berlin.

[54] Ellinger, P., and M. M. Abdel Kader. 1949. Biochem. J. 44:77.

[55] Epstein, A. A., and S. Bookman. 1912. J. Biol. Chem. 13:117.

[56] Fairhall, L. T. 1926. Ibid. 70:495.

[57] Feher, T., et al. 1967. Magy. Allatorv. Lapja. 22: 457.

[58] Feher, T., et al. 1970. Endokrinologie 56(1):55.

[59] Fiske, C. H., and M. A. Logan. 1931. J. Biol. Chem. 93:211.

[60] Folin, O., and R. D. Bell. 1917. Ibid. 29:329.

[61] Folin, O., and W. Denis. 1915. Ibid. 22:309.

[62] Folin, O., and W. Denis. 1916. Ibid. 26:497.

[63] Folin, O., and J. L. Morris. 1913. Ibid. 14:509.

[64] Forbes, E. B., et al. 1928. J. Nutr. 1:201.

[65] Foreman, J. K., et al. 1970. Analyst (London) 95(1134):797.

[66] Fraser, H. F., et al. 1940. Pub. Health Rep. 55: 280.

[67] Friedman, M. 1948. Amer. J. Physiol. 152:302.

[68] Friedman, M., and S. O. Byers. 1948. J. Biol. Chem. 175:727.

[69] Friedman, M., and S. O. Byers. 1950. Amer. J. Physiol. 163:684.

[70] Givens, M. H., and L. B. Mendel. 1917. J. Biol. Chem. 31:421.

[71] Gordon, G. S., et al. 1947. Endocrinology 40:375.

[72] Greaves, J. P., and P. P. Scott. 1960. Nature (London) 187:242.

[73] Greenwald, I., and J. Gross. 1925. J. Biol. Chem. 66:201.

[74] Griffith, J. Q. 1949. The Rat in Laboratory Investigation. Ed. 2. J. B. Lippincott, Philadelphia.

[75] Hamberg, U., and M. Savolainen. 1968. Acta Chem. Scand. 22(5):1452.

[76] Hammett, F. S. 1915. J. Biol. Chem. 22:551.

[77] Hansard, S. L., et al. 1952. J. Anim. Sci. 11:524.

[78] Hart, E. B., et al. 1931. J. Dairy Sci. 14:307.

[79] Hawk, P. B. 1910. J. Biol. Chem. 8:465.

[80] Hawkins, W. B., et al. 1946. Ibid. 166:223.

[81] Healy, D. J., et al. 1928. J. Amer. Vet. Med. Ass. 73:87.

[82] Heitzman, R. J., and K. G. Hibbitt. 1967. J. Endocrinol. 38:231.

[83] Heitzman, R. J., and G. H. Thomas. 1965. Ibid. 33: 455.

[84] Hende, C., van den, et al. 1967. Vlaams Diergeneesk. Tijdschr. 36:587.

[85] Hendricks, H. J. 1967. Tijdschr. Diergeneesk. 92: 1459.

[86] Herrin, R. C. 1947. Amer. J. Physiol. 149:492.

[87] Holtz, A. H. 1957. Acta Endocrinol. (Copenhagen) 26:75.

[88] Hooker, C. W. 1937. Endocrinology 21:655.

[89] Huff, J. W., and W. A. Perlzweig. 1942. J. Biol. Chem. 142:401.

[90] Hunter, A., and M. H. Givens. 1914. Ibid. 17:55.

[91] Hunter, A., and M. H. Givens. 1914. Ibid. 18:403.

[92] Hunter, D. L., et al. 1970. J. Anim. Sci. 30:47.

[93] Hunter, G. 1925. Biochem. J. 19:34.

[94] Imai, K., and S. Nakajo. 1966. Nippon Chikusan Gakkaiho 37:104.

[95] International Union of Biochemistry. 1965. Enzyme Nomenclature. Elsevier, New York.

[96] Jacobi, H., and R. Fontaine. 1967. Z. Versuchstierk. 9:205.

[97] Jailer, J. W. 1940. Amer. J. Physiol. 130:503.

[98] Jones, P. H., and R. E. Erb. 1968. J. Anim. Sci. 27:1054.

continued

[99] Keitt, T. E. 1916. S. C. Agr. Exp. Sta. Annu. Rep. 29.

[100] Kemp, E., and T. Laursen. 1960. Scand. J. Clin. Lab. Invest. 12:463.

[101] Kesner, L., and E. Muntwyler. 1963. J. Lab. Clin. Med. 61:604.

[102] Klyne, W., and A. A. Wright. 1959. J. Endocrinol. 18:32.

[103] Knodt, C. B., et al. 1942. J. Dairy Sci. 25:851.

[104] Kock, F. C. 1937. Physiol. Rev. 17:153.

[105] Koizumi, T., et al. 1969. Clin. Chim. Acta 26:477.

[106] Kolb, E., and U. Busse. 1956. Zentralbl. Veterinaermed. 3:697.

[107] Kostyak, J. 1941. Kozlem. Osszehas. Elet. Kort. Koreb. Budapest 29:178.

[108] Langwill, K. E., et al. 1945. J. Nutr. 30:99.

[109] Larson, H. W. 1931. J. Biol. Chem. 94:727.

[110] Larson, P. S., and I. L. Chaikoff. 1937. J. Nutr. 13:287.

[111] Leathwood, P. D., and D. T. Plummer. 1969. Enzymologia 37(4):240.

[112] Lee, Y. C., et al. 1969. J. Biol. Chem. 244(12):3277.

[113] Levin, L. 1949. Ibid. 178:229.

[114] Luecke, R. W., and P. B. Pearson. 1945. Ibid. 158:561.

[115] Machle, W., et al. 1942. J. Ind. Hyg. 24:199.

[116] Maignon, F., and E. Kinthakis. 1928. C. R. Acad. Sci. 186:463.

[117] Mandel, L. R., et al. 1966. Nature (London) 209:586.

[118] Manston, R., and M. J. Vagg. 1970. J. Agr. Sci. 74:161.

[119] Mariam, A. P., and A. Tinti. 1965. Ann. Fac. Med. Vet. Univ. Studi Pisa 18:19.

[120] Marsh, D. C., et al. 1947. J. Dairy Sci. 30:867.

[121] Martin, A. K. 1969. Proc. Nutr. Soc. 28:65A.

[122] Mayer, G. P., et al. 1966. Amer. J. Physiol. 211:1366.

[123] McCollum, E. V., and D. R. Hoagland. 1913. J. Biol. Chem. 16:299.

[124] McCollum, E. V., and H. Steenbock. 1912. Ibid. 13:209.

[125] McGreer, P. L., et al. 1961. Can. J. Comp. Med. Vet. Sci. 25:211.

[126] McIlwain, H., and F. Hawking. 1943. Lancet 1:499.

[127] McIntyre, K. H., and V. J. Williams. 1969. Aust. J. Exp. Biol. Med. Sci. 47:633.

[128] Mead, J. A. R., et al. 1955. Biochem. J. 61:569.

[129] Mellinger, T. J. 1968. Amer. J. Clin. Pathol. 49:200.

[130] Mendel, L. B., and J. F. Lyman. 1910. J. Biol. Chem. 8:115.

[131] Miettinen, T. 1961. Scand. J. Clin. Lab. Invest., Suppl. 61:101.

[132] Milenloovic, M. M. 1959. Vet. Soraj. 8:517.

[133] Miller, E. R. 1929. J. Amer. Vet. Med. Ass. 74:376.

[134] Miller, G. E., et al. 1951. Amer. J. Physiol. 164:155.

[135] Miller, H. G. 1926. J. Biol. Chem. 70:593.

[136] Misrahy, G., and S. Salams. 1947. Amer. J. Physiol. 150:420.

[137] Miyahara, T. 1934. Sei I Kai Med. J. 53(8-9).

[138] Mootse, G., et al. 1967. Amer. J. Physiol. 212:657.

[139] Morendo, G. C., and L. Flore. 1949. Minerva Med. 39(2):149.

[140] Morgulis, S., and H. C. Spencer. 1936. J. Nutr. 12:191.

[141] Morris, S., and S. C. Ray. 1939. Biochem. J. 33:1217.

[142] Musulin, R. R., et al. 1939. J. Biol. Chem. 129:437.

[143] Nehring, K., et al. 1965. Arch. Tierernaehr. 15:45.

[144] Nietsche, H. 1937. Biochem. Z. 294:174.

[145] O'Malley, B. W., and M. B. Lipsett. 1966. Steroids 8:711.

[146] Packett, L. V., and S. P. Coburn. 1965. Amer. J. Vet. Res. 26:112.

[147] Pamukcu, A. M., et al. 1959. Ibid. 20:597.

[148] Pamukcu, A. M., et al. 1959. Zentralbl. Veterinaermed. 6:361.

[149] Paschkis, K. E., et al. 1943. Proc. Soc. Exp. Biol. Med. 53:213.

[150] Pazur, J. H., and W. A. Delong. 1948. Sci. Agr. 28:39.

[151] Pearson, P. B., et al. 1949. Arch. Biochem. 22:191.

[152] Pelletier, O. 1968. J. Lab. Clin. Med. 72(4):674.

[153] Pentz, E. I. 1969. Anal. Biochem. 27(2):333.

[154] Persike, E. C. 1948. Endocrinology 42:356.

[155] Pigon, H. 1962. Bull. Acad. Pol. Sci. Ser. Sci. Biol. 10:13.

[156] Pigon, H., et al. 1961. Acta Endocrinol. (Copenhagen) 36:131.

[157] Plotka, E. D., and R. E. Erb. 1969. J. Anim. Sci. 29:934.

[158] Porter, P., and R. Kinworthy. 1969. Res. Vet. Sci. 10:440.

[159] Price, T. D., et al. 1967. Biochim. Biophys. Acta 138:452.

[160] Raab, W. 1969. Clin. Chim. Acta 25(1):21.

[161] Raab, W. 1969. Enzymologia 36(3):177.

[162] Reed, J. G. 1951. Tex. Univ. Publ. 5109:139.

[163] Rheinberger, M. B. 1936. J. Biol. Chem. 115:343.

[164] Richet, C., Jr. 1929. J. Lab. Clin. Med. 15:9.

[165] Robinson, D., et al. 1967. Biochem. J. 102:533.

[166] Robinson, F. A. 1951. The Vitamin B Complex. J. Wiley, New York.

[167] Rosenblum, C., et al. 1952. J. Biol. Chem. 198:915.

[168] Rosenthal, H. L., and L. Cravitz. 1958. J. Nutr. 64:281.

[169] Rota, E. 1961. Atti Soc. Ital. Sci. Vet. 15:283.

[170] Roy, J. K., and J. M. Price. 1959. J. Biol. Chem. 234:2759.

[171] Sairam, M. R., et al. 1966. Endocrinology 78:923.

[172] Salcedo, J., Jr., et al. 1948. J. Nutr. 36:307.

[173] Sarett, H. P., et al. 1942. Ibid. 24:295.

[174] Schomberg, D. W., et al. 1966. Steroids 8:277.

continued

[175] Schülke, B. 1965. Monatsh. Veterinaermed. 20: 458.

[176] Schülke, B. 1968. Arch. Exp. Veterinaermed. 22: 1185.

[177] Schülke, B., and G. Tegeler. 1967. Ibid. 21:1253.

[178] Schwartz, S., and R. Zagaria. 1956. U.S. At. Energy Comm. MDDC-504.

[179] Schwartz, S., and R. Zagaria. 1951. In A. E. Tannenbaum, ed. Toxicology of Uranium. McGraw-Hill, New York. p. 290.

[180] Schweigert, B. S., et al. 1947. Arch. Biochem. 12: 139.

[181] Scott, D. 1969. Quart. J. Exp. Physiol. 54:412.

[182] Self, H. L., et al. 1960. J. Nutr. 70:21.

[183] Shejibal, J., et al. 1967. Clin. Chim. Acta 16:324.

[184] Siegel, E. T. 1965. Amer. J. Vet. Res. 26:1125.

[185] Silber, R. H. 1944. J. Nutr. 27:425.

[186] Sjaastad, O. V. 1970. Acta Vet. Scand. 11(2): 305.

[187] Smuts, D. B. 1935. J. Nutr. 9:403.

[188] Sparacino, E. 1958. Atti Soc. Ital. Sci. Vet. 12: 718.

[189] Spector, H., et al. 1945. J. Biol. Chem. 161:145.

[190] Spiera, H., and C. L. Christian. 1964. Proc. Soc. Exp. Biol. Med. 116:944.

[191] Stalder, V. K., and H. Stegeman. 1967. Hoppe Seylers Z. Physiol. Chem. 348:242.

[192] Stehle, R. L. 1917. J. Biol. Chem. 31:461.

[193] Stekol, J. A. 1936. Ibid. 113:675.

[194] Suemitsu, R., et al. 1968. Bull. Chem. Soc. Jap. 41:138.

[195] Suemitsu, R., et al. 1969. Ibid. 42:2368.

[196] Swenson, M. J., ed. 1970. Dukes' Physiology of Domestic Animals. Ed. 8. Cornell Univ. Press, Ithaca. p. 806.

[197] Symington, R. B. 1965. J. Endocrinol. 32:23.

[198] Taylor, T., and H. Partington. 1964. J. Small Anim. Pract. 5:161.

[199] Tegeler, G., and B. Schülke. 1967. Arch. Exp. Veterinaermed. 21:77.

[200] Terri, A. E., et al. 1950. J. Biol. Chem. 182:509.

[201] Teuchy, H., and C. F. van Sumere. 1969. Clin. Chim. Acta 25(1):79.

[202] Tham, R. 1966. J. Chromatogr. 22:245.

[203] Thompson, J. H., et al. 1966. Amer. J. Vet. Res. 27:1093.

[204] Tidwell, H. C. 1946. Proc. Soc. Exp. Biol. Med. 63:13.

[205] Treacher, R. J. 1964. Brit. Vet. J. 120:178.

[206] Twarog, B. M., and I. H. Page. 1953. Amer. J. Physiol. 175:157.

[207] Ugolini, M. 1942. Biochim. Ter. Sper. 29:187.

[208] Underhill, F. P., and L. J. Bogert. 1916. J. Biol. Chem. 27:161.

[209] Vagtborg, H., ed. 1968. Use Nonhum. Primates Drug Eval. Symp., San Antonio, 1967.

[210] Valle, J. R., et al. 1947. Endocrinology 41:335.

[211] Vassel, B., et al. 1944. Arch. Biochem. 4:59.

[212] Walker, D. M., and G. J. Faichney. 1964. Brit. J. Nutr. 18:201.

[213] Warth, F. J., and N. C. Das Gupta. 1928. Biochem. J. 22:621.

[214] Wertz, A. W., et al. 1951. J. Nutr. 43:181.

[215] Whelan, M. 1925. J. Biol. Chem. 63:585.

[216] White, W. W., III, et al. 1970. J. Nutr. 100(9): 1053.

[217] Williamson, D. G., et al. 1969. Biochemistry 8(11): 4299.

[218] Wilson, R. B., et al. 1967. Amer. J. Vet. Res. 28: 313.

[219] Worden, A. N., et al. 1952. Vet. Rec. 64:836.

[220] Worden, A. N., et al. 1955. Biochem. J. 59:527.

[221] Worden, A. N., et al. 1960. J. Small Anim. Pract. 1:11.

[222] Wrenn, T. R., et al. 1967. J. Dairy Sci. 50:999.

[223] Wrenn, T. T., et al. 1968. J. Reprod. Fert. 16(2): 301.

[224] Yesberg, N. E., et al. 1970. Aust. J. Exp. Biol. Med. Sci. 48:115.

187. PHYSICAL PROPERTIES OF AND EXCRETION PRODUCTS IN URINE: CHICKEN

All values are for urine collections of at least 24 hr from chickens with either a colostomy or exteriorized ureters, plus a suitable collection device for the purpose of avoiding fecal contamination. Data in brackets refer to the column heading in brackets. Values in parentheses are ranges, estimate "c" unless otherwise indicated (*see* Introduction).

	Property or Constituent [Synonym]	Value	Remarks	Reference
	Physical properties			
1	Volume	(25-90) ml/kg body wt per da	Adult ♂♀	2,4,6
2	Specific gravity	1.015	Mean of 24 samples from 3 adult ♂; supernatant fraction of urine	2
	Electrolytes			
3	Calcium	(3-13.9) meq/da	In adult ♀; in some cases, values varied if hens were laying	9,13
4	Chloride	(0.2-3.6) meq/da		
5	Magnesium	(1.0-2.3) meq/da		

continued

	Property or Constituent [Synonym]	Value	Remarks	Reference
6	Phosphorus	(0.8-3.0) m atoms/da		
7	Potassium	(2-7.2) mEq/da		
8	Sodium	(0.4-8.4) mEq/da		
	Nitrogenous substances			
9	Total N	(40-1500) mg/kg body wt per da	Adult ♂ or capons receiving 96-3300 mg N·animal^{-1}·da^{-1}	1
10	Endogenous urinary N	0.65 mg/g body wt$^{0.75}$ per da	6 adult ♂; 14-da collections	1
11	Ammonia N	(8-15)% of total N	Young & adult chickens	12
12	Amino acid N	(1.7-2.2)% of total N		
13	Creatine + creatinine N	(0.2-8.0)% of total N		
14	Urea N	(5-10)% of total N		
15	Uric acid N	(60-80)% of total N		
16	Unidentified N	(1.2-2.8)% of total N		
17	Hydroxyproline	(2.4-5.6)[b] mg/24 hr	Determined on 9 adult ♀ on da when no egg was laid	10
18		(6.7-10.5)[b] mg/24 hr	Determined on 9 adult ♀ on da when egg was laid	10
19	Ornithuric acid	(68-163) µg/animal per da	6 adult ♀ receiving purified diet; 48-hr collections	11
	Steroid hormones			
20	Estradiol [Estradiol-17β; 1,3,5(10)-Estratriene-3,17β-diol]	(1.41-2.26) µg/animal per da	2 nonlaying adult ♀	5,8
21		(3.10-3.56) µg/animal per da	2 laying adult ♀	5,8
22	Estrone [1,3,5(10)-Estratrien-3-ol-17-one]	(0.27-0.93) µg/animal per da	2 nonlaying adult ♀	3,7,8
23		(2.42-3.61) µg/animal per da	2 laying adult ♀	3,7,8

Contributor: Nesheim, M. C.

References

[1] Ariyoshi, S. 1957. Nogyo Gijutsu Kenkyusho Hokoku G13:93.

[2] Ariyoshi, S., and H. Morimoto. 1956. Ibid. G12:37.

[3] Common, R. H., et al. 1965. Can. J. Biochem. Physiol. 45:539.

[4] Hart, W. M., and H. E. Essex. 1942. Amer. J. Physiol. 136:657.

[5] Hertelendy, F., et al. 1965. Can. J. Biochem. Physiol. 43:1379.

[6] Hester, H. R., H. E. Essex, and F. C. Mann. 1940. Amer. J. Physiol. 128:592.

[7] Mathur, R. S., and R. H. Common. 1969. Poult. Sci. 48:100.

[8] Mathur, R. S., et al. 1966. Ibid. 45:946.

[9] Mongin, P. 1967. C. R. Acad. Sci. 204:2479.

[10] Morriss, K. M. L., and T. G. Taylor. 1970. Ann. Biol. Anim. Biochim. Biophys. 10:185.

[11] Nesheim, M. C., and J. D. Garlich. 1963. J. Nutr. 79:311.

[12] O'Dell, B. L., et al. 1960. Poult. Sci. 39:426.

[13] Taylor, T. G., and J. Kirkley. 1967. Brit. Poult. Sci. 8:289.

XI. METABOLISM

188. ENERGY METABOLISM AT VARIOUS WEIGHTS: MAN

Part I. Basal: Infants and Children

Values for infants less than 38 months old are based on "basal" heat production, including specific dynamic action of food; measurements were made while the infant was sleeping quietly. For infants 1 week to 38 months old in the slender classification, heat production would be 1 kcal/hr higher; for those underweight, >2 SE (standard error) higher; for those overweight, >2 SE lower. All data are for subjects with normal weight-for-height (defined as within ±10% of average weight), and were derived from the following equations in which W = body weight, in kilograms, H = body height, in centimeters, and e = 2.718 (the basis of natural logarithms): for subjects under 11 months old, $W = 0.323e^{0.047\,H}$; for subjects 11 months old or over, $W = 2.6e^{0.018\,H}$. Other weight-for-height categories: slender, 80-90% of average; underweight, <80%; stocky, 110-120%; overweight, 120-140%; obese, >140%.

	Weight kg	Metabolic Rate kcal/hr $\male$[1] or $\female$[1]		Weight kg	Metabolic Rate kcal/hr			Weight kg	Metabolic Rate kcal/hr	
					$\male$[2]	$\female$[3]			$\male$[4]	$\female$[5]
	Age, 1 wk-10 mo			Age, 11-38 mo				Age, 3-16 yr		
1	3.5	8.4	17	9.0	22.0	21.2	33	15	35.8	33.3
2	4.0	9.5	18	9.5	22.8	22.0	34	20	39.7	37.4
3	4.5	10.5	19	10.0	23.6	22.8	35	25	43.6	41.5
4	5.0	11.6	20	10.5	24.4	23.6	36	30	47.5	45.5
5	5.5	12.7	21	11.0	25.2	24.4	37	35	51.3	49.6
6	6.0	13.8	22	11.5	26.0	25.2	38	40	55.2	53.7
7	6.5	14.9	23	12.0	26.8	26.0	39	45	59.1	57.8
8	7.0	16.0	24	12.5	27.6	26.9	40	50	63.0	61.9
9	7.5	17.1	25	13.0	28.4	27.7	41	55	66.9	66.0
10	8.0	18.2	26	13.5	29.2	28.5	42	60	70.8	70.0
11	8.5	19.3	27	14.0	30.0	29.3	43	65	74.7	74.0
12	9.0	20.4	28	14.5	30.8	30.1	44	70	78.6	78.1
13	9.5	21.4	29	15.0	31.6	30.9	45	75	82.5	82.2
14	10.0	22.5	30	15.5	32.4	31.7				
15	10.5	23.6	31	16.0	33.2	32.6				
16	11.0	24.7	32	16.5	34.0	33.4				

[1] Computed from the equation, kcal/hr = $2.18W + 0.737$; SE = 1.6 kcal/hr. [2] Computed from the equation, kcal/hr = $1.59W + 7.74$; SE = 2.2 kcal/hr. [3] Computed from the equation, kcal/hr = $1.63W + 6.48$; SE = 1.9 kcal/hr. [4] Computed from the equation, kcal/hr = $0.778W + 24.11$; SE = 2.4 kcal/hr. [5] Computed from the equation, kcal/hr = $0.815W + 21.09$; SE = 2.2 kcal/hr.

Contributor: Johnson, Herman L.

General References

[1] Sargent, D. W. 1961. U. S. Dep. Agr. Home Econ. Res. Rep. 14.

[2] Sargent, D. W. 1962. Ibid. 18.

Part II. Resting: Adults

There is no difference between the metabolic rates of the two sexes if the rate is expressed in units of either lean cell mass or active tissue. Resting metabolism is related to body weight and fat content. Since there is at present no agreed rapid method of measuring the fat content of the body, the following table—which presents a range of normal values

continued

Part II. Resting: Adults

for the resting rate of metabolism and includes clinical assessments of body fat content—is new and awaits confirmation. **Fat Content of Body,** ♂: 5% = thin, 10% = average, 15% = plump, >20% = fat; ♀: 5-15% = thin, 20% = average, 25% = plump, >30% = fat.

	Body Wt kg	Fat Content of Body							Body Wt kg	Fat Content of Body					
		5%	10%	15%	20%	25%	30%			5%	10%	15%	20%	25%	30%
		Metabolic Rate, kcal/min								Metabolic Rate, kcal/min					
1	45	...	...	0.82	0.78	...	...	5	65	1.19	1.14	1.09	1.05	1.00	0.95
2	50	0.99	0.94	0.89	0.84	0.80	...	6	70	1.26	1.21	1.16	1.11	1.07	1.02
3	55	1.06	1.01	0.96	0.91	0.86	0.81	7	75	1.32	1.28	1.23	1.18	1.13	1.08
4	60	1.12	1.08	1.03	0.98	0.93	0.88	8	80	1.39	1.34	1.30	1.25	1.20	1.15

Contributor: Passmore, R.

Reference: Passmore, R. 1966. Nutr. Dieta 8:163.

189. BASAL ENERGY METABOLISM AT VARIOUS AGES: MAN

Part I. Children

Basal Metabolic Rate: Values are kilocalories per day per interspecific body size (body weight in kilograms)$^{0.75}$; SD = standard deviation; SEM = standard error of the mean; v = coefficient of variation = (SD/mean) × 100. Values in parentheses are ranges, estimate "c" (*see* Introduction).

	Age	No. & Sex	Body Weight kg	Basal Metabolic Rate					Age	No. & Sex	Body Weight kg	Basal Metabolic Rate			
				Mean	SD	SEM	v, %					Mean	SD	SEM	v, %
1	9(8-12) da	5♂	3.8(3.4-4.5)	68	8.0	3.6	12	9	5.4(4.7-5.8) yr	5♂	20.4(19-24)	85	6.5	2.9	8
2	10(9-12) da	5♀	3.8(3.6-4.2)	67	5.6	2.5	8	10	4.9(4.3-5.3) yr	5♀	17.3(15-23)	86	5.7	2.2	7
3	6.2(5-7) mo	9♂	7.3(6.5-8.9)	90	5.0	1.7	6	11	9.0(8.5-9.5) yr	6♂	25.8(25-27)	89	4.1	1.7	5
4	6.4(5-7) mo	6♀	6.9(6.1-9.0)	85	5.0	1.7	6	12	9.1(8.5-9.7) yr	6♀	24.5(22-26)	86	8.1	3.3	9
5	11.7(10-14) mo	6♂	9.5(7.6-11.8)	100	8.8	3.6	9	13	10.9(10.3-11.5) yr	7♂	31.8(28-37)	84	7.4	2.8	9
6	11.5(10-13) mo	5♀	8.5(7.0-9.8)	113	7.3	3.3	6	14	10.6(10.2-11.0) yr	5♀	28.3(27-30)	76	6.6	2.2	9
7	23.4(20-25) mo	5♂	11.8(10-14)	104	2.6	1.2	2.5	15	13.6(12.7-15.0) yr	5♂	39.7(32-39)	82	8.1	3.6	10
8	24.2(20-28) mo	7♀	11.4(10-12)	100	9.1	3.4	9	16	12.1(11.0-13.3) yr	5♀	32.7(27-37)	85	6.8	3.0	8

Contributor: Kleiber, Max

Reference: Benedict, F. G., and F. B. Talbot. 1921. Carnegie Inst. Wash. Publ. 302.

Part II. Adults

In a graphic plot of metabolic rate against age as an abscissa, the line of calories per kilogram body weight declines more steeply with age for women than for men, whereas the line of calories per square meter body surface declines less steeply for women than for men [1], and the line of calories per (kilogram body weight)$^{0.75}$ for women parallels the corresponding line for men. **Age Factor:** Age factor of $M/W^{0.75}$ = $1 + 0.004(30-A)$, where M = basal metabolic rate, in kilocalories per day, W = body weight, in kilograms, for men and women of mean specific stature, and A = age, in years. **Basal**

continued

189. BASAL ENERGY METABOLISM AT VARIOUS AGES: MAN

Part II. Adults

Metabolic Rate, in kilocalories per day = $71W^{0.75}$ [1 + 0.004(30-A) + 0.010(s-43.4)] for men, and $66W^{0.75}$ [1 + 0.004(30-A) + 0.018(s-42.4)] for women, where s = specific stature, in centimeters of height divided by the cube root of the body weight in kilograms.

	Age yr	Age Factor	Basal Metabolic Rate kcal·da^{-1}·kg body wt$^{-0.75}$	
			♂	♀
1	20	1.04	74	68
2	30	1.00	71	66
3	40	0.96	68	63
4	50	0.92	66	61

	Age yr	Age Factor	Basal Metabolic Rate kcal·da^{-1}·kg body wt$^{-0.75}$	
			♂	♀
5	60	0.88	63	58
6	70	0.84	60	55
7	80	0.80	55	53

Contributor: Kleiber, Max

References

[1] Harris, J. A., and F. G. Benedict. 1919. Carnegie Inst. Wash. Publ. 279:120.

[2] Kleiber, M. 1968. In P. L. Altman and D. S. Dittmer, ed. Metabolism. Federation of American Societies for Experimental Biology, Bethesda, Md. pp. 352-353.

Part III. Summary of Values per Surface Area

Values are smoothed means of basal kilogram calories per square meter per hour from the three largest and most authoritative sets of original data: (i) The Mayo Foundation Standards of Boothby, Berkson, and Dunn [2], based on measurements of 639 males and 828 females; (ii) the British measurements of Robertson and Reid [6], 987 males and 1323 females; and (iii) The Carnegie Nutrition Laboratory data of Harris and Benedict [3], 136 males and 103 females. The height-weight formula of DuBois and DuBois was used in computing body surface area: $S = 0.007184W^{0.425}H^{0.725}$, where S = surface area, in square meters, W = weight, in kilograms, and H = height, in centimeters. Somewhat higher values are to be expected on first tests (i.e., on persons unaccustomed to the procedures). Values in parentheses are ranges (estimate "b", *see* Introduction), calculated by E. F. DuBois from an average coefficient of variation of 6.9% [1, 3-6].

Age yr	Metabolic Rate kcal·m^{-2}·hr^{-1}	
	♂	♀
3	60.1(51.8-68.3)	54.5(47.0-62.0)
4	57.9(49.9-65.9)	53.9(46.5-61.3)
5	56.3(48.5-64.1)	53.0(45.7-60.3)
6	54.0(46.5-61.5)	51.2(44.1-58.3)
7	52.3(45.1-59.5)	49.7(42.8-56.6)
8	50.8(43.8-57.8)	48.0(41.4-54.6)
9	49.5(42.7-56.3)	46.2(39.8-52.6)
10	47.7(41.1-54.3)	44.9(38.7-51.1)
11	46.5(40.1-52.9)	44.1(38.0-50.2)
12	45.3(39.0-51.6)	42.0(36.2-47.8)
13	44.5(38.4-50.6)	40.5(34.9-46.1)
14	43.8(37.8-49.8)	39.2(33.8-44.6)
15	43.7(37.7-49.7)	38.3(33.0-43.6)
16	42.9(37.0-48.8)	37.7(32.5-42.9)

Age yr	Metabolic Rate kcal·m^{-2}·hr^{-1}	
	♂	♀
17	41.9(36.1-47.7)	36.2(31.2-41.2)
18	40.5(34.9-46.1)	35.7(30.8-40.6)
19	40.1(34.6-45.6)	35.4(30.5-40.3)
20	39.8(34.3-45.3)	35.3(30.4-40.2)
21	39.4(34.0-44.8)	35.2(30.3-40.1)
22	39.2(33.8-44.6)	35.2(30.3-40.1)
23	39.0(33.6-44.4)	35.2(30.3-40.1)
24	38.7(33.4-44.0)	35.1(30.3-39.9)
25	38.4(33.1-43.7)	35.1(30.3-39.9)
26	38.2(32.9-43.5)	35.0(30.2-39.8)
27	38.0(32.8-43.2)	35.0(30.2-39.8)
28	37.8(32.6-43.0)	35.0(30.2-39.8)
29	37.7(32.5-42.9)	35.0(30.2-39.8)
30	37.6(32.4-42.8)	35.0(30.2-39.8)

continued

189. BASAL ENERGY METABOLISM AT VARIOUS AGES: MAN

Part III. Summary of Values per Surface Area

Age yr	Metabolic Rate kcal·m^{-2}·hr^{-1} ♂	Metabolic Rate kcal·m^{-2}·hr^{-1} ♀	Age yr	Metabolic Rate kcal·m^{-2}·hr^{-1} ♂	Metabolic Rate kcal·m^{-2}·hr^{-1} ♀
31	37.4(32.2-42.6)	35.0(30.2-39.8)	40	36.5(31.5-41.5)	34.3(29.6-39.0)
32	37.2(32.1-42.3)	34.9(30.1-39.7)	45	36.3(31.3-41.3)	33.9(29.2-38.6)
33	37.1(32.0-42.2)	34.9(30.1-39.7)	50	36.0(31.0-40.0)	33.4(28.8-38.0)
34	37.0(31.9-42.1)	34.9(30.1-39.7)	55	35.4(30.5-40.3)	32.9(28.4-37.4)
35	36.9(31.8-42.0)	34.8(30.0-39.6)	60	34.8(30.0-39.6)	32.4(27.9-36.9)
36	36.8(31.7-41.9)	34.7(29.9-39.5)	65	34.0(29.3-38.7)	31.8(27.4-36.2)
37	36.7(31.6-41.8)	34.6(29.8-39.4)	70	33.1(28.5-37.7)	31.3(27.0-35.6)
38	36.7(31.6-41.8)	34.5(29.7-39.3)	75+	31.8(27.4-36.2)	31.1[1](26.8-35.4)[1]
39	36.6(31.5-41.7)	34.4(29.7-39.1)			

[1] Extrapolated from smooth curve.

Contributor: DuBois, Eugene F.

References
[1] Berkson, J., and W. M. Boothby. 1938. Amer. J. Physiol. 121:669.
[2] Boothby, W. M., et al. 1936. Ibid. 116:468.
[3] Harris, J. A., and F. G. Benedict. 1919. Carnegie Inst. Wash. Publ. 279.
[4] Lewis, R. C., et al. 1937. Amer. J. Dis. Child. 53:348.
[5] Lewis, R. C., et al. 1943. J. Pediat. 23:1.
[6] Robertson, J. D., and D. D. Reid. 1952. Lancet 2: 940.

Part IV. Effect of Age on Body Potassium and Metabolic Levels

The effect of age on body potassium for 20- to 80-year-olds can be calculated from the following: men, 2.10-0.008(age-20) and women, 1.74-0.008(age-20). C_K = grams potassium per kilogram body weight. **Metabolic Level** = kilocalories per day divided by the cube root of the body weight in kilograms.

	Age	C_K ♂	C_K ♀	Metabolic Level ♂	Metabolic Level ♀		Age	C_K ♂	C_K ♀	Metabolic Level ♂	Metabolic Level ♀
1	Birth	1.7		....	....	4	20 yr	2.10	1.74	74	68
2	9 yr	......	2.4[1]	....	....	5	Annual change	0.008	0.008	0.004	0.004
3	16 yr	2.7[1]	......	....	....	6	Relative annual change	0.38%	0.46%	0.0054%	0.0059%

[1] Maximum.

Contributor: Kleiber, Max

General References
[1] Anderson, E. C., and W. H. Langham. 1959. Science 130:714.
[2] Kleiber, M. 1961. The Fire of Life. J. Wiley, New York, p. 215.
[3] Kleiber, M. 1968. In P. L. Altman and D. S. Dittmer, ed. Metabolism. Federation of American Societies for Experimental Biology, Bethesda, Md. pp. 352-353.

190. PATHWAYS OF MINERAL METABOLISM: LABORATORY MAMMALS

The course, or courses, of the various elements or ions during metabolism may be followed in the diagram on the following page by tracing the combination of letters and numbers accompanying each element or ion in the **Pathways**

continued

columns of the table. The data represent a consensus of the findings of various investigators for a variety of mammalian species. The ions were administered in the form of simple soluble compounds (some metals as oxides). In many cases the documented studies have involved the use of radioactive isotopes. It should be noted that different isotopes of the same element do not necessarily have the same tissue predilections [73, 74]; otherwise they usually do not differ in the extent of oral absorption or route of excretion. **Valence** refers to the valence state of the element or ion when administered. Valence state, whether injected carrier-free (radioactive isotopes) or with a complexing agent such as citrate, may have considerable influence on the pathways followed [81, 196]. **Other Known Pathways** are listed, so far as possible, in their order of decreasing importance. Also, where possible the data are intended to reflect the situation which exists four to six days following a single dose. **Reference:** Asterisk (*) indicates data were obtained on a species not usually classified as a laboratory mammal, but are probably applicable thereto. Data in brackets refer to the column heading in brackets.

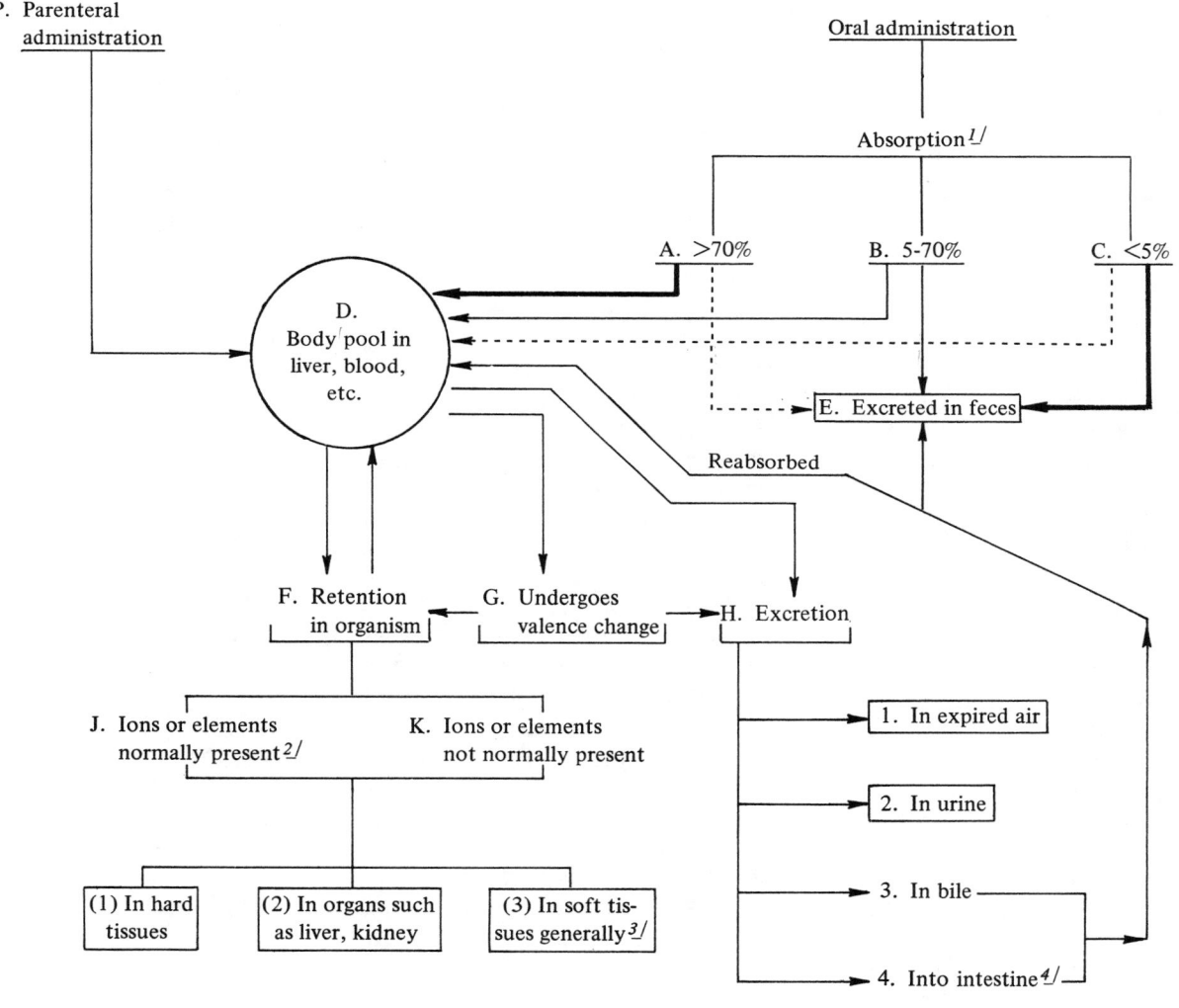

1/ Percent absorption of ions from oral administration has in some cases been rather arbitrarily classified, since the extent of absorption may depend on the amount administered and on the presence or absence of food residues in the digestive tract. 2/ Some trace elements with no known function also included. 3/ Primarily muscle, skin, and extracellular fluids. 4/ Other than in the bile, or by a route not definitely established.

continued

	Element or Ion [Valence]	Principal Oral Pathways[1]	Other Known Pathways	Reference
			Cations	
1	Actinium	CE	PDFK(1, 2), PDH4, PDH2	23,189,195
2	Aluminum	CE	PDH2, PDH3, PDFJ(2, 3)	47,78,171,177
3	Americium	CE	PDH2, PDFK(2, 1)[2], PDH3	52,73,74,76,101,111,138,154,167,168, 187,196,210
4	Antimony [3+]	BE, BDH2	BDFK(2, 3), BDH4	70,78,163,177
5	Barium	BE, BDH4	BDFK(1), BDH2	73,74,99,177,196
6	Berkelium	CE	PDFK(1, 2), PDH4, PDH2	85
7	Beryllium	CE	PDFK(1, 2, 3), PDH2, PDH4	64,116,164,177,200
8	Bismuth [3+]	CE	PDH2, PDFK(2, 1), PDH4	78,165,177
9	Cadmium	CE	PDFK(2, 3, 1)[2], PDH4, PDH2	17,54,55,78,103, 120, 140, 177, 202,208
10	Calcium	BE, BDFJ(1)	BDH4, BDH3, BDH2, BDFJ(3)	24,28,35,78,99,177,196,199,204,207
11	Californium	CE[3]	PDFK(1, 2), PDH2, PDH4	6,102,111,117,186,187,211
12	Cerium [3+]	CE	PDFK(2, 1, 3), PDH3, PDH2	2,15,29,54,55,73,74,106,108,109,118*, 122,123,165,170,197
13	Cesium	ADH2	ADH3, ADH4, ADFJ(3)	36,73,74,76,88,127-130,182,191,196
14	Chromium [3+]	CE	PDH2, PDH4, PDFK(1, 3, 2)	4,5,48,54,55,57,165,203
15	Cobalt [2+]	BE, BDH2	BDH3, BDH4, BDFJ(2, 3)	9,29,35,78,177,206
16	Copper [2+]	BE, BDH3	BDH2, BDFJ(2, 1)	4,5,29,35,39,41,78,97,114,142,143,177, 207,208
17	Curium	CE	PDFK(2, 1, 3), PDH3, PDH2	73,74,137-139,168,187,196
18	Dysprosium	CE	PDFK(1), PDH2, PDH3, PDH4	53,72
19	Einsteinium	CE	PDFK(1, 2), PDH2, PDH4	85,145,175
20	Erbium	CE	PDFK(1, 2), PDH3, PDH2, PDH4	53,72
21	Europium	CE	PDFK(1, 2), PDH4, PDH2	14,15,29,53,72
22	Francium	ADH2[3]	PDFK(2, 3)	148
23	Gadolinium	CE	PDH2, PDH3, PDFK(1, 2)	53,72
24	Gallium	CE	PDH2, PDFK(3), PDH4	94,123,177
25	Germanium	ADH2	ADH4, ADFK(3)	155,162,177
26	Gold [3+]	CE	PDFK(2, 1), PDH4, PDH2	70,73,74,78,155,165,177
27	Hafnium	CE	PDFK(2, 1), PDH2, PDH4	72,90,177
28	Holmium	CE	PDFK(2, 1, 3), PDH4, PDH3, PDH2	29,53,72,106,165
29	Indium	CE	PDFK(2, 1, 3), PDH4, PDH2	54,55,77,84,177
30	Iridium	CE	PDH2, PDFK(2, 3, 1), PDH4	54,55,69,165
31	Iron	BE	PDH4, PDFJ(2, 1), PDH2	31,35,40,78,95,110,156,177,183,207,208
32	Lanthanum	CE	PDFK(1, 2), PDH2, PDH4	4,5,29,32,53-55,72-74,78,165,177,179, 196
33	Lead [2+]	BE, BDH2	BDFK(1, 2), BDH4	54,55,70,78,101,163,165,177,190,202
34	Lithium	ADH2	ADH4, ADFJ(2, 3)	70,158,161,177
35	Lutetium	CE	PDFK(1, 2, 3), PDH4, PDH2	29,53,72,106,165
36	Magnesium	BE, BDH2	BDH3, BDFJ(1, 3)	3,21,26,27,78,171,207,208
37	Manganese [2+][4]	CE	PDH3, PDH4, PDFJ(2, 3, 1)	4,5,29,35,44,78,112,177,194
38	Mercury [2+]	BE, BDH2	PDFK(2, 3, 1), PDH4, PDH2	16,19,70,78,107,119,165,177,184,202
39	Neodymium	CE	PDFK(2, 1), PDH3, PDH2	29,53-55,72,78

[1] Ions which are well, or moderately well, absorbed when given orally may be expected to follow the same pathways when given parenterally. [2] Ion has a notable tendency to concentrate in a special tissue, such as eye, thyroid, or testis.

[3] As judged from the position of the element in the periodic table, or from the solubility of its compounds at physiological pH values, or both. [4] For information on Mn^{4+}, consult reference 165.

continued

Element or Ion [Valence]	Principal Oral Pathways[1]	Other Known Pathways	Reference
40 Neptunium	CE	PDFK(1, 3, 2), PDH2, PDH4	7,73,74,124,165,175,187
41 Nickel [2+]	BE, BDH2	PDFJ(2, 3), PDH4	49,73,74,78,174,177,206,208
42 Niobium	CE	PDFK(3, 1, 2), PDH2, PDH4	54,55,62,66,73,74,159,163,170,196
43 Palladium	CE[3]	PDH2, PDH4, PDFK(2, 3, 1)	54,55,78,115,165
44 Platinum	CE	PDH2 = PDH4, PDFK(3, 1, 2)	54,55,78,165
45 Plutonium	CE	PDFK(1, 2), PDH4, PDH2	8,20*,53,56,73,74,106,112,136,138,139, 153,156,157,165,168,187,188,196
46 Polonium	CE	PDFK(2, 1), PDH4, PDH2	63,87,125,177,180,196
47 Potassium	ADH2	ADFJ(3, 2, 1), ADH3, ADH4	29,34,35,78,127,128,165,177,199,207
48 Praseodymium	CE	PDFK(2, 3), PDH3, PDH2	53,72-74,79
49 Promethium	CE	PDFK(2, 1), PDH3, PDH2	29,53,71-74,80,176,196
50 Protactinium	CE	PDFK(1, 2, 3)	73,74,167,209
51 Radium	BE, BDFK(1, 2)[2]	BDH4, BDH2	99,111,113,132,134*,135*,141,177,196
52 Rhodium	CE	PDFK(3, 1, 2), PDH2, PDH4	54,55,165
53 Rubidium	ADH2	ADFJ(2, 3), ADH3, ADH4	25,50,88,127,177
54 Ruthenium	CE	PDFK(3, 1, 2), PDH2, PDH4	54,55,63,73,74,165,181,192,193,196
55 Samarium	CE	PDFK(2, 1), PDH3, PDH2	29,53-55,67,72,78
56 Scandium	CE[3]	PDFJ(3, 1, 2), PDH4, PDH2	10,15,73,74,118*,165
57 Silver	CE	PDH3, PDFJ(3, 2, 1), PDH2	70,78,165,166,177,208
58 Sodium	ADH2	ADFJ(2, 1, 3), ADH3, ADH4	29,35,78,165,171,177,207
59 Strontium	BE, BDFK(1, 3)	BDH2, BDH4, BDH3	4,5,51,73,74,99,111,123,126,177,191, 196,204
60 Tantalum	CE	PDH2, PDFK(1, 2, 3), PDH4	54,55,59,165
61 Terbium	CE	PDFK(1, 2, 3), PDH2, PDH3, PDH4	29,53-55,72,106,165
62 Thallium	BE	PDH4, PDFK(1, 2, 3), PDH2	53-55,78,104,106,165,177
63 Thorium	CE	PDFK(2, 1), PDH4, PDH2, PDH3	73,74,111,113,147,177,196
64 Thulium	CE	PDFK(1, 3, 2), PDH2, PDH3, PDH4	29,53,72,106,165
65 Tin [2+]	CE	PDFJ(1, 2), PDH2, PDH3	54,55,78,81,99,162,177,208
66 Tin [4+]	CE	PDH4, PDFJ(1, 2)	54,55,81
67 Titanium	CE[3]	CDFJ(2), CDH2	177,178
68 Uranium [4+]	CE	PDH4, PDFK(2, 1), PDH2	177,185,196
69 Uranium [6+]	BE, BDH2	BDFK(1), BDH4	38,65,78,177,196
70 Ytterbium	CE	PDFK(1, 2, 3), PDH3, PDH4, PDH2	15,53,72,106,165
71 Yttrium	CE	PDFK(1, 2), PDH2, PDH4	15,29,33,53,68,73,74,106,123,164,165, 196
72 Zinc	CE	PDH4, PDFJ(1, 2, 3)[2], PDH2	4,5,12,13,29,42,103,112,146*,151,160, 183,199,201,207
73 Zirconium	CE	PDFK(1, 3), PDH2, PDH4	66,73,74,159,163,170,196
Anions			
74 Arsenite[5]	BE, BDH2	BDFK(2, 3), BDH3, BDH4	70,91,98,162,177,197,198
75 Astatide	ADH2[3]	PDFK(3, 2, 1)[2], PDH2, PDH4	75,165
76 Bicarbonate	ADH2	ADH1, ADH3, ADH4, ADFJ	177
77 Borate	ADH2	PDFK(1, 2)	78,150,177

[1] Ions which are well, or moderately well, absorbed when given orally may be expected to follow the same pathways when given parenterally. [2] Ion has a notable tendency to concentrate in a special tissue, such as eye, thyroid, or testis.

[3] As judged from the position of the element in the periodic table, or from the solubility of its compounds at physiological pH values, or both. [5] For information on As^{5+}, consult reference 98.

continued

	Element or Ion [Valence]	Principal Oral Pathways[1]	Other Known Pathways	Reference
78	Bromate	ADH2	ADG(to BR⁻)	79,177
79	Bromide	ADH2	ADH3, ADH4, ADFJ [2]	29,79,177
80	Chlorate	ADH2	....	79,177
81	Chloride	ADH2	ADH3, ADH4, ADFJ	29,79,171,177
82	Chromate	BDH2	BDGH2, BDGH4, BDFK(2, 1, 3)	78,105,177,203
83	Cyanide	ADH2	ADH1, ADG(to SCN⁻, *see* entry 105)	29,70,177
84	Ferrocyanide	ADH2	....	92,93,177
85	Fluoride	BDH2	BDFJ(1, 3), BDH4	37,45,70,112,170-172,174,177
86	Hypophosphite	ADH2	....	177
87	Iodate	ADG(to I⁻)	ADH2	177
88	Iodide	ADH2	PDFJ(3, 1)[2], PDH3	29,70,73,74,79,133,165,177
89	Molybdate	BDH2	PDH2, PDFJ(2, 3, 1), PDH3	11*,29,30,43,53-55,78,165,177
90	Nitrate	ADH2	ADH3, ADH4, ADFK	79,177
91	Nitrite	ADG(to NO₃⁻)	(*see* entry 90)	177
92	Osmate [8+]	....	PDH2, PDFK(2, 3, 1), PDH4	54,55,79,165
93	Oxalate	ADH2	....	177
94	Perchlorate	ADH2	....	79
95	Permanganate	CE, CG(to MnO₂)	PDFJ(2), PDH3	79,152
96	Perrhenate	CE	PDH2, PDFK(3), PDH4	54,55,86,165
97	Pertechnetate	CE[3]	PDH2, PDH4, PDFK(2, 1)	54,55,141
98	Phosphate	BE, BDH2	BDFJ(1, 2, 3), BDH3, BDH4	35,70,149,177,207
99	Selenite	ADH2	ADFJ(2, 3), ADH4, ADGH1	22,29,46,82,100,144,169,177
100	Silicate	BE, BDH2	BDFJ(2)	50,121,177,178
101	Sulfate	BE, BDH2	BDFJ(1, 3), BDH3, BDH4, BDG	18*,29,35,58,79,96,177
102	Sulfide	ADG(to SO₄²⁻)	ADH1	29,177
103	Tellurite	BE, BDH2	BDH3, BDFK(2, 1)[2]	73,74,78,83,173,177,196
104	Thiocyanate	ADH2	ADH3, ADFJ	29,60,61,177
105	Thiosulfate	BE, BDH2	BDGH2(to SO₄²⁻), BDFJ	79,131,177
106	Tungstate	BE, BDH2	BDH4, BDFK(1, 2)	1,53-55,78,89,165,205
107	Vanadate	BE, BDH2	BDH4, BDFK(1, 2, 3)	78,165,171,177

[1] Ions which are well, or moderately well, absorbed when given orally may be expected to follow the same pathways when given parenterally. [2] Ion has a notable tendency to concentrate in a special tissue, such as eye, thyroid, or testis.

[3] As judged from the position of the element in the periodic table, or from the solubility of its compounds at physiological pH values, or both.

Contributor: McChesney, E. W.

References
[1] Aamodt, R. L. 1973. Health Phys. 24:519.
[2] Aeberhardt, A., et al. 1962. Int. J. Radiat. Biol. 5: 217.
[3] Aikawa, J. K., et al. 1959. Amer. J. Physiol. 197: 99.
[4] Anghileri, L. J. 1967. Acta Isotop. 7:281.
[5] Anghileri, L. J. 1971. J. Eur. Toxicol. 3:81.
[6] Atherton, D. R., and R. D. Lloyd. 1972. Health Phys. 22:675.
[7] Ballou, J. E., et al. 1962. Ibid. 8:685.
[8] Ballou, J. E., et al. 1972. Ibid. 22:857.
[9] Barnaby, C. F., et al. 1968. Phys. Med. Biol. 13: 421.
[10] Beck, G. 1948. Mikrochem. Ver. Mikrochim. Acta 34:62.
[11] Bell, M. C., et al. 1967. Proc. 7th Int. Congr. Nutr. 5:765 (Chem. Abstr. 70:26761, 1969).
[12] Bergman, B. 1970. Acta Radiol. Ther. Phys. Biol. 9:420.
[13] Bergman, B., and R. Soremark. 1968. J. Nutr. 94:6.

continued

[14] Berke, H. L. 1968. Health Phys. 15:301.

[15] Berke, H. L. 1969. U.S. At. Energy Comm. Rep. COD-1630-10 (Chem. Abstr. 71:110973).

[16] Berlin, M., and S. Ullberg. 1963. Arch. Environ. Health 6:589.

[17] Berlin, M., and S. Ullberg. 1963. Ibid. 7:686.

[18] Berry, R. K., et al. 1969. J. Nutr. 97:399.

[19] Brown, J. R., et al. 1967. Med. Serv. J. Can. 23:1089.

[20] Buldakov, L. A. 1968. Radiobiologiya 8:62.

[21] Burch, G. E., et al. 1965. Proc. Soc. Exp. Biol. Med. 118:581.

[22] Byard, J. L. 1969. Arch. Biochem. Biophys. 130:556.

[23] Campbell, J. E., et al. 1956. Radiat. Res. 4:294.

[24] Cartier, P. 1967. Traite Biochim. Gen. 3:495.

[25] Chertok, R. J., et al. 1968. Health Phys. 15:519.

[26] Chutkow, J. G. 1964. J. Lab. Clin. Med. 63:80.

[27] Chutkow, J. G. 1965. Ibid. 65:912.

[28] Cohn, S. H., et al. 1968. J. Nutr. 94:261.

[29] Comar, C. L., and F. Bronner, ed. 1962. Miner. Metab. 2(B).

[30] Compere, R., et al. 1968. An. Cient. 6:53 (Chem. Abstr. 73:163758, 1970).

[31] Coons, C. M. 1964. Annu. Rev. Biochem. 33:459.

[32] Cuddihy, R. G., and B. B. Boecker. 1970. Health Phys. 19:419.

[33] Daigneault, E. A. 1963. Toxicol. Appl. Pharmacol. 5:331.

[34] Danowski, T. S., and J. R. Elkinton. 1951. Pharmacol. Rev. 3:42.

[35] Davis, G. K., and J. K. Loosli. 1954. Annu. Rev. Biochem. 23:459.

[36] Dennis, M. D., and M. R. Sikov. 1969. Comp. Biochem. Physiol. 30:169.

[37] Dost, F. M., et al. 1970. Toxicol. Appl. Pharmacol. 17:573.

[38] Dounce, A. L. 1949. In C. Voegtlin and H. C. Hodge, ed. Pharmacology and Toxicology of Uranium Compounds. McGraw-Hill, New York. pp. 951-991 (Chem. Abstr. 43:9239, 1949).

[39] Dowdy, R. P., et al. 1969. Proc. Soc. Exp. Biol. Med. 130:1294.

[40] Dreyfus, J. C. 1967. Traite Biochim. Gen. 3:545.

[41] Dreyfus, J. C. 1967. Ibid. 3:562.

[42] Dreyfus, J. C. 1967. Ibid. 3:569.

[43] Dreyfus, J. C. 1967. Ibid. 3:578.

[44] Dreyfus, J. C. 1967. Ibid. 3:582.

[45] Dreyfus, J. C. 1967. Ibid. 3:609.

[46] Dreyfus, J. C. 1967. Ibid. 3:614.

[47] Dreyfus, J. C. 1967. Ibid. 3:619.

[48] Dreyfus, J. C. 1967. Ibid. 3:622.

[49] Dreyfus, J. C. 1967. Ibid. 3:623.

[50] Dreyfus, J. C. 1967. Ibid. 3:624.

[51] Dreyfus, J. C. 1967. Ibid. 3:625.

[52] Durakovic, A. B., et al. 1973. Health Phys. 24:541.

[53] Durbin, P. W., et al. 1956. Proc. Soc. Exp. Biol. Med. 91:78.

[54] Durbin, P. W., et al. 1956. U.S. At. Energy Comm. UCRL-3607.

[55] Durbin, P. W., et al. 1957. Univ. Calif. Berkeley Publ. Pharmacol. 3(1):1.

[56] Durbin, P. W., et al. 1972. Health Phys. 22:731.

[57] Edstrom, R. 1959. Acta Psychiat. Neurol. Scand. 34:26.

[58] Everett, N. B., and B. S. Simmons. 1952. Arch. Biochem. Biophys. 35:152.

[59] Fleshman, D. G., et al. 1971. Health Phys. 21:385.

[60] Funderburk, C. F., and L. van Middlesworth. 1967. Amer. J. Physiol. 213:1371.

[61] Funderburk, C. F., and L. van Middlesworth. 1968. Ibid. 215:147.

[62] Furchner, J. E., and G. A. Drake. 1971. Health Phys. 21:173.

[63] Furchner, J. E., et al. 1971. Ibid. 21:355.

[64] Furchner, J. E., et al. 1973. Ibid. 24:293.

[65] Galibin, G. P. 1969. Radioaktiv. Izotopy Org., p. 122 (Chem. Abstr. 72:63378, 1970).

[66] Gavend, M., et al. 1969. Comm. Energie At. (Fr.) Rapp. CEA-R-3703 (Chem. Abstr. 70:112141).

[67] Gensicke, F., and H. W. Nitschke. 1970. Radiobiol. Radiother. (Berlin) 11:57.

[68] Gensicke, F., et al. 1963. Fortschr. Geb. Roentgenstr. Nuklearmed. 98:338.

[69] Glaubitt, D., et al. 1971. Proc. 1st Eur. Biophys. Congr. 2:305 (Chem. Abstr. 76:82958, 1972).

[70] Goodman, L. S., and A. Gilman, ed. 1970. The Pharmacological Basis of Therapeutics. Ed. 4. Macmillan, New York.

[71] Grigorescu, S., and K. M. Weber. 1969. Atomkernenergie 14:147 (Chem. Abstr. 70:112155).

[72] Haley, T. J. 1965. J. Pharm. Sci. 54:667.

[73] Hamilton, J. G. 1947. Radiology 49:325.

[74] Hamilton, J. G. 1950. N. Engl. J. Med. 240:863.

[75] Hamilton, J. G., et al. 1953. Univ. Calif. Berkeley Publ. Pharmacol. 2:283.

[76] Hammarsten, L., and A. Nilsson. 1970. Acta Radiol. Ther. Phys. Biol. 9:433.

[77] Harrold, G. C., et al. 1943. J. Ind. Hyg. Toxicol. 25:233.

[78] Heffter, A., ed. 1927-35. Handb. Exp. Pharmakol., Bd. 3.

[79] Heffter, A., ed. 1950. Ibid., Bd. 10.

[80] Hermann, M. W., and A. J. Clark. 1973. Arch. Environ. Health 26:260.

continued

[81] Hiles, R. A. 1973. Toxicol. Appl. Pharmacol. 25: 474.

[82] Hirooka, T., and J. T. Galambos. 1966. Proc. Soc. Exp. Biol. Med. 121:743.

[83] Hollins, J. G. 1969. Health Phys. 17:497.

[84] Hor, G., et al. 1972. Int. J. Appl. Radiat. Isotop. 23:595.

[85] Hungate, F. P., et al. 1972. Health Phys. 22:653.

[86] Hurd, L. C., et al. 1933. Proc. Soc. Exp. Biol. Med. 30:96.

[87] Hursch, J. B. 1951. J. Pharmacol. Exp. Ther. 103: 450.

[88] Inaba, J., et al. 1968. Radioisotopes 17:1511 (Chem. Abstr. 69:41552).

[89] Kaye, S. V. 1968. Health Phys. 15:399.

[90] Kittle, C. F. 1951. Proc. Soc. Exp. Biol. Med. 76: 278.

[91] Klaassen, C. D. 1973. Toxicol. Appl. Pharmacol. 25:475.

[92] Kleeman, C. R., and F. H. Epstein. Proc. Soc. Exp. Biol. Med. 93:228.

[93] Kleeman, C. R., et al. 1955. Amer. J. Physiol. 182: 548.

[94] Konikowski, T., et al. 1973. J. Nucl. Med. 14:164.

[95] Konitzer, K., and K. Michalke. 1965. Acta Biol. Med. Ger. 14:489.

[96] Kulwich, R., et al. 1957. J. Nutr. 61:113.

[97] Lal, S., and T. Sourkes. 1971. Toxicol. Appl. Pharmacol. 20:269.

[98] Lanz, H., Jr., et al. 1950. Univ. Calif. Berkeley Publ. Pharmacol. 2:263.

[99] Liniecki, J. 1971. Health Phys. 21:267.

[100] Lipinski, S., and L. Sluzewa. 1968. Rocz. Panstw. Zakl. Hig. 19:405 (Chem. Abstr. 70:26944, 1969).

[101] Lloyd, R. D., et al. 1970. Health Phys. 18:149.

[102] Lloyd, R. D., et al. 1972. Ibid. 22:667.

[103] Lucis, O. J., and R. Lucis. 1969. Arch. Environ. Health 19:334.

[104] Lund, A. 1956. Acta Pharmacol. Toxicol. 12:251.

[105] Mackenzie, R. D., et al. 1959. Arch. Biochem. Biophys. 79:200.

[106] Magnusson, G. 1963. Acta Pharmacol. Toxicol. 20(Suppl. 3):25.

[107] Magos, L., and Ts. Stoichev. 1969. Brit. J. Pharmacol. 35:121.

[108] Mahlum, D. D., and M. R. Sikov. 1968. Health Phys. 14:127.

[109] Mahlum, D. D., and M. R. Sikov. 1971. Proc. 9th Rare Earth Res. Conf. 2:537.

[110] Maynard, L. A., and S. E. Smith. 1947. Annu. Rev. Biochem. 16:273.

[111] Mays, C. W., and T. F. Dougherty. 1972. Health Phys. 22:793.

[112] McClure, F. J. 1949. Annu. Rev. Biochem. 18:335.

[113] McNeill, R. G., et al. 1973. Health Phys. 24:403.

[114] Mearrick, P. T., and S. P. Mistilis. 1970. J. Lab. Clin. Med. 74:421.

[115] Meek, S. F., et al. 1943. Ind. Med. 12:447.

[116] Merville, R., et al. 1967. Bull. Pharm. Soc. Lille, p. 103 (Chem. Abstr. 68:94311, 1968).

[117] Mewhinney, J. A., et al. 1972. Health Phys. 22: 695.

[118] Miller, J. K., and W. F. Byrne. 1970. J. Nutr. 100: 1287.

[119] Miller, V. L., and E. Csonka. 1968. Toxicol. Appl. Pharmacol. 13:207.

[120] Miller, W. J., et al. 1968. J. Dairy Sci. 51:1386.

[121] Mohn, G. 1968. Beitr. Silikose-Forsch. 94:25 (Chem. Abstr. 68:112802).

[122] Morgan, B. N., et al. 1970. Amer. Ind. Hyg. Ass. J. 31:479.

[123] Morgan, R. H., et al. 1954. Amer. J. Med. Sci. 227:572.

[124] Morin, M., et al. 1973. Health Phys. 24:311.

[125] Moroz, B. B., and Yu. D. Parfenov. 1972. At. Energy Rev. 10:175 (Chem. Abstr. 77:136867).

[126] Moskalev, Yu. I., and L. Buldakov. 1968. Health Phys. 15:229.

[127] Mraz, F. R., and H. Patrick. 1957. Proc. Soc. Exp. Biol. Med. 94:409.

[128] Mraz, F. R., and H. Patrick. 1957. J. Nutr. 61: 535.

[129] Mraz, F. R., and H. Patrick. 1957. Arch. Biochem. Biophys. 71:121.

[130] Mraz, F. R., et al. 1957. Ibid. 66:177.

[131] Mudge, G. H., et al. 1969. Amer. J. Physiol. 216: 843.

[132] Mukhin, J. E. 1967. Vop. Exsp. Klin. Radiol. 3: 231 (Chem. Abstr. 69:16673, 1968).

[133] Muro, T., and K. Koecke. 1967. Endokrinologie 52:88.

[134] Nelson, N. S., and J. H. Rust. 1967. Chem. Abstr. 67:50881.

[135] Nelson, N. S., and J. H. Rust. 1968. Ibid. 68:667.

[136] Nénot, J. C., et al. 1967. Radioprotection 2:297.

[137] Nénot, J. C., et al. 1970. Health Phys. 18:613.

[138] Nénot, J. C., et al. 1971. Ibid. 20:167.

[139] Nénot, J. C., et al. 1972. Ibid. 23:635.

[140] Nordberg, G. J. 1972. Environ. Physiol. Biochem. 2:7.

[141] Oldendorf, W. H., et al. 1970. J. Nucl. Med. 11:85.

[142] Owen, C. A., Jr. 1964. Amer. J. Physiol. 207:466.

[143] Owen, C. A., Jr., and J. B. Hazelrig. 1968. Birth Defects Orig. Artic. Ser. 4:1 (Chem. Abstr. 70: 75701, 1969).

[144] Palmer, I. S., et al. 1969. Biochim. Biophys. Acta 177:336.

continued

[145] Parker, H. G., et al. 1972. Health Phys. 22:647.

[146] Pate, F. M., et al. 1970. Proc. Soc. Exp. Biol. Med. 135:653.

[147] Pavlovskaya, N. A., et al. 1971. Gig. Sanit. 36:47 (Chem. Abstr. 75:45380).

[148] Perey, M., and A. Chevallier. 1951. C. R. Soc. Biol. 145:1205.

[149] Picard, J. 1967. Traite Biochim. Gen. 3:455.

[150] Popov, T., and R. Angelieva. 1969. Gig. Sanit. 34:78 (Chem. Abstr. 70:85813).

[151] Prasad, A. S., ed. 1969. Amer. J. Clin. Nutr. Symp. 22:10.

[152] Roda, J. E., et al. 1969. J. Nucl. Med. 10:205.

[153] Romney, E. M., et al. 1970. Health Phys. 19:487.

[154] Rosen, J. C., et al. 1972. Ibid. 22:621.

[155] Rosenfeld, G. 1954. Arch. Biochem. Biophys. 48:84.

[156] Rosenthal, M. W., et al. 1972. Health Phys. 22:743.

[157] Rosenthal, M. W., et al. 1972. Ibid. 23:231.

[158] Saratikov, A. S., et al. 1971. Zh. Nevropatol. Psikhiat. S. S. Korsakova 17:1709 (Chem. Abstr. 76:68865, 1972).

[159] Sastry, V. V., et al. 1963. Fed. Proc. Fed. Amer. Soc. Exp. Biol. 22:540.

[160] Scandellari, C., and N. Conte. 1963. Acta Isotop. 3:71.

[161] Schou, M. 1957. Pharmacol. Rev. 9:17.

[162] Schroeder, H. A., et al. 1968. J. Nutr. 96:37.

[163] Schroeder, H. A., et al. 1970. Ibid. 100:59.

[164] Schubert, J., et al. 1952. J. Biol. Chem. 196:279.

[165] Scott, K. G. Unpublished. San Rafael, Calif., 1973.

[166] Scott, K. G., and J. G. Hamilton. 1950. Univ. Calif. Berkeley Publ. Pharmacol. 2:241.

[167] Scott, K. G., et al. 1948. J. Biol. Chem. 175:691.

[168] Seidel, A., and V. Volf. 1972. Health Phys. 22:779.

[169] Shearer, T. R., and D. M. Hadjimarkos. 1973. J. Nutr. 103:553.

[170] Shiraishi, Y., and R. Ichikawa. 1972. Health Phys. 22:373.

[171] Shohl, A. T. 1939. Mineral Metabolism. Reinhold, New York.

[172] Singer, L., et al. 1967. Isr. J. Med. Sci. 3:714.

[173] Slouka, V. 1971. Chem. Abstr. 75:59454.

[174] Smith, F. A. 1966. Handb. Exp. Pharmakol. 20:53.

[175] Smith, V. H. 1972. Health Phys. 22:765.

[176] Smith, V. H. 1973. Ibid. 23:31.

[177] Sollman, T. 1957. A Manual of Pharmacology. Ed. 8. W. B. Saunders, Philadelphia.

[178] Soroka, V. R. 1965. Arkh. Patol. 27:58 (Chem. Abstr. 64:2564, 1966).

[179] Spode, E., and F. Gensicke. 1958. Naturwissenschaften 45:135.

[180] Stannard, J. N., and F. A. Smith. 1964. Radiat. Res. Suppl. 5:166.

[181] Stara, J. F., et al. 1971. Intest. Absorp. Metal Ions Trace Elem. Radionucl. Symp., p. 307 (Chem. Abstr. 76:82961, 1972).

[182] Stather, J. W. 1970. Health Phys. 18:43.

[183] Suzuki, S., et al. 1967. Jap. J. Pharmacol. 17:393.

[184] Swensson, A., and U. Ulfvarson. 1968. Acta Pharmacol. Toxicol. 26:273.

[185] Tannenbaum, A., ed. 1951. Toxicology of Uranium. McGraw-Hill, New York. pp. 105, 109, 124, 128 (Chem. Abstr. 45:6748).

[186] Taylor, D. M. 1962. Health Phys. 8:679.

[187] Taylor, D. M. 1964. Brit. J. Radiol. 37:95.

[188] Taylor, D. M. 1969. Ibid. 42:44.

[189] Taylor, D. M. 1969. Health Phys. 19:411.

[190] Teisinger, J., et al. 1967. Pr. Lek. 19:251 (Chem. Abstr. 68:20593, 1968).

[191] Thomas, R. G., et al. 1968. Amer. Ind. Hyg. Ass. J. 29:253.

[192] Thompson, R. C., and O. L. Hollis. 1956. U.S. At. Energy Comm. Publ. HW-45546 (Chem. Abstr. 51:6884, 1957).

[193] Thompson, R. C., et al. 1958. Amer. J. Roentgenol. Radium Ther. Nucl. Med. 79:1026.

[194] Tichy, M., and M. Cikrt. 1972. Arch. Toxikol. 29:51.

[195] Timofeeva-Resovskaya, E. A., et al. 1971. Chem. Abstr. 74:61424.

[196] Tregubenko, I. P. 1961. Ibid. 55:1922.

[197] Tsutsumi, S. 1971. Nippon Shonika Gakkai Zasshi 75:897 (Chem. Abstr. 78:81583, 1973).

[198] Tsutsumi, S. 1972. Shika Gakuho 72:1 (Chem. Abstr. 78:817, 1973).

[199] Underwood, E. J. 1959. Annu. Rev. Biochem. 28:499.

[200] Vacher, J., and H. B. Stoner. 1968. Brit. J. Exp. Pathol. 49:315.

[201] Vallee, B. L. 1959. Physiol. Rev. 39:443.

[202] Vallee, B. L., and D. D. Ulmer. 1972. Annu. Rev. Biochem. 41:91.

[203] Visek, W. J., et al. 1953. Proc. Soc. Exp. Biol. Med. 84:610.

[204] Warren, J. M., and H. Spencer. 1971. Radiat. Res. 48:578.

[205] Wase, A. W. 1956. Arch. Biochem. Biophys. 61:272.

[206] Wase, A. W., et al. 1954. Ibid. 51:1.

[207] Widdowson, E. M. 1950. Nature (London) 166:626.

[208] Widdowson, E. M., and R. A. McCance. 1944. Proc. Nutr. Soc. 1:220.

[209] Zalikin, G. A. 1970. Chem. Abstr. 72:63377.

[210] Zalikin, G. A., et al. 1968. Radiobiologiya 8:65.

[211] Zalikin, G. A., et al. 1972. Ibid. 12:894.

The following pathways represent mainly mammalian lipid metabolism. Broken lines indicate hypothetical pathways. *Abbreviations:* ATP = adenosine 5'-triphosphate; GTP = guanosine 5'-triphosphate; CDP = cytidine 5'-diphosphate; UDP = uridine 5'-diphosphate; PAPS = phosphoadenosine phosphosulfate; NAD$^+$ and NADH = nicotinamide adenine dinucleotide (oxidized and reduced forms, respectively); NADPH = nicotinamide adenine dinucleotide phosphate (reduced form); FAD = flavin adenine dinucleotide; CoA = coenzyme A; ACP = acyl carrier protein.

FATTY ACID METABOLISM

REACTIONS

A: Occurs in mitochondria

B: Occurs in cytoplasm with soluble enzymes

C: Requires biotin, ATP, Mg^{2+}, & HCO$_3^-$; citrate & isocitrate enhance carboxylation of acetyl CoA by complexing with and activating the carboxylase enzyme

D: β-Oxidation in mitochondria; carnitine esters are involved in transporting fatty acids into mitochondria; requires FAD & NAD$^+$; ATP or GTP may participate in preliminary extramitochondrial formation of fatty acyl CoA

E: Involves transacylases, ACP's β-ketoacyl-ACP synthetase, β-ketoacyl-ACP reductase, β-hydroxyacyl-ACP dehydrase, & enoyl-ACP reductase; requires NADPH (furnished mainly by pentose phosphate pathway and by oxidation of oxalacetate to pyruvate via malic acid; NADH required for the latter produced through glycolysis); yields mainly palmitic acid

F: Occurs in microsomes

G: Includes chain elongation in microsomes involving malonyl CoA & fatty acyl CoA (analogous to de novo synthesis), chain elongation in mitochondria involving acetyl CoA & fatty acyl CoA, shortening of carbon chain by 2 carbons in microsomes, and desaturation of fatty acyl CoA coupled with chain elongation to yield polyunsaturated acids (requires NADH or NADPH) in microsomes

H: Involves mainly pancreatic & intestinal lipases and bile salts in intestinal lumen

I: ω-Oxidation in intestinal lumen

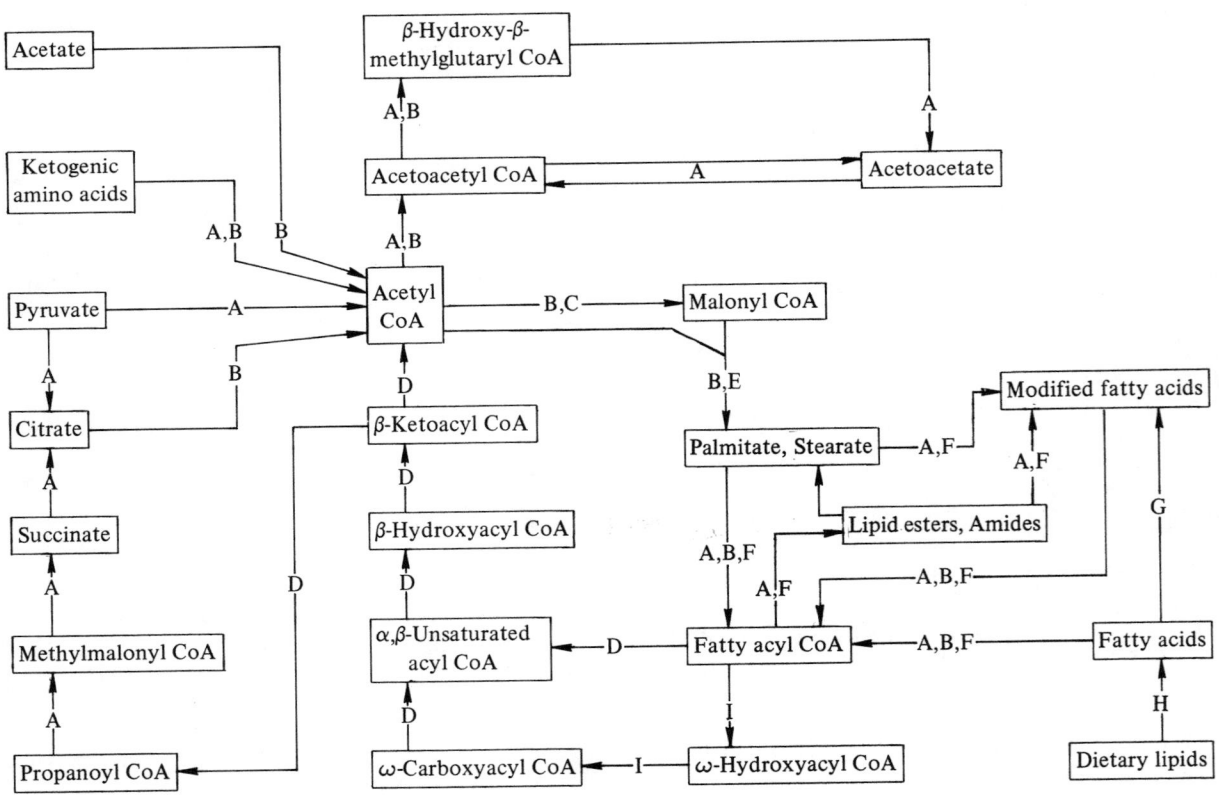

continued

191. PATHWAYS OF LIPID METABOLISM: MAMMALS

GLYCEROLIPID METABOLISM

REACTIONS		
A: Occurs in microsomes	glycerides	J: Occurs in plants
B: Occurs in mitochondria	G: Occurs in the intestinal lumen	K: Requires cholesterol as a fatty
C: Occurs in cytoplasm with soluble enzymes	H: Acylation involves mainly a primary hydroxyl group; occurs in microsomes of the intestinal mucosa & mammary glands	acid receiver; occurs in microsomes, mitochondria, lysosomes, & cell membrane of intestinal lumen & plants, and in blood plasma
D: Occurs in lysosomes		
E: Occurs in cell membrane		
F: 1,2-Diglycerides, but not 1,3-di-	I: Occurs in microsomes of brain	

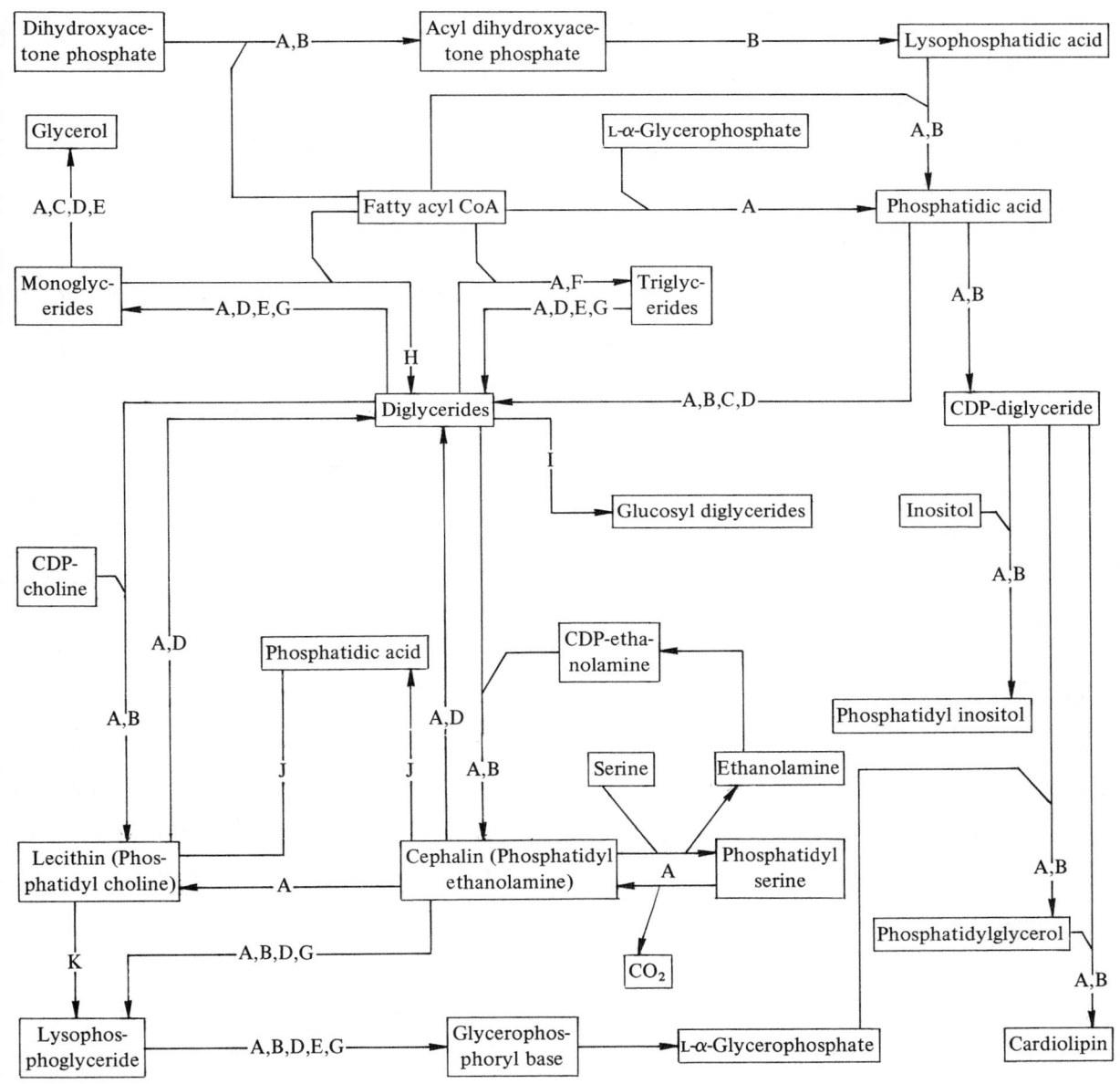

continued

SPHINGOLIPID METABOLISM

REACTIONS	
A: Occurs in microsomes	C: Requires Mn^{2+} & pyridoxal 5-phosphate
B: Requires NADPH	D: Requires a flavoprotein dehydrogenase

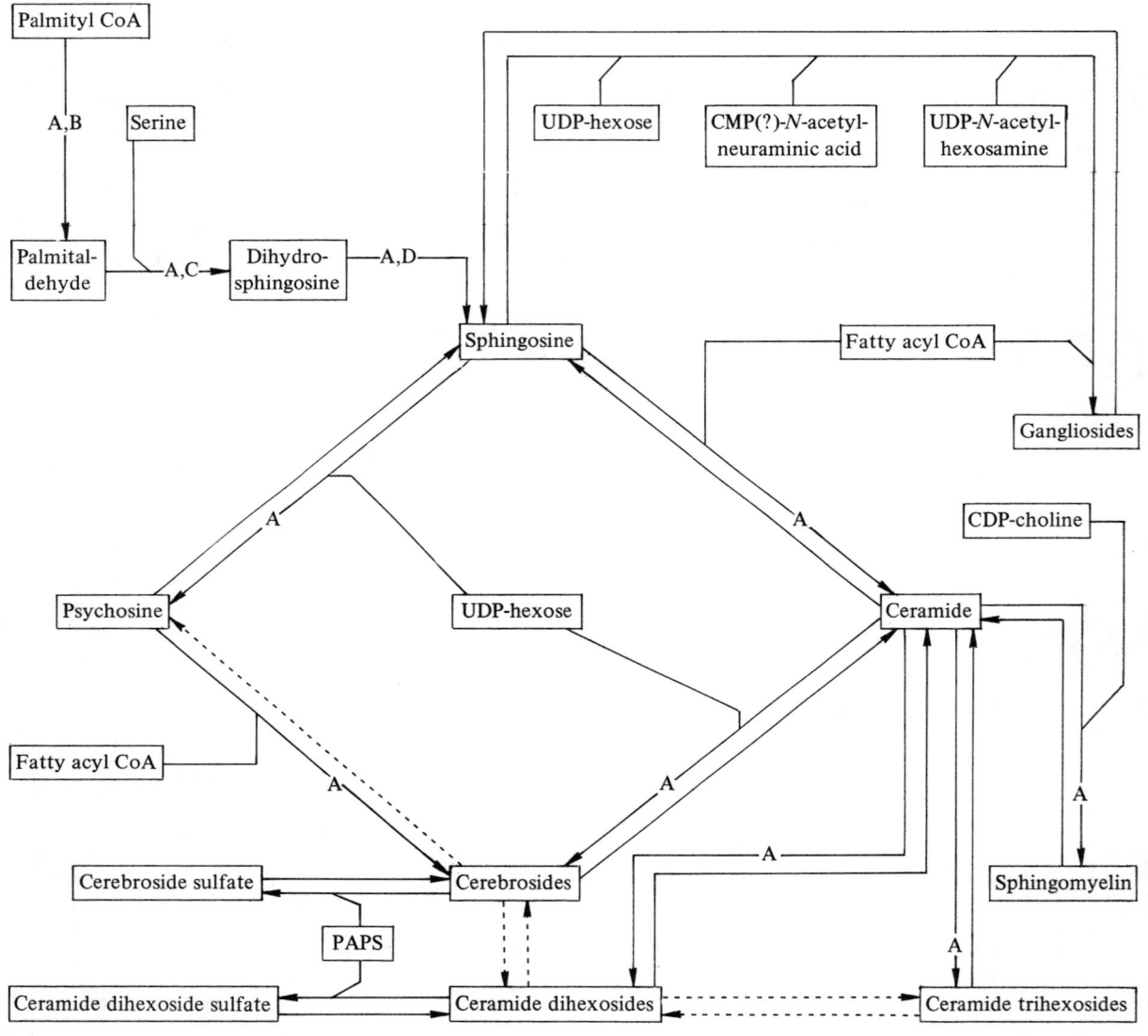

continued

STEROL METABOLISM

REACTIONS

A: Occurs in mitochondria
B: Occurs in microsomes
C: Requires NADPH; not reversible; a target process in control of biosynthesis
D: Occurs in cytoplasm with solu-

ble enzymes
E: Requires biotin, ATP, Mg^{2+}, & HCO_3^-; citrate & isocitrate enhance carboxylation of acetyl CoA by complexing with and activating the carboxylase en-

zyme
F: Requires ATP & Mn^{2+}
G: Requires NADPH & O_2
H: Occurs in blood plasma
I: Requires lecithin as the acyl donor

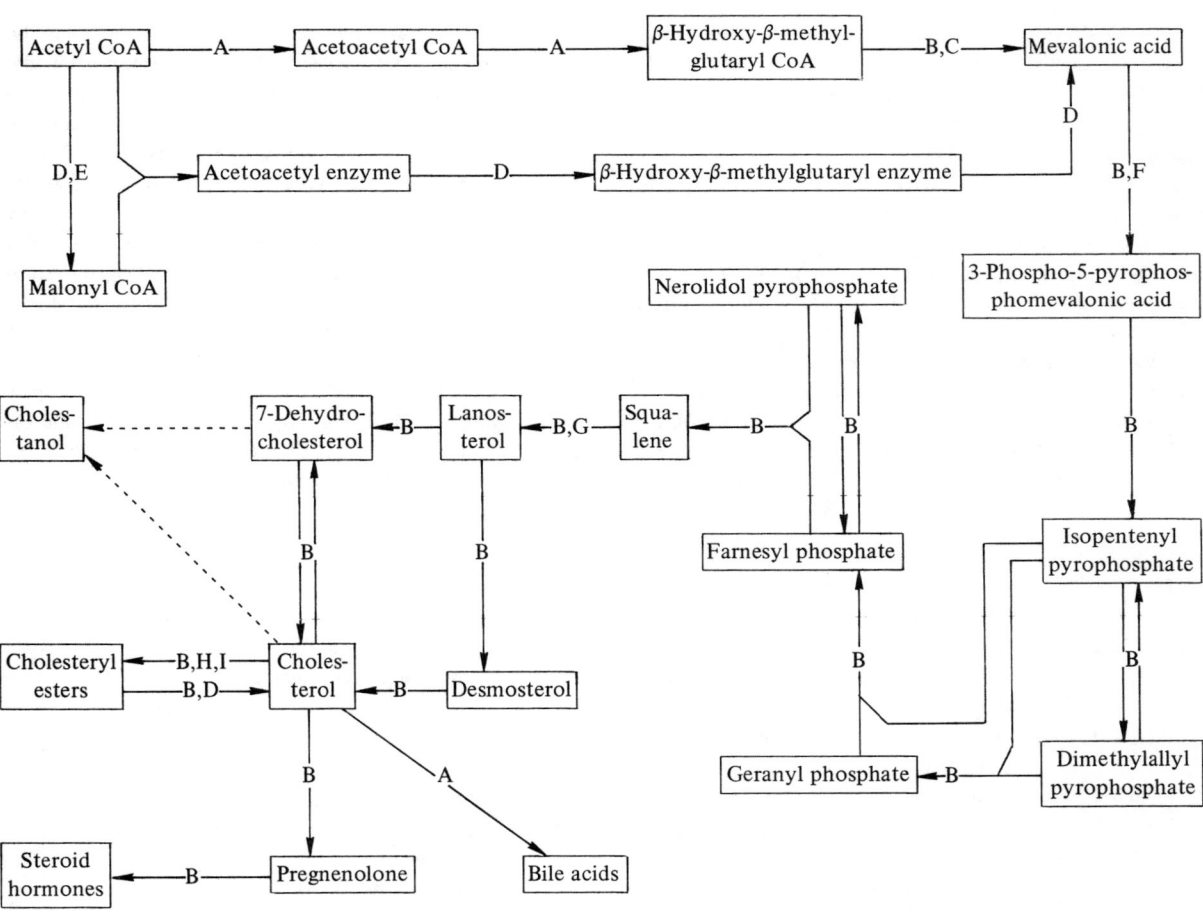

Contributor: Ellefson, Ralph D.

continued

191. PATHWAYS OF LIPID METABOLISM: MAMMALS

General References

[1] Ansell, G. B., and J. N. Hawthorne. 1964. Phospholipids. Elsevier, New York.

[2] Bloor, W. R. 1943. Biochemistry of the Fatty Acids. Reinhold, New York.

[3] Cornforth, J. W. 1959. J. Lipid Res. 1:3.

[4] Masoro, E. J. 1968. Physiological Chemistry of Lipids in Mammals. W. B. Saunders, Philadelphia.

[5] Paoletti, R., and D. Kritchevsky, ed. 1963. Advan. Lipid Res. 1.

[6] Paoletti, R., and D. Kritchevsky, ed. 1964. Ibid. 2.

[7] Paoletti, R., and D. Kritchevsky, ed. 1965. Ibid. 3.

[8] Paoletti, R., and D. Kritchevsky, ed. 1967. Ibid. 5.

[9] Paoletti, R., and D. Kritchevsky, ed. 1970. Ibid. 8.

[10] Schettler, G., ed. 1967. Lipids and Lipidoses. J. Springer, New York.

[11] Wakil, S. J., ed. 1970. Lipid Metabolism. Academic Press, New York.

192. PATHWAYS OF CARBOHYDRATE METABOLISM

The conversion of stored or ingested carbohydrate to pyruvate releases stored energy by means of anaerobic oxidation (glycolysis). Released energy is partly dissipated as heat and partly stored (temporarily) in the labile energy pool as high-energy phosphate ($\sim PO_4$) by combination of $\sim PO_4$ with continuously available ADP (adenosine 5'-diphosphate) to form ATP (adenosine 5'-triphosphate). In the conversion of 1 mole of glucose (180 grams), or of other monosaccharides, to 2 moles of pyruvate (174 grams), 2 moles of ATP are converted to ADP and 4 moles of ATP are formed from ADP, making a net gain of 2 moles of ATP, or approximately 14 kilocalories of readily available energy. If glucose-6-PO_4 has come from the metabolic breakdown of glycogen, the cost is only 1 mole of ATP, making a net gain of 3 moles of ATP (approximately 21 kilocalories). The ATP is an immediate source of energy, the utilization of which (e.g., for muscular activity) is independent of the oxygen supply. Aerobic oxidation of the reduced coenzymes formed in glycolysis and in the citric acid cycle (*see* Table 196) yields considerable amounts of energy. The reactions may be summarized as follows: glucose + 2 ATP → 2 pyruvate + 8 ATP; 2 pyruvate → 2 acetyl CoA (coenzyme A) + 6 ATP; 2 acetyl CoA → 4 CO_2 + 4 H_2O + 24 ATP; a total of 38 ATP. The complete oxidation of glucose to carbon dioxide and water releases 685.5 kilocalories of energy. The ADP system traps 266 (38 × 7) kilocalories of this energy, resulting in a possible storage of 39% (266/685) of the energy in the form of ATP. *Abbreviations:* NAD$^+$ and NADH = nicotinamide-adenine dinucleotide (oxidized and reduced forms, respectively); AMP = adenosine monophosphate; P_i = inorganic orthophosphate; PP_i = inorganic pyrophosphate; UDP = uridine diphosphate; UTP = uridine triphosphate.

ENZYME KEY [COFACTOR]

1.1.1.1 = alcohol dehydrogenase [NAD$^+$, NADH]	2.7.2.3 = phosphoglycerate kinase [Mg^{2+}]
1.1.1.27 = L-lactate dehydrogenase [NAD$^+$, NADH]	2.7.5.1 = phosphoglucomutase
1.1.99.5 = glycerolphosphate dehydrogenase [NAD$^+$, NADH]	2.7.5.3 = phosphoglyceromutase
1.2.1.12 = glyceraldehydephosphate dehydrogenase [NAD$^+$, NADH]	2.7.7.9 = glucose-1-phosphate uridylyltransferase (UDPglucose pyrophosphorylase)
2.4.1.1 = α-glucan phosphorylase [AMP, Mg^{2+}, P_i]	3.1.3.9 = glucose-6-phosphatase
2.4.1.21 = UDPglucose-starch glucosyltransferase	3.1.3.11 = hexosediphosphatase [Mg^{2+}]
2.7.1.1 = hexokinase [Mg^{2+}]	3.1.3.X = phosphoglycerol phosphatase
2.7.1.3 = ketohexokinase [Mg^{2+}]	3.2.1.1 = α-amylase
2.7.1.4 = fructokinase [Mg^{2+}]	4.1.1.1 = pyruvate decarboxylase [Mg^{2+}]
2.7.1.6 = galactokinase [Mg^{2+}]	4.1.2.13 = fructosediphosphate aldolase
2.7.1.7 = mannokinase [Mg^{2+}]	4.2.1.11 = phosphopyruvate hydratase [Mg^{2+}]
2.7.1.11 = phosphofructokinase [Mg^{2+}]	5.1.3.2 = UDPglucose epimerase [Mg^{2+}, UDP-glucose]
2.7.1.30 = glycerol kinase [Mg^{2+}]	5.3.1.1 = triosephosphate isomerase
2.7.1.40 = pyruvate kinase [K$^+$, Mg^{2+}]	5.3.1.8 = mannosephosphate isomerase
	5.3.1.9 = glucosephosphate isomerase

continued

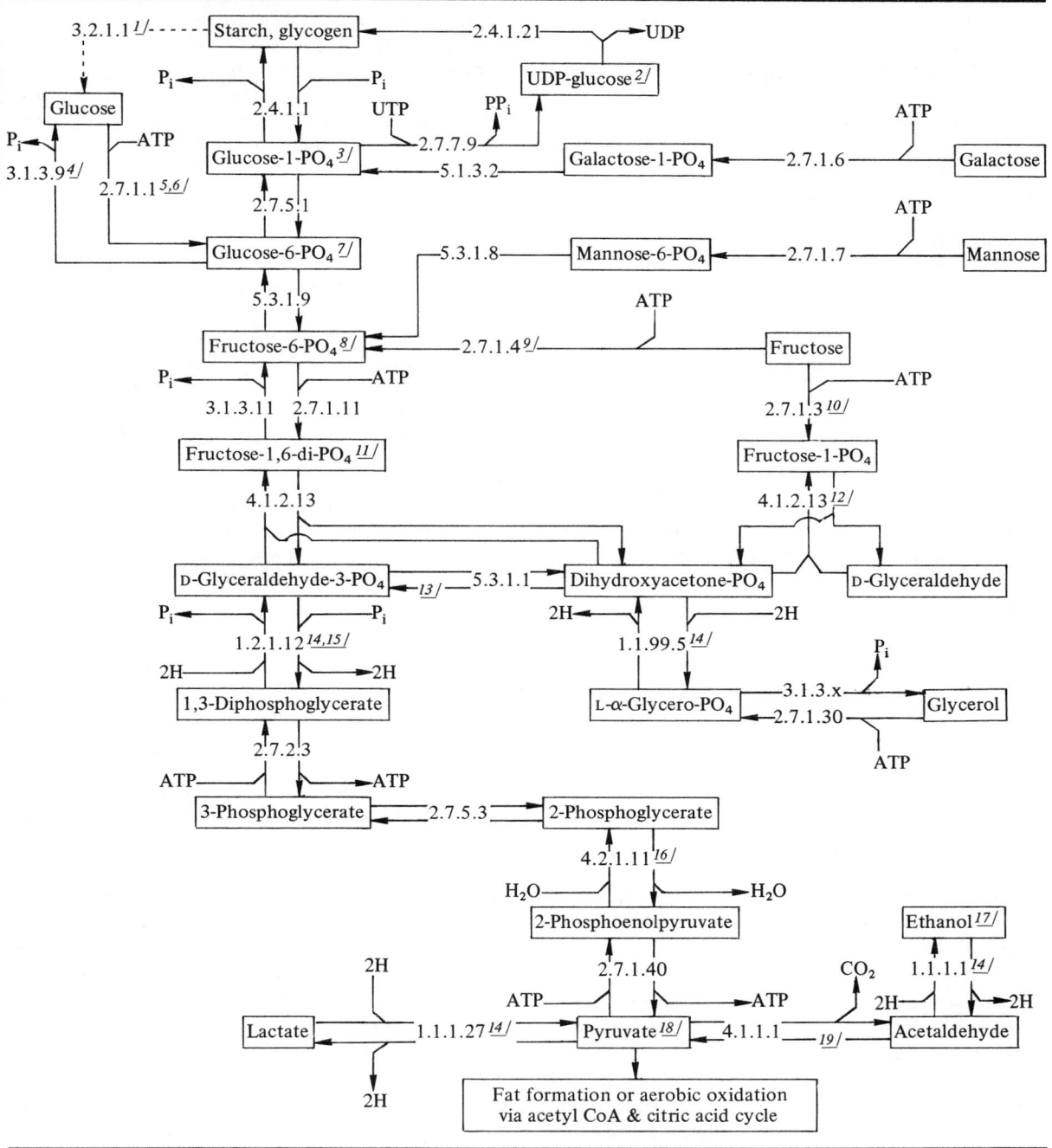

[1] Digestion; glycogen and/or starch are hydrolyzed to glucose in the intestinal lumen. [2] In plants, ADP glucose is more efficiently utilized for starch synthesis than UDP glucose. [3] Cori ester. [4] The reaction, glycogen to glucose-6-PO$_4$ to blood glucose, takes place in the liver only. [5] The reaction, glucose to glucose-6-PO$_4$ to glycogen, takes place in liver, muscle, and other tissues. [6] Reaction assumed to be inhibited by the growth hormone plus a suprarenal cor-

tical hormone; inhibition by these substances is blocked by insulin, thus favoring conversion of glucose to glucose-6-PO$_4$. [7] Robison ester. [8] Neuberg ester. [9] In all tissues. [10] In liver and muscle. [11] Harden-Young ester. [12] Liver aldolase also degrades fructose-1-PO$_4$. [13] This reaction causes each step in the conversion to pyruvate to be doubled quantitatively; thus, 1 mole of glucose gives rise to 2 moles of pyruvate. [14] NAD$^+$ acts as acceptor of released

continued

hydrogen atoms, becoming NADH in the oxidative direction of this reaction. NADH gives up hydrogen atoms and becomes NAD$^+$ in the reverse direction. Hydrogen atoms accepted by NAD$^+$ are passed on in turn to flavoprotein, cytochrome c, cytochrome oxidase, and molecular oxygen (*see* Table 197). If molecular oxygen is not sufficiently available, hydrogen atoms may be passed from NADH to pyruvate to form lactate. [15] Inhibited by iodoacetate. [16] Inhibited by fluoride. [17] End of fermentation in plant tissue. [18] Pyruvate, followed by conversion to lactate when oxygen supply is deficient (*see* footnote 14), ends glycolysis in animal tissues. If oxygen is available, pyruvate is oxidized via the citric acid cycle. [19] Thiamine pyrophosphate required as cofactor in this direction only.

Contributor: Bishop, David W.

General References

[1] Axelrod, B. 1967. In D. M. Greenberg, ed. Metabolic Pathways. Ed. 3. Academic Press, New York. v. 1, pp. 114-145.

[2] Baldwin, E. 1967. Dynamic Aspects of Biochemistry. Ed. 5. Cambridge Univ. Press, New York.

[3] Barman, T. E. 1969. Enzyme Handbook. J. Springer, New York.

[4] Bonner, J., and J. Varner, ed. 1965. Plant Biochemistry. Academic Press, New York.

[5] Cori, G. T., et al. 1951. Biochim. Biophys. Acta 7: 304.

[6] Dickens, F. 1951. In J. B. Sumner and K. Myrbäck, ed. The Enzymes. Academic Press, New York. v. 2, pp. 624-683.

[7] Krebs, H. A. 1949. Advan. Enzymol. 3:191.

[8] Lardy, H. A., ed. 1949. Respiratory Enzymes. Rev. ed. Burgess, Minneapolis.

[9] Mahler, H. R., and E. H. Cordes. 1966. Biological Chemistry. Harper, New York.

[10] Sumner, J. B., and G. F. Somers. 1953. Chemistry and Methods of Enzymes. Ed. 3. Academic Press, New York.

[11] Umbreit, W. W. 1952-60. Metabolic Maps. Burgess, Minneapolis.

[12] Werkman, C. H., and F. Schlenk. 1951. In C. H. Werkman and P. W. Wilson, ed. Bacterial Physiology. Academic Press, New York. pp. 281-324.

[13] West, E. S., et al. 1966. Textbook of Biochemistry. Ed. 4. Macmillan, New York.

193. PATHWAYS OF AMINO ACID METABOLISM

The data include enzymatic reactions, biosynthesis, utilization, and catabolism of amino acids (L-configuration, unless otherwise specified) [11,13,22]. Cofactors for many of the reactions have been omitted.

Metabolism: Two categories are shown—those which occur only in microorganisms and plants, since the resulting amino acids are essential for most animals, and those which occur in almost all living systems. Many of the biosynthetic pathways shown [1,6,9,10,11,13,19,20] are valid primarily for *Escherichia coli* and *Neurospora crassa*; some different pathways in other microorganisms are indicated [4,11]. For areas covered only briefly in this table, consult references 1, 6, 9, 10, 11, 16, 19, and 20. For utilization of amino acids in synthesis of cell constituents other than protein, consult references 11 and 13. For regulation of amino acid catabolism in animals, consult references 5 and 14, and in bacteria, consult references 7, 11, 15, and 17. For amino acid metabolism unique to plants, consult references 3, 8, and 18. For naturally occurring amino acids, consult references 3, 8, and 13. For the role of ferredoxin in amino acid metabolism, consult reference 4. For utilization of amino acids for the biosynthesis of alkaloids, consult reference 12, of antibiotics, consult references 2 and 13, and of peptides, consult references 13 and 21.

Product of Oxidative Deamination or Transamination: The deamination of amino acids in most systems involves transamination of the amino acid with an α-keto acid, usually α-ketoglutarate, to yield the α-keto analogue of the amino acid and glutamate. Glutamate is then oxidatively deaminated by glutamate dehydrogenase to yield ammonia and regenerate α-ketoglutarate. A reversal of the transamination process leads to the formation of many amino acids from their α-keto acids and ammonia. Certain amino acids, e.g., cysteine, histidine, serine, and threonine, may undergo nonoxidative deamination. In certain systems, D- or L-amino acids are involved in deamination reactions.

Decarboxylation: Data in brackets refer to the product of the decarboxylation reaction.

Pathway & Products: Oxidative deamination, transamination, and decarboxylation reactions are not included; only

continued

reactions involving further metabolism, e.g., those in which the carbon chains of the amino acids are metabolized by pathways leading to intermediates in carbohydrate or lipid metabolism, are shown. *Abbreviations:* NAD$^+$ and NADH = nicotinamide-adenine dinucleotide (oxidized and reduced forms, respectively); NADP$^+$ and NADPH = nicotinamide adenine dinucleotide phosphate (oxidized and reduced forms, respectively); CoA = coenzyme A; Fd$_{ox}$ and Fd$_{red}$ = ferredoxin (oxidized and reduced forms, respectively); P$_i$ = inorganic orthophosphate; PP$_i$ = inorganic pyrophosphate; ATP = adenosine 5'-triphosphate; ADP = adenosine 5'-diphosphate; AMP = adenosine 5'-monophosphate; IMP = inosine 5'-monophosphate; THF = tetrahydrofolate; AICAR = 5-amino-1-ribofuranosylimidazole-4-carboxamide 5'-phosphate.

	Amino Acid	Product of Oxidative De-amination or Transamination [Decarboxylation]	Metabolism	
			Type of Pathway	Pathway & Products
1	Alanine	Pyruvate	Biosynthesis	Usually by transamination
2				In *Bacillus subtilis:* Pyruvate + NH$_3$ + NADH + H$^+$ → alanine + NAD$^+$
3				Aspartate (*see* entries 20 & 25) → alanine + CO$_2$
4				In *Chlorobium thiosulfatophilum, Chromatium* D, *Clostridium kluyveri, C. pasteurianum,* & *Rhodospirillum rubrum:* Acetyl CoA + CO$_2$ + Fd$_{red}$ → pyruvate + CoA + Fd$_{ox}$; pyruvate (by transamination) → alanine
5			Utilization	In bacteria: Formation of D-alanine
6			Catabolism	By transamination
7	Arginine[1]	α-Keto-δ-guani-dovalerate [Agmatine]	Biosynthesis	Ornithine + carbamylphosphate → citrulline + P$_i$; citrulline + aspartate + ATP → argininosuccinate + AMP + PP$_i$ → arginine + fumarate
8			Utilization	Key member of ornithine-urea (Krebs-Henseleit) cycle
9				Synthesis of creatine, creatinine, & streptidine group in streptomycin (*see also* Ornithine, entries 102-107)
10			Catabolism	In animals & many microorganisms: Arginine → ornithine + urea
11				In certain microorganisms: Arginine → citrulline + NH$_3$
12				In *Streptomyces griseus:* Arginine → γ-guanidobutyramide → γ-guani-dobutyrate → γ-aminobutyrate → succinic semialdehyde
13	Asparagine	α-Ketosuccina-mate	Biosynthesis	In animal tissues: Aspartate + ATP + glutamine → asparagine + AMP + PP$_i$ + glutamate
14				In lactic acid bacteria: Aspartate + NH$_3$ + ATP → asparagine + AMP + PP$_i$
15				In plants: β-Cyanoalanine → asparagine
16			Utilization	Role in reaction of asparagine-ketoacid aminotransferase (asparagine-α-keto acid transaminase), forming α-ketosuccinamate, oxalacetate, & NH$_3$
17	Aspartic acid	Oxalacetate [α-Alanine]	Biosynthesis	Usually by transamination
18				In a few microorganisms: Reversal of aspartase
19			Utilization	Synthesis of arginine, asparagine, carbamylaspartate, & pyrimidines
20				Formation of α- & β-alanine by 2 different decarboxylase enzymes
21				Source of N-1 of purine ring (*see* Table 203. Pathways of Polynucleotide Biosynthesis, Part I. Purines) in conversion of IMP to AMP (*see* Table 195. Pathways of Nucleoprotein Catabolism)
22				In microorganisms: Synthesis of members of the aspartate biosynthetic family—aspartate → β-aspartylphosphate → aspartic β-semialdehyde → homoserine → *O*-phosphohomoserine → threonine (*see also* Isoleucine, entry 76 & 126, Lysine, entry 84, & Methionine, entry 91)
23			Catabolism	By transamination
24				In some microorganisms: Aspartate ⇌ fumarate + NH$_3$, by aspartase
25				In other bacteria: Aspartate → α- or β-alanine + CO$_2$

[1] Essential amino acid for young animals.

continued

	Amino Acid	Product of Oxidative De-amination or Transamination [Decarboxylation]	Metabolism	
			Type of Pathway	Pathway & Products
26	Citrulline	α-Keto-δ-carbami-dovalerate	Biosynthesis	Ornithine + carbamylphosphate → citrulline + P_i
27				In animals: CO_2 + NH_3 + 2 ATP + H_2O (in the presence of N-acetyl-glutamate) → carbamylphosphate + 2 ADP + P_i + H^+
28				In microorganisms: CO_2 + L-glutamine + 2 ATP → carbamylphosphate + 2 ADP + P_i + glutamate
29			Utilization	*See* Arginine, entry 7
30			Catabolism	In lactic acid bacteria: Citrulline + P_i → ornithine + carbamylphosphate; carbamylphosphate + ADP → carbamic acid + ATP → CO_2 + NH_3 (*see also* Arginine, entry 7)
31	Cysteine & cystine	β-Mercaptopyr-uvate	Biosynthesis	In animals: *see* Methionine (entry 97)
32				In bacteria: Serine + acetyl CoA → O-acetylserine + CoA + H_2S → cysteine + acetate + H_2O
33				In yeast: Serine + H_2S → cysteine + H_2O
34				In *Aspergillus nidulans:* Serine + $S_2O_3^{2-}$ → S-sulfocysteine → cysteine
35			Utilization	Formation of cystine by reversible oxidation
36				Formation of isoethionic acid, glutathione, mercapturic acids, taurine, taurocholic acid, taurocyamine, & cysteamine group in CoA
37			Catabolism	Cysteine → H_2S + NH_3 + pyruvate
38				Cysteine → cysteine sulfinic acid → (i) cysteic acid → CO_2 + taurine, (ii) CO_2 + hypotaurine, (iii) alanine + SO_2, or (iv) β-sulfinylpyruvate (by transamination) → pyruvate + SO_3^{2-}
39				β-Mercaptopyruvate → pyruvate + S
40				To trace compounds in lens: S-(1,2-Dicarboxyethyl)cysteine; to trace compounds in mammalian urines: felinine, isovalthine, homocysteine, homocysteinecysteine, & others
41	Glutamic acid	α-Ketoglutarate [γ-Aminobuty-rate]	Biosynthesis	α-Ketoglutarate + NH_3 + NADH (or NADPH) + H^+ ⇌ glutamate + NAD^+ (or $NADP^+$) + H_2O
42				Formed by catabolism of arginine & ornithine (*see* entries 7, 8, & 102)
43				In *Acetobacter suboxydans:* Glyoxylate & oxalacetate (and/or acetate & pyruvate) condense and, after subsequent transformations, form glutamate
44				In *Chlorobium thiosulfatophilum* & *Rhodospirillum rubrum:* Succinyl CoA + CO_2 + Fd_{red} → α-ketoglutarate + CoA + Fd_{ox}
45				In *Clostridium kluyveri*, some other *Clostridium* spp., & several sulfate-reducing bacteria: An atypical stereospecificity of citrate synthesis leads to an unusual ^{14}C-labeling pattern in glutamate
46			Utilization	In animals & microorganisms: Formation of glutamine & members of the glutamate biosynthetic family (arginine, citrulline, hydroxyproline, ornithine, & proline)
47				In the central nervous system: Formation of γ-aminobutyrate (GABA)
48				In bacteria: Formation of D-glutamate
49			Catabolism	By transamination & the citric acid cycle
50				In microorganisms: Glutamate → γ-aminobutyrate (by decarboxylation)
51				In *Clostridium tetanomorphum:* Glutamate ⇌ β-methylaspartate ⇌ mesaconate ⇌ citramalate ⇌ acetate + pyruvate
52	Glutamine	α-Ketoglutara-mate	Biosynthesis	Glutamate + NH_3 + ATP → glutamine + ADP + P_i + H_2O
53			Utilization	Role in glutamine-ketoacid aminotransferase (glutamine-α-keto acid transaminase)
54				Source of N-3 & N-9 of purine ring, guanylate amino group, & cytidylate amino group (*see* Table 203. Pathways of Polynucleotide Biosynthesis, Part I. Purines.)

continued

	Amino Acid	Product of Oxidative De-amination or Transamination [Decarboxylation]	Metabolism	
			Type of Pathway	Pathway & Products
55				Formation of amide N in asparagine & NAD^+, o-aminobenzoate, carbamylphosphate (see Citrulline, entry 28), glucosamine 6-phosphate, & phenylacetylglutamine
56			Catabolism	Glutamine → glutamate + NH_3
57				Glutamine + α-keto acid → α-ketoglutaramate + α-amino acid → α-ketoglutarate + NH_3
58	Glycine	Glyoxylate [5,10-Methylene-THF + NH_3 + 2 H]	Biosynthesis	Glyoxylate + glutamate (or alanine) → glycine + α-ketoglutarate (or pyruvate)
59				Usual major route: Serine + THF ⇌ glycine + 5,10-methylene-THF
60				In animal tissues: Serine + CO_2 + NH_3 + 2 H ⇌ 2 glycine + H_2O
61				Minor pathway in animal tissues: Choline → betaine → dimethylglycine → sarcosine → glycine
62				Minor route in liver, major route in Clostridium pasteurianum: Threonine → glycine + acetaldehyde
63			Utilization	Synthesis of δ-aminolevulinate & porphyrins, creatine & creatinine, glycocholate, & hippurate (see also Arginine, entry 9, & Serine, entry 119)
64				Source of N-7, C-5, & C-4 of purine ring (see Table 203. Pathways of Polynucleotide Biosynthesis: Part I. Purines)
65			Catabolism	Glycine → glyoxylate → (i) formate + CO_2, or (ii) oxalate
66				Glycine + 5,10-methylene-THF ⇌ serine + THF
67	Histidine[2]	β-Imidazolepyruvate [Histamine]	Biosynthesis	In microorganisms: 5-Phosphoribosylpyrophosphate + ATP → 5-phosphoribosyl-ATP → 5-phosphoribosyl-AMP → 5-phosphoribosylformimino-5-amino-1-(5'-phosphoribosyl)-4-imidazolecarboxamide → 5-phosphoribulosylformimino-5-amino-1-(5'-phosphoribosyl)-4-imidazolecarboxamide → AICAR + imidazoleglycerophosphate → imidazoleacetol phosphate + glutamate ⇌ histidinol phosphate + α-ketoglutarate → histidinol → histidine
68			Utilization	Synthesis of anserine, carnosine, ergothioneine, & histamine
69				Histidine → imidazoleacetate → (i) imidazoleacetate ribonucleoside, or (ii) NH_3 + formylaspartate
70				Histidine → histamine → methylhistamine
71			Catabolism	Histidine → imidazolepyruvate → imidazoleacetate
72				Histidine → NH_3 + urocanate → imidazolone propionate → (i) N-formiminoglutamate → glutamate + 5-formimino-THF (final products of formamide & formate differ among bacteria), or (ii) hydantoin-5-propionate
73	Hydroxyproline	α-Keto-2-hydroxy-δ-aminovalerate	Biosynthesis	Proline (as a proline polypeptide) → hydroxyproline in bound form → → collagen
74			Catabolism	In animals: 4-Hydroxyproline → $Δ^1$-pyrroline-3-hydroxy-5-carboxylate → γ-hydroxyglutamic semialdehyde ⇌ γ-hydroxyglutamate ⇌ 2-keto-4-hydroxyglutarate ⇌ pyruvate + glyoxylate
75				In Pseudomonas: 4-Hydroxyproline → allohydroxy-D-proline → $Δ^1$-pyrroline-4-hydroxy-2-carboxylate → α-ketoglutaric semialdehyde → α-ketoglutarate
76	Isoleucine[3]	α-Keto-β-methylvalerate [2-Methylbutylamine]	Biosynthesis	In microorganisms & plants: Pyruvate + α-ketobutyrate (see Aspartic acid, entry 22, & Threonine, entry 126) → CO_2 + α-aceto-α-hydroxybutyrate → α,β-dihydroxy-β-methylvalerate → α-keto-β-methylvalerate ⟷ isoleucine[4]
77				In rumen anaerobes: By reductive carboxylation of 2-methylbutyrate
78				In Chromatium, Clostridium pasteurianum, & Desulfovibrio desulfuricans: Propionyl CoA + CO_2 + Fd_{red} → α-ketobutyrate + CoA + Fd_{ox}

[2] Essential amino acid for many animals. [3] Essential amino acid for animals. [4] The same enzymes catalyze parallel steps in valine biosynthesis (see entry 138).

continued

	Amino Acid	Product of Oxidative Deamination or Transamination [Decarboxylation]	Metabolism	
			Type of Pathway	Pathway & Products
79			Catabolism	α-Keto-β-methylvaleric acid $\to CO_2$ + α-methylbutyryl CoA $\rightleftharpoons$ tiglyl CoA $\rightleftharpoons$ α-methyl-β-hydroxybutyryl CoA $\rightleftharpoons$ α-methylacetoacetyl CoA $\to$ acetyl CoA + propionyl CoA (for fate, *see* Valine, entry 141)
80	Leucine[3/]	α-Ketoisocaproate [Isoamylamine]	Biosynthesis	In microorganisms & plants: α-Ketoisovalerate (*see* Valine, entry 138) + acetyl CoA $\to$ β-carboxy-β-hydroxyisocaproate $\to$ α-hydroxy-β-carboxy-isocaproate $\to$ α-ketoisocaproate $\rightleftharpoons$ leucine
81				In rumen anaerobes: By reductive carboxylation of isovalerate
82			Utilization	In microorganisms: Formation of pantothenate & CoA
83			Catabolism	α-Ketoisocaproate $\to CO_2$ + isovaleryl CoA $\rightleftharpoons$ β-methylcrotonyl CoA + CO_2 $\rightleftharpoons$ β-methylglutaconyl CoA $\rightleftharpoons$ β-hydroxy-β-methylglutaryl CoA $\to$ (i) acetoacetate + acetyl CoA, or (ii) $\to \to \to$ cholesterol
84	Lysine[3/]	α-Keto-ϵ-amino-caproate [1,5-Pentanedi-amine (Cadaverine)]	Biosynthesis	In *Escherichia coli,* other bacteria, lower fungi, & green organisms[5/]: Aspartic β-semialdehyde (*see* Aspartic acid, line 22) + pyruvate $\to$ 2,3-dihydrodipicolinate $\to$ Δ^1-tetrahydrodipicolinate $\to$ N-succinyl-ϵ-keto-L-α-aminopimelate $\to$ N-succinyl-L-α,ϵ-diaminopimelate $\to$ L-α,ϵ-diamino-pimelate $\to$ *meso*-α,ϵ-diaminopimelate $\to$ lysine
85				In lower fungi, *Neurospora crassa* & other higher fungi, & euglenids[6/]: α-Ketoglutarate + acetyl CoA $\to$ homocitrate $\to$ homoaconitate $\to$ homo-isocitrate $\to$ oxaloglutarate $\to$ α-ketoadipate $\to$ α-aminoadipate $\to$ α-amino-adipic semialdehyde $\to$ L-saccharopine $\to$ lysine
86			Utilization	Formation of 5-hydroxylysine
87			Catabolism	In animals[7/]: α-Keto-ϵ-aminocaproate $\to$ Δ^1-dehydropipecolate $\to$ L-pipecolate $\to$ Δ^6-dehydropipecolate $\to$ α-aminoadipic semialdehyde $\rightleftharpoons$ α-aminoadipate $\rightleftharpoons$ α-ketoadipate $\to$ glutaryl CoA $\to$ glutaconyl CoA $\to$ crotonyl CoA
88				In anaerobic *Clostridium* spp.: By β-lysine
89				In aerobic *Pseudomonas:* By δ-aminovaleramide
90				In yeast: By ϵ-N-acetyllysine
91	Methio-nine[8/]	α-Keto-γ-methiol-butyrate	Biosynthesis	In microorganisms: Homoserine (*see* Aspartic acid, entry 22) $\to$ O-alkyl-homoserine + cysteine $\to$ cystathionine $\to$ homo-cysteine + pyruvate + NH_3
92				O-Alkylhomoserine + H_2S $\to$ homocysteine
				For methyl group synthesis
93				Main & vitamin B_{12}-independent path: Homocysteine + 5-methyltetra-hydropteroyltriglutamate $\to$ methionine + tetrahydropteroyltrigluta-mate
94				By methylcobalamin & other cofactors: Homocysteine + 5-methyl-THF $\to$ methionine + THF
95			Utilization	Methionine + ATP $\to$ PP_i + P_i + S-adenosylmethionine (active-methyl donor); S-adenosylmethionine + guanidoacetate $\to$ creatine + S-aden-osylhomocysteine (similarly, carnosine $\to$ anserine, norepinephrine $\to$ epinephrine, and many other N- & O-transmethylation reactions occur)
96				Formation of spermidine & spermine
97				In animals: S-Adenosylmethionine $\to$ adenosine + homocysteine; homo-cysteine + serine $\to$ cystathionine + homoserine
98			Catabolism	Homocysteine $\to$ α-ketobutyrate + NH_3 + H_2S; α-ketobutyrate $\to CO_2$ + propionyl CoA $\to$ methylmalonyl CoA (for fate, *see* Valine, entry 141)
99				Homocysteine $\to$ homocysteate
100				Homoserine $\to$ α-ketobutyrate + NH_3 + H_2O
101				α-Keto-γ-methiolbutyrate $\to$ methanethiol + α-ketobutyrate

[3/] Essential amino acid for animals. [5/] DAP (diaminopime-late) pathway. [6/] AAA (α-aminoadipate) pathway. [7/] Fatty acid degeneration pathway in which saccharopine may also be an intermediate. [8/] Homocysteine moiety of methionine is an essential amino acid for animals.

continued

	Amino Acid	Product of Oxidative De-amination or Transamination [Decarboxylation]	Metabolism	
			Type of Pathway	Pathway & Products
102 103 104 105 106 107	Ornithine	Glutamic semial-dehyde or α-keto-δ-aminovalerate [1,4-Butanedi-amine (Putres-cine)]	Biosynthesis	In animals: Glutamate $\to$ glutamic γ-semialdehyde $\to$ ornithine In many bacteria: Glutamate + acetyl CoA $\to$ N-acetylglutamate + CoA; ATP + N-acetylglutamate $\to$ ADP + N-acetyl-γ-glutamylphosphate $\to$ N-acetylglutamic γ-semialdehyde + glutamate $\to$ α-N-acetylornithine + α-ketoglutarate $\to$ ornithine In *Micrococcus glutamicus,* photosynthetic bacteria, & blue-green algae: α-N-Acetylornithine + glutamate $\to$ ornithine + N-acetylglutamate
			Utilization	Formation of spermidine & spermine (*see also* Arginine, entries 7 & 8; Citrulline, entry 26; Glutamic acid, entry 46; & Proline, entry 113) In birds: Formation of ornithuric acid
			Catabolism	Ornithine $\rightleftharpoons$ glutamic γ-semialdehyde $\rightleftharpoons$ glutamate
108	Phenyl-alanine[3]	Phenylpyruvate [Phenethylamine]	Biosynthesis	In microorganisms & plants: Phosphoenolpyruvate + erythrose 4-phos-phate $\to$ 3-deoxy-D-arabinoheptulosonic acid 7-phosphate $\to \to \to$ 5-dehydroquinate $\to$ 5-dehydroshikimate $\to$ shikimate $\to$ shikimate 5-phosphate $\to$ 3-enolpyruvylshikimate 5-phosphate $\to$ chorismate $\to$ pre-phenate $\to$ phenylpyruvate $\to$ phenylalanine (*see also* Tyrosine, entry 136)
109 110 111			Utilization	Phenylalanine $\to$ tyrosine Phenylpyruvic acid $\to$ (i) atrolactic acid (phenyllactic acid), or (ii) phenyl-acetic acid + CO_2
			Catabolism	*See* Tyrosine, entries 134 & 137
112 113 114	Proline	Glutamic semi-aldehyde or α-keto-δ-amino-valerate	Biosynthesis	Glutamate $\rightleftharpoons$ glutamic γ-semialdehyde $\rightleftharpoons$ Δ^1-pyrroline-5-carboxylate $\rightleftharpoons$ proline
			Utilization	*See* Hydroxyproline, entry 73, & Ornithine, entry 102
			Catabolism	Reversal of biosynthesis (*see also* Glutamic acid, entry 42)
115 116	Serine	β-Hydroxypyr-uvate	Biosynthesis	Varying in occurrence in animal tissues, microorganisms, & plants 3-Phosphoglycerate $\rightleftharpoons$ 3-phosphohydroxypyruvate $\rightleftharpoons$ serine phosphate (3-phosphoserine) $\to$ serine 3-Phosphoglycerate $\rightleftharpoons$ 2-phosphoglycerate $\rightleftharpoons$ D-glycerate $\rightleftharpoons$ 3-hydroxy-pyruvate $\rightleftharpoons$ serine
117 118 119 120			Utilization	Synthesis of glycine, cysteine, tryptophan, betaine, dihydrosphingosine, D-serineaminoethanolphosphodiester, & lombricine Synthesis of phosphatide bases: Phosphatidyl serine, cephalin (phospha-tidyl ethanolamine), & lecithin (phosphatidyl choline) Participation in many transfer reactions since the β-C of serine is a source of the 1-C derivative of THF at the —COOH, —CHO, —CH$_2$OH, & —CH$_3$ levels of oxidation, and the α-carbon & carboxyl carbon form glycine In silkworms: Formation of D-serine
121			Catabolism	Serine $\to$ pyruvate + NH_3 (*see also* Glycine, entries 59 & 60)
122 123	Threo-nine[3]	....	Biosynthesis	In microorganisms: Homoserine (*see* Aspartic acid, entry 22) $\to$ O-phosphohomoserine $\to$ threonine
			Utilization	*See* Glycine, entry 62
124 125 126			Catabolism	Threonine $\to$ acetaldehyde + glycine Threonine $\to$ aminoacetone + CO_2 Threonine $\to$ NH_3 + α-ketobutyrate $\to$ CO_2 + propionyl CoA $\to$ methyl-malonyl CoA (for fate, *see* Valine, entry 141)
127	Trypto-phan[3]	β-Indolepyr-uvate [Tryptamine]	Biosynthesis	In microorganisms: Chorismate (*see* Phenylalanine, entry 108) $\to$ o-aminobenzoate + 5-phosphoribosyl-1-pyrophosphate $\to$ N-(o-carboxy-phenyl)-D-ribosylamine 5′-phosphate $\to$ 1-(o-carboxyphenylamino)-1-de-oxyribulose 5′-phosphate $\to$ indoleglycerol 3-phosphate + serine $\to$ tryp-tophan + glyceraldehyde 3-phosphate

[3] Essential amino acid for animals.

continued

	Amino Acid	Product of Oxidative De-amination or Transamination [Decarboxylation]	Metabolism	
			Type of Pathway	Pathway & Products
128			Utilization	Synthesis of 5-hydroxytryptophan & 5-hydroxytryptamine (serotin), quinolinic acid & NAD^+, indolepyruvate & indoleacetate
129			Catabolism	Tryptophan → N-formylkynurenine → formate + kynurenine → 3-hydroxykynurenine → alanine + 3-hydroxy-o-aminobenzoate → α-amino-β-carboxymuconic semialdehyde → CO_2 + α-aminomuconic semialdehyde → α-aminomuconate → α-ketoadipate (for further degradation, *see* Lysine, entry 87)
130				Under special conditions: Kynurenic acid, quinaldate, xanthurenate, & other side products may accumulate
131				By intestinal microorganisms: Formation of indole, indoxyl, skatole, & skatoxyl
132				In the liver: Formation of metabolic indican
133				In *Pseudomonas*: Catabolic pathways by pyrocatechol & quinolinate
134	Tyrosine	p-Hydroxy-phenylpyruvate [Tyramine]	Biosynthesis	In animals: Phenylalanine → tyrosine
135				In microorganisms: Prephenate (*see* Phenylalanine, entry 108) → p-hydroxyphenylpyruvate → tyrosine
136			Utilization	Synthesis of DOPA (dihydroxyphenylalanine), norepinephrine & epinephrine, hallochrome & melanin, 3-iodotyrosine, 3,5-diiodotyrosine, thyroxine, & 3,5,3'-triiodothyronine
137			Catabolism	p-Hydroxyphenylpyruvate → CO_2 + homogentisate → maleylacetoacetate → fumarylacetoacetate → fumarate + acetoacetate
138	Valine[3/]	α-Ketoisovalerate [Isobutylamine (2-Methylpropyl-amine)]	Biosynthesis	In microorganisms & plants: Two pyruvates → α-acetolactate → α,β-dihydroxyisovalerate → α-ketoisovalerate ⇌ valine (*see also* parallel pathway for biosynthesis of isoleucine, entry 76)
139				In rumen anaerobes: By reductive decarboxylation of isobutyrate
140			Utilization	*See* Leucine, entry 80
141			Catabolism	α-Ketoisovalerate → CO_2 + isobutyryl CoA ⇌ methacrylyl CoA ⇌ β-hydroxyisobutyryl CoA → β-hydroxyisobutyrate ⇌ methylmalonic semialdehyde → (i) β-aminoisobutyrate, (ii) propionyl CoA, or (iii) L-methylmalonyl CoA ("a" form) ⇌ D-methylmalonyl CoA ("b" form) ⇌ succinyl CoA

[3/] Essential amino acid for animals.

Contributor: Wixom, Robert L.

References

[1] Atkinson, D. E. 1969. Annu. Rev. Biochem. 23:47.
[2] Bodansky, M., and D. Perlman. 1969. Science 163: 352.
[3] Bonner, J., and J. E. Varner, ed. 1965. Plant Biochemistry. Academic Press, New York. pp. 361-390.
[4] Buchanan, B. B., and D. I. Arnon. 1970. Advan. Enzymol. 33:119.
[5] Cohen, P. P. 1970. Science 168:533.
[6] Datta, P. 1969. Ibid. 165:556.
[7] Doelle, H. W. 1969. Bacterial Metabolism. Academic Press, New York. pp. 403-422.
[8] Fowden, L., et al. 1967. Advan. Enzymol. 29:89.
[9] Gibson, F., and J. Pittard. 1968. Bacteriol. Rev. 32:465.
[10] Ginsburg, A., and E. R. Stadtman. 1970. Annu. Rev. Biochem. 39:429.
[11] Greenberg, D. M., ed. 1969. Metabolic Pathways. Ed. 3. Academic Press, New York. v. 3.
[12] Leete, E. 1969. Advan. Enzymol. 32:373.
[13] Meister, A. 1965. Biochemistry of the Amino Acids. Ed. 2. Academic Press, New York.
[14] Schimke, R. T., and D. Doyle. 1970. Annu. Rev. Biochem. 39:929.
[15] Sokatch, J. R. 1969. Bacterial Physiology and Metabolism. Academic Press, New York. pp. 165-193, 251-296.
[16] Stadtman, E. R. 1966. Advan. Enzymol. 28:41.
[17] Stadtman, T. C. 1971. Science 171:859.
[18] Thompson, J. F., et al. 1969. Annu. Rev. Biochem. 38:137.
[19] Truffa-Bachi, P., and G. N. Cohen. 1968. Ibid. 37:79.
[20] Umbarger, H. E. 1969. Ibid. 38:323.
[21] Waley, S. G. 1966. Advan. Protein Chem. 21:1.
[22] White, A., et al. 1968. Principles of Biochemistry. Ed. 5. McGraw-Hill, New York. pp. 604-704.

Arrows from several amino acids abutting on the shaft of a single arrow *do not* indicate that the amino acids combine to yield a single product; each amino acid is metabolized to form eventually the same compound, e.g., arginine, hydroxyproline, and proline are metabolized separately to form glutamic acid. Slanted lines entering and/or leaving a major reaction line are drawn where two components in a reaction combine to make one compound, or where one compound is broken down into two components. Amino acids have been placed in broken-line boxes. *Abbreviations:* RNA = ribonucleic acid; TPP = thiamine diphosphate; CoA = coenzyme A.

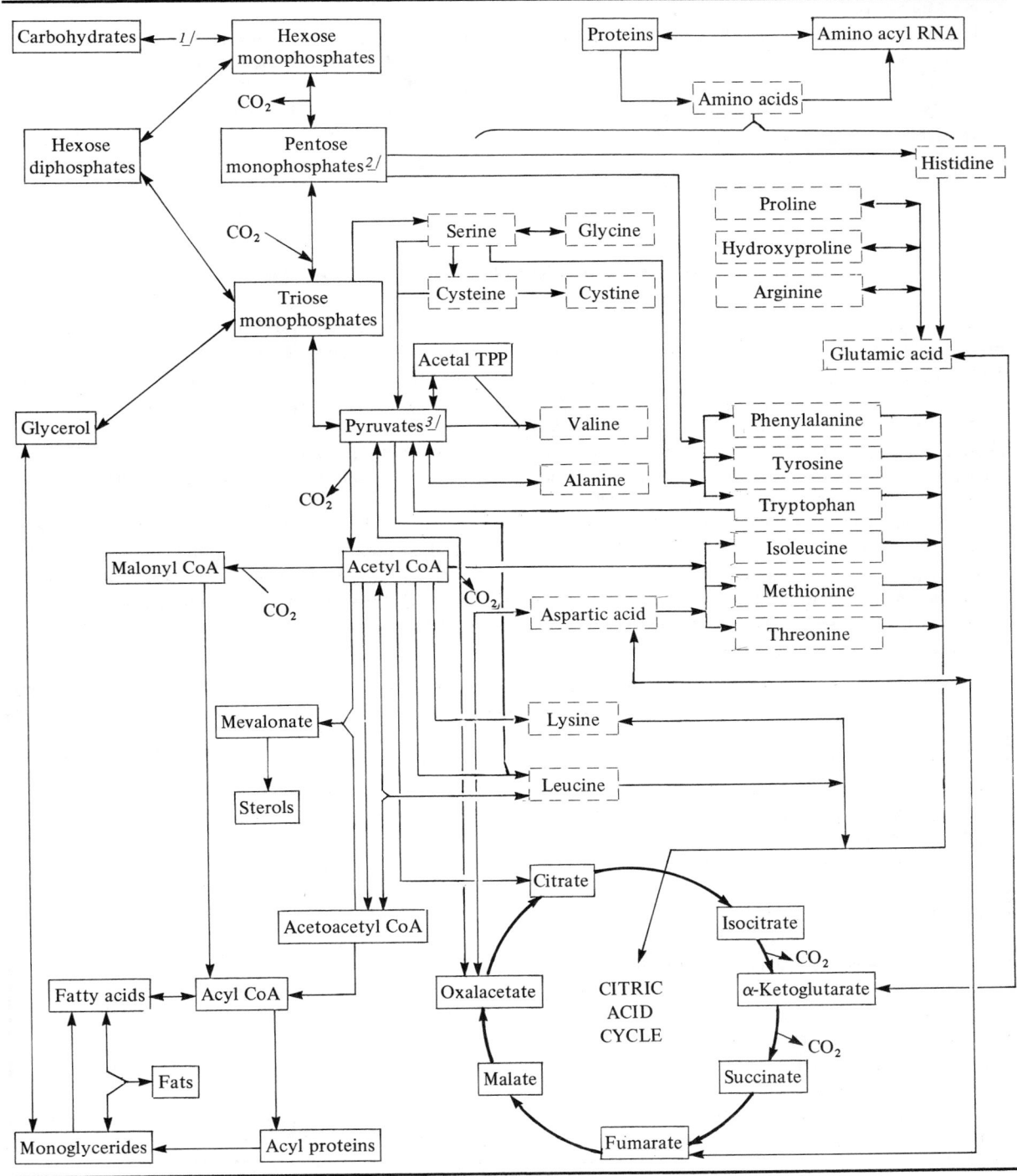

continued

[1] α-Glucan phosphorylase and hexokinase. [2] Including all the possible products of transaldolase and transketolase. CO_2 is produced during the formation of pentose mono- phosphate; in photosynthesis, pentose diphosphate will fix CO_2 to form two triose phosphates. [3] Including phospho- enolpyruvate and hydroxypyruvate.

Contributor: Koft, Bernard W.

General References

[1] Cohen, G. N. 1967. Biosynthesis of Small Molecules. Harper and Row, New York.

[2] Harper, H. A., et al. 1971. Review of Physiological Chemistry. Ed. 13. Lange, Los Altos, Calif.

[3] Mahler, H. R., and E. H. Cordes. 1971. Biological Chemistry. Ed. 2. Harper and Row, New York.

[4] West, E. S., et al. 1966. Textbook of Biochemistry. Ed. 4. Macmillan, New York.

[5] White, A., et al. 1968. Principles of Biochemistry. Ed. 4. McGraw-Hill, New York.

195. PATHWAYS OF NUCLEOPROTEIN CATABOLISM

Nucleoproteins are composed of basic proteins (histones or protamines) associated with nucleic acid in a salt linkage broken by salts, acids, and bases. Catabolism may be ini- tiated in the alimentary canal or in the tissues. Nucleic acids are composed of many nucleotide units joined by sugar- phosphate linkages. The nucleotides shown below are ob- tained by enzymatic hydrolysis of nucleic acids, although several may be obtained from other sources. Each nucleo- tide is composed of a purine or pyrimidine base linked to a pentose sugar which in turn is linked to phosphate. In ca- tabolism, nucleic acids are degraded to nucleotides which are dephosphorylated to yield inorganic phosphate plus a nucleoside; nucleosides are cleaved to yield the free base plus, usually, ribose or deoxyribose 1-phosphate. In some instances, nucleotides and free bases are interconverted through the action of phosphoribosyltransferases. Nucleo- sides and free bases are absorbed from the intestine; there is little intestinal absorption of nucleotides.

The reactions presented are for ribonucleic acid (RNA). A parallel series occurs with deoxyribonucleic acid (DNA). Enzyme Commission Numbers are those assigned by the International Union of Biochemistry on the Nomenclature and Classification of Enzymes. *Abbreviations:* $NADP^+$ = nicotinamide adenine dinucleotide phosphate (oxidized form); AMP = adenosine 5'-monophosphate; CoA = coen- zyme A.

ENZYME KEY [COENZYME]			
1.2.3.2	= xanthine oxidase	3.1.4.23	= ribonuclease II
1.2.99.1	= uracil dehydrogenase	3.2.2.1	= nucleosidase
1.3.1.2	= dihydro-uracil dehydrogenase [$NADP^+$]	3.4.4.—	= proteases
1.4.3.2	= L-amino-acid oxidase	3.5.1.6	= β-ureidopropionase
1.4.3.4	= monoamine oxidase	3.5.2.1	= barbiturase
1.7.3.3	= urate oxidase	3.5.2.2	= dihydropyrimidinase
2.4.2.3	= uridine phosphorylase	3.5.2.5	= allantoinase
2.4.2.4	= thymidine phosphorylase	3.5.3.1	= arginase
2.4.2.8	= hypoxanthine phosphoribosyltransferase	3.5.3.4	= allantoicase
2.6.1.—	= aminotransferases	3.5.4.1	= cytosine deaminase
2.6.1.18	= β-alanine aminotransferase	3.5.4.2	= adenine deaminase
2.6.1.x	= aminotransferase, uncharacterized	3.5.4.3	= guanine deaminase
3.1.3.1	= alkaline phosphatase	3.5.4.4	= adenosine deaminase
3.1.4.5	= deoxyribonuclease I	3.5.4.5	= cytidine deaminase
3.1.4.6	= deoxyribonuclease II	3.5.4.6	= AMP deaminase
3.1.4.22	= ribonuclease I	4.1.1.—	= amino acid decarboxylases

continued

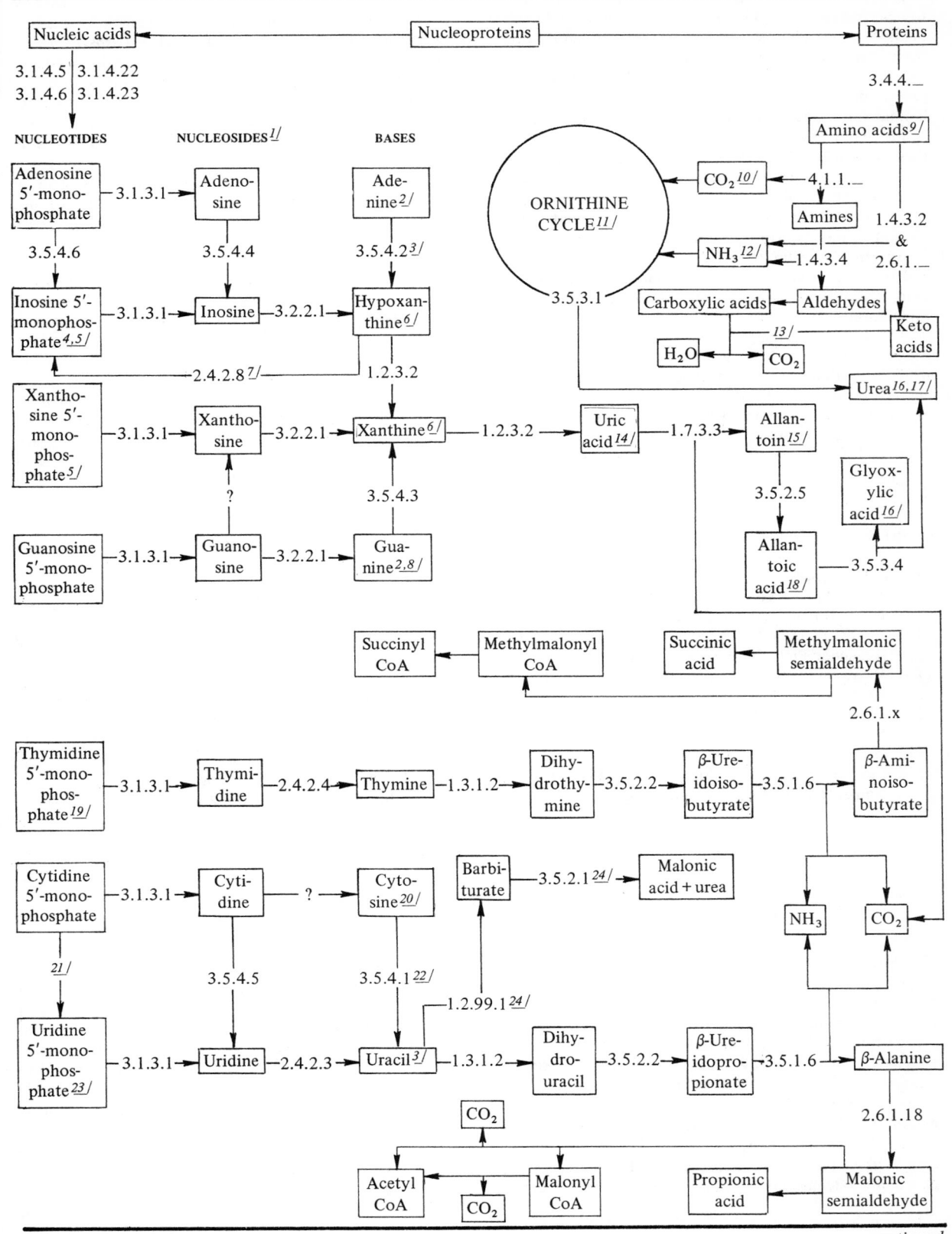

continued

1/ 6-Oxypurine nucleosides are split into purines and pentose phosphate by purine nucleoside phosphorylase present in tissues. 2/ Adenine and guanine are the major purines occurring in nucleic acids. Mammals do not require, but can synthesize, purines or pyrimidines from products of protein metabolism. 3/ The route adenine → hypoxanthine is of no importance in animals; adenine deaminase [3.5.4.4] is not found to any extent in mammals. 4/ In the biosynthesis of nucleotides, inosine 5'-monophosphate is the precursor of adenosine 5'-monophosphate and guanosine 5'-monophosphate; in uricotelic species, a portion of the inosine 5'-monophosphate is a precursor of uric acid. 5/ Important in metabolism, but does not occur in nucleic acid. 6/ Excreted to a limited extent by all mammals; primary end product of subjects with xanthinuria, congenital absence of xanthine oxidase [1.2.3.2]. In man, most of xanthine formed is excreted as uric acid. This is the source of $\sim$75% of the urinary urate; hypoxanthine, which contributes the other 25%, is primarily a metabolic intermediate. 7/ Recycle found in all normal mammalian tissues; absence resulting from inborn error leads to serious neurological disease. 8/ Excreted by swine and spiders. 9/ For more complete information on amino acid metabolism, *see* Table 193. 10/ May enter into metabolic processes, into the ornithine cycle and be incorporated into and excreted as urea, or be excreted as CO_2. 11/ Urea formation in mammalian liver occurs via the ornithine cycle (Krebs-Henseleit cycle): ornithine → citrulline → arginine succinate → arginine → ornithine. CO_2 and NH_3 enter the cycle via aspartic acid at citrulline; arginine succinate is split into arginine and fumaric acid; arginine is then converted to ornithine with the release of urea. 12/ NH_3, as in the case of CO_2, is also used to synthesize many tissue constituents; hence, it may enter into many metabolic processes, be built into amino acids, be incorporated into urea and excreted, or be excreted as NH_3 across the kidney tubule. 13/ Via the citric acid cycle (prior to entry into this cycle, sulfur-containing amino acids lose their sulfur, usually in the form of sulfate). 14/ Excreted by primates, some reptiles, and some insects as the end product of purine catabolism; excreted by birds as the end product of protein, purine, and pyrimidine catabolism (no urea formation in birds). 15/ Excreted by mammals other than primates, by gastropods, and by some insects. 16/ Excreted by amphibians, most fishes, and freshwater lamellibranchs. 17/ Excreted by mammals as the end product of amino acid metabolism. 18/ Excreted by some teleosts. 19/ Occurs in DNA. 20/ Free cytosine is excreted unchanged in animals. 21/ Cytidine 5'-monophosphate can be converted to uridine 5'-monophosphate. 22/ In yeasts and *Escherichia coli*. 23/ Occurs in RNA. 24/ In *Corynebacterium*, *Mycobacterium*, and U-i soil bacterium.

Contributors: Zbarsky, S. H.; Balis, M. Earl

General References

[1] Balis, M. E. 1968. Antagonists and Nucleic Acids. North-Holland, Amsterdam.

[2] Boyer, P. D., ed. 1970-73. The Enzymes. Ed. 3. Academic Press, New York. v. 1-8.

[3] Davidson, J. N. 1972. Biochemistry of the Nucleic Acids. Ed. 7. Methuen, London.

[4] Davidson, J. N., and W. E. Cohn, ed. 1959-70. Progr. Nucleic Acid Res. Mol. Biol., v. 1-10.

[5] Greenberg, D. M. 1969. Ibid. v. 3.

[6] International Union of Biochemistry. 1965. Enzyme Nomenclature. Elsevier, New York.

[7] Lehninger, A. L. 1970. Biochemistry. Worth, New York.

[8] Long, C., ed. 1961. Biochemists' Handbook. Van Nostrand, Princeton, N.J.

[9] Mahler, H. R., and E. H. Cordes. 1971. Biological Chemistry. Ed. 2. Harper and Row, New York.

[10] McGilvery, R. W. 1970. Biochemistry, a Functional Approach. W. B. Saunders, Philadelphia.

[11] West, E. S., et al. 1966. Textbook of Biochemistry. Ed. 4. Macmillan, New York.

[12] White, A., et al. 1973. Principles of Biochemistry. Ed. 5. McGraw-Hill, New York.

196. CITRIC ACID CYCLE

The citric acid cycle (Krebs cycle) is a major pathway for the final aerobic oxidation of carbohydrates, fats, and proteins, which are channeled into the cycle via their two key metabolites, pyruvate and acetyl CoA (active acetate). Each "revolution" of the cycle oxidizes acetate to carbon dioxide and water. One mole (59 grams) of acetate thus oxidized releases approximately 200 kilocalories of energy. A portion of the released energy (approximately 144 kilocalories) enters the phosphate pool as ATP (adenosine 5'-triphosphate). Twelve moles of ATP are formed from ADP (adenosine 5'-diphosphate) and inorganic phosphate by energizing phosphate to high-energy phosphate ($\sim$$PO_4$). The remainder of the released energy appears as heat. Oxidation of one mole (87 grams) of pyruvate, via acetyl CoA, contributes a total of 14 moles of ATP to the energy pool. Heavy lines show the main sequence of reactions. Enzyme Commission Numbers are those assigned by the International Union of Biochemistry on the Nomenclature and Classification of Enzymes. *Abbreviations:* NAD^+ and NADH = nicotinamide adenine dinucleotide (oxidized and reduced forms, respectively); $NADP^+$ and NADPH = nicotinamide adenine dinucleotide phosphate (oxidized and reduced forms, respectively); CoA = coenzyme A (ATP-pantoyl-β-alanylthioethanolamine).

continued

ENZYME KEY [COENZYME]

1.1.1.37 = malate dehydrogenase
　　　　　[NAD⁺, NADH]
1.1.1.40 = malate dehydrogenase, de-
　　　　　carboxylating [NADP⁺,
　　　　　NADPH]
1.1.1.41 = isocitrate dehydrogenase
　　　　　[NAD⁺, NADH]
1.2.4.1 = pyruvate dehydrogenase

1.2.4.2 = oxoglutarate dehydroge-
　　　　　nase (α-ketoglutarate
　　　　　dehydrogenase)
1.3.99.1 = succinate dehydrogenase
1.4.1.3 = glutamate dehydrogenase
　　　　　[NAD(P)⁺, NAD(P)H]
2.6.1.1 = aspartate aminotransferase

4.1.1.3 = oxalacetate decarboxylase
4.1.3.1 = isocitrate lyase
4.1.3.2 = malate synthase
4.1.3.7 = citrate synthase
4.2.1.2 = fumarate hydratase
4.2.1.3 = aconitate hydratase
6.2.1.4 = succinyl-CoA synthetase

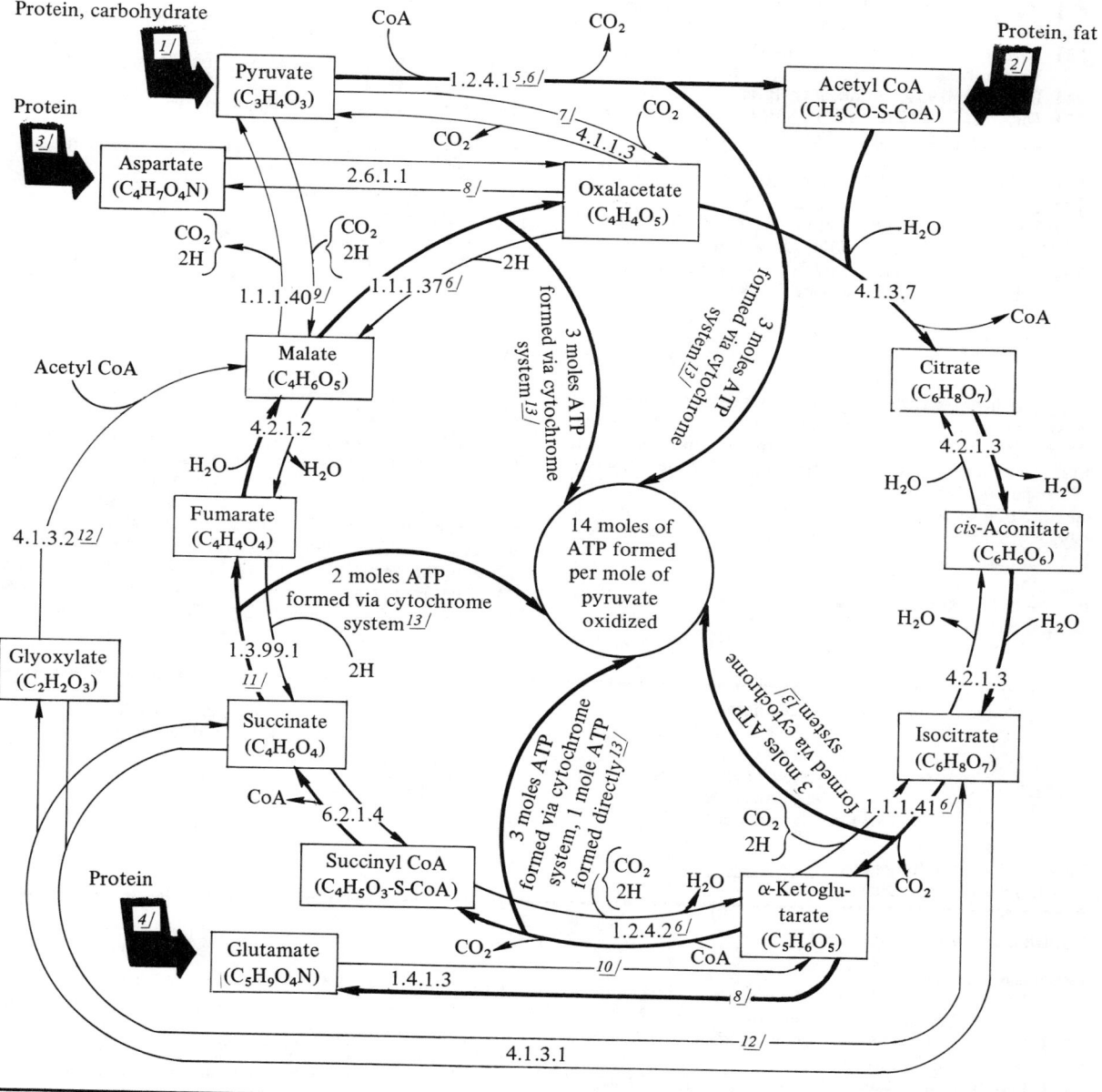

continued

1/ Glucogenic amino acid precursors of pyruvate are alanine, cysteine, glycine, methionine, serine, threonine, and valine. 2/ Ketogenic amino acid precursors of acetyl CoA are isoleucine, leucine, phenylalanine, and tyrosine. 3/ Aspartic acid occurs as a component of protein. 4/ Glutamic acid occurs as a component of protein, or may be formed from arginine, histidine, hydroxyproline, ornithine, or proline. 5/ α-Lipoic acid required. 6/ In the oxidative direction, NAD⁺ acts as the hydrogen acceptor; the hydrogen atoms thus transferred pass in turn to flavoprotein, cytochrome c, cytochrome oxidase, and finally combine with molecular oxygen. For each mole of hydrogen thus passed and finally

oxidized, 1.5 moles of ATP are formed by the addition of ~PO₄ to ADP. In the reverse direction, NADH is hydrogen donor. 7/ Biotin required as coenzyme for carboxylation. 8/ NH₃ enters the reaction by transamination. 9/ In the oxidative direction, NADP⁺ acts as hydrogen acceptor; in the reverse direction, NADPH is hydrogen donor. 10/ NH₃ then transferred from glutamate by transamination, then enters into the citric acid cycle via α-ketoglutarate. 11/ Two moles of hydrogen released and their electrons transferred to cytochrome. 12/ Cysteine and Mg²⁺ required. 13/ For details of the cytochrome system, see Table 197.

Contributor: Bishop, David W.

General References
[1] Artom, C. 1953. Annu. Rev. Biochem. 22:211.
[2] Baldwin, E. 1967. Dynamic Aspects of Biochemistry. Ed. 5. Cambridge Univ. Press, New York.
[3] Barman, T. E. 1969. Enzyme Handbook. Springer-Verlag, New York.
[4] Black, K. 1952. Annu. Rev. Biochem. 21:273.
[5] Dickens, F. 1951. In J. B. Sumner and K. Myrbäck, ed. The Enzymes. Academic Press, New York. v. 2(1), pp. 624-683.
[6] Evans, E. A., Jr. 1944. Annu. Rev. Biochem. 13:187.
[7] Frazer, A. C. 1952. Ibid. 21:245.
[8] Fruton, J. S., and S. Simmonds. 1958. General Biochemistry. Ed. 2. J. Wiley, New York.
[9] Greenberg, D. M. 1967-70. Metabolic Pathways. Ed. 3. Academic Press, New York.
[10] International Union of Biochemistry. 1965. Enzyme Nomenclature. Elsevier, New York.
[11] Krebs, H. A. 1943. Advan. Enzymol. 3:191.
[12] Ochoa, S. 1951. Physiol. Rev. 31:56.
[13] Ochoa, S., and J. R. Stern. 1952. Annu. Rev. Biochem. 21:547.
[14] Potter, V. R., and C. Heidelberger. 1950. Physiol. Rev. 30:487.
[15] Umbreit, W. W. 1952. Metabolic Maps. Burgess. Minneapolis. v. 1, pp. 90-112.
[16] Umbreit, W. W. 1960. Ibid. v. 2.
[17] West, E. S., et al. 1966. Textbook of Biochemistry. Ed. 4. Macmillan, New York.
[18] White, A., et al. 1968. Principles of Biochemistry. Ed. 4. McGraw-Hill, New York.

197. RESPIRATORY CHAIN

The cytochromes (iron porphyrin-containing compounds) in association with certain enzymes comprise the respiratory chain. The system operates as the final pathway by which an intermediate metabolite (substrate), under the influence of its specific dehydrogenase, releases hydrogen to the first member of a series of carriers for ultimate combination with oxygen to form water. Each step in the process involves both oxidation and reduction.

For each two grams of hydrogen passed through NADH, enough energy is produced to form three moles of adenosine 5'-triphosphate from adenosine 5'-diphosphate and in-

organic phosphate, whereas for each two grams of hydrogen removed from succinate, two moles of adenosine 5'-triphosphate are formed. A nonphosphorylated high-energy intermediate is indicated in energy transduction, and the intermediate may be used for the movement of ions and for transhydrogenation, as well as for the synthesis of adenosine 5'-triphosphate. The sites of energy transduction are between (1) NADH and [ubiquinone and cytochrome b], (2) [ubiquinone and cytochrome b] and cytochrome c, and (3) cytochrome c and oxygen. *Abbreviations:* NAD = nicotinamide adenine dinucleotide, NADH = nicotinamide adenine dinucleotide (reduced form).

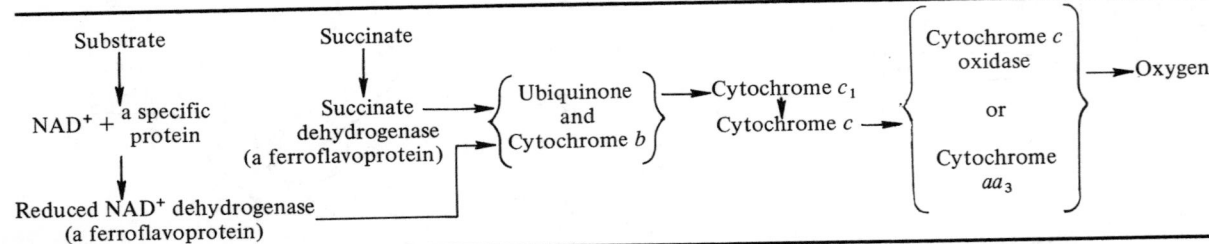

Contributor: Wainio, Walter W.

General References
[1] Chance, B. 1961. In J. E. Falk, ed. Haematin Enzymes. Pergamon Press, Oxford. v. 1, p. 597.
[2] Green, D. E., and S. Fleischer. 1963. Biochim. Biophys. Acta 70:554.
[3] Okunuki, K., et al. 1958. Proc. Int. Symp. Enzyme Chem., Tokyo-Kyoto, 1957, p. 264.
[4] Slater, E. C. 1958. Advan. Enzymol. 20:147.
[5] Pullman, M. E., and G. Schatz. 1967. Annu. Rev. Biochem. 36:539.
[6] Wainio, W. W. 1970. The Mammalian Mitochondrial Respiratory Chain. Academic Press, New York.

198. PATHWAYS OF ENERGY METABOLISM IN MUSCLE

Excitation through membrane depolarization leads to the release of Ca²⁺ from intracellular stores located in the sarcoplasmic reticulum. Ca²⁺ promotes the interaction of actin and myosin, leading to the hydrolysis of ATP by releasing the inhibition by the tropomyosin-troponin system. The ADP formed is first of all rephosphorylated by creatine phosphate. Concomitantly there is a stimulation of phosphorylase and phosphofructokinase, leading to formation of ATP and inhibition of glycogen synthesis. The role of Ca²⁺ has been demonstrated in some of these enzyme changes. Neurohormonal and hormonal control of enzymes is indicated. Under anaerobic conditions the oxidation of pyruvate leads to formation of more ATP by phosphorylation of 6 moles of ADP per mole of O₂. The energy of ATP breakdown is used for performing mechanical work. The precise relation between all phases of heat liberation and chemical change has not been completely elucidated. *Abbreviations:* ADP = adenosine diphosphate; AMP = adenosine phosphate; cAMP = cyclic adenosine 3′,5′-monophosphate; ATP = adenosine triphosphate; CoA = coenzyme A; Pᵢ = inorganic orthophosphate; PPᵢ = inorganic pyrophosphate; UDP = uridine diphosphate; UTP = uridine triphosphate.

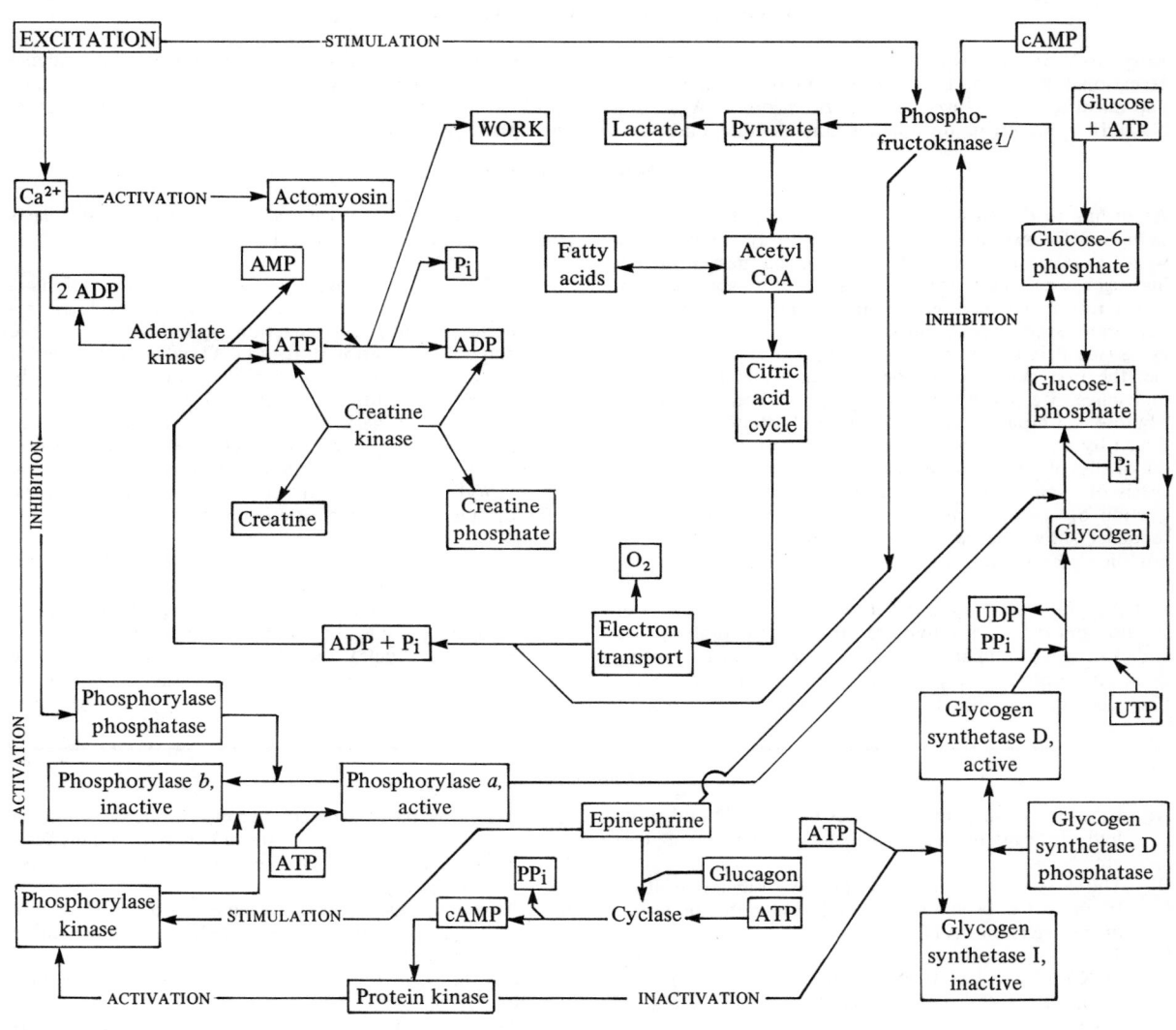

L/ This enzyme, one of several involved in the breakdown of glucose-6-phosphate to pyruvate, is essential in the regulation of glycolysis [10].

Contributor: Gergely, J.

continued

References

[1] Cold Spring Harbor Laboratory. 1972. Cold Spring Harbor Symp. Quant. Biol. 37.

[2] Ebashi, S., et al. 1969. Quart. Rev. Biophys. 2:351.

[3] Fischer, E. H., et al. 1971. Curr. Top. Cell. Regul. 4:211.

[4] Gergely, J. 1974. In J. N. Walton, ed. Diseases of Voluntary Muscle. Ed. 3. Little, Brown; Boston. p. 102.

[5] Helmreich, E., and F. C. Cori. 1965. Advan. Enzyme Regul. 3:91.

[6] Huxley, H. E. 1969. Science 164:1356.

[7] Krebs, E. G. 1972. Curr. Top. Cell. Regul. 5:99.

[8] Larner, J. 1966. Trans. N.Y. Acad. Sci., II, 29:192.

[9] Leloir, L. F., et al. 1960. Comp. Biochem. 2:97.

[10] Mansour, T. E. 1972. Curr. Top. Cell. Regul. 5:1.

[11] Mayer, S. E., and E. G. Krebs. 1970. J. Biol. Chem. 245:3153.

[12] Weber, A. 1966. Curr. Top. Bioenerg. 1:203.

[13] Weber, A., and J. M. Murray. 1973. Physiol. Rev. 53:612.

[14] Wilkie, D. R. 1968. Muscle, Inst. Biol. (London) Stud. Biol. 11.

[15] Woledge, R. C. 1971. Progr. Biophys. Mol. Biol. 22:37.

199. PATHWAYS OF PHOTOSYNTHESIS: PLANTS

Enzyme Commission Numbers are those assigned by the International Union of Biochemistry on the Nomenclature and Classification of Enzymes. *Abbreviations:* $NADP^+$ and NADPH = nicotinamide adenine dinucleotide phosphate (oxidized and reduced forms, respectively); ATP = adenosine 5'-triphosphate; ADP = adenosine 5'-diphosphate; AMP = adenosine 5'-monophosphate; P_i = inorganic orthophosphate; PP_i = inorganic pyrophosphate.

Part I. Carbon Reduction Cycle

According to the current evidence, photosynthetic carbon reduction follows the same general pathways in all plants, with the exception that in certain tropical grasses (including sugar cane and maize) and in a few other species, additional reactions utilize energy from photosynthesis to incorporate carbon dioxide into organic compounds—the C-4 cycle (*see* Part II). In the reductive pentose phosphate cycle, the first reaction (A) results in the formation of two molecules of 3-phosphoglycerate from carbon dioxide and ribulose 1,5-diphosphate. 3-Phosphoglycerate is then reduced by a series of reactions which, in effect, are a reversal of glycolysis to supply hexose phosphate for the synthesis of sucrose and polysaccharides (*see* Table 200). A portion of the intermediate compounds goes through the sequence shown below, leading to regeneration of the carbon dioxide acceptor, ribulose 1,5-diphosphate.

In light, the starting points for secondary biosynthesis of sucrose and other carbohydrates are fructose 6-phosphate and glucose 6-phosphate. The starting points for biosynthesis of fats, proteins, and many other compounds are 3-phosphoglycerate and dihydroxyacetone phosphate, both of which are known to move readily out of the chloroplasts through the limiting membrane.

In the dark, the reductive cycle within the chloroplasts is converted to an oxidative pentose phosphate cycle as a result of the inactivation of reactions A, F, I, and M. At the same time, the activation of reaction O (which is inactive in light) must occur, since 6-phosphogluconate appears only in the dark. The function of the oxidative pentose phosphate cycle in the dark is thought to be the generation of NADPH (reactions O and P), which is needed for biosynthesis in the dark. ATP is supplied in the dark by oxidative phosphorylation in the mitochondria and transfer of the ATP through the chloroplast membrane.

Heavy arrows indicate directions of material transferred during steady-state photosynthesis (reductive pentose phosphate cycle). Light arrows indicate reactions which occur in the dark inside the chloroplasts (the oxidative pentose phosphate cycle) and the reactions in which triose phosphates are oxidized to 3-phosphoglycerate (glycolysis).

REACTIONS

A: Ribulose 1,5-diphosphate adds CO_2 at C-2 and splits hydrolytically to give 2 molecules of 3-phosphoglycerate.

B: The carboxyl group of 3-phosphoglycerate is converted to an acyl phosphate in a reaction utilizing the terminal phosphate of ATP.

C: The acyl phosphate group is reduced in the presence of NADPH to give P_i & an aldehyde group, thus converting the 3-C-atom compound to glyceraldehyde 3-phosphate.

D: The aldo-sugar is converted into a keto-sugar by the transfer of 2 H atoms from C-2 to C-1.

E: The aldol condensation between aldotriose & ketotriose gives fructose 1,6-diphosphate.

F: The phosphate group on C-1 is removed by hydrolysis.

G: 2 H atoms plus the glycolyl group (C-1 & C-2) of fructose 6-phosphate are transferred to glyceraldehyde 3-phosphate to form xylulose 5-phosphate, leaving erythrose 4-phosphate.

H: An aldol condensation between erythrose 4-phosphate & dihydroxyacetone phosphate gives sedoheptulose 1,7-diphosphate.

I: Hydrolysis of the phosphate on C-1 gives sedoheptulose 7-phosphate.

J: Transfer of the glycolyl group (C-1 & C-2) plus 2 H atoms from sedoheptulose 7-phosphate to C-1 of glyceraldehyde 3-phosphate gives xylulose 5-phosphate & ribose 5-phosphate.

K: Isomerization of ribose 5-phosphate gives ribulose 5-phosphate.

continued

Part I. Carbon Reduction Cycle

L: Epimerization of C-3 of xylulose 5-phosphate gives ribulose 5-phosphate.

M: Phosphorylation of C-1 of ribulose 5-phosphate in the presence of ATP gives ribulose 1,5-diphosphate, thus completing the reductive pentose phosphate cycle.

N: Isomerization of fructose 6-phosphate gives glucose 6-phosphate.

O: Oxidation of glucose 6-phosphate in the presence of $NADP^+$ gives 6-phosphogluconate.

P: Oxidation of 6-phosphogluconate in the presence of $NADP^+$ gives ribulose 5-phosphate and CO_2.

ENZYME (SYNONYM) KEY

Reductive Pentose Phosphate Cycle (Photosynthesis) only

2.7.1.19 = phosphoribulokinase
3.1.3.11 = hexosediphosphatase (heptosediphosphatase)
4.1.1.39 = ribulosediphosphate carboxylase
4.1.2.13 = fructosediphosphate aldolase

Reductive & Oxidative Pentose Phosphate Cycle & Triose Phosphate Oxidation

1.2.1.13 = glyceraldehydephosphate dehydrogenase, $NADP^+$ (triosephosphate dehydrogenase, $NADP^+$)

2.2.1.1 = transketolase
2.7.2.3 = phosphoglycerate kinase
5.1.3.1 = ribulosephosphate 3-epimerase
5.3.1.1 = triosephosphate isomerase
5.3.1.6 = ribosephosphate isomerase

Oxidative Pentose Phosphate Cycle only

1.1.1.44 = phosphogluconate dehydrogenase, decarboxylating
1.1.1.49 = glucose-6-phosphate dehydrogenase
2.2.1.2 = transaldolase
5.3.1.9 = glucosephosphate isomerase

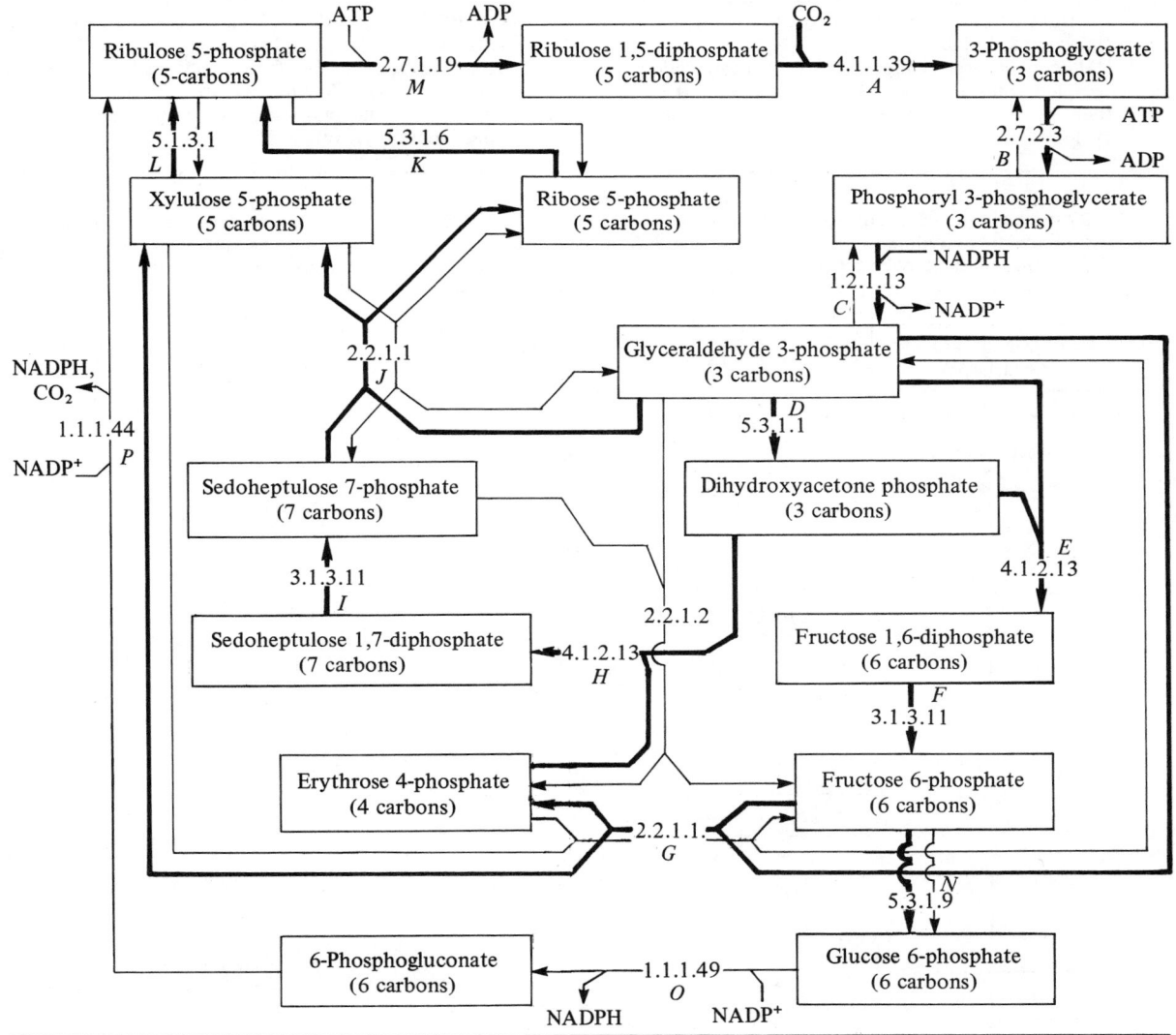

continued

199. PATHWAYS OF PHOTOSYNTHESIS: PLANTS

Part I. Carbon Reduction Cycle

Contributor: Bassham, James A.

General References

[1] Bassham, J. A. 1971. Proc. Nat. Acad. Sci. U.S. 68:2877.
[2] Bassham, J. A., and M. Calvin. 1957. The Path of Carbon in Photosynthesis. Prentice-Hall, Englewood Cliffs, N. J.
[3] Calvin, M., and J. A. Bassham. 1962. The Photosynthesis of Carbon Compounds. W. A. Benjamin, New York.

Part II. The C-4 Cycle

In certain tropical grasses (such as sugar cane and maize) and in a few other plants, the reductive pentose phosphate cycle for carbon dioxide incorporation (*see* Part I) is preceded by another cycle in which carbon dioxide is first incorporated by carboxylation of phosphoenolpyruvate.

REACTIONS

A: CO_2 is incorporated by carboxylation of phosphoenolpyruvate to give oxalacetate.

B: Oxalacetate is reduced by NADPH to give malate and $NADP^+$.

C: Oxalacetate is converted by transamination with glutamate to give aspartate.

D, One or more of the 4-C-atom acids (malate, aspartate)
E: are translocated to the parenchyma cells surrounding the vascular bundles.

F: Malate is decarboxylated to give pyruvate, which is recycled, plus CO_2 & NADPH, both of which can then be used by the reductive pentose phosphate cycle.

G: Aspartate may be converted by transamination with α-ketoglutarate to give oxalacetate & glutamate (detailed mechanism for aspartate utilization in parenchyma sheath cells not known).

H: Oxalacetate is decarboxylated to give pyruvate & CO_2.

I: Glutamate is converted by oxidative deamination with $NADP^+$ to α-ketoglutarate & NH_4^+ while also yielding NADPH & CO_2, both of which can then be used by the reductive pentose phosphate cycle.

J: The pyruvate resulting from reactions F & H presumably may be translocated back to the mesophyll cells.

K: Pyruvate is phosphorylated with ATP & P_i to give phosphoenolpyruvate & PP_i.

ENZYME KEY

1.1.1.37 = malate dehydrogenase, $NADP^+$-specific
1.1.1.40 = malate dehydrogenase, decarboxylating, $NADP^+$-specific
1.4.1.3 = glutamate dehydrogenase

2.6.1.1 = aspartate aminotransferase (aspartate transaminase)
4.1.1.38 = phosphopyruvate carboxylase

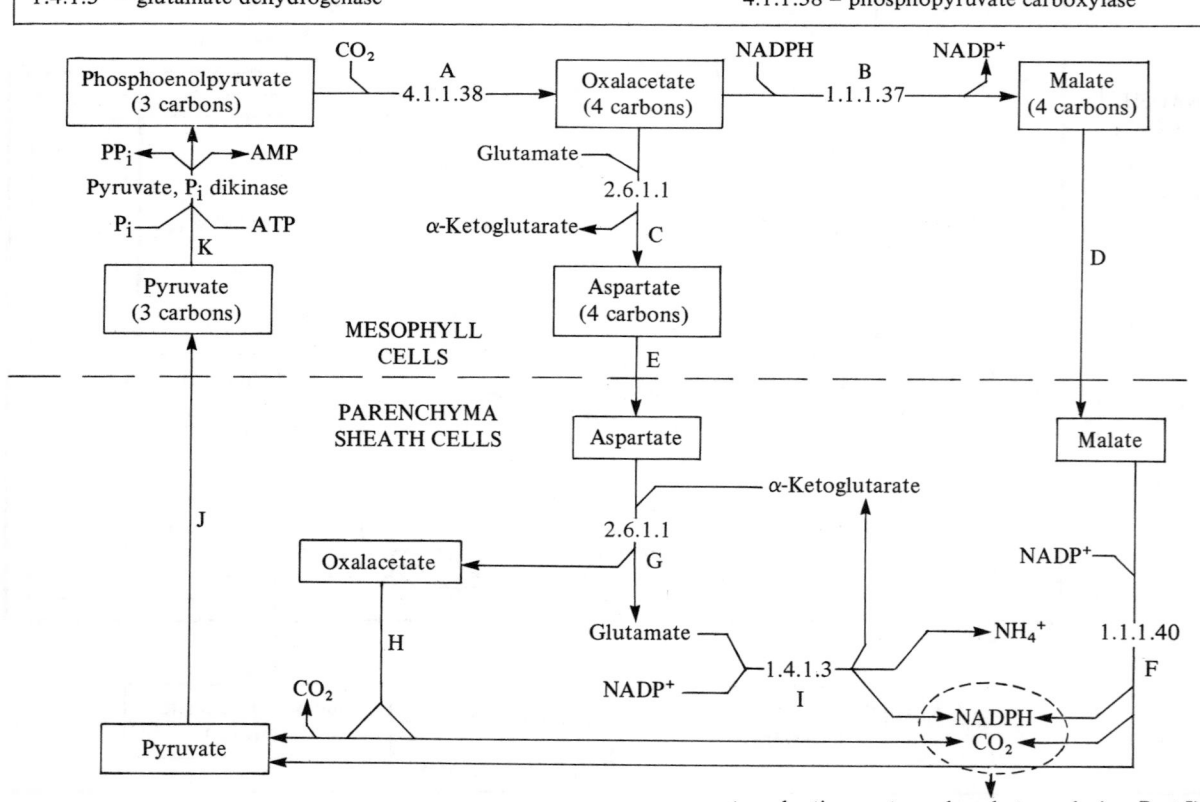

to reductive pentose phosphate cycle (*see* Part I)

continued

Contributor: Bassham, James A.

Reference: Hatch, M. D., and C. R. Slack. 1970. Annu. Rev. Plant Physiol. 21:141.

200.   PATHWAYS OF SUCROSE AND STARCH SYNTHESIS IN PLANTS: INTERMEDIATES

Sucrose and starch, common to all green plants, are formed by a series of steps involving phosphorylated intermediates. Photosynthesis phosphorylates ADP to give ATP, which in turn converts UDP to UTP. Fructose 6-phosphate is formed as an intermediate of the reductive pentose phosphate cycle of photosynthesis (*see* Table 199, Part I).   Enzyme Commission Numbers are those assigned by the International Union of Biochemistry on the Nomenclature and Classification of Enzymes. *Abbreviations:* ADP = adenosine 5'-diphosphate; ATP = adenosine 5'-triphosphate; UDP = uridine 5'-diphosphate; UTP = uridine 5'-triphosphate; PP_i = inorganic pyrophosphate.

REACTIONS

A: H atom on C-1 shifts to C-2, forming the epimer, glucose 6-phosphate; furanose ring is changed to pyranose ring.

B: Phosphate group on C-6 is transferred to C-1 through the required cofactor intermediate, glucose 1,6-diphosphate.

C: UTP reacts with glucose 1-phosphate to form UDP-glucose & PP_i.

D: Fructose 6-phosphate & UDP-glucose react to give sucrose phosphate & UDP.

E: Sucrose phosphate is hydrolyzed to give sucrose.

F: For starch synthesis, ATP reacts with glucose 1-phosphate, giving ADP-glucose & PP_i.

G: ADP-glucose reacts with glycosyl chains already present, lengthening them by 1 glucose unit.

H: Repetition of reaction G leads eventually to starch synthesis.

ENZYME (SYNONYM) KEY

2.4.1.14 = UDP glucose-fructosephosphate glucosyltransferase

2.4.1.x = ADP glucose-starch glucosyltransferase

2.7.5.1 = phosphoglucomutase

2.7.7.9 = glucose-1-phosphate uridylyltransferase (UDP-glucose pyrophosphorylase)

2.7.7.x = ADP glucose pyrophosphorylase

5.3.1.9 = glucosephosphate isomerase

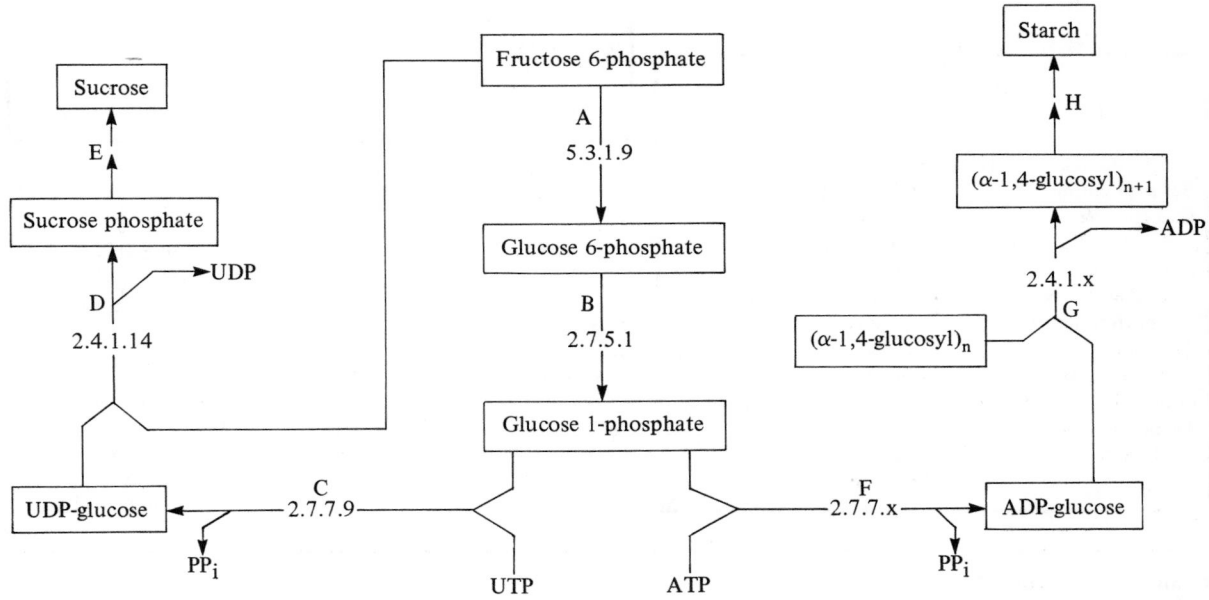

Contributor: Bassham, James A.

General References

[1] Bassham, J. A., and M. Calvin. 1957. The Path of Carbon in Photosynthesis. Prentice-Hall, Englewood Cliffs, N.J.

[2] Preiss, J., and T. Kosuge. 1970. Annu. Rev. Plant Physiol. 21:433.

Classes of compounds are indicated by initial capital letters and specific compounds by lower case. Each area of metabolic pathways for related compounds, including the formation of the monomers, is indicated by an ellipse, and is described elsewhere in this book (*see* Tables 192, 193, 195, 196, and 199). These monomers are the starting points for the flow of carbon and nitrogen into the cellular polymers and/or the formation of the major groups of "natural prod-

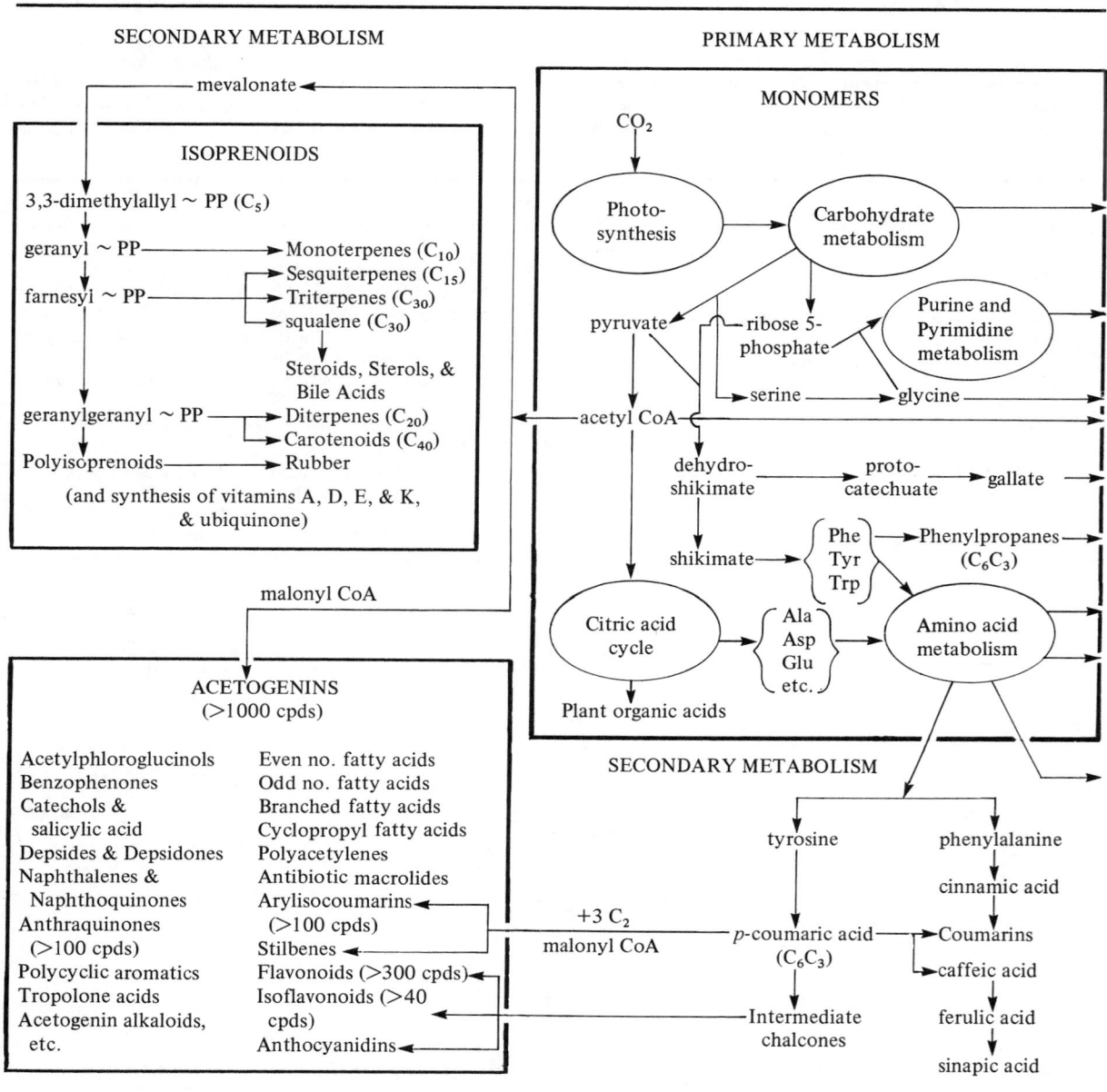

Contributor: Wixom, Robert L.

References

General Reviews:

[1] Altman, P. L., and D. S. Dittmer, ed. 1968. Metabolism. Federation of American Societies for Experimental Biology, Bethesda, Md. pp. 437-450, 455-458, 574-593.

[2] Bernfeld, P., ed. 1967. Biogenesis of Natural Compounds. Ed. 2. Pergamon Press, New York. ch. 10-19.

[3] Bu'Lock, J. D. 1965. The Biosynthesis of Natural Products. McGraw-Hill, New York.

[4] Florkin, M., and E. H. Stotz, ed. 1968. Comprehensive Biochemistry. Elsevier, Amsterdam. v. 20.

[5] Greenberg, D. M., ed. 1969-71. Metabolic Pathways. Ed. 3. Academic Press, New York. v. 1-5.

ucts," mainly in plants and microorganisms. *Abbreviations and Symbols:* cpds = compounds; ~ indicates a high-energy bond; PP = pyrophosphate; CoA = coenzyme A; and amino acids are abbreviated to the standard three-letter code. Original references may be located by a search of the appropriate cited references of reviews and books.

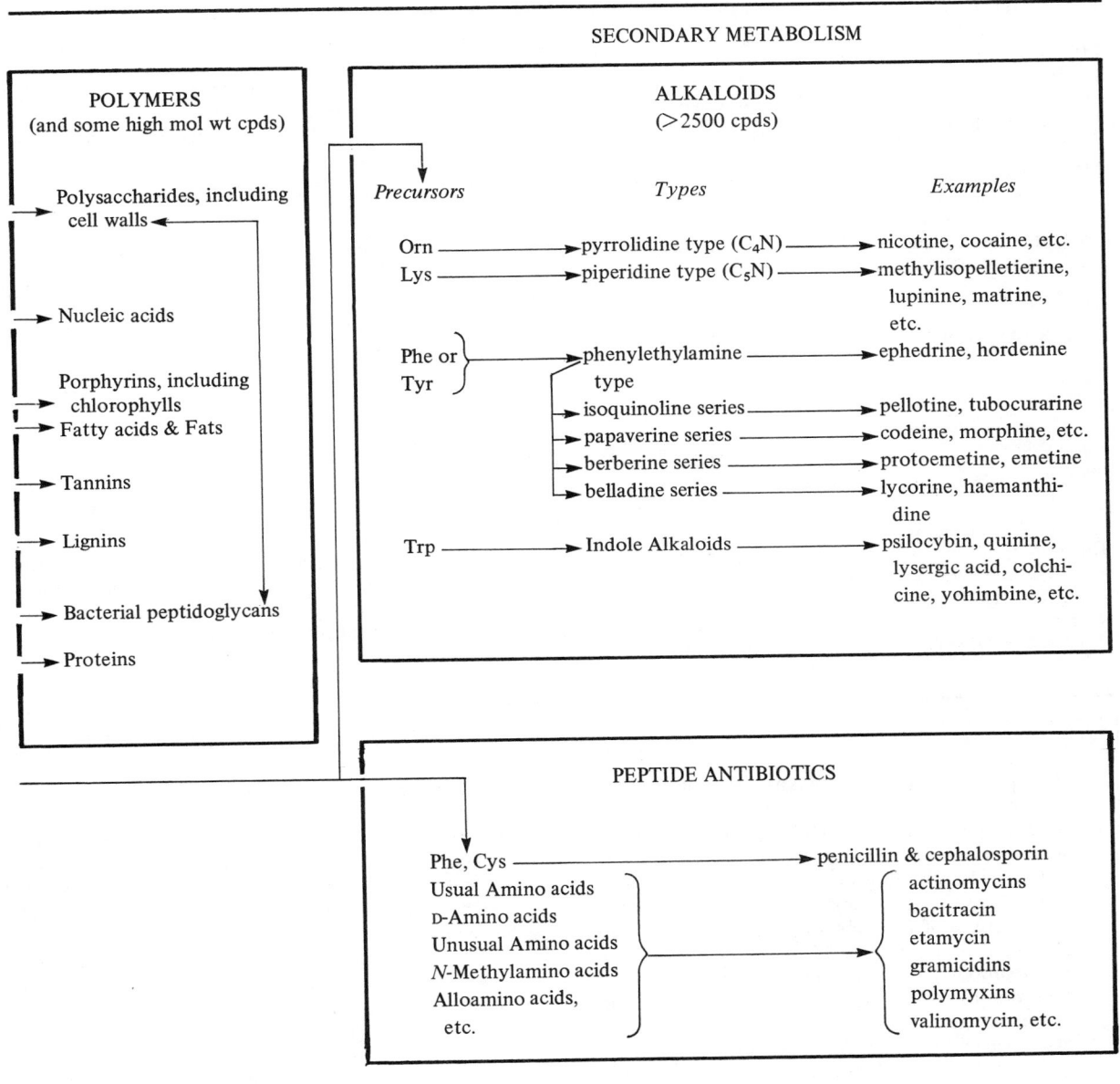

SECONDARY METABOLISM

POLYMERS
(and some high mol wt cpds)

- Polysaccharides, including cell walls
- Nucleic acids
- Porphyrins, including chlorophylls
- Fatty acids & Fats
- Tannins
- Lignins
- Bacterial peptidoglycans
- Proteins

ALKALOIDS
(>2500 cpds)

Precursors	*Types*	*Examples*
Orn	pyrrolidine type (C_4N)	nicotine, cocaine, etc.
Lys	piperidine type (C_5N)	methylisopelletierine, lupinine, matrine, etc.
Phe or Tyr	phenylethylamine type	ephedrine, hordenine
	isoquinoline series	pellotine, tubocurarine
	papaverine series	codeine, morphine, etc.
	berberine series	protoemetine, emetine
	belladine series	lycorine, haemanthidine
Trp	Indole Alkaloids	psilocybin, quinine, lysergic acid, colchicine, yohimbine, etc.

PEPTIDE ANTIBIOTICS

Phe, Cys → penicillin & cephalosporin

Usual Amino acids
D-Amino acids
Unusual Amino acids
N-Methylamino acids
Alloamino acids, etc.

→ actinomycins
bacitracin
etamycin
gramicidins
polymyxins
valinomycin, etc.

[6] Hendrickson, J. B. 1965. The Molecules of Nature. W. A. Benjamin, New York.

[7] Miller, M. W., ed. 1961. The Pfizer Handbook of Microbial Metabolites. McGraw-Hill, New York.

[8] Pridham, P. D., and T. Swain, ed. 1965. Biosynthetic Pathways in Higher Plants. Academic Press, New York.

Porphyrins and Related Compounds:

[9] Goodwin, T. W., ed. 1968. Biochem. Soc. Symp. 28.

[10] Lascelles, J. 1964. Tetrapyrrole Biosynthesis and Its Regulation. W. A. Benjamin, New York.

[11] Shemin, D. 1968. Vitam. Horm. (New York) 26: 357.

continued

Acetogenins and Isoprenoids:

[12] Archer, B. L., and B. G. Audley. 1967. Advan. Enzymol. Relat. Areas Mol. Biol. 29:221.

[13] Birch, A. J. 1967. Science 156:202.

[14] Dean, F. M. 1963. Naturally Occurring Oxygen Ring Compounds. Butterworth, London.

[15] Goodwin, T. W., ed. 1965. Chemistry and Biochemistry of Plant Pigments. Academic Press, New York.

[16] Goodwin, T. W., ed. 1970. Biochem. Soc. Symp. 29.

[17] Harbourne, J. B. 1967. Comparative Biochemistry of the Flavonoids. Academic Press, New York.

[18] Olson, R. E. 1966. Vitam. Horm. (New York) 24:551.

[19] Richards, J. H., and J. B. Hendrickson. 1964. The Biosynthesis of Steroids, Terpenes and Acetogenins. W. A. Benjamin, New York.

[20] Rudney, H., and T. S. Raman. 1966. Vitam. Horm. (New York) 24:531.

Alkaloids:

[21] Kurby, G. W. 1967. Science 155:170.

[22] Leete, E. 1965. Ibid. 147:1000.

[23] Leete, E. 1969. Advan. Enzymol. Relat. Areas Mol. Biol. 32:373.

[24] Manske, R. H. E., and H. L. Holmes, ed. 1950-67. The Alkaloids, Chemistry and Physiology. Academic Press, New York. v. 1-10.

[25] Mothes, K., and H. R. Schütte. 1969. Biosynthese der Alkaloide. Deutscher Verlag der Wissenschaften, Berlin.

[26] Pelletier, S., ed. 1970. Chemistry of the Alkaloids. Van Nostrand-Reinhold, New York.

[27] Robinson, T. 1968. The Biochemistry of Alkaloids. Springer-Verlag, New York.

[28] Taylor, W. I. 1966. Science 153:954.

Antibiotics:

[29] Bodanszky, M., and D. Perlman. 1969. Science 163:352.

[30] Katz, E. 1971. Pure Appl. Chem. 28:551.

[31] Perlman, D., and M. Bodanszky. 1971. Annu. Rev. Biochem. 40:449.

202. PROTEIN BIOSYNTHESIS

Part I. Pathways

The overall path from genetic DNA to the primary sequence of protein has been persuasively demonstrated by Khorana [21]. For recent reviews of protein biosynthesis, consult reference 14. *Abbreviations:* RNA = ribonucleic acid; tRNA = transfer ribonucleic acid; mRNA = messenger ribonucleic acid; DNA = deoxyribonucleic acid; ATP = adenosine 5'-triphosphate; AMP = adenosine 5'-monophosphate; CTP = cytidine 5'-triphosphate; GTP = guanosine 5'-triphosphate; PP$_i$ = inorganic pyrophosphate.

REACTIONS

A: "Stripped" tRNA (source unknown, molecular wt ∿30,000) is converted with ATP & CTP by unisolated enzymes [18] to tRNA's (containing anticodons) which are specific for each of the 20 different amino acids, with possibly as many as 5 different tRNA's specific for a single amino acid [16]. (For the structures of 18 tRNA's with sequence known as of 1972, consult reference 3.

B: The appropriate amino acid (1 of 20 L-amino acids) is converted by the amino acid-tRNA ligase specific for that amino acid to the corresponding amino acyl adenylate which remains tightly bound to the ligase enzyme; Mg^{2+} and probably a polyvalent cation (inferred from inhibition studies) also participate in the reaction [7,12]. This reaction is fully reversible [1,4,19]. There are 20 different ligase enzymes for each species, plus perhaps additional enzymes specific for individual organs and organelles.

C: Amino acyl adenylate and the same amino acyl ligase as in reaction B act with the specific tRNA to yield amino acyl-tRNA [2,6]. (Although chemically & enzymatically synthesized amino acyl adenylates will react in the forward or reverse directions, it is probable that under physiological conditions the synthesis of amino acyl-tRNA is concerted with no discrete amino acyl adenylate intermediate [12].) The overall reaction of amino acid, tRNA, & ATP to yield amino acyl-tRNA, AMP, & PP$_i$ is easily reversible, with an equilibrium constant near 1.0 [20].

D: mRNA (with triplet nucleotide codons [13]) is produced by RNA nucleotidyltransferase (DNA-dependent RNA polymerase) and riboside triphosphates, and is complementary to the sector of DNA involved.

E: Triplet codons of mRNA are associated with triplet anticodons of tRNA to add the next amino acid to the growing peptide chain; two enzyme fractions are involved [5,15].

F: Once the primary sequence of the protein is completed, it may undergo further reactions (e.g., formation of the α-helix or other stable conformations, formation of disulfide or other bridges, hydroxylation of proline in protocollagen, partial hydrolysis of zymogens) to become the completed functional protein.

continued

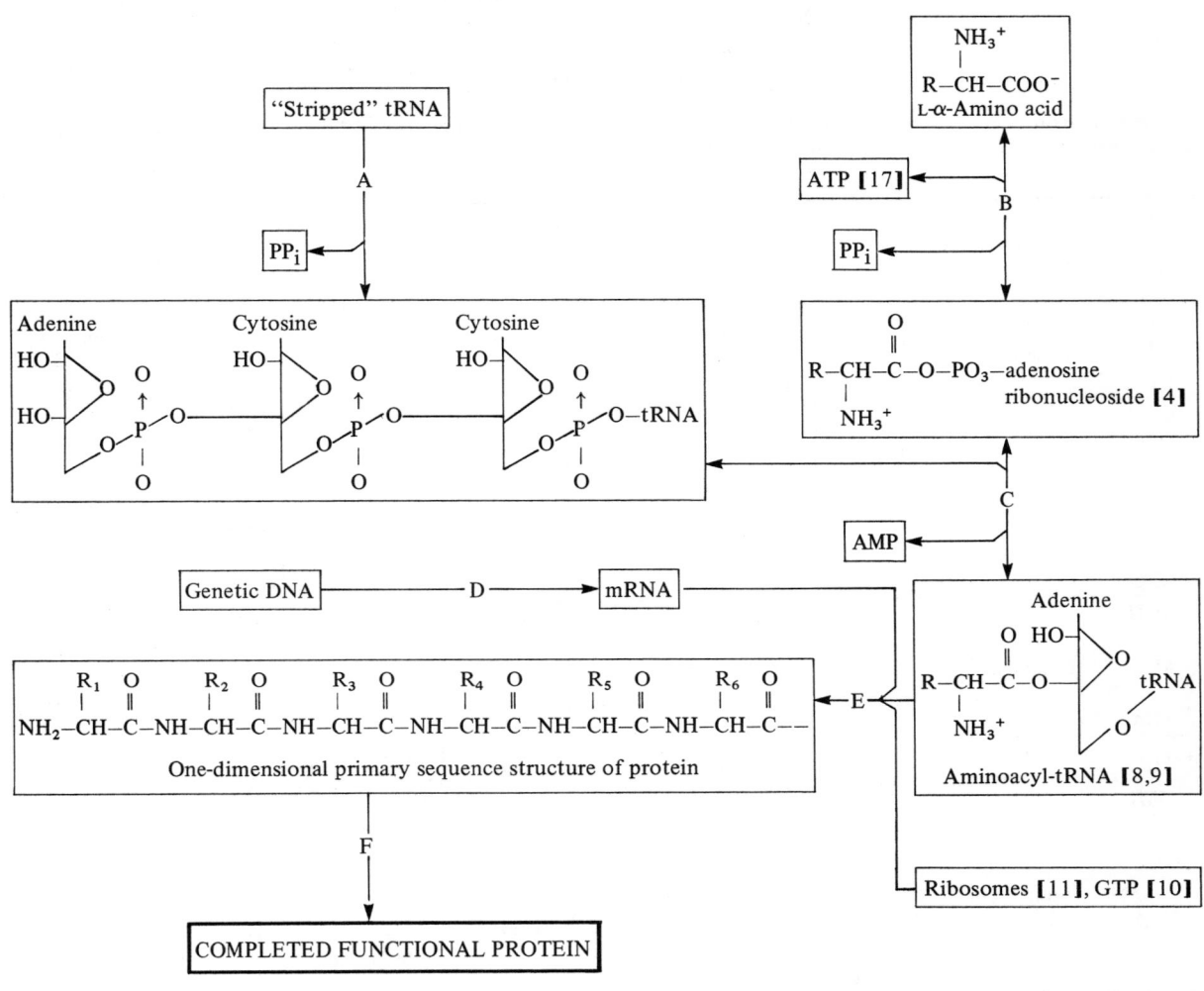

Contributor: Loftfield, Robert B.

References

[1] Berg, P. 1958. J. Biol. Chem. 233:601.

[2] Berg, P., and E. J. Offengand. 1958. Proc. Nat. Acad. Sci. U.S. 44:78.

[3] Dayhoff, M. O. 1972. Atlas of Protein Sequence and Structure. National Biomedical Research Foundation, Washington, D.C. v. 5.

[4] DeMoss, J. A., et al. 1956. Proc. Nat. Acad. Sci. U.S. 42:325.

[5] Fessenden, J. M., and K. Moldave. 1962. Biochemistry 1:485.

[6] Hecht, L. I., et al. 1959. Proc. Nat. Acad. Sci. U. S. 45:505.

[7] Hoagland, M. B., et al. 1956. J. Biol. Chem. 218:345.

[8] Hoagland, M. B., et al. 1957. Biochim. Biophys. Acta 24:215.

[9] Holley, R. W. 1957. J. Amer. Chem. Soc. 79:658.

[10] Littlefield, J. W., and E. B. Keller. 1957. J. Biol. Chem. 224:13.

[11] Littlefield, J. W., et al. 1955. Ibid. 217:111.

[12] Loftfield, R. B., and E. A. Eigner. 1969. Ibid. 244:1746.

[13] Marshall, R. E., et al. 1967. Science 155:820.

[14] McConkey, E., ed. 1971. Protein Synthesis—A Series of Advances. M. Dekker, New York.

[15] Nathans, D., and F. Lipmann. 1960. Biochim. Biophys. Acta 43:126.

[16] RajBhandary, U. L., et al. 1967. Proc. Nat. Acad. Sci. U.S. 57:751.

[17] Zamecnik, P. C., and E. B. Keller. 1954. J. Biol. Chem. 209:337.

[18] Zamecnik, P. C., et al. 1958. Proc. Nat. Acad. Sci. U.S. 44:73.

[19] Moldave, K., et al. 1959. J. Biol. Chem. 234:841.

continued

202. PROTEIN BIOSYNTHESIS

Part I. Pathways

[20] Leahy, J., et al. 1960. Ibid. 235:3209.

[21] Nishimura, S., et al. 1965. Fed. Proc. Fed. Amer. Soc. Exp. Biol. 24:409.

Part II. The Genetic Code

Nucleotide sequences of RNA (ribonucleic acid) codons are shown. *Abbreviations:* A = adenylate; C = cytidylate; G = guanylate; U = uridylate; tRNA = transfer ribonucleic acid.

UUU	Phenylalanine	UCU		UAU	Tyrosine	UGU	Cysteine
UUC		UCC	Serine	UAC		UGC	
UUA	Leucine	UCA		UAA	Terminate	UGA	Terminate
UUG		UCG		UAG		UGG	Tryptophan
CUU		CCU		CAU	Histidine	CGU	
CUC	Leucine	CCC	Proline	CAC		CGC	Arginine
CUA		CCA		CAA	Glutamine	CGA	
CUG		CCG		CAG		CGG	
AUU		ACU		AAU	Asparagine	AGU	Serine
AUC	Isoleucine	ACC	Threonine	AAC		AGC	
AUA		ACA		AAA	Lysine	AGA	Arginine
AUG	Methionine N-Formyl methionine[L]	ACG		AAG		AGG	
GUU		GCU		GAU	Aspartic acid	GGU	
GUC	Valine	GCC	Alanine	GAC		GGC	Glycine
GUA		GCA		GAA	Glutamic acid	GGA	
GUG	Valine (N-Formyl methionine[L])	GCG		GAG		GGG	

[L] N-Formylmethionyl-tRNA$_F$, an initiator of protein synthesis, binds to a different ribosomal site than methionyl-tRNA$_M$'s; hence, AUG and GUG can serve as initiators of protein synthesis or as methionine or valine codons, respectively, depending on the ribosomal codon recognition site.

Contributor: Nirenberg, Marshall W.

References: [1] Khorana, H. G., et al. 1966. Cold Spring Harbor Symp. Quant. Biol. 31:39. [2] Nirenberg, M. W., et al. 1966. Ibid. 31:11.

203. PATHWAYS OF POLYNUCLEOTIDE BIOSYNTHESIS

Part I. Purines

Abbreviations: ADP = adenosine 5'-diphosphate; AMP = adenosine 5'-monophosphate; ATP = adenosine 5'-triphosphate; Asp = aspartic acid (aspartate); Gln = glutamine; Glu = glutamic acid (glutamate); Gly = glycine; GDP = guanosine 5'-diphosphate; GTP = guanosine 5'-triphosphate; NAD$^+$ and NADH = nicotinamide adenine dinucleotide (oxidized and reduced forms, respectively); NADP$^+$ and NADPH = nicotinamide adenine dinucleotide phosphate (oxidized and reduced forms, respectively); P$_i$ = inorganic orthophosphate; PP$_i$ = inorganic pyrophosphate; THF = tetrahydrofolic acid coenzyme.

continued

Part I. Purines

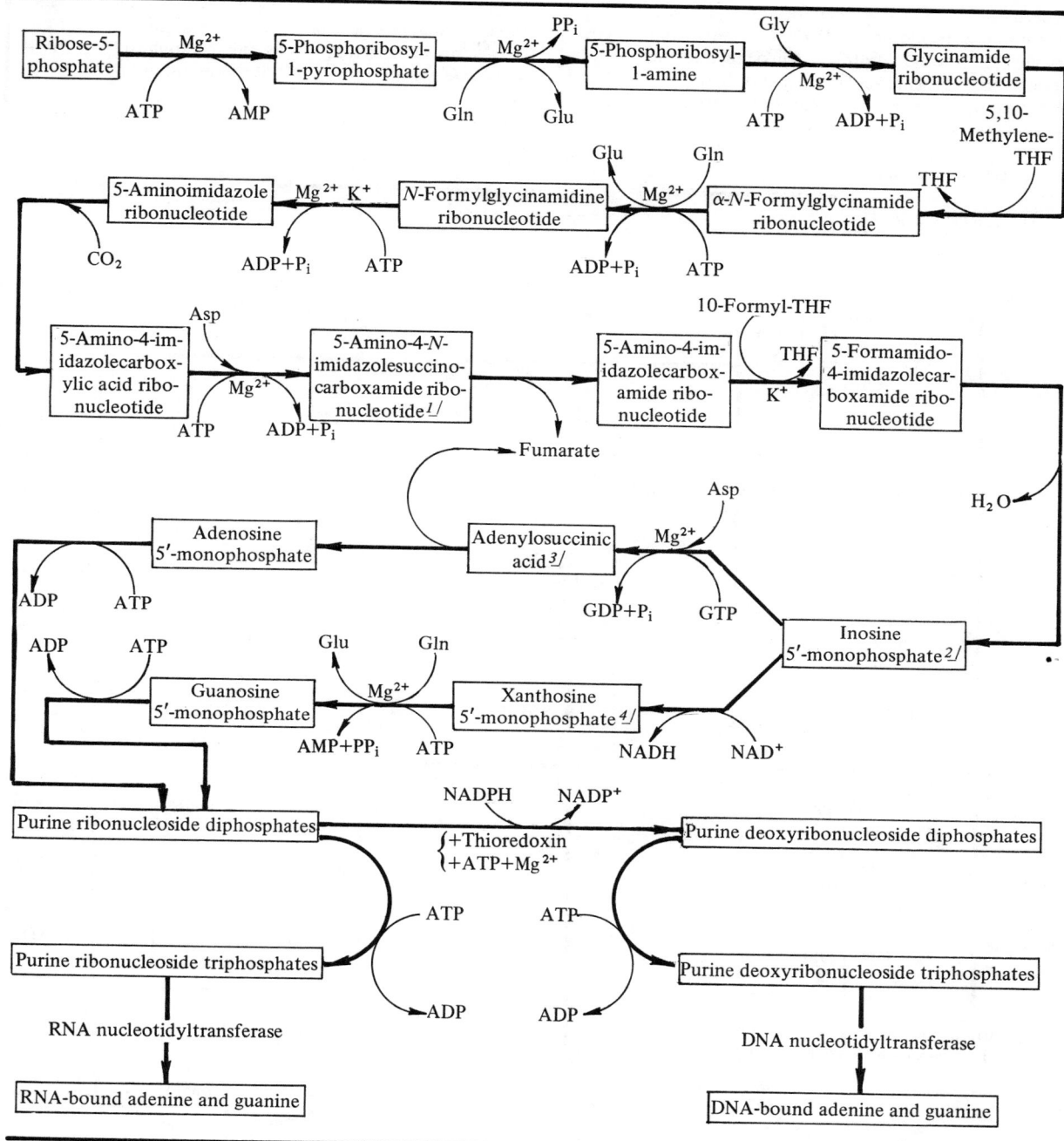

[1] Succinylaminoimidazole carboxamide ribonucleotide. [2] Inosinic acid or inosinate. [3] Adenylosuccinate. [4] Xanthylic acid.

Contributor: Lansford, Edwin M., Jr.

General References

[1] Hartman, S. C. 1967. In R. J. Williams and E. Lansford, Jr., ed. The Encyclopedia of Biochemistry. Reinhold, New York. pp. 705-708.

[2] Mahler, H. R., and E. H. Cordes. 1971. Biological Chemistry. Ed. 2. Harper and Row, New York. pp. 819-826.

[3] White, A., et al. 1973. Principles of Biochemistry. Ed. 5. McGraw-Hill, New York. pp. 705-713.

continued

Part II. Pyrimidines

Abbreviations: ADP = adenosine 5'-diphosphate; ATP = adenosine 5'-triphosphate; DHF = dihydrofolic acid coenzyme; THF = tetrahydrofolic acid coenzyme; Gln = L-glutamine; Glu = glutamic acid (glutamate); NAD$^+$ and NADH = nicotinamide adenine dinucleotide (oxidized and reduced forms, respectively); NADP$^+$ and NADPH = nicotinamide adenine dinucleotide phosphate (oxidized and reduced forms, respectively); P$_i$ = inorganic orthophosphate; PP$_i$ = inorganic pyrophosphate; PRPP = 5-phosphoribosyl-1-pyrophosphate.

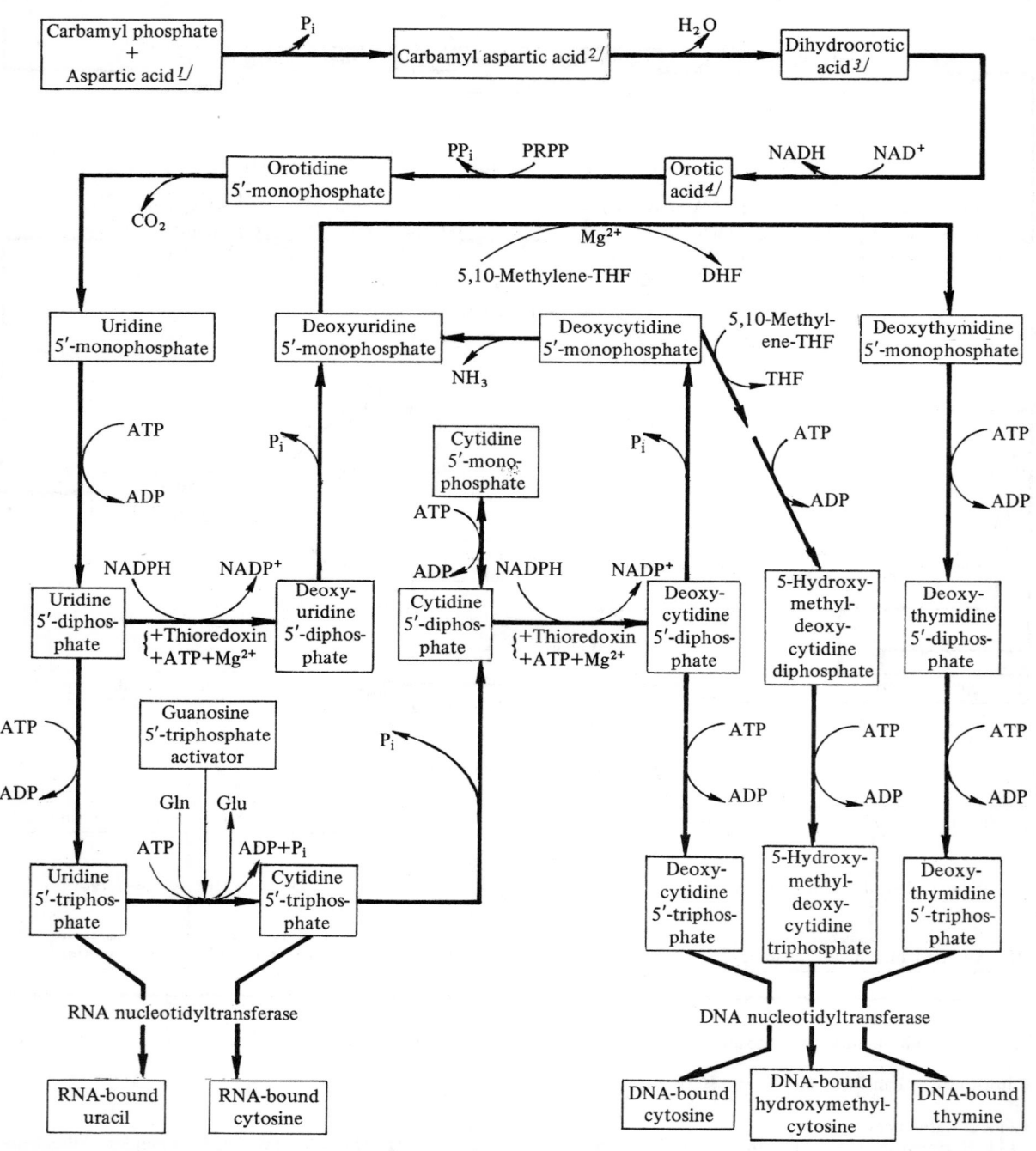

$^{1/}$ Aspartate. $^{2/}$ Ureidosuccinic acid. $^{3/}$ Dihydroorotate. $^{4/}$ Orotate.

Contributor: Lansford, Edwin M., Jr.

continued

203. PATHWAYS OF POLYNUCLEOTIDE BIOSYNTHESIS

Part II. Pyrimidines

General References

[1] Hurlbert, R. B. 1967. In R. J. Williams and E. Lansford, Jr., ed. The Encyclopedia of Biochemistry. Reinhold, New York. pp. 713-715.

[2] Mahler, H. R., and E. H. Cordes. 1971. Biological Chemistry. Ed. 2. Harper and Row, New York. pp. 826-834.

[3] White, A., et al. 1973. Principles of Biochemistry. Ed. 5. McGraw-Hill, New York. pp. 719-727.

204. NITROGEN CYCLE IN NATURE

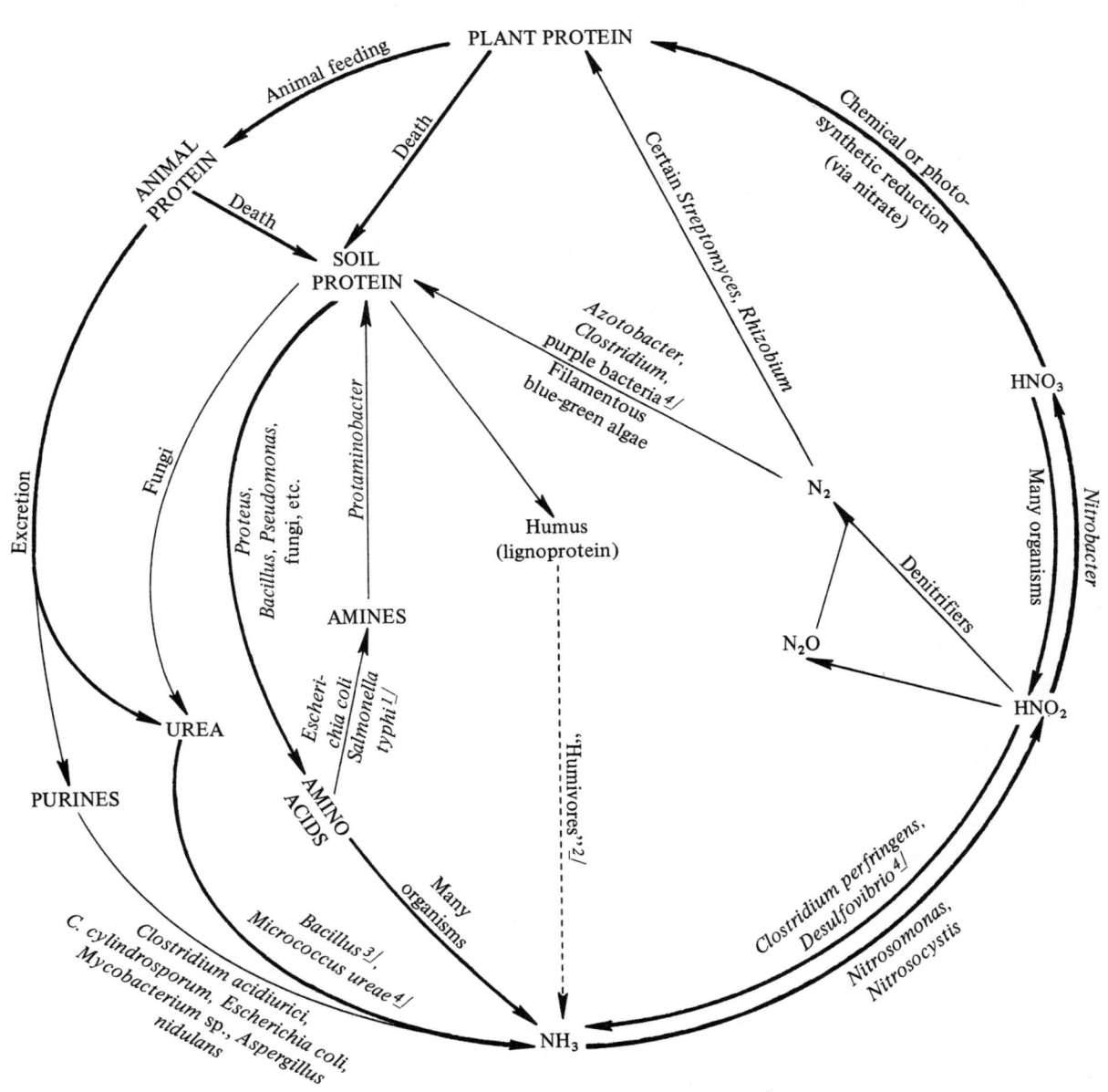

1/ Synonym: *S. typhosa.* 2/ Very slow. 3/ Synonym: *Urobacillus.* 4/ Also *Achromobacter* and several other bacteria.

Contributor: Thimann, Kenneth V.

Reference: Thimann, K. V. 1963. The life of bacteria. Ed. 2. Macmillan, New York.

XII. RESPIRATION AND CIRCULATION

205. PRINCIPLES GOVERNING BEHAVIOR OF GASES

	Law (Date)	Equation	Abbreviations & Symbols	Explanation
1	Equation of state for ideal gas	$PV = nRT$	P = pressure V = volume n = no. of moles of gas R = universal gas constant T = absolute temperature	The product of pressure times volume of a mixture of ideal gases equals the product of total number of moles present times universal gas constant times absolute temperature. The units of R depend on the units of the numerator, which has the dimension of work—i.e., $R = PV/nT = 0.08205$ atm·liter·mole^{-1}·$^{\circ}$K^{-1}; 8.314×10^7 ergs·mole^{-1}·$^{\circ}$K^{-1}; or 1.987 cal·mole^{-1}·$^{\circ}$K^{-1}.
2	Van der Waals' equation (1873)	$\left(P + \dfrac{n^2 a}{V^2}\right)(V - nb) = nRT$	P = pressure n = no. of moles of gas a = intermolecular attraction constant V = volume b = 4 times molecular volume R = universal gas constant T = absolute temperature	a & b, Van der Waals' constants, modify the preceding general equation for use with actual (nonideal) gases. a (a constant characteristic of the attractive force between molecules of each particular gas) = liter^2·atm/mole^2; b (4 times the aggregate volume occupied by all the molecules present in a given volume of gas) = liter/mole.
3	Critical point of a gas	Gas is at critical point and $P_C = f(V_C, T_C)$, if $P = f(V, T)$, $\dfrac{dP}{dV} = 0$, and $\dfrac{d^2 P}{dV^2} = 0$	P_C, V_C, T_C = pressure, volume, & absolute temperature existing at the critical point, where the curve relating pressure & volume of a given amount of gas has a point of inflection f = function relating P, V, & T in the equation of state P = pressure V = volume T = absolute temperature	Below the critical temperature, gases can be liquefied; during liquefaction, pressure remains constant as volume decreases sharply. Above the critical temperature, dP/dV never becomes 0, and liquefaction is impossible. P_C, V_C, & T_C are constants for any given gas.
4	Law of corresponding states	$\dfrac{P}{P_C} = f\left(\dfrac{V}{V_C}, \dfrac{T}{T_C}\right)$	P_C, V_C, T_C = pressure, volume, & absolute temperature—the critical constants of a gas f = a function defining the equation of state P = pressure V = volume T = absolute temperature	If f adequately describes gases with no more than 2 arbitrary constants (e.g., Van der Waals' equation), then such gases will all have the same equation of state expressed in terms of "reduced" pressure, volume, or temperature (P/P_C, V/V_C, T/T_C).
5	Boyle's law (1660)	$P_1 V_1 = P_2 V_2$, or $\dfrac{P_1}{P_2} = \dfrac{V_2}{V_1}$	P_1, P_2, V_1, V_2 = 2 pressures & corresponding volumes of a given amount of ideal gas at constant temperature	Boyle recognized that the product of pressure & volume is a constant at a fixed temperature for a given quantity of gas. This constant is nRT of equation 1, which was derived after Boyle's time.
6	Charles' (1787) & Gay-Lussac's (1802) law	$\dfrac{V_1}{V_2} = \dfrac{T_1}{T_2}$, $\dfrac{P_1}{P_2} = \dfrac{T_1}{T_2}$	$V_1, V_2, T_1, T_2, P_1, P_2$ = 2 volumes & corresponding temperatures (absolute), & pressures of a given amount of ideal gas	Either pressure or volume is directly proportional to absolute temperature of a gas if the other is held constant.

continued

	Law (Date)	Equation	Abbreviations & Symbols	Explanation
7	Avogadro's law (1811)	....	....	Equal volumes of different gases at the same temperature & pressure contain equal numbers of molecules. Avogadro's number is the number of molecules in 1 gram molecular weight and equals 6.02252×10^{23} molecules/chemical mole. The law exactly applies only for an ideal gas, 1 mole of which occupies 22.414 liters at 0°C (273.16°K) & 1 atm pressure (1.01325×10^6 dynes·cm^{-2}, or 760 mmHg).
8	Dalton's law of partial pressures (1801)	$P = P_1 + P_2 + P_3$, etc.	P = pressure P_1, P_2, P_3 = partial pressures of various gases in a mixture	The partial pressure of each gas in a mixture is independent of the other gases present; therefore the total pressure equals the sum of the partial pressures of all gases present.
9	Henry's law of gas solubility (1803)	$V_d = \alpha P_1 V_L$	α = Bunsen solubility coefficient at specified temperature P_1 = partial pressure, in atm, of that gas above the liquid V_L = volume of liquid V_d = volume of gas dissolved at STPD	The quantity of a slightly soluble gas which dissolves in a liquid at a given temperature is nearly proportional to the partial pressure of that gas in the gas phase. This law applies only to gases which do not react chemically with the solvent. Units of the Bunsen solubility coefficient are liters of gas at STPD per liter of solvent per atm.
10	Graham's law (1829)	$E \sim \sqrt{\dfrac{1}{\rho}}$	E = rate of effusion of a gas into a vacuum ρ = density of the gas	The rate of effusion of a gas into a vacuum is inversely proportional to the square root of the density of that gas. A similar relationship applies to the self-diffusion coefficient of gases.
11	Specific heat (molar)	$C_v = \dfrac{3R}{2}\,^{1/}; \dfrac{5R}{2}\,^{2/}$ $C_p = \dfrac{5R}{2}\,^{1/}; \dfrac{7R}{2}\,^{2/}$	C_v = specific heat of a gas at constant volume R = universal gas constant C_p = specific heat of a gas at constant pressure	Specific heat (molar) is the number of calories required to warm 1 mole of a gas 1°C.
12	Carnot's law (1824)	$C_p - C_v = R$	C_p = specific heat of a gas at constant pressure C_v = specific heat of a gas at constant volume R = universal gas constant	The difference between specific heats is the same for a given volume of all gases at the same pressure & temperature. For an ideal gas under standard conditions, $C_p - C_v = R$.
13	Law of adiabatic expansion or compression	$P_1 V_1{}^{\gamma} = P_2 V_2{}^{\gamma}$; $T_1 V_1{}^{\gamma-1} = T_2 V_2{}^{\gamma-1}$	P_1, P_2, V_1, V_2, T_1, T_2 = 2 corresponding pressures, volumes, & absolute temperatures of a given amount of gas $\gamma = C_p/C_v$ (ratio of specific heats) = $5/3\,^{1/}$; $7/5\,^{2/}$	Equations give the relationship of pressure or temperatures to volume of a given amount of gas when total heat content of the gas is constant—adiabatic conditions. (See Boyle's & Charles' laws.)
14	Velocity of sound in a gas	$v_s = \sqrt{\dfrac{P\gamma}{\rho}}$	v_s = velocity of sound P = pressure $\gamma = C_p/C_v$ (ratio of specific heats) = $5/3\,^{1/}$; $7/5\,^{2/}$ ρ = density of gas	Equation applies for intermediate sound frequencies, and does not apply for low pressures or for gases deviating markedly from ideal behavior.

$^{1/}$ Monatomic. $^{2/}$ Diatomic.

continued

Law (Date)	Equation	Abbreviations & Symbols	Explanation
15	Raoult's law (1888)	$P_1 = P_V x_1$	P_1 = partial pressure of substance 1 P_V = vapor pressure of pure substance 1 x_1 = mole fraction of substance 1 to total moles	The partial pressure of a volatile liquid in a mixture of liquids is proportional to the mole fraction (ratio of moles of the substance to the total number of moles in the liquid). However, molar weights of nonvolatile nonelectrolytes dissolved in a definite weight of a given solvent under the same conditions lower the solvent's freezing point, elevate its boiling point, and reduce its vapor pressure equally for all such solutes.
16	Poiseuille's law of laminar flow	$\dot{V} = \dfrac{\Delta P r^4}{8 L \eta}$	$\dot{V}$ = gas flow, in $cm^3 \cdot s^{-1}$ ΔP = pressure gradient between 2 ends of tube, in $dynes \cdot cm^{-2}$ r = radius of tube, in cm L = length of tube, in cm η = viscosity, in poise	In laminar flow, velocity is proportional to area (r^2), and volume flow is proportional to area squared (r^4). Flow is directly proportional to the driving pressure—i.e., resistance is independent of flow. This relationship does not take into account the compressibility of the gas.
17	Reynolds' number	$N_R = \dfrac{\bar{c} \cdot 2 r \cdot \rho}{\eta}$	N_R = Reynolds' number $\bar{c}$ = mean velocity of gas, in $cm \cdot s^{-1}$ r = radius of conducting tube, in cm ρ = density, in $g \cdot cm^{-3}$ η = viscosity, in poise	The tendency of a gas flowing through a tube to become turbulent is directly proportional to its velocity & density, and inversely proportional to its viscosity. Turbulence in a straight tube usually occurs when the unitless N_R reaches 1000-2000.
18	Maxwell's law	....	....	Viscosity of a gas is independent of pressure if the pressure is not extremely high or low.
19	Kinematic viscosity	$\dfrac{\eta}{\rho}$	η = viscosity, in poise ρ = density, in $g \cdot cm^{-3}$	Gases of equal kinematic viscosity will become turbulent at equal flow rates in identical airways.
20	Mach's number	$N_M = \dfrac{\bar{c}}{v_s}$	N_M = Mach's number $\bar{c}$ = mean velocity of gas v_s = velocity of sound	Flow of gas molecules escaping downstream through an orifice is limited by the velocity of sound. In practice, critical (or maximal) orifice flow occurs at approx. 0.5 atm pressure gradient.
21	Law of atmospheres	$Log \dfrac{P_o}{P_a} = \dfrac{0.4343 M g (a - o)}{RT}$	P = pressure o, a = 2 heights, in cm M = molecular weight g = acceleration of gravity, in $cm \cdot s^{-2}$ R = universal gas constant T = absolute temperature	The pressure, density, & concentration of a gas decrease exponentially with height at constant temperature. Since temperature decreases with height in the atmosphere, this relationship is only approximate.

Contributors: Severinghaus, John W.; Radford, Edward P.

General References

[1] Radford, E. P., Jr. 1964. Handb. Physiol., Sect. 3, Resp. 1:125.

[2] Glasstone, D. and D. Lewis. 1960. Elements of Physical Chemistry. Ed. 2. Van Nostrand, Princeton.

206. PRINCIPLES GOVERNING FLOW IN VESSELS

Conditions governing blood flow are not the same throughout the vascular tree. Flow is usually disturbed, but not truly turbulent, during portions of the cardiac cycle in vessels close to the heart, i.e., in the proximal aorta, main pulmonary artery, and venae cavae. Flow in the distal aorta and large arteries and veins can be regarded as linear,

continued

axisymmetric, and pulsatile. Non-Newtonian viscous properties of blood become significant in flow in terminal arteries and veins. Blood must be considered to be a two-phase fluid in flow in the microcirculation.

Part I. Quantitative Relations Pertaining to Steady Flow

The equations on the following page cannot be applied to aortic and arterial flow. They apply only to flow where (i) blood is a homogenous liquid having a constant (Newtonian) viscosity of 3-4 centipoise when it is above shear rates of approximately 100 s^{-1} and shear stress of approximately 3 dynes·cm^{-2}; (ii) flow rate is steady with time (not pulsatile); (iii) tubes are straight, with a constant cross section; and (iv) the wall of the tube does not interact with the flow by elastic expansion and contraction. Data are for Newtonian incompressible liquid in straight tubes of constant circular cross section, unless otherwise specified.

ABBREVIATIONS & SYMBOLS

τ = shear stress (drag force/unit area), in dynes·cm^{-2}

$P_{i_1} - P_{i_2}$ = dynamic pressure drop, in dynes·cm^{-2}, between sections ① and ② on page 1575 (1 dyne·cm^{-2} = 9.87 × 10^{-7} atm = 7.50 × 10^{-4} mm Hg)

r = radial distance from axis of tube, in cm

L = length of tube, in cm, between sections ① and ② on page 1575

$\dot{\gamma}$ = shear rate, or change in velocity with distance measured at 90° to flow direction [(cm/s)·cm^{-1} = 1/s]

η = viscosity, in poise (1 poise = 1 dyne·s·cm^{-2} = 1 g·cm^{-1}·s^{-1} = 100 centipoise)

N_R = Reynolds' number

a = inside radius of tube (lumen), in cm

$\bar{U}$ = mean velocity, in cm·s^{-1}

ρ = density of fluid, in g·cm^{-3}

$\dot{Q}$ = volumetric flow rate, in cm^3·s^{-1}

π = 3.14159

U_0 = velocity at axis (r = 0), in cm·s^{-1}

U_r = velocity at any distance r from axis, in cm·s^{-1}

P_i = pressure inside tube at specified section, in dynes·cm^{-2}

P_e = external pressure at same section where P_i occurs, in dynes·cm^{-2}

σ_t = tangential stress, in dynes·cm^{-2}

b = outer radius of tube, in cm

σ_r = radial stress, in dynes·cm^{-2}

σ = stress, in dynes·cm^{-2}

σ_x = axial stress, in dynes·cm^{-2}

U = velocity, in cm·s^{-1}

	Law	Equation	Explanation
1	Shear stress	$\tau = \dfrac{(P_{i_1} - P_{i_2})r}{2L}$	Shear stress varies directly with dynamic pressure drop over a given length, and varies directly with distance from axis, being zero at the axis and a maximum value at the wall
2	Shear rate at a tube wall	$\dot{\gamma} = \dfrac{(P_{i_1} - P_{i_2})r}{2\eta L}$	Local shear rate varies directly with dynamic pressure drop over a given length, and varies directly with distance from axis, being zero at the axis and a maximum value at the wall
3	Newton's equation for viscosity	$\tau = \eta\dot{\gamma}$, or $\eta = \dfrac{\tau}{\dot{\gamma}}$	Viscosity is defined as the ratio of shear stress to shear rate. Equations are limited to laminar steady flow; values for viscosity of "non-Newtonian" liquids are variable.
4	Reynolds' number	$N_R = \dfrac{2a\bar{U}\rho}{\eta} = \dfrac{2\dot{Q}\rho}{\pi a\eta}$	Reynolds' number is a ratio of inertial force to viscous drag force acting on an element of fluid. It is used as a criterion for establishing whether flow is laminar or turbulent. For steady flow in a straight cylindrical tube: if N_R <2000, the flow must be laminar and obey Poiseuille's law; if N_R >2000, the flow may be turbulent.
5	Poiseuille's law [1]	$\dot{Q} = \dfrac{\pi(P_{i_1} - P_{i_2})a^4}{8\eta L}$	Flow rate of a fluid varies directly with pressure drop, directly as the fourth power of the radius, and inversely with the tube length (limited to steady flows for Reynolds' numbers of 2000 or less)
6		$U_0 - U_r = \dfrac{(P_{i_1} - P_{i_2})}{4\eta L}\cdot(a^2 - r^2)$	Velocity varies from a maximum at the axis to zero at the wall, and as the square of the distance r from axis toward wall
7		$\bar{U} = \tfrac{1}{2}U_0$	Mean velocity is exactly one-half the velocity at the axis
8	Tangential stress in thin-walled tube	$\sigma_t = \dfrac{a(P_i - P_e)}{b - a}$	Equation shows relation between tangential wall stress & transmural pressure in thin-walled tube

[1] Cannot be applied to flow in capillaries, where blood is a two-phase fluid; particles of suspended phase (erythrocytes) are as large as lumen diameter.

continued

Part I. Quantitative Relations Pertaining to Steady Flow

	Law	Equation	Explanation
9	Tangential stress in thick-walled tube	$\sigma_t = \dfrac{a^2 P_i - b^2 P_e}{b^2 - a^2} + \dfrac{a^2 b^2 (P_i - P_e)}{r^2 (b^2 - a^2)}$	Tangential stress is a function of distance r from axis ($a < r < b$); stress is largest at a and decreases to a minimum at b
10	Radial stress in thick-walled tube	$\sigma_r = \dfrac{a^2 P_i - b^2 P_e}{b^2 - a^2} - \dfrac{a^2 b^2 (P_i - P_e)}{r^2 (b^2 - a^2)}$	Radial stress is a function of distance r from axis; also decreases with r from a maximum at a to a minimum at b

DIAGRAMS

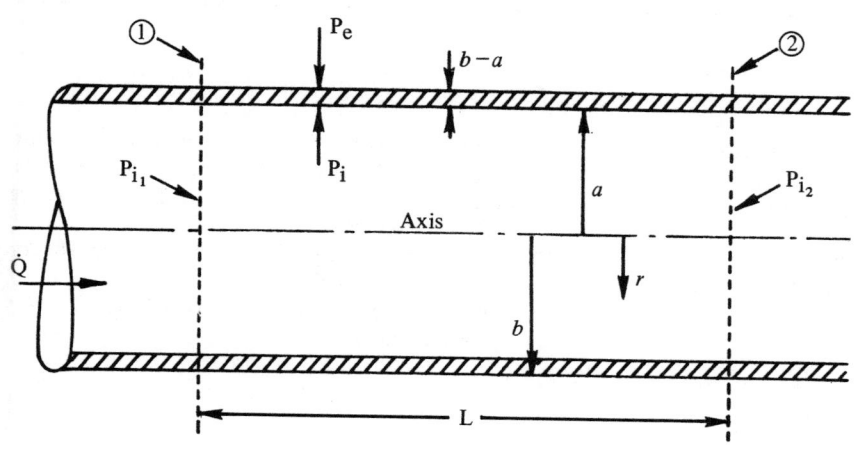

RELATION OF PRESSURE TO TUBE WALL

Pressure (P_i) is uniform across section ① or any other section, but decreases in the direction of flow (i.e., $P_{i_2} < P_{i_1}$).

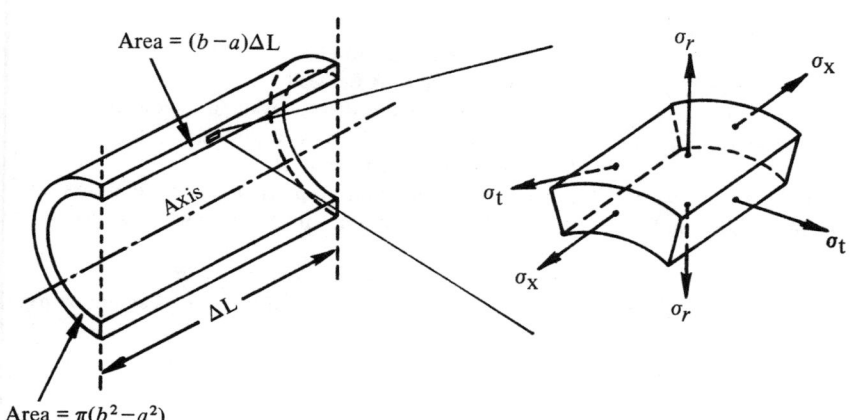

RELATION OF STRESS FACTORS TO TUBE WALL

Stress (σ) is exerted on the wall of the tube in 3 components: radial stress (σ_r), axial stress (σ_x), and tangential stress (σ_t).

continued

206. PRINCIPLES GOVERNING FLOW IN VESSELS

Part I. Quantitative Relations Pertaining to Steady Flow

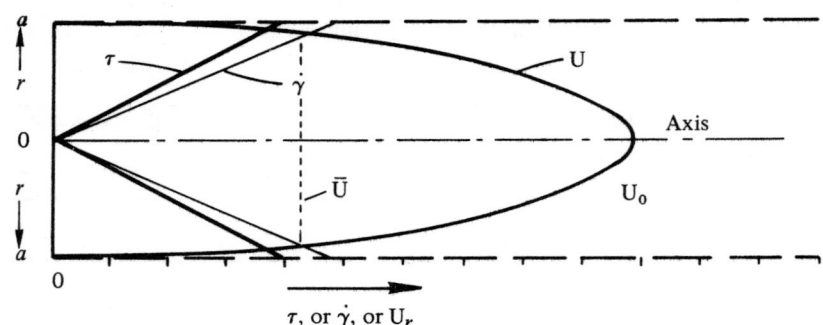

RELATION OF SHEAR STRESS, SHEAR RATE, AND POINT VELOCITY TO DISTANCE FROM AXIS AT SECTION ① FOR STEADY FLOW

Shear stress (τ), shear rate ($\dot{\gamma}$), and velocity (U) are functions of distance (r) from axis toward inner wall ($r = a$).

Contributors: Merrill, Edward W.; Cox, Robert H.

General References

[1] Haynes, R. H. 1960. Amer. J. Physiol. 198:1193.
[2] Ling, S. C., et al. 1968. Circ. Res. 23:789.
[3] McDonald, D. A. 1960. Blood Flow in Arteries. Williams and Wilkins, Baltimore.
[4] Merrill, E. W. 1969. Physiol. Rev. 49:863.
[5] Peterson, L. H., et al. 1960. Circ. Res. 8:622.

[6] Prandtl, L. 1949. Führer durch die Strömungslehre. 3 Aufl. F. Vieweg, Braunschweig. (*Translation:* Deans, W. M. 1952. Essentials of Fluid Dynamics. S. Hafner, New York.)
[7] Schlichting, H. 1955. Boundary Layer Theory. McGraw-Hill, New York.
[8] Timeshenko, S. 1956. Strength of Materials. Van Nostrand, Princeton.

Part II. Quantitative Relations Pertaining to Pulsatile Flow

ABBREVIATIONS & SYMBOLS

Q = sinusoidal flow in cm·s^{-1}

P_{i_2} = internal pressure, in dynes·cm^{-2}, at section ② on page 1575

P_{i_1} = internal pressure, in dynes·cm^{-2}, at section ① on page 1575

j = imaginary number, $\sqrt{-1}$

ω = angular frequency ($\omega = 2\pi f$, where f = circular frequency, in cycles·s^{-1}), in s^{-1}

ρ = density of fluid, in g·cm^{-3}

L = length of tube, in cm, between sections ① and ② on page 1575

J_1, J_0 = vessel functions of first kind (tabulated quantities)

z = fluid parameter = $j^{2/3}\alpha$

$\alpha = \sqrt{\omega\eta/\rho}$

η = viscosity, in poise (dyne·s·cm^{-2})

θ = complex quantity which depends on assumed coupling of blood vessel wall with surrounding environment

u_r = displacement of vessel wall in radial direction

v = Poisson ratio of vessel wall

E = Young's modulus of vessel wall, in dynes·cm^{-2}

a = inside radius of tube (lumen), in cm

b = outside radius of tube, in cm

P_i = pressure inside tube at specified section, in dynes·cm^{-2}

P_e = external pressure at same section where P_i occurs, in dynes·cm^{-2}

r = radial distance from axis of tube, in cm

σ_t = tangential stress in wall of tube (*see* diagram on page 1575)

R = viscous modulus of vessel wall, in dyne·s·cm^{-2}

t = time, in s

U = velocity, in cm·s^{-1}

U_0 = velocity at axis ($r = 0$), in cm·s^{-1}

$|z|$ = absolute value of z

continued

Part II. Quantitative Relations Pertaining to Pulsatile Flow

	Law	Equation	Explanation
1	Sinusoidal flow in tube	$Q = \dfrac{P_{i_2} - P_{i_1}}{j\omega\rho L} \cdot \left(1 - \dfrac{2J_1(z)}{zJ_0(z)} \cdot \theta\right)$	Equation shows relation between sinusoidal flow (Q) & pressure difference in oscillatory flow; $\theta = 1$ for a rigid tube
2	Radial wall displacement	$u_r = \dfrac{1-v}{E} \cdot \left[\dfrac{a^2P_i - b^2P_e}{b^2-a^2}\right] \cdot r + \dfrac{1+v}{E} \cdot \left[\dfrac{a^2b^2(P_i + P_e)}{(b^2-a^2)r}\right]$	Equation shows relation between wall displacement & changes in transmural pressures
3	Vessel wall viscoelasticity	$\sigma_t = E\left(\dfrac{u_r}{b}\right) + \dfrac{R}{b} \cdot du_r/dt$	When wall displacement is dynamic, i.e., a function of time, the stress depends upon both the displacement & the rate of change of displacement

For flows of the linear, axisymmetric, pulsatile type, flow lags the pressure difference in time (or in phase for sinusoidal variations), as contrasted with steady flow where pressure difference and flow are in phase. The graphs below show (i) the amplitude ratio (amplitude divided by the Poiseuille resistance, in dyne·s·cm^{-5}), and (ii) the phase angle of fluid impedance (a generalization of Poiseuille re-sistance, equal to $[(P_{i_1} - P_{i_2})/L]\,Q$), which determines the relation between pressure difference and pulsatile flow. For small-radius vessels or slowly varying flows, the value of α is low, and the fluid impedance approaches the Poiseuille resistance. For pulsatile flow in the larger arteries and veins, α is of the order of 6, whereas α is of the order of 0.5 for pulsatile flow occurring in terminal arteries and veins.

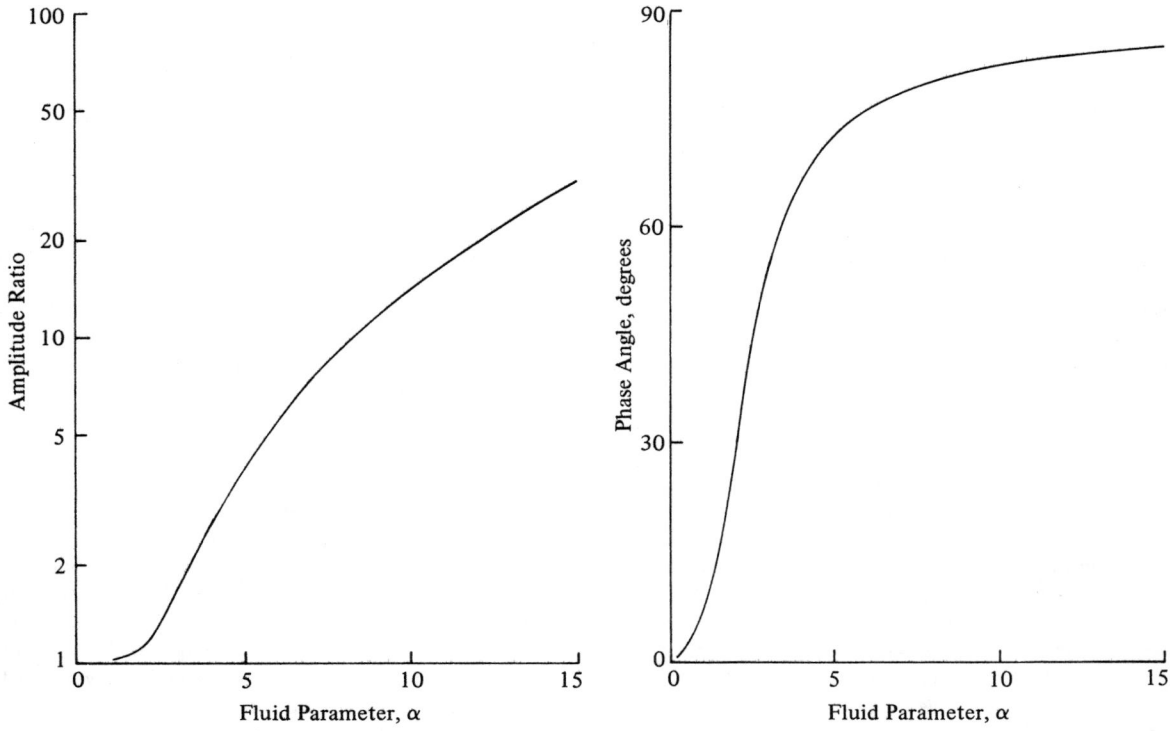

continued

Part II. Quantitative Relations Pertaining to Pulsatile Flow

More complex profiles of fluid velocity distribution occur for pulsatile flows, as compared to steady flow for which fluid velocity distribution is parabolic. At high values of α, the profile is nearly flat; at low values of α, the profile approaches a parabola.

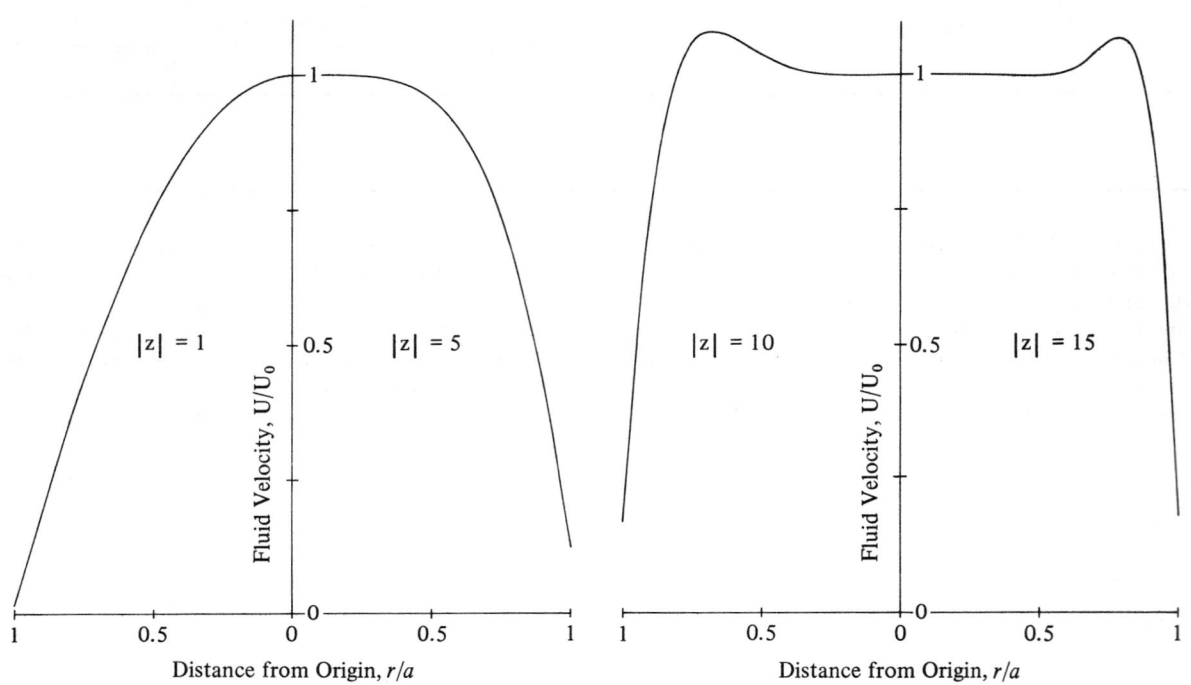

Contributor: Cox, Robert H.

General References: [1] Cox, R. H. 1968. Biophys. J. 8:691. [2] Womersley, J. R. 1955. Phil. Mag. 46:199.

Part III. Qualitative Effects Associated with Changes in Geometry

Flow separation is the most important fluid-mechanical event associated with changes in vessel geometry. Recirculating eddies are formed which may periodically detach and move downstream; a new eddy may then be formed at the original site. In physiological systems, flow separation is not possible in smaller vessels where viscous forces are much greater than the causative inertial forces. Flow separation in the venous return is far less probable than in the arterial tree. Energy dissipated by flow separation is trivial in relation to the total heart work output. Although definitive proof is lacking, the phenomenon of flow separation may be important in the formation and growth of emboli. In support of such a theory is the reasoning that during flow separation, plasma clotting factors activated in the quiescent zones of the recirculating eddy next to the vessel wall can more easily attain critical concentrations which perpetuate the clotting cascade, and that the fibrin polymer especially can evolve more readily into a network. The following drawings show physiological situations in which flow separation may occur.

continued

Part III. Qualitative Effects Associated with Changes in Geometry

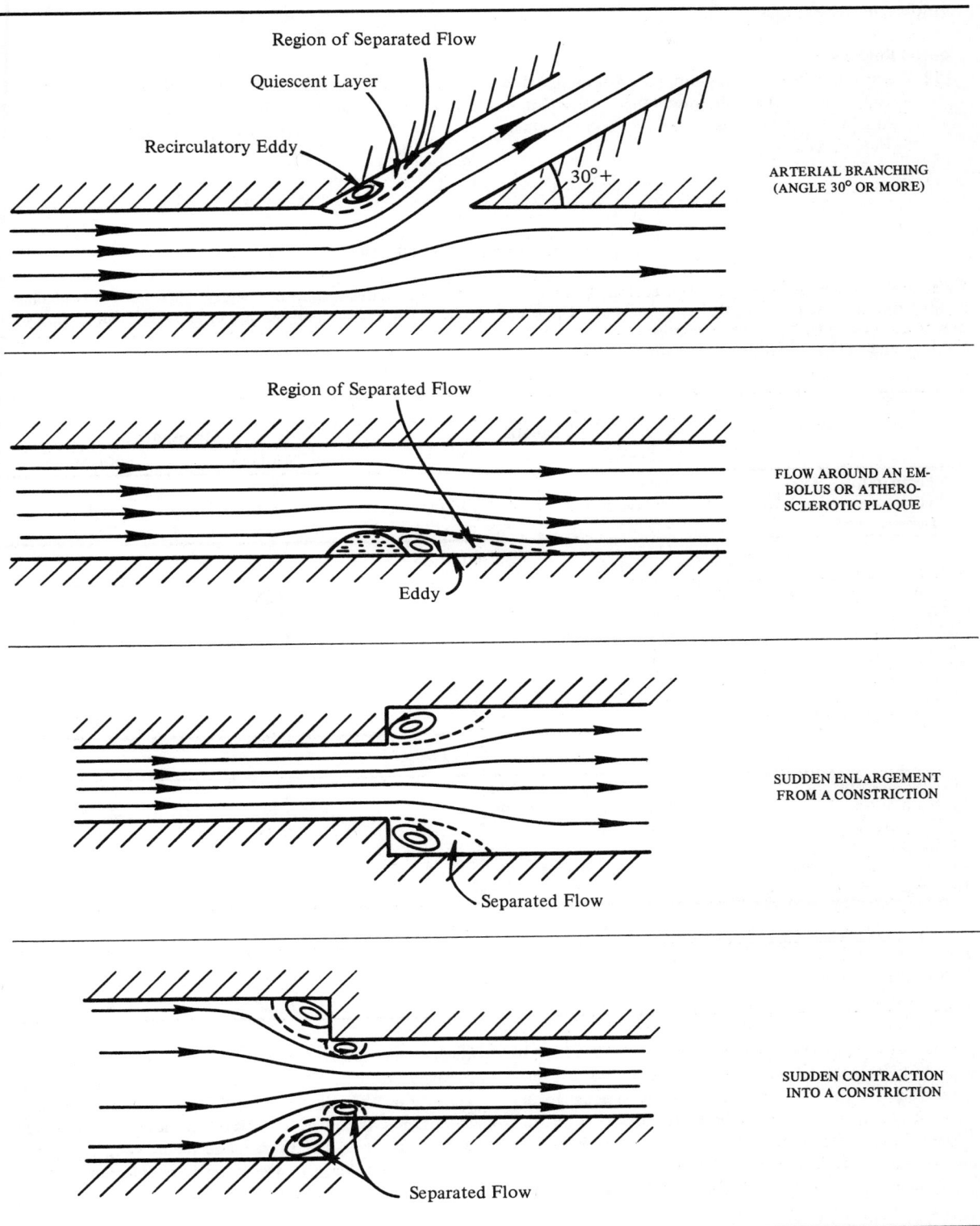

Region of Separated Flow

Quiescent Layer

Recirculatory Eddy

30°+

ARTERIAL BRANCHING
(ANGLE 30° OR MORE)

Region of Separated Flow

FLOW AROUND AN EM-
BOLUS OR ATHERO-
SCLEROTIC PLAQUE

Eddy

SUDDEN ENLARGEMENT
FROM A CONSTRICTION

Separated Flow

SUDDEN CONTRACTION
INTO A CONSTRICTION

Separated Flow

continued

Part III. Qualitative Effects Associated with Changes in Geometry

Contributor: Smith, Kenneth A.

General References

[1] Prandtl, L. 1949. Führer durch die Strömungslehre. 3 Aufl. F. Vieweg, Braunschweig. (*Translation:* Deans, W. M. 1952. Essentials of Fluid Dynamics. S. Hafner, New York.)

[2] Schlichting, H. 1965. Grenzschicht-Theorie. 5 Aufl. G. Braun, Karlsruhe. (*Translation:* Kestin, J. 1968. Boundary Layer Theory. 6th English ed. McGraw-Hill, New York.)

207. RESPIRATORY MEDIA

Water and nitrogen are the two major ecological variations in the respiratory media available to organisms. The aqueous or gaseous solvent (water or nitrogen), through which the exchange of O_2 and CO_2 occurs, is the primary substance that ventilates respiratory organs. The solvent is mechanically inspired in many species of animals. Values may vary widely; however, except for two ranges, only averages are given.

	Variable	Media			
		Aquatic		Atmospheric	
		Ocean	Fresh	Sea Level	6000 Meters
1	Temperature, °C	10[1]	15[2]	15	−24
2	Total pressure, mm Hg	760-800,000[3,4]	760-140,000[3,4]	760	354
3	Density, g·liter^{-1}	1028[5]	999	1.225	0.660
		Concentration			
4	H_2O, vol %	96.55[6]	99.99[6]	0.66[4,7]	0.66[4,7]
5	N_2, vol %	1.16[4]	1.35[4]	78.09[8]	78.09[8]
6	CO_2, vol %	0.03[4]	0.03[4]	0.03[8]	0.03[8]
7	O_2, vol %	0.64[4]	0.71[4]	20.95[8]	20.95[8]
8	Salts, ‰	34.5	0.12	·········	·········
9	pH	8.15	7	·········	·········
10	Inert gases, vol %	0.03[4]	0.03[4]	0.93[8]	0.93[8]
		Partial Pressure (Tension)[9]			
11	H_2O, mm Hg	9.2	12.8	5	2[2]
12	N_2, mm Hg	590	590	590	275[4]
13	CO_2, mm Hg	0.23	0.23	0.23	0.1[4]
14	O_2, mm Hg	158	158	158	74[4]
15	Inert gases, mm Hg	7	7	7	3[4]
16	Total pressure, mm Hg	755[8]	755[8]	760	354
		Diffusivity (Coefficient of Diffusion)			
17	N_2, cm^2·min^{-1}	·············	0.00091[4]	13[4]	22[4]
18	CO_2, cm^2·min^{-1}	·············	0.00087[4]	9.22[4]	14.8[4]
19	O_2, cm^2·min^{-1}	·············	0.00104[4]	11.7[4]	19.5[4]

[1] The surface temperature can vary from −1°C at high latitudes to 25°C at low latitudes; below 1000 meters, the temperature is 2-4°C. [2] Average assumed to be equal to the value at sea level. [3] The highest pressures occur at the greatest depths; the greatest depth for the ocean is 10,900 meters and for freshwater is 1,940 meters. [4] Calculated. [5] The density decreases slightly for a constant salinity when the temperature is increased; for ocean surface water at a temperature of 15°C the density is 1025-1027 g·liter^{-1}, depending on the salinity. [6] g·100 g^{-1}. [7] Varies but never absent, and always of biological significance. [8] Excludes water vapor. [9] For the aquatic media variables, partial pressure refers only to the water in equilibrium with the atmosphere, as at ocean or lake surface.

Contributors: Gilbert, Daniel L; McCutcheon, F. Harold

continued

General References

[1] Gilbert, D. L. 1964. Handb. Physiol., Sect. 3, Resp. 1:153.

[2] Horne, R. A. 1969. Marine Chemistry. The Structure of Water and the Chemistry of the Hydrosphere. Wiley-Interscience, New York.

[3] Linke, W. F., ed. 1958. Solubilities: Inorganic and Metal-organic Compounds. Ed. 4. Van Nostrand, New York. v. 1.

[4] Linke, W. F., ed. 1965. American Chemical Society, Washington, D. C. v. 2.

[5] Mason, B. 1966. Principles of Geochemistry. Ed. 3. J. Wiley, New York.

[6] McWhirter, N., and R. McWhirter. 1973. Guinness Book of World Records. Bantam Books, New York.

[7] Roberts, R. C. 1963. In D. E. Gray, ed. American Institute of Physics Handbook. Ed. 2. McGraw-Hill, New York. pp. 2-234.

[8] Turekian, K. K. 1969. In K. H. Wedepohl, ed. Handbook of Geochemistry. J. Springer, New York. v. 1, p. 297.

[9] Weast, R. C., ed. 1973. Handbook of Chemistry and Physics. Ed. 54. CRC Press, Cleveland.

208. RESPIRATORY FREQUENCY, TIDAL VOLUME, AND MINUTE VOLUME: VERTEBRATES

Values in parentheses are ranges, estimate "c" (*see* Introduction).

	Species (Synonym)	Body Weight[1] kg	Experimental Conditions	Respiratory Frequency breaths·min^{-1}	Tidal Volume ml[1]	Minute Volume liters·min^{-1} [1]	Reference
			Mammalia				
	Homo sapiens						
1	Premature	1.97(1.41-2.53)	....	34.4(17.2-51.6)	12.3(4.1-20.5)	0.396(0.204-0.588)	7
2	Newborn	3.4(2.5-4.3)	....	28.6(18.2-39.0)	20.7(13.5-27.9)	0.584(0.471-0.697)	7
3	Adult, ♂	68.5	....	11.7(10.1-13.1)	750(575-895)	7.43(5.8-10.3)	32
4			Light work	17.1(15.7-18.2)	1673(1510-1770)	28.6(27.3-30.9)	
5			Heavy work	21.2(18.6-23.3)	2030(1900-2110)	42.9(39.3-45.2)	
6	♀	54.0	....	11.7(10.4-13.0)	339(285-393)	4.5(4.0-5.1)	32
7			Light work	19	860(836-885)	16.3(15.9-16.8)	
8			Heavy work	30.0(25.0-35.3)	880(490-1270)	24.5(17.3-31.8)	
	Bos taurus Hereford						
9	Heifer	144	Lying	34	1400	46	13
10			Standing	32	1500	49	
11	Adult	422	Lying	30	3400	102	13
12			Standing	29	3800	109	
	Holstein						
13	Heifer	164	Lying	35	1700	59	13
14			Standing	31	2000	61	
15	Adult	514	Lying	30	3400	104	13
16			Standing	27	4200	114	
17	Guernsey,	410	Lying	30	3100	93	13
18	adult		Standing	29	3700	107	
19	Jersey, adult	403	Lying	30	2700	82	13
20			Standing	27	3400	92	
21	*Bradypus griseus*	3.1	....	6.2(4.5-8.0)	....	0.485(0.33-0.73)	21
22	*Canis familiaris*	(16.4-30.5)	Ambient temp, 24°C	18(11-37)[2]	320(251-432)[2]	5.21(3.3-7.4)[2]	16
23	♂, 6.38 ± 4.87 yr	20.99 ± 8.38	Pentobarbital Na, 30 mg·kg^{-1}, i.v.; rectal temp, 38.29 ± 0.6°C	15.5 ± 12.38	198.88 ± 81.64	2923.2 ± 2585.7	14
24	♀, 5.09 ± 4.55 yr	16.75 ± 8.16	Pentobarbital Na, 30 mg·kg^{-1}, i.v.; rectal temp, 38.29 ± 0.9°C	11.23 ± 8.02	206.77 ± 121.06	1806.4 ± 1231.4	14

[1] Unless otherwise specified. [2] Measurements made after 30-minute rest in hammock; values corrected to BTPS.

continued

	Species (Synonym)	Body Weight kg	Experimental Conditions	Respiratory Frequency breaths·min⁻¹	Tidal Volume ml	Minute Volume liters·min⁻¹	Reference
25	*Capra hircus*	....	....	19	310	5.7	1
26	*Castor canadensis*	18	....	16	....	....	18
27	*Cavia porcellus*	0.466(0.274-0.941)	....	90(69-104)	1.8(1.0-3.9)	0.16(0.10-0.38)	12
28	*(C. cobaya)*	0.69(0.43-1.05)	Thiopental Na, 32-64 mg·kg⁻¹, i.p.	42(16-67)	3.7(2.3-5.3)	0.13(0.08-0.19)	8
29	*Choloepus hoffmanni*	4.5	....	13	....	0.844(0.78-0.96)	21
30	*Equus caballus,* 7 ± 1.1 yr	486 ± 3.5	....	10.0 ± 1.2	7500 ± 370	200 ± 24.6	11
31	*Felis catus*	3.7(2.3-5.7)	Thiopental Na, 32-64 mg·kg⁻¹, i.p.	30(24-42)	34(20-42)	0.96(0.86-1.09)	8
32		2.503 ± 0.53	α-Chloralose, 80 mg·kg⁻¹, i.v.	15 ± 3	25.5 ± 5.3	0.381 ± 0.117	2
33	*Giraffa* sp.	....	Standing	31.8(17-58)	3404(3090-3580)[3]	....	27
34	*Macaca mulatta (M. rhesus)*	2.68(2.05-3.08)	....	40(31-52)	21.0(9.8-29.0)	0.86(0.31-1.41)	12
35		2.45(1.8-3.05)	Thiopental Na, 32-64 mg·kg⁻¹, i.p.	33(27-47)	20(9-29)	0.70(0.26-1.34)	8
36	*Marmota marmota*	2.13	Awake; rectal temp, 37.8°C	8.0	22	0.174	10
37			Hibernating; rectal temp, 5-6°C	0.68	13(11.3-14.8)	0.0089	
38	*Mesocricetus auratus*	0.092(0.065-0.134)	....	74(33-127)	0.8(0.42-1.2)	0.06(0.033-0.083)	12
39	*Mus musculus*	0.02(0.012-0.026)	....	163(84-230)	0.15(0.09-0.23)	0.024(0.011-0.036)	12
40		0.032(0.027-0.038)	Thiopental Na, 32-64 mg·kg⁻¹, i.p.	109(97-123)	0.18(0.09-0.38)	0.021(0.009-0.046)	8
41	*Orcinus orca*	1090	Beached	1.11	46,200(30,500-60,900)	....	29
	Oryctolagus cuniculus						
42	0.5-1 yr	4.1 ± 0.48	....	36.8 ± 10.6	21 ± 3.2	0.188 ± 0.042	9
43	3-5 yr	4.1 ± 0.56	....	26.7 ± 6.6	26 ± 1.7	0.170 ± 0.031	9
44		2.4(2.05-3.0)	Thiopental Na, 32-64 mg·kg⁻¹, i.v.	39(32-53)	15.8(11.5-24.4)	0.62(0.37-0.89)	8
45	*Ovis aries*	59.9(46.6-74.0)	Rectal temp, 39.69 (39.30-40.13)°C	20(15.7-23.6)	362(287-455)	7.10(5.95-7.69)	15
46	*Phoca vitulina*	27.5	Cheyne-Stokes respiration	9(6-12)	....	3.97	19
47	*Rattus norvegicus*	0.113(0.063-0.152)	....	85.5(66-114)	0.86(0.60-1.25)	0.073(0.05-0.101)	12
48	*Sigmodon hispidus*	0.77	....	94.5(75-115)	0.35(0.24-0.70)	0.04(0.023-0.071)	12
49	*Sus scrofa,* ♂	225	....	....	....	37	5
50	*Tachyglossus aculeatus*	2.6	....	14.4 ± 0.5	24.3 ± 1.2	0.362 ± 0.098	3
51		4.1	....	12.9 ± 0.5	27.6 ± 1.2	0.337 ± 0.142	3
52	*Tursiops truncatus*	170	In captivity	1.1(0.9-1.3)	9,000(8,000-10,000)	9.7(9.0-10.4)	20
	Aves						
53	*Anas* sp., ♂	....	Standing	42	(35-38)	....	31
54			Supine	42	30	....	
55	♀	....	....	110	....	....	31

[3] Corrected to BTPS.

continued

Species (Synonym)	Body Weight kg	Experimental Conditions	Respiratory Frequency breaths·min⁻¹	Tidal Volume ml [1]	Minute Volume liters·min⁻¹ [1]	Reference
56	*Anser* sp., ♂	....	....	20	....	....	31
57	♀	....	....	40	....	....	31
58	*Columba livia*	....	Standing	(25-30)	(4.5-5.2)	....	31
59			Supine	(25-30)	4.7	....	
	Gallus gallus (G. domesticus)						
60	♂	4.2	....	17 ± 1	46 ± 2	0.777 ± 0.039	24
61	♀	3.4	....	27 ± 2	31 ± 2	0.766 ± 0.044	24
	Meleagris gallopavo						
62	♂	....	....	28	....	....	31
63	♀	....	....	49	....	....	31
64	*Passer domesticus*, ♂♀	....	760 mm Hg; body temp, 41.2 ± 1.3°C	81 ± 20	0.0165 ml·g⁻¹	0.0011 liters·g⁻¹·min⁻¹	33
65			344 mm Hg; body temp, 39.4 ± 2°C	112 ± 12	0.0211 ml·g⁻¹	0.0008 liters·g⁻¹·min⁻¹	
66	*Serinus canarius*	....	....	(96-120)	....	....	31
67	*Struthio camelus*	100	Cloacal temp, 39.3°C; ambient temp, 12-15°C	5	....	....	6
68			Cloacal temp, 39.3°C; ambient temp, 25°C	45	....	....	

Reptilia

69	*Malaclemys terrapin centrata*	(0.65-0.72)	Ambient temp, 24-29°C	3.7	14	0.051	26
	Sauromalus obesus	(0.10-0.20)	Ambient temp		....	....	4
70			20°C	5			
71			30°C	10			
72			40°C	16.5			

Pisces

73	*Balistes capriscus*	....	In water	(40-66)	....	(0.065-0.175)	17
74	*Neoceratodus forsteri*	(4.8-8.4)	In water	28	15	....	23
75	*Polypterus senegalus*	Body length, (240-248) mm	Ambient water temp, 28-32°C	35	....	....	25
76	*Protopterus aethiopicus*	....	In room air	0.27 ± 0.05	0.02 ml·g⁻¹	....	22
77	*Salmo gairdneri*	(0.2-0.6)	In water; 1:10,000 tricaine; pre-exercise	77 ± 1.9	....	....	30
78			Exercise peak	102 ± 2.7	....	....	

Chondrichthyes

79	*Scyliorhinus stellaris*	1.86 ± 0.86	Ambient water temp, 17(15-19)°C	40 ± 2	....	248 ± 82 liters·g⁻¹·min⁻¹	28

[1] Unless otherwise specified.

Contributors: Gleysteen, John J., and Stroud, Robert C.

continued

References

[1] Barcroft, J., et al. 1919. Quart. J. Med. 13:35.

[2] Bartorelli, C., and A. Gerola. 1963. Amer. J. Physiol. 205:589.

[3] Bentley, P. J., et al. 1967. Ibid. 212:958.

[4] Boyer, D. R. 1967. Comp. Biochem. Physiol. 20: 439.

[5] Brody, S. 1945. Bioenergetics and Growth. Reinhold, New York.

[6] Crawford, E. C., Jr., and K. Schmidt-Nielsen. 1967. Amer. J. Physiol. 212-347.

[7] Cross, K. W. 1953. Ph.D. Thesis. Univ. London, England.

[8] Crossfill, M. L., and J. G. Widdicombe. 1961. J. Physiol. (London) 158:5.

[9] Davidson, J. T., et al. 1966. J. Appl. Physiol. 21: 838.

[10] Endres, G., and H. Taylor. 1930. Proc. Roy. Soc. B107:231.

[11] Gillespie, J. R., et al. 1966. J. Appl. Physiol. 21:416.

[12] Guyton, A. C. 1947. Amer. J. Physiol. 150:70.

[13] Hall, W. C., and S. Brody. 1933. Mo. Agr. Exp. Sta. Res. Bull. 180:11.

[14] Hamlin, R. L., and C. R. Smith. 1967. Amer. J. Vet. Res. 28:175.

[15] Hemingway, A., and C. Hemingway. 1966. Resp. Physiol. 1:33.

[16] Hemingway, A., and G. S. Nahas. Unpublished. Univ. California Medical School, Los Angeles, 1953.

[17] Hughes, G. M. 1967. Experientia 23:1077.

[18] Irving, L., and N. D. Orr. 1935. Science 82:569.

[19] Irving, L., et al. 1936. J. Cell. Comp. Physiol. 7:137.

[20] Irving, L., et al. 1941. Ibid. 17:145.

[21] Irving, L., et al. 1942. Ibid. 20:189.

[22] Jesse, M. J., et al. 1967. Resp. Physiol. 3:267.

[23] Johansen, K., et al. 1967. Comp. Biochem. Physiol. 20:843.

[24] King, A. S., and D. C. Payne. 1964. J. Physiol. (London) 174:342.

[25] Magid, A. M. A. 1966. Anim. Behav. 14:531.

[26] McCutcheon, F. H. 1943. Physiol. Zool. 16:255.

[27] Patterson, J. L., et al. 1965. Ann. N.Y. Acad. Sci. 127:404.

[28] Piiper, J., and D. Schumann. 1967. Resp. Physiol. 2:139.

[29] Spencer, M. P., et al. 1967. J. Appl. Physiol. 22:974.

[30] Stevens, E. D., and D. J. Randall. 1967. J. Exp. Biol. 46:309.

[31] Sturkie, P. D. 1954. Avian Physiology. Comstock, Ithaca.

[32] Taylor, C. 1941. Amer. J. Physiol. 135:27.

[33] Tucker, V. A. 1968. J. Exp. Biol. 48:55.

209. NERVOUS CONTROL OF VENTILATION: MAMMALS

Data are primarily from experiments on mammals other than man, with evidence, often indirect, that similar responses exist in man.

| | Nerve Terminals | | Afferent Pathway | Physiologic Stimulus | Response | | | Reference |
	Type	Location			Ventilatory	Broncho-motor	Cardiovascular	
				Reflexes from Respiratory Receptors				
1	Nasal irritant receptors	Nasal mucosa	Olfactory & trigeminal	Chemical & mechanical irritation	Apnea or sneeze	Dilation	Hypotension ? & bradycardia	6, 15, 17
2	Epipharyngeal receptors	Epipharyngeal mucosa	Glossopharyngeal	Mechanical deformation	Inspiratory effort	Dilation	Hypertension	4, 15
3	Laryngeal irritant receptors	Laryngeal mucosa	Superior laryngeal	Chemical & mechanical irritation	Cough	Constriction	Hypertension	4, 15, 17
4	Cough receptors, lower airway	Tracheal & large bronchial epithelium	Vagus & sympathetics	Chemical & mechanical irritation	Cough	Constriction	Hypertension	4, 15, 17

continued

Nerve Terminals		Afferent Pathway	Physiologic Stimulus	Response			Reference
Type	Location			Ventilatory	Bronchomotor	Cardiovascular	
5 Lung irritant receptors	Small airway epithelium	Vagus	Chemical & mechanical irritation; lung disease	Hyperpnea	Constriction	Unknown	4,10
6 Lung inflation receptors	Airway smooth muscle	Vagus	Airway or lung distension	Inhibition	Dilation	Unknown	4, 11, 17
7 Lung J-receptors	Alveoli	Vagus	Lung congestion & edema	Rapid, shallow breathing	Constriction?	Hypotension & bradycardia	4,12
Reflexes from Cardiovascular Receptors							
8 Venous & atrial receptors	Great veins & atria	Vagus	Increase in pressure or volume	Unknown	Unknown	Hypotension & bradycardia	8,11
9 Epicardial (Bezold reflex) receptors	Epi- & myocardium of ventricles	Vagus	Intramural tension	Inhibition	Unknown	Hypotension & bradycardia	8,14
10 Ventricular baroreceptors	Ventricles	Vagus	Distension	Unknown	Unknown	Hypotension & bradycardia	8,11
11 Pulmonary artery baroreceptors	Pulmonary artery	Vagus	Distension	Unknown	Unknown	Hypotension & bradycardia	8,11
12 Systemic arterial baroreceptors	Aortic arch	Vagus	Distension	Inhibition?	Unknown	Hypotension & bradycardia	7,8, 11
13	Carotid sinus	Glossopharyngeal	Distension	Inhibition	Dilation	Hypotension & bradycardia	7,8, 11
14 Systemic arterial chemoreceptors	Aortic body	Vagus	Hypoxia, hypercapnia, & acidemia	Weak hyperpnea	Unknown	Hypertension & tachycardia	1,16
15	Carotid body	Glossopharyngeal	Hypoxia, hypercapnia, & acidemia	Hyperpnea	Constriction	Hypertension & primary bradycardia	1,16
Reflexes from Other Viscera & Somatic System							
16 Diaphragm tension receptors	Diaphragm tendon?	Phrenic	Diaphragm tension	Inhibition	Unknown	Unknown	3,17
17 Intercostal muscle spindle receptors	Intercostal muscles	Intercostal	γ-Drive or intercostal stretch	Intercostal contraction	Unknown	Unknown	3,13
18 "Ergoreceptors"	Skeletal muscles	Somatic	Muscle contraction	Hyperpnea	Unknown	Tachycardia?	2
19 Joint receptors	Ligaments	Somatic	Joint movement	Hyperpnea	Unknown	Unknown	2
20 Swallowing receptors	Pharynx	Glossopharyngeal	Mechanical stimulus	Inhibition	Unknown	Unknown	17
21 Pain receptors	All tissues	All nerves	Noxious stimuli	Hyperpnea	Dilation?	Hypertension? & tachycardia?	17
22 Warmth receptors	Skin	Somatic	Skin warmth	Panting[1/]	Unknown	Vasodilation	5,17

[1/] Not man.

continued

	Nerve Terminals		Afferent Pathway	Physiologic Stimulus	Response			Reference
	Type	Location			Ventilatory	Broncho motor	Cardiovascular	
23	Cold receptors	Skin	Somatic	Skin cooling	Gasping	Constriction?	Hypertension	5,17
	Central Nervous Influences							
24	Thermoregulatory "receptors" 2/	Hypothalamus	Via pneumotaxic area?	Hypothalamic warmth	Panting or hyperpnea	Unknown	Vasodilation	5
25	Emotion "receptors" 2/	Frontal lobes	Via pneumotaxic area?	Emotion	Hyperpnea	Unknown	Tachycardia	2
26	Central chemoreceptors	Medullary surface	Unknown	Hydrogen ions or carbon dioxide	Hyperpnea	Constriction?	Unknown	9

2/ Little evidence of anatomical identity for these "receptors."

Contributor: Widdicombe, John G.

References

[1] Biscoe, T. J. 1971. Physiol. Rev. 51:437.

[2] Dejours, P. 1964. Handb. Physiol., Sect. 3, Resp. 1:631.

[3] Euler, C. von. 1973. Acta Neurobiol. Exp. (Warsaw) 33:329.

[4] Fillenz, M., and J. G. Widdicombe. 1971. In N. Neil, ed. Handbook of Sensory Physiology. Springer-Verlag. Heidelberg, v. 3, pp. 81-112.

[5] Hardy, J. D. 1961. Physiol. Rev. 41:521.

[6] James, J. E. A., and M. de B. Daly. 1969. Proc. Roy. Soc. Med. 62:1287.

[7] Kezdi, P., ed. 1967. Baroreceptors and Hypertension. Pergamon Press, Oxford.

[8] Korner, P. I. 1971. Physiol. Rev. 51:312.

[9] Loeschcke, H. 1973. Acta Neurobiol. Exp. (Warsaw) 33:97.

[10] Mills, J. E., et al. 1970. Breathing, Hering-Breuer Centen. Symp., pp. 77-92.

[11] Paintal, A. 1963. Ergeb. Physiol. Biol. Chem. Exp. Pharmakol. 52:74.

[12] Paintal, A. 1970. Breathing, Hering-Breuer Centen. Symp., pp. 59-71.

[13] Sears, T. A. 1971. Sci. Basis Med., p. 129.

[14] Sleight, P., and J. G. Widdicombe. 1965. J. Physiol. (London) 181:235.

[15] Tomori, Z., and J. G. Widdicombe. 1969. Ibid. 200:25.

[16] Torrance, R. W., ed. 1968. Arterial Chemoreceptors. Blackwell Scientific Publications, Oxford.

[17] Widdicombe, J. G. 1964. Handb. Physiol., Sect. 3, Resp. 1:585.

210. DIMENSIONS OF LUNG RESPIRATORY ZONES: MAMMALS

Part I. Morphometric Parameters

Values for man obtained by light microscopy; all other values derived from electron-microscopic studies. **Specification:** No. = number of subjects, Wt = body weight, V_L = lung volume, Sa = alveolar surface, Sc = capillary surface, Vc = capillary volume, τ = mean thickness of alveolar-capillary tissue barrier, τ_{ht} = harmonic mean barrier thickness, τ_{tmin} = minimal barrier thickness, τ_{hp} = harmonic mean thickness of plasma layer, DL_{max} = maximal diffusion capacity of lung, DL_{min} = minimal diffusion capacity of lung. Sc:Sa = ratio of capillary to alveolar surface, Vc/Sa = capillary volume per alveolar surface. Values in brackets were estimated indirectly.

	Specification	Man		Dog		Monkey	Rabbit	Young Rat	Mouse	Etruscan Shrew
		Short ∼155 cm	Tall ∼175 cm	Small 10-13 kg	Large 20-24 kg					
1	No.	16	9	8	6	6	5	8	5	5
2	Wt, kg	[55]	[75]	12.2 ± 0.4	22.8 ± 0.6	3.71 ± 0.8	3.6 ± 0.5	0.14 ± 0.007	0.023 ± 0.002	0.0025 ± 0.0001
3	V_L, ml	4500	7000	735 ± 25	1501 ± 74	184 ± 3.6	79 ± 12	6.3 ± 0.2	0.74 ± 0.075	0.102 ± 0.009
4	Sa, m²	55	82	41 ± 4	90 ± 7	13 ± 0.5	5.9 ± 0.5	0.39 ± 0.02	0.068 ± 0.009	0.0144 ± 0.001
5	Sc, m²	52	70	33 ± 1.6	72 ± 4.5	12 ± 0.6	4.7 ± 0.4	0.41 ± 0.02	0.059 ± 0.006	0.0125 ± 0.001

continued

Part I. Morphometric Parameters

Spec-ifica-tion	Man		Dog		Monkey	Rabbit	Young Rat	Mouse	Etruscan Shrew
	Short ∿155 cm	Tall ∿175 cm	Small 10-13 kg	Large 20-24 kg					
6 Vc, ml	120	160	50 ± 5	119 ± 14	15 ± 1.1	7.2 ± 0.8	0.48 ± 0.02	0.084 ± 0.009	0.0131 ± 0.002
7 τ, μm	[1.7]	[1.7]	1.64 ± 0.13	1.42 ± 0.08	1.52 ± 0.05	1.51 ± 0.1	1.42 ± 0.07	1.25 ± 0.08	0.80 ± 0.09
8 τ_{ht}, μm	[0.5]	[0.5]	0.46 ± 0.01	0.48 ± 0.01	0.50 ± 0.01	0.48 ± 0.02	0.38 ± 0.02	0.32 ± 0.006	0.34 ± 0.02
9 τ_{hp}, μm	[0.18]	[0.18]	0.17 ± 0.01	0.18 ± 0.01	0.18	0.18	0.18 ± 0.005	0.11 ± 0.002	0.15
10 τ_{tmin}	......	0.3	0.25	0.25	0.2	0.2	0.15	0.15	0.1
11 DL_{max}	......	169	77 ± 6	173 ± 16	24 ± 1.2	10.6 ± 1	0.83 ± 0.03	0.147 ± 0.015	0.0284 ± 0.005
12 DL_{min}	......	84	36 ± 3	83 ± 9	....	....	....	....	....
13 Sc:Sa	0.95	0.85	0.8	0.8	0.89	0.82	1.05	0.87	0.87
14 Vc/Sa, ml/m²	2.2	2.3	1.2	1.3	1.2	1.35	1.23	1.23	0.91

Contributor: Weibel, Ewald R.

Reference: Weibel, E. R. 1973. Physiol. Rev. 53:419.

Part II. Lung Volume and Body Weight

Part III. Alveolar Surface Area and Whole Body Oxygen Consumption

Lungs were measured at maximal inflation. The slope was determined by least-squares fitting.

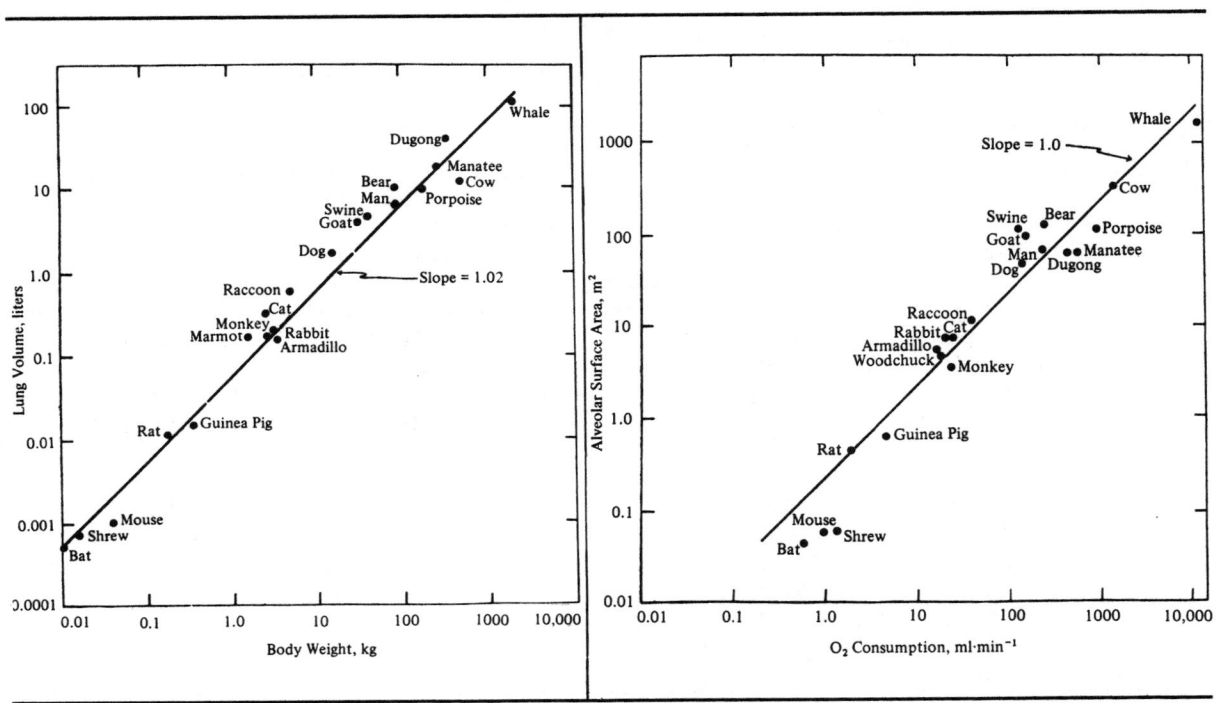

Contributor: Weibel, Ewald R.

Reference: Tenney, S. M., and J. E. Remmers. 1963. Nature (London) 197:54.

Cytochromes are intracellular chromoproteins—"chromo-" since they have as their prosthetic group a heme which absorbs light. The iron of the hemes undergoes a redox reaction during the normal physiological functioning. All of the cytochromes, with the exception of c and h, are so tightly bound to the lipoprotein membranes of the mitochondria and the endoplasmic reticulum (microsomes) that they can only be solubilized with detergents or lipases. The mitochondrion is a vesicular structure consisting of two concentric membranous vesicles, the inner and the outer membranes. The outer membrane is permeable to metabolites and inorganic ions. In general it can be said that the cytochromes of the inner membrane consist of a_3, a, c, c_1, and b (b_K and b_T) and act as redox centers in this sequence to form a respiratory chain [27]. This sequence, together with some other enzymes—substrate dehydrogenases, ubiquinone (coenzyme Q), non-heme-iron, and copper ions—allows the oxidation by molecular oxygen of such typical metabolic substrates as reduced nicotinamide adenine dinucleotide (NADH) and succinate to be coupled to the phosphorylation of adenosine 5'-diphosphate (ADP), as well as to other energy-requiring reactions such as ion translocation across the inner mitochondrial membrane [43] and the energy-linked transhydrogenase reaction [29]. The cytochromes of the microsomes (b_5 and P-450), on the other hand, are part of the complex that leads to the activation of oxygen for the hydroxylation and oxidative demethylation of a number of steroid hormones and other drugs [16].

Physical & Chemical Properties: Mol wt = molecular weight; AA = amino acid composition is known; PS = amino acid sequence is known; PG = prosthetic group; pI = isoelectric point; E_0' = oxidation-reduction midpoint potential at pH of approximately 7.0 (mV = millivolts); CCO = cytochrome c oxidase; CD = circular dichroism spectra have been determined; EPR = electron paramagnetic resonance spectra have been determined; ORD = optical rotatory dispersion spectra have been determined; NMR = nuclear magnetic resonance spectra have been determined. **Optical Absorption Spectra:** Δ = wavelength, in nanometers, of approximate maximal absorbancy of difference spectrum between reduced and oxidized samples, unless otherwise indicated (difference spectra are necessitated by the high optical turbidity of a suspension of nonsolubilized mitochondria or microsomes); O = wavelength, in nanometers, of maximal absorbancy in the spectrum of oxidized samples; R = wavelength, in nanometers, of maximal absorbancy in the spectrum of reduced samples; $E_{1\,cm}^{mM}$ [in light brackets] = millimolar extinction coefficient, or absorbancy of millimolar solutions of 1-cm thickness; λ_1, λ_2 = wavelengths, in nanometers, between which the difference in absorbancy was measured for the specified extinction coefficient. **Remarks:** K_m = Michaelis constant; ATP = adenosine 5'-triphosphate; NADP$^+$ = nicotinamide adenine dinucleotide phosphate; NADPH = reduced nicotinamide adenine dinucleotide phosphate. Figures in heavy brackets are reference numbers

Cyto-chrome	Physical & Chemical Properties	Optical Absorption Spectra [$E_{1\,cm}^{mM}$]	Remarks
		Mitochondria	
1 c oxidase	Mol wt = 200,000-500,000 [1/] [38]; AA [34]. PG = hematin a [38] bound noncovalently in two ways to protein, yields cytochromes a & a_3 which can be distinguished on basis of their reactivities [30], midpoint redox potentials [11], & optical spectra [30]; active molecule (lipoprotein) also contains one Cu ion for each heme a [38]. E_0' = +205 mV for a [11]; +365 mV for a_3 [11]; +290 mV for a_3 + ATP [53]; +225 mV for Cu [49]. Activity determined by CCO-catalyzed oxidation of cytochrome c by O_2 [38]; inhibited by azide, CO, cyanide, fluoride, hydroxylamine, NO, & sulfide [30]; CD [35], EPR [3], ORD [25]; a_3 reacts directly with O_2 & CO, a does not [30].	Δ for $a + a_3$ = 605 [26.4] & λ_1, λ_2 = 605, 630 [15]; 90% due to a & 10% to a_3 according to CO difference spectra [56], or 50% due to each according to redox titrations correlated with absorbancy changes [2/]. Δ for $a + a_3$ = 445 [164] [15]; about 40% of absorbancy due to a & 60% to a_3 [2/] [56]. Δ = 830, due mostly to Cu [19, 49].	Physiological function of membrane-bound CCO is to oxidize cytochrome c and reduce O_2 and to conserve energy, i.e., one phosphorylated ADP (ATP) for each two electrons transferred. Purified CCO [38] catalyzes only redox reactions, not energy-conserving reactions. Addition of ATP to intact mitochondria induces a structural change in CCO [57], a change in K_m for O_2 reduction [9], & an apparent change in E_0' for a_3 (see column 2); no parallel change in E_0' for a [11]. Addition of ATP to intact mitochondria causes no change in E_0' for Cu [49].

[1/] Detergent-solubilized preparation. [2/] Difficulties exist with spectral properties of a and a_3 as separate entities as extrapolated from the spectral forms of the various inhibited cytochrome c oxidases, since the influences of reduced and oxidized components on each other are insufficiently known (e.g., Cu:heme and heme:heme interactions) [59].

continued

	Cyto-chrome	Physical & Chemical Properties	Optical Absorption Spectra $[E_{1\ cm}^{mM}]$	Remarks
2	c	Mol wt = 13,700 [32]; PS [32]. PG = porphyrin c covalently bound to protein [32]. pI = 10.04 ± 0.04 [2]. E_0' = +227 mV for form bound to mitochondria [11]; +250 to +270 mV for free form [7]. EPR [42], NMR [58], ORD [50]; X-ray analysis [10].	Δ = 550 [19.9] & λ_1, λ_2 = 550, 540 [31]. O = 528 [11.2], 410 [106.1], 361 [28.5] [31]; 695 [0.85]$^{3/}$ [46]. R = 550.25 [27.7], 520.5 [15.9], 416 [129.1]; 548.3 $^{4,5/}$ [14,52].	Physiological function of cytochrome c is to oxidize cytochrome c_1 and reduce CCO and to catalyze the rapid transfer of electrons along respiratory chains [56]. It can be extracted with salt from osmotically swollen mitochondria without the use of detergents or lipases [22].
3	c_1	Mol wt = 37,000 [4]; 44,000 [61]. PG = covalently bound to protein and apparently identical to that of cytochrome c [51] (see entry 2). E_0' = +225 mV for form bound to mitochondria [11]; +220 mV for purified form $^{6/}$ [18]. CD of purified form [60].	Δ = 554 [∼19.5] & λ_1, λ_2 = 554, 540 [17]; 553.5 $^{4,7/}$ [14]. O = 558, 525, 411 [60]. R = 554 [24.1], 524 [11.6], 418 [116.0] [17]; 552.5, 522.5, 417 [60].	Physiological function of cytochrome c_1 is to oxidize cytochrome b and to reduce cytochrome c. It can be purified from the mitochondrial membrane via detergents plus other reagents & column chromatography [4,60,61]. Concentration of cytochrome c_1 can be determined in mitochondria only after salt extraction of cytochrome c [14], or from optical absorption spectra at low temperatures [55].
4	b $(b_K + b_T)$	Mol wt = 21,300 $^{L/}$ [37]. PG = iron protoporphyrin, noncovalently bound to protein [20]. E_0' = +30 mV for b_K, −30 mV for b_T, & +24 mV for b_T + ATP$^{8/}$, all measured with mitochondria & submitochondrial particles [11].	Δ for b = 564 [20 $^{9/}$] & λ_1, λ_2 = 564, 575 [5]. Δ for b_K = 561 [45]; 558$^{4/}$, 529$^{4/}$, 428$^{4/}$ [45]. Δ for b_T = 565, 558 [45]; 562.5$^{4/}$, 555$^{4/}$, 535$^{4/}$, 528$^{4/}$, 430$^{4/}$ [45]. O for purified b = 414.5 [106.2] [36]. R for purified b = 561.5 [24.7], 531 [15.4], 428.5 [148.2] [36].	Cytochrome b $(b_K + b_T)$ has been located between substrate dehydrogenases and cytochrome c_1. It has been purified with detergents [37]. Purification studies have recently identified two or three different b's on the basis of their activity & spectral properties [8]. In intact mitochondria, two b's $(b_K$ & $b_T)$ have been identified and differentiated on basis of their kinetic reactivities [6], their midpoint redox potentials [54], & their spectral properties [45]. When cytochrome b is isolated as a complex with cytochrome c_1, an apparent change in E_0' is induced when Antimycin A (an inhibitor of electron transport between b & c_1) is present together with a reductant & an oxidant [44].
5	b_5	Cytochrome b_5 has been separated from intact mitochondria only as part of mitochondrial membrane [41].	Δ = 558$^{4/}$, 551 $^{4/}$, 531 $^{4/}$, 523$^{4/}$, 423$^{4/}$ [41].	Cytochrome b_5 occurs in outer membrane of liver mitochondria [13] (almost none in heart mitochondria [12]). It is differentiated from microsomal b_5 (see entry 6) on the basis of its optical absorption spectrum [41] & its association with a lower NADPH-cytochrome c oxidoreductase activity than microsomal b_5 [13]. NADH-cytochrome c oxidoreductase activity associated with mitochondrial b_5 is more sensitive towards trypsin than that of microsomal b_5 [28].

$^{L/}$ Detergent-solubilized preparation. $^{3/}$ At 10°C. Absorption at this wavelength occurs only in the oxidized form, and its absorbancy is conformation dependent. [46] $^{4/}$ Measured at the temperature of boiling nitrogen, 77°K. $^{5/}$ The 550.25 nm band of room temperature splits at low temperature into three absorption bands, c_1, c_2, and c_3; the 548.3 band occurs at the longest wavelength and has the largest absorbancy of the three [14,52]. $^{6/}$ These two values are within each other's limits of experimental error. $^{7/}$ This absorption band does not split at low temperatures [14]. $^{8/}$ Addition of ATP to b_T of intact mitochondria may induce an apparent change in E_0' of up to +275 mV [54]. No such change in b_K. $^{9/}$ Extinction coefficient generally used before discovery of b_K and b_T.

continued

	Cyto-chrome	Physical & Chemical Properties	Optical Absorption Spectra $[E_{1\,cm}^{mM}]$	Remarks
			Microsomes	
6	b_5	Mol wt = 11,000 [21]; PS [21]. PG = iron protoporphyrin IX, noncovalently bound to protein [47]. pI = 6 [47]. $E_0' = -140$ mV in form bound to microsomes; +20 mV in purified form [23]. X-ray diffraction studies [33].	Δ = 557 [20] & λ_1, λ_2 = 557, 575 [26]. O = 560 [9], 532 [10], 413 [119] [47]; 560[4/], 532[4/] [38]. R = 557 [27], 526 [13], 422 [175]; 557.5[4/], 552.5[4/], 532[4/], 524.5[4/] [38].	No known physiological function [13]. Initial purification steps require incubation of microsomes with pancreatic lipase for release of cytochrome b_5 from the membranous microsomal structure [48].
7	P-450 (P-420)	PG = heme (protoheme) can be removed by acid-acetone treatment; P-420 contains one or two atoms of nonheme iron per mole of heme [39]. $E_0' = -20$ mV for purified P-420 [39].	Δ[10/] for P-450 = 450 [91] & λ_1, λ_2 = 450, 490; [−41] & λ_1, λ_2 = 420, 490 [39]. Δ[10/] for P-420 = 420 [111] & λ_1, λ_2 = 420, 490 [39]. O for P-420 without CO = 414 [124] [39]. R for P-420 without CO = 559 [24], 530 [13], 427 [149] [39]. R for P-420 with CO = 421 [213] [39].	Cytochrome P-450 is the microsomal CO-binding pigment [39] & the oxygen-activating enzyme for many mixed-function oxidases [40]. It occurs in the microsomes of several animal tissues & in the mitochondrial fraction of the suprarenal cortex, but not in the mitochondria of other tissues [39]. It is firmly associated with microsomal membranes and can be purified with detergents or phospholipase A [39]. This solubilization is always associated with a spectral shift of the reduced & CO-complexed cytochrome from 450 to 420 nm. P-450 occurs in a soluble form in *Rhizobium japonicum* [1].
			Other Locations	
8	h	Mol wt = 12,000 [38]; AA [38]. PG = hematoheme [38]. pI = 4.3 [38]. $E_0' = +200$ mV [24]. Not autoxidizable at neutral pH; does not combine with CO [38].	O = 409 [105.8] [38]. R = 556 [32.8], 526 [14.4], 422.5 [190.4] [38].	Physiological function is not known. It occurs in intestinal tract fluid & digestive gland of the land snail *Helix pomatia* [38].

[4/] Measured at the temperature of boiling nitrogen, 77°K. [10/] For difference spectrum between the CO-complex of the reduced form and the reduced form of the cytochrome.

Contributor: Wohlrab, Hartmut

References

[1] Appleby, C. A. 1968. Struct. Funct. Cytochromes Proc. Symp., 1967, p. 666.

[2] Barlow, G. H., and E. Margoliash. 1966. J. Biol. Chem. 241:1473.

[3] Beinert, H., et al. 1971. Probes Struct. Funct. Macromol. Membranes Proc. Colloq. Johnson Res. Found., 5th, 1969, 2:575.

[4] Bomstein, R., et al. 1961. Biochim. Biophys. Acta 50:527.

[5] Chance, B., and G. R. Williams. 1955. J. Biol. Chem. 217:395.

[6] Chance, B., et al. 1970. Proc. Nat. Acad. Sci. U.S. 66:1175.

[7] Clark, W. M. 1960. Oxidation Reduction Potentials of Organic Systems. Waverly Press, Baltimore.

[8] Davis, K. A., and Y. Hatefi. 1971. Biochem. Biophys. Res. Commun. 44:1338.

[9] Degn, H., and H. Wohlrab. 1971. Biochim. Biophys. Acta 245:347.

[10] Dickerson, R. E., et al. 1966. Hemes Hemoproteins Proc. Colloq., 3rd, p. 365.

[11] Dutton, P. L., et al. 1970. Biochemistry 9:5077.

continued

211. PROPERTIES OF CYTOCHROMES: ANIMALS

[12] Ernster, L. 1967. Mitochondrial Struct. Compartment. Proc. Round Table Discuss., p. 114.

[13] Ernster, L., and B. Kuylenstierna. 1970. Membranes Mitochondria Chloroplasts (Amer. Chem. Soc. Monogr. 165), p. 172.

[14] Estabrook, R. W. 1961. Haematin Enzymes Symp., p. 436.

[15] Gelder, B. F. van. 1966. Biochim. Biophys. Acta 118:36.

[16] Gilette, J. R., et al., ed. 1969. Microsomes and Drug Oxidation. Academic Press, New York.

[17] Green, D. E., et al. 1959. Biochim. Biophys. Acta 31:42.

[18] Green, D. E., et al. 1960. Ibid. 38:160.

[19] Griffiths, D. E., and D. C. Wharton. 1961. J. Biol. Chem. 236:1850.

[20] Hübscher, G., et al. 1954. Biochem. Z. 325:223.

[21] Huntley, T. E., et al. 1971. Probes Struct. Funct. Macromol. Membranes Proc. Colloq. Johnson Res. Found., 5th, 1969, 2:487.

[22] Jacobs, E. E., and D. R. Sanadi. 1960. J. Biol. Chem. 235:531.

[23] Kawai, Y., et al. 1963. Biochim. Biophys. Acta 67:522.

[24] Keilin, J. 1957. Nature (London) 180:427.

[25] King, T. E., et al. 1968. Struct. Funct. Cytochromes Proc. Symp., 1967, p. 204.

[26] Klingenberg, M. 1958. Arch. Biochem. Biophys. 75:376.

[27] Klingenberg, M. 1968. Biol. Oxidations, p. 3.

[28] Kuylenstierna, B., et al. 1970. Eur. J. Biochem. 12:419.

[29] Lee, C. P., and L. Ernster. 1968. Ibid. 3:385.

[30] Lemberg, M. R. 1969. Physiol. Rev. 49:48.

[31] Margoliash, E., and N. Frohwirt. 1959. Biochem. J. 71:570.

[32] Margoliash, E., and A. Schejter. 1966. Advan. Protein Chem. 21:113.

[33] Mathews, F. S., et al. 1971. Probes Struct. Funct. Macromol. Membranes Proc. Colloq. Johnson Res. Found., 5th, 1969, 2:505.

[34] Matsubara, H. 1965. Biochim. Biophys. Acta 97:61.

[35] Myer, Y. P., and T. E. King. 1969. Biochem. Biophys. Res. Commun. 34:170.

[36] Ohnishi, K. 1966. J. Biochem. (Tokyo) 59:1.

[37] Ohnishi, K. 1966. Ibid. 59:17.

[38] Okunuki, K., et al., ed. 1968. Structure and Function of Cytochromes. Univ. Tokyo Press, Tokyo.

[39] Omura, T., and R. Sato. 1967. Methods Enzymol. 10:556.

[40] Omura, T., et al. 1965. Fed. Proc. Fed. Amer. Soc. Exp. Biol. 24:1181.

[41] Parsons, D. F., et al. 1967. Mitochondrial Struct. Compartment. Proc. Round Table Discuss., p. 29.

[42] Peisach, J., and W. E. Blumberg. 1971. Probes Struct. Funct. Macromol. Membranes Proc. Colloq. Johnson Res. Found., 5th, 1969, 2:231.

[43] Pressman, B. C. 1970. Membranes Mitochondria Chloroplasts (Amer. Chem. Soc. Monogr. 165), p. 213.

[44] Rieske, J. S. 1971. Arch. Biochem. Biophys. 145:179.

[45] Sato, N., et al. 1971. Fed. Eur. Biochem. Soc. Lett. 15:209.

[46] Schejter, A., and P. George. 1964. Biochemistry 3:1045.

[47] Strittmatter, P. 1963. Enzymes, Ed. 2, 8:113.

[48] Strittmatter, P. 1967. Methods Enzymol. 10:553.

[49] Tsudzuki, T., and D. F. Wilson. 1971. Arch. Biochem. Biophys. 145:149.

[50] Urry, D. W., and P. Doty. 1965. J. Amer. Chem. Soc. 87:2756.

[51] Wada, K., et al. 1968. Struct. Funct. Cytochromes Proc. Symp., 1967, p. 309.

[52] Wilson, D. F. 1967. Arch. Biochem. Biophys. 121:757.

[53] Wilson, D. F., and P. L. Dutton. 1970. Ibid. 136:583.

[54] Wilson, D. F., and P. L. Dutton. 1970. Biochem. Biophys. Res. Commun. 39:59.

[55] Wilson, D. F., and D. Epel. 1968. Arch. Biochem. Biophys. 126:83.

[56] Wohlrab, H. 1970. Biochemistry 9:474.

[57] Wohlrab, H., and G. B. Ogunmola. 1971. Ibid. 10:1103.

[58] Wüthrich, K. 1971. Probes Struct. Funct. Macromol. Membranes Proc. Colloq. Johnson Res. Found., 5th, 1969, 2:465.

[59] Yong, F. C., and T. E. King. 1970. Biochem. Biophys. Res. Commun. 38:940.

[60] Yu, C. A., et al. 1971. Ibid. 45:508.

[61] Yu, C. A., et al. 1971. Fed. Proc. Fed. Amer. Soc. Exp. Biol. 30:1144.

212. IN VIVO AND IN VITRO CARBON DIOXIDE DISSOCIATION

Part I. Carbon Dioxide Dissociation Curves: Mammals

CO_2 dissociation curves show the relationship between CO_2 concentration and the partial pressure of CO_2 in blood or plasma at a given percent O_2 saturation of hemoglobin and at a given temperature. By subtracting the amount of physically dissolved CO_2 (which is a linear function of partial pressure), the relationship can be determined between the

continued

Part I. Carbon Dioxide Dissociation Curves: Mammals

chemically combined CO_2 of whole blood or plasma and the partial pressure of CO_2; in the case of plasma, the relationship is between HCO_3^- concentration and CO_2 tension. Data for in vitro curves can be obtained by equilibrating blood with gas mixtures of known O_2 and CO_2 tensions and determining the total CO_2 or HCO_3^- concentration of whole blood or plasma separated after equilibration; plasma thus treated is known as "true plasma." Data for in vivo curves can be obtained by equilibrating the whole animal with different CO_2 tensions. This is usually done by having the animal breathe for 10-15 minutes mixtures with CO_2 added. The CO_2 or HCO_3^- concentration in samples of whole blood or plasma is then measured.

The relationship between HCO_3^- concentration and CO_2 tension is curvilinear and difficult to deal with quantitatively. The Henderson-Hasselbalch equation expresses the relationship between HCO_3^- concentration, CO_2 tensions, and pH; any two variables may be plotted against each other, the third variable being used as a set of constant values. Both theoretical and practical reasons exist for plotting HCO_3^- concentration of true plasma against pH.

Addition or removal of carbonic acid by changing the CO_2 tension of blood may be considered as titration of the noncarbonic buffers. Since the amount of carbamino hemoglobin is independent of the CO_2 pressure over a wide range [9], one HCO_3^- appears for each H^+ added. Therefore, a graph of HCO_3^- plotted against pH is a titration curve, and its slope is the buffer value β (defined by Van Slyke [11]) of the solution being titrated: $d(HCO_3^-)/d(pH) = dB/d(pH)$. Unit of measurement for slope has been designated "slyke" (1 slyke = 1 mmole HCO_3^-·liter plasma^{-1}·pH unit^{-1}) [12]. CO_2 buffer or dissociation curves plotted in this manner are straight lines, and an expression for the slope can be derived in terms of hemoglobin and plasma protein concentrations: $d(HCO_3^-)P/d(pH) = -[2.5(Hb)_B + 10(Pr)_B]$; in which $d(HCO_3^-)_P$ = change in bicarbonate, in millimoles per liter plasma water; $(Hb)_B$ = hemoglobin, in millimoles per liter blood water; and $(Pr)_B$ = plasma proteins, in millimoles per liter blood water [2]. The slope of the in vitro CO_2 buffer curve of blood is approximately 30 slykes when Hb = 15 g/100 g blood (9 mmole/liter blood or 10.7 mmole/liter blood water); Pr = 7 g/100 g blood (0.7 mmole/liter

plasma, or $0.7 \times 0.55/0.84 = 0.46$ mmole/liter blood water); and HCO_3^- is millimoles per liter plasma. The in vitro titration curve of plasma is often represented as the relationship between log P_{CO_2} and pH. This relationship is also approximately linear, and its slope is related to the slope of the plasma HCO_3^- concentration-pH curve by the equation

$$\frac{d(\log P_{CO_2})}{d(pH)} = \frac{d(HCO_3^-)P}{2.3(HCO_3^-)P[d(pH)]} - \left[1 - \frac{d(pK')}{d(pH)}\right], \text{where } pK'$$

is the combined dissociation exponent of the Henderson-Hasselbalch equation [10].

If the HCO_3^- generated by increased CO_2 tension is assumed to be distributed only through the extracellular fluid, a similar formula can be derived for estimating in vivo CO_2 buffering of extracellular fluid: $\dfrac{d(HCO_3^-)P}{d(pH)} = -\left\{\dfrac{V_B}{V_e}[2.5(Hb)_B + 10(Pr)_B] + [\dfrac{V_e - V_B}{V_e}10(Pr)_I]\right\}$, in which V_B/V_e is the ratio of blood water volume to total extracellular water volume; $(V_e - V_B)/V_e$ is the ratio of interstitial water volume to total extracellular water volume; and $(Pr)_I$ is millimoles protein per liter of interstitial fluid [2]. The in vivo slope in adult man with normal values is approximately 11.5 slykes (see references 8 and 12 for different calculated values). References 6 and 8 indicate that the in vivo slope predicted by the equation applies only to mixed venous blood unless the arteriovenous plasma HCO_3^- difference remains constant with a change in CO_2 tension. This difference is probably not important in most clinical situations [3].

Duration of exposure to altered CO_2 pressure affects the slope of in vivo CO_2 buffer curves [2,12]. After 15 minutes the slope shows the effects mainly of chemical buffering and distribution through extracellular space; the curves at this time are primary or initial CO_2 buffer lines. Within one hour a measurable increase in slope has occurred in dogs [4,12] and rats [5,7], due to exchange between intracellular and extracellular fluids. This increase is not the result of renal activity, since it occurs in the nephrectomized animal.

Graphs are for human blood but apply equally well to other mammals.

continued

Part I.   Carbon Dioxide Dissociation Curves: Mammals

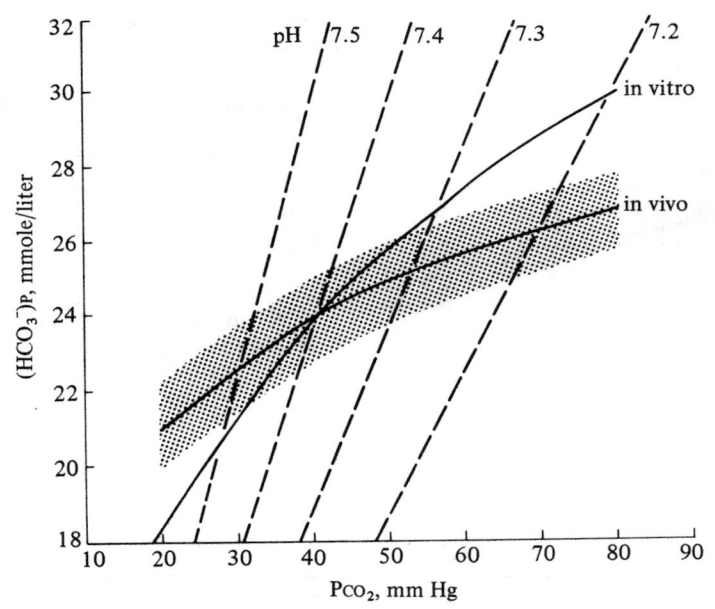

CO$_2$ DISSOCIATION CURVES FOR TRUE PLASMA, FROM BLOOD WITH NORMAL HEMOGLOBIN AND PLASMA PROTEIN CONCENTRATIONS

The shaded area encompasses 1 mmole/liter on each side of the in vivo curve.

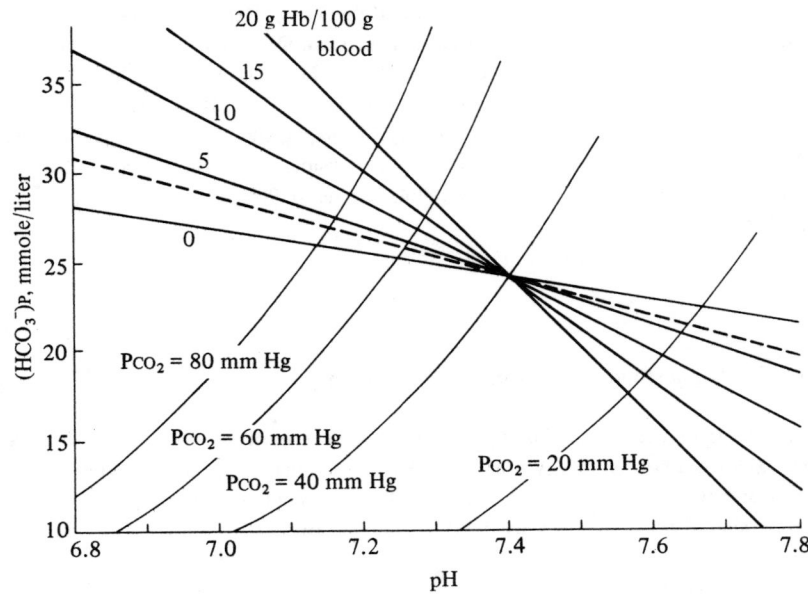

IN VITRO CO$_2$ DISSOCIATION CURVES FOR TRUE PLASMA, FROM BLOOD OF VARYING HEMOGLOBIN CONCENTRA– TIONS

The dashes represent the in vivo line for plasma, from blood with 15 g Hb/100 g.

Hemoglobin g/100 g blood	Slope slykes
0	7
5	14
10	21.5
15	30
20	38

continued

Part I.   Carbon Dioxide Dissociation Curves: Mammals

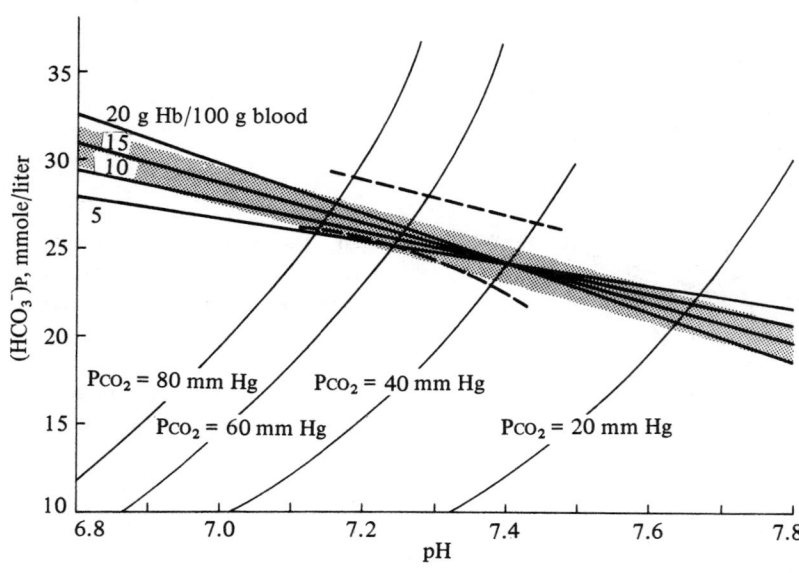

IN VIVO CO₂ DISSOCIATION CURVES, FROM BLOOD OF VARYING HEMO-GLOBIN CONCENTRATIONS

The shaded area encompasses 1 mmole/liter on each side of the 15 g/100 g buffer line. The dashes enclose the 95% confidence limits of Brackett, Cohen, and Schwartz [1].

Hemoglobin g/100 g blood	Slope slykes
5	6.4
10	9.0
15	11.6
20	14.3

Contributors: Brown, E. B., Jr., and Attebery, B. A.

References

[1] Brackett, N. C., Jr., et al. 1965. New Engl. J. Med. 272:6.

[2] Brown, E. B., Jr., and C. C. Michel. 1968. Proc. Int. Union Physiol. Sci. 6:185.

[3] Garcia, A. C., et al. 1971. Proc. Soc. Exp. Biol. Med. 137:237.

[4] Giebisch, G., et al. 1955. J. Clin. Invest. 34:231.

[5] Martin, E. D., et al. 1967. U.S. Air Force Sch. Aerosp. Med. (Brooks) TR 67-116.

[6] Michel, C. C. 1968. Resp. Physiol. 4:283.

[7] Nichols, G. 1958. J. Clin. Invest. 37:1111.

[8] Roos, A., and L. J. Thomas, Jr. 1967. Anesthesiology 28:1048.

[9] Roughton, F. J. W. 1954. U.S. Air Force Sch. Aviat. Med. (Randolph) Proj. Rep. 21-2301-0003:51.

[10] Siggaard-Andersen, O. 1964. The Acid-Base Status of the Blood. E. Munksgaard, Copenhagen.

[11] Van Slyke, D. D. 1922. J. Biol. Chem. 52:525.

[12] Woodbury, J. W. 1965. In T. C. Ruch and H. D. Patton, ed. Physiology and Biophysics. W. B. Saunders, Philadelphia, p. 905.

Part II.   Dissociation Curve Slopes: Vertebrates

Unless otherwise specified, the in vivo data are from experiments in which the CO_2 tension was increased from normal to a higher value. Slopes of dissociation or buffer curves from hyperventilation experiments are unreliable because of lactic acid accumulation [14]. The amount of increase in lactate with a corresponding decrease in HCO_3^- may be several millimoles per liter. A decrease in lactate with respiratory acidosis has little effect on the slope, since the change in lactate is usually less than 1 mmole/liter. **Experimental**

Conditions: CO_2—HV = hyperventilation; **Blood Type**— A = arterial, AV = arterialized venous, V = venous; MV = mixed venous. **Pco_2 Change:** ↑ = increased Pco_2; ↓ = decreased Pco_2. **Slope: In Vitro**—Values in brackets were calculated by the equation: $\dfrac{d(HCO_3^-)_P}{d(pH)} = -[2.5(Hb)_B + 10(Pr)_B]$, assuming plasma $(Pr)_B = 70$ g/liter (see Headnote to Part I).

continued

Part II. Dissociation Curve Slopes: Vertebrates

	Species & Condition	No. of Experiments	Hemoglobin mmole/liter blood	Experimental Conditions				P_{CO_2} Change	Slope, slykes		Reference
				Exposure Time	CO_2 %	Blood Type	Method of Measurement		In Vivo	In Vitro	
							Mammalia				
	Homo sapiens										
1	Awake	2	....	15 min	7	A	pH & plasma CO_2 content	↑	22.0	....	7
2		3	....	130 min	....	A	pH & P_{CO_2} (electrode)	↑	16.3 ± 1.0	....	15
3		7	Normal	90 min	7;10	A	pH & plasma CO_2 content	↑	11.3 ± 1.3	32	2
4		10	8.5 ± 0.17	15 min	8	AV	pH & plasma CO_2 content	↑	18.0	30 ± 1.4 [28.4]	5
5		12	8.95	30-80 min	....	AV	pH & plasma CO_2 content	↑	18.8	[29.6]	24
6		6	8.98 ± 0.19	21-30 min	7.5-7.7	A	pH & plasma CO_2 content	↑	12.5 ± 5.4	32.8 ± 0.6 [29.6]	13
7		4	9.73	15 min	7	A	pH & plasma CO_2 content	↑	13.6	[31.9]	30
8	Anesthetized	10	....	5 min	4;6;8	A	Astrup equilibration	↑	25.2 ± 1.1	....	12
9		1	4.67	40-60 min	....	A	Astrup equilibration	↑	17.8	[18.2]	32
10		5	9.25	40-60 min	....	A	Astrup equilibration	↑	18.2 ± 1.5	33.0 [30.5]	33
11		13	....	....	....	A	Astrup equilibration	↑	20.9 ± 5	....	31
12						MV	Astrup equilibration	↑	15.9 ± 3.1	28.8 ± 4.5	
13	*Arvicola terrestris,* anesthetized	5	8.64	....	....	A	pH, P_{CO_2} (electrode), & blood or plasma CO_2 content	↑	....	34.0 [28.8]	9
14	*Bos grunniens,* awake	1	9.34	....	....	V	pH & plasma CO_2 content	↑	....	23.9 [30.8]	1
15	*B. taurus* [1], anesthetized	27	....	10 min	10	A	pH & P_{CO_2} (electrode)	↑	7.2	....	18
16	*Camelus bactrianus,* awake	1	9.46	....	....	V	pH & plasma CO_2 content	....	....	27.0 [31.1]	1
	Canis familiaris										
17	Awake	21	....	2 hr	7;11;15; 18	A	pH & plasma CO_2 content	↑	15.3 ± 0.8	28.0	11
18	Anesthetized	1	....	4 min	....	V	Astrup equilibration	↑	9.4	....	23
19		8	....	10 min	9	A	pH, P_{CO_2} (electrode), & blood or plasma CO_2 content	↑	16.0	25.0	26
20		1	....	15 min	....	A	pH & plasma CO_2 content	↑	6.2	....	27
21		6	....	15 min	6;9;13; 18	A	pH, P_{CO_2} (electrode), & blood or plasma CO_2 content	↑	17.8	25.7	25
22		1	....	55 min	20	A	pH & plasma CO_2 content	↑	15.9	....	16
23		5	....	2 hr	10	A	pH & P_{CO_2} (electrode)	↑	5.6	....	20
24		7	7.80 ± 0.18	4 hr	30-40	A	pH & plasma CO_2 content	↑	14.5	[26.0]	4
25		3	8.90	3 hr	10-12	A	Astrup equilibration	↑	18.2	[28.6]	36
26		4	4.89	20 min	....	A	pH & plasma CO_2 content	↑↓	12.5	[18.8]	34
27		3	7.30	20 min	....	A	pH & plasma CO_2 content	↑↓	15.9	[25.0]	
28		3	8.70	20 min	....	A	pH & plasma CO_2 content	↑↓	17.9	[28.9]	
29		3	11.50	20 min	....	A	pH & plasma CO_2 content	↑↓	19.0	[37.1]	

[1] Calf.

continued

Part II. Dissociation Curve Slopes: Vertebrates

| | Species & Condition | No. of Experiments | Hemoglobin mmole/liter blood | Experimental Conditions | | | | Pco₂ Change | Slope, slykes | | Reference |
				Exposure Time	CO₂ %	Blood Type	Method of Measurement		In Vivo	In Vitro	
30		1	....	10 min	10	A	Astrup equilibration	↑	9.0	....	19
31			....	1 hr	10	A	Astrup equilibration	↑	12.5	....	
32			5.92	5 hr	10	A	Astrup equilibration	↑	32.3	[21.4]	
33		3	8.06	10 min	10	A	Astrup equilibration	↑	15.2	[27.2]	
34			8.26	1 hr	10	A	Astrup equilibration	↑	18.2	[27.7]	
35			8.06	5 hr	10	A	Astrup equilibration	↑	22.8	[27.2]	
36		4	8.50	10 min	HV	A	Astrup equilibration	↓	17.0	[28.4]	
37			8.85	1 hr	HV	A	Astrup equilibration	↓	26.5	[29.4]	
38			8.00	5 hr	HV	A	Astrup equilibration	↓	22.1	[27.0]	
39		5	....	40 min	HV	A	pH, Pco₂ (electrode), & blood or plasma CO₂ content	↓	12.9	....	29
40				4 hr	HV	A	pH, Pco₂ (electrode), & blood or plasma CO₂ content	↓	17.4	....	
41		7	....	1 hr	10	A	pH & Pco₂ (electrode)	↑	11.3	....	39
42			8.98	3 hr	10	A	pH & Pco₂ (electrode)	↑	17.6	[29.8]	
43		18	8.20	15 min	15;25	A	pH & plasma CO₂ content	↑	11.8 ± 0.6	24.0 ± 0.7 [27.8]	6
44		6	8.20	15 min	HV	A	pH & plasma CO₂ content	↓	24.0	24.0 ± 0.7	
45		9	....	12 min	30	A	pH & plasma CO₂ content	↑	12.2	....	38
46						MV	pH & plasma CO₂ content	↑	9.3	....	
47	*Castor fiber*, anesthetized	5	7.13	....	....	V	pH, Pco₂ (electrode), & blood or plasma CO₂ content	....	....	27.0 [24.6]	9
48	*Cervus nippon*[2/], awake	1	10.0	....	....	V	pH & plasma CO₂ content	....	....	29.3 [32.7]	1
49	*Cystophora cristata*	....	15.8	....	....	A	pH, Pco₂ (electrode), & blood CO₂ content	....	....	36	10
50	*Erinaceus europaeus*, hibernating	15	7.2	....	....	A	pH, Pco₂ (electrode), & blood or plasma CO₂ content	....	....	26.4 [24.8]	8
51	*Lama glama*, awake	1	11.2	....	....	V	pH & plasma CO₂ content	....	....	46.8 [36.2]	1
	Rattus sp.										
52	Awake	5	....	12 min	1.09	V	pH & plasma CO₂ content	↑	6.0	....	17
53					4.12	V	pH & plasma CO₂ content	↑	11.0	....	
54					8.05	V	pH & plasma CO₂ content	↑	15.6	....	
55		....	....	15 min	30	Heart	pH & plasma CO₂ content	↑	16.4	....	3
56					50	Heart	pH & plasma CO₂ content	↑	13.2	....	
57	Anesthetized	71	....	90-150 min	0-20	A	pH & plasma CO₂ content	↑	14.2	....	35
58		80	....	90-150 min	0-20	A	pH & plasma CO₂ content	↑	26.2	....	
59		9	....	20 min	10	V	pH & Pco₂ (electrode)	↑	36.1	....	22
60		9	....	45 min	10	V	pH & Pco₂ (electrode)	↑	43.1	....	
61		9	....	75 min	10	V	pH & Pco₂ (electrode)	↑	56.0	....	
62		13	....	2 hr	10	V	pH & Pco₂ (electrode)	↑	52.3	....	
63		10	....	4 hr	10	V	pH & Pco₂ (electrode)	↑	51.9	....	
64		14	....	6 hr	10	V	pH & Pco₂ (electrode)	↑	73.2	....	

[2/] Synonym: *Pseudaxis hortulorum.*

continued

Part II. Dissociation Curve Slopes: Vertebrates

	Species & Condition	No. of Experiments	Hemoglobin mmole/liter blood	Experimental Conditions				Pco2 Change	Slope, slykes		Reference
				Exposure Time	CO$_2$ %	Blood Type	Method of Measurement		In Vivo	In Vitro	
65		13	....	8 hr	10	V	pH & Pco$_2$ (electrode)	↑	68.8	....	
66		14	....	10 hr	10	V	pH & Pco$_2$ (electrode)	↑	55.6	....	
67		6	....	14 hr	10	V	pH & Pco$_2$ (electrode)	↑	74.3	....	
68		9	....	18 hr	10	V	pH & Pco$_2$ (electrode)	↑	89.3	....	
69		9	....	1 da	10	V	pH & Pco$_2$ (electrode)	↑	116.0	....	
70		9	....	36 hr	10	V	pH & Pco$_2$ (electrode)	↑	123.0	....	
71		9	....	2 da	10	V	pH & Pco$_2$ (electrode)	↑	162.5	....	
72		5	....	30 min	24	A	pH & plasma CO$_2$ content	↑	18.4	....	28
73		10	....	1 hr	24	A	pH & plasma CO$_2$ content	↑	32.9	....	
74		9	....	3 hr	24	A	pH & plasma CO$_2$ content	↑	38.0	....	
75		7	....	5 hr	24	A	pH & plasma CO$_2$ content	↑	37.2	....	
76		7	....	7 hr	24	A	pH & plasma CO$_2$ content	↑	46.3	....	
77		6	....	15 hr	24	A	pH & plasma CO$_2$ content	↑	42.0	....	
78		6	....	1 da	24	A	pH & plasma CO$_2$ content	↑	58.0	....	
79		4	....	2 da	24	A	pH & plasma CO$_2$ content	↑	90.0	....	
						Amphibia					
80	*Amphiuma tridactylum* [3/]	6	3.41	....	....	A [4/]	pH & gas chromatography	....	....	9.20	21
81	*Necturus maculosus*	6	2.68	....	....	A [4/]	pH & gas chromatography	....	....	8.00	21
82	*Rana catesbeiana,* awake	6	3.41	....	....	A [4/]	pH & gas chromatography	....	....	16.40 [15.1]	21
83	*R. temporaria,* awake	16	8.8 ± 2.3	1 da	10	Heart	Astrup equilibration	....	....	11.2	37
84		20	8.8 ± 2.3	1 da	5	Heart	Astrup equilibration	↑	32.4	20.4 [29.2]	
85				2 da	5	Heart	Astrup equilibration	↑	70.8	....	
86				5 da	5	Heart	Astrup equilibration	↑	81.6	....	

[3/] Synonym: *A. means tridactylum.* [4/] Temperature, 20-22°C.

Contributors: Brown, E. B., Jr., and Attebery, B. A.

References
[1] Bartels, H., et al. 1963. Amer. J. Physiol. 205(2): 331.
[2] Brackett, N. C., et al. 1965. N. Engl. J. Med. 272:6.
[3] Brodie, D., and D. M. Woodbury. 1958. Amer. J. Physiol. 192(1):91.
[4] Brown, E. B., Jr. 1960. J. Lab. Clin. Med. 55:767.
[5] Brown, E. B., Jr. 1966. Ann. N. Y. Acad. Sci. 133:118.
[6] Brown, E. B., Jr., and R. L. Clancy. 1965. J. Appl. Physiol. 20:885.
[7] Brown, E. B., Jr., et al. 1950. Ibid. 2:544.
[8] Claussen, G., and A. Ersland. 1968. Resp. Physiol. 5:221.
[9] Claussen, G., and A. Ersland. 1968. Ibid. 5:350.
[10] Claussen, G., and A. Ersland. 1969. Ibid. 7:1.
[11] Cohen, J. J., et al. 1964. J. Clin. Invest. 43:777.
[12] Davenport, H. T., et al. 1964. Anesthesiology 25(3): 307.
[13] Elkinton, J. R., et al. 1955. J. Clin. Invest. 25:1671.
[14] Engel, K., et al. 1969. Scand. J. Clin. Lab. Invest. 23:5.
[15] Flenley, D. C. 1964. Quart. J. Exp. Physiol. Cog. Med. Sci. 49(4):466.
[16] Giebisch, G., et al. 1955. J. Clin. Invest. 34:231.
[17] Gray, W. D., and C. E. Rauh. 1968. J. Pharmacol. Exp. Ther. 163:431.
[18] Greenburg, A. G., and C. F. Kittle. 1968. Surgery 64:315.
[19] Hurt, H., et al. 1967. Anesth. Analg. (Cleveland) 46:774.

continued

Part II. Dissociation Curve Slopes: Vertebrates

[20] Kazemi, H., et al. 1967. J. Appl. Physiol. 22(2):241.

[21] Lenfant, C., and K. Johansen. 1967. Resp. Physiol. 2:247.

[22] Martin, E., et al. 1967. U.S. Air Force Sch. Aerosp. Med. (Brooks) Proj. Res. TR 67-116.

[23] McRae, W. R., et al. 1964. Brit. J. Anaesth. 36(12): 793.

[24] Michel, C. C., et al. 1966. Resp. Physiol. 1:121.

[25] Mithoefer, J. C., et al. 1968. Ibid. 4:15.

[26] Mithoefer, J.C., et al. 1969. Anesthesiology 30:395.

[27] Nahas, G. G., and E. C. Jordan. 1960. Aerosp. Med. 31:61.

[28] Nichols, G. 1958. J. Clin. Invest. 37:1111.

[29] Norman, J., and R. J. Linden. 1965. Brit. J. Anaesth. 37(4):291.

[30] Platts, M. M., and M. Graves. 1957. Clin. Sci. 16:695.

[31] Prys-Roberts, C. 1968. Brit. J. Anaesth. 40:802.

[32] Prys-Roberts, C. Unpublished. Univ. Leeds, Dep. Anaesthesia, England, 1969.

[33] Prys-Roberts, C., et al. 1966. Brit. J. Anaesth. 38:500.

[34] Refsum, H. E., and B. M. Kim. 1967. Resp. Physiol. 2:283.

[35] Schloerb, P. R., et al. 1967. Amer. J. Physiol. 212(4):953.

[36] Siggaard-Andersen, O. 1962. Scand. J. Clin. Lab. Invest., Suppl. 66.

[37] Simkiss, K. 1968. Ibid. 214(3):627.

[38] Solberg, L., et al. Unpublished. Univ. Minnesota Medical School, Minneapolis, 1960.

[39] Veragut, U. P., and L. Smith. 1964. Surg. Gynecol. Obstet. 119:513.

213. DATA FOR CONSTRUCTING BLOOD OXYGEN DISSOCIATION CURVES: VERTEBRATES

O_2 dissociation or equilibrium curves can usually be described by Hill's equation: $y = \dfrac{(P/P_{50})^n}{1 + (P/P_{50})^n}$, in which y is the fractional saturation with O_2, P is the partial O_2 pressure ("tension"), P_{50} is the O_2 pressure required for 50% oxygenation, and n is the constant which affects the shape of the curve and is the value of the slope on a log versus log plot. If n = 1, the curves are hyperbolic; values greater than 1 indicate cooperative interactions between O_2 binding sites. (The plot should be straight, but often deviates at below 5% and above 95% oxygenation, and so is most accurately measured at 50% oxygenation.) In most hemoglobins, only P_{50} is pH-dependent (Bohr effect); in many fish hemoglobins and in some other pigments, both n and P_{50} change with pH—i.e., the shape of the curve changes with the pH.

Recent studies show that the P_{50} value (an inverse measure of O_2 affinity) in mammalian hemoglobins is greatly increased by the presence of phosphates—especially organic phosphates such as 2,3-diphosphoglycerate (DPG)—which control the O_2 pressure at which hemoglobin loses its oxygen. Since 2,3-diphosphoglycerate often declines rapidly in whole blood after it is removed from the animal, and since in vivo erythrocyte concentration varies with metabolic and environmental factors (low O_2 pressure at high altitudes may change the 2,3-diphosphoglycerate level), the values in the following tables should be used with caution.

The O_2 equilibrium of many hemoglobins and hemocyanins in free solution depends greatly on the protein concentration—e.g., the P_{50} value for lamprey hemoglobin increases 80 times when the protein concentration decreases from 3.6% to 0.1%. Meaningful comparison of different pigments should include a description of the protein concentration as an important parameter. Solvent: μ = ionic strength. P_{50} = oxygen pressure required for 50% oxygenation. Bohr Effect: calculated by the formula $\dfrac{\Delta \log P_{50}}{\Delta pH}$. n = the value which best approximates the 50% oxygenation of Hill's equation. ΔH = apparent heat of oxygenation, calculated from the van't Hoff equation: $\log \dfrac{(P_{50})_{T_2}}{(P_{50})_{T_1}} = \dfrac{\Delta H}{4.574}\left(\dfrac{T_2 - T_1}{T_1 T_2}\right)$, in which $(P_{50})_{T_1}$ and $(P_{50})_{T_2}$ are the O_2 pressures required for 50% oxygenation at absolute temperatures T_1 and T_2, respectively.

Part I. Man

Abbreviations: Tris = 2-amino-2-hydroxymethyl-1,3-propanediol; Hb = hemoglobin. Data in brackets refer to the column heading in brackets.

continued

213. DATA FOR CONSTRUCTING BLOOD OXYGEN DISSOCIATION CURVES: VERTEBRATES

Part I. Man

	Hemoglobin Specification	Blood or Blood Fraction	Solvent [Pco2, mm Hg]	pH	Temp °C	P50 mm Hg	Bohr Effect	n [ΔH]	Reference
1	Fetal	Whole blood	....	7.4	37	22.7[1]	....	....	16
2		Whole blood[2]	....		.....	Fn[3]	....	....	1
3		Free solution	0.4 M Acetate	<6.50	20	Fn[4]	....	Fn[5]	2,21,25
4			0.2 M PO4	>6.50	20	Fn[5]	Fn[5]	Fn[5]	2,21,25
5			0.1 M PO4	7.40	38	14.3[1]	....	....	32
6				7.50	15.5	1.62	−0.70	3.0	14
7		Free solution[6]	0.01 M Tris	7.00	25	4.2	....	....	38
8			0.01 M Tris[7]	7.00	25	13.8	....	....	38
9	69% Hb F	Whole blood	....	7.40	38	20.3[8]	....	....	32
10	Adult	Whole blood	....	7.1	37	26	....	....	5
11				7.4	37	24.3	....	....	16
12				7.4	37	26	....	....	12
13				7.4	37	26.8	....	....	4
14				7.4	38	26	....	2.9	9
15				7.4	38	27.2	....	....	13
16			[35]	....	37	24	....	....	27
17		Plus fluoride	....	7.4	38	28.5[1]	....	3.0	13
18		Plus iodoacetic acid	....	7.4	38	14.8[1]	....	2.8	13
19		Free solution	....	7.0	20	10	....	....	23
20				7.4	10	1.2	....	2.0	9
21			0.05 M PO4	6.5	37	26	....	2.2	26
22			0.08 M PO4	7.5	20	5.0	−0.50	2.8	20
23			0.1 M PO4	6.70	10	4.0	−0.45	2.8	24
24				6.9-7.3	.....	5.6	0.58	....	7
25				7.38	25.5	6.1	....	....	31
26				7.4	20	6.0	−0.48	3.0	19
27				7.40	38	14.7	....	....	32
28				7.5	20	4.8	−0.57	2.6	22
29				7.50	20	4.4	−0.69	3.0 [−13.6]	34
30				7.53	30	7.6	−0.67	2.7	39
31				7.7	10	1.2	−0.76	2.1	29
32				7.8	10	1.2	−0.76	2.1	29
33			0.2 M PO4	7.0	19.5	32	....	....	35
34		Free solution[6]	0.01 M NaCl	7.0	10	0.23	....	....	6
35			0.01 M NaCl[9]	7.0	10	7.4	....	....	6
36			0.01 M Tris	7.00	25	2.5	....	....	38
37			0.01 M Tris[7]	7.00	25	15.8	....	....	38
38	Young erythrocytes	Whole blood	....	7.4	37	33.5	....	3.61	11
39		Free solution[10]	....	6.60	37	34.9	....	....	11
40	Old erythrocytes	Whole blood	....	7.4	37	27.0	....	2.75	11
41		Free solution[10]	....	6.57	37	26.2	....	....	11
42	α chains	Free solution	0.1 M PO4	....	10	0.11	0.00	0.9-1.0	28
43				7.0	20	0.4	....	1.0	10
44				7.53	30	1.0[1]	0[1]	1.0[1]	39
45			0.15 M PO4	6.7	20	0.50	0.00	1.1	3

[1] Values for untreated, unmodified, adult whole blood or hemoglobin may be found among the "Adult" entries from same reference. [2] Fetal erythrocytes in adult plasma. [3] Same as for fetus. [4] Greater than for adult; i.e., the O_2 affinity of Hb F is less than that of Hb A. [5] Same as for adult. [6] "Stripped" by passing through a Sephadex column. [7] With $4 \times 10^{-4} M$ adenosine 5′-triphosphate. [8] Value for blood from fetus, containing 69% Hb F; value for blood from adult with elevated Hb F disease (also containing 69% Hb F) = 26.2 mm Hg (fetal cells contain less 2,3-DPG and so have higher oxygen affinity). [9] With $2.5 \times 10^{-3} M$ 2,3-DPG. [10] Overnight dialysis against distilled water.

continued

Part I. Man

	Hemoglobin Specification	Blood or Blood Fraction	Solvent [P_{CO_2}, mm Hg]	pH	Temp °C	P_{50} mm Hg	Bohr Effect	n [ΔH]	Reference
46	β chains	Free solution	0.1 M PO₄	7.0	20	0.5	....	1.0	10
47				7.53	30	0.5 [L]	0 [L]	1.0 [L]	39
48				7.62	15.5	0.09	0.00	1.0	14
49			0.15 M PO₄	6.6	20	0.43	0.00	1.0	3
50	γ chains	Free solution	0.1 M PO₄	7.40	15.5	0.17	0.00	1.0	14
51	A₂ [11]	Free solution	0.1 M PO₄	6.87	37	11.2	Fn [12]	1.4-2.0	18
52	H	Free solution	0.1 M PO₄	6.9-7.3	.....	0.3 [L]	0 [L]	....	7
53				7.02	30	0.6	0.00	1.0	39
54	M Hyde Park	Free solution	0.1 M PO₄	7.8	10	1.1 [L]	−0.72 [L]	1.1 [L]	29
55	M Kankakee	Free solution	0.08 M PO₄	7.5	20	50 [L]	−0.19 [L]	1.0 [L]	20
56			0.1 M PO₄	7.7	10	15 [L]	0 [L]	1.1 [L]	29
57	M Osaka	Free solution	0.2 M PO₄	7.0	19.5	10 [L]	0.00	1.2	35
58	M Random	Free solution	....	7.0	20	5 [L]	Normal	1.3	23
59	M Reserve	Whole blood	[35]	....	37	27 [L]	....	....	27
60	M Saskatoon	Free solution	0.2 M PO₄	....	.....	Normal	Normal	1.2	36
61	S	Free solution	0.1 M PO₄	7.38	25.5	8.0 [L]	....	....	31
62				7.40	38	14.3 [L]	....	....	32
63	Sickle cell anemia	Whole blood	....	7.1	37	40 [L]	....	....	5
64				7.40	37	52	....	....	15
65	Sickle cell trait	Whole blood	....	7.1	37	28 [L]	....	....	5
66	Barts	Free solution	....	....	.....	3.2	0.00	1.1	17
67			0.1 M PO₄	7.35	37	3.2	0.00	1.0	37
68	Chesapeake	Whole blood	....	7.4	38	20 [L]	....	1.8 [L]	9
69		Free solution	....	7.4	10	0.3 [L]	....	1.1 [L]	9
70			0.1 M PO₄	6.70	10	0.66 [L]	−0.45 [L]	1.3 [L]	24
71	Hiroshima	Free solution	0.1 M PO₄	7.4	20	1.8 [L]	−0.22 [L]	2.0-2.6 [L,13]	19
72				7.5	20	1.6 [L]	−0.37 [L]	2.0 [L]	22
73	Kansas	Free solution	....	7.50	20	20.9	....	1.3	8
74		Free solution [14]	0.15 M PO₄	7.37	37	40	Normal	1.1	30
75	Ranier	Free solution	....	....	.....	Fn [15]	Fn [12]	1.2	33
76	Yakima [16]	Whole blood	....	7.4	38	12	−0.52	1.1	26
77		Free solution	0.05 M PO₄	6.5	37	5.0 [L]	....	1.0 [L]	26
78	Hypoxemic erythrocytosis	Whole blood	....	7.4	37	30 [L]	....	....	12

[L] Values for untreated, unmodified, adult whole blood or hemoglobin may be found among the "Adult" entries from same reference. [11] Values same for Hb B₂, a genetic variant of Hb A₂. [12] Same as for Hb A, the chromatographically purified fraction of normal adult Hb (95% Hb A). [13] The Hill plot is biphasic below pH 7.8. [14] Hemolysate; not purified. [15] Less than for Hb A, i.e., increased oxygen affinity. [16] Blood hemolysate contains 62% Hb A; the other 38% is mostly Hb Yakima.

Contributor: Sullivan, J. Bolling

References

[1] Abrahamov, A., and C. A. Smith. 1959. Amer. J. Dis. Child. 97:375.

[2] Antonini, E., et al. 1964. Arch. Biochem. Biophys. 108:569.

[3] Antonini, E., et al. 1965. J. Mol. Biol. 12:375.

[4] Bartels, H., et al. 1961. Pfluegers Arch. Gesamte Physiol. Menschen Tiere 272:372.

[5] Becklake, M. R., et al. 1955. J. Clin. Invest. 34:751.

[6] Benesch, R., et al. 1968. Proc. Nat. Acad. Sci. U.S. 59:526.

[7] Benesch, R. E., et al. 1961. J. Biol. Chem. 236:2926.

[8] Bonaventura, J., and A. Riggs. 1968. Ibid. 243:980.

[9] Charache, S., et al. 1966. J. Clin. Invest. 45:813.

[10] De Renzo, E. C., et al. 1967. J. Biol. Chem. 242:4850.

[11] Edwards, M. J., and D. A. Rigas. 1967. J. Clin. Invest. 46:1579.

[12] Edwards, M. J., et al. 1968. Ibid. 47:1851.

[13] Engel, K., and G. Duc. 1968. Nature (London) 219:936.

continued

213. DATA FOR CONSTRUCTING BLOOD OXYGEN DISSOCIATION CURVES: VERTEBRATES

Part I. Man

[14] Enoki, Y., et al. 1968. J. Mol. Biol. 37:345.

[15] Fraimow, W., et al. 1958. Amer. J. Med. Sci. 236: 225.

[16] Hilpert, P., et al. 1963. Amer. J. Physiol. 205:337.

[17] Horton, B. F., et al. 1962. Blood 20:302.

[18] Huisman, T. H. J., et al. 1962. Nature (London) 195:1109.

[19] Imai, K. 1968. Arch. Biochem. Biophys. 127:543.

[20] Kikuchi, G., et al. 1964. Biochim. Biophys. Acta 90:199.

[21] Manwell, C. 1964. In F. Dickens and E. Neil, ed. Oxygen in the Animal Organism. Macmillan, New York. p. 49.

[22] Mihara, K., et al. 1968. Biochem. Biophys. Res. Commun. 32:763.

[23] Murawski, K., et al. 1965. Arch. Biochem. Biophys. 111:197.

[24] Nagel, R. L., et al. 1967. Biochemistry 6:2395.

[25] Nechtman, C. M., and T. H. J. Huisman. 1964. Clin. Chim. Acta 10:165.

[26] Novy, M. J., et al. 1967. J. Clin. Invest. 46:1848.

[27] Overly, W. L., et al. 1967. J. Lab. Clin. Med. 69:62.

[28] Ranney, H. M., et al. 1965. J. Biol. Chem. 240: 2442.

[29] Ranney, H. M., et al. 1968. Biochim. Biophys. Acta 160:112.

[30] Reissmann, K. R., et al. 1961. J. Clin. Invest. 40: 1826.

[31] Riggs, A., and M. Wells. 1961. Biochim. Biophys. Acta 50:243.

[32] Schruefer, J. J. P., et al. 1962. Nature (London) 196:550.

[33] Stamatoyannopoulos, G., et al. 1968. Science 159: 741.

[34] Sullivan, B. 1967. Biochem. Biophys. Res. Commun. 28:407.

[35] Suzuki, T., et al. 1965. Ibid. 19:691.

[36] Suzuki, T., et al. 1966. Biochim. Biophys. Acta 127: 280.

[37] Thompson, R. B., et al. 1965. Amer. J. Physiol. 208: 198.

[38] Tyuma, I., and K. Shimizu. 1969. Arch. Biochem. Biophys. 129:404.

[39] Tyuma, I., et al. 1966. Biochemistry 5:2957.

Part II.   Mammals Other Than Man

For additional information, consult references 1, 3, 31, 49, 52, and 60. Data in brackets refer to the column heading in brackets.

	Order & Species (Synonym)	Blood or Blood Fraction	Solvent [P_{CO_2}, mm Hg]	pH	Temp °C	P_{50} mm Hg	Bohr Effect	n [$\Delta\log P_{50}/°C$ [L/]]	Reference
	Artiodactyla								
1	*Bos taurus*	Whole blood	....	7.4	37	30.9	....	....	4
2		Type A[2/]	....	7.35	37	27.8	−0.48	....	26
3		Type B[2/]	....	7.35	37	30.6	−0.49	....	26
4		Free solution	0.1 M PO$_4$	7.50	35	20.6	−0.52	2.75	47
5		Type A[2/]	0.1 M PO$_4$	7.1	37	35.0	−0.39	....	26
6		Type B[2/]	0.1 M PO$_4$	7.1	37	38.9	−0.42	....	26
7	*Camelus bactrianus*	Whole blood	....	7.4	37	24.1	−0.49	....	5
8	*C. dromedarius*	Whole blood	....	7.2	37	25.5	....	....	45
9	Fetus	Whole blood	....	7.2	37	21	....	....	45
10	*Capra hircus*	Whole blood	....	7.40	38	30	−0.53	2.79	24
11		Type AB[2/]	....	7.35	37	27.2	−0.53	....	26
12		Type C[2/]	....	7.35	37	32.0	−0.60	....	26
		Free solution							
13		Type AB[2/]	0.1 M PO$_4$	7.1	37	31.2	−0.57	....	26
14		Type C[2/]	0.1 M PO$_4$	7.1	37	34.6	−0.63	....	26
15	Fetus	Whole blood	....	7.40	38	19	−0.62	2.66	24
16		Whole blood[3/]	....	7.35	37	20.2	−0.70	....	26
17	Kid, 1 da old	Whole blood	....	7.4	37	22.3	....	....	25
18	4 da old	Whole blood	....	7.4	37	29.1	....	....	25
19	25 da old	Whole blood	....	7.4	37	31.7	....	....	25
20	55 da old	Whole blood	....	7.4	37	35.3	....	....	25

[L/] Unless otherwise indicated. [2/] Types determined by electrophoretic properties. [3/] 92% hemoglobin F, 8% hemoglobin A.

continued

Part II. Mammals Other Than Man

	Order & Species (Synonym)	Blood or Blood Fraction	Solvent [Pco$_2$, mm Hg]	pH	Temp °C	P$_{50}$ mm Hg	Bohr Effect	n [Δlog P$_{50}$/°C]	Reference
21	Adult	Whole blood	....	7.4	37	33.0	....	....	25
22	C. hircus 4/	Whole blood	....	7.40	39	31.4	−0.53	....	41
23	C. hircus 5/	Whole blood	....	7.4	39.5	29.7	−0.50	[0.019]	9
24	Lama glama (L. peruana)	Whole blood	....	7.4	37	23.3	−0.42		5
25					38	21	−0.44	2.4	33
26	Fetus	Whole blood	....	7.4	38	18	−0.31	2.4	33
27	Ovis aries, Dorset	Whole blood	....	7.4	38	32-37	−0.48 to −0.32	2.7-2.8	34
28	Fetus	Whole blood	....	7.4	38	16	−0.54 to −0.40	2.4-2.8	34
29		Whole blood 6/	....	7.35	37	25.7	−0.71	....	26
30		Whole blood	....	7.40	39.6	20.6	....	....	8
31	Lamb, 1 da old	Whole blood	....	7.4	37	23.9	....	....	25
32	4 da old	Whole blood	....	7.4	37	25.9	....	....	25
33	30 da old	Whole blood	....	7.4	37	36.9	....	....	25
34	64 da old	Whole blood	....	7.4	37	42.5	....	....	25
35				7.40	39.6	35.0	....	....	8
36	Adult	Whole blood	....	7.4	37	33.8	....	....	4
37				7.4	37	43.5	....	....	25
38				7.40	39.6	43.7	....	....	8
39		Type A 2/	....	7.35	37	29.5	−0.51	....	26
40				7.4	38	27.7	....	2.6	35
41		Type A	[40]	...	37	29	....	....	15
42		High K$^+$	[40]	...	20	17	....	....	17
43		Low K$^+$	[40]	...	20	19	....	....	17
44		Type II 7/	[40]	7.38	37	20	....	....	27
45		Type B 2/	....	7.35	37	43.0	−0.49	....	26
46				7.4	38	37.8	....	2.6	35
47			[40]	...	37	40	....	....	15
48		High K$^+$	[40]	...	20	25	....	....	17
49		Low K$^+$	[40]	...	20	26	....	....	17
50		Type B? 2/	....	7.4	39	40	....	....	42
51		Type I 7/	[40]	7.38	37	30	....	....	27
52		Type AB 2/	....	7.4	38	37.2	....	2.7	35
53		Type C 7/	....	7.35	37	29.1	−0.60	....	26
54		Type C	[40]	...	37	29	....	....	15
		Free solution							
55		Type A 2/	0.1 M PO$_4$	7.1	37	32.7	−0.48	....	26
56		Type II 7/	....	7.2	37	28	....	....	27
57		Type B 2/	0.1 M PO$_4$	6.8	37	41.8	−0.48	....	26
58		Type I 7/	....	7.2	37	36	....	....	27
59		Type C 8/	0.1 M PO$_4$	7.1	37	32.4	−0.50	....	26
60		Free solution 9/	0.02 M NaCl	7.0	10	4.8	....	....	12
61			0.02 M NaCl 10/	7.0	10	19.0	....	....	12
62	Sus scrofa	Whole blood	....	7.4	37	30.8	....	....	4
63						31.5	....	....	18
64		Free solution	0.1 M PO$_4$	7.38	35	13.4	−0.57	2.59	47

2/ Types determined by electrophoretic properties. 4/ African pygmy goat. 5/ Mottled German goat. 6/ 82% hemoglobin F, 18% hemoglobin B. 7/ Type II probably equals type A; type I probably equals type B. 8/ 86% hemoglobin C, 14% hemoglobin A. 9/ "Stripped" by passing through a Sephadex column. 10/ Plus 2.5 × 10^{-3} M 2,3-DPG.

continued

Part II. Mammals Other Than Man

	Order & Species (Synonym)	Blood or Blood Fraction	Solvent [P_{CO_2}, mm Hg]	pH	Temp °C	P_{50} mm Hg	Bohr Effect	n [Δlog P_{50}/°C [L/]]	Reference
	Perissodactyla								
65	*Equus asinus*	Free solution	0.1 M PO$_4$	...	20	4.7	−0.53	2.3	50
66	*E. caballus*	Whole blood	....	7.4	37	25.1	−0.45	....	9
67		Free solution	0.1 M PO$_4$	7.29	35	16.4	−0.68	3.08	47
	Proboscidea								
68	*Loxodonta africana*	Whole blood	....	7.4	37	22.4	−0.40	....	5
69				7.40	37	22.5	−0.40	....	46
70	Fetus, 5 mo old	Whole blood	....	7.40	37	21.7	....	....	46
71	12 mo old	Whole blood	....	7.40	37	17.2	....	....	46
72	Adult	Free solution	0.1 M PO$_4$	7.38	35	14.2	−0.38	2.65	47
	Pinnipedia								
	Leptonychotes weddelli								
73	Fetus	Whole blood	....	7.40	37	22.1	−0.67	2.40	30
74	Adult	Whole blood	....	7.40	37	28.5	−0.61	2.56	30
75	*Phoca vitulina*	Whole blood	[10]	...	38	25	....	....	43
76			[40]	...	37	28.0	....	....	28
77					38	31	....	....	43
	Carnivora								
78	*Canis familiaris*	Whole blood	....	7.4	37	28.3	−0.57 to −0.48	....	53
79						29.1	....	....	4
80		Free solution	0.1 M PO$_4$	7.34	35	15.0	−0.65	2.85	47
81			0.2 M PO$_4$	7.02	20	5.3	Fn [11/]	2.1-2.4	2
82		Free solution [12/]	0.1 M PO$_4$	7.0	15.5	5.5	−0.75	2.8	19
83	*Felis catus*	Whole blood	....	7.4	37	36.4	....	....	4
84		Free solution	0.1 M PO$_4$	7.50	20	11.5	−0.67	3.0 [−14.9 [13/]]	55
85			0.14 M PO$_4$	7.2	20	11.3	−0.45	....	58
86		Major [14/]	0.14 M PO$_4$	7.35	20	9.8	−0.49	....	58
87		Minor [14/]	0.14 M PO$_4$	7.2	20	11.3	−0.45	....	58
88	Fetus	Whole blood	....	7.40	38	35.6	−0.47	....	37
89	Adult	Whole blood	....	7.40	38	36.2	−0.48	....	37
	Cetacea								
90	*Phocoena phocoena*	Free solution	0.1 M PO$_4$	7.32	35	17.0	−0.52	....	48
	Rodentia								
91	*Cavia porcellus*	Whole blood	....	7.4	37	27.2	....	....	4
92				7.40	37	30	....	....	23
93		Free solution	0.03 M PO$_4$	7.2	37	14	....	....	20
94			0.1 M PO$_4$	7.40	20	4.9	−0.70	....	57
95				7.44	35	12.3	−0.79	2.69	47
96	*Mesocricetus auratus*	Whole blood	....	7.40	37	29	....	....	23
97		Free solution	0.03 M PO$_4$	7.2	37	13.7	....	....	20
98	*Mus musculus*	Whole blood	....	7.40	37	52	....	....	23
99			[40]	7.4	37	41.5	....	....	21
100		Free solution	0.03 M PO$_4$	6.8	37	34.2	....	....	20
101			0.1 M PO$_4$	...	20	12.3	−0.93	2.4	50
102				7.16	35	26.0	−0.96	2.80	47
103	BALB/cJ	Free solution	0.1 M PO$_4$	7.2	20	6.3	....	2.5	51
104	C57/6J	Free solution	0.1 M PO$_4$	7.2	20	6.3	....	2.5	51
105	C57BL/6	Free solution	0.2 M PO$_4$	7.3	20	10	−0.60	3	54

[L/] Unless otherwise indicated. [11/] Same as for adult human hemolysate. [12/] After subjugation to chain hybridization conditions. [13/] ΔH. [14/] Electrophoretic components.

continued

Part II. Mammals Other Than Man

	Order & Species (Synonym)	Blood or Blood Fraction	Solvent [P_{CO_2}, mm Hg]	pH	Temp °C	P_{50} mm Hg	Bohr Effect	n [Δlog P_{50}/°C]	Reference
106	*Rattus norvegicus*	Whole blood	[40]	7.4	37	38	....	....	21
107	Long-Evans	Whole blood	[35]	...	37	49	....	....	14
108		Free solution	0.1 *M* PO$_4$	7.40	20	6.0	−0.78	....	57
109	White	Whole blood	....	7.40	37	38	....	....	23
110		Free solution	0.03 *M* PO$_4$	7.2	37	19.7	....	....	20
111	Wild	Whole blood	....	7.40	37	39	....	....	23
112		Free solution	0.03 *M* PO$_4$	7.2	37	20.3	....	....	20
113	*Sciurus carolinensis*	Whole blood	....	7.40	37	36	....	....	22,23
114		Free solution	0.03 *M* PO$_4$	6.8	37	26.2	....	....	20
115	*Spermophilus tridecemlinea-*	Whole blood	....	7.40	37	25	....	....	23
116	*tus (Citellus tridecemline-atus)*					28	....	....	22
	Lagomorpha								
117	*Oryctolagus cuniculus*	Whole blood	[40]	...	37	39	....	2.9	59
118		Free solution	0.03 *M* PO$_4$	6.8	37	24.8	....	....	20
119	Fetus	Free solution	0.1 *M* PO$_4$	7.4	20	7.5	....	2.8	59
120	Newborn, 1 da old	Whole blood	[40]	...	37	24	....	2.9	59
121	Adult	Whole blood	....	7.4	37	30.5	....	....	4
122		Free solution	0.1 *M* PO$_4$	7.32	35	14.7	−0.75	2.79	47
123				7.4	20	9.9	....	2.8	59
	Primates								
124	*Cebus apella*	Free solution	0.1 *M* PO$_4$	7.50	20	4.9	−0.79	2.7-3.0	56
125	*Cercopithecus aethiops*	Free solution	0.1 *M* PO$_4$	7.50	20	4.6	−0.69	2.7-3.0	56
126	*Erythrocebus patas*	Free solution	0.1 *M* PO$_4$	7.50	20	5.3	−0.69	2.7-3.0	56
127	*Galago senegalensis*	Free solution	0.1 *M* PO$_4$	7.50	20	6.0	−0.75	2.7-3.0	56
128	*Gorilla gorilla (Pan gorilla)*	Whole blood	....	7.4	37	25.4	−0.50	....	44
129		Free solution	0.1 *M* PO$_4$	7.50	20	4.1	−0.64	2.7-3.0	56
130	*Hylobates lar*	Whole blood	....	7.4	38	30.4	−0.57	....	40
131		Free solution	0.1 *M* PO$_4$	7.50	20	3.7	−0.67	2.7-3.0	56
132	*Lemur catta*	Free solution	0.1 *M* PO$_4$	7.50	20	9.5	−0.60	2.7-3.0	56
133	*Macaca irus*	Whole blood	....	7.4	38	32.4	−0.47	3.0	36
134	Fetus	Whole blood	....	7.4	38	18.8	−0.40	2.5	36
135	*M. mulatta*	Whole blood	....	7.4	38	32.0	−0.47	2.9	36
136	Fetus	Whole blood	....	7.4	38	19.2	−0.51	2.7	36
137				7.40	38	16	−0.58	2.63	11
138						17.4	−0.42	2.40	10
139	Adult	Whole blood	....	7.4	38	32	....	....	38
140				7.40	38	27	−0.61	2.84	11
141						32.9	−0.30	2.65	10
142	*M. nemestrina*	Whole blood	....	7.4	38	32.5	−0.49	3.1	36
143	*M. speciosa*, fetus	Whole blood	....	7.40	37	21.3	−0.55	2.64	13
144	adult	Whole blood	....	7.40	37	33.3	−0.54	2.89	13
145	*Pan troglodytes*	Whole blood	....	7.4	37	26.4	−0.59	....	44
146					38	28.0	−0.41	....	40
147		Free solution	0.1 *M* PO$_4$	7.50	20	4.1	−0.65	2.7-3.0	56
148	*Papio anubis (Chaeropithecus papio)*	Whole blood	....	7.4	38	32.1	−0.49	[0.021]	40
149	*Saguinus oedipus (Oedipomidas oedipus)*	Free solution	0.1 *M* PO$_4$	7.50	20	5.4	−0.67	2.7-3.0	56
	Chiroptera								
150	*Myotis lucifugus*	Free solution	$\mu = 0.3$, PO$_4$	7.5	23-25	8	−0.7	2.4-2.8	32

continued

Part II. Mammals Other Than Man

	Order & Species (Synonym)	Blood or Blood Fraction	Solvent [P_{CO_2}, mm Hg]	pH	Temp °C	P_{50} mm Hg	Bohr Effect	n [Δlog P_{50}/°C]	Reference
	Insectivora								
151	*Blarina brevicauda*	Free solution	0.03 M PO$_4$	6.8	37	32.8	....	....	20
152	*Crocidura russula*	Whole blood	....	7.40	37	36.9	−0.63	....	7
153	*Erinaceus europaeus*	Whole blood	....	7.40	5	8.9	−0.36	....	16
154					38	34.0	−0.62	[0.017]	16
155					37	36.2	....		7
156	Hibernating	Whole blood	....	7.40	39	23	−0.45	[−0.0167]	7
157	Nonhibernating	Whole blood	....	7.40	39	36	−0.49	[−0.0167]	7
158	*Talpa europaea*	Whole blood	....	7.40	37	24	−0.47	....	7
	Marsupialia								
159	*Macropus giganteus*	Whole blood	....	7.4	37	27.5	−0.54	....	6
	Monotremata								
160	*Ornithorhynchus anatinus*	Whole blood	....	7.40	31	27.2	−0.56	[0.014]	39
161			[15]	...	30	31	....	....	29
162			[30]	...	30	38	....	....	29

Contributor: Sullivan, J. Bolling

References

[1] Antonini, E. 1965. Physiol. Rev. 45:123.
[2] Antonini, E., et al. 1965. Biochim. Biophys. Acta 104:160.
[3] Bartels, H. 1964. Lancet 2:599.
[4] Bartels, H., and H. Harms. 1959. Pfluegers Arch. Gesamte Physiol. Menschen Tiere 268:334.
[5] Bartels, H., et al. 1963. Amer. J. Physiol. 205:331.
[6] Bartels, H., et al. 1966. Resp. Physiol. 1:145.
[7] Bartels, H., et al. 1969. Ibid. 7:278.
[8] Battaglia, F. C., et al. 1970. Amer. J. Physiol. 219:217.
[9] Baumann, P., et al. 1963. Pfluegers Arch. Gesamte Physiol. Menschen Tiere 277:120.
[10] Behrman, R. E. 1968. J. Appl. Physiol. 25:224.
[11] Behrman, R. E., et al. 1963. Quart. J. Exp. Physiol. Cog. Med. Sci. 48:258.
[12] Benesch, R., et al. 1968. Proc. Nat. Acad. Sci. U.S. 59:526.
[13] Blechner, J. N., and V. G. Stenger. 1970. Amer. J. Obstet. Gynecol. 107:38.
[14] Bullard, R. W., et al. 1966. J. Appl. Physiol. 21:994.
[15] Chamley, J. H., and R. A. B. Holland. 1969. Resp. Physiol. 7:287.
[16] Clausen, G., and A. Ersland. 1968. Ibid. 5:221.
[17] Dawson, T. J., and J. V. Evans. 1962. Aust. J. Biol. Sci. 15:371.
[18] Edwards, M. J., and R. J. Martin. 1966. J. Appl. Physiol. 21:1898.
[19] Enoki, Y., and S. Tomita. 1968. J. Mol. Biol. 32:121.
[20] Foreman, C. W. 1954. J. Cell. Comp. Physiol. 44:421.

[21] Gray, L. H., and J. M. Steadman. 1964. J. Physiol. (London) 175:161.
[22] Hall, F. G. 1965. Science 148:1350.
[23] Hall, F. G. 1966. J. Appl. Physiol. 21:375.
[24] Hellegers, A. E., et al. 1959. Quart. J. Exp. Physiol. Cog. Med. Sci. 44:215.
[25] Hilpert, P., et al. 1963. Amer. J. Physiol. 205:337.
[26] Huisman, T. H. J., and J. Kitchens. 1968. Amer. J. Physiol. 215:140.
[27] Huisman, T. H. J., et al. 1958. Nature (London) 182:171.
[28] Irving, L., et al. 1935. J. Cell. Comp. Physiol. 6:393.
[29] Johansen, K., et al. 1966. Comp. Biochem. Physiol. 18:597.
[30] Lenfant, C., et al. 1969. Amer. J. Physiol. 216:1595.
[31] Manwell, C. 1960. Annu. Rev. Physiol. 22:191.
[32] Manwell, C., and K. V. Kerst. 1966. Comp. Biochem. Physiol. 17:741.
[33] Meschia, G., et al. 1960. Quart. J. Exp. Physiol. Cog. Med. Sci. 45:284.
[34] Meschia, G., et al. 1961. Ibid. 46:95.
[35] Naughton, M. A., et al. 1963. Ibid. 48:313.
[36] Novy, M. J., et al. 1969. J. Appl. Physiol. 26:339.
[37] Novy, M. J., and J. T. Parer. 1969. Resp. Physiol. 6:144.
[38] Parer, J. T. 1967. Ibid. 2:168.
[39] Parer, J. T., and J. Metcalfe. 1967. Ibid. 3:136.
[40] Parer, J. T., and C. P. Moore. 1968. Folia Primatol. 9:154.
[41] Parer, J. T., et al. 1967. J. Appl. Physiol. 22:756.
[42] Parer, J. T., et al. 1967. Resp. Physiol. 2:196.

continued

Part II. Mammals Other Than Man

[43] Prosser, C. L., et al. 1950. Comparative Animal Physiology. W. B. Saunders, Philadelphia.

[44] Riegel, K., et al. 1966. Resp. Physiol. 1:138.

[45] Riegel, K., et al. 1967. Ibid. 2:173.

[46] Riegel, K., et al. 1967. Ibid. 2:182.

[47] Riggs, A. 1960. J. Gen. Physiol. 43:737.

[48] Riggs, A. 1961. Nature (London) 190:94.

[49] Riggs, A. 1965. Physiol. Rev. 45:619.

[50] Riggs, A., and A. E. Herner. 1962. Proc. Nat. Acad. Sci. U.S. 48:1664.

[51] Riggs, A., and M. Rona. 1969. Biochim. Biophys. Acta 175:248.

[52] Rossi-Fanelli, A., et al. 1964. Advan. Protein Chem. 19:73.

[53] Rossing, R. G., and S. M. Cain. 1966. J. Appl. Physiol. 21:195.

[54] Smith, D. B., et al. 1966. Arch. Biochem. Biophys. 113:725.

[55] Sullivan, B. 1967. Biochem. Biophys. Res. Commun. 28:407.

[56] Sullivan, B. 1971. Comp. Biochem. Physiol. 40B:359.

[57] Sullivan, B. Unpublished. Duke Univ. Medical Center, Durham, N. C., 1973.

[58] Taketa, F., and S. A. Morell. 1966. Biochem. Biophys. Res. Commun. 24:705.

[59] Tyuma, I., et al. 1964. Jap. J. Physiol. 14:573.

[60] Wyman, J. 1964. Advan. Protein Chem. 19:223.

Part III. Birds

	Order & Species	Blood or Blood Fraction	Solvent [P_{CO_2}, mm Hg]	pH	Temp °C	P_{50} mm Hg	Bohr Effect	n	Reference
	Passeriformes								
1	*Passer domesticus*	Whole blood	....	7.50	41	47.4	.....	...	17
	Columbiformes								
2	*Columba* sp.	Whole blood	....	7.10	37.5	40.0	.....	...	9
3			[40]	...	37.5	35.0	.....	...	16
	Charadriiformes								
4	*Fulmarus glacialis*	Whole blood	[40]	7.40	42	60.5	−0.48	...	7
5	*Larus argentatus*	Whole blood	[40]	7.40	42	5.75	−0.50	...	7
	Galliformes								
6	*Coturnix coturnix*	Free solution	$\mu = 0.3$, PO_4	7.7	24	6.2	.....	...	14
7	*Gallus gallus*	Free solution	$\mu = 0.6$, PO_4	7.6	25	11.0	−0.77	...	15
8	Embryo, 5 da old	Free solution	$\mu = 0.6$, PO_4	7.6	25	3.5	−0.19	...	15
9	17-21 da old	Whole blood	....	7.4	39	31.6	.....	...	3
10	Chick, 1-23 da old	Whole blood	....	7.4	39	50.5	.....	...	3
11	Adult	Whole blood	....	7.4	39	48.9	−0.50	...	3
12		Free solution	....	7.0	37	19.5	−0.67	2.5	11
13			$\mu = 0.3$, PO_4	7.44	25	13	−0.69	...	2
14				7.7	24	7.5	.....	...	14
15		Major fraction[L]	....	7.0	37	15.8	−0.55	2.5	11
16		Minor fraction[L]	....	7.0	37	8.9	−0.42	2.6	11
17		Free solution[2]	0.1 M NaCl	7.0	10	0.26	.....	...	4
18			0.1 M NaCl[3]	7.0	10	22.4	.....	...	4
19	*G. gallus*, White Rock	Whole blood	....	7.50	42	54	.....	...	5
20	*G. gallus* × *Coturnix coturnix*	Free solution	$\mu = 0.3$, PO_4	7.7	24	8.7	.....	...	14
21	*Phasianus colchicus*	Free solution	$\mu = 0.3$, PO_4	7.44	25	13	−0.69	...	2
22	Pheasant	Whole blood	....	7.10	37.5	50.0	.....	...	16
	Anseriformes								
23	*Cairina moschata*	Free solution	....	7.10	37.0	58.0	.....	...	6
24	*Chloephaga melanoptera*	Whole blood	....	7.35	40	33.0	.....	...	10

[L] Chromatographic fraction. [2] "Stripped" by passing through a Sephadex column. [3] Plus $2.5 \times 10^{-3} M$ inositol hexaphosphate.

continued

Part III. Birds

	Order & Species	Blood or Blood Fraction	Solvent [Pco2, mm Hg]	pH	Temp °C	P50 mm Hg	Bohr Effect	n	Reference
25	*Melanitta deglandi*[4]	Free solution	$\mu = 0.3$, PO_4	7.4	24-26	13.2	−0.58	2.8	13
26	Duck, domestic	Whole blood	....	7.35	42	55	−0.40	...	1
27	Goose	Whole blood	....	7.40	.....	46	−0.47	3.1	8
28	Podicipediformes *Aechmophorus occidentalis*	Free solution[5]	$\mu = 0.3$, PO_4	7.4	24-26	11.6	−0.45	2.3	13
29	Rheiformes *Rhea americana*	Whole blood	....	7.35	40	26.0	.....	...	10
30	Sphenisciformes *Pygoscelis adeliae*	Whole blood	....	7.4	38.5	35.0	−0.49	3.0	12

[4] Synonym: *Oidemia deglandi.* [5] Erythrocytes in solution had slightly lower O_2 affinity (1-2 mm Hg).

Contributor: Sullivan, J. Bolling

References

[1] Andersen, H. T., and A. Lovo. 1967. Resp. Physiol. 2:163.

[2] Baker, C. M. A. 1966. Comp. Biochem. Physiol. 17: 467.

[3] Bartels, H., et al. 1966. Resp. Physiol. 1:345.

[4] Benesch, R., et al. 1968. Proc. Nat. Acad. Sci. U. S. 59:526.

[5] Chiodi, H., and J. W. Terman. 1965. Amer. J. Physiol. 208:798.

[6] Christensen, E. H., and D. B. Dill. 1935. J. Biol. Chem. 109:443.

[7] Clausen, G., et al. 1971. Resp. Physiol. 12:66.

[8] Danzer, L. A., and J. E. Cohn. 1967. Ibid. 3:302.

[9] Drastich, L. 1928. Pfluegers Arch. Gesamte Physiol. Menschen Tiere 219:227.

[10] Hall, F. G., et al. 1936. J. Cell. Comp. Physiol. 8: 301.

[11] Huisman, T. H. J., et al. 1964. Biochim. Biophys. Acta 88:352.

[12] Lenfant, C., et al. 1969. Amer. J. Physiol. 216: 1598.

[13] Manwell, C. 1958. Science 127:705.

[14] Manwell, C. 1963. Comp. Biochem. Physiol. 10: 103.

[15] Manwell, C. 1963. Proc. Nat. Acad. Sci. U. S. 49: 496.

[16] Prosser, C. L., et al. 1950. Comparative Animal Physiology. W. B. Saunders, Philadelphia.

[17] Tucker, V. A. 1968. J. Exp. Biol. 48:67.

Part IV. Reptiles

For additional information, consult reference 1. Data in brackets refer to the column heading in brackets.

	Order & Species	Blood or Blood Fraction	Solvent [Pco2, mm Hg]	pH	Temp °C	P50 mm Hg	Bohr Effect	n [ΔH]	Reference
1	Crocodylia *Alligator mississippiensis*	Free solution	0.1 M PO_4	7.5	20	4.8	−0.50	....	7
2	*Crocodylus acutus*	Whole blood	....	7.20	29.0	38.0	......	....	2
3			[45[1]]	7.40[1]	29.0	53.0	......	....	2
4			[50[1]]	7.40[1]	29.0	26.0	......	....	2
5	Squamata— Serpentes[2] *Agkistrodon piscivorus piscivorus*	Free solution	0.1 M PO_4	7.5	20	2.4	−0.51	....	7
6	*Crotalus horridus atricaudatus*	Free solution	0.1 M PO_4	7.5	20	2.6	−0.40	....	7
7	*Natrix taxispilota*	Free solution	0.1 M PO_4	7.5	20	2.2	−0.35	2.75 [−15.5]	6

[1] Calculated from: $pH = 6.15 + \log [(\text{total } CO_2 - 0.0290\ Pco_2)/0.0290\ Pco_2]$, in which 6.15 is the negative log of the first apparent dissociation constant (pK'), and 0.0290 is the CO_2 factor for whole blood. [2] Suborder.

continued

Part IV.   Reptiles

	Order & Species	Blood or Blood Fraction	Solvent [P_{CO_2}, mm Hg]	pH	Temp °C	P_{50} mm Hg	Bohr Effect	n [ΔH]	Reference
	Squamata—Sauria [2]								
	Dipsosaurus dorsalis								
8	Juveniles	Whole blood	[38]	....	35	67.0	......	....	5
9	Fall adults	Whole blood	[38]	....	35	66.9	......	....	5
10	Spring adults	Whole blood	[38]	....	35	58.3	2.6	....	5
11	*Gerrhonotus multicarinatus*	Whole blood	[38]	....	35	72.4	......	2.3	5
12	*Heloderma suspectum*	Whole blood	[32 [1]]	7.40	37.0	59.0	......	....	3
13			[36.0]	7.40	20.0	32.0	......	....	3
14			[37.0]	7.32	20.0	31.0	......	....	3
15	*Iguana iguana*	Whole blood	....	7.4	35	51	−0.52	....	9
16	*Sceloporus occidentalis*	Whole blood	[38]	....	35	71.5	......	4.0	5
17	*Uma inornata* [3]	Whole blood	[38]	....	35	65.3	......	3.1	5
18	*U. notata notata*	Whole blood	[38]	....	35	64.5	......	....	5
19	*U. scoparia*	Whole blood	[38]	....	35	66.0	......	....	5
	Chelonia [4]								
20	*Caretta caretta*	Free solution	0.1 M PO_4	7.9-8.0	20	13.4	....	1.17	8
21	*Chelydra serpentina serpentina*	Free solution	0.1 M PO_4	7.4	20	7.2	......	....	8
22				7.9-8.0	20	4.3	−0.56	2.14 [−9.4]	8
23	*Chrysemys picta belli* [5]	Free solution	0.1 M PO_4	7.9-8.0	20	4.0	....	2.72	8
24		Form D [6]	μ = 0.3, PO_4	7.55	15	17	−0.50	S > D	4
25		Form S [6]	μ = 0.3, PO_4	7.55	15	11	−0.50	....	4
26	*C. scripta elegans* [7]	Free solution	0.1 M PO_4	7.4	20	8.9	......	....	8
27				7.9-8.0	20	4.3	−0.65	2.31 [−13.0]	8
28	*Clemmys guttata*	Free solution	0.1 M PO_4	7.4	20	20.0	......	....	8
29				7.9-8.0	20	10.7	−0.49	1.20 [−11.0]	8
30	*Gopherus polyphemus* [8]	Free solution	0.1 M PO_4	7.4	20	8.9	......	....	8
31				7.9-8.0	20	5.1	−0.41	2.26 [−10.0]	8
32	*Malaclemys terrapin littoralis*	Free solution	0.1 M PO_4	7.9-8.0	20	6.5	......	1.82	8
33	*Sternotherus odoratus*	Free solution	0.1 M PO_4	7.9-8.0	20	3.5	......	1.33	8
34	*Terrapene carolina carolina*	Free solution	0.1 M PO_4	7.9-8.0	20	5.8	......	1.43	8
35	*T. ornata ornata*	Free solution	0.1 M PO_4	7.9-8.0	20	8.4	−0.52	1.67 [−9.9]	8
36	*Trionyx ferox*	Free solution	0.1 M PO_4	7.4	20	5.3	......	....	8
37				7.9-8.0	20	2.3	−0.77	2.14 [−9.5]	8

[1] Calculated from: pH = 6.15 + log [(total CO_2 − 0.0290 P_{CO_2})/0.0290 P_{CO_2}], in which 6.15 is the negative log of the first apparent dissociation constant (pK′), and 0.0290 is the CO_2 factor for whole blood. [2] Suborder. [3] Synonym: *U. notata inornata*. [4] Turtle hemoglobin heme-heme interaction (n) values are pH-dependent, and are highest around pH 7.5. [5] Synonym: *C. picta*. [6] Electrophoretic form. [7] Synonym: *Pseudemys scripta elegans*. [8] Synonym: *G. polyphemus polyphemus*.

Contributor: Sullivan, J. Bolling

References

[1] Dessauer, H. C. 1971. In C. Gans, ed. Biology of the Reptilia. Academic Press, New York. v. 2.

[2] Dill, D. B., and H. T. Edwards. 1931. J. Biol. Chem. 90:515.

[3] Edwards, H. T., and D. B. Dill. 1935. J. Cell. Comp. Physiol. 6:21.

[4] Manwell, C., and C. V. Schlesinger. 1966. Comp. Biochem. Physiol. 18:627.

[5] Pough, F. H. 1969. Ibid. 31:885.

[6] Sullivan, B. 1967. Science 157:1308.

[7] Sullivan, B. Unpublished. Duke Univ. Medical Center, Durham, N.C., 1973.

[8] Sullivan, B., and A. Riggs. 1967. Comp. Biochem. Physiol. 23:459.

[9] Wood, S. C., and W. R. Moberly. 1970. Resp. Physiol. 10:20.

continued

Part V. Amphibians

	Order & Species (Synonym)	Blood or Blood Fraction	Solvent [P_{CO_2}, mm Hg]	pH	Temp °C	P_{50} mm Hg	Bohr Effect	n [1]	Reference
	Salientia								
1	*Bufo bufo*	Free solution	0.1 M PO$_4$	7.4	24	39	−0.21 [2]	0.0162 [3]	9
2	*B. marinus*	Whole blood	....	7.40	25	42	−0.25	....	7
3	*Rana catesbeiana*	Free solution [4]	....	...	...	13	Present	2.7	8
4	Tadpole	Free solution [4]	....	...	...	4	Absent	2.6	8
5	Adult	Whole blood	[10]	...	22	39.0	−0.29	....	10
6		Free solution Component B [5]	0.1 M PO$_4$	6.75	20	14.8	0.22	....	1
7		Component C [5]	0.1 M PO$_4$	6.75	20	7.9	0.13	....	1
8	*R. clamitans*	Erythrocytes	....	7.4	24	4.8	....	1.8-2.0	11
9	*R. esculenta*	Free solution	0.1 M PO$_4$	7.4	20	18.2	−0.34	2.2 [6]	3
10		Component I [5]	0.1 M PO$_4$	7.55	20	13.8	−0.23	2.1	3
11		Component II [5]	0.1 M PO$_4$	7.60	20	8.7	−0.19	2.3 [6]	3
12	Acclimated to: 5°C	Whole blood	....	7.4	20	42.4	....	....	5
13	20°C	Whole blood	....	7.4	20	39.1	....	....	5
14	*R. grylio*	Free solution	0.1 M PO$_4$	7.03	30	17.3	....	....	15
15	Tadpole	Free solution	0.1 M PO$_4$	7.03	30	4.7	....	....	15
	Caudata								
	Ambystoma mexicanum (Axolotl mexicanum)								
16	Neotenic form	Whole blood	....	7.4	20	25.7	−0.14	2.0; −0.023 [3]	2,6
17		Free solution	0.2 M PO$_4$	7.5	23	14.6	Fn [7]	2.0; −9.08 [8,9]	2
18	Metamorphosed form	Whole blood	....	7.4	20	28.7	−0.26	3.4; −0.017 [3]	6
19		Free solution	0.2 M PO$_4$	7.5	23	10.2	Fn [7]	2.0	2
20	*A. tigrinum tigrinum*	Free solution	0.2 M PO$_4$	7.5	23	14.6	Fn [7]	2.0; −6.3 [8]	2
21	*Amphiuma tridactylum (A. means tridactylum)*	Whole blood	[8.5]	...	22	27.0	−0.21	....	10
22	*Cryptobranchus* sp.	Whole blood	....	7.38	25.4	18.0	....	....	12,14
23	*Desmognathus* sp.	Whole blood	....	7.38	25.4	5.0	....	....	12,14
	Dicamptodon ensatus								
24	Larval form	Whole blood	....	7.8	15	21.9	−0.131	2.5; 0.032 [3]	16
25		Free solution	μ = 0.2, PO$_4$	7.8	15	8.5 [10]	−0.113	2.45	16
26	Adult form	Whole blood	....	7.8	15	31.6	−0.139	2.8; 0.029 [3]	16
27		Free solution	μ = 0.2, PO$_4$	7.8	15	8.5 [10]	−0.113	2.63	16
28	*Necturus maculosus*	Whole blood	[6.0]	...	20	14.5	−0.13	....	10
29	*Taricha granulosa (Triturus granulosa)*	Whole blood	[40]	7.4	20	34.5	−0.18	2.2	4
30	*Taricha rivularis*	Whole blood	[40]	7.4	20	37.0	−0.13	2.3	4
31	*Triturus* sp.	Whole blood	....	7.38	25.4	7.5	....	....	12,14
	T. cristatus (Triton cristatus)								
32	Acclimated to: 4°C	Free solution	0.1 M PO$_4$	7.4	20	28	Reversed	....	13
33	30°C	Free solution	0.1 M PO$_4$	7.4	20	26	Normal	....	13

[1] Unless otherwise indicated. [2] Bohr effect is pH-dependent. [3] Δlog P_{50} per °C; linear relationship breaks down outside temperature range of 4-45°C. [4] Isolated major component. [5] Chromatographic fraction. [6] Hill plot is not a straight line below pH 7.0. [7] Slightly negative below pH 7.0; slightly positive above pH 7.0. [8] ΔH. [9] ΔH is pH-dependent. [10] Depends on adenosine 5'-triphosphate:hemoglobin ratio.

Contributor: Sullivan, J. Bolling

continued

Part V. Amphibians

References

[1] Aggarwal, S. J., and A. Riggs. 1969. J. Biol. Chem. 244:2372.

[2] Amiconi, G., et al. 1970. Int. J. Biochem. 1:582.

[3] Brunori, M., et al. 1969. Comp. Biochem. Physiol. 24:519.

[4] Coates, M. L., and J. Metcalfe. 1970-71. Resp. Physiol. 11:94.

[5] Gahlenbeck, H., and H. Bartels. 1968. Z. Vergl. Physiol. 59:232.

[6] Gahlenbeck, H., and H. Bartels. 1970. Resp. Physiol. 9:175.

[7] Hall, F. G. 1966. J. Cell. Comp. Physiol. 68:69.

[8] Hamada, K., et al. 1964. J. Biochem. (Tokyo) 55:636.

[9] Leggio, T., and G. Morpurgo. 1969. Nature (London) 219:493.

[10] Lenfant, C., and K. Johansen. 1967. Resp. Physiol. 2:247.

[11] Manwell, C. 1966. Comp. Biochem. Physiol. 17:805.

[12] McCutcheon, F. H., and F. G. Hall. 1937. J. Cell. Comp. Physiol. 9:191.

[13] Morpurgo, G., et al. 1970. Nature (London) 225:76.

[14] Prosser, C. L., et al. 1950. Comparative Animal Physiology. W. B. Saunders, Philadelphia.

[15] Trader, C. D., and E. Frieden. 1966. J. Biol. Chem. 241:357.

[16] Wood, S. C. 1971. Resp. Physiol. 12:53.

Part VI. Fishes

Solvent: Tris = 2-amino-2-hydroxymethyl-1,3-propanediol; ATP = adenosine 5′-triphosphate. For additional information, consult references 8, 14, 24, and 31. Data in brackets refer to the column heading in brackets.

	Order & Species (Synonym)	Blood or Blood Fraction	Solvent [P_{CO_2}, mm Hg]	pH	Temp °C	P_{50} mm Hg	Bohr Effect	n [ΔH[1]]	Reference
			Dipnoi						
1	*Lepidosiren paradoxa*	Whole blood	[6]	....	23	10.5	....	....	15
2	*Protopterus aethiopicus*	Whole blood	[6]	....	25	10	−0.47	....	19
3			[40]	....	25	21	....	....	19
4				7.4	25	32	....	....	35
5		Free solution	0.1 M PO_4	7.00	25.5	12.6	−0.42	2.0	28
6				7.92	25.5	4.2	....	2.1	28
			Osteichthyes						
	Perciformes (Percomorphi)								
7	*Cichlasoma cyanoguttatum*	Free solution	0.1 M NaCl, 0.05 M Tris + ATP	7.2	20	4.5[2]	−1.43[2]	2.0[2]	9
8	*Lepomis macrochirus*	Free solution	$\mu = 0.3$, PO_4	7.20	24	30	....	1.88	25
9	*Pomoxis annularis*	Free solution	$\mu = 0.3$, PO_4	7.05	23	20	....	....	25
10	*Scomber scombrus*	Whole blood	[1.0]	8.0	20.0	17.0	....	....	32
11		Free solution	....	7.38	25.0	18.0	....	....	30
12	*Thunnus thynnus*	Free solution	$\mu = 0.1$, Tris	7.5[3]	.....	12.6	−0.71	[−1.8]	33
	Perciformes (Scleroparei)								
13	*Sebastes ruberrimus (Sebastodes ruberrimus)*	Erythrocytes	....	7.40[4]	.....	6.7	....	....	22
	Gadiformes (Anacanthini)								
14	*Gadus* sp.	Whole blood	[<0.3]	....	14.0	15.0	....	....	30

[1] Unless otherwise indicated. [2] Value depends on the ATP:hemoglobin ratio. [3] Below pH 6.9, n is hyperbolic. [4] Large Root effect below pH 7.0, and n is hyperbolic.

continued

Part VI. Fishes

	Order & Species (Synonym)	Blood or Blood Fraction	Solvent [P_{CO_2}, mm Hg]	pH	Temp °C	P_{50} mm Hg	Bohr Effect	n [ΔH [1]]	Reference
	Siluriformes (Ostariophysi)								
15	*Ictalurus* sp.	Whole blood	[0-1]	....	15.0	1.4	....	....	30
16			[1-2]	....	15.0	1.4	....	....	30
17			[10]	....	15.0	5.0	....	....	30
18	*I. nebulosus*	Whole blood	....	7.8	24	8.14	−0.31	1.23 [0.031]	11
19	Acclimated to: 9°C	Whole blood	....	7.8	24	12.6	−0.31	1.32	11
20	9°C; 24°C	Free solution	PO_4	7.3	20	2.7	....	2.22	11
	Cypriniformes (Ostariophysi)								
21	*Cyprinus carpio*	Whole blood	[1-2]	....	15.0	5.0	....	....	30
22			[10.0]	....	15.0	8.0	....	....	30
23			[30.0]	....	18.0	13.0	....	....	36
24		Free solution	0.05 M PO_4	7.0	20	5.5	−1.02	2.1 [5]	27
25	*Electrophorus electricus*	Whole blood	....	7.4	28	14	−0.77	2.3	16
	Salmoniformes (Isospondyli)								
26	*Oncorhynchus keta*	Free solution	0.1 M PO_4	7.60[6]	15	18	....	2.4 [−6.4]	12
27		Fast component [7]	0.1 M PO_4	7.02	15	100	−1.25	2.4 [−7.2]	12
28		Slow component [7]	0.1 M PO_4	7.02	15	18	0.00	2.4 [−4.2]	12
29	*Salmo gairdneri*	Whole blood	[0]	....	15	14	....	....	6
30			[1-2]	....	15.0	18.0	....	....	30
31			[3]	....	15	20	....	....	6
32			[10.0]	....	15.0	35.0	....	....	30
33	(*S. iridea*)	Free solution	0.2 M PO_4	7.5	20	24.3	−0.80	2.5 [5]	10
34		Component I [2]	0.2 M PO_4	7.6	20	17.8	0.00	2.6 [−3.1]	2
35		Component IV [2]	0.2 M PO_4	7.7	20	22.4	−0.91	2.1 [5] [−9.5 [5]]	2
36	*S. salar*	Whole blood	[10]	....	15	36	....	....	4
37	*S. trutta*	Whole blood	[1-2]	....	15.0	17.0	....	....	30
38			[10]	....	15.0	39.0	....	....	30
39	*Salvelinus fontinalis*	Whole blood	[10]	....	15	43	....	....	3
	Anguilliformes (Apodes)								
40	*Anguilla anguilla*	Free solution	0.1 M PO_4	6.5	18	31.0	−0.60	....	13
41		Fast hemoglobin [2]	0.1 M PO_4	6.5	18	40.0	−0.60	....	13
42		Slow hemoglobin [2]	0.1 M PO_4	6.5	18	1.7	0.00	....	13
43	*A. japonica*	Free solution	0.1 M PO_4	7.42	15	3.1	....	1.4-1.9	37
44		Whole hemolysate	0.1 M PO_4	7.0	20	6.0	−0.35	....	38
45		Component I [7]	0.1 M PO_4	7.0	20	2.1	0.00	2.4	38
46		Component II [7]	0.1 M PO_4	7.0	20	14	−0.59	1.0	38
47		Fast component [7]	0.1 M PO_4	7.26	15	6.3 [8]	....	1.0 [9]	37
48		Slow component [7]	0.1 M PO_4	6.6-8.0	15	6.5-8.0	−0.07	2.28	37
	Amiiformes (Protospondyli)								
49	*Amia calva*	Whole blood	....	7.6	27	24	−0.50	2.6 [0.034 [10]]	17
50					15	9	−0.45	1.3	17
51			[1-2]	....	15.0	4.0	....	....	30
52			[10.0]	....	15.0	9.0	....	....	30
	Chondrichthyes								
	Rajiformes (Batoidei)								
53	*Dasyatis* sp.	Free solution	....	7.40	25.0	13-15	....	....	26

[1] Unless otherwise indicated. [2] Value depends on the ATP:hemoglobin ratio. [5] pH-dependent. [6] Below pH 7.2, O_2 dissociation curve becomes discontinuous. [7] Chromatographic or electrophoretic component. [8] P_{50} is sensitive to phosphate concentration. [9] n is pH-dependent; at pH 7.96, n = 1.4. [10] $\Delta \log P_{50}$ per °C.

continued

213. DATA FOR CONSTRUCTING BLOOD OXYGEN DISSOCIATION CURVES: VERTEBRATES

Part VI. Fishes

	Order & Species (Synonym)	Blood or Blood Fraction	Solvent [P_{CO_2}, mm Hg]	pH	Temp °C	P_{50} mm Hg	Bohr Effect	n [ΔH]	Reference
54	*Raja binoculata*	Free solution	$\mu = 0.3$, PO_4	6.54	10	16	−0.40	1.5-1.8[4]	21
55	Embryo, 1.5 g	Free solution	$\mu = 0.3$, PO_4	6.54	10	11	....	1.1	21
56	Fetus, 9 g	Free solution	$\mu = 0.3$, PO_4	6.54	10	16	....	1.5-1.8	21
57	*R. eglanteria*	Free solution	0.1 M PO_4	7.5	20	21.4	−0.69	2.20	34
58	*R. ocellata (R. oscillata)*	Whole blood	[1.0]	7.80	0.2	11.0	....	....	7
59					10.4	20.0	....	....	7
60					25.0	45.0	....	....	7
61					37.0	98.0	....	....	7
	Squaliformes (Selachii)								
62	*Scyliorhinus stellaris*	Whole blood	....	....	17	16	....	1.8	29
63	*Squalus suckleyi*	Whole blood	[0.5]	7.6	11	17	0.00	1.0	18
64		Free solution	0.25 M PO_4	7.33	25	16.4	....	1.00	20
65			$\mu = 0.3$, PO_4	6.7	20	28	−0.34	1.0	23
66	Fetus	Free solution	$\mu = 0.3$, PO_4	6.7	20	20	−0.25	1.2-1.4	23
67	5 mo old	Free solution	0.25 M PO_4	7.27	26	8.2	....	1.26	20
68	6 mo old	Erythrocytes	Saline	7.30	26	15.0	....	1.13	20
69	Adult	Erythrocytes	Saline	7.30	26	29.0	....	1.00	20

Agnatha

	Order & Species (Synonym)	Blood or Blood Fraction	Solvent [P_{CO_2}, mm Hg]	pH	Temp °C	P_{50} mm Hg	Bohr Effect	n [ΔH]	Reference
	Petromyzontiformes (Petromyzones)								
70	*Lampetra fluviatilis*	Free solution	0.15 M PO_4	7.1	20	8.9	−1.17	1.2	1
71	*L. lamottei (Entosphenus lamottei)*	Erythrocytes	....	7.3	25-26	8.5	....	1.8-1.9	24
72	*Petromyzon marinus*	Free solution	0.15 M PO_4	7.1	20	6.3	−0.75	1.5-1.7	1
73		Component 1	0.1 M PO_4	6.9	20	1.5	....	1.10	1
74		Component 3	0.1 M PO_4	6.9	20	6.6	....	1.40	1
75		Component 4	0.1 M PO_4	6.9	20	9.5	....	1.55	1
76		Component 5	0.1 M PO_4	6.9	20	6.8	....	1.40	1
77		Component 6	0.1 M PO_4	6.9	20	6.3	....	1.30	1
78	Adult	Free solution hemolysate	0.1 M PO_4	7.3	25	15.9	−0.70	1.00[11]	5
	Myxiniformes (Myxini)								
79	*Myxine glutinosa*	Free solution	$\mu = 0.3$, PO_4	7.0	21-23	9.5	....	1.0	24
80				7.5	21-23	7.5	−0.21	>1.0	24

[4] Large Root effect below pH 7.0, and n is hyperbolic. [11] At high protein concentrations and at high degrees of saturation, n>1.0.

Contributor: Sullivan, J. Bolling

References

[1] Antonini, E., et al. 1964. Arch. Biochem. Biophys. 105:404.

[2] Binotti, I., et al. 1971. Ibid. 142:274.

[3] Black, E. C., et al. 1966. J. Fish. Res. Bd. Can. 23:1.

[4] Black, E. C., et al. 1966. Ibid. 23:1187.

[5] Briehl, R. W. 1963. J. Biol. Chem. 238:2361.

[6] Cameron, J. 1971. Comp. Biochem. Physiol. 38A: 699.

[7] Dill, D. B., et al. 1932. Biol. Bull. 62:23.

[8] Fry, F. E. J. 1957. In M. E. Brown, ed. The Physiology of Fishes. Academic Press, New York. v. 1, p. 1.

[9] Gillen, R. G., and A. Riggs. 1971. Comp. Biochem. Physiol. 38B:585.

[10] Giovenco, S., et al. 1970. Int. J. Biochem. 1:57.

[11] Grigg, G. C. 1969. Comp. Biochem. Physiol. 28: 1203.

[12] Hashimoto, K., et al. 1960. Nippon Suisan Gakkaishi 26:827.

continued

Part VI. Fishes

[13] Itada, N., et al. 1970. Resp. Physiol. 8:276.

[14] Johansen, K. 1971. Annu. Rev. Physiol. 33:569.

[15] Johansen, K., and C. Lenfant. 1967. J. Exp. Biol. 46:205.

[16] Johansen, K., et al. 1968. Z. Vergl. Physiol. 61: 137.

[17] Johansen, K., et al. 1970. Resp. Physiol. 9:162.

[18] Lenfant, C., and K. Johansen. 1966. Ibid. 1:13.

[19] Lenfant, C., and K. Johansen. 1968. J. Exp. Biol. 49:437.

[20] Manwell, C. 1958. Physiol. Zool. 31:93.

[21] Manwell, C. 1958. Science 128:419.

[22] Manwell, C. 1961. In C. L. Prosser and F. A. Brown, Jr., ed. Comparative Animal Physiology. Ed. 2. W. B. Saunders, Philadelphia. p. 198.

[23] Manwell, C. 1963. Arch. Biochem. Biophys. 101: 504.

[24] Manwell, C. 1963. In A. Brodal and R. Fange, ed. The Biology of Myxine. Scandinavian Univ. Books, Oslo. p. 372.

[25] Manwell, C., et al. 1963. Comp. Biochem. Physiol. 10:103.

[26] McCutcheon, F. H. 1947. J. Cell. Comp. Physiol. 29:333.

[27] Noble, R. W., et al. 1970. J. Biol. Chem. 245: 6628.

[28] Oldham, J. H., and A. Riggs. Unpublished. Univ. Texas, Dep. Zoology, Austin, 1969.

[29] Piiper, J., and D. Schumann. 1967. Resp. Physiol. 2:135.

[30] Prosser, C. L., et al., ed. 1961. Comparative Animal Physiology. Ed. 2. W. B. Saunders, Philadelphia

[31] Riggs, A. 1971. In W. S. Hoar and D. J. Randall, ed. Fish Physiology. Academic Press, New York. v. 4, p. 209.

[32] Root, R. W. 1931. Biol. Bull. 61:427.

[33] Rossi-Fanelli, A., and E. Antonini. 1960. Nature (London) 186:895.

[34] Sullivan, B. Unpublished. Duke Univ. Medical Center, Durham, N.C., 1973.

[35] Swan, H., and F. G. Hall. 1966. Amer. J. Physiol. 210:487.

[36] Wastl, H. 1928. Biochem. Z. 197:363.

[37] Yamaguchi, K., et al. 1962. Nippon Suisan Gakkaishi 28:192.

[38] Yoshioka, M., et al. 1968. J. Biochem. (Tokyo) 63: 70.

214. OXYGEN CONSUMPTION: VERTEBRATES

Part I. Mammals

Basal metabolism, expressed as oxygen consumption ($\dot{V}O_2$) in milliliters of oxygen per gram per hour, can be predicted from weight (W), in grams, from the following equations: $\dot{V}O_2 = 4.0W^{-0.27}$ for placental animals [4] (equation based on an assumed, but undesignated, body temperature of 37°C), and $\dot{V}O_2 = 2.6W^{-0.26}$ for marsupials [9,10]. O_2 Consumption: Only those values thought to have been measured at thermal neutrality have been reported. Deviation is determined by subtracting 100 from 100 times the ratio of measured to predicted values. Whenever the body temperature is significantly below 37°C, the measured metabolism (K_1) has been converted from the body temperature of measurement (T_1) to metabolism (K_2) at a body temperature of 37°C (T_2), using the equation log $K_2 =$ log $Q_{10}/10 \cdot (T_2 - T_1) + $ log K_1, assuming $Q_{10} = 2.1$ [53].

	Species (Synonym)	No. & Sex	Body Weight g	Temperature, °C		O_2 Consumption ml·g^{-1}·hr^{-1}	Deviation %	Reference
				Body	Ambient			
	Primates							
	Homo sapiens							
1	African bushmen	10♂	47,100	....	....	0.265	+21	25
2	Andean natives	10	54,500	....	....	0.246	+16.5	29
3	Australian aborigines	9	63,000	37.2	23.6-27.8	0.163	−19.3	61
4	Caucasians	6♂	71,500	....	....	0.210	+5.6	25
5		♀	60,000	....	....	0.198	−3.4	4
6	Eskimos	10♂	60,900	....	....	0.276	+35	25

continued

Part I. Mammals

Species (Synonym)	No. & Sex	Body Weight g	Temperature, °C Body	Temperature, °C Ambient	O₂ Consumption ml·g⁻¹·hr⁻¹	Deviation %	Reference
7 *Macaca mulatta*[1]	11	3,200	....	....	0.43	−5.1	49
8 *Pan troglodytes*[1]	22	38,000	....	20-29	0.249	+7	7
9 *Papio ursinus*	17	16,400	37	27	0.304	+4	18
10 *Saguinus geoffroyi*	1	225	....	∿27	1.04	+12	55
11 *Saimiri sciureus*[1]	....	840	....	....	0.83	+27.9	40
Artiodactyla							
12 *Bos taurus*, Hereford[1]	♂[2]	700,000	....	....	0.11	+3.6	4
13	♀	500,000	....	....	0.114	−2	4
14 Holstein[1]	♀	500,000	....	....	0.125	+7.8	4
15 Shorthorn	♀[3]	380,000	39.0	18	0.160	+23	36
16 *Camelus dromedarius*[1]	4	407,000	38.1		0.099	−19	54
17 *Capra* sp.	....	36,000	....	....	0.193	−18	3
18 Jamnapuri	26	20,600	....	....	0.272	−1	51
19 *Odocoileus virginianus*	4	51,200	....	−7 to +24.7	0.226	+5.5	57
20 *Ovis aries*[1]	5	51,500	....	....	0.256	+20	8
21 Dorset[4]	♂	70,000	....	....	0.179	−9	4
22	♀	60,000	....	....	0.164	−20	4
23 *Sus scrofa*	♂	250,000	....	....	0.130	+7.1	5
24	♀	250,000	....	....	0.121	−13.6	5
Perissodactyla							
25 *Equus asinus*	♀	190,000	37.2	20	0.204	+36	63
26		165,000	37.0	20	0.204	+31	63
27 *E. caballus*[1]	....	703,000	....	....	0.145	+36	3
28 Percheron[4]	♂[2]	650,000	....	....	0.110	+2	4
29	♀	675,000	....	....	0.125	+18	4
Proboscidea							
30 *Elephas maximus*[1]	2	3,833,000	....	....	0.07	+5	4
31	1	3,672,000	36.6	20.0	0.113	+66	2
Pinnipedia							
32 *Phoca vitulina*	6	27,400	....	20-29	0.475	+87.7	21
33	4	33,000	37	−9 to +25	0.496	+106.7	30
Carnivora							
34 *Canis familiaris*[1]	3	9,700	38	25.4	0.342	+2.1	19
35 Bull terrier	9	23,600	37.8	....	0.319	+20.8	11
36 Mixed breed	59	13,900	....	18-24	0.327	+6.9	15
37	31	12,400	....	18-24	0.342	+8.9	15
38	14	20,800	39	....	0.359	+31.5	41
39	5	16,300	39	....	0.363	+25.2	41
40 *Felis catus*[1]	....	3,000	....	....	0.44	−4.6	3
41 *Mustela vison*	3	700	....	25	0.738	+8.2	13
42 *Procyon cancrivorus*	1	1,160	....	∿28	0.396	−33.7	55
43 *Vulpes vulpes*	1	4,400	....	−10 to +20	0.43	+3.9	32
Cetacea							
44 *Phocoena phocoena*	1	26,000	35.7	8	0.88	+270	34

[1] Domestic animals. [2] Castrate. [3] Heifer. [4] Composite of data in reference.

continued

Part I. Mammals

Species (Synonym)	No. & Sex	Body Weight g	Temperature, °C		O₂ Consumption ml·g⁻¹·hr⁻¹	Deviation %	Reference
			Body	Ambient			
45 *Tursiops truncatus*	2	170,000	....	....	0.36	+130	31
Rodentia							
46 *Cavia porcellus* [l]	....	500	38.5	32	0.78	+4	26
47 *Chinchilla laniger* [l]	....	402	....		0.68	−14	12
48 *Dipodomys merriami*	8	36.3	37.4	30; 31	1.18	−22	6
49 *Geomys bursarius*	10	278	36.5	27.5	0.90	+1	56
50 *Marmota marmota*	3	1,868	....	28.2	0.54	+3	35
51 *Meriones unguiculatus*	....	61-81	....	30	1.4	+6 to +23	50
52 *Mesocricetus auratus*	10	116	....	35	1.25	+13.6	58
53 *Microtus pennsylvanicus*	3	30.0	....	....	2.7	+68	62
54 *Mus musculus*	47	35.7	....	32	1.59	+4.6	48
55 *Ondatra zibethicus*	....	1,130	....	8	0.92	+53.3	20
56 *Perognathus californicus*	7	22	37.0	32.5	0.98	−43	59
57 *P. hispidus*	7	39.0	36.4-38.7	30.5-33.5	1.25	−16	60
58 *Peromyscus maniculatus*	20	19.2		26.7-28.8	2.04	+14	22
59 *Rattus norvegicus* [l]	40	545	37.5	28	0.84	+15	37
60 *Sciurus carolinensis*	....	543.1	....	....	0.79	+8.2	46
61 *Sigmodon hispidus*	2	80.8		33	1.10	−8.0	28
62 *Spermophilus citellus (Citellus citellus)*	....	178	37.7	....	0.97	−2	16
63 *S. lateralis (C. lateralis)*	....	231	....	....	0.75	−18.5	46
64 *S. tridecemlineatus (C. tridecemlinea-*	14	164.7	36.3	30	0.874	−13.5	14
65 *tus)*	9	179	37.5	29-30	0.95	−5	52
66 *Tamias striatus*	14	107	38.6	28-36	1.25	+10.6	45
Lagomorpha							
67 *Oryctolagus cuniculus* [l]	20	1,520	38.4-41.0	28	0.470	−14.7	38
Edentata							
68 *Dasypus novemcinctus*	13	3,700	34-35	30	0.200-0.275	−42 to −26	33
Chiroptera							
69 *Eptesicus fuscus*	....	16.9	36	35	0.7	−59	24
70 *Myotis lucifugus*	....	6.9	....	37.0	2.89 ± 0.89	+84	27
71 *M. myotis*	10	25.0	37	27.0	2.2	+31	42
72 *Tadarida brasiliensis mexicana (T. mexicana)*	8	10.4	37-39	33-39	2.02	−6	23,24
Insectivora							
73 *Blarina brevicauda*	....	21.0	....	15-25	5.3[5]	+201	44
74	1	20.0	....	27	3.5	+97	47
75 *Erinaceus europaeus*	4	684.0	....	29.1	0.73	+6	35
76 *Sorex cinereus*	3	2.9-4.0	38.8	25	9.0[5]	+200	43
Marsupialia [6]							
77 *Cercaertus nanus*	9	35-90	34.9	31.0	0.86	−2.0	1
78 *Dasyurus viverrinus*	2	909.9	36.7	30.0	0.45	−8	39
79 *Didelphis sp. (D. didelphii)*	3	1,256.0	34.6	22.4	0.91[5]	+34	17
80 *Macropus rufus*	6	12,690-32,490	35.9 ± 0.5	26.0	0.18	0	10

[l] Domestic animals. [5] May not be basal. [6] Predicted metabolism based on Dawson-Hulbert equation [10].

continued

Part I. Mammals

Species (Synonym)	No. & Sex	Body Weight g	Temperature, °C		O_2 Consumption $ml \cdot g^{-1} \cdot hr^{-1}$	Deviation %	Reference
			Body	Ambient			
81 *Wallabia eugenii (Macropus eugenii)*	6	4,796 ± 441	36.4 ± 0.5	25.0	0.29	−6	10
Monotremata							
82 *Tachyglossus aculeatus*	3	2,500-3,500	30.7 ± 1.03	20	0.20-0.25	0 to +18[5]	53

[5] May not be basal.

Contributors: Hudson, Jack W., and Brower, James E.

References

[1] Bartholomew, G. A., and J. W. Hudson. 1962. Physiol. Zool. 35:94.

[2] Benedict, F. G. 1936. Carnegie Inst. Wash. Publ. 474.

[3] Benedict, F. G. 1938. Ibid. 503.

[4] Brody, S. 1945. Bioenergetics and Growth. Hafner, New York.

[5] Brody, S., and H. H. Kibler. 1944. Mo. Agr. Exp. Sta. Res. Bull. 380.

[6] Brower, J. E. 1969. Ph.D. Dissertation. Syracuse Univ., N.Y.

[7] Bruhn, J. M., and F. G. Benedict. 1936. Proc. Amer. Acad. Arts Sci. 71:259.

[8] Cross, K. W., et al. 1959. J. Physiol. (London) 46:316.

[9] Dawson, T. J., and A. J. Hulbert. 1969. Nature (London) 221:383.

[10] Dawson, T. J., and A. J. Hulbert. Unpublished. Univ. New South Wales, Kensington, Sydney, Australia, 1970.

[11] DeBeer, E. J., and A. M. Hjort. 1938. Amer. J. Physiol. 124:517.

[12] Drozdz, A., and A. Gorecki. 1967. Acta Theriol. 12:81.

[13] Farrell, D. J., and A. J. Wood. 1968. Can. J. Zool. 46:41.

[14] Folk, G. E., Jr. 1960. Bull. Mus. Comp. Zool. Harvard Univ. 124:209.

[15] Galvao, P. E. 1947. Amer. J. Physiol. 148:478.

[16] Gelineo, S. 1938. C.R. Soc. Biol. 127:1357.

[17] Gley, E., and A. O. de Almeida. 1924. Ibid. 90:467.

[18] Goldstone, B. W., et al. 1967. J. Appl. Physiol. 22:86.

[19] Hammel, H. T., et al. 1958. Amer. J. Physiol. 194:99.

[20] Hart, J. S. 1963. Temp. Meas. Contr. Sci. Ind. Proc. Symp., 4th, 3(3):373.

[21] Hart, J. S., and L. Irving. 1959. Can. J. Zool. 37:447.

[22] Hayward, J. S. 1965. Ibid. 43:309.

[23] Herreid, C. F., II. 1963. Science 142:1573.

[24] Herreid, C. F., II, and K. Schmidt-Nielsen. 1966. Amer. J. Physiol. 211:1108.

[25] Hildes, J. A. 1963. Fed. Proc. Fed. Amer. Soc. Exp. Biol. 22:843.

[26] Hill, J. R. 1958. J. Physiol. (London) 143:64P.

[27] Hock, R. J. 1951. Biol. Bull. 101:289.

[28] Hudson, J. W. Unpublished. Cornell Univ., Ithaca, N.Y., 1973.

[29] Hurtado, A., et al. 1956. U.S. Air Force Sch. Aviat. Med. (Randolph) Rep. 56-104.

[30] Irving, L., and J. S. Hart. 1957. Can. J. Zool. 35:497.

[31] Irving, L., et al. 1941. J. Cell. Comp. Physiol. 17:145.

[32] Irving, L., et al. 1955. Physiol. Zool. 28:173.

[33] Johansen, K. 1961. Ibid. 34:126.

[34] Kanwisher, J., and G. Sundes. 1965. Hvalradets Skr. 48:45.

[35] Kayser, C. 1950. Arch. Sci. Physiol. 4:361.

[36] Kibler, H. H. 1957. Mo. Agr. Exp. Sta. Res. Bull. 643.

[37] Kibler, H. H., et al. 1963. J. Gerontol. 18:235.

[38] Lee, R. C. 1939. J. Nutr. 18:489.

[39] MacMillen, R. E., and J. E. Nelson. 1969. Amer. J. Physiol. 217:1246.

[40] Malinow, M. R., and R. Wagner. 1966. Lab. Anim. Care 16:105.

[41] Martin, A. W., and F. A. Fuhrman. 1955. Physiol. Zool. 28:18.

[42] Mejsnar, J., and L. Jansky. 1967. Physiol. Bohemoslov. 16:147.

[43] Morrison, P., et al. 1959. Physiol. Zool. 32:256.

[44] Morrison, P. R. 1948. J. Cell. Comp. Physiol. 31:281.

[45] Neumann, R. L. 1967. In K. C. Fisher, et al., ed. Mammalian Hibernation, III. American Elsevier, New York. pp. 64-74.

[46] Neumann, R. L. 1967. Ph.D. Dissertation. Syracuse Univ., N.Y.

continued

Part I. Mammals

[47] Pearson, O. P. 1947. Ecology 28:127.

[48] Pennycuik, P. R. 1967. Aust. J. Exp. Biol. Med. Sci. 45:331.

[49] Rakieten, N. 1935. J. Nutr. 10:357.

[50] Robinson, P. F. 1959. Science 130:502.

[51] Sadhu, D. P., and S. P. Bhatnagar. 1965. Indian J. Exp. Biol. 3:263.

[52] Samolitis, J. 1971. M.S. Thesis. Northern Illinois Univ., DeKalb.

[53] Schmidt-Nielsen, K., et al. 1966. J. Cell. Physiol. 67:63.

[54] Schmidt-Nielsen, K., et al. 1967. Amer. J. Physiol. 212:341.

[55] Scholander, P. F., et al. 1950. Biol. Bull. 99:259.

[56] Sherer, R. 1971. M.S. Thesis. Northern Illinois Univ., DeKalb.

[57] Silver, H., et al. 1959. J. Wildl. Manage. 23:434.

[58] Sullivan, B. J., and J. T. Mullen. 1954. Physiol. Zool. 27:21.

[59] Tucker, V. A. 1965. J. Cell. Comp. Physiol. 65:393.

[60] Wang, L. C., and J. W. Hudson. 1970. Comp. Biochem. Physiol. 32:275.

[61] Wardlaw, H. S. H., and C. H. Horsley. 1928. Aust. J. Exp. Biol. Med. Sci. 5:263.

[62] Wiegert, R. G. 1961. Ecology 42:245.

[63] Yousef, M. K., and D. B. Dill. 1969. J. Appl. Physiol. 27:229.

Part II. Birds

Unless otherwise indicated, metabolic rates are for birds in a postabsorptive state and at rest (as nearly as possible), at thermoneutral temperatures. When values for oxygen consumption were not given in the literature, a caloric equivalent of 4.8 calories of heat produced per milliliter of oxygen used was assumed [25]. The relationship between standard metabolic rate and body weight in nonpasserines (hummingbirds to ostriches) can be determined by the equation $\log M = \log 78.3 + 0.723 \log W \pm 0.111$, where M = heat production in kilocalories per day, and W = body weight in kilograms; the $\pm$ value is standard error of estimate of $\log M$. The equation for passerines is $\log M = \log 129 + 0.724 \log W \pm 0.0806$. [27] **Heat Production:** kcal = kilocalories. *Abbreviation:* R = respiratory gas exchange ratio (CO_2 output per O_2 uptake).

	Species	Body Weight g	Heat Production kcal/24 hr	O_2 Consumption $ml \cdot g^{-1} \cdot hr^{-1}$	Reference
		Passeriformes			
1	*Corvus caurinus*	282	74.7[1]	2.3[1]	20
2		306	98.7[2]	2.8[2]	20
3	*C. corax*	850	92.1	0.94[3]	32
4		866	94.9	0.95	27
5	*Fringilla montifringilla*	24.8	9.5	3.33	33
6	*Hesperiphona vespertina*	58	16.7	2.50	11
7	*Junco hyemalis*	18.0	6.1	2.94	27
8	*Melospiza melodia*	18.6	7.8	3.64	27
9	*Parus major*	18.5	8.4	3.92	33
10	*Passer domesticus*	22.4	9.5[2]	3.68[2]	13
11		23.5	11.0[4]	4.06[4]	13
12		23.7	10.1	3.70	29
13		25.0	6.9	2.40	28
14		25.5	6.9	2.34	19
15		26.0	9.4	3.14	14
16		26.0	12.5	4.17	23
17		27.3	8.5	2.71	33
18	*P. montanus*	22	8.5	3.36	33
19	*Troglodytes aedon*	9.0	5.3	5.14[5]	22
20	*Zonotrichia albicollis*	22.5	7.1	2.74	19
21		23.6	9.5	3.49	27
22	*Z. leucophrys*	28.6	8.0	2.43	24
		Apodiformes			
23	*Archilochus alexandri*	2.8	0.145[6]	0.45[6]	26
24		3.3	1.37	3.6	26
		Caprimulgiformes			
25	*Eurostopodus guttatus*	88	8.4	0.83	10
		Strigiformes			
26	*Bubo virginianus*	1450	108	0.647	4
		Columbiformes			
27	*Columba palumbus*	150	17.0	0.98	3
28	*Zenaidura macroura*	91.4	13.4	1.27	18
29		123	15.2	1.1	30

[1] In summer. [2] In winter. [3] CO_2 production = 0.67 $ml \cdot g^{-1} \cdot hr^{-1}$; R = 0.71. [4] In spring. [5] CO_2 production = 3.75 $ml \cdot g^{-1} \cdot hr^{-1}$; R = 0.73. [6] Torpid at 23.4 °C.

continued

Part II. Birds

Species	Body Weight g	Heat Production kcal/24 hr	O_2 Consumption $ml \cdot g^{-1} \cdot hr^{-1}$	Reference
Charadriiformes				
30 *Larus hyperboreus*	1600	302	1.64 [7]	32
Gruiformes				
31 *Grus canadensis*	3890	168	0.37	4
Galliformes				
32 *Colinus virginianus*	194	23.0	1.03	27
33 *Coturnix coturnix*	97	23	2.06	16
Falconiformes				
34 *Falco tinnunculus*	108	17.0	1.37	16
35 *Vultur gryphus*	10,320	351	0.295	4
Anseriformes				
36 *Aix sponsa*	485	65	1.16	17
37 *Branta bernicla*	1130	110.6 [1]	0.85 [1]	20
38	1168	95.5 [2]	0.71 [2]	20
39 *Olor buccinator* [8]	8880	418	0.41	4
Ciconiiformes				
40 *Ardea herodias*	1880	121	0.56	4
41 *Mycteria americana*	2500	201.4 [9]	0.70 [9]	21
Pelecaniformes				
42 *Pelecanus occidentalis*	3510	264	0.65	4

Species	Body Weight g	Heat Production kcal/24 hr	O_2 Consumption $ml \cdot g^{-1} \cdot hr^{-1}$	Reference
Casuariiformes				
43 *Casuarius bennetti*	17,600	516	0.25	4
44 *Dromiceius novaehollandiae*	38,300	1032	0.23	8
Rheiformes				
45 *Rhea americana*	21,700	800	0.32	8
Struthioniformes				
46 *Struthio camelus*	100,000	2350	0.20	27
47	100,000	3140	0.273	9
48	104,000	22,500	1.88 [10]	31
Domestic Birds				
49 Chicken	2000	97.5	0.423	3
50	2006	130.7	0.57	17
51 ♀	2710	124	0.397	34
52 Rhode Island	2000	137	0.594	1
53 Red	2420	161.7	0.58	2
54 White Plymouth Rock	2510	144.5	0.50	12
55 Duck	1870	157	0.73	16
56 Goose	3300	219	0.58	15
57	5000	280	0.49	5
58	5890	271	0.40	17
59 Pigeon	266	33.7	1.1	14
60	300	30	0.87	3
61	311	32.9	0.92	6
62	315	35.9	0.99	7
63	372	35.5	0.83	17
64 Turkey	3700	184	0.43	15

[1] In summer. [2] In winter. [7] CO_2 production = 1.25 ml·$g^{-1}·hr^{-1}$; R = 0.76. [8] Synonym: *Cygnus buccinator*. [9] Respiration calculated from measured values for growth and food consumption, assuming a 90% assimilation efficiency. [10] After running.

Contributor: Lasiewski, Robert C.

References

[1] Barott, H. G., and E. M. Pringle. 1941. J. Nutr. 22: 273.
[2] Barott, H. G., and E. M. Pringle. 1946. Ibid. 31:35.
[3] Benedict, F. G. 1938. Carnegie Inst. Wash. Publ. 503.
[4] Benedict, F. G., and E. L. Fox. 1927. Proc. Amer. Phil. Soc. 66:511.
[5] Benedict, F. G., and R. C. Lee. 1937. Carnegie Inst. Wash. Publ. 489.
[6] Burckard, E., et al. 1933. Ann. Physiol. Physicochim. Biol. 9:303.
[7] Calder, W. A., and K. Schmidt-Nielsen. 1967. Amer. J. Physiol. 213:883.
[8] Crawford, E. C., and R. C. Lasiewski. 1968. Condor 70:333.
[9] Crawford, E. C., and K. Schmidt-Nielsen. 1967. Amer. J. Physiol. 212:347.
[10] Dawson, W. R., and C. D. Fisher. 1969. Condor 71: 49.
[11] Dawson, W. R., and H. B. Tordoff. 1959. Ibid. 61: 388.
[12] Dukes, H. H. 1937. J. Nutr. 14:341.

continued

Part II. Birds

[13] Fonberg, A. 1932. Spraw. Posiedzen Tow. Nauk. Warszaw., IV, 25:59.

[14] Gelineo, S. 1955. Arch. Sci. Physiol. 9:225.

[15] Giaja, J. 1931. Ann. Physiol. Physicochim. Biol. 7:13.

[16] Giaja, J., and B. Males. 1928. Ibid. 4:875.

[17] Herzog, D. 1930. Wiss. Arch. Landwirt., B, 3:610.

[18] Hudson, J. W., and A. H. Brush. 1964. Comp. Biochem. Physiol. 12:157.

[19] Hudson, J. W., and S. L. Kimzey. 1964. Amer. Zool. 4:294.

[20] Irving, L., et al. 1955. Physiol. Zool. 28:173.

[21] Kahl, M. P. 1962. Condor 64:169.

[22] Kendeigh, S. C. 1939. J. Exp. Zool. 82:419.

[23] Kendeigh, S. C. 1944. Ibid. 96:1.

[24] King, J. R. 1964. Comp. Biochem. Physiol. 12:13.

[25] King, J. R., and D. S. Farner. 1961. In A. J. Marshall, ed. Biology and Comparative Physiology of Birds. Academic Press, New York. v. 2, pp. 215-288.

[26] Lasiewski, R. C. 1963. Physiol. Zool. 36:122.

[27] Lasiewski, R. C., and W. R. Dawson. 1967. Condor 69:13.

[28] Miller, D. S. 1939. J. Exp. Zool. 80:259.

[29] Quiring, D. P., and P. H. Bade. 1943. Growth 7:309.

[30] Riddle, O., et al. 1932. Amer. J. Physiol. 101:260.

[31] Schmidt-Nielsen, K., et al. 1969. Condor 71(4):341.

[32] Scholander, P. F., et al. 1950. Biol. Bull. 99:259.

[33] Steen, J. 1958. Ecology 39:625.

[34] Winchester, C. F. 1940. Mo. Agr. Exp. Sta. Res. Bull. 315.

Part III. Reptiles

Values show only order of magnitude and should therefore be used with caution. Some of the values were obtained from data on heat production by using a caloric equivalent of 4.8 cal/ml O_2. Unless otherwise specified, subjects were mature, at rest, and fasting.

	Species [Body Weight g]	Specification	Body Temp[1] °C	O_2 Consumption ml·g fresh wt^{-1}·hr^{-1}	Reference
	Crocodylia				
	Alligator mississippiensis 2/				
1	[49.7]	Winter	28	0.0798	25
2	[87.7]	Summer	28	0.0738	25
3	[650]	....	25	0.057	11
4	[750]	....	5	0.0063	14
5			10	0.0073	
6			15	0.0094	
7			20	0.0167	
8			25	0.0323	
9			30	0.0645	
10	[1380]	....	25	0.0625	35
11			37	0.098	
12	[53,000]	Winter	20	0.0073	8
13			22	0.0087	
	Serpentes				
	Boa constrictor 3/				
14	[3532]	....	20	0.0182	21
15	[4000-	....	16	0.0035	8
16	13,000]		21	0.0087	
17			28	0.0191	

	Species [Body Weight g]	Specification	Body Temp °C	O_2 Consumption ml·g fresh wt^{-1}·hr^{-1}	Reference
18			32	0.0304	
19	*Crotalus atrox*	Summer	17	0.0078	8
20	[2000-	& winter	22	0.0156	
21	5000]		29	0.0312	
22			36	0.0608	
23			43	0.109	
	Natrix natrix 4/				
24	[84]	....	11	0.0396	26
25			16	0.0708	
26			24	0.115	
27	[133]	....	18	0.0306	32
28	*Pituophis ca-*	....	10	0.02	22
29	*tenifer*		20	0.02	
30	[396-961]		30	0.04	
31			35	0.13	
32		Measured	10	0.07	
33		during ac-	20	0.27	
34		tivity	30	0.46	
35			35	0.52	
	Python molurus bivittatus				
36	[12,370]	Nonbrood-	27	0.011	28
37		ing	30	0.020	
38			33	0.028	

[1] Unless otherwise indicated. 2/ Synonym: *A. lucius.* 3/ Synonym: *Constrictor constrictor.* 4/ Synonyms: *Coluber natrix; Tropidonotus natrix.*

continued

Part III. Reptiles

#	Species [Body Weight g]	Specification	Body Temp[1] °C	O₂ Consumption ml·g fresh $wt^{-1}·hr^{-1}$	Reference
39	[14,250]	Brooding, winter	21[5]	0.080	28
40			25[5]	0.092	
41			29[5]	0.086	
42			30[5]	0.058	
43			33[5]	0.038	
44	P. reticulatus	Winter	17	0.0078	8
45	[32,000]		22	0.0113	
46			24	0.0122	
47			26	0.0161	
48			28	0.0258	
49			30	0.0288	
50	Thamnophis	....	25	0.102[6]	42
51	sirtalis [30.5-36.9]			0.073[7]	

Sauria

#	Species [Body Weight g]	Specification	Body Temp °C	O₂ Consumption	Reference
52	Amphibolurus	....	15	0.017	5
53	barbatus		20	0.045	
54	[240-470]		30	0.10	
55			35	0.12	
56			40	0.18	
57		Measured during activity	15	0.17	
58			20	0.35	
59			30	0.25	
60			35	0.28	
61			40	0.23	
62	Anolis caro-	Spring	28	0.198	19
63	linensis	Summer	28	0.220[8]	
64	[2.8-8.0]	....	30	0.280	12
65	Cnemidopho-	Summer	4	0.014	13
66	rus tigris[9]		12	0.035	
67			20	0.103	
68			28	0.257	
69			36	0.219	
70	[18]	Measured at night	20	0.063	3
71			30	0.15	
72			35	0.26	
73			40	0.33	
74		During activity	20	0.41	
75			30	0.90	
76			35	1.50	
77			40	2.00	
78	Coleonyx va-	Summer	4	0.0108	13
79	riegatus		12	0.0257	
80			20	0.0572	

#	Species [Body Weight g]	Specification	Body Temp °C	O₂ Consumption	Reference
81			28	0.152	
82			36	0.278	
	Dipsosaurus dorsalis				
83	[34.1-94.3]	Winter[10,11]	15	0.009	37
84			20	0.050	
85			25	0.075	
86			30	0.044	
87			35	0.058	
88			40	0.11	
89		Spring & fall[11]	20	0.041	
90			25	0.055	
91			30	0.090	
92			35	0.120	
93			40	0.150	
94	[52-87]	Summer	20	0.033	17
95			25	0.059	
96			30	0.090	
97			35	0.17	
98			40	0.20	
99			45	0.36	
100	Eumeces ob-	....	15	0.042	15
101	soletus [25-		20	0.057	
102	35]		25	0.080	
103			30	0.17	
104			35	0.22	
105			40	0.48	
106	Gerrhonotus	....	5	0.009	18
107	multicari-		10	0.020	
108	natus [23-		15	0.030	
109	40]		20	0.063	
110			25	0.12	
111			30	0.15	
112			35	0.28	
113			40	0.57	
	Iguana iguana[12]				
114	[369-1220]	Measured fitted with mask	15	0.021	38
115			20	0.040	
116			25	0.058	
117			30	0.075	
118			35	0.13	
119			40	0.18	
120		During activity	15	0.095	
121			20	0.20	
122			25	0.29	
123			30	0.38	

[1] Unless otherwise indicated. [5] Ambient temperature; elevated heat production associated with skeletal muscle contractions at frequencies up to 35/min. [6] Acclimated to 8°C. [7] Acclimated to 32°C. [8] Recently fed. [9] Synonym: C. tesselatus. [10] Dormant immediately before experiment. [11] Average rate for < 24 hr. [12] Synonym: I. tuberculata.

continued

Part III. Reptiles

#	Species [Body Weight g]	Specification	Body Temp °C	O₂ Consumption ml·g fresh wt⁻¹·hr⁻¹	Reference
124			35	0.48	
125			40	0.50	
126	[507-1897]	Measured	20	0.039	43
127		fitted	30	0.090	
128		with	38	0.170	
		mask			
129		During ac-	20	0.0998	
130		tivity	30	0.191	
131			38	0.483	
132	[910-1300]	Summer	26	0.0348	8
133			31	0.0574	
134	*Lacerta viridis*	Held in rub-	10	0.15	39
135		ber dia-	20	0.30	
136		phragm for respira-	30	0.60	
137		tion measurements	35	0.75	
138	[1.7]	....	20	0.0674 [13]	33
139	[16.4]	....	20	0.0375 [13]	33
140	[19.2]	....	30	0.436	23
141	[30.5]	....	15	0.0073 [13]	34
142			20	0.0147 [13]	34
143				0.0272 [13]	33
144	*Lygosoma la-*	....	19	0.111 [11,14]	27
145	*terale* [0.8-		30	0.306 [11,14]	
146	1.3]		36	0.399 [11,14]	
	Sceloporus occidentalis				
147	[11.5]	....	35	0.291	20
148	[13-16]	Winter	20	0.20	16
149			30	0.45	
150			35	0.52	
151			40	0.85	
152	[16]	....	35	0.176	20
153	*Tiliqua scin-*	Summer	20	0.027	7
154	*coides*		30	0.090	
155	[493]		40	0.19	
156		Measured	20	0.14	
157		during ac-	30	0.26	
158		tivity	40	0.39	
159	*Uta stansburi-*	....	15	0.17	1
160	*ana*		25	0.26	
161			35	0.34	
162		Measured	15	0.64	
163		during ac-	25	0.75	
164		tivity	35	1.10	
165	[1-5]	Winter;	10	0.019	41
166		measured	15	0.032	
167		at night	20	0.069	
168			25	0.11	
169			30	0.15	
170			35	0.25	
171	[2-4]	....	20	0.35	16
172			30	0.65	
173			35	0.78	
174			40	1.20	
175	[2.4-6.8]	....	30	0.28	12
176	[5-6]	....	10	0.13	16
177			20	0.30	
178			30	0.50	
179			35	0.58	
180			40	0.90	
181	*Varanus* spp.	....	20	0.029	6
182	[714]		30	0.080	
183			40	0.32	
184		Measured	20	0.18	
185		during ac-	30	0.37	
186		tivity	40	0.72	
187	*V. gouldii*	Measured	15	0.010	9
188	[139-1280]	at night	20	0.024	
189			25	0.050	
190			30	0.081	
191			35	0.108	
192			40	0.112	
193		During ac-	15	0.237	
194		tivity	20	0.320	
195			25	0.422	
196			30	0.570	
197			35	0.760	
198			40	1.012	
199	*Xantusia vigi-*	Summer	4	0.0111	13
200	*lis*		12	0.0298	
201			20	0.0652	
202			28	0.161	
203			36	0.272	

Rhynchocephalia

Sphenodon punctatus

#	Species [Body Weight g]	Specification	Body Temp °C	O₂ Consumption ml·g fresh wt⁻¹·hr⁻¹	Reference
204	[340]	♀, measured	10	0.072	44
205		during ac-	15	0.098	
206		tivity	20	0.135	
207			25	0.160	
208			30	0.158	
209			35	0.144	
210	[340-520]	....	10	0.009	44

11/ Average rate for ≮24 hr. 13/ Fall and winter; measured at night. 14/ Values estimated for 1-g subject from metabolism-weight regression line for species.

continued

Part III. Reptiles

	Species [Body Weight g]	Specification	Body Temp °C	O₂ Consumption ml·g fresh wt⁻¹·hr⁻¹	Reference		Species [Body Weight g]	Specification	Body Temp °C	O₂ Consumption ml·g fresh wt⁻¹·hr⁻¹	Reference
211			15	0.015		228	[958-1390]	Summer	20	0.0261 [15]	4
212			20	0.022		229		& fall		0.0491 [16]	
213			25	0.030			*C. scripta* [18]				
214			30	0.048		230	[150-350]	....	24	0.0853	31
215			35	0.060		231	[160-300]	....	24	0.0875	30
	Chelonia					232	[233-1805]	Spring	10	0.009	29
						233			20	0.021	
	Chelydra serpentina					234			30	0.042	
216	[82-1433]	....	25	0.017	10	235	*Gopherus*	Summer,	22	0.0130	8
217	[1299-1930]	Summer	20	0.0195 [15]	4	236	*polyphe-*	fall, &	28	0.0191	
218		& fall		0.0582 [16]		237	*mus* [5000-6000]	winter	31	0.0270	
219	*Chrysemys*	....	5	0.0031	40	238	*Malaclemys terrapin centrata* [19] [720]	....	24	0.035	36
220	*picta* [350-450]		28	0.0361							
221				0.0621 [8]							
	C. picta marginata [17]					239	*Terrapene carolina*	....	20-23	0.1742 ± 0.0436	2
222	[100-300]	....	0	0.0071	24						
223			4	0.0170		240			35-38	0.2815 ± 0.0492	
224			11	0.0203							
225			18	0.0309							
226			22	0.0406							
227			29	0.0544							

[8] Recently fed. [15] Laboratory animals. [16] Recently captured. [17] Synonym: *C. marginata*. [18] Synonym: *Pseudemys scripta*. [19] Synonym: *M. centrata*.

Contributors: Bennett, Albert F., and Dawson, William R.

References

[1] Alexander, C. E., and W. G. Whitford. 1968. Copeia, p. 678.
[2] Altland, P. D., and M. Parker. 1955. Amer. J. Physiol. 180:421.
[3] Asplund, K. K. 1970. Herpetologica 26:403.
[4] Baldwin, F. M. 1926. Proc. Iowa Acad. Sci. 33:315.
[5] Bartholomew, G. A., and V. A. Tucker. 1963. Physiol. Zool. 36:199.
[6] Bartholomew, G. A., and V. A. Tucker. 1964. Ibid. 37:341.
[7] Bartholomew, G. A., et al. 1965. Copeia, p. 169.
[8] Benedict, F. G. 1932. Carnegie Inst. Wash. Publ. 425.
[9] Bennett, A. F. 1972. J. Comp. Physiol. 79:259.
[10] Boyer, D. R. 1963. Science 140:813.
[11] Boyer, D. R. 1966. Physiol. Zool. 39:307.
[12] Claussen, D. L. 1967. Comp. Biochem. Physiol. 20:115.
[13] Cook, S. F. 1949. Univ. Calif. Berkeley Publ. Zool. 53:367.

[14] Coulson, R. A., and T. Hernandez. 1964. Biochemistry of the Alligator. Louisiana State Univ. Press, Baton Rouge, p. 9.
[15] Dawson, W. R. 1960. Physiol. Zool. 33:87.
[16] Dawson, W. R., and G. A. Bartholomew. 1956. Ibid. 29:40.
[17] Dawson, W. R., and G. A. Bartholomew. 1958. Ibid. 31:100.
[18] Dawson, W. R., and J. R. Templeton. 1966. Ecology 47:759.
[19] Dessauer, H. C. 1953. Proc. Soc. Exp. Biol. Med. 82:351.
[20] Francis, C., and G. R. Brooks. 1970. Comp. Biochem. Physiol. 35:436.
[21] Galvao, P. E., et al. 1965. Amer. J. Physiol. 209:501.
[22] Greenwald, O. E. 1971. Copeia, p. 98.
[23] Gelineo, S., and A. Gelineo. 1955. C. R. Soc. Biol. 149:565.
[24] Hall, F. G. 1924. J. Metab. Res. 6:393.
[25] Hernandez, T., and R. A. Coulson. 1952. Proc. Soc. Exp. Biol. Med. 79:145.

continued

Part III. Reptiles

[26] Hill, A. V. 1911. J. Physiol. (London) 43:379.

[27] Hudson, J. W., and F. W. Bertram. 1966. Physiol. Zool. 39:21.

[28] Hutchison, V. H., et al. 1966. Science 151:694.

[29] Hutton, K. E., et al. 1960. J. Cell. Comp. Physiol. 55:87.

[30] Jackson, D. C. 1968. J. Appl. Physiol. 24:503.

[31] Jackson, D. C., and K. Schmidt-Nielsen. 1966. J. Cell. Physiol. 67:225.

[32] Kayser, C. 1940. Ann. Physiol. Physicochim. Biol. 16:1.

[33] Kramer, G. 1934. Z. Vergl. Physiol. 20:600.

[34] Kramer, G. 1935. Ibid. 22:39.

[35] Krehl, L., and F. Soetbeer. 1899. Pfluegers Arch. Gesamte Physiol. Menschen Tiere 77:611.

[36] McCutcheon, F. H. 1943. Physiol. Zool. 16:255.

[37] Moberly, W. R. 1963. Ibid. 36:152.

[38] Moberly, W. R. 1968. Comp. Biochem. Physiol. 27:1.

[39] Nielsen, B. 1961. J. Exp. Biol. 38:301.

[40] Rapatz, G. L., and X. J. Musacchia. 1957. Amer. J. Physiol. 188:456.

[41] Roberts, L. A. 1968. Ecology 49:809.

[42] Steward, G. R. 1965. Herpetologica 21:81.

[43] Tucker, V. A. 1966. J. Exp. Biol. 44:77.

[44] Wilson, K. J., and A. K. Lee. 1970. Comp. Biochem. Physiol. 33:311.

Part IV. Amphibians

Values in parentheses are ranges, estimate "c" (*see* Introduction).

	Species	Ambient Temp °C	Body Weight g	O₂ Consumption ml·g⁻¹·hr⁻¹	Reference		Species	Ambient Temp °C	Body Weight g	O₂ Consumption ml·g⁻¹·hr⁻¹	Reference
	Salientia					26		25 [2]	38.6	0.10208 ± 0.00816	2
1	*Bufo america-*	5	25.2	0.0242	5	27		25 [3]	35.2	0.09771 ± 0.01203	2
2	*nus*	15	19.0	0.1101	5	28		25	35.0	0.093	1
3		25	21.1	0.1217	5	29	*R. sylvatica*	5	9.0	0.0540	5
4	*B. marinus*	15	123.8	0.0374	5	30		14	8.8	0.067(0.059-0.075)	8
5		25	88.7	0.0715	5	31		15	7.4	0.0989	5
6	*B. terrestris*	5	21.4	0.0305	5	32		25	6.0	0.1080	1
7		15	16.6	0.0804	5	33			8.2	0.206(0.186-0.233)	8
8		25	19.8	0.1133	5	34	*Xenopus laevis*	15	63.6	0.0338	5
9	*Hyla crucifer*	14	0.9	0.122(0.097-0.148)	8		Caudata				
10		24	0.9	0.357(0.333-0.382)	8	35	*Ambystoma*	5	13.1	0.0241	11,13
11	*H. versicolor*	5	8.3	0.0721	5	36	*maculatum*	10	11.9	0.0511	11,13
12		15	8.3	0.1041	5	37		15	13.4	0.0753	11,13
13		25	7.6	0.2007	5	38		25	12.9	0.1329	11,13
14			4.5	0.1020	1	39		30	12.9	0.1341	11,13
15	*Leptodactylus*	10	5.1	0.038(0.032-0.046)	8		*A. tigrinum*				
16	*typhonius*	25	5.1	0.115(0.098-0.147)	8	40	Larva	20	0.31	0.1609 ± 0.0464	4
17	*Rana catesbei-*	5	80.9	0.0416	5	41	Axolotl	20	0.30	0.1664 ± 0.0236	4
18	*ana*	15	47.3	0.0571	5	42	Adult	10	15.0	0.0595	11-13
19		25	35.0	0.0430	1	43		15	16.5	0.0918	11-13
	R. pipiens pipiens					44		25	14.9	0.1052	11-13
20	Tadpole,	9	3.65	0.025	6	45	*Amphiuma*	5	161.4	0.0041 ± 0.00043	3
21	stages 9-13 [1]	27	3.65	0.140	6	46	*means*	15	213.4	0.0077 ± 0.00044	3
22	Adult	5 [2]	47.7	0.01479 ± 0.00204	2	47		25	228.1	0.0171 ± 0.00094	3
23		5 [3]	33.5	0.01579 ± 0.00378	2	48	*Cryptobran-*	5	342.7	0.0064 ± 0.00061	3
24		15 [2]	32.1	0.04653 ± 0.00403	2	49	*chus allegani-*	15	387.2	0.0135 ± 0.00091	3
25		15 [3]	31.8	0.03625 ± 0.00594	2	50	*ensis*	25	344.4	0.0236 ± 0.00123	3

[1] Taylor-Kollros stages [9]. [2] Light:dark cycle = 8:16 hr. [3] Light:dark cycle = 16:8 hr.

continued

Part IV.   Amphibians

	Species	Ambient Temp °C	Body Weight g	O$_2$ Consumption ml·g^{-1}·hr^{-1}	Reference		Species	Ambient Temp °C	Body Weight g	O$_2$ Consumption ml·g^{-1}·hr^{-1}	Reference
51	*Desmognathus*	5	16.4	0.0288	12,13	61	*P. glutinosus*	15	4.2	0.0816	12,13
52	*quadramacu-*	10	10.1	0.0444	12,13	62	*Salamandra sal-*	15	19.1	0.0804	12,13
53	*latus*	15	16.8	0.0565	12,13		*amandra*				
54		20	13.3	0.0697	12,13	63	*Taricha granu-*	5	13.3	0.0408	12,13
55		25	15.1	0.0769	12,13	64	*losa*	10	12.5	0.0494	12,13
56	*Necturus macu-*	5	132.9	0.0066 ± 0.00030	3	65		15	13.8	0.0780	12,13
57	*losus*	15	128.9	0.0119 ± 0.00043	3	66		20	10.1	0.1148	12,13
58		25	114.0	0.0184 ± 0.00058	3	67		25	11.9	0.1378	12,13
59	*Plethodon cine-*	1	0.68	0.0160 ± 0.00093	10	68	*Triturus vul-*	20	.....	0.033	7
60	*reus*	10	0.85	0.0337 ± 0.00081	10		*garis*				

Contributor: Hutchison, Victor H.

References

[1] Davison, J. 1955. Biol. Bull. 109:407.

[2] Guimond, R. W., and V. H. Hutchison. 1968. Comp. Biochem. Physiol. 27:177.

[3] Guimond, R. W., and V. H. Hutchison. Unpublished. Univ. Rhode Island, Kingston, 1969.

[4] Helff, O. M. 1927. J. Exp. Zool. 49:353.

[5] Hutchison, V. H., et al. 1968. Physiol. Zool. 41:65.

[6] Parker, G. E. 1967. Copeia (3):610.

[7] Sawaya, P. 1947. Univ. Sao Paulo Fac. Fil. Cienc. Letras Zool. Bol. 12:43.

[8] Tashian, R. E., and C. Ray. 1957. Zoologica (New York) 42:63.

[9] Taylor, A. C., and J. J. Kollros. 1946. Anat. Rec. 94:7.

[10] Vernberg, F. J. 1952. Physiol. Zool. 25:243.

[11] Whitford, W. G., and V. H. Hutchison. 1963. Biol. Bull. 124:344.

[12] Whitford, W. G., and V. H. Hutchison. 1965. Physiol. Zool. 38:228.

[13] Whitford, W. G., and V. H. Hutchison. 1967. Ibid. 40:127.

Part V.   Fishes

A major problem in most measurements of fish oxygen consumption is uncertainty as to the animal's state of activity. This problem is compounded by two other factors: (i) placement in the respiration chamber may result in near maximum oxygen consumption by the fish even when quiescent; and (ii) the investigator's avoidance of measurement-taking during the initial period of enhanced metabolism results in a lack of clearly defined metabolic limits for the fish. In most instances the fish was free in a chamber 10-40 times its volume, and the investigator assumed that he was measuring resting metabolism. However, the rates obtained are two to three times the resting rate [54]; also, the correspondence between such "routine" rates and the resting rate is not constant but varies with the temperature [17,18,47], making proper application of the Q_{10} concept difficult. The "routine" measurement, nevertheless, is probably the best estimate of the metabolic needs at a given temperature, since it measures, at least to some degree, the metabolism required to meet the stimulus for spontaneous activity at that temperature, as well as the cost of cellular repair and ancillary activity. In general (and certainly when the oxygen content of the medium was sufficiently near air saturation), the respiratory exchange ratio indicated that the metabolism was aerobic; exceptions, however, were noted [8,29,33]. Selection of data has been confined to experiments in which the temperature was the same as the temperature of the maintenance medium. **Habitat:** S = salt water, F = freshwater. **No. of Experiments:** >+ = many experiments on different fish at different times (central value for oxygen consumption given); + = several; ++ = many; <+ = few. For information on "acute" experiments, in which maintenance and experimental temperatures differed, consult reference 18. For information on oxygen consumption of eggs and embryos, consult reference 7. All data documented by Winberg have been attributed to reference 54, and not to the original citations. Data in brackets refer to the column heading in brackets.

continued

Part V. Fishes

	Order & Species (Synonym) [Habitat]	Ambient Temp °C	Body Weight g	O$_2$ Consumption ml·g^{-1}·hr^{-1} [No. of Experiments]	Reference
	Osteichthyes				
	Pleuronectiformes				
1	Cynoglossus	15	6.7	0.042 [>+]	15
2	brevis [S]	20	6.7	0.069 [>+]	15
3		25	6.7	0.098 [>+]	15
4		30	6.7	0.174 [>+]	15
5		35	6.7	0.174 [>+]	15
6		37	6.7	0.174 [>+]	15
7	Pleuronectes	5	4	1.430 L/ [5]	14
8	platessa [S]		5	0.074 [+]	14
9		10	1	0.214 [+]	14
10			2	0.181 [+]	14
11			4	0.860 L/ [5]	14
12			5	0.134 [+]	14
13		15	1	0.428 [+]	14
14			2	0.333 [+]	14
15			4	0.750 L/ [5]	14
16			5	0.260 [+]	14
17		20	1	0.928 [+]	14
18			2	0.762 [+]	14
19			4	0.430 L/ [5]	14
20			5	0.400 [+]	14
	Perciformes				
21	Chaenocephalus aceratus [S]	0.5	980	0.016 [17]	21
22	Lagodon rhom-	10.5	59.3	0.029 [1]	56
23	boides [S]	15.5	86.1	0.045 [1]	56
24		15.6	58.0	0.030 [1]	56
25		19.9	59.2	0.080 [1]	56
26		21.0	43.6	0.081 [1]	56
27		25.0	55.2	0.120 [1]	56
28		26.1	65.5	0.163 [1]	56
29		30.4	59.3	0.272 [1]	56
30	Lepomis mac-	6	100	0.070 2/ [31]	55
31	rochirus [F]	10	100	0.088 2/ [45]	55
32		13	133	0.035 [10]	51
33		15	100	0.088 2/ [40]	55
34		25	3-13; 15	0.093 [3 each]	36
35			7	0.086 [63]	34
36			10	0.113 [64]	37
37			12	0.070 [70]	34
38			45	0.037 [64]	34
39			100	0.148 2/ [22]	55
40			118	0.070 [11]	32
41			133	0.074 [11]	51
42		30	10	0.168 [19]	37
43			133	0.098 [10]	51
44		35	7	0.123 [112]	34
45			8; 15	0.134 [2 each]	36
46	Micropterus sal-	5	6-10	0.038 [3]	24
47	moides [F]			0.048 L/ [6]	24
48		10	150	0.056 3/ [>+]	5
49				0.126 L/ [>+]	5
50		12	6-10	0.130 [3]	24
51				0.198 L/ [6]	24
52		15	150	0.069 3/ [>+]	5
53				0.161 L/ [>+]	5
54		18	43	0.046 [48]	54
55		20	9	0.060 [8]	54
56			28	0.088 [20]	20
57			44	0.074 [26]	20
58			47	0.053 [8]	54
59			150	0.074 3/ [>+]	5
60				0.224 L/ [>+]	5
61		22	6-10	0.185 [3]	24
62				0.303 L/ [6]	24
63		25	12	0.070 [1]	34
64			150	0.080 3/ [>+]	5
65				0.252 L/ [>+]	5
66		29	6-10	0.320 [3]	24
67				0.450 L/ [6]	24
68		30	12	0.071 [1]	34
69			150	0.143 3/ [>+]	5
70				0.340 L/ [>+]	5
71		34	150	0.108 3/ [>+]	5
72				0.300 L/ [>+]	5
73		35	72	0.083 [1]	34
74			98	0.080 [1]	34
75	Myoxocephalus	5	99	0.037 [>+]	15
76	scorpius (Cot-	10	99	0.049 [>+]	15
77	tus scorpius)	15	99	0.059 [>+]	15
78	[S]	20	99	0.084 [>+]	15
79		23	99	0.084 [>+]	15
80	Notothenia gib- berifrons [S]	0.5	470	0.016 [6]	21
81	N. neglecta [S]	0.5	1000	0.020 [2]	21
82	Parachaenich- thys charcoti- co [S]	0.5	557	0.017 [1]	21
83	Perca fluviatilis	13	24	0.073 [6]	31
84	[F]	14	40	0.110 [3]	54

L/ Active condition—fish stimulated to some constant level of activity so that maximum rate of O$_2$ consumption was attained or approximated. 2/ Paced condition—fish in annular chamber counter, rotated to match speed at which fish swims spontaneously. 3/ Standard condition, with effect of physical activity eliminated from the determination.

continued

Part V. Fishes

	Order & Species (Synonym) [Habitat]	Ambient Temp °C	Body Weight g	O₂ Consumption ml·g⁻¹·hr⁻¹ [No. of Experiments]	Reference		Order & Species (Synonym) [Habitat]	Ambient Temp °C	Body Weight g	O₂ Consumption ml·g⁻¹·hr⁻¹ [No. of Experiments]	Reference
85		16	11	0.161 [5]	54		Siluriformes				
86			16	0.124 [1]	54	124	Ictalurus nebu-	10	100	0.014[3/] [14]	2
87		17	7	0.095 [2]	54	125	losus [F]		115	0.092[L/] [<+]	1
88			16	0.219 [3]	54	126		20	90	0.186[L/] [<+]	1
89			31	0.112 [10]	31	127			100	0.046[3/] [14]	2
90			201	0.088 [4]	54	128			181	0.050 [10]	45
91		18	69	0.151 [2]	54	129		25	24	0.058 [76]	34
92		19	15	0.158 [3]	54	130			54	0.062 [63]	34
93			26	0.189 [3]	54	131			74	0.084 [51]	34
94		20	20	0.116 [2]	54	132			75	0.070 [10]	32
95			34	0.104 [2]	54	133		30	25	0.095 [75]	34
96		23	20	0.189 [>+]	54	134			100	0.074[3/] [17]	2
97		24	9	0.252 [>+]	54	135			102	0.234[L/] [<+]	1
98	Pomoxis annu-laris [F]	17	11	0.064 [36]	54	136		35	23	0.088 [70]	34
	Gasterosteiformes					137			57	0.085 [67]	34
99	Gasterosteus aculeatus (G. leiurus) [S]	18	1.0	0.300 [2]	54	138	I. punctatus [F]	24	6.5	0.144 [8]	19
							Cypriniformes				
100	Hippocampus	18	10	0.090 [1]	54	139	Carassius aura-	5	6	0.040 [28]	28
101	brevirostris	22	1.7	0.176 [>+]	54	140	tus [F]	7-9	25	0.064 [<+]	39
102	[S]	25	3.1	0.162 [4]	54	141		9	100	0.040 [>+]	54
	Atheriniformes					142		10	55	0.030 [3]	25
103	Fundulus heter-	20	10	0.570 [27]	22	143				0.053[L/] [3]	25
104	oclitus [S]	21	13	0.136 [>+]	54	144			72	0.198[L/] [4]	1
	Gadiformes					145			100	0.011[3/] [14]	6
105	Gadus morhua	3	500	0.035 [++]	46	146				0.024[L/] [14]	6
106	[S]		1000	0.030 [++]	46	147				0.041 [1]	54
107			3000	0.024 [++]	46	148		12	36	0.046 [2]	54
108			6000	0.021 [++]	46	149			100	0.030[3/] [6]	6
109		10	500	0.052 [++]	46	150			111	0.030 [1]	54
110			1000	0.048 [++]	46	151		15	6	0.130 [28]	28
111			3000	0.042 [++]	46	152			33	0.077 [4]	54
112			6000	0.039 [++]	46	153		16	6	0.069 [>+]	54
113		15	500	0.064 [++]	46	154		18	39	0.041 [1]	54
114			1000	0.055 [++]	46	155			82	0.036 [1]	54
115			3000	0.046 [++]	46	156			130	0.039 [1]	54
116			6000	0.041 [++]	46	157		19	1.6	0.149 [3]	54
117	Melanogram-	10	156	0.042[3/] [3]	53	158			2.5	0.151 [9]	54
118	mus aeglefinus [S]			0.228[L/] [3]	53	159			21	0.101 [>+]	54
	Batrachoidiformes					160		20	3.8	0.085 [>+]	54
119	Halophryne	15	20.9	0.015 [>+]	15	161			4	0.085 [+]	54
120	dussumieri	20	20.9	0.022 [>+]	15	162			5	0.114 [2]	54
121	[S]	25	20.9	0.036 [>+]	15	163			9	0.110 [>+]	54
122		30	20.9	0.059 [>+]	15	164			29	0.133 [35]	54
123		35	20.9	0.057 [>+]	15	165			52	0.261[L/] [4]	1
						166			72	0.086 [>+]	54
						167			80	0.035[3/] [3]	50

[L/] Active condition—fish stimulated to some constant level of activity so that maximum rate of O₂ consumption was attained or approximated. [3/] Standard condition, with effect of physical activity eliminated from the determination.

continued

Part V. Fishes

#	Order & Species (Synonym) [Habitat]	Ambient Temp °C	Body Weight g	O$_2$ Consumption ml·g^{-1}·hr^{-1} [No. of Experiments]	Reference	#	Order & Species (Synonym) [Habitat]	Ambient Temp °C	Body Weight g	O$_2$ Consumption ml·g^{-1}·hr^{-1} [No. of Experiments]	Reference
168			100	0.021 [3/] [14]	6	216			35	0.030 [>+]	54
169				0.180 [L/] [14]	6	217				0.622 [L/] [<+]	1
170			110	0.055 [3/] [3]	29	218			39	0.198 [3]	54
171				0.280 [L/] [3]	29	219			100	0.035 [17]	2
172		21	51	0.080 [>+]	54	220			174	0.070 [6]	45
173		22-23	~50	0.239 [24]	42	221			602	0.091 [>+]	54
174		24	33	0.075 [>+]	54	222		21	0.003	1.000 [1]	54
175		25	5	0.136 [26]	44	223			335	0.152 [2]	54
176		30	6	0.250 [28]	28	224		22	0.026	0.545 [1]	54
177			55	0.131 [4]	25	225		24	0.560	0.601 [1]	54
178				0.189 [L/] [4]	25	226		25	0.140	0.695 [1]	54
179			74	0.369 [L/] [4]	1	227			2.7	0.392 [3]	54
180			100	0.050 [3/] [13]	6	228		30	0.700	0.659 [1]	54
181				0.120 [L/] [13]	6	229			61	0.656 [L/] [<+]	1
182		32	100	0.104 [3/] [3]	6	230			100	0.070 [19]	2
183		35	100	0.089 [3/] [14]	6	231		35	100	0.082 [14]	2
184				0.147 [L/] [14]	6		**Salmoniformes**				
185	*Cyprinus carpio*	8	320	0.039 [4]	54	232	*Coregonus*	10	1892	0.023 [2]	54
186	[F]	9	331	0.053 [4]	54	233	*muksun* [F]	20	1710	0.027 [1]	54
187		10	10	0.056 [3/] [++]	26	234	*Esox lucius* [F]	10	265	0.049 [>+]	54
188			15	0.056 [3/] [>+]	27	235		13	661	0.051 [3]	54
189				0.150 [L/] [>+]	27	236		15	250	0.040 [>+]	54
190			25	0.105 [9]	54	237			680	0.060 [1]	54
191			26	0.085 [5]	54	238			1850	0.046 [>1]	54
192			100	0.012 [17]	2	239		18	71	0.106 [2]	54
193		11	345	0.030 [10]	54	240			280	0.083 [3]	54
194		14	74	0.090 [>+]	54	241		20	130	0.096 [>1]	54
195		15	10	0.100 [3/] [++]	26	242	*Oncorhynchus*	5	50	0.028 [3/] [9]	10
196			15	0.095 [3/] [>+]	27	243	*nerka* [F]			0.360 [L/] [9]	10
197				0.280 [L/] [>+]	27	244		10	50	0.042 [3/] [11]	10
198		16	8	0.175 [5]	54	245				0.440 [L/] [11]	10
199		17	17	0.179 [2]	54	246		15	50	0.050 [3/] [10]	10
200		19	9	0.190 [9]	54	247				0.626 [L/] [10]	10
201				0.240 [9]	54	248			100	0.058 [3/] [89]	11
202			10	0.260 [>+]	54	249				0.511 [L/] [89]	11
203			17	0.240 [>+]	54	250		20	50	0.084 [3/] [9]	10
204			21	0.260 [>+]	54	251				0.596 [L/] [9]	10
205			40	0.177 [1]	54	252		24	50	0.137 [3/] [5]	10
206			113	0.113 [7]	54	253				0.594 [L/] [5]	10
207			793	0.156 [3]	54	254	*Osmerus mor-dax* [F]	15	38	0.158 [6]	54
208			2831	0.092 [1]	54	255	*Salmo gairdneri*	5	100	0.040 [3/] [17]	43
209			3487	0.123 [1]	54	256	[F]			0.248 [L/] [17]	43
210		20	2.5	0.280 [19]	54	257		8	50	0.073 [33]	16
211			4.3	0.295 [>+]	54	258		10	2	0.374 [10]	12
212			10	0.145 [3/] [++]	26	259			12	0.353 [10]	12
213			12	0.254 [2]	54	260			32	0.313 [10]	12
214			15	0.150 [3/] [>+]	27	261			65	0.228 [10]	12
215				0.410 [L/] [>+]	27						

[L/] Active condition—fish stimulated to some constant level of activity so that maximum rate of O$_2$ consumption was attained or approximated. [3/] Standard condition, with effect of physical activity eliminated from the determination.

continued

Part V. Fishes

	Order & Species (Synonym) [Habitat]	Ambient Temp °C	Body Weight g	O_2 Consumption ml·g⁻¹·hr⁻¹ [No. of Experiments]	Reference
262		12	115	0.063 [9]	32
263		14	202	0.212 [3]	54
264		15	30	0.154	30
265			80	0.060 3/ [3]	29
266				0.350 L/ [3]	29
267			100	0.078 3/ [16]	43
268				0.408 L/ [16]	43
269			210	0.057	49
270				0.070 [11]	49
271		16	50	0.134 [46]	16
272		19	900	0.119	54
273	Hatchery	5	193	0.269 L/ [12]	13
274			206	0.025 3/ [12]	13
275		10	193	0.328 L/ [12]	13
276			206	0.029 3/ [12]	13
277		15	193	0.403 L/ [12]	13
278			206	0.055 3/ [12]	13
279		20	193	0.400 L/ [12]	13
280			206	0.059 3/ [12]	13
281		25	193	0.335 L/ [12]	13
282			206	0.095 3/ [12]	13
283	Wild	5	238	0.256 L/ [12]	13
284			241	0.029 3/ [12]	13
285		10	238	0.344 L/ [12]	13
286			241	0.038 3/ [12]	13
287		15	238	0.386 L/ [12]	13
288			241	0.042 3/ [12]	13
289		20	238	0.415 L/ [12]	13
290			241	0.066 3/ [12]	13
291		25	238	0.412 L/ [12]	13
292			241	0.084 3/ [12]	13
293	S. gairdneri [S]	5	100	0.052 3/ [14]	43
294				0.279 L/ [14]	43
295		15	100	0.089 3/ [14]	43
296				0.437 L/ [14]	43
297	S. salar [F]	5	42.5	0.037 [11]	40
298			80	0.031 [20]	40
299		6	....	0.050 3/ [++]	38
300		10	42.5	0.061 [11]	40
301			80	0.053 [20]	40
302		14	0.17	0.525 [3]	54
303			2.5	0.364 [3]	54
304			10	0.176 [3]	54
305		15	0.15	0.266	54
306			1.5	0.366	54
307			5	0.214	54
308				0.280 [12]	54
309			10	0.175	54
310			20	0.147	54
311			42.5	0.120 [11]	40
312			80	0.170 [20]	40
313		18	25	0.160 3/ [++]	38
314		20	16	0.181 [>+]	54
315			25	0.160 [>+]	54
316	S. trutta fario	10	0.583	0.091 [10]	54
317	(S. fario) [F]		0.671	0.116 [10]	54
318			100	0.056 3/ [11]	2
319			350	0.040 3/ [++]	3
320				0.066 3/ [++]	3
321		20	2.15	0.354 [7]	54
322			23	0.196 [>+]	54
323			96	0.210 [>+]	54
324	Salvelinus fontinalis [F]	9-10	2	0.300 L/ [+]	48
325			16	0.250 L/ [+]	48
326			25	0.200 L/ [+]	48
327		10	100	0.035 3/ [3]	4
328				0.055 3/ [15]	2
329			164	0.234 L/ [<+]	1
330			690	0.015 3/ [++]	3
331				0.030 3/ [++]	3
332		15	100	0.075 3/ [15]	2
333			164	0.270 L/ [<+]	1
334		20	23	0.140 [>+]	54
335			100	0.103 3/ [15]	2
336			164	0.230 L/ [<+]	1
337	Anguilliformes Anguilla anguilla [F]	12	195	0.025 [6]	54
338		13	38	0.066 [4]	54
339			40	0.048 [4]	54
340		14	51	0.041 [1]	54
341			181	0.024 [6]	54
342		15	112	0.048 [1]	54
343		17	0.2	0.161 [2]	54
344			33	0.097 [2]	54
345			40	0.088 [3]	54
346			54	0.091 [6]	54
347			90	0.082	54
348			430;485	0.069	54
349			1191	0.044	54
350		18?	21	0.087 [3]	54
351		20	120	0.065 [6]	54
352			150	0.056 [>+]	54
353			223	0.063 [>+]	54
354			230	0.060 [>+]	54

L/ Active condition—fish stimulated to some constant level of activity so that maximum rate of O_2 consumption was attained or approximated. 3/ Standard condition, with effect of physical activity eliminated from the determination.

continued

Part V. Fishes

	Order & Species (Synonym) [Habitat]	Ambient Temp °C	Body Weight g	O_2 Consumption $ml \cdot g^{-1} \cdot hr^{-1}$ [No. of Experiments]	Reference
355	*A. anguilla* [S]	13	67	0.015 [5]	9
356		21	75	0.022 [2]	9
357		22	75	0.033 [2]	9
358		25	75	0.042 [2]	9
359		27	75	0.035 [2]	9
360		30	75	0.056 [2]	9
361	*Moringua linearis* [S]	30	1.5	0.175 [13]	52
	Chondrichthyes				
	Rajiformes				
362	*Torpedo torpedo (Raja torpedo)* [S]	14	410	0.049 [1]	54
363		15	315	0.045 [1]	54
	Squaliformes				
364	*Scyliorhinus caniculus* [S]	12	150	0.080 [1]	23
365		14	149	0.060 [1]	23

	Order & Species (Synonym) [Habitat]	Ambient Temp °C	Body Weight g	O_2 Consumption $ml \cdot g^{-1} \cdot hr^{-1}$ [No. of Experiments]	Reference
366	*(Scyllium catulus)* [S]	14	19	0.078 [3]	54
367			24	0.087 [3]	54
368		15	400	0.054 [1]	54
369	*Squalus suckleyi* [S]	13	100	0.105 [1]	41
370			1000	0.038 [23]	41
371			5000	0.032 [16]	41
	Agnatha				
	Petromyzontiformes				
372	*Lampetra fluviatilis* [F]	16	37	0.098 [12]	54
373	*Petromyzon marinus* [F]	18	3.9	0.129 [5]	54
374		22	3.4	0.380 [5]	54
375			3.5	0.230 [5]	54
	Myxiniformes				
376	*Eptatretus stouti* [S]	4	60.2	0.006 [13]	35
377		10	61.8	0.009 [13]	35

Contributors: Fry, F. E. J., and Brett, J. R.

References

[1] Basu, S. P. 1959. J. Fish. Res. Bd. Can. 16:175.

[2] Beamish, F. W. H. 1964. Can. J. Zool. 42:177.

[3] Beamish, F. W. H. 1964. Ibid. 42:189.

[4] Beamish, F. W. H. 1964. Trans. Amer. Fish. Soc. 93:103.

[5] Beamish, F. W. H. 1970. Can. J. Zool. 48(6):1221.

[6] Beamish, F. W. H., and P. S. Mookherjii. 1964. Ibid. 42:161.

[7] Blaxter, J. H. S. 1969. In W. S. Hoar and D. J. Randall, ed. Fish Physiology. Academic Press, New York. pp. 178-252.

[8] Blazka, P. 1958. Physiol. Zool. 31:117.

[9] Boetius, I., and J. Boetius. 1967. Medd. Dann. Fisk. Havunders. 4:339.

[10] Brett, J. R. 1964. J. Fish. Res. Bd. Can. 21:1183.

[11] Brett, J. R. 1965. Ibid. 22:1491.

[12] Coche, A. G. 1967. Hydrobiologia 29:165.

[13] Dickson, I. W., and R. H. Kramer. 1971. J. Fish. Res. Bd. Can. 28(4):587.

[14] Edwards, R. R. C., et al. 1969. J. Exp. Mar. Biol. Ecol. 3:1.

[15] Edwards, R. R. C., et al. 1970. Comp. Biochem. Physiol. 34(2):491.

[16] Evans, R. M., et al. 1962. Can. J. Zool. 40:107.

[17] Fry, F. E. J. 1957. In M. E. Brown, ed. The Physiology of Fishes. Academic Press, New York. v. 1, pp. 1-53.

[18] Fry, F. E. J., and P. W. Hochachka. 1970. In G. C. Whittow, ed. Comparative Physiology of Thermoregulation. Academic Press, New York. pp. 79-134.

[19] Gerald, J. W., and J. J. Cech, Jr. 1970. Physiol. Zool. 43:47.

[20] Glass, N. R. 1968. Ecology 49:340.

[21] Holeton, G. F. 1970. Comp. Biochem. Physiol. 34(2):457.

[22] Hoss, D. E. 1968. Proc. 21st Annu. Conf. Southeast. Ass. Game Fish Comm., 1967, p. 416.

[23] Hughes, G. M., and S. Umezawa. 1968. J. Exp. Biol. 49:557.

[24] Johnson, M. G., and W. H. Charlton. 1960. Progr. Fish Cult. 22:155.

[25] Kanungo, M. S., and C. L. Prosser. 1959. J. Cell. Comp. Physiol. 54:259.

[26] Kausch, H. 1959. Verh. Int. Ver. Limnol. 17:669.

[27] Kausch, H. 1968. Arch. Hydrobiol., Suppl. 33(3-4): 263.

[28] Klicka, J. 1965. Physiol. Zool. 38:177.

[29] Kutty, M. N. 1968. J. Fish. Res. Bd. Can. 25: 1689.

[30] Mann, H. 1968. Arch. Fischereiwiss. 19:131.

[31] Mann, K. H. 1965. J. Anim. Ecol. 34:253.

[32] Marvin, D. E., and A. G. Heath. 1968. Comp. Biochem. Physiol. 27:349.

[33] Mathur, G. B. 1967. Nature (London) 214:318.

[34] Moss, D. D., and D. C. Scott. 1961. Trans. Amer. Fish. Soc. 90:377.

[35] Munz, F. W., and R. W. Morris. 1965. Comp. Biochem. Physiol. 16:1.

[36] National Council for Stream Improvement. 1958. Nat. Counc. Tech. Bull. 111.

[37] O'Hara, J. 1968. Ecology 49:159.

[38] Peterson, R. H., and J. M. Anderson. 1969. J. Fish. Res. Bd. Can. 26:93.

[39] Picos, C. A., et al. 1969. Z. Vergl. Physiol. 63:146.

continued

[40] Power, G. 1959. Arctic 12(4):195.

[41] Pritchard, A. W., et al. 1958. J. Mar. Res. 17:403.

[42] Prosser, C. L., et al. 1957. Physiol. Zool. 30:137.

[43] Rao, G. M. M. 1968. Can. J. Zool. 46:781.

[44] Rohland, M. L. 1965. Bull. Soc. Zool. Fr. 90:347.

[45] Saunders, R. L. 1962. Can. J. Zool. 40:817.

[46] Saunders, R. L. 1963. J. Fish. Res. Bd. Can. 20: 373.

[47] Schmeing-Engberding, F. 1953. Z. Fisch. Hilfswiss. 2:125.

[48] Shepard, M. P. 1955. J. Fish. Res. Bd. Can. 12:387.

[49] Skidmore, J. F. 1970. J. Exp. Biol. 52(2):481.

[50] Smit, H. 1965. Can. J. Zool. 43:623.

[51] Spitzer, K. W., et al. 1969. Comp. Biochem. Physiol. 30:83.

[52] Subramanian, A. 1967. Proc. Indian Acad. Sci. 66(6):273.

[53] Tytler, P. 1969. Nature (London) 221:27.

[54] Winberg, G. G. 1960. Fish. Res. Bd. Can. Transl. Ser. 194.

[55] Wohlschlag, D. E., and R. O. Juliano. 1959. Limnol. Oceanogr. 4:195.

[56] Wohlschlag, D. E., et al. 1968. Contrib. Mar. Sci. 13:89.

215. DATA FOR CONSTRUCTING OXYGEN DISSOCIATION CURVES: INVERTEBRATES

O_2 dissociation or equilibrium curves can usually be described by Hill's equation: $y = (P/P_{50})^n/[1 + (P/P_{50})^n]$. For a further discussion of O_2 dissociation curves, *see* main headnote of Table 213. **Solvent:** μ = ionic strength; Tris = 2-amino-2-hydroxymethyl-1,3-propanediol. P_{50} = O_2 pressure required for 50% oxygenation. **Bohr Effect:** Calculated by the formula $\Delta \log P_{50}/\Delta pH$. n = the value which best approximates the 50% oxygenation of Hill's equation. ΔH = apparent heat of oxygenation, calculated from the van't Hoff equation: $\log [(P_{50})_{T_2}/(P_{50})_{T_1}] = (\Delta H/4.574)\cdot[(T_2 - T_1)/(T_1 T_2)]$, in which $(P_{50})_{T_1}$ and $(P_{50})_{T_2}$ are the O_2 pressures required for 50% oxygenation at absolute temperatures T_1 and T_2, respectively. For additional information on myoglobins and hemoglobins, consult references 8, 19, 26, 33, and 37; for hemocyanins, references 9, 10, 29, 26, and 33; and for hemerythrin, references 8, 9, 20, and 33. Data in brackets refer to the column heading in brackets.

	Phylum & Species (Synonym)	Specification	Solvent [P_{CO_2}]	pH	Temp °C	P_{50} mm Hg	Bohr Effect	n [ΔH[1/]]	Reference
				Myoglobins & Hemoglobins					
1	**Echinodermata** *Arhynchite pugettensis*	Coelom	μ = 0.2, PO_4	....	23-24	3.4-4.0	Slightly negative	1.0	28
2		Muscle	μ = 0.2, PO_4	....	23-24	11	0.00	1.0	28
3				7.1-7.8	21	9.0	0.00	1.0	27
4	*Cucumaria miniata*	Erythrocytes	....	7.5-9.5	10	11.5	0.00	1.48	25
5		Free solution	μ = 0.2, PO_4	6.0-7.5	10	3.7	0.00	1.33	25
6				6.6-7.5	26	8.88	0.00	1.35	25
7	**Arthropoda** *Anisops pellucens*	In vivo	....	....	24	28	0.00	[0.014[2/]]	34
8	*Chironomus thummi thummi*	Free solution[3/]	0.2 M PO_4	7.1	37	3	−0.3 to +2.0	1.1	43
9	*Cyzicus cf. heirosolymitanus*	Free solution	0.01 M Tris	7.2	28	0.035	....	2.3	2
10	*Daphnia magna*	Free solution	....	7.20	20	3.5	0.00	Sigmoid curve	15
11	*Moina macrocopa*	Free solution	....	7.20	20	2.2	0.00	Sigmoid curve	14
12	*Triops longicaudatus*	Free solution	0.1 M PO_4	7.42	23	6.6	−0.23	1.4-2.0 [0.020[2/]]	13

[1/] Unless otherwise indicated. [2/] Change in log P_{50} per degree Celsius. [3/] Five isolated fractions.

continued

215. DATA FOR CONSTRUCTING OXYGEN DISSOCIATION CURVES: INVERTEBRATES

	Phylum & Species (Synonym)	Specification	Solvent [P_{CO_2}]	pH	Temp °C	P_{50} mm Hg	Bohr Effect	n [ΔH [1]]	Reference
	Annelida								
13	*Arenicola* sp.	....	....	5.4-6.8	20	6.2	0.00	3.5	30
14		Free solution	$\mu = 0.6$, PO$_4$	6.0-7.4	20	5	0.00	4	31
15	*A. marina*	Free solution	$\mu = 0.2$, PO$_4$	7.50	.....	1.75	Normal	2.6-3.9	45
16	*Eupolymnia crescentis*	Free solution	$\mu = 0.1$, PO$_4$	5-7	10	36	0.00	1.06	25
17	*Glycera dibranchiata*	Free solution	$\mu = 0.2$, PO$_4$	7.4	.....	7.00	....	1.04	12
18		Light component	$\mu = 0.2$, PO$_4$	7.4	.....	1.45	−1.09	1.03	12
19		Heavy component	$\mu = 0.2$, PO$_4$	7.4	.....	4.60	0.03	1.22	12
20	*Lumbricus terrestris*	Whole blood [4]	Saline	7.44	25	6.8	−0.4	5.30 [−10]	4
21		Free solution	0.1 *M* PO$_4$	7.3	20	8	....	....	11
22			$\mu = 0.2$, PO$_4$	7.72	10	3.5	−0.25	1.8 [5]	25
23	*Nephtys hombergii*	Coelom	....	7.4	15	7.4	0.44	1.0 [6]	18
24			$\mu = 0.2$, PO$_4$	7.43	20	6.8	−0.09	1.7	46
25		Vascular	....	7.4	15	5.5	−0.18	1.0 [6]	18
26			$\mu = 0.2$, PO$_4$	7.48	20	6.3	−0.09	1.8	46
27	*Travisia pupa*	Coelom	$\mu = 0.2$, PO$_4$	....	22-23	0.36	0.00	....	28
28		Muscle	$\mu = 0.2$, PO$_4$	....	22-23	0.08	0.00	....	28
29		Vascular	$\mu = 0.2$, PO$_4$	....	22-23	0.5-1.1	Small [7]	....	28
30	*Tubifex tubifex*	....	[0.03%]	....	25	140	Reverse	Sigmoid curve	35
31			[5%]	....	25	25	....	Hyperbolic curve	35
32		Free solution	....	6.0-7.5	20	2.2	0.00	2.3 [8] [0.013 [2]]	42
	Mollusca								
33	*Amicula stelleri* (*Cryptochiton stelleri*)	Radula	$\mu = 0.2$, PO$_4$	5.9-7.9	10	2.6	0.00	1.63 [9]	23
34				6.5-7.9	22	4.1	0.00	1.19	27
35	*Aplysia californica; A. vaccaria*	Neuron	....	7.43	20-21	4.0	....	1.2	47
36	*A. depilans; A. fasciata* (*A. limacina*)	Free solution	....	7.2	20	2.7	−0.02	1.0	41
37	*Cardita floridana*	Whole blood	$\mu = 0.6$, PO$_4$	7.0-7.5	22-24	10	0.00	<1	31
38			$\mu = 0.6$, Tris	7.0-7.5	22	20	0.00	....	31
39	*Fusitriton oregonensis* (*Argobuccinum oregonense*)	Radula	$\mu = 0.2$, PO$_4$	6.5-7.7	25	8.5	0.00	1.35	27
40	*Ischnochiton conspicuus*	Radula	$\mu = 0.2$, PO$_4$	7.0	.....	1.1	....	1.14	27
41	*Mercenaria mercenaria*	Muscle	$\mu = 0.6$, PO$_4$	7.5	22-24	0.5	....	....	31
42	*Noetia ponderosa*	Free solution	$\mu = 0.6$, PO$_4$	6.7-8.2	22-24	13	....	1.1	31
	Nematoda (Aschelminthes)								
43	*Ascaris lumbricoides*	Body wall	....	....	.....	0.02	....	1.0 [10]	44
44		Perienteric fluid	....	....	.....	<0.1	....	3	44

Hemocyanins

	Phylum & Species (Synonym)	Specification	Solvent [P_{CO_2}]	pH	Temp °C	P_{50} mm Hg	Bohr Effect	n [ΔH [1]]	Reference
	Arthropoda								
45	*Cardisoma guanhumi*	Whole blood	....	7.55	25	3.5	−0.75	2.64 [0.0217 [2]]	38
46	*Crangon vulgaris*	Whole blood	$\mu = 0.1$, Tris	8.0	20	69.5	Normal	6.0	5
47	*Homarus americanus*	Whole blood	$\mu = 0.07$, Tris	7.7	20	76.0	....	3.6	36
48			$\mu = 0.07-0.26$ [11], Tris	7.7	20	25.2	....	3.6	36
49			$\mu = 0.26$, Tris	7.7	20	20.9	....	3.6	36

[1] Unless otherwise indicated. [2] Change in log P_{50} per degree Celsius. [4] Diluted 1:10 with saline. [5] At low O_2 saturation levels, n = 1; at high O_2 saturation levels, n rises to 4-5. [6] At high O_2 saturation levels, n = 1.2. [7] Bohr effect may be result of the change from hyperbolic to sigmoid curve. [8] At 30°C, n = 0.8. [9] After 1-da storage, n = 1.0. [10] Assumed value. [11] Including 25 m*M* Ca^{2+}.

continued

	Phylum & Species (Synonym)	Specification	Solvent [P_{CO_2}]	pH	Temp °C	P_{50} mm Hg	Bohr Effect	n [ΔH]	Reference
50	*Loligo pealei*	Whole blood	Tris [12]	7.36	23	228	-0.88	3.9 [13]	6
51	*Panulirus interruptus*	....	0.2 M Na⁺	6.6	20	1.6	0.00 [14]	3.3	17
52				8.0	20	19.1	-0.24 [15]	3.3	17
53	*Tachypleus tridentatus*	Whole blood	0.2 M Tris [16]	7.2	25-27	5.07	....	4.20	16
	Mollusca								
54	*Amicula stelleri (Cryptochiton stelleri)*	....	....	7.10	10	17.5	....	....	23
55				7.53 [17]	23-24	21	-0.12	1.0-2.2 [18]	27
56	*Chiton tuberculatus*	Whole blood	....	7.19	25	25	0.11 [19]	2.3-3.0 [20]	39
57	*Diodora aspera*	Whole blood	....	6.9-7.8	25	17	0.00	1.65 [-12.6]	40
58	*Helix pomatia*	Whole blood	0.1 M Tris	7.0	20	9.6	Normal	1 [21]	21
59			[0.3 mm Hg]	8.6	15	10	Fn [22]	Sigmoid curve [22]	40
60	*Ischnochiton conspicuus*	Whole blood	....	6.2-7.5	21	7-9	Small	1.0-1.4	27
61	*Octopus dofleini*	....	[15 mm Hg]	....	11	84 [23]	....	....	22
62		Whole blood	[3.2 mm Hg]	....	11	39			22
			Hemerythrin						
	Sipuncula								
	Phascolopsis gouldii (Golfingia gouldii)	Free solution							
63		Electrophoretic F	μ = 0.6, PO₄	7.4	25	3.3	0.00	....	32
64		Electrophoretic S	μ = 0.6, PO₄	7.4	25	4.6	0.00	....	32
65		Electrophoretic F+S	μ = 0.6, PO₄	7.4	25	3.9	0.00	....	32
66	*Phascolosoma agassizii*	Free solution	μ = 0.2, PO₄	7.23	13	2.7	0.00	1.0 [-17]	24
	Siphonosoma ingens	Free solution							
67		Coelomic	μ = 0.2, PO₄	....	18.5	1.8	....	1.0	28
68		Vascular	μ = 0.2, PO₄	....	18.5	1.0	....	1.0	28
69	*Sipunculus nudus*	Free solution	0.015 M PO₄	6-9	.....	3.5	0.0	1.0 [-13.5]	3
70	*Themiste pyroides (Dendrostomum pyroides)*	Free solution	0.1 M PO₄	7.5	25	4-5	....	1.0	7
	Brachiopoda								
71	*Lingula unguis*	Free solution	μ = 0.2, PO₄	6.7	22-24	16	....	1.0	29
72				7.6	22-24	7.5	Normal [24]	1.7-1.8	29
			Chlorocruorin						
	Annelida								
73	*Pharusa inflata (Stylarioides inflata)*	Free solution	PO₄	7.48	20	27	-0.92	4-5	33
74	*Spirographis spallanzanii*	Free solution	0.1 M Tris	7.5	20	44.6	-0.45	Fn [25] [4-5]	1

[12] 0.01 M Mg²⁺. [13] Drops to 0 at low and high pH values. [14] For pH 5.3-6.6. [15] For pH 6.7-8.0. [16] 80 mM Ca²⁺. [17] pH is adjusted with lactic acid. [18] Highest n values at higher O_2 saturation levels. [19] For pH 7.2-7.7. [20] Nonlinear Hill plot. [21] <1 at higher pH values and in presence of Ca²⁺ or Mg²⁺. [22] Reverse Bohr effect below pH 7.8 as Hill plot becomes hyperbolic. [23] Increasing P_{CO_2} caused decline in O_2-binding power. [24] Approximately two-thirds the value for man. [25] At high and low O_2 saturation levels, n = 1.0.

Contributor: Sullivan, J. Bolling

References

[1] Antonini, E., et al. 1962. Arch. Biochem. Biophys. 97:336.

[2] Ar, A., and A. Schejter. 1970. Comp. Biochem. Physiol. 33:481.

continued

[3] Bates, G., et al. 1968. Biochemistry 7:3016.
[4] Cosgrove, W. B., and J. B. Schwartz. 1965. Physiol. Zool. 38:206.
[5] DeJangmah, J. S., and D. J. Grove. 1971. Comp. Biochem. Physiol. 38A:461.
[6] DePhillips, H. A., et al. 1969. Biochemistry 8: 3665.
[7] Ferrell, R. E., and G. B. Kitto. 1970. Ibid. 9:3053.
[8] Florkin, M. 1969. In M. Florkin and B. T. Scheer, ed. Chemical Zoology. Academic Press, New York. v. 4, p. 111.
[9] Ghiretti, F. 1962. In O. Hayaishi, ed. Oxygenases. Academic Press, New York. pp. 517-553.
[10] Ghiretti, F. 1966. In K. M. Wilbur and C. M. Yonge, ed. Physiology of Mollusca. Academic Press, New York. v. 2, pp. 233-248.
[11] Haughton, T. M., et al. 1958. J. Exp. Biol. 35:360.
[12] Hoffman, R. J., and C. P. Mangum. 1970. Comp. Biochem. Physiol. 36:211.
[13] Horne, F. R., and K. W. Beyenbach. 1971. Amer. J. Physiol. 220:1875.
[14] Hoshi, T., et al. 1968. Sci. Rep. Niigata Univ. Ser. D. (Biol.) 5:87.
[15] Hoshi, T., et al. 1969. Ibid. 6:155.
[16] Hwang, J. C., and C. P. Fung. 1970. Comp. Biochem. Physiol. 37:573.
[17] Johnston, W., et al. 1967. Ibid. 22:261.
[18] Jones, J. D. 1955. J. Exp. Biol. 32:110.
[19] Jones, J. D. 1963. Probl. Biol. 1:9.
[20] Keilin, D. 1960. Acta Biochim. Pol. 7:415.
[21] Konings, W. N., et al. 1969. Biochim. Biophys. Acta 194:55.
[22] Lenfant, C., and K. Johansen. 1965. Amer. J. Physiol. 209:991.
[23] Manwell, C. 1958. J. Cell. Comp. Physiol. 52:341.
[24] Manwell, C. 1958. Science 127:592.
[25] Manwell, C. 1959. J. Cell. Comp. Physiol. 53:61.
[26] Manwell, C. 1960. Annu. Rev. Physiol. 22:191.
[27] Manwell, C. 1960. Arch. Biochem. Biophys. 89: 194.
[28] Manwell, C. 1960. Comp. Biochem. Physiol. 1:267.
[29] Manwell, C. 1960. Science 132:550.
[30] Manwell, C. 1961. In C. L. Prosser and F. A. Brown, Jr., ed. Comparative Animal Physiology. Ed. 2. W. B. Saunders, Philadelphia. p. 198.
[31] Manwell, C. 1963. Comp. Biochem. Physiol. 8:209.
[32] Manwell, C. 1963. Science 139:755.
[33] Manwell, C. 1964. Oxygen Anim. Organism Proc. Symp. 1963, p. 49.
[34] Miller, P. L. 1966. J. Exp. Biol. 44:529.
[35] Palmer, M. F., and G. Chapman. 1970. J. Zool. 161: 203.
[36] Pickett, S. M., et al. 1966. Science 151:1005.
[37] Read, K. R. H. 1966. In K. M. Wilbur and C. M. Yonge, ed. Physiology of Mollusca. Academic Press, New York. v. 2, pp. 209-232.
[38] Redmond, J. R. 1962. Biol. Bull. 122:252.
[39] Redmond, J. R. 1962. Physiol. Zool. 35:304.
[40] Redmond, J. R. 1963. Science 139:1294.
[41] Rossi-Fanelli, A., et al. 1958. Symp. Protein Struct. Proc., 1957, p. 144.
[42] Scheler, W. 1960. Biochem. Z. 332:366.
[43] Sick, H., and K. Gersonde. 1969. Eur. J. Biochem. 7:273.
[44] Smith, M. H., and D. L. Lee. 1963. Proc. Roy. Soc. B157:234.
[45] Weber, R. E. 1970. Comp. Biochem. Physiol. 35: 179.
[46] Weber, R. E. 1971. Neth. J. Sea Res. 5:240.
[47] Wittenberg, B. A., et al. 1965. Biochem. J. 96:363.

216. OXYGEN CONSUMPTION: INVERTEBRATES

Part I. Effect of Age, Sex, Size, and Stage of Development

Variable: Q_{O_2} = weight-specific oxygen consumption, in µl $O_2 \cdot mg^{-1} \cdot hr^{-1}$, unless otherwise specified; a = oxygen consumption (at the y-intercept) in µl $O_2 \cdot hr^{-1}$ for a whole animal of unit weight (1 g); b = regression coefficient (slope) of the change in total oxygen consumption (O_2) with changing body weight (W), or dry weight ([W]), in the equation $O_2 = aW^b$. Because metabolism usually increases with weight in a proportionality of less than unity, conversion of $O_2 = aW^b$ to the weight specific form, $Q_{O_2} = aW^{b-1}$, in most cases yields a negative slope value, $b-1$. **Wet Weight Value:** r = correlation coefficient. Data in brackets refer to the column heading in brackets. Values in parentheses are ranges, estimate "c" (*see* Introduction).

	Class & Species [Locality]	Stage & Sex	No. of Determinations	Ambient Temp °C	Weight [Dry Weight]	Variable	Wet Weight Value[1/] [Dry Weight Value]	Remarks	Reference
			Echinodermata						
	Asteroidea								
1	*Asterias rubens*	Mature	5	15	10 g	Q_{O_2}	0.40	*b* value calculated from original data by Farmanfarmaian	3
2					....	*a*	200		
3					....	*b*	0.31		

1/ Unless otherwise indicated.

continued

Part I. Effect of Age, Sex, Size, and Stage of Development

	Class & Species [Locality]	Stage & Sex	No. of Determinations	Ambient Temp °C	Weight [Dry Weight]	Variable	Wet Weight Value [Dry Weight Value]	Remarks	Reference
4 5	Echinoidea *Eucidaris tribuloides* [Elliott Key, Florida]	Mature	12	20	[1 g] [(0.3-4.2) g]	Q_{O_2} b	[0.4] 0.70	Measurements made in winter; weight based on dried, decalcified tissue; CO_2 not absorbed in seawater medium; pH not checked	17
6 7	Holothuroidea *Parastichopus japonicus*[2] [Pusan, Korea]	Mature	5	8.5	50 g (15-75) g	Q_{O_2} b	0.004 0.87	....	3
8 9			11	13.5	50 g (12-75) g	Q_{O_2} b	0.006 0.73		
	Arthropoda								
10 11	Crustacea *Acartia clausi* [Long Island Sound]	Mature	20	20	[4.19 mg/1000 copepods] [(3.80-7.27) mg/ 1000 copepods]	Q_{O_2} b	[6.79] 0.819	Regression equation for grouped data of 7 copepod species: $y = 13.2[W]^{0.856}(r = 0.831)$	2
12 13	*Artemia salina* [San Francisco Bay]	All stages	33	25	.... [(0.032-0.57) mg]	a b	[101] 0.754(r = 0.93)	....	20
14 15		♂	20	25	.... [(0.02-0.45) mg]	Q_{O_2} b	[1.0 ± 0.039(SE)] 0.883	Seawater concentration = 35‰	5
16 17					.... [(0.02-0.45) mg]	Q_{O_2} b	[1.0 ± 0.054(SE)] 0.624	Seawater concentration = 140‰	5
18 19		♀	20	25	.... [(0.03-0.40) mg]	Q_{O_2} b	[1.0 ± 0.083(SE)] 0.604	Seawater concentration = 35‰	4
20 21					.... [(0.03-0.40) mg]	Q_{O_2} b	[1.0 ± 0.041(SE)] 0.721	Seawater concentration = 140‰	4
22	*Daphnia pulex* [Ann Arbor, Michigan]	All stages	32	20	[(0.0027- 0.0460) mg]	b	0.881	Water bottle & Warburg methods comparable	22
23 24 25	*Homarus americanus* [Gulf of Maine]	Lobster-like stages	22	15	500 g .... (0.9-12,300) g	Q_{O_2} a b	0.024 85 0.88	Value of a given in reference probably 10 times actual value	16
26 27 28	*Pachygrapsus crassipes* [Palos Verdes, California]	Mature	22	8.5	10.0 g .... (3.0-33.0) g	Q_{O_2} a b	0.016 36.2 ± 2 SE [3] 0.665(r = 0.942)	Starved 16 da before respiration measurements; Q_{O_2} values calculated from weight-specific regression equations	23
29 30 31			24	23.5	10.0 g .... (3.0-33.0) g	Q_{O_2} a b	0.078 145 ± 10%(2 SE) 0.730(r = 0.981)		
32 33 34			26	16	10.0 g .... (3.0-40.0) g	Q_{O_2} a b	0.035 75.8 ± 2 SE [4] 0.664(r = 0.956)		
35 36 37	*Palaemonetes vulgaris* [Arkansas Pass, Texas]	Shrimp-like stages	34	20	300 mg .... (25-350) mg	Q_{O_2} a $b-1$	0.23 [5] 150 -0.37	No specific interaction between salinity & temperature found from pooled regression analysis	15

[2] Synonym: *Stichopus japonicus*. [3] 2 SE = +18%, −15% (unequal because metabolism:size relationship is logarithmic). [4] 2 SE = +15%, −13% (unequal because metabolism: size relationship is logarithmic). [5] Salinity data pooled.

continued

Part I. Effect of Age, Sex, Size, and Stage of Development

	Class & Species [Locality]	Stage & Sex	No. of Determinations	Ambient Temp °C	Weight [Dry Weight]	Variable	Wet Weight Value [L] [Dry Weight Value]	Remarks	Reference
38	*Uca pugilator* [Beaufort, North Carolina]	Zoea, 1 da	21	25	0.328 µg N	Q_{O_2}	0.0831 [6] ± 0.0035 (SE)	Laboratory-reared at 25°C; Q_{O_2} determined from group of 20 individuals in single Warburg flask	27
39		Megalops	19	25	0.360 mg	Q_{O_2}	1.207 ± 0.117(SE)	Laboratory-reared at 25°C	27
40		Young crab	6	25	0.676 mg	Q_{O_2}	1.036 ± 0.0535(SE)	Laboratory-reared at 25°C	27
41		Mature	63	28	2.35(0.95-4.87) g	Q_{O_2}	0.0800(0.0484-0.1484)	Range of Q_{O_2} covers weight range	26
42 43	[Georgia salt marshes]	Crab stages	19	29.9 35 [7]	.... (0.004-2.5) mg	Q_{O_2} $b-1$	0.146 ± 0.025(SD) −0.227($r = −0.956$)	Q_{O_2} value adjusted for animal of standard size (size not given)	25
	Annelida								
	Hirudinea [8]								
44 45	*Erpobdella octoculata* [Berkshire, England]	Immature to mature	20	20	30 mg (12-104) mg	Q_{O_2} b	0.133 1.06	2-6 leeches used for each determination [9]	14
46 47	*Glossiphonia complanata* [Berkshire, England]	Immature to mature	40	20	30 mg (4-94) mg	Q_{O_2} b	0.165 0.715	2-6 leeches used for each determination [9]	14
	Oligochaeta								
48 49	*Eisenia foetida* [Münster, Germany]	Immature to mature	24	15	(11-840) mg	a b	41 0.659	b value derived from slope angle of 33.4°	7
50 51	*Lumbricus terrestris* [Vienna, Austria]	Mature	....	20	(0.2-2.5) g	Q_{O_2} b	0.082 0.67	....	18
	Polychaeta								
52 53 54	*Arenicola marina* [Helgoland, Germany]	Mature	50	15	1 g .... (0.104-14.17) g	Q_{O_2} a b	0.062 62.01 0.77	Measurements made in autumn; b value varies seasonally from 0.7 (summer) to 0.8	9
55 56 57	*Clymenella torquata* [Vineyard Sound, Massachusetts]	Immature to mature	21	23.5	100 mg .... (7.6-223) mg	Q_{O_2} a b	0.197 59.3 0.478	5-50 worms used for each determination [9]	13
	Mollusca								
	Cephalopoda								
58 59 60	*Octopus cyanea* [Oahu, Hawaii]	All stages	28	24.5-27.5	1 g .... (0.570-2300) g	Q_{O_2} a b	0.279 279 0.833($r > 0.9$)	No influence of sex detected	12

[L] Unless otherwise indicated. [6] $\mu l\ O_2 \cdot \mu g\ N^{-1} \cdot hr^{-1}$. [7] Probable temperature for regression determinations. [8] b value for *Erpobdella testacea*, 0.81; *Helobdella stagnalis*, 0.81; *Piscicola geometra*, 0.695. [9] For a large range of sizes, it was often necessary to make group measurements on several smaller animals to obtain significantly large values; where animals were of sufficient size, reliable measurements could be made on individuals.

continued

Part I. Effect of Age, Sex, Size, and Stage of Development

	Class & Species [Locality]	Stage & Sex	No. of Determinations	Ambient Temp °C	Weight [Dry Weight]	Variable	Wet Weight Value [Dry Weight Value]	Remarks	Reference
	Bivalvia								
61	*Mercenaria mercenaria* [New Jersey estuaries]	Mature	31	25	1 g	Q_{O_2}	0.106	....	11
62					....	a	106		
63					(4.95-284) g	$b-1$	−0.344($r = -0.906$)		
64			33	25	1 g	Q_{O_2}	0.385	Total wet weight with shell	6
65					....	a	385		
66					(13.0-378) g	b	0.399($r = 0.72$)		
67					1 g	Q_{O_2}	0.89	Wet weight of drained meats without shell	6
68					....	a	890		
69					(1.11-51.6) g	b	0.379($r = 0.71$)		
70					[1 g]	Q_{O_2}	[1.80]	Dry weight of drained meats without shell	6
71					....	a	18,000		
72					[(0.156-7.80) g]	b	[0.379($r = 0.69$)]		
73	*Mytilus edulis* [Gloucester, Massachusetts]	Mature	30	15.8	[1 g]	Q_{O_2}	[0.712(0.449-1.128)]	b value varies with temperature from 0.546 to 0.745	21
74					....	a	[712]		
75					[(0.2-10) g]	b	0.635($r = 0.931$)		
76	[Sylt, Schleswig-Holstein, Germany]	Mature	50	15	1 g	Q_{O_2}	0.0765	Measurements made in January; b value varies seasonally from 0.70 to 0.93	8
77						a	76.5		
78					0.0189-8.34 g	b	0.79		
	Gastropoda								
79	*Crepidula fornicata* [Sylt, Schleswig-Holstein, Germany]	Immature to mature	30	15	1.0 g	Q_{O_2}	0.0272	Shell-free wet weight	10
80					....	a	27.2		
81					(0.03-8) g	b	0.852($r = 0.9908$)		
82	*Helix pomatia* [Germany]	Immature to mature	....	20	0.1 g	Q_{O_2}	0.27	b value grouped with 4 snails in same & other subclasses	24
83					(0.134-39.5) g	b	0.76		
84	*Littorina littorea* [Kent, England]	Immature to mature	9	11	[100 mg]	Q_{O_2}	[0.13 [10/]]	Standard rate in January	19
85					....	$b-1$	−0.77($r = 0.886$)		
86				12.5	[100 mg]	Q_{O_2}	[0.22]	Standard rate in May	
87					....	$b-1$	−0.36($r = 0.905$)		Marked seasonal differences in $b-1$ between May and earlier months
88			11	11	[100 mg]	Q_{O_2}	[0.75]	Active rate in January	
89					....	$b-1$	−0.70($r = 0.937$)		
90			15	12.5	[100 mg]	Q_{O_2}	[1.20]	Active rate in May	
91					....	$b-1$	−0.53($r = 0.868$)		
92	*Lymnaea palustris* [Jutland, Denmark]	Mature	15	18	....	a	161 ± 4%(SD)	Measurements made in June	1
93					(40-200) mg	b	0.761		Marked seasonal differences also among other pulmonates & opisthobranchs
94			24	18	....	a	1750 ± 4%(SD)	Measurements made in August	
95					(40-200) mg	b	0.452		

10/ Rates are estimates read from text figures.

continued

Part I. Effect of Age, Sex, Size, and Stage of Development

	Class & Species [Locality]	Stage & Sex	No. of Determinations	Ambient Temp °C	Weight [Dry Weight]	Variable	Wet Weight Value [Dry Weight Value]	Remarks	Reference
					Platyhelminthes				
96 97	Turbellaria *Crenobia alpina* [Westmorland, England]	Mature	96	14.5	10 mg (1.5-17.0) mg	Q_{O_2} $b-1$	0.120 ± 6.6%(SE) -0.34	1-5 animals used for each determination 9/	28
98 99	*Polycelis felina* 11/ [Worcestershire, England]	Mature	28	14.5	10 mg (1.6-9.8) mg	Q_{O_2} $b-1$	0.170 ± 6.6%(SE) -0.18	1-3 animals used for each determination 9/	28

9/ For a large range of sizes, it was often necessary to make group measurements on several smaller animals to obtain significantly large values; where animals were of sufficient size, reliable measurements could be made on individuals. 11/ Synonym: *P. cornuta*.

Contributor: Roberts, John L.

References

[1] Berg, K., and K. W. Ockelmann. 1959. J. Exp. Biol. 36:690.
[2] Conover, R. J. 1959. Limnol. Oceanogr. 4:259.
[3] Farmanfarmaian, A. 1966. Physiol. Echinodermata, p. 245.
[4] Gilchrist, B. M. 1956. Hydrobiologia 8:54.
[5] Gilchrist, B. M. 1958. Ibid. 12:27.
[6] Hamwi, A. 1969. Ph.D. Thesis. Rutgers Univ., New Brunswick, N.J.
[7] Krüger, F. 1952. Z. Vergl. Physiol. 34:1.
[8] Krüger, F. 1960. Helgolaender Wiss. Meeresunters. 7:125.
[9] Krüger, F. 1964. Ibid. 10:38.
[10] Krüger, F. 1970. Mar. Biol. 5:145.
[11] Loveland, R. E., and D. S. K. Chu. 1969. Comp. Biochem. Physiol. 29:173.
[12] Maginniss, L. A., and M. J. Wells. 1969. J. Exp. Biol. 51:607.
[13] Mangum, C. P. 1963. Comp. Biochem. Physiol. 10: 335.
[14] Mann, K. H. 1956. J. Exp. Biol. 33:615.
[15] McFarland, W. N., and P. E. Pickens. 1965. Can. J. Zool. 43:571.
[16] McLeese, D. W. 1964. Helgolaender Wiss. Meeresunters. 10:7.
[17] McPherson, B. F. 1968. Biol. Bull. 135:308.
[18] Müller, I. 1943. Biol. Zentralbl. 63:446.
[19] Newell, R. C., and V. I. Pye. 1971. J. Mar. Biol. Ass. U.K. 51:315.
[20] Packard, T. T., and P. B. Taylor. 1968. Limnol. Oceanogr. 13:552.
[21] Read, K. R. H. 1962. Comp. Biochem. Physiol. 7: 89.
[22] Richman, S. 1958. Ecol. Monogr. 28:273.
[23] Roberts, J. L., 1957. Physiol. Zool. 30:232.
[24] Schwartzkopff, J., and H. Wesemeier. 1959. Naturwissenschaften 46(8):272.
[25] Teal, J. M. 1959. Physiol. Zool. 32:1.
[26] Vernberg, F. J. 1959. Biol. Bull. 117:163.
[27] Vernberg, F. J., and J. D. Costlow, Jr. 1966. Physiol. Zool. 39:36.
[28] Whitney, R. J. 1942. J. Exp. Biol. 19:168.

Part II. Effect of Removal and Replacement of Neuroendocrine Tissues

Values are averages. Plus/minus (±) values are standard error.

	Class & Species	Stage & Sex	Temp °C	Type of Operation	Oxygen Consumption $\mu l \cdot g^{-1} \cdot hr^{-1}$ Control	Experimental	Reference
1 2	Crustacea *Astacus* sp.	....	....	Bilateral removal of eyestalk Bilateral removal of sinus gland	61.7 30.6 ± 8.3	77.7 30.2 ± 8.3	5

continued

Part II. Effect of Removal and Replacement of Neuroendocrine Tissues

	Class & Species	Stage & Sex	Temp °C	Type of Operation	Oxygen Consumption $\mu l \cdot g^{-1} \cdot hr^{-1}$		Reference
					Control	Experimental	
3	*Gecarcinus lateralis*	....	25	Bilateral removal of eyestalk	49	100[1/]	1
4		....		Bilateral removal of sinus gland	49	46[1/]	1
5	*Sesarma reticulata*	Adult ♂	25	Bilateral removal of eyestalk	57.4 ± 4.7	86.6 ± 2.8[2/]	8
6				Bilateral removal of Y organ	57.4 ± 4.7	53.2 ± 2.7[3/]	
7				Bilateral removal of eyestalk & Y organ	57.4 ± 4.7	94.4 ± 6.0[4/]	
8	*Uca pugilator*[5/]	....	20	Bilateral removal of eyestalk	39	66	3
9	*U. pugilator*[6/]	....	20	Bilateral removal of eyestalk	49	108	3
10				Eyestalk extract injected into animals without eyestalks	97	75	
11	*U. pugnax*	....	20	Bilateral removal of eyestalk	41	69	3
	Insecta						
12	*Blaberus discoidalis*	Adult ♂	25	Allatectomy	204	190[1/]	6
13				Allatectomy & cardiatectomy	204	158[1/]	
14	*Calliphora vicina*[7/]	Adult ♀	25	Allatectomy	1674 ± 54	1278 ± 54	14
15				Reimplantation of active corpora allata	....	1578 ± 60	
16	*Carausius morosus*	Adult ♀	25	Allatectomy & cardiatectomy	452 ± 12	388 ± 12	7
17	*Leptinotarsa decemlineata*	Adult ♀	25	Allatectomy	1253 ± 46	263 ± 46	15
18	*Leucophaea maderae*	Adult ♀	26	Implantation of active corpora allata	326 ± 18	443 ± 2[8/]	11
19	*Locusta migratoria*	5th instar nymph[9/]	29	Implantation of corpora allata	1040-1060	889-960	9
20		Adult ♀	29	Allatectomy	500	375	10
21	*Pyrrhocoris apterus*	Adult ♂	25	Allatectomy	480	470	12
22				Allatectomy & cardiatectomy	480	452	
23		♀	25	Allatectomy	480	430	13
24				Reimplantation of corpora allata	480	900	
25	*Tenebrio molitor*	Adult ♂	25	Allatectomy	786 ± 32	736 ± 43	4
26		♀	25	Allatectomy	745 ± 179	558 ± 118	4
	Polychaeta						
27	*Nereis diversicolor*	Adult ♀, young	15	Removal of prostomium	700	1250	2

[1/] Measurements made 30 days after operation. [2/] Measurements made not less than 14 days after operation; crabs fed. [3/] Measurements made not less than 30 days after operation; crabs fed. [4/] Measurements made not less than 14 days after removal of eyestalks; Y organs previously removed; crabs fed. [5/] From Florida. [6/] From Woods Hole, Massachusetts. [7/] Synonym: *C. erythrocephala*. [8/] Measurements made 3-5 days after operation. [9/] Gregarious phase.

Contributor: Engelmann, Franz

References

[1] Bliss, D. E. 1953. Biol. Bull. 104:275.
[2] Dhainaut, A. 1966. C. R. Soc. Biol. 160:1002.
[3] Edwards, G. A. 1950. Physiol. Comp. Oecol. 2:34.
[4] El-Ibrashy, M. T. 1965. Meded. Landbouwhogesch. Wageningen 65:1.
[5] Frost, R., et al. 1951. Anat. Rec. 111:572.
[6] Keeley, L. L., and S. Friedman. 1967. Gen. Comp. Endocrinol. 8:129.
[7] Neugebauer, W. 1961. Wilhelm Roux Arch. Entwicklungsmech. Organismen 153:314.

[8] Passano, L. M., and S. Jyssum. 1963. Comp. Biochem. Physiol. 9:195.
[9] Roussel, J. P. 1963. J. Insect. Physiol. 9:349.
[10] Roussel, J. P. 1963. Ibid. 9:721.
[11] Sägesser, H. 1960. Ibid. 5:264.
[12] Slama, K. 1964. Biol. Bull. 127:499.
[13] Slama, K., and H. Hrubesova. 1963. Zool. Jahrb. Abt. Allg. Zool. Physiol. Tiere 70:291.
[14] Thomsen, E. 1949. J. Exp. Biol. 26:137.
[15] Wilde, J. de, and D. Stegwee. 1958. Arch. Neer. Zool. 13(Suppl. 1):277.

continued

Part III. Effect of Variation in Temperature

Data in brackets refer to the column heading in brackets.

	Class & Species [Habitat]	Illumi-nation	Specification	Method	Temp °C	Oxygen Consumption		Ref-er-ence
						Value	Unit of Measurement	
	Echinodermata							
1	Echinoidea *Strongylocentro-*	....	....	Manometer	5; 10	0.0078	ml·g wet wt^{-1}·hr^{-1}	4
2	*tus purpuratus*				15	0.0130		
3	[Marine]				20	0.0261		
	Arthropoda							
4	Crustacea *Acartia clausi*	....	....	Manometer	10	0.065 ± 0.0055	μl·animal^{-1}·hr^{-1}	5
5	[Marine]				13	0.061 ± 0.006		
6					17	0.073 ± 0.005		
7					20	0.107 ± 0.006		
8	*Calanus finmar-*	....	♂	Winkler	0	0.20	μl·animal^{-1}·hr^{-1}	8
9	*chicus* [Ma-				5	0.26		
10	rine]				10	0.38		
11					15	0.61-0.62		
12					20	0.61		
13			♀	Winkler	0	0.58		
14					5	0.28		
15					10	0.31		
16					15	0.40-0.57		
17					20	0.83		
18			Larva, stage V	Winkler	0	0.13		
19					5	0.17		
20					10	0.25		
21					15	0.41-0.46		
22					20	0.61		
23	*Diaptomus ore-*	....	♀; 1.01 mm	Micro-Winkler	5	0.023	μl·animal^{-1}·hr^{-1}	2
24	*gonensis*				10	0.026		
25	[Freshwater]				15	0.042		
26					20	0.064		
27					25	0.098		
28	*Hemigrapsus*	Dark	....	Scholander microres-pirometer	10 ± 0.1	0.032	ml·g wet wt^{-1}·hr^{-1}	3
29	*nudus* [Ma-				20 ± 0.1	0.070		
30	rine]				30 ± 0.1	0.042		
31	*Metamysidopsis elongata* [Ma-rine]	....	Juveniles; 0.03 mg average dry wt	Polaro-graphic O$_2$ electrode	13.8 [1,2]	7.71	μl O$_2$·mg dry wt^{-1}·hr^{-1}	1
32			♂; 0.31 mg aver-age dry wt	Polaro-graphic O$_2$ electrode	13.8 [1,2]	3.60		
33			Immature, ♀; 0.28 mg aver-age dry wt	Polaro-graphic O$_2$ electrode	15.2 [1,2]	1.95		
34			Brooding, ♀; 0.47 mg aver-age dry wt	Polaro-graphic O$_2$ electrode	13.8 [1,2]	3.22		

[1] Acclimation temperature. [2] Experimental temperature.

continued

Part III. Effect of Variation in Temperature

	Class & Species [Habitat]	Illumination	Specification	Method	Temp °C	Oxygen Consumption		Reference
						Value	Unit of Measurement	
35	*Orconectes immunis* [Freshwater]	Reduced light	1.8 g average wt	Winkler	16	0.044	ml·g wet wt^{-1}·hr^{-1}	16
36					24	0.139		
37					30	0.212		
38					35	0.179		
39			3.45 g average wt	Winkler	16	0.064		
40					24	0.105		
41					30	0.114		
42					35	0.115		
43			8.37 g average wt	Winkler	16	0.068		
44					24	0.113		
45					30	0.124		
46					35	0.113		
47	*Panulirus interruptus* [Marine]	Dark	4-9 cm	O$_2$ electrode	12.5	0.0396	ml·g wet wt^{-1}·hr^{-1}	17
48					12.6	0.0351		
49					12.8	0.0766		
50					12.9	0.0585		
51					13.0	0.0319		
52					15.5	0.0521		
53					15.9	0.0429		
54					16.0	0.0492		
55					16.1	0.0539		
56					19.6	0.0654		
57					19.7	0.0578		
58					19.9	0.0876		
	Insecta							
59	*Acroneuria pacifica* [3] [Freshwater]	Light	Larva; 0.05-0.08 g dry wt	Warburg	5	0.498	ml·g dry wt^{-1}·hr^{-1}	7
60					10	0.747		
61					15	0.874		
62					20	0.864		
63					25	1.148		
64					30	1.316		
65			Adult, ♂; 0.0238 g average dry wt	Warburg	10	1.204		
66			Adult, ♀; 0.056 g average dry wt	Warburg	10	0.746		
67	*Anax junius* [3] [Freshwater]	Reduced light	Larva, ♂; 0.085-0.150 g dry wt	Differential respirometer	13	0.373-0.448	ml·g dry wt^{-1}·hr^{-1}	11
68					20	0.722-0.851		
69					27	1.411-1.436		
70					34	1.890-1.948		
71			Larva, ♀; 0.085-0.150 g dry wt	Differential respirometer	13	0.392-0.464		
72					20	0.701-0.799		
73					27	1.455-1.486		
74					34	2.165-2.173		
75			Adult, ♂; 0.168 g average dry wt	Differential respirometer	30	7.000		
76			Adult, ♀; 0.174 g average dry wt	Differential respirometer	30	7.269		

[3] O$_2$ consumption values for different sizes of the same species may be found in the given reference.

continued

Part III. Effect of Variation in Temperature

	Class & Species [Habitat]	Illumi-nation	Specification	Method	Temp °C	Oxygen Consumption		Ref-er-ence
						Value	Unit of Measurement	
	Mollusca							
	Gastropoda							
77	*Bithynia leachi*	Dark	....	Polarimeter	10 ± 1	85	$\mu l \cdot animal^{-1} \cdot hr^{-1}$	9
78	[Freshwater]				15 ± 1	127		
79	*Fimbria fim-*	....	....	Gas ana-lyzer	16	0.012	$ml \cdot g$ wet $wt^{-1} \cdot hr^{-1}$	14
80	*bria* [4] [Fresh-water]				20	0.015		
81	*Limax flavus*	....	....	....	0	0.047	$ml \cdot g^{-1} \cdot hr^{-1}$	12
82	[Marine]				10	0.10		
83					20	0.185		
84					30	0.225		
85	*Littorina lit-*	....	....	Volumetric gas ana-lyzer	−10	0.0002	$ml \cdot g$ wet $wt^{-1} \cdot hr^{-1}$	6
86	*torea* [Marine]				0	0.020		
87					10	0.070		
88					20	0.145		
89					30	0.070		
	Nematoda							
	Adenophorea							
90	*Eustrongylides*	....	Medium size	Warburg	5	0.009 ± 0.0008	$ml \cdot g^{-1} \cdot hr^{-1}$	15
91	sp. [Marine]				10	0.0182 ± 0.0006		
92					17	0.034 ± 0.0034		
93					22	0.070 ± 0.0082		
94					27	0.108 ± 0.0114		
95					32	0.128 ± 0.020		
96					37	0.152 ± 0.008		
97					42	0.190 ± 0.016		
98					45	0.226 ± 0.010		
99					48	0.262 ± 0.026		
	Platyhelminthes							
	Trematoda							
	Zoogonus rubellus							13
100	[Marine [5]]	....	Cercaria; average	Cartesian diver	6	3.9 ± 0.4	$ml \cdot g$ $N^{-1} \cdot hr^{-1}$	
101			8.4×10^{-8} g		12	5.2 ± 0.5		
102			N/worm		18	14.5 ± 1.3		
103					24	15.6 ± 1.4		
104					30	32.7 ± 2.0		
105					36	26.8 ± 2.0		
106	[Marine [6]]	....	Sporocyst; aver-	Cartesian diver	6	1.3 ± 0.1		
107			age 1.29 ×		12	1.8 ± 0.2		
108			10^{-6} g N/worm		18	4.1 ± 0.2		
109					24	4.2 ± 0.4		
110					30	10.2 ± 0.6		
111					36	9.6 ± 0.8		
	Protozoa							
	Rhizopodea							
112	*Amoeba chaos*	....	....	Warburg	15 ± 0.05	$(5.040 ± 0.85) \times 10^{-3}$	$\mu l \cdot animal^{-1} \cdot hr^{-1}$	10
113	*chaos* [Fresh-water]				20 ± 0.05	$(7.080 ± 0.827) \times 10^{-3}$		
114					25 ± 0.05	$(9.010 ± 0.910) \times 10^{-3}$		
115					30 ± 0.05	$(13.244 ± 1.760) \times 10^{-3}$		
116					35 ± 0.05	$(17.749 ± 1.540) \times 10^{-3}$		

[4] Synonym: *Tethys leporina.* [5] Free-living. [6] Parasitic on *Ilyanassa obsoleta (Nassarius obsoletus).*

continued

216. OXYGEN CONSUMPTION: INVERTEBRATES

Part III. Effect of Variation in Temperature

Contributors: Moshiri, Gerald A., Blanchard, Gwynn D., and Whiting, Nicholas H.; Knight, Allen W.

References

[1] Clutter, R. I., and G. H. Theilacker. 1971. U.S. Dep. Com. Nat. Mar. Fish. Serv. Fish Bull. 69:93.

[2] Comita, G. W. 1968. Limnol. Oceanogr. 13:51.

[3] Dehnel, P. A. 1960. Biol. Bull. 118:215.

[4] Farmanfarmaian, A., and A. C. Giese. 1963. Physiol. Zool. 36:237.

[5] Gauld, D. T., and J. E. G. Raymont. 1953. J. Mar. Biol. Ass. U.K. 31:447.

[6] Kanwisher, J. 1959. Biol. Bull. 116:258.

[7] Knight, A. W., and A. R. Gaufin. 1966. J. Insect Physiol. 12:347.

[8] Marshall, S. M., et al. 1935. J. Mar. Biol. Ass. U.K. 20:1.

[9] Moreira, G. S., and W. B. Vernberg. 1967. Mar. Biol. 282:284.

[10] Pace, D. M., and W. H. Belda. 1944. Biol. Bull. 86:146.

[11] Petitpren, M. F., and A. W. Knight. 1970. J. Insect Physiol. 16(3):449.

[12] Segal, E. 1961. Amer. Zool. 1:235.

[13] Vernberg, W. B. 1961. Exp. Parasitol. 11:270.

[14] Vernon, H. M. 1896. J. Physiol. (London) 19:18.

[15] von Brand, T. 1943. Biol. Bull. 84:148.

[16] Wiens, A. W., and K. B. Armitage. 1960. Physiol. Zool. 34:39.

[17] Winget, R. R. 1969. Biol. Bull. 136:301.

Part IV. Effect of Salinity Variation in External Medium

Oxygen Consumption: Values are for endogenous respiration. For general information, consult reference 14. Data in brackets refer to the column heading in brackets. Values in parentheses are ranges, estimate "c" (*see* Introduction).

	Class & Species	Normal Environmental Salinity ‰	Method	Temp °C	Experimental Salinity ‰	Oxygen Consumption μl·mg wet wt^{-1}·hr^{-1} [1] [μl·mg dry wt^{-1}·hr^{-1}]	Remarks	Reference
	— Echinodermata							
	Asteroidea							
1	*Asterias ru-*	15	Winkler	15	15	0.021 ± 0.002	....	2
2	*bens*				30	0.025 ± 0.002		
3		30	Winkler	15	30	0.014 ± 0.001	....	2
	Arthropoda							
	Crustacea							
4	*Acartia ton-*	Estua-	Modified	20	11.0	[31.906]	Great individual variation, so a	9
5	*sa*	rine	Winkler		14.7	[21.427]	standard determination was	
6		(vari-			18.2	[21.140]	made at 36.4‰ for each batch	
7		able)			21.9	[22.382]	of animals prior to exposure to	
8					25.5	[12.107]	experimental medium; no mor-	
9					29.2	[13.517]	tality until salinities ≯ 7.2‰	
10					33.0	[11.425]		
11					36.4	[12.361(9.037-15.845)]		
	Artemia salina							
12	Nauplius	35	Modified	16	10	0.166 [2]	Animals reared in the experimen-	4
13	larva		Winkler		35	0.145 [2]	tal medium	
14					50	0.096 [2]		
15	Intermedi-	35	Modified	16	10	0.083 [2]	Animals reared in the experimen-	4
16	ate		Winkler		35	0.093 [2]	tal medium	
17	form				50	0.083 [2]		

[1] Unless otherwise indicated. [2] μl O$_2$·μg N^{-1}·hr^{-1}.

continued

Part IV. Effect of Salinity Variation in External Medium

	Class & Species	Normal Environmental Salinity ‰	Method	Temp °C	Experimental Salinity ‰	Oxygen Consumption μl·mg wet wt^{-1}·hr^{-1} [1]/ [μl·mg dry wt^{-1}·hr^{-1}]	Remarks	Reference
18	♂, 0.1 mg	35	Winkler	....	35	[10.5]	Animals reared in the experimen-	7
19					140	[10.2]	tal medium	
20	0.2 mg	35	Winkler	....	35	[9.5]	Animals reared in the experimen-	7
21					140	[7.5]	tal medium	
22	0.3 mg	35	Winkler	....	35	[9.0]	Animals reared in the experimen-	7
23					140	[7.0]	tal medium	
24	♀, 0.1 mg	35	Winkler	25	35	[11.0]	Animals reared in the experimen-	6
25					140	[11.0]	tal medium	
26	0.2 mg	35	Winkler	25	35	[9.0]	Animals reared in the experimen-	6
27					140	[9.0]	tal medium	
28	0.3 mg	35	Winkler	25	35	[8.0]	Animals reared in the experimen-	6
29					140	[8.0]	tal medium	
30	Adult	35	Modified Winkler	16	10	0.055 [2]/	Animals reared in the experimen-	4
31					35	0.065 [2]/	tal medium	
32					50	0.050 [2]/		
33	*Astacus as-*	Fresh-	Winkler	17	Freshwater	0.034	....	16
34	*tacus* [3]/	water			15.00	0.024		
35	*Callinectes*	34–36	Warburg mano-metric	25	7.60	0.150	Normally tolerates brackish wa-	8
36	*sapidus*				38.00	0.097	ter of 7-12‰ salinity	
37	*Cyathura*	0.1–	Winkler	15	1.0	[0.96]	Animals placed in experimental	5
38	*polita*	28.9 [4]/			10.40	[0.63]	medium 24 hr before measure-	
39					21.70	[0.83]	ment	
40					27.60	[0.79]		
41					36.90	[1.00]		
42		21.2–	Winkler	15	1.02	[0.92]	Animals placed in experimental	5
43		29.0			8.63	[0.63]	medium 24 hr before measure-	
44					17.10	[0.50]	ment	
45					24.21	[0.83]		
46					35.94	[0.79]		
47	*Gammarus*	1.0–	Winkler	15	1.00	0.10 ± 0.007	....	18
48	*duebeni*	10.0			4.00	0.08 ± 0.008		
49					7.00	0.08 ± 0.009		
50					10.00	0.09 ± 0.015		
51					20.00	0.10 ± 0.028		
52	*Hemigrap-*	7.0–	Modified Scho-lander volu-metric	5	7.00	0.064	Acclimation temperatures given;	3
53	*sus nu-*	24.5			26.20	0.046	all O_2 measurements made at	
54	*dus*			10	7.00	0.040	10°C	
55					26.20	0.046		
56				20	7.00	0.028		
57					26.20	0.031		
58	*Palaemone-*	1.32	Winkler	15	0.17	0.74	Animals in experimental medium	10
59	*tes vari-*	aver-			4.59	0.19	24 hr before measurement; tol-	
60	*ans*	age,			12.17	0.22	erate freshwater & salinities	
61		sluice			29.52	0.42	<45‰; survival time short in	
62		pool			39.00	0.47	salinities >45‰	

[1]/ Unless otherwise indicated. [2]/ μl O_2·μg N^{-1}·hr^{-1}. [3]/ Synonym: *Potamobius fluviatilis*. [4]/ Water flooding beach.

continued

Part IV. Effect of Salinity Variation in External Medium

	Class & Species	Normal Environmental Salinity ‰	Method	Temp °C	Experimental Salinity ‰	Oxygen Consumption $\mu l \cdot mg$ wet $wt^{-1} \cdot hr^{-1}$ [1] [$\mu l \cdot mg$ dry $wt^{-1} \cdot hr^{-1}$]	Remarks	Reference
63		Salt marsh	Winkler	15	2.90	0.71	Animals in experimental medium 24 hr before measurement; survival times: 16 hr in freshwater, several days in 1.7‰ salinity, several wk in 60.0‰	10
64					6.00	0.72		
65					12.30	0.54		
66					17.40	0.43		
67					25.70	0.12		
68					34.30	0.26		
69					44.00	0.31		
70					59.20	0.42		
					Annelida			
71	Oligochaeta *Tubifex tubifex*	0-3.5	Warburg manometric	20	0	0.57 ± 0.03	Animals in experimental medium 24 hr before measurement	13
72					1.75	0.45 ± 0.02		
73					3.50	0.55 ± 0.02		
74					5.25	0.58 ± 0.04		
75					6.65	0.57 ± 0.03		
					Mollusca			
76	Bivalvia *Mytilus edulis*	15	Warburg manometric	15	15	1.380	....	15
77				15[5]	30	1.320	After 32 da, O_2 consumption changed to 0.800 $\mu l \cdot mg$ wet $wt^{-1} \cdot hr^{-1}$	
78				10[6]	30	1.020	After 28 da, O_2 consumption changed to 0.590 $\mu l \cdot mg$ wet $wt^{-1} \cdot hr^{-1}$	
79		30	Warburg manometric	15	30	0.820	....	15
80				15[5]	15	0.910	After 32 da, O_2 consumption changed to 1.440 $\mu l \cdot mg$ wet $wt^{-1} \cdot hr^{-1}$	
81				10[6]	15	0.610	After 49 da, O_2 consumption changed to 1.000 $\mu l \cdot mg$ wet $wt^{-1} \cdot hr^{-1}$	
82	Gastropoda *Potamopyrgus jenkinsi*	1.2-5.4	Polarographic	19[5]	Freshwater[7]	0.270	Animals in experimental medium 15-17 hr before measurement	12
83					Freshwater[8]	0.150		
84					5.4	0.200		
85		8.90-11.10	Polarographic	19[5]	Freshwater[8]	0.150	Animals in experimental medium 21 hr before measurement	11
86					11.10	0.200		
					Platyhelminthes			
87	Turbellaria *Procerodes ulvae*	35	Barcroft manometric	....	1.72	6.65[9]	Animals in experimental medium 20 min before measurement	1
88					3.43	6.60[9]		
89					8.60	5.30[9]		
90					11.40	5.20[9]		

[1] Unless otherwise indicated. [5] Summer. [6] Winter. [7] From river. [8] From marlpit. [9] $\mu l/hr$, since animal weight was not measured.

continued

Part IV. Effect of Salinity Variation in External Medium

	Class & Species	Normal Environmental Salinity ‰	Method	Temp °C	Experimental Salinity ‰	Oxygen Consumption $\mu l \cdot mg$ wet $wt^{-1} \cdot hr^{-1}$ [1] [$\mu l \cdot mg$ dry $wt^{-1} \cdot hr^{-1}$]	Remarks	Reference
91					17.20	4.00[2]		
92					22.90	3.05[2]		
93					28.60	3.15[2]		
94					35.00	2.83[2]		
	Coelenterata							
95	Anthozoa *Metridium senile*[10]	....	Mano-metric	....	10	0.15	Animals have some tolerance to brackish water	17
96					15	0.15		
97					30	(0.20-0.23)		
98					45	0.16		
99					60	0.15		

[1] Unless otherwise indicated. [2] $\mu l/hr$, since animal weight was not measured. [10] Synonym: *M. marginatum*.

Contributor: Palmer, Maureen F.

References

[1] Beadle, L. C. 1931. J. Exp. Biol. 8:211.

[2] Bock, K. J., and C. Schlieper. 1953. Kiel. Meeresforsch. 9:201.

[3] Dehnel, P. A. 1960. Biol. Bull. 118:215.

[4] Eliassen, E. 1953. Univ. Bergen Arbok Naturvitenskap. Rekke 11:3.

[5] Frankenberg, D., and W. D. Burbanck. 1963. Biol. Bull. 125:81.

[6] Gilchrist, B. M. 1956. Hydrobiologia 8:54.

[7] Gilchrist, B. M. 1958. Ibid. 12:27.

[8] King, E. N. 1965. Comp. Biochem. Physiol. 15:93.

[9] Lance, J. 1965. Ibid. 14:155.

[10] Lofts, B. 1956. J. Exp. Biol. 33:730.

[11] Lumbye, J. 1958. Hydrobiologia 10:245.

[12] Lumbye, J., et al. 1965. Ibid. 25:489.

[13] Palmer, M. F. 1968. J. Zool. 154:463.

[14] Potts, W. T. W., and G. Parry. 1964. Osmotic and Ionic Regulation in Animals. Pergamon Press, New York.

[15] Schlieper, C. 1955. Kiel. Meeresforsch. 11:22.

[16] Schwabe, E. 1933. Z. Vergl. Physiol. 19:183.

[17] Shoup, C. 1932. Ecology 13:81.

[18] Suomalainen, P. 1956. Verh. Int. Ver. Limnol. 13:873.

217. PROPERTIES OF CYTOCHROMES: HIGHER PLANTS

Cytochromes are intracellular chromoproteins—"chromo-", since they have a heme as their prosthetic group which absorbs light. The iron of the hemes undergoes a redox reaction during the normal physiological functioning. Almost all of the cytochromes are so tightly bound to the lipoprotein membranes of the mitochondria and the endoplasmic reticulum (microsomes) that they can be solubilized only with detergents or lipases. Higher plant cells contain two well-characterized electron transport systems: the respiratory chain of the mitochondria [11], and the photosynthetic electron transport system of the chloroplasts [5,6, 33]. The microsomal oxygen-activating and electron transport system has been demonstrated in higher plant tissue [25]. It has also been noted that plants having microsomes containing cytochrome b_{555} (b_5) also have cytochrome P-450 as microsomal pigment [25]. The functions of other intracellular b-type cytochromes have not been identified [11]. The mitochondrial respiratory chain of higher plants is essentially identical to that of mammalian mitochondria. However, plant mitochondria have also a cyanide-insensitive respiratory chain [3] that utilizes the same substrate dehydrogenase as the respiratory chain terminating with cytochrome c oxidase. The two chains separate in the region of ubiquinone or the b-type cytochromes. Plant

continued

mitochondria also have three instead of only two b-type cytochromes which belong to the respiratory chain [11]. Electron transport in the chloroplast [5,6,33] consists of the following sequence: photosystem II accepts a photon, extracts an electron from water, and reduces a component Q of unknown nature. This Q donates its electron to photosystem I (P-700) via cytochrome b_{559} and cytochrome f, phosphorylating one adenosine 5'-diphosphate (ADP) to adenosine 5'-triphosphate (ATP) for every two electrons transferred (noncyclic photophosphorylation). Photosystem I accepts a photon and reduces a pigment—ferredoxin-reducing substance (FRS), or cytochrome-reducing substance (CRS)—which may reduce ferredoxin, and which then, via ferredoxin NADP$^+$ reductase, yields the reduction of nicotinamide adenine dinucleotide phosphate (NADP$^+$). FRS (or CRS) and ferredoxin may also be oxidized by photosystem I via cytochrome b_6 (b_{563}) and phosphorylate one ADP in the process (cyclic photophosphorylation). Cyto-

chromes f, b_6, and b_{559} exist in approximately the ratios 1:2:2 [6]. **Physical & Chemical Properties:** mol wt = molecular weight; PG = prosthetic group; pI = isoelectric point; E_0' = oxidation-reduction midpoint potential at pH of approximately 7.0 unless otherwise specified; mV = millivolts. **Optical Absorption Spectra:** Δ = wavelength, in nanometers, of approximate maximal absorbency of difference spectrum between reduced and oxidized samples; **R** = wavelength, in nanometers, of maximal absorbency in the spectrum of reduced samples; **O** = wavelength, in nanometers, of maximal absorbency in the spectrum of oxidized samples; $[E_{1\,cm}^{mM}]$ = millimolar extinction coefficient, or absorbency of millimolar solutions of 1-cm thickness; λ_1, λ_2 = wavelengths, in nanometers, between which the difference in absorbency was measured for the specified extinction coefficient. Data in light brackets refer to the column heading in brackets. Figures in heavy brackets are reference numbers.

Cyto-chrome	Physical & Chemical Properties	Optical Absorption Spectra $[E_{1\,cm}^{mM}]$	Remarks
		Mitochondria	
1 c oxidase	E_0' = +380 mV for a_3; +190 mV for a [1/] [14]. Cytochrome c oxidase has many of the basic properties of mammalian cytochrome c oxidase [26].	Δ for a_3 = 605-601 [18,34]; 445 [2/] [2]. Δ for a = 605-601 [18,34]; 445 [2/], 438 [2/] [2].	Cytochrome c oxidase is the only CO-binding pigment in plant mitochondria [26]. Has not been purified.
2 c (c_{547})	Amino acid sequence is known [31]. E_0' = +235 mV [14]. Very similar properties to mammalian cytochrome c [16].	Δ = 547 [2/], 545 [2/], 515 [2/], 415 [2/] [21,23]. **R** = 550 [17].	Isolated from wheat germ; highly purified
3 c_{549} (c_1)	E_0' = +235 mV [14].	Δ = 549 [2/], 517 [2/] [23].	Detected spectrophotometrically only in saline-extracted mitochondria [23]. Spectral characterizations carried out with mitochondria from Jerusalem artichoke.
4 b_{553}	E_0' = +75 mV [14]. Kinetically identified [32].	Δ = 556 [32]; 553 [2/], 428 [2/] [23].	Kinetic studies done with mitochondria from hypocotyls of etiolated mung beans [32]. Spectral characterizations done with mitochondria from a variety of plant sources [23]. b_{557} partially purified from sweet-potato mitochondria [1]. Cytochromes b_{557} & b_7 may be identical [4,23].
5 b_{557} (b_7)	E_0' = +42 mV [14]. Kinetically identified [32].	Δ = 560 [32]; 557 [2/], 428 [2/] [23].	
6 b_{563} (b_{562})	E_0' = −77 mV [14]. Kinetically identified [32].	Δ = 565 [32]; 563 [2/], 428 [2/] [23].	
		Chloroplasts	
7 f	Mol wt = 245,000 with 4 hemes [15]; 110,000 with 2 hemes [13]. PG = cytochrome c-type heme, covalently bound to protein [13,15]. pI = 4.7 [13].	Δ = 554.5 [22.0] & λ_1, λ_2 = 554.5, 540 [15]. Δ = 554.5 [19.7] [15]. **R** = 554.5 [20.2] & λ_1, λ_2 = 554.5, 540 [15]; 532.8, 524, 422, 330,	Physiologically, cytochrome f is located on the electron transport path between cytochrome b_{559} & photosystem I [5]. Can be extracted from leaves with alkaline ethanol [20],

[1/] Measurements were carried out with mung bean mitochondria; cytochromes a and a_3 are components of cytochrome c oxidase. [2/] Measured at the temperature of boiling nitrogen, 77°K.

continued

Cyto-chrome		Physical & Chemical Properties	Optical Absorption Spectra $[E_{1\ cm}^{mM}]$	Remarks
		$E_0' = +390$ mV for intact spinach chloroplasts [22]; $+365$ mV for purified form [13].	$402 \underline{3/}$ [15]; $552 \underline{2/}$, $548 \underline{2/}$ [10].	and further purified by acetone & ammonium sulfate fractionation [13].
8	b_{559}	$E_0' = +325$ mV in intact chloroplasts, at pH 8.2 [22]. In intact chloroplasts, it is not autoxidizable and does not combine with CO [7].	$\Delta = 559, 526, 427$ [24]; $557 \underline{2/}$ [7].	Cytochrome b_{559} is generally placed on the main electron transport path between photosystems I & II [5]. Recent data, however, place it on a side path [8]. Has not been purified, and appears to be tightly bound to chloroplast lamellae [7]. Is structurally & functionally different from cytochrome b_6 [7,12,24].
9	b_6 (b_{563})	$E_0' = -60$ mV [19]. Autoxidizable; does not combine with CO [19].	$\Delta = 563$ [7].	Postulated to be part of the cyclic photophosphorylation pathway between CRS (or FRS) & P-700, or ferredoxin & P-700 [5]. Partially purified with the non-ionic detergent digitonin [7].
		Microsomes		
10	b_{555} (b_5)	Mol wt = 13,500 [29]; amino acid composition is known [29]. PG = heme (protoheme) [28]. $E_0' = +20$ mV [28]. Acidic protein [29]; does not combine with CO [27].	$\Delta = 558 \underline{2/}, 552 \underline{2/}$ [9]. O = 560 [8.5], 529, 413 [105] [29]. R = 559, 555 [22.7], 527, 423 [159] [28,29]; $559 \underline{2/}, 552 \underline{2/}, 426 \underline{2/}$ [27].	Cytochromes b_{555} & b_5 are identical [25]. Purified from soluble fraction of etiolated mung beans [9]; present at very low concentrations, or absent from cells of many other plants [29].
		Other Intracellular Sources		
11	b_{559} (b_3)	Mol wt = 28,000 [30]. PG = protohemin IX [30]. Basic protein; slowly autoxidizable [30].	O = 562, 529, 416 [30]. R = 559, 529, 425 [30].	Cytochromes b_{559} & b_3 are identical [30]. Purified from soluble fraction of etiolated mung beans & broad bean leaves [20,30].
12	b_{561}	PG = heme (protoheme) [28]. $E_0' = -30$ mV [28].	O = 558, 528, 418 [27]. R = 561, 531, 427 [27]; $560 \underline{2/}, 427 \underline{2/}$ [27].	Purified from a soluble fraction of etiolated mung bean [27].

$\underline{2/}$ Measured at the temperature of boiling nitrogen, 77°K. $\underline{3/}$ A shoulder.

Contributor: Wohlrab, Hartmut

References

[1] Baker, J. E., and P. Borchett. 1965. Plant Physiol. 40(Suppl.):55.

[2] Bendall, D. S., and W. D. Bonner, Jr. 1966. Hemes Hemoproteins Proc. Colloq., 3rd, p. 485.

[3] Bendall, D. S., and W. D. Bonner, Jr. 1971. Plant Physiol. 47:236.

[4] Bendall, D. S., and R. Hill. 1956. New Phytol. 55:206.

[5] Bishop, N. I. 1971. Annu. Rev. Biochem. 40:197.

[6] Boardman, N. K. 1968. Advan. Enzymol. Relat. Areas Mol. Biol. 30:1.

[7] Boardman, N. K., and J. M. Anderson. 1967. Biochim. Biophys. Acta 143:187.

[8] Boardman, N. K., et al. 1971. Ibid. 234:126.

[9] Bonner, W. D., Jr. 1961. Haematin Enzymes Symp. 1959, p. 491.

[10] Bonner, W. D., Jr. 1961. Ibid., p. 492.

[11] Chance, B., et al. 1968. Annu. Rev. Plant Physiol. 19:295.

[12] Cramer, W. A., and W. L. Butler. 1967. Biochim. Biophys. Acta 143:187.

[13] Davenport, H. E., and R. Hill. 1952. Proc. Roy. Soc. B139:327.

[14] Dutton, P. L., and B. T. Storey. 1971. Plant Physiol. 47:282.

[15] Forti, G., et al. 1965. Biochim. Biophys. Acta 109:33.

[16] Goddard, D. R. 1944. Amer. J. Bot. 31:270.

continued

[17] Hagihara, B., et al. 1959. J. Biochem. (Tokyo) 46: 321.

[18] Harmey, M., et al. 1963. Nature (London) 209:174.

[19] Hill, R. 1954. Ibid. 174:501.

[20] Hill, R., and R. Scarisbrick. 1951. New Phytol. 50: 98.

[21] Keilin, D., and E. F. Hartree. 1949. Nature (London) 164:259.

[22] Knaff, D. B., and D. I. Arnon. 1971. Biochim. Biophys. Acta 226:400.

[23] Lance, C., and W. D. Bonner, Jr. 1968. Plant Physiol. 43:756.

[24] Lundegardh, H. 1965. Proc. Nat. Acad. Sci. U.S. 53:703.

[25] Moore, C. W. D. 1967. Ph.D. Dissertation. Univ. Cambridge, England.

[26] Plesnicar, M., et al. 1967. Plant Physiol. 42:366.

[27] Shichi, H., and D. P. Hackett. 1962. J. Biol. Chem. 237:2955.

[28] Shichi, H., and D. P. Hackett. 1962. Ibid. 237:2959.

[29] Shichi, H., et al. 1963. Ibid. 238:1156.

[30] Shichi, H., et al. 1963. Ibid. 238:1162.

[31] Stevens, F. C., et al. 1967. Ibid. 242:2764.

[32] Storey, B. T. 1969. Plant Physiol. 44:413.

[33] Whittingham, C. P. 1970. Progr. Biophys. Mol. Biol. 21:127.

[34] Yakushiji, E. 1935. Acta Phytochim. (Tokyo) 8: 325.

218. RESPIRATION RATES: PLANTS

Part I. Bacteria

Rate of respiration differs with the strain of bacteria, culture conditions, age of cells, origin of inoculum, nature of solution used for washing, and composition of the respiratory system. Data are for bacterial suspensions in the presence of glucose, and in most instances have not been corrected for endogenous respiration. Q_{O_2} = oxygen quotient.

	Species	Temp °C	Culture Age hr	Q_{O_2} $\mu l \cdot mg$ dry $wt^{-1} \cdot hr^{-1}$ [1]	Reference
1	Aerobacter aerogenes	30	....	122[2]	11
2			48	50	1,2
3		36	17	47	1,2
4	Azotobacter agilis[3]	30	Continuous	2240	28
5	A. chroococcum	22	36	2000-10,000[4]	26
6		30	....	300-2700	13
	Bacillus cereus				
7	Short	30	....	21[2]	11
8			18	42-86	29
9	Filamentous	30	18	3-49	29
10	B. licheniformis	37	18	140-196[2]	34
11	B. macerans	37	....	21[5]	9
12				4[6]	9
13	B. psychrophilus[7]	20	21	6[8]	41
14	B. stearothermophilus	55	....	36[8,9]	12
15	B. subtilis	37	6-8	170	16
16	Spores	32	98-147	10	10
17	B. thuringiensis[7]	30	7.5	60[8]	41
18	Corynebacterium sp.	30	48-96	67	23
19	Escherichia coli	30	....	67.7[2]	11
20		32	20	272	1
21		40	20	200	22
22	Ferrobacillus ferrooxidans	25	175	0.08[10]	38
23	Haemophilus parainfluenzae	.....	....	4.5[8,11]	43
24				30[8]	39
25				40[8,12]	43
26		30	....	14[13]	42
27	Klebsiella aerogenes	30	Continuous	100	18
28	Lactobacillus bulgaricus	37	8	34	38
29		45	8	55	38
30	L. casei 58	30	....	21[2]	5
31	103	30	....	11.8	5
32	L. plantarum	30	....	19.5	5
33	Leuconostoc citrovorum	38	16	8	7
34	Micrococcus aurantiacus	35	30-34	14	30
35	M. cinnabareus	35	30-34	36	30
36	M. flavus	35	30-34	8	30
37	M. freudenreichii	35	30-34	20	30

[1] Unless otherwise indicated. [2] Data given as Q_{O_2} for nitrogen; calculated assuming 10% nitrogen. [3] Synonym: A. vinelandii. [4] $\mu l \cdot mg$ $N^{-1} \cdot hr^{-1}$. [5] Aerobic. [6] Anaerobic. [7] For data on temperatures from 5-40°C and cell-free extracts, consult reference. [8] Calculated. [9] Q_{O_2} = oxygen consumption·mg protein$^{-1} \cdot hr^{-1}$. [10] Glucose inhibits respiration slightly: at pH 5, endogenous 0.12 oxidation of sulfur = 3.47 and of thiosulfate = 18.6. [11] Aerated culture. [12] Nonaerated culture. [13] On formate, Q_{O_2} = 105; on lactate, Q_{O_2} = 56.

continued

Part I. Bacteria

	Species	Temp °C	Culture Age hr	Q_{O_2} μl·mg dry wt^{-1}·hr^{-1}	Reference		Species	Temp °C	Culture Age hr	Q_{O_2} μl·mg dry wt^{-1}·hr^{-1} [1]	Reference
38	M. luteus	35	30-34	15	30	58	P. fluorescens	26	20	58	35
39	398	30	48	5	4	59	P. fluorescens [15]	30	18	1.4 [16]	15
40	M. lysodeikticus	30	48	9	4	60	P. natriegens	30	....	268	8
41	M. roseus A	30	48	0	4	61	Rhizobium leguminosa-	30	....	33 [2]	11
42	412	30	48	21.2	4		rum				
43	416	30	48	16.4	4	62	Sarcina flava	30	48	18.3	4
44	9815	30	48	8.7	4	63	S. lutea	30	48	23.4	4
45	M. sodonensis	30	48	23.1	4	64	Staphylococcus epider-	30	8	66 [17]	19
46	Mycobacterium sp.	38	84	22	14	65	midis			67 [18]	20
47	Leprous	38	84	8	14	66	Streptococcus agalactiae	37	15	110	27
48	M. avium	37	84	1	31	67	S. faecalis	.....	....	28-58 [19]	6
49	M. phlei	38	84	28	14	68	B33A	38	18	106	36
50	M. ranae	38	84	32	14	69	10C-1	37	15	57-80	32
51	M. smegmatis [14]	38	84	23	14	70	Group D	37	12-15	?	17
52		38	84	13	14	71	S. pneumoniae [20]	37	18	27	3
53	M. stercoris	38	84	15	14	72	S. pyogenes	37.5	4	57-63	37
54	M. tuberculosis	38	252	4	14	73	S. thermophilus	37	8	4-9	40
55	Neisseria meningitidis	37	16	56	25	74		50	8	5-10	40
56	Pseudomonas aerugi-	.....	48	99-137	24	75	Psychrophilic species	30	14	127	33
57	nosa	20	....	26	21						

[1] Unless otherwise indicated. [2] Data given as Q_{O_2} for nitrogen; calculated assuming 10% nitrogen. [14] Synonym: M. butyricum. [15] For data on effect of various respiratory inhibitors on oxygen consumption, consult reference. [16] Oxygen consumption reported as μatoms O_2·mg dry wt^{-1}·hr^{-1}. [17] Cells grown aerobically at 37°C. If grown anaerobically for 16 hr, Q_{O_2} = 7; if anaerobically plus heme, Q_{O_2} = 42. [18] Cells grown aerobically at 37°C. If grown anaerobically for 16 hr, Q_{O_2} = 10. If heme added after growth, Q_{O_2} = 13; if during growth, Q_{O_2} = 37. [19] Cells grown on glucose: aerobically, Q_{O_2} = 44.7, plus hematin, Q_{O_2} = 58.2; anaerobically, Q_{O_2} = 28.6; grown with lactate and hematin, Q_{O_2} = 58.2. Endogenous 0.16 to 0.30. Other substrates, Q_{O_2} is low. [20] Synonym: Diplococcus pneumoniae.

Contributors: Umbreit, W. W.; Conti, S. F.

References

[1] Ajl, S. J. 1950. J. Bacteriol. 59:499.
[2] Ajl, S. J., and T. O. Wong. 1951. Ibid. 61:379.
[3] Bernheim, F., and M. L. Bernheim. 1943. Ibid. 46:225.
[4] Blevins, W. T., et al. 1969. Can. J. Microbiol. 15:383.
[5] Brown, J. P., and P. J. Van Demark. 1968. Ibid. 14:829.
[6] Bryan-Jones, D. G., and R. Whittenburg. 1969. J. Gen. Microbiol. 58:247.
[7] Chang, S. C., et al. 1951. J. Bacteriol. 62:753.
[8] Cho, H. W., and R. G. Eagon. 1967. Ibid. 93:866.
[9] Conti, S. F., et al. 1968. Ibid. 96:554.
[10] Crook, P. G. 1952. Ibid. 63:193.
[11] Dietrich, S. M. C., and R. H. Burris. 1967. Ibid. 93:1467.
[12] Downey, R. J., et al. 1969. Ibid. 98:1956.
[13] Drozd, J., and J. R. Postgate. 1970. J. Gen. Microbiol. 63:63.

[14] Edson, N. L., and G. J. Hunter. 1943. Biochem. J. 37:563.
[15] Faust, M. A., and R. N. Doetsch. 1969. J. Bacteriol. 97:806.
[16] Gary, N. D., and R. C. Bard. 1952. Ibid. 64:501.
[17] Gunsalus, I. C., and W. W. Umbreit. 1945. Ibid. 49:347.
[18] Harrison, D. E. F., and S. J. Pirt. 1967. J. Gen. Microbiol. 46:193.
[19] Jacobs, N. J., and S. F. Conti. 1965. J. Bacteriol. 89:675.
[20] Jacobs, N. J., et al. 1967. Ibid. 93:278.
[21] Kay, W. W., and A. F. Gronlund. 1969. Can. J. Microbiol. 15:739.
[22] Krebs, H. A. 1937. Biochem. J. 31:2095.
[23] Levine, S., and L. O. Krampitz. 1952. J. Bacteriol. 64:645.
[24] MacKelvie, R. M., et al. 1968. Can. J. Microbiol. 14:639.

continued

Part I. Bacteria

[25] Mallquia, L. P., and E. Weiss. 1970. J. Bacteriol. 101:127.

[26] Meyerhof, O., and D. Burk. 1928. Hoppe Seylers Z. Physiol. Chem. 139:117.

[27] Mickelson, M. N. 1967. J. Bacteriol. 94:184.

[28] Nagai, S., et al. 1969. J. Gen. Microbiol. 59:163.

[29] Nickerson, W. J., and F. J. Sherman. 1952. J. Bacteriol. 64:667.

[30] Nunheimer, T. D., and F. W. Fabian. 1942. Ibid. 44:215.

[31] Oginsky, E. L., et al. 1950. Ibid. 59:29.

[32] O'Kane, D. J. 1950. Ibid. 60:449.

[33] Purohit, K., and J. L. Stokes. 1967. Ibid. 93:199.

[34] Schulp, J. A., and A. H. Stouthamer. 1970. J. Gen. Microbiol. 64:195.

[35] Sebek, O. K., and C. I. Randles. 1952. J. Bacteriol. 63:693.

[36] Seeley, H. W., and P. J. Van Demark. 1951. Ibid. 61:27.

[37] Sevag, M. G., and M. Shelburne. 1942. Ibid. 43:411.

[38] Silver, M. 1970. Can. J. Microbiol. 16:845.

[39] Sinclair, P. R., and D. C. White. 1970. J. Bacteriol. 101:365.

[40] Stein, R. M., and W. L. Frazier. 1941. Ibid. 42:501.

[41] Stokes, J. L., and J. M. Larkin. 1968. Ibid. 95:95.

[42] White, D. C. 1966. Antonie van Leeuwenhoek J. Microbiol. Serol. 32:139.

[43] White, D. C., and A. N. Tucker. 1969. J. Bacteriol. 97:199.

Part II. Slime Molds and Fungi

Method: Mano = manometric; Chem = chemical; Pol = polarographic; Volu = volumetric. **Substrate:** Endo = endogenous; Org = organic compounds; CHO = carbohydrates; Com = complex substrates. Q_{O_2} = oxygen quotient; Q_{CO_2} = carbon dioxide quotient. Q_{CO_2} values in boldface are for anaerobic CO_2 production; all other Q_{CO_2} values are for aerobic CO_2 production. **R** = respiratory gas exchange ratio. Data in brackets refer to the column heading in brackets.

	Species	Material [Method]	Sub-strate	Specification	Temp °C	Q_{O_2} [Q_{CO_2}] $\mu l \cdot mg$ dry $wt^{-1} \cdot hr^{-1}$ [1]	R CO_2/O_2	Ref-er-ence
				Myxomycetes				
1	*Physarum poly-cephalum*	Plasmodia [Mano]	Endo	50 mg/vessel	22	1.4[2] [1.0[2]; **0.24**[2]]	0.75-0.85	1
2				PO₄ buffer, pH 6.0; 0 da	25	1.08[2] [0.11[2]]	0.83	38
				Phycomycetes				
3	*Achlya* sp.	Mycelia [Mano]	Endo	pH 5	21.7	19.5 (max 23)	0.88	46
4	*Allomyces arbus-cula*	Washed mycelia [Mano]	Endo	Unstarved	28	1.5	....	23
5				Starved	28	17.9	....	23
6			Org	+0.1 *M* glutamate	20	0.84	....	41
7	*A. macrogynus*	Mycelia [Mano]	Endo	Low glucose medium	.....	....	0.82-0.88	4
8			CHO	2.75 m*M* glucose	.....	....	1.09-1.22	4
9	*Mucor guilliermon-dii*	Mycelia [Mano]	Endo	Mycelial phase; endogenous	25	5.7-10.0 [3.2; 7.1]	....	25
10			CHO	Mycelial phase; glucose	25	5.6-21.4 [10.7-42.3; **18.3-82.1**]	....	25
11		Cell suspension [Mano]	CHO	Yeast phase; glucose	25	7.8-39.0 [21.9-118.0; **30.9-142.0**]	....	25
12	*Phycomyces blakes-leeanus*	Mycelia [Chem]	CHO	1.5 da	20	[27]	....	49
13				3.5 da	20	[13]	....	49
14				7 da	20	[3]	....	49
15	*Rhizopus nigricans*	Sporangiospores [Mano]	Endo	5 hr	30	4.7-8.5[3]	....	32
16			CHO	5 hr; 1% sucrose	30	4.3-9.2[3]	....	32
17	*R. sexualis*	Mycelia [Chem]	Org	52 hr	20	[25.7[4]]	....	19
18	*Saprolegnia* sp.	Mycelia [Mano]	Endo	pH 5	21.7	10.6 (max 36)	0.75	46

[1] Unless otherwise indicated. [2] $\mu l \cdot mg$ wet $wt^{-1} \cdot hr^{-1}$. [3] $\mu l \cdot mg$ wet $wt^{-1} \cdot 5 \ hr^{-1}$. [4] $mg \cdot g$ dry $wt^{-1} \cdot hr^{-1}$.

continued

Part II. Slime Molds and Fungi

	Species	Material [Method]	Sub-strate	Specification	Temp °C	Q_{O_2} [Q_{CO_2}] $\mu l \cdot mg$ dry $wt^{-1} \cdot hr^{-1}$ [1]	R CO_2/O_2	Reference
19	*Zygorhynchus*	Mycelia [Mano]	Endo	Starved 24 hr; pH 6.8	25	5.0-6.4	....	34
20	*moelleri*		CHO	Starved 24 hr; pH 6.8	25	26.4-37.0	....	34
				Ascomycetes				
21	*Candida albicans*	Yeast cells [Mano]	Endo	Normal strain; pH 7.2	30	19.4	....	48
22		Mycelia [Mano]	Endo	Filamentous mutant; pH 7.2	30	29.0	....	48
23	*Chaetomium* sp.	Pellets [Chem]	CHO	....	23-25	....	1.22	3
24	*Monilinia fructicola*	Mycelia [Mano]	Endo	5 hr	30	2.92[3]	....	31
25			CHO	5 hr; 1% sucrose	30	3.21[3]	....	31
26		Conidia [Mano]	Endo	5 hr	30	4.5-5.1[3]	....	32
27			CHO	5 hr; 0.2 mg sucrose/mg spores	30	47.2-54.2[3]	....	32
28	*Neurospora crassa*	Mycelia [Mano]	Endo	3-da mycelia	30	29.6 [21.5]	0.73	20
29			CHO	3-da mycelia; sucrose	30	40.1 [31.5]	0.79	20
30	*N. sitophila*	Conidia [Mano]	Endo	2 hr	30	0.87[5] [0.62[5]]	0.71	8
31			CHO	2 hr; 6.6 mM glucose	30	2.18[5] [2.30[5]]	1.06	8
32	*N. tetrasperma*	Ascospores [Mano]	Endo	Ascospores, dormant	25	0.25-0.55 [<0.03]	....	15
33					25	0.21-0.59	0.6	45
34				heat-activated	25	4.5-10.9 [**5.0-10.9**]	....	15
35				furfural-activated	25	0.5-20	0.8-1.2	45
36				germinating	25	9.0-22 [**1.0-2.0**]	....	15
37					25	16.4-24.2	0.59	45
38	*Saccharomyces cerevisiae*	Washed cells [Pol]	Endo	Endogenous	24	47	....	29
39			CHO	Glucose	24	74.8	....	29
40	Baker's	Washed cell suspension [Mano]	Endo	Endogenous	22-25	4.8[2]	....	21
41			CHO	Glucose	22-25	3.9[2]	....	21
42	Brewer's	Washed cell suspension [Mano]	Endo	Endogenous	22-25	4.2[2]	....	21
43			CHO	Glucose	22-25	19.5[2]	....	21
44	R	Cell suspension [Mano]	CHO	No stored reserves	.....	83-109 [370-432; 278-299]	....	24
45				Fat reserves	.....	76 [249; **322**]	....	24
46				Glycogen reserves	.....	0 [63; **116**]	....	24
47	U	Cell suspension [Mano]	CHO	No stored reserves	.....	10-137 [160-348; 276-284]	....	24
48				Fat reserves	.....	125 [151; **261**]	....	24
49				Glycogen reserves	.....	47 [82; **83**]	....	24
50	*Schizosaccharomyces octosporus*	Cell suspension [Mano]	Endo	Endogenous	30	21 [**0.1**]	....	44
51			CHO	Glucose	30	90 [**225**]	....	44
52	*S. pombe*	Cell suspension [Mano]	Endo	Endogenous	30	17.9 [**0.4**]	....	44
53			CHO	Glucose	30	36.4 [**22.0**]	....	44
54	*Sordaria* sp.	Pellets [Chem]	CHO	....	23-25	....	1.56	3
55	*S. fimicola*	Mycelia [Mano]	Endo	Endogenous	26	1.28	....	13
				Basidiomycetes				
56	*Agaricus campestris* [6]	Sporophores [Mano]	Endo	Material from nature, variable	30	2.48 [3.35; **0.28**]	0.74	39
57			CHO	Material as above; glucose	30	3.83 [3.56; **0.53**]	0.93	39

[1] Unless otherwise indicated.   [2] $\mu l \cdot mg$ wet $wt^{-1} \cdot hr^{-1}$.   [3] $\mu l \cdot mg$ wet $wt^{-1} \cdot 5$ hr^{-1}.   [5] $\mu l \cdot 10^5$ $spores^{-1} \cdot hr^{-1}$.   [6] Synonym: *Psalliota campestris*.

continued

Part II. Slime Molds and Fungi

	Species	Material [Method]	Sub-strate	Specification	Temp °C	Q_{O_2} [Q_{CO_2}] $\mu l \cdot mg$ dry $wt^{-1} \cdot hr^{-1}$ [1]	R CO_2/O_2	Ref-er-ence
58		Growing culture [Volu]	......	....	25	1.9-2.9 [2.3-4.0]	0.70-0.90	7
59	*Coprinus comatus*	Sporophores [Chem]	Endo	Endogenous	17	[2.7]	....	40
60	*Exidia glandulosa*	Mycelia [Chem]	......	....	.....	....	0.7	5
61	*Merulius lacrymans*	Mycelia [Mano]	Endo	Unstarved	22.5	10-16	0.87-1.11	16
62				Starved 24 hr	22.5	6-10	0.75-1.13	16
63			CHO	Unstarved; glucose	22.5	11-20	0.90-1.11	16
64				Starved 24 hr; glucose	22.5	11-13	0.86-1.02	16
65		Sporophores [Chem]	Endo	Endogenous	17	[1.0]	....	40
66	*Puccinia graminis*	Uredospores	Endo	Nongerminating, 30 min	22	3.0	....	27
67	*tritici*	[Pol]		Germinating, 30 min	22	11.6	....	27
	Schizophyllum	Mycelia [Mano]	CHO	Glucose growth medium				
68	*commune*			48 hr	25	∿60 [∿40]	∿1.3	50
69				96 hr	25	∿100 [∿70]	∿1.45	50
70				270 hr	25	∿20 [∿8]	∿1.1	50
71	*Ustilago avenae*	Pellets [Chem]	CHO	....	23-25	....	1.01	3
72	*U. maydis*	Teliospores	Endo	Ungerminated	29.5	1.2	....	6
73		[Mano]		∿75% germinated; 12 hr	29.5	9.0	....	6
74			CHO	Ungerminated; glucose	29.5	1.3	....	6
75				∿75% germinated; glucose	29.5	23.5	....	6
				Deuteromycetes (Fungi Imperfecti)				
76	*Alternaria* sp.	Pellets [Chem]	CHO	Mutants or strains	23-25	....	1.26-1.31	3
77	*A. oleracea*	Mycelia [Mano]	Endo	5 hr	30	2.87[3]	....	31
78			CHO	5 hr; 1% sucrose	30	4.10[3]	....	31
79		Conidia [Mano]	Endo	5 hr	30	7.1-8.2[3]	....	32
80			CHO	5 hr; 1% sucrose	30	17.4-17.7[3]	....	32
81	*Aspergillus niger*	Mycelia [Mano]	Endo	5 hr	30	2.99[3]	....	31
82			CHO	5 hr; 1% sucrose	30	4.57[3]	....	31
83		Conidia [Mano]	Endo	5 hr	30	6.3-12.8[3]	....	32
84			CHO	5 hr; 1% sucrose	30	9.7-17.7[3]	....	32
85				Germinated 10 hr in glucose medium	30	∿4[7]	....	51
86	*Blastomyces bra-*	Washed cell sus-	CHO	Starved; mycelial phase	20	2.4	....	37
87	*siliensis*	pension [Mano]		yeast phase	20	14.2	....	37
88	*B. dermatitidis*	Washed cell sus-	Endo	Starved	3	1.3	....	37
89		pension			41	13.3	....	37
90		[Mano]			45	10.3	....	37
91		Mycelia, washed	Endo	Endogenous	37	16[8]	0.80	2
92		cell suspension	CHO	Glucose	37	23[8]	0.96	2
		[Mano]						
93	*Botrytis cinerea*	Mycelia [Mano]	CHO	Starved; 2 da	26	3.0	1.5	14
94				4 da	26	2.0	1.5	14
95				6 da	26	1.5	1.5	14
96	*Candida albicans*	Cell suspension	Endo	Starved	30	5	....	35
97		[Mano]	CHO	Glucose	30	40	....	35

[1] Unless otherwise indicated. [3] $\mu l \cdot mg$ wet $wt^{-1} \cdot 5 \ hr^{-1}$. [7] $\mu l \cdot \mu g$ nitrogen$^{-1} \cdot hr^{-1}$. [8] $\mu l \cdot 10 \ \mu l$ tissue volume$^{-1} \cdot hr^{-1}$.

continued

Part II. Slime Molds and Fungi

	Species	Material [Method]	Sub-strate	Specification	Temp °C	Q_{O_2} [Q_{CO_2}] $\mu l \cdot mg$ dry $wt^{-1} \cdot hr^{-1}$ [1]	R CO_2/O_2	Reference
98	*Cephalosporium*	Conidia [Mano]	Endo	5 hr	30	1.7-2.7[3]	....	32
99	*acremonium*		CHO	5 hr; 1% sucrose	30	37.1-42.8[3]	....	32
100	*Cladosporium* spp.	Pellets [Chem]	CHO	5 strains	23-25	....	1.10-1.28	3
101	*Colletotrichum*	Mycelia [Mano]	Endo	Endogenous	30	12.6	0.9-1.0	17
102	*gloeosporioides*		CHO	Glucose	30	13.3	1.31	17
103	*Epidermophyton*	Mycelia [Mano]	Endo	pH 3.0	.....	3.0	....	36
104	*floccosum*			pH 5.0	.....	0.8	....	36
105				pH 6.0	.....	1.6	....	36
106	*Fusarium graminea-*	Pellets [Mano]	Endo	Whole cells	30	13.6	0.84	12
107	*rum*			Minced cells	30	25.9	0.72	12
108			CHO	Whole cells; glucose	30	15.7	1.24	12
109				Minced cells; glucose	30	28.0	1.11	12
110	*F. lini*	Mycelia [Mano]	Endo	Endogenous	25.5	0.52	....	22
111			CHO	Glucose	25.5	0.61	....	22
112	*F. solani phaseoli*	Macroconidia	Endo	Ungerminated; 6.0-6.7 hr	30	1.44-2.82 [0.93-1.85]	0.65	9
113		[Mano]		Germinated; 1.3 hr	30	29.1 [25.1]	0.86	9
114			CHO	Ungerminated; glucose; 2 hr	30	7.1 [0.5]	....	10
115				Germinated; glucose; 2 hr	30	18.6 [5.7]	....	10
116	*Helminthosporium* *gramineum*	Pellets [Chem]	CHO	....	23-25	....	1.31	3
117	*Microsporum canis*	Mycelia [Mano]	Endo	4-7 da old	37.5	....	1.0	33
118				11-15 da old; starved	37.5	....	0.87	18
119	*M. gypseum*	Macroconidia [Mano]	Endo	Preincubated 4 hr	25	10.8	....	30
120	*Myrothecium ver-*	Washed, homog-	Com	4 hr	30	45	....	11
121	*rucaria*	enized mycelia		24 hr	30	108	....	11
122		[Mano]		100 hr	30	22	....	11
123		Conidia [Mano]	CHO	Germinating spores; 0 hr	30	2	....	28
124				1 hr	30	65	....	28
125				3 hr	30	75	....	28
126				Glucose; 1 hr	30	[5.2]	1.15	28
127				3 hr	30	[5.2]	1.24	28
128	*Sporotrichum bom-* *bycinum*	Pellets [Chem]	CHO	....	23-25	....	1.28	3
129	*Torula* sp.	Washed cell sus-pension [Mano]	CHO	± Glutathione; ± cysteine	30	28 [9]	....	26
130	*Torulopsis utilis*	Cell suspension [Mano]	Endo	Nitrogen-starved	30	3.9[2] [3.8[2]]	0.97	43
131	*Trichophyton gyp-*	Mycelia [Mano]	Endo	pH 4.6	.....	1.06	....	36
132	*seum*			pH 7.0	.....	1.73	....	36
133				pH 8.0	.....	2.69	....	36
134	*Trichothecium ro-* *seum* [9]	Pellets [Chem]	CHO	....	23-25	....	1.19	3
	Deuteromycetes—Mycelia Sterilia							
135	*Rhizoctonia solani*	Mycelia [Mano]	Endo	4-da culture	29.5	45	....	42
136				9-da culture	29.5	15	....	42

[1] Unless otherwise indicated. [2] $\mu l \cdot mg$ wet $wt^{-1} \cdot hr^{-1}$. [3] $\mu l \cdot mg$ wet $wt^{-1} \cdot 5$ hr^{-1}. [9] Synonym: *Cephalothecium roseum*.

continued

Part II. Slime Molds and Fungi

	Species	Material [Method]	Sub-strate	Specification		Temp °C	Q_{O_2} [Q_{CO_2}] $\mu l \cdot$mg dry wt$^{-1} \cdot$hr^{-1}	R CO_2/O_2	Reference
137	*Sclerotium batati-*	Mycelia [Mano]	Endo	Age:	0-28 hr	29.5	~11.5 [4.5]	0.7	47
138	*cola*				28-57 hr	29.5	~9.5	0.7	47
139			CHO	Glucose; age:	0.28 hr	29.5	~18	0.9	47
140					28-57 hr	29.5	~16	1.0	47

Contributor: Cochrane, Vincent W.

References

[1] Allen, P. J., and W. H. Price. 1950. Amer. J. Bot. 37:393.

[2] Bernheim, F. 1942. J. Bacteriol. 44:533.

[3] Birkinshaw, J. H., et al. 1931. Phil. Trans. Roy. Soc. London B220:55.

[4] Bonner, B. A., and L. Machlis. 1957. Plant Physiol. 32:291.

[5] Bonnier, G., and L. Mangin. 1884. Ann. Sci. Natur. Bot. Biol. Veg., Ser. 6, 17:210.

[6] Caltrider, P. G., and D. Gottlieb. 1963. Phytopathology 53:1021.

[7] Chevillard, L., et al. 1930. Ann. Physiol. Physicochim. Biol. 6:506.

[8] Cochrane, V. W., and D. L. W. Tull. 1958. Phytopathology 48:623.

[9] Cochrane, V. W., et al. 1963. Amer. J. Bot. 50:806.

[10] Cochrane, V. W., et al. 1963. Plant Physiol. 38:533.

[11] Darby, R. T., and D. R. Goddard. 1950. Amer. J. Bot. 37:379.

[12] Dorrell, W. W. 1948. Doctoral Thesis. Univ. Wisconsin, Madison.

[13] Edwards, G. A., et al. 1947. Amer. J. Bot. 34:551.

[14] Gentile, A. C. 1954. Plant Physiol. 29:257.

[15] Goddard, D. R. 1939. Cold Spring Harbor Symp. Quant. Biol. 7:362.

[16] Goksøyr, J. 1960. Physiol. Plant. 13:559.

[17] Greene, G. L. 1967. Ibid. 20:580.

[18] Hawker, L. E. 1950. Physiology of Fungi. Univ. London Press, London.

[19] Hawker, L. E., and P. M. Hepden. 1962. Ann. Bot. (London) 26:619.

[20] Heplar, J. Q., and E. L. Tatum. 1954. J. Biol. Chem. 208:489.

[21] Holtz, P., et al. 1948. Naunyn Schmiedebergs Arch. Exp. Pathol. Pharmakol. 205:243.

[22] Kikuchi, G., and E. S. G. Barron. 1959. Arch. Biochem. Biophys. 84:96.

[23] Leonard, W. R. 1949. J. Cell. Comp. Physiol. 34:293.

[24] Lindegren, C. C. 1946. Arch. Biochem. 9:353.

[25] Lüers, H., et al. 1930. Biochem. Z. 217:253.

[26] Machlis, S., and K. C. Blanchard. 1937. J. Cell. Comp. Physiol. 9:207.

[27] Maheshwari, R., and A. S. Sussman. 1970. Phytopathology 60:1357.

[28] Mandels, G. R., and A. B. Norton. 1948. Quartermaster Gen. Lab. Res. Rep. Microbiol. Ser. 11.

[29] Matsunaka, S., et al. 1966. Plant Physiol. 41:1364.

[30] McBride, B. C., and J. J. Stock. 1966. Appl. Microbiol. 14:973.

[31] McCallan, S. E. A., and L. P. Miller. 1957. Contrib. Boyce Thompson Inst. 18:483.

[32] McCallan, S. E. A., et al. 1954. Ibid. 18:39.

[33] Melton, F. M. 1951. J. Invest. Dermatol. 17:27.

[34] Moses, V. 1954. Biochem. J. 57:547.

[35] Nickerson, W. J. 1946. Amer. J. Bot. 33:831.

[36] Nickerson, W. J., and J. B. Chadwick. 1946. Arch. Biochem. 10:81.

[37] Nickerson, W. J., and G. A. Edwards. 1949. J. Gen. Physiol. 33:41.

[38] Ohta, J. 1954. J. Biochem. (Tokyo) 39:489.

[39] Rast, D. 1961. Ber. Schweiz. Bot. Ges. 71:209.

[40] Richards, F. J. 1927. New Phytol. 26:187.

[41] Shoup, C. S., and F. T. Wolf. 1946. J. Cell. Comp. Physiol. 28:365.

[42] Skowronski, B. S., and D. Gottlieb. 1970. J. Bacteriol. 104:640.

[43] Sperber, E. 1945. Ark. Kemi Mineral. Geol. 21A(3):1.

[44] Spiegelman, S., and M. Nozawa. 1945. Arch. Biochem. 6:303.

[45] Sussman, A. S. 1961. Quart. Rev. Biol. 36:109.

[46] Unestam, T., and F. H. Gleason. 1968. Physiol. Plant. 21:573.

[47] Van Etten, J. L., et al. 1966. J. Bacteriol. 91:169.

[48] Ward, J. M., and W. G. Nickerson. 1958. J. Gen. Physiol. 41:703.

[49] Wassink, E. C. 1934. Rec. Trav. Bot. Neer. 31:583.

[50] Wessels, J. G. H. 1965. Wentia 13:1.

[51] Yanagita, T. 1957. Arch. Mikrobiol. 26:329.

continued

Part III. Algae, Lichens, and Bryophytes

Method: Mano = manometric; Chem = chemical; O_2 elec = O_2 electrode; Cond = conductometric. Q_{O_2} = oxygen quotient; Q_{CO_2} = carbon dioxide quotient. R = respiratory gas exchange ratio. Data in brackets refer to the column heading in brackets.

	Division or Class & Species	Method	Temp °C	Q_{O_2} $[Q_{CO_2}]$ $\mu l \cdot 100$ mg dry wt$^{-1} \cdot$ hr^{-1} [1]	R CO_2/O_2	Variable Affecting Respiration Rate	Reference
	Algae						
	Cyanophyta						
1	*Anabaena variabilis*	Mano	25	840	1.1	Control or endogenous values	20
2				170	1.0	24-hr dark starvation	
3	*Anacystis nidulans*	Mano	25	160	1.0	Control or endogenous values	20
4				30	0.9	24-hr dark starvation	
5			39	470	1.1	Control or endogenous values	
6				190	1.1	24-hr dark starvation	
7	*Nostoc muscorum*	Mano	25	440	....	Control or endogenous value	20
8				110	....	24-hr dark starvation	
	Chrysophyta						
9	*Ochromonas malhamensis*	Mano	26	20,000[2]	0.8	Starvation	28
10				30,000[2]	....	24-hr starvation	
	Chlorophyta						
11	*Chlamydomonas reinhard-*	O_2 elec	20	13[3]	....	....	24
12	*tii*			6-8[3]	....	Quinacrine (atabrine)	
13	*Chlorella pyrenoidosa*	....	....	120	....	....	39
14		Mano	3.5	150	0.98	Control or endogenous values	9
15				200	....	Carbohydrate substrate	
16			18	430	0.94	Control or endogenous values	9
17				890	....	Carbohydrate substrate	
18			20	1700	1.39	....	10
19			25	50.4[4]	....	....	21
20				43.4[4]	....	Ketoglutarate	
21				44.3[4]	....	Succinate	
22				46.4[4]	....	Pyruvate	
23				48.2[4]	....	Glycerol	
24				48.2[4]	....	Sucrose	
25				49.2[4]	....	DL-Alanine	
26				80.1[4]	....	Acetate	
27				91.2[4]	....	D-Glucose	
28	*C. vannielii*	Mano	25	580	....	3228 lux light	29
29				115.6[5]			
30				1630	....	64,560 lux light	
31				3025.9[5]			
32	*Cladophora rupestris*	Chem	20	33	....	....	11
33	*Dunaliella tertiolecta*	Mano	25	50.7[4]	....	....	21
34				47.0[4]	....	Acetate	
35				48.1[4]	....	Glycerol	
36				50.2[4]	....	Sucrose	
37				50.4[4]	....	DL-Alanine	
38				51.4[4]	....	Ketoglutarate	
39				52.8[4]	....	Pyruvate	
40				53.3[4]	....	Succinate	
41				55.1[4]	....	D-Glucose	

[1] Unless otherwise indicated. [2] μg·g dry wt$^{-1} \cdot$ hr^{-1}. [3] μmoles·mg chlorophyll$^{-1} \cdot$ hr^{-1}. [4] μl·mg protein^{-1}·4 hr^{-1}. [5] μl·mg chlorophyll$^{-1} \cdot$ hr^{-1}.

continued

Part III. Algae, Lichens, and Bryophytes

	Division or Class & Species	Method	Temp °C	Q_{O_2} [Q_{CO_2}] $\mu l \cdot 100$ mg dry wt$^{-1} \cdot$hr^{-1} [1]	R CO_2/O_2	Variable Affecting Respiration Rate	Reference
42	*Enteromorpha compressa*	Chem	20	[27]	3.6	....	25
43				67	....	....	11
44	*E. linza*	....	....	....	0.62-1.09	....	39
45				129	....	....	
46		Chem	19	[66]	0.62	....	14
47	*Scenedesmus basiliensis*	....	....	140	....	....	39
48	*Spirogyra majuscula*	Chem	10.4	0.5[6/]	....	pH	7
49	*Ulothrix flacca*	Chem	....	160	....	....	12
50	*Ulva lactuca*	....	....	....	0.67-1.28	....	39
51				81	....	....	
52		Chem	12	56	0.95	....	17
53			18	[50]	0.67	....	14
54	*Valonia utricularis*	Chem	20	[8.4]	1.5	....	25
55		....	....	....	5.7	O_2	
	Charophyceae (Charophyta)						
56	*Chara vulgaris*	Chem	18	[1.5[6/]]	....	....	18
57	*Nitella flexilis*	Chem	18	[1.6[6/]]	....	....	18
	Phaeophyta						
58	*Ascophyllum* sp.	....	....	93[7/] [175[7/]]	0.81	....	6
59	*A. nodosum*	Mano	20	1.9[6/]	0.80	....	22
60	*Ectocarpus siliculosus*	Chem	12	41[6/]	....	....	14
61	*Fucus* sp.	....	....	141[7/] [107[7/]]	0.76	....	6
62	*F. serratus*	....	....	....	0.53-0.65	....	39
63		Chem	17	19	0.99	....	17
64			18	[18]	0.54	....	14
65	*F. vesiculosus*	....	....	....	0.60-0.77	....	39
66		Chem	14	[12.7[8/]]	....	....	5
67		Mano	18	5.1[6/]	0.78	....	22
68	*Laminaria digitata*	Mano	5	[0.9[9/]]	0.67	....	19
69	*L. saccharina*	Mano	5	[2.1[9/]]	0.80	....	19
70	*Sargassum linifolium*	Chem	20	[24]	5.5	....	25
	Rhodophyta						
71	*Batrachospermum monili-forme*	Chem	20	64	....	....	11
72	*Ceramium rubrum*	....	....	....	0.89-1.02	....	39
73		Chem	17	[45]	0.89	....	14
74	*Chondrus* sp.	....	....	139[7/] [113[7/]]	0.81	....	6
75				[80-100[7/]]	....	....	
76	*C. crispus*	Mano	23	2.8[6/]	0.81	....	22
77	*Gelidium amansii*	....	....	85	....	....	39
78	*G. cartilagineum*	....	....	....	1.18	....	37
79	*G. corneum*	Chem	20	[13]	3.26	....	25
80	*Gigartina teedii*	Chem	12	49	0.98	....	17
81	*Gracilaria compressa*	Chem	20	[9]	1.4	....	25
82	*Polysiphonia violacea*	Chem	11	[107]	1.02	....	14
83	*Porphyra laciniata*	Chem	17	39	....	....	17
84	*P. tenera*	....	....	155	....	....	39
85	*Porphyridium cruentum*	Mano	20	57	....	Starvation	33
86				196	....	Light	

[1] Unless otherwise indicated. [6/] $\mu l \cdot 100$ mg wet wt$^{-1} \cdot$hr^{-1}. [7/] $\mu l \cdot g$ fresh wt$^{-1} \cdot$hr^{-1}. [8/] $\mu g \cdot 100$ g wet wt$^{-1} \cdot$hr^{-1}. [9/] $\mu l \cdot$cm$^{-2} \cdot$hr^{-1}.

continued

Part III. Algae, Lichens, and Bryophytes

	Division or Class & Species	Method	Temp °C	Q_{O_2} [Q_{CO_2}] $\mu l \cdot 100$ mg dry $wt^{-1} \cdot hr^{-1}$ [L/]	R CO_2/O_2	Variable Affecting Respiration Rate	Reference
				Lichenes			
	Ascolichenes						
87	*Alectoria nigricans*	Mano	0	8	....	....	30
88			10	14			
89			30	33			
90	*Cladonia rangiferina*	....	....	8.5 [6.1]	0.80	....	26
91			10	[10]	....		
92			18	[8]	....		
93		Mano	50	[8]	0.80	....	16
94	*C. sylvatica*	Mano	0	2.9	....	....	30
95			10	6.8			
96			30	24			
97	*Lecanora haematomma; L. subfusca*	Mano	....	....	0.80	....	16
98	*Lecidea superans*	Mano	....	....	0.85	....	16
99	*Lobaria linita*	Mano	0	10	....	....	30
100			10	22			
101			30	72			
102	*L. pulmonaria*	....	18	[18]	....	....	26
103			27.2	[77]			
104		Chem	27	[1]	....	....	36
105				[26]	....	Moisture	
106	*Parmelia acetabulum*	....	....	3.1 [2.7]	0.74	....	26
107		Mano	....	[2.3]	0.79	....	16
108	*P. caperata*	....	....	33.1 [25.1]	0.75	....	26
109	*P. nigrociliata*	Mano	0	4	....	....	30
110			10	13			
111			30	25			
112	*P. physodes*	....	....	....	0.86	....	1
113					1.0	Moisture	
114			18.5	26.7	....	....	26
115	*Peltigera aphthosa*	Mano	0	17	....	....	30
116			10	33			
117			30	90			
118	*P. canina*	....	....	[14]	....	....	26
119		Chem	20	[15.3 [2/]]	....	....	8
120	*P. polydactyla*	Mano	20	82 [52]	0.64	Control or endogenous values	32
121				120 [107]	0.87	Asparagine	
122				131 [158]	1.22	Glucose	
123				76	....	Control or endogenous value	31
124				94	....	NH_4Cl	
125				155	....	Glucose	
126				161	....	NH_4Cl & glucose	
127			25	95 [52]	....	Control or endogenous values	13
128				154 [198]	1.29	Glucose	
129				100 [68]	0.68	Control or endogenous values	
130				164 [210]	1.28	Glucose	
131				116 [103]	0.89	Control or endogenous values	

L/ Unless otherwise indicated.   2/ $\mu l \cdot cm^{-2} \cdot hr^{-1}$.

continued

Part III. Algae, Lichens, and Bryophytes

	Division or Class & Species	Method	Temp °C	Q_{O_2} [Q_{CO_2}] $\mu l \cdot 100$ mg dry $wt^{-1} \cdot hr^{-1}$ [L/]	R CO_2/O_2	Variable Affecting Respiration Rate	Reference
132				238 [311]	1.31	Sucrose	
133				104 [66]	0.64	Control or endogenous values	
134				188 [231]	1.23	Sucrose	
135	P. subamericana	Mano	0	5.7	....	....	30
136			10	19			
137			30	42			
138	Pertusaria communis	Mano	....	....	0.84	....	16
139	Umbilicaria proboscidea	Mano	0	3.5	....	....	30
140			10	6.5			
141			30	18			
142	U. pustulata	....	....	41.7 [36.3]	0.87	....	26
143			18	[13]	....		
144			28	[41]	....		
145		Chem	28	[11]	....	....	36
146				[22]	....	Moisture	
147	Usnea dasypoga	Cond	....	[60]	....	....	23
148				[90]	....	Moisture	
				Bryophyta			
	Marchantiopsida (Hepaticae)						
149	Frullania tamarisci	....	....	[32]	....	....	15
150				[47]	....	NH₄Cl & glucose	
151	Marchantia polymorpha	Chem	20	[0.6 9/]	....	....	34
152	Riccia fluitans	Mano	25	250	....	....	38
153				300	....	Inhibitors	
	Bryopsida (Musci)						
154	Bracythecium geheebii	Chem	−14	[53 10/]	....	....	2
155			−11	[46 10/]			
156			−9.5	[82.5 10/]			
157			−9.0	[41.2-63.5 10/]			
158			−8.5	[41.5 10/]			
159			−8.0	[72.5-75.0 10/]			
160			−3.5	[56.5 10/]			
161			2.0	[83.2 10/]			
162			2.5	[96.8 10/]			
163	Bryum antaricum	Mano	5	5.3; 5.6; 6.4	....	....	27
164			15	9.9; 11.3; 13.4			
165			25	16.0; 17.8; 20.2			
166			30	21.5			
167	B. argenteum	Mano	−2	8.3	....	....	27
168			2	14.0; 19.7			
169			8	28.4			
170			10	41.8			
171			15	46.7			
172			20	86.7			
173			30	125.0			
174			38	145.0			
175	Camptothecium philippeanum	Chem	−14	[40.0 10/]	....	....	2
176			−11	[42.5 10/]			

L/ Unless otherwise indicated. 9/ $\mu l \cdot cm^{-2} \cdot hr^{-1}$. 10/ mg·100 g fresh wt^{-1}.

continued

Part III. Algae, Lichens, and Bryophytes

	Division or Class & Species	Method	Temp °C	Q_{O_2} [Q_{CO_2}] $\mu l \cdot 100$ mg dry $wt^{-1} \cdot hr^{-1}$ [1]	R CO_2/O_2	Variable Affecting Respiration Rate	Reference
177			−9.5	[67.5 [10]]			
178			−9.0	[38.0-70.0 [10]]			
179			−8.5	[43.5 [10]]			
180			−8.0	[48.0-67.5 [10]]			
181			−3.5	[67.5 [10]]			
182			2.0	[114.4 [10]]			
183			2.5	[100.0 [10]]			
184	*Hylocomium parietinum;*	Chem	0	[15]	....	....	18
185	*H. proliferum*		20	[46]			
186			30	[92]			
187	*H. squarrosum*	Chem	5	[15]	....	....	18
188			20	[61]			
189			30	[100]			
190	*Hypnum cupressiforme*	Chem	18.5	2	....	....	6
191				30	....	Moisture	
192	*H. triquetrum*	....	....	5-401 [2]	....	....	35
193				....	4.69	Moisture	
194			14	4000	....	Season	
195			20	[0.8]	....	....	15
196				[30.0]	....	Moisture	
197		Mano	....	0.5	....	....	35
198				40.0	....	Moisture	
199	*Isothecium viviparum*	Chem	−14	[47.5 [10]]	....	....	2
200			−11	[37.0 [10]]			
201			−9.5	[52.0 [10]]			
202			−9.0	[38.0-73.5 [10]]			
203			−8.5	[43.0 [10]]			
204			−8.0	[37.0-65.0 [10]]			
205			−3.5	[60.0 [10]]			
206			2.0	[104.0 [10]]			
207			2.5	[112.4 [10]]			
208	*Mnium undulatum*	....	....	[7.5]	....	....	15,
209				[97.0]	....	Moisture	35
210	*Orthotrichum affine*	Mano	55	[12]	0.70	....	16
211	*Polytrichum juniperinum*	Gas analysis	0	[0.8 [11]]	....	Habitat: forest	4
212				[1.1 [11]]	....	Habitat: arctic	
213			10	[1.8 [11]]	....	Habitat: forest	
214				[2.3 [11]]	....	Habitat: arctic	
215			20	[3.2 [11]]	....	Habitat: forest	
216				[3.9 [11]]	....	Habitat: arctic	
217			30	[5.4 [11]]	....	Habitat: forest	
218				[8.7 [11]]	....	Habitat: arctic	
219		....	18	[1.2 [6,12]]	1.00 [12]	....	3
220				[0.7 [6,12]]	0.65 [12]	Growth, development, or maturation	
221	*Sphagnum girgensohnii*	Chem	5	[20]	....	....	18
222			20	[71]			
223			30	[130]			

[1] Unless otherwise indicated. [2] $\mu g \cdot g$ dry $wt^{-1} \cdot hr^{-1}$. [6] $\mu l \cdot 100$ mg wet $wt^{-1} \cdot hr^{-1}$. [10] mg $\cdot 100$ g fresh wt^{-1}. [11] Estimates by Karlander from author's graphs; mg/mg chlorophyll. [12] Shoots or tops only.

continued

Part III. Algae, Lichens, and Bryophytes

Contributor: Karlander, Edward P.

References

[1] Ahmadjian, V. 1966. In S. M. Henry, ed. Symbiosis: Its Physical and Biochemical Significance. Academic Press, New York. v. 1, pp. 35-97.

[2] Atanasiu, L. 1971. Bryologist 74:23.

[3] Bastit, E. 1891. Rev. Gen. Bot. 3:255.

[4] Bazzaz, F. A., et al. 1970. Bryologist 73:579.

[5] Bidwell, R. C. S. 1963. Can. J. Bot. 41(1):155.

[6] Blinks, L. R. 1951. In G. M. Smith, ed. Manual of Phycology. Chronica Botanica, Waltham, Mass. pp. 263-291.

[7] Bode, H. R. 1925. Jahrb. Wiss. Bot. 65:352.

[8] Boysen-Jensen, P., and D. Müller. 1929. Ibid. 70:503.

[9] French, C. S., et al. 1934. J. Gen. Physiol. 18:193.

[10] Gaffron, H. 1939. Biol. Zentralbl. 59:288.

[11] Gessner, F. 1940. Jahrb. Wiss. Bot. 89:1.

[12] Harder, R. 1915. Ibid. 56:254.

[13] Harley, J. L., and D. C. Smith. 1956. Ann. Bot. (London), n.s. 20:513.

[14] Hoffmann, C. 1929. Jahrb. Wiss. Bot. 71:214.

[15] Jönsson, B. 1894. C. R. Acad. Sci. 119:440.

[16] Jumelle, H. 1892. Rev. Gen. Bot. 4:49,103,159, 220,259,305.

[17] Kniep, H. 1914. Int. Rev. Gesamten Hydrobiol. Hydrogr. 7:1.

[18] Kolkwitz, R. 1900. Wiss. Meeresuntersuch. Abt. Helgoland 4:31.

[19] Krascheninnikoff, T. 1926. C. R. Acad. Sci. 182: 939.

[20] Kratz, W. A., and J. Myers. 1955. Plant Physiol. 30:275.

[21] Kwon, Y. M., and B. R. Grant. 1971. Plant Cell Physiol. 12:29.

[22] Kylin, H. 1911. Ark. Bot. 11:1.

[23] Neubauer, A. F. 1938. Beitr. Biol. Pflanz. 25:273.

[24] Neuman, J., and R. P. Levine. 1971. Plant Physiol. 47:700.

[25] Pantanelli, E. 1914. Ber. Deut. Bot. Ges. 32:488.

[26] Quispel, A. 1960. Encycl. Plant Physiol. 12:455.

[27] Rastorfer, J. R. 1970. Bryologist 73:544.

[28] Reazin, G. H. 1954. Amer. J. Bot. 41:771.

[29] Reger, B. J., and R. W. Krauss. 1970. Plant Physiol. 46:568.

[30] Scholander, P. F., et al. 1952. Amer. J. Bot. 39: 707.

[31] Smith, D. C. 1960. Ann. Bot. (London), n.s. 24:52.

[32] Smith, D. C. 1960. Ibid., n.s. 24:172.

[33] Speer, H. L., and R. F. Jones. 1964. Physiol. Plant. 17:287.

[34] Stalfelt, M. G. 1937. Planta 27:30.

[35] Stiles, W. 1960. Encycl. Plant Physiol. 12:461.

[36] Stocker, O. 1927. Flora (Jena) 121:334.

[37] Tseng, C. K., and B. M. Sweeney. 1946. Amer. J. Bot. 33:706.

[38] Usami, S. 1937. Acta Phytochim. (Tokyo) 9:287.

[39] Whittingham, C. P. 1960. Encycl. Plant Physiol. 12: 447.

Part IV. Vascular Plants

Method: Mano = manometric; Chem = chemical; Cond = conductometric; Elec = electrode; IR = infrared carbon dioxide analyzer; Magn = paramagnetic oxygen analyzer; Gas = gas chromatography and electrical conductivity; Color = colorimetric. Q_{O_2} = oxygen quotient; Q_{CO_2} = carbon dioxide quotient. R = respiratory gas exchange ratio. Data in brackets refer to the column heading in brackets.

	Species (Synonym)	Condition or Plant Part	Method	Temp °C	Q_{O_2} [Q_{CO_2}] $\mu l \cdot 100$ mg wet wt$^{-1} \cdot$hr^{-1} [1/]	R CO_2/O_2	Variable Affecting Respiration Rate	Reference
					Seeds			
1	*Acer saccharum*	Resting	.....	......	[14]	....	....	64
2	*Avena sativa*	Resting	Chem	37.8	[0.02 2/]	....	....	9
3					[0.17 2/]	....	Moisture	
4	*Cannabis sativa*	Resting	Mano	18	11	0.82	....	45
5		Germinating	Mano	18	10.5	0.66		
6	*Chenopodium album*	Moist	Mano	25	9.6	0.93	....	110
7	*Citrullus vulgaris*	Resting	Mano	28	....	0.90	....	103

1/ Unless otherwise indicated. 2/ $\mu l \cdot 100$ mg dry wt$^{-1} \cdot$hr^{-1}.

continued

Part IV. Vascular Plants

	Species (Synonym)	Condition or Plant Part	Method	Temp °C	Q_{O_2} $[Q_{CO_2}]$ $\mu l \cdot 100$ mg wet wt$^{-1} \cdot$hr^{-1} [1]	R CO_2/O_2	Variable Affecting Respiration Rate	Reference
8	*Cocos nucifera*	Embryo	Mano	30	400 [2]	....	....	30
9					50 [2]	....	Development	
10		Hypocotyl	Mano	30	64 [2]	....	....	
11		Endosperm	Mano	30	0 [2]	....	....	
12	*Cucurbita pepo*	Germinating	Chem	25	[10]	0.94	....	74
13	'Sutton's Long White Vegetable Marrow'				[117]	0.62	Development	
14	*Fagopyrum sagitta-*	Germinating	.....	25	[41]	0.8	....	73
15	*tum (F. esculen-tum)*				[306]	1.0	Development	
16	*Glycine max (G. so-*	Germinating	Mano	......	....	0.93	....	37
17	*ja, Soja max)*					0.87	Growth, development or maturation	
18	*Gossypium hirsu-*	Resting	Mano	26	[0.03]	0.96	Moisture	66
19	*tum* 'Delfos-3506'				[6.0]	1.12	Storage or starvation	
20	*Helianthus annuus*	Resting	Mano	28	....	1.05	....	103
21	'Simpson's Giant	Germinating	Chem	25	[41]	0.85	....	74
22	Single' & 'Sut-ton's Giant Yellow'				[407]	0.50	Development	
23	*Hordeum vulgare*	Resting	Chem	37.8	[0.002 [2]]	....	....	9
24					[0.36 [2]]	....	Moisture	
25	*Juglans regia*	Resting	Mano	28	....	0.52	....	103
26	*Juniperus virginiana*	Resting	Mano	25	[0.05]	0.76	....	98
27		Germinating	Mano	25	[6.6]	0.84	....	
28					[2.5]	0.97	Development	
29	*Lathyrus odoratus* 'Maxima Alba'	Moist	Mano	20	6.4 [2]	....	....	43
30		Seedling	Mano	20	430 [2]	....		
31					100 [2]	....	Growth, development or maturation	
32	'What Joy'	Germinating	.....	25	[46]	0.9	....	73
33					[102]	0.98	Development	
34	*Linum usitatissi-*	Resting	Chem	37.8	[0.03 [2]]	....	....	9
35	*mum*				[1.5 [2]]	....	Moisture	
36		Germinating	Mano	18	....	0.90	....	37
37						0.35	Growth, development or maturation	
38	*Malus pumila (Pyrus malus)* 'Newton Pippin'	Resting	.....	19	[2.8 [2]]	0.86	....	52
39	*Medicago sativa*	Resting	Mano	18	38	1.08	....	45
40		Germinating	Mano	18	106	0.86		
41	*Oryza sativa* 'Oobe'	Resting	Mano	......	0.03 [2]	1.15	....	38
42		Moist	Mano	......	2.8 [2]	1.96		
43		Germinating	Mano	......	4.9 [2]	1.98		
44		Seedling	Mano	......	1.06 [2]	1.00		
45	*Phaseolus vulgaris*	Germinating	.....	......	[65]	....	....	75
46	*Pinus radiata (P. in-signis)*	Resting	Mano	......	[0.0013 [2]]	....		125
47	*Pisum sativum*	Resting	Mano	28	....	1.00	....	103
48		Intact	Chem	20	[35]	1.1	....	100
49					[15]	4.9	O_2	
50	'Kelvedon Wonder'	Green	Chem	15	[15]	....	....	12
51	'Onward'	Green	Chem	15	[12.4]	....		121

[1] Unless otherwise indicated. [2] $\mu l \cdot 100$ mg dry wt$^{-1} \cdot$hr^{-1}.

continued

Part IV. Vascular Plants

	Species (Synonym)	Condition or Plant Part	Method	Temp °C	Q_{O_2} [Q_{CO_2}] $\mu l \cdot 100$ mg wet wt$^{-1} \cdot$hr^{-1} [1]	R CO_2/O_2	Variable Affecting Respiration Rate	Reference
52	*Prunus amygdalus*	Germinating	Mano	......	....	0.7	....	37
53	*(Amygdalus communis)*					0.86	Growth, development or maturation	
	P. domesticus							110
54	'Blue Gage'	Moist	Mano	25	8.0	0.70	....	
55	'Burbank'	Moist	Mano	25	4.7	0.91		
56	*P. persica*	Moist	Mano	25	5.8	0.68	....	110
57	*Raphanus sativus*	Resting	Mano	20	7.0	0.86	....	45
58		Germinating	Mano	20	1.03	0.58		
59	*Ricinus communis*	Resting	Mano	28	....	1.03	....	103
60		Germinating	Mano	......	....	0.70	....	87
61		Seedling	Mano	30	133	0.39	....	89
62			Chem	17	[25]	....	....	115
63	*Rumex crispus*	Moist	Mano	25	6.7	1.16	....	110
64	*Secale cereale*	Resting	Chem	37.8	[0.002 [2]]	....	....	9
65					[0.11 [2]]	....	Moisture	
66		Seedling	Chem	18	[12]	....	....	115
67	*Sorghum bicolor (S.*	Resting	Chem	37.8	[0.011 [2]]	....	....	9
68	*vulgare)*				[0.32 [2]]	....	Moisture	
69	*Triticum aestivum*	Resting	Chem	38	[0.005 [2]]	....	....	10
70					[0.16 [2]]	....	Moisture	
71		Germinating	Chem	38	[0.014 [2]]	....	....	10
72					[0.53 [2]]	....	Moisture	
73		Seedling	Chem	18	[21]	....	....	115
74	*Tropaeolum majus*	Germinating	Chem	25	....	0.89	Age: one seedling, 11 hr old	117
75	'Sutton's Tall Scarlet'					0.68	Age: one seedling, 148 hr old	
76	*Vicia faba*	Resting	Mano	28	....	0.99	....	103
77		Seedling	Chem	20	[13]	....	....	115
78	'Sutton's Broad Windsor'	Germinating	Chem	25	....	1.23, 0.82 [3]	....	117
79	*Zea mays*	Seedling	Chem	18	15	....	....	115
80		Scutellum	Mano	29	0.16	....	....	51
81	'Hopeland Sweet'	Resting	Chem	22	[0.24 [2]]	....	....	4
82					[1.2 [2]]	....	Moisture	
83	'Sutton's Improved Japanese Striped'	Germinating	.....	25	[10]	0.75	....	73
84					[127]	1.0	Development	
					Roots			
85	*Allium cepa*	Segment	Mano	25	1390 [2]	0.99	....	18
86					1140	1.07	Growth, development or maturation	
87	*Beta vulgaris*	Intact	Chem	25	0.9	....	O_2	27
88					0.6	0.8	Storage or starvation	
89		Segment	Mano	25	....	1.01	Aerated tap water, at 18 hr	116
90						0.85	Aerated tap water, at 642 hr	

[1] Unless otherwise indicated. [2] $\mu l \cdot 100$ mg dry wt$^{-1} \cdot$hr^{-1}. [3] Observations for 1 da; R values fell as seedling developed.

continued

Part IV. Vascular Plants

	Species (Synonym)	Condition or Plant Part	Method	Temp °C	Q_{O_2} $[Q_{CO_2}]$ $\mu l \cdot 100$ mg wet $wt^{-1} \cdot hr^{-1}$ [1]	R CO_2/O_2	Variable Affecting Respiration Rate	Reference
91	(B. saccharifera)	Slice	Mano	15	1.8	....	....	80
92				25	6.0	....		
93	Chrysanthemum morifolium (C. sinense)	Intact	Mano	28	....	0.93	....	103
94	Dahlia sp.	Intact	.....	22	[0.9]	....		112
95					[0.4]	....	Storage or starvation	
96	Daucus carota	Slice	Mano	12	4.0	....	....	80
97				25	10.5			
98	'Red Core Chantenay'	Intact	Chem	0.5	[0.44]	0.92	....	99
99					[0.22]	1.16	Storage or starvation	
100				10	[1.5]	1.08	....	
101					[0.5]	1.01	Storage or starvation	
102				24	[3.3]	1.10	....	
103					[1.5]	1.18	Storage or starvation	
104	Glycine max (G. soja, Soja max)	Nodule	Mano	28	60-430[2]	1.0-2.0	....	3
105	Gossypium roseum	Intact	Chem	38	[380[2]]	....	....	60
106					[73[2]]	....	Growth, development or maturation	
107	Hordeum vulgare 'Plumage Archer'	Intact	Cond	20	[482[2]]	....	....	128
108					[740[2]]	....	O_2	
109	Impatiens sp.	Intact	Chem	38	[625[2]]	....	....	60
110					[104[2]]	....	Growth, development or maturation	
111	Ipomoea batatas	Segment	Mano	25	96	1.0	....	122
112	'Triumph'	Intact	Chem	15	[1.4]	....		63
113				25	[3.2]			
114				35	[5.6]			
115	Lathyrus odoratus	Excised	Mano	20	[160[2]]	....	....	43
116	Lespedeza stipulacea	Nodule	Mano	28	130[2]; 550[2]	0.94; 1.4	....	3
117	Lycopersicon esculentum 'Bonny Best'	Excised root tips	Mano	25	600[2]	1.0	....	54
118					800[2]	1.0	Organic acids or metabolic poisons	
119	Malus pumila (Pyrus malus)	Intact	Chem	14	26[2]	0.73	....	124
120	Melilotus alba	Nodule	Mano	28	380[2]; 660[2]	0.95; 1.09	....	3
121	Oryza sativa	Intact	.....	15-18	180[2]	....	....	69
122					230[2]	....	Growth, development or maturation	
123	Pastinaca sativa	Intact	Chem	1.5	[1.1]	....		4
124				22	[2.7]			
125	Raphanus sativus	Intact	Mano	28	....	0.99	....	103
126	Taraxacum officinale	Intact	Chem	......	[0.04[2]]	0.94	....	104
127					[0.1[2]]	1.24	Herbicides	
128	Triticum aestivum (T. vulgare)	Intact	Chem	20	10[2]	....	....	77
129					25[2]	....	Inorganic nutrition, salts	
130	Vicia faba	Excised	Mano	26	....	1.46	....	107

[1] Unless otherwise indicated. [2] $\mu l \cdot 100$ mg dry $wt^{-1} \cdot hr^{-1}$.

continued

Part IV. Vascular Plants

	Species (Synonym)	Condition or Plant Part	Meth-od	Temp °C	Q_{O_2} $[Q_{CO_2}]$ $\mu l \cdot 100$ mg wet $wt^{-1} \cdot hr^{-1}$ [1]	R CO_2/O_2	Variable Affecting Respiration Rate	Ref-er-ence
131	*Vigna sinensis*	Nodule	Mano	28	71	1.0	....	3
132					640 [2]	1.1		
					Stems			
133	*Acer rubrum*	Xylem	Mano	25	3.7	....	....	46
134					2.3	....	Growth, development or maturation	
135		Cambium	Mano	25	22.4	....	....	
136		Phloem	Mano	25	16.9	....	....	
137	*Aesculus* sp.	Bud	.....	20	[9.7]	....	....	110
138	*Asparagus offici-*	Shoot	Chem	30	[915 [2]]	....	....	15
139	*nalis*				[254 [2]]	....	Storage or starvation	
140	'Mary Washington'	Intact	Chem	0.5	[3.0]	0.98	....	99
141					[2.0]	0.95	Storage or starvation	
142				10	[9.7]	1.03	....	
143					[3.6]	0.86	Storage or starvation	
144				24	[35.4]	1.04	....	
145					[13.2]	0.95	Storage or starvation	
146	*Dahlia pinnata (D. variabilis)*	Bulb	Mano	25	....	0.99	....	103
147	*Elodea* sp.	Shoot	.....	7	[15 [2]]		....	106
148				15	[31 [2]]			
149				25	[64 [2]]			
150	*E. canadensis*	Shoot	Mano	20	90 [2]	....	....	43
151	*Equisetum telma-*	Intact	Mano	Room	[9.6]	0.80	....	91
152	*teia*	Shoot or top	Mano	20	[6]	0.78	....	82
153		Fruiting shoot or top	Mano	20	[100]	0.83	....	82
154		Branchlet	Mano	Room	[19]	0.69	....	91
155	*Fagus sylvatica*	Intact	Mano	5	[0.07]	....	....	76
156				15	[0.15]			
157				20	[0.25]			
158	*Fraxinus nigra*	Xylem	Mano	25	[31.3]	....	....	46
159					[1.4]	....	Growth, development or maturation	
160		Cambium	Mano	25	[22]	....	Growth, development or maturation	
161		Phloem	Mano	25	[16.7]	....	Growth, development or maturation	
162	*Gladiolus* sp.	Corm	Chem	23	[8.5 [2]]	....	....	32
163	*Gossypium roseum*	Intact	Chem	38	[168 [2]]	....	....	60
164					[42 [2]]	....	Growth, development or maturation	
165	*Helianthus annuus*	Shoot	Chem	5	[76 [2]]	....	....	67
166	'Sutton's Giant			10	[141 [2]]			
167	Yellow'			25	[483 [2]]			
168	*Impatiens* sp.	Intact	Chem	38	[270 [2]]	....	....	60
169					[59 [2]]	....	Growth, development or maturation	
170	*Ipomoea batatas*	Tuber	Chem	30	[1.4]	....	....	53
171					[7.0; 2.4]	....	Storage or starvation	
172	*Lathyrus odoratus*	Intact	Mano	20	[160 [2]]	....	....	43
173		Shoot	Mano	20	[350 [2]]			

[1] Unless otherwise indicated. [2] $\mu l \cdot 100$ mg dry $wt^{-1} \cdot hr^{-1}$.

continued

Part IV. Vascular Plants

	Species (Synonym)	Condition or Plant Part	Method	Temp °C	Q_{O_2} [Q_{CO_2}] $\mu l \cdot 100$ mg wet wt$^{-1} \cdot$hr^{-1} [1]	R CO_2/O_2	Variable Affecting Respiration Rate	Reference
174	*Lycopersicon escu-*	Segment	Mano	28	[420 [2]]	0.91	....	67
175	*lentum*				[350 [2]]	0.95	Inorganic nutrition, salts	
	Malus pumila (Pyrus malus)							31
176	'Jonathan'	Intact	Chem	6	[2.3]	....	....	
177					[4.6]	....	Precooling	
178	'McIntosh'	Intact	Chem	6	[1.7]	....	....	
179					[3.8]	....	Precooling	
180	*Nicotiana glauca* × *N. langsdorffii*	Callus	Mano	30	380 [2]	1.0	pH & metabolic poisons	90
	Phaseolus vulgaris							26
181	'Black Valentine'	Shoot	Chem	24	[150 [2]]	....	....	
182					[190 [2]]	....	Herbicides	
183	'California Red	Intact	Mano	30	28 [2]	0.9	....	113
184	Kidney'				710 [2]	1.1	Herbicides & metabolic poisons	
185	*Picea abies (P. ex-*	Shoot	Mano	19	25.0	....	....	6
186	*celsa)*				6.3	....	Growth, development or maturation	
187	*Pisum sativum*	Segment	Mano	25	532	1.07	....	28
188	'Alaska'				334 [2]	0.98	Storage or starvation	
189	*Prunus laurocerasus*	Shoot	Chem	22.5	[14.4]	....	....	8
190					[2.6]	....	Storage or starvation	
191	*Quercus coccifera*	Segment	Mano	21	[31]	0.89	....	92
192					[11]	0.83	Growth, development or maturation	
193	*Ranunculus pseudo-*	Tip	Elec	10	41.2 [2]	....		97
194	*fluitans*			15	81.1 [2]			
195				20	111.0 [2]			
196	*Raphanus raphani-strum*	Intact	Mano	Room	[10.5]	0.87	....	91
197	*Ricinis communis*	Shoot	Mano	20	[19.2]	0.96	....	6
198	*Rumex pulcher*	Intact	Mano	Room	[11.8]	0.85	....	91
199	*Saccharum officina-*	Intact	Chem	28	[27 [2]]	....	....	55
200	*rum*				[4]	....	Growth, development or maturation	
201	'Pindar'	Intact	Chem	6	[0.14-0.27]	....	....	20
202				15	[0.36-0.72]			
203				35	[1.4-2.7]			
204				45	[1.6-3.1]			
205	*Salix herbacea*	Shoot	Chem	0	[2.5]	....	....	120
206				10	[9.1]			
207				20	[23.4]			
	Solanum tuberosum							
208	'King Edward VII'	Tuber	Chem	1	[0.13]	....	Storage or starvation, in air	11
209					[0.28]	....	Storage or starvation, in 5% O_2	
210					[0.40]	....	Storage or starvation, in 60% O_2	
211				10	[0.78; 0.51]	....	Storage or starvation	
212	'Rural'	Tuber	Chem	0.5	[0.07; 0.15]	0.45; 0.66	Storage or starvation	99
213				10	[0.2; 0.15]	0.86; 0.99		
214				24	[0.6; 0.3]	1.02; 0.75		
215	'Russet Burbank'	Tuber	Chem	2.5	[0.2]	....	....	4
216				22	[0.5]			

[1] Unless otherwise indicated. [2] $\mu l \cdot 100$ mg dry wt$^{-1} \cdot$hr^{-1}.

continued

Part IV. Vascular Plants

	Species (Synonym)	Condition or Plant Part	Method	Temp °C	Q_{O_2} [Q_{CO_2}] $\mu l \cdot 100$ mg wet $wt^{-1} \cdot hr^{-1}$ [1/]	R CO_2/O_2	Variable Affecting Respiration Rate	Reference
217			Mano	25	3.3	....	Age: slices, freshly cut	81
218			Elec	0	0.28			
219				5	0.26			
220				14	1.5			
221				24	3.1			
222			Mano	25	13.5	....	Age: slices, at 24 hr	
223			Elec	0	1.5			
224				5	2.6			
225				14	6.1			
226				24	12.5			
227	'Sebago'	Tuber	Chem	22	[7.3]	....	....	41
228					[1.8]	....	Growth, development or maturation	
229					[0.5]	....		
230					[1]	....	Storage or starvation	
231	*Syringa vulgaris*	Cambium	Mano	......	....	1.29	Age: young wood	107
232						1.38	Age: young bark	
233	*Taxus baccata*	Shoot	Mano	28	....	0.97	....	103
234	*Triticum aestivum*	Shoot	Mano	8	[19]	1.03	....	6
235	*(T. sativum)*			13	[29]	0.98		
236	*Vicia faba*	Intact	Mano	Room	[6.2]	....	....	91
237		Shoot	Mano	21	[62.6]	0.90		
238		Shoot, etiolated	Mano	21	[48.8]	0.87		
239	*Zea mays*	Shoot	Mano	30	[760 [2/]]	....	Light or photoperiod	48

Leaves

	Species (Synonym)	Condition or Plant Part	Method	Temp °C	Q_{O_2} [Q_{CO_2}]	R CO_2/O_2	Variable Affecting Respiration Rate	Reference
240	*Acer pseudoplatanus*	Intact	Chem	10	[33]	....	....	101
241	*Aesculus hippocastanum*	Intact	Mano	0	[6]	0.97	....	23
242				14	[25]	1.01		
243				25	[77]	0.98		
244	*Allium cepa* 'Yellow Blade'	Bulb	Chem	22	[2.1]	....	....	4
245	*Antirrhinum majus*	Intact	Mano	20	[16]	0.88	....	82
246	*Asparagus albus*	Tendril, phyllode, or cladode	Mano	Room	[22.3]	0.78	....	91
247	*Asplenium adiantum nigrum*	Frond	Mano	20	[13]	0.86	....	82
248		With sori	Mano	20	[17]	1.01		
249		Blade	Mano	Room	[13.4]	0.80	....	91
250		Petiole	Mano	Room	[8.3]	0.80	....	91
251	*Beta vulgaris*	Intact	Chem	27	[23]	....	....	85
252	*Betula nana*	Intact	Chem	10	[26]	....	....	120
253				20	[66]			
254	*Bryonia dioica*	Intact	Mano	20	[76]	0.90	....	92
255					[11]	0.60	Growth, development or maturation	

[1/] Unless otherwise indicated. [2/] $\mu l \cdot 100$ mg dry $wt^{-1} \cdot hr^{-1}$.

continued

Part IV. Vascular Plants

	Species (Synonym)	Condition or Plant Part	Method	Temp °C	Q_{O_2} [Q_{CO_2}] µl·100 mg wet wt^{-1}·hr^{-1} [1]	R CO_2/O_2	Variable Affecting Respiration Rate	Reference
256		Blade	Mano	Room	[13.2]	0.65	....	91
257		Petiole	Mano	Room	[9.4]	0.87	....	91
258		Tendril, phyllode, or cladode	Mano	Room	[11.3]	1.02	....	91
259	*Castanea* sp.	Intact	Mano	25	....	1.02	....	83
260						0.92	Growth, development or maturation	
261	*Catalpa bignonioides*	Intact	Chem	14	[18-25]	....	....	101
262	*Citrus limon*	Intact	Mano	......	7.7-9.5 [4]	....	....	123
263	*C. sinensis* 'Washington Navel'	Intact	Mano	......	9.6-12.9 [4]	....	....	123
264	*Elodea canadensis*	Intact	Mano, chem	......	....	8.4	....	105
265	*Fagus sylvatica*	Intact	Chem	20	[1-5 [4]]	....	....	24
266	*Fragaria* sp.	Intact	Chem	24.5	[10 [4]]	....	....	5
267					[5 [4]]	....	Growth, development or maturation	
268	'Huxley'	Intact	Chem	15	[10.6-15.0]	1.0	....	13
269	*Fraxinus excelsior*	Intact	Chem	20	[1 [4]]	....	....	24
270					[6 [4]]	....	Light or photoperiod	
271	*Gladiolus gandavensis*	Intact	Mano	24	[18]	0.64	....	82
272	*Gossypium roseum*	Intact	Chem	38	[224 [2]]	....	....	60
273					[94 [2]]	....	Growth, development or maturation	
274	*Helianthus annuus*	Intact	Chem	25	[9 [4]]	....	....	114
275					[3 [4]]	....	Storage or starvation	
276	*Hibiscus rosa-sinensis*	Intact	Chem	20	[1.3 [4]]	....	....	42
277	*Hordeum vulgare*	Intact	Chem	25	[76]	1.2	....	129
278	'Plumage Archer'				[15]	0.8	Storage or starvation	
279	*Ilex aquifolium*	Intact	Mano	21	[12]	....	....	115
280	*Impatiens* sp.	Intact	Chem	38	[312 [2]]	....	....	60
281					[120 [2]]	....	Growth, development or maturation	
282	*Iris germanica*	Intact	Chem	22.5	[12 [5]]	....	....	7
283					[13.6 [5]; 5 [5]]	....	Storage or starvation	
284	*Lactuca sativa* 'Imperial 44'	Intact	Chem	0.5	[0.8]	0.84	....	98
285					[0.35]	0.98	Storage or starvation	
286				10	[1.3]	1.09	....	
287					[0.73]	0.93	Storage or starvation	
288				24	[3.3]	1.12	....	
289					[2.6]	0.99	Storage or starvation	
290	*Lathyrus odoratus*	Intact	Mano	20	170 [2]	....	....	43
291	*Lycopersicon esculentum* 'Bonny Best'	Segment	Mano	28	390 [2]	0.96	....	68
292					430 [2]	0.91	Inorganic nutrition, salts	

[1] Unless otherwise indicated. [2] µl·100 mg dry wt^{-1}·hr^{-1}. [4] µl·cm^{-2}·hr^{-1}. [5] mg CO_2·3 hr^{-1}·10 g fresh wt^{-1}.

continued

Part IV. Vascular Plants

	Species (Synonym)	Condition or Plant Part	Method	Temp °C	Q_{O_2} [Q_{CO_2}] $\mu l \cdot 100$ mg wet wt$^{-1} \cdot$hr^{-1} [1]	R CO_2/O_2	Variable Affecting Respiration Rate	Reference
293	'John Baer'	Segment	Mano	30	42	1.28	....	118
294					46	1.13	Inorganic nutrition, salts	
295	'Michigan State	Intact	Mano	27	260[2]	....	....	36
296	Forcing'				320[2]	....	Light or photoperiod	
297	Malus pumila (Py-	Intact	Chem	33	8.6[4]	....	....	108
298	rus malus) 'Mc-Intosh'				43.0[4]	....	Moisture	
299	Nicotiana glauca ×	Segment	Mano	25	330[2]	1.27	....	90
300	N. langsdorffii				170[2]	1.43	Growth, development or maturation	
301	Oenothera biennis	Blade	Mano	18	[24]	0.83	....	92
302					[12]	0.70	Growth, development or maturation	
303	Phaseolus vulgaris	Intact	Mano	26	26-57	....	....	62
304	Phleum pratense	Intact	.....	21-26	124[2]	....	....	69
305	Phoenix dactylifera	Intact	Chem	20	[4.5[4]]	....	....	42
306	Phyllitis scolopen-	Frond	Mano	3	2.2	....	....	14
307	drium (Scolopen-			13	9.9	....	....	
308	drium scolopen-			22	17.5	....	....	
309	drium)			25	23	....	Age: very young leaves	
310					130	....	Age: medium-sized leaves	
311					40	....	Age: oldest leaves	
312				30	31	....	....	
313	Pinus pinea	Intact	Mano	14	[6.9]	0.82	....	23
314				24	[12]	0.83		
315	Pisum sativum	Intact	Mano	27	430[2]	....	....	36
316	'Alaska'				680[2]	....	Light or photoperiod	
317	Polypodium vulgare	Frond	Chem	16	[250]	....	....	61
318					[86]	....	Growth, development or maturation	
319			Mano	20	[10]	0.92	....	82
320		With sori	Mano	20	[19]	1.06	....	82
321	Populus deltoides × P. nigra (P. canadensis)	Intact	Chem	.....	[19]	....	....	101
322	Prunus amygdalus (Amygdalus communis)	Intact	Mano	14	[29]	1.00	....	93
323	P. laurocerasus	Intact	Chem	22.5	[20]	....	....	8
324					[3.4; 13.6]	....	Storage or starvation	
325	Pteridium aquili-	Frond	Chem	10	[15]	....	....	61
326	num (Eupteris			15.5	[265]	....	....	
327	aquilina)				[66]	....	Growth, development or maturation	
328				30	[46]	....	....	
329				48	[168]	....	....	
330	(Pteris aquilina)	Frond	Mano	22	[19]	0.84	....	82
331		With sori	Mano	22	[35]	1.01	....	
332	Quercus coccifera	Intact	Mano	21	[44]	0.87	....	92
333					[13]	0.79	Growth, development or maturation	

[1] Unless otherwise indicated. [2] $\mu l \cdot 100$ mg dry wt$^{-1} \cdot$hr^{-1}. [4] $\mu l \cdot$cm$^{-2} \cdot$hr^{-1}.

continued

Part IV. Vascular Plants

	Species (Synonym)	Condition or Plant Part	Method	Temp °C	Q_{O_2} [Q_{CO_2}] $\mu l \cdot 100$ mg wet wt$^{-1} \cdot$hr^{-1} [1]	R CO_2/O_2	Variable Affecting Respiration Rate	Reference
334	*Raphanus raphani-*	Blade	Mano	Room	[13.3]	0.73	....	91
335	*strum*	Petiole	Mano	Room	[6.2]	0.86		
336	*Rheum rhaponti-cum*	Segment	Mano	30	[29]	1.17	....	88
337	*Rhododendron far-gesii*	Intact	Chem	22.5	[13.6]	....	....	7
338					[5.1]	....	Storage or starvation	
339	*Rosa* sp.	Intact	Mano	14	[23]	0.93	....	93
340	*Rumex pulcher*	Blade	Mano	Room	[14.7]	0.76	....	91
341		Petiole	Mano	Room	[3.3]	0.80		
342	*Salix glauca*	Intact	Chem	0	[13]	....	....	120
343				10	[45]			
344				20	[78]			
345	*Secale cereale*	Intact	Mano	15	[26]			21
346				25	[44]			
347	*Solanum tuberosum*	Intact	Chem	10	10	....	....	61
348				30	[41]			
349				48	[137]			
350	*Sorghum bicolor (S. vulgare)*	Intact	Chem	.....	[1.2 [2]]	....	....	56
351					[0.2 [2]]	....	Growth, development or maturation	
352	*Spinacia oleracea*	Intact	Chem	20	[7.2]	0.82	....	100
353					[4.7]	0.87	O_2	
354		Segment	Mano	30	62	1.0	....	22
355					41	0.74	Storage or starvation	
356	*Syringa vulgaris*	Intact	Mano	18	[3.7]	0.98	....	23
357				24	[7.5]	0.94		
358				32	[28]	0.99		
359	*Taraxacum offici-nale*	Intact	Mano	19	[48.5]	0.95	....	71
360	*Taxus baccata*	Intact	Mano	16	[6]	0.86	....	23
361				34	[23]	0.80		
362				46	[55]	0.89		
363	*Tradescantia viridis*	Intact	Mano	29	....	1.01	....	103
364	*Triticum aestivum*	Intact	Mano	25	[40.2]	0.97	....	91
365	*(T. sativum)*	Intact, etiolated	Mano	25	[37.5]	0.98		
366	*Tulipa* sp. 'Le Notre'	Bulb	.....	20	[4.6 [2]]	1.2	....	2
367					[2.8 [2]]	1.1	Storage or starvation: 3 wk	
368					[8.6 [2]]	2.6	Storage or starvation: 3 mo	
369	*Ulmus glabra (U. montana)*	Intact	Chem	16	[24]	....	....	101
370	*Vicia faba*	Blade	Mano	Room	[11.1]	....	....	91
371		Petiole	Mano	Room	[4.1]			
372	*Vitis vinifera*	Blade	Chem	......	[81 [2]]	....	....	86
373	*Yucca gloriosa*	Intact	Chem	22.5	[8.5]	....	....	7
374					[3.3]	....	Storage or starvation	
375	*Zea mays*	Intact	Mano	26	[68.3]	0.99	....	91
376		Intact, etiolated	Mano	26	[54.1]	0.97		

[1] Unless otherwise indicated. [2] $\mu l \cdot 100$ mg dry wt$^{-1} \cdot$hr^{-1}.

continued

Part IV. Vascular Plants

	Species (Synonym)	Condition or Plant Part	Method	Temp °C	Q_{O_2} [Q_{CO_2}] $\mu l \cdot 100$ mg wet wt$^{-1} \cdot$hr^{-1} [1]	R CO_2/O_2	Variable Affecting Respiration Rate	Reference
					Flowers			
377	*Antirrhinum majus*	Petal	Mano	23	[82]	1.15	Age: young	82
378					[70]	1.13	Age: medium	
379					[34]	1.00	Age: mature	
380	*Cucumis sativus*	Pistil	Mano	22	[48]	....	Age: young	82
381					[43]	....	Age: medium	
382					[29]	....	Age: mature	
383	*Dahlia pinnata (D. variabilis)*	Petal	Mano	28	....	0.94	....	103
384	*Gladiolus gandaven-sis*	Petal	Mano	24	[15]	0.72	....	82
385		Stamen	Mano	24	[27]	0.77		
386		Pistil	Mano	24	[71]	0.90		
387	*Helianthus annuus*	Inflores-cence	Chem	10	[57[2]]	....	....	67
388					[43[2]]	....	Growth, development or maturation	
389	*Hibiscus rosa-sinensis*	Petal	Mano	26	[130]	1.06	Age: young	82
390					[86]	1.04	Age: medium	
391					[38]	0.96	Age: mature	
392		Sepal	Mano	24	[75]	0.81	Age: young	
393					[44]	0.90	Age: medium	
394					[29]	0.94	Age: mature	
395	*Lathyrus odoratus*	Petal	Mano	20	330[2]	....	....	43
396		Filament	Mano	20	160[2]			
397		Ovary	Mano	20	300[2]			
398		Ovule	Mano	20	420[2]			
399	*Lilium bulbiferum (L. croceum)*	Stamen	.....	......	[56]	1.14	....	49
400					[21]	0.98	Growth, development or maturation	
401		Pistil	.....	......	[58]	1.06		
402					[19]	1.12	Growth, development or maturation	
403	*L. longiflorum*	Pollen[6]	Mano	30	1267	1.0	....	34
404	*Pinus densiflora*	Pollen	Mano	25	160[2]	....	....	94,95
405	*Rosa* sp.	Intact	Mano	28	....	1.04	....	82
406	*Syringa vulgaris*	Intact	.....	20	[40]	....	....	110
407	*Tulipa gesneriana*	Intact	.....	28	....	0.95	....	103
408		Pollen	Mano	20	300[2]	....	....	94,95
409	*Yucca gloriosa*	Petal	Mano	24	[67]	0.91	Age: young	82
410					[41]	0.97	Age: medium	
411					[44]	1.07	Age: mature	
412		Pistil	Mano	16	[24]	....	Age: young	
413					[23]	....	Age: medium	
414					[22]	....	Age: mature	
					Fruits			
415	*Ananas comosus (A. sativus)*	Intact	Chem	......	3	1.2	....	72
416			IR	20	[5.0]	....	....	35
417					[1.0]	....	Growth, development or maturation	

[1] Unless otherwise indicated. [2] $\mu l \cdot 100$ mg dry wt$^{-1} \cdot$hr^{-1}. [6] On sucrose medium.

continued

Part IV. Vascular Plants

	Species (Synonym)	Condition or Plant Part	Method	Temp °C	Q_{O_2} [Q_{CO_2}] $\mu l \cdot 100$ mg wet wt$^{-1} \cdot$hr^{-1} [1]	R CO_2/O_2	Variable Affecting Respiration Rate	Reference
418	Bryonia dioica	Intact	Chem	25	[64]	....	....	119
419					[8.5]	....	Growth, development or maturation	
420	Capsicum annuum	Slices	Mano	25	8 [5]	0.6	....	57
421	'California Wonder'				3 [2]	0.6	Growth, development, & storage. Essentially no difference in R value with increasing maturity.	
422	C. frutescens 'Windsor A'	Intact	Chem	0.5	[0.44]	....	....	99
423					[0.29]	0.96	Storage or starvation	
424				10	[1.2]	1.27	....	
425					[0.58]	0.88	Storage or starvation	
426				24	[4.0]	1.12	....	
427					[1.4]	0.88	Storage or starvation	
428	Citrus limon	Intact	Magn	20	0.7	....	....	130
429					0.14	....	Storage or starvation	
430	'Eureka'	Intact	.....	0	[0.15]	1.2		50
431				21	[1.1]	1.0		
432				38	[4.1]	1.4		
433	C. sinensis 'Washington Navel'	Intact	.....	0	[0.15]	1.2		50
434				10	[0.8]	1.1		
435				21	[2.0]	1.1		
436	Cocos nucifera	Endocarp & nucellus	Mano	30	400 [2]	....	....	30
437					0 [2]	....	Growth, development or maturation	
438	Cucumis melo	Intact	Gas	20	[1.9]	....	....	79
439					[4.3]	....	Storage or starvation	
440				30	[4]	....	....	
441					[6.5]	....	Storage or starvation	
442	'Cantaloupe'	Intact	Color	20	[2.5]	....	....	84
443					[1.3; 4.5]	....	Growth, development or maturation	
444	C. sativus 'Davis Perfect'	Intact	Chem	0.5	[0.2]	0.97	....	99
445					[0.08]	0.88	Storage or starvation	
446				10	[1.0]	1.01	....	
447					[0.4]	1.10	Storage or starvation	
448				24	[2.3]	1.01	....	
449					[0.8]	0.91	Storage or starvation	
450	Fragaria sp.	Intact	Chem	20	[3.3]	0.84	....	96
451					[5.1]	0.91	Growth, development or maturation	
452	Helianthus annuus	Intact	Mano	25	....	0.96	....	103
453	Hibiscus esculentus	Intact	Chem	30	[306 [2]]	....	....	15
454					[104 [2]]	....	Storage or starvation	
455	Lycopersicon esculentum	Intact	IR	21	[3.0]	....	....	1
456					[1.3]	....	Growth, development or maturation	
457		Slices	IR	21	[4.7]	....	....	
458	(Solanum lycopersicon)	Intact	Mano	28	....	1.9	....	103
459	'Marglobe'	Intact	Chem	0.5	[0.36]	1.11	....	99
460					[0.15]	0.97	Storage or starvation	

[1] Unless otherwise indicated. [2] $\mu l \cdot 100$ mg dry wt$^{-1} \cdot$hr^{-1}.

continued

Part IV. Vascular Plants

	Species (Synonym)	Condition or Plant Part	Method	Temp °C	Q_{O_2} [Q_{CO_2}] $\mu l \cdot 100$ mg wet $wt^{-1} \cdot hr^{-1}$	R CO_2/O_2	Variable Affecting Respiration Rate	Reference
461				10	[0.77]	1.39	....	
462					[0.58]	1.06	Storage or starvation	
463				24	[2.5]	1.11	....	
464					[1.6]	1.13	Storage or starvation	
465	*Malus pumila (Pyrus malus)* 'Cox's Orange'	Intact	Chem	12	[0.7]	....	....	65
466					[1.4]	....	Growth, development or maturation	
467					[0.6]	....	....	
468					[1.2]	....	Storage or starvation	
469					[0.6]	....	....	59
470					[1.4]	....	Storage or starvation	
471				15	[0.7]	....	....	59
472					[1.6]	....	Storage or starvation	
473	'Early Victoria'	Intact	Chem	12	[2.8]	....	....	58
474					[0.7; 1.0]	....	Growth, development or maturation	
475	'Jonathan'	Intact	Chem	20	[1.7]	....	....	40
476					[0.8]	....	Growth, development or maturation	
477			Mano	27	[2.4]	0.43	....	109
478					[5.1; 0.6]	0.91	Growth, development or maturation	
479	*Nicotiana tabacum*	Intact	Mano	28	....	0.94	....	103
480	*Persea americana*	Intact	Magn	15	2.5	....	....	17,
481	(*P. gratissima*)				8.5	....	Storage or starvation	130
482				20	2	....	....	
483					12	....	Storage or starvation	
484		Peel	Magn	20	12	....	....	16
485					20	....	Storage or starvation	
486		Pulp	Magn	20	12	....	....	16
487					20	....	Storage or starvation	
488	'Fuerte'	Intact	Chem	15	[5.8]	....	....	19,
489					[3.6; 8.1]	....	Storage or starvation	102
490	*Phaseolus vulgaris*	Intact	Chem	0.5	[0.95]	0.94	....	99
491	'Tendergreen'				[0.65]	0.96	Storage or starvation	
492				10	[4.6]	1.08	....	
493					[2.0]	0.98	Storage or starvation	
494				24	[16.4]	1.14	....	
495					[6.6]	1.00	Storage or starvation	
496	*Pisum sativum* 'Laxton Progress'	Intact	Chem	0.5	[2.2]	1.07	....	99
497					[1.4]	0.96	Storage or starvation	
498				10	[7.9]	1.13	....	
499					[3.1]	1.00	Storage or starvation	
500				24	[20]	1.32	....	
501					[12]	1.06	Storage or starvation	
502	*Prunus domesticus*	Intact	Chem	4	[0.5]	....	....	29
503	'Santa Rosa'			18	[1.7]	....	....	
504					[3.6]	....	Storage or starvation	

continued

Part IV. Vascular Plants

	Species (Synonym)	Condition or Plant Part	Meth-od	Temp °C	Q_{O_2} [Q_{CO_2}] $\mu l \cdot 100$ mg wet wt$^{-1} \cdot$hr^{-1} [1]	R CO$_2$/O$_2$	Variable Affecting Respiration Rate	Ref-er-ence
505	*P. persica* 'Primrose'	Intact	Chem	4	[0.4]	....	....	29
506					[0.3]	....	Storage or starvation	
507				18	[1.4]	....	....	
508					[2.0]	....	Storage or starvation	
509	*Pyrus communis*	Intact	Chem	18	[6.3]	....	....	39
510	'Bartlett'				[1.0; 1.2]	....	Growth, development or maturation	
511	*Quercus alba*	Intact	Mano	2.5	17[2]	0.16	....	25
512				10	16[2]	0.30		
513				30	21[2]	0.71		
514	*Ribes nigrum*	Intact	Chem	1.2	[0.5]	....	....	47
515				11.2	[1.5]			
516				30.9	[7.7]			
517	*R. rubrum*	Intact	Mano	28	....	1.4	....	103
518	'Fay'	Intact	Chem	1.8	[0.3]	....	....	47
519				11.8	[0.7]			
520				32.0	[3.2]			
521	*Ricinus communis*	Intact	Mano	28	....	1.07	....	103
522	*Rosa* sp.	Intact	Mano	28	....	0.86	....	103
523	*Secale cereale* 'Ab-	Intact	Mano	28	245[2]	....	....	111
524	bruzzi'				12[2]	....	Growth, development or maturation	
525	*Triticum aestivum*	Intact	Mano	28	340[2]	....	....	111
526	(*T. vulgare*) 'Leapland'				8[2]	....	Growth, development or maturation	
527	*Vitis vinifera*	Intact	.....	0	0.15 [0.14]	0.91	....	78
528				10	0.5 [0.5]	1.05		
529				21.1	1.4 [1.7]	1.20		
530				26.7	1.6 [2.0]	1.25		
531	*Zea mays* 'Stowell's	Intact	Chem	4.5	[3.5]	....	....	4
532	Evergreen Sweet'			28	[11-17]			

Whole Plants

	Species (Synonym)	Condition or Plant Part	Meth-od	Temp °C	Q_{O_2} [Q_{CO_2}]	R CO$_2$/O$_2$	Variable Affecting Respiration Rate	Ref-er-ence
533	*Betula nana*	Intact	Mano	16	[7.0[4]]	0.93	....	70
534	*Gossypium roseum*	Intact	Chem	38	[198[4]]	....	....	60
535					[65[2]]	....	Growth, development or maturation	
536	*Helianthus annuus*	Intact	Chem	10	[148[2]]	....	....	67
537	'Sutton's Giant Yellow'				[13[2]]	....	Growth, development or maturation	
538	*Impatiens* sp.	Intact	Chem	38	390[2]	....	....	60
539					91[2]	....	Growth, development or maturation	
540	*Ipomoea batatas*	Intact	Mano	21	[1]	....	....	127
541	'Big Stem Jersey'				[2]	....	Wounding	
542	*Nicotiana tabacum*	Intact	Chem	......	7.7	....	....	44
543	'Samsun'				10.0	....	Disease	
544	*Ranunculus pseudo-fluitans*	Intact	Elec	20	100.0[2]	....	....	97

[1] Unless otherwise indicated. [2] $\mu l \cdot 100$ mg dry wt$^{-1} \cdot$hr^{-1}. [4] $\mu l \cdot$cm$^{-2} \cdot$hr^{-1}.

continued

Part IV. Vascular Plants

	Species (Synonym)	Condition or Plant Part	Method	Temp °C	Q_{O_2} [Q_{CO_2}] $\mu l \cdot 100$ mg wet $wt^{-1} \cdot hr^{-1}$ [L/]	R CO_2/O_2	Variable Affecting Respiration Rate	Reference
545	*Ricinus communis*	Intact	Mano	30	180	0.78	....	89
546	*Solanum tuberosum*	Intact	Chem	19	[10.7]	....	....	126
547	'Arran Comrade'				[14.3]	....	Disease	
548	*Triticum aestivum*	Intact	Chem	2	[38[2/]]	....	....	33
549	'Minhardi'				[13[2/]]	....	Storage or starvation	

[L/] Unless otherwise indicated. [2/] $\mu l \cdot 100$ mg dry $wt^{-1} \cdot hr^{-1}$.

Contributor: Forward, Dorothy F.

References

[1] Abdul-Baki, A. A., et al. 1965. Plant Physiol. 40: 611.

[2] Algera, L. 1936. Proc. Kon. Ned. Akad. Wetensch., Sect. Sci., 39:846, 971, 1106.

[3] Allison, F. E., et al. 1940. Bot. Gaz. 101:513.

[4] Appleman, C. O., and R. G. Brown. 1946. Amer. J. Bot. 33:170.

[5] Arney, S. E. 1947. New Phytol. 46:68.

[6] Aubert, E. 1892. Rev. Gen. Bot. 4:421.

[7] Audus, L. J. 1939. New Phytol. 38:284.

[8] Audus, L. J. 1947. Ann. Bot. (London), n.s. 11: 165.

[9] Bailey, C. H. 1940. Plant Physiol. 15:257.

[10] Bailey, C. H., and A. M. Gurjar. 1920. J. Biol. Chem. 44:17.

[11] Barker, J. 1965. New Phytol. 64:201.

[12] Barker, J. 1965. Ibid. 64:210.

[13] Barker, J., and M. E. Younis. 1965. J. Exp. Bot. 16: 59.

[14] Belehradek, J., and M. Belehradkova. 1929. New Phytol. 28:313.

[15] Benoy, M. P. 1929. J. Agr. Res. 39:75.

[16] Ben-Yehoshua, S. 1964. Physiol. Plant. 17:71.

[17] Ben-Yehoshua, S., et al. 1963. Plant Physiol. 38: 194.

[18] Berry, L. J. 1949. J. Cell. Comp. Physiol. 33:41.

[19] Biale, J. B. 1946. Amer. J. Bot. 33:363.

[20] Bieleski, R. L. 1958. Aust. J. Biol. Sci. 11:315.

[21] Blanc, L. 1916. Rev. Gen. Bot. 28:65.

[22] Bonner, J., and S. G. Wildman. 1946. Arch. Biochem. 10:497.

[23] Bonnier, G., and L. Mangin. 1884. Ann. Sci. Natur. Zool., Ser. 6, 19:217.

[24] Boysen-Jensen, P., and D. Müller. 1929. Jahrb. Wiss. Bot. 70:503.

[25] Brown, J. W. 1939. Plant Physiol. 14:621.

[26] Brown, J. W. 1946. Bot. Gaz. 107:332.

[27] Choudhury, J. K. 1939. Proc. Roy. Soc. B127: 238.

[28] Christiansen, G. S., and K. V. Thimann. 1950. Arch. Biochem. 26:248.

[29] Claypool, L. L., and F. W. Allen. 1948. Proc. Amer. Soc. Hort. Sci. 51:103.

[30] Cutter, V. M., Jr., et al. 1952. Amer. J. Bot. 39:51.

[31] DeLong, W. A., et al. 1930. Plant Physiol. 15:509.

[32] Denny, F. E. 1939. Contrib. Boyce Thompson Inst. 10:453.

[33] Dexter, S. T. 1934. Plant Physiol. 9:831.

[34] Dickinson, D. B. 1967. Physiol. Plant. 20:118.

[35] Dull, G. G., et al. 1967. Ibid. 20:1059.

[36] Elliott, B. B., and A. C. Leopold. 1952. Plant Physiol. 27:787.

[37] Ermakov, A. I., and N. N. Ivanov. 1931. Biochem. Z. 231:79.

[38] Erygin, P. S. 1936. Plant Physiol. 11:821.

[39] Ezell, B. D., and F. Gerhardt. 1938. J. Agr. Res. 56:365.

[40] Ezell, B. D., and F. Gerhardt. 1942. Ibid. 65:453.

[41] Forward, D. F. 1953. Can. J. Bot. 31:33.

[42] Gabrielsen, E. K. 1931. Planta 14:217.

[43] Genevois, L. 1927. Biochem. Z. 191:147.

[44] Glasstone, V. F. 1942. Plant Physiol. 17:267.

[45] Godlewski, E. 1882. Jahrb. Wiss. Bot. 13:491.

[46] Goodwin, R. H., and D. R. Goddard. 1940. Amer. J. Bot. 27:234.

[47] Gore, H. C. 1911. U.S. Dep. Agr. Bur. Chem. Bull. 142.

[48] Groner, M. G. 1936. Amer. J. Bot. 23:381.

[49] Guilcher, J. M. 1937. Rev. Gen. Bot. 49:235.

[50] Haller, M. H., et al. 1945. J. Agr. Res. 71:327.

[51] Hanson, J. B., et al. 1965. J. Exp. Bot. 16:282.

[52] Harrington, G. T. 1923. J. Agr. Res. 23:117.

continued

Part IV. Vascular Plants

[53] Hasselbring, H., and L. A. Hawkins. 1915. Ibid. 5: 509.

[54] Henderson, J. H., and J. F. Stauffer. 1944. Amer. J. Bot. 31:528.

[55] Hes, J. W. 1949. Proc. Kon. Ned. Akad. Wetensch., Sect. Sci., 52:915.

[56] Hover, J. M., and F. G. Gustafson. 1926. J. Gen. Physiol. 10:33.

[57] Howard, F. C., and M. Yamaguchi. 1957. Plant Physiol. 32:418.

[58] Hulme, A. C. 1951. J. Hort. Sci. 26:118.

[59] Hulme, A. C. 1954. Ibid. 29:142.

[60] Inamdar, R. S., et al. 1925. Ann. Bot. (London) 39:281.

[61] Johansson, N. 1926. Sv. Bot. Tidskr. 20:107.

[62] Johnson, C. M., and W. M. Hoskins. 1952. Plant Physiol. 27:507.

[63] Johnstone, G. R. 1925. Bot. Gaz. 80:145.

[64] Jones, H. A. 1920. Ibid. 69:127.

[65] Jones, J. D., et al. 1965. New Phytol. 64:158.

[66] Karon, M. L., and A. M. Altschul. 1946. Plant Physiol. 21:506.

[67] Kidd, F., C. West, and G. E. Briggs. 1921. Proc. Roy. Soc. B92:368.

[68] Klein, R. M. 1951. Arch. Biochem. 30:207.

[69] Kostytschev, S. 1927. Plant Respiration. Blakiston, Philadelphia.

[70] Krascheninnikoff, T. 1926. C. R. Acad. Sci. 182: 939.

[71] Kylin, H. 1911. Ark. Bot. 11:1.

[72] Langworthy, C. F., et al. 1920. J. Biol. Chem. 41: lxix.

[73] Leach, W. 1936. Proc. Roy. Soc. B119:507.

[74] Leach, W., and K. W. Dent. 1934. Ibid. B116:150.

[75] Lewin, M. 1905. Ber. Deut. Bot. Ges. 23:100.

[76] Löhr, E. 1957. Physiol. Plant. 10:340.

[77] Lundegardh, H. 1950. Nature (London) 165:513.

[78] Lutz, J. M. 1938. U.S. Dep. Agr. Tech. Bull. 606.

[79] Lyons, J. M., et al. 1962. Plant Physiol. 37:31.

[80] MacDonald, I. R., and P. C. deKock. 1958. Ann. Bot. (London), n.s. 22:429.

[81] MacDonald, I. R., and G. C. Laties. 1962. J. Exp. Bot. 13:435.

[82] Maige, G. 1911. Ann. Sci. Natur. Bot. Biol. Veg., Ser. 9, 14:1.

[83] Maquenne, L., and E. Demoussey. 1913. C. R. Acad. Sci. 156:278.

[84] McGlasson, W. B., and H. K. Pratt. 1964. Plant Physiol. 39:120.

[85] Meyer, A., and N. T. Deleano. 1911. Z. Bot. 3:657.

[86] Meyer, A., and N. T. Deleano. 1913. Ibid. 5:209.

[87] Meyer, B. S., and D. S. Rader. 1936. Plant Physiol. 11:437.

[88] Morrison, J. F. 1949. Aust. J. Exp. Biol. Med. Sci. 27:581.

[89] Murlin, J. R. 1933. J. Gen. Physiol. 17:283.

[90] Newcomb, E. H. 1950. Amer. J. Bot. 37:264.

[91] Nicolas, G. 1909. Ann. Sci. Natur. Bot. Biol. Veg., Ser. 9, 10:1.

[92] Nicolas, G. 1918. Rev. Gen. Bot. 30:209.

[93] Nicolas, G. 1919. Ibid. 31:161.

[94] Okunuki, K. 1937. Acta Phytochim. (Tokyo) 9: 267.

[95] Okunuki, K. 1939. Ibid. 11:27.

[96] Overholser, E. L., et al. 1931. Plant Physiol. 6:549.

[97] Owens, M., and P. J. Maris. 1964. Hydrobiologia 23:533.

[98] Pack, D. A. 1920. Bot. Gaz. 71:32.

[99] Platenius, H. 1942. Plant Physiol. 17:179.

[100] Platenius, H. 1943. Ibid. 18:671.

[101] Plester, W. 1912. Beitr. Biol. Pflanz. 11:249.

[102] Pratt, R., and J. B. Biale. 1944. Plant Physiol. 19: 519.

[103] Pringsheim, E. G. 1935. Jahrb. Wiss. Bot. 81:579.

[104] Rasmussen, L. W. 1947. Plant Physiol. 22:377.

[105] Ronkin, R. R., and S. C. Brooks. 1942. Science 95:231.

[106] Rosenfels, R. S. 1935. Protoplasma 23:503.

[107] Ruhland, W., and K. Ramshorn. 1938. Planta 28: 471.

[108] Schneider, G. W., and N. F. Childers. 1941. Plant Physiol. 16:565.

[109] Shaw, S. T. 1942. Ibid. 17:80.

[110] Sherman, H. 1921. Bot. Gaz. 72:1.

[111] Shirk, H. G. 1942. Amer. J. Bot. 29:105.

[112] Smith, C. L. 1936. J. Agr. Res. 53:557.

[113] Smith, F. G. 1948. Plant Physiol. 23:70.

[114] Spoehr, H. A., and J. M. McGee. 1924. Amer. J. Bot. 11:493.

[115] Stich, C. 1891. Flora (Jena) 74:1.

[116] Stiles, W., and K. W. Dent. 1947. Ann. Bot. (London), n.s. 11:1.

[117] Stiles, W., and W. Leach. 1933. Proc. Roy. Soc. B113:405.

[118] Tsui, C. 1949. Nature (London) 164:970.

[119] Ulrich, R. 1944. Bull. Soc. Bot. Fr. 91:210.

[120] Wager, H. G. 1941. New Phytol. 40:1.

[121] Wager, H. G. 1967. J. Exp. Bot. 18:672.

[122] Walter, E. M., and J. M. Nelson. 1945. Arch. Biochem. 6:131.

[123] Wedding, R. T., et al. 1952. Plant Physiol. 27: 269.

[124] White, D. G., and N. F. Childers. 1944. Ibid. 19: 699.

[125] White, J. 1909. Proc. Roy. Soc. B81:417.

[126] Whitehead, R. 1934. Ann. Appl. Biol. 21:48.

[127] Whiteman, T. M., and H. A. Schomer. 1945. Plant Physiol. 20:171.

[128] Woodford, E. K., and F. G. Gregory. 1948. Ann. Bot. (London), n.s. 12:335.

[129] Yemm, E. W. 1935. Proc. Roy. Soc. B117:504.

[130] Young, R. E., et al. 1962. Plant Physiol. 37:416.

For a comprehensive review of the subject,

Com-ponent	Agnatha [1]	Chondrichthyes, Osteichthyes, & Dipnoi [2]	Amphibia
1 Sinus venosus	Thin-walled, elongated sac or tube into which systemic veins open	Smooth, thin-walled chamber into which systemic veins open. Cardiac muscle has high intrinsic contraction rate and acts as the "pacemaker." (Although contraction is myogenic in origin, rate of beat is under nervous control, being depressed by vagal stimulation and accelerated by sympathetic stimulation.)	Caudata: Thin-walled, triangular-shaped chamber, shifted toward right side. Salientia: Separate chamber; relatively smaller than in Caudata.
2 Sinoatrial junction	Sinoatrial opening guarded by pair of valves	Sinoatrial opening guarded by pair of valves. Cardiac muscle continuous from sinus to atrium.	Approximately the same as in Osteichthyes
3 Atrium	Single muscular sac. Atrium displaced slightly to left side.	Thin, reticulate-walled chamber; no division into right & left sides, no pulmonary veins. Dipnoi: Partial septation. Pulmonary vein enters to left, and sinus venosus to right, of septum.	Caudata: Incomplete septum partially dividing chamber bilaterally, with sinus venosus opening into right atrium and single pulmonary vein into left atrium. Salientia: Complete interatrial septum.
4 Atrioventricular junction	Atrioventricular channel connects both vesicles. Two valves present.	Atrioventricular valve composed of two cusps. Cardiac muscle of atrium continuous with that of ventricle around entire circumference of atrioventricular junction. Dipnoi: Unique fibrocartilaginous plug fits into atrioventricular opening connected with interatrial & interventricular septum, serving as the only valve.	Continuity of atrial & ventricular muscles, as in Osteichthyes. Caudata: Atrioventricular valve of two or four fibrous flaps. Salientia: Four valve cusps.
5 Ventricle	Thick-walled muscular sac with smooth internal surface	Thick-walled chamber; network of muscular trabeculae; no division into right & left sides. Dipnoi: Septum present.	No interventricular septum; series of high septa create secondary chambers in ventricle
6 Bulbus cordis (embryonic) [2]	Remains as conus arteriosus; reduced to two valves in adult	Remains as conus arteriosus; reduced in teleosts to two semilunar valves & corresponding striated muscles. Chondrichthyes: Relatively long, with several valves. Dipnoi: Divided into dorsal & ventral channels.	Remains as conus arteriosus with semilunar valves, and a "spiral valve" coursing lengthwise

[1] Data are from reference 6. [2] For information on *Polypterus* and *Protopterus*, consult references 2 and 13. [3] Data for Crocodylia are from reference 23. [4] Some authorities are of the opinion that a small part of the sinus venosus is also incorporated in the left atrium [8]. [5] The view that "Purkinje-like" fibers are present in the turtle and in lower

consult references 1, 3, 7, 10, 15, 16, 18, and 22.

Reptilia[3]	Aves	Mammalia			
		Bos taurus	Canis familiaris	Homo sapiens	
Asymmetric; shifted to right side but externally obvious except in Crocodylia, in which it is partly incorporated in wall of right atrium. Chelonia: Origin of beat dependent on intrinsic ganglia [9].	Largely included in right atrium. Sinoatrial node, near base of right venous valve, not as clearly defined as in mammals.	Incorporated in right atrium. Sinoatrial node, or "pacemaker," is specialized tissue in atrial region (part of sinus in embryo).		Sinus venosus completely incorporated in right atrium[4]. Sinoatrial node same as in Bos & Canis.	1
Approximately the same as in Osteichthyes	Right valve of embryonic sinus becomes valve of inferior vena cava	Right valve of embryonic sinus becomes valve of inferior vena cava & of coronary sinus		Vestige of embryonic sinoatrial junction found in adult right atrium	2
Same as in Salientia, but interatrial septum contributes to valves dividing atrioventricular opening in two	Complete interatrial septum. Extensive distribution of specialized conduction fibers.	Complete interatrial septum. Histological characteristics of nodal fibers unusually clear in Bos & other ungulates. Physiological studies on rabbit & dog indicate impulse is conducted from sinoatrial to atrioventricular node by special tracts [10]. Cytological differences obscure between atrial conduction paths & typical muscle fibers [22].		Complete interatrial septum; occasional small remnant of foramen ovale. Sinoatrial node near opening of superior vena cava; atrioventricular node near opening of coronary sinus. Three internodal tracts described [12].	3
Chelonia: Continuity of muscle, as in Osteichthyes. Presence of "Purkinje-like" fibers controversial.[5] Crocodylia: Atrioventricular ring contains cartilage extending into base of right atrioventricular valve & similar valve of right aortic arch.	Atrial & ventricular muscles separated by ring of connective tissue, except for atrioventricular bundles of conduction fibers. Right atrioventricular valve is large & muscular, left valve is bicuspid.	Connective tissue of atrioventricular ring (anulus fibrosus) contains bone. Atrioventricular bundle usually distinct. Right atrioventricular valve usually tricuspid, left valve usually bicuspid.	Atrioventricular valves the same as in Bos. Ring of connective tissue separates atrial & ventricular muscle, except for atrioventricular bundle of His.	Atrioventricular ring of dense connective tissue. Right atrioventricular valve is tricuspid, left valve is bicuspid. Atrioventricular bundle of His present from atrioventricular node to ventricles.	4
Chelonia, Sauria, Serpentes: Ventricle partially divided by incomplete septum. Crocodylia: Complete ventricular septum containing cartilage.	Complete ventricular septum	Complete septum. Histological characteristics of Purkinje (conduction) fibers distinct.	Complete ventricular septum	Complete interventricular septum, membranous in uppermost reaches. Forms left ventricle[6].	5
Incorporated in ventricle & arterial trunks, except in Sphenodon which retains it in the form of a short, proximal conus arteriosus [20]	Proximal portion incorporated in right ventricle; distal incorporated in right aortic & pulmonary trunks	Proximal portion incorporated in right ventricle; distal incorporated in left aortic & pulmonary trunks.		Man & rat: Bulbus cordis appears to be principal source of right ventricle[6] [5,14].	6

forms is supported in reference 18, while the view that a specialized conduction system of Purkinje fibers is neomorphic for birds and mammals is supported in reference 4.

[6] For designations of postatrial chambers, consult reference 24. [7] Transposition of the great vessels was induced experimentally in rats [14] and chickens [19].

continued

	Component	Agnatha [1/]	Chondrichthyes, Osteichthyes, & Dipnoi [2/]	Amphibia
7	Truncus arteriosus [8/]	Part bordering on ventricle is enlarged to form bulbus arteriosus containing smooth muscles only. Terminal parts give off afferent branchial arteries.	Elasmobranchii: Becomes a long, strong conus arteriosus. Osteichthyes: In teleosts, part bordering on ventricle is enlarged to form a bulbus arteriosus containing smooth muscles only, into which a much reduced bulbus cordis is incorporated. Terminal parts give off afferent branchial arteries. Dipnoi: Becomes conus, divided internally by a spiral valve.	Divided internally into three (adult) or four (larva) pairs of channels, each leading to an aortic arch. Right & left sets externally separated into right & left aortas in Salientia, not in Caudata.

[1/] Data are from reference 6. [2/] For information on *Polypterus* and *Protopterus*, consult references 2 and 13. [3/] Data for Crocodylia are from reference 23. [8/] An expanded portion of the ventral aorta lying within the pericardial cavity;

Contributors: Copenhaver, W. M.; Ballard, W. W.; Andrew, Warren; Grodzinski, Z.; Monie, I. W.

References

[1] Arey, L. B. 1965. Developmental Anatomy. Ed. 7. W. B. Saunders, Philadelphia.

[2] Bugge, J. 1961. Dan. Naturhis. Foren. Videnskab. Medd. 123:193.

[3] Chiodi, V., and R. Bortolami. 1967. The Conducting System of the Vertebrate Heart. Calderini, Bologna, Italy.

[4] Davies, F., and E. T. B. Francis. 1946. Biol. Rev. Cambridge Phil. Soc. 21:173.

[5] De Vries, P. A., and J. B. de C. M. Saunders. 1962. Carnegie Inst. Wash. Publ. 621:87.

[6] Favaro, G. 1901. In H. G. Bronn, ed. Klassen und Ordnungen des Thier-Reichs. C. F. Winter, Leipzig. Bd. 6.

[7] Goodrich, E. S. 1930. Studies on the Structure and Development of Vertebrates. Macmillan, London.

[8] Hamilton, W. J., et al. 1972. Human Embryology. Rev. ed. 4. W. Heffer, Cambridge, England.

[9] Heinbecker, P., and G. H. Bishop. 1935. Amer. J. Physiol. 114:212.

[10] Hoffman, B. F., and P. F. Cranefield. 1960. The Electrophysiology of the Heart. McGraw-Hill, New York.

220. COMPARATIVE ANATOMY OF THE

Part I.

	Vessel	Agnatha	Chondrichthyes, Osteichthyes, & Dipnoi [1/]	Amphibia
			Main Longitudinal Vessels	
1	Aorta & caudal artery	Continuous vessels lying ventral to axial skeleton, from heart region to tip of tail. Caudal artery enclosed in hemal channel; aorta similarly enclosed in *Acipenser* only.		
2	Aortic arches	Six, seven, or more epibranchial arteries	Mainly four to five epibranchial arteries. Dipnoi: Pulmonary arteries present	One to four pairs of aortic arches
3	Carotid arteries	Myxini: Internal & external carotid arteries. Petromyzones: Internal carotid artery, dorsal; external carotid artery, ventral	Internal carotid arteries	Internal & external carotid arteries. Carotid ducts usually, but not always, lost in adult Caudata, and always lost in adult Salientia.

[1/] Unless otherwise indicated.

Reptilia[3]	Aves	Mammalia			
		Bos taurus	Canis familiaris	Homo sapiens	
Always completely divided into three trunks--right & left systemic & pulmonary--except in Crocodylia in which the foramen of Panizza is open between bases of right & left systemic trunks	Right aortic & left pulmonary trunks	Divided into left aortic & right pulmonary trunks. Semilunar valves at junction of embryonic bulbus cordis & truncus arteriosus.			7

also known as the bulbus arteriosus, or aortic sac [1,11,17]. For discussion on the use of this term, consult reference 21.

[11] Hyman, L. G. 1947. Comparative Vertebrate Anatomy. Univ. Chicago Press, Chicago.
[12] James, T. N. 1963. Amer. Heart J. 66:498.
[13] Magid, A. M. A. 1967. J. Zool. 152:19.
[14] Monie, I. W., et al. 1966. Anat. Rec. 156:175.
[15] Nelsen, O. E. 1953. Comparative Embryology of the Vertebrates. Blakiston, New York.
[16] Parsons, T. S., ed. 1968. Amer. Zool. 8:177.
[17] Patten, B. M. 1968. Human Embryology. Ed. 3. McGraw-Hill, New York.

[18] Robb, J. S. 1965. Comparative Basic Cardiology. Grune and Stratton, New York.
[19] Rychter, Z. 1962. Advan. Morphog. 2:333.
[20] Simmons, J. R. 1965. J. Zool. 146:451.
[21] Sissman, N. J. 1970. Cardiac Develop. Proc. Int. Symp. 1968, p. 27.
[22] Truex, R. C., and M. Q. Smythe. 1965. Ann. N.Y. Acad. Sci. 127:19.
[23] White, F. N. 1956. Anat. Rec. 125:417.
[24] O'Rahilly, R. 1971. Acta Anat. 79:70.

VASCULAR SYSTEM: VERTEBRATES

Blood Vessels

Reptilia	Aves	Mammalia	
Main Longitudinal Vessels			
A continuous vessel lying ventral to vertebrae, from heart region to tip of tail. Secondarily split into unequal right & left halves in turtles. Caudal artery enclosed in hemal arches of caudal vertebrae where such arches occur.			1
One pair of aortic arches	Right aortic arch only	Left aortic arch only	2
Internal & external carotid arteries originate from common carotids. Many Serpentes: only one common carotid. Crocodylia: Carotid duct absent.	Internal & external carotids originate from common carotid arteries, which may be symmetrical, asymmetrical, fused, or one may be obliterated	Various connections of internal & external carotids with aortic arch: brachiocephalic artery, common carotid artery, carotid trunk	3

continued

	Vessel	Agnatha	Chondrichthyes, Osteichthyes, & Dipnoi [1]	Amphibia
4	Posterior cardinal veins	In all embryos, two posterior cardinal veins present & continuous with the caudal vein. Myxini: Same as in embryo. but right posterior cardinal vein much thinner than left. Petromyzones: Same as in embryo.	Formation of kidneys causes great changes in distribution of posterior cardinals (renal portal system). Chondrichthyes: Caudal vein empties into renal portal veins; renal & hepatic veins empty into posterior cardinal veins, which are sinus-like distentions. Osteichthyes: Posterior cardinals often asymmetrical but receive renal & hepatic veins. Renal portal blood derived from caudal vein and/or segmental veins; caudal vein often leads directly to posterior cardinal. *Polypterus:* Paired posterior cardinals, connected by several anastomoses, enter separately the ducts of Cuvier; pulmonary veins open by intermediation of hepatic vein into sinus venosus [1]. *Latimeria* [2]: Posterior vena cava collects renal & hepatic blood and passes it into sinus venosus [2]. Dipnoi: Caudal vein, renal portal veins, asymmetric posterior cardinal vein, & a posterior vena cava.	Posterior cardinals rudimentary. Well-developed posterior vena cava drains kidneys. Caudata: Renal portal blood derived from iliac & caudal veins.
5	Anterior cardinal veins	Myxini: Left anterior cardinal vein (internal jugular) & inferior jugular vein (ventral) join sinus venosus. Right anterior cardinal vein opens into cor portale of liver. Petromyzones: Anterior cardinal veins unite to form common trunk and open into sinus venosus. Inferior jugular vein (ventral) present.	Chondrichthyes: Anterior cardinal veins (internal jugulars) are sinus-like distensions. Inferior jugular veins open into common cardinal sinus. Osteichthyes: Two cardinal veins. Mainly one internal jugular vein joining sinus venosus. Dipnoi: Two cardinal & two jugular veins.	Caudata: Two anterior cardinal veins (internal jugulars), two inferior jugular veins. Salientia: Anterior cardinal veins (internal jugulars) & inferior jugular veins fuse into one short trunk on each side, the anterior vena cava, which enters the sinus venosus.

		Main Segmental Vessels
6	Dorsal segmental vessels	Parietal arteries are formed from the dorsal aorta in every segment on each side, and alternate with parietal veins draining to one or several of the paired longitudinal veins (posterior cardinal, subcardinal, lateral cutaneous, etc.). Not all persist in adults, nor need arrangement remain symmetrical.
7	Dorsal rami	Supply epaxial muscles & overlying skin, spinal cord & vertebrae, & the dorsal fins where present
8	Ventral rami	Supply hypaxial muscles & overlying skin. In regions of paired limbs local members of the series enlarge as subclavian & iliac vessels.

		Secondary Longitudinal Vessels	
9	Lateral cutaneous vein	....	Chondrichthyes, Osteichthyes, Gymnophiona, Caudata: Lateral cutaneous vein in lateral line groove, below skin from tail to region of forelimb. Originates from end tips of lateral segmental veins. Salientia: Great & small cutaneous vein.

[1] Unless otherwise indicated.   [2] Class: Crossopterygii.

VASCULAR SYSTEM: VERTEBRATES

Blood Vessels

Reptilia	Aves	Mammalia	
In all embryos, two posterior cardinal veins present & continuous with the caudal vein.			4
Formation of kidneys causes great changes in distribution of posterior cardinals (renal portal system). Sauria: Caudal vein empties into two renal portal veins. Two hepatic veins join posterior vena cava. Crocodylia: Posterior vena cava emerges as single vessel from kidneys.	Rudimentary caudal & renal portal veins. Renal veins join femoral & internal iliac veins in kidney, which in turn join to form posterior vena cava. Posterior vena cava receives hepatic vein; no posterior cardinal veins persist.	No renal portal system. Posterior cardinals obliterated & replaced by supracardinal derivatives, the azygos & hemiazygos veins. Posterior vena cava is main trunk vein.	
Sphenodon: Two anterior cardinal veins (internal jugular veins). Inferior jugular veins (external) reduced & replaced by tracheal vein; these veins join subclavian vein to form anterior vena cava. Sauria: Similar in structure to *Sphenodon.*	Two anterior venae cavae, each formed by an anterior cardinal vein, vertebral vein, & subclavian vein. Right cardinal vein more prominent than left. Inferior jugular vein absent.	Two anterior venae cavae, each formed by an anterior cardinal vein, inferior jugular vein, & subclavian vein. In ungulates, right vena cava more prominent than left because blood passes from left into right by anastomosis. Insectivora, Rodentia: Brachiocephalic veins of equal size. Primates, Carnivora: Section of left vein, located between heart & anastomosis, disappears.	5
Main Segmental Vessels			
Parietal arteries are formed from the dorsal aorta in every segment on each side, and alternate with parietal veins draining to one or several of the paired longitudinal veins (posterior cardinal, subcardinal, lateral cutaneous, etc.). Not all persist in adults, nor need arrangement remain symmetrical.			6
Supply epaxial muscles & overlying skin, spinal cord & vertebrae, & the dorsal fins where present			7
Supply hypaxial muscles & overlying skin. In regions of paired limbs, local members of the series enlarge as subclavian & iliac vessels.			8
Secondary Longitudinal Vessels			
Sauria: Lateral cutaneous vein probably present in all species	....	....	9

continued

	Vessel	Agnatha	Chondrichthyes, Osteichthyes, & Dipnoi	Amphibia
10	Abdominal vein	....	Extends from region of cloaca to shoulder girdle, where it merges into sinus venosus or into hepatic portal system. Chondrichthyes: Two lateral abdominal veins, one on each side of body wall.	Caudata, Salientia: A single median, ventral abdominal vein.
11	Epigastric arteries & veins	Myxini: Netlike track	Two distinct trunks running close to each other are located on inner surface of abdominal wall between longitudinal abdominal & segmental trunk muscles	

Visceral Vessels

	Vessel	Agnatha	Chondrichthyes, Osteichthyes, & Dipnoi	Amphibia
	Visceral arteries			
12	Paired	Paired lateral branches from dorsal aorta supply kidney strips (however longitudinally subdivided), gonads & their ducts		
13	Un-paired	Myxini: Mesenteric arteries (approximately 35 in number) distributed to intestine as segmental vessels. Petromyzones: Only one artery persists as celiaco-mesenteric artery.	Chondrichthyes: Celiac artery, two or three mesenteric arteries. Osteichthyes: Mainly one celiacomesenteric artery. Dipnoi: Celiac artery, two or three mesenteric arteries.	Caudata: Celiac artery & numerous mesenteric arteries distribute to intestine. Mesenterics almost segmentally arranged in *Siren*, usually spring from complexly branching trunks in *Necturus & Salamandra*. Salientia: Only celiacomesenteric artery.
14	Visceral veins, un-paired	Subintestinal vein prominent in embryos, draining blood from yolk sac and partly from caudal vein. Remains in adult as variable component of hepatic portal vein. Prominent in lampreys. Hepatic portal vein drains alimentary tract, spleen, pancreas, & (variably) parts of ventral body wall & pelvic appendages. Hepatic veins open directly into sinus venosus, except in Dipnoi & Amphibia which are the only anamniotes to develop a posterior vena cava. Hepatic veins become tributaries of the vena cava when it is present.		

Vessels of the Forelimb

	Vessel	Agnatha	Chondrichthyes, Osteichthyes, & Dipnoi	Amphibia
15	Arteries	Forelimbs absent	Chondrichthyes: Subclavian artery arises from median aorta. Lateral & medial pterygial artery, adradial arteries. Osteichthyes: Subclavian artery originates from median aorta. Basal arteries, inter-radial arteries.	Caudata: Subclavian artery arises from median aorta. Brachial, interosseal (main vessel), radial (radiomarginal), & ulnar (ulnomarginal) arteries. Dorsal arterial arch of hand, metacarpal & digital arteries. Salientia: Subclavian arteries originate from aortic arch, brachial & deep brachial arteries. Other vessels same as in Caudata.
16	Veins	Forelimbs absent	Chondrichthyes: Adradial veins, lateral & medial pterygial vein. Subclavian vein fuses with epigastric vein and enters duct of Cuvier. Osteichthyes: Interradial veins, basal vein. Subclavian vein enters duct of Cuvier or posterior cardinal vein. Left subclavian joins abdominal vein & epigastric vein, right subclavian joins only epigastric vein (*Salmo*).	Caudata: Digital veins, interosseal vein (main vessel), ulnar vein (ulnomarginal), radial vein (radiomarginal), brachial vein. Subclavian vein, with lateral cutaneous vein, enters sinus venosus. Salientia: Digital veins, dorsal venous arch of hand, ulnar vein (ulnomarginal), radial vein (radiomarginal), interosseal vein.
			Brachial vein & great cutaneous vein unite to join subclavian vein which enters anterior vena cava (cranial). Deep brachial vein continues as subscapular vein, which with internal jugular vein forms brachiocephalic vein.	

Blood Vessels

Reptilia	Aves	Mammalia	
Abdominal vein, double or single, connects renal portal with hepatic portal system	Only anterior root of abdominal vein persists and is represented by umbilical vein in the embryo		10
Two distinct trunks running close to each other are located on inner surface of abdominal wall between longitudinal abdominal & segmental trunk muscles. Probably absent in birds.			11
Visceral Vessels			
Paired lateral branches from dorsal aorta supply kidneys (pronephros, mesonephros, metanephros), gonads & their ducts. Not strictly segmental, their number varies according to species & age of individual.			12
Sphenodon: Gastric, celiac, common mesenteric (anterior), & posterior mesenteric arteries. Sauria: Gastric, celiacomesenteric, & posterior mesenteric arteries. Serpentes: Many arteries (mesenteric) reach intestine from aorta *(Boa).* Crocodylia: Gastroesophageal, celiaco-mesenteric, & mesenteric arteries.	Celiac artery, anterior mesenteric artery (superior), posterior mesenteric artery (inferior)	Celiac artery, anterior mesenteric artery (cranial or superior), posterior mesenteric artery (caudal or inferior)	13
Subintestinal vein embryonic, with variable traces persisting in adult. Draws blood from intestine & from caudal vein; delivers blood to right omphalomesenteric, later the hepatic portal vein. Follows free ventral border of gut (in mesentery), draining it, the stomach, spleen, & pancreas, and delivering to the liver sinusoids. Hepatic vein drains liver sinusoids toward heart by way of posterior vena cava.			14
Vessels of the Forelimb			
Chelonia: Subclavian artery, with carotid artery, originates from brachiocephalic artery. Brachial artery replaced by lateral brachial artery. Two arterial arches of hand, dorsal & volar. Sauria: Both subclavian arteries arise from right aortic arch. Axillary, brachial, interosseal (main vessel), ulnar, radial, & median arteries; metacarpal & digital arteries.	Subclavian artery, with carotid artery, originates from right aortic arch (brachiocephalic artery). Axillary, brachial, ulnar (main vessel), interosseal, radial, & ulnar nerve arteries; metacarpal & digital arteries.	Right subclavian artery arises from left aortic arch, chiefly as brachiocephalic artery; left subclavian arises directly from arch or truncus communis. Axillary artery, brachial artery, median artery (main vessel in most mammals), ulnar artery (main vessel in Prosimii), radial artery, interosseal artery (main vessel in *Ornithorhynchus).* Metacarpal arteries, dorsal & volar digital arteries.	15
Emys: Only one brachial vein. Sauria: Digital veins, dorsal venous arch of hand, radial vein (main vessel, marginal radial vein in embryos), ulnar vein, interosseal vein, brachial vein, & lateral brachial vein. Lateral cutaneous vein empties into axillary vein. Subclavian vein enters internal jugular vein. *Alligator:* Only one brachial vein.	Metacarpal veins, basilic vein (main vessel), ulnar vein, interosseal vein, radial vein (radiomarginal), brachial vein. Subclavian vein enters anterior vena cava.	Digital veins, metacarpal veins, volar & dorsal venous arches, basilic vein (ulnomarginal), cephalic vein (radiomarginal), ulnar vein, radial vein, median vein, brachial vein, axillary vein, subclavian vein. (Above list valid for five-fingered appendage.)	16

continued

Contributors: Grodzinski, Z.; Ballard, W. W.; Monie, I. W.

Specific References
[1] Magid, A. M. A. 1967. J. Zool. 152:19.
[2] Robineau, D., and J. Anthony. 1971. C. R. Acad. Sci. 273:689.

General References
[3] Francis, E. T. B. 1934. The Anatomy of the Salamander. Oxford Univ. Press, London.
[4] Gelderen, C. A. 1933. Handb. Vergl. Anat. Wirbeltiere 6:685.
[5] Goodrich, E. S. 1930. Studies on the Structure and Development of Vertebrates. Macmillan, London.

[6] Gorkiewicz, C. 1947. Bull. Int. Acad. Pol. Sci. Lett. Cl. Sci. Math. Natur., B2, p. 241.
[7] Grodzinski, Z. 1926. Ibid., B, p. 955.
[8] Grodzinski, Z. 1928. Ibid., B2, p. 417.
[9] Grodzinski, Z. 1928. Mem. Int. Acad. Pol. Sci. 1: 110.
[10] Grodzinski, Z. 1933. Bull. Int. Acad. Pol. Sci. Lett. Cl. Sci. Math. Natur., B2, pp. 243, 259, 321.
[11] Grodzinski, Z. 1938. In H. G. Bronn, ed. Klassen und Ordnungen des Thier-Reichs. C. F. Winter, Leipzig. Bd. 6.

Part II.

	Component	Agnatha	Chondrichthyes, Osteichthyes, & Dipnoi	Amphibia
1	Lymph hearts	Myxini: One pair of pulsating sacs located in tail. [1] Petromyzones: Absent.	Chondrichthyes: Absent. Osteichthyes: Two elongated vesicles joined by a channel and located at base of tail. Vesicles not pulsating in ganoid fishes.	Gymnophiona: Approximately 100 spherical vesicles in trunk & tail, beneath skin in lateral line groove. Caudata: Ten to twenty rounded vesicles on each side of trunk, located as in Gymnophiona. Salientia: one pair of anterior & one to four pairs of posterior hearts.
2	Lymph sacs (other than hearts), lymph sinuses	Myxini: Three subcutaneous sacs underlie entire skin. Petromyzones: Supralabial, orbital, ocular ring, & deep labial sinuses.	Chondrichthyes: Absent. Osteichthyes: Pectoral, pineal, orbital, cephalic, occipital, & lateral sinuses.	Caudata: Orbital sinus, sinus lymphaticus cordis; axillary sinus probably in larvae only. Salientia: In tadpoles, mandibular, circumoral, pericardial, & temporal sinuses; in adults, several subcutaneous sacs.
3	Lymph nodes	....	....	....
4	Subvertebral lymphatic trunks (thoracic duct)	Myxini: Two wide trunks located on both sides of aorta; fused into wide sinus in liver region. Petromyzones: Unpaired sinus-like trunk beneath aorta & cardinal veins.	Two slender trunks located on both sides of aorta & caudal artery	Gymnophiona: One sinus-like extended trunk accompanies aorta. Caudata: One or two trunks. Salientia: Two trunks.
5	Cisterna chyli in lumbar area	....	....	Gymnophiona: Absent. Caudata: Present. Extends to thoracic region. Salientia: Absent.
6	Connections with veins	Myxini: With anterior cardinal vein. Petromyzones: Numerous connections with both posterior cardinal veins.	Chondrichthyes: With posterior cardinal vein at point where subclavian artery crosses. Osteichthyes: With anterior cardinal veins.	Caudata: With anterior cardinal veins. Salientia: With anterior lymph hearts.

[1] These sacs are regarded as venous hearts in references 1 and 2.

Blood Vessels

[12] Grodzinski, Z. 1946. Bull. Int. Acad. Pol. Sci. Lett. Cl. Sci. Math. Natur., B2, pp. 1, 22.

[13] Grodzinski, Z. 1948. Ibid., B2, p. 61.

[14] Hafferl, A. 1933. Handb. Vergl. Anat. Wirbeltiere 6:563.

[15] Magid, A. M. A. 1967. J. Zool. 152:19.

[16] Nelsen, O. E. 1953. Comparative Embryology of the Vertebrates. Blakiston, New York.

[17] Romanes, G. J., ed. 1971. Cunningham's Textbook of Anatomy. Ed. 11. Oxford Univ. Press, London.

[18] Sikorowa, L. 1947. Bull. Int. Acad. Pol. Sci. Lett. Cl. Sci. Math. Natur., B2, p. 299.

[19] Stephan, F. 1954. Traite Zool. 12:854.

[20] Szarski, H. 1947. Bull. Int. Acad. Pol. Sci. Lett. Cl. Sci. Math. Natur., B2, p. 145.

[21] Weidenreich, F. 1933. Handb. Vergl. Anat. Wirbeltiere 6:375.

Lymphatics

Reptilia	Aves	Mammalia	
Only posterior hearts. Chelonia, Crocodylia: Spherical in shape. Sauria: Two ovoid vesicles attached to both ends of transverse process of first caudal vertebra. Serpentes: Two elongated vesicles, each surrounded by bifurcated transverse processes of four to five caudal vertebrae.	In all embryos only one pair of posterior hearts, located in region between pelvis & femur. Hearts persist in some adults (*Alca, Anser, Casuarius, Podiceps, Struthio*).	Absent even in embryos	1
Chelonia: Jugular cistern. Sauria: Retrocardial, axillary, jugular, tracheal, & thyroidal sinuses. Serpentes: Mandibular sinus. Crocodylia: Absent.	....	Jugular & iliac lymph sacs in embryos only	2
Chelonia: Small nodes in lower eyelid	Microscopically discernible nodes in walls of lymph vessels. Anseriformes: Two cervicothoracic & two lumbar lymph glands macroscopically visible.	Many lymph nodes: man, approximately 465; cattle, 300; dog, 60; horse, 8000	3
Chelonia: Two trunks in tail, single in body cavity and bifurcated anteriorly. Sauria, Serpentes: Sinus surrounds aorta. Crocodylia: Two slender trunks.	Two trunks located on both sides of aorta	One or two trunks associated with aorta & caudal artery	4
Chelonia, Sauria: Present. Serpentes, Crocodylia: Absent.	....	Always present. Great variation in shape & size.	5
With anterior cardinal veins	With anterior cardinal veins	In most mammals thoracic duct connects with left anterior cardinal vein, in some with right, in few with both	6

continued

Component	Agnatha	Chondrichthyes, Osteichthyes, & Dipnoi	Amphibia
7 Jugular lymphatic trunks	Myxini: Absent. Petromyzones: Seven peribranchial sinuses, each connected with anterior cardinal vein.	Chondrichthyes: Two trunks connected with corresponding anterior cardinal veins. Osteichthyes: Two sinus-like distended vessels connected with corresponding subvertebral trunks.	Caudata: Two trunks connected with corresponding subvertebral trunks. Salientia: Two short trunks connecting head sinuses with anterior lymph hearts.
8 Lateral longitudinal lymphatic trunks	....	Chondrichthyes: Absent. Osteichthyes: Below skin in lateral line groove from base of tail fin to head; opens into some of head sinuses or directly into duct of Cuvier.	Gymnophiona, Caudata: In lateral line groove from base of tail to head. Opens into lymph hearts. Salientia: In tadpoles, from base of tail to anterior lymph heart, disappearing during metamorphosis.
9 Longitudinal lymphatic trunks (other than lateral)	....	Chondrichthyes: Absent. Osteichthyes: Dorsal trunk unpaired, located in dorsal midline of tail & body from base of tail fin to head; ventral trunk unpaired, located in ventral midline of tail & in middle of abdominal wall. Spinal trunk dorsal to spinal cord.	Caudata: Dorsal trunk unpaired, located in dorsal midline of tail & body. Ventral trunk unpaired, located in ventral midline of tail. Abdominal trunk paired in wall of abdomen. Salientia: Dorsal & ventral trunks only in fin of tadpoles.

Contributor: Grodzinski, Z.

Specific References

[1] Cole, F. J. 1925. Trans. Roy. Soc. Edinburgh 54: 309.
[2] Favaro, G. 1905. Atti Reale Inst. Veneto Sci. Lett. Arti 65:195.

General References

[3] Allen, W. F. 1906. Proc. Wash. Acad. Sci. 8:41.
[4] Allen, W. F. 1908. Amer. J. Anat. 8:49.
[5] Allen, W. F. 1913. Quart. J. Microsc. Sci. 59(2):309.
[6] Baum, H. 1912. Das Lymphgefässsystem des Rindes. A. Hirschwald, Berlin.

[7] Baum, H. 1928. Das Lymphgefässsystem des Pferdes. J. Springer, Berlin.
[8] Clark, E. R., and E. L. Clark. 1920. Carnegie Inst. Wash. Publ. 272:447.
[9] Glaser, G. 1933. Z. Anat. Entwicklungsgesch. 100: 433.
[10] Grodzinski, Z. 1929. Bull. Int. Acad. Pol. Sci. Lett. Cl. Sci. Math. Natur., B2, p. 433.
[11] Grodzinski, Z. 1932. Ibid., B2, p. 221.
[12] Hoyer, H. 1905. Anat. Anz. 27:50.

221. BASAL AND NONBASAL HEART RATE: MAN

Heart rate varies with environment (including temperature) and psychological state. Values in parentheses are ranges, estimate "b" for basal measurements, and estimate "c" for nonbasal (see Introduction).

Age yr	Sex	Heart Rate beats/min	Reference	Age yr	Sex	Heart Rate beats/min	Reference	Age yr	Sex	Heart Rate beats/min	Reference
Basal				5 3	♂	92	6	11 7	♂	85	6
				6	♀	86		12	♀	73	
1 1	♂	116	6	7 4	♀	87	6	13 8	♂	80	6
2	♀	122		8 5	♀	91	6	14	♀	77	
3 2	♂	104	6	9 6	♂	87	6	15 9	♂	81	6
4	♀	103		10	♀	80		16	♀	85	

continued

Lymphatics

Reptilia	Aves	Mammalia	
Chelonia: Two trunks enter jugular cistern which connects both subvertebral trunks. Sauria: Two trunks connected with subvertebral trunks by way of jugular sinus. Crocodylia: Two trunks enter corresponding anterior cardinal veins.	Each of two trunks joins corresponding subvertebral trunk	Irregular lymph vessels join anterior cardinal veins separately or by way of subvertebral trunks	7
Chelonia: Thoracic part well-developed. Sauria: From tip of tail to forelimb. Caudal part enters lymph heart, thoracic part enters axillary sinus. Serpentes: Lateral trunk reaches maxillary sinus. Crocodylia: Only caudal part present.	....	In adult, present only in tail. In embryos, transitory thoracic part observed.	8
....	....	....	9

[13] Hoyer, H. 1908. Bull. Int. Acad. Pol. Sci. Lett. Cl. Sci. Math. Natur., p. 451.
[14] Hoyer, H. 1928. Ibid., B2, p. 79.
[15] Hoyer, H. 1934. Mem. Int. Acad. Pol. Sci. Cl. Med. 1:205.
[16] Kampmeier, O. 1925. J. Morphol. Physiol. 41:95.
[17] Kihara, R., and E. Naito. 1933. Folia Anat. Jap. 11:405.
[18] Marcus, H. 1908. Gegenbaurs Morphol. Jahrb. 38:590.

[19] Mozejko, B. 1911. Anat. Anz. 40:469.
[20] Panizza, B. 1833. Sopra il Sistema Linfatico dei Rettili. Bizzoni, Pavia.
[21] Retzius, G. 1890. Biol. Untersuch. (Stockholm) 1:20.
[22] Sabin, F. R. 1909. Amer. J. Anat. 9:43.
[23] Tretjakoff, D. 1927. Gegenbaurs Morphol. Jahrb. 58:209.
[24] Tretjakoff, D. 1930. Ibid. 64:133.
[25] Weidenreich, F., et al. 1933. Handb. Vergl. Anat. Wirbeltiere 6:745.

221. BASAL AND NONBASAL HEART RATE: MAN

	Age yr	Sex	Heart Rate beats/min	Reference		Age yr	Sex	Heart Rate beats/min	Reference		Age yr	Sex	Heart Rate beats/min	Reference
17	10	♂	79	6	27	16	♂	62(49-75)	5	37	20-40	♂	62	6
18		♀	80		28		♀	66(51-81)		38		♀	68	
19	12	♂	70(53-88)	5	29	17	♂	59(49-62)	5	39	24	♂	61(47-75)	5
20		♀	71(56-87)		30		♀	64(50-78)		40		♀	69(52-86)	
21	13	♂	66(64-78)	5	31	18	♀	73	6	41	30	♂	59(47-72)	5
22		♀	68(52-84)		32	19	♂	65	6	42		♀	65(48-82)	
23	14	♂	67(53-81)	5	33		♀	71		43	34	♂	72(65-79)	2
24		♀	68(55-82)		34	20	♂	64	6	44	40-59	♂	61 ± 7	4
25	15	♂	65(54-76)	5	35		♀	69		45	40-60	♂	57	6
26		♀	67(50-85)		36	20-39	♂	59 ± 7	4	46		♀	70	

continued

	Age yr	Sex	Heart Rate beats/min	Reference
47	43	♂	69(63-75)	2
48	55	♂	70(64-75)	2
49	60-70	♂	66	6
50		♀	71	
51	60-79	♂	60 ± 7	4
52	65	♂	63(57-69)	2
53	>70	♂	65	6
54		♀	73	
55	73	♂	66(59-73)	2
56	>80	♂	61 ± 8	4
57	82	♂	67(52-82)	2
		Nonbasal		
58	<1	♂♀	134(101-160)	7
59	1	♂♀	111(84-136)	7
60	2	♂♀	108(84-134)	7
61	3	♂♀	108(80-124)	7
62	4	♂♀	103(80-133)	7
63	5	♂♀	98(70-128)	7
64	6	♂♀	93(72-128)	7
65	7	♂♀	94(72-112)	7
66	8	♂♀	89(72-114)	7
67	9	♂♀	91(68-120)	7

	Age yr	Sex	Heart Rate beats/min	Reference
68	10-11	♂	85 ± 13	3
69		♀	90 ± 14	
70	12-13	♂	82 ± 13	3
71		♀	88 ± 13	
72	14-15	♂	78 ± 12	3
73		♀	83 ± 14	
74	16-17	♂	76 ± 12	3
75		♀	80 ± 12	
76	18-19	♂	73 ± 13	3
77		♀	80 ± 12	
78	20	♂♀	71(59-99)	7
79	20-29	♂	76 ± 12	3
80		♀	78 ± 11	
81	20-39	♂	76 ± 9	4
82	21	♂♀	71(41-96)	7
83	22	♂♀	70(56-100)	7
84	23	♂♀	71(50-96)	7
85	24	♂♀	72(50-96)	7
86	25-30	♂♀	72(52-102)	7
87	25-44	♂♀	71(50-104)	1
88	30-35	♂♀	70(58-104)	7
89	30-39	♂	75 ± 11	3
90		♀	78 ± 11	

	Age yr	Sex	Heart Rate beats/min	Reference
91	35-40	♂♀	72(56-104)	7
92	40-45	♂♀	72(50-104)	7
93	40-49	♂	76 ± 11	3
94		♀	78 ± 11	
95	40-59	♂	75 ± 8	4
96	45-49	♂♀	72(49-100)	1
97	50-55	♂♀	72(52-94)	7
98	50-59	♂	75 ± 12	3
99		♀	77 ± 12	
100		♂♀	73(48-108)	1
101	55-60	♂♀	75(48-108)	7
102	60-65	♂♀	73(54-100)	7
103	60-69	♂	74 ± 10	3
104		♀	76 ± 8	
105	60-70	♂♀	74(52-100)	1
106	60-79	♂	74 ± 8	4
107	65-70	♂♀	75(52-96)	7
108	70-75	♂♀	75(54-104)	7
109	70-79	♂♀	75(50-104)	1
110	75-80	♂♀	72(50-94)	7
111	>80	♂	73 ± 9	4
112	>80	♂♀	77(63-98)	1

Contributors: Pool, Peter E.; Shock, Nathan W.

References

[1] Bowerman, W. G., and J. H. Brett. 1941. Quart. Rev. Biol. 16:90.

[2] Brandfonbrener, M., et al. 1955. Circulation 12:57.

[3] Montoye, H. J., et al. 1968. J. Gerontol. 23:127.

[4] Shock, N. W., et al. Unpublished. Gerontology Research Center, Baltimore, 1974.

[5] Shock, N. W. 1944. Amer. J. Dis. Child. 68:17.

[6] Sutliff, W. D., and E. Holt. 1925. Arch. Intern. Med. 35:224.

[7] Tigerstedt, R. A. 1902. In J. Mackenzie. The Study of the Pulse. Y. J. Pentland, Edinburgh and London. p. 53.

222. HEART RATE: VERTEBRATES

Heart rate in homoiotherms varies with species, age, body weight, body temperature, anesthesia, activity, and environment.

Part I. Mammals

Values in parentheses are ranges, estimate "c" unless otherwise indicated (*see* Introduction).

	Species (Synonym)	Specification	Heart Rate beats/min	Reference
1	*Alopex lagopus*	4.3 kg; 38.5°C; anesthetized [L/]	240	12
2	*Blarina brevicauda*	20-30 g; 37.5°C; awake	699(618-780)	12
3	*Bos taurus*	....	45	6,39
4		Embryo	161	16
5		Newborn	(141-160)	10

[L/] With pentobarbital sodium.

continued

Part I. Mammals

	Species (Synonym)	Specification	Heart Rate beats/min	Reference
6		Young	106(100-115)	34
7		500 kg; 38.0°C	(46-54)	5
8		♀	(60-71)	1,2,11,13
9	*Bradypus tridactyla*	Adult	90	29
10	*Camelus bactrianus*	Adult	(25-32)	34
11	*Canis familiaris*	....	(50-56)[2]	13
12		....	(70-130)	13,34
13		Embryo	(120-170)	10
14		Newborn	(160-180)	10
15		Young; 1.04 kg; anesthetized	208(145-275)	32
16		Young; 1.75 kg	180	10
17		5 kg	(105-125)	10,41
18		5-20 kg	(72-200)	10,34,41
19		6.5 kg	120	7
20		9.6 kg	96	10,49
21		15 kg	(72-82)	10,41
22		20 kg	85	10,49
23	Dachshund	....	115(96-129)	15
24	Spitz	....	106	15
25	St. Bernard	....	(74-80)	15
26	*Capra hircus*	....	(60-100)	10,13,34,41
27		Embryo	(120-246)	3
28		Newborn	(145-240)	3
29		33 kg; 39°C	81(70-135)	5,10
30	*Castor canadensis*	....	140	27
31		Diving	10	27
32		10 kg; 38.0°C; anesthetized	108	12
33	*Cavia porcellus*	....	(280-300)	7,10,13
34		0.3-0.75 kg	(230-300)	4,10,31,35,44,47
35		0.437 kg; anesthetized	269(225-312)	32
36		0.584-0.593 kg; anesthetized	(132-288)	22,34,35
37	*Clethrionomys rutilus*	30 g; 37.3°C; anesthetized [1]	684	12
38	*Dasypus novemcinctus*	2.8-4.0 kg; 32-36°C	(70-100)	43
39	*Delphinapterus leucas*	Diving	(15-16)	51
40	(*Beluga* sp.)	Diving	16(12-23)	45
41	*Delphinus delphis*	....	150	34
42	*Dicrostonyx groenlandicus rubricatus (D. rubricatus)*	50 g; 38.3°C; awake	(348-465)	12
43	*Didelphis marsupialis virginiana (D. virginiana)*	2.2-3.2 kg; 35.0°C; anesthetized [1]	187(140-228)	12
44	*Elephas maximus indicus (E. indicus)*	2000 kg	(25-41)	17,34
45		3000 kg	(26-50)	10,16
46		<4090 kg	30(22-39)	18
47	*Eptesicus fuscus*	20 g; 35.5°C; anesthetized [1]	(444-600)	12
48	*Equus asinus*	Adult	(40-56)	34
49		400 kg	(45-50)	34
50	*E. caballus*	....	(23-46)	13,15,34,38
51		Newborn	(100-120)	40
52		Young	63(60-71)	34
53		380-450 kg	(34-55)	10,20,34,49
54	Thoroughbred	....	(38-45)	13

[1] With pentobarbital sodium. [2] Basal rate.

continued

Part I. Mammals

	Species (Synonym)	Specification	Heart Rate beats/min	Reference
55	E. asinus, ♂ × E. caballus, ♀[3/]	Adult	(46-50)	34
56	Erethizon dorsatum	....	(280-320)	12
57	Erinaceus europaeus	0.485 kg; anesthetized	263(200-325)	32
58		0.5-0.9 kg; 4.0°C; hibernating	(3-24)	12
59		0.5-0.9 kg; awake	246(234-264)	12,30,48
60	Eutamias minimus	40 g; 38.7°C; awake	684(660-702)	12
61	Felis catus (F. domesticus)	....	(110-140)	10,13,34
62		Newborn	168	36
63		Young; 0.1 kg	300	10
64		0.754 kg; anesthetized	245(161-290)	32
65		2.5 kg	(110-240)	10,41
66	F. concolor	....	60	45
67	Giraffa camelopardalis	Adult	66	34
68	Hyaena sp.	Adult	(55-58)	34
69	Lepus europaeus	2.5 kg	64(60-70)	10
70	Macaca irus	Adult	215	50
71	M. mulatta	....	192	14
72	Macropus sp.	....	125	11
73	Marmota caligata	3.3-5.1 kg; 0-10°C; hibernating	(5-15)	12
74		3.3-5.1 kg; 39.6°C; anesthetized [L/]	252	12
75	M. marmota	3.6 kg	186(160-206)	10,23
76	M. monax	1.8-2.8 kg; 36.6°C; anesthetized [L/]	(180-264)	12
77	Mephitis mephitis	1.0-2.0 kg; 36.5°C; awake	166(144-192)	12
78	Mesocricetus auratus	75-103 g; anesthetized	(375-425)	35
79		103 g; anesthetized	(276-420)	32
80	Microtus arvalis	21 g; anesthetized	522	12
81	M. oeconomus	20-40 g; 38.5°C; anesthetized [L/]	(565-600)	12
82	M. pennsylvanicus	19 g; 39.3°C; anesthetized [L/]	600	12
83	Mus musculus	....	(600-655)	10,13
84		10-20 g; 38.4°C; awake	624(480-738)	12
85		17 g; anesthetized	(450-550)	32
86		29 g; anesthetized	376	35
87	White	10-30 g; 37.5°C; awake	498(402-834)	12
88	Muscardinus avellanarius	14-23 g	(580-780)	8,10,37
89	Mustela erminea	90-200 g; 41.1°C; awake	357(300-420)	12
90	M. frenata	0.2-0.4 kg; 40.0°C; awake	182(172-192)	12
91	M. putorius (Putorius sp.)	0.7-1.3 kg; 40.0°C; awake	231(216-242)	12
92	M. vison	0.7-1.4 kg; 40.5°C; anesthetized [L/]	(272-414)	12
93	Myotis lucifugus	6 g; anesthetized [L/]	588	12
94	M. myotis	Hibernating	(18-80)	33
95	Ondatra zibethicus	0.8-1.3 kg; 38.0°C; anesthetized [L/]	(148-306)	12
96	Oryctolagus cuniculus (Lepus cuniculus)	Newborn	(120-240)	10,11,34
97		1.434 kg	220	21
98		2.0 kg	(205-220)	10,24,49
99		1.34 kg; anesthetized	251(167-330)	32
100	Oryzomys palustris	90 g; 37.8°C; awake	(318-384)	12
101	Ovis aries	....	180	11
102		....	(60-80)	13,34
103		50 kg	(70-80)	10,20
104	Panthera leo (Felis leo)	Adult	40	34
105	P. pardus (F. pardus)	Adult	60	34

[L/] With pentobarbital sodium.   [3/] Mule.

continued

Part I. Mammals

	Species (Synonym)	Specification	Heart Rate beats/min	Reference
106	*P. tigris (F. tigris)*	Adult	64	34
107	*Peromyscus* sp.	22 g; anesthetized	420	35
108	*P. maniculatus*	10-30 g; 37.5°C; awake	534(324-858)	12
109	*Phoca vitulina*	20-25 kg	100	28
110		20-25 kg; diving	10	28
111	*Phocoena phocoena*	170 kg	(40-110)	27
112	*Pipistrellus pipistrellus (Vesperugo pipi-*	4 g	660(230-972)	9,10
113	*strellus)*	4 g; hibernating	30	9
114	*Plecotus auritus*	9 g	(600-900)	9,10,34
115	*Rattus* sp. *(Mus ratta)*	....	(300-550)	10,11,13,34,38,46
116		200 g	(360-520)	10,37
117	*R. norvegicus*	....	362	19
118		Embryo	(95-256)	3
119		Newborn	161(121-201)[b]	36
120		Young	(500-525)	26
121		252 g; anesthetized	352(260-450)	32
122		272 g; 36.9°C; anesthetized [1/]	(330-480)	12
123	White	6.3-8.0 g; held	301(279-317)	25
124		10 g; held	309(292-331)	25
125		18-20 g; held	488(407-624)	25
126		92-210 g; awake	305(270-350)[2/]	25
127		92-210 g; held	538	25
128		92-210 g; fettered	656	25
129		237 g; anesthetized	347	35
130	*Reithrodontomys megalotis*	10 g; 38.0°C; anesthetized [1/]	(408-615)	12
131	*Scalopus aquaticus*	70-90 g; awake	579(540-618)	12
132	*Sciurus carolinensis*	0.5-0.6 kg; 40.1°C; anesthetized [1/]	390	12
133	*S. vulgaris*	0.222 kg	320	10,49
134	*Sorex cinereus*	3-4 g; awake	782(500-1320[4/])	12
135	*Spermophilus citellus (Citellus citellus)*	0.189-0.216 kg; anesthetized	(200-325)	32,35
136	*S. columbianus (C. columbianus)*	0.7-0.8 kg; 37.2°C; anesthetized [1/]	(270-288)	12
137	*S. franklini (C. franklini)*	0.3-0.4 kg; 0-10°C; hibernating	(2[5/]-4)	12
138		0.3-0.4 kg; 36.6°C; anesthetized [1/]	396	12
139	*S. tridecemlineatus (C. tridecemlinea-*	0.1-0.3 kg; 36.9°C; awake	276(96-378)	12
140	*tus)*	0.3 kg; 0-10°C; hibernating	(3-15)	12
141	*S. undulatus parryii (C. undulatus par-*	0.6-1.0 kg; 0-10°C; hibernating	(2[5/]-7)	12
142	*ryii, C. parryi)*	0.6-1.0 kg; 38.1°C; awake	222(204-348)	12
143	*Sus scrofa*	Newborn	227	36
144	*(S. domesticus)*	100 kg	(60-86)	10,13,34
145		130 kg	(70-86)	10,41
146	*Sylvilagus floridanus*	1.4 kg; 39.7°C; anesthetized [1/]	318	12
147	*Tamiasciurus hudsonicus*	0.1-0.3 kg; 40.6°C; awake	(336-372)	12
148	*Tapirus indicus*	....	44	34
149	*Taxidea taxus*	7.9-10.9 kg; 37.5°C; awake	138(128-144)	12
150	*Trichechus* sp.	170-330 kg	50-60	42
151		170-330 kg; diving	30	42
152	*Tursiops truncatus*	140-180 kg	110	27
153		140-180 kg; diving	50	27
154	*Vulpes fulva*	4.5-4.7 kg; 38.0°C; anesthetized [1/]	180(72-300)	12

[1/] With pentobarbital sodium.   [2/] Basal rate.   [4/] Highest heart rate recorded for a mammal.   [5/] Lowest heart rate recorded for a mammal.

continued

222. HEART RATE: VERTEBRATES

Part I. Mammals

Contributors: Dawe, Albert R.; Kruta, Vladislav, and Seliger, Václav.

References

[1] Alfredson, B. V., and J. F. Sykes. 1940. Proc. Soc. Exp. Biol. Med. 43:580.

[2] Alfredson, B. V., and J. F. Sykes. 1943. J. Agr. Res. 65:61.

[3] Barcroft, J. 1936. Physiol. Rev. 16:103.

[4] Benedict, F. G. 1925. J. Biol. Chem. 20:301.

[5] Benedict, F. G., and E. G. Ritzman. 1923. Carnegie Inst. Wash. Publ. 324.

[6] Blaxter, K. L. 1943. Vet. J. 99:2.

[7] Buchanan, F. 1910. Sci. Progr. (London) 5:60.

[8] Buchanan, F. 1910. J. Physiol. (London) 40:P-xlii.

[9] Buchanan, F. 1911. Ibid. 42:P-xxi.

[10] Clark, A. J. 1927. Comparative Physiology of the Heart. Macmillan, New York. pp. 143-145.

[11] Davies, F., and E. T. B. Francis. 1950. J. Anat. 86: 302.

[12] Dawe, A. R. 1953. Ph.D. Thesis. Univ. Wisconsin, Madison.

[13] Dukes, H. H. 1947. The Physiology of Domestic Animals. Ed. 6. Comstock, Ithaca. p. 131.

[14] Eddy, N. B., and J. G. Reid. 1934. J. Pharmacol. Exp. Ther. 52:468.

[15] Ellinger, R. 1894. Thesis. Univ. Greifswald, Germany.

[16] Evans, G. H. 1910. Elephants and Their Diseases. Rangoon.

[17] Forbes, A. 1921. Amer. J. Physiol. 55:385.

[18] Gley, E., and A. Quinquaud. 1922. Arch. Neer. Physiol. 7:392.

[19] Grad, B. 1952. Endocrinology 50:94.

[20] Grossman, J. D., ed. 1953. Sisson's Anatomy of Domestic Animals. Ed. 4. W. B. Saunders, Philadelphia.

[21] Hamilton, A. F., et al. 1937. Amer. J. Physiol. 119: 206.

[22] Harrington, D. W. 1898. Ibid. 1:383.

[23] Hecht, S. 1916. Z. Gesamte Exp. Med. 4:259.

[24] Hering, H. E. 1895. Pfluegers Arch. Gesamte Physiol. Menschen Tiere 60:425.

[25] Hoskins, R. G., et al. 1927. Amer. J. Physiol. 82: 621.

[26] Hundley, J. M., et al. 1945. Ibid. 144:404.

[27] Irving, L., et al. 1941. J. Cell. Comp. Physiol. 17: 145.

[28] Irving, L., et al. 1941. Ibid. 18:283.

[29] Irving, L., et al. 1942. Ibid. 20:189.

[30] Johansson, B. 1957. Cardiologia 30(1).

[31] Koenigsfeld, H., and E. Oppenheimer. 1922. Z. Gesamte Exp. Med. 28:106.

[32] Kruta, V. 1958. Babakova Sbir. (Praha) 8.

[33] Kulzer, E. 1967. Z. Vergl. Physiol. 56:63.

[34] Lehmann, G. 1925. Tabulae Biol. 1:138.

[35] Lombard, E. A. 1952. Amer. J. Physiol. 171:189.

[36] Marcuse, F. L., and A. U. Moore. 1943. Ibid. 139: 49.

[37] Oppenheimer, E. 1922. Z. Gesamte Exp. Med. 28: 96.

[38] Prosser, C. L., et al. 1950. Animal Physiology. W. B. Saunders, Philadelphia. p. 552.

[39] Ralston, N. P. 1940. Mo. Agr. Exp. Sta. Res. Bull. 317.

[40] Reichert, A. 1909. Inaugural Dissertation. Univ. Giessen, Germany.

[41] Reichert, A. 1910. Zentralbl. Biochem. Biophys. 10:170.

[42] Scholander, P. F., and L. Irving. 1941. J. Cell. Comp. Physiol. 17:169.

[43] Scholander, P. F., et al. 1943. Ibid. 21:53.

[44] Schott, E. 1920. Arch. Exp. Pathol. Pharmakol. 87: 309.

[45] Spector, W. S., ed. 1956. Handbook of Biological Data. W. B. Saunders, Philadelphia. p. 277.

[46] Sprague, H., and M. Rappaport. 1943. Amer. Heart J. 26:662.

[47] Stübel, H. 1910. Pfluegers Arch. Gesamte Physiol. Menschen Tiere 135:249.

[48] Suomalainen, P., and S. Sarajas. 1951. Ann. Zool. Soc. Zool. Bot. Fenn. Vanamo 14(2).

[49] Vierordt, K. 1877. Grundriss der Physiologie der Menschen. Ed. 5. H. Laupp, Tübingen. p. 162.

[50] Waart, A. de, and C. J. Storm. 1934. Acta Brevia Neer. Physiol. Pharmacol. Microbiol. 4:130.

[51] White, P. D., et al. 1953. N. Engl. J. Med. 248:69.

Part II. Birds

Values in parentheses are ranges, estimate "c" (*see* Introduction).

	Species (Synonym)	Body Weight g	Heart Rate beats/min	Reference		Species (Synonym)	Body Weight g	Heart Rate beats/min	Reference
1	*Anas platyrhyn-*	....	(120-200)	7	6	*Anser* sp.	2800	144	4,15
2	*chos (A. boscas)*	770-1000	190(185-195)	3	7		4000	80	4,10
3		785	317(229-420)	8,14	8	*Archilochus colubris*	4	615[L]	11
4	*(Anatis pullus)*	2060	240	2,4					
5		2304	212(133-268)	4,14	9	*Casuarius casuarius (C. galeatus)*	60,000	70	4

[L] Basal rate.

continued

Part II. Birds

	Species (Synonym)	Body Weight g	Heart Rate beats/min	Reference		Species (Synonym)	Body Weight g	Heart Rate beats/min	Reference
10	*Columba* sp.	....	(120-360)	1,4,8	24	*Melospiza melodia*	20	450[1]; 1020[2]	11
11		237	244	9,14	25	*Parus major*	14	870	4,12
12		240-370	185(141-225)	1,2,8	26	*Passer domesticus*	....	460	8
13	*Corvus cornix*	360	378(312-492)	8,14	27		20-27	(640-910)	1,2,4,8,12
14	*C. monedula*	140	342(326-358)	8,14	28		28	350[1]; 902[2]	11
15	*Falco peregrinus*	960	347	4,14	29	*Serinus canarius*	....	690(570-840)	16
16	*F. tinnunculus*	159	367	4,14	30		16	514[1]; 1000[2]	11
17	*Fringilla monti-fringilla*	22	(900-920)	4,12	31	*Struthio camelus*	80,000	65(60-70)	4
					32	*Sturnus vulgaris*	....	388(375-400)	16
18	*Gallus gallus (G.*	....	(150-400)	5,6,9,13	33	*Troglodytes aedon*	11	450[1]; 950[2]	11
19	*domesticus)*	1920-3120	(178-458)	1,8,14	34	*Turdus merula*	58	(390-560)	4,12
20	♀	1000	354	15	35	*T. migratorius*	....	570(520-620)	16
21	*Gyps fulvus*	8310	199	8,14	36	*Zenaidura macrou-ra*	130	135[1]; 570[2]	11
22	*Larus canus*	388	401(360-483)	8,14					
23	*Meleagris gallopavo*	8750	93	8,14					

[1] Basal rate. [2] Maximum rate on nest.

Contributors: Kruta, Vladislav, and Seliger, Václav; Woodbury, Robert A.

References

[1] Buchanan, F. 1909. J. Physiol. (London) 38:P-lxii.
[2] Buchanan, F. 1910. Sci. Progr. (London) 5:60.
[3] Buchanan, F. 1913. J. Physiol. (London) 47:P-iv.
[4] Clark, A. J. 1927. Comparative Physiology of the Heart. Macmillan, New York. pp. 146-148.
[5] Dukes, H. H. 1947. The Physiology of Domestic Animals. Ed. 6. Comstock, Ithaca. p. 131.
[6] Henderson, E. W., and E. W. Hathaway. 1943. Poult. Sci. 22:44.
[7] Koppanyi, T., and N. Kleitman. 1927. Amer. J. Physiol. 82:672.
[8] Lehmann, G. 1925. Tabulae Biol. 1:137.
[9] McNally, E. H. 1941. Poult. Sci. 20:266.

[10] Mosso, A. 1901. Arch. Ital. Biol. 35:21.
[11] Odum, E. P. 1945. Science 101:153.
[12] Oppenheimer, E. 1922. Z. Gesamte Exp. Med. 28: 96.
[13] Prosser, C. L., et al. 1950. Animal Physiology. W. B. Saunders, Philadelphia. p. 552.
[14] Stübel, H. 1910. Pfluegers Arch. Gesamte Physiol. Menschen Tiere 135:249.
[15] Vierordt, K. 1877. Grundriss der Physiologie der Menschen. Ed. 5. H. Laupp, Tübingen. p. 162.
[16] Woodbury, R. A., and W. T. Hamilton. 1937. Amer. J. Physiol. 119:663.

Part III. Reptiles and Amphibians

Values in parentheses are ranges, estimate "c" (*see* Introduction).

	Species (Synonym)	Specification	Heart Rate beats/min	Reference		Species (Synonym)	Specification	Heart Rate beats/min	Reference
	Reptilia				7		23.5°C	70	8
					8	*Emys orbicularis (E. lutaria)*	....	(9-60)	8
1	*Anguis fragilis*	....	64	8	9	*Lacerta agilis*	....	50	7
2	*Caretta* sp. *(Thalassochelys* sp.*)*	....	11	8	10	*L. viridis*	15-19 g	(60-66)	3
3	*Chrysemys terrapen (Pseude-mys rugosa)*	....	(21-44)	8	11	*Natrix natrix (Coluber natrix)*	....	(60-68)	6,8
4	*Crocodylus* sp.	....	(10-60)	3,4	12		169 g	(23-41)	3,8
5		71 g	(22-47)	3	13	*Testudo denticulata*	5000 g; 28-30°C	17(11-37)	2
6		15°C	30	10					

continued

Part III. Reptiles and Amphibians

Species (Synonym)	Specification	Heart Rate beats/min	Reference		Species (Synonym)	Specification	Heart Rate beats/min	Reference
Amphibia				16 17	R. pipiens, R. temporaria	2°C 22°C	(5-9) (34-39)	1 1
14 Bufo sp.	....	(40-50)	5,8	18	Salamandra sp.	....	(30-40)	9
15 Rana pipiens	....	(37.5-60)	8					

Contributors: Kruta, Vladislav, and Seliger, Václav

References

[1] Barcroft, J., and J. J. Izquierdo. 1931. J. Physiol. (London) 71:145.

[2] Benedict, F. G. 1932. Carnegie Inst. Wash. Publ. 425.

[3] Buchanan, F. 1909. J. Physiol. (London) 39:P-xxv.

[4] Gaskell, W. H. 1883. Ibid. 4:43.

[5] Hoffmeister, F. 1888. Pfluegers Arch. Gesamte Physiol. Menschen Tiere 44:366.

[6] Hoffmeister, F. 1888. Ibid. 44:360.

[7] Laurens, H. 1920. Ibid. 182:50.

[8] Lehmann, G. 1925. Tabulae Biol. 1:136.

[9] Reinmüller, J. 1932. Pfluegers Arch. Gesamte Physiol. Menschen Tiere 230:782.

[10] Rubner, M. 1924. Biochem. Z. 148:222, 268.

Part IV. Fishes

Values in parentheses are ranges, estimate "c" (*see* Introduction).

Species (Synonym)	Heart Rate beats/min	Reference		Species (Synonym)	Heart Rate beats/min	Reference
Osteichthyes (Pisces)			13	Myoxocephalus scorpius (Cottus scorpius)	(55-74)	1
1 Anguilla sp.	(20-68)	6	14	Perca fluviatilis	(52-66)	1
2 Hibernating	(1-2)	6	15	Pleuronectes platessa	(54-76)	1
3 A. anguilla	(48-56)	1	16	Salmo trutta	(30-46)	1
4 36 cm	(46-68)	5		Chondrichthyes		
5 Carassius sp.	(36-40)	6				
6 Cyprinus carpio	(40-78)	1,9	17	Mustelus canis (Galeus canis)	(34-40)	1
7 Esox lucius	(30-54)	1,6	18	Raja sp.	(16-50)	6
8 Gadus morhua	(48-60)	1	19	Scyliorhinus sp. (Scyllium catulus)	(16-50)	6
9 30 cm; at 18°C	(24-40)	8	20	1000 g; at 16°C	44	3
10 Gasterosteus aculeatus; 2 g	(60-100)	3,7	21	Scyliorhinus caniculus (Scyllium caniculus)	(39-48)	1
11 Ictalurus sp. (Ameiurus sp.)	22(5-50)	4	22	At 26°C	65	2,6
12 Micropterus salmoides (Microcropierus salmoides)	20(5-50)	4	23	Squalus acanthias (Acanthias vulgaris)	(40-50)	1
			24	Torpedo sp.	(16-50)	6

Contributors: Kruta, Vladislav, and Seliger, Václav; Woodbury, Robert A.

References

[1] Bielig, W. 1931. Z. Vergl. Physiol. 15:488.

[2] Bottazzi, F. 1901. Zentralbl. Physiol. 14:665.

[3] Clark, A. J. 1927. Comparative Physiology of the Heart. Macmillan, New York. p. 104.

continued

Part IV.   Fishes

[4] Hart, I. J. 1944. Proc. Fla. Acad. Sci. 7:221.

[5] Kolff, W. M. 1908. Pfluegers Arch. Gesamte Physiol. Menschen Tiere 122:37.

[6] Lehmann, G. 1925. Tabulae Biol. 1:136.

[7] Rubner, M. 1924. Biochem. Z. 148:222, 268.

[8] Thesen, J. E. 1896. Arch. Zool. Exp. Gen. 3(3):122.

[9] Woodbury, R. A., and W. T. Hamilton. 1937. Amer. J. Physiol. 119:663.

223.   HEART RATE AND CARDIAC OUTPUT DURING EXERCISE: MAN

Unless otherwise indicated, all measurements were made on subjects in an upright position on a treadmill or bicycle. **Condition** (habitual level of physical activity): 0 = sedentary; U = unspecified; + = trained; + + = highly trained (endurance athletes). Values in parentheses are ranges, estimate "c" (*see* Introduction).

Part I.   Submaximal Exercise

Submaximal exercise is any level of physical activity below the level at which maximal oxygen consumption occurs. Calculation of regression equations did not include values for heart rate and cardiac output at rest and at maximal exercise level, unless otherwise indicated. **Heart Rate:** Values tend to be higher in these experiments due to use of intravascular catheters. **Cardiac Output** was determined by the direct Fick method, unless otherwise indicated. *Symbol:* $\dot{V}_{O_2}$ = oxygen consumption, in liters per minute. Data in brackets refer to the column heading in brackets.

		Subjects				Heart Rate, beats/min		Oxygen Consumption liters/min	Cardiac Output Regression Equation liters/min	Reference
	Age, yr	No. & Sex [Observations]	Height [1] cm	Weight kg	Condition	Value	Regression Equation			
1	(18-34)	18♂♀	2.0±0.1 [2]	....	0	....	....	....	$4.2+6.3\,\dot{V}_{O_2}$ [3,4]	9
2	20(16-25)	4♀ [5] [9]	166(158-174)	62(48-77)	U	100-170	$93.1+39.1\,\dot{V}_{O_2}$	0.5-2.0	$6.34+6.17\,\dot{V}_{O_2}\pm1.22$	8
3	21(19-23)	11♀ [36]	169(165-176)	63(58-68)	+	97-202	$67.7+51.9\,\dot{V}_{O_2}$	0.8-2.7	$5.48+5.34\,\dot{V}_{O_2}$ ±1.42 [4]	1
4	22(16-40)	14♂ [5] [40]	175(168-182)	66(45-78)	U	75-184	$69.5+38.7\,\dot{V}_{O_2}$	0.7-3.0	$6.93+5.74\,\dot{V}_{O_2}\pm1.53$	8
5	24(21-30)	12♂ [44]	180(169-188)	75(56-88)	+	73-189	$63.2+29.9\,\dot{V}_{O_2}$	0.9-4.2	$4.34+5.22\,\dot{V}_{O_2}$ ±1.54 [4]	1
6	26(23-41)	10♂ [19]	180(171-185)	74(63-91)	0	92-161	$66.0+37.9\,\dot{V}_{O_2}$	0.8-2.2	$4.63+5.75\,\dot{V}_{O_2}\pm0.82$	2
7		9♂ [5] [19]	180(171-183)	74(63-91)	0	91-172	$71.2+38.6\,\dot{V}_{O_2}$	0.8-2.1	$7.61+5.28\,\dot{V}_{O_2}\pm1.04$	
8	30(21-52)	16♂♀ [5] [46]	175(160-185)	73(52-96)	0	75-164	$74.9+38.9\,\dot{V}_{O_2}$	0.5-2.2	$6.93+5.34\,\dot{V}_{O_2}$	3
9	33(19-44)	10♂ [35]	178(172-187)	69(58-95)	0	83-184	$63.1+51.9\,\dot{V}_{O_2}$	0.9-2.5	$3.95+5.88\,\dot{V}_{O_2}\pm0.81$	10
10	(35-49)	18♂♀	2.0±0.1 [2]	....	0	....	....	....	$3.7+6.4\,\dot{V}_{O_2}$ [3,4]	9
11	(50-69)	18♂♀	2.1±0.1 [2]	....	0	....	....	....	$3.1+6.5\,\dot{V}_{O_2}$ [3,4]	9
12	51(38-63)	25♂ [72]	176±5	78±11	0	....	....	0.9-3.5	$4.77+5.75\,\dot{V}_{O_2}$ ±1.68 [4]	7
13	51(45-55)	9♂ [26]	173(168-180)	69(64-76)	+ +	91-179	$57.7+31.4\,\dot{V}_{O_2}$	1.2-3.0	$7.52+5.63\,\dot{V}_{O_2}$ ±2.08 [4]	6
14	71(61-83)	15♂ [5] [32]	175(163-187)	73(59-91)	0 & +	90-149	$66.4+41.7\,\dot{V}_{O_2}$	0.8-1.9	$4.12+6.27\,\dot{V}_{O_2}\pm0.98$	4,5
15		9♂ [14]	174(163-187)	76(65-91)	0 & +	90-137	$60.9+42.7\,\dot{V}_{O_2}$	0.8-1.9	$2.51+6.40\,\dot{V}_{O_2}\pm0.72$	

[1] Unless otherwise indicated. [2] Body surface area, in square meters. [3] Includes values for subjects at rest in sitting position and during exercise at self-determined maximal level. [4] Determined by indicator dilution method. [5] Subjects in supine position, using a bicycle.

continued

223. HEART RATE AND CARDIAC OUTPUT DURING EXERCISE: MAN

Part I. Submaximal Exercise

Contributors: Blomqvist, Gunnar; Saltin, Bengt; and Mitchell, Jere H.

References

[1] Åstrand, P.-O., et al. 1964. J. Appl. Physiol. 19:268.
[2] Bevegård, S., et al. 1960. Acta Physiol. Scand. 49:279.
[3] Donald, K. W., et al. 1955. Clin. Sci. 14:37.
[4] Granath, A., and T. Strandell. 1964. Acta Med. Scand. 176:447.
[5] Granath, A., et al. 1964. Ibid. 176:425.

[6] Grimby, G., et al. 1966. J. Appl. Physiol. 21:1150.
[7] Grimby, G., et al. 1969. Scand. J. Clin. Lab. Invest. 24(4):335.
[8] Holmgren, A., et al. 1960. Acta Physiol. Scand. 49:343.
[9] Julius, S., et al. 1967. Circulation 36:222.
[10] Reeves, J. T., et al. 1961. J. Appl. Physiol. 16:283.

Part II. Maximal Exercise

Maximal exercise is that level of physical activity at which maximal oxygen consumption occurs. **Mean Arterial Pressure:** Values of mean pressures were recorded at the brachial artery. **Cardiac Output** was determined by the indicator dilution method, unless otherwise indicated.

		\multicolumn{3}{c}{Subjects}		Condition	Heart Rate beats/min	Mean Arterial Pressure mm Hg	Maximal Oxygen Consumption liters/min	Cardiac Output liters/min	Reference
	Age, yr	No. & Sex	Height[1] cm	Weight kg						
1	20(18-24)	6♂	179(174-185)	69(60-82)	0	193(189-205)	92(75-123)	3.42(2.71-3.80)	22.8(20.5-25.0)	9
2	20(19-21)	5♂	184(180-188)	76(63-99)	+	191(187-193)	108(97-123)	3.88(3.23-4.91)	22.7(19.3-27.3)	10
3	(20-43)	15♂	....	....	0	187 ± 13	....	3.22 ± 0.46	23.4 ± 5.5	7
4	21(19-23)	11♀	169 ± 4 (163-176)	63 ± 3 (58-68)	+	194 ± 4 (179-207)	....	2.60 ± 0.20 (2.35-3.02)	18.4 ± 1.5 (16.0-20.9)	1
5	21(20-21)	3♂	184(182-189)	71(62-75)	0	192(182-198)	98(91-106)	2.52(2.39-2.64)	17.2(16.0-18.4)	10
6	24(19-31)	5♂[2]	1.90(1.80-2.00)[3]	....	0	178(160-188)	108(93-122)	3.18(2.74-3.85)	22.6(17.9-25.2)	8
7	24(21-30)	12♂	180 ± 7 (169-191)	75 ± 9 (56-88)	+	186 ± 8 (174-204)	....	4.05 ± 0.70 (2.66-5.39)	23.8 ± 3.7 (16.3-29.9)	1
8	26(22-34)	8♂	186 ± 5 (180-194)	75 ± 7 (64-84)	++	190 ± 10 (171-206)	116 ± 11 (100-133)	5.57 ± 0.49 (4.66-6.24)	36.0 ± 4.7 (27.8-42.0)	2
9	28(19-30)	5♂	1.81(1.74-1.86)[3]	....	0	171(161-195)	112(80-142)	2.40(1.63-2.94)	17.2(12.5-21.3)[4]	3
10	45(38-49)	11♂	176 ± 6	77 ± 12	0	185 ± 7	142 ± 21	2.80 ± 0.39	19.5 ± 2.4	6
11	51(45-55)	9♂	173 ± 4 (168-180)	69 ± 4 (64-73)	++	171 ± 13 (147-191)	134 ± 12 (119-154)	3.56 ± 0.41 (2.73-4.15)	26.8 ± 2.8 (21.9-31.1)	5
12	55(50-62)	14♂	177 ± 5	79 ± 6	0	173 ± 12	138 ± 14	2.20 ± 0.39	17.0 ± 3.6	6
13	71(61-83)[5]	6♂	175 ± 6	73 ± 10	0	128 ± 7	127 ± 17	1.47 ± 0.27	11.6 ± 1.7[4]	4

[1] Unless otherwise indicated. [2] All subjects had functional systolic murmurs. [3] Body surface area, in square meters. [4] Determined by direct Fick method. [5] Values are probably not for maximal exercise, but are included because data for this age group are scarce; higher heart rates were reached during experiments not involving catheterization.

Contributors: Mitchell, Jere H.; Blomqvist, Gunnar; and Saltin, Bengt

References

[1] Åstrand, P.-O., et al. 1964. J. Appl. Physiol. 19:268.
[2] Ekblom, B., and L. Hermansen. 1968. Ibid. 25:619.
[3] Epstein, S. E., et al. 1967. Circulation 35:1049.
[4] Granath, A., et al. 1964. Acta Med. Scand. 176:425.
[5] Grimby, G., et al. 1966. J. Appl. Physiol. 21:1150.
[6] Grimby, G., et al. 1969. Scand. J. Clin. Lab. Invest. 24(4):335.

[7] Mitchell, J. H., et al. 1958. J. Clin. Invest. 37:538.
[8] Robinson, B. F., et al. 1966. Circ. Res. 19:26.
[9] Rowell, L. B. 1962. Ph. D. Thesis. Univ. Minnesota, Minneapolis.
[10] Saltin, B., et al. 1968. Circulation 38, Suppl. 7:1.

All subjects were considered to be healthy and normal, unless otherwise specified. Plus/minus (±) values are standard deviation; where standard deviation was not given in the reference, it was calculated from the range, as described in reference 19 in Part I. **Vascular Resistance** = $(\bar{P}_A - \bar{P}_V)/Q$, where $\bar{P}_A$ = **Pulmonary Arterial** mean pressure, $\bar{P}_V$ = pulmonary venous (or "Wedge" or left atrial) mean pressure, and Q = cardiac output (or **Pulmonary Blood Flow**).

Part I.   Man

All subjects were supine unless otherwise specified. **Pulmonary Blood Flow** was determined by the Fick method, unless otherwise indicated.

	Subjects Age, yr	No.	Condition	Oxygen Consumption ml/min	Pulmonary Arterial Systolic	Pulmonary Arterial Diastolic	Pulmonary Arterial Mean	Wedge Mean	Pulmonary Blood Flow liter·min^{-1}·m^{-2}	Vascular Resistance mm Hg·liter^{-1}·min·m^{2}	Reference
							At Rest				
1	3-19	30	....	....	19 ± 3	8 ± 2	13 ± 3	7 ± 2	....	....	12
2	12 ± 4	10	....	....	14 ± 5	8 ± 3	12 ± 2	7 ± 2	4.3 ± 1.0	1.3 ± 0.9	3
3	18-42	10	Legs elevated	....	....	....	....	....	3.7 ± 0.3[1]	....	15
4	21 ± 5	18	....	....	20 ± 3[2]	9 ± 3	14 ± 2	8 ± 3	3.6 ± 0.8	1.5 ± 0.7	11
5	30 ± 6	16	....	....	....	....	....	....	3.4 ± 0.5[1]	....	17
6	36 ± 15	12	....	....	21 ± 4[2]	5 ± 1	12 ± 2	5 ± 0.6	3.6 ± 0.8	1.9 ± 1.0	8
7									2.9 ± 0.5[3]	2.4 ± 1.5	
8	37 ± 6	10	....	....	22 ± 3[2]	8 ± 2	13 ± 2	....	3.1 ± 0.5	....	4
9	Unspeci-	52	....	....	22 ± 5[4]	10 ± 3	15 ± 4	9 ± 3	4.0 ± 0.8	1.4 ± 0.8	9
10	fied								3.2 ± 0.2[3]	1.9 ± 0.6	
11		8	....	....	23 ± 2[5]	9 ± 2	15 ± 1	9 ± 2	4.2 ± 0.7	1.4 ± 0.2	5
12	25 ± 8	8	14-24 wk pregnant	....	18 ± 3	6 ± 3	10 ± 3	5 ± 2	4.1 ± 0.4	1.4 ± 0.6	1
13	25 ± 11	10	28-30 wk pregnant	....	19 ± 4	7 ± 3	12 ± 2	5 ± 2	3.9 ± 0.6	1.8 ± 0.6	1
14	23 ± 5	10	31-35 wk pregnant	....	18 ± 4	6 ± 2	11 ± 3	6 ± 1	3.6 ± 0.6	1.3 ± 0.4	1
15	22 ± 4	11	36-40 wk pregnant	....	17 ± 3	6 ± 3	11 ± 3	5 ± 2	3.4 ± 0.4	1.7 ± 0.6	1
16	Sedated, 43 ± 11	9	Premedicated with secobarbital Na, 90-180 mg	....	....	....	16 ± 3[6]	7 ± 2	3.3 ± 0.9	2.9 ± 1.3	18
							During Exercise				
17	23 ± 7	8	Rest	267 ± 51	....	....	11 ± 3	....	4.2 ± 1.0	....	10
18		8	Exercise	535 ± 116	....	....	13 ± 1	....	6.1 ± 1.7	....	10
19	26 ± 7	7	Rest	289 ± 37	19 ± 4	7 ± 2	12 ± 3	....	4.1 ± 0.8	....	2
20		8	Exercise 1[7]	1160 ± 157	28 ± 6	9 ± 3	16 ± 4	....	7.0 ± 0.5	....	2
21		8	Exercise 2[8]	1960 ± 273	36 ± 8	9 ± 4	18 ± 4	....	9.3 ± 1.0	....	2
22	26 ± 7	7	Sitting; rest	348 ± 46	14 ± 2[9]	5 ± 2	9 ± 2	....	3.0 ± 0.8	....	2
23		8	Sitting; Exercise 1[7]	1125 ± 195	21 ± 5[9]	9 ± 3	14 ± 4	....	5.6 ± 0.3	....	2
24		8	Sitting; Exercise 2[8]	1959 ± 315	27 ± 8[9]	10 ± 5	18 ± 6	....	8.3 ± 0.8	....	2
25	Unspeci-	7	Rest	237 ± 41	....	....	13 ± 2	8 ± 2	3.8 ± 0.8	1.5 ± 0.3	6
26	fied	7	Exercise	612 ± 179	....	....	19 ± 3	10 ± 3	5.1 ± 0.6	1.7 ± 0.4	6
27	Sedated[10] 35 ± 10	16	Rest	260 ± 22	....	....	18 ± 2	7.7[11]	4.4 ± 0.7	2.3 ± 0.3	7
28	26	4	Light exercise	537 ± 76	....	....	17 ± 2	9.5[11]	5.3 ± 1.0	1.4 ± 0.2	7
29	32	4	Intermediate exercise	752 ± 64	....	....	18 ± 3	9.5[11]	6.0 ± 0.5	1.4 ± 0.3	7

[1] Nitrous oxide method. [2] Zero reference level for pressures at 5 cm behind sternum. [3] Dye method. [4] Zero reference level for pressures at "center of heart." [5] Zero reference level for pressures at 10 cm anterior to back. [6] Zero reference level for pressures at 10 cm above table. [7] Work load was one-half that of Exercise 2. [8] Work load ranged from 500-900 kg·m/min, and produced a heart rate of about 150 beats/min in each subject. [9] Zero reference level for pressures at junction between fourth costal cartilage and sternum. [10] Premedicated with 400 mg amobarbital. [11] Wedge pressures not measured, but assumed equal to those in reference 6.

continued

Part I. Man

	Subjects		Condition	Oxygen Consumption ml/min	Blood Pressure, mm Hg				Pulmonary Blood Flow liter·min^{-1}·m^{-2}	Vascular Resistance mm Hg·liter^{-1}· min·m^2	Reference
	Age, yr	No.			Pulmonary Arterial			Wedge Mean			
					Systolic	Diastolic	Mean				
30	33	4	High exercise	1027 ± 82	....	....	17 ± 2	9.5[11]	6.7 ± 0.4	1.1 ± 0.5	7
31	34	4	Highest exercise	2040 ± 212	....	....	20 ± 2	9.5[11]	9.2 ± 1.0	1.1 ± 0.6	7
32	35 ± 10	16	5-min rest after exercise	288 ± 35	....	....	16 ± 2	7.7[11]	3.9 ± 0.5	2.1 ± 0.3	7
			At High Altitude [12]								
33	1-5	7	Rest	....	57 ± 17	32 ± 18	45 ± 17	7 ± 2	....	....	13
34	6-14	25	Rest	....	41 ± 10	18 ± 10	28 ± 10	5 ± 1	....	....	13
35	Adult	25	Resident at sea level; rest	....	22 ± 3	6 ± 2	12 ± 2	6 ± 2	4.0 ± 1.0	1.6 ± 0.6	13
36		38	Rest	....	41 ± 13	15 ± 8	28 ± 10	5 ± 2	3.7 ± 1.6	6.1 ± 4.0	13
37		35	Rest	260	41	15	29	5	3.6	6.5	13
38			Exercise	1300	77	40	60	6	7.5	7.2	13
39	13-17	22	Resident at 3090 m above sea level; rest	237 ± 35	....	....	24 ± 8	9 ± 2	3.6 ± 0.5	4.4 ± 1.3	16
40			Resident at 3090 m above sea level; exercise	1021 ± 36	....	....	48 ± 13	....	6.3 ± 1.2	....	16
41	Adult	6	Resident at sea level, after 1 yr at 4540 m above sea level; rest	226 ± 10	25 ± 2	12 ± 2	18 ± 2	....	3.5 ± 0.3	....	14

[11] Wedge pressures not measured, but assumed equal to those in reference 6. [12] All subjects resident at 4540 m above sea level, unless otherwise specified.

Contributor: Richardson, David W.

References

[1] Bader, R. A., et al. 1955. J. Clin. Invest. 34:1524.

[2] Bevegård, S., et al. 1960. Acta Physiol. Scand. 49: 279.

[3] Brotmacher, L., and P. Fleming. 1957. Guy's Hosp. Rep. 106:268.

[4] Cournand, A. 1950. Circulation 2:641.

[5] Dexter, L., et al. 1950. J. Clin. Invest. 29:602.

[6] Dexter, L., et al. 1951. J. Appl. Physiol. 3:439.

[7] Donald, K. W., et al. 1955. Clin. Sci. 14:38.

[8] Doyle, J. T., et al. 1951. J. Clin. Invest. 30:345.

[9] Harris, P., and D. Heath. 1962. Human Pulmonary Circulation. E. and S. Livingstone, London. pp. 49, 62, 66.

[10] Hickam, J. B., and W. H. Cargill. 1948. J. Clin. Invest. 27:10.

[11] Holmgren, A., et al. 1960. Acta Physiol. Scand. 49: 343.

[12] Kjellberg, S. R., et al. 1959. Diagnosis of Congenital Heart Disease. Year Book, Chicago.

[13] Penazola, D., et al. 1962. Med. Thorac. 19:449.

[14] Rotta, A., et al. 1956. J. Appl. Physiol. 9:328.

[15] Vermeire, P., and J. Butler. 1968. Circ. Res. 22: 299.

[16] Vogel, J. H. K., et al. 1962. Med. Thorac. 19:461.

[17] Wasserman, K., and J. H. Comroe. 1962. J. Clin. Invest. 41:401.

[18] Westcott, R. N., et al. 1951. Ibid. 30:957.

[19] Wilcoxon, F., and R. A. Wilcox. 1964. Some Rapid Approximate Statistical Procedures. Lederle Laboratories, New York. p. 16.

continued

Part II. Mammals Other Than Man

In all animals, the chest was closed. **Ventilation:** IPPB = intermittent positive pressure breathing. **Blood Pressures:**

Pulmonary Arterial [Other]—S = systolic, D = diastolic. Data in brackets refer to the column heading in brackets.

	Subjects		Anesthesia mg/kg	Ventilation	Body Position	Blood Pressures, mm Hg				Blood Flow liter/min [L] [Method]	Vascular Resistance mm Hg·liter^{-1}· min [L]	Ref-er-ence
	Animal & Body Wt kg	No. & Sex				Location of Zero Reference	Pulmonary Arterial Mean [Other]	Left Atrial Mean				
1	Baboon, 24 ± 8	7	Pentobarbital Na, 12-25	Tracheal tube; spontaneous	Supine	....	23 ± 6 [S, 33 ± 9; D, 15 ± 5]	.....	4.3 ± 0.9 [Dye]		....	4
2	Cat, 3-4	9	α-Chloralose, 10-15	Spontaneous	....	Pulmonary artery	17 ± 4	6		....	....	3
	Cattle											
3	404 ± 67	9♀	None	Normal	Standing	Olecranon	24 ± 5 [S, 33 ± 6; D, 19 ± 5]	.....	41 ± 8 [Dye]		....	2
4	407 ± 33	10♀	None	Normal	Standing	Olecranon	27 ± 4	12 ± 5	33 ± 8 [Fick]		0.8 ± 0.2	8
	Dog											
5	9 ± 2	11	Pentobarbital Na, 30	Tracheal tube; IPPB	....	....	13 ± 2 [S, 18 ± 2; D, 10 ± 2]	8 ± 2	2.2 ± 0.6 [Fick]		2.3 ± 1.2	1
6	>12	22	Pentobarbital Na, 33	Tracheal tube; spontaneous	....	Intrapleural	18 ± 4	8 ± 4	3.6 ± 1.0[2] [Fick]		2.6 ± 0.9[3]	5
7	16-18	7	None	Normal	Standing	Middle of chest	18 ± 3	6 ± 4	3.5 ± 1.2 [Fick]		3.4 ± 1.4	7
8		6	None	Normal	Standing	Intrapleural	20 ± 4	6[4]	3.9 ± 1.5 [Dye]		3.2 ± 2.2	7
9	17 ± 3	9	Urethan, 320-480; α-chloralose, 32-48	Tracheal tube; spontaneous	Supine	Back	19 ± 4	10 ± 3	2.3 ± 1.0 [Fick]		4.3 ± 2.2	6
10	20-25	16	Pentobarbital Na, 28	....	....	....	18 ± 5	4 ± 2	3.2 ± 1.1 [Fick]		4.1 ± 0.9	9
11	Unspecified	5	None	Normal	Lying on right side	Intrapleural	14 ± 2	4.7	2.7 ± 0.3 [Dye]		3.4 ± 0.8	10

[1] Unless otherwise indicated. [2] Liter·min^{-1}·m^{-2}. [3] mm Hg·liter^{-1}·min·m^2. [4] Assumed, not measured.

Contributor: Richardson, David W.

References

[1] Bergofsky, E. H., et al. 1962. J. Clin. Invest. 41: 1492.

[2] Doyle, J. T., et al. 1960. Circ. Res. 8:4.

[3] Euler, U. S. von, and G. Liljestrand. 1946. Acta Physiol. Scand. 12:301.

[4] Guenter, C. A., et al. 1968. J. Appl. Physiol. 25: 507.

[5] Haddy, F. J., et al. 1949. Amer. J. Physiol. 158: 89.

[6] Lewis, B. M., and R. Gorlin. 1952. Ibid. 170:574.

[7] Nahas, G. G., et al. 1954. J. Appl. Physiol. 6:467.

[8] Reeves, J. T., et al. 1962. Circ. Res. 10:166.

[9] Stroud, R. C., and H. Rahn. 1953. Amer. J. Physiol. 172:211.

[10] Thilenius, O. G., et al. 1964. Ibid. 206:867.

Values were determined in vivo and calculated for 10 minutes of saturation or desaturation. The cerebral blood flow in normal adults has been calculated [10] to be 43 ± 3 ml·100 g^{-1}·min^{-1} by extrapolation to infinity to include fully the white matter of the brain; this value is theoretically more accurate than those included in this table. Cerebral arteriovenous oxygen difference (the quantity of oxygen removed by the brain from each 100 ml of blood flowing through the brain) is equal to 100 times oxygen consumption, in milliliters per 100 g per minute, divided by cerebral blood flow, in milliliters per 100 g per minute. Vascular Resistance is equal to mean arterial pressure divided by cerebral blood flow. Cerebral Blood Flow Method: ^{85}Kr = radioactive krypton, intermittent samplings [9]; ^{133}Xe = radioactive xenon, intracarotid injection and extracranial γ-recording [3,11]; ^{131}I-AP = [^{131}I]iodoantipyrine accumulation as estimated by external counting; N_2O = nitrous oxide, intermittent sampling [5]; ^{79}Kr = radioactive krypton, external counting, intermittent blood sampling, and integrated arteriovenous difference. Values in parentheses are ranges, estimate "c" (see Introduction).

| | Subjects | | | O_2 Consumption ml·100 g^{-1}·min^{-1} [1] | Vascular Resistance mm Hg·ml^{-1}·100 g·min [1] | Cerebral Blood Flow ml·100 g^{-1}·min^{-1} [1] | | Reference |
	Age, yr	No. & Sex	Condition			Method	Value	
			Homo sapiens					
1	24	♂	Normal; alert; recumbent; normocapnic	3.5(3.1-4.0)	1.9	^{85}Kr	50(44-58)	10
2	~25	♂	Normal; alert; recumbent; normocapnic	....	....	^{133}Xe	50(42-54)	3
3	25	♂	Normal	76(44-115)[2]	8.5(6.4-11.8)[3]	^{131}I-AP	1097(902-1368)[4]	15
4			Normal; alert; recumbent; normocapnic	3.3(2.6-4.2)[5]	1.6(1.2-2.5)[5]	N_2O	54(40-67)[5]	4-6
5			Normal; inhaling 5-7% CO_2	3.3(2.4-3.9)	1.1(0.7-1.4)	N_2O	93(65-141)	6
6			10% O_2	3.2(2.6-3.5)	1.1(0.8-1.6)	N_2O	73(54-93)	
7			85-100% O_2	3.2(2.6-4.4)	2.2(1.8-2.7)	N_2O	45(34-55)	
8	26(23-31)	♂	Passive hyperventilation with air	4.7(4.0-5.1)	2.4(1.7-3.5)	N_2O	41(36-47)	4
9	29	♂	Normal Inhaling air	3.7(2.5-4.4)	1.7(1.3-1.8)	N_2O	56(48.2-65.9)	17
10			Inhaling 5% CO_2 + 10% O_2 + 85% N_2	4.0(2.9-4.7)	1.1(0.9-1.3)	N_2O	97(80.6-118.0)	
11		♂♀	Normal; alert; recumbent; normocapnic	3.1(2.2-3.9)	1.8	N_2O	52(40-64)	2
12	30	♂♀	Hospitalized; no brain disease	3.1(2.1-4.5)	1.7(1.2-2.4)	N_2O	51(43-56)	14
13			Inhaling 2.5% CO_2	3.1(2.5-3.4)	1.8(1.2-2.1)	N_2O	52(47-57)	
14	35	♂♀	Hospitalized; no brain disease	3.0(2.6-3.3)	2.0(1.5-2.5)	N_2O	52(30-68)	14
15			Inhaling 3.5% CO_2	3.0(2.5-3.5)	1.8(1.3-3.4)	N_2O	57(33-74)	
16	36	♂♀	Normal	63(41-90)[2]	9.0(5.4-11.1)[3]	^{131}I-AP	996(787-1263)[4]	15
17	38(17-55)	10♂, 10♀	Normal; alert; recumbent; normocapnic	3.4(2.4-4.3)	1.8(1.1-2.3)	^{85}Kr	52(33-67)	9
18	50.1	♂	Normal; breathing air	3.4(3.2-3.6)	....	^{85}Kr	49.3(35-65)	13
19	56	♂♀	Normal; alert; recumbent; normocapnic	2.9(2.0-3.9)	2.2	N_2O	46(30-64)	2
20	71	♂	Normal	3.3(2.6-4.2)	1.6(1.0-2.2)	N_2O	57.9(42-75)	1
21	Unspecified	....	Anesthetized (thiopental Na)	2.1(1.5-3.0)	1.3(0.6-2.1)	N_2O	60(33-117)	18
22		♂	Normal	....	....	^{79}Kr	83.1(60-104)	12
23						N_2O	57.1(51-68)	
24		♂	Normal	3.8(3.11-4.9)	1.33(0.9-1.7)	N_2O	64.9(52-100)	16
25			Tilted 65°	3.8(2.8-4.7)	1.1(0.77-1.4)	N_2O	51.6(42-81)	
			Papio anubis & P. cynocephalus					
26	Young adults[6]	♂♀	Anesthetized (phencyclidine, N_2O)	2.8(1.4-6.0)	2.0(1.4-2.9)	^{133}Xe	50(35-78)	19, 20

[1] Unless otherwise indicated. [2] Total cerebral O_2 consumption. [3] Total cerebral vascular resistance. [4] Total cerebral blood flow. [5] Approximately same values found in subjects with essential hypertension [7] and with schizophrenia [8]. [6] 8-15 kg.

Contributors: Raper, A. Jarrell; Lassen, N. A.

continued

References

[1] Dastur, D. K., et al. Unpublished.

[2] Heyman, A., et al. 1953. N. Engl. J. Med. 249:223.

[3] Ingvar, D. H., et al. 1965. Acta Neurol. Scand., Suppl. 14:72.

[4] Kety, S. S., and C. F. Schmidt. 1946. J. Clin. Invest. 25:107.

[5] Kety, S. S., and C. F. Schmidt. 1948. Ibid. 27:476.

[6] Kety, S. S., and C. F. Schmidt. 1948. Ibid. 27:484.

[7] Kety, S. S., et al. 1948. Ibid. 27:511.

[8] Kety, S. S., et al. 1948. Amer. J. Psychiat. 104:765.

[9] Lassen, N. A., and O. Munck. 1955. Acta Physiol. Scand. 33:30.

[10] Lassen, N. A., et al. 1960. J. Clin. Invest. 39:491.

[11] Lassen, N. A., et al. 1963. Neurology 13:719.

[12] Lewis, B. M., et al. 1960. J. Clin. Invest. 39:707.

[13] Munck, O., and N. A. Lassen. 1957. Circ. Res. 5:163.

[14] Patterson, J. L., Jr., et al. 1955. J. Clin. Invest. 27:484.

[15] Reinmuth, O. M., et al. 1965. Arch. Neurol. (Chicago) 12:49.

[16] Scheinberg, P., and E. A. Stead, Jr. 1949. J. Clin. Invest. 28:1163.

[17] Shapiro, W., et al. 1966. Circ. Res. 19:903.

[18] Wechsler, R. L., et al. 1951. Anesthesiology 12:308.

[19] Deshmukh, V. D., and A. M. Harper. 1973. Acta Neurol. Scand. 49:649.

[20] Harper, A. M., et al. 1972. Arch. Neurol. (Chicago) 27:1.

226. RENAL BLOOD FLOW: MAMMALS

Method: C_{PAH} = p-aminohippurate plasma clearance; C_D = Diodrast plasma clearance.

Part I. Man

Effective Plasma Flow (EPF) was determined from p-aminohippurate, or Diodrast plasma clearance. **Effective Blood Flow (EBF)** was calculated from effective plasma flow and hematocrit ratio (Hct) by the formula, EBF = EPF/1 −Hct unless otherwise indicated. Values in parentheses are ranges, estimate "c" unless otherwise specified (*see* Introduction).

	Subjects		No. of Observations	Method	Effective Plasma Flow ml·min^{-1}·1.73 m^{-2} body surface area[1]	Effective Blood Flow ml·min^{-1}·1.73 m^{-2} body surface area[1]	Reference
	Age yr	No. & Sex					
1	2-40	91♂	258	C_{PAH}, C_D	655(492-818)[b]	1166(910-1422)[b]	9
2	2-40	31♀	91	C_{PAH}, C_D	600(498-702)[b]	940(756-1124)[b]	
3	16-60	61♂	...	C_D	697(425-969)[b]	1209(697-1721)[b]	8,10
4	16-55	17♀	...	C_D	594(390-798)[b]	982(614-1350)[b]	
5	<20-45	19♀[2]	...	C_D	800(498-1102)[b]	1359(881-1837)[b]	2
6	<20-40	13♀[3]	...	C_D	571(393-749)[b]	919(451-1387)[b]	
7	Adult	34♀[4], 31♀[5]	...	C_D	617(397-837)[b]	962(602-1322)[b]	3
8	20-29	10♂	27	C_D	786(529-993)	1339(860-1780)	5
9	30-39	10♂	21	C_D	676(323-956)	1145(521-1622)	
10	40-49	9♂	14	C_D	689(509-846)	1150(868-1342)	
11	50-59	7♂	21	C_D	586(343-804)	987(746-1341)	
12	60-69	2♂	5	C_D	584(498-680)	997(844-1192)	
13	22-51	11♀	16	C_D	596(441-782)	973(718-1264)	
14	23-27	6♂	...	C_{PAH}	663[6]	1257[6,7]	6
15	23-57	2♂, 11♀	13	C_{PAH}	497(361-648)	881(631-1179)	7
16	24-39	13♂	38	C_{PAH}	811[8]	1385[6,8]	1
17	20-29	9♂	9	C_D	614(481-724)	1077(859-1353)	4
18	30-39	9♂	9	C_D	649(519-804)	1181(931-1493)	
19	40-49	10♂	10	C_D	574(396-736)	1008(737-1252)	
20	50-59	11♂	11	C_D	500(341-617)	849(631-1007)	
21	60-69	10♂	10	C_D	442(253-534)	775(453-941)	
22	70-79	9♂	9	C_D	354(234-519)	589(411-845)	
23	80-89	12♂	12	C_D	289(147-462)	475(237-732)	

[1] Unless otherwise indicated. [2] Pregnant, 2-8 lunar months. [3] Pregnant, 9-10 lunar months. [4] Plasma flow; subjects pregnant, near term. [5] Blood flow; subjects pregnant, near term. [6] Calculated from $\dfrac{C_{PAH}/E_{PAH}}{1 - Hct}$, where E_{PAH} = extraction ratio of p-aminohippurate. [7] Direct measurement of renal blood flow by xenon wash-out method = 4.55 ml·min^{-1}·g kidney wt^{-1}. [8] ml·min^{-1}.

continued

Part I. Man

Contributor: Selkurt, Ewald E.

References
[1] Aurell, M., et al. 1966. Clin. Sci. 31:461.
[2] Bucht, H. 1951. Scand. J. Clin. Lab. Invest., Suppl. 3.
[3] Chesley, L. C. 1951. Med. Clin. N. Amer. 35:699.
[4] Davies, D. F., and N. W. Shock. 1950. J. Clin. Invest. 29:496.
[5] Goldring, W., et al. 1940. Ibid. 19:739.
[6] Ladefoged, J., and F. Pedersen. 1967. Acta Physiol. Scand. 69:220.
[7] Pfeiffer, J. B., Jr., and H. G. Wolff. 1950. J. Clin. Invest. 29:1227.
[8] Smith, H. W. 1943. Lectures on the Kidney. Univ. Kansas Press, Lawrence.
[9] Smith, H. W. 1951. The Kidney: Structure and Function in Health and Disease. Oxford Univ. Press, New York.
[10] Smith, H. W., et al. 1943. J. Mt. Sinai Hosp. New York 10:59.

Part II. Mammals Other Than Man

Method: EPF = effective plasma flow; EBF = effective blood flow; Hct = hematocrit ratio; E_{PAH} = p-aminohippurate extraction. T or E: T = total flow; E = effective flow.

	Species	No. of Subjects	Condition	Method	Plasma or Blood	T or E	Flow ml·min^{-1} (both kidneys)	Flow ml·min^{-1}·g kidney wt^{-1}	Flow ml·min^{-1}·kg body wt^{-1}	Reference
1	*Aotus tri-*	17	Anesthetized	Electromagnetic flowmeter	Plasma	T	18.9	2.60	23.2	24
2	*virgatus*		(pentobarbital Na)	Electromagnetic flowmeter	Blood	T	36.8	5.00	45.0	
3	*Canis fa-*	6	Unanesthetized	EPF = EBF(1 − Hct)	Plasma	E	212[1]	2.20[2]	15.8	9,18
4	*miliaris*			Thermostromuhr	Blood	T	384	4.00	28.6	
5		51	Unanesthetized	EPF = EBF(1 − Hct)	Plasma	E	158[1]	1.73[2]	11.5	12-14,
6				Direct venous outflow	Blood	T	288	3.15	21.0	16
7		75	Unanesthetized	C_{PAH}	Plasma	E	166	1.90[2]	13.5[3]	10
8				EBF = EPF/(1 − Hct)	Blood	E	302[1]	3.46	24.6[4]	
9		11	Unanesthetized	EPF = EBF(1 − Hct)	Plasma	E	156[1]	2.20[5]	10.0[6]	27
10				Urea extraction	Blood	T	284	4.00	18.0[7]	
11		14	Anesthetized	Direct venous outflow	Plasma	T	226	2.40	14.0	23,25
12			(pentobarbital Na)	Direct venous outflow	Blood	T	400	3.90	21.0	
13		63	Anesthetized	EPF = EBF(1 − Hct)	Plasma	E	180[1]	2.10	11.4	17,19,
14			(pentobarbital Na)	Electromagnetic flowmeter	Blood	T	326	3.80	20.6	20,26
15		20[8]	Anesthetized (α-chloralose); splenectomized	EPF = EBF(1 − Hct)	Plasma	E	211[1]	1.60	11.2	2
16				Electromagnetic flowmeter	Blood	T	384	2.90[2]	20.2	
17	*Macaca*	4	Tranquilized (re-serpine)	C_{PAH}	Plasma	E	50.0	2.00[1]	8.06	22
18	*mulatta*			EBF = EPF/(1 − Hct)	Blood	E	91.0[1]	3.60[9]	14.7[1]	
19	*M. spe-*	6	Tranquilized (in-novarvet)	^{131}I-hippuran	Plasma	E	118.0	2.33[1]	15.1	21
20	*ciosa*			EBF = EPF/(1 − Hct)	Blood	E	214[1]	4.30[9]	27.5[1]	
21	*Oryctola-*	95	Unanesthetized	C_{PAH}	Plasma	E	55	3.13[10]	21.0[11,12]	1,5,
22	*gus cuni-culus*			Thermostromuhr, $\dfrac{C_{PAH}/E_{PAH}}{1-Hct}$	Blood	T	87	5.00	35.2[13]	11, 28
23	*Rattus*	160	Unanesthetized	C_D; C_{PAH}	Plasma	E	4.6	2.75[10]	27.7[14]	3,4,6-
24	*norvegi-cus*			EBF = EPF/(1 − Hct); ^{86}Rb uptake	Blood	T	8.4[1]	5.10	51.0[15]	8,15

[1] Calculated for an average hematocrit ratio of 0.45. [2] Kidney wt in g = 7.1 × body wt in kg. [3] Plasma flow = 266 ml·min^{-1}·m^{-2} body surface area. [4] Blood flow = 484 ml·min^{-1}·m^{-2} body surface area. [5] Kidney wt in g = 96.2 × m^{-2} body surface area. [6] Plasma flow = 248 ml·min^{-1}·m^{-2} body surface area. [7] Blood flow = 450 ml·min^{-1}·m^{-2} body surface area. [8] All values below 9.0 ml·min^{-1}·kg^{-1} rejected.

[9] Kidney wt in g = 6.4 × body wt in kg. [10] Kidney wt in g = 8.0 × body wt in kg. [11] Calculated for an average body wt of 2.9 kg. [12] Plasma flow = 327 ml·min^{-1}·m^{-2} body surface area. [13] Blood flow = 558 ml·min^{-1}·m^{-2} body surface area. [14] Plasma flow = 163 ml·min^{-1}·m^{-2} body surface area. [15] Blood flow = 296 ml·min^{-1}·m^{-2} body surface area.

continued

Part II. Mammals Other Than Man

Contributor: Selkurt, Ewald E.

References

[1] Brod, J., and J. H. Sirota. 1949. Amer. J. Physiol. 157:31.

[2] Buckley, N. M., et al. 1967. Ibid. 212:579.

[3] Dicker, S. E., and H. Heller. 1945. J. Physiol. (London) 103:449.

[4] Dicker, S. E., and H. Heller. 1946. Ibid. 104:353.

[5] Forster, R. P. 1947. Amer. J. Physiol. 150:523, 534.

[6] Friedman, M. 1947. Ibid. 148:387.

[7] Friedman, S. M., et al. 1947. Ibid. 150:340.

[8] Goldman, H. 1968. Ibid. 214:860.

[9] Herrick, J. F., et al. 1939. J. Pharmacol. Exp. Ther. 66:73.

[10] Houck, C. R. 1948. Amer. J. Physiol. 153:169.

[11] Korner, P. I. 1963. Circ. Res. 12:353.

[12] Levy, S. E., and A. Blalock. 1937. Amer. J. Physiol. 118:368.

[13] Levy, S. E., and A. Blalock. 1938. Ibid. 122:609.

[14] Levy, S. E., et al. 1938. Ibid. 122:38.

[15] Lippman, R. W. 1948. Ibid. 152:27.

[16] Mason, M. F., et al. 1937. Ibid. 118:667.

[17] McNay, J. L., et al. 1965. Circ. Res. 16:510.

[18] Medes, S., and J. F. Herrick. 1933. Proc. Soc. Exp. Biol. Med. 31:116.

[19] Navar, L. G. Unpublished. Univ. Mississippi Medical Center, Jackson, 1969.

[20] Navar, L. G., et al. 1966. Amer. J. Physiol. 211:1387.

[21] O'Dell, R., et al. 1968. J. Appl. Physiol. 24:366.

[22] Pickering, D. E., and H. H. Sussman. 1962. Amer. J. Vet. Res. 23:667.

[23] Selkurt, E. E. 1963. Amer. J. Physiol. 205:286.

[24] Selkurt, E. E. Unpublished. Indiana Univ. Medical Center, Indianapolis, 1971.

[25] Selkurt, E. E., and M. J. Elpers. 1963. Amer. J. Physiol. 205:147.

[26] Selkurt, E. E., et al. 1964. Ibid. 207:989.

[27] Van Slyke, D. D., et al. 1934. Ibid. 109:336.

[28] Walker, A. M., et al. 1937. Ibid. 118:95.

227. HEPATIC BLOOD FLOW: MAMMALS

Values in parentheses are ranges, estimate "c" (*see* Introduction).

Part I. Man

	Condition	Method[1]	Hepatic Blood Flow[2] ml·min^{-1}	Reference
1	Normal	Sulfobromophthalein	1405(1040-2080)	13,14
2			1446(865-2250)	1,2,18
3			1455(1300-1890)	11
4			1510(1108-1850)	3
5			1560(1192-1737)	12
6		Plus alcohol	2070 ± 15	21
7		Plus galactose	1630(1490-1805)	19,21
8		Plus indocyanine green[3]	1306(790-2095)	4,7,8
9		Plus rose bengal	1600	5
10			2060 ± 30	21
11		Plus urea (endogenously produced)	1395(1045-2020)	13,14
12		Colloidal [^{198}Au]gold[3]	1425(1120-2010)	20
13		[^{198}Au]gold[3,4]	1090(542-1779)	9
14		^{131}I-albumin[3,4]	1663(980-2190)	17
15	Pregnant	Sulfobromophthalein	1565(1092-2065)	12
	Anesthetized			
16	Before; after breath of 3% CO_2	Sulfobromophthalein	1148(470-2110)	6

[1] Constant infusion of indicator, and sampling from hepatic vein and peripheral artery or vein, unless otherwise indicated. [2] Unless otherwise indicated. [3] Single injection, and sampling from peripheral artery or vein. [4] Determined by disappearance of radioactivity from a limb or other portion.

continued

Part I. Man

	Condition	Method [1]	Hepatic Blood Flow [2] ml·min^{-1}	Reference
17	After; after breath of 3% CO_2	Sulfobromophthalein	976(490-1540)	6
18	Barbiturate & diethyl ether; before	Sulfobromophthalein	1258(746-2140)	16
19	after	Sulfobromophthalein	884(467-1850)	16
20	Morphine & scopolamine; before	Sulfobromophthalein	1245(1030-1620)	6
21	after	Sulfobromophthalein	1150(840-1540)	6
22	Nitrous oxide-scopolamine; before	Sulfobromophthalein	1208(820-1640)	6
23	after	Sulfobromophthalein	1351(780-2110)	6
24	Open abdomen	Electromagnetic flow probe	1004 ± 322 [5]	15
25			870 ± 1460 [6]	10

[1] Constant infusion of indicator, and sampling from hepatic vein and peripheral artery or vein, unless otherwise indicated. [2] Unless otherwise indicated. [5] Flow in hepatic artery = 258 ml·min^{-1}; flow in portal vein = 744 ml·min^{-1}. [6] Flow in portal vein.

Contributor: Iber, Frank L.

References

[1] Bearn, A. G., et al. 1951. J. Physiol. (London) 115: 430.
[2] Bearn, A. G., et al. 1951. Ibid. 115:442.
[3] Bradley, S. E., et al. 1945. J. Clin. Invest. 24:890.
[4] Caesar, J., et al. 1961. Clin. Sci. 21:43.
[5] Combes, B. 1960. J. Lab. Clin. Med. 56:537.
[6] Epstein, R. M., et al. 1961. J. Clin. Invest. 40:592.
[7] Feruglio, F. S., et al. 1964. Clin. Sci. 26:487.
[8] Feruglio, F. S., et al. 1964. Ibid. 26:493.
[9] Krook, H. 1956. Acta Med. Scand., Suppl. 318:6.
[10] Moreno, A. H., et al. 1967. J. Clin. Invest. 46:436.
[11] Mueller, R. P., et al. 1952. Circulation 6:894.
[12] Munnell, E. W., and H. C. Taylor, Jr. 1947. J. Clin. Invest. 26:952.
[13] Myers, J. D. 1947. Ibid. 24:890.
[14] Myers, J. D. 1950. Ibid. 29:1421.
[15] Schenk, W. G., Jr., et al. 1962. Ann. Surg. 156:463.
[16] Shackman, R., et al. 1953. Clin. Sci. 12:307.
[17] Shaldon, S., et al. 1961. J. Clin. Invest. 40:1346.
[18] Sherlock, S., et al. 1950. J. Lab. Clin. Med. 35:923.
[19] Tygstrup, N., and K. Winkler. 1958. Clin. Sci. 17:1.
[20] Vetter, J., et al. 1954. J. Clin. Invest. 33:1594.
[21] Winkler, K., et al. 1965. Scand. J. Clin. Lab. Invest. 17:423.

Part II. Mammals Other Than Man

Method: BSP = sulfobromophthalein; ICG = indocyanine green; PAH = p-aminohippurate. Plus/minus (±) values are standard deviations, unless otherwise indicated. Data in brackets refer to the column heading in brackets.

	Animal	Condition	Method	Hepatic Blood Flow [1] ml·min^{-1}	ml·min^{-1}·kg body wt^{-1} [ml·min^{-1}·100 g liver^{-1}]	Reference
1	Cattle, calf	Normal	Dye dilution using Evans' blue [2]	....	37.8(28.4-65.7) [3]	13
2	Dog	Unanesthetized [4]	Constant infusion of BSP [5]	....	37.5 ± 2.5 [6]	26
3					34.3 ± 13.5	14
4			Blood collected & measured	....	39.0[165]	12
5				415(266-612)	28.6(18.7-39.0) [86(58-112)]	4

[1] Unless otherwise indicated. [2] Infusion into mesenteric vein; sampling in portal vein. [3] Flow in portal vein. [4] No change with thiopental Na anesthesia or splenectomy. [5] Sampling from hepatic vein and peripheral artery or vein. [6] Standard error.

continued

227. HEPATIC BLOOD FLOW: MAMMALS

Part II. Mammals Other Than Man

	Animal	Condition	Method	Hepatic Blood Flow [1]		Reference
				$ml \cdot min^{-1}$	$ml \cdot min^{-1} \cdot kg$ body wt^{-1} [$ml \cdot min^{-1} \cdot 100$ g liver^{-1}]	
6			Constant infusion of BSP[5]	....	43.0 [130]	15
7			ICG injection	....	43 ± 2.2[6]	1
8			Local thermal dilution	....	45 ± 5.2[6]	23
9			Endogenous urea production[5]	383(241-705)	32(18-48)	20
10		Fed	Thermostromuhr	810(655-890)	(84-114)	17
11		Fasted	Thermostromuhr	487(408-522)	(52-71)	17
12		Normal	BSP & constant infusion of PAH[7]	....	44; 38[3]	18
13		Anesthetized (thiopental Na)	BSP & constant infusion of PAH[7]	....	45; 30[3]	18
14		Anesthetized (thiopental Na)	Constant infusion of BSP[5]	....	38.7 ± 11.5	27
15				....	37.0 ± 2.3[156 ± 11]	6
16				570 ± 12.2	29.5 ± 9.3	28
17				690 ± 52[6]	42 ± 2.9[6] [140 ± 8.2[6]]	29
18			Constant infusion of ICG[5]	....	36.9 ± 11	19
19			Single injection of ICG	....	37.6 ± 8.3	19
20			Constant infusion of rose bengal[5]	(318-1328)	36.4 ± 7.0[6]	8
21			Intestinal Xenon-133	....	42 ± 6.5; 22 ± 3.2[3]	25
22			Electromagnetic flowmeter	....	31.0	15
23				....	21.4 ± 8.5[3]; 11.3 ± 4.4[8]	24
24			Single injection of colloidal [^{198}Au]gold [9]	....	35.0 ± 12[6]	5
25				....	44.0 ± 7[6]	22
26			Thermostromuhr	147(52-400)[3]; 144(43-430)[8]	15.5(5-37)[3]; 7.5 (2-16)[8]	16
27		Anesthetized (thiopental Na)	Blood collected & measured	....	40.9(22-68.1); 30.1[3]	29
28	Cat	Anesthetized (pentobarbital Na)	Blood collected & measured	....	[66]	10
29			Xenon-133	....	[74]	
30	Monkey [10]	Anesthetized (thiopental Na)	....	....	25.0 ± 5.1	30
31	Mouse	Anesthetized	Single injection of colloidal [^{198}Au]gold [9]	....	63.0 [102(93-103)]	7
32			ICG injection	....	[35]	9
33	Rabbit	Normal	Thermal dilution	100 ± 5.7[3,6]	37.0[3]	32
34	Rat	Normal	Single injection of colloidal ^{131}I-albumin [9]	....	66.2 ± 0.19[6]	21
35		Normal	Thermoelectric	....	[79(75-92)]	3
36		Anesthetized	Thermoelectric	....	[42]	3
37	Sheep	Normal	....	500	....	2
38		6 hr after eating	....	1400	....	2
39		Normal; fed	BSP & constant infusion of PAH[7]	(1830-3530)	55; 43[3]	18
40		fasted	BSP & constant infusion of PAH[7]	....	42; 31[3]	18
41		Pregnant; fed	BSP & constant infusion of PAH[7]	(2430-5520)	65; 53[3]	18
42		fasted	BSP & constant infusion of PAH[7]	....	44; 34[3]	18
43		Anesthetized	Thermal dilution	....	55; 43[3]	11

[1] Unless otherwise indicated. [3] Flow in portal vein. [5] Sampling from hepatic vein and peripheral artery or vein. [6] Standard error. [7] Infusion into mesenteric vein; sampling in portal and hepatic veins. [8] Flow in hepatic artery. [9] Determination by external counting of head. [10] *Macaca mulatta.*

continued

227. HEPATIC BLOOD FLOW: MAMMALS

Part II. Mammals Other Than Man

Contributor: Iber, Frank L.

References

[1] Banaszak, E. F., et al. 1960. Amer. J. Physiol. 198: 877.

[2] Bensadoun, A., and J. T. Reid. 1962. J. Dairy Sci. 45:540.

[3] Birnie, J. H., and J. Grayson. 1952. J. Physiol. (London) 116:189.

[4] Blalock, A., and M. F. Mason. 1936. Amer. J. Physiol. 117:328.

[5] Burkle, J. S., and J. L. Gliedman. 1959. Gastroenterology 36:112.

[6] Casselman, W. G. B., and A. M. Rappaport. 1954. J. Physiol. (London) 124:173.

[7] Cheever, A. W., and K. S. Warren. 1964. Trans. Roy. Soc. Trop. Med. Hyg. 58:406.

[8] Combes, B. 1960. J. Lab. Clin. Med. 56:537.

[9] Dannielson, G. B., et al. 1971. Acta Chir. Scand. 137:621.

[10] Darle, N. 1970. Ibid., Suppl. 407:1.

[11] Fegler, G., and K. J. Hill. 1958. Quart. J. Exp. Physiol. Cog. Med. Sci. 43:189.

[12] Frank, E. D., et al. 1962. Amer. J. Physiol. 202:7.

[13] Fries, G. F., and G. H. Conner. 1961. Amer. J. Vet. Res. 22:487.

[14] Gilmore, J. P. 1958. Amer. J. Physiol. 195:465, 469.

[15] Greenway, C. V., and R. D. Stark. 1971. Physiol. Rev. 51:23.

[16] Grodins, F. S., et al. 1941. Amer. J. Physiol. 132:375.

[17] Herrick, J. F., et al. 1934. Ibid. 109:52.

[18] Katz, M. L., and E. N. Bergman. 1969. Ibid. 216: 946.

[19] Ketterer, S. G., et al. 1960. Ibid. 199:481.

[20] Lipscomb, A., and L. A. Crandall, Jr. 1947. Ibid. 148:302.

[21] Rabinovici, N., and E. Wiener. 1963. J. Surg. Res. 3:3.

[22] Restrepo, J. E., et al. 1960. Surgery 48:748.

[23] Roberts, R. J., and G. L. Plaa. 1967. J. Appl. Physiol. 23:779.

[24] Shaffey, O. A., and M. A. Hassab. 1968. Surgery 63:962.

[25] Shizgal, H. M., and M. S. Goldstein. 1972. Ibid. 72: 83.

[26] Shoemaker, W. C. 1960. J. Appl. Physiol. 15:473.

[27] Smythe, C. M. 1959. Circ. Res. 7:268.

[28] Smythe, C. M., et al. 1953. Amer. J. Physiol. 172: 737.

[29] Teramoto, S., and H. B. Shumacher, Jr. 1962. J. Surg. Res. 2:3.

[30] Waldhausen, J. A., et al. 1964. Surg. Forum 15:7.

[31] Werner, A. Y., and S. M. Horvath. 1952. J. Clin. Invest. 31:433.

[32] White, S. W., et al. 1967. Aust. J. Exp. Biol. Med. Sci. 45:453.

228. SKIN BLOOD FLOW: MAN

Venous occlusion plethysmographic measurements of the finger, hand, toe, and foot are for total blood flow (no effort being made to separate flow through superficial and deeper tissues). All other data are for measurements of blood flow through superficial tissues only. Data in brackets refer to the column heading in brackets. Values in parentheses are ranges, estimate "c" (*see* Introduction).

	Area of Skin	Condition of Blood Vessels	Ambient Temp [Skin Temp] °C	Method of Measurement	Blood Flow	Reference
1	Total	Normal	[22-29]	Helium uptake[1]	$(3-4)$[2] $ml \cdot 100\ g^{-1} \cdot min^{-1}$; 0.01 $ml \cdot cm^{-2} \cdot min^{-1}$	11
2			23-28	Local heat loss; calorimetry	0.015 $ml \cdot cm^{-2} \cdot min^{-1}$	23
3			25	Local heat loss; calorimetry	$(0.008-0.078)\ ml \cdot cm^{-2} \cdot min^{-1}$	38
4			25-27	Photoplethysmography	$(0.016-0.028)\ ml \cdot cm^{-2} \cdot min^{-1}$	24
5		Dilated	[35-36]	Helium uptake[1]	0.027 $ml \cdot cm^{-2} \cdot min^{-1}$	11
6		Constricted	27	Local heat loss; calorimetry	$0.073(0.037-0.157)\ ml \cdot cm^{-2} \cdot min^{-1}$	38
7	Finger	Normal	....	Photoplethysmography	$(0.071-0.356)\ ml \cdot cm^{-2} \cdot min^{-1}$	25
8					$(0.072-0.27)\ ml \cdot cm^{-2} \cdot min^{-1}$	24
9				Rheoplethysmography	51.8 $ml \cdot 100\ g^{-1} \cdot min^{-1}$	13
10			[15-25]	Venous occlusion with extra isolation cuffs at finger base	$(1.3-3.8)\ ml \cdot 100\ g^{-1} \cdot min^{-1}$	15

[1] Limited to cutaneous tissues. [2] Calculated from values in reference.

continued

	Area of Skin	Condition of Blood Vessels	Ambient Temp [Skin Temp] °C	Method of Measurement	Blood Flow	Reference
11			22-24	Rheoplethysmography	49.2 ± 22.3 ml·100 g^{-1}·min^{-1}	14
12			25	Venous occlusion with cuff at wrist	22.5[2]/(18-48) ml·100 g^{-1}·min^{-1}	40
13			28	Venous occlusion with cuff close to segment	47.7 ± 6.2 ml·100 g^{-1}·min^{-1}	35
14		Dilated	[0]	Venous occlusion with cuff close to segment[3]/	87[2]/(32-175) ml·100 g^{-1}·min^{-1}	17
15			22-23 [45]	Venous occlusion with cuff close to segment[4]/	84 ml·100 g^{-1}·min^{-1}	39
16			25-27	Photoplethysmography[5]/	0.60 ml·cm^{-2}·min^{-1}	24
17			30 ± 0.5	Venous occlusion with cuff close to segment[5]/	27[2]/(12.4-45.1) ml·100 g^{-1}·min^{-1}	19
18			30	Venous occlusion with extra isolation cuffs at finger base	11.2 ml·100 g^{-1}·min^{-1}	15
19		Constricted	[0]	Venous occlusion with cuff close to segment	(2.3-14) ml·100 g^{-1}·min^{-1}	17
20			[16-20]	Venous occlusion with cuff close to segment[6]/	2.3[2]/(0.2-4.5) ml·100 g^{-1}·min^{-1}	39
21	Hand	Normal	22 [32-33]	Venous occlusion with cuff close to segment	13.1 ± 5 ml·100 g^{-1}·min^{-1}	10
22			22-23 [32-33]	Venous occlusion with cuff close to segment	3.6 ± 1.8 ml·100 g^{-1}·min^{-1}	21
23			24 [35-40]	Total heat exchange	3.57 ml·100 g^{-1}·min^{-1}; 0.05 ml·cm^{-2}·min^{-1}	30
24			25 [20]	Venous occlusion with cuff close to segment	10.9 ± 7.6 ml·100 g^{-1}·min^{-1}	32
25			25 [32]	Venous occlusion with cuff close to segment	9.3 ± 2.1 ml·100 g^{-1}·min^{-1}	1
26			25-27	Photoplethysmography	(0.027-0.14) ml·cm^{-2}·min^{-1}	24
27			26 [37]	Venous occlusion with cuff close to segment	10 ml·100 g^{-1}·min^{-1}	33
28			32	Venous occlusion with cuff close to segment	5.87 ± 2.7 ml·100 g^{-1}·min^{-1}	2
29			34	Venous occlusion with cuff close to segment	6.6 ± 2.5 ml·100 g^{-1}·min^{-1}	4
30					6.6 ml·100 g^{-1}·min^{-1}	4
31					7.5 ± 2.3 ml·100 g^{-1}·min^{-1}	3
32					8.3 ± 3.1 ml·100 g^{-1}·min^{-1}	7
33					9.2 ml·100 g^{-1}·min^{-1}	6
34					10.7 ml·100 g^{-1}·min^{-1}	5
35		Dilated	24 [40-43]	Total heat exchange	0.24 ml·cm^{-2}·min^{-1}	30
36			25 [40]	Venous occlusion with cuff close to segment	25.3 ± 7.5 ml·100 g^{-1}·min^{-1}	32
37			30 [43]	Venous occlusion with cuff close to segment	39.5[2]/(29-54) ml·100 g^{-1}·min^{-1}	33
38			34	Venous occlusion with cuff close to segment[5]/	15.8 ± 4.2 ml·100 g^{-1}·min^{-1}	4
39				Venous occlusion with cuff close to segment[4]/	16.8 ± 4.7 ml·100 g^{-1}·min^{-1}	3
40					20.3 ml·100 g^{-1}·min^{-1}	6
41			41	Venous occlusion with cuff close to segment	20.5 ± 6.1 ml·100 g^{-1}·min^{-1}	7
42		Constricted	6	Venous occlusion with cuff close to segment[7]/	2.0 ± 1.2 ml·100 g^{-1}·min^{-1}	7
43			[10]	Venous occlusion with cuff close to segment	2.9 ± 0.9 ml·100 g^{-1}·min^{-1}	32
44			23	Venous occlusion with cuff close to segment	1.4 ± 0.6 ml·100 g^{-1}·min^{-1}	7
45	Forearm	Normal	18	Venous occlusion with counter pressure on segment	22.6 ± 5.9 ml·100 g^{-1}·min^{-1}; 0.32 ± 0.08[2]/ ml·cm^{-2}·min^{-1}	28
46			19-22	Xenon clearance from intracutaneous injection sites[1]/	5.1 ± 1.7 ml·100 g^{-1}·min^{-1}; 0.009 ± 0.0003[2]/ ml·cm^{-2}·min^{-1}	37
47			22	Venous occlusion with counter pressure on segment	28.5 ml·100 g^{-1}·min^{-1}; 0.4[2]/ ml·cm^{-2}·min^{-1}	26
48			22-24	^{85}Kr clearance after intra-arterial injections	3.1 ± 2.6 ml·100 g^{-1}·min^{-1}; 0.05[2]/ ml·cm^{-2}·min^{-1}	29
49			23-24 [33]	Venous occlusion before & after epinephrine iontophoresis	8.6 ± 6.8 ml·100 g^{-1}·min^{-1}; 0.12[2]/ ml·cm^{-2}·min^{-1}	31

[1]/ Limited to cutaneous tissues. [2]/ Calculated from values in reference. [3]/ Hunting reaction (cold-induced vasodilation) was used to induce vasomotor change. [4]/ Legs and other portions of body were heated to induce vasodilation. [5]/ Histamine was used to induce vasodilation. [6]/ Cold pressor was used to induce vasoconstriction. [7]/ Cold vasodilation contributed to the result.

continued

Area of Skin	Condition of Blood Vessels	Ambient Temp [Skin Temp] °C	Method of Measurement	Blood Flow	Reference
50		24[37-40]	Total heat exchange	3.5[2/] ml·100 g⁻¹·min⁻¹; 0.05 ml·cm⁻²·min⁻¹	30
51		25-27	Photoplethysmography	(0.85-2.4)[2/] ml·100 g⁻¹·min⁻¹; (0.012-0.034) ml·cm⁻²·min⁻¹	24
52		[31.5-34.5]	Photoplethysmography	1.48[2/] ml·100 g⁻¹·min⁻¹; 0.021 (0.016-0.030) ml·cm⁻²·min⁻¹	25
53		[32-34]	O₂ utilization	36 ml·100 g⁻¹·min⁻¹; 0.5[2/] ml·cm⁻²·min⁻¹	18
54	Dilated	....	Venous occlusion with counter pressure on segment[8/]	62 ml·100 g⁻¹·min⁻¹; 0.88[2/] ml·cm⁻²·min⁻¹	28
55				73.3 ml·100 g⁻¹·min⁻¹; 1.03[2/] ml·cm⁻²·min⁻¹	26
56		22-24	131I-antipyrine clearance from intracutaneous sites	20.8 ± 5.1 ml·100 g⁻¹·min⁻¹ [2/]; 0.29[2/] ml·cm⁻²·min⁻¹	29
57		24[40-43]	Total heat exchange	10.6[2/] ml·100 g⁻¹·min⁻¹; 0.15 ml·cm⁻²·min⁻¹	30
58		25-27	Photoplethysmography[5/]	42.4[2/] ml·100 g⁻¹·min⁻¹; 0.60 ml·cm⁻²·min⁻¹	24
59	Constricted	[2-15]	Photoplethysmography[9/]	10.6[2/] ml·100 g⁻¹·min⁻¹; 0.015 (0.007-0.024) ml·cm⁻²·min⁻¹	25
60	Varied	19-27[30-34.5]	Venous occlusion before & after epinephrine iontophoresis	12.2(0-70.5) ml·100 g⁻¹·min⁻¹; 0.154 ± 0.121 ml·cm⁻²·min⁻¹	16
61	Toe — Normal	....	Venous occlusion with cuff at ankle	(6-20.5) ml·100 g⁻¹·min⁻¹	40
62		20.5 ± 2[29]	Venous occlusion with cuff close to segment	10 ml·100 g⁻¹·min⁻¹	20
63		25-27	Photoplethysmography	(0.050-0.095) ml·cm⁻²·min⁻¹	24
64	Dilated	....	Venous occlusion with cuff at ankle	(22.5-42) ml·100 g⁻¹·min⁻¹	40
65		20.5 ± 2[32]	Venous occlusion with cuff close to segment	>30 ml·100 g⁻¹·min⁻¹ [10/]	20
66		25-27	Photoplethysmography[5/]	0.46 ml·cm⁻²·min⁻¹	24
67	Constricted	20.5 ± 2[24]	Venous occlusion with cuff close to segment	3 ml·100 g⁻¹·min⁻¹ [10/]	20
68	Varied	....	Venous occlusion with cuff at ankle	(1-90) ml·100 g⁻¹·min⁻¹	22
69	Foot — Normal	....	Venous occlusion with cuff close to segment	3.35 ml·100 g⁻¹·min⁻¹	34
70		22[33]	Venous occlusion with cuff close to segment	3.5 ± 1.4 ml·100 g⁻¹·min⁻¹	9
71		25-27	Photoplethysmography	(0.0246-0.0336) ml·cm⁻²·min⁻¹	24
72		26[37]	Venous occlusion with cuff close to segment	5 ml·100 g⁻¹·min⁻¹	33
73	Dilated	....	Venous occlusion with cuff close to segment	16.3[2/](15-18) ml·100 g⁻¹·min⁻¹; (2.6-2.8) ml·cm⁻²·min⁻¹	33
74		22[43]	Xenon clearance from intracutaneous injection sites[5/]	16.0 ± 6 ml·100 g⁻¹·min⁻¹	12
75	Calf — Normal	19-22	Xenon clearance from intracutaneous injection sites[L/]	6.1 ± 1.5 ml·100 g⁻¹·min⁻¹	37
76			Xenon clearance from epicutaneous sites[L/]	5.7 ± 1.2 ml·100 g⁻¹·min⁻¹	37
77		[27-29.5]	85Kr clearance after intra-arterial injections	0.34 ± 0.14 ml·cm⁻²·min⁻¹	36
78		20	Venous occlusion with counter pressure on segment	10.4 ± 5.7 ml·100 g⁻¹·min⁻¹	27
79		25-27	Photoplethysmography	(0.013-0.022) ml·cm⁻²·min⁻¹	24
80		26-27	131I clearance from intracutaneous injection sites	4.9 ± 1.3 ml·100 g⁻¹·min⁻¹	8
81	Dilated	19-22	Xenon clearance from intracutaneous injection sites[5/]	10.7 ± 2.6 ml·100 g⁻¹·min⁻¹	37
82		[30.5-33.5]	85Kr clearance after intra-arterial injections	1.1 ± 0.4 ml·100 g⁻¹·min⁻¹	36

[L/] Limited to cutaneous tissues. [2/] Calculated from values in reference. [5/] Histamine was used to induce vasodilation. [8/] Reflex heat was used to induce vasodilation. [9/] Cold air was applied locally to induce vasoconstriction. [10/] For 12 subjects.

continued

	Area of Skin	Condition of Blood Vessels	Ambient Temp [Skin Temp] °C	Method of Measurement	Blood Flow	Reference
83			22	Xenon clearance from intracutaneous injection sites [5]	6.2 ± 2.0 [11] ml·100 g^{-1}·min^{-1}	12
84					10.5 ± 2.1 [12] ml·100 g^{-1}·min^{-1}	12
85			25-27	Photoplethysmography [5]	0.15 ml·cm^{-2}·min^{-1}	24
86			35	Venous occlusion with counter pressure on segment	29.5 ± 7.1 ml·100 g^{-1}·min^{-1}	27
87	Thigh	Dilated	22	Xenon clearance from intracutaneous injection sites	7.5 ± 2.1 ml·100 g^{-1}·min^{-1}	12
88	Ab-do-men	Normal	19-22	Xenon clearance from intracutaneous injection sites [1]	(3.6-4.7) ml·100 g^{-1}·min^{-1}	37
89				Xenon clearance from epicutaneous sites [1]	(4.0-4.9) ml·100 g^{-1}·min^{-1}	37
90	Trunk	Normal	....	Photoplethysmography	(0.0122-0.0224) ml·cm^{-2}·min^{-1}	24
91	Cheek	Normal	....	Photoplethysmography	(0.09-0.2) ml·cm^{-2}·min^{-1}	24
92				Xenon clearance from epicutaneous sites [1]	9.0 ml·100 g^{-1}·min^{-1}	37
93			19-22	Xenon clearance from epicutaneous sites [1]	(12-18) ml·100 g^{-1}·min^{-1} [13]	37
94		Dilated	25-27	Photoplethysmography [5]	0.44 ml·cm^{-2}·min^{-1}	24
95	Fore-head	Normal	....	Photoplethysmography	(0.072-0.11) ml·cm^{-2}·min^{-1}	24
96			[31.5-35.5]	Photoplethysmography	(0.047-0.135) ml·cm^{-2}·min^{-1}	25
97		Dilated	25-27	Photoplethysmography	0.41 ml·cm^{-2}·min^{-1}	24
98		Con-stricted	[0-12.4]	Photoplethysmography	(0.030-0.088) ml·cm^{-2}·min^{-1}	25

[1] Limited to cutaneous tissues. [5] Histamine was used to induce vasodilation. [11] Subjects >30 yr old. [12] Subjects <30 yr old. [13] In area of hair growth.

Contributor: Abramson, D. I.

References

[1] Abramson, D. I., and S. M. Fierst. 1942. Amer. Heart J. 23:84.

[2] Abramson, D. I., et al. 1941. Ibid. 22:329.

[3] Abramson, D. I., et al. 1961. Amer. J. Phys. Med. 40:5.

[4] Abramson, D. I., et al. 1963. J. Appl. Physiol. 18:305.

[5] Abramson, D. I., et al. 1965. Arch. Phys. Med. Rehabil. 46:412.

[6] Abramson, D. I., et al. 1967. Vasc. Dis. 4:205.

[7] Abramson, D. I., et al. 1971. Arch. Phys. Med. Rehabil. 52:97.

[8] Albert, J. S., and J. D. Coffman. 1969. Amer. J. Physiol. 216(1):156.

[9] Allwood, M. J. 1958. Clin. Sci. 17(2):331.

[10] Beaconsfield, P., and J. Ginsburg. 1955. J. Physiol. (London) 130:467.

[11] Behnke, A. R., and T. L. Willmon. 1941. Amer. J. Physiol. 131(3):627.

[12] Bohr, H. 1966. Scand. J. Clin. Lab. Invest., Suppl. 99:60.

[13] Burch, G. 1955. Clin. Sci. 14:361.

[14] Caliva, F. S., et al. 1963. Circulation 28:415, 421.

[15] Catchpole, B. N., and R. P. Jepson. 1955. Clin. Sci. 14:109.

[16] Cooper, K. E., et al. 1955. J. Physiol. (London) 128(2):258.

[17] Edwards, M., and A. C. Burton. 1960. J. Appl. Physiol. 15:201.

[18] Evans, N. T. S., and P. F. D. Naylor. 1966. Resp. Physiol. 2:61.

[19] Farber, E. M., et al. 1959. Arch. Dermatol. Syphilol. 79:130.

[20] Felder, D., et al. 1954. Clin. Sci. 13:221.

[21] Gaskell, P. 1955. J. Physiol. (London) 131(3):639.

[22] Goetz, R. 1946. Amer. Heart J. 31:146.

[23] Hardy, J. D., and G. F. Soderstrom. 1938. J. Nutr. 16:493.

[24] Hertzman, A. B., and W. C. Randall. 1948. J. Appl. Physiol. 1:234.

[25] Hertzman, A. B., et al. 1947. Amer. J. Physiol. 150(1):122.

[26] Hyman, C., and T. P. Greeson. 1966. J. Invest. Dermatol. 47(4):363.

[27] Hyman, C., and W. H. Wong. 1968. Circ. Res. 22:251.

[28] Hyman, C., et al. 1964. Amer. Heart J. 68:508.

[29] Jacobsson, S. 1967. Scand. J. Plast. Reconstr. Surg., Suppl. 3.

[30] Kamon, E., and H. S. Belding. 1969. J. Appl. Physiol. 26(3):317.

[31] Kontos, H., et al. 1966. Amer. J. Physiol. 211:869.

[32] Krog, J., et al. 1969. J. Appl. Physiol. 15:654.

[33] Kunkel, P., et al. 1938. J. Clin. Invest. 17:715.

[34] McPherson, A., and A. W. L. Kessel. 1955. Clin. Sci. 14:361.

[35] Ring, G. C., et al. 1959. J. Gerontol. 14(2):189.

[36] Sejrsen, P. 1967. Circ. Res. 21(3):281.

[37] Sejrsen, P. 1969. Ibid. 25:215.

[38] Stewart, H. J., and W. F. Evans. 1943. Amer. Heart J. 26:67.

[39] Wilkins, R. W., et al. 1938. Clin. Sci. 3:403.

[40] Winsor, T. 1959. Peripheral Vascular Diseases. C. C. Thomas, Springfield, Ill.

229. LIMB BLOOD FLOW: MAN

Values in parentheses are ranges, estimate "b" unless otherwise indicated (*see* Introduction).

	Extremity	Temperature, °C Bath	Ambient	Plethysmography Method	Blood Flow ml·min⁻¹·100 ml segment⁻¹	Reference
1	Forearm	2	18-21	Strain gauge	4.6(2.3-6.9)	12
2		10	18-21	Strain gauge	2.4(0.2-4.5)	12
3		14	18-21	Strain gauge	1.1(0.2-2.1)	12
4		17	22-25	Water	0.7(0.4-1.0)	5
5		18	18-21	Strain gauge	0.9(0.2-1.5)	12
6		26	18-21	Strain gauge	1.5(0.4-2.5)	12
7		28-30	22-25	Water	1.6(0.6-2.7)	6
8		32	22-27	Water	1.9(0.4-3.3)	2,3,5
9		34	18-21	Strain gauge	3.7(1.0-6.4)	12
10		35	15-20	Water	4.2(1.5-7.0)[a]	7
11		42-45	15-25	Strain gauge, water	13.2(0.8-25.5)	5,7,12
12	Hand	5	20	Water	2.9(1.3-4.5)	9
13		5	24	Water	4.3(3.1-8.0)[c]	22
14		10	20	Water	1.0(−0.1 to +2.1)	9
15		15	24	Water	0.9(0.3-1.5)[c]	22
16		20	24	Water	1.3(1.0-1.7)[c]	22
17		25	24	Water	2.7(1.4-4.4)[c]	22
18		30	20	Water	3.8(−0.8 to +8.4)	9
19		32	20	Water	4.5(−1.5 to +10.5)	9
20		32	25-27	Water	8.7(2.9-14.4)	2,16,22
21		35	20	Water	6.1(−2.3 to +14.5)	9
22		38	20	Water	9.2(0.4-18.0)	9
23		40	25	Water	7.5(2.7-12.3)	16
24		42.5	20	Water	16.7(7.3-26.1)	9
25		44-45	42-43	Water	56.0(41.0-68.0)[c]	19
26		45	20	Water	19.7(7.9-31.5)	9
27	Fingers	....	22-23	Impedance	7.5(0.3-14.8)	8
28			22-24	Air	13.7(1.3-26.1)	11
29		27	Cold	Water	1.3(0.7-2.3)[c]	13
30			Warm	Water	4.0(2.3-6.1)[c]	13
31		44	.....	Water	(80-90)[d]	10
32	Constricted phase	9-17	Cold	Water	1.5(1.3-1.7)[c]	13
33			Warm	Water	3.7(2.9-4.5)[c]	13
34	Dilated phase	9-17	Cold	Water	15.1(8.0-20.2)[c]	13
35			Warm	Water	47.3(26.0-77.7)[c]	13
36	Leg	10-14	.....	Water	1.2(0.3-2.1)	4
37		32	.....	Water	1.4(0.4-2.4)	4
38		35	.....	Water	4.1(2.1-6.3)[c]	21
39		45	.....	Water	3.6	1
40	Calf	....	26	Air	2.8(1.2-4.4)	23
41		20	35	Water	3.0(0.4-5.6)	15
42		32	25	Water	1.4(0.4-2.4)	2
43			30	Water	3.6(1.0-6.2)	17
44		Diathermy	26	Air	6.4(0.6-12.2)	23
45	Foot	....	26	Air	1.6(0.2-3.0)	23
46		18-23	22-25	Water	0.4(−0.2 to +0.9)	14
47		30-34	22-25	Water	3.1(−0.8 to +6.9)	14
48		32	21	Water	2.0(−0.5 to +4.6)	18
49			24-27	Water	3.9(0.3-7.5)	20
50		38	24-27	Water	8.6(1.1-16.1)	20
51		45	24-27	Water	16.0(4.5-27.5)	20

continued

Contributor: Conrad, Margaret C.

References

[1] Abramson, D. I. Unpublished. Univ. Illinois, College Medicine, Chicago, 1969.

[2] Abramson, D. I., and S. M. Fierst. 1942. Amer. Heart J. 23:84.

[3] Abramson, D. I., et al. 1939. Ibid. 17:206.

[4] Abramson, D. I., et al. 1941. Ibid. 22:329.

[5] Abramson, D. I., et al. 1958. J. Clin. Invest. 37:1031.

[6] Abramson, D. I., et al. 1959. Ibid. 38:1126.

[7] Barcroft, H., and O. G. Edholm. 1943. J. Physiol. (London) 102:5.

[8] Bashour, F. A., and R. E. Jones. 1965. Dis. Chest 47:465.

[9] Brown, G. M., and J. Page. 1952. J. Appl. Physiol. 5:221.

[10] Burton, A. C. 1939. Amer. J. Physiol. 127:437.

[11] Caliva, F. S., et al. 1963. Circulation 28:415.

[12] Clarke, R. S. J., et al. 1958. Clin. Sci. 17:165.

[13] Edwards, M., and A. C. Burton. 1960. J. Appl. Physiol. 15:201.

[14] Gaskell, P., and G. M. Bray. 1967. Can. J. Physiol. Pharmacol. 45:63.

[15] Halliday, J. A. 1960. Amer. Heart J. 60:110.

[16] Hillestad, L. K. 1962. Angiology 13:161.

[17] Hillestad, L. K. 1963. Acta Med. Scand. 174:23.

[18] Hoobler, S. W., et al. 1949. J. Clin. Invest. 28:638.

[19] Roddie, I. C., and J. T. Shepherd. 1956. J. Physiol. (London) 131:657.

[20] Scheinberg, P., et al. 1948. Amer. Heart J. 35:409.

[21] Shepherd, R. C., and R. Warren. 1960. Clin. Sci. 20:99.

[22] Spealman, C. R. 1945. Amer. J. Physiol. 145:218.

[23] Wessman, H. C., and F. J. Kottke. 1967. Arch. Phys. Med. Rehabil. 48:567.

230. DIGITAL BLOOD FLOW AND ARTERIAL BLOOD PRESSURE: MAN

Values in parentheses are ranges, estimate "b" (*see* Introduction).

	Measurement	Extremity	Method	Condition	Value	Reference
1	Blood flow ml·min^{-1}· cm^{-2} skin	3rd or 4th finger, terminal phalangeal skin	Calorimetric	Subjects recumbent; room temp, 26-29°C	0.20(0.08-0.32)	6
2				Vasodilation (0.5 hr or more indirect heating)	0.28(0.22-0.34)	1,3,4,11
3				Plus autonomic ganglion blockade	0.29(0.21-0.37)	6
4				Administered via intravenous drip (5% glucose in water)	0.26(0.16-0.36)	5,7
5				Plus norepinephrine infusion, 0.026 (0.01-0.042) mg/min	0.24(0.12-0.36)	5,7
6				Subjects pregnant, 3rd trimester; recumbent; room temp, 26-29°C	0.29(0.15-0.43)	8
7				Subjects pregnant, 3rd trimester; vasodilation (0.5 hr or more indirect heating), plus autonomic ganglion blockade	0.33(0.19-0.47)	8
8				Infant recumbent; room temp, 26-29°C; vasodilation (indirect heating); 1-2 da old	0.09 ± 0.03	13
9				Infant recumbent; room temp, 26-29°C; vasodilation (indirect heating); 4-5 da old	0.13 ± 0.04	13
10		Great toe, terminal phalangeal skin	Calorimetric	Vasodilation (1 hr or more indirect heating), plus autonomic ganglion blockade	0.21(0.15-0.29)	4
11				Spinal anesthesia	0.13(0.05-0.21)	4
12	μl·5 ml digit^{-1}·s^{-1}	Finger	Digital plethysmography	Subjects fasting, reclining at 30° angle; room temp, 22-24°C	41(3.8-78.2)	2
13					16.3(7.5-25.1)	9
14				Plus hexamethonium	17.7(8.3-27.1)	9

continued

	Measurement	Extremity	Method	Condition	Value	Reference
15				Subjects resting	19(15-40)	12
16				Plus vasodilation (2 oz of whiskey & indirect heating)	56(40-80)	12
17		2nd toe	Digital plethysmography	Subjects resting	10(5-16)	12
18				Plus vasodilation (2 oz of whiskey & indirect heating)	25(19-35)	12
19	Arterial pressure, mm Hg Systolic	3rd or 4th finger, middle phalanx	Gaertner capsule ("flushing" technique)	Subjects recumbent; room temp, 26-29°C	104(70-138)	6,10
20				Vasodilation (0.5 hr or more indirect heating)	101(81-121)	4
21				Plus autonomic ganglion blockade	87(67-107)	6
22				Administered via intravenous drip (5% glucose in water)	91(62-120)	5,7
23				Plus norepinephrine infusion, 0.026 (0.01-0.042) mg/min	134(100-168)	5,7
24				Subjects pregnant, 3rd trimester; recumbent; room temp, 26-29°C	106(83-129)	8
25				Subjects pregnant, 3rd trimester; vasodilation (0.5 hr or more indirect heating), plus autonomic ganglion blockade	91(64-118)	8
26		Great toe	Gaertner capsule ("flushing" technique)	Vasodilation (1 hr or more indirect heating), plus autonomic ganglion blockade	87(57-117)	4
27	Diastolic	3rd or 4th finger, middle phalanx	Determined from point of cessation of throbbing	Subjects recumbent; room temp, 26-29°C	65(39-91)	6,10
28				Vasodilation (0.5 hr or more indirect heating)	58(35-81)	4
29				Plus autonomic ganglion blockade	52(32-72)	6
30				Administered via intravenous drip (5% glucose in water)	58(40-76)	5,7
31				Plus norepinephrine infusion, 0.026 (0.01-0.042) mg/min	83(57-109)	5,7
32				Subjects pregnant, 3rd trimester; recumbent; room temp, 26-29°C	68(48-88)	8
33				Subjects pregnant, 3rd trimester; vasodilation (0.5 hr or more indirect heating), plus autonomic ganglion blockade	58(32-84)	8
34	Mean (1/3 pulse pressure plus digital diastolic pressure)	Finger	Systolic & diastolic pressure determined by pulse wave analysis	Subjects fasting, reclining at 30° angle; room temp, 22-24°C	86(70-102)	2
35					85(76-94)	9
36				Plus hexamethonium	80(73-87)	9

Contributors: Mendlowitz, Milton, and Naftchi, N. Eric

References

[1] Arnott, W. M., and J. M. MacFie. 1948. J. Physiol. (London) 107:233.

[2] Caliva, F. S., et al. 1963. Circulation 28:415.

[3] Capriglione, L. A., and F. L. V. Duque. 1948. Arq. Clin. (Rio de Janiero) 7:3.

[4] Mendlowitz, M. 1954. The Digital Circulation. Grune and Stratton, New York.

[5] Mendlowitz, M., and N. Naftchi. 1958. J. Appl. Physiol. 13:247.

[6] Mendlowitz, M., et al. 1957. Ibid. 10:436.

[7] Mendlowitz, M., et al. 1958. Ibid. 13:252.

[8] Mendlowitz, M., et al. 1958. Amer. J. Obstet. Gynecol. 76:473.

[9] Miyahara, M. 1966. Jap. Circ. J. 30:157.

[10] Weaver, J. C., and D. F. Bohr. 1950. Amer. Heart J. 39:413.

[11] Wilson, G. M. 1952. Quart. J. Med. 21:201.

[12] Winsor, T. 1959. Peripheral Vascular Diseases; an Objective Approach. C. C. Thomas, Springfield, Ill.

[13] Yang, D. C. Y., et al. 1955. Proc. Soc. Exp. Biol. Med. 88:626.

231. ARTERIAL BLOOD PRESSURE: MAN

Part I. At Various Ages

GRAPHIC

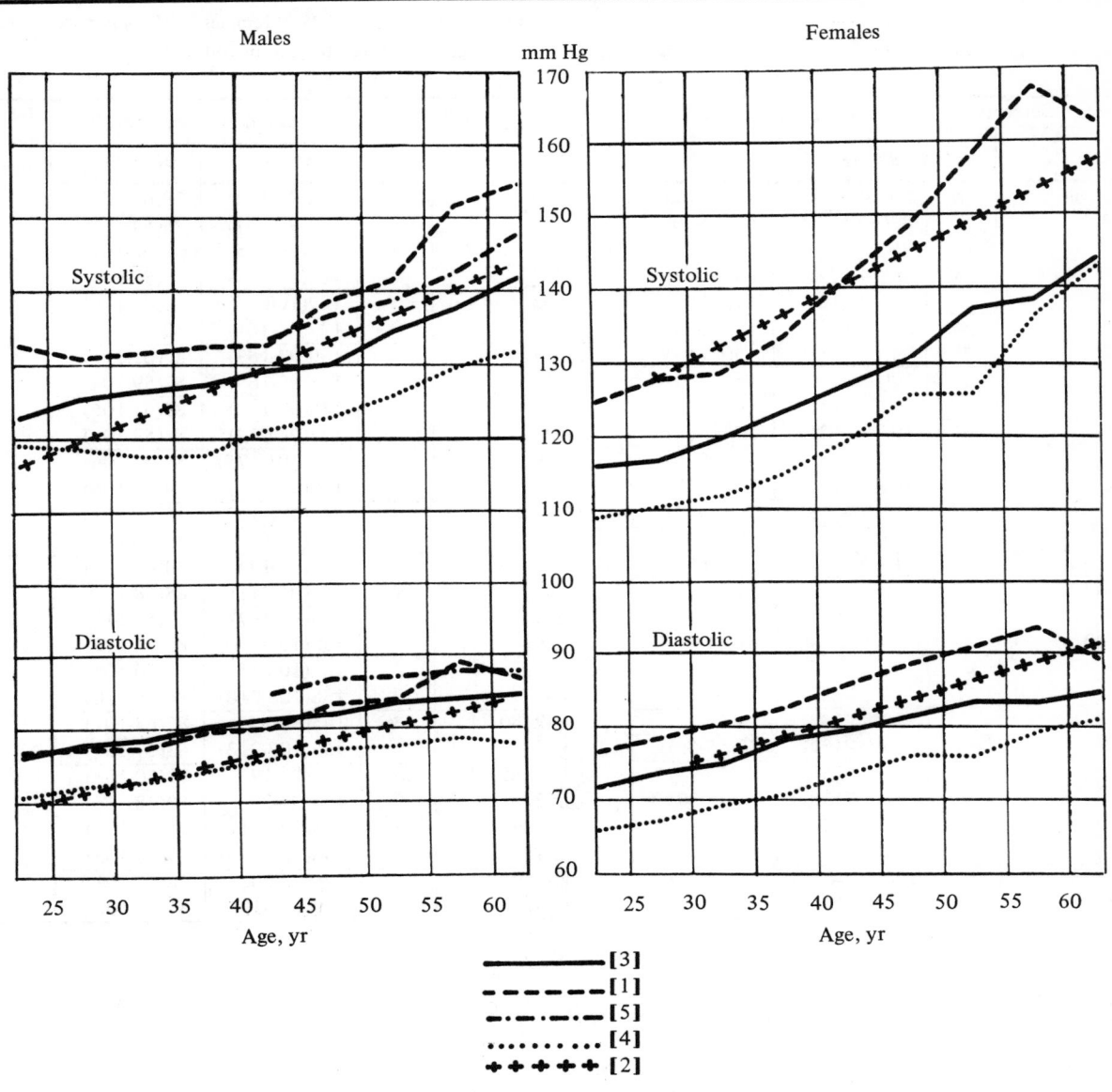

Contributors: Hartroft, W. Stanley; Dustan, Harriet P.

Specific References

[1] Gover, M. 1948. Pub. Health Rep. 63:1083.

[2] Hamilton, M., et al. 1954. Clin. Sci. 13:273.

[3] Master, A. M., et al. 1950. J. Amer. Med. Ass. 143: 1464.

[4] Robinson, S. C., and M. Brucer. 1939. Arch. Intern. Med. 64:409.

[5] Russek, H. I., and B. L. Zorman. 1946. Geriatrics 1:113.

General References

[6] Master, A. M., et al. 1952. Normal Blood Pressure and Hypertension. Lea and Febiger, Philadelphia. p. 104.

[7] Pickering, G. 1968. High Blood Pressure. Ed. 2. Grune and Stratton, New York. ch. 12.

continued

231. ARTERIAL BLOOD PRESSURE: MAN

Part I. At Various Ages

TABULAR

Number of subjects: line 1, 24 infants; lines 7-18, 3580 children; lines 19-42, 7222 males and 7984 females; lines 43-56, 2998 males and 2759 females. Values in parentheses are ranges, estimate "b" (*see* Introduction).

	Subjects		Blood Pressure, mm Hg		Reference		Subjects		Blood Pressure, mm Hg		Reference
	Age yr	Sex	Systolic	Diastolic			Age yr	Sex	Systolic	Diastolic	
1	Newborn	♂♀	80(64-96)	46(30-62)	5	29	30-34	♂	126(99-153)	79(60-98)	
2	0.5-1	♂♀	89(60-118)	60(50-70)[1]	1	30		♀	120(92-147)	75(54-96)	
3	1	♂♀	96(66-126)	66(41-91)[1]		31	35-39	♂	127(99-155)	80(60-101)	
4	2	♂♀	99(74-124)	64(39-89)[1]		32		♀	124(97-151)	78(58-98)	
5	3	♂♀	100(75-125)	67(44-90)[1]		33	40-44	♂	129(100-159)	81(63-100)	
6	4	♂♀	99(79-119)	65(45-85)[1]		34		♀	127(94-161)	80(59-100)	
7	5	♂♀	94(80-108)	55(46-64)	2	35	45-49	♂	130(97-163)	82(61-103)	
8	6	♂♀	100(85-115)	56(48-64)		36		♀	131(92-169)	82(59-104)	
9	7	♂♀	102(87-117)	56(48-64)		37	50-54	♂	135(97-172)	83(61-106)	
10	8	♂♀	105(89-121)	57(48-66)		38		♀	137(96-179)	84(59-108)	
11	9	♂♀	107(91-123)	57(48-66)		39	55-59	♂	138(101-175)	84(62-106)	
12	10	♂♀	109(93-125)	58(49-67)		40		♀	139(97-180)	84(61-106)	
13	11	♂♀	111(94-128)	59(49-69)		41	60-64	♂	142(100-183)	85(60-109)	
14	12	♂♀	113(95-131)	59(49-69)		42		♀	144(100-188)	85(60-110)	
15	13	♂♀	115(96-134)	60(50-70)		43	65-69	♂	143(92-194)	83(64-102)	4
16	14	♂♀	118(99-137)	61(51-71)		44		♀	154(97-211)	85(58-112)	
17	15	♂♀	121(102-140)	61(51-71)		45	70-74	♂	145(93-197)	82(52-112)	
18	16	♂♀	121(102-140)	61(51-71)		46		♀	159(108-210)	85(55-115)	
19	17	♂	121(96-146)	74(56-93)	3	47	75-79	♂	146(104-188)	81(56-106)	
20		♀	116(93-139)	72(54-90)		48		♀	158(106-210)	84(58-110)	
21	18	♂	120(96-143)	74(55-94)		49	80-84	♂	145(95-195)	82(63-101)	
22		♀	116(94-139)	72(55-89)		50		♀	157(102-212)	83(57-109)	
23	19	♂	122(92-151)	75(54-95)		51	85-89	♂	145(98-192)	79(50-108)	
24		♀	115(92-138)	71(54-89)		52		♀	154(99-209)	82(48-116)	
25	20-24	♂	123(96-150)	76(57-96)		53	90-94	♂	145(99-191)	78(54-102)	
26		♀	116(93-139)	72(53-91)		54		♀	150(104-196)	79(55-103)	
27	25-29	♂	125(100-150)	78(60-95)		55	95-106	♂	146(92-200)	78(53-103)	
28		♀	117(94-139)	74(56-92)		56		♀	149(103-195)	81(57-106)	

[1] Point of muffling taken as the diastolic pressure.

Contributors: Master, Arthur M.; Lindsay, Hugh A.; Hartroft, W. Stanley

References

[1] Allen-Williams, G. M. 1945. Arch. Dis. Childhood 20:125.

[2] Graham, A. W., et al. 1945. Amer. J. Dis. Child. 69:203.

[3] Master, A. M., et al. 1952. Normal Blood Pressure and Hypertension. Lea and Febiger, Philadelphia.

[4] Master, A. M., et al. 1957. Proc. Soc. Exp. Biol. Med. 94:463.

[5] Woodbury, R. A., et al. 1938. Amer. J. Physiol. 122:472.

continued

Part II. By Geographic Location and Nationality

Data in brackets refer to the column heading in brackets. Values in parentheses are ranges, estimate "b" (*see* Introduction).

#	Location [Nationality]	Age yr[1]	No. & Sex	Systolic	Diastolic	Reference
1	New England & Ontario		154	146(96-196)	82(58-106)	12
2	United States Atlantic Coast		1154	145(99-191)	81(59-103)	12
3	South	....	384	142(96-188)	82(57-107)	12
4	Midwest	....	77	147(101-193)	83(57-109)	12
5	Far West	....	139	144(92-196)	82(58-106)	12
6	Pacific Coast		404	143(95-191)	80(54-106)	12
7	Maryland[2]	19	4♂	113(77-149)	69(63-75)	13
8		20	36♂	114(92-136)	68(50-86)	
9		21	173♂	115(93-137)	70(54-86)	
10		22	379♂	115(95-135)	69(53-85)	
11		23	204♂	115(95-135)	69(53-85)	
12		24	93♂	112(92-132)	69(55-83)	
13		25	52♂	115(93-137)	70(54-86)	
14		26	46♂	114(96-132)	70(56-84)	
15		27	29♂	110(84-136)	71(55-87)	
16		28	15♂	112(92-132)	70(56-84)	
17		29	19♂	115(97-133)	70(57-85)	
18		30	11♂	114(96-132)	72(56-88)	
19		31	10♂	112(94-130)	69(55-83)	
20		32	5♂	116(94-138)	75(53-97)	
21		33	5♂	116(94-138)	75(51-99)	
22		34	3♂	117(91-143)	69(53-85)	
23		35	2♂	114(96-132)	72(72-72)	
24	Massachusetts	30-34	388♂	131(99-163)	83(61-105)	6
25		35-39	438♂	132(98-166)	85(61-109)	
26		40-44	420♂	135(99-171)	87(63-111)	
27			508♀	131(91-171)	83(59-107)	
28		45-49	352♂	138(96-180)	88(64-112)	
29			446♀	142(94-190)	87(63-111)	
30		50-54	353♂	140(96-184)	89(63-115)	
31			421♀	150(90-210)	90(62-118)	
32		55-59	262♂	145(91-199)	88(58-118)	
33			371♀	154(92-216)	91(61-121)	
34	Michigan Caucasians	6-9	45♂	106(72-140)	61(27-95)	5
35			47♀	105(83-127)	67(35-99)	
36		10-14	28♂	115(93-137)	63(39-87)	
37			36♀	117(101-133)	67(51-83)	
38		15-19	33♂	129(115-143)	71(47-95)	
39			31♀	120(100-140)	67(57-77)	
40		20-24	34♀	127(87-167)	73(53-93)	
41			43♀	123(57-189)	73(49-97)	
42		25-29	30♀	130(102-158)	74(30-118)	
43			39♀	118(72-164)	77(65-89)	
44		30-34	38♂	125(93-157)	77(65-89)	
45			33♀	123(91-155)	79(47-111)	

#	Location [Nationality]	Age yr[1]	No. & Sex	Systolic	Diastolic	Reference
46		35-39	22♂	125(79-171)	79(41-117)	
47			27♀	120(70-170)	78(68-88)	
48		40-44	22♂	135(113-157)	85(69-101)	
49			25♀	145(111-179)	86(50-122)	
50		45-49	20♂	128(96-160)	79(67-91)	
51			20♀	145(123-167)	85(61-109)	
52		50-54	14♂	139(113-165)	88(72-104)	
53			15♀	145(113-177)	87(73-101)	
54		55-59	11♂	141(85-197)	83(69-97)	
55			16♀	161(111-211)	86(62-110)	
56		60	28♂	144(70-218)	79(49-109)	
57			30♀	157(119-195)	82(70-94)	
58	Negroes	6-9	154♂	102(76-128)	64(42-86)	5
59			166♀	103(89-117)	65(45-85)	
60		10-14	143♂	109(81-137)	62(50-74)	
61			139♀	112(88-136)	67(41-93)	
62		15-19	139♂	125(101-149)	74(44-104)	
63			153♀	119(89-149)	71(41-101)	
64		20-24	123♂	128(100-156)	79(51-107)	
65			170♀	120(82-158)	74(44-104)	
66		25-29	98♂	133(97-169)	83(55-111)	
67			128♀	127(81-173)	80(52-108)	
68		30-34	58♂	136(94-178)	88(56-120)	
69			86♀	132(104-160)	85(65-105)	
70		35-39	55♂	143(69-217)	92(54-130)	
71			109♀	140(94-186)	88(54-122)	
72		40-44	67♂	142(90-194)	91(63-119)	
73			87♀	150(60-240)	91(41-141)	
74		45-49	67♂	145(99-191)	94(58-130)	
75			75♀	153(117-189)	92(76-108)	
76		50-54	37♂	156(96-216)	93(69-117)	
77			46♀	156(84-228)	92(58-126)	
78		55-59	16♂	145(71-219)	87(55-119)	
79			30♀	182(116-248)	98(82-114)	
80		60	33♂	169(71-267)	90(40-140)	
81			61♀	176(120-232)	90(64-116)	
82	Missouri	3	60♂	99(79-119)	57(29-85)	8
83			60♀	99(77-121)	58(36-80)	
84		4	79♂	98(80-116)	57(37-77)	
85			65♀	98(78-118)	60(40-80)	
86		5	90♂	101(81-121)	60(40-80)	
87			80♀	102(82-122)	60(42-78)	
88		6	89♂	105(83-127)	60(40-80)	
89			81♀	105(83-127)	64(46-82)	
90		7	77♂	106(86-126)	63(45-81)	
91			81♀	107(85-129)	63(43-83)	
92		8	61♂	108(86-130)	61(37-85)	
93			70♀	108(88-128)	65(49-81)	

[1] Unless otherwise indicated. [2] Subjects were medical students.

continued

Part II. By Geographic Location and Nationality

	Location [Nationality]	Age yr	No. & Sex	Systolic	Diastolic	Reference
94		9	61♂	111(89-133)	65(45-85)	
95			69♀	112(92-132)	67(47-87)	
96		10	53♂	114(92-136)	66(48-84)	
97			68♀	114(92-136)	64(46-82)	
98		11	53♂	114(92-136)	65(47-83)	
99			61♀	121(97-145)	69(53-85)	
100		12	51♂	116(96-136)	67(53-81)	
101			58♀	117(93-141)	65(49-81)	
102		13	47♂	120(96-144)	65(49-81)	
103			50♀	121(97-145)	69(49-89)	
104		14	41♂	120(100-140)	68(52-84)	
105			33♀	119(95-143)	67(47-87)	
106		15	33♂	125(105-145)	67(51-83)	
107			22♀	115(93-137)	67(49-85)	
108	London, England	10-14	12♂	105(77-133)	61(41-81)[3/]	4
109			15♀	111(79-143)	65(47-83)[3/]	
110		15-19	34♂	117(97-137)	68(50-86)[3/]	
111			58♀	117(95-139)	71(55-87)[3/]	
112		20-24	60♂	123(97-149)	74(54-94)[3/]	
113			68♀	119(93-145)	72(58-86)[3/]	
114		25-29	82♂	124(96-152)	74(54-94)[3/]	
115			103♀	123(97-149)	76(58-94)[3/]	
116		30-34	90♂	123(95-151)	74(54-94)[3/]	
117			108♀	121(91-151)	75(57-93)[3/]	
118		35-39	90♂	125(97-153)	78(60-96)[3/]	
119			119♀	128(94-162)	79(55-103)[3/]	
120		40-44	99♂	127(91-163)	77(51-103)[3/]	
121			122♀	134(94-174)	82(58-106)[3/]	
122		45-49	79♂	131(95-167)	80(58-102)[3/]	
123			114♀	134(88-180)	82(58-106)[3/]	
124		50-54	87♂	135(95-175)	82(58-106)[3/]	
125			131♀	147(91-203)	88(58-118)[3/]	
126		55-59	60♂	146(98-194)	87(59-115)[3/]	
127			108♀	154(96-212)	89(59-119)[3/]	
128		60-64	52♂	154(88-220)	88(50-126)[3/]	
129			87♀	159(105-213)	92(62-122)[3/]	
130		65-69	46♂	152(100-204)	85(55-115)[3/]	
131			74♀	173(119-227)	94(64-124)[3/]	
132		70-74	27♂	161(93-229)	87(51-123)[3/]	
133			60♀	175(121-229)	93(63-123)[3/]	
134		75-79	4♂	150(74-226)	83(43-123)[3/]	
135			26♀	177(111-243)	97(61-133)[3/]	
136		80-84	5♂	175(129-221)	91(73-109)[3/]	
137			11♀	198(136-260)	97(59-135)[3/]	
138	[Fijians]	10-19	352♂	111(83-139)	72(50-94)[3/]	9
139			359♀	115(91-139)	75(53-97)[3/]	
140		20-29	305♂	125(97-153)	80(60-100)[3/]	
141			461♀	123(99-147)	79(57-101)[3/]	

	Location [Nationality]	Age yr	No. & Sex	Systolic	Diastolic	Reference
142		30-39	300♂	125(97-153)	81(59-103)[3/]	
143			317♀	127(97-157)	81(59-103)[3/]	
144		40-49	293♂	127(97-157)	82(62-102)[3/]	
145			219♀	135(91-179)	84(60-108)[3/]	
146		50-59	163♂	133(89-177)	83(59-107)[3/]	
147			143♀	143(91-195)	85(61-109)[3/]	
148		60-69	75♂	133(87-179)	79(55-103)[3/]	
149			56♀	146(98-194)	82(60-104)[3/]	
150		70	48♂	136(102-170)	80(54-106)[3/]	
151			21♀	142(92-192)	84(54-114)[3/]	
152	[Fiji Indians] Rural	30-39	394♂	121(93-149)	77(55-101)	10
153		40-49	448♂	126(88-164)	79(53-105)	
154		50-59	187♂	134(82-186)	81(51-111)	
155		60-69	179♂	136(88-184)	80(58-102)	
156	Urban	30-39	394♂	126(84-168)	88(62-114)	10
157		40-49	448♂	130(88-172)	87(59-115)	
158		50-59	187♂	140(96-184)	89(63-115)	
159		60-69	179♂	145(101-189)	88(70-106)	
160	India [Bengalis]	15-19	41♂	116	68	3
161			66♀	115	66	
162		20-24	52♂	118	71	
163			65♀	117	70	
164		25-29	32♂	117	72	
165			71♀	115	71	
166		30-34	32♂	115	75	
167			86♀	114	72	
168		35-39	41♂	118	74	
169			56♀	117	75	
170		40-44	45♂	111	74	
171			62♀	120	77	
172		45-49	26♂	120	76	
173			53♀	125	79	
174		50-54	23♂	117	78	
175			55♀	128	79	
176		55-59	29♂	132	81	
177			54♀	131	77	
178		60-64	21♂	138	78	
179			25♀	137	78	
180		65-69	21♂	138	72	
181			13♀	138	80	
182		70	19♂	139	73	
183			19♀	143	73	
184	[Melanesians]	15-29	313♂	(114-121)	(85-94)	11
185			353♀	(109-115)	(67-76)	
186		30-44	352♂	(111-122)	(84-94)	
187			328♀	(108-119)	(67-77)	

3/ Fourth phase.

continued

Part II. By Geographic Location and Nationality

	Location [Nationality]	Age yr[1]	No. & Sex	Systolic	Diastolic	Reference
188		40-49	227♂	(109-120)	(83-94)	
189			209♀	(112-126)	(69-76)	
190		50-60	214♂	(101-137)	(81-96)	
191			159♀	(113-149)	(66-78)	
192	[Scandi-	15[4]	40♂♀[5]	90(72-110)[6]		2
193	navi-	30[4]	40♂♀[5]	89(70-122)[6]		
194	ans]	1[7]	40♂♀[5]	79(68-110)[6]		
195		2[7]	40♂♀[5]	81(68-104)[6]		
196		3[7]	40♂♀[5]	80(60-100)[6]		
197		1[8]	40♂♀[5]	78(64-102)[6]		
198		3[8]	40♂♀[5]	82(66-106)[6]		
199		5[8]	40♂♀[5]	90(68-124)[6]		
200		7[8]	40♂♀[5]	97(72-120)[6]		
201		15-19	724♂	115(91-139)	72(56-88)	1
202		20-29	2340♂	120(94-146)	75(57-93)	
203		30-39	2948♂	123(97-149)	78(60-96)	
204		40-49	2252♂	127(97-157)	81(61-101)	
205		50-59	1819♂	130(92-168)	83(61-105)	
206		60-69	980♂	142(96-188)	85(61-109)	
	Taiwan [Chinese]					
207	Farm-	15-19	831♂	122(92-152)	74(54-94)	15
208	ers		951♀	119(107-131)	78(58-98)	
209		20-24	390♂	124(98-152)	78(56-100)	
210			908♀	125(95-155)	79(59-99)	
211		25-29	839♂	124(98-152)	79(59-99)	
212			1013♀	121(99-143)	79(57-101)	
213		30-34	735♂	124(98-152)	79(59-99)	
214			1047♀	123(91-155)	79(58-98)	
215		35-39	689♂	123(95-151)	80(60-100)	
216			931♀	126(92-160)	80(58-102)	
217		40-44	539♂	124(88-160)	80(56-104)	
218			787♀	126(88-164)	81(57-105)	
219		45-49	491♂	124(88-160)	81(57-105)	
220			655♀	131(87-175)	83(61-105)	
221		50-54	451♂	126(90-162)	82(60-104)	
222			587♀	134(88-180)	85(57-113)	
223		55-59	411♂	131(85-177)	84(58-110)	
224			430♀	137(87-187)	86(60-112)	
225		60-64	304♂	135(85-185)	84(58-110)	
226			334♀	146(96-196)	85(57-113)	
227		65-69	238♂	138(80-196)	87(61-113)	
228			261♀	151(97-205)	89(63-115)	
229		70-74	142♂	142(84-200)	88(58-118)	
230			125♀	155(91-219)	88(58-118)	
231		75-79	66♂	140(82-198)	86(54-118)	
232			70♀	157(103-211)	91(63-119)	
233		80	31♂	149(93-205)	85(61-109)	
234			48♀	164(92-236)	92(62-122)	

	Location [Nationality]	Age yr[1]	No. & Sex	Systolic	Diastolic	Reference
235	Fisher-	15-19	302♂	124(96-152)	79(61-97)	15
236	men		286♀	125(95-155)	80(64-96)	
237		20-24	175♂	128(96-160)	81(61-101)	
238			309♀	128(96-160)	82(62-102)	
239		25-29	247♂	126(90-162)	81(61-101)	
240			436♀	125(97-153)	81(61-101)	
241		30-34	356♂	128(98-158)	81(59-103)	
242			442♀	128(92-164)	83(59-107)	
243		35-39	307♂	129(99-159)	84(62-106)	
244			433♀	129(89-169)	84(60-108)	
245		40-44	252♂	128(94-162)	84(60-108)	
246			377♀	133(89-177)	85(61-109)	
247		45-49	201♂	130(92-168)	85(61-109)	
248			248♀	134(86-182)	85(59-111)	
249		50-54	180♂	137(91-183)	88(58-118)	
250			213♀	146(86-206)	90(58-122)	
251		55-59	176♂	140(90-190)	91(61-119)	
252			139♀	149(93-205)	91(59-123)	
253		60-64	125♂	144(90-198)	91(57-125)	
254			105♀	155(99-211)	96(60-132)	
255		65-69	76♂	145(87-203)	89(65-113)	
256			72♀	156(100-212)	92(62-122)	
257		70-74	43♂	147(91-203)	91(55-127)	
258			29♀	157(95-219)	90(62-118)	
259		75-79	20♂	145(85-205)	88(56-120)	
260			20♀	168(96-240)	93(71-115)	
261		80	5♂	155(81-229)	87(55-119)	
262			11♀	166(112-220)	97(69-125)	
263	Urban	15-19	524♂	115(89-141)	67(41-93)	7
264	dwell-		404♀	110(88-132)	66(42-90)	
265	ers	20-24	768♂	118(90-146)	72(48-96)	
266			636♀	110(86-134)	67(43-91)	
267		25-29	1169♂	117(91-143)	72(50-94)	
268			616♀	109(83-135)	68(42-94)	
269		30-34	1274♂	117(89-145)	70(46-94)	
270			462♀	111(81-141)	70(44-96)	
271		35-39	822♂	117(89-145)	76(54-98)	
272			328♀	117(75-159)	75(47-103)	
273		40-44	738♂	121(85-157)	80(52-108)	
274			278♀	120(74-166)	78(48-108)	
275		45-49	513♂	126(84-168)	82(54-110)	
276			197♀	131(85-177)	83(47-119)	
277		50-54	284♂	133(77-189)	83(49-117)	
278			121♀	137(83-191)	83(53-113)	
279		55-59	163♂	139(81-197)	84(52-116)	
280			91♀	139(81-197)	82(52-112)	
281		60-64	84♂	148(80-216)	86(50-122)	
282			71♀	144(78-210)	83(53-113)	

[1] Unless otherwise indicated. [4] Minutes. [5] From a group of 40 subjects. [6] Mean blood pressure. [7] Hours. [8] Days.

continued

Part II. By Geographic Location and Nationality

	Location [Nationality]	Subjects		Blood Pressure, mm Hg		Reference		Location [Nationality]	Subjects		Blood Pressure, mm Hg		Reference
		Age yr	No. & Sex	Systolic	Diastolic				Age yr	No. & Sex	Systolic	Diastolic	
283		65	82♂	150(90-210)	85(53-117)		289		36-40	78♂	117 ± 10	79 ± 7	
284			104♀	158(100-216)	83(55-111)		290		41-45	70♂	120 ± 14	81 ± 9	
285	[Tibetans]	16-20	11♂	124 ± 13	80 ± 7	14	291		46-50	45♂	127 ± 21	86 ± 13	
286		21-25	106♂	118 ± 12	78 ± 8		292		51-55	64♂	131 ± 26	85 ± 14	
287		26-30	116♂	119 ± 14	79 ± 9		293		56-60	52♂	135 ± 22	87 ± 13	
288		31-35	85♂	118 ± 12	79 ± 8		294		<61	33♂	139 ± 23	87 ± 14	

Contributor: Lindsay, Hugh A.

References

[1] Bjerkedal, T., and H. Natrig. 1966. Acta Med. Scand. 180:257.

[2] Contis, G., and J. Lind. 1963. Acta Paediat. (Stockholm), Suppl. 146:41.

[3] Das, B. C., and B. N. Mukherjee. 1963. Gerontologia 8:92.

[4] Hamilton, M., et al. 1954. Clin. Sci. 13:11.

[5] Johnson, B. C., and R. D. Remington. 1961. J. Chronic Dis. 13:39.

[6] Kannel, W. B., et al. 1961. Ann. Intern. Med. 55:33.

[7] Lin, T. -Y., et al. 1959. Clin. Sci. 18:301.

[8] Londe, S. 1968. Clin. Pediat. 7:400.

[9] Lovell, R. R. H., et al. 1960. Australas. Ann. Med. 9:4.

[10] Maddocks, I. 1961. Circulation 24:1220.

[11] Maddocks, I. 1967. Med. J. Aust. 1:1123.

[12] Master, A. M., et al. 1961. Geriatrics 16:218.

[13] Murphy, E. A., et al. 1967. Johns Hopkins Med. J. 120:1.

[14] Sehgal, A. K., et al. 1968. Circulation 37:36.

[15] Tseng, W. -P. 1967. Amer. J. Epidemiol. 86:513.

232. ARTERIAL BLOOD PRESSURE: VERTEBRATES OTHER THAN MAN

Plus/minus (±) values are standard deviations, unless otherwise indicated. Data in brackets refer to the column heading in brackets. Values in parentheses are ranges, estimate "b" or "c" (see Introduction).

	Species (Synonym)	Method [Anesthetic]	Subjects	Blood Pressure, mm Hg		Reference
				Systolic	Diastolic	
				Mean		
			Mammalia			
1	Bos taurus	Strain gauge	12♀	160	110	14
2		Mercury manometer [None]	9 calves; (70-266) kg	100(80-120)		93
3		Direct; strain gauge [None]	Adult	135		73
4		[Chloral hydrate]	♀	166		16
5		[Local]	♀	125		15
6		[Pentobarbital sodium]	Young	(160-180)		15
7		Strain gauge [Promazine]	15 subjects; (1-12) mo	131(80-184)		50
8		Pressure transducer; implanted catheter, heart level	Adults; supine	135		72
9	Camelus dromedarius	Strain gauge [Phencyclidine]	1♂, 1♀; adults	209	169	61
10	Canis familiaris	Cuff; auscultation [None]	4; fasted 7-38 da	82(74-86)	42(35-51)	111
11			13 adults	112(95-136)	56(43-66)	
12		Hypodermic; Tycos sphygmomanometer [None]	35	108(92-120)		71

continued

	Species (Synonym)	Method [Anesthetic]	Subjects	Systolic	Diastolic	Reference
				Mean		
13		Xylol indicator [None]	52	142(104-180)	....	112
14		Strain gauge [None]	5♂ adults; trained	(95-111)		66
15		Strain gauge; implanted arterial catheters [None]	10 adults; trained, resting	(112-146)	(72-103)	31
16		Strain gauge; implanted arterial catheters [None]	26 adults; trained, resting	(74-110)		68
17		Strain gauge manometer; femoral artery [None]	20	104(100-120)		2
18		Strain gauge manometer; femoral artery [Pentobarbital sodium]	20	134(100-175)		2
19		Hypodermic; optical manometer [Morphine]	99♂, 116♀	180(100-275)	89(30-140)	36
20		Mercury manometer [Barbital sodium]	67♂ adults	134(85-190)		105
21			80♀ adults	125(60-170)		
22		Capacitance manometer [Pentobarbital sodium]	22	156(108-198)	100(75-121)	80
23		Oscillometer [Pentobarbital sodium]	22	149(108-189)	100(75-122)	80
24		Auscultation [Pentobarbital sodium]	22	149(100-187)	104(79-127)	80
25	Capra hircus	[None]	Adult	120(112-126)	84(76-90)	55
26		Electromanometer on carotid loop [None]	8♂; (18.1-49.9) kg	124(111-136)	98(86-113)	46
27		Strain gauge [None]	10♂♀ young; 14.8 kg; trained	122	85	43
28		[Urethan]	4	120		15
29	Cavia porcellus	[Diethyl ether, pentobarbital sodium, and/or procaine]	8 adults	77(28-140)	47(16-90)	56
30		Mercury or condenser manometer [Pentobarbital sodium]	Adult	(120-170)		8
31	Cercopithecus aethiops	Mercury manometer; femoral artery [Diethyl ether and/or pentobarbital sodium]	1	(110-150)	....	107
32	Didelphis marsupialis virginiana	Strain gauge; transducer indwelling carotid artery catheter [None]	9♂♀ adults	175	133	42
33			9♂♀ adults; trained	119		
34	Equus asinus	Direct; strain gauge; carotid artery [Electroanesthesia]	10	171	103	115
35	E. caballus	Cuff on tail; systolic determined by palpation; diastolic by oscillation or auscultation [None]	5♂, 3♀; 4.5 mo-1.5 yr	80	50	10
36			173♂ adults	98(90-104)	64(45-86)	
37			43♀ adults	90(86-98)	59(43-84)	
38		Strain gauge [None]	18 adults	131	89	28
39		Strain gauge [Chloral hydrate]	14 adults	130	92	28
40		Strain gauge [Promazine]	14 adults	90	65	28
41		[Local]	6 subjects; (13-18) yr	169(152-194)		15
42	Thoroughbred gelding	Direct; carotid loop [Propionylpromazine, 50 mg]	12 subjects; 7.3 yr; (228-505) kg	142(118-166)	99(77-121)	18
	Felis catus	Strain gauge; implanted arterial catheters [None]	3 adults; trained			34
43			Awake & resting	118(88-142)	70(56-85)	
44			Asleep	92	46	
45		Strain gauge transducer; cannula in femoral artery [None]	5♂, 5♀; adults	171(135-200)	123(90-145)	30
		Pressure transducer; implanted catheter	10 adults			33
46			Awake	118		
47			Asleep	85		
48			After deep sleep	105		

continued

	Species (Synonym)	Method [Anesthetic]	Subjects	Blood Pressure, mm Hg		Reference
				Systolic	Diastolic	
				Mean		
49		Strain gauge [None]	5♀ adults; trained	121	93	12
50		Cuff on carotid loop; mercury manometer [None]	4	(140-170)		54
51		Mercury manometer [Allobarbital-urethan]	19♂ adults; (1.4-4.9) kg	129(67-216)		81
52			208♀ adults; (1.4-4.9) kg	121(62-200)		
53		Optical manometer [Barbital or diethyl ether]	5 adults	120	75	113
54	*Giraffa camelopardalis*	Pressure transducer; implanted catheter, heart level	Supine	260	160	102
55			Standing	120	75	
56			Adults; supine	219		
57		Implanted transducer in carotid artery, radiotelemetered [None]	2; wild, free-ranging			104
			Supine	280	160	
58			Standing	160(150-170)	107(105-110)	
59			Walking	(140-180)	(90-120)	
60		[None]	4 adults	219		73
61		Strain gauge [Local]	4 subjects; 2 yr	(220-353)	(190-303)	29
62	*Macaca irus (M. cynomolgus)*	Mercury manometer; femoral artery [Diethyl ether and/or pentobarbital sodium]	1	(110-150)	....	107
63	*M. mulatta*	[None]	14 adults	159(137-188)	127(112-152)	88
64		Mercury manometer; iliac artery [None]	16	134(110-175)	76(65-95)	109
65		Strain gauge; implanted arterial catheters [None]	13 adults; restrained 2-34 wk	(117-136)	(71-84)	25
66		Mercury manometer; femoral artery [Diethyl ether and/or pentobarbital sodium]	10	(110-150)	....	107
67	*Macropus giganteus, M. rufus*	Strain gauge; femoral artery [Allobarbital-urethan & pentobarbital]	15♂, 3♀	122 ± 23	79 ± 18	57
68	*Mesocricetus auratus*	Strain gauge manometer [None]	28♂♀	109	....	7
69		Strain gauge manometer; carotid cannula [Pentobarbital sodium]	20♂♀	98	....	7
70		Mercury or condenser manometer [Pentobarbital sodium]	Adult	(120-170)		8
71	*Mus musculus*	Plethysmograph [None]	(2-4) mo	121(109-132)	....	39
72			(10-16) mo	123(110-136)		
73			(24-30) mo	127(115-139)		
74		Optical manometer; carotid cannula [Local]	2	147(133-160)	106(102-110)	114
75		Optical manometer; carotid cannula [Urethan or diethyl ether]	9 adults	113(95-125)	81(67-90)	114
76		Cuff; mercury manometer [Pentobarbital sodium or phenobarbital]	15 subjects; (16-25) g	(60-126)	....	58
77	Inbred strains	Plethysmograph [None]	19	(72-110)		84
78	A/J	Cuff; pneumatic pulse transducer [None]	40♂; 34(28-40) wk; 32 (24-40) g	84(58-110)	....	83
79	BALB/cJ	Cuff; pneumatic pulse transducer [None]	40♂; 36(30-42) wk; 30 (24-36) g	105(79-131)	....	83
80	CBA/J	Cuff; pneumatic pulse transducer [None]	40♂; 28(22-34) wk; 40 (32-48) g	97(71-123)	....	83
81	C57BL/6J	Cuff; pneumatic pulse transducer [None]	40♂; 34(18-50) wk; 28 (21-35) g	93(67-119)	....	83

continued

	Species (Synonym)	Method [Anesthetic]	Subjects	Blood Pressure, mm Hg		Reference
				Systolic	Diastolic	
				Mean		
82	DBA/2J	Cuff; pneumatic pulse transducer [None]	40♂; 29(27-33) wk; 30 (24-36) g	89(62-115)	....	83
83	RF/J	Cuff; pneumatic pulse transducer [None]	40♂; 25(19-31) wk; 34 (30-38) g	96(70-122)	....	83
84	SJL/J	Cuff; pneumatic pulse transducer [None]	40♂; 36(30-42) wk; 30 (24-36) g	96(70-122)	....	83
85	129/J	Cuff; pneumatic pulse transducer [None]	40♂; 33(27-39) wk; 27 (23-31) g	89(63-115)	....	83
86	*Myotis lucifugus*	Mercury manometer; carotid artery [Pentobarbital sodium]	11	(39-105)		67
87	*Ornithorhynchus* sp.	Mercury manometer; carotid artery	....	(123-136)		22
88	*Oryctolagus cuniculus*	Hypodermic manometer	1 newborn	35	1	35
89		Cuff on carotid loop; mercury manometer [None]	55	120(80-150)	....	13
90		Hamilton manometer [None]	32 adults	110(95-130)	80(60-90)	78
91		Pressure cup on central artery [None]	9	82(70-90)	....	1
92		Strain gauge; implanted catheter in ear artery [None]	18 adults; unrestrained	113 ± 2.32[1]	73 ± 1.57[1]	48
93		Manometers; carotid catheter [Pentobarbital sodium]	90 subjects; 3 hr	29		11
94			1 da	33		
95			3 da	36		
96			10 da	46		
97			17 da	54		
98		Condenser manometer; catheter in carotid artery [Pentobarbital sodium]	21♂♀; newborn	30		63
99			9♂♀; 1-3 da	34		
100			8♂♀; 4-7 da	41		
101			13♂♀; 9-14 da	57		
102			8♂♀; 21-31 da	77		
103			5♂♀; adults	96		
104	*Ovis aries*	Strain gauge [None]	4♀ adults; trained	103	85	60
105		[Local]	13 adults	114(90-140)		15
106	Rambouillet-Suffolk	Direct; carotid loop [None]	8♀; 2.4 yr	123(104-135)	93(75-103)	70
107	*Pan troglodytes*	....	2	136(125-147)	80(76-85)	59
108	*Papio leucophaeus*	Cardiac catheterization [Pentobarbital sodium]	3	115[2]; 19[3]	85[2]; 9[3]	103
109	*Phoca vitulina*	Mercury manometer	1 young	∿135		44
110		Strain gauge; catheter in flipper artery [Local]	1 adult	150	105	65
111	*Rattus* sp.	[None]	100 adults	98(82-120)	....	27
112		Strain gauge; implanted arterial catheter [None]	4 adults	(148-173)[4]	(96-110)	49
113		Plethysmograph [None]	40♀; (135-200) g	125(102-140)	....	97
114		Plethysmograph [Amobarbital, 4 mg/100 g]	40♀; (135-200) g	104(94-112)	....	97
115		Plethysmograph [Diethyl ether, shallow]	40♀; (135-200) g	117(110-126)	....	97
116		Plethysmograph [Diethyl ether, deep]	40♀; (135-200) g	104(95-110)	....	97

[1] Standard error. [2] Aortic valve pressure. [3] Pulmonary artery pressure. [4] When measurement was made by tail plethysmography, systolic pressure was 57 ± 10 mm Hg lower, and mean arterial pressure was 10-20 mm Hg lower.

continued

	Species (Synonym)	Method [Anesthetic]	Subjects	Blood Pressure, mm Hg		Reference
				Systolic	Diastolic	
				Mean		
117		Plethysmograph [Morphine, 10 mg/100 g]	40♀; (135-200) g	64(62-70)	....	97
118		Plethysmograph [Pentobarbital sodium, 4 mg/100 g]	40♀; (135-200) g	104(86-115)	....	97
119		Plethysmograph [Urethan, 20 mg/100 g]	40♀; (135-200) g	78(72-84)	....	97
120		Mercury manometer [Diethyl ether and/or amobarbital]	18♂; 6 mo	124		17
121			23♀; 6 mo	116		
122		Plethysmograph [Allobarbital 5/]	18 young adults	105(87-122)	....	6
123		Plethysmograph [Diethyl ether]	70 young adults	106(78-132)	....	6
124		Cuff; microscopy [Diethyl ether]	....	110(80-140)	....	21
125		Cuff; microscopy [Pentobarbital sodium]	....	90(60-120)	....	21
126		Cuff; foot microscopy [Pentobarbital sodium]	100	(60-140)	....	32
127		Optical manometer [Pentobarbital sodium]	6 subjects; 50 determinations	130(75-150)	....	87
128		Optical manometer [Pentobarbital sodium]	68 determinations	120(45-180)	....	69
129		Strain gauge; foot pulse [Pentobarbital sodium]	68 determinations	120(40-180)	....	69
130		Cuff on tail	13♀; 280 g	122		98
131	R. norvegicus Holtzman	Microphonic manometer [None]	....	148(147-150)	....	26
132	Norway	Optical manometer [Pentobarbital sodium]	124 adults, mostly ♂	129(88-184)	91(58-145)	85
133	Sprague-Dawley	Aortic cuff; mercury manometer [None]	20♂; (105-106) g; 540 determinations	130(108-163)	....	20
134	Sus scrofa	[None]	149 subjects; (1.9-5.5) kg	(60-80)	....	45
135		[None]	35 subjects; (40-400) kg	(100-180)	....	19
136		[None]	Adult	169(144-185)	108(98-120)	55
137		Strain gauge [α-Chloralose]	8 subjects; (8-13) wk	170	123	5
138		Mercury manometer; carotid artery [Pentobarbital sodium]	(0-2) wk	(60-70)		51
139			3 wk	100		
140	Tursiops truncatus	Catheter in external carotid artery attached to strain gauge pressure transducer [Nitrous oxide & oxygen]	4 adults; covered with towels soaked in seawater	152(142-160)	118(111-130)	90
		Aves				
141	Anas platyrhynchos, Pekin	Direct; strain gauge; carotid artery [Local]	Adult	180	134	94
142	(A. boscas)	Strain gauge; implanted arterial catheter [None]	20 adults	(100-175)		24
143	Colinus virginianus	Direct; strain gauge; carotid artery [Local]	15♂; restrained	150	136	76
144			11♀; restrained	146	129	
145	Corvus cornix	....	....	147		53
146	C. monedula	....	....	119		53
147	Coturnix coturnix japonica	Direct; strain gauge; carotid artery [Local]	12♂; restrained	158	152	76
148			12♀; restrained	156	147	

5/ Synonym: Diallyl barbituric acid.

continued

#	Species (Synonym)	Method [Anesthetic]	Subjects	Blood Pressure, mm Hg Systolic Mean	Diastolic Mean	Reference
149	Falco naumanni (F. cenchris)	....	....	103		53
150	Gallus gallus (G. domesticus)	Cuff [None]	14	130	....	9
151		Dynograph [None]	28♂; 14 mo	207	61	64
152			24 mo	200	87	
153			36 mo	213	104	
154			40 mo	234	119	
155			28♀; 14 mo	149	43	
156			24 mo	144	40	
157			36 mo	125	35	
158			40 mo	137	36	
159		Optical manometer [Barbital]	5 adults	130	85	113
160		Optical manometer [Diethyl ether or morphine]	1	130	85	113
161		Direct; strain gauge; carotid artery [Local]	♂ adult	190	150	94
162			♀ adult	150	125	
163	White Leghorn	Cuff, proximal to hock [None]	79♂; in winter	202	....	108
164			in summer	180		
165			140♀; in winter	165		
166			in summer	147		
167			35♂; (10-14) mo	164(160-168)	....	95
168			20♂; (22-30) mo	189(150-228)		
169			22♂; (34-54) mo	188(159-217)		
170			60♀; (10-14) mo	131(112-150)		
171			62♀; (19-26) mo	139(120-158)		
172			54♀; (30-38) mo	155(133-177)		
173			21♀; (42-54) mo	160(131-189)		
174		Indirect [None]	20♂ adults; 2.6 kg; in Feb	181(139-223)		106
175			16♂ adults; 3.0 kg; in Aug	177(139-215)		
176			20♀ adults; 2.0 kg; in Feb	153(121-185)		
177			19♀ adults; 2.0 kg; in Aug	147(123-171)		
178			527♀; (131-147) da	142(80-217)	....	41
179			286♀; (221-230) da	152(67-251)		
180			129♀; (384-391) da	151(93-209)		
181	Larus canus	....	....	179		53
182	Meleagris gallopavo	Mercury manometer; carotid artery [None]	20♂; 1 yr	302	204	91
183		Mercury manometer; tibial artery [None]	20♂; 1 yr	286	200	91
184	Beltsville Small White	Linear core transducer; catheter in carotid artery [None]	6♂ adults; 10.2 kg	236	142	23
185			9♀ adults; 4.2 kg	191	146	
186	Broad-Breasted Bronze	Linear core transducer; catheter in carotid artery [None]	6♂ adults; 16.8 kg	271	167	23
187			8♀ adults; 7.6 kg	223	171	
188	Bronze	Direct; strain gauge; carotid artery [Local]	♂ adult	297	222	94
189			♀ adult	257	200	
190	New Jersey Buff	Direct; strain gauge; carotid artery [Local]	♂ adult	226	152	94
191			♀ adult	212	157	
192	Serinus canarius	Optical manometer [Local]	6	175(110-250)	154(150-160)	94, 114
193	Sturnus vulgaris	Optical manometer [Local]	2	180(150-210)	130(100-160)	94, 114

continued

	Species (Synonym)	Method [Anesthetic]	Subjects	Blood Pressure, mm Hg		Refer-
				Systolic	Diastolic	
				Mean		
194	*Turdus migratorius*	Optical manometer [Local]	2	118(110-125)	80	94, 114
			Reptilia			
195	*Chrysemys scripta (Pseudemys scripta)*	Strain gauge; implanted arterial catheter [None]	Adult	30	26	110
196 197	*C. scripta elegans (P. elegans)*	Hamilton manometer	5; at 16°C at 22°C	27 31	21 25	79
198	*C. terrapen (P. rugosa)*	....	....	(18-35)		52
199	*Crocodylus* sp.	....	....	(30-50)		52
200	*Natrix natrix (Coluber natrix)*	....	....	89		52
			Amphibia			
201	*Bufo arenarum*	Strain gauge; arterial cannula [None]	13	43(32-53)	....	99
202		Strain gauge; arterial cannula [None]	18	48(34-62)	....	100
203		Strain gauge pressure transducer; catheter in aorta [20% urethan]	8 adults	(34-53)		101
204	*B. terrestris*	....	....	48		52
205	*Rana* sp.	....	....	(30-55)		52
206 207	*R. catesbeiana*	Cuff; web microscopy [None] Optical manometer [Local]	6 6	32(28-36) 43(36-56)	21(18-24) 31(24-44)	4 114
208	*R. esculenta*	....	....	(20-60)		52
209 210 211	*R. pipiens*	Cuff; web microscopy [None] Direct [None]	6 In air Submerged	31(21-36) 32(25-38) 23(16-30)	21(16-26) 21(17-25) 16(11-19)	4 86
212 213	*R. ridibunda*	Photoelectric cell & occluding cuff [None]	5 subjects; 40 g; at 14°C 6 subjects; 40 g; at 25°C	26(16-33) 30.7(24-36)	....	3
			Osteichthyes (Pisces)			
214	*Anguilla* sp.	....	....	(65-70)		52
215	*A. anguilla*	Cannulated ventral aorta [Urethan]	17	35.5(25.7-45.3)	....	62
216	*Cyprinus carpio*	Optical manometer [Local]	3	43(40-45)	....	114
217	*Esox lucius*	....	....	(35-84)		52
218	*Gadus morhua*	Direct; strain gauge; implanted catheter in bulbus arteriosus	....	29	18	47
219 220	*Ictalurus punctatus*	....	Adult	40 30	30 23	37 38
221	*Micropterus salmoides*	....	Adult	50	40	37
222 223	*Oncorhynchus nerka*	Direct; strain gauge; cannulated dorsal aorta [None]	Free-swimming Resting Swimming	. . 44 55	38 49	89
224 225	*O. tshawytscha*	Direct; strain gauge; needle in ventral aorta [Tricaine]	Immature Spawning	82(60-104) 80(50-110)	50(16-84) 46(16-76)	77
226 227		Direct; strain gauge; needle in dorsal aorta [Tricaine]	Immature Spawning	44(18-70) 40(20-60)	37(13-61) 32(12-52)	77

continued

	Species (Synonym)	Method [Anesthetic]	Subjects	Blood Pressure, mm Hg		Reference
				Systolic	Diastolic	
				Mean		
228	*Salmo gaird-*	Direct	49	80(40-120)	....	40
229	*neri*	Cannulated dorsal aorta [None]	39	29(28-30)	25(24-26)	92
230		Cannulated ventral aorta [None]	39	40(39-41)	32(31-33)	92
231		Cannulated subintestinal vein [None]	39	9(8-10)	8(7-9)	92
232		Direct; strain gauge; implanted catheter in dorsal aorta [None]	17; free-swimming	38.7 ± 2.9	34.4	75
			Chondrichthyes			
233	*Mustelus canis*	Direct; ventral aorta	13♂, 15♀; (2.5-4.5) kg; pithed	26(22-30)	19(17-21)	96
234	*Raja* sp.	....	....	20		52
235	*R. punctulata*	....	Adult	16	7	74
236	*Scyliorhinus*	....	....	33	29	74
237	*caniculus*			(30-37)		52
238	*Squalus acan-* *thias*	Direct; ventral aorta [Curare, 1.8 mg/kg]	26 subjects; (1.4-2.7) kg	30	24	82
239		Direct; dorsal aorta [Tricaine, 0.05 mg/kg]	26 subjects; (1.4-2.7) kg	17	16	82
240	*Torpedo* sp.	....	....	(16-18)		52

Contributors: Lindsay, Hugh A.; Hoversland, Arthur S.; Link, Roger P.

References

[1] Anderson, H. C. 1923. Proc. Soc. Exp. Biol. Med. 20:295.

[2] Barlow, G., and D. H. Knott. 1964. Amer. J. Physiol. 207:764.

[3] Bicher, H. I. 1962. J. Appl. Physiol. 17:173.

[4] Bieter, R. N., and F. H. Scott. 1929. Amer. J. Physiol. 91:265.

[5] Booth, N. H., et al. 1960. Ibid. 199:1189.

[6] Byrom, F. B., and C. Wilson. 1938. J. Physiol. (London) 93:301.

[7] Callahan, A. B., et al. 1959. J. Appl. Physiol. 14:1051.

[8] Chatfield, P. O., and C. P. Lyman. 1950. Amer. J. Physiol. 163:566.

[9] Collins, G. J., Jr., et al. 1963. Amer. J. Vet. Res. 24:1063.

[10] Covington, N. G., and G. W. McNutt. 1931. J. Amer. Vet. Med. Ass. 79:603.

[11] Dennis, J. 1968. Quart. J. Exp. Physiol. Cog. Med. Sci. 53:136.

[12] Dhindsa, D. S. Unpublished. Univ. Oregon Medical School, Portland, 1970.

[13] Dominguez, R. 1924. J. Metab. Res. 6:123.

[14] Doyle, J. T., et al. 1960. Circ. Res. 8:4.

[15] Dukes, H. H. 1955. The Physiology of Domestic Animals. Ed. 7. Comstock, Ithaca.

[16] Dukes, H. H., and L. H. Schwarte. 1931. J. Amer. Vet. Med. Ass. 79:37.

[17] Durant, R. R. 1927. Amer. J. Physiol. 81:679.

[18] Eberly, V. E., et al. 1964. Amer. J. Vet. Res. 25:1712.

[19] Engelhardt, W. 1966. Swine Biomed. Res. Proc. Symp., p. 307.

[20] Farrell, G. L., and E. Anderson. 1949. Proc. Soc. Exp. Biol. Med. 72:461.

[21] Farris, E. J., and J. Q. Griffith, Jr. 1949. The Rat in Laboratory Investigation. Ed. 2. J. B. Lippincott, Philadelphia.

[22] Feakes, M. J., et al. 1950. J. Exp. Biol. 27:50.

[23] Ferguson, T. M., et al. 1968. Poult. Sci. 48:1478.

[24] Folkow, B., et al. 1967. Acta Physiol. Scand. 70:347.

[25] Forsyth, R. P., and R. Baireuther. 1967. Amer. J. Physiol. 212:1461.

[26] Fregly, M. J. 1963. J. Lab. Clin. Med. 62:223.

[27] Friedman, M., and S. C. Freed. 1949. Proc. Soc. Exp. Biol. Med. 70:670.

[28] Gabel, A. A., et al. 1964. Amer. J. Vet. Res. 25:1151.

[29] Goetz, R. H., et al. 1960. Circ. Res. 8:1049.

[30] Gordon, D. B., and H. Goldblatt. 1967. Proc. Soc. Exp. Biol. Med. 125:177.

[31] Gregg, D. E., et al. 1965. Circ. Res. 16:102.

[32] Griffith, J. Q., Jr. 1934. Proc. Soc. Exp. Biol. Med. 32:394.

[33] Guazzi, M. 1965. Arch. Ital. Biol. 103:789.

[34] Guazzi, M., et al. 1968. Amer. J. Physiol. 214:969.

[35] Hamilton, W. F., et al. 1937. Ibid. 119:206.

continued

[36] Hamilton, W. F., et al. 1940. Ibid. 128:233.
[37] Hart, I. J. 1944. Proc. Fla. Acad. Sci. 7:221.
[38] Hart, J. S. 1957. Can. J. Zool. 35:195.
[39] Henry, J. P., et al. 1965. J. Gerontol. 20:239.
[40] Holeton, G. F., and D. J. Randall. 1967. J. Exp. Biol. 46:297.
[41] Hollands, K. G., et al. 1965. Brit. Poult. Sci. 6:297.
[42] Hoversland, A. S., and W. Murphy. Unpublished. Univ. Oregon Medical School, Portland, 1971.
[43] Hoversland, A. S., et al. 1965. Fed. Proc. Fed. Amer. Soc. Exp. Biol. 24:705.
[44] Irving, L., et al. 1942. Amer. J. Physiol. 135:557.
[45] Jezkova, D. 1960. Cesk. Akad. Zemedel. Ved Vet. Med. 5:93.
[46] Jha, S. K., et al. 1961. Amer. J. Vet. Res. 22:912.
[47] Johansen, K. 1962. Comp. Biochem. Physiol. 7:169.
[48] Korner, P. I. 1965. J. Physiol. (London) 180:266.
[49] Krieger, E. M. 1964. Circ. Res. 15:511.
[50] Kuida, H., et al. 1961. Amer. J. Physiol. 200:247.
[51] LeBlanc, J., and L. E. Mount. 1968. Nature (London) 217:77.
[52] Lehmann, G. 1925. Tabulae Biol. 1:142.
[53] Lehmann, G. 1925. Ibid. 1:143.
[54] Liddell, E. G. T., and H. M. Carleton. 1936. Quart. J. Exp. Physiol. 26:155.
[55] Link, R. P. Unpublished. Univ. Illinois, Urbana, 1956.
[56] Marshall, L. H., and C. H. Hanna. 1956. Proc. Soc. Exp. Biol. Med. 92:31.
[57] Maxwell, G. M., et al. 1964. Amer. J. Physiol. 206:967.
[58] McMaster, P. D. 1941. J. Exp. Med. 74:29.
[59] Meehan, J. P., et al. 1964. Fed. Proc. Fed. Amer. Soc. Exp. Biol. 23:515.
[60] Metcalfe, J., and J. T. Parer. 1966. Amer. J. Physiol. 210:821.
[61] Metcalfe, J., et al. 1968. Amer. J. Vet. Res. 29:2063.
[62] Mott, J. C. 1951. J. Physiol. (London) 114:387.
[63] Mott, J. C. 1965. Ibid. 181:728.
[64] Muller, H. D., and M. E. Carroll. 1966. Poult. Sci. 45:1195.
[65] Murdaugh, H. V., Jr., et al. 1966. Amer. J. Physiol. 210:176.
[66] Neill, W. A., et al. 1969. Ibid. 217(3):710.
[67] Nicoll, P. A. 1964. Fed. Proc. Fed. Amer. Soc. Exp. Biol. 23:253.
[68] Olmsted, F., and I. H. Page. 1965. Circ. Res. 16:134.
[69] Olmsted, F., et al. 1951. Circulation 3:722.
[70] Parker, H. E., et al. 1966. Amer. J. Vet. Res. 27:430.
[71] Parkins, W. M. 1934. Amer. J. Physiol. 107:518.
[72] Patterson, J. L., Jr. 1965. Ann. N. Y. Acad. Sci. 127:393.
[73] Patterson, J. L., Jr., et al. 1965. Ibid. 127:393.
[74] Prosser, C. L., and F. A. Brown, Jr. 1961. Comparative Animal Physiology. Ed. 2. W. B. Saunders, Philadelphia.
[75] Randall, D. J., et al. 1965. Can. J. Zool. 43:863.
[76] Ringer, R. K. 1968. Poult. Sci. 47:1602.
[77] Robertson, O. H., et al. 1966. Amer. J. Physiol. 210:957.
[78] Rodbard, S. 1940. Ibid. 129:448.
[79] Rodbard, S., and D. Feldman. 1946. Proc. Soc. Exp. Biol. Med. 63:43.
[80] Romagnoli, A. 1953. Cornell Vet. 43:161.
[81] Root, M. A. 1950. Amer. J. Physiol. 162:308.
[82] Satchell, G. H. 1962. J. Exp. Biol. 39:503.
[83] Schlager, G. 1966. Nature (London) 212:519.
[84] Schlager, G., and R. S. Weibust. 1967. Genetics 55:497.
[85] Schroeder, H. A. 1942. J. Exp. Med. 75:513.
[86] Shelton, G., and D. R. Jones. 1965. J. Exp. Biol. 42:339.
[87] Shuler, R. H., et al. 1944. Amer. J. Physiol. 141:625.
[88] Smith, C. C., and A. Ansevin. 1957. Proc. Soc. Exp. Biol. Med. 96:428.
[89] Smith, L. S., et al. 1967. J. Fish. Res. Bd. Can. 24:1775.
[90] Sommer, L. S., et al. 1968. Amer. J. Physiol. 215:1498.
[91] Speckmann, E. W., and R. K. Ringer. 1963. Can. J. Biochem. Physiol. 41:2337.
[92] Stevens, E. D., and D. J. Randall. 1967. J. Exp. Biol. 46:307.
[93] Stowe, C. M., and A. L. Good. 1960. Amer. J. Physiol. 198:987.
[94] Sturkie, P. D. 1965. Avian Physiology. Ed. 2. Bailliere, Tindall and Cassell, London. pp. 89-117.
[95] Sturkie, P. D., et al. 1953. Amer. J. Physiol. 174:405.
[96] Sudak, F. N. 1965. Comp. Biochem. Physiol. 14:689.
[97] Sulkin, N. M., and K. R. Brizzee. 1947. Proc. Soc. Exp. Biol. Med. 64:125.
[98] Thomas, R. G. 1966. Lovelace Found. At. Energy Comm. Rep. 91:7.
[99] Uranga, J. 1963. Acta Physiol. Lat. Amer. 13:177.
[100] Uranga, J. 1964. Ibid. 14:115.
[101] Uranga, J. 1967. Amer. J. Physiol. 213:1244.
[102] Van Citters, R. L. 1968. Comp. Biochem. Physiol. 24:1035.
[103] Van Citters, R. L., and J. E. Lasry. 1965. Folia Primatol. 3:13.
[104] Van Citters, R. L., et al. 1966. Science 152:384.
[105] Van Liere, E. J., et al. 1949. Ibid. 109:489.
[106] Vogel, J. A., and P. D. Sturkie. 1963. Ibid. 140:1404.
[107] Votaw, C. L., and E. W. Lauer. 1963. Exp. Neurol. 7:502.
[108] Weiss, H. S., et al. 1961. Amer. J. Physiol. 201:655.
[109] Werdegar, D., et al. 1964. J. Appl. Physiol. 19:519.
[110] White, F. N., and G. Ross. 1966. Amer. J. Physiol. 211:15.
[111] Wilhelmj, C. M., et al. 1951. Ibid. 166:296.
[112] Wilson, R. B., and T. J. Clarke. 1964. J. Amer. Vet. Med. Ass. 144:981.
[113] Woodbury, R. A., and B. E. Abreu. 1944. Amer. J. Physiol. 142:114.
[114] Woodbury, R. A., and W. F. Hamilton. 1937. Ibid. 119:663.
[115] Wykoff, M. H., and C. E. Short. 1969. Amer. J. Vet. Res. 30:73.

233. VENOUS BLOOD PRESSURE: MAN

Subjects were supine, breathing quietly (forced respiration, e.g., Valsalva's maneuver, profoundly influences venous pressure). Reference level was the phlebostatic axis. Values in parentheses are ranges, estimate "c" (*see* Introduction).

	Vein	Specification	Blood Pressure mm H_2O		Vein	Specification	Blood Pressure mm H_2O
1	Median basilic	At elbow: 3-5 yr old	46(30-63)	6	Abdominal	....	115(70-160)
2		5-10 yr old	58(33-74)	7	Femoral	....	111(98-128)
3		adult ♂	100(50-140)	8	Great saphenous	At ankle	150(110-190)
4		♀	94(60-128)	9	Dorsal pedal	....	175(124-210)
5	Dorsal metacarpal	....	130(70-170)				

Contributor: Braunwald, Eugene

Reference: Burch, G. E. 1972. A Primer of Venous Pressure. C. C. Thomas, Springfield, Ill.

234. CAPILLARY BLOOD PRESSURE: VERTEBRATES

All measurements were made at the microscopic level. **Method:** DC = direct cannulation [6]; OT = osmotic transients [14]; CT = capillary tonometry [1] with in vivo transparent chamber technique. Values in parentheses are ranges, estimate "c" (*see* Introduction).

	Species [1]	Condition	Tissue	Method	Capillary Pressure, cm H_2O Arteriolar	Venous	Reference
1	*Homo sa-*	Normal	Skin, base of fingernail	DC	43.5(28.6-65.0)[2]	16.5(8.0-24.5)[2]	8,10
2	*piens*	Hyperemic	Skin, base of fingernail	DC	86.0(71.0-93.0)	(54.5-66.5)	10
3		Hypertensive	Skin, base of fingernail	DC	48.5(10.1-95.1)	30.8(12.8-58.0)	4
4	*Cavia por-cellus*	Decerebrate; anesthetized with barbital & diethyl ether	Mesentery	DC	38.5(31.0-49.0)	17.0(13.0-19.5)	7,10
5	*Leporidae* [3]	Anesthetized with pentobarbital sodium	Omentum	DC, OT	27.0(25.0-40.0)	22.0(16.0-25.0)	5,14
6	*Rattus* sp.	....	Skin	CT	24.0(20.0-27.0)	13.0(10.0-17.0)	1
7		Anesthetized with 5-*sec*-butyl-5-ethyl-2-thiobarbituric acid [4]	Kidney Glomerular capillaries	DC	60.1(49.0-78.0)	....	2
8			Efferent capillaries	DC	14.9(9.0-25.0)	9.2(5.0-15.0)	15
9		Anesthetized with urethan	Striated muscle	DC, OT	31.0(25.0-34.0)	17.0(15.0-25.0)	11
10		Decerebrate	Mesentery	DC	30.0(22.0-34.0)	17.0(15.0-20.0)	13
11	*Bufo bufo* [5]	Anesthetized with Novonal	Mesentery	DC	27.5(23.7-37.5)	21.0(14.0-22.0)	13
12	*Rana* sp.	Normal; anesthetized with urethan	Striated muscle	DC	14.9(11.0-18.0)	9.5(7.0-12.7)	9,10
13			Web	DC	13.9(10.0-19.0)	9.6(8.5-13.0)	7,8
14		Normal; curarized	Web	DC	14.5(10.0-20.5)	10.0(8.5-15.5)	10
15		Hyperemic	Mesentery	DC	17.5(12.0-24.0)	9.5(6.0-12.0)	3
16			Striated muscle	DC	20.1(17.0-26.0)	16.0(12.0-17.5)	10
17			Web	DC	19.5(14.0-26.5)	16.5(15.0-17.5)	10
18		Pithed	Mesentery	DC	14.4(5.0-22.0)	10.1(6.7-18.0)	6,10,12

[1] Unless otherwise indicated. [2] Varies directly with arteriolar vasodilation produced by emotion, heat, or trauma and with venous pressure as affected by hydrostatic pressure or venous obstruction; varies inversely with arteriolar vasoconstriction produced by emotion or cold; varies minimally in a single capillary with time, and also from capillary to capillary. [3] Family. [4] Synonym: Inactin. [5] Synonym: *B. vulgaris*.

Contributors: Intaglietta, M.; Griffith, J. Q., Jr.; Mendlowitz, Milton, and Naftchi, N. Eric.

continued

References

[1] Algire, G. H. 1953. J. Nat. Cancer Inst. 14:865.

[2] Brenner, B. M., et al. 1971. J. Clin. Invest. 50:1776.

[3] Brown, E., and E. M. Landis. 1947. Amer. J. Physiol. 149:302.

[4] Eichna, L. W., and J. Bordley, III. 1942. J. Clin. Invest. 21:711.

[5] Intaglietta, M., et al. 1970. Microvasc. Res. 2:212.

[6] Landis, E. M. 1926. Amer. J. Physiol. 75:548.

[7] Landis, E. M. 1930. Ibid. 93:353.

[8] Landis, E. M. 1930. Heart 15:209.

[9] Landis, E. M. 1931. Amer. J. Physiol. 98:704.

[10] Landis, E. M. 1934. Physiol. Rev. 14:404.

[11] Smaje, L., et al. 1970. Microvasc. Res. 2:96.

[12] Wiederhielm, C. A., et al. 1964. Amer. J. Physiol. 207:173.

[13] Wind, F. 1937. Naunyn Schmiedebergs Arch. Exp. Pathol. Pharmakol. 186:161.

[14] Zweifach, B. W., and M. Intaglietta. 1968. Microvasc. Res. 1:83.

[15] Brenner, B. M., et al. 1972. Amer. J. Physiol. 222:246.

235. NERVOUS CONTROL OF THE CARDIOVASCULAR SYSTEM: VERTEBRATES

Symbols: ↑ = increase; ↓ = decrease

	Receptor		Afferent Nerve	Effective Stimulus	Response		Reference
	Type	Location			Cardiovascular	Pulmonary	
1	Systemic arterial pressure receptors	Carotid sinus	Branch of glossopharyngeal	↑ in transmural pressure	Bradycardia; large ↓ in peripheral resistance, both skin & muscle; small ↓ in venous tone, ↓ in splanchnic venous tone; ↑ in coronary resistance	Slowing or arrest of breathing	3,5,19,22, 23,25, 35,36
2		Aortic arch & branches	Aortic depressor branches of the vagus	↑ in transmural pressure (higher range than carotid sinus?)	Same as above plus ↓ in cardiac contractility	Slowing or arrest of breathing	29
3		Coronary arteries	Vagus	Large ↑ in transmural pressure	Small ↓ in blood pressure; heart rate unchanged	Uncertain	7
4				Coronary artery occlusion	↓ in blood pressure; ↓ in peripheral resistance (not cholinergic)	Uncertain	15
5			Cardiac sympathetic	↑ in transmural pressure, coronary sinus occlusion, ? myocardial ischemia	Uncertain	Uncertain	8
6		Mesenteric arteries (Pacinian corpuscles)	Splanchnic	↑ in transmural pressure	Uncertain	Uncertain	20
7		Thoracic aorta	Dorsal roots of thoracic 1-12	↑ in transmural pressure	Peripheral vasodilation	Uncertain	21
8	Systemic arterial chemoreceptors	Carotid body	Branch of glossopharyngeal	Asphyxia; anoxia; hypercapnia; acidemia	Complex primary bradycardia in animals, primary tachycardia in man; modest, variable venoconstriction; ↑ in peripheral resistance; tachycardia due to hyperventilation & central sympathetic stimulation	Tachypnea; ↑ in tidal volume	6,9,11,12, 16-18,37

continued

	Receptor		Afferent Nerve	Effective Stimulus	Response		Reference
	Type	Location			Cardiovascular	Pulmonary	
9		Aortic body	Aortic nerves and/or vagus	Asphyxia; anoxia; hypercapnia; acidemia	Primary tachycardia; ↑ in cardiac contractility & peripheral resistance	Tachypnea	14,16,37, 42
10	Cardiac mechanoreceptors Low pressure	Left atrium & pulmonary veins	Vagus	↑ in transmural pressure	Tachycardia without ↑ in contractility; diuresis; no change in peripheral vascular resistance	None?	10,27,28
11		Right atrium & venae cavae	Vagus	↑ in transmural pressure	Tachycardia; diuresis	Uncertain	2,24
12	High pressure	Left ventricular epi- & myocardium	Vagus, with C fibers	↑ in wall tension & contractility; coronary venous occlusion; extrasystoles; digitalis; hemorrhage	Bradycardia; hypotension; cholinergic arterial dilation; vomiting	Hypopnea	4,31-33, 38-41,43
13		Right ventricle	Vagus, myelinated	↑ in transmural pressure	Uncertain	Uncertain	34
14	Pulmonary arterial pressure receptors	Bifurcation of main pulmonary artery	Vagus	↑ in transmural pressure	Blood pressure changes variable	Hypopnea	13
15	Voluntary muscle receptors	Muscle, receptors uncertain	Somatic nerves	Static contraction	↑ in blood pressure & heart rate	Hyperpnea	1,30
16	Bronchial stretch receptors	Tracheal large bronchi	Vagus	↑ in transbronchial pressure	Tachycardia, peripheral vasodilation	Tachypnea, ↓ in tidal volume	9
17	Snout or beak receptors	Nose, beak, or snout	Trigeminal	Immersion, smoke	Variable bradycardia depending on species; vasoconstriction	Apnea or hypopnea	26,43

Contributor: Sleight, Peter

References

[1] Alam, M., and F. H. Smirk. 1937. J. Physiol. (London) 89:372.

[2] Aviado, D. M., et al. 1951. Amer. J. Physiol. 165: 261.

[3] Beiser, G. D., et al. 1970. J. Clin. Invest. 49:225.

[4] Bergel, D. H., and G. S. Makin. 1967. Cardiovasc. Res. 1:80.

[5] Brender, D., and M. M. Webb-Peploe. 1969. J. Physiol. (London) 205:257.

[6] Bristow, J. D., et al. 1971. Ibid. 216:281.

[7] Brown, A. M. 1966. Ibid. 184:825.

[8] Brown, A. M., and A. Malliani. 1971. Ibid. 212:685.

[9] Browse, N. L., and J. T. Shepherd. 1966. Amer. J. Physiol. 210:1435.

[10] Carswell, F., et al. 1970. J. Physiol. (London) 207:1.

[11] Chalmers, J. P., et al. 1967. Ibid. 188:435.

[12] Chalmers, J. P., et al. 1967. Ibid. 192:537.

[13] Coleridge, J. G., and C. Kidd. 1961. Ibid. 158:197.

[14] Comroe, J. H., Jr., and L. Mortimer. 1964. J. Pharmacol. Exp. Ther. 146:33.

[15] Constantin, L. 1963. Amer. J. Cardiol. 11:205.

[16] Daly, M. D., and B. H. Robinson. 1968. J. Physiol. (London) 195:387.

[17] Dawes, G. S., and J. H. Comroe. 1954. Physiol. Rev. 34:167.

[18] Downing, S. E. 1966. Proc. Int. Symp. Cardiovasc. Resp. Eff. Hypoxia, 1965, p. 208.

[19] Feigl, E. O. 1968. Circ. Res. 23:223.

[20] Gammon, G. D., and D. W. Bronk. 1935. Amer. J. Physiol. 114:77.

[21] Gruhzit, C. C., et al. 1953. J. Pharmacol. Exp. Ther. 109:261.

[22] Hadjiminas, J., and B. Öberg. 1968. Acta Physiol. Scand. 72:518.

[23] Intersociety Symposium on Active Neurogenic Vasodilatation. 1966. Fed. Proc. Fed. Amer. Soc. Exp. Biol. 25:1583, 1593, 1596, 1607, 1611, 1618.

[24] Kappagoda, C. T., et al. 1971. J. Physiol. (London) 235:493.

[25] Kedzi, P. 1965. Baroreceptors and Hypertension. Pergamon Press, Oxford.

[26] Korner, P. 1971. Physiol. Rev. 51:312.

[27] Ledsome, J., and R. Hainsworth. 1970. Resp. Physiol. 9:86.

[28] Ledsome, J., and R. J. Linden. 1968. J. Physiol. (London) 198:487.

continued

[29] Levy, N. M., et al. 1966. Circ. Res. 19:930.

[30] Lind, A. R., et al. 1968. Clin. Sci. 35:45.

[31] Muers, M. F., and P. Sleight. 1972. J. Physiol. (London) 221:259.

[32] Muers, M. F., and P. Sleight. 1972. Ibid. 221:283.

[33] Öberg, B., and S. White. 1970. Acta Physiol. Scand. 80:383.

[34] Paintal, A. S. 1955. Quart. J. Exp. Physiol. Cog. Med. Sci. 40:348.

[35] Ross, J. R., et al. 1961. Circ. Res. 9:75.

[36] Ross, J. R., et al. 1961. J. Clin. Invest. 40:563.

[37] Sagawa, K. 1969. Annu. Rev. Physiol. 31:295.

[38] Salisbury, P. F., et al. 1960. Circ. Res. 8:530.

[39] Sleight, P. 1964. J. Physiol. (London) 173:321.

[40] Sleight, P., and J. G. Widdicombe. 1965. Ibid. 181:235.

[41] Sleight, P., et al. 1969. Circ. Res. 25:705.

[42] Stern, S., and E. Rapaport. 1967. Ibid. 20:214.

[43] Thoren, P. 1972. M.D. Thesis, Goteborg, Sweden.

[44] White, S. W., and D. L. Franklin. 1970. Proc. Aust. Physiol. Pharmacol. Soc. 1:51.

236. ELECTRICAL PROPERTIES OF CARDIAC TISSUE: VERTEBRATES

Part I. Action Potentials of Single Fibers

Resting and action potential values (which are negative for the inside of the fiber) were obtained by direct measurement with an intracellular microelectrode filled with $3M$ potassium chloride. Extracellular potassium concentration ranged from 2.7 to 5.4 mM. Due to technical difficulties in measuring small fibers, low values for resting and action potential should be used with caution. Values for other properties were obtained with two intracellular or extra-cellular recording electrodes. Action potential duration values convey the order of magnitude only, since duration varies markedly with change in frequency of contraction. For general information on conduction velocity, consult reference 23. **Fiber Diameter:** Values in brackets are for fiber diameters determined from formalin-fixed paraffin sections [6]. Values in parentheses are ranges, estimate "c" unless otherwise indicated (see Introduction).

	Species	Tissue	Technique	No. of Observations[1]	Fiber Diameter μ	Property	Value	Reference
1	*Homo sapiens*	Atrium	In vitro	4-5[2]	....	Resting potential, mV	58	22
2						Action potential, mV	75	
3		At 27°C	In vitro	124[2]	10	Resting potential, mV	(60-75)	30
4						Action potential, mV	92(80-101)	
5		Ventricle	In situ	.....	....	Resting potential, mV	65	45
6						Action potential, mV	95	
7						Action potential duration, ms	200	
8				.....	....	Resting potential, mV	(40-90)	1
9				340	16	Resting potential, mV	73	1,36
10						Action potential, mV	94	
11				5	16	Resting potential, mV	65	45
12						Action potential, mV	95	
13						Action potential duration, ms	200	
14			In vitro	24	16	Resting potential, mV	87(71-95)	34
15						Action potential, mV	115(92-125)	
16						Conduction velocity, m/s	1.3	
17	Embryo, 7-12 wk	Atrium	In vitro	37[2]	....	Resting potential, mV	(70-85)	37
18						Action potential, mV	90(80-104)	
19		Ventricle	In vitro	37[2]	....	Resting potential, mV	(70-85)	37
20						Action potential, mV	110(95-120)	
21	*Canis familiaris*	Atrium	In situ	100	10 [10]	Resting potential, mV	85(68-94)	12
22						Action potential, mV	100(82-118)[b]	
23		At 35-37°C	....	.....	....	Action potential duration, ms	(100-200)	31
24			In vitro	50	10 [10]	Resting potential, mV	83(70-94)	
25						Action potential, mV	100(86-119)	

[1] Unless otherwise indicated.　[2] Number of hearts.

continued

Part I. Action Potentials of Single Fibers

	Species	Tissue	Technique	No. of Observations	Fiber Diameter μ	Property	Value	Reference
26		At 37-38°C	....	.....	....	Action potential duration, ms	250	14
27						Conduction velocity, m/s	1.0	
28						Depolarization rate, max, V/s	>150	
29			In vitro	100	10 [10]	Resting potential, mV	85(68-95)	13
30						Action potential, mV	105(82-120)	
31		Ventricle	In situ	33	16 [11]	Resting potential, mV	82(76-96)	32
32						Action potential, mV	102(96-114)	
33		At 37-38°C	In situ	200	16 [11]	Resting potential, mV	80(65-95)[b]	12
34						Action potential, mV	100(80-120)[b]	
35				200	16 [11]	Action potential duration, ms	(300-500)	12,29
36						Upstroke duration, ms	2.0	
37						Conduction velocity, m/s	0.88(0.34-1.65)	
38						Depolarization rate, max, V/s	150	
39		Papillary muscle	In vitro	.....	....	Action potential duration, ms	250	14
40						Conduction velocity, m/s	1.0	
41						Depolarization rate, max, V/s	>150	
42				100	16 [11]	Resting potential, mV	85(70-95)	13
43						Action potential, mV	105(82-125)	
44		Purkinje fiber	In vitro	400	30 [22]	Resting potential, mV	89(86-92)[b]	33
45						Action potential, mV	121(117-125)[b]	
46						Action potential duration, ms	(250-400)	
47						Conduction velocity, m/s	2.5	
48		At 37-38°C	In vitro	312	30 [22]	Resting potential, mV	90(78-102)[b]	7
49						Action potential, mV	121	
50						Action potential duration, ms	300	
51						Upstroke duration, ms	0.5	
52						Conduction velocity, m/s	2.0(1.3-3.2)	
53						Depolarization rate, max, V/s	610	
54		Sinus, atrial; at 35-37°C	In vitro	.....	....	Resting potential, mV	75(65-80)	31
55						Action potential, mV	84(70-98)[b]	
56						Action potential duration, ms	300	
57	Capra hircus	Purkinje fiber, at 33.5°C	In vitro	57	75 [40]	Resting potential, mV	94(78-110)[b]	7
58						Action potential, mV	135(123-147)[b]	
59						Action potential duration, ms	(240-400)	
60						Upstroke duration, ms	0.5	
61						Conduction velocity, m/s	2.2(1.7-2.7)[b]	
62						Depolarization rate, max, V/s	800	
63	Cavia porcellus	Atrium	In situ	.....	....	Resting potential, mV	57	43,44
64						Action potential, mV	68	
65						Action potential duration, ms	(100-150)	
66		Ventricle	In vitro	241	[13]	Resting potential, mV	52.8	17
67						Action potential, mV	67.2	
68						Action potential duration, ms	(70-100)	
69	Felis catus	Atrium, at 37-38°C	In vitro	625	10 [10]	Resting potential, mV	60(36-91)	2
70						Action potential, mV	65(30-95)	

continued

Part I. Action Potentials of Single Fibers

	Species	Tissue	Technique	No. of Observations	Fiber Diameter μ	Property	Value	Reference
71						Action potential duration, ms	250	
72						Conduction velocity, m/s	0.3	
73		Ventricle	In situ	.....	16 [10]	Resting potential, mV	80(65-95)[b]	12
74						Action potential, mV	100(80-120)[b]	
75						Action potential duration, ms	(200-400)	
76		Papillary muscle, at 37-38°C	In vitro	160	16 [10]	Resting potential, mV	88(86.8-89.2)[b]	35
77						Action potential, mV	116(115-117)[b]	
78						Action potential duration, ms	(120-170)	
79						Upstroke duration, ms	1.1	
80						Conduction velocity, m/s	0.96(0.9-1.0)[b]	
81		Purkinje fiber, at 37°C	In vitro	.....	[13]	Resting potential, mV	96	32
82						Action potential, mV	121	
83	*Mus musculus*	Atrium	In vitro	64	[8]	Resting potential, mV	86(73-99)[b]	5
84						Action potential, mV	98(86-110)[b]	
85						Action potential duration, ms	30	
86	*Oryctolagus cuniculus*	Atrium	In vitro	.....	[11]	Resting potential, mV	78(70.2-85.8)[b]	42
87						Action potential, mV	92(83.6-100.4)[b]	
88						Action potential duration, ms	150	
89				.....	[11]	Depolarization rate, max, V/s	250	27
90				35	[11]	Resting potential, mV	73	20
91						Action potential, mV	89	
92						Action potential duration, ms	135	
93				30	[11]	Resting potential, mV	78	38
94						Action potential, mV	97	
95		Ventricle	In vitro	50	[11]	Resting potential, mV	80	3
96						Action potential, mV	108	
97		At 37°C	....	65	....	Resting potential, mV	82	10
98						Action potential, mV	115	
99		Sinoatrial node	In vitro	.....	....	Resting potential, mV	56	42
100						Action potential, mV	57	
101						Action potential duration, ms	(200-300)	
102				30	....	Resting potential, mV	66(51-74)	31
103						Action potential, mV	79(63-94)	
104				25	....	Resting potential, mV	61	20
105						Action potential, mV	66	
106						Action potential duration, ms	189	
107		& atrioventricular node	In vitro	.....	....	Depolarization rate, max, V/s	13	27
108	*Ovis aries; Bos* sp., calf	Purkinje fiber	In vitro	.....	60	Resting potential, mV	98(91-110)	40
109						Action potential, mV	132	
110						Action potential duration, ms	400	
111	*Rattus* sp.	Atrium	In vitro	876	[8]	Resting potential, mV	62(51-73)[b]	15
112						Action potential, mV	75.2(59.6-90.8)[b]	
113		Ventricle	In vitro	128	[9]	Resting potential, mV	83(65-101)[b]	26
114						Action potential, mV	101	

continued

Part I. Action Potentials of Single Fibers

	Species	Tissue	Technique	No. of Observations	Fiber Diameter μ	Property	Value	Reference
115	*Sus scrofa*	Ventricle	In vitro	100	....	Resting potential, mV	79	9
116						Action potential, mV	106	
117						Action potential duration, ms	327	
118						Depolarization rate, max, V/s	160	
119		Purkinje fiber	In vitro	100	....	Resting potential, mV	85	9
120						Action potential, mV	123	
121						Action potential duration, ms	467	
122						Depolarization rate, max, V/s	650	
123	*Gallus gallus* [3],	Atrium, 7-da	In situ	44	....	Resting potential, mV	29.2(10-41)	8
124	embryo	embryo				Action potential, mV	39.2(11-81)	
125						Action potential duration, ms	50(30-70)[b]	
126		Ventricle, 7-da	In situ	195	....	Resting potential, mV	39.3(10-70)	8
127		embryo				Action potential, mV	53.5(13-100)	
128						Action potential duration, ms	120(100-400	
129		Heart cells, tissue	In vitro	45	....	Resting potential, mV	65	19
130		culture				Action potential, mV	85	
131				30	....	Resting potential, mV	63	4
132						Action potential, mV	90	
133						Action potential duration, ms	140	
134	Turtle	Atrium	In situ	10	....	Resting potential, mV	56(50-63)	28
135						Action potential, mV	65(55-90)	
136						Action potential duration, ms	(400-700)	
137		Ventricle	....	.....	....	Action potential duration, ms	(600-1400)	28
138			In vitro	.....	....	Resting potential, mV	85	41
139						Action potential, mV	110	
140	Frog	Atrium	In vitro	50	5	Resting potential, mV	75	11
141		Ventricle	....	.....	....	Action potential duration, ms	760	25
142						Depolarization rate, max, V/s	57	
143			In situ,	239	10	Resting potential, mV	64.5(27-112)	8,46
144			in vitro			Action potential, mV	77.2(30-132)	
145				150	10	Resting potential, mV	58.4(40-80)	18
146						Action potential, mV	74.2(50-110)	
147			In vitro	38	5	Resting potential, mV	84.5	24
148						Action potential, mV	123	
149						Action potential duration, ms	600	
150				485	10	Resting potential, mV	84.5(77-89)	39
151						Action potential, mV	102.5(95-112)	
152		At 18-19°C	....	.....	....	Upstroke duration, ms	7.4	2,21
153						Conduction velocity, m/s	0.174	
154						Depolarization rate, max, V/s	10	
155		Sinus venosus	In vitro	.....	....	Resting potential, mV	(45-60)	16
156						Action potential, mV	(50-70)	
157						Action potential duration, ms	(400-600)	

[3] Synonym: *G. domesticus.*

continued

Part I. Action Potentials of Single Fibers

	Species	Tissue	Technique	No. of Observations	Fiber Diameter μ	Property	Value	Reference
158		Truncus arteriosus	In situ	.....	....	Resting potential, mV	95	43,44
159						Action potential, mV	125	
160						Action potential duration, ms	560	

Contributors: Weidmann, Silvio; Trautwein, Wolfgang

References

[1] Bromberger-Barnea, B., et al. 1959. Circ. Res. 7: 138.

[2] Burgen, A. S. V., and K. G. Terroux. 1953. J. Physiol. (London) 119:139.

[3] Cranefield, P. F., and B. F. Hoffman. 1958. Physiol. Rev. 38:41.

[4] DeHaan, R. L., and S. H. Gottlieb. 1968. J. Gen. Physiol. 52:643.

[5] Draper, M. H., and J. F. Lamb. Unpublished. Poultry Research Centre, Edinburgh, Scotland, 1959.

[6] Draper, M. H., and M. Mya-Tu. 1959. Quart. J. Exp. Physiol. 44:91.

[7] Draper, M. H., and S. Weidmann. 1951. J. Physiol. (London) 115:74.

[8] Fingl, E., et al. 1952. J. Pharmacol. Exp. Ther. 104:103.

[9] Gettes, L. S., and B. Surawicz. 1968. Circ. Res. 23: 717.

[10] Gettes, L. S., et al. 1962. Amer. J. Physiol. 203: 1135.

[11] Haas, H. G., et al. 1966. Pfluegers Arch. Gesamte Physiol. Menschen Tiere 288:43.

[12] Hoffman, B. F., and E. E. Suckling. 1952. Amer. J. Physiol. 170:357.

[13] Hoffman, B. F., and E. E. Suckling. 1953. Ibid. 173:312.

[14] Hoffman, B. F., and E. E. Suckling. 1954. Ibid. 179:123.

[15] Hollander, P. B., and J. L. Webb. 1955. Circ. Res. 3:604.

[16] Hutter, O. F., and W. Trautwein. 1956. J. Gen. Physiol. 39:715.

[17] Johnson, E. A. 1956. J. Pharmacol. Exp. Ther. 117:237.

[18] Kleinfeld, M., et al. 1954. Circ. Res. 2:488.

[19] Lieberman, M. 1967. Ibid. 21:879.

[20] Marshall, J. M. 1957. Ibid. 5:664.

[21] Meda, E. 1955. Arch. Fisiol. 55:298.

[22] Meda, E., et al. 1960. Boll. Soc. Ital. Biol. Sper. 36:1868.

[23] Mya-Tu, M. 1957. J. Exp. Med. Sci. (Calcutta) 1: 99.

[24] Niedergenke, R., and R. K. Orkand. 1966. J. Physiol. (London) 184:291.

[25] Niedergenke, R., and R. K. Orkand. 1966. Ibid. 184:312.

[26] Otsuka, M., and H. P. Gurtner. 1957. Helv. Physiol. Pharmacol. Acta 15:73.

[27] Paes de Carvalho, A., et al. 1969. J. Gen. Physiol. 54:607.

[28] Sano, T., et al. 1956. Circ. Res. 4:444.

[29] Schaefer, H., and W. Trautwein. 1949. Pfluegers Arch. Gesamte Physiol. Menschen Tiere 251:417.

[30] Sleator, W., and T. de Gubareff. 1964. Amer. J. Physiol. 206:1000.

[31] Trautwein, W., and J. Dudel. 1958. Pfluegers Arch. Gesamte Physiol. Menschen Tiere 266:653.

[32] Trautwein, W., and K. Zink. 1952. Ibid. 256:68.

[33] Trautwein, W., et al. 1953. Ibid. 258:243.

[34] Trautwein, W., et al. 1962. Circ. Res. 10:306.

[35] Trautwein, W., et al. 1964. Pfluegers Arch. Gesamte Physiol. Menschen Tiere 260:40.

[36] Truex, R. C., and W. M. Copenhaver. 1947. Amer. J. Anat. 80:173.

[37] Tuganowski, W., and A. Cekanski. 1971. Pfluegers Arch. 323:21.

[38] Vaughan Williams, E. M. 1958. J. Physiol. (London) 140:327.

[39] Ware, F., Jr., et al. 1957. Amer. J. Physiol. 190: 194.

[40] Weidmann, S. 1955. J. Physiol. (London) 129:568.

[41] Weidmann, S. 1956. Ibid. 132:157.

[42] West, T. C. 1955. J. Pharmacol. Exp. Ther. 115:283.

[43] Woodbury, J. W., and A. J. Brady. 1956. Science 123:100.

[44] Woodbury, J. W., and A. J. Brady. Unpublished. Univ. Washington, School Medicine, Seattle, 1958.

[45] Woodbury, J. W., et al. 1957. Circ. Res. 5:179.

[46] Woodbury, L. A., et al. 1951. Amer. J. Physiol. 164:307.

continued

Part II. Electrical Constants of Fiber Tissue

Values for atrial and ventricular tissue were obtained by making current pulses flow through extracellular electrodes and measuring potential changes by means of intracellular electrodes. With Purkinje fibers from ungulates (goat and sheep), and with tissue cultures, one intracellular microelectrode provided the polarizing pulse while a second intracellular electrode recorded the change of membrane potential at various distances. λ = space constant. R_m = membrane resistance of 1 cm². C_m = membrane capacitance/cm². Specific membrane capacitance (C_m) and resistance (R_m) were usually calculated on the assumption that the "fibers" in question are circular cylinders. This procedure is reasonable in the case of atrial and ventricular tissue, but misleading in the case of Purkinje fibers of ungulates. On the grounds of morphometric data it is concluded that Purkinje cells making up a "fiber" have a specific membrane capacitance of about 1 μF/cm², and a specific resistance of 20,000 ohm·cm² [6]. T_m = membrane time constant. R_i = specific resistance of the intracellular compartment as measured in a longitudinal direction. All authors have made assumptions rather than measurements of either R_i or membrane surface. It would be misleading, therefore, to indicate a range or a standard error.

	Species	Fiber Tissue	No. of Observations	Fiber Diameter μ	λ mm	R_m ohm·cm²	C_m μF/cm²	T_m ms	R_i ohm·cm	Reference
1	*Canis familiaris*	Ventricular trabecula	5	16	1.35	....	....	2.0	....	5
2		False tendon	....	30	1.25	8900	1.68	15.0	168	7
3		Papillary muscle	....	16	1.18	5300	0.6	3.2	60	7
4		Right atrium	....	12	1.24	5600	2.61	14.6	261	7
5	*Capra hircus*	Purkinje fiber	8	75	1.9	2000	12.4	19.5	105	8
6	*Oryctolagus cuniculus*	Crista terminalis	10	....	0.99	....	1.31	3.0	....	1
7		Right atrium	10	....	0.66	3000	1.27	2.7	....	1
8		Sinoatrial node	10	2-8	0.47	....	....	....	....	2
9	*Ovis aries*	Ventricular trabecula	9	15	0.96	9100	0.81	4.4	470	9
10		Purkinje fiber	6	....	2.2	....	....	24.1	....	1
11			5	120	2.4	1400	12.0; 3.1	17	140	3
12	*Rattus* sp.	Tissue culture monolayer	25	....	0.36	1300-2600	1.3	....	502	4

Contributor: Weidmann, Silvio

References

[1] Bonke, F. I. M. 1973. Pfluegers Arch. 339:1.

[2] Bonke, F. I. M. 1973. Ibid. 339:16.

[3] Dominguez, G., and H. Fozzard. 1970. Circ. Res. 24:565.

[4] Jongsma, H. J., and H. E. von Rijn. 1972. J. Membr. Biol. 9:341.

[5] Kamiyama, A., and K. Matsuda. 1966. Jap. J. Physiol. 16:407.

[6] Mobley, B. A., and E. Page. 1972. J. Physiol. (London) 220:547.

[7] Sakamoto, Y., and M. Goto. 1970. Jap. J. Physiol. 20:30.

[8] Weidmann, S. 1952. J. Physiol. (London) 118:348.

[9] Weidmann, S. 1970. Ibid. 210:1041.

237. EVENTS DURING CARDIAC CYCLE: MAN AND DOG

Phases occurring in the right ventricle correspond to those in the left ventricle, but are asynchronous [6,13,23,31]: right atrial contraction generally precedes left atrial contraction; right ventricular contraction begins after left ventricular contraction; right ventricle has a shorter isovolumic contraction phase and begins to eject before the left ventricle; right ventricular ejection ends after left ventricular ejection; tricuspid valve opening usually occurs slightly before mitral valve opening. The schematic presentation of the left ventricular cardiac cycle does not show the exact

continued

duration of events. Left ventricular pressure exceeds aortic pressure only during the initial 45% of the ejection period [33]. The aortic valve actually closes 5-15 ms before the incisura and the aortic component of the second heart sound [25].

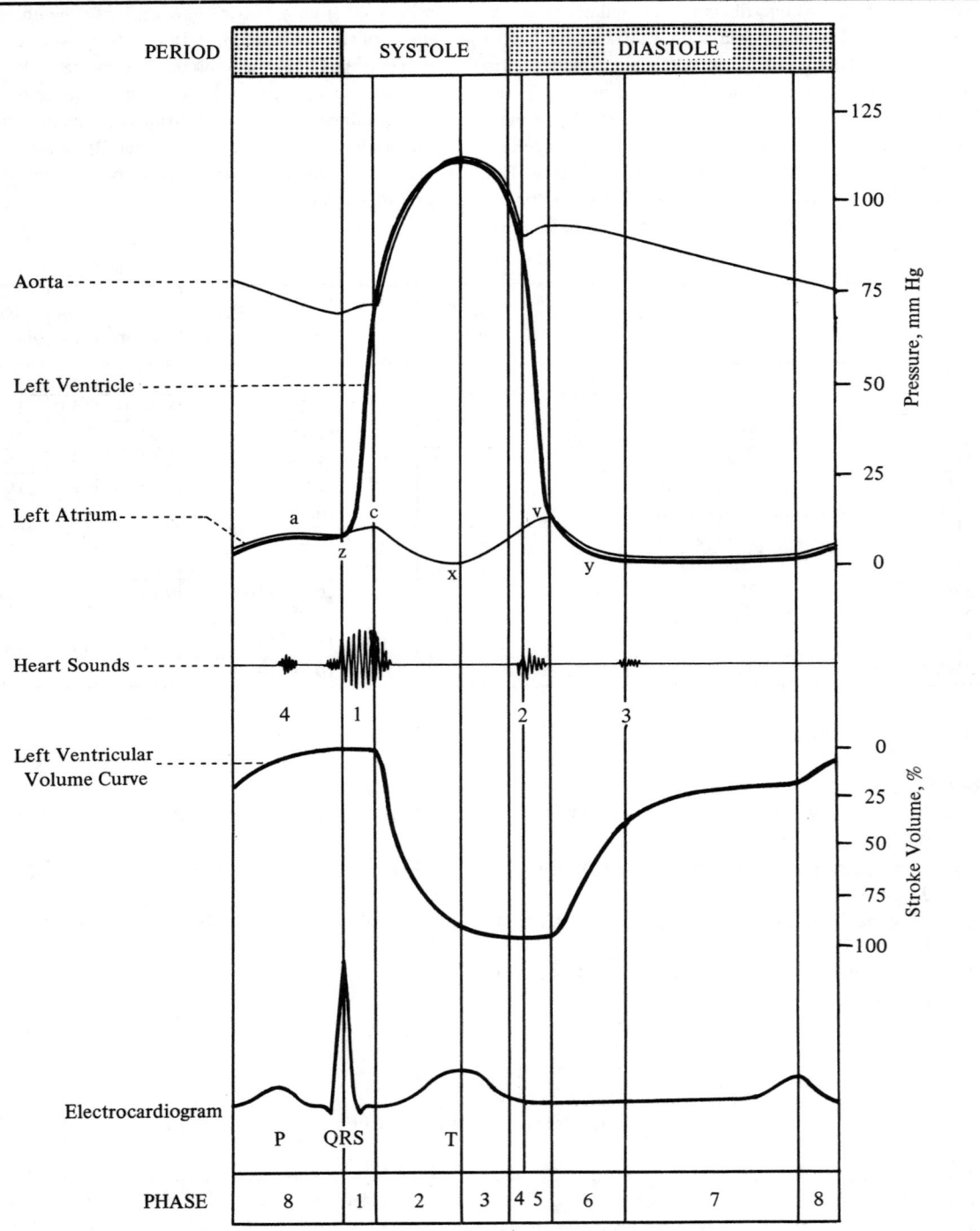

continued

Phase Duration for an assumed heart rate of 75 beats/min was obtained by extrapolation from the data: for man, from references 3,5,6,9,10,13,17,20,21,29,31,36,37,42,45; and for dog, from references 2,7,19-21,24,28,36,39,47-51.

Duration of individual phases varies with species and sex [24,40,45,46], age [12,15,17,53], heart rate [3,5,7,10,12,14-17, 19-23,26-28,30,34,35,39,40-42,44-52], posture [24], activity [4,10], preload [7,14,19-21,28-30,36,39,40,42,45,47-51], afterload [2,7,16,19-21,26,28-30,32,38-40,42,45,47-51], contractility [2,7,8,10,11,16,18,19,26-30,39-45,50,51], ventricular excitation sequence [1], time of day [40,46], and technique of measurement [18,22,34,35,46].

	Phase	Event at Onset of Phase	Main Event During Phase	Event at End of Phase	Phase Duration s	
					Man	Dog
1	Isovolumic contraction [L]	Onset of left ventricular contraction	Rapid rise of left ventricular pressure with no volume change	Opening of aortic valve	0.06	0.05
2	Maximum ejection	Opening of aortic valve	Rapid outflow of blood from left ventricle	Peak left ventricular pressure	0.12	0.10
3	Reduced ejection	Peak left ventricular pressure	Decreasing outflow of blood from left ventricle	End of left ventricular ejection	0.14	0.12
4	Protodiastole	End of left ventricular ejection	Rapid decrease in left ventricular pressure	Closure of aortic valve	0.03	0.02
5	Isovolumic relaxation [L]	Closure of aortic valve	Continued relaxation of left ventricle, with no volume change	Opening of mitral valve	0.09	0.05
6	Rapid inflow	Opening of mitral valve	Rapid flow of blood from left atrium to left ventricle	Slowing of inflow from left atrium to left ventricle	0.09	0.06
7	Diastasis	Slowing of inflow from left atrium to left ventricle	Continued slower flow from left atrium to left ventricle	Onset of left atrial contraction	0.16	0.29
8	Atrial systole	Onset of left atrial contraction	Increased flow from left atrium to left ventricle	End of left atrial contraction and onset of left ventricular contraction	0.11	0.11

[L] Isovolumic = isovolumetric = isometric = isochoric.

Contributor: Schlant, Robert C.

References

[1] Adolph, R. J., et al. 1969. Amer. Heart J. 78:585.

[2] Agress, C. M., and S. Wegner. 1968. Jap. Heart J. 9: 169.

[3] Agress, C. M., et al. 1965. Ibid. 6:497.

[4] Aronow, W. S. 1970. Amer. J. Cardiol. 26:235.

[5] Braunwald, E., et al. 1955. J. Appl. Physiol. 8:309.

[6] Braunwald, E., et al. 1956. Circ. Res. 4:100.

[7] Braunwald, E., et al. 1958. Ibid. 6:319.

[8] Büyüköztürk, K., et al. 1971. Amer. J. Cardiol. 28: 183.

[9] Coblentz, B., et al. 1947. Brit. Heart J. 11:1.

[10] Frank, M. N., and W. B. Kinlaw. 1962. Amer. J. Cardiol. 10:800.

[11] Garrard, C. L., Jr., et al. 1970. Circulation 42:455.

[12] Golde, D., and L. Burstin. 1970. Ibid. 42:1029.

[13] Gribbe, P., et al. 1958. Cardiologia 33:293.

[14] Harley, A., et al. 1969. J. Clin. Invest. 48:895.

[15] Harris, L. C., et al. 1964. Amer. J. Cardiol. 14:448.

[16] Harris, W. S., et al. 1967. J. Clin. Invest. 46:1704.

[17] Harrison, T. R., et al. 1964. Amer. Heart J. 67:189.

[18] Jezek, V. 1963. Cardiologia 43:298.

[19] Katz, L. N. 1921. J. Lab. Clin. Med. 6:291.

[20] Katz, L. N., and H. S. Feil. 1923. Arch. Intern. Med. 32:672.

[21] Katz, L. N., and H. S. Feil. 1925. Heart 12:171.

[22] Kumar, S., and D. H. Spodick. 1970. Amer. Heart J. 80:401.

[23] Leighton, R. F., et al. 1971. Amer. J. Cardiol. 27: 66.

[24] Lombard, W. P., and O. M. Cope. 1926. Amer. J. Physiol. 77:263.

[25] MacCanon, D. M., et al. 1964. Circ. Res. 14:387.

[26] Metzger, C. C., et al. 1970. Amer. J. Cardiol. 25: 434.

[27] Pouget, J. M., et al. 1971. Circulation 43:289.

[28] Remington, J. W., et al. 1948. Amer. J. Physiol. 154:6.

[29] Sambhi, M. P. 1960. Amer. J. Cardiol. 6:1042.

[30] Sawayama, T., et al. 1969. Circulation 40:327.

[31] Schlant, R. C. 1974. In J. W. Hurst, R. B. Logue, R. C. Schlant, and N. K. Wenger, ed. The Heart. Ed. 3. McGraw-Hill, New York. p. 79.

continued

[32] Shaver, J. A., et al. 1968. J. Clin. Invest. 47:217.

[33] Spencer, M. P., and F. C. Greiss. 1962. Circ. Res. 10:274.

[34] Spodick, D. H., and S. Kumar. 1968. Amer. Heart J. 76:70.

[35] Spodick, D. H., and S. Kumar. 1968. Ibid. 76:498.

[36] Sutton, G. C., et al. 1962. Amer. J. Med. Sci. 242: 323.

[37] Tafur, E., et al. 1964. Circulation 30:381.

[38] Tarazi, R. C., et al. 1969. Dis. Chest 55:214.

[39] Wallace, A. G., et al. 1963. Circ. Res. 12:611.

[40] Weissler, A. M., and C. L. Garrard, Jr. 1971. Mod. Concepts Cardiovasc. Dis. 40:1.

[41] Weissler, A. M., and C. D. Schoenfeld. 1970. Amer. J. Med. Sci. 259:4.

[42] Weissler, A. M., et al. 1961. Amer. Heart J. 62:367.

[43] Weissler, A. M., et al. 1964. Circulation 29:721.

[44] Weissler, A. M., et al. 1965. Amer. J. Cardiol. 15: 153.

[45] Weissler, A. M., et al. 1968. Circulation 37:149.

[46] Weissler, A. M., et al. 1969. Amer. J. Cardiol. 23: 577.

[47] Wiggers, C. J. 1921. Amer. J. Physiol. 56:415, 439.

[48] Wiggers, C. J. 1923. Circulation in Health and Disease. Lea and Febiger, Philadelphia.

[49] Wiggers, C. J. 1928. Pressure Pulses in the Cardiovascular System. Longmans, Green; New York.

[50] Wiggers, C. J. 1949. Physiology in Health and Disease. Ed. 5. Lea and Febiger, Philadelphia.

[51] Wiggers, C. J. 1952. Circulatory Dynamics: Physiologic Studies. Grune and Stratton, New York.

[52] Willems, J., and H. Kesteloot. 1967. Acta Cardiol. 22:401.

[53] Willems, J. L., et al. 1970. Circulation 42:37.

238. RELATION OF HEART SOUNDS TO CARDIAC CYCLE: MAN

Heart Sound: Designations are those of the Committee on Standardized Terminology [1]. Values in parentheses are ranges, estimate "c" unless otherwise indicated (*see* Introduction).

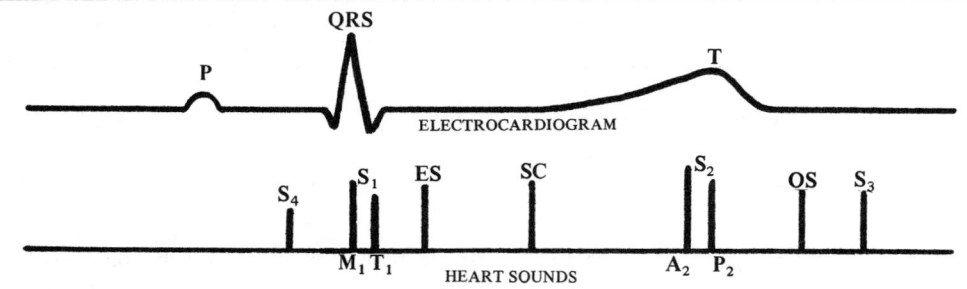

	Heart Sound	Timing	Mechanism	Remarks
1	S$_4$ (Fourth heart sound)	Left side: 0.17(0.12-0.24) s after onset of P wave Right side: 0.12(0.09-0.16) s after onset of P wave [13]	Occurs within cavity of left or right ventricle during atrial contribution to ventricular filling	Most commonly present in diseases associated with decreased ventricular compliance, such as systemic or pulmonary hypertension, aortic or pulmonic stenosis, etc. May be present in normal subjects, particularly adults beyond middle age.
2	S$_1$ (First heart sound) M$_1$ (Mitral component)	0.06(0.05-0.09) s after onset of QRS	Believed to be related to sequential closure of mitral & tricuspid valves	Normally may be either single or split
3	T$_1$ (Tricuspid component)	0.09(0.08-0.13) s after onset of QRS [4,11]		
4	ES (Ejection sound) Aortic	0.12(0.06-0.16) s after onset of QRS; 0.06(0.02-0.07) s after onset of S$_1$ [12]	May be due to normal ejection into a dilated great vessel, rapid ejection into a normal great vessel, or abrupt upward	....

continued

	Heart Sound	Timing	Mechanism	Remarks
5	Pulmonic	0.10(0.07-0.16) s after onset of QRS; 0.04(0.02-0.10) s after onset of S₁ [9,10]	movement of a mobile stenotic or bicuspid semilunar valve (usually congenital) [14]	Pulmonic ejection sounds may selectively decrease with inspiration [7]
6	SC (Systolic click)	May be single or multiple, constant or variable; occurs characteristically in mid- or late systole [2]	Believed to originate in elongated redundant mitral chordae tendineae [2]	Abnormal sound which may occur alone or may introduce a late systolic murmur of mitral incompetence
7	S₂ (Second heart sound) A₂ (Aortic component)	Coincides with dicrotic notch of aortic pressure pulse	Related to caudal movement of the aortic valve as the left ventricular pressure falls below aortic pressure	Normally the 2 components are either synchronous, or the aortic component precedes the pulmonic
8	P₂ (Pulmonic component)	Coincides with dicrotic notch of pulmonary arterial pressure pulse	Related to caudal movement of the pulmonary valve as the right ventricular pressure falls below pulmonary arterial pressure	
9	Splitting	Normal inspiratory splitting, (0.02-0.06) s, expiratory splitting, (0.00-0.02) s [6]	Inspiratory splitting is caused principally by a delay in the pulmonic component of the second heart sound; movement of the aortic component in opposite direction also contributes but to a much lesser degree	....
10	OS (Opening snap) Mitral	(0.04-0.13) s after A₂ [3]	An abnormal sound that coincides with opening movement of either mitral or tricuspid valve; such valves are usually (but not invariably) stenotic	Commonest cause is mitral stenosis. Tricuspid opening snaps are relatively rare.
11	Tricuspid	(0.07-0.12) s after P₂ [8]		
12	S₃ (Third heart sound)	(0.10-0.20) s after onset of S₂ [5]	Occurs within left or right ventricular cavity during rapid filling phase of cardiac cycle	Commonly present in normal children & young adults; occurs in disease states characterized by ventricular failure or abnormally rapid ventricular filling

Contributor: Perloff, Joseph K.

References
[1] American College of Cardiology and American Heart Association, Committee on Standardized Terminology. 1968. Amer. J. Cardiol. 21:273.
[2] Barlow, J. B., et al. 1968. Brit. Heart J. 30:203.
[3] Castle, R. F. 1964. In B. L. Segal, ed. The Theory and Practice of Auscultation. F. A. Davis, Philadelphia. p. 154.
[4] Fowler, N. O. 1968. Cardiac Diagnosis. Hoeber Medical Division, Harper and Row, New York.
[5] Grayzel, J. 1960. Amer. J. Med. 28:578.
[6] Harris, A., and G. Sutton. 1968. Brit. Heart J. 30: 739.
[7] Hultgren, H. N., et al. 1969. Circulation 40:631.
[8] Kossman, C. E. 1955. Ibid. 11:378.
[9] Leatham, A., and L. Vogelpoel. 1954. Brit. Heart J. 16:21.
[10] Minhas, K., and B. M. Gasul. 1959. Amer. Heart J. 57:49.
[11] Reinhold, J., and U. Rudhe. 1957. Brit. Heart J. 19:473.
[12] Reinhold, J., et al. 1955. Ibid. 17:327.
[13] Weitzman, D. 1955. Ibid. 17:70.
[14] Whittaker, A. V., et al. 1969. Circulation 39:475.

Part I. Physiological Variables

Condition of Subjects: U = unanesthetized; A = anesthetized; R = restrained; C = curarized.

	Animal	Variable	Condition of Subjects	Temp Site	Body Temperature, °C					Reference
					20[1]	25	30	35	37-39[2]	
1	Man	Metabolic rate, kcal·m⁻²·hr⁻¹	U	Mouth	....	....	....	200	60	33
2		Metabolic rate, observed/estimated	A	Rectum	....	1.58	1.46	2.82	1.00	14
3		O_2 consumption[3], ml/min	U	Mouth	....	....	....	200	235	11
4		Respiratory quotient, CO_2/O_2	A	Rectum	....	0.68	0.75	0.77	0.88	14
5		Respiratory volume, liter/min	A	Rectum	....	9.6	12.7	19.4	8.7	14
6		Heart rate (sinus-atrium)[4], beats/min	.....	....	40	70	100	145	157	18
7		Ventricular rate[4], beats/min	.....	....	10	20	....	40	16	18
8		Pulse pressure, mm Hg	A	Rectum	....	20	40	40	38	7
9		Mean arterial blood pressure, mm Hg	A	Rectum	....	64	80	96	78	7
10		Blood HbO_2 capacity, mmole/liter	A	Rectum	....	10.8	9.73	9.2	8.0	14
11		Blood HbO_2 content, %	A	Rectum	....	93.0	96.7	95.9	97.2	14
12		Blood total CO_2, mmole/liter	A	Rectum	....	20.0	13.5	18.6	21.5	14
13	Cat	Respiratory rate, breaths/min	U	Rectum	0	47	55	60	....	2
14		Heart rate, beats/min	U	Rectum	50	117	180	220	....	2
15			A	Rectum	35	78	126	.....	180	13
16		Perfused heart rate, beats/min	.....	....	53	100	146	.....	....	3
17		Arterial blood pressure, systolic/diastolic	A	Rectum	62/22	105/65	140/97	.....	....	13
18	Dog	O_2 consumption[5], % control	A	Rectum	20	50	70	.....	100	36
19		O_2 consumption[6], ml·kg⁻¹·min⁻¹	A	Rectum	4.1	5.4	....	.....	....	34
20		Cardiac output, ml·kg⁻¹·min⁻¹	A	Rectum	18	....	....	.....	133	6
21		Heart rate[3], beats/min	A	Esophagus	36	....	65	.....	120	7
22		Heart rate[7], beats/min	A	Esophagus	40	....	90	.....	120	7
23		Perfused heart rate, beats/min	A	Rectum	....	....	53	167	....	3
24		Duration of systole, s	A	Rectum	0.60	0.33	0.20	0.16	0.15	22
25		PR interval, s	A	Rectum	0.22	....	....	.....	0.10	6
26		QRS duration, s	A	Rectum	0.09	....	....	.....	0.05	6
27		QT interval, s	A	Rectum	1.04	....	....	.....	0.25	6
28		Mean arterial blood pressure, mm Hg	A	Rectum	....	70-120	85-130	.....	110-142	32
29		Venous blood pressure, cm H_2O	A	Rectum	5-11	1-9	1-8	.....	0.3	32
30		Blood viscosity[8]	A	....	8.78	7.23	5.52	4.42	3.50	22
31		Hematocrit[8], %	A	Rectum	60.6	56.9	54.2	54.1	43.9	22
32		Arterial P_{CO_2}, mm Hg	A	Rectum	8	15	25	.....	36	35
33		Coronary vein O_2 saturation[8], %	A	Rectum	29.0	....	....	.....	28.4	24
34		Coronary vein O_2 content[8], vol %	A	Rectum	8.3	....	....	.....	4.8	24
35		Coronary arteriovenous O_2 difference[8], vol %	A	Rectum	12.7	....	....	.....	13.8	24
36		Coronary artery blood flow, ml/min	A	Rectum	....	15.8	....	.....	38.3	31
37		Glomerular filtration rate, ml·m⁻²·min⁻¹	A	Rectum	....	22	36	47.2	63	8
38	Guinea pig	O_2 consumption, ml·kg⁻¹·min⁻¹	R	Rectum	....	13	25	35	20.8	19
39		Heart rate, beats/min	R	Rectum	....	125	213	300	....	19
40		Ventilation rate, % of normal	R	Rectum	....	75	125	170	100	19

[1] Unless otherwise indicated. [2] Control. [3] Body surface cooled. [4] Embryo heart. [5] Subjects not shivering. [6] Subjects shivering; $Q_{10} = 1.9$. [7] Blood stream cooled. [8] Arterial O_2 saturation, 95% or more.

continued

239. EFFECT OF HYPOTHERMIA ON CIRCULATION: VERTEBRATES

Part I. Physiological Variables

	Animal	Variable	Condition of Subjects	Temp Site	Body Temperature, °C					Reference
					20 [1]	25	30	35	37-39 [2]	
41	Hamster	O_2 consumption, ml·kg^{-1}·min^{-1}	U	Rectum	38	50	56	.....	....	3,4
42		Respiratory rate, breaths/min	U	Rectum	120	122	110	90	....	2
43		Heart rate, beats/min	U	Rectum	190	269	330	380	....	2
44		Perfused heart rate, beats/min	U	Rectum	47	73	105	155	....	3
45	Rabbit	O_2 consumption, ml·kg^{-1}·hr^{-1}	C	Rectum	....	200	300	.....	600	23
46		Respiratory rate, breaths/min	U	Rectum	60	20-40 [9]	....	.....	200	5
47		Heart rate, beats/min	U	Rectum	20-40	40-70	....	.....	200	5
48		Isolated atrium rate, beats/min	A	Rectum	30	65	100	145	....	10
49		Blood volume, ml/kg	A	Rectum	....	....	50	.....	72	30
50		Plasma volume, ml/kg	A	Rectum	....	....	28	.....	44	30
51		Plasma protein, g/100 ml	A	Rectum	....	....	6.0	.....	4.9	30
52		Total circulating plasma protein, g/kg	A	Rectum	....	....	1.7	.....	2.1	30
53		Hematocrit, %	A	Rectum	....	....	42	.....	41	30
54		Circulating RBC volume, ml/kg	A	Rectum	....	....	22	.....	29	30
55		Thiocyanate space, ml/kg	A	Rectum	....	....	170	.....	245	30
56		Extravascular thiocyanate space, ml/kg	A	Rectum	....	....	142	.....	202	30
57	Rat	O_2 consumption, ml·kg^{-1}·min^{-1}	U	Rectum	8 [10]	17	25	.....	18.6	1,3,27,28
		O_2 consumption (tissue slices, dry), ml·g^{-1}·hr^{-1}								
58		Cerebral cortex	.....	....	2.7	3.8	5.4	7.9	10.2	15
59		Heart ventricle	.....	....	3.3	5.1	7.2	8.3	10.0	17
60		Liver	.....	....	2.3	4.0	5.9	8.3	9.8	16
61		Striated muscle	.....	....	1.2	1.50	1.9	2.4	3.1	20
62		Respiratory rate, breaths/min	A	Rectum	18	48	68	66	....	10
63		Perfused respiratory rate, breaths/min	A	....	12 ± 7 [11]	....	....	.....	....	29
64		Cardiac output, ml·kg^{-1}·min^{-1}	U	Rectum	64 [12]	....	....	.....	286	27,28
65			A	Rectum	....	65	105	150	190	9
66		Heart rate, beats/min	U	Rectum	100 [12]	....	....	.....	420	27,28
67			R	Rectum	110	200	300	420	460	21
68			A	Rectum	120	195	270	350	....	12
69		Perfused heart rate, beats/min	.....	....	73	120	167	226		3
70			A	....	60 ± 9 [13]	....	....	.....	360-380	25
71		Arteriovenous conduction time, s	R	Rectum	0.08	0.06	0.045	0.04		21
72		Arterial blood pressure, mm Hg	U	Rectum	90 [12]	....	....	.....	130	27,28
73			A	Rectum	....	105	120	125	135	9
74		Arterial pH	U	....	6.9 [12]	....	....	.....		29
75		Hematocrit, %	U	....	60 [12]	....	....	.....	42	29
76	Squirrel, ground	O_2 consumption, ml/hr	U	....	....	....	....	.....	271.4 ± 13.3	25
77			U [14]	....	4.6 ± 0.5 [15]	....	....	.....		26
78		Cardiac output, ml·kg^{-1}·min^{-1}	U	....	....	....	....	.....	313 ± 28	26
79			U [14]	....	4.6 ± 0.6 [15]	....	....	.....	....	26
80		Hematocrit, %	U [14]	....	40 ± 2 [15]	....	....	.....		26
81		Arterial O_2 content, vol %	U	....	....	....	....	.....	18.8 ± 0.4	25
82			U [14]	....	15.9 ± 0.2 [15]	....	....	.....	....	26
83		Venous O_2 content, vol %	U	....	....	....	....	.....	12.2 ± 0.2	25
84			U [14]	....	8.6 ± 0.3 [15]	....	....	.....	....	26

[1] Unless otherwise indicated. [2] Control. [9] "Pseudohibernating" state. [10] At body temperature of 15°C, O_2 consumption was 4.2 ml·kg^{-1}·min^{-1}. [11] At body temperature of 16°C. [12] At body temperature of 15°C. [13] At body temperature of 14°C. [14] Hibernating. [15] At body temperature of 6.6°C.

continued

239. EFFECT OF HYPOTHERMIA ON CIRCULATION: VERTEBRATES

Part I. Physiological Variables

Contributor: Popovic, Vojin

References

[1] Adolph, E. F. 1950. Amer. J. Physiol. 161:359.
[2] Adolph, E. F. 1951. Ibid. 166:75.
[3] Adolph, E. F. 1951. Ibid. 166:92.
[4] Adolph, E. F., and J. W. Lawrow. 1951. Ibid. 166:62.
[5] Ariel, I., et al. 1943. Cancer Res. 3:448.
[6] Bigelow, W. G., et al. 1950. Ann. Surg. 132:849.
[7] Blair, E. 1960. Clin. Pharmacol. Ther. 1:758.
[8] Blatteis, C. M., and S. M. Horvath. 1958. Amer. J. Physiol. 192:357.
[9] Bullard, R. W. 1959. Ibid. 196:415.
[10] Clark, A. J. 1920. J. Physiol. (London) 54:275.
[11] Cooper, J. L., and D. N. Ross. 1960. Hypothermia in Surgical Practice. F. A. Davis, Philadelphia.
[12] Crismon, J. M. 1944. Arch. Intern. Med. 74:235.
[13] Dahlen, R. W. 1964. Proc. Soc. Exp. Biol. Med. 115:1.
[14] Dill, D. B., and W. H. Forbes. 1941. Amer. J. Physiol. 132:685.
[15] Field, J., et al. 1944. J. Neurophysiol. 7:117.
[16] Fuhrman, F. A., and J. Field. 1945. Arch. Biochem. 6:337.
[17] Fuhrman, G. J., et al. 1950. Amer. J. Physiol. 163:642.

[18] Garrey, W. E., and S. E. Townsend. 1948. Ibid. 152:219.
[19] Gosselin, R. E. 1949. Ibid. 157:103.
[20] Hallinger, N. F. 1944. Ph.D. Thesis. Stanford Univ., Palo Alto.
[21] Hamilton, J. B., et al. 1937. Amer. J. Physiol. 118:21.
[22] Hegnauer, A. H., et al. 1950. Ibid. 161:445.
[23] O'Connor, J. J. 1947. Proc. Roy. Irish Acad. B51:211.
[24] Penrod, K. E. 1951. Amer. J. Physiol. 164:79.
[25] Popovic, P., et al. 1968. Ann. Surg. 168:298.
[26] Popovic, V. 1964. Amer. J. Physiol. 207(6):1345.
[27] Popovic, V., and K. M. Kent. 1964. Ibid. 207:767.
[28] Popovic, V., and K. M. Kent. 1965. Ibid. 209:1069.
[29] Popovic, V., and K. M. Kent. 1966. Proc. Int. Microcirc. Conf. (Cambridge, Engl.), p. 63.
[30] Rodbard, S., et al. 1951. Amer. J. Physiol. 167:485.
[31] Sabiston, D. C., et al. 1955. Surgery 38:498.
[32] Sarajas, H. S. S. 1961. Ann. Acad. Sci. Fenn., A5 (86).
[33] Spealman, C. R. 1946. Amer. J. Physiol. 146:262.
[34] Spurr, G. B., et al. 1954. Ibid. 179:139.
[35] Mohiri, H., et al. 1966. Amer. J. Surg. 112:241.
[36] Watanabe, A., et al. 1959. Path. Biol. 7:1017.

Part II. Stroke Volume and Cardiac Output

	Animal	Experimental Conditions	No. of Subjects	Temperature		Stroke Volume ml [1]	Cardiac Output ml/min [1]	Reference
				Site	°C			
1 2	Man	Subjects premedicated and anesthetized with thiopental sodium, N_2O, diethyl ether, or cyclopropane; cooled by packing with ice in bags; artificially respired. Cardiac output measured by indicator-dilution principle.	10	Rectum	31.3 36.7	58.5 54.9	3446 4190	13
3 4 5	Dog	Subjects anesthetized with pentobarbital sodium; cooled with ice bags. Chest open; cardiac output measured by direct Fick method.	5	Esophagus	23.8 28.9 37.2	14 13 17	788 1398 2674	7
6 7 8		Subjects cooled by blankets. Barbiturates or diethyl ether anesthesia controlled shivering; below 27°C, artificial respiration with 95% O_2 & 5% CO_2. Cardiac output measured by Fick method.	3	Rectum	20 27 37	....	17[2] 45[2] 133[2]	1
9 10		Subjects, weighing 7.8-15.5 kg, anesthetized with thiopental sodium; cooled by immersion in ice water; at low temperature, artificial respiration with room air or 100% O_2. Cardiac output measured by Fick method.	8 9	Rectum Rectum	16-18 37.2-39.5	10.4 ± 2.5 9 ± 2.9	26 ± 6.5[2] 145.5 ± 40.7[2]	8

[1] Unless otherwise indicated.   [2] $ml \cdot kg^{-1} \cdot min^{-1}$.

continued

Part II. Stroke Volume and Cardiac Output

	Animal	Experimental Conditions	No. of Subjects	Temperature Site	Temperature °C	Stroke Volume ml[1]	Cardiac Output ml/min[1]	Reference
11		Subjects, with average weight of 10.5 kg, anesthetized with hexobarbital; cooled by immersion in ice water. Shivering suppressed by succinylcholine; artificial respiration. Cardiac output measured by Fick method.	10	Rectum	20	16.7	470	2
12			13	Rectum	25	13.5	840	
13			13	Rectum	30	12.8	1260	
14			13	Rectum	35	12.1	1550	
15			13	Rectum	38	9.9	1340	
16		Subjects anesthetized with diethyl ether; cooled in water at 1°C; transferred to air-conditioned room when body temperature reached 29°C. Cardiac output measured by Fick method.	6	Rectum	23.2	....	1213 ± 569[3]	6
17			7	Rectum	38.0	....	3603 ± 1628[3]	
18		Subjects anesthetized with pentobarbital sodium, supplemented with thiopental sodium to control shivering; cooled by immersion in ice water. Cardiac output measured by Fick method.	8	Rectum	26.4	11.5	831	5
19					37.6	18.2	2549	
20		Subjects anesthetized with thiopental sodium initially; cooled by arteriovenous shunts with heat exchanger. Chest open; artificial respiration with O_2. Cardiac output measured by dye dilution.	4	Rectum	25	....	388	14
21			9	Rectum	30	....	814	
22			9	Rectum	35	....	1447	
23			7	Rectum	38	....	1871	
24		Subjects deeply anesthetized with pentobarbital sodium (no shivering); cooled with chipped-ice packs. Cardiac output measured by Fick method.	3	Deep rectum	27	7.5	45[2]	11
25					29	9.5	50[2]	
26					31	9.5	55[2]	
27					33	9	60[2]	
28					35	10.5	90[2]	
29					37	14	155[2]	
30		Subjects anesthetized with thiopental sodium followed by diethyl ether; cooled by arteriovenous shunts with heat exchanger, plus crushed ice on body when necessary. Aortic flow measured by electromagnetic flowmeter.	10	Aortic blood	20	1.01[4]	33.6[2]	4
31					25	1.05[4]	68[2]	
32					30	0.94[4]	102[2]	
33					35	0.87[4]	136.2[2]	
34					38	0.92[4]	156.8[2]	
35					40	1.03[4]	170.8[2]	
36		Subjects anesthetized with pentobarbital sodium; cooled by immersion in ice water; below 30°C, artificial respiration with room air. Cardiac output measured by Fick method.	18	Deep colon	20	11.6	23[2]	10
37					25	12.5	63[2]	
38					30	14.8	116[2]	
39					37	9.2	133[2]	
40		Subjects anesthetized with thiamylal sodium followed by diethyl ether; cooled by immersion in ice water; 100% O_2 & dextran administered, and tidal volume kept normal throughout cooling. Aortic flow measured by electromagnetic flowmeter.	11	Rectum	20	0.95[4]	25[2]	12
41					25	0.85[4]	50[2]	
42					30	0.92[4]	90[2]	
43					35	0.95[4]	127[2]	
44					38	0.90[4]	140[2]	
45	Lamb	Subjects 1-7 da old. Anesthetized with chloralose; cooled by pumping blood through ice-water bath. Cardiac output measured by dye dilution.	9	Esophagus	27	....	75[2]	9
46					30	....	98[2]	
47					35	....	160[2]	
48					39	....	320[2]	
49	Rat, albino	Unanesthetized, restrained subjects, weighing 250-350 g; cooled by immersion in ice water. Cardiac output measured by dye dilution.	3-14[5]	Colon	16	....	35[2]	3
50					18	....	60[2]	
51					23	....	88[2]	
52					28	....	132[2]	
53					33	....	172[2]	
54					37	....	209[2]	

[1] Unless otherwise indicated. [2] $ml \cdot kg^{-1} \cdot min^{-1}$. [3] 2 hr after removal from cold bath. [4] ml/kg. [5] Values are averages.

continued

Part II. Stroke Volume and Cardiac Output

	Animal	Experimental Conditions	No. of Subjects	Temperature		Stroke Volume ml	Cardiac Output ml/min	Reference
				Site	°C			
55 56	Chicken	Subjects unanesthetized; cooled by immersion in water at 18-22°C. Cardiac output measured by dye dilution.	5	Rectum	27 ± 0.9 40.9 ± 0.2	1.8 ± 0.4 1.1 ± 0.3	187 ± 47 357 ± 71	15

Contributor: Badeer, Henry S.

References

[1] Bigelow, W. G., et al. 1950. Ann. Surg. 132:849.
[2] Brendel, W., et al. 1957-58. Pfluegers Arch. Gesamte Physiol. Menschen Tiere 266:341.
[3] Bullard, R. W. 1959. Amer. J. Physiol. 196:415.
[4] Delin, N. A., et al. 1964. J. Thorac. Cardiovasc. Surg. 47:774.
[5] Edwards, W. S., et al. 1954. Ann. Surg. 139:275.
[6] Fisher, B., et al. 1957. Amer. J. Physiol. 188:473.
[7] Hansen, A. T., et al. 1956. Scand. J. Clin. Lab. Invest. 8:182.
[8] Hegnauer, A. H., and H. E. D'Amato. 1954. Amer. J. Physiol. 178:138.
[9] Koivikko, A. 1970. Acta Physiol. Scand. 78:571.
[10] Kuhn, L. A., and J. K. Turner. 1959. Circ. Res. 7:366.
[11] Prec, O., et al. 1949. J. Clin. Invest. 28:293.
[12] Rittenhouse, E. A., et al. 1971. J. Thorac. Cardiovasc. Surg. 61:359.
[13] Rose, J. C., et al. 1957. Circulation 15:512.
[14] Sabiston, D. C., et al. 1955. Surgery 38:498.
[15] Whittow, G. C., et al. 1965. Nature (London) 206:200.

Part III. Heart Rate

	Animal	Experimental Conditions	No. of Subjects	Temperature		Heart Rate beats/min	Reference
				Site	°C		
1	Man	Subjects, of all ages, anesthetized with diethyl ether or cyclopropane for cardiovascular surgery & neurosurgery. Surface cooling; O₂ inhalation below 30°C.	100	Rectum	28	60	19
2					29	60	
3					30	62	
4					31	63	
5					32	65	
6					33	70	
7					34	74	
8					35	79	
9					36	83	
10					37	91	
11		Anesthetized or unanesthetized adults immersed in water at 2-12°C [1/]	103	Rectum	30	Atrial fibrillation	18
12					34	50	
13					37	80-90	
14		Infants with cardiac malformations, mean age 3.9 mo. Subjects anesthetized (anesthetic not stated) and cooled by immersion in ice water.	14	Rectum	20	42 ± 10	34
15					25	67 ± 11	
16					30	111 ± 13	
17					37	176 ± 29	
18	Cat	Decerebrate subjects cooled by applying crushed ice to bodies	15	Deep rectum	20	62	28
19					25	100	
20					30	138	
21					35	192	
22					37	220	

[1/] Immediately after immersion, heart rate was 120-140 beats/min. Lethal temperature is variable and uncertain.

continued

Part III. Heart Rate

	Animal	Experimental Conditions	No. of Subjects	Temperature Site	Temperature °C	Heart Rate beats/min	Reference
23	Dog	Subjects anesthetized with pentobarbital sodium and artificially respired with air-O_2 mixture; cooled by a heat exchanger coupled with a pump-oxygenator	6	Mid-esophagus	15	15	27
24					20	45	
25					25	70	
26					30	120	
27					35	165	
28		Subjects anesthetized with pentobarbital sodium and cooled by ice packs. O_2 & inhalation anesthetics used with respirator.	16	Rectum	22	38	17
29					24	51	
30					26	70	
31					28	89	
32					30	108	
33					32	123	
34					34	147	
35					36	175	
36		Subjects anesthetized with hexobarbital and immersed in ice water. Shivering suppressed by succinylcholine; artificial respiration.	10	Rectum	20	22 ± 13	8
37			13	Rectum	25	57 ± 13	
38			13	Rectum	30	96 ± 28	
39			13	Rectum	35	134 ± 28	
40			13	Rectum	38	141 ± 18	
41		Subjects anesthetized with pentobarbital sodium and immersed in water at 5°C. Artificial respiration at 30°C body temperature.	4	Rectum	15	21	13
42			4	Rectum	16	21	
43			6	Rectum	18	40	
44			7	Rectum	20	60	
45			9	Rectum	22	80	
46			16	Rectum	24	90	
47			16	Rectum	26	110	
48			16	Rectum	28	120	
49			16	Rectum	30	140	
50			16	Rectum	32	142	
51			16	Rectum	35	155	
52			16	Rectum	36	155	
53			16	Rectum	38	143	
54		Subjects anesthetized with pentobarbital sodium and immersed in water at 2-5°C. Artificial respiration when necessary.	19	Right heart blood	17	17	23
55					19	24	
56					21	32	
57					23	44	
58					25	63	
59					27	84	
60					29	108	
61					31	132	
62					33	147	
63					35	161	
64					37	174	
65		Subjects anesthetized with pentobarbital sodium or thiopental sodium, followed by diethyl ether. Blood cooling by arteriovenous shunts; surface cooling with crushed ice.	10	Aortic blood	20	32	16
66					25	73	
67					30	113	
68					35	153	
69					38	177	
70					40	194	

continued

Part III. Heart Rate

	Animal	Experimental Conditions	No. of Subjects	Temperature		Heart Rate beats/min	Reference
				Site	°C		
71		Subjects cooled by whole body perfusion; pump-oxygenator equilibrated with 95% O_2	8	Myocardium	10	10	20
72					15	25	
73					20	45	
74					25	70	
75					30	103	
76					34	131	
77		Subjects anesthetized with pentobarbital sodium; cooled by immersion in ice water; below 30°C, artificial respiration with room air	18	Deep colon	20	21	30
78					25	52	
79					30	101	
80					37	180	
81		Subjects anesthetized with pentobarbital sodium; cooled by refrigerated blankets; artificially respired with room air. Saline infused throughout cooling.	10	Esophagus	19	17	2
82					25	58	
83					30	103	
84					35	150	
85					37	170	
86		Subjects anesthetized with thiamylal sodium followed by diethyl ether; cooled by immersion in ice water; 100% O_2 & dextran administered, and tidal volume kept normal throughout cooling	11	Rectum	20	33	35
87					25	60	
88					30	95	
89					35	131	
90					38	152	
91	Guinea pig	Deep urethan narcosis	2	Deep rectum	30	212	4
92					32	216	
93					34	227	
94					36	240	
95					38	256	
96					40	287	
97					42	283	
98		Unanesthetized, restrained subjects placed in rubber glove and immersed in ice water	9	Colon	23[2/]	75	21
99					25	120	
100					30	210	
101					35	295	
102					38	350	
103	Hamster, golden	Unanesthetized subjects, during arousal from hibernation	6	Cheek pouch	5	14	12
104					10	50	
105					15	105	
106					20	185	
107					25	270	
108					30	380	
109					35	500	
110	Hedgehog	During arousal from hibernation	9	Dorsal skin	7.5	26	7
111					12.5	30	
112					17.5	80	
113					22.5	152	
114					27.5	150	
115					32.5	181	

[2/] Heart rate was irregular at body temperature <23°C.

continued

Part III. Heart Rate

	Animal	Experimental Conditions	No. of Subjects	Temperature		Heart Rate beats/min	Reference
				Site	°C		
116	Monkey	Subjects, 12-18 mo old, anesthetized with pentobarbital sodium and immersed in water at 3°C. Artificial respiration with 100% O_2.	20	Rectum	23	50	6
117					30	100	
118					33	140	
119					37	167	
120	Macaque	Young subjects, weighing 3-4 kg, anesthetized with diethyl ether and immersed in water bath	5	Deep rectum	20	52	10
121					23	81	
122					25	102	
123					27	124	
124					29	143	
125					31	163	
126					33	180	
127					35	198	
128	Opossum	Subjects anesthetized with pentobarbital sodium and cooled in refrigerator at −10°C	8	Colon	18	63	33
129					22	102	
130					26	138	
131					30	173	
132					34	210	
133	Rabbit	♂ subjects anesthetized with diethyl ether; cooled by packing with ice	6	Esophagus	26	150	31
134					30	205	
135					35	300	
136					37	320	
137	Albino	4 subjects anesthetized with diethyl ether, 9 with pentobarbital sodium; immersed in water at 2.5°C. Artificial respiration at <20°C body temperature.	13	Rectum	14	28	14
138					17	38	
139					20	63	
140					26	110	
141					29	158	
142					35	242	
143					38	280	
144		Unanesthetized subjects cooled by immersion [3]	....	Deep rectum	20[4]	20-40	3
145					25	40	
146					28	70	
147					39	200	
148		Subjects anesthetized with pentobarbital sodium and cooled by applying crushed ice to bodies	27	Colon	10	13	5
149					12	24	
150					14	34	
151					16	45	
152					18	59	
153					20	70	
154					22	84	
155					24	96	
156					26	115	
157					28	132	
158					30	158	
159					32	185	
160					34	211	

[3] After immersion, heart rate was 270 beats/min. [4] Heart beat was irregular at <20°C body temperature.

continued

Part III. Heart Rate

	Animal	Experimental Conditions	No. of Subjects	Temperature Site	°C	Heart Rate beats/min	Reference
161					36	234	
162					38	256	
163					40	276	
164	Rat, albino	Subjects anesthetized with pentobarbital sodium and cooled by contact with cold copper tubing. Skin moistened with glycerol.	12	Deep rectum	15	45	15
165					20	120	
166					25	195	
167					30	270	
168					35	345	
169		Unanesthetized, restrained subjects placed in icebox at 2-5°C	8	Colon	15	45	22
170					20	110	
171					25	210	
172					30	300	
173					35	405	
174					37	460	
175		Unanesthetized, restrained subjects immersed in ice water	6-30[5/]	Colon	15	24	11
176					19	100	
177					22	160	
178					25.5	210	
179					28	280	
180					31.5	315	
181					34.5	380	
182					37	420	
183		Subjects anesthetized with pentobarbital sodium and cooled by lowering ambient temperature; artificial respiration	7	Colon	17.7	50	29
184			9	Colon	18.7	80	
185			9	Colon	20.7	140	
186			9	Colon	22.3	180	
187			9	Colon	24.7	230	
188			9	Colon	27.5	290	
189			9	Colon	29.9	340	
190			9	Colon	32.9	360	
191		♂ subjects unanesthetized and unrestrained in plexiglass chamber; cooled by placing in room at 1-3°C. Heart rates measured during cooling.	14	Colon	18	79 ± 17	1
192					20	107 ± 22	
193					25	208 ± 14	
194					30	331 ± 16	
195					35	463 ± 25	
196					37	520 ± 23	
197	Squirrel, ground	During arousal from hibernation	2	Food pouch	10	38	26
198					15	102	
199					20	218	
200					25	357	
201	Arctic	During arousal from hibernation	1	Rectum	0.5	4	24
202					4	68	
203					12	180	
204					20	218	
205					33	235	
206					38	245	

5/ Body temperatures are means of 6-30 determinations.

continued

Part III. Heart Rate

	Animal	Experimental Conditions	No. of Subjects	Temperature		Heart Rate	Reference
				Site	°C	beats/min	
207	Woodchuck	Subject entering hibernation	1 6/	Subcutaneous	12	8	32
208				tissue in pos-	15	10	
209				terior flank	20	25	
210					25	40	
211					30	70	
212					37	80-95	
213	Chicken	Subjects unanesthetized; cooled by	5	Rectum	27 ± 0.9	101 ± 9	37
214		immersion in water at 18-22°C			40.9 ± 0.2	329 ± 18	
215	Reptiles	Subjects unanesthetized. Temperature	8 snakes, 8 liz-	Cloaca	7	12	25
216		of ambient air altered.	ards		10	15	
217					15	22	
218					20	39	
219					25	64	
220					30	102	
221					33	147	
222	Frog, South	Subjects unanesthetized, restrained.	4	Ventricular	2	4	36
223	African	Temperature of water changed.		blood	5	11	
224					10	20	
225					15	18	
226					20	27	
227					25	34	
228					30	31	
229					36	25	
230	Fishes (cod,	Ambient temperature changed	Large number	Ambient liq-	0	6	9
231	eel,		(exact fig-	uid	5	12	
232	flounder,		ures not giv-		12	18	
233	pollack,		en)		15	25	
234	sculpin,				20	32	
235	skate)				25	38	
236					30	45	

6/ Heart rates were variable in same animal.

Contributor: Badeer, Henry S.

References

[1] Andrews, P. M., et al. 1969. J. Appl. Physiol. 27: 539.

[2] Angelakos, E. T., and J. B. Daniels. 1969. Ibid. 26: 194.

[3] Ariel, I., et al. 1943. Cancer Res. 3:448.

[4] Barcroft, J., and J. J. Izquierdo. 1931. J. Physiol. (London) 71:364.

[5] Bartlett, R. G., Jr. 1957. J. Appl. Physiol. 10:143.

[6] Bering, E. A., Jr., et al. 1956. Surg. Gynecol. Obstet. 102:134.

[7] Biörck, G., and B. Johansson. 1955. Acta Physiol. Scand. 34:257.

[8] Brendel, W., et al. 1957-58. Pfluegers Arch. Gesamte Physiol. Menschen Tiere 266:341.

[9] Britton, S. W. 1923-24. Amer. J. Physiol. 67:411.

[10] Bryce-Smith, R., et al. 1960. J. Appl. Physiol. 15: 440.

[11] Bullard, R. W. 1959. Amer. J. Physiol. 196:415.

[12] Chatfield, P. O., and C. P. Lyman. 1950. Ibid. 163: 566.

continued

Part III. Heart Rate

[13] Covino, B. G. 1958. Cold Inj. Trans. Conf., 5th, p. 136.

[14] Covino, B. G., and W. R. Beavers. 1958. J. Appl. Physiol. 13:422.

[15] Crismon, J. M. 1944. Arch. Intern. Med. 74:235.

[16] Delin, N. A., et al. 1964. J. Thorac. Cardiovasc. Surg. 47:774.

[17] Deterling, R. A., Jr., et al. 1955. Arch. Surg. 70:87.

[18] Gagge, A. P., and L. P. Herrington. 1947. Annu. Rev. Physiol. 9:409.

[19] Gillmann, H. 1957. Verh. Deut. Ges. Kreislaufforsch. 23:162.

[20] Gollan, F. 1959. Ann. N.Y. Acad. Sci. 80:301.

[21] Gosselin, R. E. 1949. Amer. J. Physiol. 157:103.

[22] Hamilton, J. B., et al. 1937. Ibid. 118:71.

[23] Hegnauer, A. H., et al. 1950. Ibid. 161:455.

[24] Hock, R. 1958. Cold Inj. Trans. Conf., 5th, p. 106.

[25] Johansen, K. 1959. Acta Physiol. Scand. 46:346.

[26] Johnson, G. E. 1929. Biol. Bull. 57:107.

[27] Johnson, P., et al. 1960. Ann. Surg. 151:490.

[28] Klykov, N. V. 1960. The Problem of Acute Hypothermia. Pergamon Press, New York. p. 82.

[29] Krieger, E. M. 1960. Acta Physiol. Lat. Amer. 10:31.

[30] Kuhn, L. A., and J. K. Turner. 1959. Circ. Res. 7:366.

[31] Lennartz, H., and W. Grote. 1969. Anaesthesist 18:145.

[32] Lyman, C. P. 1958. Amer. J. Physiol. 194:83.

[33] Nardone, R. M., et al. 1955. Ibid. 181:352.

[34] Rittenhouse, E. A., et al. 1970. Amer. Heart J. 79:167.

[35] Rittenhouse, E. A., et al. 1971. J. Thorac. Cardiovasc. Surg. 61:359.

[36] Taylor, N. B. 1931. J. Physiol. (London) 71:156.

[37] Whittow, G. C., et al. 1965. Nature (London) 206:200.

XIII. BLOOD AND OTHER BODY FLUIDS

240. BLOOD ELECTROLYTES: PRIMATES

Part I. Man

Values in parentheses are ranges, estimate "c" unless otherwise indicated (*see* Introduction). For additional information, consult references, 3, 24, 46, 65, and 66.

	Constituent	Concentration	Reference
		Whole Blood	
1	Aluminum	(21-94) µg/100 ml	77
2		34.5 µg/100 ml	8,53,67
3	Antimony	37 µg/100 ml	8,53,67
4	Arsenic	10 µg/100 ml	63
5		45 µg/100 ml	8,53,67
6	Barium	<18 µg/100 ml	8,53,67
7	Beryllium	<0.01 µg/100 ml	8,53,67
8	Bicarbonate	20.9(19.1-22.7)[b] meq/liter	73
9	Bismuth	1 ± 1.7 µg/100 ml	8,16
10	Boron	9.5 µg/100 ml	8,53,67
11	Bromide	0.37(0.23-0.53) mg/100 ml	12
12		0.44 mg/100 ml	8,53,67
13		0.81(0.33-1.73) mg/100 ml	74
14	Cadmium	0.5 ± 0.5 µg/100 ml	16
15		0.65 µg/100 ml	8,53,67
16		0.85(0.3-5.0) µg/100 ml	63
17	Calcium	9.7 mg/100 ml	4
18	Cesium	0.27 µg/100 ml	8,53,67
19	Chloride	84(77-88) meq/liter	52
20	Chromium	2.8(1.0-5.5) µg/100 ml	63
21	Cobalt	0.35 µg/100 ml	26
22		1.7 µg/100 ml	8,53,67
23	Copper	89(64-114) µg/100 ml	56
24		98 ± 13 µg/100 ml	76
25	Fluoride	<0.01 mg/100 ml	8,53,67
26		(0.01-0.03) mg/100 ml	63
27		0.018(0.004-0.036) mg/100 ml	22
28	Gold	(0-0.1) µg/100 ml	10
	Iodine		
29	Total I	9.7(2.5-16.9) µg/100 ml	15
30	Protein-bound I	(4-8.5) µg/100 ml	50,68
31	Thyroxine I	4.35(3.9-4.8) µg/100 ml	18
32	Iron	(38-45) mg/100 ml	8,16,53,67
33	Lead	11 ± 6.5 µg/100 ml	16,39
34		20 µg/100 ml	8
35	Lithium	2.0 µg/100 ml	8
36	Magnesium	4.24 mg/100 ml	75
37	Manganese	(1.2-2.6) µg/100 ml	8,16
38	Mercury	0.5(0.2-0.9) µg/100 ml	37
39	Molybdenum	1.5 µg/100 ml	8,53,67
40	Nickel	0.26(0.11-0.46) µg/100 ml	47
41	Niobium	240 µg/100 ml	8,53,67

	Constituent	Concentration	Reference
42	Phosphate	2.95(2.4-3.5) mg/100 ml	78
	Phosphorus		
43	Total P	34.98 mg/100 ml	54
44	Inorganic P	3.3(2.4-3.76) mg/100 ml	9
45	Total acid-soluble P	23.5(20.8-25.8) mg/100 ml	38
46	Organic acid-soluble P	23.1(18.6-28.6) mg/100 ml	32
47	Adenosine triphosphate P	4.6(1.8-6.2) mg/100 ml	32
48	Diphosphoglycerate P	12.4(8.1-16.7) mg/100 ml	32
49	Hexose phosphate P	3.2(1.4-5.0) mg/100 ml	32
50	Lipid P	13.7(12.5-15.4) mg/100 ml	59
51	Nucleoprotein P	2.65 mg/100 ml	35
52	Nucleotide P	2.8(2.2-3.4) mg/100 ml	38
53	Potassium	45.5 meq/liter	41
54	Rubidium	300(260-345) µg/100 ml	6
55	Selenium	20.6(10-34) µg/100 ml	2
56	Silicon	0.83(0.35-1.31) mg/100 ml	79
57	Silver	Trace	36
58	Sodium	85.4(79.3-91) meq/liter	27
59	Strontium	3.3 µg/100 ml	8,53,67
	Sulfate (other than protein sulfur)		
60	Total, as sulfur	(3.84-5.06) mg/100 ml	61
61	Inorganic, as sulfur	(0.28-0.65) mg/100 ml	61
62	Esterified, as sulfur	(0.07-0.96) mg/100 ml	61
63	Neutral, as sulfur	(3.19-4.32) mg/100 ml	61
	Sulfur		
64	Total S	122 mg/100 ml	42
65	Protein S	118 mg/100 ml	42
66	Tellurium	3.3 µg/100 ml	8,53,67
67	Tin	12.4 µg/100 ml	8,53,67
68	Titanium	2.6 µg/100 ml	8,53,67
69	Uranium	0.08 µg/100 ml	8,53,67
70	Vanadium	1.6 µg/100 ml	8,53,67
71	Zinc	509-650 µg/100 ml	8,16,71
72	Zirconium	236 µg/100 ml	8,53,67
		Erythrocytes	
73	Aluminum	7 µg/100 ml	36
74	Antimony	5.3 µg/100 ml	8,53,67
75	Arsenic	<3.1 µg/100 ml	8,53,67
76	Barium	Nil	8,53,67

1751

continued

Part 1. Man

	Constituent	Concentration	Reference		Constituent	Concentration	Reference
77	Beryllium	Nil	8,53,63, 67	118	Titanium	3.2 µg/100 ml	8,53,67
				119	Vanadium	2.3 µg/100 ml	8,53,67
78	Bicarbonate	11.2(10.9-11.5) meq/liter	60	120	Zinc	1.24(0.88-1.6) mg/100 ml	5
79	Bromide	0.3 mg/100 ml	8,53,67	121	Zirconium	480 µg/100 ml	8,53,67
80		0.98(0.92-1.40) mg/100 ml	34			Plasma or Serum	
81	Calcium	(0.6-1.4) meq/liter	58	122	Aluminum	17(5-50) µg/100 ml	55
82		0.12(0.05-0.19) meq/kg erythrocytes	70	123		43 µg/100 ml	8,53,67
83	Chloride	67.9(58.9-76.9) meq/liter	44	124	Antimony	5.4 µg/100 ml	8,53,67
84	Chromium	1.8 µg/100 ml	8,53,67	125	Arsenic	19 µg/100 ml	8,53,67
85	Cobalt	Greater than whole blood	69	126	Barium	7.9 µg/100 ml	8,53,67
86	Copper	89(66-112)[b] µg/100 ml	11	127	Beryllium	<0.4 µg/100 ml	8,53,67
87	Fluoride	7 µg/100 ml	8,53,67	128	Bicarbonate	27(24-31) meq/liter	21
	Iodine			129	Bromine	0.3(0.07-1.3) mg/100 ml	14
88	Total I	14 µg/100 ml	8,53,67	130	Cadmium	Trace	69
89	Protein-bound I	(4.9-5.2) µg/100 ml	45	131	Calcium	5.0(4.5-5.5) meq/liter	17
	Iron			132	Ionized	2.47 meq/liter	80
90	Total Fe	96 mg/100 ml	8,53,67	133	Chloride	103(99-111) meq/liter	52
91	Nonhemoglobin Fe	2.5 µg/100 ml	1	134	Chromium	2.8 µg/100 ml	8,53,67
				135	Cobalt	0.03 µg/100 ml	48
92	Lead	48 µg/100 ml	8,53,67	136	Copper	114(81-147)[b] µg/100 ml	11
93	Lithium	2.4 µg/100 ml	8,53,67	137	Fluorine	2.8 µg/100 ml	8,53,67
94	Magnesium	4.93(3.87-5.99) meq/liter	29		Iodine		
95	Manganese	2.4 ± 0.1 µg/100 ml	13	138	Total I	7.0(5.9-7.6) µg/100 ml	62
96	Mercury	0.7 µg/100 ml	8,53,67	139	Organic I	(2.2-5.1) µg/100 ml	19
97	Molybdenum	1.5 µg/100 ml	8,53,67	140	Precipitable I	5.0(3.8-7.1) µg/100 ml	30,31, 49
98	Nickel	5.3(0-31) µg/100 ml	33	141	Protein-bound I	6.4(5.5-7.8) µg/100 ml	62
99	Niobium	520 µg/100 ml	8,53,67	142	Thyroxine I	(3-6) µg/100 ml	17
	Phosphorus			143	Iron	(50-170) µg/100 ml	17,53, 80
100	Total P	71 mg/100 ml	32	144		115 ± 42 µg/100 ml	76
101	Inorganic P	2.4(0.9-3.3) mg/100 ml	32	145	Lead	4.6 µg/100 ml	8,53,67
102	Organic acid-soluble P	49.7(38.5-58.7) mg/100 ml	32	146	Lithium	3.1 µg/100 ml	8,53,67
103	Adenosine triphosphate P	10.6(4.2-15.1) mg/100 ml	32	147	Magnesium	1.85(1.5-2.5) meq/liter	64,75
104	Diphosphoglycerate P	29.2(19-40.4) mg/100 ml	32	148	Manganese	0.142 ± 0.02 µg/100 ml	13
				149		0.83 µg/100 ml	8,53,67
105	Hexose phosphate P	7.5(3.5-10.7) mg/100 ml	32	150	Mercury	0.3 µg/100 ml	8,53,67
				151	Molybdenum	0.4 µg/100 ml	8,53,67
106	Lipid P	11.9 mg/100 ml	20	152	Nickel	3 µg/100 ml	8,53,67
107	Nucleotide P	6.2(5.1-7.1) mg/100 ml	38	153	Niobium	<8.3 µg/100 ml	8,53,67
108	Potassium	88(76-100) meq/liter	44	154	Phosphate	3.9(3.1-4.9) mg/100 ml	57
109	Rubidium	480 µg/100 ml	8,53,67		Phosphorus		
110	Silver	Trace	36	155	Total P	11.4(10.7-12.1) mg/100 ml	20,32
111	Sodium	8.7(5.1-13.1) meq/liter	44	156	Inorganic P	3.5(2.7-4.3) mg/100 ml	7,23,72
112	Strontium	0.32 µg/100 ml	8,53,67	157	Organic P	8.3(7-9) mg/100 ml	25
	Sulfur			158	Adenosine triphosphate P	0.16(0.0-0.64) mg/100 ml	32
113	Total S	190 mg/100 ml	42	159	Diphosphoglycerate P	0.03(0.0-0.30) mg/100 ml	32
114	Protein S	186 mg/100 ml	42				
115	Neutral S	0.015 mg/100 ml	51	160	Hexose phosphate P	0.04(0.0-0.22) mg/100 ml	32
116	Tellurium	3.1 ng/100 ml	8,53,67				
117	Tin	22 µg/100 ml	8,53,67	161	Lipid P	8.2(6.9-9.7) mg/100 ml	32

continued

Part I. Man

	Constituent	Concentration	Refer-ence
162	Nucleic acid P	0.54(0.44-0.65) mg/100 ml	43
163	Potassium	4.4(3.5-5.5) meq/liter	27,80
164	Rubidium	73 μg/100 ml	8,53,67
165	Selenium	1.1 μg/100 ml	8,53,67
166	Silicon	0.79 mg/100 ml	40
167	Sodium	140(133-144) meq/liter	28,80
168	Strontium	5.7 μg/100 ml	8,53,67
	Sulfate (other than protein sulfur)		
169	Total, as sulfur	3.38(2.95-3.75) mg/100 ml	61
170	Inorganic, as sul-fur	1.57(1.0-1.85) mg/100 ml	61

	Constituent	Concentration		Refer-ence
171	Esterified, as sulfur	0.39(0.25-0.65) mg/100 ml		61
172	Neutral, as sulfur	1.42(0.9-1.95) mg/100 ml		61
	Sulfur			
173	Total S	78 mg/100 ml		42
174	Protein S	74 mg/100 ml		42
175	Tellurium	3.0 μg/100 ml		8,53,67
176	Tin	3.3 μg/100 ml		8,53,67
177	Titanium	4.0 μg/100 ml		8,53,67
178	Vanadium	1.0 μg/100 ml		8,53,67
179	Zinc	1.0(0.7-1.5) mg/100 ml		5
180	Zirconium	40 μg/100 ml		8,53,67

Contributors: Smith, Carl C., and Wolfe, Geraldine F.; Cartwright, George E.

References

[1] Alcuin-Arens, M. 1940-41. Quart. J. Med. 6-7:203.
[2] Allaway, W. H., et al. 1968. Arch. Environ. Health. 16:342.
[3] Bala, Yu. M., and V. M. Liftshits. 1965. Probl. Gematol. Pereliv. Krovi 10:23 (Fed. Proc. Fed. Amer. Soc. Exp. Biol. 25(Transl. Suppl.):T370, 1966).
[4] Baumann, R., and R. Herrmann. 1953. Z. Gesamte Exp. Med. 120:172.
[5] Berfenstam, R. 1952. Acta Paediat. (Uppsala) 41, Suppl. 87.
[6] Bertrand, G., and D. Bertrand. 1951. Bull. Acad. Nat. Med. Paris 135:27.
[7] Bodansky, A., and H. L. Jaffe. 1934. Arch. Intern. Med. 54:88.
[8] Bowen, H. J. M. 1966. Trace Elements in Biochemistry. Academic Press, New York.
[9] Brain, R. T., et al. 1928. Biochem. J. 22:628.
[10] Brune, D., et al. 1966. Clin. Chim. Acta 13:285.
[11] Cartwright, G. E., and M. M. Wintrobe. 1964. Amer. J. Clin. Nutr. 14:224.
[12] Conway, E. J., and J. C. Flood. 1936. Biochem. J. 30:716.
[13] Cotzias, G. C., et al. 1968. J. Clin. Invest. 47:992.
[14] Cretius, K., and K. Beyermann. 1962. Klin. Wochenschr. 40:89.
[15] Curtis, G. M., and M. B. Fertman. 1947. Arch. Surg. (Chicago) 54:541.
[16] Delves, H. T., et al. 1971. Analyst (London) 96:260.
[17] Diem, K., and C. Lentner, ed. 1970. Geigy Scientific Tables. Ed. 7. J. R. Geigy, Basel.
[18] Elmer, A. W., et al. 1934. C. R. Soc. Biol. 115:1714.
[19] Fazio, B., et al. 1954. Arch. Maragliano Patol. Clin. 9:511.
[20] Ferranti, F., and O. Giannetti. 1933. Diagn. Tec. Lab. 4:664.
[21] Gambino, S. R. 1965. Stand. Methods Clin. Chem. 5:169.
[22] Gedalia, I., et al. 1961. Proc. Soc. Exp. Biol. Med. 106:147.
[23] Gibbs, E. L., et al. 1942. J. Biol. Chem. 144:325.
[24] Goldwater, L. J., et al. 1962. Arch. Environ. Health 5:537.
[25] Grassheim, K., and E. Lucas. 1928. Z. Klin. Med. 107:172.
[26] Haerdi, W., et al. 1960. Helv. Chim. Acta 43:869.
[27] Hald, J. 1946. J. Biol. Chem. 163:429.
[28] Hald, P. M., and W. B. Mason. 1958. Stand. Methods Clin. Chem. 2:165.
[29] Hanze, S. 1962. Der Magnesiumstoffwechsel. G. Thieme, Stuttgart.
[30] Heinemann, M., et al. 1948. J. Clin. Invest. 27:91.
[31] Heinemann, M., et al. Unpublished.
[32] Helve, O. 1946. Acta Med. Scand. 125:505.
[33] Herring, W. B., et al. 1960. Amer. J. Clin. Nutr. 8:846.
[34] Hunter, G. 1955. Biochem. J. 60:261.
[35] Javillier, M., and M. Fabrykant. 1931. Bull. Soc. Chim. Biol. 13:685.
[36] Kehoe, R. A., et al. 1940. J. Nutr. 19:579.
[37] Kellershohn, C., et al. 1965. J. Lab. Clin. Med. 66:168.
[38] Kerr, S. E., and L. Daoud. 1935. J. Biol. Chem. 109:301.
[39] Kopito, L., and H. Shwachman. 1972. Stand. Methods Clin. Chem. 7:151.
[40] Kvorning, S. A., and E. Kirk. 1949. J. Gerontol. 4:16.
[41] Lans, H. S., et al. 1952. Amer. J. Med. Sci. 223:65.
[42] Larizza, P. 1935. Fisiol. Med. 6:203.
[43] Mandel, P., and P. Metais. 1948. C. R. Soc. Biol. 142:241.

continued

Part I. Man

[44] Marongiu, F., et al. 1966. Klin. Wochenschr. 44: 1405.

[45] McClendon, J. F., and W. C. Foster. 1944. Amer. J. Med. Sci. 207:549.

[46] Niedermayer, W., et al. 1962. Arthritis Rheum. 5: 439.

[47] Nomoto, S., et al. 1971. Biochemistry 10:1647.

[48] Parr, R. M., and D. M. Taylor. 1964. Biochem. J. 91:424.

[49] Peters, J. P., et al. 1948. Obstet. Gynecol. Surv. 3: 647.

[50] Reals, W. J., et al. 1953. Mil. Surg. 113:478.

[51] Reed, L., and W. Denis. 1927. J. Biol. Chem. 73: 623.

[52] Schales, O. 1953. Stand. Methods Clin. Chem. 1:37.

[53] Schroeder, H. A., and A. P. Nason. 1971. Clin. Chem. 17:461.

[54] Sehra, K. B., and B. Ahmad. 1945. Ann. Biochem. Exp. Med. 5:145.

[55] Seibold, M. 1960. Klin. Wochenschr. 38:117.

[56] Shields, G. S., et al. 1961. J. Clin. Invest. 40:2007.

[57] Simonsen, D. G., et al. 1946. J. Biol. Chem. 166: 747.

[58] Sobel, A. E., et al. 1941. Ibid. 140:501.

[59] Sokolovitch, M. 1931. Arch. Dis. Childhood 6:183.

[60] Sommerkamp, H., and K. Bomke. 1964. Klin. Wochenschr. 42:392.

[61] Sturm, A., and A. Pothmann. 1940. Z. Klin. Med. 137:467.

[62] Taurog, A., and I. L. Chaikoff. 1946. J. Biol. Chem. 163:313.

[63] Tepper, L. B. 1972. In D. H. K. Lee, ed. Metallic Contaminants and Human Health. Academic Press, New York. p. 229.

[64] Thiers, R. E. 1965. Stand. Methods Clin. Chem. 5: 131.

[65] Thiers, R. E., et al. 1955. Anal. Chem. 27:1725.

[66] Thomas, L. C., and R. A. Chittenden. 1960. Lancet 2:209.

[67] Tipton, I. H. 1969. Int. Comm. Radiol. Protect. Handb. Rep. Subcomm. 2, ch. 2.

[68] Tommasino, P. O., and J. J. Staffieri. 1953. Rev. Asoc. Med. Argent. 67:489.

[69] Underwood, E. J. 1971. Trace Elements in Human and Animal Nutrition. Ed. 3. Academic Press, New York.

[70] Valberg, L. S., et al. 1965. J. Clin. Invest. 44:379.

[71] Vallee, B. L., and J. G. Gibson, II. 1948. J. Biol. Chem. 176:445.

[72] Wertheim, A. R., et al. 1954. J. Clin. Invest. 33: 565.

[73] West, C. D. Unpublished.

[74] Wikoff, H. L., et al. 1940. Amer. J. Clin. Pathol. 10: 234.

[75] Willis, C. E. 1965. Clin. Chem. 11:251.

[76] Wintrobe, M. M., et al. 1953. J. Nutr. 50:395.

[77] Wolff, H. 1948. Biochem. Z. 319:1.

[78] Wootten, I. D. P., and E. J. King. 1953. Lancet 264: 470.

[79] Worth, G., and G. Campen. 1951. Hoppe Seylers Z. Physiol. Chem. 288:155.

[80] Young, D. S., et al. 1971. Clin. Chem. 17:403.

Part II. Primates Other Than Man

All animals were normal, or assumed normal, unless otherwise specified. **Concentration:** Plus/minus (±) values are standard deviation, unless otherwise indicated. Values in parentheses are ranges, estimate "c" unless otherwise indicated (*see* Introduction).

	Species	Blood Component	No. of Observations	Constituent	Concentration	Reference
1	*Alouatta seniculus,* ♂♀	....	2	Calcium	(8.6-9.9) mg/100 ml	16
2			2	Phosphorus	(2.6-3.0) mg/100 ml	
3	*Aotus trivirgatus,* ♂♀	Plasma	3	Calcium	9.8 ± 0.32 mg/100 ml	71
4			3	Carbon dioxide	22.5 ± 2.40 meq/liter	
5			3	Chloride	102 ± 2.65 meq/liter	
6			3	Potassium	3.7 ± 0.42 meq/liter	
7			3	Sodium	149.5 ± 0.61 meq/liter	
8	*Ateles* sp., ♂♀	Whole blood	3	Phosphorus	6.2 ± 0.9 mg/100 ml	54
	Cebus sp.					
9	♂, young	Serum	8	Magnesium	1.3 ± 0.21 [1/] mg/100 ml	88
10			8	Potassium	5.2 ± 0.8 [1/] meq/liter	
11			8	Sodium	160 ± 2.5 [1/] meq/liter	
12	♂♀	....	11	Calcium	10.7 ± 1.08 mg/100 ml	30

[1/] Plus/minus (±) values are standard error.

continued

Part II. Primates Other Than Man

	Species	Blood Component	No. of Observations	Constituent	Concentration	Reference
13	*C. albifrons*, ♂♀; 2.0-2.5 kg	Serum	4	Calcium	10.9 ± 0.5 mg/100 ml	36
14			4	Phosphorus	6.6 ± 1.2 mg/100 ml	
	Cercocebus torquatus atys					
15	♂, 0.9-1.8 kg	....	8	Calcium	10.3 ± 0.55 mg/100 ml	70
16			8	Chloride	104.3 ± 2.23 meq/liter	
17			15	Potassium	5.7 ± 0.67 meq/liter	
18			16	Sodium	153.3 ± 5.2 meq/liter	
19	7-16 kg; fasted	Serum	19	Calcium	11.0 ± 0.6 mg/100 ml	1
20			31	Chloride	104.9 ± 3.6 meq/liter	
21			26	Phosphorus	6.2 ± 1.3 mg/100 ml	
22			27	Potassium	5.7 ± 0.8 meq/liter	
23			27	Sodium	152.9 ± 3.0 meq/liter	
24	♀, 0.9-1.8 kg	....	2	Calcium	10.9 ± 0.42 mg/100 ml	70
25			2	Chloride	103.5 ± 0.36 meq/liter	
26			17	Potassium	6.1 ± 0.23 meq/liter	
27			17	Sodium	157.7 ± 6.1 meq/liter	
28	6-12 kg; fasted	Serum	33	Calcium	10.1 ± 0.7 mg/100 ml	1
29			39	Chloride	105.3 ± 4.1 meq/liter	
30			31	Phosphorus	5.0 ± 1.3 mg/100 ml	
31			39	Potassium	5.0 ± 0.7 meq/liter	
32			39	Sodium	149.1 ± 4.5 meq/liter	
33	♂♀, 2.6-12 kg	Plasma	22	Potassium	3.7 meq/liter	78
34			25	Sodium	147.2 meq/liter	
	Cercopithecus aethiops					
35	♂, fasted	Plasma	32	Calcium	10.4 ± 1.0 mg/100 ml	62
36			16	Chloride	110 ± 1.4 meq/liter	
37			24	Phosphate	4.7 ± 0.8 mg/100 ml	
38			32	Potassium	4.4 ± 0.5 meq/liter	
39			32	Sodium	150 ± 3.4 meq/liter	
40	4.5-7.5 kg; fasted	Serum	27	Calcium	10.5 ± 0.7 mg/100 ml	1
41			34	Chloride	106.8 ± 4.4 meq/liter	
42			31	Phosphorus	5.5 ± 1.4 mg/100 ml	
43			39	Potassium	4.2 ± 0.7 meq/liter	
44			39	Sodium	154.5 ± 4.7 meq/liter	
45	♀, fasted	Plasma	32	Calcium	10.9 ± 0.3 mg/100 ml	62
46			16	Chloride	113 ± 3.5 meq/liter	
47			12	Phosphate	3.2 ± 3.2 mg/100 ml	
48			32	Potassium	4.2 ± 0.6 meq/liter	
49			32	Sodium	151 ± 4.0 meq/liter	
50	3.0-5.0 kg; fasted	Serum	34	Calcium	9.7 ± 0.7 mg/100 ml	1
51			38	Chloride	108.2 ± 3.6 meq/liter	
52			33	Phosphorus	4.7 ± 1.3 mg/100 ml	
53			42	Potassium	4.8 ± 0.6 meq/liter	
54			42	Sodium	153.3 ± 4.4 meq/liter	
55	*Galago crassicaudatus*, ♂	....	2	Potassium	5.2 ± 0.3 meq/liter	30
56			2	Sodium	152 ± 2.8 meq/liter	
57	♀	....	1	Potassium	4.6 meq/liter	
58			2	Sodium	144 ± 11.3 meq/liter	
59	♂♀	....	3	Calcium	10.6 ± 0.1 mg/100 ml	
60			2	Phosphorus	5.3 ± 1.8 mg/100 ml	

continued

Part II. Primates Other Than Man

	Species	Blood Component	No. of Observations	Constituent	Concentration	Reference
	Gorilla gorilla					
61	♂, <1 to >9 yr old; fasted	Serum	15	Calcium	9.6 ± 0.7 mg/100 ml	46
62			15	Carbon dioxide	21.3 ± 3.9 meq/liter	
63			15	Chloride	97.4 ± 4.5 meq/liter	
64			15	Phosphorus	5.2 ± 0.5 mg/100 ml	
65			15	Potassium	4.1 ± 0.3 meq/liter	
66			15	Sodium	135.9 ± 3.9 meq/liter	
67	7.5 yr old	....	1	Calcium	10.3 mg/100 ml	11
68			1	Chloride	94 meq/liter	
69			1	Phosphorus	5.2 mg/100 ml	
70			1	Potassium	4.3 meq/liter	
71			1	Sodium	135 meq/liter	
72	16 yr old	....	1	Calcium	10.9 mg/100 ml	11
73			1	Chloride	97 meq/liter	
74			1	Phosphorus	3.8 mg/100 ml	
75			1	Potassium	4.1 meq/liter	
76			1	Sodium	140 meq/liter	
77	♀, <1 to >9 yr old; fasted	Serum	29	Calcium	9.5 ± 0.7 mg/100 ml	46
78			29	Carbon dioxide	20.9 ± 2.8 meq/liter	
79			29	Chloride	98 ± 4.5 meq/liter	
80			29	Phosphorus	5.2 ± 0.8 mg/100 ml	
81			29	Potassium	4.1 ± 0.5 meq/liter	
82			29	Sodium	134.9 ± 3.9 meq/liter	
83	10.5 yr old	....	1	Calcium	9.8 mg/100 ml	11
84			1	Chloride	97 meq/liter	
85			1	Potassium	4.1 meq/liter	
86			1	Sodium	136 meq/liter	
87	♂♀	Serum	12	Chloride	97.6 ± 10 meq/liter	61
88			10	Copper	85 ± 27 μg/100 ml	
89			12	Iron	139 ± 36 μg/100 ml	
90			11	Potassium	5.6 ± 1.7 meq/liter	
91			11	Sodium	121 ± 15 meq/liter	
92	0-5 yr old; fasted	Serum	24	Calcium	9.7 ± 0.7 mg/100 ml	46
93			24	Carbon dioxide	20.8 ± 3.8 meq/liter	
94			24	Chloride	98.1 ± 4.3 meq/liter	
95			24	Phosphorus	5.4 ± 0.7 mg/100 ml	
96			24	Potassium	4.3 ± 0.4 meq/liter	
97			24	Sodium	135.3 ± 3.1 meq/liter	
98	5-10 yr old; fasted	Serum	20	Calcium	9.3 ± 0.6 mg/100 ml	46
99			20	Carbon dioxide	21.4 ± 2.4 meq/liter	
100			20	Chloride	97.4 ± 4.7 meq/liter	
101			20	Phosphorus	4.9 ± 0.5 mg/100 ml	
102			20	Potassium	3.8 ± 0.4 meq/liter	
103			20	Sodium	135.0 ± 4.8 meq/liter	
104	Lowland, ♂	....	5	Calcium	(7.5-10.9) mg/100 ml	16
105			5	Chloride	(89-114) meq/liter	
106			1	Magnesium	3.38 mg/100 ml	
107			7	Phosphorus	(3.64-5.2) mg/100 ml	
108			5	Potassium	(4.02-5.8) meq/liter	
109			3	Sodium	(115.7-160.0) meq/liter	

continued

Part II. Primates Other Than Man

	Species	Blood Component	No. of Obser-vations	Constituent	Concentration	Reference
110	♀	....	3	Calcium	(10.0-11.0) mg/100 ml	16
111			3	Chloride	(95-110) meq/liter	
112			5	Phosphorus	(3.0-5.1) mg/100 ml	
113			3	Potassium	(4.36-4.74) meq/liter	
114			2	Sodium	124.8 meq/liter	
115	Mountain, ♂	....	1	Calcium	10.6 mg/100 ml	16
116			1	Chloride	93 meq/liter	
117			1	Phosphorus	3.42 mg/100 ml	
118			1	Potassium	3.6 meq/liter	
119	♀	....	1	Calcium	10.9 mg/100 ml	16
120			1	Chloride	90 meq/liter	
121			1	Phosphorus	3.90 mg/100 ml	
122			1	Potassium	4.1 meq/liter	
123	*Hylobates lar*, ♂♀	....	2	Calcium	(8.5-9.9) mg/100 ml	16
124			2	Phosphorus	(1.2-1.9) mg/100 ml	
125		Whole blood	4	Phosphorus	3.2 ± 1.2 mg/100 ml	54
126	*Lagothrix lagotricha*, ♂♀	....	2	Calcium	(10.1-10.3) mg/100 ml	16
127			2	Phosphorus	(5.0-7.4) mg/100 ml	
128	*Lemur catta*, ♂	....	3	Chloride	112.7 ± 0.6 meq/liter	30
129			1	Potassium	6.5 meq/liter	
130			1	Sodium	164 meq/liter	
131	♀	....	2	Chloride	113.0 ± 1.4 meq/liter	30
132	*L. fulvus*, ♂	....	7	Chloride	109.4 ± 4.8 meq/liter	30
133			3	Potassium	6.9 ± 0.4 meq/liter	
134			3	Sodium	156.7 ± 5.8 meq/liter	
135	♀	....	6	Chloride	111.3 ± 4.6 meq/liter	30
136			2	Potassium	7.1 ± 0.5 meq/liter	
137			2	Sodium	160.5 ± 12.0 meq/liter	
138	♂♀	....	2	Phosphorus	6.4 ± 2.0 mg/100 ml	30
	Macaca arctoides					
139	♂	....	3	Chloride	103.3 ± 1.2 meq/liter	30
140			2	Potassium	4.1 ± 0.3 meq/liter	
141			3	Sodium	157.7 ± 5.5 meq/liter	
142	Fasted	....	24	Chloride	100 ± 8.4 meq/liter	55
143			129	Potassium	5.77 ± 0.93 meq/liter	
144			129	Sodium	145 ± 19.4 meq/liter	
145	6-15 kg; fasted	Serum	11	Calcium	5.0 ± 0.45 meq/liter	90
146			11	Chloride	111.8 ± 2.1 meq/liter	
147			11	Potassium	4.12 ± 0.69 meq/liter	
148			11	Sodium	150.5 ± 3.8 meq/liter	
149	7.5-12 kg; fasted	Serum	51	Calcium	10.34 ± 0.52 mg/100 ml	2
150			52	Carbon dioxide	19.9 ± 3.22 meq/liter	
151			52	Chloride	103.6 ± 3.14 meq/liter	
152			49	Phosphorus	5.5 ± 1.08 mg/100 ml	
153			52	Potassium	4.53 ± 0.64 meq/liter	
154			32	Sodium	148.9 ± 4.18 meq/liter	
155	♀	....	2	Chloride	109.0 ± 1.4 meq/liter	30
156			2	Potassium	4.3 ± 0.9 meq/liter	
157			2	Sodium	160 ± 5.7 meq/liter	

continued

Part II. Primates Other Than Man

	Species	Blood Component	No. of Observations	Constituent	Concentration	Reference
158	Fasted	....	16	Chloride	100 ± 5.6 meq/liter	55
159			107	Potassium	5.35 ± 0.61 meq/liter	
160			107	Sodium	150 ± 22.6 meq/liter	
161	6-10 kg; fasted	Serum	61	Calcium	10.14 ± 0.68 mg/100 ml	2
162			61	Carbon dioxide	20.4 ± 3.11 meq/liter	
163			61	Chloride	104.7 ± 3.33 meq/liter	
164			58	Phosphorus	4.6 ± 1.58 mg/100 ml	
165			61	Potassium	4.6 ± 0.59 meq/liter	
166			61	Sodium	147.2 ± 3.75 meq/liter	
167	6-15 kg; fasted	Serum	25	Calcium	5.1 ± 0.23 meq/liter	90
168			25	Chloride	114.2 ± 2.1 meq/liter	
169			25	Potassium	4.39 ± 0.47 meq/liter	
170			25	Sodium	152.2 ± 2.6 meq/liter	
171	♂♀	Serum	2	Calcium	(10.4-10.6) mg/100 ml	12
172			2	Sodium	(149-152) meq/liter	
173		....	4	Phosphorus	5.6 ± 2.7 mg/100 ml	30
174		....	6	Potassium	3.2 ± 0.2 [1/] meq/liter	66
175			6	Sodium	145.0 ± 3.7 [1/] meq/liter	
176	Adolescent	....	17	Potassium	4.8 meq/liter	67
177			21	Sodium	152 meq/liter	
178	Fasted	....	2	Potassium	4.1 meq/liter	12
	M. cyclopis, ♂♀					
179	2-10 yr old; fasted	Serum	67	Calcium	10.26 ± 0.87 mg/100 ml	84
180			79	Chloride	105.8 ± 7.3 meq/liter	
181			66	Iron	130.0 ± 40.5 μg/100 ml	
182			78	Magnesium	1.38 ± 0.73 mg/100 ml	
183			79	Phosphorus	5.1 ± 1.6 mg/100 ml	
184			79	Potassium	5.2 ± 0.6 meq/liter	
185			79	Sodium	150.0 ± 4.0 meq/liter	
186	2.3-5.17 kg	Plasma	8	Chloride	118 meq/liter	96
187			8	Potassium	2.8 meq/liter	
188			8	Sodium	156 meq/liter	
	M. fascicularis					
189	♂	Serum	8	Calcium	10.84(9.0-12.6) mg/100 ml	65
190			8	Phosphorus	2.66(1.4-4.6) mg/100 ml	
191	3 kg	Plasma	5	Calcium	10.2 ± 0.18 mg/100 ml	64
192	3.5-9.0 kg; fasted	Serum	38	Calcium	10.17 ± 0.68 mg/100 ml	2
193			38	Chloride	104.3 ± 2.85 meq/liter	
194			40	Phosphorus	5.23 ± 1.28 mg/100 ml	
195			38	Potassium	4.54 ± 0.57 meq/liter	
196			38	Sodium	149.8 ± 3.84 meq/liter	
197	Adult	Plasma	16	Chloride	109.3 ± 3.7 meq/liter	83
198			8	Chloride	109.5 meq/liter	82
199			8	Potassium	3.65 meq/liter	82
200			16	Potassium	3.7 ± 0.83 meq/liter	83
201			8	Sodium	139 meq/liter	82
202			16	Sodium	141.1 ± 5.6 meq/liter	83
203	♀	Serum	14	Calcium	10.65(9.9-11.4) mg/100 ml	65
204			14	Phosphorus	2.01(1.2-3.3) mg/100 ml	
205		....	4	Chloride	115.0 ± 5.6 meq/liter	30

[1/] Plus/minus (±) values are standard error.

continued

Part II. Primates Other Than Man

	Species	Blood Component	No. of Observations	Constituent	Concentration	Reference
206			4	Potassium	6.0 ± 1.0 meq/liter	30
207			4	Sodium	149.3 ± 3.2 meq/liter	30
208	3-6 kg; fasted	Serum	60	Calcium	9.98 ± 0.55 mg/100 ml	2
209			61	Chloride	105.6 ± 3.59 meq/liter	
210			49	Phosphorus	5.0 ± 1.19 mg/100 ml	
211			60	Potassium	4.91 ± 0.61 meq/liter	
212			61	Sodium	147.1 ± 5.42 meq/liter	
213	♂♀	Plasma	3	Calcium	11.9 mg/100 ml	44
214			3	Phosphorus	3.0 mg/100 ml	
215	M. fuscata, ♂	....	20	Chloride	107.5 ± 8.0 meq/liter	30
216			23	Potassium	4.3 ± 0.5 meq/liter	
217			24	Sodium	157.4 ± 11.0 meq/liter	
218	♀	....	17	Chloride	109.8 ± 7.9 meq/liter	30
219			16	Potassium	3.9 ± 0.6 meq/liter	
220			16	Sodium	151.5 ± 10.8 meq/liter	
221	♂♀	....	3	Calcium	(9.1-9.7) mg/100 ml	16
222			3	Phosphorus	(1.4-5.0) mg/100 ml	16
223			24	Phosphorus	4.9 ± 1.2 mg/100 ml	30
224	M. maurus, ♂	....	1	Calcium	10.0 mg/100 ml	16
225			1	Phosphorus	2.5 mg/100 ml	
226	M. mulatta ♂	....	20	Bicarbonate	29.9 ± 3.6 mg/100 ml	89
227			50	Chloride	111.3 ± 4.7 meq/liter	30
228			20	Chloride	115.1 ± 12.5 meq/liter	89
229			60	Potassium	4.4 ± 0.7 meq/liter	30
230			60	Sodium	150.6 ± 9.3 meq/liter	30
231	2-4 yr old; fasted	Serum	20	Calcium	5.3 ± 0.2[L/]-5.4 ± 0.1[L/] meq/liter	87
232			10	Chloride	112.4 ± 0.8[L/] meq/liter	
233			10	Phosphorus	5.8 ± 0.3[L/] mg/100 ml	
234			10	Potassium	5.1 ± 0.1[L/] meq/liter	
235			10	Sodium	155.1 ± 0.6[L/] meq/liter	
236	27-39 mo old	....	4	Calcium	13.8 mg/100 ml	49
237			4	Phosphorus	5.3 mg/100 ml	
238			4	Potassium	4.9 meq/liter	
239			4	Sodium	162 meq/liter	
240	Young adult	Serum	175	Calcium	5.61 ± 0.33 meq/liter	69
241			119	Phosphorus	5.92 ± 1.05 mg/100 ml	
242			175	Potassium	4.68 ± 0.56 meq/liter	
243			175	Sodium	148.7 ± 4.2 meq/liter	
244	4-6 kg	Serum	31	Chloride	105.7 ± 0.61[L/] meq/liter	28
245			33	Phosphorus	3.44 ± 0.21[L/] mg/100 ml	
246			23	Potassium	4.53 ± 0.08[L/] meq/liter	
247			24	Sodium	148.5 ± 0.99[L/] meq/liter	
248	♀	....	20	Bicarbonate	30.3 ± 3.4 mg/100 ml	89
249			20	Chloride	110.2 ± 27.6 meq/liter	89
250			212	Chloride	112.5 ± 6.3 meq/liter	30
251			252	Potassium	4.3 ± 0.9 meq/liter	30
252			256	Sodium	152.1 ± 9.2 meq/liter	30
253		Plasma	3	Potassium	4.0 meq/liter	73
254			3	Sodium	145 meq/liter	73

[L/] Plus/minus (±) values are standard error.

continued

Part II. Primates Other Than Man

	Species	Blood Component	No. of Observations	Constituent	Concentration	Reference
255	2-4 yr old; fasted	Serum	20	Calcium	4.9 ± 0.2[1]-5.4 ± 0.1[1] meq/liter	87
256			10	Chloride	114.2 ± 0.7[1] meq/liter	
257			10	Phosphorus	5.8 ± 0.3[1] mg/100 ml	
258			10	Potassium	5.1 ± 0.1[1] meq/liter	
259			10	Sodium	154.0 ± 0.8[1] meq/liter	
260	Young adult	Serum	214	Calcium	5.40 ± 0.63 meq/liter	69
261			214	Phosphorus	5.79 ± 1.11 mg/100 ml	
262			214	Potassium	4.72 ± 0.50 meq/liter	
263			214	Sodium	148.4 ± 4.4 meq/liter	
264	Adult	Serum	16	Calcium	10.9 ± 0.7 mg/100 ml	38
265			6	Iron	189 μg/100 ml	13
266			16	Phosphorus	4.7 ± 1.3 mg/100 ml	38
267	Pregnant, 16-150 da	Serum	5	Iron	295 μg/100 ml	13
268	Mature	Serum	9	Iron	170.6 ± 78.4 μg/100 ml	77
269	Pregnant, 1st trimester	Serum	6	Iron	220.7 ± 62.1 μg/100 ml	77
270	2nd trimester	Serum	7	Iron	120.4 ± 65.3 μg/100 ml	
271	2.5-4 kg	....	5	Potassium	5.93 ± 0.32 meq/liter	75
272			5	Sodium	157.8 ± 2.53 meq/liter	
273	♂♀	....	28	Calcium	9.2 ± 1.06 mg/100 ml	30
274			5	Chloride	108.3 ± 10.3 meq/liter	55
275			198	Phosphorus	5.2 ± 1.5 mg/100 ml	30
276		Whole blood	2	Bicarbonate	23.6 mmole/liter	48
277			4	Chloride	82.5 mmole/liter	48
278			16	Phosphorus	1.5 mmole/liter	48
279			49	Phosphorus	4.5 ± 1.2-4.6 ± 0.6 mg/100 ml	54
280			8	Potassium	52.3 mmole/liter	48
281			5	Sodium	93.9 mmole/liter	48
282		Erythrocytes	4	Chloride	55.5 mmole/liter	48
283			13	Phosphorus	0.9 mmole/liter	48
284			23	Potassium	102.1 ± 1.2 mmole/liter	17
285			8	Potassium	113.1 mmole/liter	48
286			5	Sodium	8.3 mmole/liter	48
287			23	Sodium	10.0 ± 0.38 mmole/liter	17
288		Plasma	2	Bicarbonate	28.0 mmole/liter	48
289			89	Calcium	6.35 meq/liter	58
290			4	Chloride	102.2 mmole/liter	48
291			89	Chloride	111.8 meq/liter	58
292			13	Phosphorus	2.1 mmole/liter	48
293			89	Phosphorus	4.59 mg/100 ml	58
294			8	Potassium	5.1 mmole/liter	48
295			5	Potassium	4.2 meq/liter	50
296			5	Sodium	157.7 mmole/liter	48
297			5	Sodium	144 meq/liter	50
298		Serum	6	Iron	87 μg/100 ml	9
299			20	Phosphorus	4.4 ± 1.52 mg/100 ml	41
300			59	Potassium	4.0 ± 0.9[1]-4.4 ± 0.1[1] meq/liter	20,40
301			71	Sodium	147 ± 3[1]-153.5 ± 5[1] meq/liter	20,40
302	Fetus, 150 da gestation	Serum	4	Calcium	8.4 mg/100 ml	10
303			4	Phosphorus	5.4 mg/100 ml	
304			4	Potassium	4.5 meq/liter	
305			4	Sodium	140.5 meq/liter	

[1] Plus/minus (±) values are standard error.

continued

Part II. Primates Other Than Man

	Species	Blood Component	No. of Observations	Constituent	Concentration	Reference
306	Infant	....	....	Calcium	9.6 mg/100 ml	59
307				Phosphorus	3.88 mg/100 ml	
308	11-14 mo old	Serum	5	Calcium	10.55 mg/100 ml	24
309			5	Phosphorus	3.48 mg/100 ml	
310	15 mo old	Plasma	21	Iron	180 μg/100 ml	63
311	2-3 yr old	Serum	8	Calcium	(11.5-12.3) mg/100 ml	60
312			8	Chloride	(107-110) meq/liter	
313			8	Phosphorus	(5.76-6.78) mg/100 ml	
314			8	Potassium	(4.36-4.46) meq/liter	
315			8	Sodium	(143-149) meq/liter	
316	2-4 yr old	Whole blood	12	Copper	(57-92) μg/100 ml	5
317			12	Iodine	(4.4-8.3) μg/100 ml	
318			12	Iron	(29-48) mg/100 ml	
319		Serum	12	Calcium	(9.3-13.2) mg/100 ml	
320	5-10 yr old	Serum	7	Calcium	(10.5-11.1) mg/100 ml	60
321			7	Chloride	104 meq/liter	
322			7	Phosphorus	(4.11-4.49) mg/100 ml	
323			7	Potassium	(4.28-4.29) meq/liter	
324			7	Sodium	(142-144) meq/liter	
325	Young	Serum	8	Calcium	10.2 mg/100 ml	86
326			8	Phosphorus	5.1 mg/100 ml	
327	1.5-2.5 kg	Serum	4	Iron	(150-300) μg/100 ml	21
328	1.8-3.2 kg	Plasma	198	Calcium	4.86 ± 0.81 meq/liter	58
329			190	Chloride	108.3 ± 10.3 meq/liter	
330			166	Phosphorus	5.00 ± 0.95 mg/100 ml	
331	2-4 kg	Serum	14	Iron	175.6 μg/100 ml	76
332	2-6 kg	....	>40	Bicarbonate	18.4 meq/liter	22
333			>40	Potassium	4.2 meq/liter	
334			>40	Sodium	148 meq/liter	
335	2.3-3.0 kg	Serum	6	Iron	185 ± 50 μg/100 ml	27
336	2.3-3.5 kg	Serum	36	Calcium	3.9 ± 0.8 meq/liter	14
337			18	Chloride	108 ± 11 meq/liter	
338			19	Phosphate	4.2 ± 2.1 mg/100 ml	
339	2.5-3.5 kg	Serum	35	Potassium	5.0 meq/liter	31
340			35	Sodium	143 meq/liter	
341	2.7-4.4 kg	....	6	Bicarbonate	23.8 meq/liter	85
342			6	Chloride	106 meq/liter	
343			7	Potassium	4.4 meq/liter	
344			7	Sodium	149 meq/liter	
345	2.8-5.3 kg	Serum	108	Chloride	114 ± 9 meq/liter	3
346			10	Phosphorus	6.4 ± 1.0 mg/100 ml	
347			83	Potassium	4.7 ± 0.8 meq/liter	
348			85	Sodium	158 ± 18 meq/liter	
349	2.8-7.2 kg	Plasma	19	Potassium	3.9 meq/liter	51
350			19	Sodium	145 meq/liter	
351	3-4.4 kg	Serum	3	Chloride	101 meq/liter	94
352			3	Potassium	4.6 meq/liter	
353			3	Sodium	146 meq/liter	
354	3-5 kg	Whole blood	152	Phosphorus	4.1 ± 0.1 [1] mg/100 ml	34
355		Serum	145	Chloride	107.7 ± 0.04 [1] meq/liter	
356			76	Potassium	4.44 ± 0.08 [1] meq/liter	

[1] Plus/minus (±) values are standard error.

continued

Part II. Primates Other Than Man

	Species	Blood Component	No. of Observations	Constituent	Concentration	Reference
357			152	Sodium	153.8 ± 0.95 [1/] meq/liter	
358	3-8 kg; fasted	Plasma	10	Chloride	110.2 ± 1.0 [1/] meq/liter	92
359			10	Potassium	4.2 ± 0.3 [1/] meq/liter	
360			10	Sodium	153.0 ± 1.7 [1/] meq/liter	
361	3.2-5.5 kg	....	89	Calcium	5.3 ± 0.5 meq/liter	6
362			89	Potassium	4.6 ± 0.7 meq/liter	
363			89	Sodium	152 ± 8.0 meq/liter	
364	3.5-4.5 kg	....	7	Potassium	3.3 ± 0.2 meq/liter	32
365			7	Sodium	147 ± 1.6 meq/liter	
366	3.8-6.5 kg	Plasma	14	Chloride	103 meq/liter	29
	M. nemestrina					
367	♂	Serum	78	Calcium	10.58(7.1-14.1) mg/100 ml	65
368			78	Phosphorus	5.22(1.4-9.1) mg/100 ml	
369		....	10	Chloride	112.6 ± 5.7 meq/liter	30
370			5	Potassium	4.0 ± 0.4 meq/liter	
371			5	Sodium	152.2 ± 1.8 meq/liter	
372	Young adult	Serum	56	Calcium	(9.5-11.7) mg/100 ml	7
373			56	Phosphorus	(4.5-5.2) mg/100 ml	
374	♀	Serum	454	Calcium	10.29(6.3-14.5) mg/100 ml	65
375			454	Phosphorus	4.45(0.5-11.0) mg/100 ml	
376		....	26	Chloride	111.3 ± 4.7 meq/liter	30
377			27	Potassium	4.2 ± 0.6 meq/liter	
378			27	Sodium	147.6 ± 8.2 meq/liter	
379	Young adult	Serum	399	Calcium	(10.1-11.0) mg/100 ml	7
380			397	Phosphorus	(4.3-5.0) mg/100 ml	
381	♂♀	....	8	Phosphorus	3.9 ± 1.7 mg/100 ml	30
	M. radiata					
382	♂, 3-7 kg	Serum	18	Calcium	12.5 ± 0.73 [1/] mg/100 ml	79
383			18	Phosphorus	4.6 ± 0.23 [1/] mg/100 ml	
384	6-10 kg; fasted	Serum	29	Calcium	10.7 ± 0.56 mg/100 ml	2
385			33	Chloride	105.3 ± 2.94 meq/liter	
386			15	Phosphorus	5.57 ± 1.14 mg/100 ml	
387			33	Potassium	4.9 ± 0.59 meq/liter	
388			33	Sodium	154.3 ± 4.07 meq/liter	
389	♀, 3.7-6 kg; fasted	Serum	64	Calcium	9.95 ± 0.57 mg/100 ml	2
390			64	Chloride	106.8 ± 3.3 meq/liter	
391			36	Phosphorus	4.0 ± 1.07 mg/100 ml	
392			64	Potassium	4.6 ± 0.57 meq/liter	
393			64	Sodium	148.8 ± 4.5 meq/liter	
394	*M. sylvana*, ♀	....	1	Calcium	9.15 mg/100 ml	16
395			1	Chloride	112 meq/liter	
396			1	Potassium	4.0 meq/liter	
397			1	Sodium	111 meq/liter	
398	♂♀	....	4	Calcium	(8.5-9.6) mg/100 ml	16
399			4	Phosphorus	(2.7-4.4) mg/100 ml	
400	*Mandrillus sphinx*, ♀	....	1	Potassium	3.2 meq/liter	16
401	♂♀	....	8	Calcium	(6.7-10.0) mg/100 ml	16
402			8	Phosphorus	(1.6-4.0) mg/100 ml	

[1/] Plus/minus (±) values are standard error.

continued

Part II. Primates Other Than Man

	Species	Blood Component	No. of Observations	Constituent	Concentration	Reference
	Pan troglodytes					
403	♂	Erythrocytes	1	Potassium	127 meq/liter	19
404			1	Sodium	28.2 meq/liter	
405		Plasma	1	Potassium	4.99 meq/liter	19
406			1	Sodium	152 meq/liter	
407		Serum	35	Chloride	101 ± 4 meq/liter	61
408			32	Copper	121 ± 26 µg/100 ml	
409			34	Iron	132 ± 41 µg/100 ml	
410			30	Phosphorus	5.12 ± 1.23 mg/100 ml	
411			31	Potassium	4.4 ± 1.1 meq/liter	
412			34	Sodium	130 ± 6 meq/liter	
413	<1 to >40 yr old; fasted	Serum	71	Bicarbonate	23.4 ± 4.2 meq/liter	46
414			71	Calcium	9.3 ± 1.0 mg/100 ml	
415			79	Chloride	98.9 ± 3.8 meq/liter	
416			70	Phosphorus	5.2 ± 1.3 mg/100 ml	
417			71	Potassium	3.7 ± 0.4 meq/liter	
418			71	Sodium	139.5 ± 3.7 meq/liter	
419	14-180 mo old; fasted	Serum	143	Bicarbonate	59.0 ± 9.8 vol %	33
420			148	Calcium	4.5 ± 0.5 meq/liter	
421			148	Chloride	101 ± 4.5 meq/liter	
422			147	Potassium	3.8 ± 0.6 meq/liter	
423			148	Sodium	139.4 ± 5.9 meq/liter	
424	28-74 mo old	....	13	Bicarbonate	59.6 ± 7.62 vol %	72
425			13	Calcium	4.74 ± 0.59 meq/liter	
426			13	Chloride	103.3 ± 5.8 meq/liter	
427			13	Phosphorus	3.63 ± 0.78 mg/100 ml	
428			13	Potassium	3.9 ± 1.07 meq/liter	
429			13	Sodium	142.8 ± 10.36 meq/liter	
430	36-70 mo old	....	13	Chloride	102 ± 1.9 meq/liter	42
431			13	Sodium	141 ± 2.4[1] meq/liter	
432	4-5 yr old	....	3	Bicarbonate	57.4 vol %	26
433			3	Sodium	142.3 meq/liter	
434	Mature	....	1	Sodium	149 meq/liter	18
435	9-18 kg	....	4	Chloride	164 meq/liter	39
436			4	Potassium	5.3 meq/liter	
437			4	Sodium	146 meq/liter	
438	♀	Erythrocytes	1	Potassium	131 meq/liter	19
439			1	Sodium	24.8 meq/liter	
440		Plasma	1	Potassium	3.83 meq/liter	19
441			1	Sodium	149 meq/liter	
442		Serum	33	Chloride	102 ± 3 meq/liter	61
443			27	Copper	129.5 ± 25 µg/100 ml	
444			33	Iron	134 ± 41 µg/100 ml	
445			31	Phosphorus	5.42 ± 1.16 mg/100 ml	
446			28	Potassium	3.9 ± 0.9 meq/liter	
447			28	Sodium	128.5 ± 4 meq/liter	
448	<1 to >40 yr old; fasted	Serum	153	Bicarbonate	23.2 ± 3.9 meq/liter	46
449			153	Calcium	9.3 ± 0.8 mg/100 ml	
450			153	Chloride	100.0 ± 4.2 meq/liter	

[1] Plus/minus (±) values are standard error.

continued

Part II. Primates Other Than Man

	Species	Blood Component	No. of Obser-vations	Constituent	Concentration	Refer-ence
451			153	Phosphorus	4.6 ± 1.2 mg/100 ml	
452			153	Potassium	3.6 ± 0.6 meq/liter	
453			153	Sodium	138.9 ± 3.4 meq/liter	
454	14-180 mo old; fasted	Serum	98	Bicarbonate	58.3 ± 10.2 vol %	33
455			102	Calcium	4.5 ± 0.9 meq/liter	
456			102	Chloride	101 ± 4.9 meq/liter	
457			101	Potassium	3.9 ± 0.6 meq/liter	
458			102	Sodium	139.3 ± 5.9 meq/liter	
459	28-74 mo old	....	7	Bicarbonate	59.9 ± 7.15 vol %	72
460			7	Calcium	4.9 ± 0.52 meq/liter	
461			7	Chloride	102.9 ± 1.98 meq/liter	
462			7	Phosphorus	3.78 ± 1.06 mg/100 ml	
463			7	Potassium	4.15 ± 0.75 meq/liter	
464			7	Sodium	140.4 ± 5.08 meq/liter	
465	36-70 mo old	....	11	Chloride	111 meq/liter	42
466			11	Sodium	156 meq/liter	
467	4-5 yr old	....	1	Bicarbonate	65.6 vol %	26
468			1	Sodium	142 meq/liter	
469	Mature	....	4	Sodium	141 meq/liter	18
470	♂♀	Whole blood	9	Phosphorus	3.1 ± 1.0-4.13 ± 1.69 mg/100 ml	54
471		Serum	3	Potassium	3.63 meq/liter	80
472			3	Sodium	136 meq/liter	
473	0-5 yr old; fasted	Serum	38	Bicarbonate	20.5 ± 3.4 meq/liter	46
474			38	Calcium	9.6 ± 0.9 mg/100 ml	
475			38	Chloride	102.1 ± 3.8 meq/liter	
476			38	Phosphorus	5.5 ± 1.2 mg/100 ml	
477			38	Potassium	4.1 ± 0.5 meq/liter	
478			38	Sodium	139 ± 4.0 meq/liter	
479	18-36 mo old	Serum	6	Calcium	13.0 mg/100 ml	68
480			6	Chloride	374 mg/100 ml	
481			6	Potassium	19.6 mg/100 ml	
482			6	Sodium	304 mg/100 ml	
483	18 mo-16 yr old	Serum	169	Bicarbonate	51.4 vol %	81
484			86	Calcium	5.05 meq/liter	
485			128	Chloride	103 meq/liter	
486			47	Phosphorus	4.6 mg/100 ml	
487			83	Potassium	4.0 meq/liter	
488			101	Sodium	144 meq/liter	
489	20-59 mo old	Serum	12	Iron	91.5 μg/100 ml	93
490	<3 yr old	Serum	7	Chloride	104.5 ± 3 meq/liter	61
491			4	Copper	111 ± 16 μg/100 ml	
492			7	Iron	134 ± 32 μg/100 ml	
493			6	Phosphorus	6.20 ± 1.51 mg/100 ml	
494			7	Potassium	4.6 ± 1.0 meq/liter	
495			7	Sodium	128 ± 3 meq/liter	
496	3-7 yr old	Serum	25	Chloride	102.5 ± 3 meq/liter	61
497			24	Copper	118 ± 26 μg/100 ml	
498			25	Iron	130 ± 22 μg/100 ml	
499			25	Phosphorus	5.57 ± 0.83 mg/100 ml	
500			24	Potassium	4.1 ± 0.5 meq/liter	
501			25	Sodium	129 ± 5 meq/liter	

continued

Part II. Primates Other Than Man

	Species	Blood Component	No. of Obser-vations	Constituent	Concentration	Refer-ence
502	4-5 yr old	....	4	Calcium	10.6 mg/100 ml	26
503			4	Chloride	101 ± 3.0 meq/liter	
504			4	Potassium	3.9 ± 0.7 meq/liter	
505	4-6 yr old	....	4	Bicarbonate	58.2 vol %	25
506			4	Calcium	10.1 mg/100 ml	
507			4	Chloride	100 meq/liter	
508			4	Phosphorus	3.72 mg/100 ml	
509			4	Potassium	3.95 meq/liter	
510			4	Sodium	142 meq/liter	
511	5-10 yr old; fasted	Serum	69	Bicarbonate	23.4 ± 4.0 meq/liter	46
512			69	Calcium	9.4 ± 0.8 mg/100 ml	
513			69	Chloride	99.4 ± 3.4 meq/liter	
514			68	Phosphorus	5.2 ± 1.3 mg/100 ml	
515			69	Potassium	3.6 ± 0.4 meq/liter	
516			69	Sodium	139.4 ± 3.4 meq/liter	
517	7-15 yr old	Serum	19	Chloride	100.5 ± 3 meq/liter	61
518			17	Copper	131 ± 19 μg/100 ml	
519			18	Iron	139 ± 38 μg/100 ml	
520			16	Phosphorus	5.56 ± 1.17 mg/100 ml	
521			16	Potassium	3.9 ± 1.0 meq/liter	
522			18	Sodium	128 ± 5 meq/liter	
523	>10 yr old; fasted	Serum	117	Bicarbonate	24.0 ± 3.8 meq/liter	46
524			117	Calcium	9.2 ± 0.9 mg/100 ml	
525			117	Chloride	99.1 ± 4.4 meq/liter	
526			117	Phosphorus	3.8 ± 1.0 mg/100 ml	
527			117	Potassium	3.5 ± 0.5 meq/liter	
528			117	Sodium	139.0 ± 3.8 meq/liter	
529	>15 yr old	Serum	6	Chloride	100 ± 3 meq/liter	61
530			5	Copper	116 ± 31 μg/100 ml	
531			6	Iron	97.5 ± 31 μg/100 ml	
532			6	Phosphorus	3.80 ± 0.74 mg/100 ml	
533			4	Potassium	3.1 ± 0.5 meq/liter	
534			4	Sodium	132 ± 3 meq/liter	
535	Juvenile	Serum	7	Calcium	4.63 ± 0.18 meq/liter	8
536			7	Chloride	102.5 ± 4.77 meq/liter	
537			7	Phosphorus	6.02 ± 0.27 mg/100 ml	
538			7	Potassium	4.53 ± 0.63 meq/liter	
539			7	Sodium	148.0 ± 1.4 meq/liter	
540	Immature	....	13	Chloride	108 ± 1.9[1] meq/liter	18
541			15	Sodium	154 ± 2.4[1] meq/liter	
542	Mature	Serum	27	Calcium	4.78 ± 0.35 meq/liter	8
543			27	Chloride	105 ± 4.31 meq/liter	
544			27	Phosphorus	3.69 ± 1.08 mg/100 ml	
545			27	Potassium	3.85 ± 0.36 meq/liter	
546			27	Sodium	137.83 ± 2.07 meq/liter	
	Papio spp.					
547	♂	....	23	Calcium	9.6 ± 0.45 mg/100 ml	56
548			23	Chloride	108 ± 2.3 meq/liter	
549			23	Phosphate	4.8 ± 1.44 mg/100 ml	

[1] Plus/minus (±) values are standard error.

continued

Part II. Primates Other Than Man

	Species	Blood Component	No. of Observations	Constituent	Concentration	Reference
550		Plasma	10	Phosphate	5.2 ± 1.4 mg/100 ml	57
551	9-14 kg	Plasma	11	Potassium	3.4 ± 0.05[1]-3.47 ± 0.14[1] meq/liter	74
552	Fasted	Plasma	59	Iron	149 ± 45 µg/100 ml	57
553			40	Iron	152 ± 53 µg/100 ml	
554			58	Magnesium	1.6 ± 0.2 mg/100 ml	
555			41	Magnesium	1.7 ± 0.3 mg/100 ml	
556			41	Zinc	112 ± 32.5 µg/100 ml	
557			58	Zinc	138 ± 29.8 µg/100 ml	
558	♀	....	77	Calcium	9.4 ± 0.45 mg/100 ml	56
559			77	Chloride	110 ± 3.2 meq/liter	
560			77	Phosphate	3.8 ± 1.30 mg/100 ml	
561	Fasted	Plasma	98	Iron	147 ± 55 µg/100 ml	57
562			99	Magnesium	1.6 ± 0.2 mg/100 ml	
563			29	Phosphate	3.5 ± 1.4 mg/100 ml	
564			30	Phosphate	3.6 ± 1.4 mg/100 ml	
565			99	Zinc	132 ± 31.0 µg/100 ml	
566	♂♀, 3-54 mo old	Serum	51	Potassium	5.0 ± 0.7 meq/liter	47
567			51	Sodium	147 ± 6 meq/liter	
568	Young-mature	Serum	38	Potassium	4.3 ± 0.5 meq/liter	47
569			38	Sodium	151 ± 8 meq/liter	
570	8.5-26.9 kg	Serum	12	Calcium	4.20 ± 0.73 meq/liter	8
571			12	Chloride	107.37 ± 3.65 meq/liter	
572			12	Phosphorus	6.97 ± 1.49 mg/100 ml	
573			12	Potassium	3.82 ± 0.53 meq/liter	
574			12	Sodium	142.41 ± 2.55 meq/liter	
575	Fasted	....	171	Calcium	9.2 ± 0.6-9.8 ± 0.6 mg/100 ml	56
576			171	Chloride	108 ± 1.6-108 ± 3.2 meq/liter	
577			171	Phosphate	4.0 ± 1.1-4.4 ± 1.4 mg/100 ml	
578			171	Potassium	3.6 ± 0.3-3.8 ± 0.4 meq/liter	
579			171	Sodium	142 ± 2.3-146 ± 1.9 meq/liter	
580		Plasma	185	Calcium	9.4 ± 0.6 mg/100 ml	57
581			190	Chloride	107.6 ± 3.3 meq/liter	
582			115	Phosphate	4.0 ± 1.1 mg/100 ml	
583			190	Potassium	3.8 ± 0.5 meq/liter	
584			190	Sodium	143 ± 2.4 meq/liter	
	P. cynocephalus					
585	♂, <1 yr old	....	34	Calcium	10.8 ± 0.64 mg/100 ml	7
586			34	Phosphorus	6.2 ± 1.2 mg/100 ml	
587	1-3 yr old	....	32	Phosphorus	5.9 ± 0.95 mg/100 ml	7
588	♀, <1 yr old	....	34	Calcium	10.5 ± 0.82 mg/100 ml	7
589			34	Phosphorus	6.0 ± 1.4 mg/100 ml	
590	1-3 yr old	....	45	Phosphorus	6.2 ± 1.5 mg/100 ml	7
591	adult; pregnant	Serum	3	Carbon dioxide	43.1 vol %	15
592			3	Chloride	121 meq/liter	
593			3	Potassium	4.0 meq/liter	
594			3	Sodium	152 meq/liter	
595	♂♀, adult	Serum	10	Iron	148 µg/100 ml	23
596	*P. cynocephalus anubis*, ♂	Serum	73	Calcium	10.88(9.8-13.1) mg/100 ml	65
597			72	Phosphorus	5.99(2.8-8.2) mg/100 ml	

[1] Plus/minus (±) values are standard error.

continued

Part II. Primates Other Than Man

	Species	Blood Component	No. of Observations	Constituent	Concentration	Reference
598	♀	Serum	86	Calcium	10.79(8.4-12.7) mg/100 ml	65
599			86	Phosphorus	6.18(1.7-9.6) mg/100 ml	
	P. hamadryas [2/]					
600	♀	Erythrocytes	1	Potassium	184 meq/liter	19
601			1	Sodium	19.0 meq/liter	
602		Plasma	1	Potassium	3.38 meq/liter	19
603			1	Sodium	163 meq/liter	
604	Adult	Serum	9	Iron	144 µg/100 ml	37
605	♂♀	Whole blood	....	Phosphorus	4.21 ± 1.1-5.13 ± 2.23 mg/100 ml	54
	P. ursinus, ♂♀					
606	Infant-adult	....	1400	Calcium	4.9 ± 0.6 meq/liter	91
607			1400	Carbon dioxide	30.1 ± 4.5 mmole/liter	
608			1400	Chloride	100 ± 6 meq/liter	
609			1400	Phosphorus	1.7 ± 0.5 mmole/liter	
610			1400	Potassium	3.3 ± 0.7 meq/liter	
611			1400	Sodium	145 ± 6 meq/liter	
612	12.5 ± 5.8 kg	....	8	Calcium	4.4 ± 0.2 mmole/liter	52
613			8	Phosphorus	1.85 ± 0.5 mmole/liter	
	Pongo pygmaeus					
614	♂	....	1	Chloride	106.4 meq/liter	16
615			1	Potassium	4.34 meq/liter	
616			1	Sodium	126 meq/liter	
617	<1 to >12 yr old; fasted	Serum	43	Calcium	9.2 ± 0.9 mg/100 ml	46
618			43	Carbon dioxide	22.2 ± 3.7 meq/liter	
619			43	Chloride	99.6 ± 3.4 meq/liter	
620			43	Phosphorus	4.4 ± 0.9 mg/100 ml	
621			43	Potassium	4.0 ± 0.6 meq/liter	
622			43	Sodium	137.7 ± 3.8 meq/liter	
623	3 yr old	....	1	Calcium	9.8 mg/100 ml	11
624			1	Chloride	100 meq/liter	
625			1	Phosphorus	6.4 mg/100 ml	
626			1	Potassium	4.1 meq/liter	
627			1	Sodium	138 meq/liter	
628	15 yr old	....	1	Calcium	9.6 mg/100 ml	11
629			1	Chloride	99 meq/liter	
630			1	Phosphorus	3.3 mg/100 ml	
631			1	Potassium	3.7 meq/liter	
632			1	Sodium	143 meq/liter	
633	♀	....	1	Calcium	10.9 mg/100 ml	16
634			2	Chloride	(91.5-100.8) meq/liter	
635			2	Phosphorus	(2.3-3.5) mg/100 ml	
636			2	Potassium	(2.2-2.55) meq/liter	
637			1	Sodium	60 meq/liter	
638	<1 to >12 yr old; fasted	Serum	48	Calcium	9.6 ± 0.9 mg/100 ml	46
639			49	Carbon dioxide	20.5 ± 3.7 meq/liter	
640			49	Chloride	101.5 ± 3.6 meq/liter	
641			49	Phosphorus	4.5 ± 1.0 mg/100 ml	
642			48	Potassium	4.2 ± 0.7 meq/liter	
643			49	Sodium	139.0 ± 3.7 meq/liter	

[2/] Synonym: *P. doguera hamadryas.*

continued

	Species	Blood Component	No. of Observations	Constituent	Concentration	Reference
644	14 yr old	....	1	Calcium	9.9 mg/100 ml	11
645			1	Chloride	97 meq/liter	
646			1	Phosphorus	3.6 mg/100 ml	
647			1	Potassium	4.3 meq/liter	
648			1	Sodium	138 meq/liter	
649	♂♀; 0-5 yr old; fasted	Serum	20	Calcium	9.3 ± 1.2 mg/100 ml	46
650			21	Carbon dioxide	18.5 ± 3.2 meq/liter	
651			21	Chloride	101.8 ± 5.2 meq/liter	
652			21	Phosphorus	4.9 ± 1.5 mg/100 ml	
653			20	Potassium	4.5 ± 0.9 meq/liter	
654			21	Sodium	138.6 ± 4.6 meq/liter	
655	5-10 yr old; fasted	Serum	44	Calcium	9.5 ± 0.8 mg/100 ml	46
656			44	Carbon dioxide	22.3 ± 4.1 meq/liter	
657			44	Chloride	100.2 ± 2.8 meq/liter	
658			44	Phosphorus	4.4 ± 0.8 mg/100 ml	
659			44	Potassium	4.0 ± 0.5 meq/liter	
660			44	Sodium	138.3 ± 3.2 meq/liter	
661	>10 yr old; fasted	Serum	27	Calcium	9.3 ± 0.8 mg/100 ml	46
662			27	Carbon dioxide	21.8 ± 2.4 meq/liter	
663			27	Chloride	100.4 ± 3.2 meq/liter	
664			27	Phosphorus	4.2 ± 0.6 mg/100 ml	
665			27	Potassium	3.9 ± 0.5 meq/liter	
666			27	Sodium	138.4 ± 4.0 meq/liter	
	Presbytis entellus					
667	♂, 12-20 kg; fasted	Serum	13	Calcium	11.4 ± 1.4 mg/100 ml	1
668			8	Chloride	103.3 ± 3.6 meq/liter	
669			15	Phosphorus	5.6 ± 1.6 mg/100 ml	
670			20	Potassium	5.9 ± 0.7 meq/liter	
671			20	Sodium	154.3 ± 5.1 meq/liter	
672	♀, 10-16 kg; fasted	Serum	24	Calcium	11.6 ± 0.9 mg/100 ml	1
673			36	Chloride	107.3 ± 3.8 meq/liter	
674			30	Phosphorus	5.0 ± 1.3 mg/100 ml	
675			37	Potassium	5.7 ± 0.7 meq/liter	
676			38	Sodium	154.1 ± 4.4 meq/liter	
677	*Saguinus nigricollis*, ♂♀	Serum	79	Calcium	10.4 mg/100 ml	35
678			70	Carbon dioxide	13.64 meq/liter	
679			82	Chloride	113.6 meq/liter	
680			31	Magnesium	2.44 meq/liter	
681			49	Phosphate	5.48 mg/100 ml	
682			95	Potassium	5.71 meq/liter	
683			90	Sodium	169.0 meq/liter	
684	Mature	Plasma	17	Iron	(29.6-256.2) μg/100 ml	4
685	*S. oedipus*, ♂♀	Serum	17	Calcium	9.95 mg/100 ml	35
686			34	Carbon dioxide	18.56 meq/liter	
687			31	Chloride	108.5 meq/liter	
688			16	Magnesium	2.14 meq/liter	
689			34	Phosphate	4.72 mg/100 ml	
690			40	Potassium	5.99 meq/liter	
691			36	Sodium	161.2 meq/liter	

continued

240. BLOOD ELECTROLYTES: PRIMATES

Part II. Primates Other Than Man

	Species	Blood Component	No. of Observations	Constituent	Concentration	Reference
692	Mature	Plasma	19	Iron	(9.6-254.0) µg/100 ml	4
693		Serum	38	Calcium	4.40 ± 0.41 meq/liter	8
694			74	Chloride	110.9 ± 6.07 meq/liter	
695			34	Phosphorus	4.82 ± 1.61 mg/100 ml	
696			62	Potassium	4.86 ± 0.79 meq/liter	
697			61	Sodium	146.9 ± 7.28 meq/liter	
	Saimiri sciureus					
698	♂	....	36	Chloride	123.4 ± 4.5 meq/liter	30
699	♂♀	....	144	Calcium	10.1 ± 0.93 mg/100 ml	30
700			7	Phosphorus	3.4 ± 0.6 mg/100 ml	30
701			105	Potassium	4.9 meq/liter	67
702			155	Sodium	155 meq/liter	67
703	6-12 mo old	Serum	12	Calcium	9.9 ± 0.49 mg/100 ml	43
704			12	Phosphorus	4.5 ± 1.23 mg/100 ml	
705	1-4 yr old	....	67	Calcium	5.1 ± 0.3 meq/liter	53
706			48	Chloride	113.6 ± 5.2 meq/liter	
707			67	Phosphorus	5.3 ± 1.4 mg/100 ml	
708			67	Potassium	5.6 ± 1.2 meq/liter	
709			67	Sodium	159.7 ± 6.1 meq/liter	
710	2-3 yr old; fasted	Serum	109	Calcium	9.6 ± 0.5 mg/100 ml	45
711			110	Chloride	118 ± 5.5 meq/liter	
712			110	Potassium	6.3 ± 1.1 meq/liter	
713			110	Sodium	148 ± 6.1 meq/liter	
714	3-4 yr old; fasted	Serum	104	Calcium	10.0 ± 0.5 mg/100 ml	45
715			105	Chloride	113 ± 5.4 meq/liter	
716			101	Phosphorus	4.9 ± 1.7 mg/100 ml	
717			105	Potassium	4.5 ± 0.9 meq/liter	
718			105	Sodium	148 ± 4.9 meq/liter	
719	4-5 yr old; fasted	Serum	85	Calcium	9.5 ± 0.7 mg/100 ml	45
720			87	Chloride	115 ± 7.9 meq/liter	
721			87	Potassium	4.3 ± 0.9 meq/liter	
722			87	Sodium	152 ± 6.6 meq/liter	
723	425-435 g	....	5	Carbon dioxide	47.1 vol %	95
724			5	Chloride	116 meq/liter	
725			5	Potassium	2.7 meq/liter	
726			5	Sodium	153 meq/liter	
727	600-900 g	Serum	12	Calcium	10.7 ± 0.57 mg/100 ml	36
728			12	Phosphorus	5.0 ± 1.43 mg/100 ml	
729	*Symphalangus syndactylus,* ♂	....	1	Calcium	10.3 mg/100 ml	16
730			1	Chloride	104 meq/liter	
731			1	Magnesium	2.60 mg/100 ml	
732			1	Potassium	6.0 meq/liter	
733	♀	....	1	Calcium	9.8 mg/100 ml	16
734			1	Chloride	104 meq/liter	
735			1	Magnesium	2.50 mg/100 ml	
736			1	Potassium	5.1 meq/liter	
737			1	Sodium	133 meq/liter	

Contributors: Smith, Frank A., Michaelson, S.M., and Lebda, Nancy J. A.

continued

240. BLOOD ELECTROLYTES: PRIMATES

Part II. Primates Other Than Man

References

[1] Altshuler, H. L., and R. E. Stowell. 1972. Lab. Anim. Sci. 22:692.

[2] Altshuler, H. L., et al. 1971. Ibid. 21:916.

[3] Anderson, D. R. 1966. Amer. J. Vet. Res. 27:1484.

[4] Anderson, E. T., et al. 1967. Lab. Anim. Care 17:30.

[5] Asatiani, V. S., et al. 1959. Bull. Exp. Biol. Med. 47:203.

[6] Bezahler, G. H., and A. Kaminskis. 1968. Edgewood Arsenal Tech. Mem. EA-TM-116-5.

[7] Blakey, G. A., and W. R. Morton. Unpublished. Univ. Washington, Regional Primate Research Center, Seattle, 1973.

[8] Burns, K. F., et al. 1967. Amer. J. Clin. Pathol. 48:484.

[9] Chatterjea, J. B. 1960. Bull. Calcutta Sch. Trop. Med. 8:9.

[10] Chez, R. A., et al. 1964. Amer. J. Obstet. Gynecol. 90:128.

[11] Clevenger, A. B., et al. 1971. Amer. J. Clin. Pathol. 55:479.

[12] Cortese, T. A., Jr., et al. 1969. J. Invest. Dermatol. 53:172.

[13] Cotes, P. M., et al. 1966. Brit. J. Pharmacol. 26:633.

[14] Crawley, G. J., et al. 1966. Appl. Microbiol. 14:445.

[15] Crosby, W. M., et al. 1968. Amer. J. Obstet. Gynecol. 101:100.

[16] D'Agostino, V. Unpublished. Bronx Zoo, N.Y., 1973.

[17] Dunn, M. J. 1969. J. Clin. Invest. 48:674.

[18] Elmadjian, F. 1963. 6571st Aeromed. Res. Lab. Tech. Doc. Rep. ARL-TDR-63-18.

[19] Emeljanov, N. A. 1966. Zh. Evol. Biokhim. Fiziol. 2:519.

[20] Faas, F. H., and A. K. Ommaya. 1968. J. Neurosurg. 28:137.

[21] Fitch, C. D., et al. 1964. Proc. Soc. Exp. Biol. Med. 116:130.

[22] Fox, C. L., Jr., and S. E. Lasker. 1961. Surg. Gynecol. Obstet. 112:274.

[23] Foy, H., et al. 1968. Acta Haematol. 39:118.

[24] Freeman, S., et al. 1943. Gastroenterology 1:199.

[25] Gleason, T. L., III, and R. H. Edwards. 1963. 6571st Aeromed. Res. Lab. Tech. Doc. Rep. ARL-TDR-63-14.

[26] Gleason, T. L., III, and R. H. Edwards. 1965. Ibid. ARL-TDR-65-16.

[27] Greenberg, L. D., and J. F. Rinehart. 1955. Proc. Soc. Exp. Biol. Med. 88:325.

[28] Greep, R. O., et al. 1952. Endocrinology 50:664.

[29] Guerra, F., and H. G. Barbour. 1943. J. Pharmacol. Exp. Ther. 79:55.

[30] Hall, A. S. 1971. Advan. Automat. Anal. 4:129.

[31] Herrero, B. A., et al. 1967. Exp. Mol. Pathol. 6:84.

[32] Herschkowitz, N., et al. 1965. Brain 88:557.

[33] Hodson, H. H., Jr., et al. 1968. Folia Primatol. 8:77.

[34] Hofmann, F. G., et al. 1954. Amer. J. Physiol. 178:361.

[35] Holmes, A. W., et al. 1967. Lab. Anim. Care 17:41.

[36] Hunt, R. D., et al. 1969. Amer. J. Clin. Nutr. 22:358.

[37] Huser, H. J., et al. 1967. In H. Vagtborg, ed. The Baboon in Medical Research. Univ. Texas Press, Austin. v. 2.

[38] King, T. O., and Gargus, J. L. 1967. Lab. Anim. Care 17:391.

[39] Klein, F., et al. 1966. J. Infec. Dis. 116:123.

[40] Knobil, E., and R. O. Greep. 1958. Endocrinology 62:61.

[41] Laird, C. W. 1972. Representative Values for Animal and Veterinary Populations and Their Clinical Significance. Hycel, Inc., Houston, Tex.

[42] Layne, D. S., et al. 1964. 6571st Aeromed. Res. Lab. Tech. Doc. Rep. ARL-TDR-63-26.

[43] Lehner, N. D. M., et al. 1967. Lab. Anim. Care 17:483.

[44] Levitt, M. F., et al. 1958. J. Clin. Invest. 37:294.

[45] Manning, P. J., et al. 1969. Lab. Anim. Care 19:831.

[46] McClure, H. M., et al. In press. In G. H. Bourne, ed. The Chimpanzee. S. Karger, Basel. v. 5.

[47] McCraw, A. P., and A. K. Sim. 1972. J. Comp. Pathol. 82:193.

[48] McKee, R. W., et al. 1946. J. Exp. Med. 84:569.

[49] Melville, G. S., Jr., et al. 1966. U.S. Air Force Sch. Aerosp. Med. Tech. Rep. (Brooks) SAM-TR-66-48.

[50] Murphy, G. P., and J. C. Sharp. 1964. J. Surg. Res. 4:550.

[51] Murphy, G. P., and S. C. Woodward. 1964. Invest. Urol. 2:235.

[52] Murphy, G. P., et al. 1968. S. Afr. Med. J. 42 (Suppl.):26.

[53] New, A. E. 1968. In L. A. Rosenblum and R. W. Cooper, ed. The Squirrel Monkey. Academic Press, New York. p. 417.

[54] Olsen, R. E., and K. F. Burns. 1971. Hycel Vet. Symp. 1:59.

[55] Oser, F., et al. 1970. Lab. Anim. Care 20:462.

[56] Pena, A. de la, and J. W. Goldzieher. 1967. In H. Vagtborg, ed. The Baboon in Medical Research. Univ. Texas Press, Austin. v. 2.

[57] Pena, A. de la, et al. 1970. Lab. Anim. Care 20:251.

[58] Petery, J. J. 1967. Ibid. 17:342.

[59] Pickering, D. E., and D. A. Fisher. 1953. Amer. J. Dis. Child. 86:1.

[60] Pickering, D. E., and T. T-H Kao. 1961. J. Amer. Vet. Med. Ass. 138:527.

[61] Planas, J., and M. Grau. 1971. Folia Primatol. 15:77.

[62] Pridgen, W. A. 1967. Lab. Anim. Care 17:463.

[63] Proehl, E. C., and C. D. May. 1952. Blood 7:671.

[64] Raman, A. 1970. Quart. J. Exp. Physiol. Cog. Med. Sci. 55:271.

[65] Reese, D. Unpublished. Univ. Washington, Regional Primate Research Center, Seattle, 1973.

[66] Reigel, D. H., et al. 1970. In F. M. Wageneder and S. Schuy, ed. Electrotherapeutic Sleep and Electroanesthesia. Excerpta Medica, Amsterdam.

continued

Part II. Primates Other Than Man

[67] Reynolds, D. V. 1969. Stanford Res. Inst. Proj. BU-6097.
[68] Robaidek, E. S., et al. 1967. 6571st Aeromed. Res. Lab. Tech. Doc. Rep. ARL-TDR-67-21.
[69] Robinson, F. R., and R. F. Ziegler. 1968. Lab. Anim. Care 18:50.
[70] Ross, M. A., and W. G. Sheldon. 1966. U.S. Army Med. Res. Lab. Rep. USAMRL-679.
[71] Schnell, J. V., et al. 1969. Mil. Med. 134:1068.
[72] Scott, R. A., Jr. 1964. 6571st Aeromed. Res. Lab. Tech. Rep. ARL-TDR-64-12.
[73] Sharp, J. C., and G. P. Murphy. 1964. Nephron 1:172.
[74] Shropshire, S., Jr., et al. 1969. Aerosp. Med. 40:237.
[75] Singh, T. I., and S. Banerjee. 1964. Indian J. Exp. Biol. 2:215.
[76] Sood, S. K., et al. 1965. Blood 26:421.
[77] Spicer, E. J. F., and C. E. Oxnard. 1967. Folia Primatol. 6:236.
[78] Spink, W. W., et al. 1963. Proc. Soc. Exp. Biol. Med. 112:795.
[79] Srikantia, S. G., and C. Gopalan. 1963. J. Appl. Physiol. 18:1231.
[80] Stafanini, P., et al. 1968. Int. Surg. 49:181.
[81] Staten, F. W., et al. 1961. U.S. Air Force Missile Develop. Cent. Tech. Rep. AFMDC-TR-61-25.
[82] Sweet, A. Y., et al. 1958. J. Clin. Invest. 37:65.
[83] Sweet, A. Y., et al. 1961. Amer. J. Physiol. 201:975.
[84] Taylor, J. F., et al. 1973. Lab. Anim. Sci. 23:582.
[85] Tisher, C. C., et al. 1969. Amer. J. Pathol. 56:469.
[86] Toomey, J. A., et al. 1942. Amer. J. Dis. Child. 64:1008.
[87] Turbyfill, C. L., et al. 1970. Lab. Anim. Care 20:269.
[88] Vitale, J. J., et al. 1963. Circ. Res. 12:642.
[89] Vogin, E. E., and F. Oser. 1971. Lab. Anim. Sci. 21:937.
[90] Vondruska, J. F. 1970. Ibid. 20:97.
[91] Weber, H. W., et al. 1971. Int. Symp. Lab. Anim., 4th, 1969, p. 529.
[92] White, R. J., et al. 1960. Proc. Staff Meet. Mayo Clin. 35:114.
[93] Wisecup, W. G., et al. 1968. Amer. J. Vet. Res. 29:1823.
[94] Wolfman, E. F., Jr., et al. 1966. J. Surg. Res. 6:2.
[95] Workman, R. D., et al. 1962. U.S. Nav. Med. Res. Lab. Rep. 374.
[96] Young, T. K., and R. A. Phillips. 1967. Proc. Soc. Exp. Biol. Med. 125:1174.

241. BLOOD ELECTROLYTES: MAMMALS OTHER THAN PRIMATES

Plus/minus (±) values are standard deviation, unless otherwise indicated.

	Species (Synonym)	Blood Component	No. of Observations	Constituent	Concentration	Reference
1	*Alcelaphus buselaphus jacksoni*, ♂	....	2	Calcium	9.5 mg/100 ml	20
2			1	Chloride	114 meq/liter	
3			2	Phosphorus	5.67-6.3 mg/100 ml	
4			1	Potassium	3.92 meq/liter	
5	*Ammotragus lervia*, ♂♀	....	1	Calcium	9.8 mg/100 ml	20
6			1	Phosphorus	7.5 mg/100 ml	
7	Adult	Serum	21	Calcium	11.4 ± 0.8 mg/100 ml	75
8			21	Chloride	120 ± 3 meq/liter	
9			21	Phosphorus	8.4 ± 2.1 mg/100 ml	
10			21	Potassium	5.1 ± 0.9 meq/liter	
11			21	Sodium	149 ± 4 meq/liter	
12	*Arctocephalus australis*, ♀	....	1	Calcium	11.8 mg/100 ml	20
13			1	Phosphorus	6.3 mg/100 ml	
14	*Bison bonasus*, ♂	....	1	Calcium	11.6 mg/100 ml	20
15			1	Chloride	96 meq/liter	
16			1	Phosphorus	10.1 mg/100 ml	
17			1	Potassium	3.96 meq/liter	
18	*Bos grunniens*, ♀	....	1	Chloride	110 meq/liter	51
19			1	Potassium	3.3 meq/liter	
20			1	Sodium	174.0 meq/liter	
21	*B. taurus* ♂	Serum	...	Chloride	97-111 meq/liter	71

continued

	Species (Synonym)	Blood Component	No. of Observations	Constituent	Concentration	Reference
22			...	Potassium	3.9 ± 5.8 meq/liter	71
23			...	Sodium	132-152 meq/liter	71
24	♀	Whole blood	29	Copper	68.0-81.2 µg/100 ml	33
25			843	Magnesium	2.3 ± 0.23-2.4 ± 0.32 mg/100 ml	66
26		Plasma	1	Iron	175 µg/100 ml	37
27			...	Magnesium	2.8 ± 0.32 mg/100 ml	66
28			11	Potassium	5.6 ± 0.9 meq/liter	16
29		Serum	275	Magnesium	2.05 ± 0.25-2.3 ± 0.17 mg/100 ml	66
30			20	Phosphorus	6.77 ± 0.19 mg/100 ml	39
31	6 mo-6 yr old	Whole blood	158	Phosphorus	6.8 mg/100 ml	81
32		Plasma	316	Calcium	8.6-11.0 mg/100 ml	81
33			158	Copper	125.8 µg/100 ml	
34			158	Magnesium	2.1 mg/100 ml	
35			158	Potassium	14.0 mg/100 ml	
36			158	Sodium	337.3 mg/100 ml	
37	Adult; day of calving	Whole blood	3-14	Potassium	61.4 mg/100 ml	80
38			3-14	Sodium	246 mg/100 ml	
39		Serum	3-14	Calcium	7.7 mg/100 ml	80
40			3-14	Chloride	382 mg/100 ml	
41	at calving	Plasma	10	Bicarbonate	27.1 ± 3.2 meq/liter	48
42			9	Chloride	107.2 ± 5.3 meq/liter	
43			10	Potassium	4.4 ± 0.4 meq/liter	
44			10	Sodium	139.3 ± 6.4 meq/liter	
45		Serum	31	Calcium	8.07 mg/100 ml	66
46	24 hr post-calving	Plasma	4	Bicarbonate	30.7 ± 3.2 meq/liter	48
47			5	Chloride	116.2 ± 6.1 meq/liter	
48			5	Potassium	4.4 ± 0.2 meq/liter	
49			5	Sodium	141.6 ± 2.7 meq/liter	
50	5 da post-calving	Whole blood	3-14	Potassium	57.0 mg/100 ml	80
51			3-14	Sodium	254 mg/100 ml	
52		Serum	3-14	Calcium	10.4 mg/100 ml	80
53			3-14	Chloride	354 mg/100 ml	
54	15 da post-calving	Whole blood	3-14	Potassium	58.0 mg/100 ml	80
55			3-14	Sodium	266 mg/100 ml	
56		Serum	3-14	Calcium	9.0 mg/100 ml	80
57			3-14	Chloride	322 mg/100 ml	
58	30 da post-calving	Whole blood	3-14	Potassium	48.3 mg/100 ml	80
59			3-14	Sodium	262 mg/100 ml	
60		Serum	3-14	Calcium	9.6 mg/100 ml	80
61			3-14	Chloride	362 mg/100 ml	
62	♂♀	Whole blood	833	Calcium	7.4 ± 0.8 mg/100 ml	66
63			11	Potassium	14.2 ± 2.7 meq/liter	16
64			11	Sodium	119.8 ± 12.5 meq/liter	16
65		Erythrocytes	11	Potassium	22.0 ± 4.5 meq/liter	16
66			11	Sodium	79.1 ± 14.6 meq/liter	
67		Plasma	11	Sodium	141.8 ± 6.3 meq/liter	16
68		Serum	275	Calcium	10.2 ± 2.8-11.08 ± 0.67 mg/100 ml	66
69			422	Phosphorus	6.62 ± 1.31 mg/100 ml	56
70	At birth	Plasma	9	Bicarbonate	28.2 ± 4.4 meq/liter	48
71			9	Chloride	101.7 ± 7.1 meq/liter	
72			10	Potassium	5.0 ± 0.2 meq/liter	
73			10	Sodium	140.9 ± 6.1 meq/liter	

continued

	Species (Synonym)	Blood Component	No. of Observations	Constituent	Concentration	Reference
74	24 hr old	Plasma	8	Bicarbonate	30.9 ± 3.4 meq/liter	48
75			9	Chloride	102.9 ± 6.3 meq/liter	
76			9	Potassium	5.2 ± 0.7 meq/liter	
77			9	Sodium	138.4 ± 6.0 meq/liter	
78	Calf	Serum	22	Calcium	10.35-12.6 mg/100 ml	14
79			22	Magnesium	1.89-2.60 mg/100 ml	
80			22	Phosphorus	5.8-7.2 mg/100 ml	
	Afrikaner					
81	♀, 4 yr old	Serum	4	Calcium	8.32 meq/liter	35
82			4	Phosphorus	7.02 mg/100 ml	
83			4	Potassium	8.62 meq/liter	
84			4	Sodium	130 meq/liter	
85	7-8 yr old	Serum	4	Calcium	8.06 meq/liter	35
86			4	Phosphorus	7.08 mg/100 ml	
87			4	Potassium	8.57 meq/liter	
88			4	Sodium	129 meq/liter	
89	>10 yr old	Serum	4	Calcium	8.00 meq/liter	35
90			4	Phosphorus	6.14 mg/100 ml	
91			4	Potassium	8.69 meq/liter	
92			4	Sodium	130 meq/liter	
93	♂♀, calf	Serum	...	Calcium	15.57 mg/100 ml	34
94				Phosphorus	11.07 mg/100 ml	
95				Potassium	33.9 mg/100 ml	
96				Sodium	307 mg/100 ml	
97	Angus, ♀	Serum	36	Phosphorus	7.83 ± 1.44 mg/100 ml	39
98	Ayrshire, ♂, 1-2 wk old	Whole blood	7	Bicarbonate	26.44 ± 2.233 meq/liter	23
99		Plasma	7	Potassium	4.78 ± 0.7 meq/liter	23
100			7	Sodium	142.5 ± 6.5 meq/liter	
	Friesland					
101	♀, 4 yr old	Serum	4	Calcium	7.48 meq/liter	35
102			4	Phosphorus	7.75 mg/100 ml	
103			4	Potassium	7.29 meq/liter	
104			4	Sodium	128 meq/liter	
105	7-8 yr old	Serum	4	Calcium	8.00 meq/liter	35
106			4	Phosphorus	8.06 mg/100 ml	
107			4	Potassium	7.90 meq/liter	
108			4	Sodium	130 meq/liter	
109	>10 yr old	Serum	4	Calcium	7.44 meq/liter	35
110			4	Phosphorus	7.16 mg/100 ml	
111			4	Potassium	7.30 meq/liter	
112			4	Sodium	125 meq/liter	
113	♂♀, calf	Serum	...	Calcium	14.30 mg/100 ml	34
114				Phosphorus	11.29 mg/100 ml	
115				Potassium	32.43 mg/100 ml	
116				Sodium	299 mg/100 ml	
	Guernsey, ♀					
117	<0.5 yr old	Serum	37	Calcium	11.68 ± 0.07[1] mg/100 ml	76
118			37	Chloride	112.7 ± 0.4[1] meq/liter	
119			37	Phosphorus	9.97 ± 0.15[1] mg/100 ml	

[1] Plus/minus (±) values are standard error.

continued

	Species (Synonym)	Blood Component	No. of Observations	Constituent	Concentration	Reference
120			37	Potassium	4.54 ± 0.08[1] meq/liter	
121			37	Sodium	137.3 ± 1.0[1] meq/liter	
122	0.5-1.5 yr old	Serum	72	Calcium	11.31 ± 0.05[1] mg/100 ml	76
123			72	Chloride	113.6 ± 0.2[1] meq/liter	
124			72	Phosphorus	8.03 ± 0.13[1] mg/100 ml	
125			72	Potassium	4.08 ± 0.06[1] meq/liter	
126			72	Sodium	137.9 ± 0.5[1] meq/liter	
127	3.5-4.5 yr old	Serum	28	Calcium	11.15 ± 0.11[1] mg/100 ml	76
128			28	Chloride	114.2 ± 0.6[1] meq/liter	
129			28	Phosphorus	5.55 ± 0.24[1] mg/100 ml	
130			28	Potassium	4.33 ± 0.10[1] meq/liter	
131			28	Sodium	138.0 ± 0.8[1] meq/liter	
132	4-6 yr old; 6-2 da pre-calving	Serum	2	Phosphorus	5.0-5.3 mg/100 ml	18
133	4-2 da pre-calving	Whole blood	2	Bicarbonate	26-27 meq/liter	18
134		Plasma	2	Chloride	102-106 meq/liter	18
135		Serum	2	Calcium	9.8 mg/100 ml	18
136	0-3 da post-calving	Serum	2	Phosphorus	2.5-3.5 mg/100 ml	18
137	1-3 da post-calving	Whole blood	2	Bicarbonate	20-24 meq/liter	18
138		Serum	2	Calcium	7.8-8.1 mg/100 ml	18
139	4 da post-calving	Plasma	2	Chloride	96 meq/liter	18
140	6.5-7.5 yr old	Serum	13	Calcium	11.24 ± 0.14[1] mg/100 ml	76
141			13	Chloride	115.2 ± 0.2[1] meq/liter	
142			13	Phosphorus	5.24 ± 0.26[1] mg/100 ml	
143			13	Potassium	4.29 ± 0.18[1] meq/liter	
144			13	Sodium	136.5 ± 1.2[1] meq/liter	
145	9.5-10.5 yr old	Serum	5	Calcium	11.14 ± 0.14[1] mg/100 ml	76
146			5	Chloride	115.2 ± 1.4[1] meq/liter	
147			5	Phosphorus	6.06 ± 0.33[1] mg/100 ml	
148			5	Potassium	4.48 ± 0.20[1] meq/liter	
149			5	Sodium	139.6 ± 1.0[1] meq/liter	
150	>10.5 yr old	Serum	10	Calcium	10.72 ± 0.10[1] mg/100 ml	76
151			10	Chloride	114.1 ± 0.9[1] meq/liter	
152			10	Phosphorus	5.35 ± 0.45[1] mg/100 ml	
153			10	Potassium	4.40 ± 0.10[1] meq/liter	
154			10	Sodium	133.8 ± 1.2[1] meq/liter	
	Hereford					
155	♀, 1 yr old	Plasma	24	Calcium	10.08 mg/100 ml	40
156			24	Magnesium	1.52 mg/100 ml	
157			24	Phosphorus	5.42 mg/100 ml	
158	3 yr old	Plasma	29	Calcium	10.64 mg/100 ml	40
159			29	Magnesium	1.5 mg/100 ml	
160			29	Phosphorus	3.50 mg/100 ml	
161	5 yr old	Plasma	28	Calcium	9.11 mg/100 ml	40
162			28	Magnesium	1.46 mg/100 ml	
163			28	Phosphorus	3.68 mg/100 ml	
164	9-10 yr old; 1 mo pre-calving	Plasma	18	Calcium	106.1 ± 8.9 ppm	30
165			...	Copper	1.29 ± 0.29 ppm	
166			18	Magnesium	21.1 ± 3.6 ppm	
167			20	Phosphorus	6.2 mg/100 ml	
168			15	Zinc	1.19 ± 0.55 ppm	
169	at calving	Plasma	15	Calcium	104.7 ± 14.3 ppm	30
170			13	Magnesium	22.2 ± 7.4 ppm	

[1] Plus/minus (±) values are standard error.

continued

	Species (Synonym)	Blood Component	No. of Observations	Constituent	Concentration	Reference
171			15	Phosphorus	5.9 mg/100 ml	
172			12	Zinc	0.99 ± 0.18 ppm	
173	1 mo post-calving	Plasma	19	Calcium	97.5 ± 12.6 ppm	30
174			...	Copper	1.30 ± 0.33 ppm	
175			18	Magnesium	20.1 ± 5.4 ppm	
176			18	Phosphorus	6.6 mg/100 ml	
177			13	Zinc	1.16 ± 0.14 ppm	
178	9 mo post-calving	Plasma	18	Calcium	123.4 ± 6.0 ppm	30
179			...	Copper	1.26 ± 0.31 ppm	
180			18	Magnesium	26.1 ± 3.8 ppm	
181			19	Phosphorus	5.0 mg/100 ml	
182			19	Zinc	1.30 ± 0.1 ppm	
183	11-12 yr old	Plasma	6	Calcium	5.09 ± 0.3-5.54 ± 0.25 meq/liter	31
184			6	Magnesium	1.48 ± 0.41-2.30 ± 0.16 meq/liter	
185	♂♀, 1-11 mo old	Whole blood	6	Phosphorus	6.07 ± 0.61 mg/100 ml	27
186		Plasma	6	Chloride	106.56 ± 1.87 meq/liter	27
187			6	Potassium	4.88 ± 0.3 meq/liter	
188			6	Sodium	139.45 ± 4.45 meq/liter	
189		Serum	6	Calcium	11.07 ± 0.66 mg/100 ml	27
190			6	Magnesium	2.20 ± 0.25 mg/100 ml	
191	25-37 mo old	Whole blood	6	Phosphorus	4.91 ± 0.48 mg/100 ml	27
192		Plasma	6	Chloride	106.82 ± 2.67 meq/liter	27
193			6	Potassium	4.29 ± 0.26 meq/liter	
194			6	Sodium	140.36 ± 4.94 meq/liter	
195		Serum	6	Calcium	11.15 ± 0.31 mg/100 ml	27
196			6	Magnesium	2.87 ± 0.17 mg/100 ml	
	Holstein					
197	♂, 1-4 wk old	Plasma	6	Calcium	10.25 mg/100 ml	59
198			6	Chloride	99.4 meq/liter	
199			6	Phosphorus	7.92 mg/100 ml	
200			6	Potassium	4.39 meq/liter	
201			6	Sodium	138.9 meq/liter	
202	♀, <0.5 yr old	Serum	26	Calcium	11.59 ± 0.1 [1] mg/100 ml	76
203			26	Chloride	115.2 ± 0.8 [1] meq/liter	
204			26	Phosphorus	9.83 ± 0.28 [1] mg/100 ml	
205			26	Potassium	4.77 ± 0.14 [1] meq/liter	
206			26	Sodium	139.9 ± 0.8 [1] meq/liter	
207	0.5-1.5 yr old	Serum	22	Calcium	11.53 ± 0.08 [1] mg/100 ml	76
208			22	Chloride	112.8 ± 0.5 [1] meq/liter	
209			22	Phosphorus	8.42 ± 0.20 [1] mg/100 ml	
210			22	Potassium	4.28 ± 0.08 [1] meq/liter	
211			22	Sodium	136.1 ± 1.0 [1] meq/liter	
212	3.5-4.5 yr old	Serum	42	Calcium	10.64 ± 0.08 [1] mg/100 ml	76
213			42	Chloride	112.8 ± 0.5 [1] meq/liter	
214			42	Phosphorus	6.00 ± 0.16 [1] mg/100 ml	
215			42	Potassium	4.47 ± 0.08 [1] meq/liter	
216			42	Sodium	137.1 ± 0.6 [1] meq/liter	
217	6.5-7.5 yr old	Serum	8	Calcium	10.62 ± 0.14 [1] mg/100 ml	76
218			8	Chloride	112.4 ± 0.8 [1] meq/liter	
219			8	Phosphorus	5.32 ± 0.24 [1] mg/100 ml	
220			8	Potassium	3.95 ± 0.18 [1] meq/liter	
221			8	Sodium	137.8 ± 1.3 [1] meq/liter	

[1] Plus/minus (±) values are standard error.

continued

	Species (Synonym)	Blood Component	No. of Observations	Constituent	Concentration	Reference
222	9.5-10.5 yr old	Serum	4	Calcium	10.68 ± 0.21[1]/ mg/100 ml	76
223			4	Chloride	115.0 ± 0.9[1]/ meq/liter	
224			4	Phosphorus	5.08 ± 0.91[1]/ mg/100 ml	
225			4	Potassium	4.48 ± 0.45[1]/ meq/liter	
226			4	Sodium	139.8 ± 0.2[1]/ meq/liter	
227	>10.5 yr old	Serum	5	Calcium	10.67 ± 0.14[1]/ mg/100 ml	76
228			5	Chloride	111.6 ± 0.7[1]/ meq/liter	
229			5	Phosphorus	5.70 ± 0.74[1]/ mg/100 ml	
230			5	Potassium	4.38 ± 0.12[1]/ meq/liter	
231			5	Sodium	142.0 ± 2.6[1]/ meq/liter	
232	Adult	Serum	88	Calcium	9.6 ± 0.9 mg/100 ml	64
233			88	Chloride	97 ± 9 meq/liter	
234			88	Phosphate	6.1 ± 1.0 mg/100 ml	
235			88	Potassium	5.1 ± 0.8 meq/liter	
236			88	Sodium	140 ± 10 meq/liter	
	Jersey					
237	♂	Whole blood	6	Calcium	2.9 meq/liter	57
238			6	Magnesium	1.3 meq/liter	
239			6	Potassium	10.0 meq/liter	
240			6	Sodium	105 meq/liter	
241		Erythrocytes	6	Calcium	1.0 meq/kg	57
242			6	Magnesium	2.4 meq/kg	
243			6	Potassium	17.4 meq/kg	
244			6	Sodium	90 meq/kg	
245		Plasma	6	Calcium	4.6 meq/kg	57
246			6	Magnesium	1.8 meq/kg	
247			6	Potassium	5.6 meq/kg	
248			6	Sodium	127 meq/kg	
	♀					
249	2-8 yr old; pre-calving	Serum	15	Bicarbonate	25 ± 5 meq/liter	60
250			14	Calcium	4.6 ± 0.2 meq/liter	
251			15	Potassium	3.9 ± 0.4 meq/liter	
252	1 wk pre-calving	Serum	7	Calcium	10.32 mg/100 ml	36
253			6	Magnesium	2.4 mg/100 ml	
254			7	Phosphorus	5.49 mg/100 ml	
255	3 da pre-calving	Serum	42	Calcium	10.1-10.9 mg/100 ml	7
256	1 da pre-calving	Serum	42	Calcium	9.9-10.4 mg/100 ml	7
257	12 hr pre-calving	Serum	5	Calcium	9.90 mg/100 ml	36
258			4	Magnesium	2.19 mg/100 ml	
259			3	Phosphorus	4.28 mg/100 ml	
260	Day of calving	Serum	37	Calcium	8.6 mg/100 ml	7
261	1-3 hr post-calving	Serum	5	Calcium	8.8 mg/100 ml	7
262	12 hr post-calving	Serum	8	Calcium	8.72 mg/100 ml	36
263			7	Magnesium	2.65 mg/100 ml	
264			7	Phosphorus	4.44 mg/100 ml	
265	1 da post-calving	Serum	42	Calcium	8.5-8.6 mg/100 ml	7
266	3 da post-calving	Serum	42	Calcium	9.7-10.1 mg/100 ml	7
267	1 wk post-calving	Serum	4	Calcium	10.31 mg/100 ml	36
268			4	Magnesium	1.70 mg/100 ml	
269			4	Phosphorus	5.88 mg/100 ml	
270	Adult, pre-calving	Serum	26	Chloride	105 ± 6 meq/liter	60
271			26	Sodium	145 ± 6 meq/liter	

[1]/ Plus/minus (±) values are standard error.

continued

	Species (Synonym)	Blood Component	No. of Obser- vations	Constituent	Concentration	Refer- ence
	♂♀					
272	Fetus	Serum	34	Chloride	101 ± 4 meq/liter	60
273			34	Sodium	142 ± 6 meq/liter	
274	187-212 da gestation	Serum	7	Bicarbonate	21 ± 7 meq/liter	60
275			8	Calcium	6.8 ± 0.4 meq/liter	
276			7	Potassium	4.3 ± 0.4 meq/liter	
277	225-259 da gestation	Serum	12	Bicarbonate	22 ± 4 meq/liter	60
278			12	Calcium	7.0 ± 0.3 meq/liter	
279			12	Potassium	4.3 ± 0.6 meq/liter	
280	1-4 da old	Serum	10	Bicarbonate	24 ± 8 meq/liter	60
281			9	Calcium	5.8 ± 0.4 meq/liter	
282			10	Chloride	97 ± 5 meq/liter	
283			9	Phosphate	1.6 ± 0.3 meq/liter	
284			10	Potassium	4.4 ± 0.4 meq/liter	
285			10	Sodium	143 ± 4 meq/liter	
286	12-23 da old	Serum	7	Bicarbonate	24 ± 6 meq/liter	60
287			8	Calcium	5.0 ± 0.2 meq/liter	
288			8	Chloride	102 ± 3 meq/liter	
289			8	Phosphate	1.9 ± 0.2 meq/liter	
290			8	Potassium	4.6 ± 0.2 meq/liter	
291			8	Sodium	143 ± 4 meq/liter	
	Bradypus sp.					
292	♂♀	....	4	Chloride	101.8 meq/liter	73
293			4	Potassium	3.6-10 meq/liter	
294			4	Sodium	128 meq/liter	
295	Mature	....	1	Calcium	4.5 meq/liter	73
296			1	Magnesium	4.35 meq/liter	
297			1	Phosphorus	6 mg/100 ml	
298	*Caluromys derbianus,* ♀	Serum	3	Phosphorus	4.25 ± 1.6 mg/100 ml	62
299	♂♀	Serum	71	Chloride	102.2 ± 6.0 meq/liter	62
300			50	Potassium	6.0 ± 0.9 meq/liter	
301			75	Sodium	143.0 ± 4.7 meq/liter	
302	*Camelus dromedarius,* ♀	....	1	Calcium	10.0 mg/100 ml	20
303			1	Chloride	112.0 meq/liter	
304			1	Phosphorus	3.0 mg/100 ml	
305			1	Potassium	4.0 meq/liter	
306			1	Sodium	111.3 meq/liter	
	Canis familiaris					
307	♂	Serum	57	Phosphorus	4.68 ± 1.87 mg/100 ml	39
308	♀	Plasma	61	Phosphorus	4.3 mg/100 ml	1
309			24	Potassium	4.1 meq/liter	
310			24	Sodium	147 meq/liter	
311		Serum	54	Phosphorus	4.41 ± 1.79 mg/100 ml	39
312	♂♀	Whole blood	4	Calcium	1.6 meq/kg	57
313			4	Magnesium	1.7 meq/kg	57
314			4	Potassium	3.7 meq/kg	57
315			12	Potassium	4.8 ± 0.6 meq/liter	16
316			4	Sodium	110 meq/kg	57
317			12	Sodium	127.9 ± 9.6 meq/liter	16
318		Erythrocytes	4	Calcium	0.8 meq/kg	57
319			4	Magnesium	27 meq/kg	57

continued

	Species (Synonym)	Blood Component	No. of Observations	Constituent	Concentration	Reference
320			4	Potassium	6.7 meq/kg	57
321			12	Potassium	5.7 ± 1.0 meq/liter	16
322			4	Sodium	96 meq/kg	57
323			12	Sodium	92.8 ± 11.1 meq/liter	16
324		Plasma	16	Bicarbonate	26.0 ± 6.2 meq/liter	67
325			4	Calcium	2.9 meq/kg	57
326			19	Calcium	5.3 ± 0.4 meq/liter	67
327			32	Chloride	111 ± 3 meq/liter	17
328			20	Chloride	118.0 ± 5.0 meq/liter	67
329			4	Magnesium	0.8 meq/kg	57
330			16	Magnesium	1.8 ± 0.3 meq/liter	67
331			16	Phosphate	2.7 ± 0.8 meq/liter	67
332			4	Potassium	3.4 meq/kg	57
333			64	Potassium	4.0 ± 0.4-4.5 ± 0.3 meq/liter	16,17, 67
334			4	Sodium	124 meq/kg	57
335			66	Sodium	147.0 ± 2.6-158.6 ± 13.1 meq/liter	16,17, 67
336		Serum	9	Calcium	10.16 ± 2.04 mg/100 ml	66
337			...	Copper	38-58 μg/100 ml	15
338			10	Magnesium	2.1 ± 0.3 meq/liter	66
339			20	Phosphorus	4.11 ± 0.14 mg/100 ml	39
340			...	Potassium	4.37-5.65 meq/liter	71
341			...	Sodium	141.1-152.3 meq/liter	71
	Beagle					
342	♂, 6-12 mo old	Serum	405	Calcium	5.53 ± 0.30 meq/liter	61
343			350	Phosphorus	6.64 ± 0.82 mg/100 ml	
344			405	Potassium	5.04 ± 0.34 meq/liter	
345			405	Sodium	147.1 ± 2.9 meq/liter	
346	13 mo old	Serum	...	Bicarbonate	13.7-22.1 meq/liter	77
347			...	Calcium	9.9-11.7 mg/100 ml	
348			...	Chloride	102-118 meq/liter	
349			...	Phosphorus	3.2-5.9 mg/100 ml	
350			...	Potassium	4.2-5.2 meq/liter	
351			...	Sodium	141-153 meq/liter	
352	1.5-10.4 yr old	Serum	17	Copper	0.88 ± 0.17 ppm	24
353			199	Iron	1.99 ± 0.53 ppm	
354	2-3 yr old	Serum	20	Calcium	5.2 ± 0.09[1]-5.3 ± 0.06[1] meq/liter	19
355	Fasted 16 hr	Serum	10	Chloride	115 ± 1.0[1] meq/liter	19
356			10	Phosphorus	3.3 ± 0.21[1] mg/100 ml	
357			10	Potassium	5.3 ± 0.16[1] meq/liter	
358			10	Sodium	155 ± 0.6[1] meq/liter	
359	♀, 6-12 mo old	Serum	404	Calcium	5.51 ± 0.31 meq/liter	61
360			352	Phosphorus	6.42 ± 0.85 mg/100 ml	
361			404	Potassium	4.96 ± 0.32 meq/liter	
362			404	Sodium	146.6 ± 2.7 meq/liter	
363	13 mo old	Serum	...	Bicarbonate	14.5-21.1 meq/liter	77
364				Calcium	9.9-12.3 mg/100 ml	
365				Chloride	102-118 meq/liter	
366				Phosphorus	3.0-6.1 mg/100 ml	
367				Potassium	4.3-5.5 meq/liter	
368				Sodium	142-154 meq/liter	

[1] Plus/minus (±) values are standard error.

continued

	Species (Synonym)	Blood Component	No. of Observations	Constituent	Concentration	Reference
369	1.5-10.4 yr old	Serum	13	Copper	0.88 ± 0.19 ppm	24
370	2-3 yr old	Serum	20	Calcium	5.2 ± 0.07[1]-5.4 ± 0.08[1] meq/liter	19
371	Fasted 16 hr	Serum	10	Chloride	114 ± 0.8[1] meq/liter	19
372			10	Phosphorus	3.8 ± 0.15[1] mg/100 ml	
373			10	Potassium	5.1 ± 0.13[1] meq/liter	
374			10	Sodium	155 ± 0.6[1] meq/liter	
375	8-10 yr old	Serum	30	Calcium	10.8 mg/100 ml	55
376			30	Chloride	106 meq/liter	
377			30	Phosphorus	3.9 mg/100 ml	
378			30	Potassium	4.7 meq/liter	
379			30	Sodium	146 meq/liter	
380	10 yr old	Serum	86	Calcium	5.94 meq/liter	61
381			86	Phosphorus	4.8 mg/100 ml	
382	Adult, 1-2 hr post-feeding	Serum	64	Calcium	11.3 ± 1.0 mg/100 ml	45
383			64	Chloride	667 ± 25 mg/100 ml	
384			64	Phosphorus	5.2 ± 1.4 mg/100 ml	
385	24 hr post-feeding	Serum	64	Calcium	12.4 ± 1.4 mg/100 ml	45
386			64	Chloride	669 ± 23 mg/100 ml	
387			64	Phosphorus	4.4 ± 0.7 mg/100 ml	
388	♂♀, <1 yr old	Serum	393	Phosphorus	5.73 ± 1.43 mg/100 ml	58
389	2-3 mo old	Serum	29	Calcium	11.0 mg/100 ml	55
390			29	Phosphorus	7.8 mg/100 ml	
391	3-24 mo old	Serum	775	Calcium	9.9 ± 1.6 mg/100 ml	44
392			916	Chloride	107 ± 9 meq/liter	
393			852	Phosphorus	5.4 ± 1.8 mg/100 ml	
394			65	Potassium	4.7 ± 0.5 meq/liter	
395			69	Sodium	182 ± 14 meq/liter	
396	4 mo old	Serum	245	Calcium	10.4 ± 1.5 mg/100 ml	44
397			213	Phosphorus	7.2 ± 1.8 mg/100 ml	
398	4-12 mo old	Serum	388	Calcium	5.44 ± 0.70 meq/liter	61
399	6-12 mo old	Serum	809	Calcium	5.40 ± 0.31 meq/liter	61
400			702	Phosphorus	6.39 ± 0.77 mg/100 ml	
401			809	Potassium	4.95 ± 0.28 meq/liter	
402			809	Sodium	146.7 ± 2.8 meq/liter	
403	6 mo-9 yr old	Serum	63	Chloride	110.0 ± 2.4 meq/liter	46
404			63	Potassium	4.73 ± 0.28 meq/liter	
405			63	Sodium	147.3 ± 3.1 meq/liter	
406	7.3-8.7 mo old	Serum	120	Phosphorus	5.5 ± 1.4 mg/100 ml	61
407	8 mo old	Serum	162	Calcium	10.4 ± 1.8 mg/100 ml	44
408			178	Phosphorus	5.1 ± 1.2 mg/100 ml	
409	11-14 mo old	Serum	635	Calcium	11.0 mg/100 ml	55
410			788	Chloride	111 meq/liter	
411			632	Phosphorus	4.4 mg/100 ml	
412			787	Potassium	4.8 meq/liter	
413			787	Sodium	148 meq/liter	
414	12 mo old	Serum	134	Calcium	9.4 ± 1.6 mg/100 ml	44
415			185	Phosphorus	4.4 ± 1.0 mg/100 ml	
416	14-18 mo old	Serum	56	Calcium	10.8 mg/100 ml	55
417			56	Chloride	111 meq/liter	
418			57	Phosphorus	4.0 mg/100 ml	
419			55	Potassium	4.6 meq/liter	
420			55	Sodium	148 meq/liter	

[1] Plus/minus (±) values are standard error.

continued

	Species (Synonym)	Blood Component	No. of Observations	Constituent	Concentration	Reference
421	18-30 mo old	Serum	48	Calcium	10.8 mg/100 ml	55
422			44	Chloride	111 meq/liter	
423			48	Phosphorus	3.6 mg/100 ml	
424			44	Potassium	4.5 meq/liter	
425			44	Sodium	148 meq/liter	
426	30-42 mo old	Serum	39	Calcium	10.7 mg/100 ml	55
427			40	Chloride	112 meq/liter	
428			39	Phosphorus	3.5 mg/100 ml	
429			39	Potassium	4.6 meq/liter	
430			39	Sodium	148 meq/liter	
431	42-54 mo old	Serum	34	Calcium	10.6 mg/100 ml	55
432			28	Chloride	112 meq/liter	
433			36	Phosphorus	3.4 mg/100 ml	
434			28	Potassium	4.7 meq/liter	
435			28	Sodium	148 meq/liter	
436	54-66 mo old	Serum	46	Calcium	10.7 mg/100 ml	55
437			23	Chloride	114 meq/liter	
438			46	Phosphorus	3.4 mg/100 ml	
439			23	Potassium	4.8 meq/liter	
440			23	Sodium	149 meq/liter	
441	66-78 mo old	Serum	31	Calcium	10.8 mg/100 ml	55
442			30	Phosphorus	3.4 mg/100 ml	
443	C. latrans	....	1	Calcium	11.2 mg/100 ml	20
444			1	Chloride	122.0 meq/liter	
445			1	Phosphorus	7.56 mg/100 ml	
446			1	Potassium	2.6 meq/liter	
447		Whole blood	3	Phosphorus	3.2 ± 1.5 mg/100 ml	51
448	C. lupus, ♂♀	Whole blood	5	Phosphorus	2.5 ± 0.6 mg/100 ml	51
	Capra hircus					
449	♂♀	Whole blood	3	Magnesium	3.7 ± 0.65 mg/100 ml	66
450		Erythrocytes	3	Magnesium	4.5 ± 1.18 mg/100 ml	66
451		Plasma	3	Magnesium	3.2 ± 0.35 mg/100 ml	66
452		Serum	30	Calcium	10.3 ± 0.7 mg/100 ml	66
453	20-22 mo old	Plasma	10	Calcium	10.9-12.9 mg/100 ml	47
454			10	Chloride	380-415 mg/100 ml	
455			10	Phosphorus	1.5-5.0 mg/100 ml	
	Angora					
456	♀, adult; 110 ± 5 da pregnant	Whole blood	4	Chloride	105-129 meq/liter	9
457			4	Potassium	5.1-7.6 meq/liter	
458			4	Sodium	142-175 meq/liter	
459	♂♀, fetus	Whole blood	4	Chloride	96-104 meq/liter	9
460			4	Potassium	4.2-6.1 meq/liter	
461			4	Sodium	125-143 meq/liter	
462	Cavia porcellus, ♂♀	Whole blood	14	Potassium	50.4 ± 4.2 meq/liter	16
463			14	Sodium	89.5 ± 8.3 meq/liter	
464		Erythrocytes	14	Potassium	107.2 ± 10.1 meq/liter	16
465			14	Sodium	24.4 ± 5.4 meq/liter	
466		Plasma	14	Potassium	8.1 ± 1.6 meq/liter	16
467			14	Sodium	137.3 ± 11.4 meq/liter	
468	Body wt, 400-650 g	Plasma	146	Calcium	4.64 ± 0.63 meq/liter	12
469			100	Chloride	92.3 ± 10.4 meq/liter	
470			144	Phosphorus	5.33 ± 1.15 mg/100 ml	
471			149	Potassium	4.8 ± 0.84 meq/liter	
472			149	Sodium	122.18 ± 9.76 meq/liter	

continued

	Species (Synonym)	Blood Component	No. of Observations	Constituent	Concentration	Reference
473	*Cephalophus maxwelli*	....	2	Calcium	10.4-12.6 mg/100 ml	20
474			2	Phosphorus	11.0-13.8 mg/100 ml	
475	*Cervus canadensis rooseveltii*, ♂	....	1	Calcium	7.4 mg/100 ml	20
476			1	Phosphorus	11.9 mg/100 ml	
477	♀	....	1	Calcium	5.4 mg/100 ml	20
478			1	Phosphorus	9.1 mg/100 ml	
479	*C. nippon taiouanus*, ♂	....	1	Calcium	10.8 mg/100 ml	20
480			1	Phosphorus	7.6 mg/100 ml	
	Choloepus didactylus					
481	♂	....	...	Bicarbonate	2.2 meq/liter	73
482				Calcium	4.9 meq/liter	
483				Chloride	102 meq/liter	
484				Phosphorus	3.0 mg/100 ml	
485				Potassium	4.8 meq/liter	
486				Sodium	140 meq/liter	
487	♀	....	...	Bicarbonate	1.8 meq/liter	73
488				Calcium	5.6 meq/liter	
489				Chloride	94 meq/liter	
490				Phosphorus	3.5 mg/100 ml	
491				Potassium	5.5 meq/liter	
492				Sodium	137 meq/liter	
493	♂♀	....	...	Chloride	99.7 meq/liter	73
494			...	Potassium	7.7 meq/liter	
495			3	Potassium	3.8-6.2 meq/liter	
496			...	Sodium	131 meq/liter	
497			3	Sodium	133-139 meq/liter	
498	Mature	....	6	Calcium	2.07-3.6 meq/liter	73
499			3	Chloride	94-96 meq/liter	
500			6	Magnesium	1.1-2.0 meq/liter	
501			3	Phosphorus	2.7-5.4 mg/100 ml	
502	*Dama dama*, ♂♀	Whole blood	16	Phosphorus	5.2 ± 1.6-5.48 ± 1.97 mg/100 ml	51
503	*Dasypus novemcinctus (D. novem-*	Serum	10	Calcium	11.29 ± 0.37[1] mg/100 ml	70
504	*cinctus mexicanus)*, ♂♀; body wt, 4.54-5.44 kg		10	Phosphorus	5.51 ± 0.24[1] mg/100 ml	
505	*Dasyurus maculatus*, ♂; adult	Erythrocytes	2	Calcium	1.0-1.7 meq/liter	52
506			2	Magnesium	3.7-5.6 meq/liter	
507			2	Potassium	53-83 meq/liter	
508		Serum	2	Calcium	4.3-4.4 meq/liter	52
509			2	Magnesium	1.6-2.3 meq/liter	
510			2	Phosphorus	1.4-5.7 mg/100 ml	
511			2	Potassium	4.6-4.7 meq/liter	
512			2	Sodium	133-141 meq/liter	
513	*D. viverrinus*, ♂♀	Erythrocytes	2	Calcium	0-1.3 meq/liter	54
514			2	Magnesium	2.4-3.9 meq/liter	
515			2	Potassium	50-65 meq/liter	
516		Serum	2	Calcium	4.2-4.5 meq/liter	54
517			2	Chloride	104-132 meq/liter	
518			2	Magnesium	1.7-2.9 meq/liter	
519			2	Phosphorus	4.0-4.6 mg/100 ml	
520			2	Potassium	3.7-7.6 meq/liter	
521			2	Sodium	132-137 meq/liter	
522	*Delphinapterus leucas*, ♂	....	9	Calcium	7.5-12.4 mg/100 ml	20
523			3	Chloride	118-128 meq/liter	

[1] Plus/minus (±) values are standard error.

continued

	Species (Synonym)	Blood Component	No. of Observations	Constituent	Concentration	Reference
524			9	Phosphorus	3.9-8.2 mg/100 ml	
525			3	Potassium	3.0-4.4 meq/liter	
526			1	Sodium	148.7 meq/liter	
527	♀	....	10	Calcium	6.6-12.1 mg/100 ml	20
528			4	Chloride	110.4-122 meq/liter	
529			10	Phosphorus	5.5-8.0 mg/100 ml	
530			4	Potassium	2.83-5.4 meq/liter	
531			2	Sodium	124.8-185.3 meq/liter	
532	*Didelphis marsupialis virginiana,* ♂	Serum	14	Calcium	10.67 ± 0.4 mg/100 ml	72
533			14	Phosphorus	6.8 ± 0.98 mg/100 ml	
534			14	Potassium	5.2 ± 0.64 meq/liter	
535			14	Sodium	146.3 ± 5.6 meq/liter	
536	*Dipodomys* sp., ♂♀; body wt,	Serum	...	Calcium	7.5 ± 0.2 [1/] mg/100 ml	26
537	36 ± 2 g			Phosphate	12.1 ± 0.9 [1/] mg/100 ml	
538	*Elaphurus davidianus,* ♀	....	2	Calcium	10.5-10.8 mg/100 ml	20
539			2	Chloride	108.6-112.6 meq/liter	
540			1	Magnesium	1.77 meq/liter	
541			2	Phosphorus	6.3-6.6 mg/100 ml	
542			2	Potassium	3.68-3.96 meq/liter	
543			2	Sodium	130.5-153.1 meq/liter	
	Elephas maximus					
544	♂; adult (Tuskers)	Serum	14	Calcium	11.80 ± 1.12 mg/100 ml	50
545			14	Chloride	488.00 ± 93.10 mg/100 ml	
546			14	Magnesium	2.60 ± 0.60 mg/100 ml	
547			14	Phosphate	4.46 ± 0.84 mg/100 ml	
548	♀, adult; nonlactating	Serum	10	Calcium	12.50 ± 1.27 mg/100 ml	50
549			10	Chloride	496.90 ± 96.44 mg/100 ml	
550			10	Magnesium	2.33 ± 0.79 mg/100 ml	
551			10	Phosphate	4.07 ± 0.64 mg/100 ml	
552	lactating	Serum	5	Calcium	11.10 ± 0.89 mg/100 ml	50
553			5	Chloride	433.00 ± 79.47 mg/100 ml	
554			5	Magnesium	2.49 ± 0.88 mg/100 ml	
555			5	Phosphate	4.27 ± 1.12 mg/100 ml	
556	♂♀, 3-14 yr old	Serum	10	Calcium	12.20 ± 0.95 mg/100 ml	50
557			11	Chloride	473.60 ± 66.32 mg/100 ml	
558			10	Magnesium	2.41 ± 0.59 mg/100 ml	
559			11	Phosphate	5.53 ± 0.49 mg/100 ml	
	Equus asinus					
560	♂, 4-7 yr old	Plasma	16	Phosphate	4.72 ± 0.69 [1/] mg/100 ml	82
561			10	Potassium	4.03 ± 0.44 [1/] meq/liter	
562			10	Sodium	138.7 ± 4.6 [1/] meq/liter	
563	♂♀	Whole blood	...	Chloride	109.8 ± 1.4 [1/] meq/liter	84
564				Phosphate	3.5 ± 0.2 [1/] mg/100 ml	
565		Plasma	...	Calcium	1.40 ± 0.26 mg/g	29
566				Chloride	1.87 ± 0.24 mg/g	
567				Copper	11.11 ± 2.18 µg/g	
568				Iron	15.0 ± 5.17 µg/g	
569				Magnesium	189.6 ± 36.2 µg/g	
570				Phosphorus	0.867 ± 0.016 mg/g	
571				Potassium	1.87 ± 0.24 mg/g	
572				Sodium	26.6 ± 5.6 mg/g	
573				Sulfur	10.1 ± 0.4 mg/g	
574				Zinc	5.21 ± 1.13 µg/g	

[1/] Plus/minus (±) values are standard error.

continued

	Species (Synonym)	Blood Component	No. of Observations	Constituent	Concentration	Reference
575	7 mo-8 yr old	Serum	11	Chloride	110.9 ± 3.77 meq/liter	85
	E. caballus					
576	♂♀	Whole blood	10	Magnesium	4.0 ± 0.62 mg/100 ml	66
577		Erythrocytes	10	Magnesium	6.8 ± 1.27 mg/100 ml	66
578		Plasma	10	Magnesium	2.4 ± 0.32 mg/100 ml	66
579		Serum	30	Calcium	12.4 ± 0.58 mg/100 ml	66
580			...	Chloride	99-109 meq/liter	71
581			30	Magnesium	2.5 ± 0.31 mg/100 ml	66
582			222	Phosphorus	3.38 ± 1.36 mg/100 ml	56
583			...	Potassium	2.4-4.7 meq/liter	71
584			...	Sodium	132-146 meq/liter	71
585	1-32 yr old	Serum	10	Chloride	104.8 ± 3.28 meq/liter	85
	Pony					
586	♂	....	1	Calcium	11.2 mg/100 ml	20
587			1	Chloride	100 meq/liter	
588			1	Potassium	3.04 meq/liter	
589			1	Sodium	133 meq/liter	
590	♀	....	1	Calcium	12.0 mg/100 ml	20
591			1	Phosphorus	2.4 mg/100 ml	
592	♂♀	Plasma	4	Calcium	4.83 ± 0.12[1] meq/liter	3
593			4	Chloride	100.9 ± 1.4[1] meq/liter	
594			4	Magnesium	1.45 ± 0.07[1] meq/liter	
595			4	Phosphorus	2.85 ± 0.07[1] mmoles/liter	
596	Fasted 1-9 da	Plasma	36	Calcium	4.49 ± 0.12[1]-4.90 ± 0.13[1] meq/liter	3
597			36	Chloride	95.5 ± 5.2[1]-103.6 ± 2.0[1] meq/liter	
598			36	Magnesium	1.02 ± 0.13[1]-1.60 ± 0.04[1] meq/liter	
599			36	Phosphorus	1.59 ± 0.22[1]-3.14 ± 0.14[1] mmoles/liter	
600	Refed 2-6 da	Plasma	12	Calcium	5.01 ± 0.24[1]-5.20 ± 0.12[1] meq/liter	3
601			12	Chloride	99.5 ± 4.6[1]-106.1 ± 3.1[1] meq/liter	
602			12	Magnesium	1.17 ± 0.11[1]-1.67 ± 0.12[1] meq/liter	
603			12	Phosphorus	2.03 ± 0.05[1]-2.6 ± 0.22[1] mmoles/liter	
604	Shetland, ♂♀	Serum	8	Calcium	10.2 ± 1.0[1] mg/100 ml	66
605			...	Magnesium	1.54 ± 0.16 mg/100 ml	
606	2 mo-11 yr old	Serum	6	Chloride	103.9 ± 3.89 meq/liter	85
607	Before work	Serum	...	Calcium	10.0 mg/100 ml	10
608				Phosphorus	3.8 mg/100 ml	
609	After 4 hr work	Serum	...	Calcium	10.8 mg/100 ml	10
610				Phosphorus	2.8 mg/100 ml	
611	*E. grevyi*, ♀	....	2	Calcium	11.0-11.5 mg/100 ml	20
612			2	Chloride	104-112 meq/liter	
613			2	Magnesium	3.06-3.38 mg/100 ml	
614			2	Phosphorus	4.7-5.2 mg/100 ml	
615			2	Potassium	3.42-3.62 meq/liter	
616			2	Sodium	135.0-154.5 meq/liter	
617	*Felis caracal*, ♂	....	1	Calcium	10.0 mg/100 ml	20
618			1	Phosphorus	5.4 mg/100 ml	
	F. catus					
619	♂; body wt, 3 kg; fasted 18-24 hr	Whole blood	55	Potassium	5.7 ± 0.1[1] meq/liter	78
620			55	Sodium	149.8 ± 1.2[1] meq/liter	
621	♂♀	Whole blood	4	Potassium	4.2 ± 0.8 meq/liter	16
622			4	Sodium	131.9 ± 8.1 meq/liter	
623		Erythrocytes	4	Potassium	5.9 ± 1.9 meq/liter	16
624			4	Sodium	105.8 ± 14.4 meq/liter	

[1] Plus/minus (±) values are standard error.

continued

	Species (Synonym)	Blood Component	No. of Obser-vations	Constituent	Concentration	Reference
625		Plasma	4	Potassium	3.2 ± 0.6 meq/liter	16
626			4	Sodium	143.0 ± 7.5 meq/liter	
627		Serum	10	Calcium	8.22 ± 0.97 mg/100 ml	66
628			...	Chloride	117-123 meq/liter	71
629			14	Phosphorus	4.75 ± 1.03 [1]/ mg/100 ml	39
630			...	Potassium	4.0-4.5 meq/liter	71
631			...	Sodium	147-156 meq/liter	71
632	*F. concolor*, ♂	....	2	Calcium	8.33-13.3 mg/100 ml	20
633			2	Phosphorus	4.72-5.9 mg/100 ml	
634			1	Potassium	3.84 meq/liter	
635	♂♀	Whole blood	6	Phosphorus	2.3 ± 0.2-2.60 ± 0.57 mg/100 ml	51
636	*F. planiceps*, ♂	....	1	Calcium	10.5 mg/100 ml	20
637			1	Chloride	118 meq/liter	
638			1	Phosphorus	7.8 mg/100 ml	
639			1	Potassium	2.5 meq/liter	
640			1	Sodium	156.8 meq/liter	
641	*F. viverrina*, ♀	....	1	Calcium	9.9 mg/100 ml	20
642			1	Phosphorus	5.2 mg/100 ml	
643	*Gazella thomsoni*	....	1	Calcium	10.4 mg/100 ml	20
644			1	Chloride	122 meq/liter	
645			1	Phosphorus	4.12 mg/100 ml	
646			1	Potassium	2.98 meq/liter	
647	♂	....	1	Calcium	10.0 mg/100 ml	20
648			1	Phosphorus	6.5 mg/100 ml	
649	*Halichoerus grypus*, ♂♀; young	Plasma	6	Calcium	11.2 ± 1.0 mg/100 ml	28
650			6	Chloride	108 ± 3.6 meq/liter	
651			6	Magnesium	3.3 ± 0.4 mg/100 ml	
652			6	Potassium	4.5 ± 0.2 meq/liter	
653			6	Sodium	159 ± 5 meq/liter	
654	*Isoodon obesulus*, ♂♀	Erythrocytes	4	Calcium	0-4.4 meq/liter	54
655			4	Magnesium	3.8-8.9 meq/liter	
656			4	Potassium	18-130 meq/liter	
657		Serum	4	Calcium	4.0-5.1 meq/liter	54
658			4	Chloride	100-157 meq/liter	
659			4	Magnesium	1.4-2.0 meq/liter	
660			3	Phosphorus	2.9-3.2 mg/100 ml	
661			4	Potassium	4.0-5.2 meq/liter	
662			4	Sodium	122-136 meq/liter	
663	*Lama guanicoe (L. huanacus)*, ♀	....	1	Calcium	8.0 mg/100 ml	20
664			1	Chloride	118 meq/liter	
665			1	Phosphorus	8.0 mg/100 ml	
666			1	Potassium	3.56 meq/liter	
667	*Lasiorhinus latifrons*	Erythrocytes	1	Calcium	2.1 meq/liter	54
668			1	Magnesium	3.45 meq/liter	
669			1	Potassium	85 meq/liter	
670		Serum	1	Calcium	5.3 meq/liter	54
671			1	Chloride	114 meq/liter	
672			1	Magnesium	2.75 meq/liter	
673			1	Phosphorus	6.5 mg/100 ml	
674			1	Potassium	6.9 meq/liter	
675			1	Sodium	160 meq/liter	
676	*Macropus robustus*, ♂♀	Serum	...	Potassium	6.4-10.3 meq/liter	54
677				Sodium	130-161 meq/liter	

[1]/ Plus/minus (±) values are standard error.

continued

	Species (Synonym)	Blood Component	No. of Observations	Constituent	Concentration	Reference
678	*M. rufus (Megaleia rufa)*, ♂♀	Serum	...	Phosphorus	4.3 mg/100 ml	54
679				Potassium	7.0-11.9 meq/liter	
680				Sodium	123-156 meq/liter	
681	*Martes zibellina*, ♂♀	Whole blood	4	Phosphorus	8.0 ± 4.1 mg/100 ml	51
	Meriones unguiculatus, adult					
682	♂	Whole blood	10	Phosphorus	5.94 ± 2.24 mg/100 ml	41
683	♀	Whole blood	10	Phosphorus	4.88 ± 0.94 mg/100 ml	41
684	♂♀	Whole blood	20	Potassium	4.54 ± 0.69 meq/liter	41
685			20	Sodium	150.9 ± 7.0 meq/liter	
	Mesocricetus auratus, ♂♀					
686	2-5 mo old	Plasma	145	Calcium	4.76 ± 0.49 meq/liter	12
687			146	Chloride	96.73 ± 5.19 meq/liter	
688			145	Phosphorus	5.29 ± 0.96 mg/100 ml	
689			199	Potassium	4.63 ± 1.32 meq/liter	
690			199	Sodium	128.59 ± 9.0 meq/liter	
691	2.5-4 mo old	Plasma	35	Calcium	11.5 mg/100 ml	5
692	Fed	Plasma	32	Chloride	100 ± 10.3 meq/liter	5
693			33	Potassium	4.8 ± 1.9 meq/liter	
694			34	Sodium	147 ± 5.5 meq/liter	
695	Fasted, 4-6 hr	Plasma	8	Chloride	114 ± 11.6 meq/liter	5
696	24 hr	Plasma	13	Potassium	4.5 ± 0.8 meq/liter	12
697			14	Sodium	150 ± 3.9 meq/liter	
	Mus musculus, adult					
698	♂; body wt, 25-35 g	Serum	60	Calcium	8.17 ± 0.18[1]/-9.00 ± 0.19[1]/ mg/100 ml	8
699	♀; body wt, 25-35 g	Serum	60	Calcium	8.26 ± 0.16[1]/-10.12 ± 0.18[1]/ mg/100 ml	8
700	♂♀; body wt, 20-25 g	Plasma	99	Calcium	2.78 ± 0.4 meq/liter	12
701			149	Chloride	107.55 ± 6.66 meq/liter	
702			146	Phosphorus	6.55 ± 1.61 mg/100 ml	
703			148	Potassium	5.25 ± 1.31 meq/liter	
704			147	Sodium	134.18 ± 9.58 meq/liter	
705	body wt, 25-35 g	Serum	235	Calcium	8.40 ± 1.09 mg/100 ml	69
706	C57BL/6J, ♂; 8-10 mo old	Serum	41	Sodium	186 ± 29.4 meq/liter	22
707	*Nandinia binotata*, ♂	....	1	Calcium	10.5 mg/100 ml	20
708			1	Phosphorus	5.8 mg/100 ml	
709	*Odocoileus virginianus*, ♀	Whole blood	5	Iron	234 ± 33 μg/100 ml	65
710	Pregnant	Whole blood	18	Iron	219 ± 43 μg/100 ml[2]/	65
711			7	Iron	288 ± 64 μg/100 ml[3]/	
712	*Oryctolagus cuniculus*, ♂♀	Whole blood	6	Calcium	5.5 meq/kg	57
713			6	Magnesium	4.3 meq/kg	57
714			7	Magnesium	5.4 ± 0.74 mg/100 ml	66
715			6	Potassium	37.2 meq/kg	57
716			16	Potassium	43.7 ± 0.5 meq/liter	16
717			6	Sodium	81 meq/kg	57
718			16	Sodium	98.5 ± 9.0 meq/liter	16
719		Erythrocytes	6	Calcium	2.0 meq/kg	57
720			6	Magnesium	8.0 meq/kg	57
721			7	Magnesium	9.4 ± 2.63 mg/100 ml	66
722			6	Potassium	83.1 meq/kg	57
723			16	Potassium	110.1 ± 6.0 meq/liter	16
724			6	Sodium	2.6 meq/kg	57
725			16	Sodium	16.8 ± 6.3 meq/liter	16

[1]/ Plus/minus (±) values are standard error. [2]/ Hemoglobin concentration ≯17 mg/100 ml. [3]/ Hemoglobin concentration >17 mg/100 ml.

continued

Species (Synonym)	Blood Component	No. of Observations	Constituent	Concentration	Reference
726	Plasma	6	Calcium	6.8 meq/kg	57
727		6	Magnesium	2.0 meq/kg	57
728		7	Magnesium	3.2 ± 0.59 mg/100 ml	66
729		6	Potassium	5.1 meq/kg	57
730		16	Potassium	4.2 ± 0.5 meq/liter	16
731		6	Sodium	139 meq/kg	57
732		16	Sodium	141.6 ± 10.8 meq/liter	16
733 Young adult	Plasma	105	Calcium	5.0 ± 1.11 meq/liter	12
734		99	Chloride	96.5 ± 6.79 meq/liter	
735		148	Phosphorus	5.47 ± 1.14 mg/100 ml	
736		143	Potassium	5.0 ± 0.93 meq/liter	
737 *Oryx gazella*	....	1	Calcium	7.4 mg/100 ml	20
738		1	Chloride	114 meq/liter	
739		1	Phosphorus	7.35 mg/100 ml	
740		1	Potassium	2.56 meq/liter	
741 ♂	....	2	Calcium	6.9-7.27 mg/100 ml	20
742		2	Phosphorus	16-18 mg/100 ml	
743		1	Potassium	7.4 meq/liter	
Ovis aries					
744 ♂; adult	Whole blood	9	Copper	0.98 ± 0.14 μg/ml	43
745	Erythrocytes	9	Copper	0.95 ± 0.16 μg/ml	43
746	Plasma	9	Copper	1.02 ± 0.11 μg/ml	43
747 1 yr old	Erythrocytes	2	Zinc	12.21 ± 0.43[1] μg/ml	63
748	Plasma	6	Iron	169 ± 12[1] μg/100 ml	79
749		2	Zinc	1.56 ± 0.09[1] μg/ml	63
750 ♀; 1 yr old	Plasma	37	Phosphorus	6.42 ± 1.5[1] mg/100 ml	82
751		48	Potassium	4.00 ± 0.37[1] meq/liter	
752		28	Sodium	150.4 ± 4.8[1] meq/liter	
753 3-4 yr old	Whole blood	149	Phosphorus	5.55 mg/100 ml	81
754	Plasma	149	Calcium	10.15 mg/100 ml	
755		149	Copper	105.1 μg/100 ml	
756		149	Magnesium	2.16 mg/100 ml	
757		149	Potassium	29.19 mg/100 ml	
758		149	Sodium	372.9 mg/100 ml	
759 ♂♀	Whole blood	10	Magnesium	3.3 ± 0.13 mg/100 ml	66
760		11	Potassium	11.6 ± 1.8 meq/liter	16
761		11	Sodium	125.7 ± 11.6 meq/liter	16
762	Erythrocytes	10	Magnesium	3.8 ± 0.29 mg/100 ml	66
763		11	Potassium	18.2 ± 4.1 meq/liter	16
764		11	Sodium	94.0 ± 10.4 meq/liter	16
765	Plasma	517	Calcium	9.2 ± 1.0 mg/100 ml	66
766		23	Copper	68.4 μg/100 ml	81
767		4	Copper	104 μg/100 ml	68
768		10	Magnesium	2.9 ± 0.13 mg/100 ml	66
769		4	Magnesium	2.1 mg/100 ml	68
770		11	Potassium	6.9 ± 1.0 meq/liter	16
771		11	Sodium	150.6 ± 11.2 meq/liter	16
772	Serum	722	Calcium	12.16 ± 0.28 mg/100 ml	66
773		...	Chloride	95-103 meq/liter	71
774		12	Magnesium	2.5 ± 0.3 mg/100 ml	66
775		...	Potassium	3.9-5.4 meq/liter	71
776		...	Sodium	139-152 meq/liter	71

[1] Plus/minus (±) values are standard error.

continued

	Species (Synonym)	Blood Component	No. of Obser- vations	Constituent	Concentration	Reference
777	Lambs, spring	Plasma	6	Calcium	11.2 mg/100 ml	42
778			6	Magnesium	2.2 mg/100 ml	
779	fall	Plasma	4	Calcium	10.2 mg/100 ml	42
780			4	Magnesium	2.4 mg/100 ml	
781	Fetus	Whole blood	10	Copper	0.45 ± 0.17 µg/ml	43
782		Erythrocytes	10	Copper	0.78 ± 0.67 µg/ml	43
783		Plasma	10	Copper	0.26 ± 0.08 µg/ml	43
784	Newborn, before suckling	Whole blood	15	Copper	0.67 ± 0.15 µg/ml	43
785		Erythrocytes	15	Copper	0.81 ± 0.22 µg/ml	43
786		Plasma	15	Copper	0.50 ± 0.16 µg/ml	43
787	15 wk old	Whole blood	244	Phosphorus	8.17 mg/100 ml	81
788		Plasma	244	Calcium	11.1 mg/100 ml	
789			224	Copper	139.2 µg/100 ml	
790			244	Magnesium	2.30 mg/100 ml	
791			224	Potassium	30.71 mg/100 ml	
792			244	Sodium	374.9 mg/100 ml	
793	1 yr old	Whole blood	...	Phosphorus	6.4 ± 1.6 mg/100 ml	83
794				Sodium	130 ± 5.0 meq/liter	
795		Plasma	4	Phosphorus	8.1 mg/100 ml	68
796	Adult	Whole blood	334	Phosphorus	5.54 mg/100 ml	81
797		Plasma	334	Calcium	9.65 mg/100 ml	
798			334	Chloride	364.9 mg/100 ml	
799			334	Magnesium	2.02 mg/100 ml	
800			334	Potassium	23.16 mg/100 ml	
801			334	Sodium	345.4 mg/100 ml	
802	Finnish Landrace, ♂♀	Plasma	39	Copper	44.2 µg/100 ml	81
803	Karoo, ♂♀	Plasma	24	Copper	0.13 mg/100 ml	11
	Merino					
804	♂	Whole blood	6	Calcium	3.4 meq/kg	57
805			6	Magnesium	2.0 meq/kg	
806			6	Potassium	6.7 meq/kg	
807			6	Sodium	107 meq/kg	
808		Erythrocytes	6	Calcium	1.3 meq/kg	57
809			6	Magnesium	2.8 meq/kg	
810			6	Potassium	9.5 meq/kg	
811			6	Sodium	107 meq/kg	
812		Plasma	6	Calcium	4.8 meq/kg	57
813			6	Magnesium	1.8 meq/kg	
814			6	Potassium	4.9 meq/kg	
815			6	Sodium	124 meq/kg	
816	♂♀	Plasma	30	Copper	77.6 µg/100 ml	81
817	Onderstepoort, ♂♀	Plasma	27	Copper	0.09 mg/100 ml	11
818	O. musimon, ♂	....	6	Calcium	9.1-12.2 mg/100 ml	20
819			2	Chloride	98-116 meq/liter	
820			6	Phosphorus	6.05-10.3 mg/100 ml	
821			2	Potassium	2.8-3.2 meq/liter	
822	♀	....	2	Calcium	10.0-11.6 mg/100 ml	20
823			3	Phosphorus	5.1-8.6 mg/100 ml	
824	Panthera leo, ♂	....	1	Calcium	11.4 mg/100 ml	20
825			1	Phosphorus	5.9 mg/100 ml	
826	♀	....	3	Calcium	10.8-12.3 mg/100 ml	20
827			3	Phosphorus	5.6-6.4 mg/100 ml	
828	♂♀	Whole blood	8	Phosphorus	3.7 ± 0.5-4.31 ± 0.7 mg/100 ml	51

continued

	Species (Synonym)	Blood Component	No. of Observations	Constituent	Concentration	Reference
829	P. nebulosa	....	1	Calcium	9.6 mg/100 ml	20
830	♂	....	1	Calcium	9 mg/100 ml	20
831			1	Chloride	116.4 meq/liter	
832			1	Phosphorus	6.0 mg/100 ml	
833			1	Potassium	2.05 meq/liter	
834			1	Sodium	152 meq/liter	
835	♀	....	1	Chloride	118 meq/liter	20
836			1	Potassium	2.88 meq/liter	
837			1	Sodium	162.6 meq/liter	
838	♂♀	....	2	Chloride	109-115 meq/liter	20
839			2	Phosphorus	5.0-5.2 mg/100 ml	
840			2	Potassium	2.1 meq/liter	
841	P. onca, ♂	....	1	Calcium	9.9 mg/100 ml	20
842			1	Phosphorus	4.4 mg/100 ml	
843	P. pardus, ♂	....	2	Calcium	7.70-12.2 mg/100 ml	20
844			1	Chloride	109 meq/liter	
845			2	Phosphorus	4.72-5.3 mg/100 ml	
846			1	Potassium	3.56 meq/liter	
847	P. tigris, ♂♀	Whole blood	12	Phosphorus	5.0 ± 1.6-6.08 ± 2.27 mg/100 ml	51
848	P. tigris altaica, ♂	....	5	Calcium	8.33-12.9 mg/100 ml	20
849			5	Chloride	109-124 meq/liter	
850			5	Phosphorus	5.3-7.9 mg/100 ml	
851			4	Potassium	2.6-3.76 meq/liter	
852			2	Sodium	155.7-165.3 meq/liter	
853	♀	....	4	Calcium	8.3-11.9 mg/100 ml	20
854			2	Chloride	108.4-120 meq/liter	
855			2	Potassium	2.8-2.9 meq/liter	
856			2	Sodium	142.2-166 meq/liter	
857	♂♀	....	2	Chloride	126-132 meq/liter	20
858			4	Phosphorus	4.8-6.9 mg/100 ml	
859			2	Potassium	3.84-3.9 meq/liter	
860	P. tigris tigris, ♀	....	2	Calcium	8.33-11.5 mg/100 ml	20
861			1	Chloride	112 meq/liter	
862			2	Phosphorus	5.4 mg/100 ml	
863			1	Potassium	3.7 meq/liter	
864	P. uncia, ♂	....	2	Calcium	8.70-12.7 mg/100 ml	20
865			1	Chloride	111 meq/liter	
866			2	Phosphorus	5.4-6.1 mg/100 ml	
867			1	Potassium	5.8 meq/liter	
868	♀	....	7	Calcium	7.70-13.4 mg/100 ml	20
869			2	Chloride	107-110 meq/liter	
870			7	Phosphorus	4.0-8 mg/100 ml	
871			2	Potassium	4.18-5.0 meq/liter	
872	Perameles gunnii, ♂♀	Erythrocytes	3	Calcium	0-2.8 meq/liter	54
873			3	Magnesium	5.8-7.5 meq/liter	
874			3	Potassium	110-233 meq/liter	
875		Serum	3	Calcium	3.9-5.0 meq/liter	54
876			3	Chloride	99-113 meq/liter	
877			3	Magnesium	1.6-2.1 meq/liter	
878			3	Phosphorus	3.2-3.9 mg/100 ml	
879			3	Potassium	3.2-3.7 meq/liter	
880			3	Sodium	140-143 meq/liter	

continued

	Species (Synonym)	Blood Component	No. of Observations	Constituent	Concentration	Reference
881	*Potorous tridactylus*, ♂♀	Erythrocytes	2	Calcium	0.5-2.2 meq/liter	54
882			2	Magnesium	4.7 meq/liter	
883			2	Potassium	155-243 meq/liter	
884		Serum	2	Calcium	5.0-5.5 meq/liter	54
885			2	Chloride	94-103 meq/liter	
886			2	Magnesium	1.3-1.7 meq/liter	
887			2	Phosphorus	3.2-3.6 mg/100 ml	
888			2	Potassium	3.4-3.7 meq/liter	
889			2	Sodium	134-138 meq/liter	
890	*Potos* sp., ♂♀	Whole blood	3	Phosphorus	4.3 ± 0.3 mg/100 ml	51
891	*Procyon lotor*, ♂♀	Whole blood	19	Phosphorus	4.7 ± 0.92-5.0 ± 0.9 mg/100 ml	51
	Rattus norvegicus, inbred					
892	♂	Plasma	66	Phosphorus	4.93 ± 1.73 mg/100 ml	39
893	12 wk old; germ free; fasted	Serum	19	Potassium	5.29 ± 1.07 meq/liter	13
894	overnight		20	Sodium	138.37 ± 3.38 meq/liter	
895	85-90 da old	Plasma	6-12	Calcium	11.0 ± 0.24[1] mg/100 ml	58
896			6-12	Magnesium	2.01 ± 0.06[1] mg/100 ml,	
897			6-12	Phosphorus	7.50 ± 0.30[1] mg/100 ml	
898	Germ free	Plasma	6-12	Calcium	11.4 ± 0.34[1] mg/100 ml	58
899			6-12	Magnesium	1.89 ± 0.05[1] mg/100 ml	
900			6-12	Phosphorus	7.56 ± 0.24[1] mg/100 ml	
901	Body wt, 285 ± 8 g	Serum	...	Calcium	10.5 ± 0.2[1] mg/100 ml	26
902				Phosphate	9.1 ± 0.3[1] mg/100 ml	
903	♀	Plasma	60	Phosphorus	5.75 ± 2.55 mg/100 ml	39
904	12 wk old; germ free; fasted	Serum	18	Potassium	4.76 ± 1.06 meq/liter	13
905	overnight		18	Sodium	134.99 ± 6.46 meq/liter	
906	♂♀	Whole blood	10	Potassium	54.1 ± 7.7 meq/liter	16
907			10	Sodium	99.9 ± 17.9 meq/liter	
908		Erythrocytes	10	Potassium	104.7 ± 15.4 meq/liter	16
909			10	Sodium	33.5 ± 3.5 meq/liter	
910		Plasma	10	Potassium	9.6 ± 0.9 meq/liter	16
911			10	Sodium	148.7 ± 8.5 meq/liter	
912	12 wk old; germ free; fasted	Serum	18	Calcium	9.7 ± 0.48 mg/100 ml	13
913	overnight		18	Phosphate	8.02 ± 1.23 mg/100 ml	
914	180-250 g	Plasma	148	Calcium	4.00 ± 0.63 meq/liter	12
915			150	Chloride	96.2 ± 6.39 meq/liter	
916			144	Phosphorus	7.29 ± 0.97 mg/100 ml	
917			100	Potassium	2.70 ± 0.46 meq/liter	
918			147	Sodium	118.29 ± 11.09 meq/liter	
	Sarcophilus harrisii					
919	♂	Serum	2	Chloride	100-102 meq/liter	53
920	Adult	Serum	2	Calcium	5.1 meq/liter	53
921			2	Magnesium	2.0-2.1 meq/liter	
922			2	Phosphorus	7.8-8.4 mg/100 ml	
923			2	Potassium	4.8-5.0 meq/liter	
924			2	Sodium	136-142 meq/liter	
925	♀; lactating	Serum	1	Calcium	3.4 meq/liter	53
926			1	Chloride	102 meq/liter	
927			1	Magnesium	2.25 meq/liter	
928			1	Phosphorus	9.1 mg/100 ml	
929			1	Potassium	4.6 meq/liter	
930			1	Sodium	135 meq/liter	

[1] Plus/minus (±) values are standard error.

continued

	Species (Synonym)	Blood Component	No. of Observations	Constituent	Concentration	Reference
931	♂♀	Erythrocytes	4	Calcium	0 meq/liter	54
932			4	Magnesium	4.7 meq/liter	
933		Serum	4	Calcium	3.4-6.7 meq/liter	54
934			3	Chloride	100-102 meq/liter	
935			4	Magnesium	1.8-2.4 meq/liter	
936			3	Potassium	4.6-5.0 meq/liter	
937			3	Sodium	135-142 meq/liter	
938	*Sigmodon hispidus*, ♂♀	Serum	...	Calcium	14.43 mg/100 ml	21
939				Phosphorus	6.7 mg/100 ml	
	Sus scrofa					
940	♂, weanling	Erythrocytes	4	Zinc	8.95 ± 0.66 μg/ml packed cells	6
	♀					
941	Pregnant	Serum	14	Calcium	10.11 ± 1.08 mg/100 ml	66
942	30 da	Serum	24	Calcium	9.1 mg/100 ml	49
943			24	Phosphorus	6.43 mg/100 ml	
944	60 da	Serum	24	Calcium	9.56 mg/100 ml	49
945			24	Phosphorus	6.54 mg/100 ml	
946	90 da	Serum	24	Calcium	9.25 mg/100 ml	49
947			24	Phosphorus	5.86 mg/100 ml	
948	96-48 hr pre-parturition	Serum	24	Calcium	9.3 mg/100 ml	49
949			24	Phosphorus	6.1 mg/100 ml	
950	48-24 hr pre-parturition	Serum	24	Phosphorus	6.5 mg/100 ml	49
951	48-0 hr pre-parturition	Serum	24	Calcium	9.2 mg/100 ml	49
952	1-24 hr post-parturition	Serum	24	Calcium	9.3 mg/100 ml	49
953			24	Phosphorus	7.0 mg/100 ml	
954	48-72 hr post-parturition	Serum	24	Calcium	10.0 mg/100 ml	49
955			24	Phosphorus	6.8 mg/100 ml	
956	♂♀	Whole blood	10	Magnesium	6.4 mg/100 ml	66
957			7	Potassium	48.1 ± 4.8 meq/liter	16
958			7	Sodium	78.0 ± 15.0 meq/liter	16
959			6	Zinc	11.0 μg/g	38
960		Erythrocytes	10	Magnesium	10.5 mg/100 ml	66
961			7	Potassium	105.9 ± 12.7 meq/liter	16
962			7	Sodium	15.6 ± 1.8 meq/liter	16
963		Plasma	31	Chloride	101 ± 3 meq/liter	17
964			10	Magnesium	3.2 mg/100 ml	66
965			31	Potassium	5.9 ± 0.8 meq/liter	17
966			7	Potassium	7.7 ± 2.7 meq/liter	16
967			7	Sodium	133.2 ± 11.0 meq/liter	16
968			31	Sodium	145 ± 3 meq/liter	17
969		Serum	50	Calcium	9.65 ± 0.99 mg/100 ml	66
970			...	Chloride	96-106 meq/liter	71
971			...	Potassium	4.4-6.7 meq/liter	71
972			...	Sodium	135-150 meq/liter	71
973	3-4 mo old	Serum	81	Calcium	5.3 ± 0.1 [1]-6.0 ± 0.1 [1] meq/liter	4
974			81	Magnesium	1.51 ± 0.05 [1]-7.79 ± 0.07 [1] meq/liter	
975			81	Phosphorus	2.3 ± 0.1 [1]-2.8 ± 0.2 [1] mmoles/liter	
976	5 mo old	Serum	6	Calcium	11.0 mg/100 ml	2
977			6	Chloride	105 meq/liter	
978			6	Magnesium	2.07 mg/100 ml	
979			6	Phosphorus	7.8 mg/100 ml	
980			6	Potassium	4.5 meq/liter	
981			6	Sodium	131 meq/liter	

[1] Plus/minus (±) values are standard error.

continued

	Species (Synonym)	Blood Component	No. of Observations	Constituent	Concentration	Reference
982	Fasted 19-115 hr	Serum	30	Calcium	10.1-10.7 mg/100 ml	2
983			30	Chloride	89-98 meq/liter	
984			30	Magnesium	1.75-2.10 mg/100 ml	
985			30	Phosphorus	5.8-7.8 mg/100 ml	
986			30	Potassium	4.6-4.8 meq/liter	
987			30	Sodium	131-146 meq/liter	
988	Refed 3 or 6 da	Serum	12	Calcium	10.4-11.3 mg/100 ml	2
989			12	Chloride	106-108 meq/liter	
990			12	Magnesium	2.0-2.2 mg/100 ml	
991			12	Phosphorus	7.8-7.9 mg/100 ml	
992			12	Potassium	4.3-4.4 meq/liter	
993			12	Sodium	138-143 meq/liter	
	Hormel miniature, 5 mo old; fasted 12 hr					
994	♂	Serum	14	Calcium	11.2 ± 0.4 mg/100 ml	74
995			14	Chloride	102 ± 2 meq/liter	
996			14	Phosphorus	8.4 ± 0.5 mg/100 ml	
997			14	Potassium	4.4 ± 0.4 meq/liter	
998			14	Sodium	145 ± 2 meq/liter	
999	♀	Serum	14	Calcium	11.6 ± 0.5 mg/100 ml	74
1000			14	Chloride	106 ± 3 meq/liter	
1001			14	Phosphorus	8.4 ± 0.5 mg/100 ml	
1002			14	Potassium	5.1 ± 0.8 meq/liter	
1003			14	Sodium	147 ± 2 meq/liter	
1004	*Tragulus napu*	....	1	Calcium	10.1 mg/100 ml	20
1005			1	Chloride	119.0 meq/liter	
1006			1	Sodium	177.4 meq/liter	
1007	*Trichosurus vulpecula,* ♂♀	Erythrocytes	4	Calcium	5.4 meq/liter	54
1008			4	Magnesium	10.2 meq/liter	
1009			4	Potassium	127 meq/liter	
1010		Serum	4	Calcium	3.4-5.8 meq/liter	54
1011			4	Chloride	87-102 meq/liter	
1012			4	Magnesium	1.4-2.25 meq/liter	
1013			4	Phosphorus	4.0-9.1 mg/100 ml	
1014			4	Potassium	4.2-5.0 meq/liter	
1015			4	Sodium	136-158 meq/liter	
1016	*Urocyon littoralis santacruzae*	....	1	Calcium	9.7 mg/100 ml	20
1017			1	Chloride	108.4 meq/liter	
1018			1	Phosphorus	4.3 mg/100 ml	
1019			1	Potassium	1.8 meq/liter	
1020			1	Sodium	127.4 meq/liter	
	Ursus americanus					
1021	♂, 4 yr old	Plasma	1	Chloride	104 meq/liter[4]	32
1022			1	Sodium	152 meq/liter[4]	
1023		Serum	1	Phosphorus	5.3 mg/100 ml[4]	32
1024	♂♀	Whole blood	10	Phosphorus	5.47 ± 1.34-5.5 ± 0.7 mg/100 ml	51
1025	3-8 yr old	Plasma	3	Chloride	118 ± 1 meq/liter[5]	32
1026			3	Sodium	147 ± 6 meq/liter[5]	
1027		Serum	3	Phosphorus	6.9 ± 0.7 mg/100 ml[5]	32
	U. arctos					
1028	♂	Plasma	1	Chloride	114 meq/liter[6]	32
1029			1	Sodium	143 meq/liter[6]	
1030		Serum	1	Phosphorus	3.1 mg/100 ml[6]	32
1031	♂♀	Whole blood	6	Phosphorus	4.6 ± 0.1-4.72 ± 0.27 mg/100 ml	51

[4] Spring. [5] Summer. [6] Autumn.

continued

	Species (Synonym)	Blood Component	No. of Observations	Constituent	Concentration	Reference
1032	1-12 yr old	Plasma	13	Chloride	106 ± 7 meq/liter[4]	32
1033			13	Sodium	145 ± 8 meq/liter[4]	
1034		Serum	13	Phosphorus	5.1 ± 1.4 mg/100 ml[4]	32
1035	5-24 yr old	Plasma	8	Chloride	108 ± 5 meq/liter[5]	32
1036			8	Sodium	141 ± 2 meq/liter[5]	
1037		Serum	8	Phosphorus	4.1 ± 1.2 mg/100 ml[5]	32
1038	*U. arctos middendorffi,* ♀	....	2	Chloride	106.8-110.8 meq/liter	20
1039			2	Phosphorus	3.86-4.22 mg/100 ml	
1040			2	Sodium	88.7-139.2 meq/liter	
1041	*Wallabia eugenii (Macropus eugenii),* ♂♀	Serum	8	Calcium	5.4 ± 0.3 meq/liter	54
1042			8	Chloride	98.8 ± 2.0 meq/liter	
1043			8	Potassium	3.9 ± 0.64 meq/liter	
1044			8	Sodium	154 ± 6 meq/liter	
1045	*Zalophus californianus,* ♂	....	1	Calcium	10.9 mg/100 ml	20
1046			1	Phosphorus	10.9 mg/100 ml	
1047	Dolphin, ♂	....	9	Calcium	8.4-11.7 mg/100 ml	20
1048			5	Chloride	104-126.0 meq/liter	
1049			9	Phosphorus	3.7-6.8 mg/100 ml	
1050			5	Potassium	2.0-4.1 meq/liter	
1051			3	Sodium	111-159.2 meq/liter	
1052	Otter, ♂♀	Whole blood	15	Phosphorus	4.94 ± 0.87-5.3 ± 0.9 mg/100 ml	51
1053	Porcupine	....	1	Calcium	12.4 mg/100 ml	20
1054			1	Phosphorus	7.2 mg/100 ml	
1055	Rabbit, ♂	....	120	Phosphorus	3.3 ± 0.2[1]-4.9 ± 0.3[1] mg/100 ml	25
1056		Serum	118	Phosphorus	4.08 ± 0.86 mg/100 ml	39
1057	♀	....	120	Phosphorus	3.5 ± 0.3[1]-5.1 ± 0.3[1] mg/100 ml	25
1058		Serum	116	Phosphorus	3.89 ± 0.80 mg/100 ml	39
1059	♂♀	Serum	20	Phosphorus	2.52 ± 0.10 mg/100 ml	39

[1] Plus/minus (±) values are standard error. [4] Spring. [5] Summer.

Contributors: Smith, Frank A., Michaelson, S. M., and Lebda, Nancy J. A.

References
[1] Baer, J. E., et al. 1957. Proc. Soc. Exp. Biol. Med. 95:80.
[2] Baetz, A. L., and W. L. Mengeling. 1971. Amer. J. Vet. Res. 32:1491.
[3] Baetz, A. L., and J. E. Pearson. 1972. Ibid. 33:1941.
[4] Baetz, A. L., et al. 1971. Ibid. 32:1479.
[5] Bannon, P. D., and G. H. Friedell. 1966. Lab. Anim. Care 16:417.
[6] Berry, R. K., et al. 1966. J. Nutr. 88:284.
[7] Blosser, T. H., and J. L. Albright. 1956. Ann. N.Y. Acad. Sci. 64:386.
[8] Bonilla, C. A., et al. 1968. Comp. Biochem. Physiol. 26:715.
[9] Boulos, B. M., and K. M. Hassanein. 1971. Urol. Int. 26:138.
[10] Brown, D. C. Unpublished. A.E.C., Oak Ridge, 1972.
[11] Brown, J. M. M. 1963. Ann. N.Y. Acad. Sci. 104: 504.
[12] Burns, K. F., and C. W. DeLannoy, Jr. 1966. Toxicol. Appl. Pharmacol. 8:429.
[13] Burns, K. F., et al. 1971. Lab. Anim. Sci. 21:415.
[14] Byrne, W. F. 1971. Thesis. Univ. Tennessee, Knoxville.
[15] Calkins, E., et al. 1956. Ann. N.Y. Acad. Sci. 64: 410.
[16] Coldman, M. F., and W. Good. 1967. Comp. Biochem. Physiol. 21:201.
[17] Coulter, D. B., and L. L. Small. 1971. Cornell Vet. 61:660.
[18] Craige, A. H., Jr., et al. 1949. J. Amer. Vet. Med. Ass. 114:136.
[19] Cramer, M. B., et al. 1969. Amer. J. Vet. Res. 30: 1183.
[20] D'Agostino, V. Unpublished. Bronx Zoo, N.Y., 1972.
[21] Dolyak, F., and C. A. Leone. 1953. Trans. Kans. Acad. Sci. 56:242.

continued

[22] Finch, C. E., and J. R. Foster. 1973. Lab. Anim. Sci. 23:339.

[23] Fisher, E. W., and G. H. De La Fuente. 1972. Res. Vet. Sci. 13:315.

[24] Fisher, G., et al. 1972. Univ. Calif. Davis Sch. Vet. Med. Radiat. Biol. Lab. Annu. Rep. UCD 472-119.

[25] Fox, R. R. 1971. Hycel Vet. Symp. 1:9.

[26] Frankel, H. M., et al. 1972. Comp. Biochem. Physiol. 43A:733.

[27] Gartner, R. J. W., et al. 1966. Res. Vet. Sci. 7:424.

[28] Greenwood, A. G., et al. 1971. J. Amer. Vet. Med. Ass. 159:571.

[29] Haley, T. J., et al. 1966. Nature (London) 212:820.

[30] Hall, R. F. Unpublished. A.E.C., Oak Ridge, 1972.

[31] Hall, R. F., and R. A. Reynolds. 1972. Amer. J. Vet. Res. 33:1711.

[32] Halloran, D. W., and A. M. Pearson. 1972. Can. J. Zool. 50:827.

[33] Hayakawa, T., and T. Takayama. 1961. Nat. Inst. Anim. Health Quart. 1:113.

[34] Heynes, H. 1971. J. Agr. Sci. 76:563.

[35] Heynes, H. 1971. S. Afr. J. Anim. Sci. 1:95.

[36] Hibbs, J. W., and W. D. Pounden. 1956. Ann. N.Y. Acad. Sci. 64:375.

[37] Kaneko, J. J. 1963. Ibid. 104:689.

[38] Klussendorf, R. C., and J. M. Pensack. 1958. J. Amer. Vet. Med. Ass. 132:446.

[39] Laird, C. W. 1972. Representative Values for Animal and Veterinary Populations and Their Clinical Significance. Hycel, Inc., Houston, Tex.

[40] Marsh, H., and K. F. Swingle. 1960. Amer. J. Vet. Res. 21:212.

[41] Mays, A., Jr. 1969. Lab. Anim. Care 19:838.

[42] McAleese, D. M., et al. 1961. J. Nutr. 74:505.

[43] McCosker, P. J. 1968. Res. Vet. Sci. 9:91.

[44] McKelvie, D. H. 1970. In A. C. Anderson, ed. The Beagle as an Experimental Dog. Iowa State Univ. Press, Ames. p. 281.

[45] McKelvie, D. H., et al. 1966. Amer. J. Vet. Res. 27:1405.

[46] Michaelson, J. M., et al. 1966. J. Amer. Vet. Med. Ass. 148:532.

[47] Millson, G. C., et al. 1960. J. Comp. Pathol. 70:194.

[48] Moore, W. E. 1969. Amer. J. Vet. Res. 30:1133.

[49] Nachreiner, R. F., and O. J. Ginther. 1972. Ibid. 33:2215.

[50] Nirmalan, G., and S. G. Nair. 1969. Res. Vet. Sci. 10:176.

[51] Olsen, R. E., and K. F. Burns. 1971. Hycel Vet. Symp. 1:59.

[52] Parsons, R. S., and E. R. Guiler. 1972. Comp. Biochem. Physiol. 43A:935.

[53] Parsons, R. S., et al. 1970. Ibid. 32:345.

[54] Parsons, R. S., et al. 1971. Ibid. 39B:209.

[55] Pickrell, J. A. Unpublished. Lovelace Foundation, Albuquerque, N. Mex., 1973.

[56] Pierce, K. R., and C. W. Laird. 1971. Hycel Vet. Symp. 1:25.

[57] Quinn, P. J., and I. G. White. 1967. Res. Vet. Sci. 8:58.

[58] Reddy, B. S. 1971. Fed. Proc. Fed. Amer. Soc. Exp. Biol. 30:1815.

[59] Reece, W. O., and J. D. Wahlstrom. 1972. Amer. J. Vet. Res. 33:2175.

[60] Reeves, J. T., et al. 1972. Ibid. 33:2159.

[61] Robinson, F. R., and R. F. Ziegler. 1968. Lab. Anim. Care 18:39.

[62] Rothstein, R., and D. Hunsaker, II. 1972. Ibid. 22:227.

[63] Sasser, L. B., et al. 1971. Radiat. Res. 46:115.

[64] Schultz, R. H., et al. 1971. J. Reprod. Fert. 27:355.

[65] Seal, U. S., and A. W. Erickson. 1969. Comp. Biochem. Physiol. 30:695.

[66] Simesen, M. G. 1970. In J. J. Kaneko and C. E. Cornelius, ed. Clinical Biochemistry of Domestic Animals. Ed. 2. Academic Press, New York. v. 1, p. 318.

[67] Snyder, J. W., et al. 1967. Amer. J. Vet. Res. 28:1705.

[68] Standish, J. F., and C. B. Ammerman. 1971. J. Anim. Sci. 33:481.

[69] Stringham, R. M., Jr., et al. 1967. Comp. Biochem. Physiol. 22:325.

[70] Strozier, L. M., et al. 1971. Lab. Anim. Sci. 21:399.

[71] Tasker, J. B. 1971. In J. J. Kaneko and C. E. Cornelius, ed. Clinical Biochemistry of Domestic Animals. Ed. 2. Academic Press, New York. v. 2, p. 95.

[72] Timmons, E. H., and P. A. Marques. 1969. Lab. Anim. Care 19:342.

[73] Toole, J. F. 1972. Lab. Anim. Sci. 22:118.

[74] Tumbleson, M. E., et al. 1969. Lab. Anim. Care 19:345.

[75] Tumbleson, M. E., et al. 1970. Ibid. 20:242.

[76] Tumbleson, M. E., et al. 1973. Cornell Vet. 63:58.

[77] Van Stewart, E., and B. B. Longwell. 1969. Amer. J. Vet. Res. 30:907.

[78] Velasco, M., et al. 1971. J. Amer. Vet. Med. Ass. 158:763.

[79] Wade, L., Jr., et al. 1971. Radiat. Res. 46:89.

[80] Ward, G. M. 1956. Ann. N.Y. Acad. Sci. 64:361.

[81] Wiener, G. Unpublished. Animal Breeding Research Organization, Edinburgh, 1972.

[82] Wykoff, M. H. 1966. Radiat. Res. 27:445.

[83] Wykoff, M. H. 1969. Health Phys. 16:804.

[84] Wykoff, M. H. Unpublished. A.E.C., Oak Ridge, 1972.

[85] Yousef, M. K., et al. 1971. Comp. Biochem. Physiol. 39B:279.

Values in parentheses are ranges, estimate "c", unless otherwise indicated (*see* Introduction).

	Species	Blood Component	Electrolyte	Concentration	Reference
1	*Anas platyrhynchos*	Whole blood	Copper	0.35(0.22-0.45) mg/liter	3
2			Phosphorus, inorganic	6.7(6.1-7.3) mg/100 ml	24
3			Potassium	52.3 meq/liter	25
4			Sodium	77.8 meq/liter	25
5		Erythrocytes	Potassium	101.6 meq/liter	25
6			Sodium	8.4 meq/liter	25
7	Mallard, ♂	Serum	Iron	159 µg/100 ml	41
8			Phosphorus, inorganic	3.8(2.8-4.8) mg/100 ml	29
9	♀, non-laying	Serum	Calcium	10.8(8.5-13.8) mg/100 ml	61
10			Iron	132 µg/100 ml	41
11			Potassium	19.3(16.6-25.7) mg/100 ml	61
12			Sodium	331(278-420) mg/100 ml	61
13	laying	Serum	Iron	1065 µg/100 ml	41
14	8 mo old; laying	Serum	Calcium	20.2 mg/100 ml	62
15			Potassium	16.6 mg/100 ml	62
16			Sodium	314 mg/100 ml	62
17	Pekin, ♂	Plasma	Calcium, total	(9.0-9.6) mg/100 ml	33
18			ultrafilterable	(6.0-6.8) mg/100 ml	33
19			Chloride	103(100-106)[b] mmole/liter	17
20			Phosphorus, inorganic	1.71(0.77-2.65)[b] mmole/liter	17
21			Potassium	3.09(2.37-3.81)[b] mmole/liter	17
22			Sodium	138(125-151)[b] mmole/liter	17
23	♀, young	Plasma	Calcium	11.0 mg/100 ml	23
24	adult	Plasma	Calcium	20.0(12.3-34.0) mg/100 ml	23
25	*Anser* sp.	Erythrocytes	Zinc	6.5 µg/g	50
26	*A. anser*	Whole blood	Potassium	48.8 meq/liter	25
27			Sodium	76.2 meq/liter	25
28		Erythrocytes	Potassium	99.6 meq/liter	25
29			Sodium	10.8 meq/liter	25
30	♂	Serum	Iron	163.8 µg/100 ml	41
31	♀, non-laying	Serum	Iron	160.0 µg/100 ml	41
32	laying	Serum	Iron	1260 µg/100 ml	41
33			Potassium	3.8 meq/liter	25
34			Sodium	140.5 meq/liter	25
35	Pilgrim [1/], 1 wk, ♂	Plasma	Calcium	8.25(7.57-8.93)[b] mg/100 ml	22
36			Chloride	99.2(93.0-105.4)[b] mg/100 ml	22
37			Phosphorus, inorganic	5.45(3.95-6.95)[b] mg/100 ml	22
38	♀	Plasma	Calcium	8.46(8.40-8.52)[b] mg/100 ml	22
39			Chloride	98.8(93.0-104.6)[b] mg/100 ml	22
40			Phosphorus, inorganic	5.56(3.78-7.34)[b] mg/100 ml	22
41	20 wk, ♂	Plasma	Calcium	11.27(11.21-11.33)[b] mg/100 ml	22
42			Chloride	106.6(102.8-110.4)[b] mg/100 ml	22
43			Phosphorus, inorganic	4.03(3.13-4.93)[b] mg/100 ml	22
44	♀	Plasma	Calcium	11.14(10.02-12.26)[b] mg/100 ml	22
45			Chloride	108.3(105.3-111.3)[b] mg/100 ml	22
46			Phosphorus, inorganic	4.09(3.33-4.85)[b] mg/100 ml	22
47	55 wk, ♂	Plasma	Calcium	10.91(10.67-11.15)[b] mg/100 ml	22
48			Chloride	103.5(98.5-108.5)[b] mg/100 ml	22
49			Phosphorus, inorganic	1.80(0.32-3.28)[b] mg/100 ml	22

[1/] For values at ages other than 1, 20, & 55 wk, consult reference 22.

continued

	Species	Blood Component	Electrolyte	Concentration	Reference
50	♀	Plasma	Calcium	33.35(18.15-48.19)[b] mg/100 ml	22
51			Chloride	99.8(95.4-104.2)[b] mg/100 ml	22
52			Phosphorus, inorganic	6.29(1.67-10.91)[b] mg/100 ml	22
53	*Anthropoides virgo*	Whole blood	Phosphorus, inorganic	4.9 mg/100 ml	47
54	*Ara macao*	Whole blood	Phosphorus, inorganic	6.4 mg/100 ml	47
55	*Carpodacus mexicanus*	Serum	Chloride	(120-142) meq/liter	45
56	*Catharacta skua*	Whole blood	Copper	0.39(0.35-0.42) mg/liter	3
57	*Ciconia ciconia*[2/]	Whole blood	Phosphorus, inorganic	5.6 mg/100 ml	47
58	*Colinus virginianus*	Plasma	Sodium	163 meq/liter	35
59	♂	Serum	Calcium	14.6(14.1-15.4) mg/100 ml	2
60	♀, non-laying	Serum	Calcium	14.2(11.0-14.8) mg/100 ml	2
61	laying	Serum	Calcium	29.3(23.0-40.2) mg/100 ml	2
62	*Columba livia*	Whole blood	Phosphorus, inorganic	6.4(5.2-7.1) mg/100 ml	47
63		Erythrocytes	Magnesium	44 mg/100 ml	42
64		Plasma	Magnesium	2.4 mg/100 ml	42
65			Potassium	3.51 meq/liter	37
66			Sodium	151.9 meq/liter	37
67		Serum	Iron	217(167-269) µg/100 ml	40
68	White Carneau, ♂	Serum	Calcium	9.9 mg/100 ml	49
69	♀, non-laying	Serum	Calcium	10.4 mg/100 ml	49
70	laying	Serum	Calcium	22.6 mg/100 ml	49
71	*Coturnix coturnix*	Whole blood	Selenium	5.8 µµmole/g	34
72		Plasma	Magnesium	1.92 meq/liter	60
73			Potassium	2.91 meq/liter	60
74			Sodium	157.3 meq/liter	60
75	6-22 mo	Plasma	Calcium	4.8 meq/liter	60
76	*C. coturnix japonica*	Whole blood	Iron	85.7 mg/100 ml	57
77			Zinc	0.5 mg/100 ml	57
78	*Cygnus atratus*	Whole blood	Phosphorus	3.9 mg/100 ml	47
79	*Diomedea immutabilis; D. nigripes*	Plasma	Potassium	5.7(4.9-7.0) meq/liter	13
80			Sodium	167(162-171) meq/liter	13
81	*Dromiceius novaehollandiae*	Whole blood	Copper	0.64(0.55-0.71) mg/liter	3
82	*Eudyptes chrysolophus*	Whole blood	Copper	0.53(0.50-0.55) mg/liter	3
83	*E. crestatus*	Whole blood	Copper	0.37(0.32-0.43) mg/liter	3
84	*Falco sparverius*	Plasma	Calcium	5 mmole/liter	6
85			Chloride	152(147-157) mmole/liter	6
86			Potassium	14(12-16) mmole/liter	6
87			Sodium	187(184-190) mmole/liter	6
88	*Forpus passerinus spengeli*[3/]	Whole blood	Phosphorus, inorganic	8.3 mg/100 ml	47
89	*Fratercula arctica*	Plasma	Chloride	133.4 meq/liter	20
90			Potassium	3.1 meq/liter	20
91			Sodium	160.7 meq/liter	20
92	*Fulica americana*	Plasma	Chloride	96.6(87.6-105.6)[b] meq/liter	8
93			Sodium	135(103-166)[b] meq/liter	8
94	*Gallus gallus (G. domesticus)*	Whole blood	Copper	0.23(0.11-0.47) mg/liter	3
95			Magnesium	5.0(4.7-5.3) mg/100 ml	12
96		Erythrocytes	Zinc	1.007 mg/100 ml	48
97		Plasma	Zinc	0.210 mg/100 ml	48
98	1 da	Plasma	Calcium	9.7 mg/100 ml	59
99			Copper	4.0 µg/100 ml	59
100			Magnesium	1.7 mg/100 ml	59
101			Phosphorus, inorganic	3.4 mg/100 ml	59

[2/] Synonym: *Ciconia alba.* [3/] Synonym: *Psittacula spengeli.*

continued

	Species	Blood Component	Electrolyte	Concentration	Reference
102			Potassium	17.7 mg/100 ml	59
103			Sodium	278.2 mg/100 ml	59
104	♂	Serum	Iron	102.5 µg/100 ml	41
105	♀, non-laying	Serum	Iron	129.0 µg/100 ml	41
106	laying	Serum	Iron	500.0 µg/100 ml	41
107	Brown Leghorn[4], ♂	Erythrocytes	Calcium	0.52 meq/liter	11
108			Chloride	52.60 meq/liter	11
109			Iron	4.32 meq/liter	11
110			Magnesium	8.31 meq/liter	11
111			Potassium	105.87 meq/liter	11
112			Sodium	9.58 meq/liter	11
113	Cornish × White Rock[5], 4 wk	Plasma	Potassium	7.1 meq/liter	58
114			Sodium	159 meq/liter	58
115	12 wk	Plasma	Calcium	13.3 mg/100 ml	31
116			Magnesium	1.5 mg/100 ml	31
117			Phosphorus, inorganic	6.4 mg/100 ml	31
118	Desi Fowl, ♂	Whole blood	Calcium	12.6 mg/100 ml	38
119			Chloride	491.6 mg/100 ml	38
120		Serum	Magnesium	1.47 mg/100 ml	38
121	♀, non-laying	Whole blood	Calcium	12.4 mg/100 ml	38
122			Chloride	479.7 mg/100 ml	38
123		Serum	Magnesium	1.52 mg/100 ml	38
124	laying	Whole blood	Calcium	18.4 mg/100 ml	38
125			Chloride	482.3 mg/100 ml	38
126		Serum	Magnesium	1.34 mg/100 ml	38
127	Leghorn × New Hampshire, 2 wk	Serum	Fluoride	0.23 µg/ml	52
128	New Hampshire[5], 3 wk	Whole blood	Molybdenum	0.032 µg/ml	28
129	New Hampshire × Leghorn	Whole blood	Potassium	41.7 meq/liter	25
130			Sodium	84.3 meq/liter	25
131	Rhode Island Red[5]	Erythrocytes	Phosphorus, inorganic	0.56 mmole/liter	14
132	♂	Erythrocytes	Potassium	88.8 meq/liter	25
133			Sodium	10.7 meq/liter	25
134	♀, adult	Plasma	Calcium, total	24.6(19.5-30.0) mg/100 ml	53
135			ultrafilterable	8.2(7.5-8.7) mg/100 ml	53
136			Magnesium, total	3.41(3.04-3.95) mg/100 ml	53
137			ultrafilterable	2.09(1.82-2.34) mg/100 ml	53
138			Phosphorus, inorganic	1.15 mmole/liter	14
139	Rhode Island Red × Wyandotte[5],	Plasma	Bicarbonate	25.79 meq/liter	36
140	♀, 13 mo		Chloride	111.14 meq/liter	36
141			Potassium	5.29 meq/liter	36
142			Sodium	168.57 meq/liter	36
	Single-comb White Leghorn[4]				
143	♂, 8 da	Plasma	Magnesium	3.1(1.3-4.9)[b] mg/100 ml	30
144	24 wk	Whole blood	Selenium	4.16 µµmole/g	34
145	1 yr	Whole blood	Selenium	8.0 µµmole/g	34
146	adult	Plasma	Calcium, total	9.4 mg/100 ml	55
147			ultrafilterable	6.2 mg/100 ml	55
148			Chloride	117(106-124) meq/liter	4
149			Phosphorus, inorganic	6.0 mg/100 ml	55
150			Potassium	3.8(3.1-4.6) meq/liter	4
151			Sodium	152(140-161) meq/liter	4

[4] Egg-producing breed. [5] Meat-producing breed.

continued

	Species	Blood Component	Electrolyte	Concentration	Reference
152	♀	Whole blood	Selenium	2.3 μμmole/g	34
153	10-12 wk	Plasma	Phosphorus, inorganic	6.65(5.41-7.89)[b] mg/100 ml	5
154	14 wk	Plasma	Calcium	17.0(14.0-19.6) mg/100 ml	7
155			Iron	159(115-220) μg/100 ml	7
156	adult, non-laying	Plasma	Calcium, total	(7.6-11.0) mg/100 ml	54
157			ultrafilterable	(4.8-5.2) mg/100 ml	54
158	laying	Plasma	Bicarbonate	27.9 mmole/liter	21
159			Calcium, total	24.7 mg/100 ml	43
160			ultrafilterable	7.0 mg/100 ml	43
161			Magnesium	2.0 mg/100 ml	31
162			Phosphorus, inorganic	3.4 mg/100 ml	31
163			Potassium[6]	14.2(11.6-17.1) mg/100 ml	15
164			Sodium	312(303-326) mg/100 ml	15
165	Capon	Plasma	Calcium, total	11.59 mg/100 ml	44
166			ultrafilterable	6.24 mg/100 ml	44
167			Phosphorus, inorganic	6.1 mg/100 ml	55
168	*Heterospizias meridionalis*	Plasma	Calcium	3 mmole/liter	6
169			Chloride	123 mmole/liter	6
170			Potassium	8 mmole/liter	6
171			Sodium	170 mmole/liter	6
172	*Larus glaucescens*	Plasma	Chloride	123.4 meq/liter	19
173	7-10 da	Plasma	Potassium	5.71 meq/liter	16
174			Sodium	151.0 meq/liter	16
175	3-6 mo	Plasma	Potassium	4.30 meq/liter	16
176			Sodium	153.9 meq/liter	16
177	*Lophortyx californicus*	Plasma	Sodium	157 meq/liter	35
178	*L. gambelii*	Plasma	Sodium	162 meq/liter	35
179	*Loxia curvirostra sitkensis*	Plasma	Sodium	161.2(148-171) meq/liter	9
180	*Macronectes giganteus*	Whole blood	Copper	0.34 mg/liter	3
181	*Meleagris gallopavo*	Whole blood	Copper	0.54 mg/liter	3
182	Broad-Breasted Bronze	Whole blood	Copper	0.23(0.18-0.28) mg/liter	3
183			Phosphorus, inorganic	5.6(5.2-6.0) mg/100 ml	47
184			Selenium	2.1 μμmole/g	34
185	♂	Plasma	Calcium	10.5(9.6-11.9) mg/100 ml	39
186			Phosphorus, inorganic	3.8(3.1-4.6) mg/100 ml	39
187		Serum	Iron	70 μg/100 ml	41
188	♀, non-laying	Plasma	Calcium	9.2(7.8-11.4) mg/100 ml	39
189			Phosphorus, inorganic	4.4(3.2-5.6) mg/100 ml	39
190		Serum	Iron	104.9 μg/100 ml	41
191	laying	Plasma	Calcium	25.2(13.8-36.9) mg/100 ml	39
192			Phosphorus, inorganic	7.1(4.9-9.4) mg/100 ml	39
193	Poults	Whole blood	Copper	1.4(1.0-1.9) ppm	27
194			Molybdenum	0.87(0.1-2.1) ppm	27
195	White Holland, 42-71 wk ♂	Plasma	Calcium	23.9(19.4-30.4) mg/100 ml	26
196			Chloride	85.0(79.0-91.0) meq/liter	26
197			Potassium	6.4(5.8-7.7) mg/100 ml	26
198			Sodium	155.0(143.0-164.0) mg/100 ml	26
199	♀, laying	Plasma	Calcium	34.5(19.6-45.2) mg/100 ml	26
200			Chloride	92.0(84.0-103.0) meq/liter	26
201			Potassium	6.0(5.1-7.2) mg/100 ml	26
202			Sodium	149.6(139.0-167.0) mg/100 ml	26

[6] For blood electrolyte values during shell formation, consult reference 15.

continued

	Species	Blood Component	Electrolyte	Concentration	Reference
203	Wild	Whole blood	Copper	0.54 mg/liter	3
204	*Melierax gabar* [7]	Plasma	Chloride	127 mmole/liter	6
205			Sodium	160 mmole/liter	6
206	*Nycticorax nycticorax*	Whole blood	Phosphorus, inorganic	6.1 mg/100 ml	47
207	*Passerculus sandwichensis beldingi*	Serum	Chloride	139(101-177)[b] meq/liter	46
208	*Phasianus colchicus*, 4 mo	Whole blood	Calcium[8]	8.9 mg/100 g	1
209			Copper	0.52 μg/g	1
210			Iron	>23 μg/g	1
211			Lead	0.22 μg/g	1
212			Magnesium	5.0 mg/100 g	1
213			Phosphorus, inorganic	119 mg/100 g	1
214			Potassium	157 mg/100 g	1
215			Sodium	224 mg/100 g	1
216			Strontium	0.0543 μg/g	1
217	adult	Whole blood	Calcium	7.4 mg/100 g	1
218			Copper	0.37 μg/g	1
219			Iron	>23 μg/g	1
220			Lead	0.26 μg/g	1
221			Magnesium	6.0 mg/100 g	1
222			Phosphorus, inorganic	129 mg/100 g	1
223			Potassium	181 mg/100 g	1
224			Sodium	203 mg/100 g	1
225			Strontium	0.0023 μg/g	1
226	*Pygoscelis papua*	Whole blood	Copper	0.50(0.43-0.58) mg/liter	3
227	*Rallus owstoni*	Plasma	Chloride	117.6(115.4-119.3) meq/liter	8
228			Sodium	178(172-185) meq/liter	8
229	*Scardafella inca*	Plasma	Chloride	109.9 meq/liter	32
230	*Serinus canarius*	Whole blood	Phosphorus, inorganic	5.6 mg/100 ml	47
231		Serum	Potassium	(21-25) mg/100 ml	56
232	*Sterna hirundo*	Plasma	Sodium	136.8(135.4-138.0) meq/liter	18
	Struthio camelus australis, 13 mo				
233	♂	Whole blood	Calcium	10.6(8.2-13.3) mg/100 ml	10
234			Magnesium	7.7 mg/100 ml	10
235			Phosphorus, inorganic	10.6(10.2-11.4) mg/100 ml	10
236			Potassium	197.0 mg/100 ml	10
237			Sodium	258.7 mg/100 ml	10
238	♀	Whole blood	Calcium	12.9(11.6-14.2) mg/100 ml	10
239			Magnesium	7.6(7.4-7.7) mg/100 ml	10
240			Phosphorus, inorganic	10.7(10.2-11.6) mg/100 ml	10
241			Potassium	201.3(189.0-212.0) mg/100 ml	10
242			Sodium	287.5(270.0-322.5) mg/100 ml	10
243	*Zenaida asiatica*	Plasma	Chloride	109.7 meq/liter	32
244	*Zenaidura macroura*	Plasma	Chloride	135.9 meq/liter	51
245			Sodium	175.6 meq/liter	51

[7] Synonym: *Micronisus gabar.* [8] For values for additional trace elements, consult reference 1.

Contributor: Hunsaker, Walter G.

References

[1] Anderson, W. L., and P. L. Stewart. 1969. J. Wildl. Manage. 33:254.

[2] Baldini, J. T., and M. X. Zarrow. 1952. Poult. Sci. 31:800.

[3] Beck, A. B. 1956. Aust. J. Zool. 4:1.

[4] Beljan, J. R., et al. 1971. Poult. Sci. 50:229.

[5] Bide, R. W., and C. le Q. Darcel. 1969. Ibid. 48:795.

[6] Cade, T. J., and L. Greenwald. 1966. Condor 68:338.

continued

[7] Campbell, E. A. 1960. Poult. Sci. 39:140.
[8] Carpenter, R. E., and M. A. Stafford. 1970. Condor 72:316.
[9] Dawson, W. R., et al. 1965. Auk 82:606.
[10] De Villiers, O. T. 1938. Onderstepoort J. Vet. Sci. Anim. Ind. 11:419.
[11] El Jack, M. H., and P. E. Lake. 1966. Brit. Poult. Sci. 7:315.
[12] Eveleth, D. F. 1937. J. Biol. Chem. 119:289.
[13] Frings, H., et al. 1958. Science 128:1572.
[14] Gourlay, D. R. H. 1957. Amer. J. Physiol. 190:536.
[15] Hodges, R. D. 1970. Ann. Biol. Anim. Biochim. Biophys. 10:199.
[16] Holmes, W. N., et al. 1961. J. Endocrinol. 23:53.
[17] Holmes, W. N., et al. 1968. J. Exp. Biol. 48:487.
[18] Hughes, M. R. 1968. Physiol. Zool. 41:210.
[19] Hughes, M. R. 1970. Comp. Biochem. Physiol. 32:315.
[20] Hughes, M. R. 1970. Can. J. Zool. 48:479.
[21] Hunt, J. R., and J. R. Aitken. 1962. Poult. Sci. 41:434.
[22] Hunt, J. R., et al. 1964. Brit. Poult. Sci. 5:257.
[23] Kaneko, T., et al. 1964. Bull. Nat. Inst. Anim. Ind. Chiba, 4 & 5 (Nutr. Abstr. Rev. 35:95, 1965).
[24] Kerr, S. E., and L. Daoud. 1935. J. Biol. Chem. 109:301.
[25] Ketz, H. A., and G. Assmann. 1960. Acta Biol. Med. Ger. 4:598.
[26] Kirshner, N., et al. 1951. Poult. Sci. 30:875.
[27] Kratzer, F. H. 1952. Proc. Soc. Exp. Biol. Med. 80:483.
[28] Kurnick, A. A., et al. 1957. Ibid. 95:353.
[29] Landauer, W., et al. 1941. Endocrinology 28:458.
[30] Lloyd, J. W., and W. E. Collins. 1970. Poult. Sci. 49:446.
[31] Lloyd, J. W., et al. 1970. Ibid. 49:1117.
[32] MacMillen, R. E., and C. H. Trost. 1966. Auk 83:441.
[33] Mandel, L., et al. 1952. C. R. Soc. Biol. 146:1805.
[34] McFarland, L. Z., et al. 1970. Poult. Sci. 49:216.
[35] McNabb, F. M. A. 1969. Comp. Biochem. Physiol. 28:1059.
[36] Mongin, P., and B. Sauveur. 1970. Ann. Biol. Anim. Biochim. Biophys. 10:141.
[37] Munday, K. A., and G. F. Blane. 1961. Comp. Biochem. Physiol. 2:8.
[38] Nirmalan, G., and M. Aravindan. 1963. Kerala Vet. 2:20 (Nutr. Abstr. Rev. 35:996, 1965).
[39] Paulsen, T. M., et al. 1950. Poult. Sci. 29:15.
[40] Planas, J., and M. C. Martin-Mateo. 1965. Rev. Espan. Fisiol. 21:1 (Nutr. Abstr. Rev. 36:109, 1966).
[41] Planas, J., et al. 1961. Nature (London) 189:668.
[42] Platner, W. S. 1945. Univ. Mich. Microfilm Publ. 1231:289.
[43] Polin, D., and P. D. Sturkie. 1957. Endocrinology 60:778.
[44] Polin, D., and P. D. Sturkie. 1958. Ibid. 63:177.
[45] Poulson, T. L., and G. A. Bartholomew. 1962. Condor 64:245.
[46] Poulson, T. L., and G. A. Bartholomew. 1962. Physiol. Zool. 35:109.
[47] Rapoport, S., and G. M. Guest. 1941. J. Biol. Chem. 138:269.
[48] Savage, J. E., et al. 1964. Poult. Sci. 43(2):420.
[49] Sendroy, J., Jr., et al. 1961. Proc. Soc. Exp. Biol. Med. 108:641.
[50] Smirnov, A. A. 1948. Biokhimiya 13:79.
[51] Smyth, M., and G. A. Bartholomew. 1966. Auk 83:597.
[52] Suttie, J. W., et al. 1964. Proc. Soc. Exp. Biol. Med. 115:575.
[53] Taylor, T. G., and F. Hertelendy. 1961. Poult. Sci. 40:115.
[54] Urist, M. R., and N. M. Deutsch. 1960. Endocrinology 66:377.
[55] Urist, M. R., and N. M. Deutsch. 1960. Ibid. 66:805.
[56] Velick, S. F., and J. Scudder. 1940. Amer. J. Hyg. 31:92.
[57] Vohra, P., and D. C. Bond. 1970. Poult. Sci. 49:565.
[58] Weber, C. W., et al. 1968. Ibid. 47:1318.
[59] Weiser, M., et al. 1965. Wien. Tieraerztl. Monatsschr. 52:237 (Nutr. Abstr. Rev. 35:996, 1965).
[60] Willoughby, E. J. 1971. Comp. Biochem. Physiol. 38:541.
[61] Wood, J. S., and W. E. Hofman. 1967. J. Wildl. Manage. 31:546.
[62] Wood, J. S., and R. L. Smoes. 1968. Ibid. 32:934.

243. PLASMA ELECTROLYTES: REPTILES

Values represent levels of electrolytes in well-hydrated, fasted animals. These values often show remarkable changes related to environmental parameters such as temperature and state of hydration, and physiological events such as feeding, diving, and reproduction (reviewed in reference 12). Data in brackets are number of subjects. Values in parentheses are ranges, estimate "c" (*see* Introduction).

Species	Electrolyte Concentration, mmole/liter								Reference
	Bicarbonate	Calcium	Chloride	Magnesium	Phosphate[1]	Potassium	Sodium	Sulfate	ence
	Crocodiles								
1 *Alligator missis-sippiensis*	19.8(14-27)[2,3] [75]	2.6(2.4-2.8) [78]	112(102-121)[4] [165]	1.5(1.3-1.7) [66]	1.3(0.8-1.7) [95]	3.83(2.85-4.00) [65]	141(133-145) [50]	Trace [22]	1,6-8

[1] Unless otherwise indicated. [2] During feeding, a bicarbonate maximum of 106 mmole/liter was observed [9]. [3] Drops as low as 5 mmole/liter during a dive [12,39].

[4] During feeding, a chloride minimum of 7 mmole/liter was observed [9].

continued

Species	Electrolyte Concentration, mmole/liter								Reference
	Bicarbonate	Calcium	Chloride	Magnesium	Phosphate [1]	Potassium	Sodium	Sulfate	
2 *Crocodylus acutus*	11 [1]	3.4 [1]	117 [1]	1.9 [1]	....	7.9 [1]	149 [1]	....	17
Snakes									
3 *Agkistrodon*	....	3.4(2.3-5.0) [8]	120(81-160) [10]	1.5(1.0-2.8) [6]	1.6(0.7-2.8)[5] [8]	5.0(4.5-5.6) [5]	152(125-173) [11]	....	15,28
4 *Coluber constrictor*	14(8-22) [3]	3.2(2.0-4.3) [5]	101(64-144) [8]	1.5(1.1-1.9) [2]	3.8(2.0-5.8)[5] [5]	4.1(3.3-4.8) [4]	151(131-167) [8]	....	15,28
5 *Crotalus*	....	3.0(2.2-3.7) [2]	130(123-137) [6]	1.4(1.0-1.8) [2]	1.7(1.0-2.3) [2]	3.7(3.6-3.7) [2]	150(146-154) [2]	....	4,15,33
6 *Lampropeltis getulus*	7(2-10) [5]	2.9(2.0-3.9) [8]	121(59-133) [12]	1.5(0.9-2.0) [2]	2.4(1.3-5.4)[5] [5]	4.5(3.4-5.6) [7]	148(112-171) [12]	....	15,28
7 *Laticauda semifasciata*	....	....	....	....	....	....	159(145-173) [2]	....	20
8 *Natrix sipedon*	....	3.8(2.0-5.1) [13]	127(59-147) [39]	1.3(0.8-2.8) [11]	2.3(1.6-2.9)[5] [6]	4.6(3.1-8.2) [36]	159(108-174) [39]	....	10,14,15,28,32
9 *Pituophis catenifer*	....	3.6 [1]	140 [4]		....	6.0 [4]	179 [5]	....	15,16
10 *Thamnophis elegans*	14(2-20) [6]	3.4(3.0-4.1) [12]	134(122-143) [8]	1.4(0.8-1.8) [12]	1.9 [1]	4.3(3.8-4.8) [12]	161(149-169) [12]		14,15
11 *T. sauritus*	....	2.7(1.4-4.4) [12]	125(123-127) [2]	2.0(1.1-2.7) [12]	1.6(1.4-2.0) [12]	5.4(5.1-5.6) [2]	159(157-161) [2]		13-15
12 ♀, during estrus[6]	....	10.9(4.5-90) [43]	....	4.0(1.2-11) [36]	2.5(1.0-18) [35]	....	....	....	13
13 *T. sirtalis*	....	3.0(2.7-4.2) [17]	130(124-137) [6]	1.5(0.6-2.2) [17]	0.7 [2]	5.9(4.1-7.2) [6]	152(143-159) [6]	....	14,15
14 *Vipera aspis*	....	....	130(128-134) [5]	....	....	6.5(5.3-7.9) [13]	170(154-194) [13]		31
Lizards									
15 *Agama*	....	2.9 [2]	....	....	....	5.7 [2]	171 [8]	....	43,48
16 *Amphibolurus ornatus*	....	....	....	....	....	5.0 [22]	150[7] [21]	....	3
17 *Anolis carolinensis*	15(10-23) [25]	2.9(2.0-4.2) [20]	127(113-133) [30]	....	2.6(1.7-3.2) [19]	4.6(2.8-5.9) [15]	157(139-186) [41]	....	11,30
18 *Ctenosaura acanthura*	15(10-22) [5]	2.9(2.3-3.5) [5]	133(128-137) [5]	1.0(0.9-1.1) [5]	2.3(1.8-3.4) [5]	2.9(2.4-3.2) [5]	159(158-163) [5]	....	26
19 *Dipsosaurus dorsalis*	....	2.3 [10]	114 [54]	0.9 [10]	....	3.1 [64]	162 [64]		5,35
20 *Heloderma*	18	....	119(109-129) [3]	....	....	4.6(3.7-5.5) [2]	158(157-159) [2]	....	21,49
21 *Iguana iguana*	24(15-33) [9]	2.7(2.6-2.8) [9]	118(110-124) [9]	0.9(0.7-1.1) [9]	2.0(1.6-2.4) [9]	3.5(2.9-4.3) [9]	157(142-165) [9]	....	26,36
22 *Sauromalus obesus*	....	....	123 [8]	....	....	4.9(1.5-9.4) [7]	169(161-180) [7]	....	18,42
23 *Trachydosaurus rugosus*	....	....	....	....	....	4.1(2.9-5.6) [22]	175(148-242)[7,8] [22]	....	2

[1] Unless otherwise indicated. [5] Phosphorus. [6] Probably occurs in reptiles of all orders [12]. [7] Markedly affected by state of hydration [2,3,23]. [8] Average value, 195 meq/liter during summer [2].

continued

Species	Electrolyte Concentration, mmole/liter								Reference
	Bicarbonate	Calcium	Chloride	Magnesium	Phosphate	Potassium	Sodium	Sulfate	
24 Varanus griseus	24(16-37) [9]	3.4(2.5-6.2) [15]	142(113-178)7/ [15]	1.4(0.9-2.3) [15]	1.5(1.1-1.9) [15]	3.8(2.6-6.4) [15]	161(122-196)7/ [15]	....	23
Turtles									
25 Caretta	30(23-36) [6]	4.0(2.7-5.2) [3]	109(108-110) [3]	2.1(1.4-2.9) [2]	3.3(3.0-3.5) [2]	2.3(1.5-6.7) [13]	158 [13]	0.3 [1]	19,27,40,44
26 Chelydra serpentina	38	3.8(2.5-6.5) [11]	76(54-90) [4]	2.7(1.5-4.5) [3]	1.3(1.0-1.9) [9]	3.2(2.5-3.8) [4]	132(123-141) [4]	0.3 [2]	15,25,34,40,45
27 Chrysemys picta belli9/	47(44-49) [7]	5.5(4.8-6.1) [2]	85(81-89) [2]	4.8(1.6-7.9) [2]	1.0(0.9-1.0) [2]	3.3(3.0-3.6) [2]	135(120-149) [2]	0.8 [1]	40
28 C. scripta10/	40(22-71)3/ [28]	2.7(1.0-5.0) [11]	81(76-85) [9]	2.2 [15]	1.1 [15]	4.1(3.3-5.1) [7]	121(100-134) [7]	0.17(0.1-0.2) [6]	24,29,34,38-41,46,47
29 Terrapene carolina	....	1.3(0.4-3.7) [14]	108(85-128) [10]	3.5(1.7-4.5) [7]	2.4(1.1-3.1) [7]	4.7(3.1-5.5) [10]	130(85-156) [11]	1.2(0.4-2.3) [3]	15,22,29
30 Testudo graeca	....	4.0	100	....	....	7.8	....	....	19,29,37
31 Trionyx ferox	....	1.7(0.6-2.9) [7]	90(85-102) [7]	1.5(1.4-1.6) [4]	2.0(1.3-3.2) [5]	6.8(4.4-7.1) [6]	113(109-120) [7]	....	15

3/ Drops as low as 5 mmole/liter during a dive [12,39]. 7/ Markedly affected by state of hydration [2,3,23]. 9/ Synonym: C. picta. 10/ Synonym: Pseudemys scripta.

Contributor: Dessauer, Herbert C.

References

[1] Austin, J. H., et al. 1927. J. Biol. Chem. 72:677.

[2] Bentley, P. J. 1959. J. Physiol. (London) 145:37.

[3] Bradshaw, S. D., and V. H. Shoemaker. 1967. Comp. Biochem. Physiol. 20:855.

[4] Carmichael, E. B., and P. W. Petcher. 1945. J. Biol. Chem. 161:693.

[5] Chan, D. K. O., et al. 1970. Gen. Comp. Endocrinol. 15:374.

[6] Coulson, R. A., and T. Hernandez. 1955. Proc. Soc. Exp. Biol. Med. 88:682.

[7] Coulson, R. A., and T. Hernandez. 1964. Biochemistry of the Alligator: A Study of Metabolism in Slow Motion. Louisiana State Univ. Press, Baton Rouge.

[8] Coulson, R. A., et al. 1950. Proc. Soc. Exp. Biol. Med. 73:203.

[9] Coulson, R. A., et al. 1950. Ibid. 74:866.

[10] Dantzler, W. H. 1967. Comp. Biochem. Physiol. 22:131.

[11] Dessauer, H. C. 1952. Proc. Soc. Exp. Biol. Med. 80:742.

[12] Dessauer, H. C. 1970. In C. Gans and T. S. Parsons, ed. Biology of the Reptilia. Academic Press, New York. v. 3, pp. 1-72.

[13] Dessauer, H. C., and W. Fox. 1959. Amer. J. Physiol. 197:360.

[14] Dessauer, H. C., et al. 1956. Proc. Soc. Exp. Biol. Med. 92:299.

[15] Dessauer, H. C., et al. Unpublished. Louisiana State Univ. Medical Center, New Orleans, 1959.

[16] Dietz, T. H., and E. D. Brodie, Jr. 1969. Comp. Biochem. Physiol. 30:673.

[17] Dill, D. B., and H. T. Edwards. 1931. J. Biol. Chem. 90:515.

[18] Dill, D. B., et al. 1935. J. Cell. Comp. Physiol. 6:37.

[19] Drilhon, A., and F. Marcoux. 1942. Bull. Soc. Chim. Biol. 24:103.

[20] Dunson, W. A., and A. M. Taub. 1967. Amer. J. Physiol. 213:975.

[21] Edwards, H. T., and D. B. Dill. 1935. J. Cell. Comp. Physiol. 6:21.

[22] Gaumer, A. E. H., and C. J. Goodnight. 1957. Amer. Midl. Natur. 58:332.

[23] Haggag, G., et al. 1965. Comp. Biochem. Physiol. 16:457.

[24] Haning, Q. C., and A. M. Thompson. 1965. Ibid. 15:17.

[25] Henderson, L. J. 1928. Blood: A Study in General Physiology. Yale Univ. Press, New Haven.

[26] Hernandez, T., and R. A. Coulson. 1951. Proc. Soc. Exp. Biol. Med. 76:175.

[27] Holmes, W. N., and R. L. McBean. 1964. J. Exp. Biol. 41:81.

[28] Hutton, K. E. 1958. J. Cell. Comp. Physiol. 52:319.

[29] Hutton, K. E., and C. J. Goodnight. 1957. Physiol. Zool. 30:198.

[30] Hutton, K. E., and R. Ortman. 1957. Proc. Soc. Exp. Biol. Med. 96:842.

[31] Izard, Y., et al. 1961. Ann. Inst. Pasteur Paris 100:539.

[32] LeBrie, S. J., and I. D. W. Sutherland. 1962. Amer. J. Physiol. 203:995.

continued

[33] Luck, J. M., and L. Keeler. 1929. J. Biol. Chem. 82: 703.

[34] Lyman, R. A., Jr. 1945. J. Cell. Comp. Physiol. 25: 65.

[35] Minnich, J. E. 1970. Comp. Biochem. Physiol. 35: 921.

[36] Moberly, W. R. 1968. Ibid. 27:1.

[37] Nera, M. C. D. 1925. Boll. Inst. Zool. Roma 3:71.

[38] Robin, E. D. 1962. Nature (London) 195:249.

[39] Robin, E. D., et al. 1964. J. Cell. Comp. Physiol. 63:287.

[40] Smith, H. W. 1929. J. Biol. Chem. 82:651.

[41] Stenroos, O. O., and W. M. Bowman. 1968. Comp. Biochem. Physiol. 25:219.

[42] Templeton, J. R. 1964. Ibid. 11:223.

[43] Tercafs, R. R., and J. M. Vassas. 1967. Arch. Int. Physiol. Biochim. 75:667.

[44] Tercafs, R. R., et al. 1963. Ibid. 71:614.

[45] Vars, H. M. 1934. J. Biol. Chem. 105:135.

[46] Williams, J. K. Unpublished. Louisiana State Univ. Medical Center, New Orleans, 1959.

[47] Wilson, J. W. 1939. J. Cell. Comp. Physiol. 13: 315.

[48] Wright, A., and I. C. Jones. 1957. J. Endocrinol. 15: 83.

[49] Zarafonetis, C. J. D., and J. P. Kalas. 1960. Copeia, p. 240.

244. PLASMA ELECTROLYTES: AMPHIBIANS

Data in brackets are number of subjects. Values in parentheses are ranges, estimate "c" (*see* Introduction).

	Species	Electrolyte Concentration, mmole/liter							Reference
		Bicarbonate	Calcium	Chloride	Magnesium	Phosphate	Potassium	Sodium	
1	*Amphiuma means*	18(14-21) [5]	3.1 [1]	85(77-95) [11]	1.1 [1]	3.5	4.3(3.3-5.6) [7]	109(95-116) [11]	10, 12
2	*Bufo bufo*	....	....	91 [10]	....	...	3.1(1.8-4.5) [40]	122(110-133) [50]	3
3	*B. marinus*	....	....	104 [5]	....		3.7(2.8-5.1) [5]	107(88-128) [5]	13
4	*B. viridis*	....	....	86 [5]	....	...	9 [5]	129 [5]	7
5	*B. woodhousei*	....	....	80(66-107) [7]	....		4.0 [2]	107 [2]	4
6	*Gastrophryne carolinensis*[1]	5 [1]	....	....	....	...	7.4 [1]	128 [1]	4
7	*Leptodactylus ocellatus*	....	....	91 [3]	....		4.8(2.1-6.7) [6]	122 [1]	8
8	*Rana areolata*	....	1.5	75	0.6	...	5.8	86	9
9	*R. catesbeiana*	....	1.6	70(55-82) [4]	3.8	2.2	4.8(4.4-5.0) [3]	105(101-113) [3]	4
10	*R. esculenta*	....	2.3	70	1.6	...	5.1	96	14
11	*R. pipiens*	....		70 [36]	....	...	1.7 [30]	111 [30]	6
12	*Xenopus laevis*	....	2.0 [9]	....	0.8 [7]	...	....	....	1
13	Frog	25	2.3	74	2.9	3.1	2.5	104	2,5
14	Toad	....	1.8	....	1.0	1.9	....	....	11
15		....	0.5[2]	....	0.4[2]	...	....	....	

[1] Synonym: *Microhyla carolinensis.* [2] Dialyzable.

Contributor: Dessauer, Herbert C.

References

[1] Charles, E. 1930. Proc. Roy. Soc. B107:504.

[2] Clark, A. J., et al. 1938. Metabolism of the Frog's Heart. Oliver and Boyd, London.

[3] Danielson, B. G. 1964. Acta Physiol. Scand., Suppl. 236:1.

[4] Dessauer, H. C., et al. Unpublished. Louisiana State Univ. Medical Center, New Orleans, 1971.

[5] Fenn, W. O. 1936. Physiol. Rev. 16:450.

[6] Gibbons, L. V., and H. M. Kaplan. 1959. Copeia, p. 176.

[7] Gordon, M. S. 1962. J. Exp. Biol. 39:261.

[8] Harris, E. J., and H. Martins-Ferreira. 1955. Ibid. 32:539.

[9] Macallum, A. B. 1926. Physiol. Rev. 6:316.

[10] McCay, C. M. 1931. J. Biol. Chem. 90:497.

[11] Ogasawara, K. 1954. Chem. Abstr. 48:2797g.

[12] Pearson, J. Unpublished.

[13] Shoemaker, V. H. 1964. Comp. Biochem. Physiol. 13:261.

[14] Urano, F. 1908. Z. Biol. (Munich) 50:212.

Values in parentheses are ranges, estimate "c" (*see* Introduction).

	Species (Synonym)	Blood Component	Constituent	Concentration	Reference
1	*Acipenser medirostris*	Serum	Calcium	2.0 mmoles/liter	13
2			Chloride	169 mmoles/liter	13
3			Magnesium	1.98 mmoles/liter	13
4			Potassium	2.5 mmoles/liter	13
5			Sodium	165 mmoles/liter	13
6			Sulfate	2.48 mmoles/liter	13
7	*Acrocheilus alutaceus*	Serum	Magnesium	3.48(3.14-3.82) mg/100 ml	12
8	*Anguilla anguilla*	Serum	Calcium	2.29 mmoles/liter	2
9			Chloride	88.25 mmoles/liter	2
10			Magnesium	2.13 mmoles/liter	2
11			Phosphate	1.81 mmoles/liter	2
12			Potassium	1.75 mmoles/liter	2
13			Sodium	150.1 mmoles/liter	2
14	*Carassius auratus*	Whole blood	Magnesium	12.27(11.5-12.8) mg/100 ml	12
15		Serum	Magnesium	2.02(1.42-2.70) mg/100 ml	12
16	*Carpiodes velifer*	Serum	Magnesium	4.52(4.15-4.97) mg/100 ml	12
17	*Catostomus catostomus pocatello (C. pocatello)*	Serum	Magnesium	3.22(2.92-3.58) mg/100 ml	12
18	*Coregonus lavaretus (C. clupeoides)*	Serum	Calcium	2.67 mmoles/liter	14
19			Chloride	116.8 mmoles/liter	14
20			Magnesium	1.69 mmoles/liter	14
21			Potassium	3.81 mmoles/liter	14
22			Sodium	140.9 mmoles/liter	14
23	*Cyprinus carpio*	Serum	Calcium	2.12 mmoles/liter	9
24			Chloride	125.2 mmoles/liter	9
25			Magnesium	1.23 mmoles/liter	9
26			Potassium	2.93 mmoles/liter	9
27			Sodium	130 mmoles/liter	9
28	*Fundulus heteroclitus*	Serum	Calcium	2.4 mmoles/liter	16
29			Chloride	149.6 mmoles/liter	16
30			Magnesium	2.2 mmoles/liter	16
31			Potassium	4.5 mmoles/liter	16
32			Sodium	202.0 mmoles/liter	16
33	*Ictalurus natalis (Ameiurus erebennus)*	Serum	Magnesium	6.32(5.8-7.8) mg/100 ml	12
34	*I. punctatus*	Serum	Magnesium	5.46(4.40-7.82) mg/100 ml	12
35	*Ictiobus niger*	Serum	Magnesium	2.58(2.1-3.1) mg/100 ml	12
36	*Lampetra fluviatilis*	Serum	Calcium	2.0 mmoles/kg serum	14
37			Chloride	95.9 mmoles/kg serum	14
38			Magnesium	2.1 mmoles/kg serum	14
39			Potassium	3.2 mmoles/kg serum	14
40			Sodium	119.6 mmoles/kg serum	14
41	*Lophius americanus*	Serum	Calcium	2.2 mmoles/liter	6
42			Chloride	177 mmoles/liter	6
43			Magnesium	0.8 mmole/liter	6
44			Potassium	3.4 mmoles/liter	6
45			Sodium	198 mmoles/liter	6
46	*L. piscatorius*	Plasma	Calcium	0.55 meq/100 ml	1
47			Chloride	16 meq/100 ml	1
48			Magnesium	0.5 meq/100 ml	1
49			Phosphate	2.1 meq/100 ml	1
50			Potassium	0.51 meq/100 ml	1
51			Sodium	20.0 meq/100 ml	1

continued

	Species (Synonym)	Blood Component	Constituent	Concentration	Reference
52	*Mustelus canis*[1]	Serum	Calcium	5 mmoles/kg serum	3
53			Chloride	270 mmoles/kg serum	3
54			Magnesium	3 mmoles/kg serum	3
55			Potassium	8 mmoles/kg serum	3
56			Sodium	288 mmoles/kg serum	3
57	*Myoxocephalus scorpius (Cottus scorpius)*	Serum	Chloride	173 mmoles/liter	4
58			Potassium	3.8 mmoles/liter	4
59			Sodium	184 mmoles/liter	4
60	*Mylocheilus caurinus (M. lateralis)*	Serum	Magnesium	4.36(3.88-4.66) mg/100 ml	12
61	*Myxine glutinosa*	Serum	Calcium	5.1 mmoles/kg serum	15
62			Chloride	508 mmoles/kg serum	15
63			Magnesium	11.9 mmoles/kg serum	15
64			Potassium	8.2 mmoles/kg serum	15
65			Sodium	486 mmoles/kg serum	15
66	*Paralabrax clathratus*	Serum	Calcium	3.0 mmoles/liter	17
67			Chloride	147 mmoles/liter	17
68			Magnesium	1.5 mmoles/liter	17
69			Potassium	5.0 mmoles/liter	17
70			Sodium	180 mmoles/liter	17
71	*Perca fluviatilis*	Serum	Calcium	4.38 mmoles/liter	10
72			Chloride	120.30 mmoles/liter	10
73			Magnesium	1.55 mmoles/liter	10
74			Potassium	3.63 mmoles/liter	10
75			Sodium	154.2 mmoles/liter	10
76	*Petromyzon marinus*	Serum	Calcium	2.4 mmoles/liter	18
77			Chloride	113.0 mmoles/liter	18
78			Magnesium	1.9 mmoles/liter	18
79			Potassium	6.2 mmoles/liter	18
80			Sodium	139.0 mmoles/liter	18
81	*Prosopium williamsoni*	Serum	Magnesium	2.95(1.8-4.3) mg/100 ml	12
82	*Raja erinacea*	Whole blood	Calcium	(9.8-14.2) meq/liter	7
83			Chloride	(236-279) meq/liter	7
84			Magnesium	(1.4-6.2) meq/liter	7
85			Potassium	(4.8-11.9) meq/liter	7
86			Sodium	(230-287) meq/liter	7
87	*Salmo gairdneri (S. iridea)*	Serum	Magnesium	4.16(3.3-5.7) mg/100 ml	12
88	*S. trutta*	Serum	Magnesium	4.78(3.7-6.1) mg/100 ml	12
89	*Salvelinus fontinalis*	Serum	Magnesium	2.69(1.33-3.87) mg/100 ml	12
90	Carp	Whole blood	Chloride	401(347-446) mg/100 ml	5
91			Manganese	(5.8-7.2) µg/100 ml	5
92			Potassium	169.5(154.0-176.5) mg/100 ml	5
93		Serum	Calcium	11.50(9.45-14.77) mg/100 ml	5
94				21.6 mg/100 ml	11
95			Iron	25(16-33) µg/100 ml	5
96			Magnesium	3.32(2.52-3.88) mg/100 ml	5
97				1.3 mg/100 ml	11
98			Phosphate	9.0 mg/100 ml	11
			Phosphorus		
99			Total P	49.0(37.3-60.6) mg/100 ml	5
100			Inorganic P	8.69(6.79-12.10) mg/100 ml	5
101			Potassium	24.6(17.5-26.9) mg/100 ml	5
102			Sodium	300(292-316) mg/100 ml	5
103			Sulfur, inorganic	0.944(0.765-1.172) mg/100 ml	5

[1] For information on other electrolytes, consult reference 8.

continued

Contributor: Nace, Paul F.

References

[1] Brull, L., and E. Nizet. 1953. J. Mar. Biol. Ass. U.K. 32:321.

[2] Chan, D. K. O., et al. 1967. J. Endocrinol. 37:297.

[3] Doolittle, R. F., et al. 1960. Science 132:36.

[4] Enger, P. S. 1964. Comp. Biochem. Physiol. 11:131.

[5] Field, J. B., et al. 1943. J. Biol. Chem. 148(2):261.

[6] Forster, R. P., and F. Berglund. 1956. J. Gen. Physiol. 39:349.

[7] Hartman, F. A., et al. 1941. Physiol. Zool. 14(4): 476.

[8] Hoar, W. S., and D. J. Randall, ed. 1969. Fish Physiology. Academic Press, New York. v. 1, p. 34.

[9] Houston, A. H., and J. A. Madden. 1968. Nature (London) 217:969.

[10] Lutz, P. L. 1972. Comp. Biochem. Physiol. 42:711.

[11] Ogasawara, K. 1953. Igaku To Seibutsugaku 29:250.

[12] Platner, W. S. 1949. Univ. Mich. Microfilm Publ. 1231:289.

[13] Potts, W. T. W., and P. P. Rudy. 1972. J. Exp. Biol. 56:703.

[14] Robertson, J. D. 1954. Ibid. 31:424.

[15] Robertson, J. D. 1966. In H. Barnes, ed. Some Contemporary Studies in Marine Science. Allen and Unwin, London. p. 631.

[16] Umminger, B. L. 1969. J. Exp. Zool. 172:283.

[17] Urist, M. R. 1962. Perspect. Biol. Med. 6:75.

[18] Urist, M. R. 1963. Ann. N. Y. Acad. Sci. 109:294.

246. BLOOD NON-PROTEIN NITROGENOUS SUBSTANCES: MAN

Concentration: Values are mg/100 ml blood, unless otherwise specified. Values in parentheses are ranges, estimate "c" unless otherwise indicated (*see* Introduction). For additional data on plasma or serum amino acids in prematures, neonates, infants, children, and adults, consult Table 3-1 in Scriver, C. R., and L. E. Rosenberg, 1973. Major Probl. Clin. Pediat. 10:42, published by W. B. Saunders, Philadelphia.

	Constituent	Concentration	Reference
	Whole blood		
1	Alloxan	0.02(0.015-0.025)	53
	Amino acids		
2	α-Alanine	(2.79-5.11)	33,70
3	Arginine	1.0(0.6-1.7)	38,70
4	Cystine	0.9(0.6-1.2)[b]	42,70
5	Glutamine	10	59,70
6	Glycine	(1.8-2.5)	1,17,18, 33
7	Histidine	1.21(1.09-1.38)	68,70
8	Isoleucine	1.3(0.9-1.5)	42,70
9	Leucine	1.7(1.4-2.0)[b]	37,70
10	Lysine	2.2(1.3-3.0)	42,70
11	Methionine	0.426(0.392-0.457)	70,73
12	Phenylalanine	1.0(0.8-1.2)[b]	38,70
13	Threonine	1.6(1.3-2.0)	42,70
14	Tryptophan	0.274(0.269-0.289)	21,70
15	Tyrosine	1.1(0.8-1.4)[b]	42,70
16	Valine	2.4(2.0-2.9)	36,70
17	Ammonia	0.047(0.02-0.07)	39,47
18	Bilirubin	(0.19-1.44)	20
19	Coproporphyrin	1.2(0-2.6) μg/100 ml	83
20	Creatine	2.7	77
21	Creatinine	0.6	77
22	Cysteamine	0.29	56
23	N,N-Dimethyltryptamine	3.9(2.7-5.1) μg/100 ml	32
24	Ergothioneine	1.2(0.24-2.19)	54,55

	Constituent	Concentration	Reference
	Glutathione		
25	Total	36.8(36.6-37.0)	14,16
26	Oxidized	4.02(3.99-4.06)	16
27	Reduced	(26.7-31.9)	60
28	Histamine	4.3(1.6-8.9) μg/100 ml	61,76
29	Indican	(0.095-0.105)	3
30	Methylguanidine	<0.2	77
	Nucleotides		
31	Total	41(31-52)	40
32	Adenine	(21-36)	11
33	Adenosine 5'-	6.2 ± 3.1 μmoles/liter[1]	7
34	monophosphate	5.1 ± 1.2 μmoles/liter[2]	7
35	Adenosine 5'-di-	47.8 ± 13 μmoles/liter[1]	7
36	phosphate	46.6 ± 7 μmoles/liter[2]	7
37	Adenosine 5'-tri-	43.3 ± 7.3 μmoles/liter[1]	7
38	phosphate	42.6 ± 5.7 μmoles/liter[2]	7
39	Guanosine 5'-tri-	24.5 ± 5.9 μmoles/liter[1]	7
40	phosphate	26.4 ± 2.1 μmoles/liter[2]	7
41	Nicotinamide ade-	29.8 ± 5.1 μmoles/liter[1]	7
42	nine dinucleotide (NAD⁺, DPN)	32.4 ± 5.3 μmoles/liter[2]	7
43	Nicotinamide ade-	11.6 ± 1.7 μmoles/liter[1]	7
44	nine dinucleotide phosphate (NADP⁺, TPN)	11.2 ± 1.2 μmoles/liter[2]	7
45	Polypeptides	<7	30
46	Porphyrin	0.0068	13
47	Protoporphyrin	0.014(0.011-0.017)	10,66,69
48	Serotonin	(0.9-1.8) μg/100 ml	19

[1] For males. [2] For females.

continued

	Constituent	Concentration	Reference
49	Spermidine	0.096(0.086-0.106)	64
50	Spermine	0.13(0.11-0.15)	64
	Nitrogen		
51	Total N	3430(3000-4100)	31
52	Non-protein N	33.8(27-47)	8,41,44
53	Amide N	(134-144)	9
54	α-Amino N	6.1(4.84-7.36)	8,33
55	Ammonia N	(0.015-0.116)	25
56	Polypeptide N	(2.7-7.5)	75
57	Residual N	(10-25)	29
58	Urea N	11.0(6-16)	8,41,45
59	Uric acid N	0.8(0.53-1.04)[1]	7
60		0.7(0.46-1.06)[2]	7
	Erythrocytes		
	Amino acids		
61	α-Alanine	(2.5-5.6)	33,70,81
62	Arginine	0.3(0.1-0.6)	38,70
63	Cystine	0.4(0.3-0.5)	42,70
64	Glycine	(1.6-3.5)	1,17,18, 33
65	Histidine	(2.2-2.8)	24,70
66	Isoleucine	0.9(0.5-1.4)	42,70
67	Leucine	1.5(1.0-1.8)	37,70
68	Lysine	1.4(0.9-1.8)	42,70
69	Methionine	0.5(0.3-0.8)	42,70
70	Phenylalanine	1.0(0.7-1.3)[b]	42,70
71	Threonine	1.6(1.3-2.1)	42,70
72	Tryptophan	0.3	23,38, 70,71
73	Tyrosine	1.1(0.7-1.5)[b]	42,70
74	Valine	2.0(1.6-2.5)	36,70
75	δ-Aminolevulinic acid	(0.025-0.045)	35
76	Coproporphyrin, free	0.5(0-2.0) µg/100 ml	79,83
77	Creatine	8.1(6.0-10.2)[b]	41,50,67
78	Creatinine	1.8(1.7-1.9)[b]	41,50,67
79	Ergothioneine	0.96(0.3-1.6)	27,28
	Glutathione		
80	Total	87	6,11,51
81	Oxidized	8.5	11,51
82	Reduced	79	11,51
83	Porphobilinogen	(0.015-0.040) µg/100 ml	35
84	Protoporphyrin, free	35(13-140) µg/100 ml	15,83
85	Uroporphyrin	(0-2) µg/100 ml	35
	Nitrogen		
86	Non-protein N	31.5(18.9-40.7)	8,84
87	α-Amino N	8.8(7.2-10.5)	8,33
88	Polypeptide N	7.0	48
89	Urea N	11(6-16)	8,84
90	Uric acid N	0.6(0.3-1.0)	26,41,50

	Constituent	Concentration	Reference
	Plasma or Serum		
91	Allantoin	0.45(0.3-0.6)	5
	Amino acids		
92	Alanine	3.41(3.01-3.73)	70,72
93		2.94(2.10-3.65)[3]	22
94	β-Alanine	0.13[3,4]	22
95	α-Aminobutyric	0.30(0.22-0.35)	70,72
96	acid	0.15(0.06-0.30)[3]	22
97	Arginine	1.51(1.22-1.93)	70,72
98		0.94(0.38-1.53)[3]	22
99	Asparagine	0.58(0.54-0.65)	70,72
100		0.60[3,4]	22
101	Aspartic acid[5]	0.03(0.01-0.07)	70,72
102		0.11(Trace-0.22)[3]	22
103	Citrulline	0.50(0.21-0.97)	5,70
104		0.28(0.15-0.50)[3]	22
105	Cysteine + cystine	1.18(1.08-1.30)	70,72
106	Cystine	1.47(0.85-2.02)[3]	22
107	Glutamic acid	0.70(0.43-1.15)	70,72
108		0.76(0.30-1.57)[3]	22
109	Glutamine	8.30(6.1-10.2)	4,70
110		11.16(7.86-14.01)[3]	22
111	Glycine	1.54(1.34-1.73)	70,72
112		2.58(1.68-3.86)[3]	22
113	Histidine	1.15(0.79-1.48)	70,72
114		1.19(0.76-1.77)[3]	22
115	Hydroxyproline	0.42[3,4]	22
116	Isoleucine	0.89(0.69-1.28)	70,72
117		0.52(0.35-0.69)[3]	22
118	Leucine	1.69(1.42-2.30)	70,72
119		0.95(0.61-1.43)[3]	22
120	Lysine	2.72(2.51-3.02)	70,72
121		2.93(1.67-3.93)[3]	22
122	Methionine	0.38(0.33-0.43)	70,72
123		0.44(0.13-0.61)[3]	22
124	1-Methylhistidine[5]	0.11(0.04-0.17)	70,72
125	3-Methylhistidine[5]	0.08(0.04-0.13)	70,72
126	Ornithine	0.72(0.62-0.80)	70,72
127		1.21(0.65-2.00)[3]	22
128	Phenylalanine	0.84(0.69-0.95)	70,72
129		1.30(0.69-1.82)[3]	22
130	Proline	2.36(2.01-3.34)	70,72
131		2.13(1.23-3.19)[3]	22
132	Serine	1.12(1.01-1.25)	70,72
133		1.72(0.99-2.55)[3,6]	22
134	Taurine	0.55(0.41-0.82)	70,72
135		1.76(0.93-2.70)[3]	22
136	Threonine	1.39(1.21-1.72)	70,72
137		2.59(1.36-3.99)[3]	22

[1] For males. [2] For females. [3] Newborn; blood samples obtained within 17 hr after birth. 25 infants (9 male and 16 female); birth weight of all <2500 g. [4] Determined on pooled plasma of 10 infants. [5] Too low in concentration to permit unequivocal identification. [6] Corrected for asparagine.

continued

	Constituent	Concentration	Reference		Constituent	Concentration	Reference
138	Tryptophan	1.11	38,70	152	Imidazoles	1.45(0-3.0)	49
139		0.65(Trace-1.37)[3/]	22	153	Indican	0.3(0.06-0.54)	57,63
140	Tyrosine	1.03(0.81-1.45)	70,72	154	Indoxylacetic acid	(0.1-0.2)	66
141		1.26(0.76-1.80)[3/]	22	155	Indoxyl-3-lactic acid	(0.01-0.1)	66
142	Valine	2.88(2.37-3.71)	70,72	156	Serotonin	1.3(0.1-2.5) μg/100 ml	19
143		1.60(0.94-2.88)[3/]	22	157	Uracil	0.08	43
144	δ-Aminolevulinic acid	0.019(0.011-0.027)	34		Nitrogen		
				158	Total N	(1200-1430)	31
145	Bilirubin	0.6(0.26-1.4)	58	159	Non-protein N	(23-37)	52
146	Coproporphyrin	0.8(0.4-1.5) μg/100 ml	83	160	α-Amino N	(3.37-4.97)	82
147	Creatine	0.45(0.28-0.62)	2,74	161	Ammonia N	0.028 ± 0.009	46
148	Creatinine	1.1(0.7-1.5)	74,78	162	Polypeptide N	2.21	48
149	Ethanolamine	0.32(0.16-0.56)[3/]	22	163	Residual N	11.0	80
150	Histamine	0.005(0.002-0.008) μg/ 100 ml	62	164	Urea N	12.5(7-18)	45
				165	Uric acid N	5.1 ± 1.0[1/]	12,65
151	Hypoxanthine	0.1	43	166		3.9 ± 0.9[2/]	12,65

[1/] For males. [2/] For females. [3/] Newborn; blood samples obtained within 17 hr after birth. 25 infants (9 male and 16 females); birth weight of all <2500 g.

Contributors: Smith, Carl C., and Wolfe, Geraldine F.; Hamilton, Paul B.

References

[1] Alexander, B., et al. 1945. J. Biol. Chem. 160:51.

[2] Allinson, M. J. C. 1945. Ibid. 157:169.

[3] Angostino, L. 1945. Boll. Soc. Ital. Biol. Sper. 20: 173.

[4] Archibald, R. M. 1944. J. Biol. Chem. 154:643.

[5] Archibald, R. M. 1944. Ibid. 156:121.

[6] Beutler, E., et al. 1963. J. Lab. Clin. Med. 61:882.

[7] Bishop, C., et al. 1959. J. Biol. Chem. 234:1233.

[8] Bjornesjo, K. B. 1963. Scand. J. Clin. Lab. Invest. 15, Suppl. 69:25.

[9] Bliss, S. 1929. J. Biol. Chem. 81:129.

[10] Brodersen, R., et al. 1963. Scand. J. Clin. Lab. Invest. 15:523.

[11] Buell, M. V. 1935. J. Biol. Chem. 108:273.

[12] Caraway, W. T. 1963. Stand. Methods Clin. Chem. 4:239.

[13] Careddu, G. 1938. Atti Soc. Med. Chir. Padova Fac. Med. Chir. Univ. Padova 16:254.

[14] Caren, R., and H. O. Carne. 1951. Amer. J. Med. Sci. 221:307.

[15] Cartwright, G. E., et al. 1948. Blood 3:501.

[16] Ceresa, F., and P. Guala. 1940. Arch. Sci. Med. 70: 369.

[17] Christensen, H. N., and E. L. Lynch. 1946. J. Biol. Chem. 163:741.

[18] Christensen, H. N., et al. 1947. Ibid. 168:191.

[19] Crawford, N. 1965. Clin. Chim. Acta 12:274.

[20] Delgado Febres, E. 1949. An. Fac. Med. Univ. Nac. Mayor San Marcos Lima 32:29.

[21] Denko, C. W., et al. 1947. Arch. Biochem. 13:483.

[22] Dickinson, J. C., et al. 1965. Pediatrics 36:2.

[23] Dunn, M. S., et al. 1945. J. Biol. Chem. 157:387.

[24] Euler, H. von, and L. Heller. 1947. Ark. Kemi Mineral. Geol. 25A:10.

[25] Folin, O. 1932. J. Biol. Chem. 97:141.

[26] Folin, O., and H. Svedberg. 1930. Ibid. 88:85, 715.

[27] Fraser, R. S., and S. Jegard. 1950. J. Lab. Clin. Med. 35:960.

[28] Fraser, R. S., and S. Jegard. 1951. Ibid. 37:199.

[29] Gettler, A. O., and W. Baker. 1916. J. Biol. Chem. 25:221.

[30] Godfried, E. G. 1939. Biochem. J. 33:955.

[31] Gram, H. C. 1924. Amer. J. Med. Sci. 168:511.

[32] Gross, H., and F. Franzen. 1965. Z. Klin. Chem. 3: 99.

[33] Gutman, G. E., and B. Alexander. 1947. J. Biol. Chem. 168:527.

[34] Haeger-Aronsen, B. 1960. Scand. J. Clin. Lab. Invest. 12, Suppl. 47:1.

[35] Heilmeyer, L. 1962. Schweiz. Med. Wochenschr. 92:1285.

[36] Henderson, L. M., et al. 1949. J. Biol. Chem. 177: 815.

[37] Hier, S. W. 1947. Ibid. 171:813.

[38] Hier, S. W., and O. Bergeim. 1946. Ibid. 163:129.

[39] Hutchinson, J. H., and D. H. Labby. 1962. J. Lab. Clin. Med. 60:170.

[40] Jackson, H., Jr. 1923. J. Biol. Chem. 57:121.

[41] Jellinek, E. M., and J. M. Looney. 1939. Ibid. 128: 621.

[42] Johnson, C. A., and O. Bergeim. 1951. Ibid. 188: 883.

[43] Jolley, R. L., and C. D. Scott. 1970. Clin. Chem. 16: 687.

[44] Josephson, B., et al. 1962. Acta Paediat. (Stockholm) 51, Suppl. 135:111.

[45] Kaplan, A. 1965. Stand. Methods Clin. Chem. 5: 245.

[46] Kingsley, G. R., and H. S. Tager. 1970. Ibid. 6: 115.

continued

[47] Labbé, M., et al. 1929. C. R. Acad. Sci. 188:738.

[48] Larizza, P. 1937. Naunyn Schmiedebergs Arch. Exp. Pathol. Pharmakol. 186:232.

[49] Loeper, M., et al. 1934. Bull. Soc. Chim. Biol. 16: 1385.

[50] Looney, J. M. 1924. Amer. J. Psychiat. 4:34.

[51] Looney, J. M., and H. M. Childs. 1934. J. Clin. Invest. 13:963.

[52] Looney, J. M., and A. I. Walsh. 1939. J. Biol. Chem. 130:635.

[53] Loubatieres, A., and P. Bouyard. 1951. Tunisie Med. 39:659.

[54] McMenamy, R. H., et al. 1960. J. Clin. Invest. 39: 1675.

[55] Melville, D. B., and R. Lubschez. 1953. J. Biol. Chem. 200:275.

[56] Mondovi, B., et al. 1961. Ital. J. Biochem. 10:42.

[57] Müting, D., et al. 1963. Z. Klin. Med. 157:538.

[58] Nosslin, B. 1960. Scand. J. Clin. Lab. Invest. 12, Suppl. 49.

[59] Örström, Å., and M. Örström. 1950. Acta Med. Scand. 138:108.

[60] Pansini, R., and E. Pire. 1953. Boll. Soc. Ital. Biol. Sper. 29:1629.

[61] Peña y de la Peña, E., et al. 1953. Bol. Sanid. Mil. (Mex.) 6:259.

[62] Pettay, O. 1950. Acta Paediat. (Stockholm) 39: 283.

[63] Pinelli, L. 1935. Biochim. Ter. Sper. 22:563.

[64] Raina, A. 1962. Scand. J. Clin. Lab. Invest. 14:318.

[65] Remp, D. G. 1970. Stand. Methods Clin. Chem. 6:1.

[66] Rodnight, R. 1961. Int. Rev. Neurobiol. 3:251.

[67] Sandberg, A. A., et al. 1953. Metab. Clin. Exp. 2: 22.

[68] Schmidt, E. G., et al. 1937. J. Biol. Chem. 120:705.

[69] Schumm, O., and G. Knop. 1939. Z. Gesamte Exp. Med. 106:252.

[70] Soupart, P. 1962. In J. T. Holden, ed. Amino Acid Pools. American Elsevier, New York. p. 220.

[71] Steele, B. F., et al. 1950. J. Nutr. 40:145.

[72] Stein, W. H., and S. Moore. 1954. J. Biol. Chem. 211:915.

[73] Tamura, E., et al. 1950-51. J. Jap. Soc. Food Nutr. 3:207.

[74] Taussky, H. H. 1961. Stand. Methods Clin. Chem. 3:99.

[75] Trovato, A. 1947. Atti Accad. Peloritana Pericolanti 48:75.

[76] Van Arsdel, P. P., Jr., and G. N. Beall. 1960. Arch. Intern. Med. 106:714.

[77] Van Pilsum, J. F., et al. 1956. J. Biol. Chem. 222: 225.

[78] Viergiver, E. 1954. Bull. Ayer Clin. Lab. 4:61.

[79] Watson, C. J. 1950. Arch. Intern. Med. 86:797.

[80] Widal, F., and M. Laudat. 1926. C. R. Soc. Biol. 95:1233.

[81] Wiss, O., and R. Kruger. 1948. Helv. Chim. Acta 31:1774.

[82] Woodruff, C. W., and E. B. Man. 1945. J. Biol. Chem. 157:95.

[83] Wranne, L. 1960. Acta Paediat. (Stockholm) 49, Suppl. 124:1.

[84] Wu, H. 1922. J. Biol. Chem. 51:27.

247. BLOOD NON-PROTEIN NITROGENOUS SUBSTANCES: VERTEBRATES OTHER THAN MAN

Concentrations are expressed as mg/100 ml blood component, unless otherwise specified. Values in parentheses are ranges, estimate "c" unless otherwise indicated (*see* Introduction).

	Species [Specification]	Blood Component	Constituent	Concentration	Reference
1	*Bos taurus*	Plasma	Histamine	0.165 µg/ml	21
2	♀	Whole blood	Creatinine	(1-2.07)	30
			Glutathione		20
3			Total	46	
4			Oxidized	6	
5			Reduced	40	
6			Uric acid	(0.05-2.08)	30
7		Plasma	Tryptophan	1.12(0.8-1.2)	29
	Canis familiaris	Whole blood	Amino acids		
8			Arginine	3.7(1.7-5.2)	12,13
9			Histidine	1.33(1.0-2.0)	12
10			Isoleucine	1.76(1.2-2.2)	12
11			Leucine	2.51(1.2-3.6)	2
12			Lysine	2.54(1.6-3.6)	2
13			Methionine	1.18(0.8-1.7)	12
14			Phenylalanine	1.47(0.9-2.5)	12,13

continued

	Species [Specification]	Blood Component	Constituent	Concentration	Reference
15			Threonine	2.4(1.2-3.3)	12
16			Tryptophan	1.17(0.6-2.4)	12
17			Tyrosine	1.2(0.7-2.0)	12
18			Valine	2.63(1.5-4.1)	12
19			Creatinine	(1-1.7)	30
			Glutathione		2
20			Total	31.3	
21			Reduced	29.2	
22			Uric acid	(0-0.5)	30
23		Erythrocytes	Arginine	4.2	12,13
		Plasma	Amino acids		
24			Arginine	3.27(1.79-4.75)[b]	12,13
25			Citrulline	(0.8-1.5)	1
26			Cystine	0.9(0.5-1.5)	12
27			Glutamic acid	<0.6	1
28			Glutamine	(7-13)	2
29			Histidine	1.24(0.90-1.58)[b]	12
30			Isoleucine	1.31(0.87-1.95)	12
31			Leucine	2.09(1.43-3.06)	12
32			Lysine	2.42(1.26-3.58)[b]	12
33			Methionine	(0.20-1.88)	12
34			Phenylalanine	1.16(0.58-1.74)[b]	12,13
35			Threonine	2.58(1.5-3.5)	12
36			Tryptophan	1.20(0.8-1.5)	12
37			Tyrosine	1.06(0.58-1.54)[b]	12
38			Valine	2.22(1.5-3.0)	12
39			Uric acid	0.33	7
40	*Capra hircus*	Whole blood	Creatinine	(0.9-1.82)	30
41			Uric acid	(0.33-1.0)	30
		Plasma	Amino acids		23
42			Lysine	1.8(1.3-2.4)	
43			Tyrosine	1.2(1.0-1.5)	
44	*Cavia porcellus*	Whole blood	Glutathione, total	(80-175)	2
45		Plasma	Glycine	2.5	9
	Equus caballus	Whole blood	Amino acids		
46			Cysteine	0.3	18
47			Cystine	1.25	2
48			Creatinine	(1.2-1.9)	30
			Glutathione		2
49			Total	60	
50			Reduced	50	
51			Uric acid	(0.90-1.09)	30
		Erythrocytes	Amino acids		
52			Cysteine	0.5	18
53			Cystine	0.6	2
		Plasma or serum	Amino acids		
54			Cysteine	0.2	18
55			Cystine	1.6	18
56			Tryptophan	1.2	25
57			Bilirubin	0.98	15
58			Urea	(28-58)	15
	Felis catus	Plasma[1/]	Amino acids		31
59			Alanine	7.0	

[1/] Blood obtained by heart puncture with heparinized syringe [27].

continued

	Species [Specification]	Blood Component	Constituent	Concentration	Reference
60			Arginine	1.4	
61			Asparagine	0.9	
62			Aspartic acid	0.1	
63			Citrulline	<0.1	
64			Cystine	0.4	
65			Glutamic acid	1.8	
66			Glycine	2.3	
67			Histidine	1.4	
68			Isoleucine	0.8	
69			Leucine	1.6	
70			Lysine	2.8	
71			Methionine	0.4	
72			3-Methylhistidine	0.1	
73			Ornithine	0.2	
74			Phenylalanine	0.9	
75			Proline	2.3	
76			Serine	2.1	
77			Taurine	0.7	
78			Threonine	1.4	
79			Tryptophan	<0.2	
80			Tyrosine	0.7	
81			Valine	2.4	
	Mus musculus	Plasma	Amino acids		26
82			Alanine	5.87(5.3-6.6)	
83			Arginine	0.97(0.9-1.0)	
84			Glutamic acid	3.33(2.9-3.6)	
85			Glycine	1.90(1.7-2.3)	
86			Histidine	1.57(1.4-1.7)	
87			Isoleucine	1.47(1.2-2.0)	
88			Leucine	2.40(2.2-2.8)	
89			Lysine	6.37(5.7-7.0)	
90			Methionine	1.9(1.7-2.2)	
91			Phenylalanine	2.4(2.0-3.2)	
92			Proline	1.83(1.6-2.1)	
93			Threonine	3.50(3.0-3.9)	
94			Tryptophan	1.23(1.1-1.4)	
95			Tyrosine	2.53(2.4-2.7)	
96			Valine	4.30(3.8-5.0)	
97	*Ovis aries*	Whole blood	Creatinine	(1.2-1.93)	30
98			Glutathione, total	26	2
99			Uric acid	(0.05-1.93)	30
100		Plasma	Tryptophan	1.1(0.8-1.3)	24
101	*Rattus norvegicus*	Plasma	Urea	34	19
102	Holtzman	Whole blood	Glutathione, reduced	40(30-45)	8
	Sprague-Dawley	Whole blood	Amino acids		
103			Alanine	12.3(8.9-15.7)[b]	5
104			Tryptophan	1.57(1.5-2.0)	11
		Plasma	Amino acids		11
105			Arginine	3.21(2.35-4.07)[b]	
106			Glycine	2.27(1.85-2.69)[b]	
107			Histidine	0.97(0.85-1.09)[b]	
108			Isoleucine	1.32(0.96-1.68)[b]	
109			Leucine	2.66(2.20-3.12)[b]	
110			Lysine	5.8(4.4-7.2)[b]	

continued

	Species [Specification]	Blood Component	Constituent	Concentration	Reference
111			Methionine	0.95(0.81-1.09)[b]	
112			Phenylalanine	1.37(1.15-1.59)[b]	
113			Proline	4.3(3.5-5.1)[b]	
114			Threonine	4.4(3.4-5.4)[b]	
115			Tryptophan	1.68(1.44-1.92)[b]	
116			Tyrosine	2.23(1.73-2.73)[b]	
117			Valine	2.67(2.27-3.07)[b]	
118	Wistar	Whole blood	Uric acid	1.5(0.5-3.4)	4
119	*Sus scrofa*	Whole blood	Creatinine	(1-2.7)	30
120			Glutathione, total	36	2
121			Uric acid	(0.05-1.95)	30
122		Erythrocytes	Ergothioneine	20.7(15.6-24)	22
		Plasma	Amino acids		
123			Cystine	(0.6-0.9)	3
124			Tryptophan	1.1(1.0-1.2)	24
125	Mouse	Whole blood	Glutathione, total	(90-115)	2
	Rabbit	Whole blood	Glutathione		2
126			Total	45(35-55)	
127			Reduced	35(26-40)	
128			Histamine	0.28	2
		Plasma	Amino acids		
129			Cystine	(0.9-1.1)	3
130			Glycine	4.0	9
131	Rat	Whole blood	Glutathione, total	(75-165)	2
132	*Gallus gallus* [Non-laying]	Whole blood	Creatine	(0.90-1.85)	28
133			Urea	5.7	10
134			Uric acid	(2.47-8.08)	28
135	*Meleagris gallopavo* [Non-	Whole blood	Creatinine	(0.86-0.94)	30
136	laying]		Uric acid	(3.41-5.19)	30
137	*Cyprinus carpio*	Whole blood	Creatine	2.58 mg/100 ml plasma	6
138			Creatinine	0.56 mg/100 ml plasma	6
139			Urea	7.6 mg/100 ml plasma	6
140			Uric acid	2.6 mg/100 ml plasma	6
	Entosphenus tridentatus	Plasma	Amino acids		16
141			Alanine	0.4	
142			Arginine	0.4	
143			Glutamic acid	0.3	
144			Glycine	0.2	
145			Histidine	0.8	
146			Isoleucine	0.4	
147			Leucine	0.6	
148			Lysine	1.1	
149			Methionine	0.3	
150			Phenylalanine	0.3	
151			Serine	0.3	
152			Threonine	0.4	
153			Tyrosine	0.2	
154			Valine	0.7	
	Ictalurus furcatus; I. punctatus; Pylodictis olivaris [Average of 10 subjects]	Plasma	Amino acids		16
155			Alanine	0.9(0.5-1.2)	
156			Arginine	0.3(0.2-0.6)	
157			Asparagine	1.2(0.6-1.7)	
158			Aspartic acid	0.09(0.06-0.11)	
159			½ Cystine	0.2(0.1-0.3)	

continued

	Species [Specification]	Blood Component	Constituent	Concentration	Reference
160			Glutamic acid	0.9(0.6-1.7)	
161			Glycine	0.5(0.3-0.8)	
162			Histidine	0.4(0.1-1.1)	
163			Isoleucine	1.7(0.9-3.2)	
164			Leucine	2.4(1.4-4.9)	
165			Lysine	1.1(0.6-1.4)	
166			Methionine	0.04(0.02-0.07)	
167			Ornithine	1.0(0.2-2.7)	
168			Phenylalanine	0.9(0.5-1.5)	
169			Proline	0.6(0.2-1.4)	
170			Serine	0.7(0.4-1.0)	
171			Taurine	3.1(2.1-4.9)	
172			Threonine	1.1(0.8-1.5)	
173			Tyrosine	1.0(0.5-1.7)	
174			Valine	1.7(1.0-3.2)	
175	*Oncorhynchus gorbuscha*, ♂	Serum	Urea	12.5 mmoles/liter	14
176	♀	Serum	Urea	6.5 mmoles/liter	14
177	*O. gorbuscha* [Average of 6♂, 6♀; spawning]	Plasma	Amino acids		16
			Alanine	5.6(4.0-8.0)	
178			Arginine	1.8(0.4-3.5)	
179			Asparagine	8.4(3.2-12.0)	
180			Aspartic acid	0.2(0.1-0.5)	
181			½ Cystine	0.1(0.1-0.2)	
182			Glutamic acid	2.0(1.2-3.5)	
183			Glycine	5.8(1.4-12.8)	
184			Histidine	1.0(0.7-1.5)	
185			Isoleucine	1.7(1.2-2.3)	
186			Leucine	2.9(1.9-3.4)	
187			Lysine	9.0(4.7-15.7)	
188			Methionine	1.6(0.6-3.2)	
189			Ornithine	0.2(0.1-0.3)	
190			Phenylalanine	1.8(1.1-2.2)	
191			Proline	0.9(0.5-1.4)	
192			Serine	2.4(1.3-4.6)	
193			Taurine	12.2(7.5-17.3)	
194			Threonine	4.5(2.5-7.7)	
195			Tyrosine	1.0(0.4-1.5)	
196			Valine	3.9(2.4-4.8)	
197	*O. kisutch* [Average of 3♂, 3♀; spawning]	Plasma	Amino acids		16
			Alanine	3.2(1.9-5.8)	
198			Arginine	1.6(1.2-2.5)	
199			Asparagine	2.3(1.2-4.1)	
200			Aspartic acid	1.3(0.5-2.0)	
201			½ Cystine	5.4(4.4-6.4)	
202			Glutamic acid	2.0(1.6-2.7)	
203			Glycine	3.5(1.4-5.2)	
204			Histidine	0.4(0.2-0.6)	
205			Isoleucine	1.4(1.1-1.6)	
206			Leucine	2.2(1.8-2.9)	
207			Lysine	2.8(1.0-3.9)	
208			Methionine	1.7(0.9-2.5)	
209			Ornithine	2.2(1.0-3.5)	
210			Phenylalanine	0.8(0.6-1.1)	
211			Serine	6.8(4.0-11.9)	

continued

	Species [Specification]	Blood Component	Constituent	Concentration	Reference
212			Taurine	16.2(11.2-21.4)	
213			Threonine	2.1(1.5-2.9)	
214			Tyrosine	0.6(0.3-0.7)	
215			Valine	0.3(0.1-0.5)	
216	*O. tshawytscha* [1 subject, 5 lb; marine habitat]	Plasma	Amino acids		17
216			Alanine	15.9	
217			Arginine	6.3	
218			Aspartic acid	1.0	
219			Isoleucine	7.3	
220			Leucine	12.6	
221			Lysine	8.7	
222			Methionine	3.3	
223			Phenylalanine	3.0	
224			Serine	4.1	
225			Taurine	4.9	
226			Threonine	5.8	
227			Tyrosine	4.0	
228			Valine	11.9	
229	*O. tshawytscha* [1 subject, 25-30 lb; spawning; fresh-water habitat]	Plasma	Amino acids		17
230			Alanine	10.1	
231			Arginine	4.0	
232			Aspartic acid	0.4	
233			Isoleucine	2.2	
234			Leucine	3.3	
235			Lysine	8.3	
236			Methionine	1.3	
237			Phenylalanine	1.7	
238			Serine	10.7	
239			Taurine	33.8	
240			Threonine	3.6	
241			Tyrosine	1.0	
241			Valine	4.9	
242	*Salmo gairdneri* [Average of 3 subjects, 3 yr old; starved 2 da]	Plasma	Amino acids		16
243			Alanine	4.4(3.9-5.1)	
244			Asparagine	4.3(3.9-4.8)	
245			Aspartic acid	0.1(0.1-0.2)	
246			Glutamic acid	1.0(0.8-1.5)	
247			Glycine	2.7(1.7-3.8)	
248			Histidine	6.5(2.7-13.6)	
249			Isoleucine	2.8(2.2-3.5)	
250			Leucine	4.3(3.6-5.6)	
251			Lysine	3.9(1.4-7.8)	
252			Methionine	0.72(0.70-0.73)	
253			Ornithine	0.5(0.4-0.7)	
254			Phenylalanine	1.0(0.8-1.1)	
255			Proline	1.2(0.3-2.6)	
256			Serine	0.8(0.7-0.8)	
257			Taurine	4.6(3.2-7.2)	
258			Threonine	2.8(2.4-3.6)	
259			Tyrosine	0.7(0.6-0.8)	
259			Valine	5.4(4.4-6.9)	
260	*S. gairdneri* [Average of 1♂, 3♀; spawning]	Plasma	Amino acids		16
260			Alanine	7.5(4.1-11.5)	
261			Arginine	3.9(2.0-4.9)	

continued

	Species [Specification]	Blood Component	Constituent	Concentration	Reference
262			Asparagine	7.4(5.6-8.9)	
263			Aspartic acid	0.5(0.2-0.9)	
264			Glutamic acid	1.2(0.9-1.6)	
265			Glycine	3.4(2.6-4.7)	
266			Histidine	1.3(0.8-1.8)	
267			Isoleucine	5.4(4.3-6.3)	
268			Leucine	7.9(6.9-9.1)	
269			Lysine	16.2(9.9-25.8)	
270			Methionine	1.5(1.3-1.8)	
271			Ornithine	1.7(0.8-2.4)	
272			Phenylalanine	3.2(2.3-5.1)	
273			Proline	1.0(0.4-1.7)	
274			Serine	2.4(1.6-3.2)	
275			Taurine	17.7(8.1-27.9)	
276			Threonine	6.5(4.7-7.7)	
277			Tyrosine	2.3(1.7-3.2)	
278			Valine	10.3(8.4-12.8)	
279	*Salvelinus fontinalis*	Whole blood	Creatine	1.32 mg/100 ml plasma	6
280			Creatinine	0.72 mg/100 ml plasma	6
281			Urea	5.5 mg/100 ml plasma	6
282			Uric acid	8.6 mg/100 ml plasma	6
283	Salmon	Whole blood	Glutathione, total	6.2 mg/100 ml plasma	2

Contributors: Beerstecher, Ernest, Jr.; Johnson, Charles L.

References

[1] Archibald, R. N. 1944. J. Biol. Chem. 154:643.

[2] Beerstecher, E., Jr. Unpublished. Univ. Texas Dental Branch, Houston, 1971.

[3] Brown, B. H., and H. B. Lewis. 1941. J. Biol. Chem. 138:705.

[4] Byers, S. O., et al. 1947. Amer. J. Physiol. 150: 677.

[5] Euler, H. von, and L. Heller. 1947. Ark. Kemi Mineral, Geol. 25A:22.

[6] Field, J. B., et al. 1943. J. Biol. Chem. 148(2):261.

[7] Friedman, M., and S. O. Byers. 1948. Ibid. 175: 727.

[8] Grunert, R. R., and P. H. Phillips. 1949. Ibid. 181: 821.

[9] Gutman, G. E., and B. Alexander. 1947. Ibid. 168: 527.

[10] Heller, V. G., and R. H. Thayer. 1948. Endocrinology 42:161.

[11] Henderson, L. M., et al. 1949. J. Biol. Chem. 177: 815.

[12] Hier, S. W. 1947. Ibid. 171:813.

[13] Hier, S. W., and O. Bergeim. 1946. Ibid. 163:129.

[14] Holmes, W. N., and E. M. Donaldson. 1969. In W. S. Hoar and D. J. Randall, ed. Fish Physiology. Academic Press, New York. v. 1, pp. 1-89.

[15] Jennings, F. W., and W. Mulligan. 1953. J. Comp. Pathol. Ther. 63:286.

[16] Johnson, C. L. Unpublished. U.S. Dep. of the Interior, Bureau of Sport Fisheries and Wildlife, Cook, Wash., 1971.

[17] Mertz, E. T. 1969. In O. W. Neuhaus and J. E. Halver, ed. Fish in Research. Academic Press, New York. pp. 233-244.

[18] Numata, I. 1940. Biochem. Z. 304:404.

[19] Persike, E. C. 1948. Endocrinology 42:356.

[20] Reid, J. T., et al. 1948. Amer. J. Physiol. 152:633.

[21] Romanelli, V. 1949. Atti Soc. Ital. Sci. Vet. 3:232.

[22] Salt, H. B. 1931. Biochem. J. 25:812.

[23] Schweigert, B. S. Unpublished. Univ. California, Dep. Food Science and Technology, Davis, 1971.

[24] Schweigert, B. S., et al. 1946. J. Biol. Chem. 164: 213.

[25] Schweigert, B. S., et al. 1947. Arch. Biochem. 12: 139.

[26] Steele, B. F., et al. 1950. Ibid. 25:124.

[27] Stein, W. H., and S. Moore. 1954. J. Biol. Chem. 211:915.

[28] Sturkie, P. D. 1954. Avian Physiology. Comstock, Ithaca.

[29] Sutton, T. S., and G. C. Esh. 1948. J. Dairy Sci. 31: 187.

[30] Swenson, M. J., ed. 1970. Dukes' Physiology of Domestic Animals. Ed. 8. Cornell Univ. Press, Ithaca. p. 52.

[31] Tallan, H. H., et al. 1954. J. Biol. Chem. 211:927.

248. BLOOD LIPIDS: MAN

For information on serum lipoprotein levels, consult references 14 and 19. Values in parentheses are ranges, estimate "c" (*see* Introduction).

Lipid (Synonym)	Concentration mg/100 ml [1]	Reference
Whole blood		
1 Lipids, total	652	11
2 Fatty acids, total	364(283-442)	17
3 Cholesterol, total	(140-215)	33
Erythrocytes		
4 Lipids, total	510(408-612)	7
Fatty acids		22
5 Palmitic (16:0)	20.0%	
6 Oleic (18:1)	13.5%	
7 Linoleic (18:2)	9.2%	
8 Eicosatrienoic (20:3) plus Behenic (22:0)	3.3%	
9 Arachidonic (20:4) plus Cetoleic (22:1)	15.2%	
10 Docosatetraenoic (22:4) plus Nervonic (24:1)	7.8%	
11 Fat, total	400(180-595)	12
Phosphatides		
12 Total	196(26-297)	12
13 Phosphatidyl serine	7.8	31
14 Phosphatidyl ethanolamine	26.8	31
15 Phosphatidyl choline (Lecithin)	68.4	31
16 Sphingomyelin	56.8	31
17 Phosphatidyl inositol	5.0	31
18 Phosphatidal ethanolamine (Phosphatidyl ethanolamine plasmalogen)	29.0	31
19 Phosphatidal choline (Lecithin plasmalogen)	2.8	31
20 Lysolecithin	3.4	31
Cholesterol		
21 Total	120(102-138)	7
22	173(118-228)	8
23 Free	140(119-161)	3
Plasma or Serum		
24 Lipids, total	(385-675)	16
25	589(521-730)	1
26	657(433-810)	32
Fatty acids		
27 Total	(150-500)	29
28	(294-341)	20
29 Non-esterified	(8-20)	16
30	19	4
Free		10,24
31 Palmitic (16:0)	(23.0-27.9)%	
32 Oleic (18:1)	(25.5-45.5)%	
33 Linoleic (18:2)	(7.0-13.1)%	
34 Triglycerides	(10-190)	16
35	(50-220)	6
36	(137-192)	25
37	160	2
Triglyceride fatty acids		10,24
38 Palmitic (16:0)	(26.5-28.1)%	
39 Oleic (18:1)	(36.8-43.6)%	
40 Linoleic (18:2)	(12.2-14.7)%	
Phosphatides		
41 Total	(110-250)	16
42	235(172-269)	26
43	267	15
44 Phosphatidyl ethanolamine	2	30
45 Phosphatidyl choline	(80-200)	16
46	146	30
47	156(106-200)	21
48 Sphingomyelin	34	30
49	56(43-80)	21
50 Plasmalogens	(7-8)	10
51 Lysolecithin	15	30
Phosphatide fatty acids		10,24
52 Palmitic (16:0)	(30.7-34.9)%	
53 Oleic (18:1)	(11.5-15.1)%	
54 Linoleic (18:2)	(18.2-21.5)%	
Steroids		
55 Estradiol	(0.23-0.26)	13
56 Estrone	(0.05-0.06)	13
57 17-Ketosteroids	0.171	5
Bile acids		
58 Total	0.081	23
59 Chenodeoxycholic acid	0.029	23
60 Deoxycholic acid	0.025	23
61 Cholic acid	0.020	23
62	(0.5-1.5)	27
Cholesterol [2]		
63 Total	(140-260)	16
64	(194-227)[3]	28
65	(197-224)[4]	28
66	(242-254)[5]	28
67	(230-272)[6]	28
68	(258-259)[7]	28
69	(275-285)[8]	28
70 Free	(30-100)	6
71	(40-70)	16
72 Ester	(90-200)	16
Cholesterol ester fatty acids		10,24
73 Palmitic (16:0)	(11.8-12.1)%	
74 Oleic (18:1)	(18.9-24.6)%	
75 Linoleic (18:2)	(47.1-50.9)%	
76 Dihydrocholesterol	0.57	18

[1] Unless otherwise specified. [2] Cholesterol levels in man and other animals tend to display a seasonal variation; peak values generally appear in winter. For a recent review, consult reference 9. [3] Males, 1-30 yr. [4] Females, 1-30 yr. [5] Males, 30-60 yr. [6] Females, 30-60 yr. [7] Males, 60-80 yr. [8] Females, 60-80 yr.

continued

Contributor: Kritchevsky, David

References

[1] Boyd, E. M. 1933. J. Biol. Chem. 101:323.

[2] Brown, D. F., et al. 1966. J. Atheroscler. Res. 6: 232.

[3] Brun, G. C. 1939. Acta Med. Scand., Suppl. 99.

[4] Castelli, W. P., et al. 1966. J. Atheroscler. Res. 6: 328.

[5] Clayton, G. W., et al. 1955. J. Clin. Endocrinol. Metab. 15:693.

[6] Drem, K., and C. Lentner. 1970. Geigy Scientific Tables. Ed. 7. J. R. Geigy, Basel. p. 600.

[7] Farquhar, J. W. 1962. Biochim. Biophys. Acta 60: 80.

[8] Foldes, F. F., and A. J. Murphy. 1946. Proc. Soc. Exp. Biol. Med. 62:215.

[9] Fyfe, T., et al. 1968. J. Atheroscler. Res. 8:591.

[10] Goodman, D. S., and T. Shiratori. 1964. J. Lipid Res. 5:307.

[11] Kaufman, H. T., and H. G. Schwarz. 1954. Fette Seifen Anstrichm. 56:17.

[12] Kirk, E. 1938. J. Biol. Chem. 123:637.

[13] Kroman, H. S., et al. 1966. J. Atheroscler. Res. 6: 247.

[14] Lindgren, F. T., and A. V. Nichols. 1960. Plasma Proteins 2:1.

[15] Lindgren, F. T., et al. 1964. J. Lipid Res. 5:68.

[16] Masoro, E. J. 1968. Physiological Chemistry of Lipids in Mammals. W. B. Saunders, Philadelphia. p. 186.

[17] McClure, C. W., and M. E. Huntsinger. 1928. J. Biol. Chem. 76:5.

[18] Mosbach, E. M. 1966. Proc. Int. Congr. Nutr., 7th, p. 469.

[19] Olson, R. E., and J. W. Vester. 1960. Physiol. Rev. 40:677.

[20] Page, E., and L. Michaud. 1951. Can. J. Med. Sci. 29:239.

[21] Peterson, V. P. 1950. Scand. J. Clin. Lab. Invest. 2: 44.

[22] Phillips, G. B., et al. 1969. Lipids 4:544.

[23] Sandberg, D. H., et al. 1965. J. Lipid Res. 6:182.

[24] Schrade, W. 1960. Med. Ernaehr. 1:267.

[25] Shaper, A. G., et al. 1966. J. Atheroscler. Res. 6: 313.

[26] Taurog, A., et al. 1944. J. Biol. Chem. 155:19.

[27] Thannhauser, S. J., et al. 1942. Trans. Ass. Amer. Physicians 57:290.

[28] Werner, M., et al. 1970. Z. Klin. Chem. Klin. Biochem. 8:105.

[29] White, A., et al. 1968. Principles of Biochemistry. Ed. 4. McGraw-Hill, New York. p. 706.

[30] Williams, J. H., et al. 1966. Lipids 1:89.

[31] Williams, J. H., et al. 1966. Ibid. 1:391.

[32] Wilson, W. R., and A. E. Hansen. 1936. J. Biol. Chem. 112:457.

[33] Wootton, I. D. P., and E. J. King. 1953. Lancet 264:470.

249. BLOOD LIPIDS: VERTEBRATES OTHER THAN MAN

Values in parentheses are ranges, estimate "c" (*see* Introduction).

	Animal	Blood Component	Lipid	Concentration mg/100 ml	Reference
1	Alpaca	Serum	Cholesterol, total	70	11
2	Armadillo	Serum	Cholesterol, total	(96-147)	22
3	Baboon	Serum	Triglyceride	73	10
4			Cholesterol, total	100	5,13
5			free	32	13
6			ester	67	13
7			α-Lipoprotein cholesterol, total	53	13
8			β-Lipoprotein cholesterol, total	43	13
9	Caribou	Whole blood	Cholesterol, total	157	9
10	Cat	Erythrocytes	Cholesterol, total	(218-246)	19
11		Plasma	Lipid, total	376(145-607)	2
12			Fat, neutral	108	2
13			Phospholipid	132(21-143)	2
14			Cholesterol, total	93(43-143)	2
15			ester	73(25-127)	2
16		Serum	Cholesterol, total	(90-110)	23
17				(95-130)	9

continued

	Animal	Blood Component	Lipid	Concentration mg/100 ml	Reference
18	Cattle Bull	Erythrocytes	Cholesterol, total	180	19
19	Cow	Plasma	Lipid, total	348(185-511)	2
20			Phospholipid, total	84(17-151)	2
21			Cholesterol, total	110(8-212)	2
22		Serum	Cholesterol, total	(50-230)	23
23				(96-245)	14
24	Ox	Erythrocytes	Cholesterol, total	340	19
25	Chimpanzee	Serum	Cholesterol, total	225	4
26	Deer	Serum	Cholesterol, total	(44-137)	9
27	Dog	Erythrocytes	Cholesterol, total	213	19
28		Serum	Lipid, total	580(470-725)	2
29			Cholesterol, total	(110-135)	9
30				(125-250)	23
31	Dromedary	Serum	Cholesterol, total	(17-29)	9
32	Elephant	Serum	Cholesterol, total	67	9
33	Gazelle	Serum	Cholesterol, total	48	9
34	Goat	Serum	Cholesterol, total	(55-200)	23
35				(80-130)	9
36	Gorilla	Serum	Cholesterol, total	322	4
37	Guanaco	Serum	Cholesterol, total	(30-50)	9
38	Guinea pig	Serum	Cholesterol, total	(30-50)	9
39	Hippopotamus	Whole blood	Cholesterol, total	38	9
40		Serum	Triglyceride	70	18
41			Phospholipid	7	18
42			Cholesterol, total	12	18
43	Horse	Serum	Cholesterol, total	(75-150)	23
44				(83-140)	9
45	Lion	Serum	Cholesterol, total	(110-160)	9
46	Llama	Serum	Cholesterol, total	(33-116)	9
47	Marmoset	Serum	Cholesterol, total	69	15
48	Monkey Capuchin	Serum	Cholesterol, total	98	15
49	Rhesus	Serum	Lipid, total	536(400-637)	1
50			Cholesterol, total	130	5
51	Ringtail	Serum	Cholesterol, total	90	15
52	Spider	Serum	Cholesterol, total	130	15
53				170	5
54	Squirrel	Serum	Cholesterol, total	105	15
55	Woolly	Serum	Cholesterol, total	133	15
56	Muskrat	Whole blood	Cholesterol, total	110	9
57	Opossum	Whole blood	Cholesterol, total	150	9
58	Orangutan	Serum	Cholesterol, total	259	4
59	Rabbit Dutch belted	Serum	Triglyceride	23	11
60			Phospholipid	71	11
61			Cholesterol, total	40(26-85)	11
62			free	8	11
63			ester	33	11
64	New Zealand	Serum	Lipid, total	(283-346)	16
65			Triglyceride	(124-156)	16
66			Phospholipid	(95-121)	16
67			Cholesterol, total	(35-53)	16
68			free	(11-14)	16
69			ester	(48-67)	16

continued

	Animal	Blood Component	Lipid		Concentration mg/100 ml	Reference
70	Rat	Serum	Cholesterol, total		(120-135)	9
71	Wistar	Serum	Triglyceride		(40-50)	12
72			Phospholipid		(70-125)	12
73			Cholesterol, total		(33-50)	12
74	Sheep	Serum	Triglyceride		18	6
75			Phospholipid		46	6
76			Cholesterol, total		89	6
77					(100-150)	23
78				free	13	6
79				ester	76	6
80	Squirrel	Serum	Cholesterol, total		(160-200)	9
81	Swine	Serum	Phospholipids		(94-126)	20
82					(121-137)	21
83			Cholesterol, total		(52-62)	3
84					(91-112)	21
85					(100-250)	23
86	Minipig	Serum	Lipid, total		224	7
87			Cholesterol, total		(67-100)	8
88					(79-100)	7
89	Fowl	Serum	Cholesterol, total		(100-200)	9
90	Chicken[1]	Serum	Phospholipids		155(84-226)	2
91			Cholesterol, total		(110-130)	17
92					(125-200)	23
93				ester	66(26-106)	2
94	Chicken[2]	Serum	Cholesterol, total		(125-200)	23
95	Turtle	Serum	Cholesterol, total		30	9
96	Frog	Serum	Cholesterol, total		129	9

[1] Non-laying. [2] Laying.

Contributor: Kritchevsky, David

References

[1] Angus, M. G. N., et al. 1971. Ann. Trop. Med. Parasitol. 65:155.

[2] Boyd, E. M. 1942. J. Biol. Chem. 143:131.

[3] Bragdon, J. H., et al. 1957. Proc. Soc. Exp. Biol. Med. 95:282.

[4] Clevenger, A. B., et al. 1971. Amer. J. Clin. Pathol. 55:479.

[5] Eggen, D. A., et al. 1969. Ann. N.Y. Acad. Sci. 162:110.

[6] Garton, G. A., and W. R. H. Duncan. 1964. Biochem. J. 92:472.

[7] Harman, D. 1969. J. Atheroscler. Res. 10:77.

[8] Hill, E. G., et al. 1958. Proc. Soc. Exp. Biol. Med. 99:586.

[9] Kritchevsky, D. 1958. Cholesterol. J. Wiley, New York. p. 279.

[10] Kritchevsky, D. 1970. Trans. N.Y. Acad. Sci. 32:821.

[11] Kritchevsky, D., and S. A. Tepper. 1968. J. Atheroscler. Res. 8:357.

[12] Kritchevsky, D., and S. A. Tepper. 1969. Med. Exp. 19:329.

[13] Kritchevsky, D., et al. 1967. Nutr. Dieta 9:283.

[14] Lennon, H. D., Jr., and J. P. Mixner. 1957. J. Dairy Sci. 40:1424.

[15] Lofland, H. B., et al. 1967. Arch. Pathol. 83:211.

[16] Lutton, C. E., and T. T. Tsaltas. 1965. Proc. Soc. Exp. Biol. Med. 118:1048.

[17] Malinow, M. R., et al. 1963. J. Atheroscler. Res. 3:321.

[18] McKinney, B., and C. P. Luck. 1964. Nature (London) 202:705.

[19] Ponder, E. 1948. Hemolysis and Related Phenomena. Grune and Stratton, New York.

[20] Reiser, R., et al. 1959. Circ. Res. 7:833.

[21] Rowsell, H. C., et al. 1960. Can. Med. Ass. J. 83:1175.

[22] Strozier, L. M., et al. 1971. Lab. Anim. Sci. 21:399.

[23] Swenson, M. J., ed. 1970. Dukes' Physiology of Domestic Animals. Ed. 8. Cornell Univ. Press, Ithaca. p. 52.

Values in parentheses are ranges, estimate "c" unless otherwise indicated (*see* Introduction).

	Carbohydrate	Concentration mg/100 ml	Method	Remarks	Reference
			Whole Blood		
1	Fructose	(0-1)	....	Fetus	5
2		(0.5-5.0)	....	....	23
3	Glucosamine	(60-82)	....	....	12
4	Glucose	75(55-90)	Glucose oxidase	....	21
5		(36-116)	Calculated from fermentable sugar in cord blood	Fetus	5
6		(20-30)	Zinc hydroxide filtrate, ferricyanide iodometric titration	Newborn	10
7		90(80-100)[b]	Zinc hydroxide filtrate, copper-iodometric titration	Arterial blood, fasting subjects	18
8		85.5(75.5-95.5)[b]	Zinc hydroxide filtrate, copper-iodometric titration	Venous blood, fasting subjects	18
9		90(71-109)[b]	....	Fasting subjects	7
10	Glucuronic acid	6.7(4.1-9.3)[b]	Tungstate-sulfuric acid filtrate, color development with naphthoresorcinol	....	11
11	Glycogen	5.5(1.2-16.2)	Copper-iodometric titration	....	22
			Erythrocytes		
12	Glucose	74(46-102)[b]	Defibrinated blood; tungstic acid filtrate, fermentation	....	17
13	Glucuronic acid	0.6(0.0-2.0)	Color development with naphthoresorcinol, with preliminary hydrolysis but without deproteinization	....	1
			Plasma or Serum		
14	Glucosamine	(76-110)	....	....	24
15		48(42-55)	Color development with acetylacetone on hydrolysate of alcohol precipitate	Fetus	15
16		63(52-69)	Color development with acetylacetone on hydrolysate of alcohol precipitate	Subjects, 3-8 yr old	15
17		67(61-78)	Color development with acetylacetone on hydrolysate of alcohol precipitate	Subjects, 21-49 yr old	15
18		81(70-89)	Color development with acetylacetone on hydrolysate of alcohol precipitate	Subjects, 61-85 yr old	15
19	Acetyl-	(80-100)	....	....	19
20	Glucuronic acid	0.8(0-1.6)	Color development with naphthoresorcinol, with preliminary hydrolysis but without deproteinization	....	1
21		1.71(1.13-2.29)[b]	....	....	20
22		3.2(2.0-4.4)	Naphthoresorcinol	....	9
23	Glycogen	6.8(4.8-8.9)	....	....	16
24	Hexoses Fructose	0.87 ± 0.28	High-resolution column chromatography	....	4
25		<7.5	Zinc hydroxide filtrate, fermentation, color development with diphenylamine	....	14
26	Galactose	0.70 ± 0.22	High-resolution column chromatography	....	4
27	Glucose	74.9 ± 12.3	High-resolution column chromatography	....	4
28		80(67-93)	Glucose oxidase	....	21
29		91(75-107)	Glucose oxidase	....	13
30		99(82-117)	Somogyi-Nelson	....	13
31	Lactose	(0-trace)	Destruction of non-lactose sugar by *Bacillus proteus*; tungstic acid filtrate, copper-molybdate color formation	Males, females (pregnant & non-pregnant)	3

continued

	Carbohydrate	Concentration mg/100 ml	Method	Remarks	Reference
32		(0-2)	Destruction of non-lactose sugar by *B. proteus;* tungstic acid filtrate, copper-molybdate color formation	During lactation, 3-8 da postpartum	3
33	Pentoses Total	0.7(0.02-1.3)	Orcinol	....	8
34		3.7(2.6-4.8)[b]	Trichloroacetic acid filtrate, quantitative orcinol reaction	....	2
35		2.55(1.75-3.35)[b]	Saline extract of acetone precipitate	....	2
36	Phosphorylated	2.1	Trichloroacetic acid filtrate	....	2
37		2.2(1.6-2.8)[b]	Saline extract of acetone precipitate	....	2
38	L-Xylulose	0.14(0-0.5)	....	....	25
39	Polysaccharides Non-glucosamine	80(62-103)	Absorption at 500 mμ by product of tryptophan reaction with acidified alcohol precipitate	Fetus	15
40		105(94-118)	Absorption at 500 mμ by product of tryptophan reaction with acidified alcohol precipitate	Subjects, 3-8 yr old	15
41		(93-126)	Absorption at 500 mμ by product of tryptophan reaction with acidified alcohol precipitate	Subjects, 21-49 yr old	15
42		129(104-138)	Absorption at 500 mμ by product of tryptophan reaction with acidified alcohol precipitate	Subjects, 61-85 yr old	15
43	Protein-bound carbohydrates (Glycoproteins) Total	273	....	....	20, 26
44	Hexoses	121(117-125)	....	....	26
45	Hexosamines	83(75-91)	....	....	26
46	Sialic acid	60(52.6-67.4)	....	....	26
47	Fucose	8.9(7.7-10.1)	....	....	26
48	Uronic acids	0.23(0.08-0.38)	....	....	6

Contributors: Smith, Carl C., and Wolfe, Geraldine F.

References

[1] Deichmann, W. B., and M. Dierker. 1946. J. Biol. Chem. 163:753.

[2] Green, H. M., et al. 1949. Clin. Sci. 8:65.

[3] Hubbard, R. S., and H. J. Brock. 1935. J. Biol. Chem. 110:411.

[4] Jolley, R. L., et al. 1970. Amer. J. Clin. Pathol. 53: 793.

[5] Karvonen, M. J. 1949. Acta Paediat. (Stockholm) 37:68.

[6] Kerby, G. P. 1958. J. Clin. Invest. 37:962.

[7] Lozner, E. L., et al. 1941. Ibid. 20:507.

[8] McKay, E. 1964. Clin. Chim. Acta 10:320.

[9] Muting, D., et al. 1963. Z. Klin. Med. 157:538.

[10] Pedersen, J. 1949. Acta Paediat. (Stockholm), Suppl. 77, p. 201.

[11] Ratish, H. D., and J. G. M. Bullowa. 1943. Arch. Biochem. 2:381.

[12] Rivano, R., and G. Mannetti. 1950. Arch. Maragliano Patol. Clin. 5:1099.

[13] Saifer, A., and S. Gerstenfeld. 1958. J. Lab. Clin. Med. 51:448.

[14] Seibert, F. B., et al. 1948. Arch. Biochem. 18: 279.

[15] Shetlar, M. R., et al. 1948. Proc. Soc. Exp. Biol. Med. 69:507.

[16] Sikinami, Y., et al. 1940. Tohoku J. Exp. Med. 38: 371.

[17] Somogyi, M. 1928. J. Biol. Chem. 78:117.

[18] Somogyi, M. 1948. Ibid. 174:189, 597.

[19] Stary, Z., et al. 1950. Bull. Fac. Med. Istanbul 13: 233.

[20] Südhof, H. 1954. Deut. Arch. Klin. Med. 201:89.

[21] Sunderman, F. W., and F. W. Sunderman, Jr. 1961. Amer. J. Clin. Pathol. 36:75.

[22] Wagner, R. 1946. Arch. Biochem. 11:249.

[23] Wallenfals, K. 1951. Naturwissenschaften 38:238.

[24] West, R., and D. H. Clarke. 1938. J. Clin. Invest. 17:173.

[25] Winegrad, A. I., and V. J. DePratti. 1965. Diabetes 14:311.

[26] Winzler, R. J. 1960. Plasma Proteins 1:309.

Numerous factors influence blood carbohydrate levels in vertebrates, including analytical technique, strain, sex, age, nutritional status, environmental conditions, anesthesia, methods of handling animals, etc. Values therefore should be used with caution. **Concentration:** Plus/minus (±) values are standard deviation, unless otherwise indicated; values in parentheses are ranges, estimate "c", unless otherwise indicated (*see* Introduction). For additional information on zoo animals, consult reference 60.

	Order[1] & Species (Synonym)	Blood Component	Carbohydrate	Concentration mg/100 ml	Method	Remarks	Reference
	Mammalia						
	Artiodactyla						
1	*Bos taurus*	Whole blood	Glucose	62	Glucose oxidase	8 calves, 1-2 hr old; fasted	95
2				95	Glucose oxidase	8 calves, 1 da old, milk fed; fasted 6 hr	
3			Fructose	52	Roe	8 calves, 1-2 hr old; fasted	
4				2.8	Roe	8 calves, 1 da old, milk fed; fasted 6 hr	
5		Erythrocytes	Glucose	17 ± 3	Glucose oxidase	8 subjects	12
6		Plasma	Glucose	65 ± 10	Glucose oxidase	8 subjects	12
7	*Capra hircus*	Whole blood	Glucose	54(47-60)	Somogyi-Shaffer-Hartman	2 subjects; fed ad lib.	64
8				78(58-92)	Somogyi-Shaffer-Hartman	6 sucklings, 4-7 wk old; fed ad lib.	
9	*Ovis aries*	Whole blood	Glucose	46.8 ± 7.2	o-Toluidine	15 subjects	97
10				82(65-108)	Somogyi-Shaffer-Hartman	4 lambs, 25-32 da old	64
11		Erythrocytes	Glucose	14 ± 6	Glucose oxidase	8 subjects	12
12		Plasma	Glucose	63 ± 10	Glucose oxidase	8 subjects	12
13	Merino	Whole blood	Glucose	88(74-100)	Nelson	9 lambs, 2-3 wk old	58
14				52(50-57)	Nelson	5♀, 1-3 yr old	
15	*Sus scrofa*	Whole blood	Fructose	187	Resorcinol-ferric chloride	2 subjects, fetal, 82 da gestation	1
16				76	Resorcinol-ferric chloride	2 subjects, fetal, 112 da gestation	
17				1.8	Resorcinol-ferric chloride	1♀, 82 da pregnant	
18		Erythrocytes	Glucose	2 ± 2	Glucose oxidase	6 subjects	12
19				45(28-88)	Somogyi	7 subjects, fetal & newborn; concentration decreases 2 wk postnatal	33
20			Fructose	54(33-70)	Seliwanoff	7 subjects, fetal & newborn	33
21		Plasma	Glucose	95 ± 17	Glucose oxidase	6 subjects	12
22				60(42-121)	Somogyi	7 subjects, fetal & newborn	33
23			Fructose	70(53-85)	Seliwanoff	7 subjects, fetal & newborn	33
24	*(S. domesticus)*	Whole blood	Glucose	64.4 ± 10.1	o-Toluidine	15 subjects	97
25	Perissodactyla *Equus caballus*	Whole blood	Glucose	78.5 ± 10.2	o-Toluidine	15 subjects	97
26		Serum	Glucose	83 ± 23(37-129)[b]	o-Toluidine	192 subjects	72

[1] Unless otherwise indicated.

continued

	Order & Species (Synonym)	Blood Component	Carbohydrate	Concentration mg/100 ml	Method	Remarks	Reference
	Carnivora						
27	Canis familiaris	Whole blood	Glucose	62.5 ± 11.0	o-Toluidine	7 subjects	97
28		Erythrocytes	Glucose	12 ± 5	Glucose oxidase	9 subjects	12
29		Plasma	Glucose	84 ± 8	Glucose oxidase	9 subjects	12
30	Beagle	Serum	Glucose	91 ± 16(59-123)	o-Toluidine	429 subjects	72
31	Mongrel	Plasma	Glucose	84 ± 7[2/] (33-120)	Glucose oxidase	34 subjects, 3-24 hr old; anesthetized	50
32				120 ± 8[2/] (52-167)	Glucose oxidase	8 subjects, 48-110 hr old; anesthetized	
33	Felis catus (F. domesticus)	Whole blood	Glucose	75.2 ± 9.3	o-Toluidine	5 subjects	97
34		Erythrocytes	Glucose	8 ± 2	Glucose oxidase	4 subjects	12
35		Plasma	Glucose	102 ± 14	Glucose oxidase	4 subjects	12
	Rodentia[3/]						
36	Cavia porcellus	Whole blood	Glucose	95 ± 14(60-125)	Somogyi	39♂; fasted 14-18 hr	59
37		Erythrocytes	Glucose	28 ± 3	Glucose oxidase	6 subjects	12
38		Plasma	Glucose	125 ± 13	Glucose oxidase	6 subjects	12
39			Inositol	1.70 ± 1.32(0.93-3.7)	Kampling & Nixon	4 subjects	17
40	Cricetulus griseus	Whole blood	Glucose	107 ± 1.2[2/] (80-135)	Glucose oxidase	88 subjects; fed ad lib.	6
41		Plasma	Glucose	92.3 ± 2.8	Somogyi	26♂, 28-30 da old; ether anesthesia	83
42				88.9 ± 3.7	Somogyi	24♂, 80-120 da old; ether anesthesia	
43	Mesocricetus auratus	Whole blood	Glucose	111.2 ± 6.4[2/] (77-187)	Ferri-ferrocyanide	29♂; fasted 24 hr; 22°C, 12:12 light:dark regimen	53
44				89.8 ± 5.4(54-150)	Ferri-ferrocyanide	25♂; fasted 24 hr; 4°C, 12:12 light:dark regimen	53
45				132.0 ± 19.4[2/]	Glucose oxidase	4♀, virgins, 2-3 mo old; fasted 24 hr	67
46				154.8 ± 8.5[2/]	Glucose oxidase	10♀, 10-16 mo old; fasted 24 hr	67
47				57.0 ± 4.4[2/]	Glucose oxidase	5♀, pregnant; fasted 24 hr	67
	Mus musculus						
48	C57BL/Ks	Whole blood	Glucose	91 ± 2[2/]	Glucose oxidase	14 subjects, 1 wk old	62
49				116 ± 13(90-142)	Ferri-ferrocyanide	43 subjects, 5.5-30 wk old; fed ad lib.	10
50				134 ± 6[2/]	Glucose oxidase	11 subjects, 34 wk old	62
51	LP/J	Serum	Glucose	66.6 ± 6.4[2/] (38.0-95.2)[b]	o-Toluidine	5♀	84
52	Swiss-Purdue	Whole blood	Glucose	173.8 ± 5.9[2/]	Ferri-ferrocyanide	61 subjects; fed ad lib.; non-anesthetized	45
53				108.9 ± 3.6[2/]	Ferri-ferrocyanide	22 subjects; fasted 24 hr; non-anesthetized	
54				70.1 ± 3.5[2/]	Ferri-ferrocyanide	24 subjects; fed ad lib.; nembutal anesthesia	

[2/] Plus/minus (±) value is standard error. [3/] For more inclusive data on genetic strains of diabetic rodents, consult reference 79; on hibernating rodents, consult reference 86.

continued

	Order & Species (Synonym)	Blood Component	Carbohydrate	Concentration mg/100 ml	Method	Remarks	Reference
55	*Rattus norvegicus; R. rattus*	Erythrocytes	Glucuronic acid	0.4(0-1.0)	Naphthoresorcinol	7 subjects	19
56		Plasma	Glucuronic acid	0.9(0.5-1.1)	Naphthoresorcinol	7 subjects	19
57			Pentoses, total	5.27(5.05-5.44)	Meybaum (modification)	Subjects fasted 18 hr	40
58			Glucose	80.9 ± 2.8[2/]	Glucose oxidase	10♀, 19 da pregnant; fed ad lib.	49
59				51.3 ± 3.2[2/]	Glucose oxidase	8♀, 19 da pregnant; fasted 48 hr	
60	Albino	Plasma	Glucose	128 ± 5[2/]	Glucose oxidase	7♂, cesarean birth; fed ad lib.	48
61				91 ± 7[2/]	Glucose oxidase	7♂, cesarean birth; fasted 120 hr	
62	Holtzman	Plasma	Glucose	78 ± 1.5[2/]	Nelson-Somogyi	12♀, 21 da pregnant; fed ad lib.	5
63	Porton-Wistar, albino	Erythrocytes	Glucose	52 ± 9	Boehringer colorimetric	30♂; fasted 2-3 hr	44
64		Plasma	Glucose	152.5 ± 15.5	Boehringer colorimetric	42♂; fasted 2-3 hr	44
65	Sprague-Dawley	Plasma	Inositol	1.14 ± 0.45(0.22-1.8)	Kampling & Nixon	31 subjects; fed ad lib.	17
66		Serum	Polysaccharide, non-glucosamine	164	Tryptophan reaction	36♂; 6 pooled samples	81
67	Albino	Serum	Hexoses, protein-bound	156 ± 10	Orcinol	15♂	82
68			Hexosamine, protein-bound	144 ± 25	Boas (modification)	15♂	
69			Methyl pentoses, protein-bound	10.8 ± 2.6	Dische & Shettles	15♂	
70			Sialic acid, protein-bound	153 ± 19	Thiobarbituric acid assay	15♂	
71	Wistar, albino	Whole blood	Glucose	94.2 ± 4.6[2/] (55-140)	Ferri-ferrocyanide	32 subjects; 22°C, 15:12 light:dark regimen	53
72				92.0 ± 3.5[2/] (64-127)	Ferri-ferrocyanide	25 subjects; 4°C, 12:12 light:dark regimen	
73	*Spermophilus lateralis (Citellus lateralis)*	Whole blood	Glucose	183 ± 20(166-220)	Glucose oxidase	9 subjects; active non-hibernating; fasted 18 hr	86
74				118 ± 20(83-153)	Glucose oxidase	25 subjects; hibernating; no variations during hibernation	
75	*S. undulatus (C. undulatus)*	Whole blood	Glucose	153.2(102-194)	....	5 subjects; active	68
76				147.5(100-190)	....	10 subjects; hibernating	
77				44.4(31-58)	....	7 subjects; fasted 6 wk	
78	*S. undulatus plesius*	Plasma	Glucose	129 ± 36	Ferricyanide	41 subjects; summer; active, nonhibernating	32
79				112 ± 43	Ferricyanide	38 subjects; winter; hibernating; concentration decreases during hibernation	

2/ Plus/minus (±) value is standard error.

continued

	Order & Species (Synonym)	Blood Component	Carbohydrate	Concentration mg/100 ml	Method	Remarks	Reference
	Lagomorpha						
80	*Oryctolagus*	Erythrocytes	Glucose	16 ± 5	Glucose oxidase	13 subjects	12
81	*cuniculus*		Glucuronic acid	0.7(0.0-1.6)	Naphthoresorcinol	12 subjects	19
82		Plasma	Glucose	134 ± 11	Glucose oxidase	13 subjects	12
83			Glucuronic acid	1.4(0.5-2.6)	Naphthoresorcinol	11 subjects	19
84			Inositol	$0.77 \pm 0.23(0.55-1.2)$	Kampling & Nixon	6 subjects	17
			Pentose				40
85			Total	4.17(3.51-4.83)	Meybaum (modification)	6 subjects; fasted 18 hr	
86			Phosphorylated	2.49(1.87-3.63)	Meybaum (modification)	6 subjects; fasted 18 hr	
87		Serum	Glucosamine	70.8 ± 9.7	Acetylacetone reaction	30 subjects	91
88	Inbred	Serum	Glucose	117.1 ± 3.0[2/]	*o*-Toluidine	24♂; sampled at 1200 hr	27
89				147.5 ± 13.0[2/]	*o*-Toluidine	24♂; sampled at 0400 hr	
90	Strain A	Serum	Glucose	110.1 ± 5.8[2/]	*o*-Toluidine	10♂	27
91	Strain C	Serum	Glucose	144.1 ± 10.7[2/]	*o*-Toluidine	10♂	27
	Primates						
92	*Cercopithecus aethiops*	Whole blood	Glucose	125(100-164)	Folin-Wu	4 subjects; non-anesthetized	78
93				37(15-55)	Folin-Wu	4 subjects; 120 min post-pentobarbital anesthesia	
94	*Hylobates lar*	Serum	Glucose	$57 \pm 15(27-87)$[b]	*o*-Toluidine	4 subjects; zoo population	69
95	*Macaca mulatta*	Whole blood	Fructose	(0-3)	Resorcinol (modification)	9♀; pregnant	11
96		Plasma	Glucose	53 ± 3.9[2/] (40-88)	Glucose oxidase	14♀; fasted 12 hr; anesthetized	92
97				57(40-78)	Glucose oxidase	15♀, pregnant	9
98				44(32-63)	Glucose oxidase	15 subjects, fetal, 141-153 da gestation	9
99	*M. speciosa*	Whole blood	Glucose	$69.1 \pm 15.9(48.8-106.3)$	Glucose oxidase	23♀; femoral vein samples	51
100	*Pan troglodytes*	Serum	Glucose	$97 \pm 44(9-185)$[b]	*o*-Toluidine	5 subjects; zoo population	69
101	*Papio anubis*	Plasma	Glucose	76.7 ± 1.07[2/] (62-100)	Ferricyanide	27♂; fasted 20-24 hr	13
102	*Saimiri sciureus*	Plasma	Glucose	82.0 ± 5.0[2/] (58-139)	Glucose oxidase	20♀; fasted 12 hr; anesthetized	92
	Marsupialia						
103	*Wallabia eugenii*	Whole blood	Glucose	$53.5 \pm 15.5(35-87)$	Glucose oxidase	20♀; fasted 0-45 min	76
104	*(Macropus eugenii)*	Plasma	Glucose	$121.3 \pm 39.9(60-200)$	Glucose oxidase	20♀; fasted 0-45 min	76
105		Serum	Glucose	$59.9 \pm 20.2(26-100)$	Glucose oxidase	50♀, pregnant; fasted 10-24 hr; anesthetized	75, 76

[2/] Plus/minus (±) value is standard error.

continued

	Order[1] & Species (Synonym)	Blood Component	Carbohydrate	Concentration mg/100 ml	Method	Remarks	Reference
				Aves			
106	Strigiformes *Bubo virginianus*	Whole blood	Glucose	213 ± 37.7(160-315)	o-Toluidine	20 subjects; fasted 18 hr	35, 37
107	Galliformes *Coturnix coturnix japonica*	Plasma	Glucose	295 ± 7[2]	Haslewood & Strookman	37♂, 6 wk old	30
108	*Gallus gallus* Meat-type strain	Whole blood	Glucose	210.7 ± 3.3[2]	o-Toluidine	24♂, 4-8 wk old; fed ad lib.; sampled at 1200 hr	87
109				180.8 ± 2.2[2]	o-Toluidine	24♂, 4-8 wk old; fed ad lib.; sampled at 2000 hr	
110	Rhode Island Red	Plasma	Glucose	173 ± 3[2]	Haslewood & Strookman	15 embryos, 19 da old	28
111				297 ± 9[2]	Haslewood & Strookman	10 subjects, 28 da old	29
112	Thornber 606	Plasma	Glucose	288 ± 13[2]	Glucose oxidase	5♂; fed ad lib.; concentration decreased with fasting	61
113				268 ± 11[2]	Glucose oxidase	5♀; fed ad lib.; concentration decreased with fasting	
114				282 ± 2[2]	Glucose oxidase	50♂♀, 6-10 wk old; fed ad lib.	
115	*Meleagris gallopavo*	Whole blood	Glucose	216 ± 20.6(200-256)	Nelson	6♂, 1 yr old; fasted 18 hr; concentration decreased with age	34, 37
116	Anseriformes *Anas platyrhynchos*	Whole blood	Glucose	124 ± 18.4(75-173)	o-Toluidine	240♂; fasted 18 hr	20, 37
117		Erythrocytes	Glucose	25.9 ± 19.4	o-Toluidine	47♂	2,37
118		Plasma	Glucose	197 ± 23.7	o-Toluidine	47♂	2,37
119	*A. platyrhynchos domesticus*	Whole blood	Glucose	114 ± 7.42(104-130)	Nelson	16 subjects; fasted 18 hr	36, 37
120	*Anser anser (A. domesticus),*	Whole blood	Glucose	122 ± 14.9(72-183)	o-Toluidine	89 subjects; fasted 18 hr; non-anesthetized	21, 37
121	Emden & Toulouse strains			116 ± 13.7(86-176)	o-Toluidine	108 subjects; fasted 18 hr; anesthetized	
				Reptilia[4]			
122	Crocodilia *Alligator mississippiensis*	Whole blood	Glucose	99(21-205)	Folin-Wu	25 subjects; seasonal variation	16
123	Serpentes[5] *Bothrops jararaca*	Whole blood	Glucose	67.4 ± 20.5	Hagedorn-Jensen	♂ subjects; fasted 5 da	73
124				59.6 ± 19.0	Hagedorn-Jensen	♀ subjects; fasted 5 da	
125	*Naja naja*	Whole blood	Glucose	28.8(24-34)	Glucose oxidase	5 subjects; fasted 1 wk	96

[1] Unless otherwise indicated. [2] Plus/minus (±) value is standard error. [4] For more inclusive data on reptiles, consult reference 23. [5] Suborder.

continued

Order[1] & Species (Synonym)	Blood Component	Carbohydrate	Concentration mg/100 ml	Method	Remarks	Reference
126 *Philodryas* sp.	Whole blood	Glucose	63.3 ± 19.4	Hagedorn-Jensen	44 subjects; fasted 5 da	73
127 *Xenodon merremii*	Whole blood	Glucose	41 ± 3.5[2]	Somogyi-Nelson	10 subjects	52
Sauria[5]						
128 *Anolis carolinensis*	Whole blood	Glucose	172(58-305)	Folin-Wu	715 subjects; fasted 3-4 da; seasonal variation	22
129 *Ctenosaura acanthura*	Whole blood	Glucose	192(151-250)	Folin-Wu	5 subjects	47
130 *Eumeces obsoletus*	Whole blood	Glucose	98.1(84.2-113.9)	Somogyi	7 subjects; fasted 7-28 da; no variation with sex	65
131 *Iguana iguana (I. iguana rhinolopha)*	Whole blood	Glucose	155(132-195)	Folin-Wu	9 subjects	47
132 *Uromastix hardwicki*	Whole blood	Glucose	124 ± 1.1[2] (105-140)	Glucose oxidase	10 subjects; active	96
133			120.3 ± 10.8[2] (46-280)	Glucose oxidase	40 subjects; hibernating	
134 *Varanus griseus*	Whole blood	Glucose	95.3 ± 4.6(84-120)	Kemp & Kitz	7 subjects; sampled in summer	41
135			35.9 ± 2.3(31.2-40.0)	Kemp & Kitz	4 subjects; sampled in winter	
Chelonia						
136 *Chrysemys dorbignyi*	Whole blood	Glucose	91 ± 11[2]	Somogyi-Nelson	6 subjects; fasted 15 hr; no seasonal variation	15
137 *C. picta*	Whole blood	Glucose	76 ± 9.9[2]	Somogyi-Nelson	18 subjects; 22°C	74
138			49 ± 2.2[2]	Somogyi-Nelson	17 subjects; fasted 6-8 wk; 22°C	
139			68 ± 8.8[2]	Somogyi-Nelson	19 subjects; 4°C, 4-8 wk	
140 *C. scripta elegans (Pseudemys scripta elegans)*	Whole blood	Glucose	210 ± 27(178-246)	Folin-Wu	10 subjects; 4-6°C, 1 da	55
141			53 ± 39(20-115)	Folin-Wu	10 subjects; 4-6°C, 56 da	
142	Plasma	Glucose	70 ± 6(44-96)	Folin-Wu	120 subjects; no seasonal variation	54
143 *Terrepene carolina carolina*	Whole blood	Glucose	36.2 ± 13.3(21-64)	Folin-Wu	6 subjects; active	57
144			110 ± 34.9(66-157)	Folin-Wu	7 subjects; hibernating	
Amphibia						
Salientia						
145 *Bufo bufo*	Whole blood	Glucose	14.0 ± 0.5[2]	Hexokinase	Subjects fasted; 20-22°C, 4 da	46
146			8.8 ± 0.5[2]	Hexokinase	Subjects fasted; 2°C, 4 da	

[1] Unless otherwise indicated. [2] Plus/minus (±) value is standard error. [5] Suborder.

continued

	Order & Species (Synonym)	Blood Component	Carbohydrate	Concentration mg/100 ml	Method	Remarks	Reference
147	*Rana catesbeiana*	Whole blood	Glucose	13.5(0-70)	Nelson	154 subjects; no variation with nutritional state or season	93
148	*R. clamitans*	Whole blood	Glucose	24 ± 1.9[2/] (17-35)	Anthrone	8 subjects, larval stage V	31
149				40 ± 2.7[2/] (28-58)	Anthrone	10♂; adults	
150	*R. temporaria*	Whole blood	Glucose	19.4	Glucose oxidase	279 subjects; fasted 3 wk	43
151	*Xenopus laevis*	Whole blood	Glucose	(13-18)	Glucose oxidase	Subjects fasted 24 hr; larval stage 55	42
	Caudata						
152	*Ambystoma mexicanum*	Whole blood	Glucose	60.3 ± 2.8[2/]	Glucose oxidase	8 subjects; well fed	80
153				24.5 ± 1.3[2/]	Glucose oxidase	8 subjects; fasted 3 wk	
154	*Necturus maculosus*	Plasma	Glucose	14.1 ± 2.5[2/] (6.3-26.2)	Glucose oxidase	8 subjects; cannulated; 3 da post-operation	14
155	*Taricha torosa*	Whole blood	Glucose	25 ± 0.7[2/] (9-58)	Somogyi	54 subjects; fasted 4 da	94

Osteichthyes[6/]

	Order & Species (Synonym)	Blood Component	Carbohydrate	Concentration mg/100 ml	Method	Remarks	Reference
	Perciformes						
156	*Lepomis macrochirus*	Whole blood	Glucose	88.3 ± 20.3(53.0-130.0)	Glucose oxidase	11 subjects; fasted 3 da; summer, 20°C	18
157				50.2 ± 12.0(32.5-77.5)	Glucose oxidase	16 subjects; fasted 3 da; winter, 5°C	
158	*Myoxocephalus scorpius (Cottus scorpius)*	Whole blood	Glucose	42.0 ± 0.9[2/] (14.7-69.3)[7/]	Hagedorn-Jensen	145 subjects	24
159				9.3 ± 0.4[2/] (0-19.8)[7/]	Glucose oxidase	96 subjects	
	Atheriniformes						
160	*Fundulus heteroclitus*	Serum	Glucose	70.8	Glucose oxidase	24 subjects; salt water, 10°C	88
161				348	Glucose oxidase	24 subjects; salt water, −1.5°C, 8-15 da	88
162				50.1 ± 2.8[2/]	Glucose oxidase	7 subjects; freshwater, 11°C, 9 wk	89
163				1066.6 ± 193.5[2/] (362.8-1687.8)	Glucose oxidase	7 subjects; freshwater, 0.1°C, 2 wk	89
	Batrachoidiformes						
164	*Opsanus tau*	Whole blood	Glucose	42 ± 6[2/]	Glucose oxidase	16 subjects; fasted 2-3 mo; June	85
165				20 ± 5[2/]	Glucose oxidase	12 subjects; fasted 2-3 mo; August	
	Siluriformes						
166	*Ictalurus nebulosus*	Serum	Glucose	40.7 ± 3.5[2/]	Glucose oxidase	7 subjects; 20°C	90
167				75.4 ± 30.5[2/]	Glucose oxidase	7 subjects; 0.5°C, 39 da	
	Cypriniformes						
168	*Carassius auratus*	Serum	Glucose	28.5 ± 9.6(12.9-91.4)	Glucose oxidase	300 subjects; 1.5-5.0 g; 25°C, at least 4 da	8

[2/] Plus/minus (±) value is standard error. [6/] For more inclusive data on teleost fishes, consult reference 8. [7/] Range is mean ±2.58 standard deviations.

continued

	Order & Species (Synonym)	Blood Component	Carbohydrate	Concentration mg/100 ml	Method	Remarks	Reference
169	*Cyprinus carpio*	Whole blood	Glucose	100 ± 3.1[2]/ (67-154)	Hagedorn-Jensen	45 subjects; wild; 22°C	66
170				75 ± 2.0[2]/ (43-121)	Hagedorn-Jensen	81 subjects; cultured; 22°C	
171	Salmoniformes *Esox lucius*	Plasma	Glucose	131 ± 51.1(59-240)	Glucose oxidase	11♂; sampled June-July from trap net	63
172	*Oncorhynchus gorbuscha*	Plasma	Glucose	75 ± 30(23-167)	Folin-Wu	59 subjects; concentration decreased with imminence of spawning	56
173	*O. tshawytscha*	Plasma	Glucose	210(121-286)	....	14 subjects; spring-run migrating adults; freshwater	77
174	*Salmo gairdneri*	Whole blood	Glucose	53.4 ± 12.4(40.2-74.9)	Nelson-Somogyi	13 subjects, 1.5 yr old; anesthetized with tricaine (MS-222); 11.5°C	4
175	*S. salar*	Whole blood	Glucose	74 ± 5.1[2]/ (64.1-85.5)	Hagedorn-Jensen	4♀; spawning	26
176	Anguilliformes *Anguilla rostrata*	Whole blood	Glucose	77.8 ± 5.6[2]/	Nelson-Somogyi	9♀, immature; fasted 2 mo; 12°C	7
177	Acipenseriformes *Polyodon spathula*	Serum	Glucose	29.8 ± 6.1[2]/	Glucose oxidase	8♂; spawning	38
	Holocephali						
178	Chimaeriformes *Hydrolagus colliei*	Whole blood	Glucose	62.2 ± 1.6[2]/	Glucose oxidase	173 subjects; no variation with sex	71
	Chondrichthyes						
179	Rajiformes *Raja eglanteria*	Plasma	Glucose	138 ± 13	Glucose oxidase	4 subjects, freshly caught	70
180	*R. erinacea*	Plasma	Glucose	51.0 ± 16.8(20.1-88.6)	Glucose oxidase or Folin-Malmross	128 subjects; no variation with sex or fasting	39
181	*R. laevis*	Plasma	Glucose	47.8 ± 15.9(20.0-70.0)	Glucose oxidase or Folin-Malmross	8 subjects; no variation with sex	39
182	*R. ocellata*	Plasma	Glucose	43.9 ± 16.8(27.1-77.2)	Glucose oxidase or Folin-Malmross	6♀	39
183	Squaliformes *Squalus acanthias*	Whole blood	Glucose	49.2 ± 1.6[2]/	Glucose oxidase	198 subjects; no variation with sex	71
184		Plasma	Glucose	91.2 ± 25.1(52.5-191)	Glucose oxidase	23 subjects; fasted 1-3 da	70

[2]/ Plus/minus (±) value is standard error.

continued

Order & Species (Synonym)	Blood Component	Carbohydrate	Concentration mg/100 ml	Method	Remarks	Reference
Agnatha						
Petromyzontiformes						
185 *Lampetra fluviatilis*	Whole blood	Glucose	43 ± 2.1[2/]	Glucose oxidase	14 subjects	3
186 *Myxine glutinosa*	Whole blood	Glucose	15.8 ± 6.0(0.4-31.2)[7/]	Glucose oxidase	2-14 da after capture	25

[2/] Plus/minus (±) value is standard error.   [7/] Range is mean ±2.58 standard deviations.

Contributor: Young, Jack E.

References

[1] Aherne, F. X., et al. 1969. J. Anim. Sci. 29:906.

[2] Assimacopoulos, C. A., et al. 1966. Fed. Proc. Fed. Amer. Soc. Exp. Biol. 25:442.

[3] Bentley, P. J., and B. K. Follet. 1965. J. Endocrinol. 31:127.

[4] Black, E. C., and S. J. Tredwell. 1967. J. Fish. Res. Bd. Can. 24:939.

[5] Blake, C. A., and R. L. Hazelwood. 1971. Proc. Soc. Exp. Biol. Med. 136:632.

[6] Boquist, L. 1967. Acta Soc. Med. Upsal. 72:358.

[7] Butler, D. G. 1968. Gen. Comp. Endocrinol. 10:85.

[8] Chavin, W., and J. E. Young. 1970. Comp. Biochem. Physiol. 33:629.

[9] Chez, R. A., et al. 1970. J. Clin. Invest. 49:1517.

[10] Chick, W. L., and A. A. Like. 1970. Diabetologia 6:243.

[11] Chinard, F. P., et al. 1956. J. Physiol. (London) 132:289.

[12] Coldman, M. F., and W. Good. 1967. Comp. Biochem. Physiol. 21:201.

[13] Conway, M. J., et al. 1969. J. Clin. Invest. 48:1349.

[14] Copland, D. L., and R. DeRoss. 1971. J. Exp. Zool. 178:35.

[15] Correa, P. R., et al. 1960. Endocrinology 66:731.

[16] Coulson, R. A., et al. 1950. Proc. Soc. Exp. Biol. Med. 73:203.

[17] Dawson, R. M. C., and N. Freinkel. 1961. Biochem. J. 78:606.

[18] Dean, J. M., and C. J. Goodnight. 1964. Physiol. Zool. 37:280.

[19] Deichmann, W. B., and M. Dierker. 1946. J. Biol. Chem. 163:753.

[20] DeOya, M., et al. 1971. Amer. J. Physiol. 221:25.

[21] DeOya, M., et al. 1971. Proc. Soc. Exp. Biol. Med. 136:107.

[22] Dessauer, H. C. 1952. Ibid. 80:742.

[23] Dessauer, H. C. 1970. In C. Gans and T. S. Parsons, ed. Biology of the Reptilia. Academic Press, New York. pp. 1-72.

[24] Falkmer, S. 1961. Acta Endocrinol. 37(Suppl. 59):1.

[25] Falkmer, S., and A. J. Matty. 1966. Gen. Comp. Endocrinol. 6:334.

[26] Fontaine, M., and J. Hatey. 1963. Physiol. Comp. Oecol. 3:37.

[27] Fox, R. R., et al. 1970. J. Hered. 61:261.

[28] Freeman, B. M. 1967. Comp. Biochem. Physiol. 20:179.

[29] Freeman, B. M. 1969. Ibid. 30:993.

[30] Freeman, B. M. 1970. Ibid. 34:871.

[31] Frye, B. E. 1964. J. Exp. Zool. 155:215.

[32] Galster, W. A., and P. Morrison. 1970. Amer. J. Physiol. 218:1228.

[33] Goodwin, R. F. W. 1956. J. Physiol. (London) 134:88.

[34] Grande, F. 1969. Proc. Soc. Exp. Biol. Med. 131:740.

[35] Grande, F. 1970. Ibid. 133:540.

[36] Grande, F. 1971. Ibid. 137:548.

[37] Grande, F. Unpublished. Mt. Sinai Hospital, Minneapolis, Minn., 1972.

[38] Grant, B. F., et al. 1970. Comp. Biochem. Physiol. 37:321.

[39] Grant, W. C., Jr., et al. 1969. Physiol. Zool. 42:231.

[40] Green, H. N., et al. 1949. J. Pathol. Bacteriol. 61:101.

[41] Haggag, G., et al. 1966. Comp. Biochem. Physiol. 17:341.

[42] Hanke, W., and K. H. Leist. 1971. Gen. Comp. Endocrinol. 16:137.

[43] Hanke, W., et al. 1969. Z. Vergl. Physiol. 65:351.

[44] Heath, D. F., and J. G. Rose. 1969. Biochem. J. 112:373.

[45] Heistand, W. A., et al. 1947. Proc. Soc. Exp. Biol. Med. 65:324.

[46] Hermansen, B., and C. B. Jorgenson. 1969. Gen. Comp. Endocrinol. 12:313.

[47] Hernandez, T., and R. A. Coulson. 1951. Proc. Soc. Exp. Biol. Med. 76:175.

[48] Herrera, E., and N. Freinkel. 1968. Biochim. Biophys. Acta 170:244.

[49] Herrera, E., et al. 1969. J. Clin. Invest. 48:2260.

[50] Hetenyi, G., Jr., et al. 1972. Brit. Med. J. 2:625.

[51] Hinkley, C. M., et al. 1969. Amer. J. Obstet. Gynecol. 104:893.

[52] Houssay, B. A., and J. C. Penhos. 1960. Acta Endocrinol. 35:313.

[53] Howland, R. J. Unpublished. Univ. Surrey, Guilford, England, 1972.

continued

[54] Hutton, K. E. 1960. Copeia (4):360.

[55] Hutton, K. E. 1964. Herpetologica 20:129.

[56] Hutton, K. E. 1968. U.S. Fish Wildl. Serv. Fish. Bull. 66:195.

[57] Hutton, K. E., and C. J. Goodnight. 1957. Physiol. Zool. 30:198.

[58] Jarret, I. G., et al. 1964. Biochem. J. 90:189.

[59] Johnson, D. D. 1950. Endocrinology 46:135.

[60] Laird, C. W., ed. 1971. Proc. Hycel's Annu. Vet. Symp., Houston, 1st.

[61] Langslow, D. R., et al. 1970. J. Endocrinol. 46: 243.

[62] Lavine, R. L., et al. 1971. Diabetes 20:134.

[63] MacKay, W. C., and D. D. Beatty. 1968. Can. J. Zool. 46:797.

[64] McCandless, E. L., and J. A. Dye. 1950. Amer. J. Physiol. 162:434.

[65] Miller, M. R., and D. H. Wurster. 1956. Endocrinology 58:114.

[66] Motelica, I. 1965. Rev. Roum. Biol., Ser. Zool. 10: 159.

[67] Musacchia, X. J., and A. H. Hartner. 1970. Proc. Soc. Exp. Biol. Med. 135:307.

[68] Musacchia, X. J., and C. G. Wilber. 1952. J. Mammal. 33:356.

[69] Olsen, R. E. 1971. Proc. Hycel's Annu. Vet. Symp., Houston, 1st, p.

[70] Oppelt, W. W., et al. 1963. Life Sci. 7:497.

[71] Patent, G. J. 1970. Gen. Comp. Endocrinol. 14: 215.

[72] Pierce, K. 1971. Proc. Hycel's Annu. Vet. Symp., Houston, 1st, p.

[73] Prado, J. L. 1946. Mem. Inst. Butantan 19:59.

[74] Rapatz, G. L., and X. J. Musacchia. 1957. Amer. J. Physiol. 188:456.

[75] Renfree, M. B. 1970. J. Reprod. Fert. 22:483.

[76] Renfree, M. B. 1972. Ph.D. Thesis. Australian National Univ., Zoology Dep., Canberra.

[77] Robertson, O. H., et al. 1961. Endocrinology 68: 733.

[78] Rodriguez-Torres, R., and S. Berkovich. 1968. Med. Surg. 26:40.

[79] Schmidt, S. L., et al. 1970. Diabetologia 6:154.

[80] Schultheiss, H. 1970. Thesis. Univ. Frankfurt am Main, Zool. Inst., Germany.

[81] Shetlar, M. R., et al. 1950. Cancer Res. 10:445.

[82] Smith, C. J., and P. C. Kellcher. 1969. Comp. Biochem. Physiol. 28:1467.

[83] Sullivan, R. E., and F. G. Everett. 1952. J. Dent. Res. 31:151.

[84] Taft, S. T. 1969. Summer Report. Jackson Laboratory, Bar Harbor, Maine.

[85] Tashima, L., and G. F. Cahill, Jr. 1968. Gen. Comp. Endocrinol. 11:262.

[86] Twente, J. W., and J. A. Twente. 1967. J. Mammal. 48:381.

[87] Twiest, G., and C. J. Smith. 1970. Comp. Biochem. Physiol. 32:371.

[88] Umminger, B. L. 1969. J. Exp. Zool. 172:409.

[89] Umminger, B. L. 1971. Comp. Biochem. Physiol. 38A:141.

[90] Umminger, B. L. 1971. Physiol. Zool. 44:20.

[91] Werner, I. 1949. Acta Physiol. Scand. 19:27.

[92] Wilson, R. B., et al. 1971. Diabetes 20:151.

[93] Wright, P. A. 1959. Endocrinology 64:551.

[94] Wurster, D. H., and M. R. Miller. 1960. Comp. Biochem. Physiol. 1:101.

[95] Young, J. W., et al. 1970. J. Nutr. 100:1267.

[96] Zain-ul-Abedein, M., and M. H. Qazi. 1965. Can. J. Biochem. Physiol. 43:831.

[97] Zelnicek, E. 1968. Comp. Biochem. Physiol. 25: 1117.

252. ACID-BASE BALANCE OF BLOOD AND PLASMA: MAN

Part I. Acid-Base and Blood Gas Values for Various Ages

All values refer to blood at 37°C. The source of blood was arterial, unless otherwise indicated. "Excess base concentration" of blood ($\Delta c_{\text{base (B)}}$) is the concentration of titratable base minus the concentration of titratable acid when titrating the blood with strong acid or base to a plasma pH of 7.40, at a carbon dioxide pressure of 40 mm Hg and a temperature of 37°C. The excess base concentration of blood can be derived approximately by means of the following equation: $\Delta c_{\text{base (B)}} = [1 - 0.023 \text{ (liter/mmole)} \cdot c_{\text{Hb (B)}}] \cdot [\Delta c_{\text{HCO}_3^- \text{(Pl)}} + (2.30 c_{\text{Hb (B)}} + 7.7 \text{ mmoles/liter}) \cdot \Delta \text{pH(Pl)}]$, where $c_{\text{Hb (B)}}$ is hemoglobin concentration

in blood, $\Delta c_{\text{HCO}_3^- \text{(Pl)}}$ is excess bicarbonate concentration in plasma and is equal to $c_{\text{HCO}_3^- \text{(Pl)}} - 24.1$ mmoles/liter, and $\Delta \text{pH(Pl)}$ is equal to plasma pH − 7.40. "Standard bicarbonate concentration" ($c_{\text{HCO}_3^- \text{(Pl)}}$) is the concentration of bicarbonate in the plasma phase of blood equilibrated with a gas mixture where carbon dioxide pressure is 40 mm Hg, oxygen pressure is greater than 100 mm Hg, and temperature is 37°C. *Abbreviation:* Hb = hemoglobin (molecular weight = 16,114 g/mole). Values in parentheses are ranges, estimate "b" unless otherwise indicated (*see* Introduction).

continued

Part I. Acid-Base and Blood Gas Values for Various Ages

	Subjects	Variable	Value	Reference
			Blood	
1	1-7 da old, ♂♀	Hb concentration	(8.6-11.4) mmoles/liter	10
2		CO_2 pressure	(26.1-44.7) mm Hg	4
3		Total CO_2 concentration	(11.0-19.6) mmoles/liter[1]	10
4		Excess base concentration	(−6.1 to +2.7) mmoles/liter	4
5	1-4 wk old, ♂♀	Hb concentration	(6.5-11.7) mmoles/liter	7
6		O_2 pressure	(71-101) mm Hg	
7		O_2 saturation fraction (Hb)	(0.90-1.00)	
8		CO_2 pressure	(29-45) mm Hg	
9		Excess base concentration	(−7 to +1) mmoles/liter[1]	
10	4-16 mo old, ♂♀	Hb concentration	(4.5-7.8) mmoles/liter	7
11		O_2 pressure	(55-101) mm Hg	
12		O_2 saturation fraction (Hb)	(0.86-0.99)	
13		CO_2 pressure	(25-40) mm Hg	
14		Excess base concentration	(−5 to +2) mmoles/liter[1]	
15	3 mo-3 yr old, ♂♀	CO_2 pressure	(27-45) mm Hg	11
16		Excess base concentration	(−6.8 to +0.6) mmoles/liter	
17	3-15 yr old, ♂♀	Hb concentration	(4.2-11.0) mmoles/liter	3
18		CO_2 pressure	(31-44) mm Hg	11
19		Total CO_2 concentration	(18.2-23.4) mmoles/liter	3
20		Excess base concentration	(−3.6 to +3.0) mmoles/liter	11
21	Adult, ♂	Erythrocyte packed volume	(40-54) ml/100 ml	2
22		Hb concentration	(8.7-11.1) mmoles/liter	2
23		O_2 pressure	(74-110) mm Hg	6
24		O_2 saturation fraction (Hb)	(0.934-0.978)	9
25		CO_2 pressure	(35-45) mm Hg	8
26		Total CO_2 concentration	(19.2-24.0) mmoles/liter[1]	8
27		Excess base concentration	(−1.0 to +3.1) mmoles/liter	8
28	♀	Erythrocyte packed volume	(37-47) ml/100 ml	2
29		Hb concentration	(7.4-9.9) mmoles/liter	2
30		O_2 pressure	(74-110) mm Hg	6
31		O_2 saturation fraction (Hb)	(0.934-0.978)	9
32		CO_2 pressure	(32-43) mm Hg	8
33		Total CO_2 concentration	(18.2-24.0) mmoles/liter[1]	8
34		Excess base concentration	(−1.8 to +2.8) mmoles/liter	8
35	♂♀[2]	Erythrocyte packed volume	(37-54) ml/100 ml	2
36		Hb concentration	(7.4-11.1) mmoles/liter	2
37		O_2 pressure	36 mm Hg[3]	8
38		O_2 saturation fraction (Hb)	0.7[3]	8
39		CO_2 pressure	(37-51) mm Hg[1]	5
40		Total CO_2 concentration	(19.9-25.1) mmoles/liter[1]	5
41		Excess base concentration	(−1.0 to +4.5) mmoles/liter[1]	5
			Plasma	
42	1-7 da old, ♂♀	pH	(7.33-7.52)	4
43		Total CO_2 concentration	(14.5-23.5) mmoles/liter[1]	10
44		HCO_3^- concentration	(13.7-22.3) mmoles/liter[1]	4
45		Standard HCO_3^- concentration	(16-25) mmoles/liter[1]	4

[1] Estimated or calculated value. [2] Source was venous blood. [3] Estimated value for mixed venous blood.

continued

Part I. Acid-Base and Blood Gas Values for Various Ages

	Subjects	Variable	Value	Reference
46	1-4 wk old, ♂♀	pH	(7.33-7.45)	7
47		Total CO_2 concentration	(17.5-26.2) mmoles/liter[1]	
48		HCO_3^- concentration	(16.6-25.0) mmoles/liter[1]	
49		Standard HCO_3^- concentration	(17.8-24.4) mmoles/liter	
50	4-16 mo old, ♂♀	pH	(7.38-7.51)	7
51		Total CO_2 concentration	(18.0-27.0) mmoles/liter[1]	
52		HCO_3^- concentration	(17.2-25.8) mmoles/liter[1]	
53		Standard HCO_3^- concentration	(19.0-23.0) mmoles/liter	
54	3 mo-3 yr old, ♂♀	pH	(7.32-7.44)	11
55		Total CO_2 concentration	22.1 mmoles/liter[1]	
56		HCO_3^- concentration	21.0 mmoles/liter[1]	
57		Standard HCO_3^- concentration	(18.5-24.5) mmoles/liter	
58	3-15 yr old, ♂♀	pH	(7.35-7.48)	11
59		Total CO_2 concentration	(21.0-28.3) mmoles/liter[1]	
60		HCO_3^- concentration	(20.0-27.0) mmoles/liter[1]	
61		Standard HCO_3^- concentration	(21.1-26.8) mmoles/liter	
62	Adult, ♂	pH	(7.38-7.45)	8
63		Total CO_2 concentration	(23.8-29.0) mmoles/liter	
64		HCO_3^- concentration	(22.7-27.8) mmoles/liter	
65		Standard HCO_3^- concentration	(23.2-26.8) mmoles/liter	
66	♀	pH	(7.39-7.46)	8
67		Total CO_2 concentration	(22.3-28.3) mmoles/liter	
68		HCO_3^- concentration	(21.2-27.0) mmoles/liter	
69		Standard HCO_3^- concentration	(22.8-26.4) mmoles/liter	
70	♂♀[2]	pH	(7.35-7.44)	5
71		Total CO_2 concentration	(24.2-30.5) mmoles/liter[1]	5
72		HCO_3^- concentration	(23.0-29.0) mmoles/liter[1]	5
73		Standard HCO_3^- concentration	(18.5-26.5) mmoles/liter	1

[1] Estimated or calculated value. [2] Source was venous blood.

Contributor: Siggaard-Andersen, Ole

References

[1] Funder, J., and J. O. Wieth. 1966. Scand. J. Clin. Lab. Invest. 18:167.

[2] Hathaway, W. E. 1971. In P. L. Altman and D. S. Dittmer, ed. Respiration and Circulation. Federation of American Societies for Experimental Biology, Bethesda, Md. pp. 147-148.

[3] Kennedy, C., and L. Sokoloff. 1957. J. Clin. Invest. 36:1130.

[4] Kildeberg, P. 1968. Clinical Acid-Base Physiology. E. Munksgaard, Copenhagen.

[5] Leeuwen, A. M. van. 1964. Net Cation Equivalency ("Base Binding Power") of the Plasma Proteins. Scheltema and Holkema, Amsterdam.

[6] Mellemgaard, K. 1966. Acta Physiol. Scand. 67:10.

[7] Riegel, K. 1963. Klin. Wochenschr. 41:249.

[8] Siggaard-Andersen, O. 1974. The Acid-Base Status of the Blood. Rev. ed. Williams and Wilkins, Baltimore.

[9] Siggaard-Andersen, O., et al. 1972. Clin. Chim. Acta 42:85.

[10] Singer, R. B. 1964. In P. L. Altman and D. S. Dittmer, ed. Biology Data Book. Federation of American Societies for Experimental Biology, Washington, D. C. p. 259.

[11] Várrová, V., et al. 1969. Poumon Coeur 25:1121.

continued

Part II. Acid-Base Values for Normal Human Plasma and Erythrocyte Fluid

All values are assumed to refer to arterial blood at 37°C, although some of the values were actually measured on venous blood, e.g., sodium ion, potassium ion, and chloride ion concentrations, and others. **Specification:** c = molar concentration; P = (partial) pressure; Pr = protein (total); tCO_2 = total carbon dioxide; $\Delta pH(Pl)$ = plasma pH − 7.40; m = molality; Pr^- = net protein anion; ρ = mass concentration. *Abbreviation:* Pl = plasma.

	Constituent	Variable	Specification	System	Value mmole/liter[1]	Reference
1	Bicarbonate	Molar concentration	Includes carbonate & carbamate	Pl	25.2 ± 1.3	9
2			Includes carbonate	RBC	13.0	9
3	Buffer, non-bicar-	Buffer value, β	$\beta = dc_{base}/dpH$. $P_{CO_2} = 0$, i.e., the sys-	Pl	7.7	9
4	bonate		tem is bicarbonate-free	RBC	64	9
5	Carbamate	Molar concentration	Carbamate is CO_2 bound primarily to	Pl	0.2	9
6			terminal amino groups of the peptide chains: $Pr-NH-COO^-$	RBC	0.8; 2.4[2]	10
7	Carbon dioxide	Molar concentration	Includes H_2CO_3	Pl	1.2 ± 0.12	9
8				RBC	1.0	9
9		Solubility coefficient, α	$\alpha = c/P$	Pl	0.0306 ± 0.0002 mmole· liter^{-1}·mm Hg^{-1}	2
10				RBC	0.026 mmole·liter^{-1}·mm Hg^{-1}	11
11	Total	Molar concentration	$c_{tCO_2(RBC)}/c_{tCO_2(Pl)} = 0.590 - 0.2913 \times$	Pl	26.4 ± 1.3	9
12			$\Delta pH(Pl) - 0.0844\ [\Delta pH(Pl)]^2$, for oxygenated blood	RBC	15.6	7
13	Carbonic acid	First apparent dissociation constant, pK_1' (overall)	$pK_1' = -\log(a_{H^+}\cdot c_{HCO_3^-}/c_{CO_2})$, where a_{H^+} = hydrogen ion activity	Pl	6.103 ± 0.002[3]	9
14				RBC	6.10; 6.12[2,3]	10
15	Chloride	Molar concentration	$m_{Cl^-(RBC)}/m_{Cl^-(Pl)} = 3.319 - [0.359$	Pl	106.0 ± 1.7	6
16			$pH(Pl)]$, for oxygenated blood	RBC	54	5
17	2,3-Diphospho-	Molar concentration	Charge number = 4.1 at pH(RBC) = 7.2	Pl	0	1
18	glycerate			RBC	4.5 ± 0.5	3
19	Hydrogen ion	pH	pH(RBC) = 7.19 + 0.77 $\Delta pH(Pl)$, for	Pl	7.415 ± 0.025[3,4]	9
20			oxygenated blood	RBC	7.205 ± 0.025[4]; 7.240[2,3]	9
21	Potassium ion	Molar concentration	....	Pl	3.7 ± 0.31	6
22			Corrected for 3.19% trapped plasma	RBC	102 ± 4	6
23	Protein	Mass concentration	....	Pl	68.3 ± 3.7 g/liter	8
24			Mainly hemoglobin	RBC	328 ± 14 g/liter	4
25	Net protein anion	Molar concentration	$c_{Pr^-}/\rho_{Pr} = 103(pH - 5.66)$ mmole/kg	Pl	12.5 ± 1.3	8
26			....	RBC	30	9
27	Sodium ion	Molar concentration	....	Pl	139.4 ± 3.1	6
28			Corrected for 3.19% trapped plasma	RBC	7.4 ± 0.9	6
29	Water	Mass concentration	$\rho_{H_2O(Pl)} = 995.3$ g/liter − 0.814 $\rho_{Pr(Pl)}$	Pl	940 ± 7 g/liter	8
30			....	RBC	726 ± 10 g/liter	6

[1] Unless otherwise specified. [2] Completely deoxygenated. [3] Dimensionless quantity. [4] ± one standard deviation.

Contributor: Siggaard-Andersen, Ole

References

[1] Alberti, K. G., et al. 1972. Lancet 2:7774.
[2] Bartels, H., and R. Wrbitzky. 1960. Pfluegers Arch. Gesamte Physiol. Menschen Tiere 271:162.
[3] Bauer, C., and E. Schröder. 1972. J. Physiol. (London) 227:457.
[4] Dittrich, H. 1963. Med. Klin. (Munich) 58:1882.

continued

Part II. Acid-Base Values for Normal Human Plasma and Erythrocyte Fluid

[5] Funder, J., and J. O. Wieth. 1966. Acta Physiol. Scand. 68:234.

[6] Funder, J., and J. O. Wieth. 1966. Scand. J. Clin. Lab. Invest. 18:167.

[7] Kelman, G. R. 1967. Resp. Physiol. 3:111.

[8] Leeuwen, A. M. van. 1964. Net Cation Equivalency ("Base Binding Power") of the Plasma Proteins. Scheltema and Holkema, Amsterdam.

[9] Siggaard-Andersen, O. 1974. The Acid-Base Status of the Blood. Rev. ed. Williams and Wilkins, Baltimore.

[10] Siggaard-Andersen, O., et al. 1972. Scand. J. Clin. Lab. Invest. 29:303.

[11] Van Slyke, D. D., et al. 1928. J. Biol. Chem. 78:765.

Part III. Siggaard-Andersen Alignment Nomogram

This chart is the most commonly used and convenient method of computing the metabolic, or nonrespiratory, component of acid-base abnormalities. A straight line drawn through observed values for pH and carbon dioxide pressure (P_{CO_2}), measured at 37-38°C, intersects the vertical hemoglobin concentration lines of the grid at the value for base excess (BE). Base excess, or deficit, is the concentration difference from the normal value of whole blood buffer base, in milliequivalents per liter of blood; it equals the number of milliequivalents of strong acid or base which would be required to titrate the blood to pH 7.4 while continuously equilibrating the blood with a gas containing a P_{CO_2} of 40 mm Hg and an oxygen pressure (P_{O_2}) which holds the O_2 saturation constant at 37°C. If pH and P_{CO_2} are known at some other temperature, correct them to 37°C, using Table 262 for P_{CO_2} and the formula $\Delta pH = -0.0147\Delta T$, where T = temperature.

To Determine Base Excess: If the Astrup equilibration method has been used to prepare blood of known P_{CO_2} at 37-38°C, the known P_{CO_2} and measured pH may be used to determine base excess. However, base excess is decreased by the equilibration if O_2 saturation is increased, with a change of 0.3 meq/liter per g saturated Hb/100 ml.

Example: P_{O_2} = 36, pH = 7.50, Hb = 18 g. After equilibration at 37°C with P_{CO_2} = 20, pH = 7.66. Compute BE. From P_{CO_2} and pH values, BE of sample saturated by equilibration = +5.0. From Table 261 f_{pH} = 1.12; 1.12 × 36 = 40.4, and this saturation = 75%. The change in saturation is 25% during equilibration, and this is 0.25 × 18 = 4.5 g Hb. The change in BE during the equilibration was 0.2 × 4.5 = 0.9 meq/liter. The BE of the original sample was +5.0 + 0.9 = 5.9 meq/liter.

To Predict Buffer Base: This nomogram may also be used to predict the buffer base of the blood which would exist in vivo if P_{CO_2} were altered and, especially, restored to a normal value of 40 mm Hg. When P_{CO_2} is altered in vivo by ventilatory changes, the base of the blood exchanges with extracellular fluid. Since extracellular fluid lacks protein buffers (in particular, hemoglobin), the blood in vivo behaves in the same manner as blood in vitro diluted to about one-fourth to one-third of its actual hemoglobin concentration. As P_{CO_2} is changed in vivo, straight lines through values for simultaneously sampled pH and P_{CO_2} all pivot, or intersect, on a hemoglobin line of one-fourth or one-third of the actual blood hemoglobin value. To estimate base excess which would be found in vivo after correcting P_{CO_2} to 40 mm Hg, draw a straight line through pH and P_{CO_2} values and find its intersection with one-third of the actual hemoglobin value; then, from this intersection, draw a straight line to P_{CO_2} = 40 mm Hg, and read the base excess where this new line intersects the actual hemoglobin value.

Example: At 37°C, P_{CO_2} = 80.0, pH = 6.92, Hb = 15 g. Compute base excess of sample and of predicted in vivo blood after correction of P_{CO_2} to 40. BE of sample = −20.4. Pivot point at 5 g Hb = −15.2. Predicted normocapnic base excess at 15 g Hb = −17.0. Predicted pH at P_{CO_2} = 40 is 7.11. Standard bicarbonate predicted in vivo = 12. Sample plasma HCO_3^- = 15.2. Sample standard HCO_3^- determined in vitro = 10.4 meq/liter. Of these numbers, the predicted in vivo BE of −15.2 meq/liter most closely approximates the magnitude of the metabolic acid-base abnormality in the extracellular fluid.

Contributor: Severinghaus, John W.

Reference: Siggaard-Andersen, O. 1963. Scand. J. Clin. Lab. Invest. 15:211.

continued

Part III. Siggaard-Andersen Alignment Nomogram

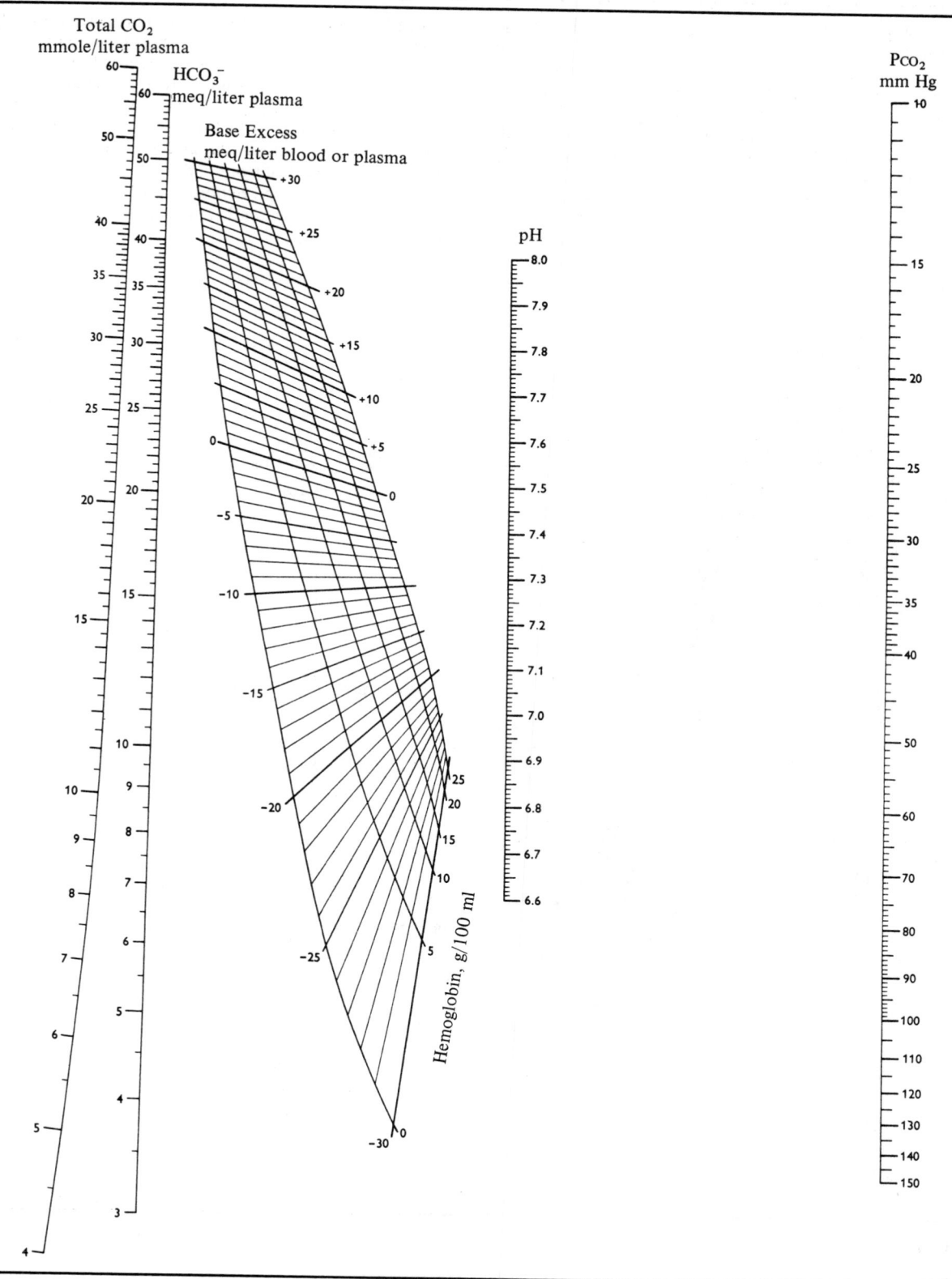

continued

252. ACID-BASE BALANCE OF BLOOD AND PLASMA: MAN

Part IV. Singer-Hastings Nomogram

For oxygenated blood at 37°C (scales 1-5), a straight line through points on two of the scales intersects the remaining scales at simultaneously occurring values for other variables. The position of this line indicates the kind and magnitude of any disturbance of the acid-base balance (as indicated by proximity of line to conditions shown in small capital letters). For venous blood, or blood with an O_2 saturation of less than 90%, the true values of whole blood carbon dioxide, $(CO_2)_B$, and buffer base, $(BB)_B$, rarely differ by more than 2 mmole/liter or 3 meq/liter, respectively, from those values obtained by means of the nomogram. Scales 5, 6, and 7 may be used to correct for this

effect of O_2 unsaturation. Use scales 6 and 7 with P_{CO_2} only to obtain factors for correction of whole blood buffer base (f_{BB}) from scale 3 and whole blood carbon dioxide (f_{CO_2}) from scale 1 when blood is not fully oxygenated, by using the formulas $(CO_2)_{B\ (corrected)} = (CO_2)_B + (f_{CO_2} \cdot U \cdot Hct)$ and $(BB)_{B\ (corrected)} = (BB)_B - (f_{BB} \cdot U \cdot Hct)$, where U ($O_2$ unsaturation) $= 1 - (\%$ saturation/100) and Hct (hematocrit) $= \%$ RBC's/100. The normal range, indicated by broken lines, is for arterial blood. *Abbreviations:* $(HCO_3^-)_P$ = plasma bicarbonate; pH_P = plasma pH; $(H_2CO_3)_P$ = plasma carbonic acid.

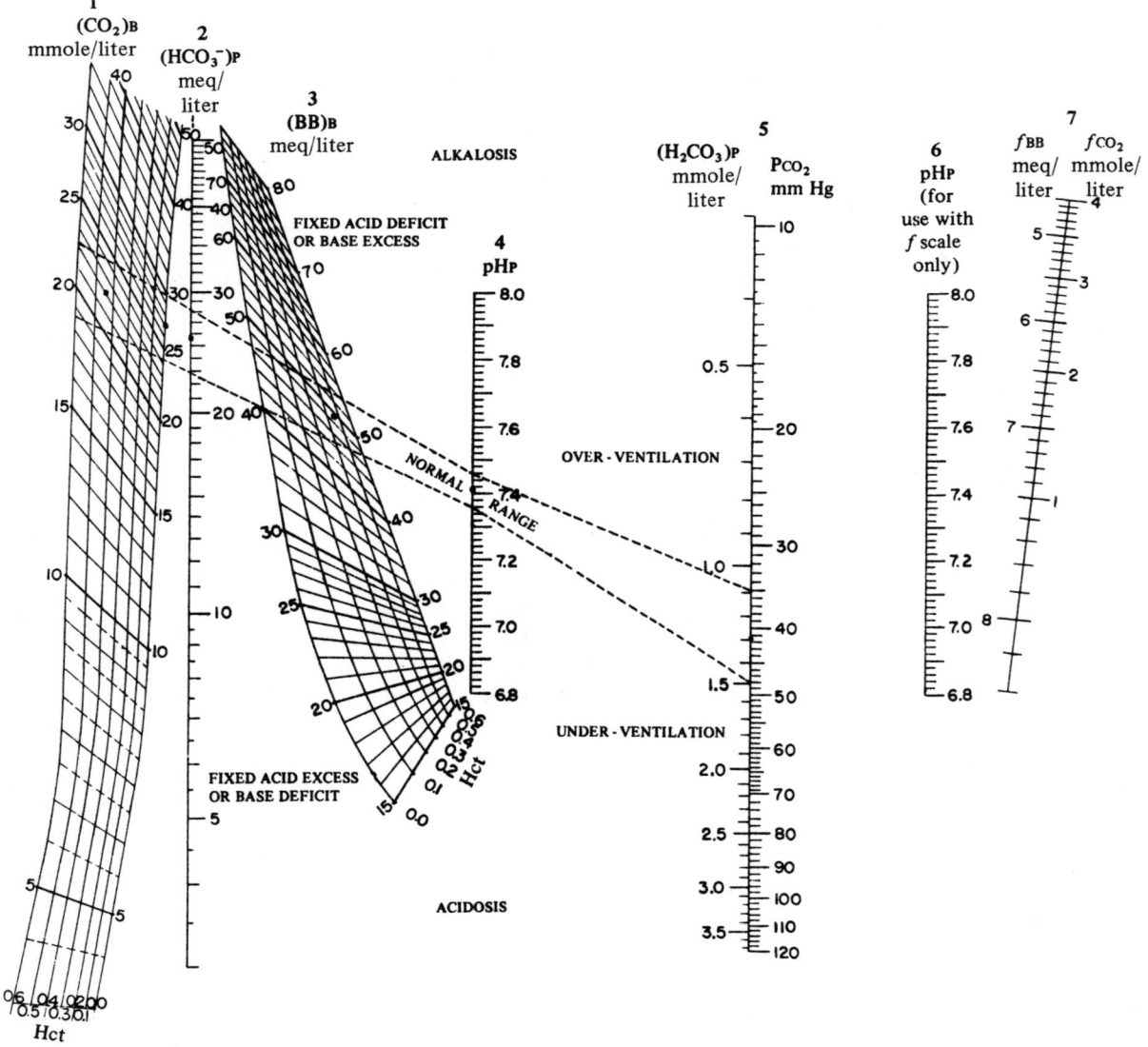

Contributor: Severinghaus, John W.

Reference: Singer, R. B., and A. B. Hastings. 1948. Medicine (Baltimore) 27:223.

continued

252. ACID-BASE BALANCE OF BLOOD AND PLASMA: MAN

Part V. Normal Ionic Patterns in Arterial Blood

Values are for adult males, and are based on the literature. Values are concentrations of the constituents multiplied by their charge number, in mmole/liter. X⁻ = undetermined anion residue (mainly sulfate, lactate, and non-esterified carboxylate). 2,3-DPG = 2,3-diphosphoglycerate. HbO₂⁻ includes the undetermined anions of the erythrocyte fluid.

The concentration of "Buffer base" is equivalent to the sum of the concentrations of buffer anions, i.e., proteinate, bicarbonate, hemoglobinate, organic phosphate, and other buffer anions. Changes in the buffer base concentration equal changes in excess base concentration (*see* Part I).

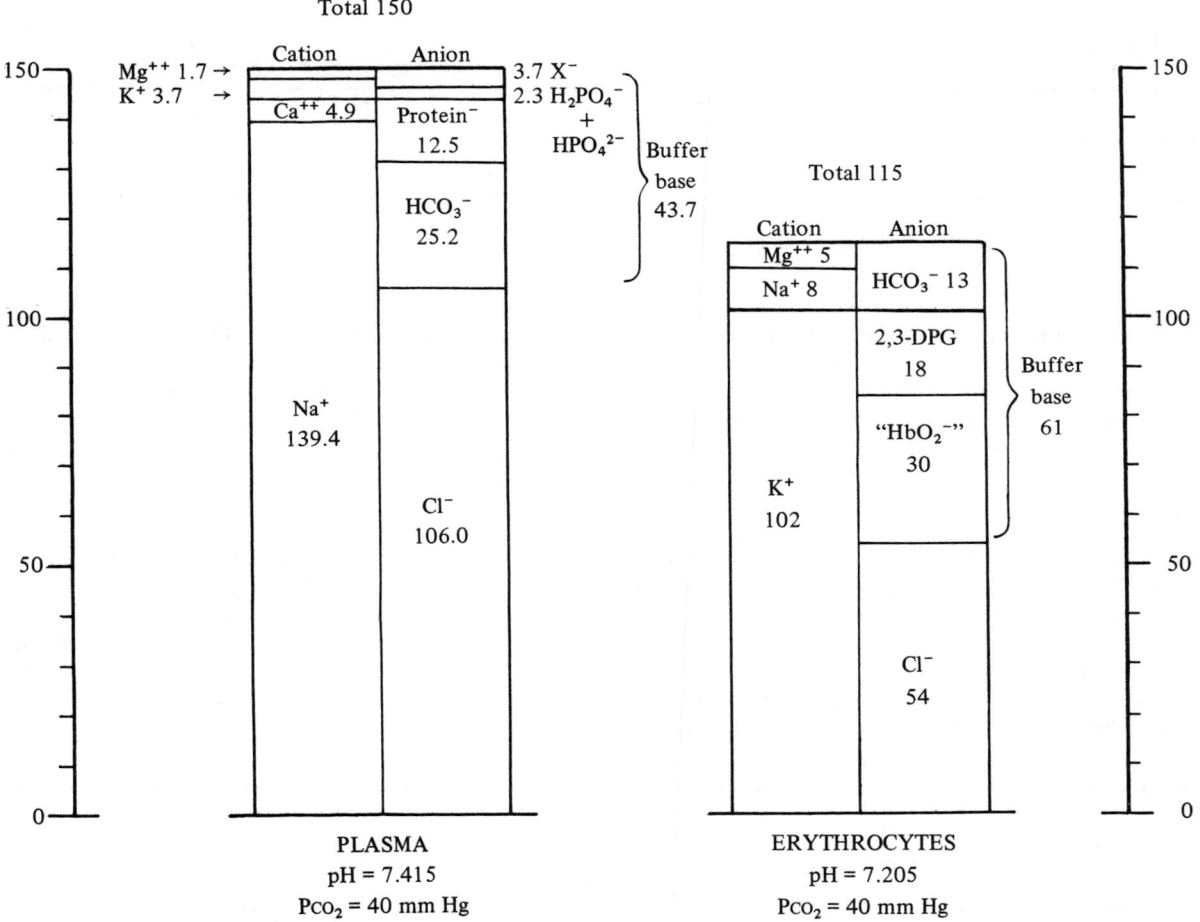

Contributors: Singer, Richard B.; Siggaard-Andersen, Ole

General References

[1] Siggaard-Andersen, O. Unpublished. Rigshospitalet, Copenhagen, Denmark, 1974.

[2] Singer, R. B. 1961. In P. L. Altman and D. S. Dittmer, ed. Blood and Other Body Fluids. Federation of American Societies for Experimental Biology, Washington, D. C. p. 189.

continued

252. ACID-BASE BALANCE OF BLOOD AND PLASMA: MAN

Part VI. Temperature Variation of Some Acid-Base Quantities

Equation of Temperature Variation: Pl = plasma; T = temperature of system in degrees Kelvin (°K); and $\Delta T = T - 273.15$, in °K.

	Dependent Variable	System	Equation of Temperature Variation
1	pH	Blood, plasma phase	$dpH(Pl)/dT = -0.015/°K$
2		Plasma	$dpH/dT = -0.012/°K$
3	Carbon dioxide pressure [Pco_2], in	Blood	$d\log Pco_2/dT = 0.021/°K$
4	mm Hg	Plasma	$d\log Pco_2/dT = 0.019/°K$
5	Solubility coefficient [α_{CO_2}], in mmole·liter^{-1}·mm Hg^{-1}	Plasma	$\log(\alpha_{CO_2}) = \log 0.0306 - 0.0092(\Delta T) + 0.00009(\Delta T)^2$
6	First apparent dissociation constant for carbonic acid [pK_1']	Plasma	$pK_1' = 6.125 + \log[1 + \exp(pH - 8.7)] - 0.0026(\Delta T) + 0.00012(\Delta T)^2$

Contributor: Siggaard-Andersen, Ole

Reference: Siggaard-Andersen, O. 1974. The Acid-Base Status of the Blood. Rev. ed. Williams and Wilkins, Baltimore.

253. ACID-BASE BALANCE OF BLOOD AND PLASMA: DOMESTIC AND LABORATORY ANIMALS

All values refer to the actual temperature of the animal. **Blood Source:** A = arterial; V = venous. Figures in heavy brackets are reference numbers. Values in parentheses are ranges, estimate "b" unless otherwise indicated (*see* Introduction).

Part I. Blood

Hb = hemoglobin (molecular weight = 16,114 g/mole). **Excess Base Concentration** ($\Delta c_{base(B)}$) is the concentration of titratable base minus the concentration of titratable acid when titrating the blood with strong acid or base to a plasma pH of 7.40, at a carbon dioxide pressure of 40 mm Hg and a temperature of 37°C. The excess base concentration of the blood can be derived approximately by means of the following equation: $\Delta c_{base(B)} = [1 - 0.023 \text{ (liter/mmole)} \cdot c_{Hb(B)}] \cdot [\Delta c_{HCO_3^-(Pl)} + (2.30\, c_{Hb(B)} + 7.7 \text{ mmoles/liter}) \cdot \Delta pH(Pl)]$, where $c_{Hb(B)}$ is hemoglobin concentration in blood, $\Delta c_{HCO_3^-(Pl)}$ is excess bicarbonate concentration in plasma and is equal to $c_{HCO_3^-(Pl)} - 24.1$ mmoles/liter, and $\Delta pH(Pl)$ is equal to plasma pH − 7.40.

	Animal	Specification	Blood Source	Temp, °C	Erythrocyte Packed Volume ml/100 ml blood	Hb Concentration mmole/liter	Po_2 mm Hg	Pco_2 mm Hg	Excess Base Concentration mmole/liter
1	Cat	Adult, ♂♀	A	(38.2-39.6) [11]	....	(4.0-7.2) [11]	(90-126) [11]	(29-37) [11]	−2[1/] [11]
2			V	(38.2-39.6) [11]	40 [17]	6.8 [17]	(32-47) [11]	(35-47) [11]	−2[1/] [11]
3	Cattle	Calf, ♂♀ 7- to 21-da-old	V	(38.0-39.0) [9]	....	....	(7-63) [9]	(42-54) [9]	+3[1/] [9]
4		21-da-old	A	38.5 [18]	(20-49) [7]	....	(78-109) [7]	(36-50) [7]	0[1/] [7]
5		Adult, ♀	V	38.5 [17]	40 [17]	7.0 [17]	....	50[1/] [14]	+3[1/] [14]
6	Dog	Adult, ♂♀	A	(38.6-39.6)[1/] [8]	(27-52) [8]	....	(77-102) [8]	(31-43) [8]	(−4 to +4)[1/] [8]

[1/] Estimated or calculated values.

continued

253. ACID-BASE BALANCE OF BLOOD AND PLASMA: DOMESTIC AND LABORATORY ANIMALS

Part I. Blood

	Animal	Specification	Blood Source	Temp, °C	Erythrocyte Packed Volume ml/100 ml blood	Hb Concentration mmole/liter	Po$_2$ mm Hg	Pco$_2$ mm Hg	Excess Base Concentration mmole/liter
7	Guinea pig	Adult	A	38.6 [10]	42 [1]	8.7 [1]	....	(21-59)[1/] [10]	−3[1/] [10]
8	Horse	Foal, 4- to 42-da-old	V	(37.2-39.1) [16]	....	....	....	(52-60) [16]	+3[1/] [16]
9		Adult	A	37.8 [17]	33 [1]	6.8 [1]	(83-109) [13]	(39-51) [13]	+4[1/] [13]
10	Monkey, rhesus	Adult	A	(37.6-39.2) [15]	....	....	(81-120) [15]	(40-45) [15]	(−0.2 to +9.8) [15]
11	Rabbit	Adult	A	39.6 [3]	42 [3]	....	....	(20-46)[1/] [3]	−8[1/] [3]
12	Rat, albino	Adult	A	38.2 [5]	46 [1]	9.0 [1]	....	(35-49)[1/] [5]	−2[1/] [5]
13	Sheep	♀, pregnant	A	38.5 [4]	....	....	(95-103) [4]	(30-37) [4]	+1[1/] [4]
14		Adult, ♂♀	V	39.1 [6]	32 [1]	7.6 [1]	....	38[1/] [6]	+2[1/] [6]
15	Chicken	♂	A	40 [2]	28.5 [12]	6.0 [12]	(75-105) [2]	(29-39) [2]	+4[1/] [2]

[1/] Estimated or calculated values.

Contributor: Siggaard-Andersen, Ole

References

[1] Albritton, E. C., ed. 1952. Standard Values in Blood. W. B. Saunders, Philadelphia.

[2] Besch, E. L., et al. 1971. Amer. J. Physiol. 220: 1379.

[3] Cole, W. H. 1944. Ibid. 141:165.

[4] Comline, R. S., and M. Silver. 1970. J. Physiol. (London) 209:587.

[5] Cooke, R. E., et al. 1952. J. Clin. Invest. 31:1006.

[6] Denton, D. A., et al. 1952. Acta Med. Scand., Suppl. 261.

[7] Donawick, W. J., and A. E. Baue. 1968. Amer. J. Vet. Res. 29:561.

[8] Feigl, E. O., and L. G. d'Alecy. 1972. J. Appl. Physiol. 32:152.

[9] Gates, J. B., et al. 1971. J. Amer. Vet. Med. Ass. 158:1678.

[10] Hawkins, J. A. 1924. J. Biol. Chem. 61:147.

[11] Herbert, D. A., and R. A. Mitchell. 1971. J. Appl. Physiol. 30:434.

[12] Hodges, R. D. Unpublished. Wye College, Univ. London, 1965.

[13] Littlejohn, A. 1969. Res. Vet. Sci. 10:263.

[14] McSherry, B. J., and J. Grinyer. 1954. Amer. J. Vet. Res. 15:509.

[15] Munson, E. S., et al. 1970. J. Appl. Physiol. 28:108.

[16] Rossdale, P. D., and P. A. Mullen. 1970. Brit. Vet. J. 126:82.

[17] Singer, R. B. 1964. In P. L. Altman and D. S. Dittmer, ed. Biology Data Book. Federation of American Societies for Experimental Biology, Washington, D.C. pp. 259-261.

[18] Tennant, B., et al. 1969. Cornell Vet. 59:594.

Part II. Plasma

	Animal	Specification	Blood Source	Temp, °C	pH	Total CO$_2$ Concentration mmole/liter	HCO$_3^-$ Concentration mmole/liter	Na$^+$ Concentration mmole/liter	Cl$^-$ Concentration mmole/liter	Protein Concentration g/liter
1	Cat	Adult, ♂♀	A	(38.2-39.6) [11]	(7.39-7.46) [11]	(18.3-25.6)[1/] [11]	(17.5-24.5) [11]	....	....	....
2			V	(38.2-39.6) [11]	(7.32-7.40) [11]	(19.0-28.1)[1/] [11]	(18.0-26.8) [11]	(150-156)[1/] [25]	(105-111)[1/] [24]	76 [20]

[1/] Estimated or calculated values.

continued

Part II. Plasma

	Animal	Specification	Blood Source	Temp, °C	pH	Total CO_2 Concentration mmole/liter	HCO_3^- Concentration mmole/liter	Na^+ Concentration mmole/liter	Cl^- Concentration mmole/liter	Protein Concentration g/liter
3	Cattle	Calf, ♂♀ 7- to 21-da-old	V	(38.0-39.0) [9]	(7.30-7.46) [9]	28.9 L/ [9]	27.5 L/ [9]	....	....	....
4		21-da-old	A	38.5 [22]	(7.34-7.42) [7]	24.8 L/ [7]	(19.6-27.6) [7]	....	....	....
5		Adult, ♀	V	38.5 [17]	(7.27-7.49) [15]	(29-33) [15]	....	(132-152) [15]	(97-111) [15]	83 [20]
6	Dog	Adult, ♂♀	A	(38.6-39.6) L/ [8]	(7.34-7.51) [8]	24.5 L/ [8]	23.5 L/ [8]	(139-155) [18]	(106-116) L/ [19]	(50-65) L/ [19]
7	Guinea pig	Adult	A	38.6 [10]	(7.17-7.53) [10]	(18-26) [10]	....	(138-144) [12]	(100-108) [12]	47 [1]
8	Horse	Foal, 4- to 42-da-old	V	(37.2-39.1) [17]	(7.29-7.39) [17]	31.3 L/ [17]	(26.0-33.4) [17]	....	....	....
9		Adult	A	37.8 [17]	(7.37-7.47) [14]	29.6 L/ [14]	(24.3-32.3) [14]	135 [23]	96 [23]	68 [1]
10	Monkey, rhesus	Adult	A	(37.6-39.2) [16]	(7.34-7.58) [16]	29.6 L/ [16]	28.5 L/ [16]	....	....	....
11	Rabbit	Adult	A	39.6 [3]	(7.28-7.36) L/ [3]	(11-25) L/ [3]	17 L/ [3]	(130-146) L/ [3]	(94-114) L/ [3]	62 [3]
12	Rat, albino	Adult	A	38.2 [5]	(7.26-7.44) L/ [5]	(20.0-28.0) L/ [5]	22.8 L/ [5]	(135-155) L/ [5]	(99-112) L/ [5]	63 [21]
13	Sheep	♀, pregnant	A	38.5 [4]	(7.41-7.55) [4]	25.5 L/ [4]	24.6 L/ [4]	....	....	....
14		Adult, ♂♀	V	39.1 [6]	7.44 [6]	26.2 [6]	25.1 L/ [6]	153 [6]	103 [6]	57 [6]
15	Chicken	♂	A	40 [2]	(7.47-7.57) [2]	27.3 L/ [2]	26.5 L/ [2]	154 [12]	117 [12]	52.5 [13]

L/ Estimated or calculated values.

Contributor: Siggaard-Andersen, Ole

References

[1] Albritton, E. C., ed. 1952. Standard Values in Blood. W. B. Saunders, Philadelphia.

[2] Besch, E. L., et al. 1971. Amer. J. Physiol. 220: 1379.

[3] Cole, W. H. 1944. Ibid. 141:165.

[4] Comline, R. S., and M. Silver. 1970. J. Physiol. (London) 209:587.

[5] Cooke, R. E., et al. 1952. J. Clin. Invest. 31:1006.

[6] Denton, D. A., et al. 1952. Acta Med. Scand., Suppl. 261.

[7] Donawick, W. J., and A. E. Baue. 1968. Amer. J. Vet. Res. 29:561.

[8] Feigl, E. O., and L. G. d'Alecy. 1972. J. Appl. Physiol. 32:152.

[9] Gates, J. B., et al. 1971. J. Amer. Vet. Med. Ass. 158:1678.

[10] Hawkins, J. A. 1924. J. Biol. Chem. 61:147.

[11] Herbert, D. A., and R. A. Mitchell. 1971. J. Appl. Physiol. 30:434.

[12] Hernandez, T., and R. A. Coulson. Louisiana State Univ., New Orleans, 1955.

[13] Hodges, R. D. Unpublished. Wye College, Univ. London, 1965.

[14] Littlejohn, A. 1969. Res. Vet. Sci. 10:263.

[15] McSherry, B. J., and J. Grinyer. 1954. Amer. J. Vet. Res. 15:509.

[16] Munson, E. S., et al. 1970. J. Appl. Physiol. 28: 108.

[17] Rossdale, P. D., and P. A. Mullen. 1970. Brit. Vet. J. 126:82.

[18] Safarova, A. A., et al. 1969. Bull. Exp. Biol. Med. (USSR) 68:28.

[19] Siggaard-Andersen, O. 1962. Scand. J. Clin. Lab. Invest., Suppl. 66.

continued

253. ACID-BASE BALANCE OF BLOOD AND PLASMA: DOMESTIC AND LABORATORY ANIMALS

Part II. Plasma

[20] Singer, R. B. 1964. In P. L. Altman and D. S. Dittmer, ed. Biology Data Book. Federation of American Societies for Experimental Biology, Washington, D.C. pp. 259-261.

[21] Smith, P. K., and A. H. Smith. 1934. J. Biol. Chem. 107:673.

[22] Tennant, B., et al. 1969. Cornell Vet. 59:594.

[23] Van Slyke, D. D., et al. 1925. J. Biol. Chem. 65: 701.

[24] Wallace, W. M., and A. B. Hastings. 1942. Ibid. 144: 637.

[25] Yannet, H. 1940. Ibid. 136:265.

254. BLOOD VOLUMES: VERTEBRATES

Part I. Man

Regression Equations: Best fit describing relations between circulating volumes in milliliters of erythrocytes, plasma, and whole blood (V_{RBC}, V_P, and V_{WB}), and common parameters of body size (H, W, and S). **Subjects:** Healthy and unanesthetized infants, children, and adults, at sea level and comfortable environmental temperature, unless otherwise specified. **Method:** ^{51}Cr or ^{32}P = erythrocyte volume calculated from large vessel hematocrit and radioactivity of whole blood samples with ^{51}Cr- or ^{32}P-tagged erythrocytes; EB = plasma volume determined by dilution in plasma or serum of Evans' blue dye; ^{131}I = plasma or blood volume determined by dilution of ^{131}I-labeled human serum albumin in plasma or blood; Hct = large vessel hematocrit (venous or arterial); V_{RBC} = erythrocyte volume, in milliliters; V_P = plasma volume, in milliliters; V_{WB} = whole blood volume, in milliliters. *Abbreviations:* H = height, in centimeters; W = weight, in kilograms; S = body surface area, in square meters, calculated from height and weight by Dubois' equation.

	Subjects			Method	Regression Equation	SD	Reference
	Age, yr	No. & Sex	Specification				
			Erythrocyte Volume, ml				
1	New-born	70♂♀	Infants within 72 hr of birth; gestational age, 220 to 295 da	^{51}Cr[1,2], or calculated[3] from Hct[1,2] & V_P (by EB or ^{131}I)	$89.52W - 7.26W^2 - 60.27$[4,5]	....	3
2	16-77	101♀	....	^{51}Cr[6]	$7.49H + 14.32W - 603$	134	4
3					$1138S - 397$	134	
4	17-71	33♂	Hospital patients, convalescent or free of illness thought likely to affect blood volume	^{51}Cr[1]	$1070S + 56$	218	2
5					$17.3W + 774$	200	
6	19-79	38♀	Hospital patients, convalescent or free of illness thought likely to affect blood volume	^{51}Cr[1]	$749S + 168$	180	2
7					$9.9W + 772$	184	
8	16-40	56♀	Indians from low socio-economic group attending hospital for minor complaints	^{51}Cr[1]	$4.64H + 20.06W - 561$	193	26
9					$1288S$[7]-958	193	
10	20-50	93♂	Indians from low socio-economic group; preoperative cases for minor surgical procedures, & professional blood donors[8]	^{51}Cr[1]	$1.04H + 19.31W + 139$	213	26
11					$982S$[7]$- 320$	221	

[1] Hematocrit corrected for trapped plasma. [2] Hematocrits measured in capillary tubes. [3] Allowance made for a difference between venous and body hematocrit. [4] W = birth weight. [5] Calculations based on original measurements and data from other authors. [6] Hematocrit not corrected for trapped plasma. [7] Surface area calculated from formula of Banerjee [26]. [8] Hemoglobin over 12.0 g/100 g, and no blood donated for at least 10 weeks.

continued

Part I. Man

	Subjects			Method	Regression Equation	SD	Reference
	Age, yr	No. & Sex	Specification				
12	Unspecified	25♂	Healthy Indian volunteers from high socio-economic group	^{51}Cr[1]	$5.82H + 27.74W - 953$	271	26
13	18-21	50♂	Clinically examined healthy Indian medical students, mostly vegetarians	Calculated[3] from Hct[6] & Vp (by EB)	$2.47H + 1223$	....	19
14					$558S + 673$	....	
15	18-20	35♀	Clinically examined healthy Indian medical students, mostly vegetarians	Calculated[3] from Hct[6] & Vp (by EB)	$11.4H + 1242$	....	19
16	19-52	201♂	....	^{51}Cr[6]	$8.6H + 18.6W - 830$	190	27
17					$1550S - 890$	190	
18	19-54	39♂	Ambulatory volunteers; life insurance company employees	^{51}Cr[6]	$16.7W + 894$	257	16
19	70-89	39♂	Active ambulatory Spanish-American War veterans[9]	^{51}Cr[6]	$23.8W + 161.1$	303	16
20	20-64	38♀	....	^{51}Cr[1]	$12.1W + 654$	149	21
21					$16.4H + 5.7W - 1649$	129	
22	22-66	40♂	....	^{51}Cr[1]	$19.2W + 609$	253	21
23					$8.2H + 17.3W - 693$	252	
24	20-74	15♀	....	^{51}Cr[6]	$20.03W + 65$	159	13
25	20-84	17♂	....	^{51}Cr[6]	$14.36W + 822$	255	13
26	22[10]	19♂	Seminary novitiates in good health	^{51}Cr[6]	$25W + 380$	....	17
27	82[10]	91♂	Active ambulatory veterans, some under treatment for chronic disease	^{51}Cr[6]	$17.6W + 521.7$	....	17
28	Unspecified	30♂	Ambulatory patients hospitalized for minor complaints and receiving no medication	^{32}P[1]	$1299S - 469$	206	22
29					$18.6W + 603$	209	
30		30♀	Ambulatory patients hospitalized for minor complaints and receiving no medication	^{32}P[1]	$618.7S + 267$	126	22
31					$8.55W + 751$	136	
32		20♂	Residents for < 1 yr at altitude of 5740 ft	^{51}Cr; Hct[2,6]	$0.00023H^3 + 17W - 210$	....	8
	Plasma Volume, ml						
33	1-17	11♂♀	Healthy volunteers & hospital convalescents; S, between 0.4 & 0.8 m²	EB	$1374S - 162.6$	63	14
34		36♂♀	Healthy volunteers & hospital convalescents; S, between 0.8 & 1.4 m²	EB	$2044S - 650$	148	
35		30♂	Healthy volunteers & hospital convalescents; S, between 1.4 & 2.0 m²	EB	$2457S - 1192$	268	

[1] Hematocrit corrected for trapped plasma. [2] Hematocrits measured in capillary tubes. [3] Allowance made for a difference between venous and body hematocrit. [6] Hematocrit not corrected for trapped plasma. [9] Remeasurements on some members of the octogenarian population reported by Piomelli [17]. [10] Average.

continued

Part I. Man

	Age, yr	No. & Sex	Specification	Method	Regression Equation	SD	Reference
36	3.5-	20♂	Healthy volunteers, mostly chil-	EB[11]	$1587S - 304$	190	5
37	41		dren & youths		$0.007367H + 2.1515$[12]	0.01957[12]	
38		21♀	Healthy volunteers, mostly chil-	EB[11]	$1423S - 194$	169	
39			dren & youths		$0.00698H + 2.1651$[12]	0.0518[12]	
40	14-76	13♂,	Hospital patients free of illness	EB	$1389S + 244$	255	7
41		12♀	thought likely to affect blood volume		$19.5W + 1358$	260	
42	16-40	56♀	Indians from low socio-economic	Calculated[3] from	$1.66H + 34.17W + 319$	346	26
43			group attending hospital for minor complaints	Hct[1] & V$_{RBC}$ (by ^{51}Cr)	$1979S$[7] $- 984$	351	
44	16-77	101♀	....	Calculated[13] from	$9.03H + 24.13W - 766$	209	4
45				Hct[6] & V$_{RBC}$ (by ^{51}Cr)	$1747S - 733$	209	
46	16-90	222♂	....	EB	$31.47W + 927$[5]	437	13
47		135♀	....	EB	$25.86W + 849$[5]	325	
48	17-66	22♂	Ambulatory hospital patients	^{131}I	$2294S - 928$	....	12
49			with disorders not expected to affect blood volume		$34.1W + 890$	....	
50	17-71	30♂	Hospital patients, convalescent	^{131}I	$1846S - 522$	297	2
51			or free of illness thought likely to affect blood volume		$27.2W + 894$	306	
52	19-79	31♀	Hospital patients, convalescent	^{131}I	$1241S + 353$	277	2
53			or free of illness thought likely to affect blood volume		$13.3W + 1540$	296	
54	18-21	50♂	Clinically examined healthy In-	EB	$97.6H - 14,093$	....	19
55			dian medical students, mostly vegetarians		$2110S - 995$	....	
56	18-20	35♀	Clinically examined healthy In- dian medical students, mostly vegetarians	EB	$1.3W + 2415$	....	19
57	19-52	201♂	....	Calculated[13] from	$19.9H + 13.1W - 2000$	240	27
58				Hct[6] & V$_{RBC}$ (by ^{51}Cr)	$1580S - 520$	240	
59	20-50	93♂	Indians from low socio-economic	Calculated[3] from	$13.03H + 35.4W - 1575$	300	26
60			group; preoperative cases for minor surgical procedures, & professional blood donors[8]	Hct[1] & V$_{RBC}$ (by ^{51}Cr)	$1903S$[7] $- 749$	337	
61	Un-spec-ified	25♂	Healthy Indian volunteers from high socio-economic group	Calculated[3] from Hct[1] & V$_{RBC}$ (by ^{51}Cr)	$33.0H + 7.94W - 3414$	411	26
62	20-64	38♀	....	EB	$48.1H - 5550$	203	21
63					$40.5H + 8.4W - 4811$	196	
64	22-66	40♂	....	EB	$30.2H - 2119$	364	21
65					$23.7H + 9W - 1709$	358	

[1] Hematocrit corrected for trapped plasma. [3] Allowance made for a difference between venous and body hematocrit. [5] Calculations based on original measurements and data from other authors. [6] Hematocrit not corrected for trapped plasma. [7] Surface area calculated from formula of Banerjee [26]. [8] Hemoglobin over 12.0 g/100 g, and no blood donated for at least 10 weeks. [11] Vp multiplied by a factor of 0.935 to correct for indicator loss of 6.5%. [12] Equation yields log values. To find SD in milliliters, calculate the log value of the mean predicted volume at a given body size, add or subtract the listed log SD, and take the antilog. The SD is the arithmetic difference between this value and the antilog of the calculated mean volume. [13] No allowance for a difference between venous and body hematocrit.

continued

Part I. Man

	Subjects			Method	Regression Equation	SD	Reference
	Age, yr	No. & Sex	Specification				
66	Adult	32♂	Apparently normal volunteers & hospital outpatients	EB	$32.59W + 1066$	388	24
67		30♂	Ambulatory patients hospitalized for minor complaints and receiving no medication	EB	$1487S + 68$	283	22
68					$32.95W + 497$	274	
69		30♀	Ambulatory patients hospitalized for minor complaints and receiving no medication	EB	$1667S - 324$	260	22
70					$22.4W + 1046$	292	
71		20♂	Residents for at least 1 yr at altitude of 5740 ft	^{131}I	$0.000266H^3 + 25W - 233$	....	8
72		18♂	....	EB	$828S + 1580$	236	6
73					$19W + 1810$	239	
74		19♀	....	EB	$1490S + 114$	248	6
75					$17W + 1491$	258	
76		51♂♀	....	EB	$1770S - 460$	267	11
77					$30W + 668$	273	
78		44♀	Women with uncomplicated singleton pregnancies	EB or ^{131}I	$1857.2S + 32.0G$[14] $+ 673$	160	23
79		35♀	Apparently normal volunteers & hospital outpatients	EB	$27.54H + 26.64W - 3302$	242	25
80					$2596S - 1451$	246	

Whole Blood Volume, ml

	Subjects			Method	Regression Equation	SD	Reference
	Age, yr	No. & Sex	Specification				
81	1-17	11♂♀	Healthy volunteers & hospital convalescents; S between 0.4 & 0.8 m²	Calculated[13] from Hct[6] & Vp (by EB)	$2267S - 268.8$	89	14
82		36♂♀	Healthy volunteers & hospital convalescents; S between 0.8 & 1.4 m²	Calculated[13] from Hct[6] & Vp (by EB)	$3511S - 1173$	235	
83		30♂	Healthy volunteers & hospital convalescents; S between 1.4 & 2.0 m²	Calculated[13] from Hct[6] & Vp (by EB)	$5074S - 3339$	427	
84	3.5-41	20♂	Healthy volunteers, mostly children & youths	Calculated[3] from Hct[1,2] & Vp (by EB)[11]	$3187S - 1136$	299	5
85					$0.008578H + 2.1900$[12]	0.02827[12]	
86		21♀	Healthy volunteers, mostly children & youths	Calculated[3] from Hct[1,2] & Vp (by EB)[11]	$2379S - 405$	271	
87					$0.007173H + 2.3457$[12]	0.0501[12]	
88	14-76	13♂, 12♀	Hospital patients free of illness thought likely to affect blood volume	Calculated[13] from Hct[1] & Vp (by EB)	$2416S + 237$	379	7
89					$32.5W + 2261$	418	
90	16-40	56♀	Indians from low socio-economic group attending hospital for minor complaints	^{51}Cr[1,3]	$14.41H + 54.03W - 1486$	520	26
91					$3611S - 1485$	511	
92	16-65	177♂	Pre-operative surgical cases suffering from minor ailments	^{131}I[13]	$51.5W + 1790$	470	20
93					$3434S - 890$	430	

[1] Hematocrit corrected for trapped plasma. [2] Hematocrits measured in capillary tubes. [3] Allowance made for a difference between venous and body hematocrit. [6] Hematocrit not corrected for trapped plasma. [11] Vp multiplied by a factor of 0.935 to correct for indicator loss of 6.5%. [12] Equation yields log values. To find SD in milliliters, calculate the log value of the mean predicted volume at a given body size, add or subtract the listed log SD, and take the antilog. The SD is the arithmetic difference between this value and the antilog of the calculated mean volume. [13] No allowance for a difference between venous and body hematocrit. [14] G = coded weeks of gestation [23].

continued

Part I. Man

	Age, yr	No. & Sex	Specification	Method	Regression Equation	SD	Reference
94	16-50	40♀	Pre-operative surgical cases suffering from minor ailments	^{131}I [13]	$27.6W + 2720$	350	20
95					$2080S + 1050$	340	
96	16-77	101♀	....	^{51}Cr [6,13]	$16.52H + 38.46W - 1369$	308	4
97					$2885S - 1131$	308	
98	17-60	55♂	Some subjects with unusual build	Calculated [3] from Hct [1] & Vp (by EB), or from Hct & VRBC (by ^{51}Cr), or from sum of Vp & VRBC	$56.7H - 4860$	535	9
99		10♀			$46.6H + 21.6W - 4670$	483	
100	17-66	22♂	Ambulatory hospital patients with disorders not expected to affect blood volume	Calculated [3] from Hct [1] & Vp (by ^{131}I)	$3456S - 1020$	....	12
101					$56.3W + 1383$	....	
102	17-71	26♂	Hospital patients, convalescent or free of illness thought likely to affect blood volume	Sum [1] of VRBC (by ^{51}Cr) & Vp (by ^{131}I)	$2855S - 359$	415	2
103					$39.8W + 1993$	403	
104	19-79	30♀	Hospital patients, convalescent or free of illness thought likely to affect blood volume	Sum [1] of VRBC (by ^{51}Cr) & Vp (by ^{131}I)	$37.68H - 2285$	494	2
105					$1848S + 749$	438	
106					$21.5W + 2415$	445	
107	17-90	92♂	Ambulatory volunteers & hospital patients with disorders not expected to affect blood volume	Calculated [3] from Hct [15] & Vp (by ^{131}I)	$0.0003669H^3 + 32.19W + 604$	506	10, 15
108					$3290S - 1229$	507	
109		63♀	Ambulatory volunteers & hospital patients with disorders not expected to affect blood volume	Calculated [3] from Hct [15] & Vp (by ^{131}I)	$0.0003561H^3 + 33.09W + 183$	479	
110					$3470S - 1954$	486	
111	18-21	50♂	Clinically examined healthy Indian medical students, mostly vegetarians	Calculated [3] from Hct [6] & Vp (by EB)	$44.8H - 3382$	....	19
112					$309S + 2532$	....	
113		35♀	Clinically examined healthy Indian medical students, mostly vegetarians	Calculated [3] from Hct [6] & Vp (by EB)	$557H - 82,935$	....	
114					$92S + 3836$	....	
115	19-52	201♂	....	^{51}Cr [6,13]	$28.5H + 31.6W - 2820$	370	27
116					$3140S - 1410$	360	
117	20-50	93♂	Indians from low socio-economic group; pre-operative cases for minor surgical procedures, & professional blood donors [8]	^{51}Cr [1,3]	$11.88H + 55.38W - 1110$	459	26
118					$3167S - 1525$	486	
119	Un-specified	25♂	Healthy Indian volunteers from high socio-economic group	^{51}Cr [1,3]	$26.42H + 39.94W - 2516$	656	26
120	20-74	15♀	....	Sum [6] of VRBC (by ^{51}Cr) & Vp (by EB)	$42.6W + 1124$ [5]	381	13
121	20-84	17♂	....	Sum [6] of VRBC (by ^{51}Cr) & Vp (by EB)	$26.87W + 2937$ [5]	733	13
122	21-36	20♂	....	Calculated [13] from Hct [6] & Vp (by EB)	$78.34H - 7881$	886	18
123	22-32	20♀	....	Calculated [13] from Hct [6] & Vp (by EB)	$27.7H - 149$	428	18

[1] Hematocrit corrected for trapped plasma. [3] Allowance made for a difference between venous and body hematocrit. [5] Calculations based on original measurements and data from other authors. [6] Hematocrit not corrected for trapped plasma. [8] Hemoglobin over 12.0 g/100 g, and no blood donated for at least 10 weeks. [13] No allowance for a difference between venous and body hematocrit. [15] Hematocrit computed from counted radioactivity of whole blood and plasma as $(V_{WB} - V_P)/V_{WB}$.

continued

Part I. Man

	Subjects		Method	Regression Equation	SD	Reference
	Age, yr	No. & Sex	Specification				

	Age, yr	No. & Sex	Specification	Method	Regression Equation	SD	Reference
124	Adult	32♂	Apparently normal volunteers & hospital outpatients	Calculated[13] from Hct[1] & V_P	$54.7W + 2016$	665	24
125		20♂	Resident for at least 1 yr at altitude of 5740 ft	Sum[2,6] of V_{RBC} (by ^{51}Cr) & V_P (by ^{131}I)	$0.000496H^3 + 42W - 443$	....	8
126		18♂	....	Calculated[3] from Hct[1] & V_P (by EB)	$3053S - 178$	338	6
127					$8W + 4657$	482	
128		19♀	....	Calculated[3] from Hct[1] & V_P (by EB)	$2600S - 87$	426	6
129					$34W + 2063$	404	
130		35♀	Apparently normal volunteers & hospital outpatients	Calculated[13] from Hct[1] & V_P	$56.98W + 1261$	400	25
131					$42.15W + 41.98H - 4772$	340	
132	Unspecified	321♂	62 children; 82 residents of China & Taiwan; some of unusual build; 57 determinations under subtropical or tropical conditions	Calculated[1,3] from results published by several authors using various methods	$0.000417H^3 + 45.0W - 30$	....	1
133		107♀	Some hospital patients; twelve 12-yr-old convalescent girls; 26 residents of Taiwan under subtropical or tropical conditions	Calculated[1,3] from results published by several authors using various methods	$0.000414H^3 + 32.8W - 30$	....	1

[1] Hematocrit corrected for trapped plasma. [2] Hematocrits measured in capillary tubes. [3] Allowance made for a difference between venous and body hematocrit. [6] Hematocrit not corrected for trapped plasma. [13] No allowance for a difference between venous and body hematocrit.

Contributor: Brown, Ellen

References
[1] Allen, T. H., et al. 1956. Metab. Clin. Exp. 5:328.
[2] Brassine, A. 1968. Pathol. Biol. 16:257.
[3] Bratteby, L. E. 1968. Acta Paediat. Scand. 57:132.
[4] Brown, E., et al. 1962. J. Clin. Invest. 41:2182.
[5] Cropp, G. J. A. 1971. J. Pediat. 78:220.
[6] Davis, H. A. 1962. Blood Volume Dynamics. C. C. Thomas, Springfield, Ill.
[7] Edwards, K. D. G., and H. M. Whyte. 1960. Clin. Sci. 19:399.
[8] Heerden, P. D. R. van, et al. 1963. S. Afr. J. Med. Sci. 28:137.
[9] Hicks, D. A., et al. 1956. Clin. Sci. 15:557.
[10] Hidalgo, J. U., et al. 1962. J. Nucl. Med. 3:94.
[11] Inkley, S. R., et al. 1955. J. Lab. Clin. Med. 45:841.
[12] Moens, R. S., et al. 1962. Schweiz. Med. Wochenschr. 92(2):1660, 1697.
[13] Moore, F. D., et al. 1963. The Body Cell Mass and Its Supporting Environment. W. B. Saunders, Philadelphia.
[14] Morse, M., et al. 1947. Amer. J. Physiol. 151:448.

[15] Nadler, S. B., et al. 1962. Surgery 51:224.
[16] Nathan, D. G., et al. 1963. Ann. N.Y. Acad. Sci. 110:965.
[17] Piomelli, S., et al. 1962. Blood 19:89.
[18] Porat, B. von. 1951. Acta Med. Scand., Suppl. 256.
[19] Purohit, G. L., and R. M. Bhatty. 1970. Indian J. Med. Sci. 24:66.
[20] Rao, B. N. B., et al. 1970. Indian J. Med. Res. 58:884.
[21] Retzlaff, J. A., et al. 1969. Blood 33:649.
[22] Samet, P., et al. 1957. Medicine (Baltimore) 36:211.
[23] Smith, R. W., and C. J. Yarbrough. 1967. Amer. J. Obstet. Gynecol. 99:18.
[24] Steinbeck, A. W. 1950. Aust. J. Exp. Biol. Med. Sci. 28:477.
[25] Steinbeck, A. W. 1954. Ibid. 32:95.
[26] Vyas, G. N., et al. 1965. Indian J. Med. Res. 53:122.
[27] Wennesland, R., et al. 1959. J. Clin. Invest. 38:1065.

Part II. Vertebrates Other Than Man

Subjects were normal adult animals. **Method:** Erythrocyte and plasma volumes were obtained by calculation or by various dilution methods, using as a label either Evans' blue (EB), ^{51}Cr, ^{131}I, ^{32}P, or ^{59}Fe, as specified; Hct (Hct$_V$)--hematocrit (venous); V_{RBC}--total volume of erythrocytes (RBC), in milliliters; V_P--volume of plasma, in milliliters; V_{WB}--volume of whole blood, in milliliters. **Venous Hematocrit:** values were obtained by centrifugation of the blood sample at 3000 revolutions per minute (18-cm radius) for 30 minutes. For further information on blood volume methods and interpretations, consult references 1 and 7. The literature has been covered through 1971. Values in parentheses are ranges, estimate "c" (*see* Introduction).

continued

Part II. Vertebrates Other Than Man

	Class & Species (Synonym)	No. & Sex	Erythrocyte Volume ml/kg		Plasma Volume ml/kg		Venous Hematocrit % cells	Whole Blood Volume ml/kg		Reference
			Method	Value	Method	Value		Method	Value	
	Mammalia									
1	*Bos taurus*	10♀	....	....	EB	38.8(36.3-40.6)	32.4(30.3-34.9)[1]	$\dfrac{V_P}{100-Hct_V}\cdot100$	57.4(52.4-60.6)	25
2	*Bubalus bubalis*	54♂	....	....	EB	34.8	32.4	$\dfrac{V_P}{100-Hct_V}\cdot100$	51.4	21
3		41♀	....	....	EB	35.6	31.1	$\dfrac{V_P}{100-Hct_V}\cdot100$	51.8	
4	*Camelus dromedarius*	19♂	....	....	EB	59(47-70)	29	$\dfrac{V_P}{100-Hct_V}\cdot100$	83(68-100)	3
5	*Canis familiaris*	26[2]	51Cr[3]	36.2	EB	50.0	43.5[4]	$V_P + V_{RBC}$	86.2	13
6	*Capra hircus*	20	51Cr[3]	14.7(9.7-19.3)	EB	55.9(42.6-75.1)	24.3(18.5-30.8)[5]	$V_P + V_{RBC}$	70.5(56.8-89.4)	17
7	*Cavia* sp.	13	....	....	131I[6]	39.4(35.1-48.4)	....	$\dfrac{V_P}{100-Hct_V}\cdot100$	75.3(67.0-92.4)	19
8	*Didelphis* sp.	10[2]	32P	19.2(14.2-29.2)	EB	37.8(29.6-52.2)	....	$V_P + V_{RBC}$	57.0(44.5-69.8)	6
	Equus caballus									
9	Draft	12	$V_{WB}-V_P$	19.3(15.1-22.2)	59Fe	42.4(36.4-49.4)	34(30-37)	$\dfrac{V_P}{100-Hct_V}\cdot100$	61.7(56.0-71.5)	18
10	Saddle	5	$V_{WB}-V_P$	25.8(20.6-30.1)	59Fe	50.5(45.5-55.0)	37(32-42)	$\dfrac{V_P}{100-Hct_V}\cdot100$	75.9(71.3-79.4)	18
11	Thoroughbred	17	$V_{WB}-V_P$	41.4(37.4-48.9)	59Fe	61.8(46.4-77.6)	45(40-52)	$\dfrac{V_P}{100-Hct_V}\cdot100$	103.1(81-118.1)	18
12	*Felis catus*	5♂[2]	51Cr[3]	14.8(12.2-17.7)[8]	EB	40.7(34.6-52.0)	....	$V_P + V_{RBC}$	55.5(47.3-65.7)	9
13	*Lagenorhynchus obliquidens*	4	$V_{WB}-V_P$	57	131I	51	53(50-59)[7]	$\dfrac{V_P}{100-Hct_V}\cdot100$	108(95-118)	26
14	*Macaca mulatta*	15♂, 3♀	32P	17.7(14.3-20.0)	EB	36.4(30.0-48.4)	39.6(35.6-42.8)[8]	$V_P + V_{RBC}$	54.1(44.3-66.6)	10
15	*Macropus* spp.[9]	19	....	....	EB	....	42.6	$\dfrac{V_P}{100-Hct_V}\cdot100$	87.5	20
16	*Marmota flaviventris*	3[2]	$V_{WB}-V_P$	50	EB	51	49.4[7]	$\dfrac{V_P}{100-Hct_V}\cdot100$	100	5
17	*Myotis lucifugus*	123[2]	....	....	EB	65	49.3[7,10]	$\dfrac{V_P}{100-Hct_V}\cdot100$	130	16
18	*Oryctolagus cuniculus*	29	32P	16.8(13.7-25.5)	EB	38.8(27.8-51.4)	....	$V_P + V_{RBC}$	55.6(44.0-70.0)	2
19	*Ovis aries*	5	51Cr[3]	19.7(16.3-23.8)	EB	46.7(43.4-52.9)	....	$V_P + V_{RBC}$	66.4(59.7-73.8)	12
20	*Phocoenoides dalli*	3	$V_{WB}-V_P$	81	131I	62	57(52-63)[7]	$\dfrac{V_P}{100-Hct_V}\cdot100$	143(130-153)	26
21	*Rattus norvegicus*	....	32P	23.7(18.4-26.0)	EB	40.4(36.3-45.3)[11]	50.3(42.3-61.5)[4,11]	$V_P + V_{RBC}$	64.1(57.5-69.9)	31
22	*Spermophilus lateralis* (*Citellus lateralis*)	9[2]	$V_{WB}-V_P$	53.9	EB	59.0	47.8[7]	$\dfrac{V_P}{100-Hct_V}\cdot100$	113	5

[1] Corrected for trapped plasma by a factor of 0.94. [2] Anesthetized. [3] As $Na_2CrO_4\cdot4\ H_2O$. [4] Corrected for trapped plasma by a factor of 0.95. [5] Corrected for trapped plasma by a factor of 0.81. [6] 131I-rabbit globulin; calculated from an average hematocrit of 47.6 obtained from 10 other guinea pigs. [7] Microhematocrit method; capillary tubes at 10,000 × gravity for 10 minutes. [8] Corrected for trapped plasma by a factor of 0.96. [9] 8 *Macropus giganteus*, 1 *M. robustus*, and 10 *M. rufus*. [10] Cardiac blood. [11] Blood from carotid artery or tail vein.

continued

Part II. Vertebrates Other Than Man

	Class & Species (Synonym)	No. & Sex	Erythrocyte Volume ml/kg		Plasma Volume ml/kg		Venous Hematocrit % cells	Whole Blood Volume ml/kg		Reference
			Method	Value	Method	Value		Method	Value	
23	*Sus scrofa*	4	^{32}P	25.9(20.2-29.0)	....	....	39.1(30.3-43.1)[4]	$\frac{V_{RBC}}{Hct_V} \cdot 100$	65(61-68)	11
24	*Tursiops truncatus*	4	$V_{WB} - V_P$ 32		^{131}I	39	45(40-48)[7]	$\frac{V_P}{100 - Hct_V} \cdot 100$	71(65-83)	26
25	*Wallabia eugenii*	10	....	....	EB	....	37	$\frac{V_P}{100 - Hct_V} \cdot 100$	93.5	20
	Aves									
26	*Anas platyrhynchos domesticus*	42	....	....	^{131}I	65.5	....	$\frac{V_P}{100 - Hct_V} \cdot 100$	102	23
27		2♂	^{51}Cr[3]	30	....	....	38.5	....	....	27
28		2♀	^{51}Cr[3]	25	....	....	43.5	....	....	27
29	*Columba livia*	6	Consult reference 4	49	EB	44	52	Consult reference 4	92	4
	Gallus gallus (G. domesticus)									
30	New Hampshire	110♂, 113♀	....	....	EB	....	....	$\frac{V_P}{100 - Hct_V} \cdot 100$	90	22
31	White Leghorn	18♂	....	....	EB	88.8	47.7	$\frac{V_P}{100 - Hct_V} \cdot 100$	137.1	29
32	*Phasianus colchicus*	4♂	Consult reference 4	22	EB	45	33	Consult reference 4	67	4
33		2♀	Consult reference 4	16	EB	32	34	Consult reference 4	48	4
	Reptilia									
34	*Alligator mississippiensis*	10[2,12]	^{51}Cr	12.6(10.4-13.8)[10]	^{131}I	60.1(44.2-76.3)[10]	22.7(18.3-28.5)[10]	$V_P + V_{RBC}$	72.7	15
35	*Chrysemys scripta elegans (Pseudemys scripta elegans)*	26[13]	....	....	EB[14]	74.0(58.2-90.8)	18.5(12.0-25.4)	$\frac{V_P}{100 - Hct_V} \cdot 100$	90.8(72.5-110.2)	28
	Amphibia									
36	*Rana catesbeiana*	2	....	....	EB	80[10]	15.5[10]	$\frac{V_P}{100 - Hct_V} \cdot 100$	95	24
	Pisces									
37	*Ictalurus natalis*	6	....	....	EB	12.5[10]	30.1[10]	....	17.7	24
38	*Salmo gairdneri*	6[2]	^{51}Cr	12(7-22)	^{131}I	16(9-26)	....	$V_P + V_{RBC}$	28(16-47)	8
39	*Salvelinus fontinalis*	15	....	....	EB	39	37.2	$\frac{V_P}{100 - Hct_V} \cdot 100$	57	14
	Chondrichthyes									
40	*Raja rhina*	8[2]	....	....	EB	59(34-79)[10]	16.8(12.0-21.5)[10,15]	....	72(40-95)	30
41	*Squalus acanthias*	24[2]	....	....	EB	55(25-90)	18.2(14-24)	....	68(31-109)	30

[1] Corrected for trapped plasma by a factor of 0.94. [2] Anesthetized. [4] Corrected for trapped plasma by a factor of 0.95. [7] Microhematocrit method; capillary tubes at 10,000 × gravity for 10 minutes. [10] Cardiac blood. [12] 2 different groups of 10 animals each for total erythrocyte volume and plasma volume determinations; both groups were combined for venous hematocrit and whole-blood volume determinations. [13] Unfed for 3-8 wk. [14] Plus high molecular weight dextran. [15] 11 subjects.

continued

Part II. **Vertebrates Other Than Man**

Contributor: Reynolds, Monica

References

[1] Altman, P. L., and D. S. Dittmer, ed. 1961. Blood and Other Body Fluids. Federation of American Societies for Experimental Biology, Washington, D.C. pp. 3-8.

[2] Armin, J., et al. 1952. J. Physiol. (London) 116:59.

[3] Banerjee, S., and R. C. Bhattacharjee. 1963. Amer. J. Physiol. 204:1045.

[4] Bond, C. F., and P. W. Gilbert. 1958. Ibid. 194:519.

[5] Bullard, R. W., et al. 1966. J. Appl. Physiol. 21:994.

[6] Burke, J. D. 1954. Physiol. Zool. 27:1.

[7] Chien, S., and M. I. Gregersen. 1962. Phys. Tech. Biol. Res. 4:1.

[8] Conte, F. P., et al. 1963. Amer. J. Physiol. 205:533.

[9] Farnsworth, P. N., et al. 1960. Proc. Soc. Exp. Biol. Med. 104:729.

[10] Gregersen, M. I., et al. 1959. Amer. J. Physiol. 196:184.

[11] Hansard, S. L., et al. 1951. Proc. Soc. Exp. Biol. Med. 78:544.

[12] Hodgetts, V. E. 1961. Aust. J. Exp. Biol. Med. Sci. 39:187.

[13] Hoff, H. E., et al. 1966. Proc. Soc. Exp. Biol. Med. 122:630.

[14] Houston, A. H., and M. A. DeWilde. 1969. Comp. Biochem. Physiol. 28:877.

[15] Huggins, S. W. 1961. Proc. Soc. Exp. Biol. Med. 108:231.

[16] Kallen, F. C. 1960. Amer. J. Physiol. 198:999.

[17] Klement, A. W., Jr., et al. 1955. Ibid. 181:15.

[18] Marcilese, N. A., et al. 1965. Amer. J. Physiol. 209:727.

[19] Masouredis, S. P., and L. R. Melcher. 1951. Proc. Soc. Exp. Biol. Med. 78:264.

[20] Maxwell, G. M., et al. 1964. Amer. J. Physiol. 206:967.

[21] Murti, T. L., and D. N. Mullick. 1961. Ann. Biochem. Exp. Med. 21:91.

[22] Newell, G. W., and C. S. Shaffner. 1950. Poult. Sci. 29:78.

[23] Portman, O. W., et al. 1952. Proc. Soc. Exp. Biol. Med. 81:599.

[24] Prosser, C. L., and S. J. F. Weinstein. 1950. Physiol. Zool. 23:113.

[25] Reynolds, M. 1953. Amer. J. Physiol. 173:421.

[26] Ridgway, S. H., and D. G. Johnston. 1966. Science 151:456.

[27] Rodnan, G. P., et al. 1957. Blood 12:355.

[28] Semple, R. E. 1960. Fed. Proc. Fed. Amer. Soc. Exp. Biol. 19:79.

[29] Sturkie, P. D., and J. M. Eiel. 1966. J. Appl. Physiol. 21:1927.

[30] Thorson, T. B. 1958. Physiol. Zool. 31:16.

[31] Wang, L. 1959. Amer. J. Physiol. 196:188.

255. ERYTHROCYTE AND HEMOGLOBIN VALUES: VERTEBRATES

Erythrocyte Packed Volume is equivalent to hematocrit. **Erythrocyte Volume** is mean corpuscular volume. **Erythrocyte Dimensions** (dry film): For mammals, dimensions are diameters; for other vertebrates, dimensions are length times width. Plus/minus (±) values are standard errors. Values in parentheses are ranges, estimate "c" unless otherwise indicated (*see* Introduction). For additional information, consult reference 3.

Species (Synonym)	Erythrocyte Count million/μl blood	Erythrocyte Packed Volume ml/100 ml blood	Erythrocyte Volume μ^3	Hemoglobin Concentration		Erythrocyte Hemoglobin Content pg	Erythrocyte Dimensions μ	Reference
				g/100 ml blood	g/100 ml RBC			
Mammalia								
Homo sapiens[1]								
1 Fetus, 10 wk	1.4	31.6	180	9.0	33	60.5	....	7,8,11-
2 22 wk	3.2	40	140	14.5	33	47	....	13,17,
3 36 wk	3.7	45	120	15.0	33	40	....	18
4 At birth[2]	5.25(3.5-6.7)	53(47-58)	113	16.8(13.7-20)	32.6	36.9	....	21
5 1 da	5.8(3.9-7.0)	60(53-73)[3]	110	18.4(15-23.5)	33	37	....	

[1] Measurements were made on venous blood, unless otherwise indicated. [2] Cord blood. [3] Capillary blood.

continued

	Species (Synonym)	Erythrocyte Count million/μl blood	Erythrocyte Packed Volume ml/100 ml blood	Erythrocyte Volume μ^3	Hemoglobin Concentration g/100 ml blood	Hemoglobin Concentration g/100 ml RBC	Erythrocyte Hemoglobin Content pg	Erythrocyte Dimensions μ	Reference
6	1 wk	5.2(4.1-6.3)	55(49-64)[3]	106	17.0(12.5-19)	33.5	36	....	
7	2 wk	5.1(4.0-6.5)	52(44-60)[3]	102	16.8(12.5-19.5)	34.3	34	....	
8	3 wk[3]	4.9(4.0-6.1)	50(42-62)	100	15.7(13.0-20)	33.2	30	....	
9	4 wk[3]	4.35(3.2-5.8)	45(34-64)	101	15.0(12-20)	32.8	30.4	....	
10	2 mo[3]	3.75(3.0-5.6)	37.7(30-48)	88	11.5(9.5-15.5)	33	30.2	....	
11	3 mo[3]	3.88(2.8-5.8)	36.7(32-45.7)	82	11.0(9.0-15)	34	28	....	
12	4 mo[3]	4.3(3.4-5.6)	35.3(32-48)	82	11.5(9.5-15)	33.5	27.7	....	
13	6 mo[3]	4.21(3.0-5.4)	38.5(33-47)	78	11.5(10.4-14)	33.5	26.1	....	
14	10 mo[3]	4.35(3.4-5.2)	39(34-48)	73	12.0(10.2-13.8)	33	23.7	....	
15	12 mo[3]	4.44(3.8-5.6)	39.3(34-48)	73	11.9(10.5-14.5)	32.5	23.5	....	
16	2 yr	4.77(3.2-5.2)	35.8(34-46)	75	11.7(10.5-13.5)	32.6	24.7	....	
17	3 yr	4.5(3.9-5.5)	37.0(33.5-47)	78	12.5(10.8-14.2)	34	26.6	....	
18	4 yr	4.7(3.8-5.4)	37.1	80	12.6(9.6-15.5)	34.0	27	....	
19	6 yr	4.7(3.8-5.4)	37.9	80	12.7(10.0-15.5)	33.5	27	....	
20	8 yr	4.7(3.8-5.4)	38.9	80	12.9(10.3-15.5)	33.2	27	....	
21	10 yr	4.8(3.8-5.4)	39.0	80	13.0(10.7-15.5)	33.3	27	....	
22	12 yr	4.8(3.8-5.4)	39.6	81	13.4(11.0-16.5)	33.8	28	....	
23	14 yr and over, ♂	5.4(4.6-6.2)[b]	47(40-54)[b]	87	16.0(14-18)[b]	34	29	....	
24	♀	4.8(4.2-5.4)[b]	42(37-47)[b]	87	14.0(12-16)[b]	34	29	....	
25	Pregnant, 6 mo	4.0(3.5-4.8)	37(32-42)	92	11.4(10.2-14.0)	31	28.5	....	4
26	9 mo	4.2(3.7-5.0)	37.5(33-43)	89	12.0(10.8-14.4)	32	28.5	....	
27	Postpartum, 10 da	4.5(4.0-5.0)	40(35-45)	89	12.8(11.4-14.4)	32	28.4	....	
28	*Bos* sp.	8.1(6.1-10.7)	40(33-47)[b]	50(47-54)	11.5(8.7-14.5)[b]	29.0	....	5.9	1
29	*Canis familiaris*	6.3(4.5-8.0)	45.5(38-53)	66(59-68)	14.8(11.0-18.0)	33(30-35)	23(21-25)	7.0(6.2-8.0)	1
30	*Capra hircus*	16.0(13.3-17.9)	33(27.0-34.6)	19.3	10.5(8.8-11.4)	34(33-36)	6.7	4.0	20

[3] Capillary blood.

continued

Species (Synonym)	Erythrocyte Count million/μl blood	Erythrocyte Packed Volume ml/100 ml blood	Erythrocyte Volume μ^3	Hemoglobin Concentration g/100 ml blood	Hemoglobin Concentration g/100 ml RBC	Erythrocyte Hemoglobin Content pg	Erythrocyte Dimensions μ	Reference
31 *Cavia porcellus*	5.6(4.5-7.0)	42(37-47)	77(71-83)	14.4(11.0-16.5)	34(33-35)	26.0(24.5-27.5)	7.4(7.0-7.5)	1
32 *Equus caballus*	9.3(8.21-10.35)[b]	33.4(28-42)[b]	....	11.1(8-14)[b]	33.0	....	5.5	1
33 *Felis catus*	8.0(6.5-9.5)	40(28-52)	57(51-63)	11.2(7.0-15.5)	28(23-31)	14(12-16)	6.0(5.0-7.0)	1
34 *Macaca mulatta*	5.2(3.6-6.8)[b]	42(32-52)[b]	....	12.6(10-16)[b]	30.0	....	....	1
35 *Meriones unguiculatus*	8.1(7.0-8.9)	47(41-51)	....	13.9(12.1-15.4)	....	....	....	15
36 *Mus musculus*	9.3(7.7-12.5)	41.5	49(48-51)	14.8(10-19)	36(33-39)	16(15.5-16.5)	6.0	1
37 *Oryctolagus cuniculus*	5.7(4.5-7.0)	41.5(33-50)	61(60-68)	11.9(8.0-15.0)	29(27-31)	21(19-23)	7.5(6.5-7.5)	1
38 *Ovis aries*	10.3(9.4-11.1)	31.7(29.9-33.6)	31(30-32)	10.9(10.0-11.8)	34.5(34-35)	11.0	4.8	20
39 *Pan troglodytes*	5.1(3.4-6.0)	41.6(24-51)	81.4(70-91)	12.3(6.5-15.1)	30.6(29-34)	24.5(20-27)	7.4	20
40 *Rattus* sp.	8.9(7.2-9.6)	46(39-53)	61(57-65)	14.8(12.0-17.5)	32(30-35)	17(15-19)	7.5(6.0-7.5)	1
41 *Sus scrofa*	6.4	39.0(38.0-40.0)	61.1(59-63)	13.7(13.2-14.2)	35.0	21.5(21-22)	....	20
42 Hamster	6.96(3.96-9.96)[b]	49(39-59)[b]	70.0	16.0(2.0-30.0)[b]	32.0	23.0	5.6(5.4-5.8)[b]	6
Aves								
43 *Chen caerulescens*	2.8(2.6-3.0)	44.7(43.1-46.2)	160(145-174)	12.7(11.9-13.4)	28.5(28-29)	45.5(40-51)	12.2 × 7.2	20
44 *Gallus gallus (G. domesticus)*	2.8(2.0-3.2)	35.6(24.0-43.3)	127(120-137)	10.3(7.3-12.9)	29(27-30)	36.6(33-41)	11.2 × 6.8	20
45 *Meleagris gallopavo*	2.3	38.0	....	11.2	23.5	....	15.5 × 7.5	16
46 Duck[4/]	2.8	39.5	....	14.8(9-21)	38.1	52.1(32-71)	12.8 × 6.6	16
Reptilia								
47 *Alligator mississippiensis*	0.67	30.0	450.0	8.2	27.0	123.0	23.2 × 12.1	20
48 *Chrysemys scripta elegans (Pseudemys scripta elegans)*	0.45 ± 0.08	18.1 ± 3.5	401 ± 22	5.6 ± 1.0	....	124 ± 6	....	9
49 *Heterodon platyrhinos (H. contortrix)*	0.57(0.50-0.63)	18.7(13.3-24.1)	324.5(266-383)	5.6(3.7-7.5)	29.5(28-31)	95.5(74-119)	16.0 × 9.5	20
50 *Natrix sipedon*	0.77	35.5	465.0	10.0	28.0	131.0	19.6 × 11.0	20
51 *Terrapene carolina*	0.70 ± 0.02	26.9 ± 0.5	....	6.2 ± 0.3	....	....	....	2
52 *Thamnophis sirtalis*	1.05(0.71-1.39)	28(19-37)	267(266-268)	8.5(5.8-11.3)	31.0	82.0	18.1 × 10.3	20

[4/] Hematology values progressively increase as duck matures.

continued

Species (Synonym)	Erythrocyte Count million/μl blood	Erythrocyte Packed Volume ml/100 ml blood	Erythrocyte Volume μ^3	Hemoglobin Concentration		Erythrocyte Hemoglobin Content pg	Erythrocyte Dimensions μ	Reference
				g/100 ml blood	g/100 ml RBC			
Amphibia								
53 Ambystoma tigrinum	1.68(1.13-1.94)	42(27-48)	250	8.6(5.6-10.9)	20.4	51.1	....	14
54 Amphiuma means	0.03	40(39-41)	13,857 (13,200-14,513)	9.4(7.7-11.0)	24(21-27)	3287(2750-3823)	62.5 × 36.3	20
55 Cryptobranchus alleganiensis	0.07	49.0	7425	13.3	27.0	2010	40.5 × 21.0	20
56 Necturus maculosus (N. maculatus)	0.02	21.4	10,070	4.6	22.0	2160	52.8 × 28.2	20
57 Rana catesbeiana	0.44(0.43-0.45)	29.3(26.6-32.0)	670(625-716)	7.8(7.4-8.2)	27(26-28)	179(174-184)	24.8 × 15.3	20
Osteichthyes								
58 Anguilla rostrata	2.48	37.9(36.0-39.8)	156(141-170)	9.0(8.0-10.0)	23.5(22-25)	36.5(35-38)	13.0 × 8.0	20
59 Carassius auratus	2.02 ± 0.11	....	....	....	....	....	8.8 × 13.4	19
60 Cyprinus carpio	0.84(0.65-1.13)	31.3(21-40)	311(278-340)	10.5(9.4-12.4)	33.5	72(63-78)	....	5
61 Gadus morhua (G. callarias)	1.55(1.49-1.60)	29.1(23.8-32.6)	186(159-201)	5.9(5.2-6.4)	20(19-22)	38(35-40)	12.2 × 9.0	20
62 Ictalurus catus (Ameirus catus)	2.65	15.4	123	9.2	2.8	35	10.4 × 8.7	20
63 Limanda ferruginea	1.23(0.78-1.61)	14.6(8.4-18.2)	117.7(107-138)	3.2(2.1-4.2)	22.7(19-25)	26.7(26-28)	10.3 × 7.7	20
64 Morone americana (Roccus americanus)	3.17(2.70-3.63)	35.3(32.7-37.8)	112.5(104-121)	8.2(6.7-9.7)	23.5(21-26)	26(25-27)	10.3 × 7.2	20
65 Salvelinus fontinalis	1.01(0.74-1.50)	27.2(22-36)	314(284-348)	8.5(6.2-11.5)	31.2	75(61-82)	....	5
66 Scomber scombrus	3.94(3.68-4.20)	57.5(56-59)	146(140-152)	14.9(14.5-15.2)	26.0	37.5(36-39)	12.5 × 8.3	20
67 Sebastes marinus	1.88	56.0	298	7.8	14	42	12.4 × 8.2	20
Chondrichthyes								
68 Dasyatis centroura	0.30	19.0	612	3.0	....	....	20.6 × 14.3	10
69 Mustelus canis	0.46	23.3	541.0	4.6	....	....	19.1 × 13.8	10
70 Raja eglanteria	0.30	24.0	823	4.5	....	....	23.7 × 14.4	10
71 R. erinacea	0.09(0.07-0.11)	7.2(4.7-9.6)	778(646-910)	1.4(0.9-1.8)	19.5(19-20)	148.5(125-172)	24.3 × 13.9	20
72 Sphyrna zygaena	0.44	23.1	526	5.4	....	....	15.2 × 11.2	10
73 Squalus acanthias	0.24	18.9	820.0	3.8	....	....	22.7 × 15.2	10
74 Torpedo nobiliana	0.15	23.5	1593	3.3	....	....	29.8 × 23.1	10
Agnatha								
75 Myxine glutinosa	0.15(0.12-0.19)	22.2(19.3-27.6)	1530(1470-1560)	4.6(4.0-5.7)	21.0	318.3(303-330)	26.4 × 18.3	20
76 Petromyzon marinus	0.33	23.5	710.0	5.8	....	....	14.3 × 14.3	10

continued

255. ERYTHROCYTE AND HEMOGLOBIN VALUES: VERTEBRATES

Contributors: Altland, Paul D.; Hathaway, William E.

References

[1] Albritton, E. C., ed. 1952. Standard Values in Blood. W. B. Saunders, Philadelphia. pp. 42-43.

[2] Altland, P. D., and E. C. Thompson. 1958. Proc. Soc. Exp. Biol. Med. 99:456.

[3] Altman, P. L., and D. S. Dittmer, ed. 1971. Respiration and Circulation. Federation of American Societies for Experimental Biology, Bethesda, Md. pp. 147-153.

[4] Bethell, F. H., et al. 1939. Ann. Intern. Med. 13:91.

[5] Field, J. B., et al. 1943. J. Biol. Chem. 148:261.

[6] Fulton, G. P., et al. 1954. Blood 9:622.

[7] Gatti, R. 1967. J. Pediat. 70:117.

[8] Guest, G. M., and E. W. Brown. 1957. Amer. J. Dis. Child. 93:486.

[9] Hirschfeld, W. J., and A. S. Gordon. 1965. Anat. Rec. 153:317.

[10] Kisch, B. 1951. Exp. Med. Surg. 9:125.

[11] Marks, J., et al. 1955. Arch. Dis. Childhood 30:117.

[12] Moe, P. J. 1965. Acta Paediat. Scand. 54:69.

[13] Oski, F. A., and J. L. Naiman. 1972. Hematologic Problems in the Newborn. W. B. Saunders, Philadelphia.

[14] Roofe, P. G. 1961. Anat. Rec. 140:337.

[15] Ruhrun, R. 1965. Lab. Anim. Care 15:313.

[16] Sturkie, P. D. 1954. Avian Physiology. Comstock, Ithaca.

[17] Turnbull, E. P. N., and J. Walker. 1955. Arch. Dis. Childhood 30:102.

[18] Walker, J., and E. P. N. Turnbull. 1953. Lancet 2: 312.

[19] Watson, L. J., et al. 1963. Cytologia 28:118.

[20] Wintrobe, M. M. 1934. Folia Haematol. (Leipzig) 51:32.

[21] Wintrobe, M. M. 1967. Clinical Hematology. Ed. 6. Lea and Febiger, Philadelphia.

256. BLOOD PLATELET COUNTS: MAMMALS

Values in parentheses are ranges, estimate "c" unless otherwise indicated (*see* Introduction). For information on additional species, consult reference 1.

	Species	No. & Sex [No. of Observations]	Platelets thousands/μl	Method	Reference
	Homo sapiens				
	Infant			Direct method of Wood, Vogel, and Famulener; cutaneous blood	8,19
1	At birth	[73]	227(140-290)		
2	1 wk	[69]	233(160-320)		
3	2 wk	[19]	242(170-370)		
4	3 wk	[23]	269(160-380)		
5	1 mo	[48]	277(200-370)		
6	2 mo	[59]	320(200-470)		
7	4 mo	[56]	324(180-450)		
8	6 mo	[47]	350(200-480)		
9	8 mo	[28]	346(220-480)		
10	10 mo	[23]	340(200-450)		
11	1 yr	[15]	339(250-470)		
12	Adult	50♂	250(140-440)	Direct method, phase microscopy; venous blood	2
13		♂♀ [185]	260(145-375)	Direct method, phase microscopy; venous and capillary blood	9
14	*Bos taurus*	....	350(250-600)	....	12
15		....	(550-600)	....	3
16	*Canis familiaris*	....	326	Direct method, phase microscopy	15
17		....	300(100-600)	....	12
18	*Capra hircus*	....	350(250-600)	....	12
19	*Cavia porcellus*	4 [8]	783(525-900)	Direct method; blood from ear	16
20		....	773(680-865)	....	18
21	*Equus caballus*	....	250(100-500)	....	12

continued

	Species	No. & Sex [No. of Observations]	Platelets thousands/μl	Method	Reference
22	*Felis catus*	....	250(100-500)	....	12
23	*Macaca mulatta*	57	344(250-750)	....	7
24		....	414	Direct method, no phase microscopy	13
25	*Mesocricetus auratus*	10♂	688(504-880)	Direct method	11
26		12♀	742(500-870)		
27	*Mus musculus* [L/]	97♂	937	Direct method, phase microscopy	10
28		73♀	924		
29	*Oryctolagus cuniculus*	24	400	Direct method, phase microscopy	4
30		12	(380-520)	....	14
31	*Rattus norvegicus*	60	1240(1100-1380)[b]	Direct method, phase microscopy	5
32		18	1190(1000-1300)	....	6
33	*Sus scrofa*	....	445(383-507)	....	17
34		....	350(250-600)	....	12

[L/] Rf/Un strain, 100-299 da old.

Contributors: Brecher, George; Odell, T. T.

References

[1] Altman, P. L., and D. S. Dittmer, ed. 1961. Blood and Other Body Fluids. Federation of American Societies for Experimental Biology, Washington, D.C. pp. 132-134.

[2] Brecher, G., et al. 1950. J. Appl. Physiol. 3:365.

[3] Brown, D. G., et al. 1961. Radiat. Res. 15:675.

[4] Cooney, D. P., et al. 1961. Acta Haematol. 26:317.

[5] Cronkite, E. P., et al. 1960. In S. A. Johnson, ed. Blood Platelets. Little, Brown; Boston. p. 595.

[6] Hjort, P. F., and H. Paputchis. 1960. Blood 15:45.

[7] Krise, G. M., et al. 1958. J. Appl. Physiol. 12:482.

[8] Merritt, K. K., and L. T. Davidson. 1933. Amer. J. Dis. Child. 46:1008.

[9] Miale, J. B. 1972. Laboratory Medicine: Hematology. Ed. 4. C. V. Mosby, St. Louis.

[10] Odell, T. T. Unpublished. Oak Ridge National Laboratory, Oak Ridge, Tenn., 1968.

[11] Otis, K., et al. 1952. Blood 7:948.

[12] Pearman, V. Unpublished. Univ. Minnesota, College Veterinary Medicine, Minneapolis.

[13] Pitcock, J. P., et al. 1962. Radiat. Res. 16:692.

[14] Rodriguez-Erdmann, F., et al. 1961. Thromb. Diath. Haemorrh. 5:518.

[15] Sorensen, D. K., et al. 1960. Radiat. Res. 13:669.

[16] Tocantins, L. M. 1938. Medicine (Baltimore) 17:202.

[17] Trum, B. F., et al. 1959. Radiat. Res. 11:326.

[18] Upton, A. C., and T. T. Odell, Jr. 1956. Arch. Pathol. 62:194.

[19] Wood, F. C., et al. 1929. Laboratory Technique. Ed. 3. T. Dougherty, New York. p. 26.

257. LEUKOCYTE COUNTS: MAN

Values are normal counts in healthy individuals, and are given as thousands per microliter of blood and as percent of total leukocytes. Values in parentheses are ranges, estimate "c", unless otherwise indicated (*see* Introduction).

Part I. Full-Term and Premature Infants

Myelocytes were found in small numbers during the first few days after birth. An occasional promyelocyte, or blast cell, was also found during this period, more often in premature than in full-term infants. About five nucleated erythrocytes per 100 leukocytes were found in the first day after birth, the number being higher in prematures.

	Age	Leukocytes, Total	Neutrophils		Eosinophils	Lymphocytes	Monocytes
			Segmented + Band	Metamyelocytes			
			Full-Term Infants [L/]				
1	0 hr	16.1(10.1-27.0)	8.0(4.4-13.2) 50%	0.75(0.30-2.00) 4.7%	0.80(0.20-2.20) 4.8%	5.6(3.5-8.6) 35%	0.95(0.55-1.60) 5.9%

[L/] 15 subjects, unless otherwise indicated.

continued

257. LEUKOCYTE COUNTS: MAN

Part I. Full-Term and Premature Infants

	Age	Leukocytes, Total	Neutrophils		Eosinophils	Lymphocytes	Monocytes
			Segmented + Band	Metamyelocytes			
2	6 hr	19.2(13.3-29.7)	11.6(7.4-18.0) 60%	0.75(0.25-2.10) 3.9%	0.75(0.25-1.90) 3.9%	4.6(3.0-7.4) 24%	1.40(0.70-2.00) 7.3%
3	12 hr	21.7(14.1-29.2)	13.2(9.0-18.5) 62%	0.70(0.30-1.65) 3.2%	0.80(0.15-1.90) 3.7%	5.3(3.4-7.9) 25%	1.40(0.95-2.00) 6.5%
4	18 hr	20.3(13.5-28.1)	12.3(8.1-17.1) 61%	0.70(0.25-1.70) 3.4%	0.80(0.15-2.15) 3.9%	4.9(2.9-7.7) 24%	1.30(0.90-2.50) 6.3%
5	24 hr	17.6(12.3-26.5)	10.5(7.1-15.3) 60%	0.55(0.15-1.10) 3.1%	0.75(0.10-2.15) 4.2%	4.4(3.1-6.6) 25%	1.15(0.75-2.00) 6.5%
6	2 da	12.2(7.8-17.8)	6.6(4.1-10.2) 54%	0.30(0.10-0.85) 2.5%	0.70(0.15-1.55) 5.7%	3.6(2.0-5.5) 30%	0.80(0.60-1.10) 6.5%
7	3 da	8.7(6.6-12.4)	4.2(1.9-6.9) 48%	0.20(0-0.50) 2.3%	0.45(0.20-1.00) 5.2%	3.3(2.2-5.2) 38%	0.60(0.30-1.05) 6.9%
8	4 da[2]	9.8(4.7-17.8)	4.1(1.4-10.2); (1.4-6.9)[b] 41%	0.15(0-0.45) 1.6%	0.70(0.20-1.80); (0.2-1.9)[b][3] 7.2%	3.9(2.0-9.1); (2.2-7.1)[b][3] 40%	1.00(0.30-2.10); (0.20-1.80)[b] 10.1%
9	5 da	8.3(4.7-12.4)	3.3(1.3-5.0) 40%	0.15(0-0.50) 1.8%	0.45(0.15-0.95) 5.3%	3.5(2.7-4.8) 42%	0.85(0.45-1.60) 10.2%
10	6 da	8.7(5.2-12.5)	3.2(1.0-5.6) 37%	0.10(0-0.40) 1.25%	0.45(0.20-1.10) 5.2%	4.0(2.9-5.9) 46%	0.85(0.50-1.60) 9.8%
11	7 da	9.6(5.2-13.0)	3.2(1.1-4.8) 34%	0.10(0-0.50) 1.1%	0.45(0.20-0.90) 4.7%	4.9(3.4-6.6) 51%	0.85(0.45-1.70) 8.9%
12	8 da	11.3(9.5-13.4)	3.8(1.2-4.7) 34%	0.10(0-0.40) 0.9%	0.55(0.30-0.95) 4.8%	5.8(4.4-6.5) 51%	1.00(0.75-1.50) 8.9%
13	10 da	11.6(9.5-13.4)	3.2(1.1-4.8) 28%	0.05(0-0.30) 0.5%	0.40(0.20-0.65) 3.5%	6.8(5.7-8.5) 59%	1.05(0.65-1.60) 9.0%
			Premature Infants[4]				
14	0 hr	10.7(5.9-16.7)	5.2(2.0-8.7) 49%	0.8(0.25-2.40) 7.5%	0.40(0.10-0.75) 3.7%	3.7(2.6-6.2) 34%	0.55(0.30-1.00) 5.1%
15	6 hr	12.2(5.5-17.5)	6.5(2.5-10.5) 53%	1.05(0.20-2.40) 8.6%	0.40(0.30-0.65) 3.3%	3.6(2.0-5.5) 30%	0.65(0.35-0.90) 5.3%
16	12 hr	14.0(6.1-18.6)	8.0(3.3-11.1) 57%	0.90(0.20-2.35) 6.4%	0.50(0.15-1.20) 3.6%	3.6(1.7-5.3) 26%	0.95(0.25-1.45) 6.8%
17	18 hr	13.1(5.5-19.2)	7.5(2.7-11.0) 57%	0.60(0.15-1.60) 4.6%	0.60(0.15-1.10) 4.6%	3.5(1.6-4.8) 27%	0.85(0.30-1.50) 6.5%
18	24 hr	12.6(5.4-17.0)	7.5(2.4-9.3) 59%	0.45(0.10-1.10) 3.6%	0.55(0.15-1.40) 4.4%	3.3(2.0-4.8) 26%	0.80(0.40-1.35) 6.3%
19	2 da	9.6(4.9-14.5)	5.2(2.2-8.3) 54%	0.30(0.05-0.65) 3.1%	0.50(0.15-1.15) 5.2%	2.9(1.7-4.5) 30%	0.70(0.35-1.15) 7.3%
20	3 da	8.7(4.9-12.3)	4.3(2.2-6.8) 50%	0.20(0.05-0.60) 2.2%	0.45(0.15-0.90) 5.2%	2.9(1.6-4.6) 33%	0.70(0.35-1.25) 7.9%
21	4 da	8.5(4.9-11.5)	3.8(2.2-6.2) 45%	0.15(0.05-0.60) 1.8%	0.45(0.10-1.05) 5.3%	3.2(1.9-4.2) 38%	0.85(0.40-1.50) 10.0%
22	5 da	9.4(5.7-11.3)	3.7(2.5-5.5) 40%	0.20(0-0.55) 2.0%	0.55(0.20-1.00) 5.8%	3.9(2.2-5.2) 42%	1.00(0.45-1.30) 10.6%
23	6 da	9.5(5.0-13.0)	3.5(1.5-5.7) 37%	0.15(0-0.50) 1.6%	0.60(0.15-1.15) 6.3%	4.2(2.1-5.2) 44%	1.05(0.50-1.55) 11.1%
24	7 da	10.5(4.9-14.0)	3.5(1.5-5.2) 33%	0.20(0-0.50) 1.9%	0.65(0.20-1.15) 6.2%	5.0(2.4-7.2) 48%	1.15(0.55-1.60) 11.0%
25	8 da	11.2(5.6-14.4)	3.6(1.7-6.7) 32%	0.20(0.05-0.45) 1.8%	0.70(0.25-1.15) 6.2%	5.4(2.9-7.6) 48%	1.25(0.55-1.85) 11.1%

[2] 53 subjects. [3] Values showed a logarithmically normal distribution. [4] 14 subjects.

continued

Part I. Full-Term and Premature Infants

	Age	Leukocytes, Total	Neutrophils		Eosinophils	Lymphocytes	Monocytes
			Segmented + Band	Metamyelocytes			
26	10 da	11.3(7.1-15.5)	3.4(1.5-5.9) 30%	0.15(0-0.45) 1.4%	0.70(0.25-1.30) 6.2%	5.8(3.8-7.9) 51%	1.20(0.75-1.65) 10.6%
27	20 da	10.8(8.2-16.0)	2.7(1.6-4.4) 25%	0.05(0-0.35) 0.5%	0.90(0.30-2.55) 8.3%	5.8(4.5-7.4) 54%	1.15(0.80-1.90) 10.6%
28	31 da	10.1(7.0-14.0)	1.9(1.6-2.3) 19%	0.05(0-0.30) 0.5%	0.95(0.35-1.85) 9.4%	6.2(4.1-7.6) 61%	1.00(0.50-1.25) 9.9%

Contributor: Xanthou, Maria

Reference: Xanthou, M. 1970. Arch. Dis. Childhood 45:242.

Part II. All Ages

Leukocytes, Total: Mean value is the sum of the means for neutrophils, eosinophils, basophils, lymphocytes, and monocytes. Values for entries 1-23 were derived from smoothed curves plotted from data given in references 2, 4-16, 18 and 19. For additional information, consult reference 1.

	Age	Leukocytes, Total	Neutrophils			Eosinophils	Basophils	Lymphocytes	Monocytes
			Total	Band[1]	Segmented				
1	At birth	18.1(9.0-30.0)[2]	11.0(6.0-26.0) 61%	1.65 9.1%	9.4 52%	0.40(0.02-0.85) 2.2%	0.10(0-0.64) 0.6%	5.5(2.0-11.0) 31%	1.05(0.40-3.1) 5.8%
2	12 hr	22.8(13.0-38.0)	15.5(6.0-28.0) 68%	2.33 10.2%	13.2 58%	0.45(0.02-0.95) 2.0%	0.10(0-0.50) 0.4%	5.5(2.0-11.0) 24%	1.20(0.40-3.6) 5.3%
3	24 hr	18.9(9.4-34.0)	11.5(5.0-21.0) 61%	1.75 9.2%	9.8 52%	0.45(0.05-1.00) 2.4%	0.10(0-0.30) 0.5%	5.8(2.0-11.5) 31%	1.10(0.20-3.1) 5.8%
4	1 wk	12.2(5.0-21.0)	5.5(1.5-10.0) 45%	0.83 6.8%	4.7 39%	0.50(0.07-1.10) 4.1%	0.05(0-0.25) 0.4%	5.0(2.0-17.0) 41%	1.10(0.30-2.7) 9.1%
5	2 wk	11.4(5.0-20.0)	4.5(1.0-9.5) 40%	0.63 5.5%	3.9 34%	0.35(0.07-1.00) 3.1%	0.05(0-0.23) 0.4%	5.5(2.0-17.0) 48%	1.00(0.20-2.4) 8.8%
6	4 wk	10.8(5.0-19.5)	3.8(1.0-9.0) 35%	0.49 4.5%	3.3 30%	0.30(0.07-0.90) 2.8%	0.05(0-0.20) 0.5%	6.0(2.5-16.5) 56%	0.70(0.15-2.0) 6.5%
7	2 mo	11.0(5.5-18.0)	3.8(1.0-9.0) 34%	0.49 4.4%	3.3 30%	0.30(0.07-0.85) 2.7%	0.05(0-0.20) 0.5%	6.3(3.0-16.0) 57%	0.65(0.13-1.8) 5.9%
8	4 mo	11.5(6.0-17.5)	3.8(1.0-9.0) 33%	0.45 3.9%	3.3 29%	0.30(0.07-0.80) 2.6%	0.05(0-0.20) 0.4%	6.8(3.5-14.5) 59%	0.60(0.10-1.5) 5.2%
9	6 mo	12.0(6.0-17.5)	3.8(1.0-8.5) 32%	0.45 3.8%	3.3 28%	0.30(0.07-0.75) 2.5%	0.05(0-0.20) 0.4%	7.3(4.0-13.5) 61%	0.58(0.10-1.3) 4.8%
10	8 mo	12.2(6.0-17.5)	3.7(1.0-8.5) 30%	0.41 3.3%	3.3 27%	0.30(0.07-0.70) 2.5%	0.05(0-0.20) 0.4%	7.6(4.5-12.5) 62%	0.58(0.08-1.2) 4.7%
11	10 mo	12.0(6.0-17.5)	3.6(1.0-8.5) 30%	0.40 3.3%	3.2 27%	0.30(0.06-0.70) 2.5%	0.05(0-0.20) 0.4%	7.5(4.5-11.5) 63%	0.55(0.05-1.2) 4.6%
12	12 mo	11.4(6.0-17.5)	3.5(1.5-8.5) 31%	0.35 3.1%	3.2 28%	0.30(0.05-0.70) 2.6%	0.05(0-0.20) 0.4%	7.0(4.0-10.5) 61%	0.55(0.05-1.1) 4.8%
13	2 yr	10.6(6.0-17.0)	3.5(1.5-8.5) 33%	0.32 3.0%	3.2 30%	0.28(0.04-0.65) 2.6%	0.05(0-0.20) 0.5%	6.3(3.0-9.5) 59%	0.53(0.05-1.0) 5.0%

[1] Includes a small percentage of myelocytes during first few days after birth. [2] Approximately 3 nucleated erythrocytes per 100 leukocytes have been found at birth.

continued

Part II. All Ages

Age		Leukocytes, Total	Neutrophils			Eosinophils	Basophils	Lymphocytes	Monocytes
			Total	Band	Segmented				
14	4 yr	9.1(5.5-15.5)	3.8(1.5-8.5) 42%	0.27 3.0%	3.5 39%	0.25(0.02-0.65) 2.8%	0.05(0-0.20) 0.6%	4.5(2.0-8.0) 50%	0.45(0-0.8) 5.0%
15	6 yr	8.5(5.0-14.5)	4.3(1.5-8.0) 51%	0.25 3.0%	4.0 48%	0.23(0-0.65) 2.7%	0.05(0-0.20) 0.6%	3.5(1.5-7.0) 42%	0.40(0-0.8) 4.7%
16	8 yr	8.3(4.5-13.5)	4.4(1.5-8.0) 53%	0.25 3.0%	4.1 50%	0.20(0-0.60) 2.4%	0.05(0-0.20) 0.6%	3.3(1.5-6.8) 39%	0.35(0-0.8) 4.2%
17	10 yr	8.1(4.5-13.5)	4.4(1.8-8.0) 54%	0.24 3.0%	4.2 51%	0.20(0-0.60) 2.4%	0.04(0-0.20) 0.5%	3.1(1.5-6.5) 38%	0.35(0-0.8) 4.3%
18	12 yr	8.0(4.5-13.5)	4.4(1.8-8.0) 55%	0.24 3.0%	4.2 52%	0.20(0-0.55) 2.5%	0.04(0-0.20) 0.5%	3.0(1.2-6.0) 38%	0.35(0-0.8) 4.4%
19	14 yr	7.9(4.5-13.0)	4.4(1.8-8.0) 56%	0.24 3.0%	4.2 53%	0.20(0-0.50) 2.5%	0.04(0-0.20) 0.5%	2.9(1.2-5.8) 37%	0.38(0-0.8) 4.7%
20	16 yr	7.8(4.5-13.0)	4.4(1.8-8.0) 57%	0.23 3.0%	4.2 54%	0.20(0-0.50) 2.6%	0.04(0-0.20) 0.5%	2.8(1.2-5.2) 35%	0.40(0-0.8) 5.1%
21	18 yr	7.7(4.5-12.5)	4.4(1.8-7.7) 57%	0.23 3.0%	4.2 54%	0.20(0-0.45) 2.6%	0.04(0-0.20) 0.5%	2.7(1.0-5.0) 35%	0.40(0-0.8) 5.2%
22	20 yr	7.5(4.5-11.5)	4.4(1.8-7.7) 59%	0.23 3.0%	4.2 56%	0.20(0-0.45) 2.7%	0.04(0-0.20) 0.5%	2.5(1.0-4.8) 33%	0.38(0-0.8) 5.0%
23	21 yr	7.4(4.5-11.0)	4.4(1.8-7.7) 59%	0.22 3.0%	4.2 56%	0.20(0-0.45) 2.7%	0.04(0-0.20) 0.5%	2.5(1.0-4.8) 34%	0.30(0-0.8) 4.0%
24	15->70 yr[3]	(4.1-10.9)[a]	(2.27-7.68)[a] (47.0-79.5)[a]%	....	....	(0-0.49)[a] (0-7.5)[a]%	(0-0.16)[a] (0-2.0)[a]%	(0.83-3.14)[a] (12.5-40.0)[a]%	(0.12-0.80)[a] (2.0-11.0)[a]%
25	>21 yr[4] White	7.1(3.9-10.3)	4.5(1.8-7.5) 63%	0.08(0-0.5) 1.1%	4.4(1.8-7.0) 62%	0.12(0-0.37) 1.7%	0.02(0-0.09) 0.3%	2.3(0.9-3.7) 32%	0.22(0-0.6) 3.1%
26	Black[5]	6.6(3.1-10.1)	4.0(1.0-7.1) 60%	0.05(0-0.3) 0.7%	3.9(1.0-6.8) 58%	0.12(0-0.40) 1.8%	0.02(0-0.14) 0.3%	2.4(1.0-3.7) 36%	0.23(0-0.6) 3.4%

[3] Values were extracted from reference 20. No differences in counts due to age or sex could be detected. [4] Values were derived from reference 3. [5] For information on blacks in Africa, consult reference 17.

Contributors: Broun, Goronwy O., Sr., Broun, Goronwy O., Jr., and Herbig, Francis; Jenkins, David E., Jr.; Wintrobe, M. M.

References

[1] Altman, P. L., and D. S. Dittmer, ed. 1961. Blood and Other Body Fluids. Federation of American Societies for Experimental Biology, Washington, D.C. pp. 125-127.

[2] Broun, G. O., Sr. Unpublished. St. Louis Univ., School Medicine, St. Louis, 1950.

[3] Broun, G. O., Jr., et al. 1966. N. Engl. J. Med. 275: 1410.

[4] Glaser, K., et al. 1950. Pediatrics 6:789.

[5] Hamre, C. J., and K. K. L. Wong. 1940. Amer. J. Dis. Child. 60:22.

[6] Hutaff, L. W., and G. T. Harrell. 1946. N.C. Med. J. 7:641.

[7] Lippman, H. S. 1924. Amer. J. Dis. Child. 27:473.

[8] Lucas, W. P. 1921. Ibid. 22:525.

[9] Osgood, E. E., et al. 1939. Ibid. 58:61.

[10] Osgood, E. E., et al. 1939. Ibid. 58:282.

[11] Osgood, E. E., et al. 1939. Arch. Intern. Med. 64:105.

[12] Osgood, E. E., et al. 1939. J. Lab. Clin. Med. 24:905.

[13] Smith, C. A. 1959. The Physiology of the Newborn Infant. Ed. 3. C. C. Thomas, Springfield, Ill.

[14] Sturgis, C. C., and F. H. Bethell. 1943. Physiol. Rev. 23:279.

[15] Sunderman, F. W., and F. Boerner. 1949. Normal Values in Clinical Medicine. W. B. Saunders, Philadelphia.

[16] Washburn, A. H. 1935. Amer. J. Dis. Child. 50:413.

[17] Wasserman, H. P. 1966. S. Afr. Med. J. 40(Suppl.).

[18] Wegelius, R. 1948. Acta Paediat. (Stockholm), Suppl. 4.

[19] Wintrobe, M. M. 1974. Clinical Hematology. Ed. 7. Lea and Febiger, Philadelphia.

[20] Zacharski, L. R., et al. 1971. Amer. J. Clin. Pathol. 56:148.

Part I. Mammals, Birds, Reptiles, and Amphibians

Values are given as thousands per microliter of blood and as percent of total leukocytes. Values in parentheses are ranges, estimate "c" (*see* Introduction).

	Species (Synonym)	Leukocytes, Total	Neutrophils	Eosinophils	Basophils	Lymphocytes	Monocytes	Reference
			Mammalia					
1	*Bos taurus*	9.2(6.0-12.0)	2.9(1.9-3.7) 31.9(20-40)%	0.7(0.3-1.3) 7.7(3-15)%	0.06(0-0.09) 0.62(0-1)%	5.09(4.1-5.9) 55.4(45-65)%	0.48(0.27-1.40) 5.2(3-15)%	11
2	*Canis familiaris*	12.0(8.0-18.0)	8.2(6.0-12.5) 68(62-80)%	0.6(0.2-2.0) 5.1(2-14)%	0.085(0-0.3) 0.7(0-2)%	2.5(0.9-4.5) 21(10-28)%	0.65(0.3-1.5) 5.2(3-9)%	1
3	*Capra hircus*	(5.0-14.0)	(2.10-3.35)	(0-1.1)	(0-0.6)	(2.10-11.25)	(0.05-0.60)	4
4	*Cavia* sp.	10.0(7.0-19.0)	4.2(2.0-7.0) 42(22-50)%	0.4(0.2-1.3) 4(2-12)%	0.07(0-0.3) 0.7(0-2)%	4.9(3.0-9.0) 49(37-64)%	0.43(0.25-2.00) 4.3(3-13)%	1
5	*Equus caballus*	(5.0-11.0)	(3.0-6.9)	(0.05-0.60)	(0-0.1)	(1.2-4.8)	(0.10-1.45)	4
6	*Felis catus*	16.0(9.0-24.0)	9.5(5.5-16.5) 59.5(44-82)%	0.85(0.2-2.5) 5.4(2-11)%	0.02(0-0.1) 0.1(0-0.5)%	5.0(2.0-9.0) 31(15-44)%	0.65(0.05-1.40) 4(0.5-7.0)%	1
7	*Macaca* spp.[1]	14.0(7-18)	4.75 (21-47)%	0.42 (0-6)%	0.14 (0-2)%	8.55 (47-75)%	0.12 (0.1-1.5)%	12
8	*Mesocricetus auratus*	6.2(3.4-7.6)	1.45 (3-43)%	0.06 (0-2)%	0	4.52 (50-96)%	0.03 (0-1)%	12
9	*Mus* sp.[2]	8.0(4.0-12.0)	2.0(0.7-4.0) 25.5(12-44)%	0.15(0-0.5) 2(0-5)%	0.05(0-0.1) 0.5(0-1)%	5.5(3.0-8.5) 68(54-85)%	0.3(0-1.3) 4(0-15)%	1
10	*Oryctolagus cuniculus*	9.0(6.0-13.0)	4.1(2.5-6.0) 46(36-52)%	0.18(0-0.4) 2(0.5-3.5)%	0.45(0.15-0.75) 5(2-7)%	3.5(2.0-5.6) 39(30-52)%	0.725(0.3-1.3) 8(4-12)%	1
11	*Ovis aries*	7.8(5-10)	2.8(1.6-3.5) 35.7(20-45)%	0.19(0.08-0.5) 2.5(1-7)%	0.03(0-0.15) 0.4(0-2)%	4.4(3.9-5.5) 56.9(50-70)%	0.47(0.08-0.60) 6(1-8)%	11
12	*Papio cyno-cephalus*	13.0(5.8-20.2)	4.1(0.1-8.1) 31%	0.14(0-0.3) 1%	0.03(0-0.06) 0.25%	8.3(3.4-13.4) 65%	0.25(0.05-0.45) 2.75%	15
13	*Rattus* sp.	14.0(5.0-25.0)	3.1(1.1-6.0) 22(9-34)%	0.3(0-0.7) 2.2(0-6)%	0.1(0-0.2) 0.5(0-1.5)%	10.2(7.0-16.0) 73(65-84)%	0.3(0-0.65) 2.3(0-5)%	1
14	*Sus scrofa*	(7.0-20.0)	(2.4-10.0)	(0.05-2.00)	(0-0.8)	(3.2-12.0)	(0.05-2.00)	4
			Aves[3]					
15	*Anas* sp.	23.4	24.3%	2.1%	1.0(0-4.5)%	45.8(13-73.5)%	4.4(0.5-11.5)%	7,13
16	*Gallus gallus* (*G. domesticus*)	32.6(9.1-56.0)	9.1(3.0-18.2)[4] 27.8(9.1-56.0)%	0.05(0-0.23)[5] 1.5(0-7)%	0.9(0-2.6) 2.7(0-8)%	17.6(7.8-27.3) 54(24-84)%	4.4(0-9.7) 13.7(0-30)%	14
17 18	*Meleagris gallo-pavo*	19.0(16.0-25.5)	44.5(35-65)%[6,7] 45.4(39-52)%[7,9]	7.5(1-24)%[6,8] 2.3(0-5)%[8,9]	6.9(3-11)%[6] 5.1(1-9)%[9]	36.3(22-46)%[6] 40.9(35-48)%[9]	7.3(2-11)%[6] 6.5(3-10)%[9]	5
			Reptilia					
19	*Cordylus vit-tifer*	24.5(20-27.5)	8.3%	16.6%	7.3%	64.3%	3.5%	9
20	*Pituophis sayi*	50.2[10]	2.7[4,5] 5.4%	....	0.01 0.2%	19.7 39.4%	3.4 6.9%	10
21	*Terrapene caro-lina*	37.5(24.0-48.0)	0.01[10] 0.3%	4.1 10.8%	3.0 8%	21.0 56.1%	3.5 9.4%	2,3
			Amphibia					
22	*Rana* sp.	6.1(4.9-7.3)	(24-72)%	(7-22)%	(1-15)%	(17-48)%	(2-20)%	12

[1] Statistical analysis indicates no significant differences in cell counts among various species; leukocyte counts within species show large variations. [2] For additional information on inbred strains of mice, consult reference 6. [3] For more recent information on avian hematology, consult reference 8. [4] Heterophils with rod-shaped eosinophilic bodies. [5] Heterophils with granular eosinophilic bodies. [6] Supravital stain. [7] Polymorphic myelocytes with eosinophilic rods. [8] Polymorphic myelocytes with pseudoeosinophilic granules. [9] Wright's stain. [10] Includes thrombocytes.

continued

Part I. Mammals, Birds, Reptiles, and Amphibians

Contributors: Altland, Paul D.; Dunlap, J. S.; Dabrowski, Z.; Rigdon, R. H.

References

[1] Albritton, E. C., ed. 1951. Standard Values in Blood. W. B. Saunders, Philadelphia. p. 53.

[2] Altland, P. D., and M. Parker. 1955. Amer. J. Physiol. 180:421.

[3] Bernstein, R. E. 1938. S. Afr. J. Sci. 35:327.

[4] Craige, A. H., Jr. Unpublished. Univ. Pennsylvania, School Veterinary Medicine, Philadelphia, 1950.

[5] Dunlap, J. S. Unpublished. Washington State College, College Veterinary Medicine, Pullman, 1956.

[6] Green, E. L., ed. 1966. Biology of the Laboratory Mouse. McGraw-Hill, Blakiston Division, New York.

[7] Hewitt, R. 1942. Amer. J. Hyg. 36:6.

[8] Lucas, A. M., and C. Jamroz. 1961. U.S. Dep. Agr. Agr. Monogr. 25.

[9] Pienaar, U. D. V. 1962. Haematology of Some South African Reptiles. Witwatersrand Press, Johannesburg. p. 126.

[10] Ryerson, D. L. 1949. J. Entomol. Zool. 41(4):49.

[11] Scarborough, R. A. 1932. Yale J. Biol. 4:69.

[12] Schermer, S. 1967. The Blood Morphology of Laboratory Animals. Ed. 3. F. A. Davis, Philadelphia.

[13] Sturkie, P. D. 1954. Avian Physiology. Comstock, Ithaca.

[14] Twisselmann, N. M. 1939. Poult. Sci. 18:151.

[15] Vagtborg, H. 1965. The Baboon in Medical Research. Univ. Texas Press, Austin.

Part II. Fishes

Values are percent of total leukocytes, unless otherwise indicated. Plus/minus (±) values are standard error. Data in brackets refer to the column heading in brackets.

Order & Species	Hemocytoblasts	Neutrophils	Eosinophils	Basophils [Heterophils]	Lymphocytes	Macrophages [Monocytes]	Thrombocytes	Reference
Dipnoi								
Ceratodiformes								
1 Neoceratodus forsteri	1	6	46	0	4	1	42	1
Osteichthyes								
Pleuronectiformes								
2 Achirus lineatus	1	9	6	0	31	0	53	1
3 Paralichthys lethostigma	4	5	3	3	32	3	50	
Perciformes								
4 Archosargus probatocephalus	0	11	5	1	37	0	46	1
5 Caranx crysos	1	10	6	3	40	0	40	
6 Chaetodipterus faber	1	5	3	1	36	1	53	
7 Cynoscion arenarius	1	4	12	2	33	0	48	
8 C. nebulosus	0	7	6	3	32	1	51	
9 Lagodon rhomboides	0	8	11	1	31	1	48	
10 Larimus fasciatus	0	5	11	5	35	1	43	
11 Lepomis cyanellus	1	12	10	2	26	0	49	
12 Micropogon undulatus	0	9	1	5	32	1	52	
13 Mugil cephalus	5	2	2	3	37	0	51	
14 M. curema	2	2	11	0	46	0	39	
15 Orthopristis chrysopterus	0	8	3	1	36	1	51	
16 Peprilus alepidotus	2	7	23	3	38	1	26	
17 P. burti[1]	0	14	5	2	31	0	48	
18 Pogonias cromis	1	6	12	0	34	1	46	
19 Polydactylus octonemus	1	16	12	0	24	0	47	
20 Rachycentron canadum	0	8	4	3	29	0	56	

[1] Synonym: Poronotus burti.

continued

Part II. Fishes

	Order & Species	Hemocy-toblasts	Neutro-phils	Eosino-phils	Basophils [Hetero-phils]	Lympho-cytes	Macro-phages [Mono-cytes]	Throm-bocytes	Refer-ence
21	*Sciaenops ocellata*	1	3	25	6	25	1	39	
22	*Scomberomorus maculatus*	2	8	26	2	30	1	31	
23	*Trachinotus carolinus*	2	1	16	0	38	2	41	
24	*Trichiurus lepturus*	0	14	4	2	31	0	49	
	Batrachoidiformes								1
25	*Opsanus beta*	2	18	4	0	30	1	45	
26	*Porichthys porosissimus*	2	8	4	1	30	1	54	
	Siluriformes								1
27	*Arius felis* [2]	1	7	7	3	31	0	51	
28	*Bagre marinus*	0	10	13	2	30	0	45	
29	*Clarias batrachus*	2	9	2	0	40	0	47	
	Cypriniformes								2
30	*Carassius auratus* [3]	..	5.1	2.2	0.02	92.6	[0]	....	
31		..	(1.13 ± 0.14) [4]	(0.48 ± 0.06) [4]	(0.04 ± 0.02) [4]	(20.3 ± 1.8) [4]	[0] [4]	....	
	Salmoniformes								1
32	*Esox americanus vermiculatus*	2	0	4	2	37	1	54	
33	*Synodus foetens*	1	9	6	1	32	1	50	
	Anguilliformes								1
34	*Anguilla rostrata*	1	10	32	0	27	0	30	
	Semionotiformes								1
35	*Lepisosteus osseus*	1	0	40	2	12	1	44	
36	*L. spatula*	1	6	2	0	42	2	47	
	Chondrichthyes								
	Rajiformes								1
37	*Dasyatis* sp.	2	1	11	[6]	29	[4]	47	
	Squaliformes								1
38	*Carcharhinus limbatus*	6	6	10	[12]	30	[0]	36	
39	*Rhizoprionodon terraeno-vae* [5]	2	6	9	[6]	36	[0]	41	
40	*Sphyrna tiburo*	0	4	27	[16]	29	[0]	24	

[2] Synonym: *Galeichthys felis.* [3] Total leukocyte count for a male subject was 21.9 ± 1.5 thousands/µl blood. [4] Values are given in terms of thousands/µl blood. [5] Synonym: *Scoliodon terraenovae.*

Contributors: Ward, James W.; Altland, Paul D.

References
[1] Ward, J. W. Unpublished. Univ. South Florida, Dep. Anatomy, Tampa, 1973.

[2] Watson, L. J., et al. 1963. Cytologia 28:116.

259. BONE MARROW DIFFERENTIAL CELL COUNTS

Part I. Rib: Dog

Values in parentheses are ranges, estimate "c" unless otherwise indicated (*see* Introduction).

	Specification	Values from				
		Mulligan	Mulligan	Rekers & Coulter	Stasney & Higgins [1]	Van Loon & Clark
1	Number of subjects	21	35	36	35	81

[1] Ranges are estimate "b" (*see* Introduction).

continued

Part I. Rib: Dog

	Specification	Values from				
		Mulligan	Mulligan	Rekers & Coulter	Stasney & Higgins[1]	Van Loon & Clark
2	Age of subjects	0.5-2.5 da	Adult	19-24 mo	Adult	Adult
3	Cells, % of total count Proerythroblasts	1.3(0.4-3.2)[2]	0.5(0-1.4)[2]	0.3(0-1.3)[3]	59(40-78)	0.6(0.2-2.7)[2]
4	Normoblasts Early	5.8(3.0-9.5)[4]	1.5(0.4-3.8)[5]	28.2(8.0-53.9)[4]		7.8(6.4-10.0)[5]
5	Intermediate	45.1(33.0-56.6)[6]	38.1(18.6-63.6)[6]			16.4(11-26)[7]
6	Late			4.6(0-11.2)[6]		17.4(9-26)[8]
7	Myeloblasts	....	0.6(0-1.8)	1.9(0.2-3.7)	2.4(0-5.1)[9]	0.6(0.2-1.0)
8	Promyelocytes	0.8(0-2.2)	1.5(0.2-4.6)	0.7(0-3.3)	2.8(0-5.8)	1.6(0.7-2.8)
9	Myelocytes	....	....	2.7(0-9.5)	....	6.0(2.7-10.0)
10	Neutrophilic	4.3(2.0-6.6)	4.7(2.2-11.2)	....	8.9(2.8-15.0)	....
11	Eosinophilic	....	....	....	1.2(0-2.4)	....
12	Metamyelocytes	9.7(7.2-12.0)	10.5(5.6-20.0)	5.1(0-24.4)[10]	15.3(7.2-23.0)	3.4(1.1-4.6)
13	Band cells	20.6(14.8-28.4)[11]	31.0(16.8-53.8)[11]	42.4(16.5-62.9)[11]	....	11.7(6.8-17.0)
14	Segmented cells Neutrophilic	3.4(0.8-6.6)	3.9(0.2-8.6)	5.0(0.2-14.3)	5.1(0-12.5)	30.1(17-44)
15	Eosinophilic	2.4(0-5.2)	3.7(1.0-6.8)	4.7(0.2-19.3)	2.8(0-6.8)	2.0(0.4-3.8)
16	Basophilic	....	....	0.2(0-1.3)	0.1(0-0.3)	....
17	Lymphocytes	3.3(1.6-6.0)	1.9(0-6.6)	0.7(0-8)	1.2(0.2-2.3)	0.9(0.2-2.7)
18	Monocytes	....	....	....	....	0.2(0-0.3)
19	Megakaryocytes	....	....	0.6(0-1.1)	0.1(0-0.5)	0.5(0-1.4)
20	Plasma cells	....	....	0.4(0-2.1)	....	....
21	Reticulum cells	....	....	....	1.0(0-2.1)	....
22	Unclassified cells	3.1(0.8-5.4)	2.1(0.8-6.1)	3.0(0-15.7)	0.2(0-0.7)[12]	....
	References	1	2	3	4	5

[1] Ranges are estimate "b" (*see* Introduction). [2] Pronormoblasts. [3] Megaloblasts. [4] Erythrocytes. [5] Basophilic normoblasts. [6] Normoblasts. [7] Polychromic normoblasts. [8] Orthochromic normoblasts. [9] Includes leukoblasts. [10] Juvenile cells. [11] Stab cells. [12] Includes heterophils.

Contributor: Rekers, Paul E.

References
[1] Mulligan, R. M. 1941. Anat. Rec. 79:101.
[2] Mulligan, R. M. 1945. Ibid. 91:161.
[3] Rekers, P. E., and M. Coulter. 1948. Amer. J. Med. Sci. 216:643.
[4] Stasney, J., and G. M. Higgins. 1937. Ibid. 193:462.
[5] Van Loon, E. J., and B. B. Clark. 1943. Clin. Med. 28:1575.

Part II. Sternum: Man

All values are for adults. For values for children, consult reference 6, p. 328. For values from other sources, consult references 1, 4, 5, 7, and 9. Values in parentheses are ranges, estimate "c" unless otherwise specified (*see* Introduction).

	Specification	Values from					
		Diggs	Israëls	Miale	Rebuck	Whitby & Britton	Wintrobe
1	Marrow aspirated, ml	(0.1-0.2)	0.2	....	.....	0.25	(1.0-2.0)

continued

Part II. Sternum: Man

	Specification	Values from					
		Diggs	Israëls	Miale	Rebuck	Whitby & Britton	Wintrobe
	Cells, % of total count						
2	Proerythroblasts	(0-1)[1]	(0.5-4.0)	(0.2-4.0)	0.5	(0-4)	4(1-8)[2]
3	Normoblasts	....	....	....	.....	....	18(7-32)
4	Early	(1-4)[3]	(1-5)	(1.5-5.8)	2	(4-15)	....
5	Intermediate	(10-20)[4]	(12-20)	(5.0-26.4)	12	....	....
6	Late	(5-10)[5]	(6-10)	(1.6-21.0)	4	(7-19)	....
7	Myeloblasts	(0-1)	(0.3-2.0)	(0.3-5.0)	1	(0-2.5)	2(0.3-5)
8	Promyelocytes	(1-5)	(1-8)	(1.0-8.0)	6	(0.5-5.0)	5(1-8)
	Myelocytes						
9	Neutrophilic	(2-10)	(5-20)	(5-19)	13	(2-8)	12(5-19)
10	Eosinophilic	....	....	(0.5-3.0)	1	(0-1)	1.5(0.5-3)
11	Basophilic	....	....	(0-0.3)	<1	....	0.3(0-0.5)
12	Metamyelocytes	....	....	....	.....	....	22(13-32)
13	Neutrophilic	(5-15)	(13-32)[6]	(13-32)	15	(10-25)	....
14	Eosinophilic	....	....	(0.3-3.7)	1	(0-2.5)	....
	Band cells						
15	Neutrophilic	(10-40)	....	(15-30)	16	....	....
	Segmented cells						
16	Neutrophilic	(10-30)	(7-30)	(7-30)	15	(10-40)[6,7]	20(7-30)[7]
17	Eosinophilic	(0-3)	(0.5-4.0)	(0.5-4.0)	1	(0-4)[6,7]	2(0.5-4)[7]
18	Basophilic	(0-1)	(0-1)	(0-0.7)	0.5	(0-1)[7]	0.2(0-0.7)[7]
19	Lymphocytes	(5-15)	(3-20)	(2.7-24.0)	10	(5-20)	10(3-17)
20	Monocytes	(0-2)	(0.5-5.0)	(0.7-2.8)	1	(0-5)	2(0.5-5)
21	Megakaryocytes	....	±[8]	(0.03-0.4)	<0.2	....	0.4(0.03-3)
22	Plasma cells	(0-1)	(0-2)	(0.1-1.5)	1	(0-1)	0.4(0-2)
23	Reticulum cells	....	±[8]	(0.2-2.0)	<0.2	....	0.2(0.1-2)
24	Unclassified cells	....	....	(0.02-3.3)	.....	....	....
25	Disintegrated cells	....	....	(1.1-20.8)	.....	....	....
	Reference	2	3	6	8	10	11

[1] Rubriblasts. [2] Pronormoblasts. [3] Prorubricytes. [4] Rubricytes. [5] Metarubricytes. [6] Includes band cells. [7] Polymorphonuclear cells. [8] Occasionally present.

Contributors: Rebuck, John W.; Diggs, Lemuel W.

References

[1] Berman, L. 1949. Blood 4:511.

[2] Diggs, L. W. In S. E. Miller and J. M. Weller, ed. 1971. Textbook of Clinical Pathology. Ed. 8. Williams and Wilkins, Baltimore. p. 43.

[3] Israëls, M. C. G. 1971. An Atlas of Bone Marrow Pathology. Ed. 4. Grune and Stratton, New York.

[4] Leitner, S. M. 1945. Die intravitale Knochenmarksuntersuchung. B. Schwabe, Basel.

[5] Lucia, S. P., and M. L. Hunt. 1947. Amer. J. Med. Sci. 213:686.

[6] Miale, J. B. 1972. Laboratory Medicine: Hematology. Ed. 4. C. V. Mosby, St. Louis. p. 327.

[7] Osgood, E. E., and A. J. Seaman. 1944. Physiol. Rev. 24:46.

[8] Rebuck, J. W. 1974. Current Values. Henry Ford Hospital, Detroit.

[9] Vaughan, S. L., and F. Brockmyre. 1947. Blood, Spec. Issue 1:54.

[10] Whitby, L. E. H., and C. J. C. Britton. 1969. Disorders of the Blood. Ed. 10. Grune and Stratton, New York.

[11] Wintrobe, M. M. 1967. Clinical Hematology. Ed. 6. Lea and Febiger, Philadelphia.

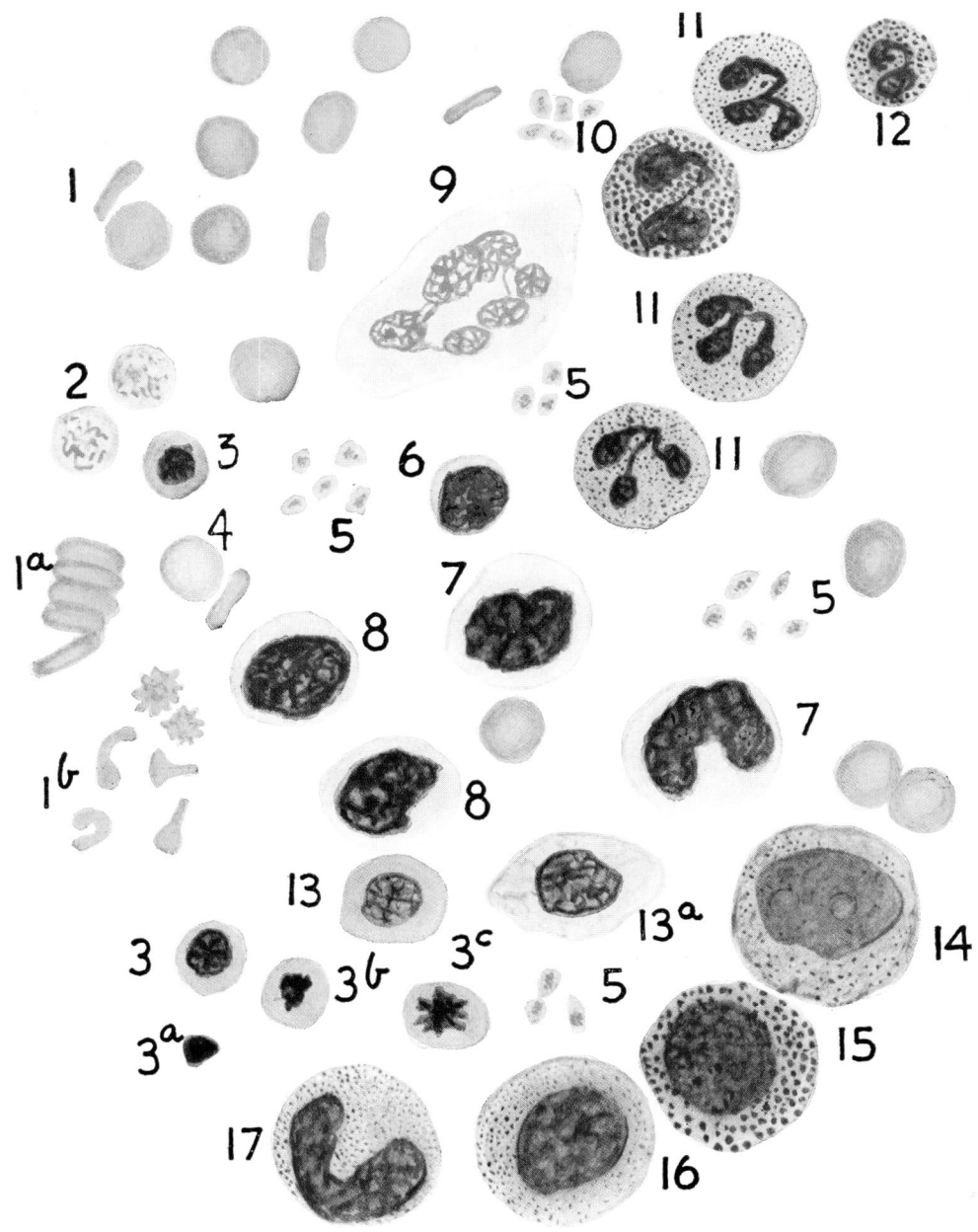

1 Erythrocytes	3^c Normoblast in mitosis	11 Neutrophil leukocytes
1^a Erythrocytes in rouleau	4 Hemolyzed red cells	12 Basophil leukocyte
1^b Deformed cells (poikilocytes),	(ghosts)	13 Polychromatophil
crenated forms	5 Platelets	erythroblast
2 Reticulocytes stained with	6 Small lymphocyte	13^a Hemocytoblast
dilute solution of cresyl blue	7 Monocytes	14 Megaloblast
3 Early normoblasts	8 Large lymphocytes	15 Eosinophil myelocyte
3^a Extruded nucleus	9 Megakaryocyte	16 Neutrophil myelocyte
3^b Late normoblast	10 Eosinophil leukocyte	17 Neutrophil metamyelocyte

Reference: Best, C. H., and N. B. Taylor. 1966. The Physiological Basis of Medical Practice. Ed. 8. Williams and Wilkins, Baltimore.

Oxygen dissociation curves show the relationship between the amount of O_2 which remains chemically combined with hemoglobin, and the O_2 pressure of the blood at a definite temperature and pH. Blood is exposed to O_2, CO_2, and N_2 in tonometers containing gas mixtures. The O_2 content is then measured by manometric or recently developed micromanometric gas-analysis apparatus. After the amount of physically dissolved O_2 is calculated from O_2 pressure and solubility, the amount of O_2 combined with hemoglobin may be determined by subtraction of the dissolved O_2 from the measured O_2 content. At a definite O_2 pressure, the proportion of hemoglobin-bound oxygen (HbO_2) to the maximum binding capacity of hemoglobin for oxygen (O_2 capacity) equals the percent of O_2 saturation of hemoglobin:

$$\frac{HbO_2, \text{vol \%}}{O_2 \text{ capacity, vol \%}} \times 100 = \% \; O_2 \text{ saturation of hemoglobin.}$$

If percent O_2 saturations are compared at different O_2 pressures, the pH for all O_2 saturations must be the same. Therefore the pH values of the individual blood tests must be determined, and the blood O_2 pressures calculated according to pH values. Conversion factor for human blood: $\Delta \log O_2$ pressure = -0.48/unit of serum pH (serum pH = 0.1 pH units).

Method of Measurement: Mixed = O_2 content determined by measuring the pH and O_2 pressure resulting from the quantitative mixing of deoxygenated and oxygenated blood volumes [14,21]. P_{50} = pressure at which hemoglobin is 50% saturated. **Bohr Effect** is calculated by the formula $\frac{\Delta \log P_{50}}{\Delta pH}$. Unless otherwise indicated, determinations were made on blood at a fixed pH of 7.40.

Part I. Adult

A small but significant shift to the right in the oxygen dissociation curves was observed in adaptation to altitude [1, 22,25]. A definite shift to the right was observed in sickle cell anemias [10] and congenital cyanotic heart disease [24]. The literature has been covered through 1971.

BLOOD OBSERVATIONS

	Species (Synonym)	No. of Subjects	Method of Measurement	Temp °C	P_{50} [1] mm Hg	O_2 Capacity ml O_2/100 ml blood	Bohr Effect	Reference
1	*Homo sapiens*	14[2]	Manometric	37.0	27	20	0.48	4
2	*Bos* sp.	6	Manometric	37.0	31	18	0.49	2,18
3	*Camelus bactrianus*	1	Manometric	37.0	24	21	0.49	5
4	*Canis familiaris*	5	Manometric	37.0	29	14	0.50	2,18
5	*Capra hircus* [3]	...	Manometric	39.0	31	14	....	28
6	*C. hircus* [4]	3[5]	Manometric	37.0	30	13	0.50	3,18
7	*Cavia porcellus*	12	Manometric	37.0	27	14	0.47	2,18
8	*Chinchilla laniger*	8	Manometric	37.0	27	...	0.53	17
9	*Cystophora cristata*	2	Micromanometric	38	24	...	0.66	11
10	*Equus caballus*	5	Manometric	37.0	25	...	....	9
11	*Erinaceus europaeus* [6]	10	Micromanometric	37.0	36	19	0.49	7
12	*Eschrichtius gibbosus*	8	Mixed	37.5	30	17	0.46	19
13	*Felis catus*	8	Manometric	37.0	36	17	0.54	2,18
14	*Gorilla gorilla*	2	Manometric	37.0	25	16	0.47	30
15	*Lama glama*	1	Manometric	37.0	23	25	0.42	5
16	*L. vicugna*	1	Manometric	39 & 40 [7]	20[8]	...	....	16
17	*Loxodonta africana*	4	Manometric	37.0	22	16	0.40	31
18	*Macaca mulatta*	6	Manometric	38.0	32	17	....	26
19	*M. nemestrina*	8	Mixed	37.5	37	17	0.52	20
20	*Macropus* sp.	1	Manometric	37.0	28	24	0.54	6
21	*Mesocricetus auratus*	9	Micromanometric	37.0	28	19	0.41	34
22	*Mus musculus*, white	31	Micromanometric	37.0	34	19	0.63	34

[1] Additional estimations of P_{50}: *Homo sapiens*, 26.6 mm Hg [33], 26.5 mm Hg [36], and 24 mm Hg [32]; *Bos* sp., 25 mm Hg [32]; *Canis familiaris*, 29 mm Hg [13] and 31 mm Hg [32]; *Capra hircus*, 28.5 mm Hg [32]; *Cavia porcellus*, 25.4 mm Hg [35] and 34 mm Hg [32]; *Equus caballus*, 23 mm Hg [32]; *Felis catus*, 39 mm Hg [32]; *Ovis aries*, 27 mm Hg [32]. [2] Curve is average of 54 dissociation curves with 207 single points. Significant differences occurred among individuals, with the difference between the lowest and highest P_{50} values being 5.8 mm Hg. [3] African pygmy goat. [4] German deer-goat. [5] 14 dissociation curves with 42 determinations. [6] Nonhibernating. [7] At altitudes of 2.81 and 4.71 km, respectively. [8] Serum pH was calculated from intracellular pH with factors in reference 7.

continued

260. BLOOD OXYGEN DISSOCIATION CURVES: MAMMALS

Part I. Adult

	Species (Synonym)	No. of Subjects	Method of Measurement	Temp °C	P_{50}[9] mm Hg	O$_2$ Capacity ml O$_2$/100 ml blood	Bohr Effect	Refer- ence
23	*Orcinus orca*	6	Mixed	37.5	31	22	0.74	23
24	*Ornithorhynchus anatinus*	3	Micromanometric	37.0	33	23	0.56	27
25	*Oryctolagus cuniculus*	10	Micromanometric	37.0	31	16	0.45	8,18
26	*Ovis aries*	7	Manometric	37.0	34	15	....	2
27	Hemoglobin A	...	Manometric	38.0	32	13[10]	....	12
28	Hemoglobin B	4	Manometric	39.0	41	11	....	29
29	*Pan troglodytes*	1	Manometric	37.0	26	17	0.52	30
30	*Papio anubis (P. doguera)*	8	Mixed	37.5	37	15	0.55	20
31	*Phoca vitulina*	4	Mixed	37.5	31	26	0.53	19
32	*Rattus norvegicus*, Wistar I	16	Micromanometric	37.0	35	23	....	15
33	*Saimiri sciureus*	4	Mixed	37.5	36	18	0.54	20
34	*Sus scrofa*	8	Manometric	37.0	31	22	0.42	2,18
35	*Tursiops truncatus*	3	Mixed	37.5	27	21	0.66	19

[9] Additional estimation of P_{50}: *Sus scrofa*, 32.5 mm Hg [32]. [10] Determination was made at a fixed Pco_2 of 40 mm Hg, rather than at a fixed pH of 7.40.

GRAPHS

Numbers in graph and in legend refer to corresponding line numbers or footnote number ($\_/$) in table. Numbers in heavy brackets are reference numbers.

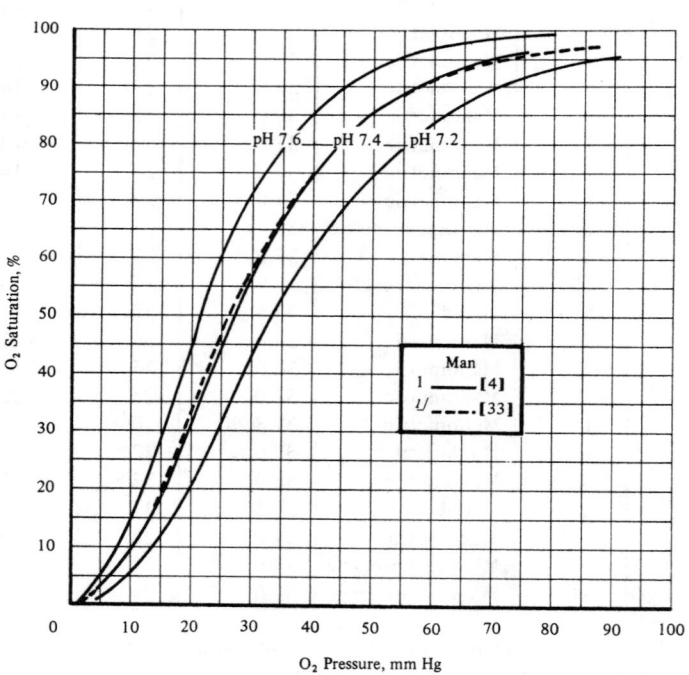

continued

Part I. Adult

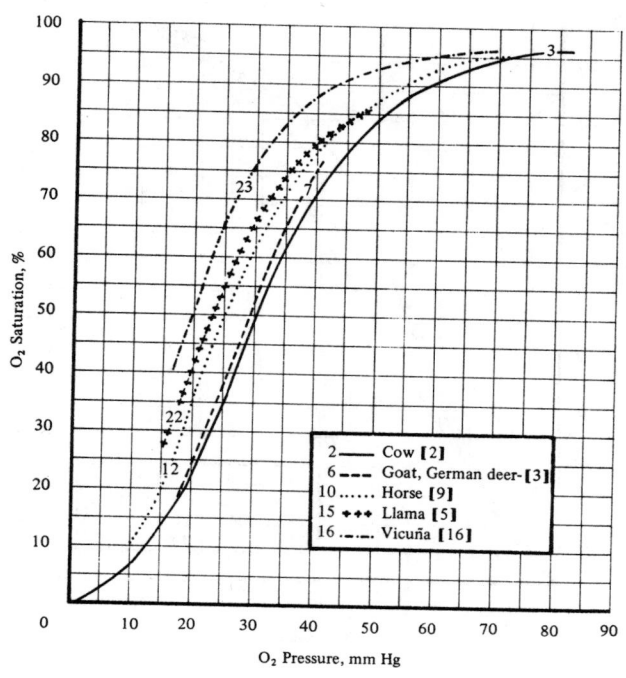

Legend:
- 2 —— Cow [2]
- 6 – – – Goat, German deer- [3]
- 10 ...... Horse [9]
- 15 ✦✦✦ Llama [5]
- 16 .—.—. Vicuña [16]

O₂ Saturation, %

O₂ Pressure, mm Hg

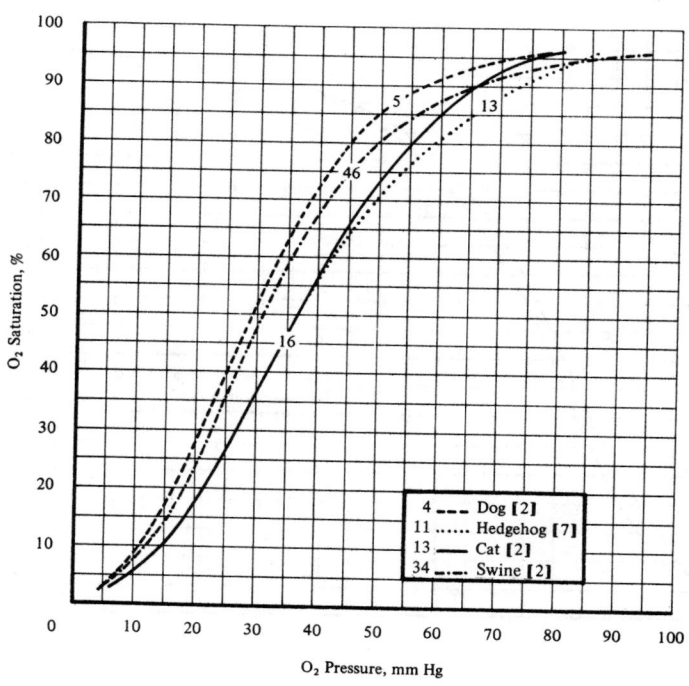

Legend:
- 4 – – – Dog [2]
- 11 ...... Hedgehog [7]
- 13 —— Cat [2]
- 34 .—.—. Swine [2]

O₂ Saturation, %

O₂ Pressure, mm Hg

continued

Part I. Adult

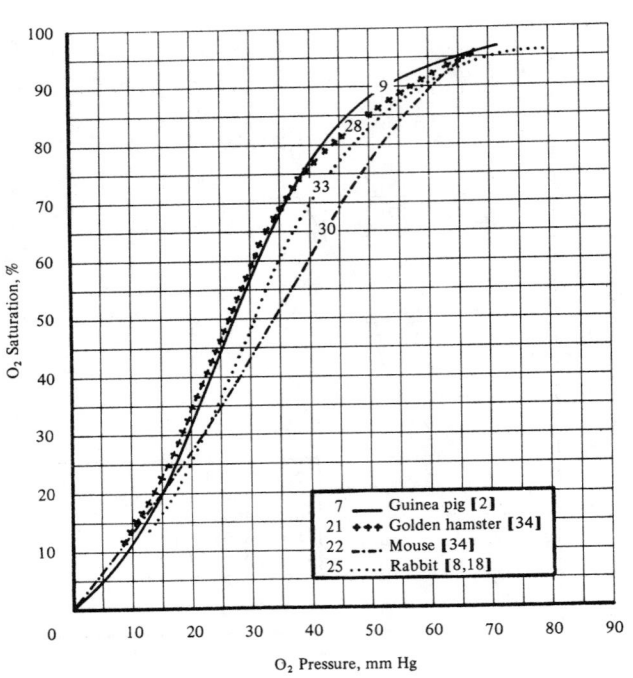

7 —— Guinea pig [2]
21 ◆◆◆ Golden hamster [34]
22 —··— Mouse [34]
25 ····· Rabbit [8,18]

O₂ Saturation, %

O₂ Pressure, mm Hg

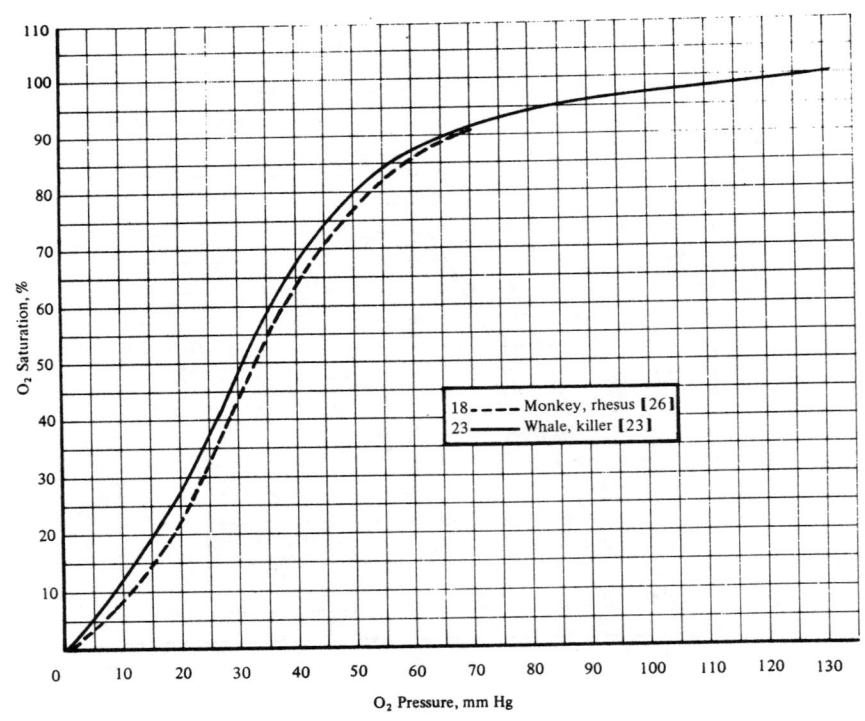

18 ---- Monkey, rhesus [26]
23 —— Whale, killer [23]

O₂ Saturation, %

O₂ Pressure, mm Hg

continued

Part I. Adult

Contributor: Bartels, Heinz

References

[1] Aste-Salazar, H., and A. Hurtado. 1944. Amer. J Physiol. 142:733.

[2] Bartels, H., and H. Harms. 1959. Pfluegers Arch. Gesamte Physiol. Menschen Tiere 268:334.

[3] Bartels, H., et al. 1960. Ibid. 271:169.

[4] Bartels, H., et al. 1961. Ibid. 272:372.

[5] Bartels, H., et al. 1963. Amer. J. Physiol. 205:331.

[6] Bartels, H., et al. 1966. Resp. Physiol. 1:145.

[7] Bartels, H., et al. 1969. Ibid. 7:278.

[8] Bauer, C., and A. M. Rathschlag-Schaefer. 1968. Ibid. 5:360.

[9] Baumann, P., et al. 1963. Pfluegers Arch. Gesamte Physiol. Menschen Tiere 277:120.

[10] Becklake, M. R., et al. 1955. J. Clin. Invest. 34:751.

[11] Clausen, G., and A. Ersland. 1969. Resp. Physiol. 7:1.

[12] Dawson, T. J., and J. V. Evans. 1965. Amer. J. Physiol. 209:593.

[13] Dill, D. B., et al. 1932. J. Biol. Chem. 95:143.

[14] Edwards, M. J., and R. J. Martin. 1966. J. Appl. Physiol. 21:1898.

[15] Gahlenbeck, H., et al. 1968. Resp. Physiol. 6:16.

[16] Hall, F. G., et al. 1936. J. Cell. Comp. Physiol. 8:301.

[17] Hall, F. G. 1965. Proc. Soc. Exp. Biol. Med. 119:1071.

[18] Hilpert, P., et al. 1963. Amer. J. Physiol. 205:337.

[19] Lenfant, C. 1969. In H. T. Andersen, ed. The Biology of Marine Mammals. Academic Press, New York. pp. 95-116.

[20] Lenfant, C., and C. Aucutt. 1969. Resp. Physiol. 6:284.

[21] Lenfant, C., and K. Johansen. 1965. Amer. J. Physiol. 209:991.

[22] Lenfant, C., et al. 1968. J. Clin. Invest. 47:2652.

[23] Lenfant, C., et al. 1968. Amer. J. Physiol. 215:1506.

[24] Morse, M., et al. 1950. J. Clin. Invest. 29:1098.

[25] Mulhausen, R. O., et al. 1968. Scand. J. Clin. Lab. Invest., Suppl. 103:9.

[26] Parer, J. T. 1967. Resp. Physiol. 2:168.

[27] Parer, J. T., and J. Metcalfe. 1967. Ibid. 3:136.

[28] Parer, J. T., et al. 1967. J. Appl. Physiol. 22:756.

[29] Parer, J. T., et al. 1967. Resp. Physiol. 2:196.

[30] Riegel, K., et al. 1966. Ibid. 1:138.

[31] Riegel, K., et al. 1967. Ibid. 2:182.

[32] Schmidt-Nielsen, K., and J. L. Larimer. 1958. Amer. J. Physiol. 195:424.

[33] Severinghaus, J. W. 1966. J. Appl. Physiol. 21:1108.

[34] Ulrich, S., et al. 1963. Pfluegers Arch. Gesamte Physiol. Menschen Tiere 277:150.

[35] Valtis, D. J., and A. G. Baikie. 1955. Brit. J. Haematol. 1:146.

[36] Valtis, D. J., and A. C. Kennedy. 1953. Glasgow Med. J. 34:521.

Part II. Maternal, Fetal, and Postnatal

The standard bicarbonate in fetal blood differs from that in maternal blood, and differs among species; therefore, curves with equal CO_2 pressures may have different pH values. The literature has been covered through 1971.

BLOOD OBSERVATIONS

	Species	No. of Subjects	Method of Measurement	Temp °C	P_{50} mm Hg	O_2 Capacity ml $O_2 \cdot 100$ ml blood^{-1}	Bohr Effect	Reference
1	*Homo sapiens*, mother	14	Manometric	37.0	26	15	0.48	5,17
2	fetus, near term	10	Manometric	37.0	22	22	0.41	5
3	postnatal, 5 day old	12	Manometric	37.0	23	23	....	3
4	61 day old	11	Manometric	37.0	25	13	....	3
5	81 day old	12	Manometric	37.0	28	14	....	3

continued

Part II. Maternal, Fetal, and Postnatal

	Species	No. of Subjects	Method of Measurement	Temp °C	P_{50} mm Hg	O_2 Capacity ml $O_2 \cdot 100$ ml blood^{-1}	Bohr Effect	Refer- ence
6	*Bos* sp., mother	11	Micromanometric	37.0	31	15	0.49	6
7	fetus, 180 day old	3	Micromanometric	37.0	20	11	....	6
8	255 day old	5	Micromanometric	37.0	23	12	....	6
9	*Camelus bactrianus*, mother	1	Manometric	37.0	21	15	....	15
10	fetus, near term	1	Manometric	37.0	16	17	....	15
11	*Capra hircus* [1], postnatal, 34 day old	1	Manometric	39.0	35	10	0.41	14
12	76 day old	1	Manometric	39.0	35	11	0.50	14
13	124 day old	1	Manometric	39.0	33	14	0.47	14
14	*C. hircus* [2], mother	3	Manometric	37.0	30	13	0.50	3,7
15	at birth	6	Manometric	37.0	20	14	0.40	3,7
16	postnatal, 5 day old	6	Manometric	37.0	27	13	0.57	3,7
17	11 day old	6	Manometric	37.0	29	11	....	3,7
18	21 day old	6	Manometric	37.0	32	10	....	3,7
19	31 day old	6	Manometric	37.0	34	14	....	3,7
20	42 day old	4	Manometric	37.0	36	15	....	3,7
21	56 day old	6	Manometric	37.0	35	16	0.42	3,7
22	72 day old	6	Manometric	37.0	33	17	....	3,7
23	91 day old	6	Manometric	37.0	32	16	0.61	3,7
24	111 day old	4	Manometric	37.0	32	16	....	3,7
25	137 day old	6	Manometric	37.0	33	16	....	3,7
26	*Cavia porcellus*, mother	9	Micromanometric	37.0	30	15	....	4
27	fetus, near term	12	Micromanometric	37.0	19	16	....	1
28	*Eschrichtius gibbosus*, mother	8	Mixed	37.0	30	17	0.46	8
29	fetus, near term	4	Mixed	37.0	19	17	0.54	8
30	*Felis catus*, mother	3	Mixed	38.0	36	12	0.48	11
31	fetus, near term	4	Mixed	38.0	36	16	0.47	11
32	*Lama glama*, mother	3	Manometric	38.0	21	18	....	10
33	fetus, near term	3	Manometric	38.0	18	19	....	10
34	*Leptonychotes weddelli*, mother	4	Mixed	37.0	29	32	0.61	9
35	fetus, near term	4	Mixed	37.0	22	28	0.67	9
36	*Loxodonta africana*, mother	1	Manometric	37.0	23	20	....	16
37	fetus, 155 day old	1	Manometric	37.0	22	13	....	16
38	365 day old	1	Manometric	37.0	17	17	....	16
39	*Macaca irus; M. mulatta; M. nemestrina* Mother	25	Mixed	38.0	32	.....	0.48	13
40	Fetus, near term	15	Mixed	38.0	19	.....	0.45	13
41	*Oryctolagus cuniculus*, mother	5	Micromanometric	37.0	31	15	....	2
42	fetus, near term	6	Micromanometric	37.0	27	14	....	2
43	*Ovis aries*, mother	7	Manometric	37.0	34	15	0.43	3,7
44	at birth	...	Manometric	37.0	17	17	0.46	3,7
45	postnatal, 3 day old	4	Manometric	37.0	28	17	....	3,7
46	10 day old	4	Manometric	37.0	32	16	....	3,7
47	22 day old	4	Manometric	37.0	36	18	....	3,7
48	35 day old	4	Manometric	37.0	39	18	0.43	3,7
49	53 day old	2	Manometric	37.0	43	20	0.39	3,7
50	*Sus scrofa*, mother	...	Mixed	38.0	33	.....	....	12
51	fetus, near term	...	Mixed	38.0	22	.....	....	12

[1] African pygmy goat. [2] German deer-goat.

continued

Part II. Maternal, Fetal, and Postnatal

GRAPHS

Numbers in graph and in legend refer to corresponding line numbers in tables. Numbers in heavy brackets are reference numbers.

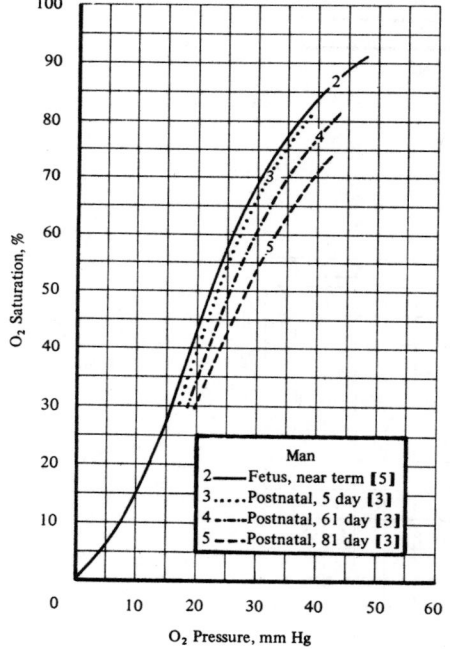

Man
2 ——— Fetus, near term [5]
3 ..... Postnatal, 5 day [3]
4 —··—··· Postnatal, 61 day [3]
5 —·—·— Postnatal, 81 day [3]

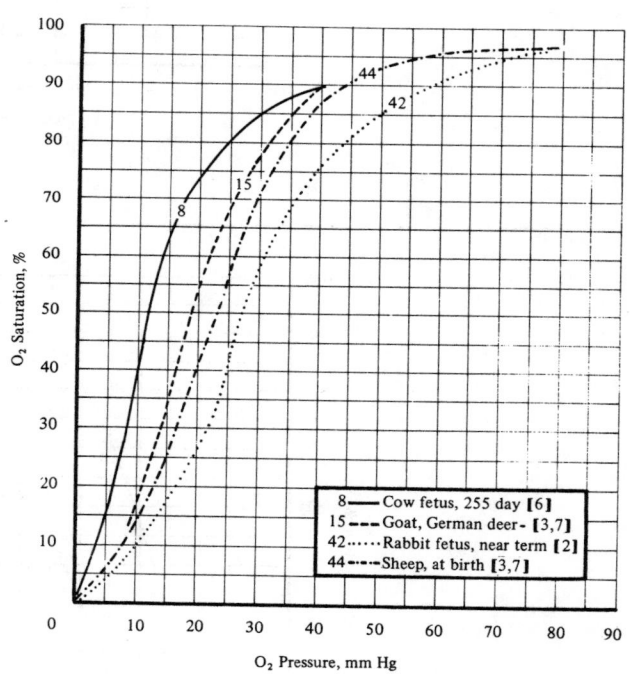

8 ——— Cow fetus, 255 day [6]
15 – – – Goat, German deer- [3,7]
42 ...... Rabbit fetus, near term [2]
44 —··—·· Sheep, at birth [3,7]

continued

Part II. Maternal, Fetal, and Postnatal

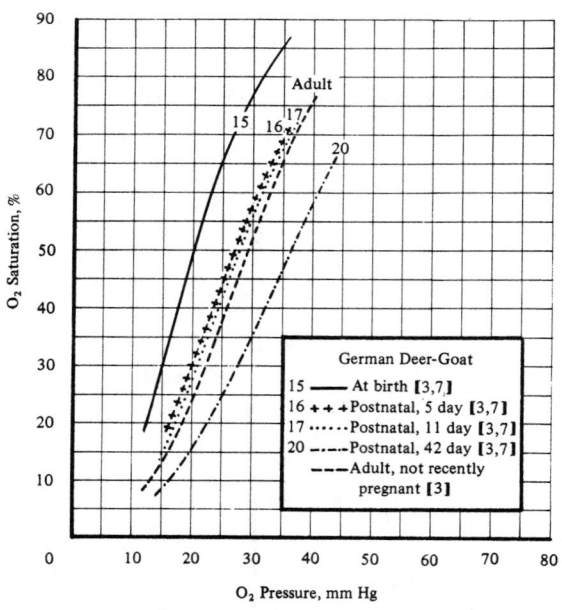

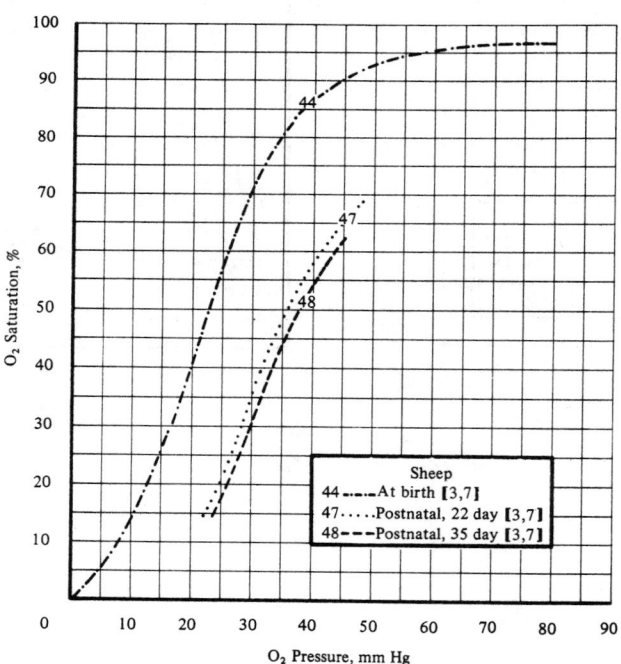

continued

260. BLOOD OXYGEN DISSOCIATION CURVES: MAMMALS

Part II. Maternal, Fetal, and Postnatal

Contributor: Bartels, Heinz

References

[1] Bartels, H. 1966. Develop. Lung Ciba Found. Symp., p. 276.

[2] Bartels, H., and J. Metcalfe. 1965. Excerpta Med. Found. Int. Congr. Ser. 87:34.

[3] Bartels, H., et al. 1960. Pfluegers Arch. Gesamte Physiol. Menschen Tiere 271:169.

[4] Bartels, H., et al. 1967. Resp. Physiol. 2:149.

[5] Beer, R., et al. 1955. Klin. Wochenschr. 33:221.

[6] Gahlenbeck, H., et al. 1968. Resp. Physiol. 4: 119.

[7] Hilpert, P., et al. 1963. Amer. J. Physiol. 205: 337.

[8] Lenfant, C. 1969. In H. T. Andersen, ed. The Biology of Marine Mammals. Academic Press, New York. pp. 95-116.

[9] Lenfant, C., et al. 1969. Amer. J. Physiol. 216: 1595.

[10] Meschia, G., et al. 1960. J. Exp. Physiol. 45:284.

[11] Novy, M. J., and J. T. Parer. 1969. Resp. Physiol. 6:144.

[12] Novy, M. J., et al. 1968. Fed. Proc. Fed. Amer. Soc. Exp. Biol. 26:485.

[13] Novy, M. J., et al. 1969. J. Appl. Physiol. 26: 339.

[14] Parer, J. T., et al. 1967. Ibid. 22:756.

[15] Riegel, K., et al. 1967. Resp. Physiol. 2:173.

[16] Riegel, K., et al. 1967. Ibid. 2:182.

[17] Rossier, P. H., and M. Hotz. 1953. Schweiz. Med. Wochenschr. 83:897.

261. BLOOD OXYGEN DISSOCIATION LINE CHARTS: MAN

These charts were designed to permit calculation of saturation (So_2) from blood Po_2 and pH at any temperature between 22 and 40°C. The calculation includes a small correction for base excess (BE), which is possible because over most of the curve the effects of pH, base excess, and temperature on affinity are independent of saturation, and alter the Po_2 by constant factors. The charts (drawn and published by Kelman) are based on the human blood dissociation curve data compiled by Severinghaus in 1966 [2]. (These curves differ from the Dill curve contributed by Severinghaus to several of the Biological Handbooks published prior to 1965. The saturation is slightly higher around 90% and lower below 20% in the new curve.)

To Determine Saturation: On the left line, find f_{temp} for the electrode temperature (not body temperature), at which pH and Po_2 were determined. If pH and Po_2 were determined at different temperatures, correct the pH to the O_2 electrode temperature. pH of blood rises 0.0147 unit per degree of cooling. Base excess is determined from pH and Pco_2, measured at 37°C, using the alignment nomogram of Siggaard-Andersen (Table 252, Part III). On the second and third lines, find f_{pH} and f_{BE} for the observed values of pH and BE. (BE is defined in terms of 37°C measurements but

is independent of temperature.) Multiply all the factors by the observed Po_2. The product is the Po_2 corrected to 37°C, pH 7.4 and BE = 0. This Po_2 will indicate the calculated saturation on the two lines at the right, the far right line being the expanded upper 9% of saturation.

To Calculate Po_2 from Saturation: If saturation has been measured, use the lines at the right to find the Po_2 of the standard curve (pH 7.4, 37°C, BE = 0). Divide this Po_2 by the factors obtained from the lines at the left for temperature, pH, and base excess. Saturation is independent of temperature except above 95% saturation, where small shifts of oxygen between hemoglobin and water occur with temperature as hemoglobin affinity changes. pH must be expressed at the temperature used for obtaining f_{temp}. *Note—* There is an alternative and usually simpler method of determining Po_2 at some body temperature other than 37°C: (i) use measured saturation to determine the standard Po_2; (ii) divide this Po_2 by the f_{pH} determined from the line chart, using the pH measured at 37°C; (iii) use Table 262, Part I or II, to correct Po_2 to body temperature.

Example: Measured at 38°C: pH = 7.335, Pco_2 = 28.1, Po_2 = 46.2, Hb = 10 g. From Table 252, Part III (alignment

continued

nomogram of Siggaard-Andersen): BE = −9.8. From the line charts below: f_{temp} = 0.947, f_{pH} = 0.930, f_{BE} = 1.03.

Compute: 46.2 × 0.947 × 0.930 × 1.03 = 41.9. From line 4: So$_2$ = 76.5%.

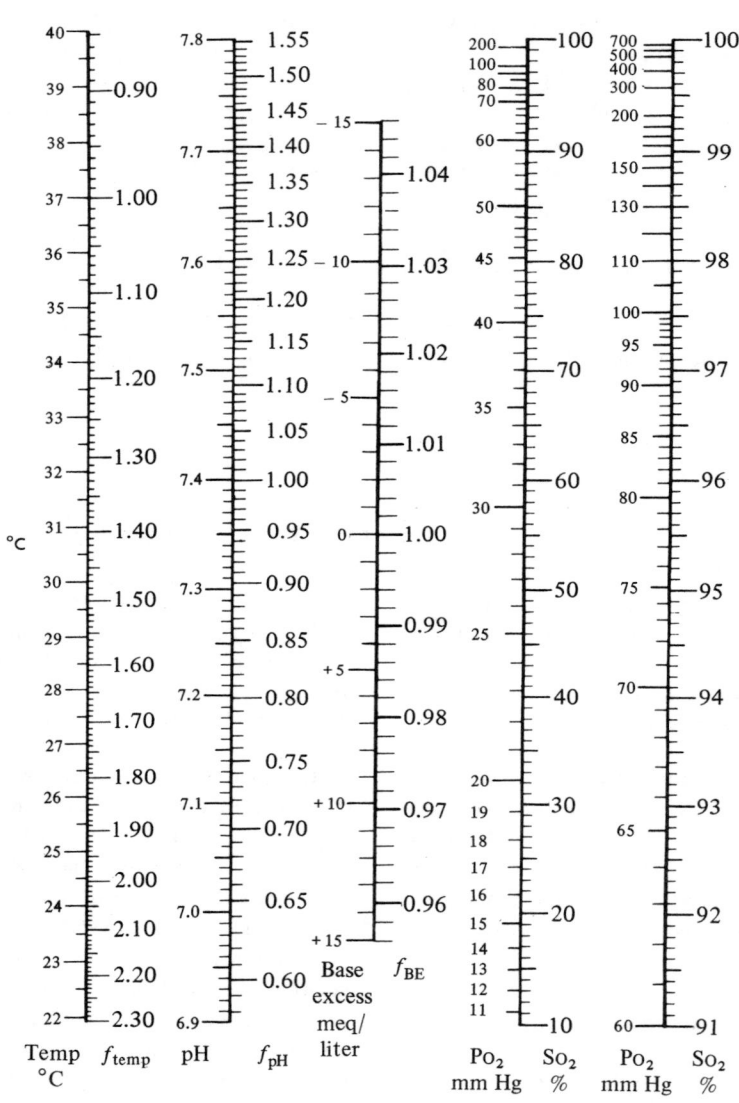

Correction Factors   Dissociation Curve

continued

261. BLOOD OXYGEN DISSOCIATION LINE CHARTS: MAN

Contributor: Severinghaus, John W.

References

[1] Kelman, G. R., and J. F. Nunn. 1966. J. Appl. Physiol. 21:1484.

[2] Severinghaus, J. W. 1966. Ibid. 21:1108.

262. EFFECT OF TEMPERATURE CHANGE ON BLOOD OXYGEN AND CARBON DIOXIDE PRESSURES: MAN AND DOG

The chart prepared by Kelman and Nunn and the line nomogram for oxygen correct two errors in the oxygen anaerobic correction factor nomograms published as Table 64 in the *Handbook of Respiration* and Table 60 in *Blood and Other Body Fluids*. At low saturation the correction is about 7.2% per °C, as compared to the previous value of 5.6% per °C. The decrease of this factor, as saturation rises above 80%, is given in the new chart and nomogram, whereas it was ignored in the previous tables. The correction at low saturation (less than 80%) may be calculated from the formula: $\Delta \log P_{O_2} = 0.031\ \Delta T$. Above 80% saturation, as temperature changes, less oxygen exchanges between hemoglobin and the dissolved phase. Then at full saturation no exchange occurs, and P_{O_2} changes as in water, 1.3% per °C, for small temperature changes near 37°C. A better approximation at full saturation is $\Delta \log P_{O_2} = 0.0054\ \Delta T$.

Part I and Part II present two methods for correcting P_{O_2} for temperature changes. The general method uses the Kelman and Nunn chart, whereby one first calculates an approximate saturation, finds the appropriate line for that saturation, determines the factor for the body temperature in question, and multiplies it by the observed P_{O_2}. In Part II, the single line nomogram for oxygen makes use of the relation of P_{O_2} to both saturation and to the final multiplier, and eliminates several steps. It is accurate only for blood of normal pH and over temperature ranges of a few degrees Celsius. Both methods assume the temperature of measurement to be 37°C.

Part I. Use of Kelman and Nunn Temperature Correction Chart

Locate the desired temperature on the abscissa. Locate the diagonal line having a saturation (numbers 90-100) that approximates the sample's calculated saturation (use Table 261). At the intersection of this line with the vertical temperature line, read the factor along the ordinate and multiply the measured P_{O_2} by this factor. The single interrupted line for carbon dioxide is used similarly to compute P_{CO_2} at 19-41°C from values obtained at 37°C. The chart may also be used to correct from other measurement temperatures to 37°C, in which case the observed P_{O_2} or P_{CO_2} should be divided by the factor. A second correction can then be made to some other temperature by multiplying by the appropriate factor obtained as described above. If electrodes are not at 37°C, note particularly the directions for temperature adjustment in calculating saturation in Table 261.

Example 1: Measured at 37°C: $P_{O_2} = 91.5$ mm Hg, pH = 7.22. Compute P_{O_2} at a body temperature of 25°C. From Table 261: $f_{pH} = 0.82$, $f_{temp} = 1.00$. Corrected $P_{O_2} = 91.5 \times 0.82 = 75.0$ mm Hg. From Table 261: Saturation = 95% at 75.0 mm Hg. From chart on following page: Correction factor for 25°C, 95% saturation = 0.49. P_{O_2} at 25°C then = $91.5 \times 0.49 = 44.9$ mm Hg. (It may be computed that the saturation at 26°C rises to 95.5% at the expense of dissolved oxygen.)

Example 2: Using electrodes at 23°C: $P_{O_2} = 30$ mm Hg, pH = 7.60. Compute P_{O_2} at 39°C. From Table 261: $f_{temp} = 2.17$ and $f_{pH} = 1.25$. $30 \times 2.17 \times 1.25 = 81.3$ mm Hg, and saturation = 96.0%. From chart on following page: Factors for 23°C and 39°C at 96% saturation = 0.47 and 1.12, respectively. P_{O_2} at 39°C = $30 \times 1.12 \div 0.47 = 71.5$ mm Hg.

continued

262. EFFECT OF TEMPERATURE CHANGE ON BLOOD OXYGEN AND CARBON DIOXIDE PRESSURES: MAN AND DOG

Part I. Use of Kelman and Nunn Temperature Correction Chart

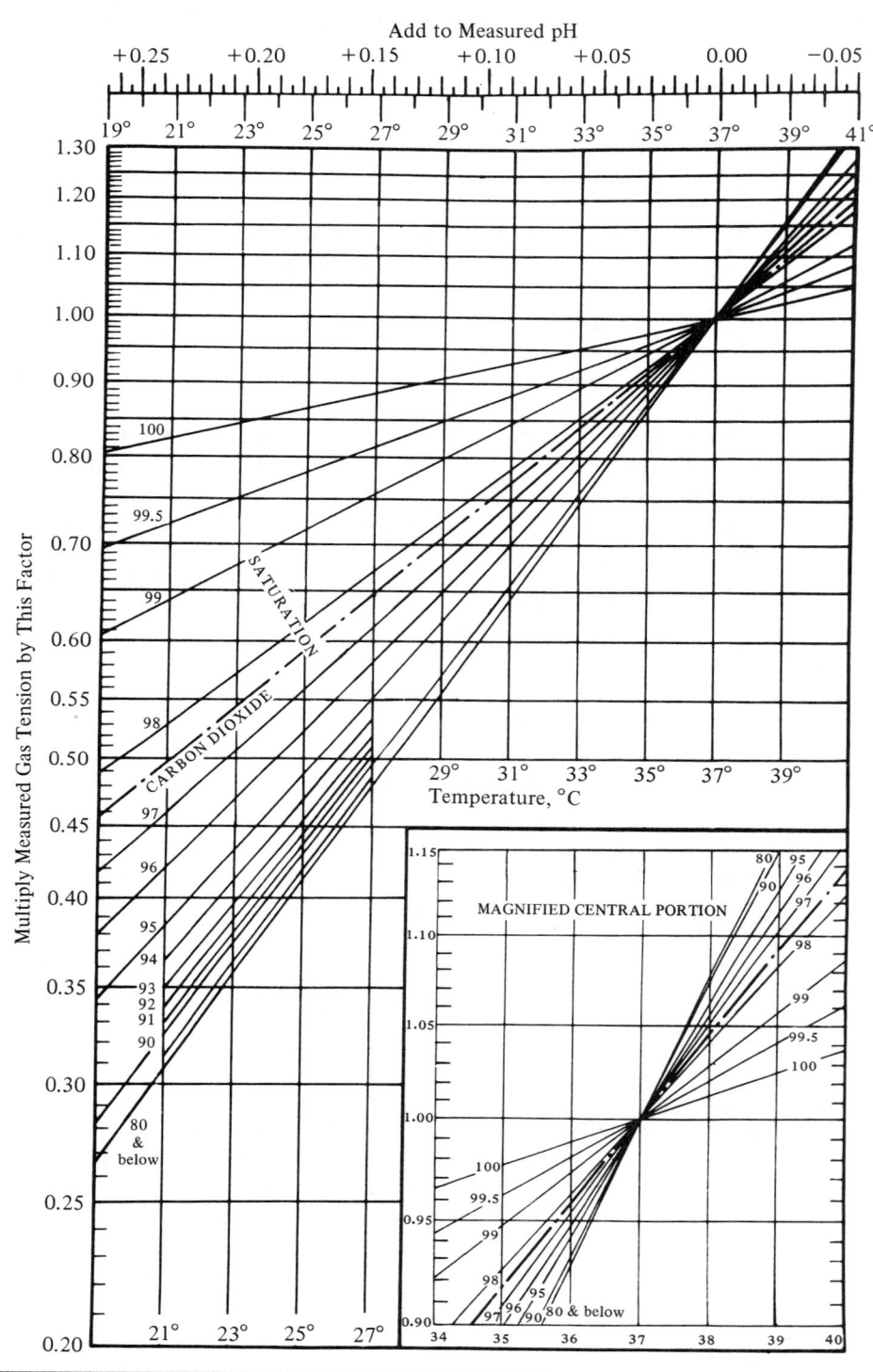

Contributor: Severinghaus, John W.

Reference: Kelman, G. R., and J. F. Nunn. 1966. J. Appl. Physiol. 21:1484.

continued

Part II.   Use of Single-Line Nomograms

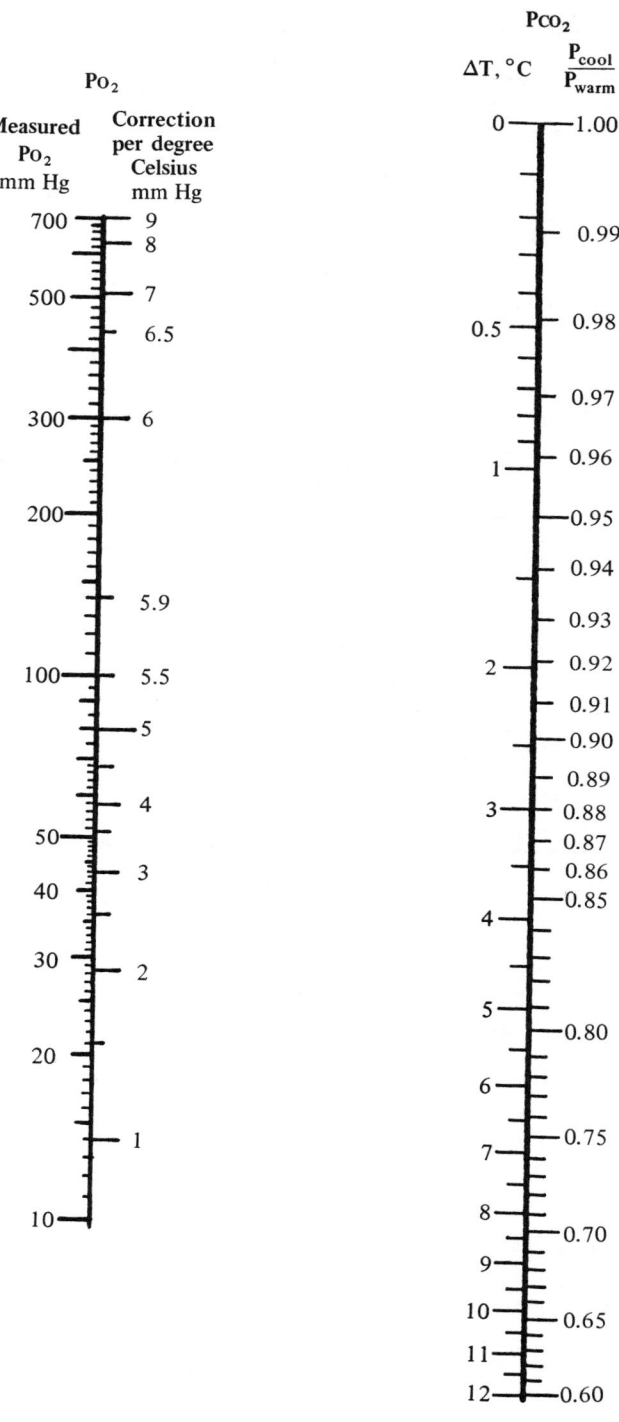

Po$_2$: Locate the observed value of Po$_2$ on the left side of the line, and opposite it read the correction in mm Hg (torr) per °C temperature difference between the measurement and the blood source. Multiply by the temperature difference, and add to observed Po$_2$ for higher temperatures, or subtract for lower temperatures. Accuracy of correction decreases with severe pH variations from 7.4 and with large temperature ranges.

Pco$_2$: Read the Pco$_2$ factor opposite the difference in temperature between the electrode and blood source. Multiply observed Pco$_2$ by this factor if source (body) is cooler than electrode, and divide if source is warmer.

Contributor: Severinghaus, John W.

Reference: Severinghaus, J. W. 1966. J. Appl. Physiol. 21:1108.

263. CARBON DIOXIDE SOLUBILITY AND FIRST DISSOCIATION CONSTANT (pK′) OF CARBONIC ACID IN PLASMA AND CEREBROSPINAL FLUID: MAN

Solubility and pK′ values are based on newly revised National Bureau of Standards buffer values, taking into account the liquid junction potentials of the potassium chloride to the buffer. Carbon dioxide was determined gasometrically.

	Temperature °C	CO_2 Solubility mmole·liter^{-1}·mm Hg^{-1}	Carbonic Acid pK′[1], at pH						
			7.0	7.1	7.2	7.3	7.4	7.5	7.6
	Plasma								
1	10	0.0629	6.246	6.238	6.230	6.221	6.213	6.204	6.194
2	15	0.05384	6.222	6.215	6.208	6.200	6.192	6.184	6.175
3	20	0.0464	6.197	6.191	6.185	6.178	6.171	6.163	6.155
4	25	0.0404	6.173	6.168	6.162	6.156	6.150	6.143	6.136
5	30	0.0356	6.148	6.144	6.139	6.134	6.129	6.123	6.116
6	35	0.0319	6.124	6.121	6.117	6.113	6.108	6.103	6.097
7	36	0.0312	6.119	6.116	6.112	6.108	6.104	6.099	6.093
8	37	0.0306	6.114	6.111	6.108	6.104	6.099	6.094	6.089
9	38	0.0300	6.109	6.106	6.103	6.099	6.095	6.090	6.085
10	39	0.0294	6.104	6.102	6.099	6.095	6.090	6.085	6.081
11	40	0.0289	6.099	6.097	6.094	6.090	6.086	6.082	6.077
	Cerebrospinal Fluid								
12	25	0.0425	6.181	6.180	6.176	6.167	6.157	6.146	6.136
13	30	0.0373	6.165	6.164	6.160	6.153	6.145	6.136	6.127
14	35	0.0333	6.149	6.148	6.144	6.139	6.133	6.125	6.118
15	36	0.0325	6.146	6.144	6.141	6.136	6.130	6.123	6.116
16	37	0.0318	6.143	6.141	6.138	6.133	6.128	6.121	6.114
17	38	0.0312	6.140	6.138	6.135	6.130	6.125	6.119	6.112
18	39	0.0306	6.137	6.135	6.132	6.127	6.123	6.117	6.110
19	40	0.0300	6.134	6.132	6.129	6.124	6.120	6.115	6.108
20	10-40	......	0.0031[2]	0.0032[2]	0.0031[2]	0.0029[2]	0.0025[2]	0.0021[2]	0.0019[2]
21	30	......	0.010[3]	0.025[3]	0.055[3]	0.075[3]	0.085[3]	0.090[3]	0.095[3]
22	38	......	0.010[3]	0.025[3]	0.040[3]	0.050[3]	0.055[3]	0.065[3]	0.070[3]

[1] Unless otherwise indicated. [2] ΔpH/Δtemp, where temp measured in °C. [3] ΔpK′/ΔpH unit.

Contributor: Severinghaus, John W.

Reference: Severinghaus, J. W. 1965. Handb. Physiol., Sec. 3, Resp. 2:1480.

264. EFFECTS OF ALTITUDE ON BLOOD VALUES: MAN

Mean Corpuscular Hemoglobin = 10 × Hemoglobin/Erythrocyte Count. Sa_{O_2} = arterial oxygen saturation. Data in brackets refer to the column heading in brackets. Values in parentheses are ranges, estimate "c" unless otherwise indicated (see Introduction).

Part I. Residents: Long-Term Effects

All subjects were resident at the altitude given, unless otherwise indicated.

continued

Part I. Residents: Long-Term Effects

Altitude m [Po_2, mm Hg; Sa_{O_2}, %]	Location	Subjects	Erythrocyte Volume [Blood Volume] ml/kg[1]	Hematocrit ml Erythrocytes/100 ml blood	Erythrocyte Count millions/μl blood	Hemoglobin g/100 ml blood	Mean Corpuscular Hemoglobin pg	Reference
Sea level	New Orleans, Louisiana	115♂	....	....	5.26	15.6	29.7	9
		100♂	....	....	5.85	15.9	27.2	35
	Kansas	350♂	....	....	5.11	15.0	29.4	24
	Kansas City, Kansas	20♂, 18-30 yr	....	49	5.08	15.6	.....	11
		20♂, 30-50 yr	....	47	4.87	15.6	.....	
		12♀, 20-40 yr	....	41	4.26	13.3	.....	
	Omaha, Nebraska	100♂	....	....	4.69	15.0	32.0	28
	Portland, Oregon	259♂	....	....	5.42	15.8	29.2	25
	Honolulu, Hawaii	137♂	....	44.2	5.08	15.1	29.2	12
	Calcutta, India	50♂	....	....	5.36	14.8	27.6	23
	Bombay, India	121♂	....	....	5.11	15.4	30.1	30
	Jena, Germany	52♂	....	....	5.06	16.0	31.6	13
	Giessen, Germany	40♂	....	....	4.96	16.0	32.3	14
	Copenhagen, Denmark	60♂	....	....	5.07	15.0	29.6	2
	Oslo, Norway	50♂	....	....	5.52	16.2	29.3	18
	Buenos Aires, Argentina	50♂	....	....	5.50	15.4	28.0	26
		50♂	....	....	5.30	14.8	27.9	33
	Lima, Peru	7102♂♂[2]	....	....	5.23	15.4	.....	16
		175♂	....	46.8	5.14(4.46-5.82)[b]	16.0(14.4-17.6)[b][3]	31.1	
		20♂	....	46.0(42.5-50.0)	....	....	.....	21
		15♀	....	39.8(26.0-41.0)	....	....	.....	
[Sa_{O_2} = 97]	Lima, Peru	14♂[4]	32.0; 1.88[5,6]; 2.12[5,7]	45(40.0-49.0)	5.0(4.3-5.6)	15.1(13.4-16.2)[3]	30.2	15
150	Lima, Peru	7♂[4]	28.3 [74.5]	42.3	....	....	.....	29
[Po_2 = 750]	Lima, Peru	250♂	....	46.6	5.11	15.6	30.9	17
		20♂	37.2 [49.6]	....	....	....	.....	
427	Tucumán, Argentina	153♂	....	48.7	5.31	16.12	30.3	20
500	Zurich, Switzerland	139♂	....	....	5.00	15.0	30.0	3,4
	Saskatchewan, Canada	20♂	....	....	5.52	15.6	28.3	7
1520	Denver, Colorado	40♂	....	48.4(43.8-53.6)	5.42(4.83-6.07)	16.5(15.0-18.3)	30.4	1
		40♀	....	43.2(37.1-46.1)	4.63(4.41-5.00)	14.5(12.7-15.7)	31.1	
[Po_2 = 625]	Denver, Colorado	9♂	....	....	....	15.9[8]	.....	8
		4♀	....	....	....	14.1[8]	.....	

[1] Unless otherwise indicated. [2] Unspecified whether residents or not. [3] Van Slyke O_2 capacity method, or Evelyn photoelectric colorimeter calibrated by the O_2 capacity method. [4] Medical students. [5] Liters, total volume. [6] Erythrocytes labeled with phosphorus-32. [7] Erythrocytes labeled with iron-59. [8] Haldane-Gower hemoglobinometer.

continued

Part I. Residents: Long-Term Effects

Altitude m [Po$_2$, mm Hg; Sa$_{O_2}$, %]	Location	Subjects	Erythrocyte Volume [Blood Volume] ml/kg	Hematocrit ml Erythrocytes/100 ml blood	Erythrocyte Count millions/μl blood	Hemoglobin g/100 ml blood	Mean Corpuscular Hemoglobin pg	Reference
33 [Po$_2$ = 615]	Colorado Springs, Colorado	8♂	....	....	....	15.0[8/]	.....	8
34		4♀	....	....	....	14.4[8/]	.....	
35 1750	Johannesburg, South Africa	10	....	....	....	14.7	.....	31
36		60♂	....	....	5.99	14.7	24.5	19
37 1830-1890	Coonoor & Wellington, India	80♂	....	49.0(38.0-65.0)	5.33(3.95-6.04)	15.9(13.1-20.3)	29.8	27
38 [Po$_2$ = 590]	Ridgway, Colorado	4♂	....	....	....	16.3[8/]	.....	8
39 2300	Ootacamund, India	20♂	....	49.4(46.0-53.0)	5.38(4.75-6.02)	15.8(14.8-16.8)	29.4	27
40	Mexico City, Mexico	23♂; 20♀[9/]	....	43.0(37.5-49.0)	5.26(4.37-6.14)[b]	14.2(13.1-15.3)[b]	27.0	34
41		100♂	....	51.2(45.0-58.5)	5.38(4.53-6.17)	17.7(14.4-20.1)	32.9	10
42		100♀	....	45.5(41.5-50.0)	5.01(4.27-6.01)	15.2(12.8-17.7)	30.3	
43 [Po$_2$ = 573]	Ouray, Colorado	13♂	....	....	....	16.4[8/]	.....	8
44		6♀	....	....	....	16.4[8/]	.....	
45 [Po$_2$ = 550]	Telluride, Colorado	5♂	....	....	....	16.4[8/]	.....	8
46 2939 [Po$_2$ = 536; Sa$_{O_2}$ = 91.2]	Argentina	45♂, 16-68 yr	....	51.1	5.47	16.8[3/]	30.7	6
47 [Po$_2$ = 533]	Camp Bird Mill, Colorado	12♂	....	....	....	17.0[8/]	.....	8
48 [Po$_2$ = 519]	Portland Mine, Colorado	10♂	....	....	....	17.1[8/]	.....	8
49 [Po$_2$ = 515]	Portland Mill, Colorado	10♂	....	....	....	16.7[8/]	.....	8
50 [Po$_2$ = 502]	Camp Bird Mine, Colorado	22♂	....	....	....	17.0[8/]	.....	8
51		2♀	....	....	....	15.6[8/]	.....	
52 [Po$_2$ = 496]	Tom Boy Mine, Colorado	4♀	....	....	....	16.6[8/]	.....	8
53 3730	Peru	20	....	....	6.88	....	.....	21
54 3870[10/]	La Paz, Bolivia	4250♂	....	54.0	5.55	18.0	33.0	22
55		6357♀	....	46.5	5.15	16.0	31.0	
56		2093[11/]	....	46.0	5.15	15.5	31.0	
57 [Po$_2$ = 480]	Lewis Mine, Colorado	6♂	....	....	....	17.0[8/]	.....	8
58 3990 [Po$_2$ = 476; Sa$_{O_2}$ = 86.9]	Argentina	15♂, 24-56 yr	....	53.9	5.84	18.0[3/]	30.9	6
59 4390	Cerro de Pasco, Peru	13♂[12/]	51.7 [85.2]	62.0	....	....	.....	29
60 4515	Mina Aguilar, Argentina	81♂	....	59.5(50.5-73.6)	6.46(5.07-9.43)	19.4(15.7-24.9)	30.0	5
61 [Po$_2$ = 446; Sa$_{O_2}$ = 82.8]	Argentina	84♂, 21-54 yr	....	59.5	6.46	19.4[3/]	29.9	6

[3/] Van Slyke O$_2$ capacity method, or Evelyn photoelectric colorimeter calibrated by the O$_2$ capacity method. [8/] Haldane-Gower hemoglobinometer. [9/] Resident 4-6 yr.

[10/] Data collected over 20-yr period. [11/] Children. [12/] Miners.

continued

Part I. Residents: Long-Term Effects

Altitude m [P_{O_2}, mm Hg; Sa_{O_2}, %]	Location	Subjects	Erythrocyte Volume [Blood Volume] ml/kg	Hematocrit ml Erythrocytes/100 ml blood	Erythrocyte Count millions/μl blood	Hemoglobin g/100 ml blood	Mean Corpuscular Hemoglobin pg	Reference
62 4540	Morococha, Peru	83♂	....	59.5	6.44	20.1	31.5	17
63		20♂	61.1 [110.5]	....	....	....	.....	
64 5340 [P_{O_2} = 401]	Aucanquilcha, Chile	6♂[12]	....	69.4	7.37	22.9[3]	32.2	32

[3] Van Slyke O_2 capacity method, or Evelyn photoelectric colorimeter calibrated by the O_2 capacity method. [12] Miners.

Contributors: Dill, David B.; Root, Walter S.

References

[1] Andresen, M. I., and E. R. Mugrage. 1936. Arch. Intern. Med. 58:136.

[2] Bierring, E., and G. Sørensen. 1936. Ugeskr. Laeg. 98:822.

[3] Burgi, K. 1933. Schweiz. Med. Wochenschr. 63:662.

[4] Burgi, K. 1933. Ibid. 63:685.

[5] Chiodi, H. 1950. J. Appl. Physiol. 2:431.

[6] Chiodi, H., and C. Pozzi. 1961. Acta Physiol. Lat. Amer. 11:51.

[7] Fiddes, J., and C. Witney. 1936. Can. Med. Ass. J. 35:654.

[8] FitzGerald, M. P. 1913. Phil. Trans. Roy. Soc. London B203:351.

[9] Foster, F. C., and J. R. Johnson. 1931. Proc. Soc. Exp. Biol. Med. 28:929.

[10] Gil, J. R., and D. G. Teran. 1948. Blood 3:660.

[11] Haden, R. L. 1925. Folia Haematol. (Leipzig) 31:113.

[12] Hamre, C. J., and M. H. Au. 1942. J. Lab. Clin. Med. 27:1231.

[13] Heilmeyer, L., and L. Hansold. 1936. Deut. Arch. Klin. Med. 179:94.

[14] Horneffer, L. 1928. Pfluegers Arch. Gesamte Physiol. Menschen Tiere 220:703.

[15] Huff, R. L., et al. 1951. Medicine (Baltimore) 30:197.

[16] Hurtado, A., et al. 1945. Arch. Intern. Med. 75:284.

[17] Hurtado, A., et al. 1956. U.S. Air Force Sch. Aviat. Med. (Randolph) Rep. 56-1.

[18] Jervell, O., and J. H. M. Waaler. 1934. Nor. Mag. Laegevidensk. 95:1141.

[19] Liknaitzky, I. 1934. Quart. J. Exp. Physiol. 24:161.

[20] Moglia, J. L., and O. A. Fonio. 1944. Rev. Soc. Arg. Biol. 20:581.

[21] Monge, C., et al. 1928. An. Fac. Med. Univ. Nac. Mayor San Marcos Lima 11(1 & 2).

[22] Morales, O. S. 1963. An. Acad. Nac. Cienc. Cuad. 2 Ser. Cienc. Natur. La Paz.

[23] Napier, L. E., and C. R. Das Gupta. 1935. Indian J. Med. Res. 23:305.

[24] Nelson, C. F., and R. Stoker. 1937. Folia Haematol. (Leipzig) 58:333.

[25] Osgood, E. E. 1935. Arch. Intern. Med. 56:849.

[26] Parodi, A. S. 1930. Rev. Soc. Arg. Biol. 6:426.

[27] Ramalingaswami, V., and P. A. Venkatachalam. 1950. Indian J. Med. Res. 38:17.

[28] Sachs, A., et al. 1935. Arch. Intern. Med. 55:226.

[29] Sanchez, C., et al. 1970. J. Appl. Physiol. 28:775.

[30] Sokhey, S. S., et al. 1937. Indian J. Med. Res. 25:505.

[31] Stammers, A. J. 1933. J. Physiol. (London) 78:21P.

[32] Talbott, J. H., and D. B. Dill. 1936. Amer. J. Med. Sci. 192:626.

[33] Tenconi, J. 1931. C. R. Soc. Biol. 108:133.

[34] Vasquez, J., et al. 1958. Bol. Med. Hosp. Infant. (Mex.) 15:53.

[35] Wintrobe, M. M., and M. W. Miller. 1929. Arch. Intern. Med. 43:96.

Part II. Transients: Short-Term Effects

Altitude: Arrow indicates travel to different altitude.

	Altitude, m [P_{O_2}, mm Hg; Sa_{O_2}, %]	Location	Subjects	Exposure Time	Erythrocyte Volume [Blood Volume] ml/kg[1]	Hematocrit ml Erythrocytes/ 100 ml blood	Erythrocyte Count millions/μl blood	Hemoglobin g/100 ml blood[1] [Mean Corpuscular Hemoglobin, pg]	Reference
					Single Altitude				
1	2390 [Sa_{O_2} = 91.0]	Matucana, Peru	15♂	2 hr	....	46.5	4.97	16.2	7
2	3140 [Sa_{O_2} = 89.6]	San Mateo, Peru	16♂	2 hr	....	46.8	5.14	16.3	7
3	3260	Peru	10	....	....	....	5.82	....	7
4	3660	La Paz, Bolivia	200	Residents	....	....	7.50	....	7
5	....	....	60[2]	....	....	47.4	5.02	16.5	
6	3730	....	13[3]	....	46.5[4]	51.8	5.42	18.1	7
7	[Sa_{O_2} = 87.6]	La Oroya, Peru	40♂	Residents	59.7; 3.36[5]	54.1(47.8-65.4)	5.67(4.89-6.45)[b]	18.8(15.9-21.7)[b]; 1150[6]	
8	4000 [P_{O_2} = 474]	Peru	....	32 da	37.0 [73.4]	....	....	....	2
9	4165 [Sa_{O_2} = 80.2]	Casapalca, Peru	18♂	2 hr	....	46.9	5.05	16.2	7
10	4540	Morococha, Peru	6♂	Residents	74.1; 4.29[5]	59.9	6.15	20.7; 1464[6]	7
11			6	2 hr	47.1; 2.36[5]	....	....	783[6]	
12			11♂	Residents	....	57.0(46.0-71.0)	6.70(5.30-9.30)	19.3(17.4-24.0) [28.8]	6
13		....	7	Residents	67.2; 3.59[4,5]	66.7	7.88	22.6; 1215[6]	8
14			6	7-21 da	47.2; 2.81[4,5]	55.6	6.43	18.6; 966.5[6]	
15	[Sa_{O_2} = 79]	....	14	....	31-33; 1.81-1.91[5,7]	48.0	5.5	16.5[8]	6
					Changes in Altitude				
16	800 →	Boulder City,	3♂	20+ da	2.42[5,9]	....	....	14.8[10]	9
17		Nevada	2♀	20+ da	1.50[5,9]	....	....	13.8[10]	
18	3800	Barcroft Lab.,	3♂	20 da	2.42[5,9]	....	....	16.1[10]	
19		White Mt. Research Station, California	2♀	20 da	1.56[5,9]	....	....	15.0[10]	
20	0 →	....	6♂	Residents	2.22[5,9]	....	....	15.1[10]	3
21	3800	Barcroft Lab., White Mt. Research Station, California	6♂	10 da	2.29[5,9]	....	....	17.0[10]	
22	[P_{O_2} = 760] →	Oxford, England	2♂	Residents	46.9[4]	....	4.78	13.8[11]	4
23	[P_{O_2} = 460] →	Pike's Peak, Colorado	2♂	34 da	48.6	....	4.82	16.7[11]	

[1] Unless otherwise indicated. [2] Subjects had 60-90 hr/mo flying time. [3] Railroad personnel; alternate nights at sea level. [4] Brilliant vital red dye and hematocrit method. [5] Total volume, in liters. [6] Total hemoglobin in g. [7] Erythrocytes labeled with radioactive phosphorus. [8] Evelyn colorimeter. [9] CO method. [10] Van Slyke O_2 capacity method or Evelyn photoelectric colorimeter. [11] Haldane-Gower CO method (100% = 20 vol %).

continued

Part II. Transients: Short-Term Effects

	Altitude, m [Po_2, mm Hg; Sa_{O_2}, %]	Location	Subjects	Exposure Time	Erythrocyte Volume [Blood Volume] ml/kg[1]	Hematocrit ml Erythrocytes/100 ml blood	Erythrocyte Count millions/μl blood	Hemoglobin g/100 ml blood[1] [Mean Corpuscular Hemoglobin, pg]	Reference
24	[Po_2 = 760]	Oxford, England	2♂	28 da	50.3	....	4.45	13.8[11]	
25	230 →	Columbia, Missouri	8♀[12]	Residents	2.55[5]	43.0	....	13.7[10]	5
26	4300	Pike's Peak, Colorado	8♀[12]	30 da	1.87[5]	48.2	....	16.3[10]	
27	1520 →	Denver, Colorado	5♂	Residents	2.46[5] [5.57[5]]	....	....	....	14
28	4300 [Po_2 = 453]	Pike's Peak, Colorado	5♂	8 da	2.11[5] [4.53[5]]	....	....	....	
29	[Po_2 = 618] →	Colorado Springs, Colorado	2♂	....	41.7	....	6.00	14.5[11]	4
30	[Po_2 = 460] →	Pike's Peak, Colorado	2♂	5-10 da	45.5	....	....	17.1[11]	
31	[Po_2 = 618]	Colorado Springs, Colorado	2♂	5-20 da	43.4	....	6.45	16.0[11]	
32	150 →	Lima, Peru	6♂	Residents	....	47.9	5.10	15.8[13]	13
33	4270	....	6♂	10 da	....	55.9	6.07	18.5	
34	150 →	Lima, Peru	10♂	Residents	42.0 [77.0]	....	....	....	12
35	4540	Morococha, Peru	10♂[14]	45 da	44.0 [76.0]	....	....	....	
36				100 da	49.0 [83.0]	....	....	....	
37				160 da	51.0 [87.0]	....	....	....	
38				240 da	57.0 [93.0]	....	....	....	
39				360 da	56.0 [96.0]	....	....	....	
40	4540 →	Morococha, Peru	3♂	Residents	54.0 [88.0]	....	....	....	12
41	150	Lima, Peru	3♂[15]	13 da	49.0 [88.0]	....	....	....	
42				60 da	37.0 [85.0]	....	....	....	
43				120 da	35.0 [83.0]	....	....	....	
44	850 →	Dyushambe, U.S.S.R.	26♂	Residents[16]	....	39.0	4.58	13.2[17] [28.8]	1
45	4540 →	Eastern Pamirs	48♂	1 wk	....	45.2	4.98	14.0[17] [28.1]	
46				2 wk	....	46.2	5.65	14.3[17] [25.3]	
47				3 wk	....	50.8	5.47	15.5[17] [28.3]	
48				4 wk	....	51.9	5.82	16.0[17] [27.5]	
49				5 wk	....	53.5	5.88	16.7[17] [28.4]	
50				6 wk	....	54.1	5.91	16.3[17] [27.6]	
51				7 wk	....	54.0	6.02	17.2[17] [28.6]	
52				8 wk	....	54.3	6.29	17.5[17] [27.8]	
53				10 wk	....	54.0	6.30	17.2[17] [27.3]	
54				11 wk	....	53.0	6.28	17.5[17] [27.9]	
55				12 wk	....	53.6	6.31	17.3[17] [27.4]	
56				13 wk	....	54.2	6.32	17.4[17] [27.5]	
57				14 wk	....	54.0	6.30	17.5[17] [27.8]	
58	850	Dyushambe, U.S.S.R.	26♂	4 wk[18]	....	42.5	5.25	15.6[17] [29.7]	
59			26♂	10 wk[18]	....	40.2	4.72	13.8[17] [29.2]	

[1] Unless otherwise indicated. [5] Total volume, in liters. [9] CO method. [10] Van Slyke O_2 capacity method or Evelyn photoelectric colorimeter. [11] Haldane-Gower CO method (100% = 20 vol %). [12] College girls, University of Missouri. [13] Modification of Drabkin method. [14] Residents of Lima (same as in entry 34) who spent 1 yr at Morococha. [15] Residents of Morococha (same as in entry 40) who spent 4 mo at Lima. [16] Before ascent. [17] Estimated from the color index. [18] After descent.

continued

Part II. Transients: Short-Term Effects

	Altitude, m [P_{O_2}, mm Hg; $S_{a_{O_2}}$, %]	Location	Subjects	Exposure Time	Erythrocyte Volume [Blood Volume] ml/kg[1]	Hematocrit ml Erythrocytes/100 ml blood	Erythrocyte Count millions/μl blood	Hemoglobin g/100 ml blood[1] [Mean Corpuscular Hemoglobin, pg]	Reference
60	0 →	London	6♂	Residents[19]	33.4[9]; 2.43[5] [77.9; 5.65[5]]	43.0	....	14.7[20]	11
61	4000-5800	Himalayas	4♂	126 da	+16.5%[9,21] [−8.8%[21]]	....	....	+30.4%[20,22]	
62	5800 →	Himalayas	5♂	21-42 da	+30.1%[9,21] [−1.8%[21]]	....	....	+35.4%[20,22]	
63	5800+	Himalayas	5♂	56-98 da	+49.3%[9,21] [+9.3%[21]]	....	....	+38.9%[20,22]	
64	0 [P_{O_2} = 760]→	Chile[23]	7♂	Residents	....	44.3	....	14.8[10]	15
65	2800 [P_{O_2} = 543]→		9♂	14-55 da	....	49.0	5.29	16.4[10] [31.0]	
66	3660 [P_{O_2} = 489]→		9♂	1-7 da	....	49.3	5.49	17.2[10] [31.3]	
67	4710 [P_{O_2} = 429]→		9♂	4-11 da	....	52.6	5.92	18.1[10] [30.6]	
68	5340 [P_{O_2} = 401]→		9♂	1-16 da	....	54.1	5.86	18.4[10] [31.4]	
69	6140 [P_{O_2} = 358]		6♂	0-6 da	....	54.3	5.72	18.4[10] [32.2]	
70	305 →	India	8♂[24]	Residents	....	....	....	14.9[20]	10
71			6♂[25]	15 da	....	....	....	13.6[20]	
72	5790 →	Himalayas	8♂[24]	....	....	....	....	20.3(18.3-22.0)[20]	
73			6♂[25]	....	....	....	....	19.0(17.6-20.0)[20]	
74	7620 →	Himalayas	12♂[24]	....	....	....	....	20.9(19.3-23.3)[20]	
75			18♂[25]	....	....	....	....	19.3(15.1-23.6)[20]	
76	7880	Himalayas	5♂[24]	....	....	....	....	20.5(19.1-21.6)[20]	
77			3♂[25]	....	....	....	....	17.9(16.8-18.9)[20]	

[1] Unless otherwise indicated. [5] Total volume, in liters. [9] CO method. [10] Van Slyke O_2 capacity method or Evelyn photoelectric colorimeter. [19] Prior to Himalayan expedition. [20] Oxyhemoglobin method, using photoelectric colorimeter. [21] Percentage change in volume. [22] Percentage change in hemoglobin concentration. [23] International High Altitude Expedition. [24] Europeans. [25] Sherpas.

Contributors: Dill, David B.; Root, Walter S.

References

[1] Bododzhanov, Yu. R. 1964. Nauch. Tr. Ryazan. Med. Inst. 18:158.

[2] Buskirk, E. R. 1966. Physiol. Work Cold Altitude Proc. Symp. Arctic Biol. Med., 6th, p. 375.

[3] Dill, D. B., et al. 1969. J. Appl. Physiol. 27:514.

[4] Douglas, G. C., et al. 1913. Phil. Trans. Roy. Soc. London B203:276.

[5] Hannon, J. J., et al. 1969. J. Appl. Physiol. 26:540.

continued

264. EFFECTS OF ALTITUDE ON BLOOD VALUES: MAN

Part II. Transients: Short-Term Effects

[6] Huff, R. L., et al. 1951. Medicine (Baltimore) 30: 197.

[7] Hurtado, A., et al. 1945. Arch. Intern. Med. 75: 284.

[8] Merino, C. F. 1950. Blood 5:1.

[9] Myhre, L. G., et al. 1970. Clin. Chem. 16:7.

[10] Pugh, L. G. C. E. 1954. J. Physiol. (London) 126: 38P.

[11] Pugh, L. G. C. E. 1964. Ibid. 170:344.

[12] Reynafarje, C. 1957. Brookhaven Symp. Biol. 10: 132.

[13] Reynafarje, C., et al. 1954. Proc. Soc. Exp. Biol. Med. 87:101.

[14] Surks, M. I., et al. 1966. J. Appl. Physiol. 21:174.

[15] Talbott, J. H. 1936. Folia Haematol. (Leipzig) 55: 23.

265. EFFECTS OF ALTITUDE ON BLOOD VALUES: VERTEBRATES OTHER THAN MAN

Erythrocytes: d = diameter. **Erythrocytes** and **Hemoglobin:** Units of kg or 100 g refer to body weight. **Remarks:** O_2 cap = oxygen capacity; Sa_{O_2} = arterial oxygen saturation; Ret = reticulocytes; WBC = white blood cells.

	Animal	Altitude or Pressure [Breathing Medium]	No. of Subjects	Exposure Time	Erythrocytes millions/μl[1] [Hematocrit, % Erythrocytes]	Hemoglobin	Remarks	Reference
					Mammalia			
1	Dog	Sea level [Air]	1[2]	....	5.0 (d = 6.94 μ)	68%	Hb measured with Haldane-Gower hemoglobinometer (100% = 20 vol %)	18
2		460 mm Hg	1[2]	4 mo	7.35 (d = 6.93 μ)	88%		
3		Sea level [Air]	1[3]	....	5.25 (d = 6.84 μ)	68%		
4		460 mm Hg	1[3]	1 mo	7.34 (d = 6.92 μ)	75%		
5		Sea level [Air]	1[4]	....	6.5	90%		
6		460 mm Hg	1[4]	31 da	9.0	98%		
7		Sea level	2	....	6.3	13.5 g/100 ml	Hb measured by Sahli method	20
8		3622 m	2	4 wk (6.5 hr/da, 5 da/wk)	6.3	15.0 g/100 ml		
9		4830 m	2	4 wk (7-8 hr/da, 6 da/wk)	7.4	18.0 g/100 ml		
10		5430 m	2	16 wk (9 hr/da, 6 da/wk)	11.2	24.0 g/100 ml		
11		Sea level	2	....	6.5	14.0 g/100 ml		
12		3622 m	2	8 wk (7 hr/da, 6 da/wk)	8.0	17.2 g/100 ml		
13		5434 m	2	16 wk (9 hr/da, 6 da/wk)	12.5	25.0 g/100 ml		
14		5486.4 m	5	88 da (8 hr/da, 6 da/wk)	+67% change	53%	Hb measured by Sahli method	21
15		Sea level	8	....	34.6 ml/kg	11.0 g/kg	Hb measured spectrophotometrically as oxyhemoglobin at 560 & 541 nm	17
16		4560 m	9	....	50.0 ml/kg	15.4 g/kg		
17		Sea level	1	Initial	37.4 ml/kg; 0.618 liter [43.0]	14.8 g/100 ml		

[1] Unless otherwise specified. [2] 6 wk old. [3] 11 wk old. [4] Adult.

continued

	Animal	Altitude or Pressure [Breathing Medium]	No. of Sub-jects	Exposure Time	Erythrocytes millions/μl[1] [Hematocrit, % Erythrocytes]	Hemoglobin	Remarks	Ref-er-ence
18				1 wk later	35.2 ml/kg; 0.582 liter [40.7]	14.0 g/100 ml		
19		6096 m	1	2 da	43.4 ml/kg; 0.717 liter [49.0]	16.7 g/100 ml		
20				8 da	47.5 ml/kg; 0.785 liter [54.7]	18.8 g/100 ml		
21				19 da	60.3 ml/kg; 0.995 liter [62.6]	22.1 g/100 ml		
22				28 da	72.1 ml/kg; 1.191 liter [67.3]	23.7 g/100 ml		
23				40 da	74.2 ml/kg; 1.225 liter [68.2]	24.1 g/100 ml		
24				50 da	71.9 ml/kg; 1.187 liter [68.1]	24.2 g/100 ml		
25				63 da	75.5 ml/kg; 1.246 liter [71.6]	25.2 g/100 ml		
26		Sea level	1	Initial	23.6 ml/kg; 0.267 liter [27.7]	9.1 g/100 ml		
27				1 wk later	21.5 ml/kg; 0.243 liter [25.7]	8.4 g/100 ml		
28		6096 m	1	11 da	30.0 ml/kg; 0.339 liter [34.3]	11.7 g/100 ml		
29				19 da	33.1 ml/kg; 0.375 liter [39.3]	13.7 g/100 ml		
30				26 da	36.3 ml/kg; 0.411 liter [40.2]	13.8 g/100 ml		
31				32 da	37.7 ml/kg; 0.426 liter [39.3]	13.8 g/100 ml		
32				39 da	38.5 ml/kg; 0.436 liter [39.3]	13.5 g/100 ml		
33				45 da	37.3 ml/kg; 0.422 liter [40.2]	14.0 g/100 ml		
34				55 da	40.6 ml/kg; 0.459 liter [40.2]	14.1 g/100 ml		
35				61 da	43.3 ml/kg; 0.490 liter [43.5]	15.3 g/100 ml		
36				68 da	40.5 ml/kg; 0.458 liter [40.1]	14.1 g/100 ml		
37				70 da	41.4 ml/kg; 0.468 liter [40.0]	13.4 g/100 ml		
38				84 da	45.3 ml/kg; 0.512 liter [42.1]	14.6 g/100 ml		
39				98 da	47.0 ml/kg; 0.532 liter [42.1]	14.7 g/100 ml		
40				103 da	48.1 ml/kg; 0.545 liter [42.6]	15.0 g/100 ml		
41				117 da	48.4 ml/kg; 0.548 liter [44.0]	15.5 g/100 ml		
42		Sea level	4	35-70 da	[55.9]	....	....	22
43				....	9.2 [54.5]	....	O_2 cap = 23.7 ml/100 ml	
44		7620 m	4	18-55 da (4 hr/da, 5 da/wk)	12.6 [69.4]	....	O_2 cap = 28.4 ml/100 ml	

[1] Unless otherwise specified.

continued

	Animal	Altitude or Pressure [Breathing Medium]	No. of Subjects	Exposure Time	Erythrocytes millions/μl [1] [Hematocrit, % Erythrocytes]	Hemoglobin	Remarks	Reference
45	Guinea pig	Sea level	27	....	5.3	....	....	13
46		380 mm Hg	27	6 da	6.3			
47				10 da	6.9			
48				14 da	7.6			
49		380 mm Hg [Air]	1	....	5.0	....	Ret = 0.8%	
50				6 da	6.3	....	Ret = 6.5%	
51				8 da	5.8	....	....	
52				16 da	5.3	....	....	
53				24 da	4.9	....	....	
54			2	....	5.4	....	Ret = 0.65%	
55				8 da	6.3	....	....	
56				10 da	6.9	....	Ret = 8.5%	
57				16 da	5.85	....	....	
58				24 da	5.35	....	....	
59			1	....	5.4	....	Ret = 0.2%	
60				8 da	6.8	....	....	
61				14 da	7.6	....	Ret = 8.2%	
62				16 da	6.0	....	....	
63				24 da	5.2	....	....	
64		300 mm Hg	13	10 da	+30% change	....	....	11
65		[Air]	6	....	4.73	98%	Hb measured with Klett-Summerson photoelectric colorimeter	5
66		[70% O_2]	6	9 da	4.69	92.3%		
67				16 da	4.35	84.5%		
68				28 da	4.35	85%		
69	Llama	Sea level	4	....	11.4 [38.6]	10.45 mmole/liter	Sa_{O_2} = 97.0%; O_2 cap = 23.5 vol %	16
70		2810 m	1	....	12.31 [28.2]	7.64 mmole/liter	Sa_{O_2} = 97.2%; O_2 cap = 17.1 vol %	
71		4710 m	1	....	12.90 [28.6]	7.25 mmole/liter	Sa_{O_2} = 88.6%	
72		5340 m	1	....	11.10 [25.8]	6.66 mmole/liter	Sa_{O_2} = 78.8%; O_2 cap = 14.9 vol %	
73	Mouse, C57BL/6	[Air]	19	20 da	7.27 [35.1]	10.66 g/100 ml	Exposure started at birth	15
74		[Air]	73	30 da	8.04 [39.8]	10.69 g/100 ml		
75		[98-100% O_2]	55	30 da	6.84 [35.1]	10.03 g/100 ml		
76	Rabbit	Sea level	7	....	[42.0]	10.7 g/100 ml	Hb measured by acid hematin method with Klett-Summerson colorimeter	1
77		Sea level	6	....	5.12	11.7 g/100 ml	Hb measured by Sahli method. Ret = 0.9%.	2
78		Sea level	5	....	4.9	76%	Hb measured with Haldane hemoglobinometer. Ret = 2.5%.	4
79		Sea level	7	....	5.56 (d = 6.71 μ)	71%	Hb measured with Fleischl-Meischer hemoglobinometer	18
80		600 mm Hg	1	10 da	7.40	74%		
81		500 mm Hg	1	15 da	7.33	84%		
82		480 mm Hg	1	52 da	8.10	81%		
83		460 mm Hg	1	9 mo	6.35	74%		
84		450 mm Hg	1	6 da	7.40	70%		
85			1	9 da	6.07	70%		

[1] Unless otherwise specified.

continued

	Animal	Altitude or Pressure [Breathing Medium]	No. of Sub-jects	Exposure Time	Erythrocytes millions/μl[1] [Hematocrit, % Erythrocytes]	Hemoglobin	Remarks	Ref-er-ence
86		4981 m	8	130-203 hr	+11.1% change [+10.5% change]	....	+9% change in arterial O_2	14
87		Sea level	3	....	4.55 [35.4]	....	Sa_{O_2} = 90.8%; O_2 cap = 15.6 vol %	16
88		2810 m	1	....	6.42 [44.8]	....	....	
89		3660 m	1	....	8.69 [47.3]	....	....	
90		4710 m	1	....	8.53 [52.2]	....	....	
91		5340 m	1	....	7.00 [57.1]	....	Arterial O_2 = 57.0 vol %	
92		Sea level	11	....	5.33 (d = 2.79 μ)	101%[5]	Hb measured by Palmer method. Ret = 0.8%	7
93		6096 m; 411 mm Hg	1	3 hr	6.14; 59 μ^3, vol each cell	....	Ret = 0.4%	
94			1	5 hr	5.28; 58 μ^3, vol each cell	....	Ret = 0.8%	
95			1	8 hr	4.81; 61 μ^3, vol each cell	....	Ret = 1.0%	
96			1	2 da	5.58; 60 μ^3, vol each cell	....	Ret = 3.4%	
97			2	4 da	6.50; 58 μ^3, vol each cell	....	Ret = 12.0%	
98			5	5 da	7.29; 59 μ^3, vol each cell	111%	Ret = 9.1%	
99		2020 m	2	1 wk	+3.5% change	−1.0% change	Hb measured with Fleischl-Meischer hemo-globinometer	6
100		3500 m	6	1 wk	+5.6% change	+7.8% change		
101		4730 m	2	1 wk	+21.8% change	+55.1% change		
102		6060 m	6	1 da	+2.7% change	+2.9% change		
103			6	2 da	+1.7% change	+5.7% change		
104			2	4 da	+0.5% change	+27.8% change		
105			4	4-5 da	+6.2% change	+27.0% change		
106			2	5 da	+12.0% change	+26.1% change		
107		[16% O_2]	4	1 wk	+4.6% change	−2.0% change	Constant barometric pressure. Hb measured with Fleischl-Meischer hemoglobinometer.	6
108		[14% O_2]	8	1 wk	+15.2% change	+17.4% change		
109		[12% O_2]	5	1 wk	+14.4% change	+16.8% change		
110		[10% O_2]	13	1 wk	+17.5% change	+26.4% change		
111		[9% O_2]	2	1 wk	+7.7% change	+12.5% change		
112		[8% O_2]	1	1 wk	+20.3% change	+22.5% change		
113		[6% O_2]	2	1 wk	+18.0% change	+35.2% change		
114		79 mm Hg[6]	1	....	7.7 [100]	....	....	3
115		141 mm Hg[6]	1	....	6.0 [85]			
116		291 mm Hg[6]	1	18 da	4.2 [72]			
117		416 mm Hg[6]	1	20 da	3.0 [55]			
118		53 mm Hg[6]	1	10 da	9.5 [120]			
119		71 mm Hg[6]	1	14 da	9.0 [115]			
120		85 mm Hg[6]	1	19 da	7.5 [105]			
121		144 mm Hg[6]	1	....	5.5 [90]			
122		420 mm Hg[6]	1	4 wk	3.0 [60]			
123	Rat	Sea level	10	....	[40.8]	13.1 g/100 ml; 2.39 g, total	Hb determined by CO method; 63 determina-tions at sea level, & at 6000 m	24
124		6000 m	12	1-2 da	[47.1]	14.7 g/100 ml; 2.68 g, total		

[1]/ Unless otherwise specified. [5]/ Value for 5 rabbits. [6]/ Respiratory oxygen pressure.

continued

	Animal	Altitude or Pressure [Breathing Medium]	No. of Subjects	Exposure Time	Erythrocytes millions/μl [1] [Hematocrit, % Erythrocytes]	Hemoglobin	Remarks	Reference
125		Sea level	53	....	9.1 ml [49.4]	15.0 g/100 ml	Hb determined by CO method	23
126		2000 m	18	14-28 da	11.8 ml [60.3]	18.0 g/100 ml		
127		4000 m	6	68 da	10.5 ml [61.0]	18.7 g/100 ml		
128		5000 m	6	63 da	14.4 ml [70.0]	22.3 g/100 ml		
129		6000 m	40	40-100 da	18.4 ml [77.6]	24.4 g/100 ml		
130		7000 m	4	90 da	18.3 ml [75.0]	23.6 g/100 ml		
131	White	422 mm Hg	14♂	0	....	14.6 g/100 ml	Hb measured with Haden-Hauser hemoglobinometer. Ret = 2.0%	19
132				3-12 da	+700,000	16.7 g/100 ml	Ret = 7.0%	
133			7♂ [7]	0	....	14.6 g/100 ml	Ret = 0.1%	
134				....	+1,300,000	16.8 g/100 ml	Ret = 0.2%	
135			7♂ [8]	0	+8,410,000	13.2 g/100 ml	Ret = 0.3%	
136				....	+8,545,000	13.5 g/100 ml	Ret = 0.1%	
137	Curtis-Dunning	4572 m	40♂	....	2.3 ml/100 g	0.53 g/100 g	Hb determined by Turner's method	9
138				5 da	2.7 ml/100 g	0.77 g/100 g		
139				10 da	4.0 ml/100 g	0.91 g/100 g		
140				15 da	4.0 ml/100 g	0.98 g/100 g		
141				20 da	4.0 ml/100 g	0.99 g/100 g		
142				25 da	4.0 ml/100 g	1.00 g/100 g		
143				30 da	4.0 ml/100 g	....		
144	Long-Evans [9]	[Air]	94♂	....	4.48 ml [37.4]	10.2 g/100 ml; 1.243 g, total	Erythrocyte volume measured with ^{59}Fe	10
145		[9% O_2]	94♂	14 da (6 hr/da)	5.92 ml [45.5]	11.73 g/100 ml; 1.56 g, total		
146		[Air]	3♀ [10]	....	7.37 ml; 2.51 ml/100 g [43.6]	12.0 g/100 ml; 0.690 g/100 g; 2.03 g, total		
147		[9% O_2]	3♀ [10]	14 da (6 hr/da)	9.20 ml; 3.59 ml/100 g [55.3]	15.0 g/100 ml; 0.969 g/100 g; 2.48 g, total		
148		[Air]	11♂ [11]	....	0.52 ml; 1.22 ml/100 g [19.0]	5.1 g/100 ml; 0.324 g/100 g; 0.137 g, total		
149		[9% O_2]	11♂ [11]	14 da (6 hr/da)	0.47 ml; 1.24 ml/100 g [20.7]	5.2 g/100 ml; 0.308 g/100 g; 0.118 g, total		
150		[Air]	21♂	0	7.94 ml [46.3]	....		
151		[7% O_2]	5♂	1 da (6 hr/da)	8.2 ml [51.0]			
152			5♂	2 da (6 hr/da)	8.23 ml [50.8]			
153			8♂	3 da (6 hr/da)	9.40 ml [48.2]			
154			5♂	4 da (6 hr/da)	8.10 ml [50.5]			
155			8♂	5 da (6 hr/da)	8.25 ml [49.8]			
156			5♂	6 da (6 hr/da)	11.13 ml [54.0]			

[1] Unless otherwise specified. [7] Hypophysectomized rats tested 8-9 da after operation. [8] Hypophysectomized rats tested 23-32 da after operation. [9] 5-264 da old. [10] Lactating. [11] Unweaned.

continued

	Animal	Altitude or Pressure [Breathing Medium]	No. of Subjects	Exposure Time	Erythrocytes millions/μl [1] [Hematocrit, % Erythrocytes]	Hemoglobin	Remarks	Reference
157			8♂	7 da (6 hr/da)	9.74 ml [51.8]			
158			7♂	8 da (6 hr/da)	9.57 ml [54.4]			
159			6♂	9 da (6 hr/da)	9.38 ml [51.8]			
160			6♂	11 da (6 hr/da)	11.26 ml [54.9]			
161			5♂	15 da (6 hr/da)	11.99 ml [56.0]			
162			6♂	20 da (6 hr/da)	12.15 ml [57.9]			
163	Sprague-Dawley	422 mm Hg	4♂	0	8.5 ± 0.6	129 ± 2.5%	Hb measured with Klett photoelectric colorimeter, using a Klett standard (14.5 g/100 ml = 100% Hb)	8
164				7 da (6 hr/da)	10.1 ± 0.6 (+19.6% change)	147 ± 2.2% (+14.9% change)		
165				14 da (6 hr/da)	10.0 ± 0.3 (+18.4% change)	168 ± 3.7% (+30.4% change)		
166			4♂ [12]	0	6.2 ± 0.1	90.5 ± 3.0%		
167				7 da (6 hr/da)	5.8 ± 0.4 (−7.7% change)	93.0 ± 6.5% (+2.8% change)		
168				14 da (6 hr/da)	7.1 ± 0.5 (+14.2% change)	94.6 ± 8.0% (+4.5% change)		
169		321 mm Hg	10♂	0	8.9 ± 0.2	113.9 ± 1.6%		
170				7 da (6 hr/da)	10.7 ± 0.4 (+19.2% change)	143.8 ± 2.9% (+26.4% change)		
171				14 da (6 hr/da)	11.6 ± 0.2 (+28.2% change)	142.9 ± 4.2% (+26.0% change)		
172			10♂ [12]	0	5.8 ± 0.2	79.5 ± 3.0%		
173				7 da (6 hr/da)	7.2 ± 0.3 (+24.2% change)	98.0 ± 3.7% (+23.3% change)		
174				14 da (6 hr/da)	8.1 ± 0.3 (+39.6% change)	100.5 ± 5.5% (+26.5% change)		
175	Wistar & Hooded	[Air]	10♂	....	7.9 ml [44.1]	2.26 g; 0.67 g/100 g; 12.64 g/100 ml	Hb determined by alveolar CO method	25
176		[21% O_2]	5♂	....	....	3.34 g; 0.77 g/100 g		
177		[30% O_2]	5♂	51 da	....	3.15 g; 0.69 g/100 g		
178		[50% O_2]	5♂	23 da	....	3.16 g; 0.67 g/100 g		
179		[60-70% O_2]	5♂	46 da	....	3.27 g; 0.68 g/100 g		
180		[80% O_2]	10♂	60 da	7.0 ml [42.4]	2.17 g; 0.62 g/100 g; 13.10 g/100 ml		
181		[80-90% O_2]	5♂	76 da	....	3.08 g; 0.66 g/100 g		
182		[100% O_2]	8♂	45 da	9.4 [53]	3.17 g; 0.75 g/100 g; 15.39 g/100 ml		
183			8♂	67 da	7.0 [43.2]	2.98 g; 0.75 g/100 g; 12.31 g/100 ml		
184			5♂	72 da	....	3.18 g; 0.71 g/100 g		
185	Sheep	Sea level	2	....	10.53 [35.3]	6.0 mmole/liter	Sa_{O_2} = 91.4%; O_2 cap = 15.9 vol %	16
186		2810 m	1	....	9.33 [26.7]	5.4 mmole/liter	Sa_{O_2} = 80.7%	
187		3050 m	2	....	11.49 [41.5]	8.2 mmole/liter	Sa_{O_2} = 79.0%	

[1] Unless otherwise specified. [12] Hypophysectomized rats tested 2 mo after operation.

continued

	Animal	Altitude or Pressure [Breathing Medium]	No. of Subjects	Exposure Time	Erythrocytes millions/μl [1] [Hematocrit, % Erythrocytes]	Hemoglobin	Remarks	Reference
188		4710 m	1	....	12.05 [50.2]	8.4 mmole/liter	Sa_{O_2} = 70.6%; O_2 cap = 18.9 vol %	
189		5340 m	1	....	16.00 [67.4]	9.7 mmole/liter	Sa_{O_2} = 56.1%	
190	Vicuña	2810 m	1	....	14.05 [29.9]	7.55 mmole/liter	Sa_{O_2} = 95.3%	16
191		4710 m	1	....	16.61 [31.9]	8.16 mmole/liter	Sa_{O_2} = 82.2%; O_2 cap = 18.2 vol %	
192	Vizcacha	3660 m	1	....	7.12 [31.8]	6.60 mmole/liter	Sa_{O_2} = 89.8%; O_2 cap = 14.8 vol %	16
					Aves			
193	Huallata[13]	5340 m	1	....	3.27 [59.1]	10.56 mmole/liter	Sa_{O_2} = 77.1%; O_2 cap = 23.6 vol %	16
194	Ostrich	3660 m	1	....	2.18 [33.8]	6.21 mmole/liter	Sa_{O_2} = 86.4%; O_2 cap = 13.9 vol %	16
195	Pigeon	Sea level	1	....	4.47	....	....	18
196		450 mm Hg	1	1 mo	5.00			
197		Sea level	1	....	4.37			
198		450 mm Hg	1	1 mo	4.92			
199		Sea level	1	....	3.25			
200		480-400 mm Hg	1	9 da	5.07			
					Amphibia			
201	Mud puppy	Sea level	28	....	4200 μl	....	440 WBC/μl	12
202		330 mm Hg	4	7 wk	5800 μl	+30% change	1520 WBC/μl	

[1] Unless otherwise specified. [13] *Chloephaga melanoptera.*

Contributor: Root, Walter S.

References

[1] Bancroft, R. W. 1949. Amer. J. Physiol. 156:158.

[2] Bell, R., and D. W. Northrup. 1950. Ibid. 163:125.

[3] Campbell, J. A. 1927. J. Physiol. (London) 62:211.

[4] Campbell, J. A. 1927. Ibid. 63:325.

[5] Cooperberg, A., and K. Singer. 1951. J. Lab. Clin. Med. 37:936.

[6] Dallwig, H. C., et al. 1916. Amer. J. Physiol. 39:77.

[7] Dubin, M. 1934. Quart. J. Exp. Physiol. 24:31.

[8] Feigin, W. M., and A. S. Gordon. 1950. Endocrinology 47:364.

[9] Fryers, G. R. 1952. Amer. J. Physiol. 171:459.

[10] Garcia, J. F. 1957. Ibid. 190:25.

[11] Goldbloom, A., and R. Gottlieb. 1929. J. Clin. Invest. 8:375.

[12] Gordon, A. S. 1935. Proc. Soc. Exp. Biol. Med. 32:820.

[13] Gordon, A. S., and W. Kleinberg. 1937. Ibid. 37:507.

[14] Grant, W. C. 1951. Amer. J. Physiol. 164:226.

[15] Gyllensten, L., and G. Swanbeck. 1959. Acta Pathol. Microbiol. Scand. 45:229.

[16] Hall, F. G., et al. 1936. J. Cell. Comp. Physiol. 8:301.

[17] Reissman, K. 1951. Amer. J. Physiol. 167:52.

[18] Schauman, P., and E. Rosenquist. 1898. Z. Klin. Med. 35:126.

[19] Stewart, G. E., et al. 1936. Proc. Soc. Exp. Biol. Med. 33:112.

[20] Stickney, J. C., and E. J. Van Liere. 1942. J. Aviat. Med. 13:170.

[21] Stickney, J. C., et al. 1943. Proc. Soc. Exp. Biol. Med. 54:151.

[22] Thorn, G. W., et al. 1942. Amer. J. Physiol. 137:606.

[23] Tribukait, B. 1963. Acta Physiol. Scand. 57:1.

[24] Tribukait, B. 1963. Ibid. 57:90.

[25] Tribukait, B. 1963. Ibid. 57:407.

Where only altitude was given by an investigator, the corresponding barometric pressure was added from *U.S. Standard Atmosphere, 1962* (reference 21 in Part I). Variations in altitude (in meters) as related to barometric pressure (in mm Hg) are due to temperature differences and to method of calculation. Data in brackets refer to the column heading in brackets.

Part I. Simulated Altitude

Subjects were adult males and females, resting during ascent to altitude. Values in lines 1-40 and lines 66-85 were obtained while subjects breathed air; values in lines 41-65 and 86-98 were obtained while subjects breathed 100% O_2. **Method:** Ast = Astrup method; Calc = calculated from observed saturation value and assumed O_2 capacity of 21.5 ml/100 ml blood (assumed O_2 capacity based on uniform, assumed hemoglobin content of 15.8 g/100 ml, where 15.8 g hemoglobin/100 ml blood $\times$ 1.36 = ml oxygen); $CC = \dfrac{O_2 \text{ content-free } O_2}{O_2 \text{ capacity}}$; $CO_2E = CO_2$ electrode; DC = determinations from CO_2 dissociation curves; HB = arterial pressure from Hill-Barcroft formula; HP = arterial pressure assumed equal to alveolar pressure, as determined by Haldane-Priestly method; O_2E = oxygen electrode; Or = oximeter readings, ground level setting of 96-97% saturation; OR = oximeter readings, ground level setting of 100% saturation; PA = arterial pressure assumed equal to alveolar pressure of alveolar samples; PE = platinum electrode; T = tonometric analysis; VA = Van Slyke analysis; VM = Van Slyke manometric analysis; VS = Van Slyke and spectrophotometric analyses. Values in parentheses are ranges, estimate "b" unless otherwise indicated (*see* Introduction).

	Altitude, m [Pressure, mm Hg]	No. of Subjects	Method	Variable	Value	Reference
				Oxygen		
1	Sea level [760]	>21	T	Pressure	96 mm Hg	3,9,14
2		>21	Calc	Content	21.2 vol %	3,9,14
3		51	VS	Saturation	98%	4,10,23
4	607 [707]	16	PE	Pressure	94.0 ± 5.9 mm Hg	22
5		16	Or	Saturation	98.7 ± 0.7 %	
6	1524 [632]	.....	....	Pressure	66 mm Hg	2
7		.....	Calc	Content	19.6 vol %	2
8		10	Or	Saturation	91(87-95) %	12
9	2250 [578]	6	PE	Pressure	61.1 mm Hg	18
10	2458 [564]	.....	....	Pressure	60 mm Hg	2
11		.....	Calc	Content	19.1 vol %	2
12		10	Or	Saturation	89(84.5-93.5) %	12
13	3048 [523]	.....	....	Pressure	53 mm Hg	2
14		.....	Calc	Content	18.4 vol %	2
15		16	Or	Saturation	85.4(79-92) %	12
16	3353 [503]	16	PE	Pressure	63.1 ± 4 mm Hg	22
17		16	Or	Saturation	92.4 ± 2.2 %	
18	3400 [500]	6	PE	Pressure	50.8 mm Hg	18
19	3658 [483]	.....	....	Pressure	52 mm Hg	2
20		.....	Calc	Content	18.3 vol %	2
21		11	Or	Saturation	84.9(77-92.5) %	12
22	4267 [446]	.....	....	Pressure	44 mm Hg	2
23		.....	Calc	Content	17.0 vol %	2
24		17	Or	Saturation	79.2(71-87.5) %	12
25	4572 [430-425]	7	PE	Pressure	35 ± 5 mm Hg[1]	17
26		5	PE	Pressure	46 ± 3 mm Hg[2]	
27	[429]	5	PE	Pressure	47 ± 6 mm Hg[3]	16
28		16	PE	Pressure	43.9 ± 4.6 mm Hg	22
29		16	Or	Saturation	78.9 ± 8.3 %	22

[1] Supine. [2] Sitting. [3] Standing.

continued

Part I. Simulated Altitude

	Altitude, m [Pressure, mm Hg]	No. of Subjects	Method	Variable	Value	Reference
30	4877 [412]	.....	....	Pressure	41 mm Hg	2
31		.....	Calc	Content	16.4 vol %	2
32		17	Or	Saturation	76.2(65-87.5) %	12
33	5486 [379]	.....	....	Pressure	36 mm Hg	2
34		.....	Calc	Content	15.3 vol %	2
35		13	Or	Saturation	71.2(57-85.5) %	12
36	6000 [354]	12	PE	Pressure	40.7(38.2-45)^c mm Hg	15
37	6096 [349]	.....	....	Pressure	35 mm Hg	2
38		.....	Calc	Content	15.2 vol %	2
39		9	Or	Saturation	70.8(57.5-84) %	12
40	8000 [267]	12	PE	Pressure	33.5(30.1-36.8)^c mm Hg	15
41	10,668 [179]	.....	Calc	Content	19.8 vol %	12
42		22	OR	Saturation	92(84-100) %	
43	11,430 [159]	3	....	Pressure	74 mm Hg	5
44		4	Calc	Content	20.2 vol %	
45		4	....	Saturation	94%	
46	11,979 [146]	5	VM, HB	Pressure	57 mm Hg	1
47			Calc	Content	19.1 vol %	
48			VM, CC	Saturation	88.7%	
49	12,192 [141]	8	....	Pressure	55 mm Hg	5
50			Calc	Content	18.9 vol %	
51			....	Saturation	88.1(81-95) %	
52	12,497 [134]	3	....	Pressure	54 mm Hg	5
53			Calc	Content	18.6 vol %	
54			....	Saturation	86.4(85-88) %	
55	12,802 [128]	3	....	Pressure	49 mm Hg	5
56			Calc	Content	17.8 vol %	
57			....	Saturation	83(71-95) %	
58	13,106 [122]	2	....	Pressure	42 mm Hg	5
59		4	Calc	Content	16.9 vol %	
60		4	....	Saturation	78.5(65-92) %	
61	13,411 [116]	3	....	Pressure	36 mm Hg	5
62			Calc	Content	15.5 vol %	
63			....	Saturation	72.2(58-86) %	
64	13,716 [111]	.....	Calc	Content	14.6 vol %	2
65				....	Saturation	68(53-83) %	
			Carbon Dioxide			
66	Sea level [760]	341	T, PA, DC	Pressure	43 mm Hg	6-8,11, 13,14, 19
67		226	VA, DC	Content	49 vol %	6-8,13, 20,23
68	607 [707]	16	CO_2E	Pressure	29.7 ± 1.8 mm Hg	22
69	1524 [632]	62[4]	HP	Pressure[5]	36.5 mm Hg	2
70	2250 [578]	6	CO_2E	Pressure	36.5 mm Hg	18
71	2458 [564]	10[4]	HP	Pressure[5]	37.4 mm Hg	2
72	3048 [523]	92[4]	HP	Pressure[5]	35.8 mm Hg	2
73	3353 [503]	16	CO_2E	Pressure	24.6 ± 2.37 mm Hg	22

[4] Acclimated to 305 m.   [5] Alveolar pressure.

continued

Part I. Simulated Altitude

	Altitude, m [Pressure, mm Hg]	No. of Subjects	Method	Variable	Value	Reference
74	3400 [500]	6	CO_2E	Pressure	35.5 mm Hg	18
75	3658 [483]	61[4]	HP	Pressure[5]	34.8 mm Hg	2
76	4267 [446]	26[4]	HP	Pressure[5]	35.4 mm Hg	2
77	4572 [430-425]	7	CO_2E	Pressure	27 ± 2 mm Hg[1]	17
78		5	CO_2E	Pressure	31 ± 6 mm Hg[2]	
79	[429]	5	CO_2E	Pressure	28 ± 4 mm Hg[3]	16
80		16	Ast	Pressure	23.2 ± 1.80 mm Hg	22
81	4877 [412]	9[4]	HP	Pressure[5]	33.8 mm Hg	2
82	5486 [379]	55[4]	HP	Pressure[5]	31.8 mm Hg	2
83	6000 [354]	12	CO_2E	Pressure	31.9(27.8-36.2)c mm Hg	15
84	6096 [349]	81[4]	HP	Pressure[5]	29.4 mm Hg	2
85	8000 [267]	12	CO_2E	Pressure	18.6(14.5-24.3)c mm Hg	15
86	11,430 [159]	3	....	Pressure	40.6 mm Hg	5
87				Content	46.3 vol %	
88	11,979 [146]	5	VM, DC	Pressure	39.4 mm Hg	1
89			VM	Content	50.0 vol %	
90	12,192 [141]	8	....	Pressure	35(26-44) mm Hg	5
91				Content	42.7(35-50) vol %	
92	12,497 [134]	3	....	Pressure	38.1 mm Hg	5
93				Content	44.8 vol %	
94	12,802 [128]	3	....	Pressure	40(36-44) mm Hg	5
95				Content	47.1(45-50) vol %	
96	13,106 [122]	3	....	Content	41.5(31-52) vol %	5
97	13,411 [116]	3	....	Pressure	33.2 mm Hg	5
98				Content	44.9 vol %	

[1] Supine. [2] Sitting. [3] Standing. [4] Acclimated to 305 m. [5] Alveolar pressure.

Contributors: Luft, Ulrich C.; Weber, Kenneth C.

References

[1] Barach, A. L., et al. 1947. J. Aviat. Med. 18:139.

[2] Committee on Aviation Medicine. 1944. Handbook of Respiratory Data in Aviation. National Research Council, Washington, D.C. Charts A-1, B-1, B-3.

[3] Comroe, J. H., Jr., and R. D. Dripps, Jr. 1944. Amer. J. Physiol. 142:700.

[4] Comroe, J. H., Jr., and P. Walker. 1948. Ibid. 152: 365.

[5] Dill, D. B., and F. G. Hall. 1942. J. Aeronaut. Sci. 9:220.

[6] Dill, D. B., et al. 1927. J. Biol. Chem. 73:251.

[7] Dill, D. B., et al. 1937. Ibid. 118:635.

[8] Dill, D. B., et al. 1940. Ibid. 136:449.

[9] Drabkin, D. L. 1949. In F. J. W. Roughton and J. C. Kendrew, ed. Haemoglobin. Interscience, New York. p. 35.

[10] Drabkin, D. L., and C. F. Schmidt. 1945. J. Biol. Chem. 157:69.

[11] Hamilton, J. A., and N. W. Shock. 1936. Amer. J. Psychol. 48:467.

[12] Henson, M., et al. 1947. J. Aviat. Med. 18:149.

[13] Hurtado, A., and H. Aste-Salazar. 1948. J. Appl. Physiol. 1:304.

[14] Lilienthal, J. L., Jr., et al. 1946. Amer. J. Physiol. 147:199.

[15] Nagasaka, T., and T. Satake. 1969. Fed. Proc. Fed. Amer. Soc. Exp. Biol. 28:1312.

[16] Reeves, J. T., and F. Daoud. 1970. Advan. Cardiol. 5:41.

[17] Reeves, J. T., et al. 1969. J. Appl. Physiol. 27:658.

[18] Roskamm, H., et al. 1969. Ibid. 27:840.

[19] Shock, N. W. 1941. Amer. J. Physiol. 133:610.

[20] Shock, N. W., and A. B. Hastings. 1934. J. Biol. Chem. 104:585.

[21] U.S. Committee on Extension to the Standard Atmosphere. 1962. U.S. Standard Atmosphere, 1962. U.S. Government Printing Office, Washington, D.C.

[22] Vogel, J. A., and C. W. Harris. 1967. U.S. Army Med. Res. Nutr. Lab. (Denver) Lab. Rep. 303.

[23] Wood, E. H. 1949. J. Appl. Physiol. 1:567.

continued

Part II. Incomplete Acclimation

Subjects were unaccustomed to altitude. **Method:** Ast = Astrup method; CC = $\dfrac{O_2 \text{ content-free } O_2}{O_2 \text{ capacity}}$; $CO_2E = CO_2$ electrode; CS = calculated from capacity and saturation; DC = derived from O_2 dissociation curve by means of O_2 saturation and pH; H = hemoglobin $\times$ 1.36; HH = calculated from Henderson-Hasselbalch equation by measurement of plasma CO_2 content and pH; HM = Haldane blood gas method; PE = platinum electrode; PH = calculated from O_2 pressure and pH; VM = Van Slyke manometric analysis. Plus/minus ($\pm$) values are standard error, unless otherwise indicated. Values in parentheses are ranges, estimate "c" unless otherwise indicated (*see* Introduction).

	Altitude, m [Pressure, mm Hg]	No. of Subjects	Method	Variable	Value	Reference
				Oxygen		
1	Sea level [760]	10[1]	DC	Pressure	94 mm Hg	1
2			VM	Content	21.1 vol %	
3			VM	Capacity	21.5 vol %	
4			CC	Saturation	98%	
5	2250 [578]	106	PE[2]	Pressure	66 ± 2.9[3] mm Hg	3
6	2810 [543]	10[1]	DC	Pressure	60(47.4-73.6)[b] mm Hg	7
7			VM	Content	20.0 vol %	
8			VM	Capacity	22.0 vol %	
9			CC	Saturation	91(86.8-95.2)[b] %	
10	3100 [535]	10	PE	Pressure	58.2 ± 0.96 mm Hg	4
11	3600 [488]	4[4]	PE	Pressure	51.7(44.0-52.6) mm Hg	9
12			CS	Content	18.5(16.4-20.0) vol %	
13			H	Capacity	21.3(20.0-22.8) vol %	
14			PH	Saturation	86.7(81.5-88.4) %	
15	3660 [489]	10[1]	DC	Pressure	47.6(42.2-53.0) mm Hg	7
16			VM	Content	19.6 vol %	
17			VM	Capacity	23.0 vol %	
18			CC	Saturation	84.5(80.5-89.0) %	
19	3735 [493]	2[5]	PE	Pressure	51.4 mm Hg	10
20	3800 [480]	4[5]	PE	Pressure	49.5(43.5-55.5)[b] mm Hg	6
21	4300 [445]	16[6]	PE	Pressure	44 mm Hg	5
22		16[7]	PE	Pressure	53 mm Hg	
23	4330 [442]	12	PE	Pressure	47.1 ± 1.4 mm Hg	8
24	4340 [458]	2[5]	PE	Pressure	47.9 mm Hg	10
25	4509 [446]	2[5]	PE	Pressure	46.3 mm Hg	10
26	4700 [429]	10[1]	DC	Pressure	44.6(36.4-47.5) mm Hg	7
27			VM	Content	19.3 vol %	
28			VM	Capacity	24.2 vol %	
29			CC	Saturation	78(70.8-85.0) %	
30	5340 [401]	10[1]	DC	Pressure	43.1(37.6-50.4) mm Hg	7
31			VM	Content	18.6 vol %	
32			VM	Capacity	24.4 vol %	
33			CC	Saturation	76.2(65.4-81.6) %	
34	5475 [380]	4[8]	DC	Pressure	34(33-36) mm Hg	11
35			CS	Content	17.5(15.8-19.3) vol %	
36			H	Capacity	26.5(24.7-28.1) vol %	
37			HM	Saturation	66(64-69) %	
38	6140 [356]	10[1]	DC	Pressure	35(26.9-40.1) mm Hg	7
39			VM	Content	16.4 vol %	
40			VM	Capacity	25.0 vol %	
41			CC	Saturation	65.6(55.5-73.0) %	

[1] 29-44 yr old. [2] "Arterialized" capillary blood. [3] Plus/minus (±) value is standard deviation. [4] 7 determinations; 4-9 da at altitude. [5] 3 da at altitude. [6] 1-3 da at altitude. [7] 15-18 da at altitude. [8] 14 wk at altitude.

continued

Part II. Incomplete Acclimation

	Altitude, m [Pressure, mm Hg]	No. of Subjects	Method	Variable	Value	Reference
				Carbon Dioxide		
42	Sea level [760]	10[1]	HH	Pressure	41 mm Hg	1
43			VM	Content	49 vol %	
44	2250 [578]	106	CO_2E[2]	Pressure	38.7 ± 1.3[3] mm Hg	3
45	2810 [543]	10[1]	HH	Pressure	33.9(31.3-36.5)[b] mm Hg	2
46			VM	Content	42.3(39.3-45.3)[b] vol %	
47	3100 [535]	10	CO_2E	Pressure	31.7 ± 0.63 mm Hg	4
48	3600 [488]	4[4]	PE	Pressure	28.8(27.7-32.4) mm Hg	9
49	3660 [489]	10[1]	HH	Pressure	29.5(23.5-34.3) mm Hg	2
50			VM	Content	40.7(36.9-44.1) vol %	
51	3735 [493]	2[5]	CO_2E	Pressure	32.0 mm Hg	10
52	3800 [480]	4[5]	PE	Pressure	29.5(24.5-34.5)[b] mm Hg	6
53	4300 [445]	16[9]	Ast	Pressure	25.4 mm Hg	5
54		16[7]	Ast	Pressure	23.6 mm Hg	
55	4330 [442]	12	CO_2E	Pressure	32.4 ± 0.8 mm Hg	8
56	4340 [458]	2[5]	CO_2E	Pressure	30.7 mm Hg	10
57	4509 [446]	2[5]	CO_2E	Pressure	30.0 mm Hg	10
58	4700 [429]	10[1]	HH	Pressure	27.1(22.9-34.0) mm Hg	2
59			VM	Content	38.3(34.9-42.5) vol %	
60	5340 [401]	10[1]	HH	Pressure	25.7(21.7-29.7) mm Hg	2
61			VM	Content	35.0(30.9-40.0) vol %	
62	6140 [356]	10[1]	HH	Pressure	22.0(19.2-24.8) mm Hg	2
63			VM	Content	30.2(26.6-33.3) vol %	

[1] 29-44 yr old. [2] "Arterialized" capillary blood. [3] Plus/minus (±) value is standard deviation. [4] 7 determinations; 4-9 da at altitude. [5] 3 da at altitude. [7] 15-18 da at altitude. [9] 1-4 da at altitude.

Contributors: Luft, Ulrich C.; Weber, Kenneth C.

References

[1] Committee on Aviation Medicine. 1944. Handbook of Respiratory Data in Aviation. National Research Council, Washington, D.C. Charts A-1, B-1, B-3.

[2] Dill, D. B., et al. 1937. J. Biol. Chem. 118:649.

[3] Doll, E., et al. 1967. Sportarzt. Sportmed. 18:317.

[4] Forster, H. V., et al. 1969. Fed. Proc. Fed. Amer. Soc. Exp. Biol. 28:1274.

[5] Hansen, J. E., et al. 1967. J. Appl. Physiol. 23:511.

[6] Kronenberg, R. S., et al. 1971. J. Clin. Invest. 50: 827.

[7] McFarland, R. A., and D. B. Dill. 1938. J. Aviat. Med. 9:1.

[8] Moncloa, F., et al. 1970. J. Appl. Physiol. 28:151.

[9] Severinghaus, J. W., et al. 1963. Ibid. 18:1155.

[10] Torrance, J. D., et al. 1970. Resp. Physiol. 11:1.

[11] West, J. B., et al. 1962. J. Appl. Physiol. 17:617.

Part III. Complete Acclimation

Subjects were adult male residents, unless otherwise indicated, resting and fasting. Values near sea level are included for comparison purposes. **Method:** Ast = Astrup method; Av = average of CO_2 electrode value and that calculated from Henderson-Hasselbalch equation using pH and HCO_3^- values; Calc = calculated from saturation value, serum pH and chart B-3 of reference 3; $CC = \dfrac{O_2 \text{ content-free } O_2}{O_2 \text{ capacity}}$; $Cco_2 =$ calculated from CO_2 content and CO_2 dissociation curve; $Co_2 =$ calculated from O_2 content and O_2 dissociation curve; $CO_2E = CO_2$ electrode; DC = determined from dissociation curves; Der = calculated from O_2 pressure and dissociation

continued

Part III. Complete Acclimation

curve; HbC = hemoglobin cyanmethemoglobin; O₂E = oxygen electrode; Or = oximeter reading, ground level setting of 96-97% saturation; PE = platinum electrode; R = with 2% correction of Roughton, et al [12]; T = tonometric analysis;

VM = Van Slyke manometric analysis. Plus/minus (±) values are standard error. Values in parentheses are ranges, estimate "b" unless otherwise indicated (*see* Introduction).

	Altitude, m [Pressure, mm Hg]	No. of Subjects	Method	Variable	Value	Reference
				Oxygen		
1	150 [746]	....	....	Pressure	90 mm Hg	3
2				Content	20.7 vol %	
3				Capacity	21.7 vol %	
4				Saturation	95.4%	
5	150 [750]	80	....	Pressure	(95-97)^c mm Hg	7
6			VM	Content	20.7(17.0-23.5)^c vol %	
7			VM	Capacity	20.8(17.4-23.6)^c vol %	
8			CC	Saturation	97.9(95.3-99.7)^c %	
9	1575 [628]	20	T	Pressure	74.8(69-86)^c mm Hg	1
10		95	HbC	Capacity	22.6(19.6-25.0)^c vol %	9
11		100♀	HbC	Capacity	20.1(17.0-22.6)^c vol %	9
12		20	VM	Saturation	94.1(89-97)^c %	1
13	1600 [625]	19	PE	Pressure	69.0 ± 1.2 mm Hg	10
14		19	Or	Saturation	93.9 ± 0.31 %	
15	2390 [568]	....	....	Pressure	68 mm Hg	6
16		12	VM	Content	21.2(18.5-24) vol %	
17		12	VM	Capacity	23.1(19-27.5) vol %	
18		12	CC	Saturation	91.7(86.5-97) %	
19	3100 [530]	39	PE	Pressure	57.2 ± 0.68 mm Hg	10
20		9	PE	Pressure	60.7 ± 0.49 mm Hg	5
21		39	Or	Saturation	89.1 ± 0.34 %	10
22	3140 [517]	....	....	Pressure	66 mm Hg	3
23		11	VM	Content	21.9(19-25) vol %	6
24		11	VM	Capacity	24.0(22-26) vol %	6
25		11	CC	Saturation	91.0(87-95) %	6
26	3700 [485]	11	PE	Pressure	60.2 ± 1.6 mm Hg	16
27	3720 [484]	10	O₂E	Pressure	57(51-59)^c mm Hg	13
28			....	Saturation	89.6(86.4-91.7)^c %	
29	3730 [479]	....	....	Pressure	57 mm Hg	3
30		15	VM	Content	21.9(18.5-25) vol %	6
31		15	VM	Capacity	25.0(21.5-28.5) vol %	6
32		15	CC	Saturation	87.6(84.5-91.5) %	6
33	3735 [493]	6	O₂E	Pressure	48.3 ± 1.0 mm Hg	17
34		6	Der	Saturation	80.2 ± 1.0 %	
35	3990 [463]	4	Calc	Pressure	55 mm Hg	2
36			VM	Content	21.1 vol %	
37			VM, R	Capacity	24.2 vol %	
38			CC	Saturation	86.9%	
39	4250 [447]	6	PE	Pressure	45.5(38.9-52.1) mm Hg	8
40	4330 [442]	15	PE	Pressure	43.6 ± 0.8 mm Hg	15
41		5	PE	Pressure	46.4 ± 1.2 mm Hg	14
42		4	PE	Pressure	50.8(47.8-54.7) mm Hg	11
43	4340 [458]	6	O₂E	Pressure	45.2 ± 1.0 mm Hg	17
44		6	Der	Saturation	74.7 ± 1.2 mm Hg	
45	4509 [446]	4	O₂E	Pressure	44.1 mm Hg	17

continued

Part III. Complete Acclimation

	Altitude, m [Pressure, mm Hg]	No. of Subjects	Method	Variable	Value	Reference
46	4515 [432]	22	Calc	Pressure	49 mm Hg	2
47			VM	Content	21.6(18-25) vol %	
48			VM, R	Capacity	26.1(21-31) vol %	
49			CC	Saturation	82.8(75-90) %	
50	4540 [431]	....	....	Pressure	47 mm Hg	3
51		18	VM	Content	23.0(19.5-26.5) vol %	6
52		18	VM	Capacity	28.3(24-32.5) vol %	6
53		18	CC	Saturation	81.4(75.5-87.0) %	6
54		40	VM	Content	22.4(18.8-27.1)[c] vol %	7
55			VM	Capacity	27.3(22.3-33.0)[c] vol %	
56			CC	Saturation	81.0(75.6-86.7)[c] %	
57	4545 [448]	6	O_2E	Pressure	47(45-50)[c] mm Hg	13
58			....	Saturation	84.2(82.6-86.4)[c] %	
59	4820 [432]	4	O_2E	Pressure	43(41-47)[c] mm Hg	13
60			....	Saturation	80.7(78.2-84.3)[c] %	
61	4860 [413]	....	....	Pressure	46 mm Hg	3
62		12	VM	Content	23.4(20.5-26.5) vol %	6
63		12	VM	Capacity	29.0(25-33) vol %	6
64		12	CC	Saturation	80.7(76-85) %	6
65	5340 [387]	7	Co_2	Pressure	43 mm Hg	4
66			VM	Content	23.0 vol %	
67			VM	Capacity	30.2 vol %	
68			CC	Saturation	76.2%	

<table>
<tr><td colspan="7" align="center">Carbon Dioxide</td></tr>
</table>

	Altitude, m [Pressure, mm Hg]	No. of Subjects	Method	Variable	Value	Reference
69	150 [750]	80	DC	Pressure	40.1(35.3-46.0)[c] mm Hg	7
70			VM	Content	48.3(43.5-53.8)[c] vol %	
71	150 [746]	....	....	Pressure	41 mm Hg	3
72				Content	46 vol %	
73	1575 [628]	20	T	Pressure	32.8(23.0-39.5)[c] mm Hg	1
74			VM	Content	42.1(36.6-47.5)[c] vol %	
75	1600 [625]	19	CO_2E	Pressure	35.6 ± 0.57 mm Hg	10
76	2390 [568]	12	DC	Pressure	37.8(34-42) mm Hg	6
77			VM	Content	41.1(37-45) vol %	
78	3100 [530]	19	CO_2E	Pressure	33.3 ± 0.47 mm Hg	10
79		9	CO_2E	Pressure	32.0 ± 0.81 mm Hg	5
80	3140 [517]	11	DC	Pressure	36.4(31-42) mm Hg	6
81			VM	Content	39.3(34.5-44) vol %	
82	3700 [485]	11	Ast	Pressure	34.7 ± 0.65 mm Hg	16
83	3720 [484]	10	Av	Pressure	32.4(30.5-35.4)[c] mm Hg	13
84	3730 [479]	15	VM	Content	36.0(33-39) vol %	6
85	3735 [493]	6	CO_2E	Pressure	34.5 ± 0.4 mm Hg	17
86	3990 [463]	4	T	Pressure	34.7 mm Hg	2
87			VM	Content	39.8 vol %	
88	4330 [442]	8	CO_2E	Pressure	32.8 ± 1.0 mm Hg	15
89		5	CO_2E	Pressure	32.4 mm Hg	14
90		4	CO_2E	Pressure	32.9(31.3-36.0) mm Hg	11
91	4340 [458]	6	CO_2E	Pressure	31.6 ± 0.9 mm Hg	17
92	4509 [446]	4	CO_2E	Pressure	32.2 mm Hg	17
93	4515 [432]	22	T	Pressure	33.8(28-40) mm Hg	2
94			VM	Content	37.9(33-43) vol %	

continued

Part III. Complete Acclimation

	Altitude, m [Pressure, mm Hg]	No. of Subjects	Method	Variable	Value	Reference
95 96	4540 [431]	18	T VM	Pressure Content	34.7(29-40) mm Hg 33.5(32-35) vol %	6
97 98		40	DC VM	Pressure Content	33.0(28.5-37.1)^c mm Hg 35.4(30.8-41.0)^c vol %	7
99	4545 [448]	6	Av	Pressure	32.5(30.9-33.6)^c mm Hg	13
100	4820 [432]	4	Av	Pressure	32.3(31.0-33.2)^c mm Hg	13
101 102	4860 [413]	12	T VM	Pressure Content	33.0(28-38) mm Hg 34.0(31-37) vol %	6
103 104	5340 [387]	7	Cco_2 VM	Pressure Content	29.3 mm Hg 31.8 vol %	4

Contributors: Luft, Ulrich C.; Weber, Kenneth C.; Hurtado, Alberto

References

[1] Anderson, L. L., et al. 1953. J. Clin. Invest. 32: 490.
[2] Chiodi, H. 1957. J. Appl. Physiol. 10:81.
[3] Committee on Aviation Medicine. 1944. Handbook of Respiratory Data in Aviation. National Research Council, Washington, D.C. Charts A-1, B-1, B-3.
[4] Dill, D. B., et al. 1936. Amer. J. Physiol. 115:530.
[5] Forster, H. V., et al. 1969. Fed. Proc. Fed. Amer. Soc. Exp. Biol. 28:1274.
[6] Hurtado, A., and H. Aste-Salazar. 1948. J. Appl. Physiol. 1:304.
[7] Hurtado, A., et al. 1956. U.S. Air Force Sch. Aviat. Med. (Randolph) Rep. 56-104.
[8] Kreuzer, F., et al. 1964. J. Appl. Physiol. 19:13.

[9] Okin, J. T., et al. 1965. Cardiopulmon. Physiol. Data Healthy Denver-Acclim. Man Proc. Symp. (Denver), p. 40.
[10] Okin, J. T., et al. 1966. Rocky Mt. Med. J. 63:44.
[11] Rennie, D., et al. 1971. J. Appl. Physiol. 30:450.
[12] Roughton, F. J. W., et al. 1944. Amer. J. Physiol. 142:708.
[13] Severinghaus, J. W., and A. Carcelen B. 1964. J. Appl. Physiol. 19:319.
[14] Severinghaus, J. W., et al. 1966. Resp. Physiol. 1: 308.
[15] Sørensen, S. C., and J. S. Milledge. 1971. J. Appl. Physiol. 31:28.
[16] Spievogel, H., et al. 1969. Respiration (Basel) 26: 369.
[17] Torrance, J. D., et al. 1970. Resp. Physiol. 11:1.

267. BLOOD COAGULATION TESTS: MAN

Part I. Skin Bleeding Time

Skin bleeding time varies with temperature, circulation, and thickness of the skin, with the area punctured and depth of the puncture, and with psychic influences. Values in parentheses are ranges, estimate "c" unless otherwise indicated (see Introduction).

	Method	Technique	Area Punctured	Wound Depth mm	Bleeding Time s	Reference
1 2	Duke	Blood absorbed every 15-30 s	Ear, finger	3	(60-180)	5,13
			Volar surface of forearm	3-4	147(0-450)[1]	12
3	Copley & Lalich	Wound immersed in physiological saline, 37°C	Finger	6	(17-340)[2]	3
4	Ivy	Sphygmomanometer cuff maintained at 40 mm Hg pressure; blood absorbed every 10 s	Volar surface of forearm	3	(0-240)	8

[1] Less than 374 s in 95% of population. [2] Less than 180 s in 95% of population.

continued

267. BLOOD COAGULATION TESTS: MAN

Part I. Skin Bleeding Time

	Method	Technique	Area Punctured	Wound Depth mm	Bleeding Time s	Reference
5		Sphygmomanometer cuff maintained at 40 mm Hg pressure; blood absorbed every 15-30 s	Volar surface of forearm	2	192(0-384)[b]	1
6				3-4	248(30-570)	7,12
7				3	240(30-730)[3/]	4,7
8		2 horizontal incisions >2 cm apart, 2-3 mm long	Volar surface of forearm	½-1	372(120-950)	6
9		3 transverse incisions, 10-14 mm long; results averaged	Volar surface of forearm	1	390(180-690)	10
10		Incision 9 mm long	Volar surface of forearm	1	300 ± 75	9
11		Blood washed off continuously with distilled water and quantitated for the amount of bleeding	Volar surface of forearm	1-2	191(100-260)	11
12		....	Volar surface of forearm	3-4	364 ± 121[4/]	2
13		24 hr after primary bleeding, crust gently lifted off, and standard Ivy bleeding time determined from same wound	Volar surface of forearm	...	90(0-360)[5/]	2

[3/] Frank bleeding should stop within 360 s; blood-tinged oozing may last another 360 s. [4/] Primary bleeding time. [5/] Secondary bleeding time.

Contributors: Owen, Charles A., and Bowie, E. J. W.

References

[1] Aggeler, P. M., et al. 1946. Blood 1:472.
[2] Borchgrevink, C. F., and B. A. Waaler. 1958. Acta Med. Scand. 162:361.
[3] Copley, A. L., and J. J. Lalich. 1942. J. Clin. Invest. 21:145.
[4] Diggs, L. W. Unpublished.
[5] Duke, W. W. 1910. J. Amer. Med. Ass. 55:1185.
[6] Hjort, P., and H. Stormorken. 1957. Scand. J. Clin. Lab. Invest. 9, Suppl. 29.
[7] Ivy, A. C., et al. 1935. Surg. Gynecol. Obstet. 60: 781.
[8] Ivy, A. C., et al. 1941. J. Lab. Clin. Med. 26:1812.
[9] Mielke, C. H., Jr., et al. 1969. Blood 34:204.
[10] Nilson, I. M., et al. 1963. Thromb. Diath. Haemorrh. 10:223.
[11] Sutor, A. H., et al. 1971. Amer. J. Clin. Pathol. 55: 541.
[12] Tocantins, L. M. 1946. Med. Clin. N. Amer. 130: 1361.
[13] Wintrobe, M. M. 1967. Clinical Hematology. Ed. 6. Lea and Febiger, Philadelphia.

Part II. Clotting Time

Values in parentheses are ranges, estimate "c" unless otherwise indicated (see Introduction).

	Method	Technique	Surface	Temp °C	No. of Subjects	Clotting Time min[1/]	Reference
			Whole Blood				
1	Aggeler, et al.	2-syringe; 2 ml in each of 2 tubes (8 × 75 mm)	Glass	Room	64	8.9(3.5-14.3)[b]	1
2				37	64	7.5(4.7-10.4)[b]	
3	Allen & Attyah	2-syringe; 1 ml in each of 10 tubes, paired (9.5 × 40 mm)	Glass	37	52	(20-35)	2

[1/] Unless otherwise specified.

continued

Part II. Clotting Time

Method	Technique	Surface	Temp °C	No. of Subjects	Clotting Time min[1]	Reference
4 Hirschboeck	1-syringe; 2 ml in 1 tube (11 mm diameter)	Glass	37	12	6.33(4-10)	9
5		Collodion	37	12	22.2(12-31)	
6		Paraffin	37	12	16.7(10-26)	
7 Kadish	1-syringe; 1 ml in 1 tube (8 mm diameter)	Glass	24-26	50	(5-10)	12
8	1-syringe; 2 ml in 1 tube (12.5 mm diameter)	Lusteroid	24-26	50	19(14-28)	
9 Lee & White	1-syringe; 1 ml in 1 tube (8 mm diameter)	Glass	Room	......	6.5(5-8)	13
10 Lewis, et al.	2-syringe; 2 ml in 2 tubes (13 × 100 mm)	Glass	37	53	9(5-13)	14
11		Silicone	37	53	34(22-50)	
12 Margulies & Barker	Equivalent of 2-syringe; 1 ml in 1 tube (8 mm diameter)	Glass	37	50	11.66(5-19)	16
13	Equivalent of 2-syringe; 1 ml in 3 tubes	Silicone	37	50	38.58(25-57)	
14 Mayer	Equivalent of 2-syringe; venous blood in capillary tubes	Glass	21	40	11.9(10.0-13.7)[b]	17
15 Pohle & Taylor	1-syringe; 2 ml in each of 2 tubes (13 × 100 mm)	Glass	37.5	......	(6-12)	19
Quick, et al.	1-syringe; 1 ml in each of 2 tubes					21
16	13 × 100 mm	Glass	37	6	(5-10)	
17	11 × 100 mm	Glass	37	6	(5.5-8.0)	
18	8 × 100 mm	Glass	37	6	(4.5-5.0)	
19	11 × 100 mm	Glass	22	6	(10.5-16.0)	
20	11 × 100 mm	Collodion	37	6	(23-29)	
21	13 × 100 mm	Lusteroid	37	6	(10.5-16.5)	
22	11 × 100 mm	Silicone	37	6	(36-52)	
23 Tocantins	1-syringe; 1 ml in 1 tube (15 mm in diameter)	Glass	37	40	11.5(8-16)	22
24		Paraffin	37	56	29.3(15-45)	
25 Wintrobe	Equivalent of 2-syringe; 1 ml in each of 2 tubes	Glass	37	......	(6-17)	23
26		Silicone	37	......	(19-60)	

Activated Whole Blood

27 Belko & Warren	Citrated blood, recalcified	Glass	25	83	3.54 ± 0.73	3
28 Hattersley	Blood drawn into "evacuated diatomite tube"	Diatomite	37	5000	107 ± 13 s	8

Native Plasma

29 Jaques, et al.	Platelet-rich plasma. Equivalent of 2-syringe; 1 ml in 1 tube (8 mm diameter).	Glass	20	7	0.75(0.3-1.0)	11
30		Silicone	20	7	1.7(1.3-6.5)	
31 Lozner & Taylor	Platelet-poor plasma. 1-syringe; 2 ml in each of 2 tubes (13 × 100 mm); all equipment oiled or siliconized.	Glass	37.5	......	11	15
32		Collodion	37.5	......	64	
33		Paraffin	37.5	......	44	
34		Lusteroid	37.5	......	49	

Recalcified Plasma

35 Beller & Graeff	Citrated, platelet-rich plasma. 2-syringe; 0.2 ml in 3 tubes.	Silicone	37	......	(2.6-4.3)	4
36 Cheney	Oxalated, platelet-poor plasma. 1-syringe; 0.2 ml in each of 2 tubes.	Glass	23-26	340	5.3(3-8)	5
37 Lozner & Taylor	Citrated, platelet-rich plasma, recalcified after 1 hr on specified surface. 1-syringe; 2 ml in each of 2 tubes (13 × 100 mm).	Glass	37.5	......	6	15
38		Collodion	37.5	......	18	
39		Paraffin	37.5	......	20	
40		Lusteroid	37.5	......	20	

[1] Unless otherwise specified.

continued

267. BLOOD COAGULATION TESTS: MAN

Part II. Clotting Time

	Method	Technique	Surface	Temp °C	No. of Subjects	Clotting Time min[1]	Reference
41	Owen, et al.	Oxalated, platelet-rich plasma. 1-syringe; 0.2 ml in 2 tubes.	Glass	37	......	(1.50-1.83)	18
42	Quick	Oxalated, platelet-rich plasma. 1-syringe; 0.1 ml in 1 tube.	Glass	37	......	(1.5-2.3)	20
	Activated Plasma						
43	Franco	Platelet-rich plasma plus celite in saline, 10-20 min at 37°C	Glass	37	......	(40-45) s	6
44	Hardisty & Hutton	Citrated, platelet-rich plasma plus kaolin in buffered saline, 20 min at 37°C	Glass	37	20	26(25-28) s	7
45	Hunter & Allensworth	Platelet-rich plasma plus celite in H$_2$O, 6+ min at 37°C	Glass	37	65	(32-48) s	10

[1] Unless otherwise specified.

Contributors: Davis, Walter E., and Brinkhous, K. M.; Owen, Charles A., and Bowie, E. J. W.

References

[1] Aggeler, P. M., et al. 1946. Blood 1:472.

[2] Allen, G. W., and A. M. Attyah. 1953. J. Lab. Clin. Med. 41:767.

[3] Belko, J. S., and R. Warren. 1958. Arch. Surg. 76: 210.

[4] Beller, F. K., and H. Graeff. 1971. Thrombosis and Bleeding Disorders. Academic Press, New York.

[5] Cheney, G. 1942. Amer. J. Med. Sci. 203:325.

[6] Franco, J. 1965. Clin. Res. 13:272.

[7] Hardisty, R. M., and R. A. Hutton. 1965. Brit. J. Haematol. 11:258.

[8] Hattersley, P. G. 1966. J. Amer. Med. Ass. 196:436.

[9] Hirschboeck, J. S. 1940. Proc. Soc. Exp. Biol. Med. 45:122.

[10] Hunter, D. T., and J. L. Allensworth. 1967. J. Clin. Pathol. 20:244.

[11] Jaques, L. B., et al. 1946. Can. Med. Ass. J. 55:26.

[12] Kadish, A. H. 1947. Amer. Heart J. 34:212.

[13] Lee, R. I., and P. D. White. 1913. Amer. J. Med. Sci. 145:495.

[14] Lewis, J. H., et al. 1957. J. Lab. Clin. Med. 49:211.

[15] Lozner, E. L., and F. H. L. Taylor. 1942. J. Clin. Invest. 21:241.

[16] Margulies, H., and N. W. Barker. 1949. Amer. J. Med. Sci. 218:42.

[17] Mayer, G. A. 1957. J. Lab. Clin. Med. 49:938.

[18] Owen, C. A., Jr., et al. 1955. Amer. J. Clin. Pathol. 25:1417.

[19] Pohle, F. J., and F. H. L. Taylor. 1937. J. Clin. Invest. 16:741.

[20] Quick, A. J. 1957. The Hemorrhagic Diseases and the Physiology of Hemostasis. C. C. Thomas, Springfield, Ill.

[21] Quick, A. J., et al. 1948. Blood 3:1121.

[22] Tocantins, L. M. 1946. Med. Clin. N. Amer. 30: 1361.

[23] Wintrobe, M. M. 1967. Clinical Hematology. Ed. 6. Lea and Febiger, Philadelphia. p. 329.

Part III. One-Stage Prothrombin Time

The results of different methods are not comparable, due to differences in concentration of the reacting substances.

Values in parentheses are ranges, estimate "b" unless otherwise indicated (see Introduction).

continued

Part III. One-Stage Prothrombin Time

	Method	Temp °C	Source of Thromboplastin	Blood	Clotting Time s	Reference
	Whole Blood					
1	0.03-0.04 ml blood (no anticoagulant)	Room	Beef lung or rabbit brain, fresh	Cutaneous	(20-30)c	3
2	0.9 ml oxalated blood	Room	Beef lung or rabbit brain, acetone-dehydrated	Venous	(25-50)c	12
3	0.1 ml oxalated blood plus CaCl$_2$	Room	Rabbit brain, acetone-dehydrated	Cutaneous	20(18-22)	4
	Whole Plasma					
4	0.1 ml oxalated plasma, plus CaCl$_2$, plus 0.1 ml thromboplastin	37	Human brain[1]	Venous	12(11-13)	8
5			Human brain, acetone-dehydrated	Venous	11.5(10-13)	1
6			Rabbit brain, acetone-dehydrated	Venous	(11-12)c	9
7				Venous	24(20-27)	10
8			Rabbit brain, dried at 37°C	Venous	(17-19)c	5
9			Commercial thromboplastins[2]	Venous	(12.7-24.1)c	6
10	0.1 ml citrated plasma, plus CaCl$_2$, plus 0.1 ml thromboplastin	37	Human brain, acetone-dehydrated	Venous	(11-20)c	2
	Diluted Plasma					
11	0.1 ml 10% oxalated plasma, plus prothrombin-free oxalated plasma, plus CaCl$_2$	37	Human brain, saline extract	Venous	35(30-40)	7
12	0.1 ml 10% oxalated plasma, plus prothrombin-free oxalated plasma (CaCl$_2$ included in thromboplastin)	37	Human or rabbit brain, acetone-dehydrated	Venous	25(20-30)	11
13	0.1 ml 12.5% oxalated plasma, plus prothrombin-free oxalated plasma[3], plus CaCl$_2$	37	Rabbit brain, acetone-dehydrated	Venous	41(34-48)	10
14	0.1 ml 25% oxalated plasma, plus prothrombin-free oxalated plasma[3], plus CaCl$_2$	37	Human brain, acetone-dehydrated	Venous	28(21-35)	1
15	0.1 ml 50% oxalated plasma, plus prothrombin-free oxalated plasma[3], plus CaCl$_2$	37	Human brain, acetone-dehydrated	Venous	16(13-19)	1

[1] National survey in Great Britain. [2] National survey in U.S. [3] Diluted with physiological saline.

Contributors: Owen, Charles A., and Bowie, E. J. W.; Davis, Walter E., and Brinkhous, K. M.

References

[1] Aggeler, P. M., et al. 1946. Blood 1:220.

[2] Biggs, R., and R. G. MacFarlane. 1966. Treatment of Haemophilia and Other Coagulation Disorders. Spottiswoode, Ballantyne; London. p. 344.

[3] Karabin, J. E., and E. R. Anderson. 1941. J. Lab. Clin. Med. 26:723.

[4] Kato, K., and H. G. Poncher. 1940. J. Amer. Med. Ass. 114:749.

[5] Magath, T. B. 1939. Amer. J. Clin. Pathol. (Tech. Suppl. 3):187.

[6] Miale, J. B., and D. LaFond. 1967. Ibid. 47:40.

[7] Owren, P. A. 1949. Scand. J. Clin. Lab. Invest. 1: 81.

[8] Poller, L. 1969. In L. Poller, ed. Recent Advances in Blood Coagulation. Little, Brown; Boston. pp. 137-154.

[9] Quick, A. J. 1945. Amer. J. Clin. Pathol. 15:560.

[10] Shapiro, S., et al. 1942. Proc. Soc. Exp. Biol. Med. 50:85.

[11] Ware, A. G., and R. Stragnell. 1952. Amer. J. Clin. Pathol. 22:791.

[12] Ziffren, S. E., et al. 1940. Ibid. (Tech. Suppl. 4):13.

continued

Part IV. Fibrinogen Levels

Values in parentheses are ranges, estimate "c" unless otherwise indicated (*see* Introduction).

	Method	No. of Subjects	Fibrinogen Level mg/100 ml plasma [1/]	Reference
	Gravimetric			
1	Recalcification	4	335(316-364)	4
2		25♂	270(200-360)	5
3		25♀	290(210-380)	5
4	Heat coagulation, 56°C	7	(300-600)	16
5	Thrombin coagulation	50	332(240-540)	10
6	Volumetric; thrombin coagulation	7	225(160-300)	14
	Nitrogen analysis			
7	Recalcification	19♂	250(190-330)	6
8		9♀	290(220-290)	6
9		80	(0.028-0.233)[2/]	7
10	Na_2SO_4 precipitation	80	(0.022-0.232)[2/]	7
11	Folin-Wu method for protein; Na_2SO_3 precipitation	12	(400-731)	2
12	Folin-Ciocalteu analysis; thrombin precipitate on crushed glass	41♂	265(177-415)	12
13		36♀	294(164-485)	12
14	Biuret analysis; thrombin precipitate on stick	66♂♀	281±42	11
	Turbidometric			
15	Thrombin precipitate	......	(150-450)	3
16	$(NH_4)_2SO_4$ precipitation	72	(125-380)	9
17		40	(180-415)	8
18	Clot absorbance; thrombin coagulation	20	(193-674)	13
19	Dilution method; thrombin coagulation	65	1/200(1/400-1/100)[3/]	1
20	Isotope dilution	......	360±50[4/]	15

[1/] Unless otherwise indicated. [2/] g fibrinogen N/100 ml plasma. [3/] "Titer." [4/] Normal values in Denver, Colorado; altitude, 5300 ft.

Contributors: Davis, Walter E., and Brinkhous, K. M.; Owen, Charles A., and Bowie, E. J. W.

References

[1] Bowan, H. S., and M. B. Yelito. 1957. Amer. J. Obstet. Gynecol. 74:670.

[2] Campbell, W. P., and M. I. Hanna. 1937. J. Biol. Chem. 119:15.

[3] Ellis, B. C., and A. Stransky. 1961. J. Lab. Clin. Med. 58:477.

[4] Foster, D. P., and G. H. Whipple. 1921. Amer. J. Physiol. 58:407.

[5] Gram, H. C. 1921. J. Biol. Chem. 49:279.

[6] Ham, T. H., and F. C. Curtis. 1938. Medicine (Baltimore) 17:413.

[7] Howe, P. E. 1923. J. Biol. Chem. 57:235.

[8] Hunter, P. T., and J. L. Allensworth. 1965. Tech. Bull. Regist. Med. Tech. 35:145.

[9] Johnson, M. L., et al. 1953. Arch. Biochem. Biophys. 46:470.

[10] Lewis, J. H., et al. 1957. J. Lab. Clin. Med. 49:211.

[11] Owen, C. A., Jr., et al. 1969. The Diagnosis of Bleeding Disorders. Little, Brown; Boston. pp. 100-101.

[12] Ratnoff, O. D., and C. Menzie. 1964. In L. M. Tocantins and L. A. Kazal, ed. Blood Coagulation, Hemorrhage and Thrombosis. Ed. 2. Grune and Stratton, New York. pp. 224-226.

[13] Rosenfeld, L. 1968. J. Lab. Clin. Med. 72:329.

[14] Shadid, J. N. 1964. Angiology 15:201.

[15] Takeda, Y. 1966. J. Clin. Invest. 45:103.

[16] Whipple, G. H. 1914. Amer. J. Physiol. 33:50.

continued

267. BLOOD COAGULATION TESTS: MAN

Part V. Clot Retraction Volume and Time

Values in parentheses are ranges, estimate "c" unless otherwise indicated (*see* Introduction).

	Method	Variable	Value	Remarks	Reference
			Blood		
1	Aggeler and Lucia	Extracorpuscular clot volume	7.9(−4.1 to +19.9)[b] % of volume of blood specimen[1/]	Fluid volume of clot, exclusive of erythrocytes, leukocytes, and platelets, after clot retraction for 1 hr at 37°C	1
2	MacFarlane	Serum volume expressed from clot	54.7(48-64)% of total serum present in blood specimen	Venous blood in glass centrifuge tube, 1 hr at 37°C. Amount of serum initially present calculated from hematocrit.	4
3	Tocantins	Serum volume expressed from clot	78.1(62-94)[b] % of total serum present in blood specimen	Venous blood in paraffin or silicone tube, 13 mm diameter, 2 hr at 37°C. Amount of serum initially present calculated from hematocrit.	5
4	Hirschboeck	Time of clot retraction	33(20-45) min	Drop of blood in castor oil; room temperature	3
			Plasma		
5	Friedman, et al.	Relative volume of clot (estimated)	Grade 4: 15%	Platelet-rich plasma plus thrombin, 1 hr at 37°C. Most clots grade 3-4; of 42 subjects, 91% were grade 4 which is normal. Grades 3 to 1 are progressively more abnormal.	2
6			Grade 3: 25%		
7			Grade 2: 50%		
8			Grade 1: 75%		

[1/] Negative values may occur owing to discrepancies between methods of measurement of formed elements and total clot volume.

Contributors: Davis, Walter E., and Brinkhous, K. M.; Owen, Charles A., and Bowie, E. J. W.

References
[1] Aggeler, P. M., et al. 1946. Blood 1:472.

[2] Friedman, L. L., et al. 1964. Mayo Clin. Proc. 39: 908.

[3] Hirschboeck, J. S. 1948. J. Lab. Clin. Med. 33:347.

[4] MacFarlane, R. G. 1939. Lancet 1:1199.

[5] Tocantins, L. M. 1946. Med. Clin. N. Amer. 130: 1361.

Part VI. Summary of Normal Values

Methods: RVV = Russell's viper venom; PTT = partial thromboplastin time; TGT = thromboplastin generation time. Values in parentheses are ranges, estimate "c" (*see* Introduction).

	Test	Method	No. of Observations	Value	Reference
1	Clotting time	2 tubes, glass (8 × 75 mm); 37°C	64	7.5(4.7-10.4) min	1
2		2 tubes, silicone (8 × 75 mm); 37°C	50	36.4(25-56) min	23

continued

Part VI. Summary of Normal Values

	Test	Method	No. of Observations	Value	Reference
3	Stypven time	0.2 ml oxalated plasma, plus 0.2 ml CaCl$_2$, plus 0.2 ml 10% RVV; room temp	50	21.7(18-25) s	37
4	One-stage prothrombin time	0.1 ml oxalated plasma, plus CaCl$_2$, plus 0.1 ml thromboplastin from rabbit brain	53	11.68(9.7-13.0) s	28
5	Two-stage prothrombin time	Oxalated plasma	10	336 ± 32 units	36
6	Prothrombin consumption	One-stage method, 1 hr	3	(27-30) s	30
7		Two-stage method, 1 hr	5	<10 units	9
8	Thrombin time	0.1 ml oxalated plasma, plus 0.1 ml thrombin	53	15(13-17) s	21
9	Thrombotest	0.1 ml citrated plasma, plus 0.5 ml thrombotest reagent; pooled plasma	......	40 s	26
10	Partial thromboplastin time	Non-activated	206	76(64-98) s	33
11		Kaolin-activated	118	39.8(32-47.6) s	22
12		Plus inosthitin	42	33.7(29-38) s	24
13	Thromboplastin generation time	With platelets	40	10 s at 5 min	3
14		With isolecithin	121	11 s at 6 min	34
15		With inosthitin	......	10 s at 4 min	8
16	Fibrinogen (Factor I)	Gravimetric; thrombin coagulation	50	332(240-540) mg/100 ml blood	21
17		Nitrogen analysis; recalcification	19♂	250(190-330) mg/100 ml blood	14
18			9♀	290(220-290) mg/100 ml blood	
19		Turbidometric	72	(125-380) mg/100 ml blood	32
20		Dilution method	65	1/200(1/400-1/100)	7
21	Factor V	One-stage prothrombin time with deficient plasma	45	(85-110) %	29
22		One-stage with Stypven	46	(70-150) %	5
23		Two-stage prothrombin time with deficient plasma	48	(60->100) %	21
24	Factor VII	One-stage using congenitally deficient plasma	92	(69-144) %	21
25		One-stage using artificially deficient plasma	7	(70-140) %	10
26	Factor VIII	Recalcification of dilute plasma	116	(50-170) %	15
27		PTT with deficient plasma	12	(64-132) %	20
28		TGT	162	(54-195) %	27
29	Factor IX	Recalcification with deficient plasma	53	(60-130) %	21
30		PTT with deficient plasma	......	(50-180) %	2
31		TGT	37	(68-120) %	6
32	Factor X	Prothrombin time with RVV and Al(OH)$_3$ adsorbed plasma	10	(65-180)%	17
33		Prothrombin time with RVV and filtered, adsorbed plasma	......	(80-120) %	11
34	Factor XI	PTT with congenitally deficient plasma	30	(91-108) %	13
35		PTT with artificially deficient plasma	20	(70->200) %	16
36		PTT with congenitally deficient plasma, kaolin-activated	45	(63-136) %	31
37	Factor XII	Recalcification with congenitally deficient plasma and kaolin-Gliddex activated sample	64	(65-175) %	35

continued

Part VI. Summary of Normal Values

Test	Method	No. of Observations	Value	Reference
38	TGT with kaolin-activated sample	31	(42-205) %	18
39 Factor XIII	Inverse of titer of clot dissolution in 1% monoiodoacetate	20	(64-128)	25
40	Rate of insoluble clot formation with monoiodoacetate inhibition	54	(86-110) %	19
41	Antibody inhibition of factor XIII activity	25	(50-150) %	4
42	Rate of incorporation of labeled amine into casein	25	(43->100) %	12

Contributors: Coon, William W., and Penner, John A.; Davis, Walter E., and Brinkhous, K. M.

References

[1] Aggeler, P. M., et al. 1946. Blood 1:472.

[2] Barrow, E. M., et al. 1960. J. Lab. Clin. Med. 55: 936.

[3] Biggs, R., and A. S. Douglas. 1953. J. Clin. Pathol. 6:23.

[4] Bohn, H., and H. Haupt. 1968. Thromb. Diath. Haemorrh. 19:308.

[5] Borchgrevink, C. F., et al. 1960. J. Lab. Clin. Med. 55:625.

[6] Boulton, F. G., and J. E. Clark. 1959. Brit. J. Haematol. 5:396.

[7] Bowan, H. S., and M. B. Yelito. 1957. Amer. J. Obstet. Gynecol. 74:670.

[8] Bowie, E. J. W., et al. 1965. Amer. J. Clin. Pathol. 44:673.

[9] Brinkhous, K. M. 1939. Amer. J. Med. Sci. 198:509.

[10] Denson, K. W. 1961. Acta Haematol. 25:105.

[11] Duckert, F., and F. Koller. 1964. In L. M. Tocantins and L. A. Kazal, ed. Blood Coagulation, Hemorrhage and Thrombosis. Ed. 2. Grune and Stratton, New York. p. 129.

[12] Dvilansky, A., et al. 1971. Brit. J. Haematol. 18: 399.

[13] Egeberg, O. 1961. Scand. J. Clin. Lab. Invest. 13: 140.

[14] Ham, T. H., and F. C. Curtis. 1938. Medicine (Baltimore) 17:413.

[15] Hardisty, R. M., and J. C. McPherson. 1962. Thromb. Diath. Haemorrh. 7:215.

[16] Horowitz, H. I., et al. 1963. Blood 22:35.

[17] Hougie, C. 1962. Proc. Soc. Exp. Biol. Med. 109: 754.

[18] Iatridis, S. G., and J. H. Ferguson. 1962. Thromb. Diath. Haemorrh. 8:46.

[19] Janssen, C. L., and R. Masure. 1970. Pathol. Eur. 5:315.

[20] Langdell, R. D., et al. 1953. J. Lab. Clin. Med. 41: 637.

[21] Lewis, J. H., et al. 1957. Ibid. 49:211.

[22] Lurie, A., and S. Smith. 1968. S. Afr. Med. J. 42: 438.

[23] Margulies, H., and N. W. Barker. 1949. Amer. J. Med. Sci. 218:42.

[24] Matchett, M. O., and G. I. C. Ingram. 1965. J. Clin. Pathol. 18:465.

[25] McDonagh, J., et al. 1969. J. Clin. Invest. 48:940.

[26] Owren, P. A. 1959. Lancet 2:754.

[27] Pudlak, P., and E. Deimlova. 1969. Brit. J. Haematol. 12:409.

[28] Quick, A. J. 1951. Physiology and Pathology of Hemostasis. Lea and Febiger, Philadelphia.

[29] Quick, A. J. 1960. J. Clin. Pathol. 13:457.

[30] Quick, A. J. 1966. Amer. J. Clin. Pathol. 45:105.

[31] Rapaport, S. I., et al. 1961. Blood 18:149.

[32] Ratnoff, O. D., and C. Menzie. 1951. J. Lab. Clin. Med. 37:316.

[33] Rodman, R. H., et al. 1958. Amer. J. Clin. Pathol. 29:525.

[34] Seaman, A. J., and K. M. Karlsen. 1959. Thromb. Diath. Haemorrh. 4:83.

[35] Veltkamp, J. J., et al. 1965. Ibid., Suppl. 17:181.

[36] Wagner, R. H., et al. 1964. In L. M. Tocantins and L. A. Kazal, ed. Blood Coagulation, Hemorrhage and Thrombosis. Ed. 2. Grune and Stratton, New York. p. 159.

[37] Witts, L. J., and C. G. Hobson. 1942. Brit. Med. J. 1:575.

Part I. Volume: Arachnids, Crustaceans, and Insects

Hemolymph volume varies according to sex, stage of development, age, nutrition, rearing status, method of blood extraction, coagulability, and method of volume determination. For additional information, consult reference 7.

Hemolymph Volume: Plus/minus (±) values are standard error, unless otherwise indicated. Values in parentheses are ranges, estimate "c" unless otherwise indicated (*see* Introduction).

	Order & Species (Synonym)	Specification	Method	Hemolymph Volume	Reference
			Arachnida		
1	Scorpionida *Heterometrus fulvipes*	♂	Congo red dilution	1.65(1.19-2.10) ml/animal, or 34.9 (25.4-45.1) ml/100 g body wt	35
2		♀	Congo red dilution	2.07(1.33-2.78) ml/animal, or 34.0 (27.6-41.2) ml/100 g body wt	
			Crustacea		
3	Decapoda *Barytelphusa guerini* (*Paratelphusa guerini*)	....	Congo red	27.8% body wt	37
4	*Panulirus polyphagus*	....	Congo red	17.0% body wt	37
5	*Scylla serrata*	....	Congo red	12.7% body wt	37
			Insecta		
6	Hymenoptera *Apis mellifera*	Larva	Exsanguination	0.04 g/insect, or (25-30)% body wt	5
7		Adult worker; anesthetized; unfixed	....	0.002 ml/insect	15
8	(*A. mellifica*)	Adult worker	Exsanguination ?	(11-17.5) μl	26
9	(*A. mellifica ligustica*)	Adult	....	0.02 ml/insect	28
10	Diptera *Aedes aegypti*	Larva	Exsanguination	(0.3-0.4) μl/insect	47
11	*Culex pipiens*	Larva	Exsanguination	(0.3-0.4) μl	47
12	*Gasterophilus intestinalis*	Larva, mature; untreated	....	(0.1-0.15) ml/larva	29
13	*Musca domestica*	Adult, 0-4 da old: ♂	Evans' blue	(3.4-4.0) μl	6
14		♀	Evans' blue	(3.9-6.0) μl	
15	*Phormia regina*	Larva	....	20 μl/insect	12
16		2-5 da old	Evans' blue	(2.5-31.1) μl/larva	9
17		"White pupa"	Evans' blue	18.1 μl/pupa	9
18		Adult	....	(1-4) μl/larva	12
19			Dye dilution	(6.6-10.2) μl/insect, or 20% body wt	14
20		Early, middle, & late pharate	Evans' blue	15.2 μl/adult	9
21		Newly emerged	Evans' blue	12.2 μl/adult	9
22	*Sarcophaga bullata*	Larva	Dye dilution	(35.0-42.6)% body wt	23
23		Pupa	Dye dilution	(23.8-33.4)% body wt	23
24		Adult	^{14}C-inulin	21.72 ± 4.71 μl [1/]	41
25			Amaranth dye	17 mg/fly	48
26			Exsanguination	(0.5-7.0) mg/fly	48

[1/] Based on the assumption that all tyrosine phosphate is in the hemolymph.

continued

Part I. Volume: Arachnids, Crustaceans, and Insects

	Order & Species (Synonym)	Specification	Method	Hemolymph Volume	Reference
	Lepidoptera				
27	*Bombyx mori*	Larva	Exsanguination	0.35 ml/insect	13
28				(0.15-0.22) ml/g body wt	4
29				31.2(27.6-34.8)[b] % body wt	38
30				28.6(25.6-31.6)[b] % body wt (dry)	38
31		Pupa	Exsanguination	(0.09-0.35) ml/insect	13
32				(0.11-0.31) ml/g body wt	4
33		Adult	Exsanguination	0.05 ml/insect	13
34	*Galleria mellonella*	Larva	Exsanguination	41(36.6-45.4)[b] % body wt (dry)	38
35		Fresh	Exsanguination	42.8 ± 6.4 ml/100 g body wt	21
36		Stored for 55-56 da [2/]	Exsanguination	48.7 ± 11.2 ml/100 g body wt	21
37		15-21 da old, untreated	Amaranth dye	(16-36)% body wt	25
38		Pupa; 0-1 da old	Amaranth dye	16.4(16-18)% body wt	25
39	*Hyalophora cecropia*	Pupa	Exsanguination	0.25 ml/g body wt	8
40	*Spodoptera eridania*	Larva	^{14}C-inulin	0.19 ml/insect	30
41	*(Prodenia eridania)*		Exsanguination	0.12(0.07-0.20) ml/insect	1
	Coleoptera				
42	*Dytiscus* sp.	....	Exsanguination	0.1 ml/insect	13
43	*Hydrophilus* sp.	....	Exsanguination	0.3 ml/insect	13
44	*Popillia japonica*	Larva	Exsanguination	0.03 ml/insect	32
45				(0.9-40.8)% body wt	3
46			Manganese dilution	40.9(38.5-42.9)% body wt	3
47	*Tenebrio molitor*	Larva	Chloride	0.22 ml/g body wt	33
48			Dye dilution	10% body wt	24
	Hemiptera				
49	*Rhodnius prolixus*	Nymph, 5th instar	....	19 μl/insect	34
50		Day of full blood meal	Exsanguination	8.0 ± 1.0[3/] μl	10
51		3 da after full blood meal	Exsanguination	27.5 ± 2.5[3/] μl	
52		6 da after full blood meal	Exsanguination	26.5 ± 2.5[3/] μl	
53		9 da after full blood meal	Exsanguination	26.0 ± 2.5[3/] μl	
54		13 da after full blood meal	Exsanguination	18.0 ± 2.5[3/] μl	
55		16 da after full blood meal [4/]	Exsanguination	17.0 ± 2.5[3/] μl	
	Orthoptera				
56	*Acheta domesticus*	♂	Specific gravity	14.0(3-21)% body wt	36
57		♀	Specific gravity	15.6(12-21)% body wt	
58	*Blattella germanica*	....	Assumed or calculated	20% body wt	16
59	*Leucophaea maderae*	Adult, ♀	^{14}C-inulin	0.22 ml/g fresh wt	40
60	*Locusta migratoria*	Nymph, 4th instar: young	....	34.1 ± 7.1 mg/100 mg fresh tissue	19
61		old	....	110.5 ± 8.2 mg/100 mg fresh tissue	
62		5th instar	....	22.3 ± 3.7 mg/100 mg fresh tissue	20
63		Young	....	69.1 ± 9.1 mg/100 mg fresh tissue	19
64		Old	....	262.1 ± 30.2 mg/100 mg fresh tissue	19
65		Adult	....	125 μl	39
66		♂; 1 da old	....	128.0 ± 29.7 mg/100 mg fresh tissue	19
67		30 da old	....	113.8 ± 6.1 mg/100 mg fresh tissue	
68		♀; 1 da old	....	199.6 ± 32.5 mg/100 mg fresh tissue	19
69		30 da old	....	233.8 ± 18.1 mg/100 mg fresh tissue	

[2/] At 11°C, 76% relative humidity. [3/] Plus/minus (±) values are 2 standard errors. [4/] Ecdysis on 18th day.

continued

Part I. Volume: Arachnids, Crustaceans, and Insects

	Order & Species (Synonym)	Specification	Method	Hemolymph Volume	Reference
70	*L. migratoria migratorioides*	Nymph	Exsanguination	<0.2 ml/insect	22
71		4th instar; 1 da old	^{14}C-inulin	58.5 ± 4.5 μl	17
72		2 da old	^{14}C-inulin	71.2 ± 7.1 μl	
73		3 da old	^{14}C-inulin	172.0 ± 13.9 μl	
74		4 da old	^{14}C-inulin	200.1 ± 28.6 μl	
75		5th instar; 1 da old	^{14}C-inulin	117.9 ± 6.1 μl	17
76		2 da old	^{14}C-inulin	120.0 ± 11.3 μl	17
77		3 da old	^{14}C-inulin	184.2 ± 16.8 μl	17
78		4 da old	^{14}C-inulin	286.6 ± 20.7 μl	17
79		5 da old	^{14}C-inulin	353.6 ± 19.2 μl	17
80			Evans' blue	0.4 ml/insect	43
81		6 da old	^{14}C-inulin	278.8 ± 27.1 μl	17
82		8 da old	Evans' blue	0.8 ml/insect	43
83		Adult	Exsanguination	0.1 μl/insect	22
84		1 da old	^{14}C-inulin	253.2 ± 17.9 μl	17
85		37 hr old	Exsanguination	207.6 ± 10.6 μl, or 18.1 ± 0.6% body wt	2
86		♂	^{14}C-inulin	359 ± 151 μl	31
87		♀	^{14}C-inulin	595 ± 338 μl	31
88		2 da old	^{14}C-inulin	373.1 ± 18.5 μl	18
89		4 da old	^{14}C-inulin	468.6 ± 17.0 μl	18
90		6 da old	^{14}C-inulin	568.7 ± 37.1 μl	18
91		8 da old	^{14}C-inulin	696.1 ± 42.7 μl	18
92		10 da old	^{14}C-inulin	755.2 ± 33.9 μl	18
93		12 da old	^{14}C-inulin	797.7 ± 85.4 μl	18
94		14 da old	^{14}C-inulin	741.2 ± 44.1 μl	18
95		16 da old	^{14}C-inulin	861.3 ± 48.3 μl	18
96		18 da old	^{14}C-inulin	856.7 ± 79.8 μl	18
97	*Periplaneta americana*	Nymph, hydrated	Inulin dilution	17.5 ± 1.4 μl/100 mg experimental wt	11
98		dehydrated	Inulin dilution	13.5 ± 1.1 μl/100 mg experimental wt	11
99		♂	Cell dilution	15.7(13.2-18.2)^{b}% body wt	49
100			Chloride	20(16.3-23.7)^{b}% body wt [5]	
101				16.8(14.8-18.8)^{b}% body wt [6]	
102			Dye dilution	19.6(18.8-20.4)^{b}% body wt	
103		♀	Cell dilution	16.8(12.3-21.3)^{b}% body wt	49
104			Chloride	18.6(14.5-22.7)^{b}% body wt [5]	
105				19.5(17.2-21.8)^{b}% body wt [6]	
106			Dye dilution	19.8(19.1-20.5)^{b}% body wt	
107		5th instar; fed	^{14}C-inulin	34.9 ± 0.6% body wt	45
108		starved	^{14}C-inulin	33.7 ± 0.6% body wt	
109		7th instar; fed	^{14}C-inulin	38.6 ± 0.8% body wt	45
110		starved	^{14}C-inulin	36.1 ± 0.8% body wt	
111		12th instar; fed	^{14}C-inulin	35.2 ± 0.6% body wt	45
112		starved	^{14}C-inulin	32.5 ± 0.7% body wt	
		Last instar; heat fixed at 60°C for 1 min			46
113		Intermolt	Amaranth dye	17(11-30)% body wt	
114		Molting	Amaranth dye	14(10-26)% body wt	

[5] Individual. [6] Pooled.

continued

Part I. Volume: Arachnids, Crustaceans, and Insects

	Order & Species (Synonym)	Specification	Method	Hemolymph Volume	Reference
115		Adult	Exsanguination	(5-20) mg/insect, or 17% body wt	42,44
116		♂	Chloride	15.3(12.9-17.7)[b] % body wt	49
117			Dye dilution	27.5(23.8-31.2)[b] % body wt	
118		2 wk old	^{14}C-inulin	33.9(29.5-39.8)% body wt	45
119		♀	Chloride	16.9(11.9-21.9)[b] % body wt	49
120			Dye dilution	20.9(18.8-23.0)[b] % body wt	
121		Heat fixed, at ecdysis	Amaranth dye	21(13-35)% body wt	46
122		24 hr old	Amaranth dye	15(13-19)% body wt	
123		>24 hr old	Amaranth dye	19(14-27)% body wt	
124	*Schistocerca gregaria*	Nymph, 3rd instar	Amaranth dye	(53.6-109.3) μl/insect	27
125		4th instar	Amaranth dye	(74.2-142.6) μl/insect	
126		5th instar	Amaranth dye	(138.8-343.9) μl/insect	
127		Adult	Amaranth dye	(176.0-304.1) μl/insect	

Contributor: Jones, Jack Colvard

References

[1] Babers, F. H. 1938. J. Agr. Res. 57:697.

[2] Bayer, R. 1968. Z. Vergl. Physiol. 58:76.

[3] Beard, R. L. 1949. J. N.Y. Entomol. Soc. 57:79.

[4] Bialaszewicz, K., and C. Landau. 1938. Acta Biol. Exp. (Warsaw) 12:307.

[5] Bishop, G. H. 1923. J. Biol. Chem. 58:567.

[6] Bodnaryk, R. P., and P. E. Morrison. 1966. J. Insect Physiol. 12:963.

[7] Buck, J. B. 1953. In K. D. Roeder, ed. Insect Physiology. J. Wiley, New York. pp. 147-190.

[8] Buck, J. B., and S. Friedman. 1958. J. Insect Physiol. 2:52.

[9] Chen, P. S., and L. Levenbook. 1966. Ibid. 12:1595.

[10] Coles, G. C. 1966. Ibid. 12:1029.

[11] Edney, E. B. 1968. Comp. Biochem. Physiol. 25:149.

[12] Evans, D. R., and V. G. Dethier. 1957. J. Insect Physiol. 1:3.

[13] Florkin, M. 1937. Mem. Acad. Roy. Med. Belg. 16:1.

[14] Friedman, S. Unpublished. Nat. Institutes of Health, Bethesda, Md., 1960.

[15] Gary, N. D., et al. 1948. J. Econ. Entomol. 41:661.

[16] Haber, V. R. 1926. Bull. Brooklyn Entomol. Soc. 21:61.

[17] Hill, L., and G. J. Goldsworthy. 1968. J. Insect Physiol. 14:1085.

[18] Hill, L., et al. 1968. Ibid. 14:1.

[19] Hoffmann, J. A. 1967. Arch. Zool. Exp. Gen. 108:251.

[20] Hoffmann, J. A. 1969. J. Insect Physiol. 15:1375.

[21] House, H. L., and L. E. Rollins. 1961. Can. Entomol. 93:653.

[22] Hoyle, G. 1954. J. Exp. Biol. 31:260.

[23] Jones, J. C. 1956. J. Morphol. 99:233.

[24] Jones, J. C. 1957. J. Cell. Comp. Physiol. 50:423.

[25] Jones, J. C. 1967. Biol. Bull. 132:211.

[26] Koenig, M. 1953. Naturwissenschaften 40:583.

[27] Lee, R. M. 1961. J. Insect Physiol. 6:36.

[28] Lensky, Y. 1964. Ibid. 10:279.

[29] Levenbook, L. 1950. Biochem. J. 47:336.

[30] Levenbook, L. 1958. J. Insect Physiol. 52:329.

[31] Loughton, B. G., and S. S. Tobe. 1969. Can. J. Zool. 47:1333.

[32] Ludwig, D. 1951. Physiol. Zool. 24:329.

[33] Munson, S. C., and J. F. Yeager. 1945. J. Econ. Entomol. 38:634.

[34] Nunez, J. A. 1962. Nature (London) 194:704.

[35] Padmanabhanaidu, B. 1966. Comp. Biochem. Physiol. 17:157.

[36] Patton, R. L. 1962. J. Insect Physiol. 8:537.

[37] Rangnekar, P. V. 1954. J. Anim. Morphol. Physiol. 1:62.

[38] Richardson, C. H., et al. 1931. Ann. Entomol. Soc. Amer. 24:503.

[39] Roussel, J. P., and M. Cazal. 1969. C. R. Acad. Sci. 268(D):581.

[40] Scheuer, R., and R. Leuthold. 1969. J. Insect Physiol. 15:1067.

[41] Seligman, M., et al. 1969. Ibid. 15:1085.

[42] Smith, H. W. 1938. N.H. Agr. Exp. Sta. Tech. Bull. 71:1.

[43] Tobe, S. S., and B. G. Loughton. 1967. Can. J. Zool. 45:975.

[44] Tobias, J. M. 1948. J. Cell. Comp. Physiol. 31:125.

[45] Wharton, D. R. A., et al. 1965. J. Insect Physiol. 11:391.

[46] Wheeler, R. E. 1962. Fed. Proc. Fed. Amer. Soc. Exp. Biol. 21:123.

[47] Wigglesworth, V. B. 1938. J. Exp. Biol. 15:235.

[48] Wilkens, J. L. 1969. J. Insect Physiol. 15:1015.

[49] Yeager, J. F., and S. C. Munson. 1950. Arthropoda 1:255.

continued

268. PHYSICAL PROPERTIES OF HEMOLYMPH: ARTHROPODS

Part II. pH: Insects

Values in parentheses are ranges, estimate "c" (*see* Introduction).

	Species	Stage	Method	pH	Reference
		Hymenoptera			
1	*Apis mellifera*	Larva	Hydrogen electrode	(6.77-6.93)	3
2		Adult	Colorimetric	6.70	15
3	*Diprion hercyniae*	Larva, 5th instar	Glass electrode	6.50(6.45-6.57)	12
4	*Neodiprion lecontei*	Larva, 6th instar	Glass electrode	6.88(6.83-6.93)	12
		Diptera			
5	*Drosophila melanogaster*	Larva	Glass electrode	(7.03-7.15)	4
6	*Gasterophilus intestinalis*	Larva	Glass electrode	6.8	18
7	*Musca domestica*	Adult	Colorimetric	(7.2-7.6)	10
		Lepidoptera			
8	*Antheraea polyphemus*	Larva, last instar	Glass electrode	6.46(6.43-6.49)	13
9	*Bombyx mori*	Larva	Colorimetric	(6.4-7.2)	10
10		5th-6th instar	Glass electrode	6.77(6.70-6.83)	12
11		Pupa	....	6.51	1
12	*Carpocapsa pomonella*	Larva	Quinhydrone electrode	6.75	20
13	*Choristoneura fumiferana*	Larva, 2nd to last instar	Glass electrode	5.66(5.60-5.73)	13
14		last instar	Glass electrode	6.98(6.96-7.02)	
15	*Galleria mellonella*	Pupa	Glass electrode	(5.8-6.4)	21
16	*Hyles euphorbiae*[1]	Larva + pupa	Quinhydrone electrode	(6.36-6.64)	14
17	*Hyphantria cunea*[2]	Larva, last instar	Glass electrode	6.53(6.46-6.60)	13
18	*Malacosoma disstria*	Larva, 5th-6th instar	Glass electrode	(6.59-6.79)	12
19	*M. pluviale*	Larva, last instar	Glass electrode	6.55(6.52-6.58)	13
20	*Pieris brassicae*	Pupa	Hydrogen electrode	(6.50-6.77)	7
21	*P. rapae*	Larva	Glass electrode	(6.76-7.56)	8
22		Pupa	Colorimetric	(5.9-6.4)	9
23	*Schizura concinna*	Larva, last instar	Glass electrode	6.32(6.29-6.35)	13
24	*Spodoptera eridania*[3]	Larva	Quinhydrone electrode	(6.40-6.67)	2
		Trichoptera			
25	*Limnephilus flavicornis*	Larva	Quinhydrone electrode	(7.04-7.18)	17
		Coleoptera			
26	*Calosoma inquisitor*	Adult	Colorimetric	(6.6-6.8)	16
27	*Carabus cancellatus*	Adult	Colorimetric	(6.6-7.3)	16
28	*Dytiscus marginalis*	Adult	Colorimetric	(6.8-7.3)	16
29	*Leptinotarsa decemlineata*	Larva + pupa	Colorimetric	(5.9-6.8)	11
30	*Melolontha melolontha*[4]	Adult	Colorimetric	(6.0-6.6)	16
31	*Popillia japonica*	Larva	Hydrogen electrode	7.07	19
32		Pupa	Hydrogen electrode	6.95	
33	*Tenebrio molitor*	Adult	Colorimetric	(6.2-7.3)	16
		Orthoptera			
34	*Dissosteira carolina*	Adult[5]	Colorimetric	(6.8-6.9)	5
35	*Melanoplus bivattatus*	Adult[5]	Colorimetric	(6.0-6.7)	5

[1] Synonym: *Deilephila euphorbiae.* [2] Synonym: *H. textor.* [3] Synonym: *Prodenia eridania.* [4] Synonym: *M. vulgaris.*
[5] Stage not specified; probably adult.

continued

268. PHYSICAL PROPERTIES OF HEMOLYMPH: ARTHROPODS

Part II. pH: Insects

	Species	Stage	Method	pH	Reference
36	*M. differentialis*	Nymph	Hydrogen electrode	(6.42-6.98)	6
37		Adult	Colorimetric	(6.4-7.0)	5
38				(7.2-7.6)	10
39	*M. femur-rubrum*	Nymph + adult	Hydrogen electrode	(6.4-6.8)	6
40		Adult [5]	Colorimetric	(6.7-6.86)	5
41	*Periplaneta americana*	Nymph + adult	Colorimetric	(7.5-8.0)	10
42	*Romalea microptera*	Nymph + adult	Hydrogen electrode	(6.4-6.8)	6
43	*Schistocerca americana*	Adult [5]	Colorimetric	6.6	5

[5] Stage not specified; probably adult.

Contributor: Buck, John B.

References
[1] Akao, A. 1931. J. Chosen Med. Ass. 21:769.
[2] Babers, F. H. 1938. J. Agr. Res. 57:697.
[3] Bishop, G. H. 1923. J. Biol. Chem. 58:543.
[4] Boche, R. D., and J. B. Buck. 1942. Physiol. Zool. 15:293.
[5] Bodine, J. H. 1925. Biol. Bull. 48:79.
[6] Bodine, J. H. 1926. Ibid. 51:363.
[7] Brecher, L. 1925. Z. Vergl. Physiol. 2:691.
[8] Craig, R., and J. R. Clark. 1938. J. Econ. Entomol. 31:51.
[9] Fink, D. E. 1925. J. Gen. Physiol. 7:527.
[10] Glaser, R. W. 1925. Ibid. 7:599.
[11] Harnisch, O. 1929. Verh. Deut. Zool. Ges. 33:57.
[12] Heimpel, A. M. 1955. Can. J. Zool. 33:99.
[13] Heimpel, A. M. 1956. Ibid. 34:210.
[14] Heller, J., and A. Moklowska. 1930. Biochem. Z. 219:473.
[15] Hoskins, W. M., and H. S. Harrison. 1934. J. Econ. Entomol. 27:924.
[16] Kocian, V., and M. Špaček. 1934. Zool. Jahrb. 54:180.
[17] Krey, J. 1937. Ibid. 58:201.
[18] Levenbook, L. 1950. J. Exp. Biol. 27:158.
[19] Ludwig, D. 1934. Ann. Entomol. Soc. Amer. 27:429.
[20] Marshall, J. 1939. J. Econ. Entomol. 32:838.
[21] Taylor, I. R., et al. 1934. Physiol. Zool. 7:593.

Part III. Specific Gravity: Insects

Values in parentheses are ranges, estimate "c" (*see* Introduction).

	Species	Stage	Specific Gravity	Reference		Species	Stage	Specific Gravity	Reference
	Hymenoptera					Lepidoptera			
1	*Apis* sp.	Larva	1.045	3	6	*Bombyx* sp.	Larva	(1.032-1.041)	4,9
	Diptera				7	*Deilephila* sp.	Larva	1.0307	5,8
					8	*Galleria mellonella*	Larva	1.0546	10
2	*Calliphora* sp.	Larva	1.021	6	9	*Prodenia* sp.	Larva	1.032	1
3	*Gasterophilus* sp.	Larva	1.062	7		Coleoptera			
4	*Musca domestica*	Larva	1.0479	10					
5	*Phormia* sp.	Larva	1.018	6	10	*Dytiscus* sp.	Adult	1.026	2
					11	*Hydrophilus* sp.	Adult	1.012	2

continued

Part III. Specific Gravity: Insects

	Species	Stage	Specific Gravity	Reference
	Hemiptera			
12	*Oncopeltus fasciatus*	Nymph, ♂♀	1.0243	10
	Orthoptera			
13	*Acheta domesticus*	Nymph, ♂	1.0188	10
14		♀	1.0192	

	Species	Stage	Specific Gravity	Reference
15		Adult, ♂	1.0215	
16		♀	1.0195	
17	*Leucophaea maderae*	Nymph, ♂♀	1.0293	10
18	*Periplaneta ameri-*	Nymph	1.0182	11
19	*cana*	♂♀	1.0297	10
20		Adult	1.0162	11

Contributors: Patton, Robert L.; Buck, John B.

References

[1] Babers, F. H. 1938. J. Agr. Res. 57:697.

[2] Barratt, J. O., and G. Arnold. 1910. Quart. J. Microsc. Sci. 56:149.

[3] Bishop, G. H. 1923. J. Biol. Chem. 58:543.

[4] Ducceschi, V. 1902. Atti Reale Accad. Georgofili 80:365.

[5] Heller, J., and A. Moklowska. 1930. Biochem. Z. 219:473.

[6] Hopf, H. S. 1940. Biochem. J. 34:1396.

[7] Levenbook, L. 1950. Ibid. 47:336.

[8] Moklowska, A. 1929. Acta Biol. Exp. (Warsaw) 3: 241.

[9] Nazari, A. 1902. Atti Reale Accad. Georgofili 80: 356.

[10] Patton, R. L., et al. Unpublished, 1960.

[11] Yeager, J. F., and R. W. Fay. 1935. Proc. Soc. Exp. Biol. Med. 32:1667.

Part IV. Freezing Point Depression: Insects

Values in parentheses are ranges, estimate "c" (*see* Introduction).

	Species	Stage	Freezing Point Depression °C	Reference
	Hymenoptera			
1	*Apis mellifera*	Larva	0.86	5
2	*Vespa crabro*	Adult	0.87	12
	Diptera			
3	*Aedes aegypti*	Larva	(0.4-0.5)	13
4	*Anopheles maculipennis*	Larva, pupa, adult	(0.57-0.74)	14
5	*Culex pipiens*	Larva	(0.4-0.5)	13
6	*Gasterophilus intestinalis*	Larva	0.872	8
7	*Phaenicia cuprina* [1]	Adult	0.812	4
	Lepidoptera			
8	*Bombyx mori*	Larva	0.48	6,7,11,15

	Species	Stage	Freezing Point Depression °C	Reference
9	*Ephestia elutella*	Larva	1.12	12
10	*Galleria mellonella*	Larva	1.14	12
11		Pupa	1.06	
12	*Spodoptera eridania* [2]	Larva	0.84	1
	Coleoptera			
13	*Carabus intricatus*	Adult [3]	0.94	12
14	*Dytiscus circumcinctus*	Adult	0.56	3
15	*Melolontha melolontha* [4]	Larva	0.81	12
16	*Popillia japonica*	Larva	1.03	9
17	*Silpha carinata*	Adult [3]	0.88	12
18	*Tenebrio molitor*	Larva	(1.16-1.34)	10,12
19		Adult	0.97	12
	Hemiptera			
20	*Notonecta glauca*	Adult [3]	0.59	12

[1] Synonym: *Lucilia cuprina.* [2] Synonym: *Prodenia eridania.* [3] Stage not specified; probably adult. [4] Synonym: *M. vulgaris.*

continued

Part IV. Freezing Point Depression: Insects

Species	Stage	Freezing Point Depression °C	Reference
Orthoptera			
21 *Blatta orientalis*	Adult	0.75	12
22 *Carausius morosus*	Adult	0.56	12
23 *Gryllotalpa gryllotalpa*	Adult	0.83	12

Species	Stage	Freezing Point Depression °C	Reference
24 *Tettigonia viridissima* 5/	Adult	0.74	12
Odonata			
25 *Aeshna* sp.	Larva	0.56	2

5/ Synonym: *Locusta viridissima.*

Contributors: Waterhouse, D. F., and Grace, T. D. C.; Buck, John B.

References

[1] Babers, F. H. 1938. J. Agr. Res. 57:697.

[2] Backman, E. L. 1911. Zentralbl. Physiol. 25:835.

[3] Backman, E. L. 1912. Pfluegers Arch. Gesamte Physiol. Menschen Tiere 149:93.

[4] Barton Browne, L., and A. Dudzinski. 1968. J. Insect Physiol. 14:1423.

[5] Bishop, G. H. 1923. J. Biol. Chem. 58:543.

[6] Ducceschi, V. 1902. Atti Reale Accad. Georgofili 80:365.

[7] Gamo, T., and S. Yamaguchi. 1927. J. Sci. Agr. Soc. (Tokyo) 295:243.

[8] Levenbook, L. 1950. Biochem. J. 47:336.

[9] Ludwig, D. 1951. Physiol. Zool. 24:329.

[10] Patton, R. L., and R. Craig. 1939. J. Exp. Zool. 81: 437.

[11] Polimanti, O. 1915. Biochem. Z. 70:74.

[12] Rouschal, W. 1940. Z. Wiss. Zool., A, p. 196.

[13] Wigglesworth, V. B. 1938. J. Exp. Biol. 15:235.

[14] Winogradskaja, O. N. 1936. Z. Parasitenk. 8:697.

[15] Yagi, N. 1924. Zool. Mag. 36:319.

Part V. Hemocytes: Insects

Cell nomenclature is according to Jones [18]. Because there is no clear synonymy among the various hemocyte classifications in the literature, some of the data for this table was necessarily interpreted and modified from the original for ease of comparison. Cells: "Adipohemocytes" include spheroidocytes and some granular hemocytes and cystocytes; "Cystocytes" are included in this table only where so identified by the original author (cystocytes are a poorly characterized category and are possibly synonymous with some granular hemocytes, or with oenocytoids or coagulocytes); "Granular hemocytes" include granulocytes, granular leukocytes, "powdery" leukocytes, leukocytes with coin-shaped inclusions, and some micronucleocytes; "Oenocytoids" include crystal cells; "Plasmatocytes" include cells with basophilic cytoplasm, fusiformocytes, lamellocytes and podocytes of Rizki [30,31], leukocytes, some macronucleocytes, phagocytes, and podocytes and vermiform cells of Yeager [44]; "Prohemocytes" include leukoblasts, some macronucleocytes, mother cells, and proleukocytes; "Spherule cells" include cells with fuchsinophilic inclusions, eruptive cells, and some granulocytes and spheroidocytes; "Other cells" include unidentified, transitional, and degenerating cells. Data in brackets refer to the column heading in brackets.

Species [Stage]	Cells	Concentration % of total cells [cells/μl]	Reference
Hymenoptera			
Apis mellifera 1/			
1 [Larva]	Total cells	[10,040-10,280]	11, 20, 25, 42
2	Plasmatocytes	15	
3	Prohemocytes	85	

Species [Stage]	Cells	Concentration % of total cells [cells/μl]	Reference
4 [5 da old]	Total cells	[2947-10,000] 2/	12
5 [Worker, 1 da old]	Total cells	[29,914]	11, 20, 25, 42
6	Oenocytoids	Present	
7	Plasmatocytes	Present	
8	Prohemocytes	Present	
9	Spherule cells	Present	

1/ Synonym: *A. mellifica.* 2/ Related to altitude.

continued

Part V. Hemocytes: Insects

	Species [Stage]	Cells	Concentration % of total cells [cells/μl]	Reference
10	[Drone]	Total cells	[2990]	
11		Plasmatocytes	Present	
12		Prohemocytes	Present	
13	[Queen]	Total cells	[3232]	
14		Prohemocytes	Present	

		Diptera		

	Species [Stage]	Cells	Concentration % of total cells [cells/μl]	Reference
	Calliphora vicina[3/]			1
15	[Larva,	Plasmatocytes	7	
16	large]	Prohemocytes	89	
17		Other cells	4	
18	[Prepupa]	Granular hemocytes	77	
19		Plasmatocytes	1	
20		Prohemocytes	17	
21		Spherule cells	0.90	
22		Other cells	5	
	Culex hortensis			2
23	[Larva]	Granular hemocytes	94.0	
24		Plasmatocytes	2.0	
25		Prohemocytes	2.0	
26	[Adult]	Granular hemocytes	88.5	
27		Plasmatocytes	10.3	
28		Prohemocytes	1.2	
29	*Drosophila*	Oenocytoids	16.8	26
30	*euronotus*	Plasmatocytes + prohemocytes	47.0	
31	[Larva, 3rd instar, late]	Lamellocytes	11.6	
32		Podocytes	24.7	
33	*D. melanogas-*	Total cells	[26,364]	28,
34	*ter* [Larva,	Oenocytoids	3.1	31
35	162 hr old]	Plasmatocytes	97.1	
36		Prohemocytes	Present	
37		Other cells	0-2	
38	*D. willistoni*	Adipohemocytes	1.0-1.4	30
39	[Larva,	Oenocytoids	0.4-2.8	
40	large]	Plasmatocytes	94.9-100	
41		Prohemocytes	Present	
42		Other cells	6.9	
43	*Musca domes-*	Oenocytoids	11.0	27
44	*tica* [Larva,	Plasmatocytes + prohemocytes	88.9	
	4 da old]			
45	*Sarcophaga*	Total cells	[23,250]	16
46	*bullata*	Granular hemocytes	57.5	
47	[Larva, last	Plasmatocytes	41.9	
48	instar]	Prohemocytes	Present	
49		Spherule cells	0.6	

		Lepidoptera		

	Anagasta kuehniella			3
50	[Larva, 6th	Total cells	[65,320]	
51	instar]	Adipohemocytes	43.8-53.7	

	Species [Stage]	Cells	Concentration % of total cells [cells/μl]	Reference
52		Oenocytoids	0.1	
53		Plasmatocytes	44.5-53.1	
54		Prohemocytes	0.6-1.3	
55		Other cells	1.2-1.8	
56	[Adult,	Total cells	[6000]	
57	young]	Adipohemocytes	63.9	
58		Oenocytoids	0	
59		Plasmatocytes	30.5	
60		Prohemocytes	3.2	
61		Other cells	2.4	
62	*Bombyx mori*	Adipohemocytes	Present	29
63	[Larva]	Granular hemocytes	Present	
64		Oenocytoids	Present	
65		Plasmatocytes	Present	
66		Prohemocytes	Present	
67		Spherule cells	Present	
68	*Galleria mel-*	Total cells	[33,700 ± 3,300]	33-35
69	*lonella*	Adipohemocytes	0.2-1.3	
70	[Larva, 7th instar]	Cystocytes	13.2-33.5	
71		Oenocytoids	0.5-1.0	
72		Plasmatocytes	63.7-79.2	
73		Prohemocytes	0.05-0.10	
74		Spherule cells	1.9-4.1	
75		Other cells	1.9-2.3	
76	*Heliothis zea*	Total cells	[31,461 ± 5,103]	36
77	[Larva, 9 da old]	Plasmatocytes	[5663 ± 787]	
78		Prohemocytes	Present	
79		Spherule cells	[7236 ± 2989]	
	Hyalophora cecropia			
80	[Larva &	Adipohemocytes	Present	22
81	adult]	Oenocytoids	Present	
82		Plasmatocytes	Present	
83		Prohemocytes	Present	
84		Spherule cells	Present	
85	[Larva, 5th instar]	Total cells	[10,066 ± 1,605]	21
86		Granular hemocytes	31.8 ± 7.04	
87		Oenocytoids	1.5 ± 0.41	
88		Plasmatocytes + prohemocytes	56.5 ± 7.2	
89		Spherule cells	10.2 ± 2.88	
90	[Pupa,	Total cells	[70]	39
91	newly	Granular hemocytes	44	
92	formed]	Plasmatocytes	55	
93	[Adult,	Total cells	[9201 ± 1445]	21
94	young]	Granular hemocytes	23.9 ± 3.53	
95		Oenocytoids	0.1 ± 0.04	
96		Plasmatocytes + prohemocytes	75.4 ± 3.69	
97		Spherule cells	0.6 ± 0.21	

[3/] Synonym: *C. erythrocephala.*

continued

Part V. Hemocytes: Insects

	Species [Stage]	Cells	Concentration % of total cells [cells/µl]	Reference
98	*Pectinophora gossypiel-la* [Larva, 4th instar]	Total cells	[17,615-21,350]	8
99		Adipohemocytes	Present	
100		Cystocytes	Present	
101		Oenocytoids	Present	
102		Plasmatocytes	Present	
103		Prohemocytes	Present	
104		Spherule cells	Present	
105	*Pseudaletia unipuncta* [Larva, 6th instar]	Total cells	[14,952]	43
106		Cystocytes	Present	
107		Plasmatocytes	79.0	
108		Prohemocytes	3.7	
109		Spherule cells	15.0	
110		Other cells	1.9	
	Spodoptera eridania [4]			32, 44
111	[Larva, 6th instar]	Total cells	[17,185 ± 1,671] [5]	
112		Adipohemocytes	9.6-31.4	
113		Cystocytes	1.7-11.8	
114		Oenocytoids	2.2-8.3	
115		Plasmatocytes	24.3-55.8	
116		Prohemocytes	0-5.5	
117		Spherule cells	8.9-30.7	
118		Other cells	1.7-12.6	
119	[Adult, young]	Total cells	[27,734 ± 1,400] [6]	
120		Adipohemocytes	0-3.5	
121		Cystocytes	0	
122		Oenocytoids	0	
123		Plasmatocytes	59.5-89.7	
124		Prohemocytes	0-7.9	
125		Spherule cells	0-17.3	
126		Other cells	2.2-40.2	
	Coleoptera			
	Leptinotarsa decemlineata [7]			6
127	[Larva, 4th instar]	Total cells	[7220 ± 169]	
128		Granular hemocytes	79.9 ± 1.43	
129		Plasmatocytes	16.9 ± 1.33	
130		Prohemocytes	0.8 ± 0.13	
131		Spherule cells	2.4 ± 0.12	
132	[Adult]	Total cells	[3540 ± 85]	
133		Granular hemocytes	81.6 ± 0.50	
134		Plasmatocytes	16.3 ± 0.55	
135		Prohemocytes	0.2 ± 0.08	
136		Spherule cells	1.9 ± 0.16	
137	*Melolontha melolon-tha* [Larva, 3rd instar]	Granular hemocytes	8.22	9
138		Plasmatocytes	47.29	
139		Prohemocytes	13.04	
140		Spherule cells	31.44	

	Species [Stage]	Cells	Concentration % of total cells [cells/µl]	Reference
	Tenebrio molitor			15, 17
141	[Larva, full-grown]	Total cells	[28,000 [5]; 44,500 [6]]	
142		Cystocytes	50.7-67.1	
143		Oenocytoids	0-1.5	
144		Plasmatocytes	31.0-47.1	
145		Prohemocytes	0-0.4	
146		Spherule cells	0.1-2.8	
147		Other cells	0.1-1.8	
148	[Adult, young]	Cystocytes	49.4-57.6	
149		Oenocytoids	0.1-1.1	
150		Plasmatocytes	38.9-49.6	
151		Prohemocytes	0.1-0.2	
152		Spherule cells	0.2-1.4	
153		Other cells	0.3-0.9	
	Hemiptera			
154	*Oncopeltus fasciatus* [Nymph, 5th instar]	Total cells	[670-1336]	10
	Rhodnius prolixus			19
155	[Nymph, 5th instar]	Granular hemocytes	6.0-75.0	
156		Oenocytoids	0-14.6	
157		Plasmatocytes	22.0-85.0	
158		Prohemocytes	0-30.0	
159	[Adult, young]	Granular hemocytes	5.0-62.0	
160		Oenocytoids	0-9.0	
161		Plasmatocytes	26.0-90.0	
162		Prohemocytes	0-12.0	
	Dermaptera			
	Forficula auricularia			5
163	[Nymph, last instar]	Cystocytes	3.5-20.0	
164		Granular hemocytes	66.5-83.0	
165		Plasmatocytes	8.0-18.0	
166		Prohemocytes	0-0.5	
167	[Adult]	Cystocytes	10.0	
168		Granular hemocytes	79.0	
169		Plasmatocytes	11.0	
170		Prohemocytes	0	
	Orthoptera			
171	*Blaberus gi-ganteus* [Adult, young]	Granular hemocytes	73.6-84.9	4
172		Plasmatocytes	8.5-10.9	
173		Prohemocytes	0.6-2.8	
174		Spherule cells	6.0-16.5	
175	*Gryllus assim-ilis* [8] [Adult]	Total cells	[70,118]	14, 37
176		Cystocytes	1.1	
177		Granular hemocytes	3.9	
178		Plasmatocytes	50.8	
179		Prohemocytes	12.4	

[4] Synonym: *Prodenia eridenia.* [5] Unfixed blood. [6] Heat-fixed blood. [7] Synonym: *Chrysomela decemlineata.* [8] Synonym: *Acheta assimilis.*

continued

Part V.   Hemocytes: Insects

	Species [Stage]	Cells	Concentration % of total cells [cells/μl]	Reference
180		Spherule cells	4.2	
181		Other cells	30.4	
182	*Locusta mi-*	Total cells	[9100 ± 1840]	13,
183	*gratoria*	Cystocytes	53.7	38,
184	[Nymph,	Granular hemocytes	20.0	40
185	5th instar]	Oenocytoids	2.8	
186		Plasmatocytes	18.8	
187		Prohemocytes	4.7	
	Mantis religiosa			7
188	[Nymph]	Total cells	[11,700-12,750]	
189		Granular hemocytes	90.5-99.0	
190		Plasmatocytes	6.5-8.5	
191		Prohemocytes	0.5-1.0	
192	[Adult]	Total cells	[4300-8020]	
193		Granular hemocytes	91.0-98.0	
194		Plasmatocytes	1.5-8.5	
195		Prohemocytes	0-0.5	
	Periplaneta americana			41
196	[Nymph, last in-	Total cells	[96,160 ± 12,973]	
197	star]	Cystocytes	24 ± 2.1	

	Species [Stage]	Cells	Concentration % of total cells [cells/μl]	Reference
198		Granular hemocytes	Present	
199		Plasmatocytes	Present	
200		Prohemocytes	Present	
201	[Adult, 24 hr old]	Total cells	[80,272 ± 10,107]	
202		Cystocytes	19 ± 3.9	
203		Granular hemocytes	Present	
204		Plasmatocytes	Present	
205		Prohemocytes	Present	
	Schistocerca gregaria			23,
206	[Nymph,	Total cells	[5000]	24
207	5th instar]	Granular hemocytes	Present	
208		Plasmatocytes	Present	
209		Prohemocytes	Present	
210	[Adult]	Total cells	[5,872-11,862]	
211		Granular hemocytes	Present	
212		Plasmatocytes	Present	
213		Prohemocytes	Present	

Contributor: Arnold, John W.

References

[1] Åkesson, B. 1954. Ark. Zool. 6:203.

[2] Amouriq, L. 1960. Bull. Soc. Entomol. Fr. 65:135.

[3] Arnold, J. W. 1952. Can. J. Zool. 30:352.

[4] Arnold, J. W. 1969. Can. Entomol. 101:68.

[5] Arvy, L., and J. Lhoste. 1945. Bull. Soc. Zool. Fr. 70:144.

[6] Arvy, L., et al. 1948. Bull. Biol. Fr. Belg. 82:1.

[7] Arvy, L., et al. 1949. Rev. Can. Biol. 8:184.

[8] Clark, E. W., and D. S. Chadbourne. 1960. Ann. Entomol. Soc. Amer. 53:682.

[9] Collin, N. 1963. Rev. Pathol. Veg. Entomol. Agr. Fr. 42:161.

[10] Feir, D. 1964. Nature (London) 202:1136.

[11] Gilliam, M., and H. Shimanuki. 1967. J. Invertebr. Pathol. 9:387.

[12] Gilliam, M., and H. Shimanuki. 1970. Experientia 26:929.

[13] Hoffmann, J. A. 1969. J. Insect Physiol. 15:1375.

[14] Hrdy, I. 1958. Cas. Cesk. Spolecn. Entomol. 55:301.

[15] Jones, J. C. 1950. Iowa State Coll. J. Sci. 24:355.

[16] Jones, J. C. 1956. J. Morphol. 99:233.

[17] Jones, J. C. 1957. J. Cell. Comp. Physiol. 50:423.

[18] Jones, J. C. 1962. Amer. Zool. 2:209.

[19] Jones, J. C. 1967. J. Insect Physiol. 13:1133.

[20] Kostecki, R. 1965. J. Apicult. Res. 4:49.

[21] Lea, M. S. 1964. Ph.D. Thesis. Northwestern Univ., Evanston, Ill.

[22] Lea, M. S., and L. I. Gilbert. 1966. J. Morphol. 118:197.

[23] Lee, R. M. 1961. J. Insect Physiol. 6:36.

[24] Mathur, C. B., and B. N. Soni. 1937. Indian J. Agr. Sci. 7:317.

[25] Metalnikov, S., and C. Toumanoff. 1930. C. R. Soc. Biol. 103:965.

[26] Nappi, A. J. 1970. Ann. Entomol. Soc. Amer. 63:1217.

[27] Nappi, A. J., and J. G. Stoffolano, Jr. 1971. Exp. Parasitol. 29:116.

[28] Nappi, A. J., and F. A. Streams. 1969. J. Insect Physiol. 15:1551.

[29] Raichoudhury, D. P., and K. Sen Gupta. 1960. Indian J. Entomol. 21:6.

[30] Rizki, M. T. M. 1953. J. Exp. Zool. 123:397.

[31] Rizki, M. T. M. 1957. J. Morphol. 100:437.

[32] Rosenberger, C. R., and J. C. Jones. 1960. Ann. Entomol. Soc. Amer. 53:351.

[33] Shapiro, M. 1967. J. Invertebr. Pathol. 9:111.

[34] Shapiro, M. 1968. Ibid. 10:230.

[35] Shapiro, M. 1969. Ibid. 13:63.

[36] Shapiro, M., et al. 1969. Ibid. 14:28.

[37] Tauber, O. E., and J. F. Yeager. 1934. Iowa State Coll. J. Sci. 9:13.

continued

Part V.   Hemocytes: Insects

[38] Tobe, S. S., and B. G. Loughton. 1969. J. Insect Physiol. 15:1659.

[39] Walters, D. R. 1970. J. Exp. Zool. 174:441.

[40] Webley, D. P. 1951. Proc. Roy. Entomol. Soc. London A26:25.

[41] Wheeler, R. E. 1963. J. Insect Physiol. 9:223.

[42] Wille, H., and M. A. Vecchi. 1966. Mitt. Schweiz. Entomol. Ges. 39:69.

[43] Wittig, G. 1966. J. Invertebr. Pathol. 8:461.

[44] Yeager, J. F. 1945. J. Agr. Res. 71:1.

269.   INORGANIC IONS AND AMINO ACIDS IN HEMOLYMPH: INSECTS

Because of the following factors, values should be used only as a guide to approximate levels of ions in the hemolymph: (i) Insects, unlike vertebrates, control the composition of their circulating body fluids only within wide limits; variations in the diet and in the environment can cause quantitatively large changes in the concentration of ions in the hemolymph. [9] (ii) The ionic composition of the hemolymph of insects kept under constant dietary and environmental conditions depends on the insects' physiological state [15].

(iii) Hemolymph samples taken from different regions of the body at the same time have different compositions [15]. (iv) Most analyses of insect hemolymph are based on samples of whole hemolymph which may contain varying numbers of hemocytes; such variations would be expected to have substantial effects on measurements of hemolymph ions, especially potassium. [3] All insects are terrestrial, unless otherwise indicated.

	Order & Species (Synonym)	Stage	Osmotic Pressure mmole NaCl/liter	Concentration, mmole/liter								Reference
				Na	K	Ca	Mg	Cl	PO₄	HCO₃	Amino Acids	
	Hymenoptera											
1	Apis mellifera (A. mellifica)	Larva	246	11	31	18	21	33	10	....	103	4,7,8
2		Adult	....	47	27	18	1	....	....	....	....	9
3	Vespula germanica	Pupa	....	23	61	11	19	....	....	....	....	8
	Diptera											
4	Calliphora vicina (C. erythrocephala)	Pupa	....	140	26	21	34	....	....	....	....	8
5	Gasterophilus intestinalis [1]	Larva	249	206	13	7	38	17	40	17	62	10
6	Stomoxys calcitrans	Adult	....	128	11	....	....	....	....	....	....	8
	Lepidoptera											
7	Bombyx mori	Larva	129	14	40	18	50	21	3	....	89	2,4,10,22,24
8		Pupa	....	22	55	30	88	....	....	....	....	8
9		Adult	....	14	36	14	45	....	....	....	....	2
	Trichoptera											
10	Limnephilus stigma [2]	Larva	106	83	14	....	....	10	18	10	41	20
	Neuroptera											
11	Osmylus fulvicephalus	Adult	226	92	40	....	....	62	....	....	....	21
12	Sialis lutaria [2]	Larva	170	109	5	8	19	31	15	15	85	19,20
	Mecoptera											
13	Panorpa communis	Adult	186	94	38	....	....	34	....	....	....	21
	Coleoptera											
14	Dytiscus marginalis [2]	Adult	208	126	14	23	38	44	....	....	....	8,20
15	Popillia japonica	Larva	281	20	9	16	39	19	25	....	171	12

[1] Parasite. [2] Freshwater habitat.

continued

Order & Species (Synonym)	Stage	Osmotic Pressure mmole NaCl/liter	Concentration, mmole/liter								Reference
			Na	K	Ca	Mg	Cl	PO$_4$	HCO$_3$	Amino Acids	
Hemiptera											
16 *Rhodnius prolixus*	Larva	179	174	....	....	....	....	....	....	....	13
17	Adult	193	162	5	....	....	....	....	....	.....	16
Plecoptera											
18 *Dinocras cephalotes* [2/]	Larva	163	117	10	....	.....	111	6	....	39	20
Dermaptera											
19 *Forficula auricularia*	Adult	207	96	13	17	....	90	....	....	.....	6,21
Isoptera											
20 *Cryptotermes havilandi*	Larva	196	103	28	.....	....	82	....	....	....	21
21 *Zootermopsis angusticollis*	Adult	....	....	....	8	17	....	....	....	....	5
Orthoptera											
22 *Carausius morosus*	Adult	160	9	28	16	145	93	120	....	35	7,8,17,18
23 *Gryllotalpa gryllotalpa*	Adult	....	234	7	28	10	....	....	....	....	8
24 *Periplaneta americana*	Adult	241	157	8	4	5	144	....	....	163	1
25 *Schistocerca gregaria*	Larva	....	81	5	18	35	....	....	....	....	8
26	Adult	211	108	11	....	....	115	....	....	105	14,23
Odonata											
27 *Aeshna grandis* [2/]	Larva	206	145	9	14	9	110	6	15	39	8,20
28 *Calopteryx virgo (Agrion virgo)*	Adult	221	145	28	....	....	109	....	....	....	20
Ephemeroptera											
29 *Ephemera danica* [2/]	Larva	141	103	18	....	....	77	....	....	....	20
Thysanura											
30 *Petrobius maritimus*	Adult	232	208	6	....	....	194	....	....	....	11

[2/] Freshwater habitat.

Contributor: Maddrell, S. H. P.

References

[1] Asperen, K. van, and I. van Esch. 1956. Arch. Neer. Zool. 11:342.

[2] Bialaszewicz, K., and C. Landau. 1938. Acta Biol. Exp. (Warsaw) 12:307.

[3] Brady, J. 1967. J. Exp. Biol. 47:313.

[4] Buck, J. B. 1953. In K. D. Roeder, ed. Insect Physiology. J. Wiley, New York. pp. 147-190.

[5] Clark, E. W. 1958. Ann. Entomol. Soc. Amer. 51:142.

[6] Clark, E. W., and R. Cray. 1953. Physiol. Zool. 26:101.

[7] Duchateau, G., and M. Florkin. 1958. Arch. Int. Physiol. 66:573.

[8] Duchateau, G., et al. 1953. Ibid. 61:518.

[9] Florkin, M., and C. Jeuniaux. 1964. In M. Rockstein, ed. The Physiology of Insecta. Academic Press, New York. v. 3, pp. 109-152.

[10] Levenbook, L. 1950. Biochem. J. 47:336.

[11] Lockwood, A. P. M., and P. C. Croghan. 1959. Nature (London) 184:370.

[12] Ludwig, D. 1951. Physiol. Zool. 24:329.

[13] Maddrell, S. H. P. 1964. J. Exp. Biol. 41:163.

[14] Phillips, J. E. 1964. Ibid. 41:15.

[15] Pichon, Y. 1970. Ibid. 53:195.

[16] Ramsay, J. A. 1953. Ibid. 29:110.

[17] Ramsay, J. A. 1955. Ibid. 32:183.

[18] Rouschal, W. 1940. Z. Wiss. Zool. A153:196.

[19] Shaw, J. 1955. J. Exp. Biol. 32:353.

[20] Sutcliffe, D. W. 1962. Ibid. 39:325.

[21] Sutcliffe, D. W. 1963. Comp. Biochem. Physiol. 9:121.

[22] Tobias, J. M. 1948. J. Cell. Comp. Physiol. 31:143.

[23] Treherne, J. E. 1959. J. Exp. Biol. 36:533.

[24] Wyatt, G. R., et al. 1956. J. Gen. Physiol. 39:853.

Part I. Common Amino Acids: Insects

Concentration: Tr = trace. **Method:** For more detailed information on microbiological assay, consult reference 5. Plus/minus (±) values are standard deviation, unless otherwise indicated. Figures in heavy brackets are reference numbers. Data in light brackets refer to the column heading in brackets. For information on other species and also crossing of species, consult reference 5.

AMINO ACIDS
(L-α-Amino acids, unless otherwise indicated)

Ala = alanine	Gln = glutamine	Leu = leucine	Ser = serine
Arg = arginine	Glu = glutamic acid	Lys = lysine	Thr = threonine
Asn = asparagine	Gly = glycine	Met = methionine	Trp = tryptophan
Asp = aspartic acid	His = histidine	Phe = phenylalanine	Tyr = tyrosine
Cys = cysteine	Hyp = hydroxyproline	Pro = proline	Val = valine
CyS = cystine	Ile = isoleucine		

Total = total of the immediately preceding amino acids, unless otherwise indicated.

	Species (Synonym)	Amino Acid	Concentration	Unit of Measurement [Method]
	Hymenoptera			
1	*Apis mellif-*	Ala	58	mg/100 ml
2	*era (A.*	Arg	50-74	[Microbio-
3	*mellifica);*	Asp	32-33	logical as-
4	larva [5,	Glu	308-347	say; hy-
5	6]	Gly	72-84	drolyzed
6		His	17-30	hemo-
7		Ile	20-24	lymph
8		Leu	25-30	plasma
9		Lys	74-104	dialysate]
10		Met	19-23	
11		Phe	8-12	
12		Pro	368-418	
13		Thr	27-49	
14		Tyr	3	
15		Val	58-59	
16		Total	1239.0	
17	*Diprion*	Ala	99	mg/100 ml
18	*hercyniae;*	Arg	20	[Paper
19	larva [17]	Asn	63	chroma-
20		Asp	12	tography]
21		Cys + CyS	43	
22		Gln	146	
23		Glu	17	
24		Gly	108	
25		His	92	
26		Ile + Leu	22	
27		Lys	43	

	Species (Synonym)	Amino Acid	Concentration	Unit of Measurement [Method]
28		Met	68	
29		Phe	10	
30		Pro	262	
31		Ser	200	
32		Thr	34	
33		Tyr	38	
34		Val	34	
35		Total [1]	1311	
36	*Neodiprion pratti pratti;* larva, 3rd-5th instar [13]	Fn [2]	Present	[Paper chromatography]
	Diptera			
	Calliphora augur [8]			mM [Paper chromatography]
37	Larva	Ala	13.29 ± 0.49 [3]	
38		Arg	Tr	
39		Asn	2.65 ± 0.17 [3]	
40		Asp	1.08 ± 0.11 [3]	
41		Cys	Tr	
42		Gln	7.45 ± 0.42 [3]	
43		Glu	3.27 ± 0.14 [3]	
44		Gly	3.93 ± 0.10 [3]	
45		Hyp	Tr	
46		Leu &/ or Ile	1.51 ± 0.06 [3]	
47		Lys	Tr	
48		Met	Tr	
49		Phe	1.18 ± 0.12 [3]	
50		Pro	8.01 ± 0.20 [3]	
51		Ser	2.43 ± 0.08 [3]	

[1] Total includes other compounds which may be found in Part III. [2] Ala, Arg, Asp, Gln, Glu, Gly, His, Ile, Leu, Lys, Phe, Pro, Ser, Tyr, and Val are present in hemolymph, independent of diet. [3] Standard error.

continued

Part I. Common Amino Acids: Insects

#	Species (Synonym)	Amino Acid	Concentration	Unit of Measurement [Method]
52		Thr	Tr	
53		Tyr	7.41 ± 0.05 [3/]	
54		Val	1.36 ± 0.05 [3/]	
55	Prepupa	Ala	4.88 ± 0.13 [3/]	
56		Arg	Tr	
57		Asn	2.22 ± 0.15 [3/]	
58		Asp	0.57 ± 0.10 [3/]	
59		Cys	Tr	
60		Gln	3.12 ± 0.18 [3/]	
61		Glu	1.65 ± 0.15 [3/]	
62		Gly	1.82 ± 0.11 [3/]	
63		Hyp	Tr	
64		Leu &/ or Ile	1.46 ± 0.06 [3/]	
65		Lys	Tr	
66		Met	Tr	
67		Phe	1.16 ± 0.12 [3/]	
68		Pro	1.80 ± 0.04 [3/]	
69		Ser	1.61 ± 0.09 [3/]	
70		Thr	Tr	
71		Tyr	3.94 ± 0.03 [3/]	
72		Val	1.30 ± 0.05 [3/]	
73	Pupa, early	Ala	3.44 ± 0.12 [3/]	
74		Arg	Tr	
75		Asn	1.89 ± 0.16 [3/]	
76		Asp	0.98 ± 0.11 [3/]	
77		Cys	Tr	
78		Gln	4.42 ± 0.40 [3/]	
79		Glu	4.28 ± 0.15 [3/]	
80		Gly	3.25 ± 0.10 [3/]	
81		Hyp	Not present	
82		Leu &/ or Ile	0.84 ± 0.06 [3/]	
83		Lys	Tr	
84		Met	Tr	
85		Phe	1.76 ± 0.11 [3/]	
86		Pro	5.50 ± 0.11 [3/]	
87		Ser	2.93 ± 0.09 [3/]	
88		Thr	Tr	
89		Tyr	5.23 ± 0.03 [3/]	
90		Val	0.87 ± 0.04 [3/]	
91	*Drosophila melanogaster;* larva, 96 hr old [3]	Ala	14.5	% total content [Chromatography]
92		Arg	1.9	
93		Asp	0.1	
94		Cys	0.2	
95		Gln	18.1	
96		Glu	4.3	
97		Gly	2.4	
98		His	4.2	

#	Species (Synonym)	Amino Acid	Concentration	Unit of Measurement [Method]
99		Leu	1.2	
100		Lys	6.1	
101		Ser	5.8	
102		Thr	4.8	
103		Tyr	2.7	
104		Val	2.1	
105	*Gasterophilus* sp.; larva [5]	Ala	0.0	mg/100 ml [Microbiological assay; hydrolyzed hemolymph plasma dialysate]
106		Arg	8	
107		Asp	14	
108		Glu	314	
109		Gly	5	
110		His	1	
111		Ile	8	
112		Leu	7	
113		Lys	8	
114		Met	7	
115		Phe	7	
116		Pro	16	
117		Thr	23	
118		Tyr	22	
119		Val	15	
120		Total	455	
	Phormia regina [4/]; larva, 3rd instar [9]			μmole/g larva [Chromatography]
121	Early	Ala	3.20 [5/]; 4.19 [6/]	
122		Arg	1.87 [5/]; 2.53 [6/]	
123		Asp	0.13 [5/]; 11.39 [6/]	
124		Gln	14.32 [5/]; 0.00 [6/]	
125		Glu	0.97 [5/]; 19.46 [6/]	
126		Gly	5.55 [5/]; 10.36 [6/]	
127		His	1.41 [5/]; 18.69 [6/]	
128		Ile	0.31 [5/]; 0.88 [6/]	
129		Leu	0.26 [5/]; 0.62 [6/]	
130		Lys	1.28 [5/]; 22.04 [6/]	
131		Met	0.48 [5/]; 0.73 [6/]	
132		Pro	5.75 [5/]; 6.19 [6/]	
133		Ser	1.79 [5/]; 3.14 [6/]	
134		Thr	1.67 [5/]; 2.31 [6/]	
135		Tyr	0.82 [5/]; 0.60 [6/]	
136		Val	0.60 [5/]; 1.34 [6/]	
137		Total [1/]	55.26 [5/]; 127.91 [6/]	
138	Late	Ala	7.84 [5/]; 8.58 [6/]	
139		Arg	0.56 [5/]; 1.34 [6/]	
140		Asp	Tr [5/]; 2.89 [6/]	
141		Gln	8.81 [5/]; 0.00 [6/]	
142		Glu	0.40 [5/]; 8.49 [6/]	
143		Gly	2.51 [5/]; 5.60 [6/]	
144		His	0.81 [5/]; 2.44 [6/]	
145		Ile	0.60 [5/]; 0.96 [6/]	
146		Leu	0.60 [5/]; 1.32 [6/]	

[1/] Total includes other compounds which may be found in Part III. [3/] Standard error. [4/] For information on late 2nd instar and middle 3rd instar, consult reference 9. [5/] Unhydrolyzed. [6/] Hydrolyzed.

continued

Part I. Common Amino Acids: Insects

	Species (Synonym)	Amino Acid	Concentration	Unit of Measurement [Method]
147		Lys	1.61[5]; 3.09[6]	
148		Met	0.20[5]; 0.00[6]	
149		Pro	3.49[5]; 4.26[6]	
150		Ser	2.28[5]; 2.80[6]	
151		Thr	1.68[5]; 1.80[6]	
152		Tyr	4.59[5]; 3.49[6]	
153		Val	1.75[5]; 2.51[6]	
154		Total[1]	42.07[5]; 54.43[6]	
	Lepidoptera			
	Antheraea pernyi[7] [10]			mM [Paper chromatography]
155	Larva	Ala[8]	5.40[9]	
156		Arg	2.00[9]	
157		Asn	1.72[9]	
158		Asp	3.13[9]	
159		Cys + CyS	1.35[9]	
160		Gln	6.34[9]	
161		Glu	10.02[9]	
162		Gly	8.16[9]	
163		His	9.32[9]	
164		Ile + Leu	3.31[9]	
165		Lys	4.84[9]	
166		Met	1.10[9]	
167		Phe	0.74[9]	
168		Pro	9.34[9]	
169		Thr	6.21[9]	
170		Trp	0.42[9]	
171		Tyr	0.37[9]	
172		Val	4.60[9]	
173		Total	78.37[9]	
174	Pupa	Ala[8]	8.64[10]; 25.70[9,11]; 5.40[9,12]	
175		Arg	4.85[10]; 9.14[9,11]; 3.10[9,12]	
176		Asn	2.14[10]; 2.84[9,11]; 1.91[9,12]	
177		Asp	2.94[10]; 3.74[9,11]; 2.95[9,12]	
178		Cys + CyS	1.31[10]; 1.43[9,11]; 1.34[9,12]	
179		Gln	7.64[10]; 9.25[9,11]; 6.55[9,12]	
180		Glu	6.02[10]; 6.04[9,11]; 9.73[9,12]	
181		Gly	8.21[10]; 10.34[9,11]; 7.85[9,12]	
182		His	6.50[10]; 14.28[9,11]; 9.86[9,12]	
183		Ile + Leu	2.64[10]; 5.55[9,11]; 3.24[9,12]	
184		Lys	7.99[10]; 12.05[9,11]; 6.01[9,12]	
185		Met	1.13[10]; 1.15[9,11]; 1.21[9,12]	
186		Phe	0.99[10]; 1.00[9,11]; 0.85[9,12]	
187		Pro	10.26[10]; 34.54[9,11]; 10.84[9,12]	
188		Thr	8.42[10]; 9.93[9,11]; 6.84[9,12]	
189		Trp	0.56[10]; 0.48[9,11]; 0.54[9,12]	
190		Tyr	0.61[10]; 0.52[9,11]; 0.41[9,12]	
191		Val	4.62[10]; 5.01[9,11]; 4.72[9,12]	
192		Total	85.47[10]; 152.99[9,11]; 83.35[9,12]	
193	Adult, pharate; 12 da after initiation of development	Ala[8]	5.70[9]	
194		Arg	12.23[9]	
195		Asn	1.86[9]	
196		Asp	3.18[9]	
197		Cys + CyS	1.52[9]	
198		Gln	5.67[9]	
199		Glu	10.62[9]	
200		Gly	7.62[9]	
201		His	6.94[9]	
202		Ile + Leu	3.62[9]	
203		Lys	14.24[9]	
204		Met	1.72[9]	
205		Phe	1.10[9]	
206		Pro	18.45[9]	
207		Thr	11.24[9]	
208		Trp	0.54[9]	
209		Tyr	0.44[9]	
210		Val	4.70[9]	
211		Total	111.39[9]	
212	*A. pernyi;* pupa, hibernating [5]	Ala	197.6-199.1	mg/100 ml [Microbiological assay; hemolymph plasma]
213		Arg	194.0-200.0	
214		Asp	16.0-17.9	
215		Glu	115.4-124.8	
216		Gly	73.5-76.8	
217		His	148.7-196.4	
218		Ile	53.6-55.6	
219		Leu	48.7-50.4	
220		Lys	157.3-186.4	
221		Met	30.8-47.2	
222		Phe	22.6-24.8	
223		Pro	376.1-478.4	
224		Thr	135.2-136.8	
225		Tyr	4.0-4.3	
226		Val	65.8-73.6	
227		Total	1646.6-1865.2	

[1] Total includes other compounds which may be found in Part III. [5] Unhydrolyzed. [6] Hydrolyzed. [7] No difference between diapausing and non-diapausing forms. [8] α-Ala plus β-Ala. [9] Means of 3 replicates; deviation from mean was 5-14%. [10] Means of 3 replicates; deviation from mean was 5-10%. [11] Diapausing, held at 6°C for 12 wk. [12] Pharate.

continued

Part I.   Common Amino Acids: Insects

	Species (Synonym)	Amino Acid	Concentration	Unit of Measurement [Method]
228	*Bombyx mori* [13]; larva, 5th instar [6]	Ser	173	mg/100 g H₂O [Microbiological assay]
229		Ala	42.5	mg/100 ml [Microbiological assay]
230		Arg	56.0	
231		Asp	58.8	
232		Glu	275.0	
233		Gly	79.4	
234		His	151.4	
235		Ile	15.1	
236		Leu	17.6	
237		Lys	83.4	
238		Met	14.3	
239		Phe	7.1	
240		Pro	27.7	
241		Thr	40.6	
242		Tyr	5.1	
243		Val	39.4	
244		Total	913.4	
	B. mori, race Nd [14] [2]			mg/100 ml [Microbiological assay]
245	Larva	Ala	30.8 [15]; 26.4 [16]	
246		Arg	15.8 [15]; 16.1 [16]	
247		Asp	92.1 [15]; 25.9 [16]	
248		Glu	318.7 [15]; 208.0 [16]	
249		Gly	246.3 [15]; 143.7 [16]	
250		His	137.9 [15]; 92.0 [16]	
251		Ile	15.8 [15]; 16.7 [16]	
252		Leu	14.8 [15]; 17.2 [16]	
253		Lys	111.1 [15]; 48.3 [16]	
254		Met	15.8 [15]; 49.4 [16]	
255		Phe	14.0 [15]; 9.2 [16]	
256		Pro	17.7 [15]; 18.4 [16]	
257		Ser	153.7 [15]; 132.2 [16]	
258		Thr	76.8 [15]; 9.2 [16]	
259		Tyr	10.3 [15]; 19.5 [16]	
260		Val	20.2 [15]; 12.6 [16]	
261	Pupa, 4-5 da old	Ala	29.1	
262		Arg	26.7	
263		Asp	19.4	
264		Glu	382.2	
265		Gly	74.5	
266		His	81.0	
267		Ile	25.9	

	Species (Synonym)	Amino Acid	Concentration	Unit of Measurement [Method]
268		Leu	24.3	
269		Lys	114.2	
270		Met	87.0	
271		Phe	12.1	
272		Pro	72.9	
273		Ser	105.3	
274		Thr	47.0	
275		Tyr	40.5	
276		Val	42.9	
277	*Galleria mellonella;* larva [17]	Ala	225	mg/100 ml [Paper chromatography]
278		Arg	39	
279		Asn	13	
280		Asp	38	
281		Cys + CyS	0	
282		Gln	369	
283		Glu	22	
284		Gly	51	
285		His	136	
286		Ile + Leu	42	
287		Lys	68	
288		Met	27	
289		Phe	11	
290		Pro	520	
291		Ser	47	
292		Thr	62	
293		Tyr	76	
294		Val	29	
295		Total [L]	1826	
296	*Hyalophora cecropia;* pupa, hibernating [5]	Ala	66.3	mg/100 ml [Microbiological assay]
297		Arg	149.0	
298		Asp	4.9	
299		Glu	83.1	
300		Gly	31.3	
301		His	85.6	
302		Ile	45.7	
303		Leu	53.1	
304		Lys	198.8	
305		Met	33.7	
306		Phe	0.0	
307		Pro	421.8	
308		Thr	62.6	
309		Tyr	2.5	
310		Val	98.8	

[L] Total includes other compounds which may be found in Part III. [13] Consult reference 7 for review of evolution of amino-acidemia in relation to growth and silk production.

[14] Mutant; does not produce fibroin (0.6% of cocoon weight) while quantity and composition of sericin is normal. [15] 4th instar, 10 da old. [16] 2-3 da after last defecation.

continued

Part I. Common Amino Acids: Insects

	Species (Synonym)	Amino Acid	Concentration	Unit of Measurement [Method]
311	*Papilio machaon;*	Ala	103-213	mg/100 ml
312	pupa, hibernating	Arg	126-127	[Microbiological assay; hydrolyzed hemolymph plasma dialysate]
313	[5]	Asp	14-19	
314		Glu	202-226	
315		Gly	48	
316		His	71-89	
317		Ile	40-56	
318		Leu	56-80	
319		Lys	325-401	
320		Met	122-163	
321		Phe	24-43	
322		Pro	146-256	
323		Thr	47-57	
324		Tyr	4-5	
325		Val	101-120	
326		Total	1575-1769	
327	*Samia cynthia* [17]	Ala	258.5[5]; 253.0[6]	mg/100 ml
328	*(Philosamia cynthia);* pupa [4]	Arg	167.0[5]; 165.6[6]	[Microbiological assay]
329		Asp	3.7[5]; 11.9[6]	
330		Glu	14.1[5]; 95.2[6]	
331		Gly	48.9[5]; 51.9[6]	
332		His	100.0[5]; 89.3[6]	
333		Ile	78.5[5]; 81.5[6]	
334		Leu	105.6[5]; 108.1[6]	
335		Lys	238.5[5]; 247.4[6]	
336		Met	22.2[5]; 64.4[6]	
337		Phe	27.4[5]; 28.1[6]	
338		Pro	238.9[5]; 244.1[6]	
339		Thr	76.7[5]; 80.0[6]	
340		Tyr	4.8[5,6]	
341		Val	122.5[5]; 127.0[6]	
342		Total	1507.3[5]; 1652.3[6]	
	Sphinx ligustri; pupa [4,6]			mg/100 ml
343		Ala	294.1[5]; 165.9-294.1[6]	[Microbiological assay]
344		Arg	303.9[5]; 226.6-262.1[6]	
345		Asp	7.2[5]; 0.0-9.2[6]	
346		Glu	13.1[5]; 160.7-222.2[6]	
347		Gly	52.3[5]; 0.0-44.4[6]	
348		His	128.8[5]; 112.4-116.8[6]	
349		Ile	55.6[5]; 29.5-54.2[6]	
350		Leu	71.2[5]; 69.9-79.8[6]	
351		Lys	381.0[5]; 324.9-367.3[6]	
352		Met	32.0[5]; 65.4-85.0[6]	
353		Phe	32.0[5]; 32.0-40.5[6]	
354		Pro	183.0[5]; 175.8-178.0[6]	
355		Thr	83.7[5]; 80.9-81.0[6]	
356		Tyr	5.2[5]; 8.5-25.4[6]	
357		Val	109.8[5]; 105.2-109.8[6]	
358		Total	1752.9[5]; 1623.8-1903.7[6]	

	Species (Synonym)	Amino Acid	Concentration	Unit of Measurement [Method]
359	Hibernating, ♂	Ala	158.5-206.7	
360	[5]	Arg	190.8-255.0	
361		Asp	9.7-9.8	
362		Glu	62.1-150.7	
363		Gly	37.7-57.7	
364		His	108.6-118.4	
365		Ile	42.5-50.6	
366		Leu	48.3-62.1	
367		Lys	294.7-321.5	
368		Met	59.9-68.3	
369		Phe	32.8-39.9	
370		Pro	94.2-150.8	
371		Thr	74.4-76.3	
372		Tyr	9.7-40.8	
373		Val	88.9-91.4	
374		Total	1411.2-1601.6	
375	Hibernating, ♀	Ala	200.7-250.4	
376	[5]	Arg	211.6-223.9	
377		Asp	5.8-7.8	
378		Glu	79.1-104.9	
379		Gly	41.4-42.6	
380		His	91.3-110.9	
381		Ile	54.5-54.7	
382		Leu	69.2-71.3	
383		Lys	310.9-311.6	
384		Met	64.3-67.2	
385		Phe	44.1-49.5	
386		Pro	176.8-230.4	
387		Thr	81.2-82.5	
388		Tyr	12.8-16.5	
389		Val	94.7-98.0	
390		Total	1622.9-1637.7	

Coleoptera

	Species (Synonym)	Amino Acid	Concentration	Unit of Measurement [Method]
	Anthonomus grandis; adult [11]			μmole/ml [Chromatography]
391	Newly emerged, ♂	Ala	3.0[5]; 22.3[6]	
392		Arg	3.6[5]; 7.9[6]	
393		Asp	1.1[5]; 24.6[6]	
394		Cys	1.2[5]; 0.0[6]	
395		Glu	2.2[5]; 58.8[6]	
396		Gly	3.0[5]; 25.6[6]	
397		His	6.9[5]; 10.4[6]	
398		Ile	1.1[5]; 10.7[6]	
399		Leu	1.1[5]; 13.2[6]	
400		Lys	2.8[5]; 12.1[6]	
401		Met	0.0[5]; 0.7[6]	
402		Phe	3.1[5]; 6.8[6]	
403		Pro	9.7[5]; 44.8[6]	
404		Ser	4.0[5]; 17.7[6]	

[5] Unhydrolyzed. [6] Hydrolyzed. [17] For information on subspecies of *Samia cynthia,* consult references 5 and 6.

continued

Part I. Common Amino Acids: Insects

	Species (Synonym)	Amino Acid	Concentration	Unit of Measurement [Method]
405		Thr	7.7[5]; 15.5[6]	
406		Trp	1.4[5]	
407		Tyr	0.4[5]; 15.6[6]	
408		Val	2.8[5]; 15.3[6]	
409		Total[L]	85.5[5]; 419.3[6]	
410	Newly emerged, ♀	Ala	3.3[5]; 27.0[6]	
411		Arg	4.1[5]; 7.2[6]	
412		Asp	1.0[5]; 23.5[6]	
413		Cys	1.3[5]; 1.4[6]	
414		Glu	2.2[5]; 53.9[6]	
415		Gly	2.8[5]; 29.7[6]	
416		His	8.6[5]; 12.0[6]	
417		Ile	1.1[5]; 10.2[6]	
418		Leu	1.3[5]; 14.4[6]	
419		Lys	3.7[5]; 16.1[6]	
420		Met	Tr[5]; 1.8[6]	
421		Phe	3.3[5]; 8.7[6]	
422		Pro	7.0[5]; 21.3[6]	
423		Ser	5.3[5]; 18.0[6]	
424		Thr	8.3[5]; 17.3[6]	
425		Trp	1.1[5]	
426		Tyr	10.3[5]; 16.7[6]	
427		Val	3.2[5]; 14.1[6]	
428		Total[L]	73.2[5]; 397.9[6]	
429	5 da old, ♂	Ala	2.9[5]; 9.0[6]	
430		Arg	1.0[5]; 4.3[6]	
431		Asp	1.1[5]; 11.2[6]	
432		Cys	1.0[5]; 4.2[6]	
433		Glu	2.3[5]; 16.9[6]	
434		Gly	4.0[5]; 15.0[6]	
435		His	3.3[5]; 3.9[6]	
436		Ile	1.0[5]; 5.2[6]	
437		Leu	1.5[5]; 7.8[6]	
438		Lys	6.2[5]; 11.0[6]	
439		Met	0.3[5]; Tr[6]	
440		Phe	1.0[5]; 2.3[6]	
441		Pro	6.7[5]; 26.7[6]	
442		Ser	1.7[5]; 4.9[6]	
443		Thr	2.4[5]; 6.3[6]	
444		Trp	0.3[5]	
445		Tyr	Tr[5]; 0.8[6]	
446		Val	1.5[5]; 5.5[6]	
447		Total[L]	44.3[5]; 219.7[6]	
448	5 da old, ♀	Ala	1.6[5]; 5.7[6]	
449		Arg	0.7[5]; 2.4[6]	
450		Asp	0.5[5]; 8.3[6]	
451		Cys	0.9[5]; 2.1[6]	
452		Glu	1.2[5]; 14.4[6]	
453		Gly	2.8[5]; 6.6[6]	

	Species (Synonym)	Amino Acid	Concentration	Unit of Measurement [Method]
454		His	2.7[5]; 2.2[6]	
455		Ile	0.5[5]; 1.9[6]	
456		Leu	0.5[5]; 3.1[6]	
457		Lys	4.2[5,6]	
458		Met	0.3[5]; 0.0[6]	
459		Phe	0.5[5]; 3.0[6]	
460		Pro	9.4[5]; 39.0[6]	
461		Ser	1.2[5]; 3.5[6]	
462		Thr	1.3[5]; 3.5[6]	
463		Trp	Tr[5]	
464		Tyr	Tr[5]; 2.8[6]	
465		Val	0.7[5]; 3.4[6]	
466		Total[L]	36.8[5]; 184.9[6]	
467	Leptinotarsa decemlineata; adult [12]	Ala	34.0	mg/100 ml [Microbiological assay; hydrolyzed dialysate]
468		Arg	19.3	
469		Asp	21.2	
470		Glu	611.0	
471		Gly	16.7	
472		His	42.8	
473		Ile	0.0	
474		Leu	12.1	
475		Lys	42.2	
476		Met	0.0	
477		Phe	9.1	
478		Pro	637.0	
479		Thr	20.6	
480		Tyr	0.0	
481		Val	24.5	
482	Popillia japonica; larva [14]	Ala	146-187	mg/100 ml [Chromatography; hydrolyzed plasma]
483		Arg	48-81	
484		Asp	42-47	
485		Glu	309-526	
486		Gly	288-325	
487		His	169-225	
488		Ile	36-54	
489		Leu	20-25	
490		Lys	29-94	
491		Met	3-12	
492		Phe	13-17	
493		Pro	264-507	
494		Ser	0	
495		Thr	11-29	
496		Tyr	11-37	
497		Val	94-150	
		Orthoptera		
498	Carausius morosus; adult [5,	Ala	10-60	mg/100 ml [Microbiological as-
499		Arg	17-19	
500		Asp	6-14	

[L] Total includes other compounds which may be found in Part III. [5] Unhydrolyzed. [6] Hydrolyzed.

continued

Part I. Common Amino Acids: Insects

	Species (Synonym)	Amino Acid	Concentration	Unit of Measurement [Method]
501	6]	Glu	50-77	say; hy-
502		Gly	23-31	drolyzed
503		His	55-58	hemo-
504		Ile	7-13	lymph
505		Leu	10-14	plasma
506		Lys	20-28	dialysate]
507		Met	9-13	
508		Phe	6-9	
509		Pro	10-16	
510		Thr	29-40	
511		Tyr	5-8	
512		Val	22-25	
513		Total	293-424	
514	*Leucoph-*	Ala	6.2	mg amino
515	*aea made-*	Arg	13.16	acid/100
516	*rae* [16]	Asp	Tr	mg amino
517		Cys	Tr	N [Paper
518		Gly	6.62	chroma-
519		His	5.05	tography]
520		Met	3.60	
521		Phe	5.5	
522		Pro	Tr	
523		Ser	2.60	
524		Thr	2.48	
525		Tyr	2.55	
526		Val	3.60	
527		Total[1]	92.66	
528	*Locusta mi-*	Ala	34[18]; 27.6[19]	mg/100 ml
529	*gratoria;*	Arg	24[18]; 16.8[19]	[Microbio-
530	nymph	Asp	13[18]; 16.8[19]	logical as-
531	[5]	Glu	166[18]; 129.7[19]	say]
532		Gly	97[18]; 70.3[19]	
533		His	30[18]; 24.3[19]	
534		Ile	21[18]; 24.9[19]	
535		Leu	21[18]; 20.5[19]	
536		Lys	47[18]; 39.5[19]	
537		Met	6[18]; 0.0[19]	
538		Phe	11[18]; 13.5[19]	
539		Pro	62[18]; 113.0[19]	
540		Ser	49[18]	
541		Thr	20[18]; 13.5[19]	
542		Tyr	28[18]; 5.4[19]	
543		Val	48[18]; 34.0[19]	
544	*Periplaneta*	Ala	7.3±0.5[3,20]	mg/100 ml
545	*america-*	Asp	2.3±0.8[3,20]	[Column
546	*na;* adult	Glu	23.8±8.2[3,20]	chroma-

	Species (Synonym)	Amino Acid	Concentration	Unit of Measurement [Method]
547	[15]	Gly	52.9±4.0[3,20]	tography]
548		Ile	5.6±0.7[3,20]	
549		Leu	6.8±0.9[3,20]	
550		Met	4.2±1.0[3,20]	
551		Phe	6.3±0.9[3,20]	
552		Pro	42.5±7.0[3,20]	
553		Ser[21]	14.1±2.4[3,20]	
554		Thr[21]	7.6±0.8[3,20]	
555		Tyr	25.1±2.1[3,20]	
556		Val	10.8±0.7[3,20]	
557		Total[1]	223.1±12.0[3,20]	
558		Arg	18.9±2.5[3,22]	
559		His	23.1±2.9[3,22]	
560		Lys	10.9±2.0[3,22]	
561		Total	52.9±7.2[3,22]	
	Schistocerca gregaria[23] [1]			μmole/100
	Nymph			ml [Chro-
562	3rd in-	Ala	216±11	matogra-
563	star	Arg	83±2	phy[24]]
564		Asp + Glu	274±11	
565		Gln	340±7	
566		Gly	843±11	
567		His	167±6	
568		Ile + Leu	201±10	
569		Lys	0	
570		Met	123±8	
571		Phe	84±4	
572		Pro	350±11	
573		Ser	193±9	
574		Thr	221±9	
575		Trp	138±20	
576		Tyr	254±21	
577		Val	263±14	
578		Total	3750	
579	5th in-	Ala	804±20	
580	star, ♂	Arg	117±3	
581		Asp + Glu	533±26	
582		Gln	1656±92	
583		Gly	4507±139	
584		His	269±32	
585		Ile + Leu	717±27	
586		Lys	73±40	

[1] Total includes other compounds which may be found in Part III. [3] Standard error. [18] Hydrolyzed hemolymph plasma dialysate. [19] 5th instar; plasma. [20] Average of 7 pools of hemolymph. [21] Overlapping with Asn and Gln peaks. [22] Average of 3 pools of hemolymph. [23] Pigmented grasshopper; for information on albinos, consult reference 1. [24] Of dinitrophenyl amino acids.

continued

Part I. Common Amino Acids: Insects

	Species (Synonym)	Amino Acid	Concentration	Unit of Measurement [Method]		Species (Synonym)	Amino Acid	Concentration	Unit of Measurement [Method]
587		Met	231 ± 15		633		Gln	671 ± 33	
588		Phe	57 ± 11		634		Gly	1811 ± 101	
589		Pro	1147 ± 40		635		His	32 ± 1	
590		Ser	604 ± 20		636		Ile + Leu	187 ± 23	
591		Thr	663 ± 80						
592		Trp	170 ± 11		637		Lys	Tr	
593		Tyr	1583 ± 51		638		Met	Tr	
594		Val	823 ± 34		639		Phe	Tr	
595		Total	13,954		640		Pro	807 ± 30	
596	5th in-	Ala	475 ± 19		641		Ser	187 ± 19	
597	star, ♀	Arg	104 ± 5		642		Thr	192 ± 22	
598		Asp + Glu	1000 ± 19		643		Trp	96 ± 21	
599		Gln	153 ± 9		644		Tyr	51 ± 3	
600		Gly	4259 ± 32		645		Val	275 ± 29	
601		His	337 ± 6		646		Total	5670	
602		Ile + Leu	463 ± 19		647	Mature,	Ala	104 ± 10	
603		Lys	78 ± 35		648	♂	Arg	58 ± 8	
604		Met	256 ± 5		649		Asp + Glu	290 ± 11	
605		Phe	Tr						
606		Pro	810 ± 40		650		Gln	Tr	
607		Ser	376 ± 19		651		Gly	684 ± 52	
608		Thr	423 ± 5		652		His	152 ± 5	
609		Trp	148 ± 7		653		Ile + Leu	101 ± 8	
610		Tyr	903 ± 21						
611		Val	652 ± 51		654		Lys	Tr	
612		Total	10,437		655		Met	Tr	
	Adult				656		Phe	Tr	
613	Imma-	Ala	339 ± 23		657		Pro	574 ± 58	
614	ture, ♂	Arg	53 ± 2		658		Ser	170 ± 18	
615		Asp + Glu	820 ± 22		659		Thr	76 ± 10	
616		Gln	852 ± 39		660		Trp	Tr	
617		Gly	1375 ± 45		661		Tyr	217 ± 16	
618		His	30 ± 3		662		Val	184 ± 9	
619		Ile + Leu	225 ± 14		663		Total	2648	
620		Lys	140 ± 69		664	Mature,	Ala	48 ± 2	
621		Met	140 ± 3		665	♀	Arg	Tr	
622		Phe	64 ± 8		666		Asp + Glu	219 ± 13	
623		Pro	545 ± 21		667		Gln	179 ± 5	
624		Ser	257 ± 32		668		Gly	703 ± 180	
625		Thr	215 ± 13		669		His	Tr	
626		Trp	115 ± 16		670		Ile + Leu	57 ± 4	
627		Tyr	384 ± 26						
628		Val	357 ± 44		671		Lys	Tr	
629		Total	5641		672		Met	93 ± 2	
630	Imma-	Ala	347 ± 28		673		Phe	Tr	
631	ture, ♀	Arg	358 ± 19		674		Pro	474 ± 11	
632		Asp + Glu	656 ± 23		675		Ser	102 ± 4	
					676		Thr	Tr	
					677		Trp	54 ± 8	
					678		Tyr	168 ± 14	
					679		Val	69 ± 4	

continued

Part I.   Common Amino Acids: Insects

	Species (Synonym)	Amino Acid	Concentration	Unit of Measurement [Method]		Species (Synonym)	Amino Acid	Concentration	Unit of Measurement [Method]
680		Total	2166		688		Leu	22-29	
	Odonata				689		Lys	6-14	
					690		Met	4-13	
681	*Aeshna* sp.;	Ala	46	mg/100 ml	691		Phe	5-11	
682	larva [5]	Arg	19-27	[Hydro-	692		Pro	12-41	
683		Asp	4-13	lyzed he-	693		Ser	24	
684		Glu	32-63	molymph	694		Thr	12-23	
685		Gly	22-54	plasma	695		Tyr	3-13	
686		His	7-21	dialysate]	696		Val	23-29	
687		Ile	16-18						

Contributor: Schoffeniels, E.

References

[1] Benassi, C. A., et al. 1961. Biochem. J. 80:332.

[2] Bricteux-Gregoire, S., et al. 1964. Arch. Int. Physiol. Biochim. 72:489.

[3] Chen, P. S. 1966. Advan. Insect Physiol. 3:53.

[4] Duchateau, G., and M. Florkin. 1954. Arch. Int. Physiol. Biochim. 62:272.

[5] Duchateau, G., and M. Florkin. 1958. Ibid. 66:573.

[6] Duchateau, G., et al. 1952. Ibid. 60:103.

[7] Florkin, M. 1965. Bull. Cl. Sci. Acad. Roy. Belg. 51:441.

[8] Hackman, R. H. 1956. Aust. J. Biol. Sci. 9:400.

[9] Levenbook, L. 1966. Comp. Biochem. Physiol. 18:341.

[10] Mansingh, A. 1967. J. Insect Physiol. 13:1645.

[11] Mitlin, N., et al. 1968. Comp. Biochem. Physiol. 25:139.

[12] Sarlet, H., et al. 1952. Biochim. Biophys. Acta 8:571.

[13] Schaefer, C. H. 1964. J. Insect Physiol. 10:363.

[14] Shotwell, O., et al. 1963. Ibid. 9:35.

[15] Stevens, T. M. 1961. Comp. Biochem. Physiol. 3:304.

[16] Todd, M. E. 1958. J. N.Y. Entomol. Soc. 66:135.

[17] Wyatt, G. R., et al. 1956. J. Gen. Physiol. 39:853.

Part II.   Common Amino Acids: Invertebrates Other Than Insects

Concentration: Tr = trace. **Method**: For more detailed information on microbiological assay, consult reference 3.

Figures in heavy brackets are reference numbers. Data in light brackets refer to the column heading in brackets.

AMINO ACIDS
(All are L-α-amino acids)

Ala = alanine	Gln = glutamine	Leu = leucine	Pro = proline
Arg = arginine	Glu = glutamic acid	Lys = lysine	Ser = serine
Asp = aspartic acid	Gly = glycine	Met = methionine	Thr = threonine
Cys = cysteine	His = histidine	Orn = ornithine	Tyr = tyrosine
CyS = cystine	Ile = isoleucine	Phe = phenylalanine	Val = valine

Total = total of the immediately preceding amino acids, unless otherwise indicated.

continued

Part II. Common Amino Acids: Invertebrates Other Than Insects

#	Class & Species	Amino Acid	Concentration	Unit of Measurement [Method]
			Arthropoda	
	Merostomata			
1	Limu-	Ala	0.14-0.18	mg/100 ml [Column chromatography]
2	lus	Asp	0.16-0.21	
3	poly-	Glu	0.26-0.33	
4	phe-	Gly	0.22-0.29	
5	mus;	Ile	0.10-0.12	
6	pool	Leu	0.17-0.21	
7	of 2-	Met	Tr	
8	10 an-	Phe	0.04-0.09	
9	imals	Pro	0.83-1.50	
10	[6]	Ser 1/	0.62-0.66	
11		Thr 1/	0.15-0.17	
12		Tyr	0.06-0.08	
13		Val	0.17-0.35	
14		Total 2/	3.28-4.16	
15		Arg	0.49-0.56	
16		His	Present	
17		Lys	0.46-0.74	
18		Total	1.02-1.23	
	Crustacea			
19	Astacus	Ala	10.2	mg/100 ml [Microbiological assay; hydrolyzed dialysate]
20	asta-	Arg	3.6	
21	cus 3/	Asp	2.3	
22	[2]	Glu	29.8	
23		Gly	6.0	
24		His	1.1	
25		Ile	6.0	
26		Leu	3.0	
27		Lys	3.0	
28		Met	0.0	
29		Phe	1.0	
30		Pro	3.3	
31		Thr	3.3	
32		Tyr	1.7	
33		Val	6.0	
34		Total	80.3	
35	Calli-	Ala	0.350 4/; 0.370 4/; 0.193 5/	µmole/ml [Column chromatography]
36	nectes	Arg	0.098 4/; 0.103 4/; 0.090 5/	
37	sapi-	Asp	0.083 4/; 0.044 4/; 0.057 5/	
38	dus;	Cys	0.000 4/	
39	adult	½ CyS	Tr 4,5/	
40	[4]	Glu	0.088 4/; 0.083 4/; 0.041 5/	
41		Gly	0.574 4/; 0.720 4/; 0.606 5/	
42		His	0.011 4/; 0.020 4/; 0.007 5/	
43		Ile	0.022 4/; 0.028 4/; 0.023 5/	
44		Leu	0.033 4/; 0.048 4/; 0.034 5/	
45		Lys	0.025 4/; 0.041 4/; 0.058 5/	
46		Met	0.000 4/; Tr 4,5/	
47		Phe	0.019 4/; 0.043 4/; 0.027 5/	
48		Pro	0.376 4/; 0.711 4/; 0.411 5/	
49		Ser	0.215 4/; 0.180 4/; 0.263 5/	
50		Thr	0.077 4/; Not present 4,5/	
51		Tyr	0.021 4/; 0.022 4/; 0.026 5/	
52		Val	0.040 4/; 0.063 4/; 0.043 5/	
53	Cancer	Ala	1.42-1.89	mg/100 ml [Column chromatography]
54	irrora-	Asp	0.23-0.33	
55	tus;	Glu	0.59-1.44	
56	pool	Gly	3.00-3.67	
57	of 2-	Ile	0.78-0.91	
58	10 an-	Leu	1.06-1.23	
59	imals	Met	0.14-0.46	
60	[6]	Phe	0-0.56	
61		Pro	3.36-4.16	
62		Ser 1/	1.99-3.48	
63		Thr 1/	0.75-1.12	
64		Tyr	1.48-1.53	
65		Val	1.37-1.64	
66		Total 2/	22.78-27.01	
67		Arg	3.26-3.80	
68		His	0.62-0.66	
69		Lys	1.91-1.93	
70		Total	5.83-6.35	
71	Erio-	Ala	0.839 4/; 0.576 6/; 0.563 7/; 0.426 8/	µmole/ml [Column chromatography]
72	cheir	Arg	0.093 4/; 0.059 6/; 0.084 7/; 0.074 8/	
73	sinen-	Asp	0.066 4/; 0.068 6/; 0.096 7/; 0.040 8/	
74	sis [7]	Glu	0.183 4/; 0.172 6/; 0.154 7/; 0.063 8/	
75		Gly	0.649 4/; 0.452 6/; 0.749 7/; 0.221 8/	
76		His	0.021 4/; 0.023 6/; 0.012 7/; 0.016 8/	
77		Ile	0.048 4/; 0.035 6/; 0.024 7/; 0.012 8/	
78		Leu	0.082 4/; 0.047 6/; 0.037 7/; 0.019 8/	
79		Lys	0.050 4/; 0.027 6/; 0.025 7/; 0.019 8/	
80		Met	Tr 4,6,8/; 0.011 7/	
81		Phe	0.052 4/; 0.031 6/; 0.019 7/; 0.012 8/	
82		Pro	2.436 4/; 2.921 6/; 8.667 7/; 0.514 8/	
83		Ser	0.198 4/; 0.141 6/; 0.196 7/; 0.090 8/	
84		Thr	0.109 4/; 0.105 6/; 0.139 7/; 0.028 8/	
85		Tyr	0.016 4/; 0.008 6/; 0.009 7/; 0.010 8/	
86		Val	0.099 4/; 0.092 6/; 0.118 7/; 0.028 8/	
87		Total 2/	5.673 4/; 5.431 6/; 11.588 7/; 1.835 8/	

1/ Overlapping with Asn and Gln peaks. 2/ Total includes other compounds which may be found in Part IV. 3/ Synonym: A. fluviatilis. 4/ In seawater. 5/ After 4 da in 50% seawater. 6/ After 3 hr in freshwater. 7/ After 4 da in freshwater. 8/ After 12 da in freshwater.

continued

Part II. Common Amino Acids: Invertebrates Other Than Insects

	Class & Species	Amino Acid	Concentration	Unit of Measurement [Method]
88	Homa-	Ala	2.83	mg/100 ml
89	rus	Asp	0.69	[Column
90	ameri-	Glu	0.16	chroma-
91	canus;	Gly	2.12	tography]
92	pool	Ile	0.69	
93	of 5	Leu	0.87	
94	ani-	Met	0.31	
95	mals	Phe	0.30	
96	[6]	Pro	6.90	
97		Ser[1]	2.38	
98		Thr[1]	0.65	
99		Tyr	0.96	
100		Val	0.93	
101		Total[2]	21.92	
102		Arg	1.00-1.01	
103		His	0.18-0.19	
104		Lys	0.42-0.49	
105		Total	1.62-1.67	
106	H. gam-	Ala	8.7	mg/100 ml
107	ma-	Arg	1.6	[Microbio-
108	rus[9]	Asp	7.0	logical as-
109	[1]	Glu	3.5	say; hy-
110		Gly	24.0	drolyzed
111		His	3.5	dialysate]
112		Ile	0.0	
113		Leu	4.2	
114		Lys	2.1	
115		Met	0.0	
116		Phe	0.2	
117		Pro	6.0	
118		Thr	0.0	
119		Tyr	3.3	
120		Val	0.0	
121		Total	64.1	
	Mollusca			
	Bivalvia			
122	Ano-	Ala	0.02	mg/100 ml
123	donta	Arg	<0.06	[Microbio-
124	cyg-	Asp	0.09	logical as-
125	nea	Glu	0.39	say; hy-
126	[3]	Gly	0.50	drolyzed
127		His	0.30	dialysate]
128		Ile	0.09	
129		Leu	0.09	
130		Lys	0.15	
131		Met	0.01	
132		Phe	0.03	
133		Pro	0.03	
134		Thr	0.25	
135		Tyr	0.04	
136		Val	0.08	
137		Total	~2.13	
138	Crass-	Ala	229[10]; 104[11]; 330[12]; 263[13]	nmole/ml hemolymph
139	sos-	Arg	27[10]; 17[11]; 24[12,13]	
140	trea	Asp	Present[10,11]; 7[12]; 3[13]	
141	virgin-	Glu	12[10]; 32[11]; 114[12]; 57[13]	
142	ica [4]	Gly	124[10]; 106[11]; 109[12]; 136[13]	
143		Ile	3[10]; Present[11,13]; 6[12]	
144		Leu	8[10]; 7[11]; 5[12]; Present[13]	
145		Lys	20[10]; 7[11]; 17[12]; 23[13]	
146		Met	Not present[10,13]; Present[11,12]	
147		Orn	69[10]; 14[11]; 111[12]; 97[13]	
148		Ser	120[10]; 53[11]; 87[12]; 339[13]	
149		Thr	Present[10,11,12]; 1[13]	
	Gastropoda			
150	Helix	Ala	0.2-0.3	μmole/ml
151	asper-	Arg	Tr-0.03	[Chromato-
152	sa	Asp	0.03-0.11	graphy[14];
153	[5]	Cys	Tr-0.05	dry or
154		Gln	0.08-0.34	dehy-
155		Glu	0.06-0.17	drated]
156		Gly	0.04-0.16	
157		Leu	0.04-0.07	
158		Ser	0.07-0.17	
159		Thr	Tr-0.08	
160		Val	0.03-0.11	
	Nematoda			
	Secernentea			
161	Paras-	Ala	9.5	mg/100 ml
162	caris	Arg	5.1	[Microbio-
163	equo-	Asp	7.8	logical as-
164	rum	Glu	21.4	say; hy-
165	[3]	Gly	5.7	drolyzed
166		His	0.7	dialysate]
167		Ile	4.2	
168		Leu	5.7	
169		Lys	6.7	

1/ Overlapping with Asn and Gln peaks. 2/ Total includes other compounds which may be found in Part IV. 9/ Synonym: H. vulgaris. 10/ Summer; Cape shore. 11/ Summer; Monmouth Beach. 12/ Winter; Cape shore. 13/ Winter; Monmouth Beach. 14/ Ascending, two-dimensional.

continued

Part II.   Common Amino Acids: Invertebrates Other Than Insects

	Class & Species	Amino Acid	Concentration	Unit of Measurement [Method]		Class & Species	Amino Acid	Concentration	Unit of Measurement [Method]
170		Met	4.4		174		Tyr	1.8	
171		Phe	4.4		175		Val	4.9	
172		Pro	6.2		176		Total	94.7	
173		Thr	6.2						

Contributor: Schoffeniels, E.

References

[1] Camien, M. N., et al. 1951. J. Biol. Chem. 193:881.

[2] Duchateau, G., and M. Florkin. 1954. Arch. Int. Physiol. Biochim. 62:487.

[3] Duchateau, G., and M. Florkin. 1958. Ibid. 66:573.

[4] Gérard, J.-F., and R. Gilles. 1972. J. Exp. Mar. Biol. Ecol. 10:125.

[5] Kerkut, G. A., and G. A. Cottrell. 1962. Comp. Biochem. Physiol. 5:227.

[6] Stevens, T. M., et al. 1961. Ibid. 3:310.

[7] Vincent-Marique, C., and R. Gilles. 1970. Ibid. 35: 479.

Part III.   Unusual Amino Acids and Other Nitrogenous Compounds: Insects

Method: For more detailed information on colorimetric method, consult reference 4. Plus/minus (±) values = standard deviation, unless otherwise indicated. Values in parentheses are ranges, estimate "c" (see Introduction).

	Species (Synonym)	Compound	Method	Concentration	Reference
			Hymenoptera		
1	*Apis mellifera*; late larva & pupa	D-Serine	Enzymatic assay	<24 nmole/insect [1/]	2
2	*Diprion hercyniae*; larva	β-Alanine	Paper chromatography	0 mg/100 ml	15
			Diptera		
3	*Calliphora augur*; larva, prepupa, & early pupa	Taurine	Paper chromatography	Trace	5
4	*Drosophila melanogaster*; larva, 96 hr old	β-Alanine	Chromatography	0.3% total content	1
5		Taurine	Chromatography	0.3% total content	
6		Peptides	Chromatography	28.6% total content	
7		Unknown substances	Chromatography	2.2% total content	
	Phormia regina; larva[2/], 3rd instar				6
8	Early	β-Alanine or phenylalanine	Chromatography	4.89[3/]; 17.79[4/] μmole/g larva	
9		β-Aminoisobutyric acid	Chromatography	2.05[3,4/] μmole/g larva	
10		Cysteic acid + homocysteic acid	Chromatography	0.00[3/]; 2.78[4/] μmole/g larva	
11		Methionine sulfoxide	Chromatography	5.29[3/]; 0.00[4/] μmole/g larva	
12		Taurine	Chromatography	0.86[3/]; 0.82[4/] μmole/g larva	
13		Phosphoethanolamine	Chromatography	1.76[3/]; 0.00[4/] μmole/g larva	
14		Ammonia	Chromatography	0.00[3/]; 24.02[4/] μmole/g larva	

[1/] <10% of total serine.   [2/] For information on late 2nd instar and middle 3rd instar, consult reference 6.   [3/] Unhydrolyzed.   [4/] Hydrolyzed.

continued

Part III.   Unusual Amino Acids and Other Nitrogenous Compounds: Insects

	Species (Synonym)	Compound	Method	Concentration	Reference
15	Late	β-Alanine or phenyl-alanine	Chromatography	1.39[3]; 1.84[4] μmole/g larva	
16		β-Aminoisobutyric acid	Chromatography	Trace[3,4]	
17		Cysteic acid or homo-cysteic acid	Chromatography	0.00[3]; 1.77[4] μmole/g larva	
18		Methionine sulfoxide	Chromatography	Trace[3]; 0.00[4] μmole/g larva	
19		Taurine	Chromatography	1.23[3]; 1.25[4] μmole/g larva	
20		Phosphoethanolamine	Chromatography	0.72[3]; 0.00[4] μmole/g larva	
21		Ammonia	Chromatography	7.08[3]; 16.35[4] μmole/g larva	
	Lepidoptera				
22	*Antheraea pernyi;* larva	Serine, total	Enzymatic assay	2.8 mM	2
23		D-Serine	Enzymatic assay	1.0 mM	
24	larva & pupa	D-Alanine	Enzymatic assay	<24 nmole/insect[5]	
	A. pernyi (Attacus pernyi); larva				3
25	4th instar, 10th da	Amino N	....	(0.29-0.77) g/kg	
26	5th instar, 8th da	Amino N	....	(0.86-2.50) g/kg	
	Bombyx mori				2
27	Larva, last instar, 6th da	Serine, total	Enzymatic assay	(6-18) mM	
28		D-Serine	Enzymatic assay	(0-1)% of total serine	
29	Larva & pupa	D-Alanine	Enzymatic assay	<24 nmole/insect[5]	
30	Pupa, 4 da old	Serine, total	Enzymatic assay	(6-26) mM	
31		D-Serine	Enzymatic assay	(15-50)% of total serine	
	Danaus plexippus				2
32	Larva & pupa	D-Alanine	Enzymatic assay	>24 nmole/insect[6]	
33	Late larva & pupa	D-Serine	Enzymatic assay	>24 nmole/insect[7]	
34	*Galleria mellonella;* larva	β-Alanine	Paper chromatography	51 mg/100 ml	15
35	*Heliothis zea;* late larva & pupa	D-Serine	Enzymatic assay	>24 nmole/insect[7]	2
	Hyalophora cecropia				2
36	Late larva & pupa	D-Alanine	Enzymatic assay	<24 nmole/insect[5]	
37	Pupa	Serine, total	Enzymatic assay	17 mM	
38		D-Serine	Enzymatic assay	12 mM	
	Malacosoma americanum				2
39	Larva	Serine, total	Enzymatic assay	18 mM	
40		D-Serine	Enzymatic assay	0.24 mM	
41	Late larva & pupa	D-Alanine	Enzymatic assay	<24 nmole/insect[5]	
42	Pupa	Serine, total	Enzymatic assay	3.4 mM	
43		D-Serine	Enzymatic assay	0.05 mM	
	Manduca quinquemaculata (Proto-parce quinquemaculata)				2
44	Late larva & pupa	D-Alanine	Enzymatic assay	<24 nmole/insect[5]	
45	Pupa	Serine, total	Enzymatic assay	7.4 mM	
46		D-Serine	Enzymatic assay	3.0 mM	
	Ostrinia nubilalis				2
47	Larva	Serine, total	Enzymatic assay	7.2 mM	
48		D-Serine	Enzymatic assay	1.9 mM	
49	Late larva & pupa	D-Alanine	Enzymatic assay	<24 nmole/insect[5]	
50	*Papilio polyxenes;* late larva & pupa	D-Serine	Enzymatic assay	>24 nmole/insect[7]	2

[3] Unhydrolyzed.   [4] Hydrolyzed.   [5] <10% of total alanine.   [6] >10% of total alanine.   [7] >10% of total serine.

continued

Part III. Unusual Amino Acids and Other Nitrogenous Compounds: Insects

	Species (Synonym)	Compound	Method	Concentration	Reference
	Porthetria dispar				2
51	Late larva & pupa	D-Alanine	Enzymatic assay	<24 nmole/insect[5]	
52	Pupa	Serine, total	Enzymatic assay	2.7 mM	
53		D-Serine	Enzymatic assay	0.0 mM	
	Samia cynthia (Attacus cynthia); larva				3
54	4th instar, 10th da	Amino N	....	(0.32-0.80) g/kg	
55	5th instar, 8th da	Amino N	....	(0.90-3.30) g/kg	
	Sphinx ligustri; larva				3
56	4th instar, 10th da	Amino N	....	(0.22-0.45) g/kg	
57	5th instar, 8th da	Amino N	....	(0.80-3.22) g/kg	
			Coleoptera		
	Anthonomus grandis; adult				9
58	Newly emerged: ♂	β-Alanine	Chromatography	0.1[3] μmole/ml; trace[4]	
59		Hydroxylysine	Chromatography	3.5[3]; 0.5[4] μmole/ml	
60		Ethanolamine	Chromatography	7.9[3]; 22.8[4] μmole/ml	
61		Glucosamine	Chromatography	1.4[3] μmole/ml; trace[4]	
62		Ammonia	Chromatography	17.5[3]; 94.0[4] μmole/ml	
63	♀	β-Alanine	Chromatography	0.6[3] μmole/ml; trace[4]	
64		Hydroxylysine	Chromatography	0.8[3] μmole/ml; trace[4]	
65		Ethanolamine	Chromatography	Trace[3]; 22.6[4] μmole/ml	
66		Glucosamine	Chromatography	0.2[3] μmole/ml; trace[4]	
67		Ammonia	Chromatography	3.7[3]; 82.0[4] μmole/ml	
68	5 da old: ♂	β-Alanine	Chromatography	Trace[3,4]	
69		Hydroxylysine	Chromatography	Trace[3,4]	
70		Ethanolamine	Chromatography	1.9[3]; 30.8[4] μmole/ml	
71		Glucosamine	Chromatography	0.9[3] μmole/ml; trace[4]	
72		Ammonia	Chromatography	3.3[3]; 51.9[4] μmole/ml	
73	♀	β-Alanine	Chromatography	Trace[3,4]	
74		Hydroxylysine	Chromatography	Trace[3,4]	
75		Ethanolamine	Chromatography	Trace[3]; 26.4[4] μmole/ml	
76		Glucosamine	Chromatography	0.7[3] μmole/ml; trace[4]	
77		Ammonia	Chromatography	7.1[3]; 53.0[4] μmole/ml	
78	*Dytiscus marginalis;* adult	Amino N as leucine	....	1.14[8]; 2.2[9] mg/ml	10
	Popillia japonica				8
79	Larva[10]	Amino N	....	236(218-270) ⎱	
80	1 wk of inanition	Amino N	....	253(226-273) ⎰ mg amino N/	
81	2 wk of inanition	Amino N	....	371(333-441) } 100 ml he-	
82	3 wk of inanition	Amino N	....	398(365-470) ⎱ molymph	
83	4 wk of inanition	Amino N	....	438(422-460) ⎰	
84	3rd instar	Amino N	....	(215-245); 262[11] ⎱ mg amino N/	7
85	Prepupa, early	Amino N	....	263 } 100 ml he-	
86	Pupa	Amino N	....	(173-227) ⎰ molymph	
			Orthoptera		
87	*Leucophaea maderae*	Amino acid N	....	85.44(76.15-97.27) mg %	14
88		β-Alanine	Paper chromatography	Trace	
89		Citrulline	Paper chromatography	8.06 mg%	
90		Norleucine	Paper chromatography	13.16 mg %	

[3] Unhydrolyzed. [4] Hydrolyzed. [5] <10% of total alanine. [8] In tap water. [9] In distilled water. [10] 6-7 tests. [11] Fed 5 wk.

continued

Part III.   Unusual Amino Acids and Other Nitrogenous Compounds: Insects

	Species (Synonym)	Compound	Method	Concentration	Reference
91		Ornithine	Paper chromatography	5.3 mg %	
92		Taurine	Paper chromatography	Trace	
93	*Periplaneta americana*	Amino acid N	....	78(67.4-109) mg %	13
94	Adult	Methionine sulfoxide	Column chromatography	9.1 ± 1.3 [12] mg/100 ml	11
95		Taurine	Column chromatography	4.7 ± 1.1 [12] mg/100 ml	
	Odonata				
96	*Aeshna* spp.; larva	Amino N as leucine	....	1.28 [13]; 1.42 [8]; 2.03 [9] mg/ml	10
97	*A. cyanea;* larva [14]	α-Amino N as glycine	Colorimetric	34 ± 13 mmole/liter	12
98	*A. grandis;* larva [15]	α-Amino N as glycine	Colorimetric	39 ± 14 mmole/liter	12
99	*Libellula* sp.; larva	Amino N as leucine	....	1.14 [8]; 2.2 [9] mg/ml	10

[8] In tap water.   [9] In distilled water.   [12] Standard error; values are averages of 7 pools of hemolymph.   [13] In 25% seawater.   [14] Large size.   [15] Medium and large size.

Contributor: Schoffeniels, E.

References

[1] Chen, P. S. 1966. Advan. Insect Physiol. 3:53.
[2] Corrigan, J. J., and N. G. Srinivasan. 1966. Biochemistry 5:1185.
[3] Courtois-Drilhon, A. 1931. Ann. Physiol. Physicochim. Biol. 7(4).
[4] Danielson, I. S. 1933. J. Biol. Chem. 101:505.
[5] Hackman, R. H. 1956. Aust. J. Biol. Sci. 9:400.
[6] Levenbook, L. 1966. Comp. Biochem. Physiol. 18:341.
[7] Ludwig, D. 1954. Physiol. Zool. 27:325.
[8] Ludwig, D., and M. Wugmeister. 1953. Ibid. 26:254.
[9] Mitlin, N., et al. 1968. Comp. Biochem. Physiol. 25:139.
[10] Schoffeniels, E. 1960. Arch. Int. Physiol. Biochim. 68:507.
[11] Stevens, T. M. 1961. Comp. Biochem. Physiol. 3:304.
[12] Sutcliffe, D. W. 1962. J. Exp. Biol. 39:325.
[13] Todd, M. E. 1957. J. N.Y. Entomol. Soc. 65:85.
[14] Todd, M. E. 1958. Ibid. 66:135.
[15] Wyatt, G. R., et al. 1956. J. Gen. Physiol. 39:853.

Part IV.   Unusual Amino Acids and Other Nitrogenous Compounds: Invertebrates Other Than Insects

Compound: NPS = free ninhydrin-positive substance; NPN = non-protein nitrogen; GABA = γ-aminobutyric acid. Method: CChr = column chromatography; Nin = ninhydrin method; Col = colorimetric method (for more detailed information, consult reference 12). Concentration: Hl = hemolymph.

	Class & Species	Compound	Method	Concentration	Remarks	Reference
				Echinodermata		
1	Echinoidea *Strongylocentrotus droebachiensis*	NPS as taurine	....	1.5 mmole/liter	Kept in seawater	9
				Arthropoda		
2	Merostomata *Limulus polyphemus*	Methionine sulfoxide	CChr	0.00-0.04 mg/100 ml	Pool of 2-10 animals	11
3		Taurine	CChr	0.12-0.17 mg/100 ml		

continued

Part IV. Unusual Amino Acids and Other Nitrogenous Compounds: Invertebrates Other Than Insects

	Class & Species	Compound	Method	Concentration	Remarks	Reference
	Crustacea					
4	*Callinectes sapidus*	NPS as leucine	....	2.79-18.34 μmole/g[1]	In 1-20.7‰ salinity	2
5		as N₂	....	8.6-102.9 mg/100 ml[1]	....	7
6	Adult	Ornithine	CChr	0.0 μmole/ml	In seawater	6
7		Taurine	CChr	0.290 μmole/ml		
8				0.920 μmole/ml		
9		Ammonia	CChr	0.008 μmole/ml		
10				0.040 μmole/ml		
11		Taurine	CChr	0.127 μmole/ml	After 4 da in 50% seawater	
12		Ammonia	CChr	0.101 μmole/ml		
13	*Cancer irroratus*	Methionine sulfoxide	CChr	0.26-0.59 mg/100 ml	Pool of 2-10 animals	11
14		Taurine	CChr	4.20-6.15 mg/100 ml		
15	*Carcinus maenas*	NPN	....	10-40 mmole/liter	Wt <35 g; NPN for ♂ >NPN for ♀	5
16				10-30 mmole/liter	Wt >35 g; NPN for ♂ <NPN for ♀	
17		α-Amino N as glycine	....	8.3 ± 0.4 mmole/liter[2]	Freshly captured, in 100% seawater	1,2
18				48.3 ± 5.18 mmole/liter	After 40 hr in 50% seawater	
19				25.9 ± 4.24 mmole/liter	After 112 hr in 50% seawater	
20				9.06 ± 2.16 mmole/liter	After 189 hr in 50% seawater	
21	*Eriocheir sinensis*	Ornithine	CChr	0.044 μmole/ml	Adapted to seawater	13
22		Taurine	CChr	0.536 μmole/ml		
23		Ammonia	CChr	0.152 μmole/ml		
24		Ornithine	CChr	0.033 μmole/ml	After 3 hr in freshwater	
25		Taurine	CChr	0.532 μmole/ml		
26		Ammonia	CChr	0.109 μmole/ml		
27		Ornithine	CChr	0.029 μmole/ml	After 4 da in freshwater	
28		Taurine	CChr	0.589 μmole/ml		
29		Ammonia	CChr	0.067 μmole/ml		
30		Ornithine	CChr	0.025 μmole/ml	After 12 da in freshwater	
31		Taurine	CChr	0.141 μmole/ml		
32		Ammonia	CChr	0.097 μmole/ml		
33	*Homarus americanus*	Methionine sulfoxide	CChr	0.23 mg/100 ml	Pool of 5 animals	11
34		Taurine	CChr	1.90 mg/100 ml		
				Annelida		
	Polychaeta					
35	*Eunice biannulata*	Amino acid N	Nin	66.72[3]; 72.60[4] mg/100 ml	In 100% seawater	3
36				90.39[3]; 48.85[4] mg/100 ml	In 75% seawater	
37				63.14[3]; 65.84[4] mg/100 ml	In 50% seawater	
38	*Nephtys caecoides*	Amino acid N	Nin	44.55 mg/100 ml[4]	In 100% seawater	3
39				38.25 mg/100 ml[4]	In 75% seawater	
40				52.77 mg/100 ml[4]	In 50% seawater	
41	*N. ciliata*	Amino acid N	Nin	71.34[3]; 35.43[4] mg/100 ml	In 100% seawater	3
42				62.40[3]; 19.14[4] mg/100 ml	In 75% seawater	
43				69.90[3]; 68.91[4] mg/100 ml	In 50% seawater	
44	*Nereis vexillosa*	Amino acid N	Nin	19.68[3]; 18.13[4] mg/100 ml	In 100% seawater	3
45				29.01[3]; 13.41[4] mg/100 ml	In 75% seawater	
46				13.41[3]; 18.74[4] mg/100 ml	In 50% seawater	

[1] Independent of salinity. [2] 57 samples; range, 2.8-23.0 mmole/liter. [3] First day. [4] Second day.

continued

Part IV. Unusual Amino Acids and Other Nitrogenous Compounds: Invertebrates Other Than Insects

	Class & Species	Compound	Method	Concentration	Remarks	Reference
				Sipuncula		
47	*Phascolopsis goul-dii* [5]	NPS	Col	0.079 ± 0.022 mole/liter coelomic fluid	10 subjects in 100% seawater	14
48				0.056 ± 0.009 mole/liter coelomic fluid	6 subjects in 90% seawater	
49				0.046 ± 0.006 mole/liter coelomic fluid	6 subjects in 80% seawater	
50				0.011 ± 0.004 mole/liter coelomic fluid	6 subjects in 50% seawater	
				Mollusca		
	Bivalvia					
51	*Anodonta cygnea*	Amino acid as CO_2 [6]	....	0.47 ± 0.04 μmole/kg total H_2O	....	10
52	*Crassostrea virgin-ica*	β-Alanine	CChr	71 [7]; 43 [8] nmole/ml Hl	Summer; cystine, histidine, phenylalanine, proline, tyrosine, & valine are not present	4
53		GABA	CChr	3 [7]; 2 [8] nmole/ml Hl		
54		Serine phosphate [9]	CChr	62 [7]; 76 [8] nmole/ml Hl		
55		Taurine	CChr	250 [7]; 152 [8] nmole/ml Hl		
56		Phosphoethanolamine	CChr	72 [7]; 57 [8] nmole/ml Hl		
57		Urea	CChr	725 [7]; 1980 [8] nmole/ml Hl		
58		Ammonia	CChr	520 [7]; 512 [8] nmole/ml Hl		
59		β-Alanine	CChr	104 [7]; 68 [8] nmole/ml Hl	Winter; cystine, histidine, phenylalanine, proline, tyrosine, & valine are not present	
60		GABA	CChr	11 [7]; 33 [8] nmole/ml Hl		
61		Serine phosphate [9]	CChr	142 [7]; 101 [8] nmole/ml Hl		
62		Taurine	CChr	112 [7]; 68 [8] nmole/ml Hl		
63		Phosphoethanolamine	CChr	434 [7]; 416 [8] nmole/ml Hl		
64		Urea	CChr	Not present [7]; 1030 [8] nmole/ml Hl		
65		Ammonia	CChr	299 [7]; 399 [8] nmole/ml Hl		
66	*Mytilus edulis*	NPS	Col	12 g/100 g wet tissue	In seawater, salinity 34.1‰	8
67				51 g/100 g wet tissue	In seawater, salinity 32.6‰	
68				22 g/100 g wet tissue	In seawater, salinity 30.3‰	
69		Amino acid as CO_2 [6]	....	2.5 ± 1 mmole/kg total water	In 100% seawater	10
70				5.4 ± 2 mmole/kg total water	In 50% seawater	
71		Taurine	CChr	0.03 g/100 g wet tissue	....	8

[5] Synonym: *Golfingia gouldii.* [6] From decarboxylation; except aspartic acid and taurine. [7] Cape shore. [8] Monmouth Beach. [9] Synonym: Phosphoserine.

Contributor: Schoffeniels, E.

References

[1] Ballard, B. S., and W. Abbott. 1969. Comp. Biochem. Physiol. 29:671.
[2] Binns, R. 1969. J. Exp. Biol. 51:29.
[3] Clark, M. E. 1968. Biol. Bull. 134:252.
[4] Feng, S. Y., et al. 1970. Comp. Biochem. Physiol. 34:547.
[5] Gilbert, A. B. 1959. J. Exp. Biol. 36:495.
[6] Gilles, R. Unpublished. Univ. Liège, Belgium, 1971.
[7] Jeffries, H. P. 1966. Chesapeake Sci. 7:164.
[8] Lange, R. 1963. Comp. Biochem. Physiol. 10:173.
[9] Lange, R. 1964. Ibid. 13:205.
[10] Potts, W. T. W. 1958. J. Exp. Biol. 35:749.
[11] Stevens, T. M., et al. 1961. Comp. Biochem. Physiol. 3:310.
[12] Troll, W., and R. K. Cannan. 1952. J. Biol. Chem. 200:803.
[13] Vincent-Marique, C., and R. Gilles. 1970. Comp. Biochem. Physiol. 35:479.
[14] Virkar, R. A. 1966. Ibid. 18:617.

Values are in glucose equivalents per 100 ml whole blood or hemolymph. Plus/minus (±) values are standard error, unless otherwise indicated. Values in parentheses are ranges, estimate "c" (*see* Introduction).

	Class & Species	No. & Sex	Method	Carbohydrate	Concentration	Remarks	Reference
	Echinodermata						
1	Echinoidea *Strongylocentrotus purpuratus*	240	Somogyi	Total reducing (Cu)	(0-13)	....	26
	Arthropoda						
2	Arachnida *Heterometrus fulvipes*	40	Somogyi & Shaffer-Hartman	Total reducing (Cu)	38.8 ± 20.2 [1]	....	38
3	Merostomata *Limulus* sp.	5	Folin & Wu	Total reducing (Cu)	(5-34)	....	36
	Crustacea *Artemia salina*						5
4	Eggs just visible	36♀	Glucose oxidase	Glucose	(48-51)	Yeast or liver-extract medium	
5	in lateral sac	22♀	Glucose oxidase	Glucose	(58-62)		
6	moving to ovisac	18♀	Glucose oxidase	Glucose	(57-61)		
7	Dormant embryos present	34♀	Glucose oxidase	Glucose	(46-49)		
8	Nondormant embryos present	30♀	Glucose oxidase	Glucose	(50-55)		
9	*Astacus* sp. [2]	....	Hagedorn & Jensen	Total reducing (SCN)	(1-4)	Controls	15
10					16	Maximum after epinephrine injection	
11	*Callinectes sapidus*	16♂	Glucose oxidase	Glucose	15.87 ± 1.37	....	8
12	Immature	8♀	Glucose oxidase	Glucose	16.71 ± 1.34	....	
13	Mature	7♀	Glucose oxidase	Glucose	18.41 ± 2.36	Early spring	
14	Early ovigerous	7♀	Glucose oxidase	Glucose	37.61 ± 2.77	....	
15	Late ovigerous	9♀	Glucose oxidase	Glucose	10.52 ± 1.03	....	
16	*Cancer magister*	1	Chromatography & anthrone	Total carbohydrate	44.3	Whole blood	35
17				Oligosaccharides	10.9	....	
18				Glycoprotein	13.2		
19				Glucose-6-phosphate	7.2		
20			Glucose oxidase	Glucose	5.7	....	
21	*Carcinus maenas*	....	Chromatography	Maltotriose	2	Pooled blood	46
22				Trehalose	1.5		
23				Fructose	1.5		
24				Maltose	3		
25	Postmolt (A)	5	Folin & Malmros	Total reducing	7.9	....	
26			Glucose oxidase	Glucose	5.8		
27	Late postmolt (B)	2	Folin & Malmros	Total reducing	8.0	....	
28			Glucose oxidase	Glucose	5.7		
29	Intermolt (C_1-C_3)	19	Folin & Malmros	Total reducing	13.5 ± 1.07	....	
30			Glucose oxidase	Glucose	8.4 ± 0.090		
31	Late intermolt (C_4-D_0)	23	Folin & Malmros	Total reducing	13.8 ± 0.72	....	
32			Glucose oxidase	Glucose	9.9 ± 0.81		
33	Premolt (D)	11	Folin & Malmros	Total reducing	17.1 ± 1.41	....	
34			Glucose oxidase	Glucose	12.2 ± 1.37		

[1] Standard deviation. [2] European freshwater crayfish.

continued

	Class & Species	No. & Sex	Method	Carbohydrate	Concentration	Remarks	Reference
	Hemigrapsus nudus						34
35	Postmolt (A$_2$)	6	LePage & Muller	Glucose	1.55 ± 0.33	....	
36	Late postmolt (B$_2$)	10	LePage & Muller	Glucose	1.12 ± 0.36	....	
37	Intermolt (C$_1$)	7	LePage & Muller	Glucose	2.55 ± 0.17	....	
38		7	LePage & Muller	Glucose	1.87 ± 0.35	Eyestalks removed	
39	Intermolt (C$_2$)	19	LePage & Muller	Glucose	1.22 ± 0.23	Eyestalks removed	
40	Late intermolt (C$_4$)	8	LePage & Muller	Glucose	1.70 ± 0.29	....	
41	Early premolt (D$_1$)	3	LePage & Muller	Glucose	2.45	....	
42	Late premolt (D$_3$)	2	LePage & Muller	Glucose	2.11	....	
43	*Homarus americanus*	....	Anthrone	Total carbohydrate	11.0(9.7-12.3)	4-da captivity; pooled blood	45
44					9.1(8.0-9.9)	8-da captivity; pooled blood	
45		194♂	Folin & Malmros	Total reducing (Cu)	13.2 ± 0.44	After handling	47
46			Glucose oxidase	Glucose	10.7 ± 0.46		
47		194♀	Folin & Malmros	Total reducing (Cu)	14.7 ± 0.57		
48			Glucose oxidase	Glucose	12.8 ± 0.69		
49		12♂	Folin & Malmros	Total reducing (Cu)	7.6 ± 1.03	10-wk captivity	
50			Glucose oxidase	Glucose	6.6 ± 1.07		
51		20♀	Folin & Malmros	Total reducing (Cu)	9.2 ± 0.75		
52			Glucose oxidase	Glucose	9.0 ± 0.67		
53	Postmolt (B)	31	Folin & Malmros	Total reducing (Cu)	6.8 ± 0.39 [L/]	August	48
54			Glucose oxidase	Glucose	4.8 ± 0.31 [L/]		
55	Intermolt	194♂	Folin & Malmros	Total reducing (Cu)	12.3 ± 0.35	....	47
56			Glucose oxidase	Glucose	7.9 ± 0.34		
57		194♀	Folin & Malmros	Total reducing (Cu)	11.9 ± 0.44		
58			Glucose oxidase	Glucose	7.9 ± 0.30		
59	(C$_1$-C$_2$)	74	Folin & Malmros	Total reducing (Cu)	11.0 ± 0.39 [L/]	September	48
60	(C$_1$-C$_3$)	74	Glucose oxidase	Glucose	7.1 ± 0.30 [L/]	September	48
61	(C$_4$)	96	Folin & Malmros	Total reducing (Cu)	11.7 ± 0.39 [L/]	April	48
62			Glucose oxidase	Glucose	7.6 ± 0.27 [L/]		
63		98	Folin & Malmros	Total reducing (Cu)	13.0 ± 0.49 [L/]	June	
64			Glucose oxidase	Glucose	7.5 ± 0.30 [L/]		
65		73	Folin & Malmros	Total reducing (Cu)	12.1 ± 0.41 [L/]	August	
66			Glucose oxidase	Glucose	7.6 ± 0.32 [L/]		
67		69	Folin & Malmros	Total reducing (Cu)	10.9 ± 0.48 [L/]	September	
68			Glucose oxidase	Glucose	8.3 ± 0.44 [L/]		
69	Premolt (D)	25	Folin & Malmros	Total reducing (Cu)	15.4 ± 0.75 [L/]	August	48
70			Glucose oxidase	Glucose	10.0 ± 0.72 [L/]		
71		33	Folin & Malmros	Total reducing (Cu)	15.3 ± 0.62 [L/]	September	
72			Glucose oxidase	Glucose	10.3 ± 0.63 [L/]		
73	*Libinia emarginata*	6	Miller & Van Slyke	Total reducing (Cu)	8.3 ± 1.3	....	24
74				Nonfermentable	6.3 ± 0.7		
75		7♀	Glucose oxidase	Glucose	12.74 ± 1.41	Early spring	8
76	Ovigerous	4♀	Glucose oxidase	Glucose	31.35 ± 1.42	....	8
	Orconectes virilis						33
77	Late intermolt	13	Folin & Wu	Total reducing (Cu)	19.2(9.6-35)	....	
78			Glucose oxidase	Glucose	7.0(0.8-24.1)		
79		13	Folin & Wu	Total reducing (Cu)	13.6(0.5-31.4)	Eyestalks removed	
80			Glucose oxidase	Glucose	4.4(0.9-11.1)		

[L/] Standard deviation.

continued

	Class & Species	No. & Sex	Method	Carbohydrate	Concentration	Remarks	Reference
81	Premolt	12	Folin & Wu	Total reducing (Cu)	29.0(6.0-46.8)	....	
82			Glucose oxidase	Glucose	4.2(2.2-9.3)		
83		12	Folin & Wu	Total reducing (Cu)	18.3(7.2-29.2)	Eyestalks removed	
84			Glucose oxidase	Glucose	4.7(4.1-5.5)		
85	*Panulirus penicillatus*	26	Hagedorn & Jensen	Total reducing (SCN)	22(20-56)	Normal	41
86				Fermentable, reducing (SCN)	(4-40)		
87				Total reducing (SCN)	12.0	Eyestalks removed	
88	*Uca minax*	15	Folin & Wu	Total reducing (Cu)	4	Acclimated to 4°C	7
89					10	Acclimated to 15°C	
90					13	Acclimated to 25°C	
91					32	Acclimated to 30°C	
	Insecta						
92	*Anagasta kuehniella*	....	....	Trehalose	1153 ± 149 [L/]	−6°C	43
93			Glucose oxidase	Glucose	160 ± 19.1 [L/]		
94			....	Glycerol	270 ± 53 [L/]		
95			....	Trehalose	1820 ± 127 [L/]	0°C	
96			Glucose oxidase	Glucose	50.4 ± 13.6 [L/]		
97			....	Glycerol	130 ± 28 [L/]		
98			....	Trehalose	1700 ± 43.7 [L/]	6°C	
99			Glucose oxidase	Glucose	39.6 ± 5.9 [L/]		
100			....	Glycerol	0		
101			....	Trehalose	1170 ± 229 [L/]	20°C	
102			Glucose oxidase	Glucose	30.6 ± 7.4 [L/]		
103			....	Glycerol	0		
104			....	Trehalose	1378 ± 154 [L/]	24-hr anoxia	
105			Glucose oxidase	Glucose	160 ± 34.0 [L/]		
106			....	Glycerol	171 ± 23 [L/]		
107	*Antheraea polyphemus* [3/], larva & pupa	....	....	Trehalose	500	....	52
	Apis mellifera [4/]						
108	Worker	552	Hagedorn & Jensen	Total reducing	2,300(0-11,500)	....	2
109		45	Hagedorn & Jensen	Total reducing	1700	Undisturbed	2
110		....	Chromatography	Total carbohydrate	(1700-3700)	....	6
111	Newly emerged	....	Chromatography	Total carbohydrate	(2000-2300)	....	6
112				Fructose	(800-1000)		
113	Queen, young	♀	Chromatography	Fructose	1200		
114	old	♀	Chromatography	Fructose	700	....	6
	Bombus agrorum						
115	Worker	6	Hagedorn & Jensen	Total reducing	1900(1000-2800)	....	2
116	Drone	2♂	Hagedorn & Jensen	Total reducing	(900-1100)		
117	Queen	1♀	Hagedorn & Jensen	Total reducing	800		
	Bombyx mori						
118	Larva	....	Anthrone	Total carbohydrate	1420	Pooled hemolymph	40
119		16	Anthrone	Total carbohydrate	(166-635)	....	53
120		....	Chromatography	Sucrose	(0.6-1.4)		
121		16	Anthrone	Fructose	(0-39)		
122		....	Chromatography	Fructose	(1.0-1.9)		
123		....	Chromatography	Glucose	(1.2-5.2)		

[L/] Standard deviation. [3/] Synonym: *Telea polyphemus.* [4/] Synonym: *A. mellifica.*

continued

	Class & Species	No. & Sex	Method	Carbohydrate	Concentration	Remarks	Reference
124		....	Anthrone	Trehalose	1230	Pooled hemolymph	40
125		....	Anthrone	Trehalose	715	Fed; pooled hemolymph	3
126					740	Starved; pooled hemolymph	
127	3rd premolt	1	....	Trehalose	300	Pooled hemolymph	10
128	4th postmolt	1	....	Trehalose	60		
129	4th intermolt	1	....	Trehalose	220		
130	4th premolt	1	....	Trehalose	120		
131	Nymph, postmolt	1	....	Trehalose	280	Pooled hemolymph	10
132	intermolt	1	....	Trehalose	120		
133	Pupa	5	Phenol	Total carbohydrate	(890-1150)	Brain removed	25
134	*Carausius morosus*	16	....	Trehalose	5600 ± 500[L]	Injected with extract of brain	11
135		16	....	Trehalose	5000 ± 600[L]	Injected with extract of corpora allata	
136		16	....	Trehalose	7600 ± 500[L]	Injected with extract of corpora cardiaca	
137	Adult	73	....	Trehalose	3700 ± 200[L]	....	
138	*Diprion hercyniae*, larva	2	Anthrone	Total carbohydrate	1288	....	53
139				Fructose	46		
140	*Galleria mellonella*, larva	1	Anthrone	Total carbohydrate	2120	....	53
141				Fructose	37		
142	*Gasterophilus intestinalis*, larva	3	Miller & Van Slyke	Total reducing (Cu)	356	38°C	28
143				Nonfermentable, reducing	95		
144			Roe & Seliwanoff	Fructose	95		
145			Glucose oxidase	Glucose	64.5		
146			Glucose oxidase	Glucose	10	0°C	
147	*Locusta migratoria* 4th instar, 1st da	5	Nelson	Trehalose	3800 ± 500	....	20
148	2nd da	5	Nelson	Trehalose	2300 ± 400		
149	4th da	5	Nelson	Trehalose	3400 ± 100		
150	5th instar, 1st da	5	Nelson	Total reducing (Cu)	49.8 ± 6.8		
151				Trehalose	2900 ± 200		
152	2nd da	5	Nelson	Total reducing (Cu)	189.1 ± 25.2		
153	4th da	5	Nelson	Total reducing (Cu)	26.3 ± 6.4		
154				Trehalose	4100 ± 100		
155	6th da	5	Nelson	Total reducing (Cu)	36.6 ± 7.6		
156				Trehalose	5200 ± 200		
157	Imago, 1st da	5	Nelson	Trehalose	3400 ± 500		
158	*Periplaneta americana*	2	....	Trehalose	(1077-1090)	....	44
159					(3021-4080)	Injected with extract of corpora cardiaca	
160	*Phormia regina*	12	....	Trehalose	2360(1260-3510)	Controls	16
161					2510(580-4610)	Normal; injected with extract of corpora allata & cardiaca	
162					3040(280-6000)	Starved 48 hr	

[L] Standard deviation.

continued

	Class & Species	No. & Sex	Method	Carbohydrate	Concentration	Remarks	Reference
163					6,120(4,520-10,720)	Starved 48 hr; injected with extract of corpora allata & cardiaca	
164	Larva	....	Anthrone	Total carbohydrate	(100-160)	....	12
165				Glucose	(70-125)		
166	Adult	....	Anthrone	Total carbohydrate	(200-3000)	....	12
167				Trehalose	(125-3000)		
168				Glucose	600		
169	Popillia japonica, larva	10	Hagedorn & Jensen	Total reducing (SCN)	248(227-283)	....	29
170		8	Hagedorn & Jensen	Nonfermentable, reducing (SCN)	179(160-200)		
171	Schistocerca gregaria	8	Anthrone	Trehalose	694.5 ± 99.3 [L]	....	49
172	5th instar	....	Hagedorn & Jensen	Total reducing (SCN)	(800-1500)	....	22
173	Adult	8♂	Anthrone	Glucose	24.1 ± 12.9 [L]	....	49

Annelida

	Class & Species	No. & Sex	Method	Carbohydrate	Concentration	Remarks	Reference
174	Oligochaeta Eisenia foetida	....	Chromatography	Glucose	23.2 ± 4.2	....	32
175	Pheretima posthuma	5	Folin & Wu	Total reducing (Cu)	91.8(70-107)	Blood	1
176		7	Hagedorn & Jensen	Total reducing (SCN)	108.5(71-135)		
177		5	Folin & Wu	Total reducing (Cu)	0	Coelomic fluid	
178		7	Hagedorn & Jensen	Total reducing (SCN)	0		
179	Polychaeta Arenicola marina	1	Hagedorn & Jensen	Total reducing (SCN)	15	Blood	13
180				Nonfermentable	3		
181				Total reducing (SCN)	0	Coelomic fluid	
182	Nephtys hombergii	....	Chromatography	Maltose	(9-102)	Pooled samples of coelomic fluid	4
183				Glucose	(22-98)		

Echiura

	Class & Species	No. & Sex	Method	Carbohydrate	Concentration	Remarks	Reference
184	Echiurida Urechis caupo	10	Somogyi	Total reducing (Cu)	21.3 ± 11.4	Whole blood	27
185					42.5 ± 8.7	Plasma	
186			Glucose oxidase	Glucose	18.7 ± 8.1	Whole blood	
187					43.0 ± 9.3 [L]	Plasma	

Sipuncula

	Class & Species	No. & Sex	Method	Carbohydrate	Concentration	Remarks	Reference
188	Phascolopsis gouldii [5]	....	Folin & Wu	Total reducing (Cu)	17.3(15-22)	Coelomic fluid	50
189			Somogyi & Shaffer-Hartman	Total reducing (Cu)	4.6(3-7)		
190	Sipunculus nudus	8	Hagedorn & Jensen	Total reducing (SCN)	(7.5-16.2)	Coelomic fluid	13
191				Nonfermentable	(2.2-8.7)		
192		11	Hagedorn & Jensen	Total reducing (SCN)	(2-7)	Coelomic fluid; fed	23
193					(3-4)	Coelomic fluid; starved	

Mollusca

	Class & Species	No. & Sex	Method	Carbohydrate	Concentration	Remarks	Reference
194	Cephalopoda Octopus dofleini	14	Glucose oxidase	Glucose	41.6(15-92)	....	19
195		1♂	Glucose oxidase	Glucose	56.61 ± 2.76 [L]	High value, repeated determinations	17
196		1♀	Glucose oxidase	Glucose	64.13 ± 1.58 [L]		
197		1♂	Glucose oxidase	Glucose	5.44 ± 0.77 [L]	Low value, repeated determinations	
198		1♀	Glucose oxidase	Glucose	10.58 ± 1.02 [L]		

[L] Standard deviation. [5] Synonym: Golfingia gouldii.

continued

	Class & Species	No. & Sex	Method	Carbohydrate	Concentration	Remarks	Reference
199	*Sepia officinalis*	6	Hagedorn & Jensen	Total reducing (SCN)	(8.0-37.0)	....	9
200		5	Hagedorn & Jensen	Total reducing (SCN)	58.3 ± 11.7	....	39
	Bivalvia						
201	*Anodonta* sp.	14	Hagedorn & Jensen	Nonfermentable	(2-5)	Freshly collected	14
202		16	Hagedorn & Jensen	Total reducing (SCN)	(23-76)	Freshly collected; cardiac blood	
203		14	Hagedorn & Jensen	Total reducing (SCN)	(22-78)	Freshly collected; mantle blood	
204		11	Hagedorn & Jensen	Total reducing (SCN)	(50-105)	Starved 1 yr	
205		11	Hagedorn & Jensen	Nonfermenting	(19-26)		
	Gastropoda						
206	*Aplysia* sp.	....	....	....	(2-14)	....	31
207		5	Hagedorn & Jensen	Total reducing (SCN)	(2-7)	....	23
208	*Haliotis rufescens*	4	Lewis & Benedict	....	56.5(37-91)	....	37
209		4	Mokrash (anthrone)	Total carbohydrate	11.1(8.4-14.4)	....	18
210	*Helix pomatia*	5	Fujita & Iwatake	Total reducing (Cu)	11.5(6.1-20.5)	Summer	30
211					10.3(4-18)	Winter	
212		15	Hagedorn & Jensen	Total reducing (SCN)	22.2(14-29)	Summer	51
213		12	Hagedorn & Jensen	Total reducing (SCN)	11.3(6-19)	Winter	
214		10-12	Hagedorn & Jensen	Total reducing (SCN)	35(29-47)	Spring, on emergence	21
215					14(4-35)	Summer	
216					16(7-30)	Winter	
217		5	Hagedorn & Jensen	Total reducing (SCN)	8(5-12)	April	42
218					33(14-50)	September	
	Polyplacophora						
219	*Amicula stelleri*[6]	1	Lewis & Benedict	....	41	....	37

[6] Synonym: *Cryptochiton stelleri.*

Contributor: Scheer, Bradley T.

References

[1] Bahl, K. N. 1946. Quart. J. Microsc. Sci. 87:357.
[2] Beutler, R. 1936. Z. Vergl. Physiol. 24:71.
[3] Bricteux-Gregoire, S., et al. 1965. Comp. Biochem. Physiol. 16:333.
[4] Clark, M. E. 1964. Biol. Bull. 127:63.
[5] Clegg, J. S. 1965. Comp. Biochem. Physiol. 14:135.
[6] Czarnowski, C. V. 1954. Naturwissenschaften 24:577.
[7] Dean, J. M., and F. J. Vernberg. 1965. Biol. Bull. 129:87.
[8] Dean, J. M., and F. J. Vernberg. 1965. Comp. Biochem. Physiol. 14:29.
[9] Derrien, Y. 1938. C. R. Soc. Biol. 127:1011.
[10] Duchateau-Bosson, G., et al. 1963. Arch. Int. Physiol. Biochim. 71:566.
[11] Dutrieu, J., and L. Gourdaux. 1967. C. R. Acad. Sci. 265D:1067.
[12] Evans, D. R., and V. G. Dethier. 1957. J. Insect Physiol. 1:3.
[13] Florkin, M. 1936. C. R. Soc. Biol. 123:1022.
[14] Florkin, M., and G. Bosson. 1936. Ibid. 121:1348.
[15] Florkin, M., and G. Duchateau. 1939. Ibid. 132:484.
[16] Friedman, S. 1967. J. Insect Physiol. 13:397.
[17] Goddard, C. K. 1968. Comp. Biochem. Physiol. 27:275.
[18] Harrison, F. M. 1962. J. Exp. Biol. 39:179.
[19] Harrison, F. M., and A. W. Martin. 1965. Ibid. 42:71.
[20] Hill, L., and G. J. Goldsworthy. 1968. J. Insect Physiol. 14:1085.
[21] Holtz, F., and T. von Brand. 1940. Biol. Bull. 79:423.
[22] Howden, G. F., and B. A. Kilby. 1956. Chem. Ind. (London), p. 1453.
[23] Kisch, B. 1929. Biochem. Z. 211:292.
[24] Kleinholz, L. H., and B. C. Little. 1949. Biol. Bull. 96:218.
[25] Kobayashi, M., and S. Kimura. 1967. J. Insect Physiol. 13:545.
[26] Lasker, P., and A. C. Giese. 1954. Biol. Bull. 106:328.

continued

[27] Lawrence, A. L., et al. 1971. Comp. Biochem. Physiol. 38(2B):463.

[28] Levenbook, L. 1950. Biochem. J. 47:336.

[29] Ludwig, D. 1951. Physiol. Zool. 24:329.

[30] Lustig, B., et al. 1937. Biochem. Z. 290:95.

[31] Martin, A. W. 1961. In A. W. Martin, ed. Comparative Physiology of Carbohydrate Metabolism in Heterothermic Animals. Univ. Washington Press, Seattle. pp. 35-64.

[32] McLaughlin, J. 1971. Comp. Biochem. Physiol. 38(1B):179.

[33] McWhinnie, M. A., and P. N. Saller. 1960. Ibid. 1: 110.

[34] McWhinnie, M. A., and B. T. Scheer. 1958. Science 128:90.

[35] Meenakshi, V. R., and B. T. Scheer. 1961. Comp. Biochem. Physiol. 3:30.

[36] Morgulis, S. 1922. J. Biol. Chem. 50:1ii.

[37] Myers, R. G. 1920. Ibid. 41:119.

[38] Padmanabhanaidu, B. 1966. Comp. Biochem. Physiol. 17:157.

[39] Robertson, J. D. 1965. J. Exp. Biol. 42:153.

[40] Saito, S. 1963. J. Insect Physiol. 9:509.

[41] Scheer, B. T., and M. A. R. Scheer. 1951. Physiol. Comp. Oecol. 2:108.

[42] Schwarz, K. 1935. Biochem. Z. 275:262.

[43] Sømme, L. 1966. J. Insect Physiol. 12:1069.

[44] Steele, J. E. 1963. Gen. Comp. Endocrinol. 3:46.

[45] Stewart, J. E., et al. 1966. Can. J. Biochem. 44:1447.

[46] Telford, M. 1968. Biol. Bull. 135:574.

[47] Telford, M. 1968. Can. J. Zool. 46:819.

[48] Telford, M. 1968. Comp. Biochem. Physiol. 26:917.

[49] Treherne, J. E. 1958. J. Exp. Biol. 35:611.

[50] Wilber, C. G. 1948. J. Biol. Chem. 173:141.

[51] Wolf-Heidegger, G. 1935. Biochem. Z. 279:55.

[52] Wyatt, G. R., and G. F. Kalf. 1956. Fed. Proc. Fed. Amer. Soc. Exp. Biol. 15:388.

[53] Wyatt, G. R., et al. 1956. J. Gen. Physiol. 39:853.

272. CHEMICAL COMPOSITION AND PHYSICAL PROPERTIES OF LYMPH: MAMMALS

Lymph forms part of the extracellular fluid system of the body. Since its basic chemical structure closely resembles that of blood plasma (or serum) and comparisons of the two are so often necessary, data, where available, are given for both lymph and plasma (or serum). **Constituent or Property:** Fatty acids—Figures in ⟨broken brackets⟩ show the relationship of carbon atoms to double bonds; Enzymes—Numbers in [light brackets] are those assigned by the International Union of Biochemistry on the Nomenclature and Classification of Enzymes [13]. For additional information on lymph, consult references 19, 29, and 30 in Part I.

Part I. Man

Human subjects from whom lymph has been obtained have been patients suffering from some disorder. The original papers should be consulted for details of the clinical condition of each subject. Enzyme values are in units (for a definition of "unit," consult reference); relationships between levels of activity in lymph and plasma are true, regardless of differences in "unit" definitions. Values in parentheses are ranges, estimate "c" (see Introduction).

	Source of Lymph	Constituent or Property (Synonym)	No. of Subjects	Value Lymph	Value Plasma or Serum	Reference
				Electrolytes		
1	Thoracic	Bicarbonate	10	22(15-27) meq/liter	20(14-25) meq/liter	6
2	duct		38	24(14-35) meq/liter	23(14-39) meq/liter	23
3		Calcium	10	3.9(2.9-4.8) meq/liter	4.6(4.0-5.2) meq/liter	6
4			40	4.2(2.9-5.0) meq/liter	4.7(4.1-5.7) meq/liter	23
5			5	4.2(3.4-5.6) meq/liter	5.0(4.3-5.9) meq/liter	3
6			1	4.4 meq/liter	4.8 meq/liter	17
7			10	10.9(6.8-12.9) mg/100 ml	9.7(7.2-11.8) mg/100 ml	15
8		Chloride	13	82(54-104) meq/liter	100(94-104) meq/liter	15
9			1	97 meq/liter	98 meq/liter	17
10			5	98(87-103) meq/liter	96(94-98) meq/liter	3
11			10	100(78-107) meq/liter	99(88-108) meq/liter	6
12			35	103(85-112) meq/liter	101(84-112) meq/liter	23

continued

Part I. Man

	Source of Lymph	Constituent or Property (Synonym)	No. of Subjects	Value Lymph	Value Plasma or Serum	Reference
13		Copper	3	116(85-145) µg/100 ml	113(89-154) µg/100 ml	21
14		Magnesium	10	1.67(1.41-2.06) meq/liter	1.83(1.56-2.06) meq/liter	6
15			17	1.74(1.32-2.93) meq/liter	1.88(1.38-2.62) meq/liter	23
16		Phosphorus, inorganic	5	2.4(2.0-3.6) meq/liter	2.5(2.1-3.5) meq/liter	3
17			1	2.7 mg/100 ml	2.9 mg/100 ml	17
18			37	3.0(1.4-4.4) mg/100 ml	3.1(1.4-4.6) mg/100 ml	23
19			10	3.1(2.0-4.4) mg/100 ml	3.1(2.4-4.3) mg/100 ml	6
20			10	4.7(3.6-6.0) mg/100 ml	4.7(2.8-6.4) mg/100 ml	15
21		Potassium	1	3.3 meq/liter	4.7 meq/liter	17
22			10	3.5(2.5-4.4) meq/liter	4.0(3.0-4.8) meq/liter	6
23			39	3.8(2.5-4.7) meq/liter	4.3(3.0-5.8) meq/liter	23
24			5	4.7(3.9-5.6) meq/liter	5.0(4.1-5.9) meq/liter	3
25			13	5.1(3.2-7.4) meq/liter	4.9(4.2-5.8) meq/liter	15
26		Sodium	5	127(118-132) meq/liter	127(113-135) meq/liter	3
27			10	136(119-152) meq/liter	140(122-152) meq/liter	6
28			1	138 meq/liter	142 meq/liter	17
29			31	138(119-151) meq/liter	141(122-152) meq/liter	23
30			4	138(133-144) meq/liter	144(141-149) meq/liter	10
31			13	153(132-176) meq/liter	137(126-152) meq/liter	15

Lipids & Carbohydrates

	Source of Lymph	Constituent or Property (Synonym)	No. of Subjects	Value Lymph	Value Plasma or Serum	Reference
32	Thoracic duct	Total lipids	14	4.6 mg/ml	7.2 mg/ml	22
		Fatty acids[1]				
33		Free[2]	14	0.2 mg/ml	0.4 mg/ml	22
		In triglycerides				24
34		Myristic ⟨14:0⟩	9[3]	2.0(1.6-3.3)%	2.1(1.0-3.9)%	
35		Palmitic ⟨16:0⟩	9[3]	26.6(23.2-31.0)%	26.0(22.8-29.3)%	
36		cis-9-Palmitoleic ⟨16:1⟩	9[3]	5.1(2.6-6.7)%	6.6(4.2-9.0)%	
37		Stearic ⟨18:0⟩	9[3]	8.1(5.8-11.4)%	3.5(2.1-5.9)%	
38		Oleic ⟨18:1⟩	9[3]	38.1(32.6-44.6)%	46.9(37.7-58.2)%	
39		Linoleic ⟨18:2⟩	9[3]	16.2(11.7-20.6)%	11.7(9.5-16.2)%	
40		Arachidonic ⟨20:4⟩	1[3]	2.0%	1.1%	
		In phospholipids				24
41		Myristic ⟨14:0⟩	5[3]	0.5(0.4-1.6)%	0.7(0.5-1.0)%	
42		Palmitic ⟨16:0⟩	9[3]	33.5(28.2-43.9)%	37.3(31.4-41.9)%	
43		cis-9-Palmitoleic ⟨16:1⟩	5[3]	3.0(1.9-3.7)%	1.6(1.3-3.7)%	
44		Stearic ⟨18:0⟩	9[3]	16.9(13.0-21.5)%	14.7(11.1-17.4)%	
45		Oleic ⟨18:1⟩	9[3]	17.5(15.1-19.9)%	16.5(13.9-21.8)%	
46		Linoleic ⟨18:2⟩	9[3]	19.8(6.3-28.8)%	18.4(15.7-21.6)%	
47		Arachidonic ⟨20:4⟩	9[3]	7.8(1.9-12.0)%	8.5(4.7-12.4)%	
		In cholesterol esters				24
48		Myristic ⟨14:0⟩	9[3]	1.5(0.6-3.9)%	0.9(0.5-1.8)%	
49		Palmitic ⟨16:0⟩	9[3]	15.4(10.4-20.3)%	10.8(8.3-12.6)%	
50		cis-9-Palmitoleic ⟨16:1⟩	9[3]	5.6(4.5-6.8)%	4.6(2.9-6.6)%	
51		Stearic ⟨18:0⟩	8[3]	1.9(1.2-3.3)%	2.3(0.9-5.0)%	
52		Oleic ⟨18:1⟩	9[3]	29.8(26.5-36.9)%	25.3(18.7-30.2)%	
53		Linoleic ⟨18:2⟩	9[3]	39.4(34.6-44.8)%	49.1(40.7-58.3)%	
54		Arachidonic ⟨20:4⟩	9[3]	5.0(4.0-7.1)%	5.4(2.7-8.9)%	

[1] For the effect of different dietary fats on fatty acid pattern in lymph, consult reference 24. [2] For percentages of individual fatty acids, consult reference 22. [3] Patients in fasting state.

continued

Part I. Man

	Source of Lymph	Constituent or Property (Synonym)	No. of Subjects	Value		Reference
				Lymph	Plasma or Serum	
55		Triglycerides[2,4]	14	1.7 mg/ml	0.9 mg/ml	22
56			19[3]	218(60-385) mg/100 ml	181(66-364) mg/100 ml	23
57		Phospholipids[2,5]	14	0.7 mg/ml	1.1 mg/ml	22
58		Cholesterol	14	0.3 mg/ml	0.6 mg/ml	22
59		Total	1	60 mg/100 ml	207 mg/100 ml	17
60			5	72(34-106) mg/100 ml	119(83-167) mg/100 ml	18
61			40	116(60-186) mg/100 ml	254(135-392) mg/100 ml	23
62		Free	5	34(15-51) mg/100 ml	38(28-56) mg/100 ml	3
63			1	36 mg/100 ml	57 mg/100 ml	17
64		Cholesterol esters[2,6]	14	1.3 mg/ml	2.3 mg/ml	22
65		Glucose	9	95(76-115) mg/100 ml	89(67-110) mg/100 ml	23
66			14	120(88-166) mg/100 ml	104(74-153) mg/100 ml	16
67			1	136 mg/100 ml	117 mg/100 ml	3
68			1	140 mg/100 ml	110 mg/100 ml	17
69	Leg lymphatics	Total lipids	14	3.95 mg/ml	7.2 mg/ml	22
70		Fatty acids, free[2]	14	0.24 mg/ml	0.4 mg/ml	
71		Triglycerides[2]	14	1.77 mg/ml	0.9 mg/ml	
72		Phospholipids[2]	14	0.84 mg/ml	1.1 mg/ml	
73		Cholesterol	14	0.1 mg/ml	0.6 mg/ml	
74		Cholesterol esters[2]	14	0.46 mg/ml	2.3 mg/ml	
		Nitrogenous Substances				
75	Thoracic duct	Protein Total	1	(2.80-3.60) g/100 ml	6.0 g/100 ml	8
76			10	3.80(2.25-5.20) g/100 ml	6.51(5.80-7.60) g/100 ml	18
77			4	3.88(1.45-5.68) g/100 ml	6.50(5.80-7.30) g/100 ml	10
78			10	4.04(0.90-7.10) g/100 ml	7.73(4.95-10.00) g/100 ml	1
79			12	4.37(3.0-5.3) g/100 ml	6.64(4.9-7.9) g/100 ml	2
80			5	4.89(2.91-7.33) g/100 ml	7.08(5.38-9.40) g/100 ml	3
81			1	5.1 g/100 ml	7.6 g/100 ml	17
82			14[7]	5.05 g/100 ml	7.0 ± 0.9 g/100 ml	28
83			12[8]	6.39 g/100 ml	7.7 ± 1.2 g/100 ml	28
84			16[9]	3.04 g/100 ml	6.6 ± 1.2 g/100 ml	28
85			3[10]	3.85 g/100 ml	5.5 ± 1.5 g/100 ml	28
86			13[7]	5.0 g/100 ml	7.0 ± 0.9 g/100 ml	27
87			19[11]	5.2 g/100 ml	7.3 ± 1.0 g/100 ml	27
88			11[12]	3.1 g/100 ml	6.1 ± 1.3 g/100 ml	27
89			39[13]	1.8 g/100 ml	5.9 ± 1.2 g/100 ml	27
90		Albumin	1	(1.64-2.45) g/100 ml	3.50 g/100 ml	8
91			10	2.12(0.43-4.08) g/100 ml	3.79(1.78-5.74) g/100 ml	1
92			10	2.14(1.10-3.24) g/100 ml	2.95(1.97-4.27) g/100 ml	18
93			4	2.32(0.54-3.45) g/100 ml	3.05(2.10-4.60) g/100 ml	10
94			5	2.34(1.50-2.67) g/100 ml	2.86(2.00-3.50) g/100 ml	3
95			12	2.67(1.57-3.42) g/100 ml	3.37(2.18-4.22) g/100 ml	2
96			1	3.42 g/100 ml	4.30 g/100 ml	17

[2] For percentages of individual fatty acids, consult reference 22. [3] Patients in fasting state. [4] For percentages of individual fatty acids, see entries 34-40. [5] For percentages of individual fatty acids, see entries 41-47. [6] For percentages of individual fatty acids, see entries 48-54. [7] Controls. [8] Patients with acute congestive heart failure. [9] Patients with chronic congestive heart failure. [10] Patients with compensated congestive heart failure. [11] Patients with early hepatic cirrhosis. [12] Patients with moderate hepatic cirrhosis. [13] Patients with late hepatic cirrhosis.

continued

Part I. Man

Source of Lymph	Constituent or Property (Synonym)	No. of Subjects	Value		Reference
			Lymph	Plasma or Serum	
97		10 [7/]	2.54 g/100 ml	3.76 g/100 ml	28
98		6 [8/]	3.11 g/100 ml	3.66 g/100 ml	28
99		4 [9/]	1.41 g/100 ml	3.14 g/100 ml	28
100		2 [10/]	2.75 g/100 ml	3.42 g/100 ml	28
101	Globulin, total	1	(1.15-1.16) g/100 ml	2.50 g/100 ml	8
102		4	1.57(0.90-2.26) g/100 ml	3.37(2.70-3.80) g/100 ml	10
103		1	1.68 g/100 ml	3.30 g/100 ml	17
104		10	1.69(1.15-2.14) g/100 ml	3.26(2.12-4.23) g/100 ml	18
105		12	1.70(1.04-2.22) g/100 ml	3.27(2.43-4.32) g/100 ml	2
106		10	1.92(0.45-3.63) g/100 ml	3.94(2.04-5.22) g/100 ml	1
107		5	2.56(1.50-4.80) g/100 ml	4.16(3.10-6.92) g/100 ml	3
108		10 [7/]	1.76 g/100 ml	3.24 g/100 ml	28
109		6 [8/]	3.28 g/100 ml	4.04 g/100 ml	28
110		4 [9/]	1.63 g/100 ml	3.46 g/100 ml	28
111		2 [10/]	1.10 g/100 ml	2.08 g/100 ml	28
112	α_1-Globulin	10	0.24(0.15-0.32) g/100 ml	0.34(0.18-0.47) g/100 ml	18
113		1	0.26 g/100 ml	0.34 g/100 ml	17
114	α_2-Globulin	10	0.24(0.15-0.26) g/100 ml	0.89(0.75-1.13) g/100 ml	18
115		1	0.25 g/100 ml	0.62 g/100 ml	17
116	β-Globulin	1	0.40 g/100 ml	0.68 g/100 ml	17
117		10	0.52(0.39-0.58) g/100 ml	0.94 (0.68-1.54) g/100 ml	18
118	γ-Globulin	10	0.71(0.46-0.98) g/100 ml	1.36(0.93-1.73) g/100 ml	18
119		1	0.78 g/100 ml	1.46 g/100 ml	17
120	Transferrin Fe complex	31	71(24-135) μg/100 ml	90(39-206) μg/100 ml	23
121	Bilirubin	37	0.5(0.1-3.5) mg/100 ml	0.6(0.1-4.2) mg/100 ml	23
122		1	0.8 mg/100 ml	1.0 mg/100 ml	17
123	Coagulation factors Prothrombin consumption test	22	25.7(10.5-142.5) s	>180(20.4 to >180) s	7
124	Thromboplastin time	22	37(10-74)%	91(45-104)%	7
125	Thrombin time	21	17.9(11.4-25.6) s	15.1(9.3-20.1) s	7
126	Fibrinogen (Factor I)	4	0.109(0.044-0.178) g/100 ml	0.473(0.275-0.705) g/100 ml	20
127		18	0.138(0.050-0.300) g/100 ml	0.363(0.125-0.600) g/100 ml	7
128		2	0.42(0.37-0.46) g/100 ml	0.73(0.58-0.87) g/100 ml	5
129	Prothrombin (Factor II)	4	19(4-41) units/ml	66(46-101) units/ml	20
130		17	63(42-86)%	97(72-100)%	7
131	Factor V	4	42(2-100) units/ml	386(346-450) units/ml	20
132		21	25(8-76)%	94(44-110)%	7
133		2	29(22-35)%	150(100-200)%	5
134	Factor VII complex	16	37(15-76)%	91(72-104)%	7
135	Factor VIII	4	11(4-16) units/ml	151(56-334) units/ml	20
136	Factor X	17	48(18-78)%	89(62-115)%	7
137	Antithrombin globulin	4	99(77-116) units/ml	155(116-191) units/ml	20
138	Creatinine	44	0.83(0.46-1.92) mg/100 ml	0.88(0.50-1.82) mg/100 ml	23
139		4	3.0(0.8-8.9) mg/100 ml	3.05(0.8-9.0) mg/100 ml	3
140	Haptoglobin	2	63(35-91) mg/100 ml	236(166-306) mg/100 ml	5
141	Uric acid	32	3.8(1.1-7.2) mg/100 ml	3.6(0.9-6.5) mg/100 ml	23
142		1	4.1 mg/100 ml	4.2 mg/100 ml	17
143		4	4.2(2.5-6.0) mg/100 ml	3.8(1.6-5.5) mg/100 ml	16
144		5	5.0(1.7-10.8) mg/100 ml	5.1(1.6-10.9) mg/100 ml	3

[7/] Controls. [8/] Patients with acute congestive heart failure. [9/] Patients with chronic congestive heart failure. [10/] Patients with compensated congestive heart failure.

continued

Part I. Man

Source of Lymph	Constituent or Property (Synonym)	No. of Subjects	Value		Reference
			Lymph	Plasma or Serum	
145	Nitrogen, non-protein	1	23 mg/100 ml	29 mg/100 ml	17
146		11	30(21-54) mg/100 ml	33(20-50) mg/100 ml	16
147		5	46.5(13.4-139.0) mg/100 ml	48.8(15.8-141.0) mg/100 ml	3
	Hepatic lymph duct — Protein				
148	Total	2 [7/]	6.20 g/100 ml	6.60 g/100 ml	28
149		4 [8/]	8.70 g/100 ml	8.00 g/100 ml	28
150		3 [9/]	6.30 g/100 ml	6.50 g/100 ml	28
151		2 [7/]	6.2 g/100 ml	7.0 g/100 ml	27
152		1 [11/]	5.9 g/100 ml	7.4 g/100 ml	27
153		8 [13/]	3.4 g/100 ml	5.9 g/100 ml	27
154	Albumin	2 [7/]	3.98 g/100 ml	3.76 g/100 ml	28
155		4 [8/]	4.20 g/100 ml	3.67 g/100 ml	
156		3 [9/]	2.94 g/100 ml	3.14 g/100 ml	
157	Globulin	2 [7/]	2.22 g/100 ml	2.84 g/100 ml	28
158		4 [8/]	4.50 g/100 ml	4.33 g/100 ml	
159		3 [9/]	3.36 g/100 ml	3.36 g/100 ml	
	Intestinal lymph duct — Protein				28
160	Total	2 [7/]	4.10 g/100 ml	6.60 g/100 ml	
161		3 [8/]	5.20 g/100 ml	8.00 g/100 ml	
162		3 [9/]	3.00 g/100 ml	6.50 g/100 ml	
163	Albumin	2 [7/]	2.55 g/100 ml	3.76 g/100 ml	
164		3 [8/]	2.39 g/100 ml	3.67 g/100 ml	
165		3 [9/]	1.24 g/100 ml	3.14 g/100 ml	
166	Globulin	2 [7/]	1.55 g/100 ml	2.84 g/100 ml	
167		3 [8/]	2.81 g/100 ml	4.33 g/100 ml	
168		3 [9/]	1.76 g/100 ml	3.36 g/100 ml	
	Leg lymphatics — Protein				14
169	Total	1	0.6 g/100 ml	5.6 g/100 ml	
170	Albumin	1	0.37 g/100 ml	2.8 g/100 ml	

Enzymes

171	Thoracic duct — Lactate dehydrogenase [1.1.1.27, 1.1.2.3]	41	27(8-375) units/ml	35(11-425) units/ml	23
172	Aspartate aminotransferase (Glutamic oxalacetic transaminase; GOT) [2.6.1.1]	1	12 units/ml	13 units/ml	17
173		43	23(4-136) units/ml	38(16-244) units/ml	23
174	Alanine aminotransferase (Glutamic pyruvic transaminase; GPT) [2.6.1.2]	43	21(2-114) units/ml	32(10-185) units/ml	23
175	Lipase [14/] [3.1.1.3]	2	(0.3-2.4) mg/100 ml	....	9
176		5	1.6(0.3-3.8) mg/100 ml	1.9(0.6-4.0) mg/100 ml	11
177	Alkaline phosphatase [3.1.3.1]	9	1.36(0.49-2.08) units/ml	1.93(1.20-3.58) units/ml	4
178		44	1.7(0.2-7.2) units/ml	2.8(1.0-17.0) units/ml	23
179		1	1.9 units/ml	2.3 units/ml	17
180	Acid phosphatase [3.1.3.2]	28	0.5(0.1-1.5) units/ml	1.0(0.3-2.2) units/ml	23
181		1	0.7 units/ml	0.3 units/ml	17
182	Amylase [14/] [3.2.1.1, 3.2.1.2]	4	(110-310) units/100 ml	....	9
183		7	262(120-325) units/100 ml	315(110-525) units/100 ml	11

[7/] Controls. [8/] Patients with acute congestive heart failure. [9/] Patients with chronic congestive heart failure. [11/] Patients with early hepatic cirrhosis. [13/] Patients with late hepatic cirrhosis. [14/] For effect of secretin, consult reference 11.

continued

Part I. Man

Source of Lymph	Constituent or Property (Synonym)	No. of Subjects	Value		Reference
			Lymph	Plasma or Serum	
184	Ketose-1-phosphate aldolase (Aldolase) [4.1.2.7]	1	10 units/ml	6 units/ml	17
		Other Properties			
185	Thoracic duct	Oxygen pressure	4 [15/]	34(20-41) mm Hg	....	12
186		4 [16/]	99(71-150) mm Hg	....	12
187		5 [7/]	55 mm Hg	85 mm Hg [17/]; 35 mm Hg [18/]	26
188		9 [19/]	30 mm Hg	66 mm Hg [17/]; 32 mm Hg [18/]	26
189		7 [15,19/]	31(18-41) mm Hg	65(62-68) mm Hg	25
190	Carbon dioxide pressure	6 [15,19/]	29(24-32) mm Hg	28(26-29) mm Hg	25
191	pH	6 [15,19/]	7.47(7.46-7.48)	7.48(7.46-7.50)	25
192	Osmolality	14	285(270-302) mosmole/kg	295(265-355) mosmole/kg	23

[7/] Controls. [15/] Breathing air. [16/] Breathing 100% oxygen. [17/] In artery. [18/] In right atrium. [19/] Patients with hepatic cirrhosis.

Contributors: Courtice, F. C.; Heath, Trevor J., and Reynolds, John D.

References

[1] Aresu, R., et al. 1962. Boll. Soc. Ital. Biol. Sper. 38:16.

[2] Bergström, K., and B. Werner. 1966. Acta Chir. Scand. 131:413.

[3] Bierman, H. R., et al. 1953. J. Clin. Invest. 32:637.

[4] Blomstrand, R., and B. Werner. 1965. Acta Chir. Scand. 129:177.

[5] Blomstrand, R., et al. 1963. Scand. J. Clin. Lab. Invest. 15:248.

[6] Blomstrand, R., et al. 1965. The Transport of Lymph in Man. Appelberg, Uppsala.

[7] Chroback, L., et al. 1967. Amer. J. Med. Sci. 253:69.

[8] Courtice, F. C., et al. 1951. Aust. J. Exp. Biol. Med. Sci. 29:201.

[9] Dumont, A. E., and J. H. Mulholland. 1960. Gastroenterology 38:954.

[10] Dumont, A. E., and J. H. Mulholland. 1960. N. Engl. J. Med. 263:471.

[11] Dumont, A. E., et al. 1960. Ann. Surg. 152:403.

[12] Groth, C. G., et al. 1965. Acta Chir. Scand. 129:586.

[13] International Union of Biochemistry. 1965. Enzyme Nomenclature. Elsevier, Amsterdam.

[14] Jacobsson, S. 1967. Acta Chir. Scand. 133:79.

[15] Liguori, G., et al. 1962. Boll. Soc. Ital. Biol. Sper. 38:14.

[16] Liguori, G., et al. 1962. Ibid. 38:19.

[17] Linder, E., and R. Blomstrand. 1958. Proc. Soc. Exp. Biol. Med. 97:653.

[18] Manenti, A. 1961. Boll. Soc. Ital. Biol. Sper. 37:646.

[19] Rusznyak, I., et al. 1967. Lymphatics and Lymph Circulation. Pergamon Press, London.

[20] Stutman, L. J., et al. 1965. Amer. J. Med. Sci. 250:292.

[21] Trip, J. A. J., et al. 1969. Clin. Chim. Acta 26:371.

[22] Voigt, K. D., et al. 1967. Experientia 23:355.

[23] Werner, B. 1966. Acta Chir. Scand. 132:63.

[24] Werner, B. 1966. Ibid. 132:77.

[25] Witte, C. L., et al. 1967. Ann. Surg. 166:254.

[26] Witte, C. L., et al. 1968. Lymphology 1:109.

[27] Witte, C. L., et al. 1968. Trans. Amer. Surg. Ass. 86:256.

[28] Witte, C. L., et al. 1969. Circulation 40:623.

[29] Yoffey, J. M., and F. C. Courtice. 1956. Lymphatics, Lymph and Lymphoid Tissue. Ed. 2. E. Arnold, London.

[30] Yoffey, J. M., and F. C. Courtice. 1970. Lymphatics, Lymph and the Lymphomyeloid Complex. Academic Press, London and New York.

continued

Part II. Dog

Enzyme values are in units (for a definition of "unit," consult reference); relationships between levels of activity in lymph and plasma are true, regardless of differences in

"unit" definitions. Plus/minus (±) values are standard error, unless otherwise indicated. Values in parentheses are ranges, estimate "c" unless otherwise indicated (*see* Introduction).

	Source of Lymph	Constituent or Property (Synonym)	No. of Subjects	Value Lymph	Value Plasma or Serum [1]	Reference
				Electrolytes		
1	Thoracic duct	Calcium	1	4.6 meq/liter	5.2 meq/liter	2
2		Carbon dioxide	6[2]	56(51-60) ml/100 ml	54(49-57) ml/100 ml [11]	3
3			6[3]	51(40-55) ml/100 ml	45(36-51) ml/100 ml [11]	
4		Chloride	1	116 meq/liter	110 meq/liter	2
5			8	121(107-132) meq/liter	119(81-132) meq/liter	35
6		Phosphorus, inorganic	1	2.0 meq/liter	2.4 meq/liter	2
7		Potassium	7	4.0(3.5-4.4) meq/liter	4.0(3.7-4.5) meq/liter	35
8			....	4.7 meq/liter	....	14
9			....	4.8 meq/liter	....	37
10		Sodium	....	144 meq/liter	....	37
11			15	146(117-155) meq/liter	145(138-152) meq/liter	35
12	Lymphatics Cardiac	Calcium	2[4]	4.6 meq/liter	4.6 meq/liter	1
13		Chloride	9	112.4 ± 2.0 meq/liter	113.7 ± 2.4 meq/liter	41
14			13	122.2 ± 0.7 meq/liter	117.0 ± 0.6 meq/liter	40
15			....	129 meq/liter	119 meq/liter	14
16			6[5]	126 ± 1.7(122-133) meq/liter	119 ± 1.6(114-124) meq/liter	58
17			6[6]	115 ± 6.4(93-130) meq/liter	115 ± 2.8(104-120) meq/liter	58
18		Potassium	9	3.9 ± 0.09 meq/liter	3.69 ± 0.13 meq/liter	41
19			12	4.65 ± 0.29 meq/liter	4.77 ± 0.03 meq/liter	40
20			8[4]	5.80 meq/liter	3.90 meq/liter	1
21			6[5]	2.8 ± 0.13(2.5-3.1) meq/liter	3.0 ± 0.1(2.8-3.2) meq/liter	58
22			6[6]	3.1 ± 0.29(2.1-4.0) meq/liter	3.1 ± 0.24(2.1-3.8) meq/liter	58
23		Sodium	9	149.0 ± 2.2 meq/liter	147.4 ± 2.5 meq/liter	41
24			12	151.2 ± 0.4 meq/liter	148.3 ± 0.5 meq/liter	40
25			6[4]	148 meq/liter	144 meq/liter	1
26			6[5]	151 ± 2.6(144-160) meq/liter	148 ± 1.7(141-152) meq/liter	58
27			6[6]	154 ± 2.8(147-166) meq/liter	149 ± 1.4(144-153) meq/liter	58
28	Cervical	Calcium	11	4.9(4.46-5.42) meq/liter	5.8(5.42-6.47) meq/liter	24
29		Carbon dioxide	10	58.8(46.4-67.2) ml/100 ml	56.8(46.2-67.0) ml/100 ml	25
30		Phosphorus, total	6	11.8(10.2-13.7) mg/100 ml	22.0(18.3-26.1) mg/100 ml	24
31		inorganic	3	3.3(2.6-4.0) meq/liter	3.1(2.4-3.8) meq/liter	24
32		Potassium	....	4.2 meq/liter	....	37
33		Sodium	....	150 meq/liter	....	37
34				157 meq/liter	163 meq/liter	37
35	Renal	Chloride	5	129(122-136) meq/liter	120 meq/liter	56
36		Phosphorus, inorganic	5	5.3 mg/100 ml	4.7 mg/100 ml	56
37		Potassium	5	5.9(4.5-7.2) meq/liter	4.5 meq/liter	56
38		Sodium	5	140 meq/liter	148 meq/liter	56
39	Capsular	Chloride	14	140(114-164) meq/liter	110(81-132) meq/liter	35
40		Potassium	12	4.0(3.5-5.3) meq/liter	4.0(3.2-4.8) meq/liter	35
41		Sodium	27	162(126-206) meq/liter	146(138-160) meq/liter	35

[1] Unless otherwise indicated. [2] Volume of expired air = 100-200 ml·min⁻¹·kg body wt⁻¹. [3] Volume of expired air = 200-300 ml·min⁻¹·kg body wt⁻¹. [4] During heart-lung perfusion. [5] Controls. [6] Subjects with congestive heart failure. [11] Arterial whole blood.

continued

Part II. Dog

	Source of Lymph	Constituent or Property (Synonym)	No. of Subjects	Value — Lymph	Value — Plasma or Serum [1]	Reference
42	Hilar	Calcium	11	3.92(3.43-4.44) meq/liter	4.74(4.02-6.21) meq/liter	31
43		Carbon dioxide	5	22.6(20.6-25.0) mmoles/liter	22.0(20.5-23.3) mmoles/liter	31
44		Chloride	14	123.6 ± 4.3 [7] meq/liter	112.7 ± 3.9 [7] meq/liter	44
45		Magnesium	11	1.60(1.18-2.26) meq/liter	1.61(1.34-1.80) meq/liter	31
46		Potassium	14	2.94(2.35-3.60) meq/liter	3.14(2.65-3.46) meq/liter	31
47			6	3.25 ± 0.41 [7] meq/liter	3.22 ± 0.49 [7] meq/liter	44
48		Sodium	13	142(130-156) meq/liter	147(140-154) meq/liter	31
49			14	152.4 ± 2.9 [7] meq/liter	146.8 ± 3.6 [7] meq/liter	44

Lipids & Carbohydrates

	Source of Lymph	Constituent or Property (Synonym)	No. of Subjects	Value — Lymph	Value — Plasma or Serum [1]	Reference
	Thoracic duct [8]	Lipids				
50		Total	....	(235-583)[b] mg/100 ml	(319-642)[b] mg/100 ml	22
51		Fatty acids, total	4	13.1 ± 1.9 meq/liter	14.0 ± 0.2 meq/liter	10
52		Triglycerides	5 [9]	92(10.6-366) mg/100 ml	....	19
53		Phospholipids	4	223 ± 15.0 mg/100 ml	400 ± 10.0 mg/100 ml	10
54			5 [9]	137(123-178) mg/100 ml	....	19
55		Cholesterol, total	4	124 ± 7.9 mg/100 ml	258 ± 29 mg/100 ml	10
56			5 [9]	155(125-196) mg/100 ml	....	19
		Carbohydrates				
57		Glucose	1	124 mg/100 ml	123 mg/100 ml	2
58		Lactate	4	10 mg/100 ml	8 mg/100 ml [10]	4
59			2	24.5(24.0-25.0) mg/100 ml H_2O	18.6(18.0-19.2) mg/100 ml H_2O	3
	Lymphatics Cervical	Lipids				
60		Total	11	305(105-505)[b] mg/100 ml	589(359-819)[b] mg/100 ml	38
61		Fatty acids, total	11	239(69-409)[b] mg/100 ml	438(258-618)[b] mg/100 ml	38
62			4	5.3 ± 0.7 meq/liter	14.0 ± 0.2 meq/liter	10
63		Phospholipids	4	103 ± 5.0 mg/100 ml	400 ± 10.0 mg/100 ml	10
64		Cholesterol, total	11	56(26-86)[b] mg/100 ml	137(73-201)[b] mg/100 ml	38
65			4	67 ± 8.4 mg/100 ml	258 ± 29 mg/100 ml	10
		Carbohydrates				
66		Glucose	9	102(84-125) mg/100 ml	104(70-135) mg/100 ml	30
67			16	132(107-144) mg/100 ml	123(112-143) mg/100 ml	24
68		Lactate	1	13.0 mg/100 ml H_2O	19.0 mg/100 ml H_2O [11]	3
69		Reducing substances, nonfermentable	10	5.8(3.3-8.3)[b] mg/100 ml	5.5(1.4-9.6)[b] mg/100 ml	26
70	Hepatic	Fatty acids, esterified	5	3.59(2.53-4.94) mg/ml	4.26(3.04-6.40) mg/ml	11
71	Intestinal [8]	Fatty acids, esterified	4 [9]	4.29(3.27-5.50) mg/ml	4.26(3.04-6.40) mg/ml	11
72	Leg	Glucose	10	115(100-130) mg/100 ml	111(100-122) mg/100 ml	26
73	Renal	Glucose	5	28 mg/100 ml	109 mg/100 ml	56
74			9	93(70-115) mg/100 ml	104(70-135) mg/100 ml	30

Nitrogenous Substances

	Source of Lymph	Constituent or Property (Synonym)	No. of Subjects	Value — Lymph	Value — Plasma or Serum [1]	Reference
	Thoracic duct	Protein				
75		Total	2	3.08 g/100 ml	7.30 g/100 ml	16
76			6	3.23(2.61-3.85)[b] g/100 ml	5.91(4.93-6.89)[b] g/100 ml	43
77			4	3.44 ± 0.42 g/100 ml	5.65 ± 0.26 g/100 ml	10
78			19	4.29 g/100 ml	7.55 g/100 ml	39
79			6	3.67 g/100 ml	6.11 g/100 ml	22

[1] Unless otherwise indicated. [7] Plus/minus (±) value is standard deviation. [8] For additional information, consult reference 67. [9] Fasted. [10] In right atrium. [11] Arterial whole blood.

continued

Part II. Dog

	Source of Lymph	Constituent or Property (Synonym)	No. of Subjects	Value		Reference
				Lymph	Plasma or Serum	
80			9	3.92 g/100 ml	5.78 g/100 ml	48
81			4	3.93(3.17-4.82) g/100 ml	8.30(7.20-8.84) g/100 ml	13
82			11	4.00(1.92-5.58) g/100 ml	6.20(5.62-7.64) g/100 ml	17
83			5	4.3 ± 0.3 [7/](3.4-5.4) g/100 ml	5.6 ± 0.3 [7/](4.7-7.2) g/100 ml	5
84			4	4.75(3.9-5.5) g/100 ml	7.95(7.0-9.1) g/100 ml	28
85			20	4.88 g/100 ml	7.31 g/100 ml	50
86			14 [5/]	4.3 ± 0.3 [7/] g/100 ml	6.1 ± 0.6 [7/] g/100 ml	66
87			15 [12/]	4.0 ± 0.7 [7/] g/100 ml	5.6 ± 0.5 [7/] g/100 ml	66
88			5 [13/]	1.1 ± 0.8 [7/] g/100 ml	5.7 ± 0.5 [7/] g/100 ml	66
89		Albumin	6	2.04(1.66-2.42)[b] g/100 ml	3.33(2.61-4.05)[b] g/100 ml	43
90			4	2.11(1.54-2.66) g/100 ml	3.29(2.60-4.15) g/100 ml	28
91			4	2.38 ± 0.23(1.31-2.40)[b] g/100 ml	3.67 ± 0.23(1.86-5.25)[b] g/100 ml	10
92			11	2.46(1.21-3.39) g/100 ml	3.56(3.19-4.36) g/100 ml	17
93			7	3.44(1.99-4.54) g/100 ml	4.44(2.80-5.87) g/100 ml	20
94		Globulin	6	0.88(0.64-1.12)[b] g/100 ml	2.08(1.70-2.46)[b] g/100 ml	43
95			4	1.08 ± 0.21 g/100 ml	1.97 ± 0.26 g/100 ml	10
96			11	1.54(0.71-2.95) g/100 ml	2.63(1.91-4.45) g/100 ml	17
97		α_1-Globulin	4	0.39(0.31-0.51) g/100 ml	0.64(0.52-0.81) g/100 ml	28
98		α_2-Globulin	4	0.57(0.50-0.71) g/100 ml	1.13(0.91-1.50) g/100 ml	28
99		β-Globulin	4	1.01(0.82-1.16) g/100 ml	1.69(1.50-1.94) g/100 ml	28
100		γ-Globulin	4	0.68(0.42-0.91) g/100 ml	1.20(1.04-1.33) g/100 ml	28
101		Immunoglobulin A	3	0.42(0.25-0.57) mg/ml	0.25(0.06-0.46) mg/ml	59
102		Immunoglobulin G_{2ab}	3	6.09(3.94-8.10) mg/ml	10.55(7.14-12.60) mg/ml	59
103		Amino acids	1	2.4 mg/100 ml	....	46
		Coagulation factors Clotting time				
104		In glass	7	8(3-15) min	....	32
105		In silicone	6	83(25-180) min	....	32
106		Recalcified	6	57(21-85) s	....	32
107			28	139 ± 63.5 [7/] s	80 ± 29.7 [7/] s	33
108		One-stage prothrombin time	7	11.5(8.2-16.2) s	....	32
109			33	13.9 ± 2.8 [7/] s	16 ± 6.7 [7/] s	33
110		Partial thromboplastin time	7	36(21-60) s	....	32
111		Fibrinogen (Factor I)	14	46 ± 14.6(26-70)% of plasma activity	....	32
112		Fibrinogen A	40	0.16 ± 0.09 [7/] g/100 ml	0.42 ± 0.16 [7/] g/100 ml	33
113		Fibrinogen B	14	0.16 ± 0.10 [7/] g/100 ml	0.42 ± 0.13 [7/] g/100 ml	33
114		Prothrombin (Factor II)	15	45 ± 8.3(31-60)% of plasma activity	....	32
115		Factor VIII (Antihemophilic factor)	15	33 ± 14.1(12-60)% of plasma activity	....	32
116		Factor IX (Plasma thromboplastic component)	12	54 ± 13.1(33-74)% of plasma activity	....	32
117		Plasminogen	21	9 ± 3.9 [7/] units/ml	18 ± 3.8 [7/] units/ml	33
118		Euglobulin clot lysis time	17	294 ± 173 [7/] min	280 ± 170 [7/] min	33

[5/] Controls. [7/] Plus/minus (±) value is standard deviation. [12/] Subjects anesthetized with local anesthetic only. [13/] Subjects anesthetized with pentobarbital sodium.

continued

Part II. Dog

Source of Lymph	Constituent or Property (Synonym)	No. of Subjects	Value		Reference
			Lymph	Plasma or Serum	
119	Histamine	8 [9]	13.8(11.8-15.3) μg/100 g	11.7(7.0-18.0) μg/100 g	54
120		8 [14]	16.0(13.7-18.0) μg/100 g	16.8(8.4-25.8) μg/100 g	51
121	Nitrogen, non-protein	1	27.0 mg/100 ml	27.2 mg/100 ml	2
122		4	33.0 mg/100 ml	33.0 mg/100 ml	9
123		10	39.0(28-50)[b] mg/100 ml	40.0(26-56)[b] mg/100 ml	17
124 Lymphatics Cardiac	Protein, total	6	3.83(2.94-4.70) g/100 ml	5.94(4.67-8.31) g/100 ml	15
125		12	3.92 ± 0.07 g/100 ml	5.63 ± 0.07 g/100 ml	40
126		9	4.30 ± 0.23 g/100 ml	5.94 ± 0.22 g/100 ml	41
127		6 [5]	3.80 ± 0.17(3.3-4.3) g/100 ml	5.08 ± 0.28(3.8-5.8) g/100 ml	58
128		6 [6]	2.90 ± 0.38(1.5-4.4) g/100 ml	4.80 ± 0.59(3.7-7.6) g/100 ml	58
129	albumin	6	2.20(1.60-2.60) g/100 ml	2.98(2.37-3.56) g/100 ml	15
130	globulin	6	1.63(1.31-2.40) g/100 ml	2.96(1.86-5.25) g/100 ml	15
131 Cervical	Protein [15], total	11	2.16(1.22-3.80) g/100 ml	7.67(6.34-8.84) g/100 ml	13
132		4	2.57 ± 0.36 g/100 ml	5.65 ± 0.26 g/100 ml	10
133		16	3.22(1.38-4.57) g/100 ml	6.18(5.54-7.23) g/100 ml	24
134		8	3.5 ± 0.3 [7](2.4-4.8) g/100 ml	5.6 ± 0.3 [7](4.7-7.2) g/100 ml	5
135		13	3.63(2.58-4.97) g/100 ml	6.25(5.62-7.64) g/100 ml	17
136		11 [12]	2.50(1.81-4.25) g/100 ml	6.26(5.68-7.13) g/100 ml	47
137		11 [13]	2.66(1.94-4.27) g/100 ml	6.43(5.34-8.06) g/100 ml	47
138		11 [16]	2.74(1.63-4.64) g/100 ml	6.42(5.54-7.33) g/100 ml	47
139	albumin	4	1.72 ± 0.39 g/100 ml	3.67 ± 0.23 g/100 ml	10
140		13	2.36(1.69-3.52) g/100 ml	3.61(3.19-4.36) g/100 ml	17
141		3	2.60(2.14-3.41) g/100 ml	4.07(2.80-5.30) g/100 ml	20
142	globulin	4	0.85 ± 0.10 g/100 ml	1.97 ± 0.26 g/100 ml	10
143		13	1.26(0.85-2.30) g/100 ml	2.63(1.91-4.45) g/100 ml	17
144	Amino acids	1	4.84 mg/100 ml	4.90 mg/100 ml	24
145	Creatinine	7	1.40(1.28-1.49) mg/100 ml	1.37(1.22-1.54) mg/100 ml	24
146	Urea	7	23.5(19.8-33.0) mg/100 ml	21.7(17.9-28.0) mg/100 ml	24
147	Nitrogen, non-protein	10	34.8(19.8-45.4) mg/100 ml	32.6(21.1-46.0) mg/100 ml	24
148		8	37.4(24.2-50.6)[b] mg/100 ml	37.5(26-49)[b] mg/100 ml	17
149 Hepatic	Protein Total	2	3.95(3.51-4.38) g/100 ml	5.40(4.96-5.83) g/100 ml	23
150		5	4.23(3.58-5.00) g/100 ml	4.99(4.12-5.72) g/100 ml	11
151		13	4.39(4.07-4.71)[b] g/100 ml	5.67(5.25-6.09)[b] g/100 ml	43
152		8	4.9 ± 0.3 [7](4.4-6.2) g/100 ml	5.6 ± 0.3 [7](4.7-7.2) g/100 ml	5
153		3	5.40(4.45-6.20) g/100 ml	6.57(5.91-7.64) g/100 ml	17
154		14 [5]	5.5 ± 0.5 [7] g/100 ml	6.1 ± 0.6 [7] g/100 ml	66
155		15 [12]	5.0 ± 0.4 [7] g/100 ml	5.6 ± 0.5 [7] g/100 ml	66
156		6 [13]	4.7 ± 0.2 [7] g/100 ml	5.7 ± 0.5 [7] g/100 ml	66
157	Albumin	13	2.74(2.46-3.02)[b] g/100 ml	3.41(3.17-3.65)[b] g/100 ml	43
158		3	2.89(2.71-3.18) g/100 ml	3.40(3.19-3.55) g/100 ml	17
159		12	2.89(2.18-3.94) g/100 ml	3.49(2.70-4.67) g/100 ml	12
160		4	3.94(2.95-5.41) g/100 ml	4.54(3.21-5.87) g/100 ml	20
161	Globulin	13	1.28(1.10-1.46)[b] g/100 ml	1.80(1.62-1.98)[b] g/100 ml	43
162		3	2.51(1.74-3.42) g/100 ml	3.17(2.45-4.45) g/100 ml	17

[5] Controls. [6] Subjects with congestive heart failure. [7] Plus/minus (±) value is standard deviation. [9] Fasted. [12] Subjects anesthetized with local anesthetic only. [13] Subjects anesthetized with pentobarbital sodium. [14] Postprandial. [15] For information on lymph-plasma ratios of other proteins, consult reference 20. [16] Subjects anesthetized with diethyl ether.

continued

Part II. Dog

	Source of Lymph	Constituent or Property (Synonym)	No. of Subjects	Value		Reference
				Lymph	Plasma or Serum	
163		Immunoglobulin G	12	620(231-847) mg/100 ml	1023(440-1595) mg/100 ml	12
164		Immunoglobulin M	12	42.5(7.0-104.0) mg/100 ml	83.8(44.8-130.0) mg/100 ml	12
165		α_2-Macroglobulin	12	106(15-393) mg/100 ml	231(41-763) mg/100 ml	12
166		Orosomucoid	9	51.6(12.1-100.3) mg/100 ml	58.6(21.6-112.5) mg/100 ml	12
167		Transferrin	12	221(144-295) mg/100 ml	306(125-545) mg/100 ml	12
	Intestinal	Protein				
168		Total	10	2.79(1.17-4.42)[b] g/100 ml	5.67(4.27-7.07)[b] g/100 ml	43
169			10	2.97(1.67-4.55) g/100 ml	5.98(4.65-7.12) g/100 ml	63
170			2	3.36(3.21-3.51) g/100 ml	6.86(6.41-7.30) g/100 ml	23
171			2	3.98(3.89-4.08) g/100 ml	6.23(6.16-6.30) g/100 ml	17
172			4[9/]	2.94(2.36-3.55) g/100 ml	4.99(4.12-5.72) g/100 ml	11
173			14[5/]	4.3 ± 0.5 [7/] g/100 ml	6.1 ± 0.6 [7/] g/100 ml	66
174			15[17/]	3.1 ± 0.3 [7/] g/100 ml	5.6 ± 0.5 [7/] g/100 ml	66
175			5[18/]	0.7 ± 0.5 [7/] g/100 ml	5.7 ± 0.5 [7/] g/100 ml	66
176		Albumin	10	1.72(0.83-2.85) g/100 ml	3.18(2.50-4.39) g/100 ml	63
177			10	1.90(1.50-2.30)[b] g/100 ml	3.47(3.09-3.85)[b] g/100 ml	43
178			2	2.42(2.37-2.48) g/100 ml	3.67 g/100 ml	17
179			2	3.14(2.50-3.77) g/100 ml	5.64(5.41-5.87) g/100 ml	20
180		Globulin	10	0.64(0.48-0.80)[b] g/100 ml	1.62(1.34-1.90)[b] g/100 ml	43
181			10	1.25(0.84-1.85) g/100 ml	2.80(1.96-3.80) g/100 ml	63
182			2	1.56(1.52-1.60) g/100 ml	2.57 g/100 ml	17
183		Immunoglobulin A	5	59(33-99) mg/100 ml	25(5-47) mg/100 ml	59
184		Immunoglobulin G$_{2ab}$	5	704(605-946) mg/100 ml	1290(900-1930) mg/100 ml	59
185	Leg	Protein, total	6	1.08 g/100 ml	6.15 g/100 ml	48
186			4	1.41(0.70-1.86) g/100 ml	7.38 g/100 ml	13
187			11	1.70(1.0-2.4)[b] g/100 ml	5.50(4.0-7.0)[b] g/100 ml	9
188			5	1.8(1.2-2.2) g/100 ml	5.9(5.2-7.4) g/100 ml	29
189			8	1.91(1.11-2.53) g/100 ml	6.46(5.91-7.64) g/100 ml	17
190			7[19/]	1.25(0.66-1.89) g/100 ml	5.76(5.07-6.38) g/100 ml	62
191			5[13/]	2.06(0.74-3.45) g/100 ml	6.75(5.60-7.89) g/100 ml	62
192			8[20/]	0.20(0.04-0.22) g/100 ml	2.90(2.10-3.38) g/100 ml	62
193		albumin	8	1.20(0.76-1.63) g/100 ml	3.62(3.19-4.01) g/100 ml	17
194			8	1.32(0.81-2.85) g/100 ml	4.58(2.80-5.87) g/100 ml	20
195		globulin	8	0.71(0.35-1.12) g/100 ml	2.84(2.11-4.45) g/100 ml	17
196		Nitrogen, non-protein	11	26.7(20-34)[b] mg/100 ml	27.2(19-35)[b] mg/100 ml	9
197			1	37.3 mg/100 ml	36.0 mg/100 ml	17
198	Lung	Protein, total	18	3.66(2.81-4.65) g/100 ml	....	61
199		albumin	4	3.12(2.34-3.57) g/100 ml	4.44(3.21-5.30) g/100 ml	20
200	Renal	Protein, total	14	1.71(0.84-2.71) g/100 ml	5.04(4.59-6.50) g/100 ml	31
201			11	1.84(0.44-4.21) g/100 ml	5.8(5.18-6.88) g/100 ml	55
202			9	2.59(1.64-3.87) g/100 ml	5.94(4.51-7.65) g/100 ml	45
203			5	3.2(2.2-5.8) g/100 ml	6.4 g/100 ml	56
204			3	4.21(3.81-4.29) g/100 ml	6.14(5.82-6.41) g/100 ml	27
205			....	4.25 g/100 ml	....	57
206		Urea	5	46 mg/100 ml	33 mg/100 ml	56
207			11	69.7 mg/100 ml	53.1[21/]; 51.1[22/] mg /100 ml	55

[5/] Controls. [7/] Plus/minus (±) value is standard deviation.
[9/] Fasted. [13/] Subjects anesthetized with pentobarbital sodium. [17/] Chronic inferior vena cava constriction. [18/] Aorta-portal vein shunt with portal vein constriction. [19/] Subjects unanesthetized, walking. [20/] Edema produced by plasmapheresis and limitation of dietary protein. [21/] Arterial. [22/] Venous.

continued

Part II. Dog

	Source of Lymph	Constituent or Property (Synonym)	No. of Sub-jects	Value — Lymph	Value — Plasma or Serum [1]	Reference
208	Capsular	Protein, total	39	2.3(0.6-3.4) g/100 ml	6.4(3.9-8.6) g/100 ml	34
209			11	2.91(1.5-4.0) g/100 ml	5.83(4.6-6.8) g/100 ml	35, 36
210		albumin	11	0.58 g/100 ml	1.23 g/100 ml	36
211		α_1-globulin	11	0.30 g/100 ml	0.51 g/100 ml	36
212		α_2-globulin	11	0.37 g/100 ml	0.71 g/100 ml	36
213		β-globulin	11	1.12 g/100 ml	2.14 g/100 ml	36
214	Hilar	Protein, total	18	3.42 ± 0.42 [7] g/100 ml	5.81 ± 0.47 [7] g/100 ml	44
215		albumin	15	2.33 ± 0.44 [7] g/100 ml	3.59 ± 0.52 [7] g/100 ml	44
216		globulin, total	15	1.09 ± 0.47 [7] g/100 ml	2.28 ± 0.49 [7] g/100 ml	44
217		Urea	7	48(33-56) mg/100 ml	55(41-66) mg/100 ml	31
218	Right lymphatic duct	Protein, total	21	3.69(3.05-4.35)[b] g/100 ml	5.50(4.24-6.76)[b] g/100 ml	9
219		Nitrogen, non-protein	20	31.0(20.0-42.0)[b] mg/100 ml	30.0(18.5-41.5)[b] mg/100 ml	9
220	Splenic	Protein, total	7	3.88(2.34-4.73) g/100 ml	6.30(5.25-7.30) g/100 ml	23

Hormones & Enzymes

	Source of Lymph	Constituent or Property (Synonym)	No. of Sub-jects	Value — Lymph	Value — Plasma or Serum [1]	Reference
221	Thoracic duct	Corticosterone	8	8.9 ± 3.5 [7] µg/100 ml	6.0 ± 1.7 [7] µg/100 ml	54
222		Hydrocortisone	8	15.8 ± 10.4 [7] µg/100 ml	14.8 ± 6.0 [7] µg/100 ml	54
223		Diamine oxidase [1.4.3.6]	11	1.81 ± 0.54 µg histamine inactivated·ml lymph^{-1}·hr^{-1}	....	21
224		(Histaminase)	5	0.32(0.13-0.64) µg histamine inactivated·ml lymph^{-1}·hr^{-1}	<0.02 µg·ml^{-1}·hr^{-1}	6
225		Lipase [3.1.1.3]	12	0.83(0.20-1.81) units/ml	0.66(0.24-1.53) units/ml	60
226		Cholinesterase [3.1.1.8]	10	4.9(3.2-8.6) units	9.2(5.7-11.2) units	18
227			5	77 ± 13.5 [7] (44-113) units	117 ± 11.2 [7] (78-162) units	5
228		Amylase [3.2.1.1, 3.2.1.2]	12	44.7(11.92-109.0) units/ml	50.2(2.0-106.7) units/ml	60
229	Lymphatics Cervical	Cholinesterase [3.1.1.8]	9	2.2(1.1-4.8) units	9.2(5.7-11.2) units	18
230			8	35 ± 5.2 [7] (19-62) units	117 ± 11.2 [7] (78-162) units	5
231	Hepatic	Lipase [3.1.1.3]	19	2.4 ± 0.3 units/ml	1.2 ± 0.5 units/ml	52, 53
232		Amylase [3.2.1.1, 3.2.1.2]	19	72.2 ± 8.2 units/ml	31.9 ± 3.1 units/ml	52, 53
233	Intestinal	Lipase [3.1.1.3]	16	1.9 ± 0.2 units/ml	1.2 ± 0.5 units/ml	52, 53
234		Amylase [3.2.1.1, 3.2.1.2]	16	60.3 ± 8.7 units/ml	31.9 ± 3.1 units/ml	52, 53
235	Leg	Peptidyl dipeptidase (Kininase II) [3.4.15.1]	5	14(12-16) min [23]	7(6-8) min [23]	29

Other Properties

	Source of Lymph	Constituent or Property (Synonym)	No. of Sub-jects	Value — Lymph	Value — Plasma or Serum [1]	Reference
236	Thoracic duct	Oxygen pressure	22	31.1 mm Hg	38.1 mm Hg [24]	42
237			15	34 ± 20 [7] mm Hg	75 ± 20 [7,11] mm Hg	49
238			8	44 ± 8 [7] mm Hg	101 ± 9 [7,11]; 59 ± 10 [7,24] mm Hg	8
239			5	45 mm Hg	63 [21]; 25 [10] mm Hg	4

[1] Unless otherwise indicated. [7] Plus/minus (±) value is standard deviation. [10] In right atrium. [11] Arterial whole blood. [21] Arterial. [23] Inactivation time of bradykinin. [24] Venous whole blood.

continued

Part II. Dog

	Source of Lymph	Constituent or Property (Synonym)	No. of Sub-jects	Value Lymph	Value Plasma or Serum [1]	Ref-er-ence
240			15	47 mm Hg	74 [21]; 34 [10]; 37 [25]; 39 [26] mm Hg	65
241			6 [2]	8(4-12) mm Hg	87(67-100) mm Hg [11]	3
242			6 [3]	10(3-14) mm Hg	86(74-100) mm Hg [11]	3
243			22 [27]	53(43-66) mm Hg	93(75-110) mm Hg [11]	64
244			3 [28]	125 mm Hg	575 mm Hg [11]	64
245		Carbon dioxide pressure	10	29(22-34) mm Hg	24(22-27) mm Hg	64
246			6	81(63-102) mm Hg	50(33-64) mm Hg	7
247			6 [2]	53(48-59) mm Hg	44(37-50) mm Hg [11]	3
248			6 [3]	42(28-55) mm Hg	32(22-44) mm Hg [11]	3
249		pH	6	7.09(6.91-7.21)	7.26(7.17-7.35)	7
250			10 [27]	7.42(7.39-7.46)	7.46(7.42-7.52)	64
251			6 [2]	7.27(7.22-7.30)	7.34(7.31-7.36)	3
252			6 [3]	7.34(7.27-7.40)	7.41(7.34-7.47)	3
253	Lymphatics Cervical	Oxygen pressure	1	7 mm Hg	22 mm Hg [11]	3
254		Carbon dioxide pressure	10	40.3(31.3-49.3)[b] mm Hg	46.4(29.4-63.4)[b] mm Hg	25
255		pH	10	7.41(7.33-7.49)[b]	7.34(7.25-7.43)[b]	25
256	Leg	Oxygen pressure	2	(5-12) mm Hg	(26-30) mm Hg [11]	3
257	Renal Capsular	Oxygen pressure	7	78 ± 6 mm Hg	104 ± 5 [21]; 60 ± 8 [22] mm Hg	8
258	Hilar	Oxygen pressure	6	60 ± 8 mm Hg	109 ± 8 [21]; 54 ± 6 [22] mm Hg	8
259		pH	5	7.45(7.34-7.54)	7.45(7.42-7.47)	31
260		Osmolality	13	289(282-312) mosmoles/kg	296(283-312) mosmoles/kg	31
261	Right lym-phatic duct	Oxygen pressure	15	75 ± 18 [7] mm Hg	75 ± 20 [7] mm Hg	49

[1] Unless otherwise indicated. [2] Volume of expired air = 100-200 ml·min⁻¹·kg body wt⁻¹. [3] Volume of expired air = 200-300 ml·min⁻¹·kg body wt⁻¹. [7] Plus/minus (±) value is standard deviation. [10] In right atrium. [11] Arterial whole blood. [21] Arterial. [22] Venous. [25] In hepatic vein. [26] In portal vein. [27] Subjects breathing air. [28] Subjects breathing 100% oxygen.

Contributors: Courtice, F. C.; Heath, Trevor J., and Reynolds, John D.

References

[1] Areskog, N. H., et al. 1965. Biochem. Pharmacol. 14:783.

[2] Arnold, R. M., and L. B. Mendel. 1927. J. Biol. Chem. 72:189.

[3] Bergofsky, E. H., et al. 1962. J. Clin. Invest. 41:1971.

[4] Bergofsky, E. H., et al. 1964. J. Amer. Med. Ass. 189:841.

[5] Brauer, R. W., and E. Hardenbergh. 1947. Amer. J. Physiol. 150:746.

[6] Carlsten, A. 1950. Acta Physiol. Scand. 20(Suppl. 70):5.

[7] Carlsten, A., and B. Söderholm. 1960. Ibid. 48:29.

[8] Cockett, A. T. K. 1967. Invest. Urol. 5:260.

[9] Courtice, F. C. Unpublished. Australian National University, John Curtin School of Medical Research, Canberra, 1971.

[10] Courtice, F. C., and B. Morris. 1955. Quart. J. Exp. Physiol. Cog. Med. Sci. 40:138.

[11] Coxon, R. V., and D. S. Robinson. 1962. Ibid. 47:252.

[12] Dive, C. C., et al. 1971. Lymphology 4:133.

[13] Drinker, C. K., and M. E. Field. 1931. Amer. J. Physiol. 97:32.

[14] Drinker, C. K., and J. M. Yoffey. 1941. Lymphatics, Lymph and Lymphoid Tissue. Harvard Univ. Press, Cambridge.

[15] Drinker, C. K., et al. 1940. Amer. J. Physiol. 130:43.

[16] Field, M. E., and C. K. Drinker. 1931. Ibid. 98:378.

[17] Field, M. E., et al. 1934. Ibid. 110:174.

[18] Friend, D. G., and O. Krayer. 1941. J. Pharmacol. Exp. Ther. 71:246.

continued

Part II. Dog

[19] Furneaux, R. W., and J. M. Ham. 1970. Experientia 26:272.

[20] Ganrot, P. O., et al. 1970. Acta Physiol. Scand. 79:280.

[21] Gesler, R. M., et al. 1956. J. Pharmacol. Exp. Ther. 116:356.

[22] Glenn, W. W. L., et al. 1949. Surg. Gynecol. Obstet. 89:200.

[23] Hatta, H., et al. 1955. Jap. J. Physiol. 5:208.

[24] Heim, J. W. 1933. Amer. J. Physiol. 103:553.

[25] Heim, J. W., and O. C. Leigh. 1935. Ibid. 112:699.

[26] Heim, J. W., et al. 1935. Ibid. 113:548.

[27] Henry, L. P., et al. 1969. Ibid. 217:411.

[28] Ismail, A. A., et al. 1967. Ibid. 213:1391.

[29] Jacobsen, S. 1966. Brit. J. Pharmacol. 27:213.

[30] Kaplan, A., et al. 1942. Amer. J. Physiol. 138:553.

[31] Keyl, M. J., et al. 1965. Ibid. 209:1031.

[32] Langdell, R. D., et al. 1960. Ibid. 199:626.

[33] Leandoer, L., et al. 1968. Thromb. Diath. Haemorrh. 19:127.

[34] Lebrie, S. J. 1968. Amer. J. Physiol. 215:116.

[35] Lebrie, S. J., and H. S. Mayerson. 1959. Proc. Soc. Exp. Biol. Med. 100:378.

[36] Lebrie, S. J., and H. S. Mayerson. 1960. Amer. J. Physiol. 198:1037.

[37] Manery, J. F. 1954. Physiol. Rev. 34:352.

[38] Marble, A., et al. 1934. Amer. J. Physiol. 109:467.

[39] Meyer-Bisch, R., and F. Gunther. 1925. Pfluegers Arch. Gesamte Physiol. Menschen Tiere 209:81, 92, 107.

[40] Miller, A. J., et al. 1964. Amer. J. Physiol. 206:63.

[41] Miller, A. J., et al. 1964. Proc. Soc. Exp. Biol. Med. 116:392.

[42] Nagy, S., et al. 1969. Acta Physiol. 35:87.

[43] Nix, J. T., et al. 1951. Amer. J. Physiol. 164:119.

[44] O'Morchoe, C. C. C., et al. 1970. Circ. Res. 26:469.

[45] Papp, M. 1963. Acta Med. (Budapest) 19:127.

[46] Peterson, W. H., and T. P. Hughes. 1925. J. Biol. Chem. 66:229.

[47] Polderman, H., et al. 1943. J. Pharmacol. Exp. Ther. 78:400.

[48] Rényi-Vámos, F. 1967. In I. Rusznyak, et al. Lymphatics and Lymph Circulation. Pergamon Press, London. p. 576.

[49] Said, S. I., et al. 1965. Proc. Soc. Exp. Biol. Med. 119:12.

[50] Saito, H., and F. Nakazawa. 1932. Tohoku J. Exp. Med. 19:233.

[51] Schmidt, N., and G. F. Bonder. 1965. Surg. Forum 16:333.

[52] Singh, H., et al. 1969. Ann. Surg. 169:233.

[53] Singh, H., et al. 1969. Arch. Surg. (Chicago) 99:80.

[54] Stark, E., et al. 1962. Acta Physiol. 21:347.

[55] Sugarman, J., et al. 1942. Amer. J. Physiol. 138:108.

[56] Swann, H. G., et al. 1958. Proc. Soc. Exp. Biol. Med. 97:517.

[57] Tormene, A., et al. 1963. Urol. Int. 16:341.

[58] Uhley, H. N., et al. 1969. Proc. Soc. Exp. Biol. Med. 131:379.

[59] Vaerman, J. P., and J. F. Heremans. 1970. Immunology 18:27.

[60] Vega, R. E., et al. 1967. Ann. Surg. 166:995.

[61] Warren, M. F., and C. K. Drinker. 1942. Amer. J. Physiol. 136:207.

[62] Weech, A. A., et al. 1934. J. Exp. Med. 60:63.

[63] Wells, H. S. 1932. Amer. J. Physiol. 101:421.

[64] Witte, C. L., et al. 1967. Ann. Surg. 166:254.

[65] Witte, C. L., et al. 1968. Lymphology 1:109.

[66] Witte, C. L., et al. 1969. Ann. Surg. 170:1002.

[67] Yoffey, J. M., and F. C. Courtice. 1970. Lymphatics, Lymph and the Lymphomyeloid Complex. Academic Press, London and New York.

Part III. Domestic and Laboratory Mammals Other Than Dog

Source of Lymph: RLD = right lymph duct; TD = thoracic duct. **Constituent or Property:** TIBC = total iron-binding capacity. Enzyme values are in units (for a definition of "unit," consult reference); relationships between levels of activity in lymph and plasma are true, regardless of differences in "unit" definitions. Plus/minus (±) values are standard error unless otherwise indicated. Values in parentheses are ranges, estimate "c" unless otherwise indicated (*see* Introduction).

	Animal	Source of Lymph	No. of Subjects	Constituent or Property (Synonym)	Value Lymph	Value Plasma or Serum	Reference
				Electrolytes			
1	Cat	Leg lymphatics	7	Potassium, meq/liter	2.79 ± 0.31	3.33 ± 0.23	49
2			3	Potassium, meq/liter	3.50 ± 0.25	3.87 ± 0.17	
3			4	Potassium, meq/liter	3.90 ± 0.50	3.70 ± 0.40	
4	Cattle Non-lactating	Mammary gland lymphatics	3	Calcium, meq/liter	3.73(3.70-3.80)	4.33(4.20-4.60)	47
5			3	Magnesium, meq/liter	1.50(1.30-1.60)	1.70(1.60-1.80)	
6			3	Potassium, meq/liter	4.06(3.92-4.30)	3.87(3.80-3.92)	

continued

Part III. Domestic and Laboratory Mammals Other Than Dog

	Animal	Source of Lymph	No. of Sub-jects	Constituent or Property (Synonym)	Value		Ref-er-ence
					Lymph	Plasma or Serum	
7			3	Sodium, meq/liter	145(139-148)	142(138-148)	
8	Lactat-ing	Mammary gland lym-phatics	8	Bicarbonate, meq/liter	21.9 ± 3.9[1](16.0-28.7)	25.9 ± 3.9[1](19.9-31.0)	36
9			3	Calcium, meq/liter	3.03(2.30-3.60)	4.00(3.50-4.60)	47
10			8	Calcium, meq/liter	3.8 ± 0.5[1](3.2-4.8)	4.4 ± 0.3[1](3.8-4.8)	36
11			8	Chloride, meq/liter	109 ± 5.3[1](104-118)	101 ± 5.6[1](94-112)	36
12			10[2]	Iodine, total, μg/100 ml	2.93 ± 1.54[1]	4.16 ± 1.57[1]	35
13			10[2]	Iodine, inorganic, μg/100 ml	0.78 ± 0.81[1]	0.75 ± 0.63[1]	35
14			10[2]	Iodine, protein-bound, μg/100 ml	2.15 ± 0.87[1]	3.41 ± 1.03[1]	35
15			3	Magnesium, meq/liter	1.53(1.30-1.70)	1.77(1.60-2.00)	47
16			8	Magnesium, meq/liter	2.0 ± 0.4[1](1.6-2.6)	1.7 ± 0.3[1](1.3-2.2)	36
17			8	Phosphorus, inorganic, meq/liter	3.0 ± 0.6[1](2.1-3.8)	2.5 ± 0.6[1](1.7-3.2)	36
18			11	Phosphorus, inorganic, mg/100 ml	6.0(3.9-9.3)	5.1(3.1-7.4)	37
19			3	Potassium, meq/liter	3.90(3.75-4.10)	3.92(3.90-3.95)	47
20			8	Potassium, meq/liter	8.3 ± 1.9[1](6.5-12.5)	3.9 ± 0.3[1](3.6-4.5)	36
21			8	Sodium, meq/liter	146 ± 5.0[1](139-154)	143 ± 6.3[1](135-150)	36
22			3	Sodium, meq/liter	146(142-150)	148(139-152)	47
23	Goat, lac-tating	Mammary gland lym-phatics	4	Bicarbonate, meq/liter	25.6(23.6-27.6)	24.1 ± 0.5[3]; 26.1 ± 0.6[4]	53
24			4	Bicarbonate, meq/liter	26 ± 1[1]	25 ± 1[1]	67
25			4	Calcium, meq/liter	2.77(2.61-3.09)	4.38 ± 0.21	53
26			11	Calcium, meq/liter	4.1 ± 0.4[1]	4.6 ± 0.2[1]	67
27			11	Chloride, meq/liter	111 ± 5[1]	107 ± 4[1]	67
28			4	Chloride, meq/liter	116.6(112.9-120.4)	109.3 ± 0.8	53
29			2	Magnesium, meq/liter	1.4 ± 0.1[1]	1.9 ± 0.2[1]	67
30			4	Magnesium, meq/liter	2.07(1.88-2.33)	2.29 ± 0.33	53
31			4	Phosphorus, inorganic, meq/liter	2.17(1.90-3.25)	3.50 ± 0.22	53
32			4	Potassium, meq/liter	4.60(4.47-4.80)	4.23 ± 0.08	53
33			9	Potassium, meq/liter	4.9 ± 0.4[1]	4.5 ± 0.3[1]	67
34			9	Sodium, meq/liter	146 ± 4[1]	146 ± 3[1]	67
35			4	Sodium, meq/liter	150(148-151)	153 ± 1.3	53
36	Rabbit	Thoracic duct	4	Iron, μg/100 ml	89.7 ± 7.6	200.0 ± 23.8	57
37			4	TIBC, μg/100 ml	195.6 ± 18.8	391.3 ± 23.9	
38			4	Saturation of TIBC, %	46.8 ± 4.0	50.4 ± 6.2	
39		Leg lym-phatics	6	Iron, μg/100 ml	86.5 ± 14.3	204.7 ± 21.5	
40			6	TIBC, μg/100 ml	147.5 ± 20.9	339.3 ± 12.1	
41			6	Saturation of TIBC, %	58.2 ± 5.48	60.2 ± 5.01	
42	Rat	Thoracic duct	14	Calcium, meq/liter	5.9	7.4	81
43			7[5,6]	Calcium, meq/liter	5.4 ± 0.3	5.6 ± 0.2	44
44			7[5,6]	Chloride, meq/liter	103 ± 2	101 ± 2	44
45			7[5,6]	Magnesium, meq/liter	$1.7 \pm <0.1$	$1.7 \pm <0.1$	44
46			14	Potassium, meq/liter	5.1	4.9	81
47			7[5,6]	Potassium, meq/liter	5.2 ± 0.2	5.4 ± 0.2	44
48			14	Sodium, meq/liter	158	154	81
49			7[5,6]	Sodium, meq/liter	145 ± 2	145 ± 1	44
50	Sheep	Renal lym-phatics	14	Calcium, mg/100 ml	8.1 ± 0.09	9.4 ± 0.07	56
51			12	Magnesium, meq/liter	1.2 ± 0.02	1.5 ± 0.02	
52			13	Potassium, meq/liter	4.0 ± 0.04	4.3 ± 0.03	
53			13	Sodium, meq/liter	148.8 ± 1.3	144.8 ± 0.9	

[1] Plus/minus ($\pm$) value is standard deviation. [2] Samples taken after slaughter. [3] Arterial. [4] In mammary vein. [5] Fasted. [6] Anesthetized.

continued

Part III. Domestic and Laboratory Mammals Other Than Dog

	Animal	Source of Lymph	No. of Sub-jects	Constituent or Property (Synonym)	Value		Ref-er-ence
					Lymph	Plasma or Serum	
54		Testicular	6	Bicarbonate, meq/liter	28.6 ± 0.70	26.2 ± 0.42	82
55		lympha-	11	Calcium, meq/liter	4.33 ± 0.37	4.76 ± 0.17	
56		tics	12	Chloride, meq/liter	111.3 ± 1.80	107.8 ± 1.10	
57			11	Magnesium, meq/liter	1.50 ± 0.04	1.69 ± 0.06	
58			17	Phosphorus, inorganic, meq/liter	3.19 ± 0.26	2.99 ± 0.26	
59			11	Potassium, meq/liter	3.79 ± 0.10	3.80 ± 0.14	
60			11	Sodium, meq/liter	144.4 ± 1.9	144.3 ± 1.5	
61	Non-lac-tating	Mammary gland lym-phatics	4	Calcium, meq/liter	4.3(4.0-4.5)	4.8(4.6-5.6)	45
62			4	Chloride, meq/liter	115(113-116)	111(108-112)	
63			4	Magnesium, meq/liter	1.8(1.1-2.1)	2.3(1.4-2.5)	
64			4	Phosphorus, inorganic, meq/liter	2.8(2.4-3.0)	2.8(2.5-3.3)	
65			4	Potassium, meq/liter	4.4(4.2-4.6)	4.6(4.4-4.9)	
66			4	Sodium, meq/liter	141(140-145)	144(142-145)	
67	Lactat-ing	Mammary gland lym-phatics	4	Calcium, meq/liter	3.6(3.1-4.1)	4.4(4.1-4.7)	45
68			4	Chloride, meq/liter	114(111-116)	110(102-114)	
69			4	Magnesium, meq/liter	1.5(1.3-1.8)	1.7(1.4-2.0)	
70			4	Phosphorus, inorganic, meq/liter	3.2(2.6-4.4)	3.2(3.0-3.6)	
71			4	Potassium, meq/liter	4.3(4.0-4.7)	4.4(4.2-4.6)	
72			4	Sodium, meq/liter	144(140-146)	145(142-148)	
				Lipids			
73	Cat	Thoracic	20	Fatty acids, total, meq/liter	13.1 ± 1.9	14.0 ± 0.2	12
74		duct	20	Phospholipid, mg/100 ml	233 ± 15	400 ± 10	
75			20	Cholesterol, total, mg/100 ml	43.6 ± 3.3	98.4 ± 7.3	
76		Lymphatics Cervical	20	Fatty acids, total, meq/liter	5.2 ± 0.9	10.8 ± 0.9	12
77			20	Phospholipid, mg/100 ml	97.5 ± 20.0	193 ± 7.5	
78			20	Cholesterol, total, mg/100 ml	35.0 ± 6.4	98.4 ± 7.3	
79		Hepatic	9	Fatty acids, total, meq/liter	7.01	7.06	58
80			18	Phospholipid, mg/100 ml	173	200	59
81			18	Cholesterol, total, mg/100 ml	100	118	59
82		Intestinal	10	Fatty acids, total, meq/liter	6.9 ± 0.3	7.8 ± 0.3	59
83			10	Phospholipid, mg/100 ml	166 ± 8	208 ± 11	
84			10	Cholesterol, total, mg/100 ml	62 ± 4.6	122 ± 6.9	
85		Leg	5	Phospholipid, mg/100 ml	62(49-80)	198(125-308)	8
86			5	Cholesterol, total, mg/100 ml	34(14-52)	147(64-347)	
87	Cattle	Thoracic	3	Total lipid, mg/100 ml	1137(911-1315)	353(271-437)	28
88		duct	3	Fatty acids, free, mg/100 ml	16(13-18)	7(3-12)	28
89			1[6]	Fatty acids, free[7], mg/100 ml	26.2	31.6	48
90			3	Fatty acids, esterified, mg/100 ml	980(807-1111)	187(154-250)	28
91			3	Triglycerides, mg/100 ml	777(580-919)	7(7-9)	28
92			1[6]	Triglycerides[7], mg/100 ml	369.2	12.2	48
93			3	Neutral lipid, mg/100 ml	803(624-927)	75(44-110)	28
94			3	Phospholipid, mg/100 ml	226(182-263)	163(123-202)	28
95			1[6]	Phospholipid[7], mg/100	82.7	78.5	48
96			3	Cholesterol, free, mg/100 ml	21(19-22)	16(9-24)	28
97			1[6]	Cholesterol, free, mg/100 ml	13.5	17.5	48
98			3	Cholesterol esters, mg/100 ml	88(81-99)	155(116-194)	28
99			1[6]	Cholesterol esters[7], mg/100 ml	48.1	106.5	48

[6] Anesthetized. [7] For percentage fatty acid composition, consult the reference.

continued

Part III. Domestic and Laboratory Mammals Other Than Dog

	Animal	Source of Lymph	No. of Subjects	Constituent or Property (Synonym)	Value		Reference
					Lymph	Plasma or Serum	
100		Lymphatics Hepatic	2	Total lipid, mg/100 ml	248(227-268)	283(275-291)	73
101			2	Fatty acids, free, mg/100 ml	10(9-11)	6(4-8)	
102			2	Triglycerides, mg/100 ml	110(90-130)	33(31-35)	
103			2	Phospholipid, mg/100 ml	68(60-76)	124(122-125)	
104			2	Cholesterol, free, mg/100 ml	9(8-10)	14(14-14)	
105			2	Cholesterol esters, mg/100 ml	38(37-39)	82(73-91)	
106		Intestinal	2	Total lipid, mg/100 ml	3437(3330-3545)	317(277-356)	73
107			2	Fatty acids, free, mg/100 ml	17(15-19)	9(7-10)	73
108			2	Triglycerides, mg/100 ml	2515(2465-2565)	22(19-25)	73
109			1[6]	Triglycerides[7], mg/100 ml	1536	14.3	48
110			2	Phospholipid, mg/100 ml	265(218-312)	127(105-148)	73
111			1[6]	Phospholipid[7], mg/100 ml	230.5	84.1	48
112			2	Cholesterol, free, mg/100 ml	23(20-26)	17(14-20)	73
113			1	Cholesterol, free, mg/100 ml	41.6	31.7	48
114			2	Cholesterol esters, mg/100 ml	57(56-57)	116(92-140)	73
115			1[6]	Cholesterol esters[7], mg/100 ml	119	192	48
116		Leg	1	Fatty acids, free[7], mg/100 ml	9.3	12.3	48
117			1[6]	Fatty acids, free[7], mg/100 ml	7.7	31.6	
118			1	Triglycerides[7], mg/100 ml	3	10.2	
119			1[6]	Triglycerides[7], mg/100 ml	4.4	12.2	
120			1	Phospholipid[7], mg/100 ml	50.9	174.8	
121			1[6]	Phospholipid[7], mg/100 ml	12.4	78.5	
122			1	Cholesterol, free, mg/100 ml	18.8	46	
123			1[6]	Cholesterol, free, mg/100 ml	5	17.5	
124			1	Cholesterol esters[7], mg/100 ml	61.3	204	
125			1[6]	Cholesterol esters[7], mg/100 ml	19.6	106.5	
126	Non-lactating	Mammary gland lymphatics	3	Fatty acids, free, mg/100 ml	11.9(6.4-16.0)	12.0(8.6-16.8)	47
127			3	Fatty acids, esterified, mg/100 ml	65(57-70)	140(132-149)	
128			3	Phospholipid, mg/100 ml	68(60-74)	156(127-199)	
129			3	Cholesterol, total, mg/100 ml	111(95-121)	238(230-248)	
130	Lactating	Mammary gland lymphatics	10	Fatty acids, total, mg/100 ml	35.3 ± 12.9[1]	173.9 ± 48.0[1]	34
131			3	Fatty acids, free, mg/100 ml	6.1(5.0-6.7)	11.0(7.9-15.9)	47
132			3	Fatty acids, esterified, mg/100 ml	39(28-48)	134(86-206)	47
133			10	Glycerides, mg/100 ml	1.4 ± 0.7[1]	4.9 ± 1.4[1]	34
134			10	Glycerides, mg/100 ml	14.3 ± 20.0[1]	36.1 ± 19.8[1]	32
135			10	Phospholipid, total, mg/100 ml	28.0 ± 28.7[1]	143.3 ± 44.6[1]	32
136			10	Phospholipid, total, mg/100 ml	29.3 ± 12.6[1]	170.1 ± 51.9[1]	34
137			3	Phospholipid, total, mg/100 ml	69(51-89)	164(141-207)	47
138			10	Phosphatidyl choline (Lecithin), mg/100 ml	21.8 ± 10.3[1]	134.6 ± 43.9[1]	34
139			10	Phosphatidyl ethanolamine (Cephalin), mg/100 ml	2.3 ± 1.0[1]	14.2 ± 3.8[1]	34
140			10	Sphingomyelin, mg/100 ml	5.2 ± 2.8[1]	21.3 ± 10.7[1]	34
141			10	Cholesterol, total, mg/100 ml	28.3 ± 20.5[1]	113.7 ± 44.9[1]	32
142			3	Cholesterol, total, mg/100 ml	78(48-118)	229(152-320)	47
143			10	Cholesterol, free, mg/100 ml	6.5 ± 2.5[1]	26.2 ± 4.5[1]	32

[1] Plus/minus (±) value is standard deviation. [6] Anesthetized. [7] For percentage fatty acid composition, consult the reference.

continued

Part III. Domestic and Laboratory Mammals Other Than Dog

| | Animal | Source of Lymph | No. of Subjects | Constituent or Property (Synonym) | Value | | Reference |
					Lymph	Plasma or Serum	
144			10	Cholesterol, free, mg/100 ml	6.9 ± 2.8 [1]	32.3 ± 11.4 [1]	34
145			10	Cholesterol esters, mg/100 ml	15.6 ± 10.6 [1]	63.4 ± 26.9 [1]	32
146			10	Cholesterol esters, mg/100 ml	37.5 ± 12.4 [1]	142.4 ± 41.6 [1]	34
147	Calves	Thoracic duct	15 [8]	Total lipid, mg/100 ml	1450 ± 120	....	69
148			15 [9]	Total lipid, mg/100 ml	500 ± 100	....	
149		Intestinal lymphatics	15 [8]	Total lipid, mg/100 ml	3140 ± 130	....	
150			15 [9]	Total lipid, mg/100 ml	790 ± 160	....	
151	New-born	Thoracic duct	6 [10]	Total lipid, mg/100 ml	359 ± 78	....	75
152			4 [11]	Total lipid, mg/100 ml	1063 ± 177	....	
153			6 [10]	Fatty acids, free, mg/100 ml	23 ± 3	....	
154			4 [11]	Fatty acids, free, mg/100 ml	18 ± 2	....	
155			6 [10]	Triglycerides, mg/100 ml	194	54	
156			4 [11]	Triglycerides, mg/100 ml	794	143	
157			6 [10]	Phospholipid, mg/100 ml	92 ± 17	....	
158			4 [11]	Phospholipid, mg/100 ml	150 ± 14	....	
159			6 [10]	Cholesterol, free, mg/100 ml	9 ± 2	....	
160			4 [11]	Cholesterol, free, mg/100 ml	8 ± 1	....	
161			6 [10]	Cholesterol esters, mg/100 ml	9 ± 1	....	
162			4 [11]	Cholesterol esters, mg/100 ml	14 ± 2	....	
163		Lymphatics Hepatic	2 [10]	Fatty acids, esterified, mg/100 ml	80 ± 19	77	46
164			1 [6,10]	Fatty acids, esterified, mg/100 ml	20	31	
165			3 [6,10]	Fatty acids, esterified, mg/100 ml	74 ± 11	72 ± 7	
166			3 [10]	Phospholipid, mg/100 ml	28 ± 7	49 ± 9	
167			2 [10]	Phospholipid, mg/100 ml	30 ± 7	44	
168		Intestinal	2 [10]	Fatty acids, free, mg/100 ml	16 ± 6	14	
169			2 [6,10]	Fatty acids, free, mg/100 ml	27 ± 6	22	
170			3 [10]	Fatty acids, esterified, mg/100 ml	357 ± 120	58 ± 5	
171			4 [6,10]	Fatty acids, esterified, mg/100 ml	539 ± 132	63 ± 9	
172			3 [10]	Phospholipids, mg/100 ml	98 ± 22	29 ± 3	
173			4 [6,10]	Phospholipid, mg/100 ml	164 ± 35	38 ± 6	
174	1- to 3-wk-old	Thoracic duct	3 [12]	Total lipid, mg/100 ml	2171	....	72
175			3 [13]	Total lipid, mg/100 ml	2966		
176			3 [12]	Fatty acids, mg/100 ml	18		
177			3 [13]	Fatty acids, mg/100 ml	25.5		
178			3 [12]	Triglycerides, mg/100 ml	1820		
179			3 [13]	Triglycerides, mg/100 ml	2396		
180			3 [12]	Phospholipid, mg/100 ml	260		
181			3 [13]	Phospholipid, mg/100 ml	300		
182			3 [12]	Cholesterol, free, mg/100 ml	15.8		
183			3 [13]	Cholesterol, free, mg/100 ml	21.7		
184			3 [12]	Cholesterol esters, mg/100 ml	34		
185			3 [13]	Cholesterol esters, mg/100 ml	46.6		

[1] Plus/minus (±) value is standard deviation. [6] Anesthetized. [8] Milk-fed. [9] Fed grain and hay. [10] Before suckling or first feed. [11] 24-32 hr after first feed. [12] Before feeding. [13] Fed whole milk.

continued

Part III. Domestic and Laboratory Mammals Other Than Dog

	Animal	Source of Lymph	No. of Subjects	Constituent or Property (Synonym)	Value		Reference
					Lymph	Plasma or Serum	
186	Goat, lactating	Mammary gland lymphatics	4	Fatty acids, volatile, meq/liter	0.77(0.68-0.91)	1.43 ± 0.1 [3]; 0.36 ± 0.1 [4]	53
187	Rabbit	Thoracic duct	7 [5]	Fatty acids, free [7], mg/100 ml	21.9 ± 2.2	15.1 ± 3.2	43
188			10 [14]	Fatty acids, esterified, meq/liter	13.8 ± 2.1	11.4 ± 2.0	60
189			7 [5]	Triglycerides [7], mg/100 ml	100.9 ± 10.5	49.0 ± 5.3	43
190			10 [14]	Phospholipid, mg/100 ml	107 ± 13.8	105 ± 18.0	60
191			7 [5]	Phospholipid [7], mg/100 ml	44.2 ± 9.1	31.2 ± 6.5	43
192			10 [14]	Cholesterol, total, mg/100 ml	43 ± 4.8	46 ± 8.8	60
193			7 [5]	Cholesterol, free, mg/100 ml	13.7 ± 2.5	11.0 ± 1.2	43
194			7 [5]	Cholesterol esters [7], mg/100 ml	40.5 ± 2.4	31.5 ± 4.0	43
195		Lymphatics Hepatic	11	Phospholipid, mg/100 ml	109 ± 6	153 ± 13	9
196			19 [15]	Phospholipid, mg/100 ml	242 ± 24	511 ± 37	
197			11	Cholesterol, total, mg/100 ml	79 ± 11	130 ± 18	
198			19 [15]	Cholesterol, total, mg/100 ml	430 ± 71	1153 ± 143	
199		Leg	6	Phospholipid, mg/100 ml	47 ± 4	143 ± 16	10
200			9 [15]	Phospholipid, mg/100 ml	83 ± 10	407 ± 36	10
201			24 [15]	Phospholipid, mg/100 ml	75 ± 7	434 ± 36	14
202			6	Cholesterol, total, mg/100 ml	35 ± 6	149 ± 22	10
203			9 [15]	Cholesterol, total, mg/100 ml	98 ± 11	798 ± 117	10
204			24 [15]	Cholesterol, total, mg/100 ml	103 ± 14	879 ± 100	14
205	Rat	Thoracic duct	5	Fatty acids, meq/liter	9.6	10.4	58
206			4	Fatty acids, mg/100 ml	(742-1460)	....	3
207			6 [5,6]	Fatty acids, free [7], mg/100 ml	39.9	23.1	44
208			4 [5]	Fatty acids, esterified, μeq/ml	11.75 ± 1.24	....	76
209			6 [5,6]	Triglycerides [7], mg/100 ml	273.2	74.3	44
210			5	Phospholipid, mg/100 ml	203	138	58
211			6 [5,6]	Phospholipid [7], mg/100 ml	86.5	70.6	44
212			4	Cholesterol, total, mg/100 ml	(23.3-62.4)	....	3
213			5	Cholesterol, total, mg/100 ml	72	51	58
214			6 [5,6]	Cholesterol, total, mg/100 ml	37.8 ± 5.3	50 ± 10.5	44
215			6 [5,6]	Cholesterol, free, mg/100 ml	9.2 ± 1.5	8.2 ± 1.7	44
216			6 [5,6]	Cholesterol esters [7], mg/100 ml	28.7 ± 4.5	41.8 ± 9.5	44
217		Lymphatics Hepatic	7	Total lipid, mg/100 ml	240(148-399)	267(202-290)	26
218			4	Cholate, mg/100 ml	1.5(0.7-1.9)	2.6(2.4-3.0)	26
219			28	Cholesterol, total, mg/100 ml	33(12-48)	65(52-71)	26
220			11	Cholesterol, total, mg/100 ml	36.0 ± 4.2	47.7 ± 2.8	4
221		Intestinal	12 [16]	Total lipid, mg/100 ml	1150	220	2
222			10 [5]	Total lipid, mg/100 ml	1590	378	2
223			3	Fatty acids, mg/100 ml	(1000-1572)	....	4
224			9	Cholesterol, total, mg/100 ml	55.2 ± 6.2	47.7 ± 2.8	4
225			3	Cholesterol, total, mg/100 ml	(62.1-69.2)	....	3
226			12 [16]	Cholesterol, free, mg/100 ml	27	17	2
227			10 [5]	Cholesterol, free, mg/100 ml	34	24	2
228			12 [16]	Cholesterol esters, mg/100 ml	86	41	2
229			10 [5]	Cholesterol esters, mg/100 ml	120	49	2

[3] Arterial. [4] In mammary vein. [5] Fasted. [6] Anesthetized. [7] For percentage fatty acid composition, consult the reference. [14] Rabbits fed low-fat diet of vegetable leaves for 2 wk prior to test. [15] Hypercholesterolemia resulting from addition of cholesterol to diet. [16] Fed.

continued

Part III. Domestic and Laboratory Mammals Other Than Dog

	Animal	Source of Lymph	No. of Subjects	Constituent or Property (Synonym)	Value Lymph	Value Plasma or Serum	Reference
230	Sheep	Thoracic duct	1	Total lipid, mg/100 ml	892	....	24
231			11	Fatty acids, free, μeq/ml	0.57 ± 0.05	0.78 ± 0.07	29
232			1	Fatty acids, free [z/], mg/100 ml	8.0	....	24
233			11	Fatty acids, esterified, μeq/ml	12 ± 1.6	2.7 ± 0.5	29
234			1	Triglycerides [z/], mg/100 ml	705	....	24
235			11	Phospholipid, mg/100 ml	119 ± 19	103 ± 5	29
236			1	Phospholipid [z/], mg/100 ml	142	....	24
237			11	Cholesterol, total, mg/100 ml	99 ± 19	101 ± 10	29
238			1	Cholesterol, free, mg/100 ml	8.0	....	24
239			1	Cholesterol, esterified [z/], mg/100 ml	20.5	....	24
240		Lymphatics Cervical	1	Total lipid, mg/100 ml	27		24
241			1	Fatty acids, free, mg/100 ml	2.0		
242			1	Triglycerides, mg/100 ml	0.3		
243			1	Phospholipids, mg/100 ml	13.9		
244			1	Cholesterol, free, mg/100 ml	4.0		
245			1	Cholesterol esters, mg/100 ml	6.9		
246		Hepatic	11	Fatty acids, free, μeq/ml	0.64 ± 0.05	0.78 ± 0.07	29
247			11	Fatty acids, esterified, total; μeq/ml	1.6 ± 0.2	2.7 ± 0.5	29
248			4	Fatty acids in triglycerides, % Palmitic ⟨16:0⟩	20.7	20.9	1
249				Stearic ⟨18:0⟩	24.9	26.2	
250				Oleic ⟨18:1⟩	34.1	33.0	
251				Linoleic ⟨18:2⟩	5.9	5.7	
252				Octadecatrienoic ⟨18:3⟩	1.9	2.1	
253			4	Fatty acids in phospholipid, % Palmitic ⟨16:0⟩	23.6	24.8	1
254				Stearic ⟨18:0⟩	30.5	31.3	
255				Oleic ⟨18:1⟩	24.5	22.8	
256				Linoleic ⟨18:2⟩	6.8	7.0	
257				Octadecatrienoic ⟨18:3⟩	1.5	1.4	
258			4	Fatty acids in cholesterol esters, % Palmitic ⟨16:0⟩	14.2	13.6	1
259				Stearic ⟨18:0⟩	5.7	6.2	
260				Oleic ⟨18:1⟩	38.3	38.1	
261				Linoleic ⟨18:2⟩	24.2	25.1	
262				Octadecatrienoic ⟨18:3⟩	4.7	4.7	
263			5	Triglycerides, mg/100 ml	27	38	1
264			5	Phospholipid, mg/100 ml	35	46	1
265			11	Phospholipid, mg/100 ml	74 ± 5	103 ± 5	29
266			11	Cholesterol, total, mg/100 ml	61 ± 9	101 ± 10	29
267			5	Cholesterol, free + esters, mg/100 ml	48	70	1
268		Intestinal	1	Total lipid, mg/100 ml	1029	....	24
269			1	Fatty acids, free [z/], mg/100 ml	7	....	24
270			11	Fatty acids, free, μeq/100 ml	89 ± 5	78 ± 7	29
271			11	Fatty acids, esterified, total; μeq/100 ml	4100 ± 320	270 ± 50	29

[z/] For percentage fatty acid composition, consult the reference.

continued

Part III. Domestic and Laboratory Mammals Other Than Dog

	Animal	Source of Lymph	No. of Subjects	Constituent or Property (Synonym)	Value Lymph	Value Plasma or Serum	Reference
272			1	Fatty acids, esterified, μeq/100 ml Total [z]	770	....	30
273				Palmitic ⟨16:0⟩	213		
274				Stearic ⟨18:0⟩	136		
275				Oleic ⟨18:1⟩	223		
276				Linoleic ⟨18:2⟩	96		
277				Octadecatrienoic ⟨18:3⟩	28		
278			1	Triglycerides [z], mg/100 ml	761	....	24
279			1	Phospholipid [z], mg/100 ml	180	....	24
280			11	Phospholipid, mg/100 ml	400 ± 80	103 ± 5	29
281			11	Cholesterol, total, mg/100 ml	130 ± 6	101 ± 10	29
282			1	Cholesterol, free, mg/100 ml	17	....	24
283			1	Cholesterol esters [z], mg/100 ml	59	....	24
284		Leg	4	Fatty acids in triglycerides, % Palmitic ⟨16:0⟩	20.7	20.9	1
285				Stearic ⟨18:0⟩	24.9	26.2	
286				Oleic ⟨18:1⟩	34.1	33.0	
287				Linoleic ⟨18:2⟩	5.9	5.7	
288				Octadecatrienoic ⟨18:3⟩	1.9	2.1	
289			4	Fatty acids in phospholipid, % Palmitic ⟨16:0⟩	24.8	24.8	
290				Stearic ⟨18:0⟩	23.0	31.3	
291				Oleic ⟨18:1⟩	22.4	33.8	
292				Linoleic ⟨18:2⟩	12.0	7.0	
293				Octadecatrienoic ⟨18:3⟩	2.1	1.4	
294			4	Fatty acids in cholesterol esters, % Palmitic ⟨16:0⟩	15.6	13.6	
295				Stearic ⟨18:0⟩	5.7	6.2	
296				Oleic ⟨18:1⟩	32.1	38.1	
297				Linoleic ⟨18:2⟩	27.8	25.1	
298				Octadecatrienoic ⟨18:3⟩	5.0	4.7	
299			5	Triglycerides, mg/100 ml	13	38	
300			5	Phospholipid, mg/100 ml	11	46	
301			5	Cholesterol, free + esters, mg/100 ml	24	70	
302		Testicular	5	Fatty acids, free, mg/100 ml	7.1(5.52-10.9)	13.4(5.9-32.5)	82
303			5	Fatty acids, esterified, mg/100 ml	37.2(26.7-43.2)	89.7(76.0-104.1)	
304			5	Phospholipid, mg/100 ml	44.7(27.3-58.8)	94.0(65.1-114.3)	
305			5	Cholesterol, total, mg/100 ml	81.9(61.4-112.8)	126.5(115.2-192.0)	
306	Non-lactating	Mammary gland lymphatics	4	Fatty acids, free, mg/100 ml	8.0(6.1-8.8)	9.2(7.7-10.5)	45
307			4	Fatty acids, volatile, mg/100 ml	7.2(5.5-8.5)	8.5(6.6-9.3)	
308			4	Fatty acids, esterified, mg/100 ml	39.4(21.3-59.0)	97.0(75.9-118.2)	
309			4	Phospholipid, mg/100 ml	43.6(34.4-51.5)	106.6(95.4-130.5)	
310			4	Cholesterol, total, mg/100 ml	43.0(37.1-49.6)	110.7(105.6-121.1)	
311	Lactating	Mammary gland lymphatics	4	Fatty acids, free, mg/100 ml	12.7(4.6-17.9)	24.0(6.5-33.0)	45
312			3	Fatty acids, volatile, mg/100 ml	5.8(5.3-6.3)	6.3(5.6-7.6)	45
313			4	Fatty acids, esterified, mg/100 ml	48.8(28.5-75.6)	172.6(99.4-283.1)	45

[z] For percentage fatty acid composition, consult the reference.

continued

Part III. Domestic and Laboratory Mammals Other Than Dog

	Animal	Source of Lymph	No. of Subjects	Constituent or Property (Synonym)	Value Lymph	Value Plasma or Serum	Reference
314			4	Fatty acids in triglycerides, % Palmitic ⟨16:0⟩	20.4	23.5	1
315				Stearic ⟨18:0⟩	26.6	27.7	
316				Oleic ⟨18:1⟩	33.3	27.2	
317				Linoleic ⟨18:2⟩	5.8	5.1	
318				Octadecatrienoic ⟨18:3⟩	1.8	2.8	
319			4	Fatty acids in phospholipid, % Palmitic ⟨16:0⟩	28.9	22.3	1
320				Stearic ⟨18:0⟩	25.6	25.6	
321				Oleic ⟨18:1⟩	23.1	22.3	
322				Linoleic ⟨18:2⟩	8.6	14.9	
323				Octadecatrienoic ⟨18:3⟩	1.5	3.4	
324			4	Fatty acids in cholesterol esters, % Palmitic ⟨16:0⟩	16.1	17.6	1
325				Stearic ⟨18:0⟩	5.0	6.2	
326				Oleic ⟨18:1⟩	38.5	37.9	
327				Linoleic ⟨18:2⟩	23.2	24.9	
328				Octadecatrienoic ⟨18:3⟩	2.6	3.2	
329			4	Triglycerides, mg/100 ml	14	76	1
330			4	Phospholipid, mg/100 ml	19	119	1
331			4	Phospholipid, mg/100 ml	44.6(39.5-54.1)	119.3(108.5-144.1)	45
332			4	Cholesterol, total, mg/100 ml	25.3(17.3-32.0)	88.9(55.6-112.1)	45
333			4	Cholesterol, free + esters, mg/100 ml	27	134	1
				Carbohydrates & Related Compounds			
334	Cat	Intestinal lymphatics	1	Glucose, mg/100 ml	219	219	31
335	Cattle Non-lactating	Mammary gland lymphatics	3	Glucose, mg/100 ml	69(58-76)	82(74-88)	47
336	Lactating	Mammary gland lymphatics	11	Glucose, mg/100 ml	48.2 ± 11.0[1]	70.6 ± 12.1[1]	38
337			3	Glucose, mg/100 ml	77(68-84)	79(70-85)	47
338			11	Fructose, mg/100 ml	0.65 ± 0.43[1]	1.16 ± 0.64[1]	38
339			11	Lactose, mg/100 ml	12.5 ± 7.6[1]	5.3 ± 5.1[1]	38
340			11	Acetone, mg/100 ml	0.46 ± 0.48[1]	0.31 ± 0.31[1]	38
341			11	Lactic acid, mg/100 ml	87.6 ± 15.2[1]	7.0 ± 3.6[1]	38
342			11	Pyruvic acid, mg/100 ml	0.42 ± 0.07[1]	0.71 ± 0.34[1]	38
343			11	Acetoacetic acid, mg/100 ml	0.19 ± 0.14[1]	0.22 ± 0.12[1]	38
344			11	α-Ketoglutaric acid (α-Oxoglutaric acid), mg/100 ml	0.17 ± 0.07[1]	0.10 ± 0.05[1]	38
345			11	Citric acid, mg/100 ml	4.05 ± 1.67[1]	2.63 ± 1.32[1]	38
346	Goat, lactating	Mammary gland lymphatics	4	Glucose, mg/100 ml	69(53-82)	61 ± 1.7[3]; 40 ± 1.0[4]	53
347			4	Lactate, meq/liter	0.56(0.35-0.78)	0.2 ± 0.05	
348	Rat	Thoracic duct	15	Fucose, mg/100 ml	5.9	....	5
349			10	Glucose, mg/100 ml	121	105	81
350			4	Glucose, mg/100 ml	209(200-220)	192(165-230)	65

[1] Plus/minus (±) value is standard deviation. [3] Arterial. [4] In mammary vein.

continued

Part III. Domestic and Laboratory Mammals Other Than Dog

	Animal	Source of Lymph	No. of Subjects	Constituent or Property (Synonym)	Value Lymph	Value Plasma or Serum	Reference
351			6[5,6]	Glucose, mg/100 ml	133.9 ± 12.4	125.8 ± 21.2	44
352			15	Hexosamines, mg/100 ml	37.47	....	5
353			15	Sialic acids, mg/100 ml	35.21	....	5
354			15	Sugar, protein-bound, mg/100 ml	67.4	....	5
355			10	Lactic acid, mg/100 ml	15.0	30.2	81
356		Hepatic lymphatics	9	Glucose, mg/100 ml	232(165-450)	173(157-202)	26
357			13[5]	Glucose, mg/100 ml	150(80-190)	119(92-130)	
358	Sheep	Testicular lymphatics	5	Reducing sugars, mg/100 ml	52.7(45.8-63.4)	64.2(59.6-66.5)	82
359			5	Glucose, mg/100 ml	47.6(43.7-52.4)	62.9(58.7-67.7)	
360			5	Lactate, mg/100 ml	9.8(5.9-12.7)	18.6(14.0-25.6)	
361			4	Citrate, mg/100 ml	1.00(0.54-1.19)	0.94(0.46-1.27)	
362	Non-lactating	Mammary gland lymphatics	1	Glucose, mg/100 ml	75.0	78.6	45
363	Lactating	Mammary gland lymphatics	1	Glucose, mg/100 ml	80.7	80.1	45

Nitrogenous Substances

	Animal	Source of Lymph	No. of Subjects	Constituent or Property (Synonym)	Value Lymph	Value Plasma or Serum	Reference
364	Cat	Thoracic duct	66	Protein, total, g/100 ml	4.53 ± 0.1	....	59
365			20	Protein, total, g/100 ml	4.63 ± 0.19	7.09 ± 0.14	12
366			....	Protein, total, g/100 ml	4.80(4.00-5.60)[b]	7.60(6.20-9.00)[b]	42
367			20	Albumin, g/100 ml	2.74 ± 0.12	3.65 ± 0.14	12
368			20	Globulin, g/100 ml	1.88 ± 0.15	3.44 ± 0.05	12
369			3	Nitrogen, non-protein, mg/100 ml	44.0	45.0	77
370		Lymphatics Cervical	20	Protein, total, g/100 ml	3.02 ± 0.28	7.09 ± 0.14	12
371			12	Protein, total, g/100 ml	3.50	....	23
372			2	Protein, total, g/100 ml	4.09	....	23
373			20	Albumin, g/100 ml	1.97 ± 0.22	3.65 ± 0.14	12
374			20	Globulin, g/100 ml	1.05 ± 0.07	3.44 ± 0.05	12
375		Gall-bladder	2	Protein, total, g/100 ml	5.01	5.43	54
376			2	Albumin, g/100 ml	3.18	3.38	
377			2	Globulin, g/100 ml	1.83	2.06	
378		Hepatic	2	Protein, total, g/100 ml	5.17	5.43	54
379			38	Protein, total, g/100 ml	6.06 ± 0.05	6.82	59
380			5	Albumin, g/100 ml	2.92	3.11	58
381			2	Albumin, g/100 ml	3.15	3.38	54
382			2	Globulin, g/100 ml	2.02	2.06	54
383			5	Globulin, g/100 ml	3.20	3.49	58
384		Intestinal	30	Protein, total, g/100 ml	4.19 ± 0.1	6.71	59
385			5	Albumin, g/100 ml	2.62	3.11	58
386			5	Globulin, g/100 ml	2.64	3.49	58
387		Leg	12	Protein, total, g/100 ml	2.64 ± 0.09	9.13 ± 1.1	49
388			5	Protein, total, g/100 ml	2.94 ± 0.20	8.60	49
389			4	Protein, total, g/100 ml	3.30 ± 0.20	9.20 ± 1.5	49
390			....	Protein, total, g/100 ml	3.31	....	23

[5] Fasted. [6] Anesthetized.

continued

Part III. Domestic and Laboratory Mammals Other Than Dog

	Animal	Source of Lymph	No. of Subjects	Constituent or Property (Synonym)	Value		Reference
					Lymph	Plasma or Serum	
391			4	Protein, total, g/100 ml	3.50 ± 0.10	7.30 ± 1.2	49
392			4	Protein, total, g/100 ml	3.9(3.0-4.7)	7.8(6.6-8.8)	8
393			....	Nitrogen, non-protein, mg/100 ml	37	36	25
394		Muscle [17]	11	Protein, total, g/100 ml	3.43(1.38-4.26)	6.20(4.95-7.05)	41
395		Skin	11	Protein, total, g/100 ml	3.06(1.53-4.90)	6.20(4.95-7.05)	41
396			10	Bilirubin, mg/100 ml	0.12 ± 0.07 [L]	0.12 ± 0.04 [L]	7
397		Right lymphatic duct	10	Protein, total, g/100 ml	4.90	7.40	11
398	Cattle	Lymphatics Cervical	8	Protein, total, g/100 ml	2.64(2.20-3.34)	6.28(5.39-7.04)	27
399		Hepatic	2	Protein, total, g/100 ml	5.73(4.99-6.47)	7.09(6.63-7.54)	73
400			2	Albumin, g/100 ml	2.25(2.23-2.27)	2.40(2.34-2.46)	
401			2	Globulin, g/100 ml	3.48(2.76-4.20)	4.69(4.17-5.20)	
402		Intestinal	3	Protein, total, g/100 ml	3.79(2.97-4.26)	6.64(5.88-7.23)	73
403			3	Albumin, g/100 ml	1.90(1.76-1.98)	2.67(2.58-2.82)	
404			3	Globulin, g/100 ml	1.89(1.21-2.28)	3.97(3.28-4.41)	
405		Leg	5	Protein, total, g/100 ml	2.7	6.2	64
406			5	Albumin, g/100 ml	1.7	3.4	64
407			5	Globulin, g/100 ml	1.0	2.8	64
408			5	α-Globulin, g/100 ml	0.31	0.91	64
409			5	β-Globulin, g/100 ml	0.37	0.92	64
410			5	γ-Globulin, g/100 ml	0.33	0.86	64
411			8	Creatine, mg/100 ml	3.0(2.2-3.9)	2.8(1.8-4.1)	27
412			8	Creatinine, mg/100 ml	1.1(0.9-1.5)	1.1(0.9-1.3)	27
413			5	Urea, mg/100 ml	23.0(10.3-36.0)	23.6(10.2-36.9)	27
414			8	Nitrogen, non-protein, mg/100 ml	20.3(13.7-27.6)	20.4(14.3-28.6)	27
415			7	Nitrogen, amino, mg/100 ml	6.1	5.6	27
416	Calves	Thoracic duct	15 [8]	Protein, total, g/100 ml	4.04 ± 0.16	....	69
417			15 [9]	Protein, total, g/100 ml	3.66 ± 0.15		
418		Intestinal lymphatics	15 [8]	Protein, total, g/100 ml	4.63 ± 0.19	....	69
419			15 [9]	Protein, total, g/100 ml	4.89 ± 0.23		
420	Newborn	Thoracic duct	3 [18]	Protein, total, g/100 ml	2.38	....	74
421			3 [19]	Protein, total, g/100 ml	3.56		
422			3 [20]	Protein, total, g/100 ml	3.55		
423			3 [21]	Protein, total, g/100 ml	3.64		
424			3 [18]	Albumin, g/100 ml	1.61 ± 0.05		
425			3 [19]	Albumin, g/100 ml	1.44 ± 0.02		
426			3 [20]	Albumin, g/100 ml	1.53 ± 0.03		
427			3 [21]	Albumin, g/100 ml	1.84 ± 0.03		
428			3 [18]	Globulin, g/100 ml	0.77 ± 0.06		
429			3 [19]	Globulin, g/100 ml	2.12 ± 0.16		
430			3 [20]	Globulin, g/100 ml	2.02 ± 0.17		
431			3 [21]	Globulin, g/100 ml	1.80 ± 0.09		

[L] Plus/minus (±) value is standard deviation. [8] Milk-fed. [9] Fed grain and hay. [17] During passive movements of limb. [18] Before first feeding; 6 samples. [19] 1-12 hr after first feeding; 27 samples. [20] 13-24 hr after first feeding; 18 samples. [21] 145-156 hr after first feeding; 36 samples.

continued

Part III. Domestic and Laboratory Mammals Other Than Dog

	Animal	Source of Lymph	No. of Subjects	Constituent or Property (Synonym)	Value Lymph	Value Plasma or Serum	Reference
		Lymphatics					46
432		Hepatic	2 [10]	Protein, total, g/100 ml	3.17 ± 0.28	4.20	
433			3 [6,10]	Protein, total, g/100 ml	3.31 ± 0.12	4.93 ± 0.60	
434		Intestinal	3 [10]	Protein, total, g/100 ml	2.71 ± 0.03	4.41 ± 0.25	
435			4 [6,10]	Protein, total, g/100 ml	3.15 ± 0.19	4.85 ± 0.51	
436	Young	Thoracic duct	4	Protein, total, g/100 ml	3.88(2.94-5.07)	6.78(5.60-7.91)	73
437			4	Albumin, g/100 ml	1.84(1.69-2.14)	2.77(2.49-3.17)	
438			4	Globulin, g/100 ml	2.04(1.22-3.38)	4.01(2.86-5.42)	
439	Adult, ♀	Thoracic duct	3	Protein, total, g/100 ml	3.31(2.91-3.95)	7.42(6.86-7.80)	28
440	Non-lactating	Mammary gland lymphatics	3	Protein, total, g/100 ml	4.4(3.7-4.9)	8.3(8.1-8.7)	47
441			3	Albumin, g/100 ml	2.1(1.5-2.4)	3.1(2.3-3.6)	
442			3	Globulin, g/100 ml	2.3(2.2-2.5)	5.2(4.5-5.9)	
443	Lactating	Mammary gland lymphatics	11	Protein, total, g/100 ml	2.86 ± 1.00 [1]	8.41 ± 0.66 [1]	38
444			3	Protein, total, g/100 ml	3.2(2.8-3.6)	9.0(8.2-9.4)	47
445			10	Protein, total, g/100 ml	3.23 ± 1.25 [1]	8.92 ± 0.39 [1]	32
446			11	Protein, total, g/100 ml	3.75(2.84-5.51)	8.54(7.58-9.64)	37
447			10 [2]	Protein, total, g/100 ml	3.09 ± 0.82 [1]	8.17 ± 0.53 [1]	35
448			10	Albumin, g/100 ml	1.27	2.39	32
449			3	Albumin, g/100 ml	1.4(1.0-1.6)	2.9(2.6-3.1)	47
450			3	Globulin, g/100 ml	1.9(1.2-2.3)	6.1(5.2-6.8)	47
451			10	Globulin, g/100 ml	1.96	6.53	32
452			10	α_1-Globulin, g/100 ml	0.23	0.82	32
453			10	α_2-Globulin, g/100 ml	0.28	0.90	32
454			10	α_3-Globulin, g/100 ml	0.11	0.37	32
455			10	β_1-Globulin, g/100 ml	0.22	0.79	32
456			10	β_2-Globulin, g/100 ml	0.50	1.85	32
457			10	γ_1-Globulin, g/100 ml	0.33	1.09	32
458			10	γ_2-Globulin, g/100 ml	0.29	0.71	32
459			3	Alanine, mg/100 ml	1.87(1.22-2.56)	1.52 ± 0.09	80
460			10	Alanine, μg N/100 ml	510 ± 149 [1]	243 ± 69 [1]	33
461			3	α-Amino-n-butyric acid, mg/100 ml	0.11(0.10-0.12)	0.22 ± 0.07	80
462			3	Arginine, mg/100 ml	0.71(0.46-0.97)	0.72 ± 0.14	80
463			3	Asparagine, mg/100 ml	0.53(0.45-0.59)	0.42 ± 0.05	80
464			3	Aspartic acid, mg/100 ml	0.14(0.11-0.16)	0.13 ± 0.02	80
465			10	Aspartic acid, μg N/100 ml	91 ± 38 [1]	38 ± 15 [1]	33
466			3	Citrulline, mg/100 ml	0.95(0.40-1.31)	0.97 ± 0.15	80
467			3	Glutamic acid, mg/100 ml	0.62(0.41-0.90)	0.80 ± 0.05	80
468			10	Glutamic acid, μg N/100 ml	257 ± 122 [1]	94 ± 77 [1]	33
469			3	Glutamine, mg/100 ml	3.74(2.98-4.21)	2.63 ± 0.23	80
470			3	Glycine, mg/100 ml	2.94(2.32-3.59)	3.05 ± 0.43	80
471			10	Glycine, μg N/100 ml	891 ± 641 [1]	535 ± 347 [1]	33
472			3	Histidine, mg/100 ml	0.99(0.58-1.47)	0.90 ± 0.05	80
473			3	Isoleucine, mg/100 ml	1.65(1.58-1.80)	1.47 ± 0.17	80
474			3	Leucine, mg/100 ml	1.89(1.64-2.19)	1.70 ± 0.19	80
475			10	Leucines, μg N/100 ml	342 ± 149 [1]	138 ± 63 [1]	33
476			3	Lysine, mg/100 ml	0.88(0.61-1.23)	0.93 ± 0.10	80
477			10	Lysine, μg N/100 ml	357 ± 113 [1]	137 ± 71 [1]	33

[1] Plus/minus (±) value is standard deviation. [2] Samples taken after slaughter. [6] Anesthetized. [10] Before suckling or first feed.

continued

Part III. Domestic and Laboratory Mammals Other Than Dog

	Animal	Source of Lymph	No. of Subjects	Constituent or Property (Synonym)	Value		Reference
					Lymph	Plasma or Serum	
478			3	Methionine, mg/100 ml	0.42(0.29-0.54)	0.21 ± 0.03	80
479			3	Ornithine, mg/100 ml	0.34(0.27-0.48)	0.54 ± 0.07	80
480			3	Phenylalanine, mg/100 ml	0.88(0.60-1.08)	0.65 ± 0.03	80
481			3	Proline, mg/100 ml	0.85(0.65-1.05)	0.81 ± 0.11	80
482			3	Serine, mg/100 ml	0.73(0.67-0.85)	0.82 ± 0.09	80
483			10	Serine, μg N/100 ml	235 ± 58 [L/]	98 ± 32 [L/]	33
484			3	Taurine, mg/100 ml	0.20(0.15-0.26)	0.36 ± 0.06	80
485			3	Threonine, mg/100 ml	1.01(0.93-1.09)	0.85 ± 0.07	80
486			10	Threonine, μg N/100 ml	220 ± 84 [L/]	93 ± 54 [L/]	33
487			3	Tyrosine, mg/100 ml	0.65(0.47-0.77)	0.54 ± 0.04	80
488			10	Tyrosine, μg N/100 ml	205 ± 89 [L/]	120 ± 62 [L/]	33
489			3	Valine, mg/100 ml	3.13(2.87-3.31)	2.47 ± 0.29	80
490			10	Valine, μg N/100 ml	324 ± 95 [L/]	162 ± 52 [L/]	33
491			10	Urea, mg/100 ml	22.7 ± 4.0 [L/]	21.9 ± 4.2 [L/]	33
492			3	Urea, mg/100 ml	27.9(17.5-44)	30.7 ± 3.6	80
493			10	Uric acid, mg/100 ml	1.68 ± 0.60 [L/]	0.55 ± 0.16 [L/]	33
494			10	Nitrogen, total amino acid, μg/100 ml	3432 ± 1123 [L/]	1658 ± 562 [L/]	33
495	Goat	Thoracic duct	....	Protein, total, g/100 ml	4.10	5.30	11
496			....	Albumin, g/100 ml	1.30	1.60	
497			....	Globulin, g/100 ml	2.80	3.70	
498	Lactating	Mammary gland lymphatics	4	Protein, total, g/100 ml	2.48(1.88-3.18)	7.55 ± 0.2	53
499			9	Protein, total, g/100 ml	3.3 ± 0.6 [L/]	6.6 ± 0.5 [L/]	67
500			1	Albumin, g/100 ml	1.36	3.36	53
501			1	Globulin, total, g/100 ml	1.11	4.19	53
502			1	α-Globulin, g/100 ml	0.54	1.94	53
503			1	β-Globulin, g/100 ml	0.18	0.51	53
504			1	γ-Globulin, g/100 ml	0.39	1.74	53
505			7	Nitrogen, non-protein, mg/100 ml	24 ± 6 [L/]	28 ± 4 [L/]	67
506			3	Nitrogen, α-amino, mg/100 ml	3.88(3.12-4.42)	5.0 ± 0.31 [3/]; 3.4 ± 0.34 [4/]	53
507	Guinea pig	Thoracic duct	1	Protein, total, g/100 ml	4.16	4.72	23
508		Cervical lymphatics	1	Protein, total, g/100 ml	3.37	4.64	
509	Horse	Cervical lymphatics	....	Protein, total, g/100 ml	3.8	....	22
510	Monkey, rhesus	Thoracic duct	2	Protein, total, g/100 ml	3.66	5.87	23
511		Cervical lymphatics	4	Protein, total, g/100 ml	3.48	5.12	
512	Rabbit	Thoracic duct	10	Protein, total, g/100 ml	3.43	5.46	13
513			15	Protein, total, g/100 ml	3.53	....	23
514			10	Albumin, g/100 ml	2.22	3.56	13
515			10	Globulin, g/100 ml	1.20	1.89	13

[L/] Plus/minus (±) value is standard deviation. [3/] Arterial. [4/] In mammary vein.

continued

Part III. Domestic and Laboratory Mammals Other Than Dog

	Animal	Source of Lymph	No. of Subjects	Constituent or Property (Synonym)	Value Lymph	Value Plasma or Serum	Reference
516		Lymphatics Cervical	8	Protein, total, g/100 ml	3.18	....	23
517		Hepatic	7	Protein, total, g/100 ml	5.82 ± 0.20	6.76 ± 0.18	9
518			12	Protein, total, g/100 ml	5.90 ± 0.29	6.94 ± 0.19	83
519			9 [15]	Protein, total, g/100 ml	5.28 ± 0.33	6.66 ± 0.25	9
520			25 [15]	Protein, total, g/100 ml	5.68 ± 0.24	6.90 ± 0.25	15
521			7	Albumin, g/100 ml	3.56 ± 0.13	3.69 ± 0.11	9
522			12	Albumin, g/100 ml	3.63 ± 0.16	3.84 ± 0.10	83
523			9 [15]	Albumin, g/100 ml	3.06 ± 0.24	3.49 ± 0.23	9
524			25 [15]	Albumin, g/100 ml	3.47 ± 0.11	3.79 ± 0.10	15
525			7	Globulin, g/100 ml	2.26 ± 0.13	3.07 ± 0.16	9
526			12	Globulin, g/100 ml	2.27 ± 0.13	3.10 ± 0.14	83
527			25 [15]	Globulin, g/100 ml	2.21 ± 0.14	3.11 ± 0.14	15
528			9 [15]	Globulin, g/100 ml	2.22 ± 0.24	3.17 ± 0.23	9
529			7	α-Globulin, g/100 ml	0.54 ± 0.04	0.72 ± 0.05	9
530			12	α-Globulin, g/100 ml	0.56 ± 0.04	0.75 ± 0.04	83
531			9 [15]	α-Globulin, g/100 ml	0.49 ± 0.04	0.70 ± 0.06	9
532			25 [15]	α-Globulin, g/100 ml	0.57 ± 0.03	0.77 ± 0.03	15
533			12	β-Globulin, g/100 ml	0.57 ± 0.04	0.80 ± 0.04	83
534			7	β-Globulin, g/100 ml	0.81 ± 0.08	1.01 ± 0.08	9
535			25 [15]	β-Globulin, g/100 ml	0.63 ± 0.04	0.92 ± 0.05	15
536			9 [15]	β-Globulin, g/100 ml	0.77 ± 0.07	1.19 ± 0.08	9
537			7	γ-Globulin, g/100 ml	0.90 ± 0.13	1.33 ± 0.17	9
538			12	γ-Globulin, g/100 ml	1.14 ± 0.16	1.55 ± 0.16	83
539			9 [15]	γ-Globulin, g/100 ml	0.97 ± 0.13	1.28 ± 0.17	9
540			25 [15]	γ-Globulin, g/100 ml	1.01 ± 0.10	1.42 ± 0.11	15
541		Leg	2	Protein, total, g/100 ml	1.26	....	23
542			3	Protein, total, g/100 ml	2.2(2.1-2.4)	6.2(6.0-6.4)	40
543			69	Protein, total, g/100 ml	2.22 ± 0.08	5.72 ± 0.08	68
544			17	Protein, total, g/100 ml	2.28 ± 0.10	6.43 ± 0.18	14
545			10	Protein, total, g/100 ml	2.3 ± 1.6 [L]	6.25 ± 0.86 [L]	70
546			6	Protein, total, g/100 ml	2.52	6.36	57
547			8	Protein, total, g/100 ml	2.57 ± 0.28	6.70 ± 0.16	16
548			9	Protein, total, g/100 ml	2.78 ± 0.26	6.66 ± 0.25	10
549			6	Protein, total, g/100 ml	2.81 ± 0.30	6.76 ± 0.18	10
550			12	Protein, total, g/100 ml	2.9 ± 0.1	5.7 ± 0.2	50
551			10	Albumin, g/100 ml	1.29 ± 0.10 [L]	3.34 ± 0.44 [L]	70
552			17	Albumin, g/100 ml	1.35 ± 0.09	3.46 ± 0.07	14
553			60	Albumin, g/100 ml	1.38 ± 0.04	3.30 ± 0.07	68
554			6	Albumin, g/100 ml	1.43 ± 0.15	3.23 ± 0.19	57
555			9	Albumin, g/100 ml	1.68 ± 0.25	3.49 ± 0.23	10
556			6	Albumin, g/100 ml	1.75 ± 0.16	3.70 ± 0.11	10
557			60	Globulin, g/100 ml	0.86	2.42	68
558			17	Globulin, g/100 ml	0.93 ± 0.09	2.97 ± 0.18	14
559			4	Globulin, g/100 ml	1.09	3.13	57
560			60	α-Globulin, g/100 ml	0.18 ± 0.01	0.49 ± 0.01	68
561			6	α-Globulin, g/100 ml	0.21 ± 0.03	0.44 ± 0.07	57
562			9	α-Globulin, g/100 ml	0.27 ± 0.03	0.70 ± 0.06	10
563			6	α-Globulin, g/100 ml	0.28 ± 0.03	0.72 ± 0.05	10
564			10	α-Globulin, g/100 ml	0.28 ± 0.05 [L]	0.92 ± 0.11 [L]	70

[L] Plus/minus (±) value is standard deviation. [15] Hypercholesterolemia resulting from addition of cholesterol to diet.

continued

Part III. Domestic and Laboratory Mammals Other Than Dog

	Animal	Source of Lymph	No. of Sub-jects	Constituent or Property (Synonym)	Value Lymph	Value Plasma or Serum	Ref-er-ence
565			10	β-Globulin, g/100 ml	0.30 ± 0.06 [L]	0.85 ± 0.24 [L]	70
566			9	β-Globulin, g/100 ml	0.36 ± 0.04	1.19 ± 0.08	10
567			6	β-Globulin, g/100 ml	0.39 ± 0.05	0.96 ± 0.08	10
568			60	β-Globulin, g/100 ml	0.42 ± 0.02	1.22 ± 0.03	68
569			6	β-Globulin, g/100 ml	0.45 ± 0.04	1.08 ± 0.07	57
570			60	γ-Globulin, g/100 ml	0.26 ± 0.01	0.71 ± 0.03	68
571			10	γ-Globulin, g/100 ml	0.40 ± 0.07 [L]	1.14 ± 0.24 [L]	70
572			6	γ-Globulin, g/100 ml	0.40 ± 0.09	1.37 ± 0.17	10
573			6	γ-Globulin, g/100 ml	0.43 ± 0.08	1.61 ± 0.08	57
574			9	γ-Globulin, g/100 ml	0.47 ± 0.06	1.28 ± 0.17	10
575	Rat	Thoracic duct	5	Protein, total, g/100 ml	1.94	5.68	58
576			10	Protein, total, g/100 ml	$3.06(1.64-4.48)^b$	$5.82(4.40-7.24)^b$	63
577			9	Protein, total, g/100 ml	4.1	5.7	81
578			19	Protein, total, g/100 ml	4.18	....	66
579			10 [5,6]	Protein, total, g/100 ml	3.94 ± 0.16	5.69 ± 0.11	44
580			5	Albumin, g/100 ml	1.29	3.20	58
581			9	Albumin, g/100 ml	1.96	2.42	81
582			10 [5,6]	Albumin, g/100 ml	2.01 ± 0.06	2.73 ± 0.10	44
583			5	Globulin, g/100 ml	0.65	2.47	58
584			9	Globulin, g/100 ml	2.15	3.31	81
585			10 [5,6]	α-Globulin, g/100 ml	0.68 ± 0.03	1.44 ± 0.04	44
586			9	α_1-Globulin, g/100 ml	0.46	0.85	81
587			9	α_2-Globulin, g/100 ml	0.20	0.32	81
588			9	β-Globulin, g/100 ml	0.92	1.26	81
589			10 [5,6]	β-Globulin, g/100 ml	0.81 ± 0.08	1.10 ± 0.09	44
590			9	γ-Globulin, g/100 ml	0.57	0.88	81
591			10 [5,6]	γ-Globulin, g/100 ml	0.44 ± 0.22	0.42 ± 0.05	44
			20 [22]	Amino acids, mg/100 ml			44
592				Alanine	2.0	3.8	
593				Arginine	1.3	1.8	
594				Aspartic acid	Trace	0.2	
595				Cysteine + cystine	Trace	Trace	
596				Glutamic acid	0.7	1.1	
597				Glycine	2.1	2.7	
598				Histidine	1.2	1.3	
599				Isoleucine	1.4	1.2	
600				Leucine	2.2	2.0	
601				Lysine	4.2	4.8	
602				Methionine	0.5	0.8	
603				Phenylalanine	1.1	1.1	
604				Proline	1.1	1.5	
605				Taurine	1.5	3.8	
606				Threonine	1.7	2.4	
607				Tyrosine	0.9	1.3	
608				Valine	2.1	2.1	
			4	Purine derivatives, mg/100 ml		....	21
609				Adenine + uracil	0.223(0.205-0.230)		
610				Cytosine	0.230(0.200-0.260)		
611				Guanine	0.127(0.100-0.140)		
612				Uric acid	0.416(0.371-0.520)		

[L] Plus/minus (±) value is standard deviation. [5] Fasted. [6] Anesthetized. [22] Pooled lymph of 20 anesthetized, fasted rats.

continued

Part III. Domestic and Laboratory Mammals Other Than Dog

	Animal	Source of Lymph	No. of Subjects	Constituent or Property (Synonym)	Value Lymph	Value Plasma or Serum	Reference
613			6 [5,6]	Urea, mg/100 ml	20.8	22.6	44
614			6 [5,6]	Nitrogen, non-protein, mg/100 ml	38.4 ± 3.3	40.2 ± 3.0	44
		Lymphatics					
615		Cervical	9	Protein, total, g/100 ml	3.07	....	66
616			18 [23]	Thyroglobulin, ng/ml	(<10-2000)	(<10-170)	20
617		Cisterna chyli	12 [23]	Thyroglobulin, ng/ml	(10-70)	(<10-170)	20
618		Hepatic	6	Protein, total, g/100 ml	4.10(3.7-4.9)	6.10(5.3-6.8)	26
619			6	Albumin, g/100 ml	2.10(1.8-2.7)	2.70(2.1-3.1)	
620			6	Globulin, g/100 ml	2.00(1.6-2.3)	3.40(2.4-4.1)	
621			6	Urea, mg/100 ml	33(25-47)	30(11-67)	
622	Sheep	Thoracic duct	1	Protein, total, g/100 ml	2.3	4.85	55
623			11	Protein, total, g/100 ml	3.0 ± 0.29	6.0 ± 0.22	29
624			11	Albumin, g/100 ml	0.72 ± 0.13	1.7 ± 0.1	29
		Lymphatics					
625		Hepatic	....	Protein, total, g/100 ml	5.74	7.55	58
626			11	Protein, total, g/100 ml	6.3 ± 0.18	7.9 ± 0.11	29
627			11	Albumin, g/100 ml	2.7 ± 0.15	3.3 ± 0.14	29
628		Intestinal	2	Protein, total, g/100 ml	3.79(3.77-3.81)	4.85	55
629			11	Protein, total, g/100 ml	4.3 ± 0.10	7.9 ± 0.1	29
630			11	Albumin, g/100 ml	2.1 ± 0.26	3.3 ± 0.14	29
631		Leg	10	Protein, total, g/100 ml	1.28 ± 0.04	6.47 ± 0.07	56
632			9	Creatinine, mg/100 ml	0.87 ± 0.03	0.88 ± 0.04	
633			13	Urea, mg/100 ml	48.3 ± 1.0	48.2 ± 1.2	
634		Ovarian	13	Protein, total, g/100 ml	5.17(3.96-6.44)	7.09(6.54-8.02)	61
635		Renal	10	Protein, total, g/100 ml	2.80 ± 0.07	6.47 ± 0.07	56
636			9	Creatinine, mg/100 ml	0.78 ± 0.06	0.88 ± 0.04	
637			13	Urea, mg/100 ml	47.5 ± 1.0	48.2 ± 1.2	
638		Testicular	5	Protein, total, g/100 ml	5.52(4.26-6.37)	8.95(6.90-10.67)	17
639			5	Albumin, g/100 ml	2.07(1.71-2.58)	2.58(2.03-3.27)	
640			5	Globulin, g/100 ml	3.44(1.68-4.57)	6.37(3.63-8.24)	
641	Fetus	Thoracic duct	5 [24]	Protein, total, g/100 ml	2.30	....	78
		Lymphatics					78
642		Intestinal	4 [24]	Protein, total, g/100 ml	2.37	....	
643		Lumbar	3 [24]	Protein, total, g/100 ml	2.12	....	
644	Immature	Lung lymphatics Draining to RLD	6	Protein, total, g/100 ml	3.24 ± 0.33	3.61 ± 0.40	39
645		Draining to TD	6	Protein, total, g/100 ml	3.34 ± 0.21		
646	Intermediate	Lung lymphatics Draining to RLD	5	Protein, total, g/100 ml	3.30 ± 0.24	4.10 ± 0.18	39
647		Draining to TD	5	Protein, total, g/100 ml	3.29 ± 0.18		

[5] Fasted. [6] Anesthetized. [23] Subjects given priming dose of thyrotropic hormone. [24] In utero.

continued

Part III. Domestic and Laboratory Mammals Other Than Dog

	Animal	Source of Lymph	No. of Subjects	Constituent or Property (Synonym)	Value		Reference
					Lymph	Plasma or Serum	
648	Mature	Lung lymphatics Draining to RLD	6	Protein, total, g/100 ml	2.69 ± 0.24	4.09 ± 0.26	39
649		Draining to TD	6	Protein, total, g/100 ml	3.27 ± 0.41		
650	Newborn	Lung lymphatics Draining to RLD	9	Protein, total, g/100 ml	5.00 ± 0.26	8.67 ± 0.32	39
651		Draining to TD	9	Protein, total, g/100 ml	5.72 ± 0.30		
652	Adult	Lung lymphatics	11	Protein, total, g/100 ml	3.9	5.6	79
653		Draining to RLD	6	Protein, total, g/100 ml	3.78 ± 0.21	8.56 ± 0.66	39
654	Pregnant	Uterine lymphatics	....	Protein, total, g/100 ml	2.32	5.93	62
655				Albumin, g/100 ml	1.41	2.96	
656				Globulin, g/100 ml	0.91	2.97	
657	Non-lactating	Mammary gland lymphatics	4	Protein, total, g/100 ml	4.93(4.34-5.51)	8.54(8.09-9.15)	45
658			4	Albumin, g/100 ml	2.48(2.12-2.67)	3.77(3.46-4.05)	
659			4	Globulin, g/100 ml	2.45(1.81-2.90)	4.77(4.04-5.38)	
660	Lactating	Mammary gland lymphatics	4	Protein, total, g/100 ml	2.51(1.46-3.24)	7.58(6.90-7.87)	45
661			4	Albumin, g/100 ml	1.45(0.83-1.94)	3.61(3.17-4.29)	
662			4	Globulin, g/100 ml	1.06(0.63-1.30)	3.97(3.58-4.54)	
				Hormones & Enzymes			
663	Cat	Thoracic duct	5	Diamine oxidase (Histaminase) [1.4.3.6], μg histamine inactivated·ml lymph^{-1}·hr^{-1}	0.42(0.09-1.10)	<0.02	6
664		Leg lymphatics	3	Lactate dehydrogenase [1.1.1.27, 1.1.2.3], units/ml	35 ± 9	18 ± 6	49
665			9	Lactate dehydrogenase, units/ml	47 ± 20	225 ± 100	
666			4	Lactate dehydrogenase, units/ml	364 ± 142	269 ± 192	
667			6	Lactate dehydrogenase, units/ml	390 ± 120	116	
668			5	Aspartate aminotransferase (Glutamic oxalacetic transaminase; GOT) [2.6.1.1], units/liter	37 ± 7	42 ± 10	
669			9	Aspartate aminotransferase, units/liter	38.0 ± 7	32.0 ± 8	
670			12	Aspartate aminotransferase, units/liter	40.8 ± 5.5	25.6 ± 5.8	
671			4	Aspartate aminotransferase, units/liter	53 ± 21	46 ± 12	
672			3	Alanine aminotransferase (Glutamic pyruvic transaminase; GPT) [2.6.1.2], units/liter	11 ± 7	21 ± 7	
673			11	Alanine aminotransferase, units/liter	13.4 ± 5.3	14.0 ± 5.3	

continued

Part III.   Domestic and Laboratory Mammals Other Than Dog

	Animal	Source of Lymph	No. of Subjects	Constituent or Property (Synonym)	Value		Reference
					Lymph	Plasma or Serum	
674			8	Alanine aminotransferase, units/liter	19.3 ± 6	33.0 ± 24	
675			4	Alanine aminotransferase, units/liter	22 ± 9	30 ± 13	
676			7	Acid phosphatase [3.1.3.2], units/ml	4.2 ± 1.4	1.0 ± 0.4	
677			4	Acid phosphatase, units/ml	6.1 ± 1.8	2.1 ± 1.1	
678			4	Acid phosphatase, units/ml	7.0 ± 2	2.7 ± 1.0	
679			4	Acid phosphatase, units/ml	13.6 ± 6	1.8	
680			4	β-Glucuronidase [3.2.1.31], units/ml	694 ± 290	990 ± 420	
681			4	β-Glucuronidase, units/ml	944 ± 177	618 ± 111	
682			2	β-Glucuronidase, units/ml	1190 ± 638	1150 ± 506	
683			4	β-Glucuronidase, units/ml	2223 ± 61	2530 ± 800	
684	Cattle, lactating	Mammary gland lymphatics	10	Total steroids, µg/100 ml	6.76 ± 2.21 [L]	8.93 ± 1.65 [L]	35
685			10	Corticosterone, µg/100 ml	2.23 ± 1.34 [L]	2.42 ± 1.15 [L]	35
686			10	Hydrocortisone, µg/100 ml	4.53 ± 1.99 [L]	6.51 ± 2.19 [L]	35
687			5	Diamine oxidase (Histaminase) [1.4.3.6], units/100 ml	1.6(0.7-3.0)	5.7(3.2-7.1)	37
688			9	Lipase [3.1.1.3], units/100 ml	17(10-22)	32(24-40)	37
689			11	Alkaline phosphatase [3.1.3.1], units/100 ml	6.6(1.2-32.3)	12.4(3.0-53.1)	37
690			11	Acid phosphatase [3.1.3.2], units/100 ml	1.7(0.2-3.8)	1.5(0.4-2.8)	37
691			11	Amylase [3.2.1.1, 3.2.1.2], units/100 ml	227(68-388)	736(308-1105)	37
692			11	Ketose-1-phosphate aldolase (Aldolase) [4.1.2.7], units/100 ml	889(631-1369)	1652(1138-2629)	37
693			11	Glucosephosphate isomerase (Phosphohexose isomerase) [5.3.1.9], units/100 ml	139(53-253)	185(63-256)	37
694	Monkey, rhesus	Thoracic duct	6	Insulin, µ units/ml	17.3 ± 1.1 [L]	23.3 ± 2.1 [L,25]; 41.8 ± 5.3 [L,26]	19
695	Rabbit	Thoracic duct	6	Insulin, µ units/ml	22.0 ± 1.6 [L]	28.8 ± 2.5 [L,25]	19
696			30	Insulin, µ units/ml	26.8 ± 8.6 [L]	24.5 ± 6.4 [L]	18
697			8	Testosterone, µg/100 ml	0.80 ± 0.11	0.21 ± 0.04 [27]; 1.74 ± 0.30 [28]	71
698			8	Androstenedione, µg/100 ml	0.06 ± 0.02	0.03 ± 0.02 [27]; 0.06 ± 0.02 [28]	71
699			7	Dehydroepiandrosterone, µg/100 ml	0.18 ± 0.04	0.04 ± 0.01 [27]; 0.13 ± 0.06 [28]	71
700			3	Diamine oxidase (Histaminase) [1.4.3.6], µg histamine inactivated·ml lymph^{-1}·hr^{-1}	0.37(0.08-0.63)	0.05	6

[L] Plus/minus (±) value is standard deviation.   [25] In vena cava.   [26] In portal vein.   [27] In carotid artery.   [28] In inferior vena cava.

continued

Part III. Domestic and Laboratory Mammals Other Than Dog

	Animal	Source of Lymph	No. of Subjects	Constituent or Property (Synonym)	Value		Reference
					Lymph	Plasma or Serum	
701		Lymphatics Leg	17	Lactate dehydrogenase [1.1.1.27, 1.1.2.3], m units/ml	316 ± 73	291 ± 38	50
702			9	Isocitrate dehydrogenase [1.1.1.41, 1.1.1.42], m units/ml	25 ± 5	23 ± 4	50
703			14	Aspartate aminotransferase (Glutamic oxalacetic transaminase; GOT) [2.6.1.1], m units/ml	36 ± 3	24 ± 5	50
704			16	Alanine aminotransferase (Glutamic pyruvic transaminase; GPT) [2.6.1.2], m units/ml	5 ± 1	11 ± 2	50
705			13	Acid phosphatase [3.1.3.2], m units/ml	14	18 ± 3	50
706			14	β-Glucuronidase [3.2.1.31], units/100 ml	743 ± 141	3635 ± 735	50
707			6	Cathepsin [3.4.4.9, 3.4.4.23], units/ml	5.5 ± 0.3	5.5 ± 0.7	50
708			3	Peptidyl dipeptidase (Kininase II) [3.4.15.1], min; inactivation time of bradykinin	6(5-6)	4(3-4)	40
709		Lumbar	3	Testosterone, μg/100 ml	1.99 ± 0.24	0.21 ± 0.04[27]; 1.74 ± 0.30[28]	71
710			3	Androstenedione, μg/100 ml	0.02 ± 0.02	0.03 ± 0.02[27]; 0.06 ± 0.02[28]	
711			4	Dehydroepiandrosterone, μg/100 ml	0.13 ± 0.05	0.04 ± 0.01[27]; 0.13 ± 0.06[28]	
712	Rat	Thoracic duct	4	Insulin, immuno-reactive, μ units/ml	38(23-50)	48(36-65)	65
713			4	Insulin-like activity, μ units/ml	84(50-140)	278(190-450)	65
714			12	Aspartate aminotransferase (Glutamic oxalacetic transaminase; GOT) [2.6.1.1], units/ml	62.0	125.0	81
715			12	Alanine aminotransferase (Glutamic pyruvic transaminase; GPT) [2.6.1.2], units/ml	15.0	36.5	81
716			11	Alkaline phosphatase [3.1.3.1], units/liter	3.62	3.13	81
717			10	Acid phosphatase [3.1.3.2], units/liter	0.70	1.85	81
718			10	Ketose-1-phosphate aldolase (Aldolase) [4.1.2.7], units/ml	36.4	74.3	81
719	Sheep	Testicular lymphatics	10	Testosterone, μg/100 ml	(2.6-61.4)	(<1.5-7.9)[3]; (3.6-90.1)[29]	51
720			3	Androstenedione, μg/100 ml	(<5-6.6)	(3.4-10.0)[29]	

[3] Arterial. [27] In carotid artery. [28] In inferior vena cava. [29] In testicular vein.

continued

Part III. Domestic and Laboratory Mammals Other Than Dog

	Animal	Source of Lymph	No. of Sub-jects	Constituent or Property (Synonym)	Value		Ref-er-ence
					Lymph	Plasma or Serum	
721	Non-preg-nant, luteal phase	Ovarian lympha-tics	1	Progesterone, μg/100 ml	137.6(71.1-204.7)	....	52
722			1	20α-Hydroxypregn-4-en-3-one	Not detected	Not detected	
723			1	17α-Hydroxyprogesterone, μg/100 ml	1.2	....	
724	Pregnant 63-97 da	Ovarian lympha-tics	5	Progesterone, μg/100 ml	115.0(55.3-163.0)	0.9(0.5-1.2)	52
725			5	20α-Hydroxypregn-4-en-3-one, μg/100 ml	1.0(0.6-1.6)	0.5(0.3-0.7)	
726			5	17α-Hydroxyprogesterone, μg/100 ml	3.9(1.1-6.3)	Not detected	
727	130 da	Ovarian lympha-tics	1	Progesterone, μg/100 ml	24.6(20.0-29.2)	0.4	
728			1	20α-Hydroxypregn-4-en-3-one	Not detected	Not detected	
729			1	17α-Hydroxyprogesterone	Not detected	Not detected	
	Other Properties						
730	Goat, lac-tating	Mammary gland lym-phatics	1	pH	7.342 ± 0.015	7.40 ± 0.015[3/]; 7.35 ± 0.065[4/]	53
731			4	pH	7.47 ± 0.02[1/]	7.45 ± 0.03[1/]	67
732	Sheep	Thoracic duct	1	Conductivity, ohm^{-1}/cm	0.0127	0.0123	55
733		Intestinal lympha-tics	2	Conductivity, ohm^{-1}/cm	0.0122(0.0120-0.0123)	0.0123	

[1/] Plus/minus (±) value is standard deviation. [3/] Arterial. [4/] In mammary vein.

Contributors: Courtice, F. C.; Heath, Trevor J., and Reynolds, John D.

References

[1] Adams, E. P. Unpublished. Australian Nat. Univ., Canberra, 1971.

[2] Apostolakis, M., et al. 1962. Biochem. Z. 336:1.

[3] Bloom, B., et al. 1951. J. Biol. Chem. 189:261.

[4] Bollman, J. L., and E. V. Flock. 1951. Amer. J. Physiol. 164:480.

[5] Budavari, I. 1965. Acta Physiol. 26(Suppl.):73.

[6] Carlsten, A. 1950. Acta Physiol. Scand. 29(Suppl. 70):5.

[7] Carlsten, A., et al. 1961. Ibid. 53:58.

[8] Courtice, F. C. 1959. Aust. J. Exp. Biol. Med. Sci. 37:465.

[9] Courtice, F. C. 1960. Ibid. 38:403.

[10] Courtice, F. C. 1961. J. Physiol. (London) 155:456.

[11] Courtice, F. C. Unpublished. Australian Nat. Univ., Canberra, 1971.

[12] Courtice, F. C., and B. Morris. 1955. Quart. J. Exp. Physiol. Cog. Med. Sci. 40:138.

[13] Courtice, F. C., and B. Morris. Unpublished. Australian Nat. Univ., Canberra, 1955.

[14] Courtice, F. C., and M. S. Sabine. 1966. Aust. J. Exp. Biol. Med. Sci. 44:23.

[15] Courtice, F. C., et al. 1962. Ibid. 40:111.

[16] Courtice, F. C., et al. 1964. Quart. J. Exp. Physiol. Cog. Med. Sci. 49:441.

[17] Cowie, A. T., et al. 1964. J. Physiol. (London) 171:176.

[18] Daniel, P. M., and J. R. Henderson. 1966. Ibid. 184:36P.

[19] Daniel, P. M., and J. R. Henderson. 1967. Lancet 1:1256.

[20] Daniel, P. M., et al. 1967. Quart. J. Exp. Physiol. Cog. Med. Sci. 52:184.

continued

Part III. Domestic and Laboratory Mammals Other Than Dog

[21] Dietrich, L. S., and G. J. Siegel. 1960. Amer. J. Physiol. 199:198.

[22] Drinker, C. K., and M. E. Field. 1933. Lymphatics, Lymph and Tissue Fluid. Williams and Wilkins, Baltimore.

[23] Drinker, C. K., and J. M. Yoffey. 1941. Lymphatics, Lymph and Lymphoid Tissue. Harvard Univ. Press, Cambridge.

[24] Felinski, G. A., et al. 1964. Biochem. J. 90:154.

[25] Field, M. E., et al. 1934-35. Amer. J. Physiol. 110:174.

[26] Friedman, M., et al. 1956. Ibid. 184:11.

[27] Glenn, W. W. L., et al. 1943. J. Clin. Invest. 22:451.

[28] Hartmann, P. E., and A. K. Lascelles. 1966. J. Physiol. (London) 184:193.

[29] Heath, T. J. Unpublished. Univ. Queensland, School of Veterinary Science, St. Lucia, 1971.

[30] Heath, T. J., et al. 1964. Biochem. J. 92:511.

[31] Heim, J. W., et al. 1935. Amer. J. Physiol. 113:548.

[32] Heyndrickx, G. V. 1959. Quart. J. Exp. Physiol. Cog. Med. Sci. 44:264.

[33] Heyndrickx, G. V. 1961. Amer. J. Physiol. 200:835.

[34] Heyndrickx, G. V. 1961. Quart. J. Exp. Physiol. Cog. Med. Sci. 46:33.

[35] Heyndrickx, G. V. 1962. Ibid. 47:302.

[36] Heyndrickx, G. V., and G. J. Peeters. 1958. Ibid. 43:174.

[37] Heyndrickx, G. V., and G. J. Peeters. 1958. Enzymologia 20:161.

[38] Heyndrickx, G. V., and G. J. Peeters. 1960. Biochem. J. 75:1.

[39] Humphreys, P. W., et al. 1967. J. Physiol. (London) 193:1.

[40] Jacobsen, S. 1966. Brit. J. Pharmacol. 27:213.

[41] Jacobsson, S., and I. Kjellmer. 1964. Acta Physiol. Scand. 60:278.

[42] Korner, P. I., and W. J. Simmonds. Unpublished, Univ. Sydney, Dept. Medicine, 1971.

[43] Kotani, M., et al. 1967. J. Lipid Res. 8:181.

[44] Kotani, M., et al. 1968. Jap. Circ. J. 32:995.

[45] Lascelles, A. K., and B. Morris. Quart. J. Exp. Physiol. Cog. Med. Sci. 46:206.

[46] Lascelles, A. K., and J. C. Wadsworth. 1971. J. Physiol. (London) 214:443.

[47] Lascelles, A. K., et al. 1964. Res. Vet. Sci. 5:190.

[48] Leat, W. M. F., and J. G. Hall. 1968. J. Agr. Sci. 71:189.

[49] Lewis, G. P. 1967. J. Physiol. (London) 191:591.

[50] Lewis, G. P. 1969. Ibid. 205:619.

[51] Lindner, H. R. 1963. Endocrinology 25:483.

[52] Lindner, H. R., et al. 1964. J. Endocrinol. 30:361.

[53] Linzell, J. L. 1960. J. Physiol. (London) 153:510.

[54] McCarrell, J. D., et al. 1941. Amer. J. Physiol. 133:79.

[55] McDougall, E. I. 1964. Biochem. J. 90:160.

[56] McIntosh, G. H., and B. Morris. 1971. J. Physiol. (London) 214:365.

[57] Morgan, E. H. 1963. Ibid. 169:339.

[58] Morris, B. Unpublished. Australian Nat. Univ., Canberra, 1971.

[59] Morris, B. 1956. Quart. J. Exp. Physiol. Cog. Med. Sci. 41:318.

[60] Morris, B., and F. C. Courtice. 1955. Ibid. 40:149.

[61] Morris, B., and M. B. Sass. 1966. Proc. Roy. Soc. B164:577.

[62] Morris, B., and M. B. Sass. Unpublished, 1971.

[63] Nix, J. T., et al. 1951. Amer. J. Physiol. 164:117.

[64] Perlmann, G. E., et al. 1943. J. Clin. Invest. 22:627.

[65] Rasio, E. A., et al. 1965. Diabetologia 1:125.

[66] Reinhardt, W. O., and C. H. Li. 1945. Proc. Soc. Exp. Biol. Med. 58:321.

[67] Reynolds, M. 1962. J. Dairy Sci. 45:742.

[68] Roberts, J. C., and F. C. Courtice. 1969. Aust. J. Exp. Biol. Med. Sci. 47:421.

[69] Romsos, D. R., and A. D. McGilliard. 1970. J. Dairy Sci. 53:1483.

[70] Rymaszewska, T., et al. 1965. Transplantation 3:114.

[71] Seiki, K., et al. 1968. J. Endocrinol. 42:157.

[72] Shannon, A. D., and A. K. Lascelles. 1967. Aust. J. Biol. Sci. 20:669.

[73] Shannon, A. D., and A. K. Lascelles. 1968. Quart. J. Exp. Physiol. Cog. Med. Sci. 53:194.

[74] Shannon, A. D., et al. 1968. Ibid. 53:415.

[75] Shannon, A. D., et al. 1969. Aust. J. Biol. Sci. 22:189.

[76] Shrivastava, B. K., et al. 1967. Quart. J. Exp. Physiol. Cog. Med. Sci. 52:305.

[77] Simmonds, W. J. Unpublished. Univ. W. Australia, 1971.

[78] Smeaton, T. C., et al. 1969. Aust. J. Exp. Biol. Med. Sci. 47:565.

[79] Staub, N. C. Unpublished. Univ. Calif., San Francisco, 1971.

[80] Verbecke, R., et al. 1965. Biochem. J. 94:183.

[81] Vogel, G., and I. Stoeckert. 1963. Pfluegers Arch. Gesamte Physiol. Menschen Tiere 277:236.

[82] Wallace, J. C., and A. K. Lascelles. 1964. J. Reprod. Fert. 8:235.

[83] Woolley, G., and F. C. Courtice. 1962. Aust. J. Exp. Biol. Med. Sci. 40:121.

273. PHYSICAL PROPERTIES AND CHEMICAL COMPOSITION OF CEREBROSPINAL FLUID: MAMMALS

Part I. Man

Values in parentheses are ranges, estimate "c" (*see* Introduction).

#	Property or Constituent	Value	Reference
	Physical Properties and General Chemical Components		
1	Freezing point depression	0.569(0.540-0.603) °C	14
2	pH	7.48(7.35-7.70)	7
3	Pressure	150(70-180) mm H_2O	26
4	Refractive index	1.3351	32
5	Specific gravity	1.0069(1.0062-1.0082)	38
6	Volume	(90-150) ml	26
7	Lymphocytes	(0-10) cells/μl	26
8	Solids, total	1.08(0.85-1.70) %	14
9	Water	99%	27
	Electrolytes		
10	Aluminum	0.1 μg/ml	23
11	Arsenic	<0.0005 μg/ml	23
12	Barium	Trace	33
13	Bicarbonate	48.3 mg/100 ml	27
14	Boron	Trace	33
15	Bromide	0.23(0.14-0.38) mg/100 ml	20
16	Calcium	4.56(3.9-5.1) mg/100 ml	21
17	Carbon dioxide	59(57-62) vol %	31
18	Chloride	438(418-452) mg/100 ml	10
19	Cobalt	0.0002 μg/ml	23
20	Copper	0.016 μg/ml	23
21	Gold	6.2×10^{-6} μg/ml	23
22	Iodine	0.005 μg/ml	17
23	Iron	(0.01-0.02) μg/ml	23
24	Lead	≯0.010 μg/ml	9
25	Magnesium	2.71(2.40-2.95) mg/100 ml	21
26	Manganese	(0.00083-0.0015) μg/ml	8
27	Mercury	<0.001 μg/ml	23
28	Phosphorus	1.53(1.25-2.10) mg/100 ml	25
29	Potassium	9.8(8.5-11.5) mg/100 ml	16
30	Silver	<0.001 μg/ml	23
31	Sodium	524(501-543) mg/100 ml	24
32	Strontium	Trace	33
33	Sulfur	0.6 mg/100 ml	36
34	Zinc	0.016 μg/ml	23
	Vitamins		
35	Inositol	2.7 mg/100 ml	30
36	Ascorbic acid (vitamin C)	1.8 mg/100 ml	34
	Lipids, Carbohydrates, Miscellaneous Organic Acids		
37	Fatty acids	(1-3) mg/100 ml	4

#	Property or Constituent	Value	Reference
38	Cholesterol	(0.24-0.50) mg/100 ml	4
39	Reducing substances, total	65(45-93) mg/100 ml	14
40	Fructose	3.4(2.0-7.5) mg/100 ml	12,19
41	Hexosamine	9(5-18) mg/100 ml	12
42	Polysaccharides	3.4(2.3-6.8) mg/100 ml	12
43	Acetic acid	13.6(0.28-26.97) mg/100 ml	24
44	Lactic acid	19(11-27) mg/100 ml	15
45	Pyruvic acid	1.02 mg/100 ml	1
46	Citric acid	0.04 mg/100 ml	3
	Nitrogenous Substances		
	Protein		
47	Total	28(12-43) mg/100 ml	14
48	Lumbar	25(20-40) mg/100 ml	27
49	Cisternal	15 mg/100 ml	27
50	Ventricular	10 mg/100 ml	27
51	Prealbumin	7(2-15) % of total protein	5,18, 28
52	Albumin	55(40-70) % of total protein	5,18
	Globulin		5,18
53	α-	10(5-20) % of total protein	
54	β-	12(5-20) % of total protein	
55	γ-	11(5-20) % of total protein	
56	τ-Component [1]	5(0-10) % of total protein	5,18
57	Fibrinogen	0	5,18, 22
	Amino acids		
58	Alanine	27.9 ± 9.9 μmoles/liter	35
59	α-Aminobutyric acid	2.6 ± 0.8 μmoles/liter	35
60	Arginine	14.2 ± 7.4 μmoles/liter	35
61	Aspartic acid	2.9 ± 2.7 μmoles/liter	35
62	Citrulline	2.1 ± 0.7 μmoles/liter	35
63	Cystine	0.2 ± 0.3 μmoles/liter	11
64	Glutamic acid	7.0 ± 4.9 μmoles/liter	11
65	Glutamine	509 ± 144 μmoles/liter	11
66	Glycine	8.5 ± 2.5 μmoles/liter	35
67	Histidine	11.1 ± 2.9 μmoles/liter	35
68	Homocarnosine	2.7 ± 1.2 μmoles/liter	35
69	Isoleucine	5.0 ± 0.9 μmoles/liter	35
70	Leucine	11.6 ± 2.4 μmoles/liter	35
71	Lysine	18.6 ± 6.4 μmoles/liter	35
72	Methionine	3.2 ± 1.0 μmoles/liter	35
73	Ornithine	8.4 ± 2.3 μmoles/liter	35
74	Phenylalanine	7.5 ± 2.2 μmoles/liter	35
75	Proline	0.6 ± 1.6 μmoles/liter	11

[1] Component migrating between β- and γ- globulins on electrophoresis.

continued

Part I.   Man

	Property or Constituent	Value	Reference
76	Serine + asparagine	35.7 ± 9.6 μmoles/liter	35
77	Taurine	5.3 ± 1.4 μmoles/liter	35
78	Threonine	26.6 ± 9.3 μmoles/liter	35
79	Tryptophan	0.8 ± 1.4 μmoles/liter	11
80	Tyrosine	9.1 ± 5.0 μmoles/liter	11
81	Valine	14.3 ± 4.0 μmoles/liter	35
82	Ammonia	(0.096-0.097) mg/100 ml	32
83	Creatinine	1.11(0.54-1.91) mg/100 ml	6
84	Ethanolamine	6.7 ± 3.3 μmoles/liter	35
85	Urea	11.7(7.4-16.0) mg/100 ml	24
86	Uric acid	(0.5-2.8) mg/100 ml	13

	Property or Constituent	Value	Reference
	Nitrogen		
87	Non-protein N	19(12-28) mg/100 ml	14
88	α-Amino N	(0.96-1.47) mg/100 ml	37
89	Urea N	14 mg/100 ml	27
	Hormones, Enzymes		
90	Cortisone	(0.1-0.2) μg/100 ml	2
91	Hydrocortisone	(0.2-0.4) μg/100 ml	2
92	17-Hydroxycortico-steroids	<2 μg/100 ml	24
93	Creatine phospho-kinase	(0-1.5) IU/liter	29

Contributors: Cumings, J. N., and Lascelles, Peter T.;   Hamilton, Paul B.

References

[1] Amatuzio, D. S., and S. Nesbitt. 1950. J. Clin. Invest. 29:1486.

[2] Baron, D. N., and D. Abelson. 1954. Nature (London) 173:174.

[3] Benni, B. 1932. Acta Med. Scand., Suppl. 50:167.

[4] Brown, W. T., et al. 1939. Arch. Neurol. Psychiat. 42:260.

[5] Bücher, T., et al. 1952. Klin. Wochenschr. 30:325.

[6] Cockrill, J. R. 1931. Arch. Neurol. Psychiat. 25:1297.

[7] Cohen, E. N., and R. T. Knight. 1947. Anesthesiology 8:594.

[8] Cotzias, G. C., and P. S. Papavasiliou. 1962. Nature (London) 195:823.

[9] Cumings, J. N. 1959. Heavy Metals and the Brain. B. H. Blackwell, Oxford.

[10] Dailey, M. E. 1931. J. Biol. Chem. 93:5.

[11] Dickinson, J. C., and P. B. Hamilton. 1966. J. Neurochem. 13:1179.

[12] Eastham, M. D., and K. R. Keay. 1952. J. Clin. Pathol. 5:319.

[13] Flexner, L. B. 1934. Physiol. Rev. 14:161.

[14] Fremont-Smith, F., et al. 1931. Arch. Neurol. Psychiat. 25:1271.

[15] Glaser, J. 1926. J. Biol. Chem. 69:539.

[16] Helmsworth, J. A. 1947. J. Lab. Clin. Med. 32:1486.

[17] Henly, A. A. 1961. In C. Long, ed. Biochemists' Handbook. E. and F. N. Spon, London. p. 894.

[18] Hoch, H., and A. Chanutin. 1952. Proc. Soc. Exp. Biol. Med. 81:628.

[19] Hubbard, R. S., and N. M. Russell. 1937. J. Biol. Chem. 119:647.

[20] Hunter, G. Unpublished. United Oxford Hospitals, Oxford, England, 1960.

[21] Hunter, G., and H. V. Smith. 1960. Nature (London) 186:161.

[22] Kabat, E. A., et al. 1942. J. Clin. Invest. 21:571.

[23] Kjellin, K. J. 1965. Nord. Med. 74:804.

[24] Klingman, W. O. Unpublished. Titus Harris Clinic, Galveston, Texas, 1960.

[25] Merritt, H. H., and W. Bauer. 1931. J. Biol. Chem. 90:215.

[26] Merritt, H. H., and F. Fremont-Smith. 1937. The Cerebrospinal Fluid. W. B. Saunders, Philadelphia.

[27] Merritt, H. H., et al. 1947. Fundamentals of Clinical Neurology. Blakiston, New York.

[28] Monseu, G., and J. N. Cumings. 1965. J. Neurol. Neurosurg. Psychiat. 28:56.

[29] Nathan, M. J. 1967. Ibid. 30:52.

[30] Nixon, D. A. 1953. J. Physiol. (London) 119:18.

[31] Pincers, J. B., and B. Kramer. 1923. J. Biol. Chem. 57:463.

[32] Roeder, F., and O. Rehm. 1942. Die Cerebrospinalflüssigkeit: Untersuchungsmethoden und Klinik für Artze und Tierärtze. Springer Verlag, Berlin.

[33] Scott, G. H., and J. H. McMillen. 1936. Proc. Soc. Exp. Biol. Med. 32:287.

[34] Spiegel-Adolph, M., et al. 1951. J. Nerv. Ment. Dis. 113:529.

[35] Van Sande, M., et al. 1970. J. Neurochem. 17:125.

[36] Watchorn, E., and R. A. McCance. 1935. Biochem. J. 29:2291.

[37] Williams, E. M., and D. M. Matthews. 1965. J. Clin. Pathol. 18:771.

[38] Wohnan, I. J., et al. 1946. Amer. J. Clin. Pathol., Tech. Sect. 10:33.

continued

Part II. Mammals Other Than Man

Values in parentheses are ranges, estimate "c" (*see* Introduction).

	Property or Constituent	Value	Reference		Property or Constituent	Value	Reference
	Cat				**Dog**		
1	Appearance	Clear & colorless	10	39	Appearance	Clear & colorless; some fibrin	10
2	pH	7.45	19	40	pH	7.37(7.35-7.39)	27
3	Pressure	100 mm H_2O	10	41	Pressure	86.5(24-172) mm H_2O	27
4	Osmotic pressure	1.017 g NaCl/100 g H_2O	1	42	Freezing point depression	(0.61-0.63) °C	10
5	Refractive index	1.33435	18	43	Refractive index	1.3342	18
6	Colloidal reaction	1110000000	10	44	Specific gravity	1.0065(1.0056-1.0125)	27
7	Nonne-Apelt reaction	Negative	10	45	Colloidal reaction	1110000000	10
8	Pandy test	Negative	10	46	Nonne-Apelt reaction	Negative	10
9	Cells	(0-1) lymphocytes/μl	10	47	Pandy test	±	10
10	Calcium	5.2 mg/100 ml	17	48	Volume	(0.9-16.0) ml	10
11	Chloride	150 meq/liter	7	49	Cells; pups <7 mo	5(1-8) lymphocytes/μl [l]	10
12	Potassium	5.9 meq/liter	7	50	adults	2.9(0-8) lymphocytes/μl	10
13	Sodium	162 meq/liter	7	51	Calcium	5.6 ± 0.12 mg/100 ml	20
14	Ascorbic acid (vitamin C)	3.8 mg/100 ml	16	52	Chloride	808(761-883) mg/100 ml	27
15	Sugar	85 mg/100 ml	10	53	Phosphorus	1.1(0.6-1.6) mg/100 ml	28
16	Protein	25 mg/100 ml	7	54	Potassium	3.1(2.8-3.4) meq/liter	28
	Cattle			55	Sodium	156.3(142-170) meq/liter	28
17	Appearance	Clear, watery	10	56	Ascorbic acid (vitamin C)	6.6 mg/100 ml	16
18	pH	(7.0-7.6)	24	57	Sugar	74(61-116) mg/100 ml	27
19	Pressure	105(80-150) mm H_2O	26	58	Protein, total	27.5(11-55) mg/100 ml	10
20	Freezing point depression	(0.54-0.55) °C	9	59	Albumin	27(16.5-37.5) mg/100 ml	10
21	Specific gravity	(1.005-1.008)	10	60	Globulin	9.0(5.5-16.5) mg/100 ml	10
22	Colloidal gold	1111000000	10	61	Protein quotient	0.35(0.14-0.75) mg/100 ml	10
23	Volume	(310-320) ml	10	62	Allantoin	0.3(0.25-0.47) mg/100 ml	4
24	Cells	(0-3) lymphocytes/μl	10	63	Uric acid	0.23(0.13-0.35) mg/100 ml	4
25		(10-20) lymphocytes/μl	24		**Goat**		
26	Calcium	(5.1-6.3) mg/100 ml	9	64	Appearance	Clear & colorless	10
27	Chloride	(650-725) mg/100 ml	9	65	Specific gravity	1.0049	13
28	Magnesium	2.1 mg/100 ml	14	66	Colloidal gold	1111000000	10
29	Phosphorus, inorganic	(0.9-3.2) mg/100 ml	24	67	Nonne-Apelt reaction	Negative	10
30	Potassium	(11.2-13.8) mg/100 ml	10	68	Pandy test	Negative	10
31	Sugar	(35-70) mg/100 ml	9	69	Cells	1 lymphocyte/μl	10
32	Protein, total	(20-33) mg/100 ml	10	70	Chloride	681 mg/100 ml	13
33	Albumin	(10-20) mg/100 ml	10	71	Sugar	71 mg/100 ml	9
34	Globulin	(2-8) mg/100 ml	10	72	Protein, total	12 mg/100 ml	9,13
35	Protein quotient	(0.11-0.25) mg/100 ml	10		**Guinea pig**		
36	Creatine	(2.4-3.8) mg/100 ml	24	73	Calcium	3 meq/liter	6
37	Creatinine	(0.5-1.7) mg/100 ml	24	74	Chloride	122 meq/liter	7
38	Urea N	11 mg/100 ml	5				

[l] Lymphocytes are 65(15-95)% small, 21(5-40)% large, and 14(0-40)% degenerate forms [3].

continued

Part II. Mammals Other Than Man

	Property or Constituent	Value	Reference		Property or Constituent	Value	Reference
75	Magnesium	2 meq/liter	6	109	Pressure	(40-110) mm H_2O	10
76	Potassium	4 meq/liter	7	110	Specific gravity	1.005	9,23
77	Sodium	150 meq/liter	7	111	Nonne-Apelt reaction	Negative	10
78	Protein	20 meq/liter	7	112	Pandy test	Negative	10
79	Nitrogen, non-protein	21 meq/liter	7	113	Carbon dioxide	(41.2-48.5) vol %	23
				114	Chloride	(600-730) mg/100 ml	9,23
	Horse			115	Sugar	(50-57) mg/100 ml	9
80	pH	7.25(7.13-7.36)	2	116	Lactic acid	(1.4-4.0) mg/100 ml	23
81	Pressure	379(272-490) mm H_2O	2	117	Protein, total	(15-19) mg/100 ml	9
82	Specific gravity	1.006(1.004-1.008)	2	118	Albumin	(15-19) mg/100 ml	23
83	Colloidal gold	1223333221	10	119	Globulin	0	23
84	Volume	(170-300) ml	12	120	Nitrogen, non-protein	(5.6-16.8) mg/100 ml	9
85	Cells	4(2-7) lymphocytes & histio-cytes/μl[2]	10				
86	Calcium	6.26(5.55-6.98) mg/100 ml	2		**Sheep**		
87	Chloride	737(691-792) mg/100 ml	2	121	Appearance	Clear & colorless	10
88	Magnesium	1.98(1.07-2.95) mg/100 ml	2	122	pH	7.35(7.3-7.4)	22
89	Phosphorus, in-organic	1.44(0.87-2.20) mg/100 ml	2	123	Pressure	(60-270) mm H_2O	10
90	Potassium	12.66(10.65-14.20) mg/100 ml	2	124	Specific gravity	1.007(1.004-1.008)	22
91	Ascorbic acid (vitamin C)	1.7 mg/100 ml	8	125	Colloidal gold	1111000000	10
92	Cholesterol	(0.25-0.65) mg/100 ml	10	126	Nonne-Apelt reaction	Negative	10
93	Sugar	57.2(40-78) mg/100 ml	2	127	Pandy test	Negative	10
94	Protein, total	47.58(28.75-71.75) mg/100 ml	2	128	Cells	(0-15) lymphocytes/μl	9
95	Albumin	38.64(22.62-67.94) mg/100 ml	2	129	Calcium	5.6 ± 0.3 mg/100 ml	21
96	Globulin	9.34(3.37-18.37) mg/100 ml	2	130	Chloride	832(750-868) mg/100 ml	9
97	Urea	(23-31) mg/100 ml	11	131	Magnesium	2.88 mg/100 ml	10
98	Nitrogen, non-protein	26.88(13.72-39.20) mg/100 ml	2	132	Sugar	(48-109) mg/100 ml	9
				133	Protein, total	(8-70) mg/100 ml	9
	Monkey			134	Nitrogen, non-protein	29(9.6-42.0) mg/100 ml	9
99	Cells, cisternal	(1-3) lymphocytes/μl	9				
100	lumbar	(4-10) lymphocytes/μl	9		**Swine**		
101	Chloride	(420-500) mg/100 ml	9	135	Appearance	Clear & colorless	10
102	Ascorbic acid (vitamin C)	2.3 mg/100 ml	16	136	Pressure	(80-145) mm H_2O	25
103	Sugar	60 mg/100 ml	9	137	Colloidal gold	1111000000	10
104	Protein, cisternal	(8-15) mg/100 ml	9,23	138	Nonne-Apelt reaction	Negative	10
105	lumbar	(20-30) mg/100 ml	9,23	139	Pandy test	Negative	10
106	Globulin	(0.4-6.3) mg/100 ml	15	140	Cells	(1-20) lymphocytes/μl	9
				141	Sugar	(45-87) mg/100 ml	9
	Rabbit			142	Protein, total	(24-29) mg/100 ml	9
107	Appearance	Clear & colorless	10	143	Albumin	(17-24) mg/100 ml	10
108	pH	(7.40-7.85)	23	144	Globulin	(5-10) mg/100 ml	10

[2] Cells are 50% lymphocytes and 50% histiocytes and degenerate forms.

Contributors: Cumings, J. N., and Lascelles, Peter T.

continued

273. PHYSICAL PROPERTIES AND CHEMICAL COMPOSITION OF CEREBROSPINAL FLUID: MAMMALS

Part II. Mammals Other Than Man

References

[1] Aldred, P., et al. 1940. J. Physiol. (London) 98: 446.

[2] Behrens, H. 1953. Proc. 15th Int. Vet. Congr. 2(1): 1031.

[3] Bindrich, H., and D. Schmidt. 1952. Arch. Exp. Vet. Med. 6:162.

[4] Byers, S. O., and M. Friedman. 1949. Amer. J. Physiol. 157:394.

[5] Carmichael, J., and E. R. Jones. 1939. J. Comp. Pathol. 52:222.

[6] Citron, L., and D. Exley. 1957. Proc. Roy. Soc. Med. 50:697.

[7] Citron, L., et al. 1956. Brit. Med. Bull. 12:101.

[8] Errington, B. J., et al. 1942. Amer. J. Vet. Res. 3: 242.

[9] Fankhauser, R. 1953. Zentralbl. Veterinaermed. 1(2):156.

[10] Fankhauser, R. 1962. In J. R. M. Innes and L. Z. Saunders, ed. Comparative Neuropathology. Academic Press, New York. pp. 21-54.

[11] Fedotov, A. I. 1937. Sb. Rab. Leningrad. Vet. Inst., p. 263.

[12] Fedotov, A. I. 1939. Vet. Bull. (London) 9:583.

[13] Fujisawa, Y. 1927. Osaka Igakkai Zasshi 26.

[14] Josland, S. W. 1934. N. Z. Dep. Agr. Annu. Rep. 1933-34 (Chem. Abstr. 29:6290-9, 1935).

[15] Kabat, E. A., et al. 1951. J. Exp. Med. 93:615.

[16] Kasahara, M., and Y. Fujisawa. 1930. Z. Gesamte Exp. Med. 73:11.

[17] Katzenelbogen, S. 1934. J. Pharmacol. Exp. Ther. 51:435.

[18] Ledoux, A. 1941. Acta Biol. Belg. 4:506.

[19] Ledoux, A. 1943. Bull. Soc. Roy. Sci. Liege 4:254.

[20] Magalhaes, L. M., et al. 1960-61. Arq. Esc. Vet. Univ. Minas Gerais 13:217.

[21] Millo, A., and A. Begliomini. 1960. Arch. Vet. Ital. 11(6):199.

[22] Nikitin, N. A. K. 1942. Vet. Bull. (London) 12:473.

[23] Roeder, F., and O. Rehm. 1942. Die Cerebrospinal-flüssigkeit: Untersuchungsmethoden und Klinik für Artze and Tierärtze. Springer Verlag, Berlin.

[24] Soliman, M. K., et al. 1965. Zentralbl. Veterinaermed. A12:769.

[25] Sorensen, D. K., et al. 1954. Amer. J. Vet. Res. 15:258.

[26] Sykes, J. F., and L. A. Moore. 1942. Amer. J. Vet. Res. 3:364.

[27] Teunissen, G. H. B., and M. A. J. Verwer. 1953. Proc. 15th Int. Vet. Congr. 2(1):1022.

[28] Yeary, R. A., et al. 1960. Amer. J. Vet. Res. 21: 306.

274. PHYSICAL PROPERTIES AND CHEMICAL COMPOSITION OF SEROUS FLUIDS: VERTEBRATES

In transudates the concentration of blood constituents depends on the plasma concentration of the constituent, the membrane permeability of the constituent, the charge of the ion (electrolytes), and the concentrations of nondiffusible ions (proteins) in the plasma and in the transudate. For non-electrolytes readily passing through the membrane, the concentration in transudate water will equal that in plasma water, provided a steady state is present. In the case of electrolytes, the concentrations in the transudate will differ from those in plasma according to the Gibbs-Donnan law for heterogeneous solutions. Figures in heavy brackets are reference numbers. Values in parentheses are ranges, estimate "c" unless otherwise indicated (*see* Introduction).

Part I. Man

Property or Constituent	Plasma	Transudates	Pleural Fluid	Pericardial Fluid	Peritoneal Fluid
		Physical Properties & General Chemical Components			
1 pH	7.39(7.33-7.45)[b] [6, 10,22]	(7.45-7.68) [15]	7.64(7.60-7.68) [35]	....	7.4(6.8-9.8) [15]
2 Specific gravity	1.027(1.025-1.029)[b] [28]	(1.005-1.015) [4]	1.013 [8]	....	1.012 [8]

continued

274. PHYSICAL PROPERTIES AND CHEMICAL COMPOSITION
OF SEROUS FLUIDS: VERTEBRATES

Part I. Man

	Property or Constituent	Plasma	Transudates	Pleural Fluid	Pericardial Fluid	Peritoneal Fluid
3	Conductivity, mho × 1000	(10.5-12.4) [34]	14.2(11.3-15.5) [34]	....	....	13.4(13.2-13.5) [24]
4	Ash, %	(0.6-1.0) [14]	....	0.76 [21]	0.67 [11]	0.98 [21]
5	Solids, %	8.6(7.9-9.1) [27]	18(3.7-59.3) [14]		....	2.5(2.0-3.0) [14]
6	Water, %	93(91-95) [34]	94(90.4-99.1) [14,15]	98(96.4-99.0) [12,15]	....	(95-99) [12]
	Electrolytes					
7	Calcium, meq/liter	(4.2-5.1) [29]	4.0(2.6-4.9) [12]	4.3(2.8-5.4) [8,30]	....	4.0(2.0-4.9) [8,15,24]
8	Carbon dioxide, meq/liter	(24-34) [17]	28.7(22.2-37.3) [12,15]	23.8(21.3-30.9) [30]	....	26.7(23.8-29.3) [15,24]
9	Chloride, meq/liter	102.4(98-108) [12]	(120-130) [4]	100(92.3-136.0) [8,30]	124.5 [14]	109(91-121) [8,15,24]
10	Magnesium, meq/liter	(1.4-2.4) [4]	2.0(1.6-2.4) [12]	1.71(0.72-2.41) [30]	....	0.5 [15]
	Phosphorus, mg/100 ml					
11	Total	23(18.6-29.0) [16]	....	11.4(6.2-30.7) [30]	....	....
12	Inorganic	(2.5-4.9) [29]	3.0(1.2-4.4) [2,15]	3.8(2.07-5.07) [8,30]	....	4.0(1.2-5.3) [8,15]
13	Potassium, meq/liter	4.7(3.6-5.5) [12]	3.4(2.8-6.0) [7,12]	4.8(2.5-6.6) [7,12,30]	....	4.1(2.0-5.6) [7,24]
14	Sodium, meq/liter	138(133-148) [7]	140(122-156) [7,12,15]	140(136-148) [12,24,30]	....	138(127-155) [12,15,24]
	Lipids					
15	Lipids, total, mg/100 ml	(450-1000) [17]	1500(700-2500) [14]	....	....	....
16	Cholesterol, mg/100 ml	(137-292) [29]	40(13-60) [14]	147(20-329) [8,30]	....	60(5-148) [8]
17	Fatty acids, mg/100 ml	316(149-483)[b] [3]	....	268(129-429) [30]	....	....
18	Lecithin, mg/100 ml	110(80-200) [4]	(20-100) [4]	50(0-125) [8]	....	40(0-140) [8]
19	Phosphatide, mg/100 ml	(125-300) [17]	....	142 [18]	....	164 [18]
	Carbohydrates, Miscellaneous Organic Acids, Hormones					
20	Sugar, mg/100 ml	(75-129) [29]	....	92(70-122) [8]	....	114(86-131) [8]
21	Lactic acid, mg/100 ml	(5-20) [4]	(17-32) [18]	17.8(10.7-47.3) [30]	....	....
22	17-Hydroxy-cortico-steroids, µg/100 ml	13(2-34) [1]	3(0-11) [32]	8(0-16) [32]	(5-16) [32]	4.2(0-9) [32]
	Nitrogenous Substances					
23	Protein, total[1/], g/100 ml	(5.7-7.9) [29]	0.85(0.4-1.3) [15,33]	1.77(0.3-4.1) [19,24,35]	3.3(0.8-4.9) [14,26]	2.1(0.02-4.50) [14,15,19,24]

[1/] Some higher than normal values probably included.

continued

Part I. Man

	Property or Constituent	Plasma	Transudates	Pleural Fluid	Pericardial Fluid	Peritoneal Fluid
24	Albumin, g/100 ml	(2.8-5.2) [29]	2.23 [18]	0.97(0.80-1.22) [8]	2.23 [14]	0.88(0.32-1.64) [8]
25	Globulin, g/100 ml	2.3(1.5-3.3) [13]	0.59 [18]	0.79(0.33-1.23) [8]	0.6 [14]	0.81(0.21-1.69) [8]
26	Fibrinogen, g/100 ml	0.28(0.20-0.39) [34]	0.03(0-0.8) [14]	0.1(0-0.3) [8,14]	0.03 [14]	0.1(0-0.2) [8]
27	Bilirubin, mg/100 ml	0.4(0.1-0.8)[d] [5]	(0-0.2) [23]	(0.1-0.7) [23]	....	0.5 [23]
28	Creatine, mg/100 ml	1.25(1.0-1.6) [20]	3.20 [18]	3.02(2.1-4.9)[2/] [30]	....	....
29	Creatinine, mg/100 ml	0.92(0.5-1.5) [20]	2.43 [18]	1.2(0.7-2.1) [8,30]	....	1.25(1.0-2.0) [8]
30	Histamine, μg/100 ml	6.4 [9]	....	(0.5-2400) [18]	....	(0.5-2.5) [18]
31	Uric acid, mg/100 ml	5.04(2.6-7.5)[3/]; 3.84(2.0-5.7)[4/] [20, 31]	....	4.0(1.9-8.0) [8,30]	....	4.2(1.8-5.3) [8]
32	Nitrogen Total N, mg/100 ml	1140(1050-1230) [2]	(318-837) [18]	287(260-339) [8]	....	150(45-554) [8]
33	Non-protein N, mg/100 ml	27(15-42) [2]	(27.5-30.0) [18]	31(20.3-42.5) [8,24, 30]	....	30.2(20.0-42.8) [8]
34	Amino acid N, mg/100 ml	4.0(3.5-6.0) [4]	6.38 [18]	5.6(4.21-8.86) [30]	....	....
35	Ammonia N, μg/100 ml	96.5 ± 3.2 [25]	1200 [18]	....	....	....
36	Urea N, mg/100 ml	(7-25) [29]	14.39 [18]	13(9.8-22.0) [8,30]	....	16(11.9-21.0) [8]

[2/] Includes creatinine. [3/] Males. [4/] Females.

Contributors: Young, Joel E.; Bowman, Russel O.

References

[1] Bliss, E. L., et al. 1953. J. Clin. Invest. 32:818.

[2] Bowman, R. O. Unpublished, 1955.

[3] Boyd, E. M. 1942. J. Biol. Chem. 143:131.

[4] Cantarow, A., and M. Trumper. 1962. Clinical Biochemistry. Ed. 6. W. B. Saunders, Philadelphia.

[5] Cantarow, A., et al. 1942. Arch. Intern. Med. 69:986.

[6] Cournand, A., et al. 1945. J. Clin. Invest. 24:106.

[7] Folk, B. P., et al. 1948. Amer. J. Physiol. 153:381.

[8] Foord, A. G., et al. 1929. J. Lab. Clin. Med. 13:417.

[9] Gefter, V. A., et al. 1968. Ter. Arkh. 40(2):68.

[10] Gibbs, E. L., et al. 1942. J. Biol. Chem. 144:325.

[11] Gorup-Besanez, E. F. von. 1878. Lehrbuch der physiologischen Chemie. Ed. 4. F. Vieweg, Braunschweig.

[12] Greene, C. H., et al. 1931. J. Biol. Chem. 91:203.

[13] Gutman, A. B., et al. 1941. J. Clin. Invest. 20:765.

[14] Hammarsten, O. 1893. A Textbook of Physiological Chemistry. J. Wiley, New York.

[15] Hastings, A. B., et al. 1927. J. Gen. Physiol. 8:701.

[16] Helve, O. 1946. Acta Med. Scand. 125:505.

[17] Henry, R. J. 1964. Clinical Chemistry. Harper and Row, New York.

[18] Hoppe-Seyler, F., and H. Thierfelder. 1953. Handbuch der physiologisch- und pathologisch-chemischen Analyse für Arzte, Biologen und Chemiker. Ed. 10. Springer Verlag, Berlin. v. 5.

[19] Iverson, P., and A. H. Johansen. 1929. Klin. Wochenschr. 8:1311.

[20] Jellinek, M., and J. M. Looney. 1939. J. Biol. Chem. 128:621.

[21] Junk, W., et al. 1925. Tabulae Biol. 2:527.

[22] Lambertsen, C. J., et al. 1950. Fed. Proc. Fed. Amer. Soc. Exp. Biol. 9:73.

continued

Part I. Man

[23] Layne, J. A., et al. 1950. Gastroenterology 16:91.

[24] Loeb, R. F., et al. 1922. J. Gen. Physiol. 4:591.

[25] Long, C., ed. 1968. Biochemists' Handbook. Van Nostrand, Princeton.

[26] Maurer, F. W., et al. 1940. Amer. J. Physiol. 129: 635.

[27] Miller, A. T., Jr. 1942. J. Biol. Chem. 143:65.

[28] Moore, N. S., and D. D. Van Slyke. 1930. J. Clin. Invest. 8:337.

[29] O'Kell, R. T., and J. R. Elliott. 1970. Clin. Chem. 16(3):161.

[30] Pinner, M., and G. Moerke. 1930. Amer. Rev. Tuberc. 22:121.

[31] Praetorius, E., and H. Poulsen. 1953. Scand. J. Clin. Lab. Invest. 5:273.

[32] Sandberg, A. A., et al. 1954. J. Lab. Clin. Med. 43: 874.

[33] Stead, E. A., and J. V. Warren. 1944. J. Clin. Invest. 23:283.

[34] Sunderman, F. W., and F. Boerner. 1949. Normal Values in Clinical Medicine. W. B. Saunders, Philadelphia.

[35] Yamada, S., et al. 1933. Z. Gesamte Exp. Med. 90: 342.

Part II. Vertebrates Other Than Man

	Animal	Property or Constituent	Plasma	Transudates	Pericardial Fluid	Peritoneal Fluid
1	Cat	Chloride, meq/liter	(117-123) [3]	....	....	80 [20]
2		Sugar, mg/100 ml	(60-100) [4]	....	....	48 [20]
3		Protein, total[1], g/100 ml	(5.3-7.6) [3]	....	2.4(2.17-2.67) [17]	(0.6-2.5) [17,20]
4		Urea nitrogen, mg/100 ml	(20-30) [3]	....	....	(7-32) [20]
5	Dog	pH [21]	....	....	....	7.26(7.13-7.40)
6		Osmotic pressure, mm H_2O [17]	....	....	66(48-90)	....
7		Water, % [8]	93(91-95)	98.9(98.3-99.3)	....	....
8		Calcium, meq/liter	4.9(4.5-5.7) [8]	3.5(3.2-4.1) [1,11,18,19]	....	4.0(2.0-4.9) [4,10,15]
9		Carbon dioxide, meq/liter	24(17.3-27.4) [8]	26.1(21.0-30.8) [8,9]	....	21.4(9.8-30.2) [21]
10		Chloride, meq/liter	122.5(115.0-136.4) [1,8,10,11,18,19]	126(118.8-127.5) [8]	....	124(111-143) [21]
11		Magnesium, meq/liter [8]	2.2(1.4-2.9)	1.7(1.4-2.2)	....	....
12		Phosphorus, mg/100 ml Total	26 [14]	12(11.8-18.4) [1,11]	....	....
13		Inorganic	4.4(3.2-6.0) [6]	5.6(3.6-7.3) [11,18]	....	....
14		Potassium, meq/liter [8]	5.3(4.7-6.2)	5.0(4.2-6.1)	....	....
15		Sodium, meq/liter [8]	159(152-169)	150(144-156)	....	....
16		Sugar, mg/100 ml	(55-90) [3]	....	....	180(160-200) [21]
17		Protein, total[1], g/100 ml	(6.1-7.8) [11]	3.0(0.17-4.8) [1,8,11,18,19]	1.75(0.8-2.9) [17]	2.6(1.63-3.71) [17]

[1] Some higher than normal values probably included.

continued

Part II. Vertebrates Other Than Man

	Animal	Property or Constituent	Plasma	Transudates	Pericardial Fluid	Peritoneal Fluid
18		Albumin, g/100 ml	3.57 [12]	....	1.03(0.75-1.52) [17]	....
19		Globulin, g/100 ml	2.63 [12]	....	0.75(0.45-1.54) [17]	....
20		Creatinine, mg/100 ml	(1.0-1.7) [3]	1.4(1.28-1.49) [11]	....	....
21		Uric acid, mg/100 ml	0.33 [7]	Trace [11]	....	....
		Nitrogen, mg/100 ml				
22		Total N	1100 [2]	....	....	149(26-295) [21]
23		Non-protein N	27(15-40) [2]	34(19.8-45.4) [11]	....	....
24		Amino acid N	....	(2.4-4.8) [11,19]	....	....
25		Urea N [11]	....	11(9.9-16.5)	....	....
26	Guinea pig	Chloride, meq/liter [21]	....	....	....	109(104-113)
27		Sugar, mg/100 ml	95(60-125) [13]	....	....	130 [21]
28	Horse	Water, % [9]	....	(93.5-95.8) [9]	....	....
29		Chloride, meq/liter	(98-106) [3]	99 [9]	....	....
30		Lipid, total, % [9]	....	(0.3-3.4)	....	....
31		Protein, total[1], g/100 ml	6.72 [3]	(3.5-4.2) [9]	....	....
32		Fibrinogen, g/100 ml	0.34 [12]	(0.04-2.20) [9]	....	....
33	Monkey [17]	Protein, total[1], g/100 ml	....	....	1.71(1.35-2.22)	....
34	Rabbit [17]	Protein, total[1], g/100 ml	....	....	2.16(1.48-3.65)	1.53
35	Rat	Protein, total[1], g/100 ml	6.0 ± 0.2 [16]	....	2.07 [17]	....
36	Duck [17]	Protein, total[1], g/100 ml	....	....	2.51(2.42-2.59)	2.51
37	Hen	Protein, total[1], g/100 ml	4.6 ± 0.1 [16]	....	3.53 [17]	....
38	Turtle	pH	7.72(7.46-7.80)	....	8.25(7.9-8.5)	8.12(7.85-8.42)
39	[23]	Calcium, meq/liter	4.6(3.1-6.5)	2.4	2.1(0.6-4.5)	3.4(2.4-5.2)
40		Carbon dioxide, meq/liter	40.4(23.2-52.5)	44	88.5(29-131)	68.9(24-128)
41		Chloride, meq/liter	86.4(54.5-109.8)	75.6	55.1(15-129)	70.8(33-124)
42		Magnesium, meq/liter	3.0(0.5-7.9)	0.8	1.1(0.3-3.5)	2.1(0.3-5.0)
43		Phosphate, meq/liter	1.7(0.9-3.5)	....	1.4(0.7-2.0)	1.3(0.7-2.4)
44		Potassium, meq/liter	4.0(2.4-6.7)	2.0	3.15(1.1-6.1)	3.2(2.4-4.3)
45		Sodium, meq/liter	138(120-163)	123	140(128-152)	137(120-152)
46		Sulfate, meq/liter	0.5(0.1-1.3)	....	0.35	0.5(0.1-1.2)

[1] Some higher than normal values probably included.

continued

Part II. Vertebrates Other Than Man

	Animal	Property or Constituent	Plasma	Transudates	Pericardial Fluid	Peritoneal Fluid
47	Elasmo-	pH	7.36(7.20-7.63)	7.45(7.15-7.64)	6.12(5.30-6.86)	5.80(5.40-6.35)
48	branchs[2]/ [22]	Calcium, meq/liter	4.9(2.9-6.0)	4.6(3.0-6.9)	1.4(0.5-3.5)	3.4(1.7-6.6)
49		Carbon dioxide, meq/liter	8.2(5.6-11.6)	7.3(4.6-10.5)	0.4(trace-0.5)	0.3(trace-0.4)
50		Chloride, meq/liter	236(227-266)	262(244-282)	370(366-373)	274(188-332)
51		Magnesium, meq/liter	2.8(1.7-3.5)	1.0(0.9-1.0)	2.6(1.0-5.0)	17.8(8.0-25.0)
52		Phosphate, meq/liter	2.0(0.7-3.5)	1.2(0.9-1.7)	0.4(0-0.7)	0.7(0-0.9)
53		Potassium, meq/liter	5.3(4.5-6.8)	4.8(3.8-6.0)	16.6(8.5-22.0)	6.6(5.2-8.9)
54		Sodium, meq/liter	259(236-275)	266(262-270)	314(290-321)	246(145-304)
55		Sulfate, meq/liter	1.0(trace-3.1)	0.4(trace-1.0)	Trace	5.0(trace-14.0)
56		Creatine, mg/100 ml	2.88(1.8-4.2)	2.4	....	3.9(3.6-4.2)
57		Creatinine, mg/100 ml	(0-0.5)	....	0	(0-0.7)
		Nitrogen, mg/100 ml				
58		Non-protein N	1090(1070-1125)	681	....	870(758-1015)
59		Amino acid N	7.5(5.6-9.4)	....	....	(0-2.6)
60		Ammonia N	....	(0-1)	3.3	23(8.6-60.4)
61		Urea N	1179(1045-1300)	971(555-1240)	1067(692-1346)	1013(900-1100)

[2]/ Head fluid considered a transudate.

Contributors: Young, Joel E.; Bowman, Russel O.

References

[1] Arnold, R. M., and L. B. Mendel. 1927. J. Biol. Chem. 72:189.

[2] Bowman, R. O. Unpublished, 1955.

[3] Coles, E. H. 1967. Veterinary Clinical Pathology. W. B. Saunders, Philadelphia.

[4] De Bodo, R. C., et al. 1937. J. Pharmacol. Exp. Ther. 61:48.

[5] Foord, A. G., et al. 1929. J. Lab. Clin. Med. 14: 417.

[6] Freeman, S., and C. J. Farmer. 1935. Amer. J. Physiol. 113:200.

[7] Friedman, M., and S. O. Byers. 1948. J. Biol. Chem. 175:727.

[8] Greene, C. H., et al. 1931. Ibid. 91:203.

[9] Hammarsten, O. 1893. A Textbook of Physiological Chemistry. Ed. 1. J. Wiley, New York.

[10] Hastings, A. B., et al. 1927. J. Gen. Physiol. 8:701.

[11] Heim, J. W. 1933. Amer. J. Physiol. 103:553.

[12] Howe, P. E. 1925. Physiol. Rev. 5:439.

[13] Johnson, D. D. 1950. Endocrinology 46:135.

[14] Kerr, S. E., and L. Daoud. 1935. J. Biol. Chem. 109:301.

[15] Loeb, R. F., et al. 1922. J. Gen. Physiol. 4:591.

[16] Long, C., ed. 1968. Biochemists' Handbook. Van Nostrand, Princeton.

[17] Maurer, F. W., et al. 1940. Amer. J. Physiol. 129: 635.

[18] Meyer-Bisch, R., and F. Günther. 1925. Pfluegers Arch. Gesamte Physiol. Menschen Tiere 109:81.

[19] Petersen, W. H., and T. P. Hughes. 1927. J. Biol. Chem. 66:229.

[20] Putnam, T. J. 1923. Amer. J. Physiol. 63:548.

[21] Schechter, A. J. 1931. Yale J. Biol. 4:167.

[22] Smith, H. W. 1929. J. Biol. Chem. 81:407.

[23] Smith, H. W. 1929. Ibid. 82:651.

Total body water, i.e., water in the extracellular and intracellular compartments, is usually measured as the volume of distribution in the body of an appropriate indicator after a single intravenous injection. The most reliable, commonly-used indicators are antipyrine and the heavy isotopes, deuterium oxide, or tritium oxide. During fetal life and early childhood there is a rapid decrease in total body water, after which the water content remains nearly constant at 72% ± 2 of the fat-free weight. From birth to puberty there is no apparent difference between male and female in body water content; following puberty, however, the proportion of body water increases in the male and decreases in the female.

Part I. Antipyrine Determination

In the presence of edema, equilibration may be slowed. In some instances, the concentration of antipyrine in pleural and ascitic fluid may be greater than the concentration in plasma water, necessitating direct, continued analysis of each compartment to prevent error. [4,8,10,16] Values in parentheses are ranges, estimate "b" unless otherwise indicated (see Introduction).

	Subjects		Total Body Water ml/kg body wt	Reference		Subjects		Total Body Water ml/kg body wt	Reference
	Age	No. & Sex				Age	No. & Sex		
1	Premature-28 da old	6	712	11	16	50-59 yr old	61♂	531	1-3,5,12, 14-17
2	Newborn	5	754(647-861)	8	17	50-60 yr old	21♀	441	19
3	Newborn-6 mo old	......	(720-830)ᶜ	7	18	60-70 yr old	19♀	422	15,17,19
4	1-12 mo old	8	627(504-750)	8	19	70-79 yr old	21♂	544	12
5	6 mo-11 yr old	......	(530-630)ᶜ	7	20	80-89 yr old	4♂	560	12
6	1-10 yr old	8	569(491-647)	8	21	>80 yr	4♀	488	15,17
7	16-30 yr old	94♀	516.6	19	22	Adult	16[2]	506[3]	18
8	17-39 yr old	23♂	548	1-3,5,14-17	23		16[2]	506[4]	18
9	18-46 yr old	81♂[1]	611(430-729)ᶜ	13	24		10[2]	549	9
10	20-29 yr old	4♂	554	12	25		57♂	527(403-682)ᶜ	8,17
11	20-39 yr old	18♀	444	15,17	26		33♂	585	6
12	30-39 yr old	20♂	541	12	27		31♀	446(292-528)ᶜ	1,17
13	30-40 yr old	26♀	493	19	28		......	557[5]	10
14	40-49 yr old	34♂	527	12	29	<70 kg	26♂	559(450-668)	1,17
15	40-50 yr old	27♀	486	19	30	>70 kg	22♂	549(435-663)	1,17

[1] Navy personnel. [2] Number of observations. [3] 4-Iodoantipyrine. [4] N-Acetyl-4-aminoantipyrine. [5] Edematous subjects.

Contributors: Calcagno, Philip L., Hollerman, Charles E., and Jose, Pedro A.

References

[1] Berger, E. Y., et al. 1950. Amer. J. Physiol. 162: 318.

[2] Brodie, B. B., et al. 1951. Proc. Soc. Exp. Biol. Med. 77:794.

[3] Deane, N. 1951. J. Clin. Invest. 30:1469.

[4] Deane, N. 1952. Methods Med. Res. 5:159.

[5] Deane, N., and H. W. Smith. 1952. J. Clin. Invest. 31:197.

[6] Faller, I. L., et al. 1955. J. Lab. Clin. Med. 45:748.

[7] Friis-Hansen, B. J., et al. 1950. Amer. J. Dis. Child. 80:515.

[8] Friis-Hansen, B. J., et al. 1951. Pediatrics 7:321.

[9] Grunner, O. 1957. Klin. Wochenschr. 35:347.

[10] Hurst, W. W., and F. R. Sherum. 1951. Amer. J. Med. 10:516.

[11] Kagan, B. M., et al. 1963. Ann. N. Y. Acad. Sci. 110:830.

[12] Norris, A. H., et al. 1963. Ibid. 110:623.

[13] Osserman, E. F., et al. 1950. J. Appl. Physiol. 2: 633.

[14] Prentice, T. C., et al. 1952. J. Clin. Invest. 31:412.

[15] Scribante, P., et al. 1952. Helv. Physiol. Pharmacol. Acta 10:224.

[16] Soberman, R. J., et al. 1949. J. Biol. Chem. 179:31.

[17] Steele, J. M., et al. 1950. Amer. J. Physiol. 162: 313.

[18] Talso, P. J., et al. 1955. J. Lab. Clin. Med. 46:619.

[19] Young, C. M., et al. 1963. Ann. N. Y. Acad. Sci. 110:589.

continued

Part II. Deuterium Oxide and Tritium Oxide Determinations

Deuterium oxide and tritium oxide are useful indicators in measuring total body water because of their rapid equilibration time. Since there is a change in the molecular weight of these substances as compared to water, there is a possibility that their rate of exchange in the body may not be the same as that of non-isotopic water. The error introduced through exchange of the isotope deuterium oxide with hydrogen atoms of organic molecules has been estimated to give results as high as 1.0-1.5% of the body weight. [16,21] Values in parentheses are ranges, estimate "c" unless otherwise indicated (*see* Introduction).

	Subjects Age	No. & Sex	Total Body Water ml/kg body wt	Reference
	Deuterium Oxide			
1	Newborn	41♂	784 ± 13	6-9,22
2		55♀	745 ± 23	
3	2-7 da old	12♂	743 ± 10	4,8,9,11
4		10♀	788 ± 11	
5	8-27 da old	11♂	726 ± 52	4,7,8,11
6		11♀	707 ± 17	
7	1 mo old	23♂	720 ± 39	4,8,11
8		22♀	671 ± 53	
9	2 mo old	9♂	670 ± 49	8
10		7♀	627 ± 56	
11	3 mo old	19♂	625 ± 20	8,11
12		18♀	618 ± 55	4,8,9,11
13	4 mo old	11♂	646 ± 62	4,8,9
14		11♀	614 ± 70	4,8,9,18
15	5 mo old	10♂	640 ± 47	4,8,18
16		5♀	604 ± 24	
17	6 mo old	21♂	587 ± 28	8,11,18
18		16♀	572 ± 27	
19	7 mo old	6♂	605 ± 66	8,18
20		7♀	570 ± 21	
21	8 mo old	12♂	608 ± 60	4,8
22		5♀	584 ± 56	
23	9 mo old	4♂	572 ± 12	4,8,9
24		3♀	531 ± 20	4,8,9
25	12 mo old	14♂	573 ± 60	8,11
26		8♀	571 ± 40	
27	2 yr old	9♂	616 ± 42	4,8,9
28		4♀	629 ± 53	
29	3 yr old	10♂	590 ± 32	4,8,9
30	7 yr old	6♂	583 ± 12	4,8,9
31		3♀	603 ± 9	
32	10-14 yr old	11♂	572 ± 34	4,8,12
33		11♀	562 ± 42	
34	14-18 yr old	7♂	618 ± 18	4,8,12
35		3♀	596 ± 2	
36	19-34 yr old	76♂	611	4,15,20,21
37		18♀	512	4
38	35-54 yr old	10♂	554	4
39		6♀	482	
40	>55 yr old	6♂	543	4,15
41		5♀	462	
42	Adult	47♂	598(420-720)	3,5,9,16,17
43		13♀	510(420-599)	
	Pregnant			
44	10 wk	39	543[1]	14
45		54	538[2]	
46	20 wk	......	542[1]; 534[2]	14
47	30 wk	......	546[1]; 541[2]	14
48	38 wk	......	478[1]	14
49			565[2]	10,14
50	Postpartum	......	526[1]	14
51			524[2]	13,14
	Tritium Oxide			
52	10-36 mo old	2♂	585 ± 70	1
53		19♂	686 ± 52[3]	
54		19♂	700 ± 68[4]	
55	20-25 yr	4♂	603(575-630)	19
56	23-49 yr	13♂	607(511-703)[b]	2
57	34-56 yr	15♂	521(479-569)	19

[1] Primipara. [2] Multipara. [3] Kwashiorkor without edema. [4] Kwashiorkor with edema.

Contributors: Calcagno, Philip L., Hollerman, Charles E., and Jose, Pedro A.

References

[1] Brinkman, G. L., et al. 1965. Pediatrics 34:94.
[2] Cooper, J. A., et al. 1958. J. Lab. Clin. Med. 52: 129.
[3] Edelman, I. S. 1952. Amer. J. Physiol. 171:279.
[4] Edelman, I. S., et al. 1952. Surg. Gynecol. Obstet. 95:1.
[5] Edelman, I. S., et al. 1952. Science 115:447.
[6] Flexner, L. B., et al. 1947. J. Pediat. 30:413.
[7] Friis-Hansen, B. 1957. Acta Paediat. (Stockholm) 46, Suppl. 110.
[8] Friis-Hansen, B. 1965. In J. Brozek, ed. Human Body Composition. Pergamon Press, Oxford. pp. 191-209.
[9] Friis-Hansen, B. J., et al. 1951. Pediatrics 7:321.

continued

Part II. Deuterium Oxide and Tritium Oxide Determinations

[10] Haley, H. B., and J. W. Woodbury. 1952. J. Clin. Invest. 31:635.

[11] Hanna, F. M. 1963. Ann. N.Y. Acad. Sci. 110:840.

[12] Hunt, E. E., Jr., and F. P. Heald. 1963. Ibid. 110: 532.

[13] Hutchinson, D. L., et al. 1953. J. Clin. Invest. 33: 235.

[14] Hytler, F. E., and M. A. Thomson. 1966. J. Obstet. Gynaecol. Brit. Commonw. 73:553.

[15] London, I. M., and D. Rittenberg. 1950. J. Biol. Chem. 184:687.

[16] Moore, F. G. 1946. Science 104:157.

[17] Moore, F. G. 1947. J. Amer. Med. Ass. 141:646.

[18] Owen, G. M., et al. 1963. Ann. N.Y. Acad. Sci. 110: 861.

[19] Prentice, T. C., et al. 1952. J. Clin. Invest. 31:412.

[20] Schwartz, I. L., et al. 1952. Fed. Proc. Fed. Amer. Soc. Exp. Biol. 11:142.

[21] Soberman, R., et al. 1949. J. Biol. Chem. 179:31.

[22] Yssing, M., and B. Friis-Hansen. 1965. Acta Paediat. Scand., Suppl. 159:117.

Part III. Desiccation and Specific Gravity Determinations

Desiccation determination: Intact subject weighed before and after drying to constant weight, usually at a temperature of 105°C ± 5. Specific gravity determination: Body water calculated from an empirical relationship between percent of body water, percent of body fat, and body specific gravity. Values in parentheses are ranges, estimate "b" unless otherwise indicated (see Introduction).

Subjects Specification	No. & Sex	Total Body Water ml/kg body wt	Reference		Subjects Specification	No. & Sex	Total Body Water ml/kg body wt	Reference
		Desiccation		8			740	
				9			796	
Fetus					Infants of diabetic mothers			
1 <100 g	35	914(871-957)	7,8,10,11, 15,17	10	1000-1499 g	3	800(774-818)	7
2 100-499 g	39	882(837-927)	7,8,10,11, 15,17,21	11	1500-2499 g	4	760(681-832)	7
				12	2500-3500 g	3	680(645-734)	7
3 500-999 g	17	852(792-912)	3,7,8,11,13, 15,17,21	13	Adult	....	679	16
				14		....	676	2
4 1000-1499 g	11	832(798-866)	3,7,8,10,11, 13,15	15		5	648(580-678)c	1,16,18
				16		4♂	635	4,16,19,20
5 1500-2499 g	14	783(710-856)	5-8,11,21	17		1♀	560	20
6 Fetus or newborn, >2500 g	19	708(598-818)	4,6-8,11,12, 15,21			Specific Gravity		
7 Newborn	....	664	9	18	Adult	9	543(444-596)c	14

Contributors: Calcagno, Philip L., Hollerman, Charles E., and Jose, Pedro A.

References

[1] Aron, H. 1917. In S. Hatai. Amer. J. Anat. 21:23.

[2] Aron, H. 1927. In C. Oppenheimer, ed. Handbuch der Biochemie des Menschen und der Tiere. Ed. 2. G. Fischer, Jena. v. 7, pp. 152-234.

[3] Bezold, A. von. 1857. Z. Wiss. Zool. 8:487.

[4] Bischoff, E. 1863. Z. Ration. Med., Ser. 3, 20:75.

[5] Brubacher, H. 1890. Z. Biol. 27:517.

[6] Camerer, W., Jr. 1902. Ibid. 43:1.

[7] Fee, B. A., and W. B. Weil, Jr. 1963. Ann. N.Y. Acad. Sci. 110:869.

[8] Fehling, H. 1877. Arch. Gynaekol. 11:523.

[9] Friis-Hansen, B. J., et al. 1951. Pediatrics 7:321.

[10] Givens, M. H., and I. G. Macy. 1933. J. Biol. Chem. 102:7.

[11] Iob, V., and W. W. Swanson. 1934. Amer. J. Dis. Child. 47:302.

[12] Klose, E. 1914. Jahrb. Kinderheilk. Phys. Erzieh. 80:154.

[13] Langstein, L., and F. Edelstein. 1917. Ibid. 15:49.

[14] Messinger, W. J., and J. M. Steele. 1949. Proc. Soc. Exp. Biol. Med. 70:316.

[15] Michel, C. 1900. Obstetrique 5:252.

continued

275. TOTAL BODY WATER: MAN

Part III. Desiccation and Specific Gravity Determinations

[16] Mitchell, H. H., et al. 1945. J. Biol. Chem. 158: 625.

[17] Schmitz, E. 1924. Arch. Gynaekol. 121:1.

[18] Skelton, H. 1927. Arch. Intern. Med. 40:140.

[19] Volkmann, A. W. 1874. Ber. Verh. Saechs. Akad. Wiss. Leipzig Math. Naturwiss. Kl. 26:202.

[20] Widdowson, E. M., et al. 1951. Clin. Sci. 10:113.

[21] Widdowson, E. M., and C. M. Spray. 1951. Arch. Dis. Childhood 26:205.

276. TOTAL BODY WATER: MAMMALS OTHER THAN MAN

For information on methods, *see* Table 275. Values in parentheses are ranges, estimate "b," "c," or "d" as indicated (*see* Introduction).

	Animal	Specification	No.[1] & Sex	Method	Total Body Water ml/kg body wt[1]	Reference
1	Cat	Newborn	7	Desiccation	807	54,58
2		2 wk old	1	Desiccation	738	53
3		12 wk old	1	Desiccation	666	53
4		Adult	1	Deuterium oxide	615	11
5			1	Desiccation	580	55
6			3	Desiccation	677(642-724)[c]	4,41,56
7			8[2]	Sodium chloride	500(420-560)[c]	12
8			11	Urea	630(565-715)[c]	12
9	Cattle	1-4 da old	6	Tritium oxide	875 ± 21	46
10		1 wk old	5	Antipyrine	730	39
11		1-12 mo old	90	Tritium oxide	704 ± 15	31
12		13-24 mo old	90	Tritium oxide	688 ± 23	21
13		25-36 mo old	90	Tritium oxide	669 ± 19	31
14		37-48 mo old	90	Tritium oxide	651 ± 15	31
15		>48 mo old	90	Tritium oxide	609 ± 20	31
16		Adult	28	Tritium oxide	641 ± 25[3]	32
17			28	Tritium oxide	669 ± 16[4]	32
18			19	Desiccation	710(680-730)[c5]	41
19			30	Specific gravity	537(431-633)[c]	33
20			5	Urea	625(580-686)[c]	44
21		Fattened	30	Antipyrine	539(431-647)[b]	33
22	Deer	1-7 yr	6	Tritium oxide	634(580-699)	35
23	Dog	Newborn	7	Desiccation	779(737-803)[c]	22,54
24			5	Desiccation	812(806-820)[c5]	4,41
25		42 da old	.....	Desiccation	705	5
26		100 da old	.....	Desiccation	689	5
27		Young	11	Desiccation	700(670-730)[b]	44,51,54
28		Adult	14	Antipyrine	583(532-679)[c]	28,52
29			8[2]	Antipyrine	599(539-679)[c]	28
30			40	Deuterium oxide	589(350-900)[c]	11,18,20,49
31			33	Deuterium oxide	619(525-713)[d]	20,45
32			6	Desiccation	628(550-662)[c]	13,14,26,44
33		Lean	7	Antipyrine	734(639-795)[c]	28,51
34			4	Desiccation	700(619-756)[c]	45,57
35		Obese	14	Desiccation	596(503-690)[b]	44,45,57

[1] Unless otherwise indicated. [2] No. of observations. [3] Spring. [4] Summer. [5] ml/kg fat-free body weight.

continued

Subjects		No.[1] & Sex	Method	Total Body Water ml/kg body wt [1]	Reference
Animal	Specification				
36 Guinea pig	Fetus <12 g	4	Desiccation	894(863-966)[c]	21
37	27-52 g	5	Desiccation	822(808-839)[c]	
38	71-112 g	4	Desiccation	716(684-754)[c]	
39	Newborn	11	Desiccation	710	28,58
40	15 da old	5	Desiccation	779	53
41	Adult	5[2]	Deuterium oxide	650(600-670)[c]	17
42		50	Desiccation	635(464-708)[c]	42,47
43		6♂	Desiccation	727(711-743)[b]	8
44		6♀	Desiccation	718(686-750)[b]	8
45 Hamster	Adult	1♂	Desiccation	674	8
46 Monkey	Adult	5	Antipyrine	695(628-721)[c]	51
47		7	Desiccation	691(650-720)[c]	26,51
48 Mouse	Fetus, half-term	5	Desiccation	871	7
49	Newborn	69	Desiccation	833	7,53
50	15 da old	31	Desiccation	757	53
51	30 da old	39	Desiccation	766	53
52	Adult	4	Desiccation	747(700-783)[c5]	4,41
53		6♂	Desiccation	727(687-767)[b]	8
54		6♀	Desiccation	685(600-765)[b]	8
55		16♀	Desiccation	740(712-768)[b5]	3
56 Rabbit	Fetus <1 g	2	Desiccation	915(914-915)[c]	15
57	10-50 g	14	Desiccation	840(784-896)[b]	
58	>50 g	2	Desiccation	816(815-818)[c]	
59	Newborn	16	Desiccation	830(772-888)[d]	5,15,58
60	Young	6	Desiccation	720(651-767)[c]	5,15
61	Adult	4	Antipyrine	743(688-778)[c]	50,51
62		9	Deuterium oxide	728(676-774)[c]	40
63		2	Deuterium oxide	741(702-779)[c]	29
64		2	Tritium oxide	559(545-573)[c]	43
65		20	Desiccation	708(590-830)[b]	26,40,43,45,51
66		10	Desiccation	729(692-770)[c5]	4,26,41,50
67		8♂	Desiccation	704(646-762)[b]	8
68		8♀	Desiccation	668(622-714)[b]	8
69 Rat	Fetus <0.2 g	165	Desiccation	922(918-926)[b]	2,24
70	0.2-0.5 g	147	Desiccation	912(903-921)[d]	2,24
71	0.5-1.0 g	96	Desiccation	900(892-908)[b]	2,24
72	1.0-2.5 g	150	Desiccation	885(876-894)[d]	2,24
73	2.5-5.0 g	12	Desiccation	874(867-881)[b]	2
74	Newborn	177	Desiccation	868(851-885)[d]	2,24,27,30,36,58
75	2 da old	43	Desiccation	832(809-855)[b]	24
76	4 da old	38	Desiccation	822(807-837)[b]	24
77	6 da old	36	Desiccation	814(773-855)[b]	24
78	7-9 da old	47	Desiccation	797(757-837)[d]	24,27,36
79	10-15 da old	25	Desiccation	757(719-795)[d]	24,27
80	20-30 da old	25	Desiccation	712(676-748)[d]	24,27,36
81	Weanling	3	Desiccation	747(742-753)[b5]	3
82	1-2 mo old	28	Desiccation	697(662-732)[d]	24,27,34,36
83	2-3 mo old	13	Desiccation	684(643-725)[d]	24,36

[1] Unless otherwise indicated. [2] No. of observations. [5] ml/kg fat-free body weight.

continued

Subjects			Method	Total Body Water ml/kg body wt[1]	Reference
Animal	Specification	No.[1] & Sex			
84		Adult	2	Deuterium oxide	655(635-675)[c]	38
85			313	Desiccation	638(536-740)[d]	6,9,23,24,27,34,36,48
86			9	Desiccation	670(653-697)[c]	10,27,34,41
87			12♂	Desiccation	666(622-710)[b]	8
88			7♂	Desiccation	730(715-744)[b][5]	3
89			12♀	Desiccation	683(653-713)[b]	8
90		Lean, <5.5% fat	25♂	Desiccation	690(676-704)[d]	48
91			24♀	Desiccation	684(670-698)[d]	
92		Average, 8-14%	48♂	Desiccation	660(620-700)[d]	48
93			34♀	Desiccation	650(610-690)[d]	
94		Obese, 15-26% fat	40♂	Desiccation	558(508-608)[d]	48
95			38♀	Desiccation	586(516-656)[d]	
96	Sheep	Young	34[2]	Antipyrine	618(450-720)[c]	25
97			44[2]	[131I] Iodoantipyrine	623(480-740)[c]	
98		Adult	16[2]	Antipyrine	553(370-630)[c]	25
99			18[2]	[131I] Iodoantipyrine	562(350-650)[c]	
100		2-5 yr old	6	Tritium oxide	533(471-585)[c]	35
101		2½-14 yr old	8	Tritium oxide	546	1
102		Pregnant	6	Desiccation	736	19
103	Swine	Newborn	19	Desiccation	834	58,59
104		3-6 da old	7	Deuterium oxide	724	60
105		7-21 da old	12	Deuterium oxide	664	60
106		17 da old	3	Desiccation	799(796-802)[c]	59
107		22-42 da old	12	Deuterium oxide	652	60
108		43-65 da old	12	Deuterium oxide	649	60
109		8 wk old	12	Desiccation	513	16
110		Adult	.....	Specific gravity	462	37

[1] Unless otherwise indicated. [2] No. of observations. [5] ml/kg fat-free body weight.

Contributors: Calcagno, Philip L., Hollerman, Charles E., and Jose, Pedro A.

References

[1] Amand, R. S., and H. R. Parker. 1966. Amer. J. Vet. Res. 27:899.

[2] Angulo y Gonzalez, A. W. 1932. Anat. Rec. 52:117.

[3] Annegers, J. 1954. Proc. Soc. Exp. Biol. Med. 87:454.

[4] Aron, H. 1917. In S. Hatai. Amer. J. Anat. 21:23.

[5] Aron, H. 1927. In C. Oppenheimer, ed. Handbuch der Biochemie des Menschen und der Tiere. Ed. 2. G. Fischer, Jena. v. 7, pp. 152-234.

[6] Ashworth, U.S., and G. R. Cowgill. 1938. J. Nutr. 15:73.

[7] Bezold, A. von. 1857. Z. Wiss. Zool. 8:487.

[8] Cizek, L. J. 1954. Amer. J. Physiol. 179:104.

[9] DaCosta, E., and R. Clayton. 1950. J. Nutr. 41:597.

[10] Drake, T. G. H., et al. 1930. J. Exp. Med. 51:867.

[11] Edelman, I. S. 1952. Amer. J. Physiol. 171:279.

[12] Eggleton, M. G. 1951. J. Physiol. (London) 115:482.

[13] Engels, W. 1904. Arch. Exp. Pathol. Pharmakol. 51:346.

[14] Falck, C. P., and T. Scheffer. 1854. Arch. Physiol. Heilk. 13:508.

[15] Fehling, H. 1877. Arch. Gynaekol. 11:523.

[16] Filer, L. J., Jr., and T. D. D. Groves. 1963. Ann. N.Y. Acad. Sci. 110:349.

[17] Flexner, L. B., et al. 1942. J. Biol. Chem. 144:35.

[18] Fogelman, M. J., et al. 1952. Amer. J. Physiol. 169:94.

[19] Foot, J. Z. 1969. J. Reprod. Fert., Suppl. 9:9.

[20] Gaudino, M., and M. F. Levitt. 1949. J. Clin. Invest. 28:1487.

[21] Gellhorn, A., and L. B. Flexner. 1942. Amer. J. Physiol. 136:750.

[22] Gerhartz, H. 1910. Pfluegers Arch. Gesamte Physiol. Menschen Tiere 135:104.

[23] Haldi, J., et al. 1944. Amer. J. Physiol. 141:83.

[24] Hamilton, B., and M. M. Dewar. 1938. Growth (Montreal) 2:13.

[25] Hansard, S. L., and W. A. Lyke. 1956. Proc. Soc. Exp. Biol. Med. 93:263.

[26] Harrison, H. E., et al. 1936. J. Biol. Chem. 113:515.

continued

[27] Hatai, S. 1917. Amer. J. Anat. 21:23.

[28] Herrold, M., and L. A. Saperstein. 1952. Proc. Soc. Exp. Biol. Med. 79:419.

[29] Hevesy, G., and C. F. Jacobsen. 1940. Acta Physiol. Scand. 1:11.

[30] Inaba, R. 1911. Arch. Anat. Physiol., Physiol. Abt., p. 1.

[31] Kamal, H. T., and S. M. Seif. 1970. J. Dairy Sci. 52:1650.

[32] Kamal, H. T., and S. M. Seif. 1970. Ibid. 52:1657.

[33] Kraybill, H. F., et al. 1951. J. Appl. Physiol. 3:681.

[34] Light, A. E., et al. 1934. J. Biol. Chem. 107:689.

[35] Longhurst, W. M., et al. 1970. Amer. J. Vet. Res. 31:673.

[36] Lowrey, L. G. 1913. Anat. Rec. 7:143.

[37] Lynch, G. P., and G. H. Wellington. 1963. Ann. N.Y. Acad. Sci. 110:318.

[38] McDougall, E. J., et al. 1934. Nature (London) 134:1006.

[39] McFadden, D. L., and C. R. Richards. 1956. J. Dairy Sci. 39:1438.

[40] Moore, F. D. 1946. Science 104:157.

[41] Moulton, C. R. 1923. J. Biol. Chem. 57:79.

[42] Pace, N., and E. N. Rathbun. 1945. Ibid. 158:685.

[43] Pace, N., et al. 1947. Ibid. 168:459.

[44] Painter, E. 1940. Amer. J. Physiol. 129:744.

[45] Pfeiffer, L. 1887. Z. Biol. (Munich), n. F. 5, 23:340.

[46] Philips, R. W., and R. L. Knox. 1970. J. Dairy Sci. 52:1664.

[47] Rathbun, E. N., and N. Pace. 1945. J. Biol. Chem. 158:667.

[48] Scheer, B. T., et al. 1947. J. Nutr. 34:581.

[49] Schwartz, I. L., et al. 1952. Fed. Proc. Fed. Amer. Soc. Exp. Biol. 11:142.

[50] Soberman, R. J. 1949. Proc. Soc. Exp. Biol. Med. 70:172.

[51] Soberman, R. J. 1950. Ibid. 74:789.

[52] Soberman, R. J., et al. 1951. Amer. J. Physiol. 164:450.

[53] Spray, C. M., and E. M. Widdowson. 1950. Brit. J. Nutr. 4:332.

[54] Thomas, K. 1911. Arch. Anat. Physiol., Physiol. Abt., p. 9.

[55] Voit, C. von. 1866. Z. Biol. (Munich) 2:307.

[56] Voit, C. von. 1927. In H. Skelton. Arch. Intern. Med. 40:140.

[57] Weigert, R. 1905. Jahrb. Kinderheilk. 61:178.

[58] Widdowson, E. M. 1950. Nature (London) 166:626.

[59] Wilson, M. B. 1902. Amer. J. Physiol. 8:197.

[60] Wood, A. J., and T. D. D. Groves. 1963. Ann. N.Y. Acad. Sci. 110:349.

277. RENAL FUNCTION TESTS: VERTEBRATES

Part I. Man

Values in parentheses are ranges, estimate "b" unless otherwise indicated (*see* Introduction).

	Specification	Method or Condition	Subjects		Value	Reference
			Age	No. & Sex		
1	Renal blood flow, ml· min^{-1}·1.73 m^2 body surface area^{-1}	Calculated from renal plasma flow divided by 1 minus hematocrit	16-55 yr	17♀	982(614-1350)	48,50
2			16-60 yr	61♂	1209(697-1721)	48,50
3			<20-45 yr	27♂	1076(660-1492)	9
4				23♀	973(503-1443)	
5				19♀[1]	1359(881-1837)	
6			<20-40 yr	13♀[2]	919(451-1387)	9
7			20-29 yr	9♂	1077(777-1377)	15
8			30-39 yr	9♂	1181(727-1635)	15
9			40-49 yr	10♂	1008(596-1420)	15
10			50-59 yr	11♂	849(603-1095)	15
11			60-69 yr	10♂	775(497-1053)	15
12			70-79 yr	9♂	589(323-855)	15
13			80-89 yr	12♂	475(193-757)	15
14			Adult	31♀[3]	962(602-1322)	12
15	Renal plasma flow, ml· min^{-1}·1.73 m^2 body surface area^{-1}	Determined by diodone[4] clearance without correction for extraction ratio	2-8 da	5	73	16
16		Determined by *p*-aminohippurate clearance without correction for extraction ratio	1-3 hr	4	50(16-90)[c]	52
17			4-28 da	7[5]	149	1
18			10-22 da	4	229	44

[1] Pregnant, 2-8 lunar mo. [2] Pregnant, 9 and 10 lunar mo. [3] Pregnant, near term. [4] Synonym: Diodrast. [5] Premature infants.

continued

Part I. Man

Specification	Method or Condition	Subjects		Value	Reference
		Age	No. & Sex		
19		37-95 da	8[5]	203	2
20		1-6 mo	8	326	44
21		6-12 mo	10	480	44
22		12-19 mo	11	519(320-718)	44
23		2-12 yr	19	654(413-895)	44
24	Determined by diodone[4] clearance; constant infusion technique	16-55 yr	17♀	594(390-798)	48,50
25		16-60 yr	61♂	697(425-969)	48,50
26		19-27 yr	10♀	628(428-828)	7
27		<20-45 yr	19♀[1]	800(498-1102)	9
28		<20-40 yr	13♀[2]	571(393-749)	9
29		20-29 yr	9♂	614(464-763)	15
30		21-25 yr	10♂	600(388-812)	7
31		30-39 yr	9♂	649(415-884)	15
32		40-49 yr	10♂	574(351-797)	15
33		50-59 yr	11♂	500(326-674)	15
34		60-69 yr	10♂	442(282-603)	15
35		70-79 yr	9♂	354(187-521)	15
36		80-89 yr	12♂	289(112-466)	15
37		Adult	34♀[3]	617(397-837)	12
38	Determined by p-aminohippurate clearance; constant infusion technique	16-49 yr	30♂	654(328-980)	49
39		21-32 yr	9♂	613(399-827)	11
40		Adult	8♂	628(538-718)	8
41			8♂	603(435-771)	11
42			11♀	592(286-898)	49
43	Determined by p-aminohippurate clearance; subcutaneous injection technique	<20-45 yr	27♂	557(251-863)	9
44			23♀	557(271-843)	
45	Determined by [131I] o-iodohippurate sodium[6] clearance; single injection technique	22-46 yr	9	622(512-750)	51
46	Renal plasma flow, ratio of o-iodohippurate sodium clearance to p-aminohippurate clearance	Determined by plasma disappearance curve of [131I] o-iodohippurate sodium, single injection technique	16 mo-16 yr	20	1.02	47
47	Renal plasma flow, extraction ratio for p-aminohippurate, %	Determined by catheterization of renal artery and renal vein	8 da-3 mo	7	68(50-86)	10
48			5 mo-10 yr	7	91(79-109)	10
49	Glomerular filtration rate, ml·min⁻¹·1.73 m² body surface area⁻¹	Determined by inulin or mannitol clearance	2-8 da	14	39(17-60)	16,37, 43,44
50			4-28 da	20[5]	45(26-64)	1,2,55
51			10-22 da	18	50(32-69)	37,44
52			37-95 da	11[5]	58(30-86)	2,55
53			1-6 mo	14	77(39-114)	43,44
54			6-12 mo	10	103(49-157)	44
55			12-19 mo	11	127(62-191)	44
56			2-12 yr	37	127(89-165)	3,43,44
57		Determined by inulin clearance; constant infusion technique	16-49 yr	34♂	124(72-176)	49
58			16-55 yr	10♀	115(89-141)	48,50
59				21♀	117(86-148)	
60			16-60 yr	67♂	131(88-174)	48,50
61			18-45 yr	25♂	140(76-204)	33

[1] Pregnant, 2-8 lunar mo. [2] Pregnant, 9 and 10 lunar mo. [3] Pregnant, near term. [4] Synonym: Diodrast. [5] Premature infants. [6] Synonym: Hippuran.

continued

Part I. Man

	Specification	Method or Condition	Subjects		Value	Reference
			Age	No. & Sex		
62			19-27 yr	10♀	118(90-146)	7
63			<20-40 yr	10♀[2/]	156(95-217)	9
64			20-29 yr	9♂	123(90-156)	15
65			21-25 yr	10♂	125(116-134)	7
66			28-60 yr	24♂	136(97-175)	48,50
67			30-39 yr	9♂	115(93-137)	15
68			40-49 yr	10♂	121(75-168)	15
69			50-59 yr	11♂	99(70-128)	15
70			60-69 yr	10♂	96(45-147)	15
71			70-79 yr	9♂	89(49-129)	15
72			80-89 yr	12♂	65(24-106)	15
73			Adult	8♂	130(99-161)	8
74				26♂	126(92-160)	4
75				16♀	109(82-136)	49
76				57♀[3/]	126(69-183)	12
77				10♀[3/]	131(67-195)	13
78				8♀[7/]	126(94-158)	13
79		Determined by inulin clearance; single intravenous injection technique	1-3 hr	6	19(3.3-31)c	52
80			<20-45 yr	27♂	118(79-157)	9
81				23♀	122(73-171)	
82				17♀[1/]	170(124-216)	
83			20-50 yr	36♂	124(97-151)	30
84				20♀	119(93-145)	
85		Determined by polyfructosan clearance, constant infusion technique	1-5 da	11[5/]	69(37-101)	27
86				20[8/]	81(53-109)	
87			5-21 da	11[5/]	89(61-118)	27
88			5-22 da	13[8/]	87(59-115)	
89			6 wk-18 mo	19	107(87-127)	
90			18 mo-15 yr	28	116(96-136)	
91		Determined by [51Cr] ethylenediamine-tetraacetic acid (EDTA)	15-63 yr	8	117(96-197)	51
92		Determined by [131I] diatrizoate[9/], single intravenous injection technique	15-63 yr	8	134(125-217)	51
93	Glomerular filtration rate, ml/min	Determined by [131I] diatrizoate[9/], single intravenous injection technique	20-39 yr	....	127	17
94			40-49 yr	....	110	
95			50-69 yr	....	108	
96	Glomerular filtration rate, ratio of sodium iothalamate clearance to inulin clearance	Determined by plasma disappearance curve of [125I] sodium iothalamate, single intravenous injection technique	16 mo-16 yr	36[10/]	1.12	47
97	Glomerular filtration rate, ratio of inulin clearance to sodium iothalamate clearance	Determined by [131I] sodium iothalamate, single intravenous injection technique	5-15 yr	10[11/]	1.03(0.83-1.23)	14
98	Glomerular filtration rate, ratio of creatinine clearance to sodium iothalamate clearance	....	1-17 yr	25[12/]	0.998(0.64-1.35)	45

[1/] Pregnant, 2-8 lunar mo. [2/] Pregnant, 9 and 10 lunar mo. [3/] Pregnant, near term. [5/] Premature infants. [7/] From group of 10 subjects in preceding line of data; 2nd wk postpartum. [8/] Full-term infants. [9/] Synonym: Hypaque.

[10/] Inulin clearance, 14-140 ml·min^{-1}·1.73 m^2 body surface area^{-1}. [11/] Patients with renal disease; inulin clearance, 5-97 ml·min^{-1}·1.73 m^2 body surface area^{-1}. [12/] Creatinine clearance, 29-188 ml·min^{-1}·1.73 m^2 body surface area^{-1}.

continued

Part I. Man

	Specification	Method or Condition	Subjects Age	No. & Sex	Value	Reference
99	Filtration fraction, %	Calculated from glomerular filtration rate divided by renal plasma flow	2-8 da	5	49	16
100			4-28 da	7[5]	34	1
101			10-22 da	3	24	44
102			37-95 da	8[5]	33	2
103			1-6 mo	6	24	44
104			6-12 mo	10	22(8-36)	44
105			12-19 mo	11	25(15-35)	44
106			2-12 yr	19	20(12-28)	44
107			16-49 yr	31♂	19(12-26)	49
108			16-55 yr	17♀	20(14-26)	48,50
109			16-60 yr	61♂	19(14-24)	48,50
110			19-27 yr	10♀	19(16-22)	7
111			20-29 yr	9♂	20(18-23)	15
112			<20-40 yr	10♀[2]	29(21-37)	9
113			<20-45 yr	27♂	22(15-28)	9
114				23♀	23(13-32)	
115				17♀[1]	22(12-33)	
116			21-25 yr	10♂	21(14-28)	7
117			30-39 yr	9♂	18(11-26)	15
118			40-49 yr	10♂	21(15-28)	15
119			50-59 yr	11♂	21(15-27)	15
120			60-69 yr	10♂	22(15-28)	15
121			70-79 yr	9♂	26(10-42)	15
122			80-89 yr	12♂	23(15-31)	15
123			Adult	11♀	19(12-27)	49
124				26♀[3]	20	12
125		Calculated from inulin clearance divided by *p*-aminohippurate clearance without correction for extraction ratio	1-3 hr	4	41(21-51)[c]	52
126			1-5 da	11[5]	57(35-79)	27
127				20[8]	59(41-77)	
128			5-21 da	11[5]	52(32-72)	27
129			5-22 da	13[8]	47(27-67)	27
130			6 wk-18 mo	19	29(19-39)	27
131			18 mo-15 yr	28	25(17-33)	27
132		Calculated from inulin clearance divided by *p*-aminohippurate clearance with correction for extraction ratio	8-16 da	3	23	10
133			8 mo	1	25	
134	Urine volume, ml/24 hr	....	1 da	35	20(0-68)[c]	53
135			2 da	29	21(0-82)[c]	
136			3 da	26	36(0-96)[c]	
137			4 da	26	65(5-180)[c]	
138			5 da	23	103(1-217)[c]	
139			6 da	19	124(42-268)[c]	
140			8 da	17	151(59-330)[c]	
141			10 da	6	190(106-320)[c]	
142			12 da	2	222(207-246)[c]	
143	Concentrating capacity (maximal urinary osmolality), mosmoles/kg H_2O	Determined after 12-18 hr of water deprivation	7-40 da	25	(600-1100)[c]	18,19
144			2 mo-3 yr	42	Fn[13]	56
145			2-16 yr	250	1089(870-1309)	21
146			3-15 yr	16	1069(813-1325)	56

[1] Pregnant, 2-8 lunar mo. [2] Pregnant, 9 and 10 lunar mo. [3] Pregnant, near term. [5] Premature infants. [8] Full-term infants. [13] mosmoles/kg = 416 log(age in days) + 63.

continued

Part I. Man

	Specification	Method or Condition	Subjects		Value	Refer-ence
			Age	No. & Sex		
147			Adult	63	1027(807-1247)	31
148				26	1058(762-1354)	32
149				32	1076(741-1411)	25
150		Determined after 24 hr of water deprivation	Adult	14	1189(967-1342)	35
151	Urinary pH	Determined after 3-5 da of ammonium chloride administration	11-45 da	3[4,14]	4.8(4.7-4.9)[c]	28
152			51-122 da	3[14]	4.9(4.6-5.0)[c]	28
153			2-6 mo	4[14]	5.0(4.6-5.4)[c]	24
154			2-12 mo	12[14]	(4.6-6.4)[c]	41
155			3-4 mo	4[15]	4.7(4.3-5.0)[c]	24
156			2-16 yr	11	(4.7-5.6)[c]	41
157			Adult	20	5.1(4.6-5.6)[c]	23
158		Determined 5-8 hr after acute administration of ammonium or calcium chloride	7 da	8[15]	5.2	29
159			1-16 mo	11[14]	4.83(4.5-5.05)[c]	20
160			4-15 yr	52	4.8(4.55-5.1)[c]	22
161			Adult	9	4.8(4.6-5.2)[c]	57
162				8	4.85	29
	Urea clearance, ml·min⁻¹·1.73 m² body surface area⁻¹					
163	Whole blood	Calculated from urea concentration in urine times urine flow, divided by urea concentration in blood	2-28 da	26	(17-34)[c]	36
164			54-356 da	21	(35-55)[c]	
165			2-13 yr	69	(72-78)[c]	
166		Calculated from urea concentration in urine times urine flow (2 ml·min⁻¹·1.73 m² body surface area⁻¹), divided by urea concentration in blood	2-8 da	4	23	16
167			4-28 da	21[5]	32(21-43)	1
168			10-22 da	6	36	44
169			37-95 da	8[5]	40	2
170			1-6 mo	10	55(23-88)	44,46
171			6-12 mo	8	68	44,46
172			12-19 mo	8	71	44
173			2-12 yr	24	75(38-112)	38,44
174		Calculated as maximal or standard clearance according to Møller, McIntosh, & Van Slyke [40]	40-49 yr	20♂	95(66-124)	34
175			50-59 yr	20♂	86(45-127)	
176			60-69 yr	20♂	82(47-117)	
177			70-79 yr	20♂	65(30-100)	
178			80-89 yr	20♂	61(11-111)	
179	Plasma	Determined simultaneously with inulin clearance; urine flow greater than 2 ml/min	....	10♀[3]	79(21-137)	13
180				8♀[7]	77(45-109)	
181	Urea clearance, ml/min; whole blood	Calculated from urea concentration in urine times urine flow, divided by urea concentration in blood; urine flow, 2.0-13.7 ml/min	....	46	(55-147)	6
182	Urinary hydrogen excretion (titratable acid), µeq·min⁻¹·1.73 m² body surface area⁻¹	Determined after 3-5 da of ammonium chloride administration	11-45 da	3[5,14]	43(36-46)[c]	28
183			51-122 da	3[14]	62(59-64)[c]	28
184			2-6 mo	4[14]	79(58-95)[c]	24
185			2-12 mo	12[14]	42(21-72)[c]	41
186			3-4 mo	4[15]	15(9-18)[c]	24
187			2-16 yr	11	27(14-43)[c]	41
188			Adult	20	34(26-47)[c]	23

[3]/ Pregnant, near term. [4]/ Synonym: Diodrast. [5]/ Premature infants. [7]/ From group of 10 subjects in preceding line of data; 2nd wk postpartum. [14]/ Cow's milk diet. [15]/ Human milk diet.

continued

Part I. Man

	Specification	Method or Condition	Age	No. & Sex	Value	Reference
189		Determined during 5-8 hr after acute administration of ammonium or calcium chloride	7 da	8[15/]	3.5(0-8.1)	29
190			1-16 mo	11[14/]	62(43-111)c	20
191			4-15 yr	52	52(33-71)c	22
192			Adult	9	38(24-51)c	57
193				8	29(18-41)	29
194	Urinary hydrogen excretion (ammonium), μeq·min^{-1}·1.73 m^2 body surface area^{-1}	Determined after 3-5 da of ammonium chloride administration	11-45 da	3[4,14/]	48(44-51)c	28
195			51-122 da	3[14/]	82(76-92)c	28
196			2-6 mo	4[14/]	118(106-141)c	24
197			2-12 mo	12[14/]	62(20-111)c	41
198			3-4 mo	4[15/]	50(37-58)c	24
199			2-16 yr	11	59(46-73)c	41
200			Adult	20	91(34-154)c	23
201		Determined 5-8 hr after acute administration of ammonium or calcium chloride	7 da	8[15/]	15(5-25)	29
202			1-16 mo	11[14/]	57(42-79)c	20
203			4-15 yr	52	73(46-100)c	22
204			Adult	9	50(33-75)c	57
205				8	38(19-56)	29
206	p-Aminohippurate tubular maxima (excretory), mg·min^{-1}·1.73 m^2 body surface area^{-1}	Calculated as rate of p-aminohippurate excretion in urine minus rate of p-aminohippurate filtration	4-28 da	7[5/]	12.9	1
207			10-22 da	6	21.4	44
208			37-95 da	8	17.2	2
209			1-6 mo	9	51.4	44
210			6-12 mo	8	50.5	44
211			12-19 mo	9	61.2(18.8-103.6)	44
212			2-12 yr	18	73.7(35.9-111.5)	44
213			16-49 yr	35♂	79.8(46.4-113.2)	49
214			Adult	8♂	65.6(48.2-83.0)	8
215				43♂	77.2	49
216				16♀	77.2(55.6-98.8)	49
217	Diodone[4/] tubular maxima (excretory), mg I·min^{-1}·1.73 m^2 body surface area^{-1}	Calculated as rate of diodone excretion in urine minus rate of diodone filtration	16-55 yr	14♀	42.6(23.6-61.6)	48,50
218			16-60 yr	40♂	51.8(34.4-69.2)	48,50
219			19-27 yr	10♀	44.2(34.6-53.8)	7
220			20-29 yr	9♂	54.6(35.6-73.6)	15
221			21-25 yr	10♂	50.6(37.6-63.6)	7
222			30-39 yr	9♂	51.0(33.8-68.2)	15
223			40-49 yr	10♂	49.9(30.3-69.5)	15
224			50-59 yr	11♂	45.3(32.7-57.9)	15
225			60-69 yr	10♂	44.5(26.3-62.7)	15
226			70-79 yr	9♂	39.0(24.4-53.6)	15
227			80-89 yr	12♂	30.8(11.2-50.4)	15
228			Adult	82♂	50	49
229	Glucose tubular maxima (absorptive), mg·min^{-1}·1.73 m^2 body surface area^{-1}	Calculated as rate of glucose filtration minus rate of glucose excretion in urine	4-28 da	3[5/]	77	55
230			37-95 da	3[5/]	104	55
231			2-12 yr	6	543(285-801)	26
232			16-55 yr	11♀	303(193-413)	48,50
233			20-29 yr	3♂	359(324-395)c	39
234			28-60 yr	24♂	375(215-535)	48,50
235			30-39 yr	9♂	334(221-446)	39
236			40-49 yr	12♂	315(225-406)	39
237			50-59 yr	14♂	308(178-438)	39
238			60-69 yr	14♂	260(131-389)	39

[4/] Synonym: Diodrast. [5/] Premature infants. [14/] Cow's milk diet. [15/] Human milk diet.

continued

Part I. Man

Specification	Method or Condition	Subjects		Value	Reference
		Age	No. & Sex		
239		70-79 yr	15♂	239(147-332)	39
240		80-89 yr	9♂	219(119-320)	39
241 242 243 Bicarbonate tubular maxima (absorptive), mmole/ 100 ml glomerular filtrate	Calculated as rate of bicarbonate filtration minus rate of bicarbonate excretion in urine	8-36 da	4[5/]	(2.5-2.6)[c]	57
		1-12 mo	6	(2.6-2.9)[c]	54
		Adult	3	(2.8-3.0)[c]	42
244 245 246 Renal bicarbonate threshold, mmole/liter serum bicarbonate	Determined during continuous infusion of sodium bicarbonate	8-36 da	4[5/]	(22-25)[c]	54
		1-12 mo	6	(22-23)[c]	20
		Adult	3	(26-28)[c]	42
247 248 249 Phosphate tubular reabsorption, %	Calculated from one minus phosphate clearance divided by inulin clearance	Newborn	5	86(80-90)[c]	37
		16 da-4 mo	12	74(62-86)	5
		2-13 yr	11	92(82-102)	5

[5/] Premature infants.

Contributors: Heinemann, Henry O.; Nash, Martin A., and Edelmann, Chester M., Jr.

References

[1] Barnett, H. L., et al. 1948. J. Clin. Invest. 27:691.
[2] Barnett, H. L., et al. 1948. Proc. Soc. Exp. Biol. Med. 69:55.
[3] Barnett, H. L., et al. 1949. Pediatrics 3:418.
[4] Berger, E. Y., et al. 1947. Proc. Soc. Exp. Biol. Med. 66:62.
[5] Brodehl, J., and K. Gellisson. 1968. Pediatrics 42: 395.
[6] Brulles, A., et al. 1969. Clin. Chim. Acta 24:261.
[7] Brun, C., et al. 1947. Acta Med. Scand. 127:464.
[8] Brun, C., et al. 1947. Ibid. 127:471.
[9] Bucht, H. 1951. Scand. J. Clin. Lab. Invest., Suppl. 3.
[10] Calcagno, P. L., and M. I. Rubin. 1963. J. Clin. Invest. 42:1632.
[11] Chapman, C. B., et al. 1948. Ibid. 27:639.
[12] Chesley, L. C. 1951. Med. Clin. N. Amer. 35:699.
[13] Chesley, L. C., and L. O. Williams. 1945. Amer. J. Obstet. Gynecol. 50:367.
[14] Cohen, M. L., et al. 1969. Pediatrics 43:407.
[15] Davies, D. F., and N. W. Shock. 1950. J. Clin. Invest. 29:496.
[16] Dean, R. F. A., and R. A. McCance. 1947. J. Physiol. (London) 106:431.
[17] Denneberg, T. 1965. Acta Med. Scand., Suppl. 442:1.
[18] Edelmann, C. M., Jr., and H. L. Barnett. 1960. J. Pediat. 56:154.
[19] Edelmann, C. M., Jr., et al. 1960. J. Clin. Invest. 39:1062.
[20] Edelmann, C. M., Jr., et al. 1967. Ibid. 46:1309.
[21] Edelmann, C. M., Jr., et al. 1967. Amer. J. Dis. Child. 114(6):639.
[22] Edelmann, C. M., Jr., et al. 1967. Pediat. Res. 1: 452.

[23] Elkinton, J. R., et al. 1960. Amer. J. Med. 29:554.
[24] Fomons, S. J., et al. 1959. Pediatrics 23:113.
[25] Frank, M. N., et al. 1957. Amer. J. Med. Sci. 233: 121.
[26] Galan, E., et al. 1947. Arch. Med. Enfants 26:102.
[27] Geisert, J., et al. 1969. Arch. Fr. Pediat. 26:125.
[28] Gordon, H. H., et al. 1948. Pediatrics 2:290.
[29] Hatemi, N., and R. A. McCance. 1961. Acta Paediat. (Stockholm) 50:603.
[30] Hogeman, O. 1948. Acta Med. Scand., Suppl. 216a.
[31] Isaacson, L. C. 1960. Lancet 1:467.
[32] Jacobson, M. H., et al. 1962. Arch. Intern. Med. 110:121.
[33] Josephson, B., and O. Lindahl. 1943-44. Acta Med. Scand. 116:20.
[34] Lewis, W. H., Jr., and A. S. Alving. 1938. Amer. J. Physiol. 123:500.
[35] Lindeman, R. D., et al. 1960. N. Engl. J. Med. 262: 1306.
[36] McCance, R. A., and E. M. Widdowson. 1952. Lancet 263:860.
[37] McCrory, W. W., et al. 1952. J. Clin. Invest. 31:357.
[38] McIntosh, J. F., et al. 1929. Ibid. 6:467.
[39] Miller, J. H., et al. 1952. J. Gerontol. 7:196.
[40] Møller, E., et al. 1929. J. Clin. Invest. 6:427.
[41] Peonides, A., et al. 1965. Arch. Dis. Childhood 40: 33.
[42] Pitts, R. F., et al. 1949. J. Clin. Invest. 28:35.
[43] Richmond, J. B., et al. 1951. Proc. Soc. Exp. Biol. Med. 77:83.
[44] Rubin, M. I., et al. 1949. J. Clin. Invest. 28:1144.
[45] Sakai, T., et al. 1969. Pediatrics 44:905.
[46] Schoenthal, L. 1933. Amer. J. Dis. Child. 45:41.
[47] Silkalns, G. I. 1970. Pediat. Res. 4:450.

continued

Part I. Man

[48] Smith, H. W. 1943. Lectures on the Kidney. Univ. Kansas, Lawrence.

[49] Smith, H. W. 1951. The Kidney. Oxford Univ. Press, New York.

[50] Smith, H. W., et al. 1943. J. Mt. Sinai Hosp. New York 10:59.

[51] Speck, B. 1967-69. Helv. Med. Acta 34:486.

[52] Strauss, J., et al. 1965. Amer. J. Obstet. Gynecol. 91:286.

[53] Thomson, J. 1944. Arch. Dis. Childhood 19:169.

[54] Tudvad, F., et al. 1954. Pediatrics 13:4.

[55] Weintraub, D. H., et al. 1952. Proc. Soc. Exp. Biol. Med. 81:542.

[56] Winberg, J. 1959. Acta Paediat. (Stockholm) 48: 318.

[57] Wrong, O., and H. E. F. Davies. 1959. Quart J. Med. 28:259.

Part II. Homoiothermic Animals Other Than Man

Specification: C_I = inulin clearance; C_{PAH} = p-aminohippurate clearance; C_C = creatinine clearance; C_D = diodone clearance; E_{PAH} = extraction ratio of p-aminohippurate.

Values in parentheses are ranges, estimate "c" unless otherwise indicated (*see* Introduction).

	Animal	Specification	Subjects Age, Condition, or Breed	No. & Sex	Value	Reference
1	Anteater, spiny[1]	Creatinine clearance, $ml \cdot min^{-1} \cdot kg^{-1}$	....	....	1.17	6
2	Baboon	Inulin clearance, $ml \cdot min^{-1} \cdot m^{-2}$	Adult	2	60.5(49.1-71.9)	77
3		Creatinine clearance, $ml \cdot min^{-1} \cdot m^{-2}$	Adult	2	69.3(57.1-81.6)	77
4	Cat	Inulin clearance, ml/min	Adult	9	12.4(9.6-20.4)	62
5		Creatinine clearance, ml/min	....	2	18.8(17.6-19.9)	22
6			Adult	9	18.6(3.5-14.8)	62
7		p-Aminohippurate clearance, ml/min	....	2	59.5(59.3-59.8)	22
8			Adult	9	47.4(30.4-62.3)	62
9		Filtration fraction, C_I/C_{PAH}	Adult	9	0.27(0.15-0.48)	62
10		C_C/C_{PAH}	....	7	0.31(0.23-0.46)	22
11		Tubular maxima, p-aminohippurate, mg/min	....	....	4.2	22
12	Cattle	Inulin clearance, ml/min	1-2 wk	3♀	112(100-128)	71
13			6-10 wk	4♀	169(139-186)	
14			1.5-2.5 yr; non-pregnant, non-lactating	4♀	151(142-216)	
15		$ml \cdot min^{-1} \cdot kg^{-1}$	Adult; prepartum, non-lactating	10♀	1.84(1.30-2.20)	67
16		Creatinine clearance, ml/min	1-2 wk	3♀	129(103-148)	71
17			6-10 wk	4♀	179(160-227)	
18			1.5-2.5 yr; non-pregnant, non-lactating	4♀	189(156-217)	
			Adult			
19			Prepartum, non-lactating	6♀	191(171-237)	
20			7-14 da postpartum	6♀	191(140-240)	
21			7-21 da postpartum	5♀	211(207-255)	
22		$ml \cdot min^{-1} \cdot kg^{-1}$	Adult	19♀	1.68(1.32-2.23)	67
23		$liters \cdot hr^{-1} \cdot 100\ lb^{-1}$	Heifer	4	4.29(2.13-6.45)[b]	91
24				4	5.51(3.77-7.25)[b]	
25		Thiosulfate clearance, $ml \cdot min^{-1} \cdot kg^{-1}$	Adult	15♀	1.45(1.20-2.19)	67
26		p-Aminohippurate clearance, $ml \cdot min^{-1} \cdot kg^{-1}$	1-2 wk	3♀	541(501-590)	71
27			6-10 wk	4♀	779(720-909)	
28			1.5-2.5 yr; non-pregnant, non-lactating	4♀	887(701-1108)	

[1] *Tachyglossus aculeatus.*

continued

Part II. Homoiothermic Animals Other Than Man

	Animal	Specification	Subjects		Value	Ref-er-ence
			Age, Condition, or Breed	No. & Sex		
29			Adult			
			Prepartum, non-lactating	6♀	892(763-1220)	
30			7-14 da postpartum	6♀	975(672-1308)	
31			7-21 da postpartum	5♀	699(613-920)	
32		Diodone[2/] clearance, ml·min^{-1}·kg^{-1}	Adult	6♀	9.11(5.82-12.60)	67
33		Phenol red clearance, ml·min^{-1}·kg^{-1}	Calf	28♀	7.48(2.28-13.2)	1
34				4♀	7.58	2
35				20♀	7.89	2
36			Adult	22♀	7.77	2
37				24♀	8.00(4.70-10.9)	1
38				4♀	8.02	2
39		Urea clearance, ml·min^{-1}·kg^{-1}	Adult	3♀	0.84(0.56-1.00)	67
40		Filtration fraction, C_C/C_{PAH}	1-2 wk	3♀	0.24(0.21-0.27)[b]	71
41			6-10 wk	4♀	0.23(0.22-0.25)[b]	
42			1.5-2.5 yr; non-pregnant, non-lactating	4♀	0.20(0.18-0.22)[b]	
			Adult			
43			Prepartum, non-lactating	6♀	0.21(0.19-0.23)[b]	
44			7-14 da postpartum	6♀	0.20(0.18-0.22)[b]	
45			7-21 da postpartum	5♀	0.30(0.26-0.34)[b]	
46		C_C/C_D	Adult	6♀	0.16(0.11-0.22)	67
47		Tubular maxima, p-aminohippurate, mg/min	Adult	6♀	150(123-174)	71
48				6♀	153(159-178)	
49				5♀	231(180-289)	
50		Diodone[2/], mg·min^{-1}·kg^{-1}	Adult	3♀	0.94(0.67-1.33)	67
51	Chimpan-zee	Inulin clearance, ml·min^{-1}·m^{-2}	Adult	5	76(62-103)	31
52				2♀	103.0(73.3-132.6)	77
53		Creatinine clearance, ml·min^{-1}·m^{-2}	Adult	5	105(77-156)	31
54				2♀	124(90-158.3)	77
55		p-Aminohippurate clearance, ml·min^{-1}·m^{-2}	Adult	3	254(213-301)	31
56		Filtration fraction, C_I/C_{PAH}	Adult	3	0.26(0.22-0.31)	31
57	Chinchilla	Inulin clearance, ml/min	Adult	7	5.2(2.8-7.8)	93
58	Dog	Inulin clearance, ml/min	2 da	7	0.63(0.44-0.82)[b]	42
59			8 da	9	1.50(0.6-2.4)[b]	
60			13 da	8	3.06(2.61-3.51)[b]	
61			21 da	11	4.42(0.16-8.68)[b]	
62			27 da	7	4.77(4.00-5.54)[b]	
63			32 da	8	5.33(4.42-6.24)[b]	
64			39 da	9	7.81(6.36-9.26)[b]	
65			49 da	8	8.83(6.67-10.99)[b]	
66			55 da	11	11.1(7.86-14.3)[b]	
67			62 da	3	16.4(15.5-17.2)[b]	
68			69 da	5	21.2(16.6-25.7)[b]	
69			77 da	8	28.8(26.3-31.3)[b]	
70			Adult	9	36.2(24.8-49.6)	12
71		ml·min^{-1}·m^{-2}	Adult	7	61(51-76)	82
72				7	69(40-98)[b]	13
73				8♀	50(36-64)[b]	8
74				4♀	87(71-109)	94

[2/] Synonym: Diodrast.

continued

Part II. Homoiothermic Animals Other Than Man

	Animal	Specification	Subjects Age, Condition, or Breed	No. & Sex	Value	Reference
75		ml·min^{-1}·kg^{-1}	Adult	32	3.77(1.74-5.86)	3
76			non-Dalmatian	4	3.8(2.6-4.8)	95
77			Dalmatian	3	4.0(2.5-5.8)	95
78		ml·min^{-1}·g kidney wt^{-1}	2 da	7	0.13(0.09-0.17)[b]	42
79			8 da	9	0.20(0.08-0.32)[b]	
80			13 da	8	0.27(0.23-0.31)[b]	
81			21 da	11	0.27(0.01-0.53)[b]	
82			27 da	7	0.37(0.31-0.43)[b]	
83			32 da	8	0.35(0.29-0.41)[b]	
84			39 da	9	0.43(0.35-0.51)[b]	
85			49 da	8	0.49(0.37-0.61)[b]	
86			55 da	11	0.55(0.39-0.71)[b]	
87			62 da	3	0.78(0.74-0.82)[b]	
88			69 da	5	0.83(0.65-1.01)[b]	
89			77 da	8	0.91(0.83-0.99)[b]	
90		Creatinine clearance, ml/min	....	18♀	37.3(19.7-69.0)	55
91				7	70.6(48.9-90.0)	96
92				8	58.2(25.4-81.6)	96
93			Adult	5	53.5(32.8-60.9)	38
94				6	69(56-84)	81
95		ml·min^{-1}·m^{-2}	Adult	6	86.5(68-139)	52
96				32	88.4(63-119)	52
97				5	101(65-128)	45
98				31♀	94(58-130)[b]	68
99		ml·min^{-1}·kg^{-1}	Adult	17	4.2(3.2-4.9)	56
100				10♀	3.81(3.3-5.8)	20
101				75♀	4.3(2.2-8.3)	43
102				6♀	4.4(4.0-4.7)	23
103		p-Aminohippurate clearance, ml/min	Adult	5	148(100-203)	35
104				6	195(150-228)	81
105				7	303(180-370)	82
106		ml·min^{-1}·m^{-2}	Adult	32	286(203-425)	52
107				6	279(210-420)	52
108				4♀	247(189-343)	30
109				12♀	238(105-371)[b]	68
110		ml·min^{-1}·kg^{-1}	....	17	11.2(7.8-15.5)	56
111			Adult	32	12.9(6.3-21.2)	3
112				6♀	11.6(10.6-13.2)	23
113				75♀	13.5(8.1-22.4)	43
114				10♀	13.8(10.9-16.9)	20
115		p-Aminohippurate clearance, not corrected for extraction ratio, ml·min^{-1}·g kidney wt^{-1}	2 da	7	0.15(0.11-0.19)[b]	42
116			8 da	9	0.29(0.11-0.47)[b]	
117			13 da	8	0.44(0.34-0.54)[b]	
118			21 da	11	0.45(0.03-0.87)[b]	
119			27 da	7	0.74(0.66-0.82)[b]	
120			32 da	8	0.55(0.45-0.65)[b]	
121			39 da	9	0.77(0.67-0.87)[b]	
122			49 da	8	0.91(0.85-0.97)[b]	
123			55 da	11	1.46(1.06-1.86)[b]	
124			62 da	3	1.87(1.71-2.03)[b]	
125			69 da	5	2.40(2.18-2.62)[b]	
126			77 da	8	2.38(1.88-2.88)[b]	

continued

Part II. Homoiothermic Animals Other Than Man

	Animal	Specification	Subjects Age, Condition, or Breed	No. & Sex	Value	Reference
127		p-Aminohippurate extraction ratio, %	2 da	7	16.8	42
128			8 da	9	29.1	
129			13 da	8	38.5	
130			21 da	11	36.6	
131			27 da	7	50	
132			32 da	8	46.3	
133			39 da	9	53	
134			49 da	8	52.1	
135			55 da	11	81	
136			62 da	3	69	
137			69 da	5	81.5	
138			77 da	8	78.6	
139		p-Aminohippurate clearance, corrected for extraction ratio (measure of renal plasma flow), ml·min^{-1}·g kidney wt^{-1}	2 da	7	0.91(0.65-1.17)[b]	42
140			8 da	9	1.00(0.38-1.62)[b]	
141			13 da	8	1.14(0.88-1.40)[b]	
142			21 da	11	1.23(0.09-2.37)[b]	
143			27 da	7	1.47(1.31-1.63)[b]	
144			32 da	8	1.18(0.98-1.38)[b]	
145			39 da	9	1.46(1.26-1.66)[b]	
146			49 da	8	1.75(1.65-1.85)[b]	
147			55 da	11	1.8(1.3-2.3)[b]	
148			62 da	3	2.71(2.49-2.93)[b]	
149			69 da	5	2.95(2.69-3.21)[b]	
150			77 da	8	3.03(2.39-3.67)[b]	
151		Phenol red clearance, ml·min^{-1}·m^{-2}	Adult	7	118(68-168)[b]	13
152				8♀	300(172-428)[b]	8
153		Urate clearance, ml/min	....	18♀	37.9(21.4-66.6)	55
			Adult			
154			Non-pregnant, non-lactating	8♀	70.5(28.3-98.2)	96
155			Prepartum, non-lactating	7♀	45.4(20.4-70.8)	
156		ml·min^{-1}·kg^{-1}	Non-Dalmatian	4	5.3(4.3-6.0)	95
157			Dalmatian	4	3.9(2.4-5.9)	
158		Urea clearance, ml/min	Adult	9	19.9(11.7-28.1)	12
159				23	36.6(20.1-48.4)	84
160				11	55.6(28.2-83.0)	43
161		Xenon-133 washout (measure of renal blood flow), ml·min^{-1}·g kidney wt^{-1}	6 wk	5	1.2(0.3-2.1)[b]	46
162			8-10 wk	10	1.50(0.24-2.76)[b]	
163			10-12 wk	6	2.20(1.22-3.18)[b]	
164			14-16 wk	4	3.50(3.42-3.58)[b]	
165			Adult	10	3.50(2.04-4.96)[b]	
166		Filtration fraction, C_I/C_{PAH}	Adult	32	0.31(0.10-0.44)	3
167				8♀	0.17(0.13-0.21)[b]	8
168		C_C/C_{PAH}	Adult	7	0.30(0.20-0.52)	82
169				32	0.31(0.26-0.40)	52
170				6	0.31(0.28-0.34)	52
171				6	0.35(0.31-0.47)	81
172				5	0.37(0.33-0.41)	35
173				75♀	0.32(0.23-0.47)	43
		Tubular maxima, p-Aminohippurate				
174		mg·min^{-1}·m^{-2}	Adult	4♀	18(15-24)	94
175		mg·min^{-1}·kg^{-1}	Adult	12	0.78(0.54-1.03)	56

continued

Part II. Homoiothermic Animals Other Than Man

	Animal	Specification	Subjects		Value	Reference
			Age, Condition, or Breed	No. & Sex		
176				32	1.21(0.43-1.89)	3
177				6♀	0.6(0.54-0.7)	23
178	Gibbon	Inulin clearance, ml·min⁻¹·m⁻²	Adult	1♂	78.3	77
179		Creatinine clearance, ml·min⁻¹·m⁻²	Adult	1♂	95.9	
180	Goat	Inulin clearance, ml/min	Adult	5	105(75-145)	54
181		Creatinine clearance, ml/min	Adult	5	137(115-179)	54
182		ml·min⁻¹·kg⁻¹	....	....	2.2	21
183	Horse	Inulin clearance, ml·min⁻¹·m⁻²	Adult	....	69.4(47.2-91.6)b	48
184		ml·min⁻¹·kg⁻¹	Adult	1	1.40	67
185				12	1.66(1.00-2.32)b	49
186		Creatinine clearance, ml·min⁻¹·kg⁻¹	Adult	12	1.46(1.02-1.90)b	49
187		Diodone 2/ clearance, ml·min⁻¹·kg⁻¹	Adult	1♀3/	6.91(5.29-8.53)b	50
188		Urea clearance, ml·min⁻¹·kg⁻¹	Adult	6	0.76(0.56-0.96)b	49
189		Filtration fraction, C_I/C_D	Adult	1♀	0.24	50
190	Macaque4/	Inulin clearance, ml/min	Adult	12♂	12.9(9.0-15.3)	85
191		ml·min⁻¹·kg⁻¹	Adult	12♂	3.1(2.2-3.8)	
192	Macaque5/	Inulin clearance, ml·min⁻¹·kg⁻¹	Immature	6	2.18(1.00-3.60)	63
193			Adult	12	1.96(1.18-3.03)	
194		Creatinine clearance, ml·min⁻¹·kg⁻¹	Adult	10	3.08(1.73-5.22)	63
195			Left kidney only	4	1.1(0.9-1.3)b	89
196		[57Co] Vitamin B₁₂ clearance, ml·min⁻¹·kg⁻¹	....	8	2.1(0.9-3.3)b	92
197		p-Aminohippurate clearance, ml·min⁻¹·kg⁻¹	Adult	4	8.06(6.71-10.90)	63
198		[125I] o-Iodohippurate sodium6/ clearance, ml·min⁻¹·kg⁻¹	....	8	11.9(9.5-14.4)b	92
199	Macaque7/	[131I] Diatrizoate sodium8/ clearance, ml·min⁻¹·kg⁻¹	Adult	4♀	3.3(2.2-4.3)	61
200		[131I] o-Iodohippurate sodium6/, ml·min⁻¹·kg⁻¹	Adult	6♀	15.1(13.8-17.2)	
201	Monkey cebus	Inulin clearance, ml·min⁻¹·m⁻²	Adult	5	35.5(21.7-53.0)	75
202		ml·min⁻¹·kg⁻¹	....	♂	3.19(2.94-3.46)	25
203				♀	3.97(3.41-4.53)	
204		Creatinine clearance, ml·min⁻¹·m⁻²	Adult	4	37.4(30.8-43.9)	75
205		p-Aminohippurate clearance, ml·min⁻¹·kg⁻¹		♂	14.2(13.6-14.7)	25
206				♀	17.1(15.6-18.7)	
207		Urate clearance, ml·min⁻¹·m⁻²	Adult	5	1.7(1.4-2.4)	75
208		ml·min⁻¹·kg⁻¹		♂	0.28(0.23-0.35)	25
209				♀	0.38(0.26-0.49)	
210		Filtration fraction, C_I/C_{PAH}		♂	0.23(0.22-0.24)	25
211				♀	0.23(0.22-0.24)	
212	squirrel	Inulin clearance, ml·min⁻¹·g kidney wt⁻¹		7	0.59(0.35-0.83)b	69
213		p-Aminohippurate clearance, ml·min⁻¹·g kidney wt⁻¹		7	1.03(0.73-1.33)b	69
214		Filtration fraction		7	0.52(0.35-0.68)b	69
215	Orangutan	Inulin clearance, ml·min⁻¹·m⁻²	Adult	1♀	76.2	77
216		Creatinine clearance, ml·min⁻¹·m⁻²	Adult	1♀	112.5	63
217	Rabbit	Inulin clearance, ml·min⁻¹·m⁻²	Young adult	♂	50.2(22-70)	47
218		ml·min⁻¹·kg⁻¹	....	....	5.0	18
219				....	7.0(5.0-8.4)	44
220				46	2.7(1.4-4.0)b	5

2/ Synonym: Diodrast. 3/ 7 occasions. 4/ *Macaca irus.* Synonym: *M. cynomolgus.* 5/ *Macaca mulatta.* 6/ Synonym: Hippuran. 7/ *Macaca speciosa.* 8/ Synonym: Hypaque.

continued

Part II. Homoiothermic Animals Other Than Man

	Animal	Specification	Subjects Age, Condition, or Breed	No. & Sex	Value	Reference
221		Creatinine clearance, ml/min	Adult	15♂	10.1(6.3-15.2)	11
222		ml·min⁻¹·kg⁻¹	Adult	22♂	3.2(2.2-4.2)[b]	37
223				2♂	5.3	27
224		[51Cr] Ethylenediaminetetraacetic acid[9/],	Mannitol diuresis	12	12.4(8.4-20.7)	4
225		ml/min	Saline diuresis	12	13.9(9.0-24.5)	
226		p-Aminohippurate clearance, ml/min	Adult	15♂	60.1(21.5-199.0)	11
227		Diodone clearance, ml/min	....	....	36.2(30.9-45.7)	44
228		[125I] o-Iodohippurate sodium[6/] clearance,	Mannitol diuresis	14	45.8(28.0-76.2)	4
229		ml/min	Saline diuresis	14	55.9(37.9-90.7)	
230		Urea clearance, ml·min⁻¹·m⁻²	....	25	25.5	76
231			Young adult	♂	14.3(3-28)	47
232		Tubular maxima, Diodone[2/], ml·min⁻¹·m⁻²	....	....	33.4(29.1-37.7)[b]	53
233		glucose, ml·min⁻¹·m⁻²	....	....	78.7(51.9-105.5)[b]	
234	Rat	Inulin clearance, ml/min	3 wk	7	0.71(0.39-1.03)[b]	66
235			4-5 wk	12	1.46(0.96-1.96)[b]	
236			7 wk	14	2.28(1.04-3.52)[b]	
237			10 wk	18	2.93(1.39-4.47)[b]	
238			13 wk	17	3.29(2.19-4.39)[b]	
239			Adult	14	0.36(0.28-0.44)	30
240		ml·min⁻¹·kg⁻¹	Adult	20	3.2(1.1-4.7)[10/]	28
241				134	3.5(2.6-4.3)[b]	19
242				19	4.8(3.5-6.5)[11/]	28
243				84	6.0(5.4-6.6)	10
244				16	6.1(4.8-7.8)[12/]	28
245				10	6.9(4.7-9.5)[13/]	28
246				31♂	2.7(1.5-3.9)[b]	29
247				26♂	9.4(6.2-17.3)	40
248				10♀	10.5(5.5-16.0)	40
249		ml·hr⁻¹·100 g body wt⁻¹	2 da	8	7.1(2.5-11.7)[b]	24
250			4 da	4	13.8(8.2-19.4)[b]	
251			12-13 da	8	21.7(17.7-25.7)[b]	
252			16-19 da	10	27.9(16.5-39.3)[b]	
253		μl·min⁻¹·g kidney wt⁻¹	1-3 da	4	44.7(0.7-88.7)[b]	41
254			8-10 da	8	159(63-255)[b]	
255			16-18 da	8	327(180-474)[b]	
256		Creatinine clearance, ml·min⁻¹·kg⁻¹	Adult	12	3.1(2.0-4.9)[10/]	28
257				27	5.6(3.0-6.5)[11/]	28
258				39	6.1(2.9-9.3)[b]	15
259				22	6.5(4.2-11.0)[12/]	28
260				9	7.0(6.0-8.6)[13/]	28
261				171	7.0	60
262				26♂	10.8(7.0-17.9)	40
263				10♀	10.8(5.5-16.7)	40
264		p-Aminohippurate clearance ml/min	....	7	6.21(5.34-6.96)	9
265			Adult	14	2.31(1.95-2.63)	30
266		ml·min⁻¹·kg⁻¹	Adult	6	15.7(10.0-24.8)[10/]	28
267				13	21.5(11.8-35.7)[11/]	
268				15	25.8(16.0-35.3)[12/]	
269				10	34.8(29.2-40.0)[13/]	

[2/] Synonym: Diodrast. [6/] Synonym: Hippuran. [9/] Synonym: Edetic acid. [10/] Urine flow: 0-0.5 ml/hr. [11/] Urine flow: 0.5-1.0 ml/hr. [12/] Urine flow: 1.0-1.5 ml/hr. [13/] Urine flow: 1.5-2.0 ml/hr.

continued

Part II. Homoiothermic Animals Other Than Man

	Animal	Specification	Age, Condition, or Breed	No. & Sex	Value	Reference
			Subjects		**Value**	**Reference**
270		$\mu l \cdot min^{-1} \cdot g$ kidney wt^{-1}	1-3 da	4	355(99-612)[b]	41
271			8-10 da	8	618(246-990)[b]	
272			16-18 da	8	936(742-1130)[b]	
273		p-Aminohippurate extraction ratio, %	1-3 da	7	21.3(10.7-31.9)[b]	41
274			8-10 da	11	40.4(32.4-48.4)[b]	
275			16-18 da	9	73.9(63.7-84.1)[b]	
276		p-Aminohippurate clearance, corrected for	1-3 da	4	1670(1080-2260)[b]	41
277		extraction ratio, $\mu l \cdot min^{-1} \cdot g$ kidney wt^{-1}	8-10 da	8	1521(698-2344)[b]	
278			16-18 da	8	1267(995-1539)[b]	
279		Diodone[2] clearance, ml·min^{-1}·kg^{-1}	Adult	134	22.2(16.6-27.8)[b]	19
280				31	13.3(6.1-17.1)	14
281		Urea clearance, ml·min^{-1}·m^{-2}	Adult	8	10.9(4.7-17.1)[b]	26
282		ml·min^{-1}·kg^{-1}	....	171	7.0	60
283		Mannitol clearance, ml·min^{-1}·kg^{-1}	Adult	20	5.5(3.8-7.2)	14
284		Filtration fraction, C_I/C_{PAH}	....	35	0.17(0.10-0.24)[b]	18
285			Adult	14	0.16(0.11-0.21)	30
286				31♂	0.20	29
287		Filtration fraction corrected for p-amino-	1-3 da	4	0.03(0-0.07)[b]	41
288		hippurate extraction ratio, $C_I \cdot C_{PAH}^{-1} \cdot$	8-10 da	8	0.10(0.04-0.16)[b]	
289		E_{PAH}^{-1}	16-18 da	8	0.26(0.14-0.38)[b]	
		Tubular maxima				
290		p-Aminohippurate, mg/min	Adult	14	0.10(0.08-0.12)	30
291		mg·min^{-1}·kg^{-1}	....	39	2.9(2.8-3.0)[b]	15
292			Sprague-Dawley	20	3.27	14
293			Wistar	20	2.36	14
294		Diodone, mg·min^{-1}·kg^{-1}	....	134	1.32(0.96-1.68)[b]	19
295				30	1.83(1.6-2.1)	10
296		Glucose, mg/min	8 wk	9	5.17(3.11-7.23)[b]	66
297			13 wk	10	15.3(10.9-19.7)[b]	
298		Ammonia excretion after acid load, μmole·	9 da	5	12.2(11.4-13.0)[b]	36
299		hr^{-1}·100 g body wt^{-1}	14 da	4	11.1(6.54-15.66)[b]	
300			16 da	4	27.3(3.3-51.3)[b]	
301			21 da	9	39.0(27.6-50.4)[b]	
302			Adult	4	37.2(23.6-50.8)[b]	
303		Titratable acid excretion after acid load,	9 da	5	4.12(1.32-6.92)[b]	36
304		μeq·hr^{-1}·100 g body wt^{-1}	14 da	4	8.62(4.26-12.98)[b]	
305			16 da	4	16.4(6.0-26.8)[b]	
306			21 da	9	15.1(0-31.9)	
307			Adult	4	14.5(8.9-20.1)[b]	
308		Maximum depression of urine pH after	9 da	5	5.8(5.0-6.6)[b]	36
309		acid load, pH	14 da	4	6.0(5.6-6.4)[b]	
310			16 da	4	6.0(5.6-6.4)[b]	
311			21 da	9	5.9	
312			Adult	4	6.2(5.8-6.6)[b]	
313		Maximum urine osmolality after 8-hr fast,	10 da	10	938(762-1114)[b]	88
314		mosmole/liter	20 da	9	1449(1023-1875)[b]	
315	Sheep	Inulin clearance, ml/min	Adult	1♀	59	72
316				5♀	101	33
317				6♀	111	32
318			Before feeding	4♀	78(64-92)	79
319			After feeding	4♀	78(65-95)	79

[2] Synonym: Diodrast.

continued

Part II. Homoiothermic Animals Other Than Man

	Animal	Specification	Subjects Age, Condition, or Breed	No. & Sex	Value	Reference
320			High protein intake	3♀	112(94-139)	34
321			Low protein intake	3♀	49(39-57)	34
322		ml·min⁻¹·kg⁻¹	Adult	2♀	1.80(1.72-1.87)	70
323		Creatinine clearance, ml/min	Adult	14♀	33(16-50)ᵇ	90
324				1♀	60.0	70
325			Normal ureter	1♀	30.6	80
326			Exteriorized ureter	1♀	31.3	80
327		ml·min⁻¹·kg⁻¹	Adult	2♀	1.75(1.70-1.79)	70
328		p-Aminohippurate clearance, ml/min	Adult	14♀	1052(557-1547)ᵇ	90
329			Before feeding	4♀	469(434-534)	79
330			After feeding	4♀	489(413-571)	79
331			High protein intake	3♀	639(479-823)	34
332			Low protein intake	3♀	190(170-228)	34
333		Phenol red clearance, ml/min	Adult	6♀	400(110-704)	57
334		Urea clearance, ml/min	Adult	1♀	32	72
335				5♀	56	80
336				6♀	62	80
337				14♀	86(49-123)ᵇ	90
338	Swine	Inulin clearance, ml·min⁻¹·kg⁻¹	Immature	....	3.7	16
339			Adult	4	5.06(4.87-5.32)	58
340				14♀	2.1(1.8-2.5)	39
341				6♀	3.3(2.4-4.4)	83
342		Creatinine clearance, ml·min⁻¹·kg⁻¹	Adult	4	4.15(4.07-4.40)	58
343				26♀	2.2(1.5-3.4)	39
344				8♀	3.3(2.4-3.8)	83
345		p-Aminohippurate clearance, ml·min⁻¹·kg⁻¹	Adult	2	19.5(19.3-19.7)	58
346				8♀	6.4(5.2-8.4)	39
347		Urea clearance, ml·min⁻¹·kg⁻¹	Adult	26♀	1.2(0.9-1.8)	39
348				8♀	2.0(1.1-3.2)	83
349		Scandium-46 microspheres (measure of renal blood flow), ml·min⁻¹·m⁻²	24 hr	12	43(10-80)	68
350			14 da	6	350(250-500)	
351			45 da	3	760(700-830)	
352		Filtration fraction, C_I/C_{PAH}	Adult	2	0.26(0.25-0.28)	58
353		Tubular maxima, p-aminohippurate, mg·min⁻¹·kg⁻¹	Adult	2	3.11(3.00-3.21)	58
354				7♀	2.5(1.7-3.7)	39
355	Chicken	Inulin clearance, ml·min⁻¹·kg⁻¹	Adult	43♀	1.8(0.2-3.4)ᵇ	7
356				11♀	1.84(1.04-2.83)	86
357				6♀	2.5(1.8-3.5)	59
358			Normal	....	1.87	73
359				....	2.45	51
360				5	2.03	74
361				5	2.04	65
362				13♀	1.84	64
363			During water loading	....	1.37	51
364			During dehydration	....	0.60	51
365				♀	3.0	78
366		Creatinine clearance, ml·min⁻¹·kg⁻¹	Adult	♀	3.90(2.0-6.8)[14]	87
367				♀	2.25(1.3-2.6)[15]	
368		p-Aminohippurate clearance, ml/min	Adult	6♀	30.7(20.8-40.6)	59
369				7♀	67.6(53.4-104.4)	86

[14] Exogenous creatinine. [15] Endogenous creatinine.

continued

Part II. Homoiothermic Animals Other Than Man

Animal	Specification	Subjects		Value	Reference
		Age, Condition, or Breed	No. & Sex		
370	Diodone clearance, ml·min⁻¹·kg⁻¹	Adult	6♀	18.0(10.5-25.8)	86
371	Phenol red clearance	Adult	13♀	25.0	64
372	Urea clearance	....	5	1.50	65
373	Uric acid clearance, ml·min⁻¹·kg⁻¹	Adult	43♀	11.3(0-23.0)	7
374			6♀	19.8(8.7-30.0)	59
375			5♀	25.1(15.6-35.1)	86
376	Tubular maxima, p-aminohippurate, mg·min⁻¹·kg⁻¹	Adult	2♀	1.58(1.08-1.93)	17

Contributors: Osbaldiston, G. W.; Nash, Martin A., and Edelmann, Chester M., Jr.

References

[1] Anderson, R. R., and J. P. Mixner. 1959. J. Diary Sci. 42:545.

[2] Anderson, R. R., and J. P. Mixner. 1960. Ibid. 43:1476.

[3] Asheim, A., et al. 1961. Acta Physiol. Scand. 51:150.

[4] Barraclough, N. A., et al. 1970. J. Appl. Physiol. 28:209.

[5] Beechwood, E. C., et al. 1964. Amer. J. Physiol. 207:1265.

[6] Bentley, P. J., and K. Schmidt-Nielsen. 1967. Comp. Biochem. Physiol. 20:285.

[7] Berger, L., et al. 1960. Amer. J. Physiol. 198:575.

[8] Blatteis, C. M., and S. M. Horvath. 1958. Ibid. 192:353.

[9] Blaufox, M. D., et al. 1967. Ibid. 212:629.

[10] Braun-Menendez, E., and H. Chiodi. 1946. Rev. Soc. Arg. Biol. 22:314.

[11] Brod, J., and J. H. Sirota. 1949. Amer. J. Physiol. 157:31.

[12] Clapp, J. R. 1965. Proc. Soc. Exp. Biol. Med. 120:521.

[13] Corcoran, A. C., and I. H. Page. 1939. Amer. J. Physiol. 126:354.

[14] Corcoran, A. C., and I. H. Page. 1947. Fed. Proc. Fed. Amer. Soc. Exp. Biol. 6:91.

[15] Corcoran, A. C., et al. 1948. Amer. J. Physiol. 154:170.

[16] Dalgaard-Mikkelsen, S., et al. 1953. Nord. Vet. Med. 5:965.

[17] Dantzler, W. H. 1966. Amer. J. Physiol. 210:640.

[18] Dicker, S. E., and H. Heller. 1945. J. Physiol. (London) 103:449.

[19] Dicker, S. E., and H. Heller. 1946. Ibid. 104:353.

[20] Duncan, H., et al. 1965. Proc. Soc. Exp. Biol. Med. 120:293.

[21] Dziemian, A. J., et al. 1950. U.S. Army Med. Cent. Chem. Corps Res. Rep. 29:1.

[22] Eggleton, M. G., and Y. A. Habib. 1950. J. Physiol. (London) 110:458.

[23] Ewald, B. H. 1967. Amer. J. Vet. Res. 28:741.

[24] Falk, G. 1955. Amer. J. Physiol. 181:157.

[25] Fanelli, G. M., et al. 1970. Ibid. 218:627.

[26] Farr, L. E., and J. E. Smadel. 1936. Ibid. 116:349.

[27] Forster, R. P. 1952. Ibid. 168:666.

[28] Friedman, S. M. 1947. Ibid. 148:387.

[29] Friedman, S. M., and C. A. Livingstone. 1942. Ibid. 137:564.

[30] Friedman, S. M., et al. 1947. Ibid. 150:340.

[31] Gagnon, J. A., and R. W. Clarke. 1957. Ibid. 190:117.

[32] Gans, J. H. 1964. Amer. J. Vet. Res. 25:914.

[33] Gans, J. H. 1964. Ibid. 25:924.

[34] Gans, J. H., and P. F. Mercer. 1962. Ibid. 23:230.

[35] Glauser, K. F., and E. E. Selkurt. 1952. Amer. J. Physiol. 168:469.

[36] Goldstein, L. 1970. Ibid. 218:394.

[37] Grant, R. 1953. Ibid. 174:79.

[38] Gruskin, A. B., et al. 1970. Pediat. Res. 4:7.

[39] Gyrd-Hansen, N. 1968. Acta Vet. Scand. 9:183.

[40] Harvey, A., and R. L. Malvin. 1965. Amer. J. Physiol. 209:849.

[41] Horster, M., and J. E. Lewy. 1970. Ibid. 219:1061.

[42] Horster, M., and H. Valtin. 1971. J. Clin. Invest. 50:779.

[43] Houck, C. R. 1948. Amer. J. Physiol. 153:169.

[44] Hughes-Jones, N. C., et al. 1949. J. Physiol. (London) 109:288.

[45] Jolliffe, N., and H. W. Smith. 1931. Amer. J. Physiol. 98:572.

[46] Jose, P. A., et al. 1971. Pediat. Res. 5:335.

[47] Kaplan, B., and H. W. Smith. 1935. Amer. J. Physiol. 113:354.

[48] Ketz, H. A., et al. 1956. Monatsh. Veterinaermed. 11:575.

[49] Knudsen, E. 1959. Acta Vet. Scand. 1:52.

[50] Knudsen, E. 1959. Ibid. 1:188.

[51] Korr, I. M. 1939. J. Cell. Comp. Physiol. 13:175.

[52] Kubicek, W. G., et al. 1953. Amer. J. Physiol. 174:397.

[53] Laake, H. 1945. Acta Med. Scand., Suppl. 168.

[54] Ladd, M., et al. 1957. J. Appl. Physiol. 10:249.

[55] Lathen, W., et al. 1960. Amer. J. Physiol. 199:9.

[56] Low, D. G., et al. 1956. J. Infec. Dis. 98:260.

continued

Part II. Homoiothermic Animals Other Than Man

[57] Manning, J. P., et al. 1959. Amer. J. Vet. Res. 20: 858.

[58] Mundsick, R. A., et al. 1958. Endocrinology 63: 688.

[59] Nechay, B. R., and L. Nechay. 1959. J. Pharmacol. Exp. Ther. 126:291.

[60] Lippman, R. W. 1948. J. Physiol. (London) 152:27.

[61] O'Dell, R. M., et al. 1968. J. Appl. Physiol. 24:366.

[62] Osbaldiston, G. W., and W. Fuhrman. 1970. Can. J. Comp. Med. 34:138.

[63] Pickering, D. E., and H. H. Sussman. 1962. Amer. J. Vet. Res. 23:667.

[64] Pitts, R. F. 1938. J. Cell. Comp. Physiol. 11:99.

[65] Pitts, R. F., and I. M. Korr. 1938. Ibid. 11:117.

[66] Potter, D., et al. 1969. Pediat. Res. 3:51.

[67] Poulsen, E. 1957. Kgl. Vet. Landbohoejsk. Arsskr., p. 97.

[68] Russo, H. F., et al. 1952. Proc. Soc. Exp. Biol. Med. 80:736.

[69] Selkurt, E. E., and R. L. Wathen. 1967. Amer. J. Physiol. 213:191.

[70] Schmidt-Nielsen, B., et al. 1958. Ibid. 194:221.

[71] Sellers, A. F., et al. 1958. Amer. J. Vet. Res. 19: 580.

[72] Shannon, J. A. 1937. Proc. Soc. Exp. Biol. Med. 37:379.

[73] Shannon, J. A. 1938. J. Cell. Comp. Physiol. 11: 108.

[74] Shannon, J. A. 1938. Ibid. 11:135.

[75] Skeith, M. D., and L. A. Healey. 1968. Amer. J. Physiol. 214:582.

[76] Smith, H. W. 1951. The Kidney. Oxford Univ. Press, New York. p. 541.

[77] Smith, H. W., and R. W. Clarke. 1938. Amer. J. Physiol. 122:132.

[78] Sperber, I. 1960. In A. J. Marshall, ed. Biology and Comparative Physiology of Birds. Academic Press, New York. pp. 469-492.

[79] Stacy, B. P., and A. H. Brook. 1964. Aust. J. Agr. Res. 15:289.

[80] Stacy, B. P., and A. H. Brook. 1964. Quart. J. Exp. Physiol. Cog. Med. Sci. 49:301.

[81] Stamler, J., et al. 1949. J. Exp. Med. 90:511.

[82] Stevens, C. E., et al. 1956. Amer. J. Vet. Res. 17: 710.

[83] Suarez, C. A., et al. 1968. Ibid. 29:995.

[84] Summerville, W. W., et al. 1932. Amer. J. Physiol. 102:1.

[85] Sweet, A. Y., et al. 1961. Ibid. 201:975.

[86] Sykes, A. H. 1960. Res. Vet. Sci. 1:308.

[87] Sykes, A. H. 1960. Ibid. 1:315.

[88] Trimble, M. E. 1970. Amer. J. Physiol. 219:1089.

[89] Vander, A. J., and E. J. Cafruny. 1962. Ibid. 202: 1105.

[90] Webb, K. E., et al. 1970. J. Anim. Sci. 30:941.

[91] Weeth, H. J., and A. L. Lesperance. 1965. Ibid. 24: 441.

[92] Weigel, W. W., et al. 1968. Fed. Proc. Fed. Amer. Soc. Exp. Biol. 25:198.

[93] Weisser, F., et al. 1970. Amer. J. Physiol. 219:1706.

[94] White, H. L., et al. 1948. J. Physiol. (London) 156: 67.

[95] Yu, T. F., et al. 1960. Amer. J. Physiol. 199:1199.

[96] Yu, T. F., et al. 1961. Proc. Soc. Exp. Biol. Med. 107:905.

Part III. Poikilothermic Animals

Specification: c_U = concentration in urine; c_{Pl} = concentration in plasma. Values in parentheses are ranges, estimate "b" unless otherwise indicated (*see* Introduction).

	Class & Species	Specification	No. of Subjects	Value	Reference
	Reptilia				
1	*Natrix* spp.	Inulin clearance, ml·hr⁻¹·kg⁻¹	3	28.4(12.6-43.2)[c]	4
2	*N. sipedon*	Inulin clearance, ml·hr⁻¹·kg⁻¹	27	19.4(14.2-24.6)	2
3	*Pituophis melanoleucus*	Inulin clearance, ml·hr⁻¹·kg⁻¹	11	10.8(7.8-15.0)[c]	4
	Amphibia				
4	*Bufo paracnemis*	Inulin clearance, ml·hr⁻¹·kg⁻¹	2	15.8(9.9-21.6)	1
5	*Ceratophrys ornata*[1]	Inulin clearance, ml·hr⁻¹·kg⁻¹	2	101(24-178)	1
6	*Phyllomedusa sauvagei*	Inulin clearance, ml·hr⁻¹·kg⁻¹	1	57	1
7	*Rana catesbeiana*	Inulin clearance, ml·hr⁻¹·kg⁻¹	4♂	28(18-37)	8
8	*R. esculenta*	Inulin clearance, ml·hr⁻¹·kg⁻¹	...	52.6(38.0-67.2)	3
	Dipnoi				
9	*Protopterus aethiopicus*	Inulin clearance, ml·hr⁻¹·kg⁻¹	2	17.5(14-21)	7

[1] Synonym: *Ceratophis ornata.*

continued

277. RENAL FUNCTION TESTS: VERTEBRATES

Part III. Poikilothermic Animals

	Class & Species	Specification	No. of Subjects	Value	Reference
	Agnatha				
10	*Myxine glutinosa*	Inulin, c_U/c_{Pl}	8	0.85(0.32-1.35)[c]	6
11		Phenol red, c_U/c_{Pl}	6	1.0(0.3-1.7)[c]	
12	*Petromyzon marinus*	Inulin clearance, $ml \cdot min^{-1} \cdot kg^{-1}$	5[2/]	0.60(0.19-0.74)[c]	5
13		Creatinine clearance, $ml \cdot min^{-1} \cdot kg^{-1}$	5[2/]	0.34(0.17-0.49)[c]	

[2/] Adult.

Contributor: Osbaldiston, G. W.

References

[1] Carlisky, N. J., et al. 1968. Comp. Biochem. Physiol. 26:573.
[2] Dantzler, W. H. 1967. Amer. J. Physiol. 212:83.
[3] Jard, S., and F. Morel. 1963. Ibid. 204:222.
[4] Komadina, S., and S. Solomon. 1970. Comp. Biochem. Physiol. 32:333.
[5] Malvin, R. L., et al. 1970. Amer. J. Physiol. 218:1506.
[6] Rall, D. P., and J. W. Burger. 1967. Ibid. 212:354.
[7] Sawyer, W. H. 1966. Ibid. 210:191.
[8] Uranga, J., and W. H. Sawyer. 1960. Ibid. 198:1287.

278. CHEMICAL COMPOSITION AND PHYSICAL PROPERTIES OF AQUEOUS HUMOR: VERTEBRATES

Values in parentheses are ranges, estimate "c" (*see* Introduction).

Part I. Man

Plus/minus (±) values are standard deviation, unless otherwise indicated.

Constituent or Property	Value		Reference
	Aqueous Humor	Plasma	
Electrolytes			
1 Bicarbonate, $\mu mole/g$	19.64 ± 1.4	26.5 ± 2.64	4
2 $\mu mole/g$ H_2O	21.5	....	3
3 Chloride, $\mu mole/ml$	121.2(115.9-122.8)	....	12
4 $\mu mole/g$ H_2O	126	....	3
5 $\mu mole/g$	134.0 ± 22.4	109.0 ± 18.4	4
6 Copper, $nmole/ml$	(2.54-3.18)		10
7 Phosphate, $\mu mole/ml$	0.62	1.11	22
8 Sodium, $\mu mole/g$ H_2O	162.9 ± 4.3[1/]	176.4	5
9 Zinc, ppm dry mass	1.84	....	9
Vitamins & Related Compounds			
10 Trigonelline, $nmole/eye$	73.0	....	7
11 Trigonellinamide, $nmole/eye$	137.0	....	7
12 Vitamin B_{12}, pg/ml	29.9[2/]	271.9	17
13 Ascorbate, $\mu mole/ml$	1.06 ± 0.31[3/]	0.042 ± 0.023	4

[1/] Plus/minus (±) value is standard error. [2/] *Euglena* assay. [3/] Non-cataractous eyes.

continued

278. CHEMICAL COMPOSITION AND PHYSICAL PROPERTIES OF AQUEOUS HUMOR: VERTEBRATES

Part I. Man

	Constituent or Property	Value — Aqueous Humor	Value — Plasma	Reference
		Aqueous Humor	**Plasma**	
	Carbohydrates & Related Compounds			
14	Glucose, μmole/g	3.00 ± 2.04	6.33 ± 2.45	4
15	μmole/ml	$(3.70\text{-}4.78)$[4]	$(4.72\text{-}6.55)$[4]	18
16	Hexosamine, μg/g	$16.0(14.9\text{-}18.3)$	....	15
17	Mucopolysaccharide, μg/ml	240	....	2
18	Citrate, μmole/ml	$0.133(0.085\text{-}0.167)$[5]	$0.132(0.103\text{-}0.149)$	11
19	Lactate, μmole/g	4.28 ± 1.30	1.78 ± 0.80	4
	Nitrogenous Substances			
20	Protein, total, mg/100 g	$(31\text{-}1000)$	....	13
21		55[6]	....	19
22	Prealbumin$_1$, % of total protein	4.1[6]	....	19
23	Prealbumin$_2$, % of total protein	8.2[6]	....	
24	Albumin, % of total protein	31.0[6]	....	
25	α_1-Globulin, % of total protein	10.6[6]	....	
26	α_2-Globulin, % of total protein	11.2[6]	....	
27	β-Globulin, % of total protein	20.1[6]	....	
28	γ-Globulin, % of total protein	12.7[6]	....	
29	τ-fraction, % of total protein	2.1[6]	....	
30	Glycoprotein, μg/ml	$(63\text{-}75)$	....	6
	Amino acids, μmole/liter			8
31	Alanine	294 ± 66.1	....	
32	α-Aminobutyric acid	31.4 ± 7.8	....	
33	Arginine	133 ± 26.0	....	
34	Asparagine	49.2 ± 11.5	....	
35	Aspartic acid	1.0 ± 1.5	....	
36	Citrulline	9.8 ± 4.8	....	
37	Cystine	11.2 ± 3.5	....	
38	Glutamic acid	12.0 ± 3.4	....	
39	Glutamine	717 ± 134	....	
40	Glycine	16.7 ± 3.5	....	
41	Histidine	77.9 ± 12.7	....	
42	Isoleucine	79.8 ± 16.9	....	
43	Leucine	192 ± 39.6	....	
44	Lysine	155 ± 23.5	....	
45	Methionine	44.4 ± 9.9	....	
46	Ornithine	25.3 ± 4.6	....	
47	Phenylalanine	119 ± 14.0	....	
48	Proline	16.0 ± 5.3	....	
49	Serine	179 ± 38.1	....	
50	Taurine	39.1 ± 11.3	....	
51	Threonine	152 ± 41.4	....	
52	Tryptophan	31.9 ± 10.0	....	
53	Tyrosine	123 ± 16.5	....	
54	Valine	388 ± 84.5	....	
55	Urate, μmole/ml	$(0.065\text{-}0.268)$	$(0.131\text{-}0.304)$	22
56	Urea, μmole/g H_2O	6.0	....	1

[4] 23 subjects, 40 yr old. [5] Mainly eyes with senile cataracts. [6] One case with secondary cataract.

continued

278. CHEMICAL COMPOSITION AND PHYSICAL PROPERTIES OF AQUEOUS HUMOR: VERTEBRATES

Part I. Man

Constituent or Property	Value		Ref-er-ence
	Aqueous Humor	Plasma	
Enzymes			
57 Lactate dehydrogenase; activity, Bucher units/ml	0.31 ± 0.21	....	16
Physical Properties			
58 Volume, μl	347	....	20
59	350	....	14
60 Oxygen pressure, mm Hg	59.68(53.0-68.0)[7,8]	....	21
61 Carbon dioxide pressure, mm Hg	38.6(35.0-44.5)[9]	....	21
62 pH	7.21	....	3
63	7.38(7.31-7.42)[7,9]	....	20

[7] Patients 64-90 yr old. [8] Cataractous eyes. [9] Eyes with 16 cataract points.

Contributors: Langham, Maurice E.; Cole, D. F.; Hamilton, Paul B.

References

[1] Adler, F. H. 1953. Physiology of the Eye. H. Kimpton, London.

[2] Balazs, E. A. 1960. Importance Vitreous Body Retina Surg. Retina Found. Conf., 2nd, 1958, p. 29.

[3] Becker, B. 1957. Arch. Ophthalmol. 57:793.

[4] Cagianut, B. 1957. Doc. Ophthalmol. 11:173.

[5] Cardia, L., and G. Coriglione. 1962. G. Ital. Oftalmol. 15:24.

[6] Ciusa, W., et al. 1964. Exp. Eye Res. 3:169.

[7] De Bernardinis, E., et al. 1965. Exp. Eye Res. 4:179.

[8] Durham, D. G., et al. 1971. Clin. Chem. 17:285.

[9] Galin, M. A., et al. 1962. Invest. Ophthalmol. 1:142.

[10] Gerhard, J. P., and P. Calme. 1964. Bull. Soc. Ophtalmol. Fr. 64:929.

[11] Grönvall, H. 1937. Acta Ophthalmol., Suppl. 14:279.

[12] Kinsey, V. E. 1949. J. Gen. Physiol. 32:329.

[13] Kronfeld, P. C., et al. 1941. Amer. J. Ophthalmol. 24:401.

[14] Mestrezat, W., and A. Magitot. 1921. C. R. Soc. Biol. 84:185.

[15] Meyer, K., et al. 1938. Amer. J. Ophthalmol. 21:1083.

[16] Munich, W. 1959. Ber. Deut. Ophthalmol. Ges. 62:36.

[17] Phillips, C. I., et al. 1968. Nature (London) 217:67.

[18] Pohjola, S. 1966. Acta Ophthalmol., Suppl. 88.

[19] Praus, R. 1961. Exp. Eye Res. 1:67.

[20] Steindorf, K. 1947. Tabulae Biol. 22(l-a):222.

[21] Thiel, H. J. 1967. Albrecht von Graefes Arch. Ophthalmol. 174:127.

[22] Walker, A. M. 1933. J. Biol. Chem. 101:269.

Part II. Mammals Other Than Man

Constituent or Property: c_A = concentration in aqueous humor; c_{Pl} = concentration in plasma water. Plus/minus (±) values are standard error, unless otherwise indicated.

Species	Constituent or Property	Value		Ref-er-ence
		Aqueous Humor	Plasma	
Electrolytes				
1 *Bos taurus*	Bicarbonate, μmole/g H_2O	36.0	....	19
2	Calcium, μmole/ml	1.85	....	13
3	Carbon dioxide, μmole/ml	19.8	....	13

continued

Part II. Mammals Other Than Man

Species	Constituent or Property	Value — Aqueous Humor	Value — Plasma	Reference
4	Chloride, μmole/ml	114.6	....	13
5	μmole/g H_2O	124.0	....	19
6	ratio of c_A/c_{Pl}	1.15		20
7	Copper, nmole/ml	(2.2-2.9)	....	56
8	Iron, nmole/ml	1.9	....	55
9		2.9	....	73
10	Manganese, nmole/ml	0.218(0.18-0.27)	....	73
11	Phosphorus, μmole/ml	1.74	....	13
12	Potassium, μmole/ml	5.13	....	13
13		7.1	....	19
14	Sodium, μmole/g H_2O	146	....	5
15		147	....	74
16		149.5	....	19
17	ratio of c_A/c_{Pl}	0.94		20
18	Sulfur, μmole/ml	1.94	....	13
19	Zinc, nmole/g H_2O	0.4	....	56
20	*Canis familiaris* — Calcium, μeq/g H_2O	2.96 ± 0.06[1]; 2.92 ± 0.08[2]	5.24 ± 0.12	7
21	Carbon dioxide, μmole/g H_2O	29.5 ± 2.6[3]	26.2 ± 2.1[3]	24
22	vol %	60.2(58.3-62.5)		47
23	Chloride, μeq/g H_2O	124.8	115.9	26
24	Magnesium, μeq/g H_2O	1.07 ± 0.02[1]; 1.06 ± 0.02[2]	1.55 ± 0.06	7
25	Phosphate, μmole/ml	0.52	1.26	78
26	Potassium, μeq/g H_2O	4.72 ± 0.06[1]; 5.32 ± 0.05[2]	4.42 ± 0.19	18
27	Sodium, μmole/g H_2O	149.4 ± 0.5	154.8 ± 0.7	27
28	*Capra hircus* — Bicarbonate, μmole/g H_2O	21.8 ± 1.6[3]	32.9 ± 4.7[3]	24
29	Chloride, ratio of c_A/c_{Pl}	1.09		28
30	Sodium, ratio of c_A/c_{Pl}	0.93		20
31	*Cavia porcellus* — Carbon dioxide, μmole/g H_2O	40.0 ± 2.4[3]	29.8 ± 1.6[3]	24
32	Chloride, ratio of c_A/c_{Pl}	0.935		20
33	Sodium, ratio of c_A/c_{Pl}	0.98[4]		20
34	*Cercopithecus* — Carbon dioxide, μmole/g H_2O	28.9 ± 3.3[3]	35.2 ± 3.4[3]	24
35	*aethiops* — Chloride, μmole/g H_2O	122.0	110	25
36	*Equus caballus* — Calcium, μmole/g H_2O	1.55	2.53	32
37		1.97	3.02	70
38	Carbon dioxide, μmole/g H_2O	23.9 ± 3.3[3]	29.2 ± 2.0[3]	24
39	Chloride, μmole/g H_2O	123.6	110.7	32
40	ratio of c_A/c_{Pl}	1.19		28
41	Copper, nmole/g H_2O	0.3	....	56
42	Magnesium, μmole/ml	0.75	0.78	70
43	μmole/g H_2O	1.1	1.25	32
44	Phosphate, μmole/g H_2O	1.06	1.05	32
45	Potassium, μmole/g H_2O	4.86	5.15	32
46	Sodium, μmole/g H_2O	121.5	155.8	32
47	ratio of c_A/c_{Pl}	0.935		20
48	Sulfate, μmole/g H_2O	1.94	1.94	32
49	*Felis catus* — Bicarbonate, μmole/g H_2O	30.4	25.3	25
50	Calcium, μeq/g H_2O	2.70 ± 0.08[1]; 2.78 ± 0.08[2]	4.80 ± 0.10	7
51	Chloride, μmole/g H_2O	131.0	124	25
52	Magnesium, μeq/g H_2O	0.99 ± 0.05[1]; 0.89 ± 0.03[2]	1.95 ± 0.15	7

[1] Anterior chamber. [2] Posterior chamber. [3] Plus/minus (±) value is standard deviation. [4] From sodium-24 equilibrium.

continued

Part II. Mammals Other Than Man

	Species	Constituent or Property	Value — Aqueous Humor	Value — Plasma	Reference
53		Phosphate, μmole/ml	0.48	1.87	78
54		Potassium, μeq/g H_2O	4.15 ± 0.09[1]; 4.70 ± 0.08[2]	4.08 ± 0.24	7
55		Sodium, μmole/g H_2O	158.5 ± 1.50	163.6 ± 1.53	18
56	*Hippopotamus*	Carbon dioxide, μmole/g H_2O	30.7(27.3-34.5)	37.33(36.5-37.9)	50
57	*amphibius*	Chloride, μmole/g H_2O	121.0(116-128)	111.7(107-113)	
58		Potassium, μeq/g H_2O	5.03(5.0-5.85)	9.45(8.3-11.9)	
59	*Macaca fascicularis*	Sodium, ratio of c_A/c_{Pl}	0.97[4]		23
60	*M. mulatta*	Calcium, μeq/g H_2O	2.54 ± 0.05[1]; 2.54 ± 0.12[2]	4.87 ± 0.10	7
61		Magnesium, μeq/g H_2O	1.17 ± 0.04[1]; 1.30 ± 0.03[2]	1.23 ± 0.07	7
62		Potassium, μeq/g H_2O	3.59 ± 0.18[1]; 4.12 ± 0.16[2]	4.23 ± 0.20	27
63	*Ovis aries*	Chloride, ratio of c_A/c_{Pl}	1.16		28
64		Sodium, μmole/g H_2O	142.0 ± 1.2	151 ± 2.0	15
65		ratio of c_A/c_{Pl}	0.94		20
66	*Rattus norvegicus*	Carbon dioxide, μmole/g H_2O	33.8 ± 1.2[3]	30.0 ± 3.3[3]	24
67		Chloride, ratio of c_A/c_{Pl}	1.025		20
68		Sodium, ratio of c_A/c_{Pl}	0.99		20
69	*Sus scrofa*	Sodium, ratio of c_A/c_{Pl}	0.93		20
70	Rabbit	Bicarbonate, μmole/g H_2O	27.4 ± 5.80[3]	....	29
71			27.7[1]; 34.1[2]	24.0	46
72			28.7 ± 7.87[3]	....	29
73			32.4	28.1	25
74		Calcium, μeq/g H_2O	3.48 ± 0.04[1]	6.22 ± 0.18	7
75		Carbon dioxide, μmole/g H_2O	30.2[1]; 37.5[2]	20.6	46,64
76			31.4 ± 2.4[3]	24.9	24
77		Chloride, μmole/g H_2O	105.1[1]; 100.1[2]	111.8	46
78		Magnesium, μeq/g H_2O	1.41 ± 0.03[1]; 1.50 ± 0.03[2]	1.87 ± 0.08	7
79		Phosphate, μmole/ml	0.86[1]; 0.57[2]	1.11	16
80		μmole/g H_2O	0.89[1]; 0.52[2]	1.49	46
81		Potassium, μeq/g H_2O	4.26 ± 0.17[1]; 4.69 ± 0.09[2]	4.57 ± 0.22	7
82		Sodium, μeq/ml H_2O	153.1 ± 4.4[1]; 158.9 ± 1.2[2]	163.3 ± 1.2	14
83		μmole/g H_2O	146.5[1]; 144.5[2]	146.0	46
84		Zinc, ppm dry mass	2.05	....	39
		Vitamins & Related Compounds			
85	*Bos taurus*	Riboflavin, nmole/ml	(0.025-0.031)	....	58
86		Nicotinic acid, nmole/ml	0.31	16.25	68
87		Trigonelline, nmole/eye	146	....	12
88		Trigonellinamide, nmole/eye	131	....	12
89		Ascorbate, μmole/ml	1.21	....	52
90	*Canis familiaris*	Ascorbate, μmole/ml	0.295	....	60
91		Ascorbic acid, mg/100 ml	(5-6)	....	21
92	*Cavia porcellus*	Ascorbate, μmole/ml	1.25	....	60
93		Ascorbic acid, mg/100 ml	(5-25)	....	21
94	*Equus caballus*	Ascorbate, μmole/ml	1.06	....	60
95		Ascorbic acid, mg/100 ml	(18-24)	....	21
96	*Felis catus*	Ascorbate, μmole/g H_2O	0.1	....	48
97	*Macaca mulatta*	Ascorbate, μmole/ml	(0.93-1.11)	....	45
98	*Ovis aries*	Inositol, μmole/ml	0.59	0.072	57
99		Ascorbate, μmole/ml	0.966	....	76
100			1.42	....	60

[1] Anterior chamber. [2] Posterior chamber. [3] Plus/minus (±) value is standard deviation. [4] From sodium-24 equilibrium.

continued

Part II. Mammals Other Than Man

	Species	Constituent or Property	Value		Ref-er-ence
			Aqueous Humor	Plasma	
101	Lamb	Inositol, μmole/ml	0.6	0.155	57
102	*Rattus norvegicus*	Ascorbate	0	....	53
103	*Sus scrofa*	Ascorbate, μmole/ml	0.28	....	44
104			(0.51-0.85)	....	76
105	Monkey	Ascorbic acid, mg/100 ml	(16-19)	....	21
106	Rabbit	Thiamine, free, nmole/ml	9.0	13.7	67
107		ester, nmole/ml	5.0	52.7	
108		Ascorbate, μmole/ml	0.96 ± 0.21[3]	....	29
109			1.37 ± 0.20[3]	....	
110		μmole/g H$_2$O	0.96[1]; 1.30[2]	0.02	46
		Carbohydrates & Related Compounds			
111	*Aotus trivirgatus*	Hexosamine, μg/ml	5.0	....	3
112	*Bos taurus*	Glucose, μmole/g H$_2$O	3.30 ± 0.186	....	65
113		Hexosamine, μg/ml	0.4	83.9	72
114			(3.0-5.0)	....	3
115		μg/g H$_2$O	13.3(11.9-15.5)	....	52
116		Lactate, μmole/ml	2.1	....	13
117	Calf	Hyaluronic acid, neq /ml	10.6 ± 1.1[3]	....	49
118	1-2 da old	Citrate, μmole/ml	0.094	0.192	40
119	Adult	Hyaluronic acid, neq/ml	17.7 ± 1.1[3]	....	49
120		Citrate, μmole/ml	0.080	0.158	40
121	*Canis familiaris*	Glucose, μmole/ml	4.14	....	47
122			5.11	7.00	31
123		Hexosamine, μg/g	16.7(12-20)	....	52
124		Citrate, μmole/ml	0.196	0.282	40
125	*Capra hircus*	Citrate, μmole/ml	0.091	0.149	40
126	*Cavia porcellus*	Mucopolysaccharide, μg/ml	37	....	2
127		Citrate, μmole/ml	0.348	0.524	40
128	*Equus asinus*	Oxalate, nmole/ml	0.8	....	4
129	*E. caballus*	Glucose (total reducing sugars), μmole/g H$_2$O	5.48	....	32
130		Citrate, μmole/ml	(0.067-0.154)	0.136	40
131	*Felis catus*	Glucose, μmole/ml	4.55	5.65	22
132		Hexosamine, μg/g	(20-47)	....	52
133		Citrate, μmole/ml	0.123	0.149	40
134	*Macaca fascicularis*	Hyaluronic acid, neq/ml	1.7 ± 0.6[3]	....	49
135	*Ovis aries*	Hexosamine, μg/ml	17	....	3
136		μg/g	12.6	....	52
137		Sialic acid, μg/ml	11	....	3
138		Oxalate, nmole/ml	1.0	....	4
139		Citrate, μmole/ml	0.124	0.201	40
140		Hexuronic acid, μg/ml	9	....	3
141	*Sus scrofa*	Hexosamine, μg/g	14.3	....	52
142		Citrate, μmole/ml	0.154	0.148	40
143	Monkey	Mucopolysaccharide, μg/ml	423	....	2
144	Long-tailed	Citrate, μmole/ml	0.147	....	40
145	Rabbit	Glucose, μmole/ml	6.10 ± 1.00[3]	....	10
146			6.91 ± 1.24[3]	....	
147		μmole/g	6.86 ± 0.36	7.22 ± 0.32	65

[1] Anterior chamber. [2] Posterior chamber. [3] Plus/minus (±) value is standard deviation.

continued

Part II. Mammals Other Than Man

	Species	Constituent or Property	Value		Ref-er-ence
			Aqueous Humor	Plasma	
148		μmole/g H_2O	5.4[1]; 5.6[2]	5.7	46
149		Hexosamine, μg/ml	24.7(21.7-26.7)	....	52
150		Mucopolysaccharide, μg/ml	31	....	2
151		Lactate, μmole/g H_2O	9.16 ± 1.04[3]	....	10
152			9.3[1]; 9.9[2]	10.3	46
153			9.47 ± 1.61[3]	....	10
154		Pyruvate, mmole/kg H_2O	0.66	....	21
155		Citrate, μmole/ml	0.381	0.31	40

Nitrogenous Substances

	Species	Constituent or Property	Aqueous Humor	Plasma	Ref-er-ence
156	*Bos taurus*	Protein, total, mg/100 ml	22.1	....	13
157		Prealbumin, % of total protein	1.6	....	37
158		Albumin, % of total protein	59.0	....	37
159		α-Globulin, % of total protein	23.4	....	37
160		β-Globulin, % of total protein	10.3	....	37
161		γ-Globulin, % of total protein	6.2	....	37
162		Creatinine, μmole/ml	0.115	....	13
163		Urate, μmole/ml	(0.10-0.24)	....	13
164		Urea, μmole/ml	2.83	....	13
		Nitrogen, mg/100 ml			13
165		Total	20.1	....	
166		Protein N	3.5	....	
167		Non-protein N	16.4	....	
168		Amino acid N	5.5	....	
	Canis familiaris	Amino acids, μmole/g H_2O			8
169		Alanine	0.452	0.294	
170		Arginine	0.142	0.114	
171		Aspartate	0.012	0.020	
172		Cystine	0.150	0.155	
173		Glutamate	0.196	0.132	
174		Glycine	0.108	0.292	
175		Histidine	0.068	0.068	
176		Isoleucine	0.104	0.100	
177		Leucine	0.190	0.118	
178		Lysine	0.176	0.230	
179		Methionine	0.060	0.043	
180		Phenylalanine	0.092	0.048	
181		Serine	0.127	0.207	
182		Threonine	0.077	0.137	
183		Tyrosine	0.135	0.068	
184		Valine	0.135	0.085	
185		Creatinine, μmole/ml	0.150(0.089-0.168)	....	47
186		Urea, μmole/ml	7.45	7.88	6
		Nitrogen, mg/100 ml			47
187		Total	40(27-55)	....	
188		Protein N	15(5-25)	....	
189		Non-protein N	24(12-40)	....	
190		Amino acid N	9(8.0-10.3)	....	
191		Urea N	12(11-15)	....	

[1] Anterior chamber. [2] Posterior chamber. [3] Plus/minus (±) value is standard deviation.

continued

Part II. Mammals Other Than Man

	Species	Constituent or Property	Value		Reference
			Aqueous Humor	Plasma	
192	*Cavia porcellus*	Histamine, µg/ml	1.77	1.81	35
193	*Equus caballus*	Protein, total, mg/100 ml	20.1	....	32
194		Albumin, % of total protein	43	....	77
195		β-globulin, % of total protein	42.5	....	77
196		γ-globulin, % of total protein	15.0	....	77
197		Amino acids, mg/100 ml	29.0	....	33,34
198		Creatinine, µmole/ml	0.18	0.18	32
199		Urea, µmole/ml	4.67	4.50	32
		Nitrogen, mg/100 ml			
200		Total N	(22.9-29.8)	....	13
201			23.3	....	51
202			26.8	....	33,34
203		Protein N	(3.3-3.7)	....	13
204		Non-protein N	(19.0-25.0)	....	13
205			23.6	....	33,34
206		Amino acid N	4.7	....	13
	Felis catus	Amino acids, µmole/g H_2O			62
207		Alanine	0.375	0.363	
208		Aspartate	<0.001	<0.001	
209		Citrulline	<0.001	<0.001	
210		Cystine	<0.001	<0.001	
211		Glutamate	0.055	0.057	
212		Glycine	0.081	0.282	
213		Isoleucine	0.070	0.122	
214		Leucine	0.117	0.160	
215		Methionine	0.047	0.059	
216		Phenylalanine	0.100	0.137	
217		Proline	<0.001	0.122	
218		Serine	0.173	0.185	
219		Taurine	0.045	0.105	
220		Threonine	0.166	0.225	
221		Valine	0.175	0.235	
222		Urea, µmole/ml	5.16	5.59	6
223		µmole/g	(6.8-9.0)	....	66
	Macaca fascicularis	Amino acids, µmole/g H_2O			63
224		Alanine	0.180	0.170	
225		Aspartate	0.012	0.022	
226		Citrulline	<0.001	0.033	
227		Cystine	<0.001	<0.001	
228		Glutamate	0.028	0.081	
229		Glycine	0.048	0.339	
230		Histidine	0.033	0.071	
231		Isoleucine	0.048	0.063	
232		Leucine	0.120	0.116	
233		Lysine	0.105	0.115	
234		Methionine	0.018	0.019	
235		Ornithine	0.031	0.044	
236		Proline	0.042	0.398	
237		Serine	0.108	0.134	
238		Threonine	0.054	0.055	
239		Valine	0.146	0.181	

continued

Part II. Mammals Other Than Man

Species	Constituent or Property	Value		Reference
		Aqueous Humor	Plasma	
Rattus norvegicus	Amino acids, μmole/g H_2O			63
240	Alanine	0.371	0.603	
241	Arginine	0.064	0.125	
242	Aspartate	0.052	<0.001	
243	Citrulline	<0.001	0.090	
244	Glutamate	0.054	0.239	
245	Glycine	0.158	0.227	
246	Histidine	0.070	0.074	
247	Isoleucine	0.106	0.128	
248	Leucine	0.176	0.208	
249	Lysine	0.419	0.629	
250	Methionine	0.054	0.069	
251	Ornithine	0.039	0.056	
252	Proline	0.166	0.512	
253	Serine	0.270	0.338	
254	Taurine	0.095	0.183	
255	Threonine	0.350	0.518	
256	Valine	0.195	0.295	
257	Histamine, μg/ml	1.88	1.70	35
258 Rabbit	Protein, total, mg/100 ml	61.30 ± 7.07[3]	....	29
259		63.96 ± 9.74[3]	....	
260	Albumin, % of total protein	50.2	....	61
261	α_1-Globulin, % of total protein	7.7	....	
262	α_2-Globulin, % of total protein	8.7	....	
263	β_0-Globulin, % of total protein	7.6	....	
264	β_1-Globulin, % of total protein	10.0	....	
265	β_2-Globulin, % of total protein	4.0	....	
266	γ-Globulin, % of total protein	9.5	....	
267	τ-fraction, % of total protein	2.3	....	
	Amino acids, μmole/g H_2O			63
268	Alanine	0.480[1]; 0.445[2]	0.302	
269	Arginine	0.272[1]; 0.276[2]	0.096	
270	Aspartate	0.055[1]; 0.087[2]	0.029	
271	Cystine	0.030[1]; 0.008[2]	0.054	
272	Glutamate	0.295[1]; 0.401[2]	0.178	
273	Glycine	0.614[1]; 0.314[2]	1.190	
274	Histidine	0.210[1]; 0.181[2]	0.116	
275	Isoleucine	0.116[1]; 0.121[2]	0.112	
276	Leucine	0.174[1]; 0.191[2]	0.163	
277	Lysine	0.423[1]; 0.397[2]	0.212	
278	Methionine	0.023[1]; 0.026[2]	0.014	
279	Phenylalanine	0.097[1]; 0.141[2]	0.097	
280	Proline	0.267[1]; 0.223[2]	0.323	
281	Serine	0.585[1]; 0.597[2]	0.420	
282	Threonine	0.138[1]; 0.149[2]	0.165	
283	Tryptophan	0.024[1]; 0.004[2]	0.013	
284	Tyrosine	0.101[1]; 0.161[2]	0.058	
285	Valine	0.230[1]; 0.214[2]	0.195	
286	Creatine, μmole/ml	0.027	....	38

[1] Anterior chamber. [2] Posterior chamber. [3] Plus/minus (±) value is standard deviation.

continued

Part II. Mammals Other Than Man

Species	Constituent or Property	Value — Aqueous Humor	Value — Plasma	Reference
287		Creatinine, μmole/ml	0.11	....	38
288		Histamine, μg/ml	0.48	1.47	35
289		Urea, μmole/ml	8.9	....	9
290		μmole/g H_2O	6.3[1/]; 5.8[2/]	7.3	46
291		Nitrogen, non-protein, mmole/kg H_2O	13.5	....	46

Enzymes

	Species	Constituent or Property	Aqueous Humor	Plasma	Reference
292	*Bos taurus*	Cholinesterase activity, μmole acetylcholine	3.09	....	30
293		hydrolyzed·ml^{-1}·hr^{-1}	(6.6-8.1)	(120-160)	11
294	*Equus caballus*	Cholinesterase activity, μmole acetylcholine	0.66	....	11
295		hydrolyzed·ml^{-1}·hr^{-1}	0.89		30

General Physical & Chemical Properties

	Species	Constituent or Property	Aqueous Humor	Plasma	Reference
296	*Bos taurus*	Volume, ml	1.7[1/]; 1.5[2/]	....	69
297			1.70	....	75
298			1.73	....	51
299			3.1	....	54
300	*Canis familiaris*	Volume, μl	400[1/]; 200[2/]	....	69
301			(400-500)	....	36
302			430	....	51
303			850	....	54
304		Refractive index	1.33504(1.33478-1.33532)	....	47
305		Oxygen pressure, mm Hg	(40-50)	....	59
306	*Cavia porcellus*	Volume, μl	20	....	71
307	*Equus caballus*	Volume, ml	2.4	....	51
308			2.4[1/]; 1.6[2/]	....	69
309		Oxygen pressure, mm Hg	(20-40)	....	41
310	*Felis catus*	Volume, μl	600	....	36
311			600[1/]; 300[2/]	....	69
312	*Ovis aries*	Volume, μl	800[1/]; 500[2/]	....	69
313			900	....	51
314	*Sus scrofa*	Volume, μl	300[1/]; 300[2/]	....	69
315			335	....	51
316			450	....	54
317	Rabbit	Volume, μl	250[1/]	....	46
318			57[2/]	....	17
319			250	....	54
320			300	....	36
321		Oxygen pressure, mm Hg	31.0 ± 6.12[3/]	....	43
322			55.2(50.8-59.6)[5/]	....	42
323			48.2(43.0-53.4)[6/]	....	42
324		pH	7.60[1/]; 7.57[2/]	7.40	46
325		Osmolarity, difference between aqueous humor and plasma, mosmole/g H_2O	4.28 ± 0.45[1,3/]; 6.9 ± 1.3[2,3/]		1

[1/] Anterior chamber. [2/] Posterior chamber. [3/] Plus/minus (±) value is standard deviation. [5/] Unanesthetized. [6/] Anesthetized.

Contributors: Cole, D. F.; Langham, Maurice E.

continued

278. CHEMICAL COMPOSITION AND PHYSICAL PROPERTIES OF AQUEOUS HUMOR: VERTEBRATES

Part II. Mammals Other Than Man

References

[1] Auricchio, G., and P. Wistrand. 1958. Acta Physiol. Scand. 44:118.

[2] Balazs, E. A. 1960. Importance Vitreous Body Retina Surg. Retina Found. Conf., 2nd, 1958, p. 29.

[3] Balazs, E. A., et al. 1959. Arch. Biochem. Biophys. 81:464.

[4] Baratta, O. 1936. Arch. Ottalmol. 43:44.

[5] Baurmann, M. 1929. Ber. Deut. Ophthalmol. Ges. 47:156.

[6] Benham, G. H. 1937. Biochem. J. 31:1157.

[7] Bito, L. Z. 1970. Exp. Eye Res. 10:102.

[8] Bito, L. Z., et al. 1965. Ibid. 4:374.

[9] Bleeker, G. M., et al. 1968. Ibid. 7:30.

[10] Bonomi, L., and P. DiComite. 1965. Minerva Oftalmol. 7:147.

[11] Bruckner, R. 1943. Ophthalmologica 105:37.

[12] Ciusa, W., et al. 1964. Exp. Eye Res. 3:169.

[13] Cohen, M., et al. 1926. Contrib. Ophthalmic Sci. 9.

[14] Cole, D. F. 1959. Brit. J. Ophthalmol. 43:268.

[15] Cole, D. F. Unpublished. Univ. London, Inst. Ophthalmology, 1971.

[16] Constant, M. E., and J. Falch. 1963. Invest. Ophthalmol. 2:332.

[17] Copeland, R. L., and V. E. Kinsey. 1950. Arch. Ophthalmol. 44:515.

[18] Davson, H. 1939. J. Physiol. (London) 96:194.

[19] Davson, H. 1949. Brit. J. Ophthalmol. 33:175.

[20] Davson, H. 1955. J. Physiol. (London) 129:111.

[21] Davson, H. 1969. The Eye: Vegetative Physiology and Biochemistry. Ed. 2. Academic Press, New York and London. v. 1, p. 97.

[22] Davson, H., and W. S. Duke-Elder. 1948. J. Physiol. (London) 107:141.

[23] Davson, H., and C. P. Luck. 1956. Amer. J. Ophthalmol. 41:809.

[24] Davson, H., and C. P. Luck. 1956. J. Physiol. (London) 132:454.

[25] Davson, H., and C. P. Luck. 1957. Ibid. 137:279.

[26] Davson, H., and C. B. Weld. 1941. Amer. J. Physiol. 134:1.

[27] Davson, H., et al. 1949. J. Physiol. (London) 109:32.

[28] Davson, H., et al. 1952. Ibid. 116:46p.

[29] D'Ermo, F., et al. 1967. Ophthalmologica 153:385.

[30] De Roetth, A. 1950. Arch. Ophthalmol. 43:1004.

[31] Derrien, Y., and P. Frizet. 1938. Bull. Soc. Chim. Biol. 20:1238.

[32] Duke-Elder, W. S. 1927. Brit. J. Ophthalmol., Monogr. Suppl. 3:13.

[33] Duke-Elder, W. S. 1930. Ibid. 4:25.

[34] Duke-Elder, W. S. 1942. Textbook of Ophthalmology. C. V. Mosby, St. Louis. v. 1.

[35] Emmelin, N. 1945. Acta Physiol. Scand. 11(Suppl. 34).

[36] Emmert, E. 1886. Z. Vergl. Augenheilk. 4:40.

[37] Francois, J., et al. 1958. Arch. Ophthalmol. 59:692.

[38] Furuichi, C. 1961. Acta Soc. Ophthalmol. Jap. 65:561.

[39] Galin, M. A., et al. 1962. Invest. Ophthalmol. 1:142.

[40] Grönvall, H. 1937. Acta Ophthalmol., Suppl. 14.

[41] Haan, J. de 1922. Arch. Neer. Physiol. 7:245.

[42] Heald, K., and M. E. Langham. 1956. Brit. J. Ophthalmol. 40:705.

[43] Jacobi, K. W. 1966. Albrecht von Graefes Arch. Ophthalmol. 169:350.

[44] Johnson, S. W. 1936. Biochem. J. 30:1430.

[45] Kinsey, V. E., and B. Jackson. 1949. Amer. J. Ophthalmol. 32:374.

[46] Kinsey, V. E., and D. V. N. Reddy. 1964. In J. H. Prince, ed. The Rabbit in Eye Research. C. C. Thomas, Springfield, Ill. ch. 9.

[47] Krause, A. C., and A. M. Yudkin. 1930. J. Biol. Chem. 88:471.

[48] Langham, M. E. 1950. J. Physiol. (London) 111:388.

[49] Laurent, T. C., et al. 1969. Anal. Biochem. 31:133.

[50] Luck, C. P., and P. G. Wright. 1959. Nature (London) 183:1595.

[51] Mestrezat, W., and A. Magitot. 1921. C. R. Soc. Biol. 84:185.

[52] Meyer, K., et al. 1938. Amer. J. Ophthalmol. 21:1083.

[53] Muller, H. K., and W. Buschke. 1934. Arch. Augenheilk. 108:368.

[54] Niesnamoff, E. 1896. Albrecht von Graefes Arch. Ophthalmol. 42:1.

[55] Nitzescu, J. J., and J. Georgescu. 1930. C. R. Soc. Biol. 105:751.

[56] Nitzescu, J. J., and J. Georgescu. 1935. Klin. Wochenschr. 1:97.

[57] Nixon, D. A. 1959. Nature (London) 184:906.

[58] Philpot, F. J., and A. Pirie. 1943. Biochem. J. 37:250.

[59] Pierce, H. F., et al. 1933. Amer. J. Physiol. 104:553.

[60] Podesta, H. H., and J. Baucke. 1938. Albrecht von Graefes Arch. Ophthalmol. 139:720.

[61] Praus, R. 1961. Exp. Eye Res. 1:67.

[62] Reddy, D. V. N. 1967. Invest. Ophthalmol. 6:478.

[63] Reddy, D. V. N. 1968. Biochem. Eye Symp. 1966, p. 167.

[64] Reddy, D. V. N., and V. E. Kinsey. 1960. Arch. Ophthalmol. 63:715.

[65] Reim, M., et al. 1967. Ophthalmologica 154:39.

[66] Robertson, J. D., and P. C. Williams. 1939. J. Physiol. (London) 95:139.

[67] Shirakami, T. 1959. Acta Soc. Ophthalmol. Jap. 63:843.

[68] Simonelli, M. 1940. Boll. Ocul. 20:163.

[69] Spector, W. S., ed. 1956. Handbook of Biological Data. W. B. Saunders, Philadelphia.

[70] Stary, Z., and R. Winternitz. 1932. Hoppe Seylers Z. Physiol. Chem. 212:215.

[71] Steindorf, K. 1947. Tabulae Biol. 22(1-a):189.

[72] Takki-Luukkainen, I. T., and T. Miettinen. 1959. Acta Ophthalmol. 37:138.

continued

278. CHEMICAL COMPOSITION AND PHYSICAL PROPERTIES OF AQUEOUS HUMOR: VERTEBRATES

Part II. Mammals Other Than Man

[73] Tauber, F. W., and A. C. Krause. 1943. Amer. J. Ophthalmol. 26:260.

[74] Tron, E. 1926. Albrecht von Graefes Arch. Ophthalmol. 177:677.

[75] Vitello, E. 1931. Boll. Soc. Ital. Biol. Sper. 6:514.

[76] Vladesco, R., and H. Stefanesco. 1939. C. R. Soc. Biol. 132:169.

[77] Von Sallmann, L., and D. H. Moore. 1948. Arch. Ophthalmol. 40:279.

[78] Walker, A. M. 1933. J. Biol. Chem. 101:269.

Part III. Birds, Amphibians, and Fishes

Constituent or Property: c_A = concentration aqueous humor; c_{Pl} = concentration in plasma. Plus/minus (±) values are standard error, unless otherwise indicated.

	Species	Constituent or Property	Value — Aqueous Humor	Value — Plasma[1]	Reference
			Aves		
1	*Bubo virginianus*	Hexosamine, mg/100 ml	1.7	....	2
2		Hexuronic acid, mg/100 ml	2.2	....	
3			12.4[2]; 0.7[3]	....	
4		Viscosity, specific	0.82	....	
5			2.93[2]; 0.12[3]	....	
6	*Columba livia*	Citrate, μmole/ml	1.69	0.351	8
7	*Gallus gallus*[4]	Phosphate, μmole/ml	0.31	0.80	16
8		Citrate, μmole/ml	1.39	0.293	8
9		Glucose (reducing substances), μmole/ml	12.08	13.06	16
10		Hexosamine, mg/100 ml	3.65	....	2
11		Hexuronic acid, mg/100 ml	1.5	....	2
12		Urate, μmole/ml	0.157	0.236	16
13		Volume, μl	30	....	15
14	*Meleagris gallopavo*	Citrate, μmole/ml	1.82	0.38	8
15		Hexuronic acid, mg/100 ml	0.8	....	2
16		Volume, μl	160	....	15
17	*Phasianus* sp.	Citrate, μmole/ml	1.30 ± 0.026	....	8
18	*Strix aluco*	Citrate, μmole/ml	1.34	....	8
19	*S. varia*	Hexuronic acid, mg/100 ml	2.3	....	2
20		Viscosity, specific	0.45	....	2
21	Duck	Citrate, μmole/ml	1.95	0.514	8
22	Sparrow	Volume, μl	10	....	15
23	Thrush	Volume, μl	20	....	15
			Amphibia		
24	*Bufo marinus*	Bicarbonate, μeq/ml H_2O	12.5 ± 1.9[5]	14.7 ± 1.1[5]	4
25		Calcium, μmole/ml H_2O	1.51 ± 0.2[5]	2.09 ± 0.2[5]	
26		Chloride, μeq/ml H_2O	82.8 ± 0.3	79.2 ± 1.5	
27		Magnesium, μmole/ml H_2O	1.19 ± 1.0[5]	1.49 ± 0.09[5]	
28		Potassium, μeq/ml H_2O	3.6 ± 0.1	5.9 ± 0.2	
29		Sodium, μeq/ml H_2O	108.5 ± 0.9	106.5 ± 3.5	
30		Volume, μl	86	....	
31	*Rana catesbeiana*	Chloride, μeq/ml	82 ± 1	....	14
32		Potassium, μeq/ml	2.44 ± 0.08	....	
33		Sodium, μeq/ml	100 ± 1	....	

[1] Unless otherwise indicated. [2] Anterior chamber. [3] Posterior chamber. [4] Synonym: *Gallus domesticus*. [5] Plus/minus (±) value is standard deviation.

continued

278. CHEMICAL COMPOSITION AND PHYSICAL PROPERTIES OF AQUEOUS HUMOR: VERTEBRATES

Part III. Birds, Amphibians, and Fishes

	Species	Constituent or Property	Value		Reference
			Aqueous Humor	Plasma[1]	
34	*R. esculenta; R. temporaria*	Ascorbate, μmole/ml	(0.057-0.17)	....	12
35	*R. pipiens*	Phosphate, μmole/ml	0.38	0.99	16
36		Glucose, μmole/ml	1.37	2.44	16
	Crossopterygii				
37	*Latimeria chalumnae*	Magnesium, μmole/ml H_2O	3.65	28.7[6]	13
38		Urea, μmole/ml	303	355[6]	13
39		Volume, ml	1.61	....	3
40		Osmolarity, μosmole/ml	952	(981-1181)[6]	13
	Osteichthyes [7]				
41	*Gadus* sp.	Citrate, μmole/ml	(0.07-0.14)	....	8
42	*Salmo gairdneri*	Potassium, μeq/ml	3.12 ± 0.17	....	7
43		Sodium, μeq/ml	152.3 ± 1.77	....	7
44		Viscosity, kinematic, at 20°C centistoke	37.44	....	10
45	*Salvelinus namaycush*	Bicarbonate, μmole/ml	6.19	6.4[6]	9
46		Chloride, μmole/ml	93.5	117.3[6]	
	Chondrichthyes [7]				
47	*Mustelus canis*	Bicarbonate, μmole/g H_2O	15.0	6.0	6
48		Calcium, μmole/g H_2O	3.0	5.0	
49		Chloride, μmole/g H_2O	256	270	
50		Magnesium, μmole/g H_2O	3.0	3.0	
51		Phosphate, μmole/g H_2O	10	2.0	
52		Potassium, μmole/g H_2O	7.0	8.0	
53		Sodium, μmole/g H_2O	279.0	268.0	
54		Sulfate, μmole/g H_2O	4.0	3.0	
55		Ascorbate, μmole/g H_2O	0.136	0.045	
56		Glucose, μmole/g H_2O	7.0	13.0	
57		Protein, mg/100 ml	22	2850	
58		Trimethylamine oxide, μmole/g H_2O	85	97	
59		Urea, μmole/g H_2O	320	342	
60		pH	7.86	7.33	
61		Osmolarity, μosmole/ml	935	962	
62	*Scyliorhinus stellaris*	Urea, ratio, c_A/c_{Pl}	0.87		5
63	*Squalus acanthias*	Carbon dioxide, μmole/ml	8.61 ± 0.32	7.96 ± 0.18	11
64		Chloride, μmole/ml	251 ± 5	239 ± 2	
65		Potassium, μmole/ml	7.5 ± 1.0[5]	6.6 ± 0.5[5]	
66		Sodium, μmole/ml	276 ± 6	255 ± 3	
67		pH	7.63	7.56	
68		Osmolarity, μmole/g H_2O	972 ± 27	973 ± 13	

[1] Unless otherwise indicated. [5] Plus/minus (±) value is standard deviation. [6] In blood. [7] In various species of fishes, polysaccharide content of aqueous humor varies from 80 to 1000 μg/ml [1].

Contributor: Cole, D. F.

References

[1] Balazs, E. A. 1965. In E. A. Balazs and R. W. Jean-loz, ed. The Amino Sugars. Academic Press, New York. v. 2A, pp. 401-460.

[2] Balazs, E. A., et al. 1959. Arch. Biochem. Biophys. 81:464.

[3] Cole, D. F. 1968. Brit. J. Ophthalmol. 52:415.

continued

Part III. Birds, Amphibians, and Fishes

[4] Cole, D. F. 1968. Comp. Biochem. Physiol. 26:353.

[5] Derrien, Y. 1939. C. R. Soc. Biol. 130:1411.

[6] Doolittle, R. F., et al. 1960. Science 123:36.

[7] Edelhauser, H. G., et al. 1965. Invest. Ophthalmol. 4:290.

[8] Grönvall, H. 1937. Acta Ophthalmol., Suppl. 14.

[9] Hoffert, J. R., and P. O. Fromm. 1966. Comp. Biochem. Physiol. 18:333.

[10] Hoffert, J. R., and P. O. Fromm. 1969. Ibid. 28:1411.

[11] Maren, T. H. 1962. Ibid. 5:193.

[12] Muller, H. K., and W. Buschke. 1934. Arch. Augenheilk. 108:368.

[13] Pickford, G. E., and F. Blake Grant. 1967. Science 155:568.

[14] Shanbour, L. L., et al. 1970. Proc. Soc. Exp. Biol. Med. 133:11.

[15] Steindorf, K. 1947. Tabulae Biol. 22(1-a):189.

[16] Walker, A. M. 1933. J. Biol. Chem. 101:269.

279. CHEMICAL COMPOSITION AND PHYSICAL PROPERTIES OF VITREOUS HUMOR: VERTEBRATES

Values in parentheses are ranges, estimate "c" (*see* Introduction).

Part I. Man

Levels of some substances (e.g., potassium, phosphorus, glucose) change in proportion to the postmortem interval, but the scattering of values prevents an accurate timing of death. Manual determinations were made on 2-5 ml of vitreous humor pooled from both eyes of 211 males (average age 58 years), examined approximately nine hours after death. Automated values from three series of more than 500 coroner and hospital cases were analyzed at comparable postmortem intervals of approximately nine hours.

	Constituent or Property	Value	Method	Reference
	Electrolytes			
1	Bicarbonate, μeq/ml	15(4-20)[1]	CO_2-phenolphthalein	5,17
2	Calcium, μeq/ml	3.6(2.8-5.2)[2]	Clark-Collip	13
3		3.4(3.05-4.0)[1]	Cresolphthalein	5,17
4	Chloride, μeq/ml	114(89-145)[2]	Van Slyke-Hiller-Sendroy	13
5		119(105-132)[1]	Mercuric thiocyanate	5,17
6	Phosphate, μeq/ml	1.2(0.1-3.3)[2]	Fiske-Subbarow	13
7	Potassium, μeq/ml	7.7(3.3-12.0)[2]	Flame photometry	13
8		7.0(5.7-13.5)[1]	Flame photometry	10,16,17
9	Sodium, μeq/ml	144(118-154)[2]	Flame photometry	13
10		143(128-158)[1]	Flame photometry	10,16,17
11	Zinc, nmole/ml	8.7	....	6
	Vitamins			
12	Ascorbate, μmole/ml	2.21	....	18
	Lipids & Carbohydrates			
13	Lipids, μmole/g H_2O	40	....	15
14	Glucose, μmole/ml	3.89	....	18
15		3.44(0.94-5.83)[2]	Folin-Wu-Somogyi	13
16		3.28(1.55-4.95)[1]	Cupric-neocuproine	9,17
17	Hexosamine, μg/g	37[2]	Hydrolysis, acetyl acetone, Ehrlich's reaction	12
18	Mucopolysaccharide, μg/ml	240	....	1

[1] Automated; values obtained with Technicon Autoanalyzer, model SMA-12. [2] Manual determinations.

continued

279. CHEMICAL COMPOSITION AND PHYSICAL PROPERTIES OF VITREOUS HUMOR: VERTEBRATES

Part I. Man

	Constituent or Property	Value	Method	Reference
19	Hyaluronic acid, μg/ml	40[3,4]; 33[3,5]	....	3
20		217[4,6]; 144[5,6]	....	3
21		140[7]	....	2
22		240[4,8]; 163[5,8]	....	3
23		338[9]	....	2
24	Lactate, μmole/ml	7.78	....	6
25	Lactic acid, μmole/g H_2O	70	....	15
26	Pyruvate, μmole/ml	0.81	....	6
27	Pyruvic acid, μmole/g H_2O	7.3	....	15
28	Citrate, μmole/ml	0.089[10]	....	8
29	μmole/g H_2O	1.9	....	15

			Nitrogenous Substances		

	Constituent or Property	Value	Method	Reference
30	Protein, μmole/g H_2O	40	....	15
31	Collagen, μg/ml	286	....	1
	Amino acids, μmole/liter			7
32	Alanine	126 ± 15.6	Ion exchange chromatography	
33	α-Aminobutyric acid	14.4 ± 1.7	Ion exchange chromatography	
34	Arginine	71.9 ± 10.2	Ion exchange chromatography	
35	Asparagine	26.3 ± 4.3	Ion exchange chromatography	
36	Aspartic acid	1.8 ± 1.5	Ion exchange chromatography	
37	Citrulline	8.3 ± 1.6	Ion exchange chromatography	
38	Cystine	6.5 ± 6.0	Ion exchange chromatography	
39	Glutamic acid	14.5 ± 11.0	Ion exchange chromatography	
40	Glutamine	664 ± 13.4	Ion exchange chromatography	
41	Glycine	8.7 ± 2.6	Ion exchange chromatography	
42	Histidine	40.8 ± 13.8	Ion exchange chromatography	
43	Isoleucine	37.6 ± 3.4	Ion exchange chromatography	
44	Leucine	96.1 ± 20.5	Ion exchange chromatography	
45	Lysine	105 ± 14.4	Ion exchange chromatography	
46	Methionine	24.7 ± 5.0	Ion exchange chromatography	
47	Ornithine	16.0 ± 1.1	Ion exchange chromatography	
48	Phenylalanine	56.8 ± 13.6	Ion exchange chromatography	
49	Proline	4.0 ± 5.6	Ion exchange chromatography	
50	Serine	106 ± 24.4	Ion exchange chromatography	
51	Taurine	28.8 ± 5.0	Ion exchange chromatography	
52	Threonine	73.6 ± 10.3	Ion exchange chromatography	
53	Tryptophan	18.3 ± 7.0	Ion exchange chromatography	
54	Tyrosine	51.8 ± 12.3	Ion exchange chromatography	
55	Valine	174 ± 41.3	Ion exchange chromatography	
56	Bilirubin	0	Malloy-Evelyn	14
57	Creatinine, μmole/ml	0.106(0.027-0.27)[2]	Modified Jaffe reaction	13
58		0.056(0.027-0.093)[1]	Modified Jaffe reaction	5,17
59	Urea, μmole/ml	13.2	....	4
60	Nitrogen, total, μmole/g H_2O	23.5	....	15
61	urea, μmole/ml	6.2(0.7-12.9)[2]	Direct nesslerization[11]	13
62		1.3(0.3-2.6)[1]	Diacetyl monoxime	5,17

[1] Automated; values obtained with Technicon Autoanalyzer, model SMA-12. [2] Manual determinations. [3] 0-2 yr old. [4] Cortical zone. [5] Central zone. [6] 13-45 yr old. [7] 31-65 yr old. [8] 50-85 yr old. [9] 65-83 yr old. [10] Serum concentration, 0.131 μeq/ml. [11] Results obtained by the specific diacetyl monoxime method reveal that the urease-nesslerization method yields falsely high postmortem values.

continued

Part I. Man

	Constituent or Property	Value	Method	Reference
	Physical Properties			
63	Volume, ml	3.9	....	11

Contributors: Naumann, Hans N.; Langham, Maurice E.; Cole, D. F.; Hamilton, Paul B.

References

[1] Balazs, E. A. 1960. Importance Vitreous Body Retina Surg. Retina Found. Conf., 2nd, 1958, p. 29.

[2] Balazs, E. A. 1965. In E. A. Balazs and R. W. Jeanloz, ed. The Amino Sugars. Academic Press, New York. v. 2A, pp. 401-460.

[3] Berman, E. R., and I. C. Michaelson. 1964. Exp. Eye Res. 3:9.

[4] Berman, E. R., and M. Voaden. 1970. In C. N. Graymore, ed. The Biochemistry of the Eye. Academic Press, New York and London. pp. 373-463.

[5] Coe, J. I. 1969. Amer. J. Clin. Pathol. 51:741.

[6] de Vincentiis, M. 1951. Boll. Soc. Ital. Biol. Sper. 27:309.

[7] Durham, D. G., et al. 1971. Clin. Chem. 17:285.

[8] Grönvall, H. 1937. Acta Ophthalmol., Suppl. 14.

[9] Leahy, M. S., and E. R. Farber. 1967. J. Forensic Sci. 12:214.

[10] Lie, J. T. 1967. Amer. J. Med. Sci. 254:136.

[11] Mestrezat, W., and A. Magitot. 1921. C. R. Soc. Biol. 84:185.

[12] Meyer, K., et al. 1938. Amer. J. Ophthalmol. 21:1083.

[13] Naumann, H. N. 1959. Arch. Ophthalmol. 62:356.

[14] Naumann, H. N., and J. M. Young. 1960. Proc. Soc. Exp. Biol. Med. 105:70.

[15] Nordmann, J. 1968. In A. Brini, et al., ed. Biologie et chirurgie du corps vitre. G. Masson, Paris. ch. 3.

[16] Sturner, W. Q., and G. E. Gantner, Jr. 1964. Amer. J. Clin. Pathol. 42:137.

[17] Technicon Instrument Company. 1967. Instruction Manual. Tarrytown, N.Y.

[18] Van Heyningen, R. 1961. In C. Long, et al., ed. Biochemists' Handbook. E. and F. N. Spon, London. p. 711.

Part II. Mammals Other Than Man

	Species	Constituent or Property	Value		Reference
			Vitreous Humor	Plasma [1]	
		Electrolytes			
1	Bos taurus	Aluminum, μmole/ml	(0.11-0.93)	....	31
2		Barium, nmole/ml	2.41	....	38
3		Calcium, μmole/ml	1.8	....	41
4		μmole/g H_2O	(3.2-3.5)	....	17
5		Carbon dioxide, μmole/ml	20.9	....	8
6		Chloride, μmole/ml	(116-124)	....	29
7		μmole/g H_2O	(109-113)	....	17
8			116	....	43
9		Copper, nmole/g	4.12(2.87-5.40)	....	39
10		Iron, nmole/ml	36	....	31
11		nmole/g	2.14(1.07-3.57)	....	39
12		Lead, nmole/ml	2.42	....	31
13		Magnesium, μmole/ml	0.39	....	41
14			0.87	....	44
15		μmole/g H_2O	0.4	....	40
16		Molybdenum, μmole/ml	(0.073-1.04)	....	31

[1] Unless otherwise indicated.

continued

Part II. Mammals Other Than Man

	Species	Constituent or Property	Value Vitreous Humor	Value Plasma [1]	Reference
17		Nickel, nmole/ml	1.7	....	31
18		Phosphate, μmole/g H_2O	(0.1-0.3)	....	17
19		Potassium, μmole/ml	4.9	....	29
20			5.6	....	41
21		μmole/g H_2O	(4.28-8.2)	....	36
22			(7.7-10.0)	....	17
23		Silicon, μmole/ml	0.286	....	31
24		Silver, nmole/ml	5.6	....	31
25		Sodium, μmole/ml	(131-144)	....	29
26			148	....	41
27		μmole/g H_2O	(139-142)	....	17
28		Sulfur, total, μmole/ml	1.25	....	8
29		Tin, nmole/ml	0.67	....	31
30		Zinc, nmole/g	4.46(3.86-6.46)	....	39
31		nmole/eye	53.9	....	7
32	♀	Bicarbonate, μeq/g H_2O	(19.6-32.4)	....	30
33	*Canis familiaris*	Carbon dioxide, μmole/g H_2O	25.1 ± 1.4	26.2 ± 2.1	10
34	*Cercopithecus aethiops; Erythrocebus patas*	Carbon dioxide, μmole/g H_2O	24.1 ± 3.4	35.2 ± 3.4	10
35	*Equus caballus*	Calcium, μmole/ml	(2.02-2.20)	....	8
36		μmole/g H_2O	1.7	2.7	12
37		Carbon dioxide, μmole/ml	22.0	....	8
38		Chloride, μmole/ml	(109.8-115.7)	....	8
39		μmole/g H_2O	118	111	12
40		Magnesium, μmole/g H_2O	0.83	1.25[2]	12
41		Phosphate, inorganic, μmole/g H_2O	1.0	1.04[2]	12
42		Potassium, μmole/ml	(6.14-6.31)	....	8
43		μmole/g H_2O	4.95	5.51[2]	12
44		Sodium, μmole/ml	(133.5-136.0)	....	8
45		μmole/g H_2O	119.0	156[2]	12
46		Sulfate, inorganic, μmole/g H_2O	1.93	1.97[2]	12
47	*Ovis aries*	Copper, nmole/ml	4.75	....	7
48		Magnesium, μmole/ml	1.22	....	44
49		Potassium, μmole/ml	5.60	....	41
50		Zinc, nmole/ml	4.45	....	7
51	*Physeter catodon*	Copper, nmole/g dry wt	94	....	7
52		Zinc, nmole/g dry wt	172	....	7
53	*Sus scrofa*	Calcium, μmole/ml	(1.95-2.03)	....	8
54			2.0	....	41
55		Carbon dioxide, μmole/ml	(19.6-21.4)	....	8
56		Chloride, μmole/ml	121	....	29
57		Magnesium, μmole/ml	1.25	....	41
58		Phosphate, total, μmole/ml	1.07	....	8
59		Potassium, μmole/ml	7.29	....	41
60			(7.3-9.1)	....	29
61		Sodium, μmole/ml	138.1	....	8
62			139.1	....	41

[1] Unless otherwise indicated. [2] Serum concentration.

continued

Part II. Mammals Other Than Man

Species	Constituent or Property	Value Vitreous Humor	Value Plasma[1]	Reference
63 Rabbit	Bicarbonate, μeq/ml	31.3[3]; 24.8[4]; 23.9[5]	....	19
64	Total, μmole/g H_2O	26.2 ± 3.2	24.9 ± 3.8	10
65	μeq/g H_2O	(18.6-32.4)	....	30
66	Calcium, μmole/g H_2O	1.5	....	30
67	Carbon dioxide, μmole/g H_2O	26.0	20.6	33,34
68	Chloride, μmole/g H_2O	104.3	....	30
69		104.7	108.8	33
70	Phosphate, μmole/ml	0.31	....	41
71	μmole/g H_2O	0.40	....	30
72	Potassium, μmole/g H_2O	(5.1-10.2)	....	30
73		9.5	5.6	33
74	Sodium, μmole/g H_2O	134	143	33
75		(133.9-152.2)	....	30
76	Zinc, nmole/ml	9.56	....	41

Vitamins

Species	Constituent or Property	Value Vitreous Humor	Value Plasma[1]	Reference
77 *Bos taurus*	Riboflavin, nmole/ml	21.3	....	32
78	Nicotinic acid, nmole/ml	2.76	....	41
79	Ascorbate, μmole/ml	(0.54-1.59)	....	41
80 *Cavia porcellus*	Ascorbate, μmole/ml	1.20	....	41
81 *Equus caballus*	Ascorbate, μmole/ml	(0.43-0.98)	....	41
82 *Felis catus*	Ascorbate, μmole/ml	0.124	....	41
83 *Ovis aries*	Ascorbate, μmole/ml	0.631	....	41
84 *Rattus norvegicus*	Ascorbate, μmole/ml	0.086	....	41
85 *Sus scrofa*	Ascorbate, μmole/ml	0.338	....	41
86 Rabbit	Ascorbate, μmole/ml	0.417	....	4
87	μmole/g H_2O	0.46	0.04	34

Lipids, Carbohydrates, and Related Compounds

Species	Constituent or Property	Value Vitreous Humor	Value Plasma[1]	Reference
88 *Aotus* sp.	Hyaluronic acid, μg/ml	737[6]; 448[7]	....	3
89 *Bos taurus*	Glucose, μmole/ml	(2.22-3.3)	....	41
90	Hexosamine, μg/g	(125-206)	....	28
91	Sialic acid, μg/ml	10.4[8]; 20.7[4]; 29.2[9]	....	2
92	Mucopolysaccharide[10], μg/ml	710	....	2
93	Hyaluronic acid, μg/ml	251[8]; 532[4]; 1190[9]	....	2
94	Lactate, μmole/ml	1.64	....	8
95	Citrate, μmole/ml	(0.043-0.058)	....	25
96 1-2 da old	Citrate, μmole/ml	0.06	0.194[2]	20
97 8 mo-6 yr old	Hyaluronic acid, μg/ml	(432-480)		37
98 3-10 yr old	Citrate, μmole/ml	0.043	0.159[2]	20
99 >7 yr old	Hyaluronic acid, μg/ml	(295-353)		37
100 ♀	Lipids, mg/100 ml H_2O	0.6	....	30
101	Pyruvic acid, μmole/ml H_2O	0.136	....	
102	Citrate, μmole/ml H_2O	0.714	....	
103 *Canis familiaris*	Hexosamine, μg/ml	(19-44)		28
104	Hyaluronic acid, μg/ml	35	....	3
105	Citrate, μmole/ml	0.113	0.286	20
106 *Capra hircus*	Citrate, μmole/ml	0.072	0.148[2]	20

[1] Unless otherwise indicated. [2] Serum concentration. [6] In gel phase. [7] In liquid phase. [8] In anterior zone.
[3] In ciliary zone. [4] In central zone. [5] In peripheral zone. [9] In posterior zone. [10] From hexuronic acid values.

continued

Part II. Mammals Other Than Man

	Species	Constituent or Property	Value Vitreous Humor	Value Plasma[1]	Reference
107	*Cavia porcellus*	Hyaluronic acid, μg/ml	20	....	3
108		Citrate, μmole/ml	0.107	0.525[2]	20
109	*Cercopithecus pygerythrus*	Hyaluronic acid, μg/ml	237	....	5
110	*Equus caballus*	Fats, mg/100 ml	7.0	....	13
111		Cholesterol, mg/100 ml	5.0	....	12,13
112		Reducing sugars, μmole/g H_2O	5.41	5.05[2]	12
113		Glucose, μmole/ml	(3.50-4.25)	....	8
114			5.55	....	41
115		Lactate, μmole/ml	1.95	....	41
116		μmole/g H_2O	2.11	....	12
117		Citrate, μmole/ml	(0.054-0.082)	(0.136-0.174)[2]	20
118	*Felis catus*	Glucose, μmole/ml	3.56	....	41
119		μmole/g H_2O	2.5	....	14
120			3.17	5.96	9
121		Hexosamine, μg/ml	(17-40)	....	28
122		Hyaluronic acid, μg/ml	(31-53)	....	18
123			(39-73)	....	28
124		Citrate, μmole/ml	0.091	0.149	20
125	*Ovis aries*	Hexosamine, μg/ml	(48-81)	....	28
126		Hyaluronic acid, μg/ml	260	....	3
127		Citrate, μmole/ml	0.041	0.13[2]	20
128	*Sus scrofa*	Glucose, μmole/ml	1.67	....	8,14
129		Hexosamine, μg/ml	(41-63)	....	27,28
130		Hyaluronic acid, μg/ml	124	....	3
131		Lactate, μmole/ml	1.95	....	8,14
132		Citrate, μmole/ml	0.075	0.10[2]	20
133	Monkey	Mucopolysaccharide, μg/ml	25	....	30
134	Rabbit	Glucose, μmole/g H_2O	4.06	8.14	9
135		Hexosamine, μg/g	(28-35)	....	28
136		Mucopolysaccharide, μg/ml	81	....	2
137			104	....	2
138		Hyaluronic acid, μg/ml	(64-82)	....	28
139		Lactate, μmole/ml	7.22	....	11,30
140		Pyruvic acid, μmole/ml H_2O	(0.57-0.68)	....	30
141		Citrate, μmole/ml	0.0705	0.310	20
142			0.094	....	30
		Nitrogenous Substances			
143	*Bos taurus*	Protein, soluble, μg/ml	379[8]; 619[4]; 960[9]	....	2
144		Albumin, μg/ml	145	....	1
145		Globulin, μg/ml	317	....	1
146		Collagen, μg/ml	112[8]; 52[4]; 63[9]	....	2
		Amino acids, μmole/ml			45
147		Alanine	0.146	0.28	
148		Arginine	0.064		
149		Asparagine	0.089	0.106	
150		Aspartate	0.015	0.007	
151		Glutamate	0.170	0.088	
152		Glycine	0.080	0.369	

[1] Unless otherwise indicated. [2] Serum concentration. [4] In central zone. [8] In anterior zone. [9] In posterior zone.

continued

Part II. Mammals Other Than Man

	Species	Constituent or Property	Value — Vitreous Humor	Value — Plasma [1]	Reference
153		Histidine	0.019	0.019	
154		Isoleucine	0.059	0.061	
155		Leucine	0.082	0.122	
156		Lysine	0.032	0.020	
157		Methionine	0.010	0.013	
158		Phenylalanine	0.048	0.073	
159		Serine	0.111	0.133	
160		Taurine	0.165	0.056	
161		Threonine	0.036	0.059	
162		Tyrosine	0.033	0.028	
163		Valine	0.125	0.188	
164		Carnosine, mg/100 g	0.24(0.16-0.29)	....	23
165		Creatine, μmole/ml	0.122	....	8
166		Creatinine, μmole/ml	(0.10-0.12)	....	8
167		Urate, μmole/ml	(0.166-0.203)	....	8
168		Urea, μmole/ml	(3.3-3.4)	....	8
		Nitrogen, mg/100 ml			8
169		Total N	(22.7-24.6)	....	
170		Protein N	(6.9-7.0)	....	
171		Non-protein N	(15.7-17.6)	....	
172		Amino acid N	1.8	....	
	Canis familiaris	Amino acids, μmole/g H_2O			6
173		Alanine [11]	0.12[8]; 0.05[9]	0.26	
174		Arginine [12]	0.07[8]; 0.035[9]	0.14	
175		Aspartate [12]	0.35[8]	0.025	
176		Cystine [12]	0.15[8]; 0.035[9]	0.10	
177		Glutamate [13]	0.14[8]; 0.06[9]	0.15	
178		Glutamine [11]	0.27[8]; 0.13[9]	0.02	
179		Glycine [13]	0.13[8]; 0.047[9]	0.10	
180		Histidine [13]	0.023[8]; 0.023[9]	0.077	
181		Isoleucine [13]	0.053[8]; 0.03[9]	0.093	
182		Leucine [13]	0.063[8]; 0.06[9]	0.120	
183		Lysine [13]	0.10[8]; 0.093[9]	0.26	
184		Methionine [12]	0.03[8]; 0.015[9]	0.04	
185		Phenylalanine [12]	0.055[8]; 0.035[9]	0.045	
186		Serine [11]	0.11[8]; 0.06[9]	0.15	
187		Threonine [12]	0.01[9]	0.115	
188		Tyrosine [12]	0.07[8]; 0.035[9]	0.06	
189		Valine [11]	0.10[8]; 0.06[9]	0.14	
	Equus caballus	Protein, mg/ml			12
190		Total	0.652	73.7[2]	
191		Albumin	0.077	29.6[2]	
192		Globulin	0.115	44.1[2]	
193		Amino acids, μg/g H_2O	300	375[2]	12
194		Creatinine, μmole/g H_2O	0.0883	0.166[2]	12
195		Urate, μmole/ml	(0.059-0.125)	....	8
196		Urea, μmole/ml	(2.66-6.67)	....	8
197		μmole/g H_2O	4.83	4.5[2]	12,13

[1] Unless otherwise indicated. [2] Serum concentration. [8] In anterior zone. [9] In posterior zone. [11] One animal. [12] Two animals. [13] Three animals.

continued

279. CHEMICAL COMPOSITION AND PHYSICAL PROPERTIES OF VITREOUS HUMOR: VERTEBRATES

Part II. Mammals Other Than Man

	Species	Constituent or Property	Value		Ref-er-ence
			Vitreous Humor	Plasma	
		Nitrogen, mg/100 ml			
198		Total N	(14.2-35.7)	....	8
199			30.1	....	12,13
200		Protein N	(3.4-3.6)	....	8
201		Non-protein N	(14.2-32.3)	....	8
202			26.4	....	12,13
203		Amino acid N	2.1	....	8
204	Felis catus	Protein, mg/ml	7.7	....	15
205		Urea, μmole/ml	8.5	....	41
206		μmole/g H_2O	7.83	....	15
207	Ovis aries	Glutamate, μmole/ml	0.87	....	26
208	Sus scrofa	Protein, total, mg/ml	1.975	....	41
209		Urate, μmole/ml	0.027	....	8
210		Urea, μmole/ml	(2.1-3.9)	....	8
		Nitrogen, mg/100 ml			8
211		Total N	(18.3-22.3)	....	
212		Protein N	(5.3-7.3)	....	
213		Non-protein N	(13.2-15.0)	....	
214		Amino acid N	(2.7-3.0)	....	
215	Rabbit	Collagen, μg/ml	104	....	2
		Amino acids, μmole/g H_2O			33
216		Alanine	0.074	0.302	
217		Arginine	0.045	0.096	
218		Aspartate	0.019	0.029	
219		Cystine	Trace	0.054	
220		Glutamate	0.169	0.178	
221		Glycine	0.065	1.190	
222		Histidine	0.020	0.116	
223		Isoleucine	0.010	0.112	
224		Leucine	0.018	0.163	
225		Lysine	0.070	0.212	
226		Methionine	Trace	0.014	
227		Phenylalanine	0.011	0.097	
228		Proline	0.011	0.323	
229		Serine	0.130	0.420	
230		Threonine	0.025	0.165	
231		Tryptophan	Trace	0.013	
232		Tyrosine	0.021	0.058	
233		Valine	0.045	0.195	
234		Urea, μmole/g H_2O	7.63	9.85	35
		Nitrogen			
235		Total N, mg/100 ml H_2O	13	....	30
236		Non-protein N, μmole/g H_2O	17	....	34
		General Physical & Chemical Properties			
	Bos taurus				
237	Calf	Volume, ml	11.82	....	27
238	Cow	Volume, ml	20.3	....	27
239		Water, mg/100 ml vitreous fluid	99,000	....	30
240	Ox	Volume, ml	20.9	....	27

continued

Part II. Mammals Other Than Man

| | Species | Constituent or Property | Value | | Reference |
			Vitreous Humor	Plasma	
241	*Canis familiaris*	Volume, ml	3.2	....	27
242	*Equus caballus*	Volume, ml	28.8	....	27
243	*Felis catus*	Oxygen pressure, mm Hg	53	....	24
244	*Ovis aries*	Volume, ml	7.0	....	27
245	*Sus scrofa*	Volume, ml	3.2	....	27
246	Rabbit	Volume, ml	1.5	....	22
247			1.7	....	16
248			2.0	....	27
249		Oxygen pressure, mm Hg	(1.0-5.2)[4/]; (6.5-15.8)[5/]; (17.0-32.8)[14/]	....	21
250		Water, mg/100 ml vitreous fluid	99,000	....	30
251		pH	(7.0-7.1)	....	42

[4/] In central zone. [5/] In peripheral zone. [14/] Pupillary zone.

Contributors: Langham, Maurice E.; Cole, D. F.

References

[1] Balazs, E. A. 1954. Amer. J. Ophthalmol. 38:21.

[2] Balazs, E. A. 1960. Importance Vitreous Body Ret. ina Surg. Retina Found. Conf., 2nd, 1958, p. 29.

[3] Balazs, E. A. 1965. In E. A. Balazs and R. W. Jean-loz, ed. The Amino Sugars. Academic Press, New York. v. 2A, pp. 401-460.

[4] Balazs, E. A., et al. 1959. Arch. Biochem. Biophys. 81:464.

[5] Berman, E. R., and M. Voaden. 1970. In C. N. Gray-more, ed. The Biochemistry of the Eye. Academic Press, New York and London. pp. 373-463.

[6] Bito, L. Z., et al. 1965. Exp. Eye Res. 4:374.

[7] Bowness, J. M., et al. 1952. Biochem. J. 51:521.

[8] Cohen, M., et al. 1926. Contrib. Ophthalmic Sci. 9:216.

[9] Davson, H., and W. S. Duke-Elder. 1948. J. Physiol. (London) 107:141.

[10] Davson, H., and C. P. Luck. 1956. Ibid. 132:454.

[11] de Vincentiis, M. 1951. Boll. Soc. Ital. Biol. Sper. 27:309.

[12] Duke-Elder, W. S. 1930. Brit. J. Ophthalmol., Monogr. Suppl. 4:25.

[13] Duke-Elder, W. S. 1942. Textbook of Ophthalmol-ogy. C. V. Mosby, St. Louis. v. 1.

[14] Duke-Elder, W. S., and H. Davson. 1949. Brit. J. Ophthalmol. 33:21.

[15] Duke-Elder, W. S., and A. J. B. Goldsmith. 1951. Recent Advances in Ophthalmology. Ed. 4. J. and A. Churchill, London.

[16] Emmert, E. 1886. Z. Vergl. Augenheilk. 4:40.

[17] Fischer, F. P. 1949. In H. Davson, ed. Physiology of the Eye. Blakiston, Philadelphia. p. 42.

[18] Gombos, G. M., and E. R. Berman. 1967. Acta Oph-thalmol. 45:794.

[19] Green, H., et al. 1957. Arch. Ophthalmol. 57:85.

[20] Grönvall, H. 1937. Acta Ophthalmol. (Suppl. 14).

[21] Jacobi, K. W. 1966. Albrecht von Graefes Arch. Ophthalmol. 169:350.

[22] Kinsey, V. E., and D. V. N. Reddy. 1964. In J. H. Prince, ed. The Rabbit in Eye Research. C. C. Thomas, Springfield, Ill. p. 218.

[23] Krause, A. C. 1936. Arch. Ophthalmol. 16:986.

[24] Krause, A. C., and B. S. Gonen. 1956. Amer. J. Oph-thalmol. 42:764.

[25] Krause, A. C., and A. M. Stack. 1939. Arch. Oph-thalmol. 22:66.

[26] Krebs, H. A., et al. 1949. Biochem. J. 44:159.

[27] Mestrezat, W., and A. Magitot. 1921. C. R. Soc. Biol. 84:185.

[28] Meyer, K., et al. 1938. Amer. J. Ophthalmol. 21:1083.

[29] Naumann, H. 1959. Arch. Ophthalmol. 62:356.

[30] Nordmann, J. 1968. In A. Brini, et al., ed. Biologie et chirurgie du corps vitre. G. Masson, Paris. ch. 3.

[31] Oksala, A. 1954. Acta Ophthalmol. 32:235.

[32] Philpot, F. J., and A. Pirie. 1943. Biochem. J. 37:250.

[33] Reddy, D. V. N. 1968. Biochem. Eye Symp. 1966, p. 167.

[34] Reddy, D. V. N., and V. E. Kinsey. 1960. Arch. Ophthalmol. 63:715.

[35] Ross, E. J. 1949. Brit. J. Ophthalmol. 33:310.

[36] Salit, P. W. 1939. Biochem. Z. 301:253.

[37] Schweer, G. 1956. Albrecht von Graefes Arch. Oph-thalmol. 158:190.

[38] Snowden, E., and A. Pirie. 1958. Biochem. J. 70:716.

[39] Tauber, F. W., and A. C. Krause. 1943. Amer. J. Ophthalmol. 26:260.

continued

Part II. Mammals Other Than Man

[40] Tron, E. 1926. Albrecht von Graefes Arch. Ophthalmol. 117:677.

[41] Van Heyningen, R. 1961. In C. Long, et al., ed.
Biochemists' Handbook. E. and F. N. Spon, London.
p. 711.

[42] Von Sallmann, L. 1945. Arch. Ophthalmol. 33:32.

[43] Von Sallmann, L. 1951. Tabulae Biol. 22.

[44] Wolff, R., and A. Bourquard. 1937. C. R. Soc. Biol.
124:319.

[45] Wooton, J. F., et al. 1954. Arch. Ophthalmol. 51:
589.

Part III. Vertebrates Other Than Mammals

Value: Unlabeled values are in vitreous humor; G = in gel phase of vitreous; L = in liquid phase of vitreous; S = in serum;
P = in plasma. Plus/minus (±) values are standard error.

	Species	Constituent or Property	Value	Reference
		Aves		
1	*Bubo virginianus*	Ascorbate, μmole/ml	0.031	4
2		Hexosamine, μg/ml	(10-21)	
3		Hexuronic acid, μg/ml	(13-25)	
4		Collagen, μg/ml	(67-149)	
5	*Columba livia*	Ascorbate, μmole/ml	0.135	4
6		Hexosamine, μg/ml	17 G; 30 L	4
7		Lactate, μmole/ml	15.65	8
8		Pyruvate, μmole/ml	0.97	8
9		Citrate, μmole/ml	0.48; 0.35 S	7
10		Hexuronic acid, μg/ml	<10	4
11	*Gallus gallus*	Zinc, nmole/g dry wt	6.6	5
12		Ascorbate, μmole/ml	(0.043-0.074) G; 0.043 L	4
13		Hexosamine, μg/ml	(17-46) G; (10-78) L	4
14		Mucopolysaccharide, μg/ml	21 G; 17 L	2
15		Hyaluronic acid, μg/ml	10 G; 22 L	3
16		Lactate, μmole/ml	5.26	8
17		Pyruvate, μmole/ml	1.17	8
18		Citrate, μmole/ml	0.33; 0.29 S	7
19		Hexuronic acid, μg/ml	(3-12)	4
20		Collagen, μg/ml	209 G; 1.5 L	2
21		Mass, g	1.355	1
22	*Meleagris gallopavo*	Hexosamine, μg/ml	(15-38) G; (28-38) L	4
23		Hyaluronic acid, μg/ml	16 G; 28 L	3
24		Citrate, μmole/ml	0.31; 0.38 S	7
25		Hexuronic acid, μg/ml	(7-16)	4
26	*Phasianus* sp.	Citrate, μmole/ml	0.4	7
27	*Strix varia*	Mucopolysaccharide, μg/ml	35	2
28		Hexuronic acid, μg/ml	12	4
29		Collagen, μg/ml	90	2
30	Duck	Citrate, μmole/ml	0.21; 0.51 S	7
		Reptilia		
31	*Chrysemys scripta elegans*[1/]	Ascorbate, μmole/ml	0.368	4

[1/] Synonym: *Pseudemys scripta elegans.*

continued

279. CHEMICAL COMPOSITION AND PHYSICAL PROPERTIES OF VITREOUS HUMOR: VERTEBRATES

Part III. Vertebrates Other Than Mammals

	Species	Constituent or Property	Value	Reference
			Amphibia	
32	*Bufo marinus*	Chloride, μmole/ml H_2O	70.2 ± 1.7; 79.2 ± 1.5 P	6
33		Magnesium, μmole/ml H_2O	1.06 ± 0.11; 1.49 ± 0.09 P	
34		Potassium, μmole/ml H_2O	5.8 ± 0.2; 5.9 ± 0.2 P	
35		Sodium, μmole/ml H_2O	100.7 ± 1.1; 106.5 ± 3.5 P	
36		Volume, ml	0.482	
37	*Rana catesbeiana*	Hexosamine, μg/ml	46	2
38		Sialic acid, μg/ml	28	4
39		Mucopolysaccharide, μg/ml	<1	2
40		Collagen, μg/ml	182	2
			Osteichthyes	
41	*Cyprinus carpio*	Mucopolysaccharide, μg/ml	575	2
42		Hyaluronic acid, μg/ml	663 G; 623 L	
43		Collagen, μg/ml	690	
44	*Gadus* sp.	Citrate, μmole/ml	0.043	7
45	*Sphyraena* sp.	Hyaluronic acid, μg/ml	239 G; 234 L	2
46	*Thunnus thynnus*	Mucopolysaccharide, μg/ml	660	2
47		Hyaluronic acid, μg/ml	660	
48		Collagen, μg/ml	217	

Contributor: Cole, D. F.

References

[1] Abelsdorf, G., and K. Wessely. 1909. Arch. Augenheilk. 64(Suppl. 65).

[2] Balazs, E. A. 1960. Importance Vitreous Body Retina Surg. Retina Found. Conf., 2nd, 1958, p. 29.

[3] Balazs, E. A. 1965. In E. A. Balazs and R. W. Jeanloz, ed. The Amino Sugars. Academic Press, New York. v. 2A, pp. 401-460.

[4] Balazs, E. A., et al. 1959. Arch. Biochem. Biophys. 81:464.

[5] Bowness, J. M., et al. 1952. Biochem. J. 51:521.

[6] Cole, D. F. 1968. Comp. Biochem. Physiol. 26:353.

[7] Grönvall, H. 1937. Acta Ophthalmol. (Suppl. 14).

[8] de Vincentiis, M. 1951. Boll. Soc. Ital. Biol. Sper. 27:309.

280. PHYSICAL PROPERTIES AND CHEMICAL COMPOSITION OF TEARS: MAN

Tears vary in physical and chemical compositions, depending on whether the fluid is collected from the ducts of the lacrimal gland or from the conjunctival sac. Fluid from the latter is slightly opalescent as it includes all the products of the conjunctival secretions, including mucus and epithelial debris [44]. Electrophoretic analysis of tears demonstrates the presence of four to six components [70], and indicates that tear and serum proteins are different substances with differences in the absolute and relative sizes of their fractions [37]. The presence of certain amino acids [2,70] and mucus polysaccharides [37] has also been observed. **Value:** Ig = immunoglobulin; SGPT = serum glutamic pyruvic transaminase; SGOT = serum glutamic oxalacetic transaminase. Values in parentheses are ranges, estimate "b" or "c" (*see* Introduction).

continued

	Property or Constituent	Subjects		No. of Determinations	Value	Method	Remarks	Reference
		Age	No. & Sex					
					Physical Properties			
1	Conductivity	....	....	50	0.90% NaCl	....	....	61
2	Freezing point depression	Adult	3	3	0.551°C	Beckmann thermometer	Samples collected 3 times daily in Wright's capsules and pooled	65
3	pH	....	....	.....	7.35	Brown's colorimetric	....	33
4		....	....	50	7.4	....	....	28, 61
5		....	100	50	7.48(7.20-7.80)[b]	Electric pH meter	Lacrimal fluid obtained with capillary glass tubes from excretory ducts	47
6				50	7.85(7.50-8.20)[b]	....	Lacrimal fluid obtained from conjunctival sac	
7		....	8	8	(7.2-8.5)[1]	Microglass electrode & a contact lens	8 subjects examined 15-60 s. pH decreased under contact lens by 0.15-1.0.	30
8		....	35	19	>6.8	Bromthymol blue colorimetric	pH is independent of sex & presumably also of age	60
9				16	7.0			
10		Adult	77	77	7.4(7.3-7.7)[c]	Beckmann pH meter	....	32
11	Refractive index	22-40 yr[2]	16	40	1.3369(1.3361-1.3379)[c]	Refractometer	....	66
12	Vapor pressure	....	....	50	0.93% NaCl	....	....	28, 61
13		14-87 yr	53	.....	0.903-1.014% NaCl water solution	Baldes vapor pressure osmometer	Tears obtained from lower cul-de-sac with 10⁻ lambda (0.01 ml) micropipette. In 70% of subjects, 0.930-0.980% NaCl water solution.	46
14		35 yr	5♂, 5♀	10	0.90(0.87-0.92)[c] % NaCl	Krogh modification of Hill method	Lacrimation stimulated by placing capillary tube along inner side of lower lid	38
15	Volume or flow	....	....	.....	6.4 g/24 hr	....	Lacrimal fluid collected with capillary glass tube	44
16		....	5	.....	(0.50-0.67)[c] g/16 hr	....	During waking hours	69
17		....	....	.....	<15 mm	Schirmer test	....	13
18		....	....	494 eyes	26.6 ± 12.4 mm	Schirmer test I	....	35
19		....	93	186 eyes	15-30 ml/24 hr	Lacrimal streak dilution test	Tear secretion greatest between 10 & 20 yr	57
20		....	....	950 eyes	9.5 ml/24 hr	Modified lacrimal dilution test (Norn)	Value depends on age	15
		....	....	186 (total)	Dilution in 5 min:	Lacrimal streak dilution test	In normal subjects, tear production corresponds to a dilution, in the course of 5 min, of 1:366 (average)	58
21				1	1:4			
22				18	1:16			
23				54	1:64			
24				113	1:256 or more			

[1] Initial value. [2] Age range for all but 2 subjects.

continued

	Property or Constituent	Subjects		No. of Determinations	Value	Method	Remarks	Reference
		Age	No. & Sex					
25		....	....	.....	0.01 ml or 10 μl	Dye dilution	Conjunctival fluid	59
26		....	....	.....	2.4 μl/min	Determined from turnover of corneal epithelial cells & concentration of non-keratinized nucleated squamous cells in conjunctival fluid	Average tear flow	20, 59
27		....	....	.....	(14.4-28.8)[c] ml/24 hr	Tear production per unit of time can be calculated: $r = \dfrac{V}{t} \ln a$	Normal subjects. Rate of secretion causing overflow in normal drainage system: $\sim$100 μl/min	57, 59
28		....	♂	.....	34.0 ± 1.6 mg/hr	Difference in weight with a torsion balance	....	71
29			♀	.....	34.8 ± 1.7 mg/hr			
		....	162 (total)			Schirmer test I	Schirmer test I & II standardized with filter paper Whatman N. 41: 5 × 80 mm strips. Lacrimal production decreases with age.	18
30			11♂, 26♀	37	>15 mm/5 min			
31			27♂, 25♀	52	(16-30)[c] mm/5 min			
32			23♂, 50♀	73	>30 mm/5 min			
			111 (total)			Schirmer test II		
33			10♂, 17♀	27	(0-10)[c] mm/2 min			
34			16♂, 30♀	46	(11-20)[c] mm/2 min			
35			8♂, 20♀	28	(21-30)[c] mm/ 2 min			
36			2♂, 8♀	10	>30 mm/2 min			
37		....	12-29♂	.....	13 mm/5 min	Schirmer test	Test measures linear distance; tears absorbed on strip of filter paper when one end is placed in conjunctival sac	31
38			15-29♀	.....	20 mm/5 min			
39		Infant Premature	202	.....	In 60%, tears appeared before 30 da	Observation for evidence of lacrimation	....	62
40		Full-term	1326	.....	In 13.2%, overflow of tears as early as 5½ hr after birth			
41		Premature	100	.....	Normal in 14%[3/]	Schirmer test I	Non-crying infants; body wt, <1500 g	1,2, 4
42					Normal in 63%[3/]	Schirmer test I	Non-crying infants; body wt, 2000-2500 g	
43			....	.....	Normal in 67%[3/]	Schirmer test I	Crying infants; body wt, <1500 g	
44					Normal in 78%[3/]	Schirmer test I	Crying infants; body wt, 2000-2500 g	
45		Full-term	249	140 eyes	Normal in 82% 1 da after birth	Schirmer test I	After 1st wk, normal tear secretion in 95%	
46				180 eyes	Normal in 96% 1 da after birth	Schirmer test I	In 2 da-1 wk, normal tear secretion in 94-100%	

[3/] Proportionate to body weight.

continued

	Property or Constituent	Subjects		No. of Deter- mina- tions	Value	Method	Remarks	Ref- er- ence
		Age	No. & Sex					
47		½-11 yr	25	.....	1.35 g/1 da	Colorimetric	....	36
48		10-19 yr	600	.....	28.3 μl	Colorimetric method	Amount of fluid present in non-irritated conjunctival sac	75
49		70-90 yr	600	.....	2.7 μl			
50		10-39 yr	....	98	17.50 mm	Standardized Schirmer test	....	74
51		40-80 yr	....	102	12.33 mm			
52		20-45 yr	12	17	1.2(0.5-2.2)[c] μl/min[4/]	Objective fluoro- photometry	Rate of secretion causing overflow in normal drain- age system: $\sim$100 μl/min	54
53					15(6-28)[c] %/min[5/]	Objective fluoro- photometry		
54			16	39	16(9-25)[c] %/min[5/]	Subjective fluoro- photometry		
55		50-89 yr	24	27	18(3-40)[c] %/min[5/]	Subjective fluoro- photometry		
56		20-89 yr	16♂, 21♀	.....	6.2 ± 2.0 μl	Dilution method & calculations	In upright position, max capacity of cul-de-sac to hold tears: $\sim$30 μl	
57		26-77 yr	25	.....	0.61 g/1 da	....	....	36
58		>40 yr	....	.....	10-15 mm	No. 589 black rib- bon filter paper	Standardized Schirmer tear test kit	29
59	Specific weight	....	....	.....	(1.004-1.005)[c]	....	....	42
60	Surface tension	20-35 yr	6	.....	46.24 dynes/cm² [6/]	Surface tension measurements, using fine wire rings	Surface tension of tear- film as distinguished from lacrimal gland secre- tion	53
61	Temperature	....	....	.....	(30-35)[c] °C	....	Closed eyelids raise temper- ature of tears 0.5°C	42
62	Thickness of conjunctival fluid	....	13	134	(3-4)[c] μ	Pipette constructed by author	Measurements outside of palpebral fissure	56, 59
63	Thickness of precorneal film	....	....	.....	6.5 μ	Fluorometer	....	48
64	Thickness of oily layer of precorneal film	....	....	.....	(1000-1750)[c] Å	Interference pat- terns used for calculations	....	49

General Chemical Components

	Property or Constituent	Age	No. & Sex	No. of Deter- mina- tions	Value	Method	Remarks	Ref- er- ence
65	Ash	Adult	2	2	1.05 g/100 ml	Gravimetric	Samples collected 3 times daily in Wright capsule and pooled	65
66	Solids, total	....	215	1	1.87%	1 ml of tears col- lected in weigh- ing bottle; water removed by evap- oration, and solids weighed	Benzyl bromide used fre- quently as a lacrimating agent	70

[4/] Average tear flow. [5/] Mean turnover rate. [6/] Ratio of surface tension between tears and water at 32°C.

continued

	Property or Constituent	Subjects		No. of Determinations	Value	Method	Remarks	Reference
		Age	No. & Sex					
67		....	....	.....	1.84%	Evaporation of tears; solid residue cooled in desiccator, then weighed	Lacrimation induced by tear gas	26
68		Adult	2	2	1.8 g/100 ml	Gravimetric	Samples collected 3 times daily in Wright capsule and pooled	65
69	Water	Adult	2	2	98.2 g/100 ml	Gravimetric	Samples collected 3 times daily in Wright capsules and pooled	65

Electrolytes

	Property or Constituent	Age	No. & Sex	No. of Determinations	Value	Method	Remarks	Reference
70	Bicarbonate	....	....	.....	26 meq/liter	....	....	28
71	Chloride	....	20	2	135.5(134.5-136.5)[b] meq/liter	Sendroy technique	No artificial lacrimator used	26
72		Young	2♂	19	128.0(117.6-138.4)[b] meq/liter	Modification of differential potentiometric titrations of Mac-Innes & Dole	Lacrimation induced by sliced onions	73
73		8-12 yr & 5 adult ♀	32	32	(101.8-168.2)[c] meq/liter	Keys titration	Lacrimation induced by sliced onions	19
74	Phosphorus	30 yr	....	.....	2.49 μg	Modified colorimetric method	Average amount of tears: 37.43 mg	5
75	Organic	....	....	.....	250(35-320)[c] mg/liter	....	No correlation between level of tear & serum phosphorus	42
76	Inorganic	15-85 yr	30	.....	0.1206 ng	Lowery-Lopez spectrometric	Tears collected on filter paper	3
77	Potassium	Young	2♂	36	14.9(7.7-22.1)[b] meq/liter	Perkin-Elmer photometer	Lacrimation induced by sliced onions	19
78		8-12 yr & 5 adult ♀	32	32	29.0(22.8-35.2)[b] meq/liter	Flame photometry	Lacrimation induced by sliced onions	19
79		22-85 yr	30	60	30.3 μg/mg	Flame photometry	Tears collected on filter paper	6
80	Sodium	Young	2♂	42	146(126-166)[b] meq/liter	Perkin-Elmer photometer	Lacrimation induced by sliced onions	73
81		8-12 yr & 5 adult ♀	32	32	142.0(108.4-175.6)[b] meq/liter	Flame photometry	Lacrimation induced by sliced onions	19

Nitrogenous Substances

	Property or Constituent	Age	No. & Sex	No. of Determinations	Value	Method	Remarks	Reference
82	Protein, total	....	....	9	1.044 g/100 ml	Lowery, et al.	....	12
83		Adult	3	3	0.669 g/100 ml	Calculated from nitrogen content	Varies with rate of tear flow. Samples collected 3 times daily in Wright capsules and pooled.	8,9, 65
84		5-64 yr	30	30	0.360(0.136-0.592)[c] g/100 ml	Nephelometry	Varies with rate of tear flow	8,9, 34

continued

	Property or Constituent	Subjects Age	Subjects No. & Sex	No. of Determinations	Value	Method	Remarks	Reference
85	Albumin	....	....	.....	20-30% of total tear protein	Acrylamide disc electrophoresis	....	68
86		....	....	.....	20 mg/ml	Spinco Model R paper electrophoresis system	Samples collected on ordinary filter paper strips $\sim 5 \times 25$ mm	50
87		....	....	.....	30%	Electrophoresis	Lacrimal specimen collected by placing bent indicator filter paper under lower lid	22
88		....	104	.....	48.48%	Electrophoresis	....	67
89		....	....	50	Equation: A = 0.8930- 0.007271 x	Paper electrophoresis	Secretion curve of albumin; x = actual amount of tears for equation. Average amount of tears 30.08 mg	7
90		....	....	.....	Albumin I: 31.08% Ia: 0.55%	Paper electrophoresis	Healthy subjects	72
91		....	....	.....	18%	Paper electrophoresis	Schirmer test tear collection	23
92		....	21	.....	38.8%[7]	Paper electrophoresis	Tears obtained from conjunctival sac with Kirk-type ultramicropipette	16
93			12	.....	19.3%[8]			
94		....	29	124	14.7% or 52.3 mg/100 ml	Paper electrophoresis	....	37
95		....	....	.....	20.2%	Paper electrophoresis	Tears collected with capillary pipette; irritation to eyeball avoided as much as possible	25
96					30%	Agar microelectrophoresis		
97		....	42	.....	49% of total protein	Disc electrophoresis	Fractions grossly classified into 7 groups against those of human serum protein	55
98		15-75 yr	49♂, 54♀	.....	28.6 ± 3.9 (18.0- 38.1)c %	Paper electrophoresis	Schirmer test tear collection for 10 min	52
99			3	.....	29.9%	Paper electrophoresis	Lacrimation induced by crushed onion	
100		Adult	3	3	0.394 g/100 ml	Hawk & Bergeim	Samples collected 3 times daily in Wright capsule and pooled	65
101	Serum albumin	....	....	.....	5% of tear protein	Acrylamide disc electrophoresis	....	68
102	Amino acids	....	....	.....	11 free amino acids identified	1- & 2-dimension paper chromtography	Tears from lower conjunctival sac removed with capillary tube	21
103	Globulin	....	103	.....	48.7 ± 5.3 (37.5- 61.8)c %	Paper electrophoresis	Schirmer test tear collection	52
104			3	.....	42.4%	Paper electrophoresis	Lacrimation induced by crushed onion; tears collected with micropipette	
105		....	....	50	Equation: G = 1.3619- 0.010518 x	Paper electrophoresis	Secretion curve of globulins. Relations stated graphically and documented by statistical estimation	7

[7]/ Normal. [8]/ Irritant-induced tears.

continued

	Property or Constituent	Subjects		No. of Determinations	Value	Method	Remarks	Reference
		Age	No. & Sex					
106		....	....	.....	56.9%	Paper electrophoresis	Tears collected with capillary pipette	25
107					Globulins are not (or seldom) obtained	Agar microelectrophoresis		
108		....	42	.....	α_1: 4.2%	Disc electrophoresis	....	55
109					α_2: 2.5%			
110					Slow α_2: 2.6%			
111		....	104	.....	38.78%	Cellulose acetate electrophoresis	....	67
112		....	....	8	γ_{1A}: 7 mg/100 ml	Immunoelectrophoresis & gel diffusion technique with antiserums	γ_{1A} represents major fraction of γ- globulin in tears. γ_2 detected in too small amount for quantitative measurements.	17
113		....	6	.....	IgA: 88 mg/100 ml	Electrophoresis & immunoelectrophoresis	....	10
114					IgG: 31 mg/100 ml			
115					IgM: not found			
116		....	....	9	IgA: 79 mg/100 ml	Immunoelectrophoresis; double immunodiffusion precipitin test; immunoglobulin levels estimated (Mancini)	....	12, 45
117					IgG: 23 mg/100 ml			
118					IgM: none			
119					IgA/IgG: 3.5/1			
120		....	7	.....	IgA: 49 mg/100 ml	Electrophoresis, immunoelectrophoresis & agar bi-dimensional immunodiffusion	....	11
121					IgG: 38 mg/100 ml			
122					IgM: not found			
123		....	....	.....	IgA: 450 μg/ml	Radial diffusion precipitin	....	68
124					IgG: 750 μg/ml			
125		20-30 yr	12	231	IgA: 10-100 μg/ml	Radial diffusion precipitin	No lacrimator	43
126		Infant	94	205	γ_A: >0.5 mg/100 ml[9/]	Electroimmunodiffusion	Lacrimal fluid collected from conjunctival sac using fine glass capillary tubes	51
127		4 wk	4	6	γ_M detected			
128		20-30 yr	....	231	IgA: 36.8(15-137)[c] mg/100 ml	Single radial diffusion precipitin, in agar (Fahey, et al.)	Tears collected without lacrimator	24, 43
129		Adult	3	3	0.275 g/100 ml	Calculated by subtraction	....	65
130	Ceruloplasmin	....	....	.....	40 μg/ml	Radial diffusion precipitin	....	68
131	Transferrin	....	....	.....	100 μg/ml	Radial diffusion precipitin	....	68
132	Ammonia	....	....	.....	0.005 g/100 ml	....	Samples collected 3 times daily in Wright capsule and pooled	65

[9/] In 90% of infants, γ_A-globulin first detected.

continued

	Property or Constituent	Subjects		No. of Determinations	Value	Method	Remarks	Reference
		Age	No. & Sex					
133	Urea	....	2	36	1.02(0.88-1.16)[b] g/ 100 ml × plasma concentration	Micromodification of Archibald colorimetric	Lacrimation induced by sliced onion	73
134		Adult	2	2	0.03 g/100 ml	Marshall urease	Samples collected 3 times daily in Wright capsule and pooled	65
135	Nitrogen, total	Adult	6	6	0.158 g/100 ml	Folin micro-Kjeldahl	Samples collected 3 times daily in Wright capsule and pooled	65
136	Non-protein nitrogen	Adult	4	4	0.051 g/100 ml	Folin micro-Kjeldahl	Samples collected 3 times daily in Wright capsule and pooled	65
					Carbohydrates			
137	Reducing substances (as glucose)	....	12	.....	6.06(2.8-7.7)[c] mg/100 ml	....	Greatly reduced by prolonged tearing	26
138	Glucose	....	12	24	2.5(0-5.0)[c] mg/100 ml	Fermentation	Lacrimation induced by tear gas	26
139		....	....	.....	206 nmole/g	Hexokinase reaction	Students. Lacrimation induced by brown acetone.	64
140		16-79 yr	24♀	.....	6.91 mg/100 ml	Folin's colorimetric	....	4
141		38-78 yr	6♂	.....				
					Miscellaneous Organic Acids, Vitamins, & Enzymes			
142	Citric acid	Adult	1♂, 1♀	6	(0.5-0.7)[c] mg/100 ml	Enzymatic	No artificial lacrimator used	27
143	Ascorbic acid (Vitamin C)	....	....	.....	0.14 mg/100 ml	....	Pre-corneal & pre-conjunctival film	39
144	Amylase	10-59 yr	9♂, 16♀	.....	48.6 units of Wohlgemuth	Wohlgemuth's	Lacrimation artificially stimulated	40
145	Lysozyme	....	104	.....	12.74%	Cellulose acetate electrophoresis	....	67
146		....	103	.....	22.7 ± 3.9 (14.5-35.9)[c] %	Paper electrophoresis	....	52
147				3	29.7%	Paper electrophoresis	Lacrimation induced by onion	
148		....	....	.....	(10-3400)[c] μg/ml	Lysis of *Micrococcus lysodeikticus*	....	68
149		Premature infants-85 yr	306	612	(700-2000)[c] μg/ml	Lysis of *Micrococcus lysodeikticus*	Lowest values in infants <1 yr old & in adults >80 yr old	14
150		17 yr	35	.....	1438(800-2500)[c] U/ml	Viscosimetric	U = amount of enzyme required to reach half viscosity in 10 min	63
151	Phosphatase acid	15-59 yr	5♂, 8♀	13	50.9 IU	....	One IU phosphatase activity = activity that liberates 1 microgram of phosphorus per min & per liter	41
152	alkaline	15-72 yr	9♂, 7♀	16	40.2 IU			
153	Transaminase	10-66 yr	8♂, 11♀	19	SGPT and SGOT	Karmen's	Lacrimation induced by inhalation of Formol fumes	41

continued

280. PHYSICAL PROPERTIES AND CHEMICAL COMPOSITION OF TEARS: MAN

Contributors: Leopold, Irving H.; Harris, John E.

References

[1] Apt, L., and B. F. Cullen. 1964. J. Amer. Med. Ass. 189:951.
[2] Balik, J. 1952. Cesk. Oftalmol. 8:167.
[3] Balik, J. 1960. Amer. J. Ophthalmol. 49:941.
[4] Balik, J. 1961. Cesk. Oftalmol. 17:508.
[5] Balik, J. 1962. Sb. Lek. 64:275.
[6] Balik, J. 1968. Klin. Monatsbl. Augenheilk. 153:705.
[7] Balik, J., and M. Eliskova. 1961. Cesk. Oftalmol. 17:503.
[8] Balik, J., and F. Hradecky. 1953. Ibid. 9:102.
[9] Balik, J., and F. Hradecky. 1953. Ibid. 9:495.
[10] Bazzi, C., et al. 1967. Folia Allergol. 14:385.
[11] Bazzi, C., et al. 1968. G. Mal. Infet. Parassit. 20:229.
[12] Bazzi, C., et al. 1970. Progr. Immunobiol. Stand. 4:333.
[13] Beetham, W. P. 1935. Trans. Amer. Ophthalmol. Soc. 33:413.
[14] Bonavida, B., and A. T. Sapse. 1968. Amer. J. Ophthalmol. 66:70.
[15] Brandt, H. P., and G. Fritsche. 1967. Acta Ophthalmol. 45:166.
[16] Brunish, R. 1957. Arch. Ophthalmol. 57:554.
[17] Chodirker, W. B., and T. B. Tomasi, Jr. 1963. Science 142:1080.
[18] De Roetth, A. 1941. Amer. J. Ophthalmol. 24:20.
[19] Di Sant' Agnese, P. A., et al. 1958. Pediatrics 22:507.
[20] Ehlers, N. 1967. Acta Ophthalmol. 45:273.
[21] Erdei, Z. 1968. Szemeszet 105:30.
[22] Erickson, O. F. 1957. Amer. J. Ophthalmol. 43:295.
[23] Erickson, O. F., et al. 1958. Ibid. 46:12.
[24] Fahey, J. L., and E. M. McKelvey. 1965. J. Immunol. 94:84.
[25] Francois, J., and M. Rabaey. 1960. Amer. J. Ophthalmol. 50:793.
[26] Giardini, A., and J. R. E. Roberts. 1950. Brit. J. Ophthalmol. 34:737.
[27] Grönvall, H. 1937. Acta Ophthalmol. (Suppl. 14).
[28] Grove-Rasmussen, K. V., et al. 1953. Acta Pharm. Int. 2:343.
[29] Halberg, G. P., and C. Berens. 1961. Amer. J. Ophthalmol. 51:840.
[30] Hamano, H., et al. 1966. J. Jap. Contact Lens Ass. 8:90.
[31] Henderson, J. W., and W. A. Prough. 1950. Arch. Ophthalmol. 43:224.
[32] Hind, H. W., and F. M. Goyan. 1949. J. Amer. Pharm. Ass. Sci. Ed. 38:477.
[33] Hosford, G. N., and A. M. Hicks. 1935. Arch. Ophthalmol. 13:14.
[34] Junnola, K. 1953. Ann. Med. Exp. Biol. Fenn. 31(Suppl. 1).
[35] Kim, C. W. 1962. J. Korean Med. Ass. 5:1785.
[36] Kirchner, C. 1964. Klin. Monatsbl. Augenheilk. 144:412.
[37] Krause, U. 1959. Acta Ophthalmol. (Suppl. 53).
[38] Krogh, A., et al. 1945. Acta Physiol. Scand. 10:88.
[39] Kronfeld, P. C. 1952. Trans. Amer. Ophthalmol. Soc. 50:347.
[40] Liotet, S. 1967. Ann. Ocul. 200:526.
[41] Liotet, S. 1967. Ibid. 200:1258.
[42] Liotet, S., and P. Cochet. 1967. Arch. Ophtalmol. 27:251.
[43] Little, J. M., et al. 1969. Amer. J. Ophthalmol. 68:898.
[44] Magaard, H. 1882. Virchows Arch. Pathol. Anat. Physiol. Klin. Med. 89:258.
[45] Mancini, G., et al. 1965. Int. J. Immunochem. 2:235.
[46] Mastman, G. J., et al. 1961. Arch. Ophthalmol. 65:509.
[47] Matthäus, W. 1962. Klin. Monatsbl. Augenheilk. 141:899.
[48] Maurice, D. M. 1967. Invest. Ophthalmol. 6:464.
[49] McDonald, J. E. 1969. Amer. J. Ophthalmol. 67:56.
[50] McDonald, P. R., et al. 1957. Trans. Amer. Ophthalmol. Soc. 55:49.
[51] McKay, E., and H. Thom. 1969. J. Pediat. 75:1245.
[52] Mikowski, S., and S. Zajaczkowski. 1970. Wiad. Lek. 23:1725.
[53] Miller, D. 1969. Arch. Ophthalmol. 82:368.
[54] Mishima, S., et al. 1966. Invest. Ophthalmol. 5:264.
[55] Mukai, M. 1969. Folia Ophthalmol. Jap. 20:466.
[56] Norn, M. S. 1960. Acta Ophthalmol. (Suppl. 59).
[57] Norn, M. S. 1965. Ibid. 43:567.
[58] Norn, M. S. 1966. Ibid. 44:25.
[59] Norn, M. S. 1966. Ibid. 44:212.
[60] Norn, M. S. 1968. Ibid. 46:189.
[61] Pedersen-Bjergaard, K., and B. C. Smidt. 1952. Acta Dermato-Venereol. 32:261.
[62] Penbharkkul, S., et al. 1962. J. Pediat. 61:857.
[63] Regan, E. 1950. Amer. J. Ophthalmol. 33:600.
[64] Reim, M., et al. 1967. Ophthalmologica 154:39.
[65] Ridley, F. 1930. Brit. J. Exp. Pathol. 11:217.
[66] Rötth, A. von. 1922. Klin. Monatsbl. Augenheilk. 68:598.
[67] Sakurai, M. 1969. Acta Soc. Ophthalmol. Jap. 73:826.
[68] Sapse, A., et al. 1967. Bull. Soc. Ophtalmol. Fr. 80:236.
[69] Schirmer, O. 1903. Albrecht von Graefes Arch. Ophthalmol. 56:197.
[70] Smolens, J., et al. 1949. Amer. J. Ophthalmol. 32:153.
[71] Tanaka, S. 1963. J. Clin. Ophthalmol. (Tokyo) 17:129.
[72] Tapaszto, I., et al. 1965. Albrecht von Graefes Arch. Klin. Exp. Ophthalmol. 168:468.
[73] Thaysen, J. H., and N. A. Thorn. 1954. Amer. J. Physiol. 178:160.
[74] Wright, J. C. 1962. Arch. Ophthalmol. 67:564.
[75] Zintz, R., and T. Schilling. 1964. Klin. Monatsbl. Augenheilk. 144:393.

Method of determination: *Interstitial fluid* calculated by subtracting plasma volume from thiocyanate diffusion space[1]. *Intracellular fluid* calculated by subtracting thiocyanate diffusion space[1] from total body water. *Intercellular solids*[2] estimated by the method of McCance [2]

(intracellular water = 67% intracellular mass). *Bone*[2] estimated from the data of Iob and Swanson [1], Mitchell, et al. [3], Widdowson and Dickerson [4], and Widdowson, et al. [5]. *Fat*[2] estimated by difference between total body weight and all other components.

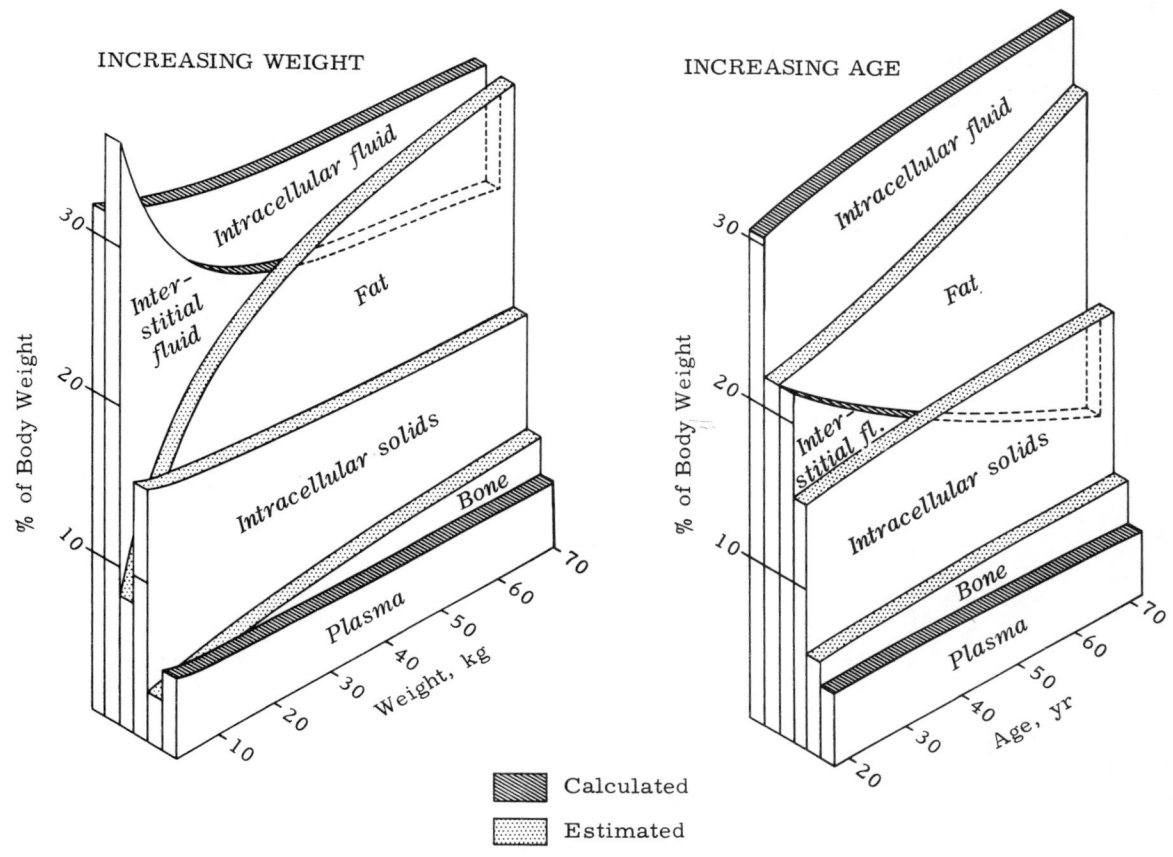

[1] The use of thiocyanate diffusion space as a measure of extracellular fluid is based on the probability that in normal persons the thiocyanate and other similar diffusion spaces are in fairly constant proportion in that nebulous entity, extracellular fluid, and that therefore the rate of change of the curves should not vary (although the absolute values may). [2] Because of the lack of data, only orders of magnitude are indicated.

Contributors: Henschel, Austin, Bass, David E., and Wedgwood, Ralph J.

References

[1] Iob, V., and W. W. Swanson. 1934. Amer. J. Dis. Child. 47:302.

[2] Ling, W. S. M., and H. Sprinz. 1948. Amer. J. Med. Sci. 215:555.

[3] Mitchell, H. H., et al. 1945. J. Biol. Chem. 158:625.

[4] Widdowson, E. M., and J. W. T. Dickerson. 1964. In C. L. Comar and F. Bronner, ed. Mineral Metabolism. Academic Press, New York. v. 2(A), pp. 1-249.

[5] Widdowson, E. M., et al. 1951. Clin. Sci. 10:113.

APPENDIXES

Appendix I. SCIENTIFIC NAMES AND CORRESPONDING COMMON NAMES

Protozoa and nonvascular plants have not been included.

Part I. Animals

Scientific Name	Common Name
Acartia clausi	Calanoid copepod
A. tonsa	Calanoid copepod
Acheta domesticus	House cricket
Achirus lineatus	Lined sole
Acipenser medirostris	Green sturgeon
Acrocheilus alutaceus	Chiselmouth
Acroneuria pacifica	Stonefly
Aechmophorus occidentalis	Western grebe
Aedes aegypti	Yellow-fever mosquito
Aeshna cyanea	Southern dragonfly
A. grandis	European dragonfly
Agama sp.	Agama
Agkistrodon piscivorus piscivorus	Eastern cottonmouth
Aix sponsa	North American wood duck
Alca sp.	Auk
Alcelaphus buselaphus jacksoni	Jackson hartebeest
Alligator mississippiensis	American alligator
Alopex lagopus	Arctic fox
Alouatta seniculus	Red howler monkey
Ambystoma maculatum	Spotted salamander
A. mexicanum	Axolotl, or Mexican salamander
A. tigrinum	Tiger salamander
A. tigrinum tigrinum	Eastern tiger salamander
Amia calva	Bowfin
Amicula stelleri	Giant Pacific chiton
Ammotragus lervia	Aoudad, or North African wild sheep
Amphibolurus barbatus	Australian bearded lizard
A. ornatus	Ornate lizard
Amphiuma means	Amphiuma
A. tridactylum	Three-toed amphiuma
Anagasta kuehniella	Mediterranean flour moth
Anas platyrhynchos	Mallard duck
A. platyrhynchos domesticus	Pekin or domestic duck
Anax junius	Green darner
Anguilla anguilla	Eel
A. japonica	Japanese eel
A. rostrata	American eel
Anguis fragilis	Slowworm
Anisops pellucens	Backswimmer
Anodonta cygnea	Swan mussel
Anolis carolinensis	Green anole lizard
Anopheles maculipennis	Malaria mosquito
Anser anser	Greylag goose
Antheraea pernyi	Giant silkworm moth
A. polyphemus	Polyphemus moth
Anthonomus grandis	Boll weevil
Anthropoides virgo	Demoiselle crane
Aotus trivirgatus	Three-banded douroucouli
Apis mellifera	Honey bee

Scientific Name	Common Name
Aplysia californica	California sea hare
A. depilans	Mediterranean sea hare
A. fasciata	Sea hare
A. vaccaria	Giant black sea hare
Ara macao	Scarlet macaw
Archilochus alexandri	Black-chinned hummingbird
A. colubris	Ruby-throated hummingbird
Archosargus probatocephalus	Sheepshead
Arctocephalus australis	South American fur seal
Ardea herodias	Great blue heron
Arenicola marina	Lugworm
Arhynchite pugettensis	Echiuroid
Arius felis	Sea catfish
Artemia salina	Brine shrimp
Arvicola terrestris	Water vole
Ascaris lumbricoides	Large roundworm
Astacus astacus	Crayfish
Asterias rubens	Starfish
Ateles sp.	Spider monkey
Bagre marinus	Gaff-topsail catfish
Balistes capriscus	Gray triggerfish
Barytelphusa guerini	Guerin's freshwater crab
Bison bonasus	European wisent
Bithynia leachi	North American freshwater snail
Blaberus discoidalis	Large tropical cockroach
B. giganteus	Cockroach
Blarina brevicauda	Short-tailed shrew
Blatta orientalis	Oriental cockroach
Blattella germanica	German cockroach
Boa constrictor	Boa constrictor
Bombus agrorum	European bumblebee
Bombyx mori	Silkworm moth
Bos grunniens	Yak
B. taurus	Cattle
Bothrops jararaca	Jararaca, or fer-de-lance
Bradypus griseus	Three-toed sloth
B. tridactyla	Three-toed sloth
Branta bernicla	Brant
Bubalus bubalis	Asiatic water buffalo
Bubo virginianus	Great horned owl
Bufo americanus	American toad
B. arenarum	Argentine toad
B. bufo	Common European toad
B. marinus	Marine toad
B. paracnemis	Rococo toad
B. terrestris	Southern toad
B. viridis	Mediterranean green toad
B. woodhousei	Woodhouse's toad
Cairina moschata	Muscovy duck

continued

Appendix I. SCIENTIFIC NAMES AND CORRESPONDING COMMON NAMES

Part I. Animals

Scientific Name	Common Name	Scientific Name	Common Name
Calanus finmarchicus	Calanoid copepod	*C. scripta*	Red-eared turtle
Callinectes sapidus	Blue crab	*C. scripta elegans*	Red-eared turtle
Calliphora vicina	Bluebottle blow fly	*C. terrapen*	Antilles terrapin
Calopteryx virgo	Damselfly	*Cichlasoma cyanoguttatum*	Rio Grande perch
Calosoma inquisitor	Ground beetle	*Ciconia ciconia*	White stork
Caluromys derbianus	Colombian opossum	*Clarias batrachus*	Walking catfish
Camelus bactrianus	Bactrian camel	*Clemmys guttata*	Spotted turtle
C. dromedarius	Arabian camel or dromedary	*Clethrionomys rutilus*	Ruddy vole
Cancer irroratus	Rock crab	*Clymenella torquata*	Bamboo worm
C. magister	Edible crab	*Cnemidophorus tigris*	Western whiptail lizard
Canis familiaris	Dog	*Coleonyx variegatus*	Variegated ground gecko
C. latrans	Coyote	*Colinus virginianus*	Bobwhite
C. lupus	Gray or timber wolf	*Coluber constrictor*	Black snake
Capra hircus	Goat	*Columba livia*	Street pigeon
Carabus cancellatus	Carab beetle	*C. palumbus*	Wood pigeon
C. intricatus	Carab beetle	*Cordylus vittifer*	South African armadillo lizard
Caranx crysos	Blue runner		
Carassius auratus	Goldfish	*Coregonus lavaretus*	Whitefish
Carausius morosus	Stick insect	*C. muksun*	Muksun
Carcharhinus limbatus	Small Atlantic blacktip shark	*Corvus caurinus*	Northwestern crow
Carcinus maenas	Green crab	*C. corex*	Common raven
Cardisoma guanhumi	West Indies land crab	*C. cornix*	Hooded crow
Cardita floridana	Bird shell	*C. monedula*	European jackdaw
Caretta caretta	Atlantic loggerhead turtle	*Coturnix coturnix*	European quail
Carpiodes velifer	High-fin carp sucker	*C. coturnix japonica*	Japanese quail
Carpocapsa pomonella	Codling moth	*Crangon vulgaris*	Shrimp
Carpodacus mexicanus	House finch	*Crassostrea virginica*	Virginia oyster
Castor canadensis	North American beaver	*Crenobia alpina*	Alpine planarian
C. fiber	Old World beaver	*Crepidula fornicata*	Slipper limpet
Casuarius bennetti	Bennett's cassowary	*Cricetulus griseus*	Gray long-tailed hamster
C. casuarius	Australian cassowary	*Crocidura russula*	White-toothed shrew
Catharacta skua	Antarctic skua	*Crocodylus acutus*	Common American crocodile
Catostomus catostomus pocatello	Long-nosed sucker	*Crotalus atrox*	Western diamondback rattlesnake
Cavia porcellus	Guinea pig	*C. horridus atricaudatus*	Canebrake rattler
Cebus albifrons	White-fronted capuchin	*Cryptobranchus alleganiensis*	Hellbender salamander
C. apella	Brown or tufted capuchin		
Ceratophrys ornata	Horned frog	*Cryptotermes havilandi*	Drywood termite
Cercaertus nanus	Dormouse possum	*Ctenosaura acanthura*	Spiny-tailed iguana
Cercocebus torquatus atys	Sooty mangabey	*Cucumaria miniata*	Sea cucumber
Cercopithecus aethiops	Grivet monkey	*Culex pipiens*	Northern house mosquito
C. pygerythrus	Vervet monkey	*Cyathura polita*	Estuarine isopod
Cervus canadensis roosevelti	Roosevelt elk	*Cygnus atratus*	Black swan
		Cynoglossus brevis	Indo-Pacific tonguefish
C. nippon	Japanese deer, or sika	*Cynoscion arenarius*	Sand sea trout
C. nippon taiouanus	Formosan sika deer	*C. nebulosus*	Spotted sea trout
Chaenocephalus aceratus	Ice fish	*Cyprinus carpio*	Carp
Chaetodipterus faber	Atlantic spadefish	*Cystophora cristata*	Hooded or bladdernose seal
Chelydra serpentina	Common snapping turtle	*Cyzicus* cf. *heirosolymitanus*	Clam shrimp
C. serpentina serpentina	Common snapping turtle		
Chen caerulescens	Blue goose		
Chinchilla laniger	Chinchilla		
Chironomus thummi thummi	Midge	*Dama dama*	Fallow deer
		Danaus plexippus	Milkweed butterfly
Chiton tuberculatus	Chiton	*Daphnia magna*	Waterflea
Chloephaga melanoptera	Andean goose, or huallata	*Dasyatis centroura*	Roughtail stingray
Choloepus didactylus	Two-toed sloth	*Dasypus novemcinctus*	Nine-banded armadillo
C. hoffmanni	Hoffman's two-toed sloth	*Dasyurus maculatus*	Tiger cat
Choristoneura fumiferana	Spruce budworm	*D. viverrinus*	Eastern native cat
Chrysemys dorbignyi	South American red-eared turtle	*Delphinapterus leucas*	Beluga or white whale
		Delphinus delphis	Dolphin
C. picta	Painted turtle	*Desmognathus quadramaculatus*	Black-bellied salamander
C. picta belli	Painted turtle		
C. picta marginata	Midland painted turtle		

continued

Part I. Animals

Scientific Name	Common Name	Scientific Name	Common Name
Diaptomus oregonensis	Calanoid copepod	*F. tinnunculus*	Kestrel
Dicamptodon ensatus	Pacific giant salamander	*Felis caracal*	Caracal cat
Dicrostonyx groenlandicus rubricatus	Varying lemming	*F. catus*	Cat
		F. concolor	Puma
Didelphis marsupialis virgiana	Common opossum	*F. planiceps*	Flat-headed cat
		F. viverrina	Fishing cat
Dinocras cephalotes	European stonefly	*Fimbria fimbria*	Sea hare
Diodora aspera	Rough keyhole limpet	*Forficula auricularia*	European earwig
Diomedea immutabilis	Laysan albatross	*Forpus passerinus spengeli*	Green-runt parrotlet
D. nigripes	Black-footed albatross	*Fratercula arctica*	Common puffin
Dipodomys merriami	Merriam's kangaroo rat	*Fringilla montifringilla*	Brambling
Diprion hercyniae	European spruce sawfly	*Fulica americana*	American coot
Dipsosaurus dorsalis	Desert iguana	*Fulmarus glacialis*	Fulmar
Dissosteira carolina	Carolina grasshopper	*Fundulus heteroclitus*	Mummichog
Dromiceius novaehollandiae	Emu	*Fusitriton oregonensis*	Oregon triton
Drosophila euronotus	Fruit fly		
D. melanogaster	Fruit fly	*Gadus morhua*	Atlantic cod
D. pachea	Fruit fly	*Galago crassicaudatus*	Thick-tailed galago
D. willistoni	Vinegar fly	*G. senegalensis*	Galago
Dytiscus circumcinctus	Predacious diving beetle	*Galleria mellonella*	Greater wax moth
D. marginalis	Diving beetle	*Gallus gallus*	Chicken
		Gammarus duebeni	Scud
		Gasterophilus intestinalis	Horse bot fly
Eisenia foetida	Manure worm, or brandling	*Gasterosteus aculeatus*	Threespine stickleback
Elaphurus davidianus	Père David's deer	*Gastrophryne carolinensis*	Eastern narrow-mouthed toad
Electrophorus electricus	Electric eel		
Elephas maximus	Indian elephant	*Gazella thomsoni*	Thomson's gazelle
E. maximus indicus	Indian elephant	*Gecarcinus lateralis*	Purple land crab
Emys orbicularis	European pond turtle	*Geomys bursarius*	Pocket gopher
Entosphenus tridentatus	Pacific lamprey	*Gerrhonotus multicarinatus*	Southern alligator lizard
Ephemera danica	Mayfly	*Giraffa camelopardalis*	Giraffe
Ephestia elutella	Tobacco moth	*Glossiphonia complanata*	Leech
Eptatretus stouti	Pacific hagfish	*Glycera dibranchiata*	Blood worm
Eptesicus fuscus	Big brown bat	*Gopherus polyphemus*	Gopher tortoise
Equus asinus	Donkey	*Gorilla gorilla*	Gorilla
E. caballus	Horse	*Grus canadensis*	Sandhill crane
E. grevyi	Grevy's zebra	*Gryllotalpa gryllotalpa*	Mole cricket
Erethizon dorsatum	North American porcupine	*Gryllus assimilis*	Field cricket
Erinaceus europaeus	European hedgehog	*Gyps fulvus*	Griffon vulture
Eriocheir sinensis	Mitten crab		
Erpobdella octoculata	Worm leech	*Halichoerus grypus*	Gray seal
E. testacea	Leech	*Haliotis rufescens*	Abalone
Erythrocebus patas	Patas monkey	*Halophryne dussumieri*	Toadfish
Eschrichtius gibbosus	Gray whale	*Heliothis zea*	Corn earworm or bollworm
Esox americanus vermiculatus	Grass pickerel	*Helix aspersa*	Dented garden snail, or petit-gris
E. lucius	Northern pike	*H. pomatia*	Edible snail
Eucidaris tribuloides	Sea urchin	*Helobdella stagnalis*	Leech
Eudyptes chrysolophus	Macaroni penguin	*Heloderma suspectum*	Gila monster
E. crestatus	Rockhopper	*Hemigrapsus nudus*	Purple shore crab
Eumeces obsoletus	Great Plains skink	*Hesperiphona vespertina*	Evening grosbeak
Eunice biannulata	Eunicid worm	*Heterodon platyrhinos*	Hog-nosed snake
Eupolymnia crescentis	Terebellid worm	*Heterometrus fulvipes*	Whip scorpion
Eurostopodus guttatus	Spotted nightjar	*Heterospizias meridionalis*	Savannah hawk
Eustrongylides sp.	Roundworm of birds & fish	*Hippocampus brevirostris*	Short-nosed seahorse
Eutamias minimus	Least chipmunk	*Hippopotamus amphibius*	Nile hippopotamus
		Homarus americanus	American lobster
Falco naumanni	Lesser kestrel	*H. gammarus*	European lobster
F. peregrinus	Peregrine falcon	*Homo sapiens*	Man
F. sparverius	Falcon	*Hyaena* sp.	Hyena

continued

Scientific Name	Common Name	Scientific Name	Common Name
Hyalophora cecropia	Cecropia moth	*Limanda ferruginea*	Yellowtail flounder
Hydrolagus colliei	Ratfish	*Limax flavus*	Slug
Hydrophilus sp.	Diving beetle	*Limnephilus flavicornis*	Caddisfly
Hyla crucifer	Spring peeper	*L. stigma*	European caddisfly
H. versicolor	Gray tree frog	*Limulus polyphemus*	Horseshoe or king crab
Hyles euphorbiae	Spurge hawkmoth	*Lingula unguis*	Tongue shell
Hylobates lar	White-headed gibbon	*Littorina littorea*	Periwinkle
Hyphantria cunea	Fall webworm	*Locusta migratoria*	Migratory locust
		L. migratoria migratorioides	African migratory locust
		Loligo pealei	Common American or Atlantic squid
Ictalurus catus	White catfish		
I. furcatus	Blue catfish	*Lophius americanus*	Goosefish
I. natalis	Yellow catfish	*L. piscatorius*	Monkfish
I. nebulosus	Brown bullhead catfish	*Lophortyx californicus*	California quail
I. punctatus	Channel catfish	*L. gambelii*	Gambel's quail
Ictiobus niger	Black buffalo fish	*Loxia curvirostra sitkensis*	Red crossbill
Iguana iguana	Common iguana	*Loxodonta africana*	African elephant
Ilyanassa obsoleta	Common mud snail	*Lumbricus terrestris*	Earthworm
Ischnochiton conspicuus	Conspicuous chiton	*Lygosoma laterale*	Little brown skink
Isoodon obesulus	Short-nosed bandicoot	*Lymnaea palustris*	Freshwater snail
Junco hyemalis	Slate-colored junco	*Macaca arctoides*	Stump-tailed macaque
		M. cyclopis	Formosan rock macaque
		M. fascicularis	Crab-eating macaque
Lacerta agilis	European fence lizard	*M. fuscata*	Japanese macaque
L. viridis	Green lacerta lizard	*M. irus*	Philippine or crab-eating monkey
Lagenorhynchus obliquidens	Pacific white-sided dolphin	*M. maurus*	Moor macaque
Lagodon rhomboides	Pinfish	*M. mulatta*	Rhesus monkey
Lagothrix lagotricha	Woolly monkey	*M. nemestrina*	Pig-tailed macaque
Lama glama	Llama	*M. radiata*	Bonnet macaque
L. guanicoe	Guanaco	*M. speciosa*	Stump-tailed macaque
L. vicugna	Vicuña	*M. sylvana*	Barbary ape
Lampetra fluviatilis	Pacific American lamprey	*Macronectes giganteus*	Giant petrel
L. lamottei	American brook lamprey	*Macropus giganteus*	Great gray kangaroo
Lampropeltis getulus	King snake	*M. robustus*	Wallaroo or euro
Larimus fasciatus	Banded drum	*M. rufus*	Red kangaroo
Larus argentatus	Herring gull	*Malaclemys terrapin centrata*	Diamondback terrapin
L. canus	Mew gull		
L. glaucescens	Glaucous-winged gull	*M. terrapin littoralis*	Texas diamondback terrapin
L. hyperboreus	Glaucous gull	*Malacosoma americanum*	Eastern tent caterpillar
Lasiorhinus latifrons	Wombat	*M. disstria*	Forest tent caterpillar
Laticauda semifasciata	Broadbanded blue sea snake, or erabu	*M. pluviale*	Western tent caterpillar
		Mandrillus sphinx	Mandrill
Latimeria chalumnae	Coelacanth	*Manduca quinquemaculata*	Tomato hornworm
Lemur catta	Ring-tailed lemur	*Mantis religiosa*	European mantid
L. fulvus	Brown lemur	*Marmota caligata*	Hoary marmot
Lepidosiren paradoxa	South American lungfish	*M. flaviventris*	Yellow-bellied marmot
Lepisosteus osseus	Longnose gar	*M. marmota*	Eurasian marmot
L. spatula	Alligator gar	*M. monax*	Woodchuck
Lepomis cyanellus	Green sunfish	*Martes zibellina*	Sable
L. macrochirus	Common bluegill	*Melanitta deglandi*	White-winged scoter
Leptinotarsa decemlineata	Colorado potato beetle	*Melanogrammus aeglefinus*	Haddock
Leptodactylus ocellatus	South American leopard frog	*Melanoplus bivittatus*	Two-striped grasshopper
L. typhonius	South American thread-toed frog	*M. differentialis*	Differential grasshopper
		M. femur-rubrum	Red-legged grasshopper
Leptonychotes weddelli	Weddell seal	*Meleagris gallopavo*	Turkey
Lepus europaeus	European hare	*Melierax gabar*	Gabar goshawk
Leucophaea maderae	Madeira cockroach	*Melolontha melolontha*	European scarab beetle
Libellula sp.	Common skimmer dragonfly	*Melospiza melodia*	Song sparrow
Libinia emarginata	Spider crab	*Mephitis mephitis*	Striped skunk

continued

Scientific Name	Common Name
Mercenaria mercenaria	Northern quahog
Meriones unguiculatus	Clawed jird
Mesocricetus auratus	Golden or Syrian hamster
Metamysidopsis elongata	Opossum-shrimp
Metridium senile	Sea anemone
Micropogon undulatus	Atlantic croaker
Micropterus salmoides	Largemouth bass
Microtus arvalis	Common vole
M. oeconomus	Tundra vole
M. pennsylvanicus	Meadow mouse
Moina macrocopa	Waterflea
Moringua linearis	Indo-Pacific worm eel
Morone americana	White perch
Mugil cephalus	Striped mullet
M. curema	White mullet
Mus musculus	House mouse
Musca domestica	House fly
Muscardinus avellanarius	Common dormouse
Mustela erminea	Ermine
M. frenata	Long-tailed weasel
M. putorius	Polecat
M. vison	Mink
Mustelus canis	Smooth dogfish
Mycteria americana	Wood ibis or wood stork
Mylocheilus caurinus	Pea-mouth
Myotis lucifugus	Little brown bat
M. myotis	Common brown bat
Myoxocephalus scorpius	Shorthorn sculpin
Mytilus edulis	Edible mussel
Myxine glutinosa	Atlantic hagfish
Myzus persicae	Green peach aphid
Naja naja	Oriental common cobra
Nandinia binotata	African palm civet
Natrix natrix	Common European grass or ringed snake
N. sipedon	North American water snake
N. taxispilota	Brown water snake
Necturus maculosus	Mud puppy
Neoceratodus forsteri	Australian lungfish
Neodiprion lecontei	Conifer sawfly
N. pratti pratti	Pine sawfly
Nephtys caecoides	Nephtyid worm
N. ciliata	Nephtyid worm
N. hombergii	Shimmy worm
Nereis diversicolor	Clam worm
Noetia ponderosa	Ark shell
Notonecta glauca	Backswimmer
Notothenia gibberifrons	Notothenid
N. neglecta	Notothenid
Nycticorax nycticorax	Black-crowned night heron
Octopus cyanea	Octopus
O. dofleini	Octopus
Odocoileus virginianus	White-tailed deer
Olor buccinator	Trumpeter swan
Oncopeltus fasciatus	Large milkweed bug
Oncorhynchus gorbuscha	Pink salmon
O. keta	Chum salmon
O. kisutch	Coho salmon
O. nerka	Sockeye salmon

Scientific Name	Common Name
O. tshawytscha	Chinook salmon
Ondatra zibethicus	Muskrat
Opsanus beta	Gulf toadfish
O. tau	Oyster toadfish
Orcinus orca	Killer whale
Orconectes immunis	Freshwater crayfish
O. virilis	Freshwater crayfish
Ornithorhynchus anatinus	Platypus
Orthopristis chrysopterus	Pigfish
Oryctolagus cuniculus	European rabbit
Oryx gazella	Gemsbok
Oryzomys palustris	Rice rat
Osmerus mordax	Rainbow smelt
Osmylus fulvicephalus	Lacewing
Ostrinia nubilialis	European corn borer
Ovis aries	Sheep
O. musimon	Mouflon
Pachygrapsus crassipes	Striped rock crab
Palaemonetes varians	Shrimp
P. vulgaris	Common prawn
Pan troglodytes	Chimpanzee
Panorpa communis	Scorpionfly
Panthera leo	Lion
P. nebulosa	Clouded leopard
P. onca	Jaguar
P. pardus	Leopard
P. tigris	Tiger
P. tigris altaica	Siberian tiger
P. tigris tigris	Bengal tiger
P. uncia	Snow leopard
Panulirus interruptus	Pacific coast spiny lobster
P. penicillatus	Olivier's spiny lobster
P. polyphagus	Banded spiny lobster
Papilio machaon	Swallowtail butterfly
P. polyxenes	Black swallowtail butterfly
Papio anubis	Olive baboon
P. cynocephalus	Yellow baboon
P. cynocephalus anubis	Olive baboon
P. hamadryas	Hamadryas or sacred baboon
P. leucophaeus	Baboon
P. ursinus	Baboon
Paralabrax clathratus	Kelp bass
Paralichthys lethostigma	Southern flounder
Parascaris equorum	Roundworm of horse
Parastichopus japonicus	Sea cucumber
Parus major	Great tit
Passer domesticus	House sparrow
P. montanus	European tree sparrow
Passerculus sandwichensis beldingi	Savannah sparrow
Pectinophora gossypiella	Pink bollworm
Pelecanus occidentalis	Brown pelican
Peprilus alepidotus	Southern harvestfish
P. burti	Gulf butterfish
Perameles gunnii	Bandicoot
Perca fluviatilis	European perch
Periplaneta americana	American cockroach
Perognathus californicus	California pocket mouse
P. hispidus	Plains or pale pocket mouse
Peromyscus maniculatus	Deer mouse

continued

Part I. Animals

Scientific Name	Common Name	Scientific Name	Common Name
Petrobius maritimus	Bristletail or silverfish	*R. ocellata*	Winter or big skate
Petromyzon marinus	Sea lamprey	*R. punctulata*	Skate
Phaenicia cuprina	Flesh fly	*R. rhina*	Longnose skate
Pharusa inflata	Flabelligerid	*Rallus owstoni*	Guam rail
Phascolopsis gouldii	Peanut worm	*Rana areolata*	Crawfish frog
Phascolosoma agassizii	Peanut worm	*R. catesbeiana*	Bullfrog
Phasianus colchicus	Ring-necked pheasant	*R. clamitans*	Bronze frog
Pheretima posthuma	Earthworm	*R. esculenta*	European edible frog
Philodryas sp.	South American colubrid	*R. grylio*	Pig frog
Phoca vitulina	Harbor seal	*R. pipiens*	Leopard frog
Phocoena phocoena	Harbor porpoise	*R. pipiens pipiens*	Leopard frog
Phocoenoides dalli	Dall's porpoise	*R. ridibunda*	Laughing or marsh frog
Phormia regina	Black blow fly	*R. sylvatica*	Wood frog
Phyllomedusa sauvagei	Argentinian tree frog	*R. temporaria*	Common European frog
Physeter catodon	Sperm whale	*Rattus norvegicus*	Norway rat
Pieris brassicae	European cabbageworm	*R. rattus*	Black rat
P. rapae	Imported cabbageworm	*Reithrodontomys mega-lotis*	Western harvest mouse
Pinna nobilis	Pen shell		
Pipistrellus pipistrellus	European brown bat	*Rhea americana*	Common rhea
Piscicola geometra	Leech	*Rhizoprionodon terraenovae*	Atlantic sharpnose shark
Pituophis catenifer	Bull snake	*Rhodnius prolixus*	Assassin bug
P. melanoleucus	Gopher snake	*Romalea microptera*	Short-horned walking stick
P. sayi	Bull snake		
Plecotus auritus	Long-eared bat		
Plethodon cinereus	Red-backed salamander	*Saguinus geoffroyi*	Marmoset, or squirrel monkey
P. glutinosus	Slimy salamander		
Pleuronectes platessa	European plaice	*S. nigricollis*	Black and red tamarin
Podiceps sp.	Grebe	*S. oedipus*	Cotton-top marmoset
Pogonias cromis	Black drum	*Saimiri sciureus*	Squirrel monkey
Polycelis felina	Freshwater planarian	*Salamandra salamandra*	Common fire salamander
Polydactylus octoneumus	Atlantic threadfin	*Salmo gairdneri*	Rainbow trout
Polyodon spathula	Paddlefish	*S. salar*	Atlantic salmon
Polypterus senegalus	Bichir	*S. trutta*	Brown trout
Pomoxis annularis	White crappie	*S. trutta fario*	Brown trout
Pongo pygmaeus	Orangutan	*Salvelinus fontinalis*	Eastern brook trout
Popillia japonica	Japanese beetle	*S. namaycush*	Lake trout
Porichthys porosissimus	Atlantic midshipman	*Samia cynthia*	Cynthia moth
Porthetria dispar	Gypsy moth	*Sarcophaga bullata*	Flesh fly
Potamopyrgus jenkinsi	Marine snail	*Sarcophilus harrisii*	Tasmanian devil
Potorous tridactylus	Rat kangaroo	*Sauromalus obesus*	Chuckwalla lizard
Potos sp.	Kinkajou	*Scalopus aquaticus*	Eastern American mole
Presbytis entellus	Hanuman langur	*Scardafella inca*	Inca dove
Procerodes ulvae	Marine planarian	*Sceloporus occidentalis*	Pacific fence lizard, or iguana
Procyon cancrivorus	Crab-eating raccoon	*Schistocerca gregaria*	Desert locust
P. lotor	Raccoon	*Schizura concinna*	Red-humped caterpillar
Prosopium williamsoni	Mountain whitefish	*Sciaenops ocellata*	Red drum
Protopterus aethiopicus	African lungfish	*Sciurus carolinensis*	Eastern gray squirrel
Pseudaletia unipuncta	Armyworm	*S. vulgaris*	European red squirrel
Pygoscelis adeliae	Adélie penguin	*Scomber scombrus*	Atlantic mackerel
P. papua	Gentoo penguin	*Scomberomorus maculatus*	King mackerel
Pylodictis olivaris	Flathead catfish	*Scyliorhinus caniculus*	Cat shark
Pyrrhocoris apterus	European firebug	*S. stellaris*	European spotted dogfish
Python molurus bivittatus	Burmese or East Indian python	*Scylla serrata*	Serrate swimming crab
		Sebastes marinus	Ocean perch, or red fish
P. reticulatus	Reticulated python	*S. ruberrimus*	Rasphead rockfish
		Sepia officinalis	Cuttlefish
		Serinus canarius	Canary
Rachycentron canadum	Cobia	*Sesarma reticulata*	Marsh crab
Raja binoculata	Big skate	*Sialis lutaria*	Common alderfly
R. eglanteria	Clearnose skate	*Sigmodon hispidus*	Cotton rat
R. erinacea	Little skate	*Silpha carinata*	Carrion beetle
R. laevis	Barndoor skate	*Siphonosoma ingens*	Peanut worm

continued

Part I.   Animals

Scientific Name	Common Name
Sipunculus nudus	Marine worm
Siren sp.	Mud eel, or siren
Sorex cinereus	Masked shrew
Spermophilus citellus	Souslik
S. columbianus	Columbian ground squirrel
S. franklini	Franklin ground squirrel
S. lateralis	Golden-mantled ground squirrel
S. tridecemlineatus	Thirteen-lined ground squirrel
S. undulatus	Arctic ground squirrel
Sphenodon sp.	Tuatara
Sphinx ligustri	Privet hawkmoth
Sphyraena sp.	Barracuda
Sphyrna tiburo	Atlantic bonnethead shark
S. zygaena	Smooth hammerhead shark
Spirographis spallanzanii	Peacock fan worm
Spodoptera eridania	Southern armyworm
Squalus acanthias	Spiny dogfish
S. suckleyi	Pacific spiny dogfish
Sterna hirundo	Common tern
Sternotherus odoratus	Musk turtle
Stomoxys calcitrans	Stable fly
Strix aluco	Tawny owl
S. varia	Barred owl
Strongylocentrotus droebachiensis	Sea urchin
S. purpuratus	Western purple sea urchin
Struthio camelus	African ostrich
S. camelus australis	Ostrich
Sturnus vulgaris	Common starling
Sus scrofa	Swine
Sylvilagus floridanus	Eastern cottontail rabbit
Symphalangus syndactylus	Siamang gibbon
Synodus foetens	Inshore lizardfish
Tachyglossus aculeatus	Spiny anteater
Tachypleus tridentatus	Indo-Pacific king crab
Tadarida brasiliensis mexicana	Mexican free-tail bat
Talpa europaea	Mole
Tamias striatus	Eastern chipmunk
Tamiasciurus hudsonicus	Eastern red squirrel
Tapirus indicus	Asiatic tapir
Taricha granulosa	Rough-skinned newt
T. rivularis	Red-bellied newt
T. torosa	California newt
Taxidea taxus	American badger
Tenebrio molitor	Yellow mealworm
Terrapene carolina	Eastern box turtle
T. ornata ornata	Ornate box turtle
Testudo denticulata	South American tortoise
T. graeca	European tortoise
Tettigonia viridissima	European katydid
Thamnophis elegans	Western terrestrial garter snake
T. sauritus	Ribbon snake
T. sirtalis	Common garter snake
Themiste pyroides	Peanut worm
Thunnus thynnus	Bluefin tuna
Tiliqua nigrolutea	Australian blotched blue-tongued skink
T. rugosus	Australian shingle-back skink
T. scincoides	Blue-tongued skink

Scientific Name	Common Name
Torpedo nobiliana	Atlantic torpedo
T. torpedo	Electric ray torpedo
Trachinotus carolinus	Florida pompano
Trachydosaurus rugosus	Shingle-backed lizard
Tragulus napu	Large Malayan mouse deer
Travisia pupa	Opheliid
Trichechus sp.	Manatee
Trichiurus lepturus	Atlantic cutlassfish
Trichosurus vulpecula	Brush-tail possum
Trionyx ferox	Florida softshell turtle
Triops longicaudatus	Tadpole shrimp
Triturus cristatus	European newt
T. vulgaris	Smooth newt
Troglodytes aedon	Northern house wren
Tubifex tubifex	Tubificid oligochaete
Turdus merula	Blackbird
T. migratorius	Robin
Tursiops truncatus	Atlantic bottle-nosed porpoise
Uca minax	Fiddler crab
U. pugilator	Atlantic fiddler crab
U. pugnax	Fiddler crab
Uma inornata	Fringe-toed lizard
U. notata notata	Colorado desert fringe-toed lizard
U. scoparia	Mojave fringe-toed lizard
Urechis caupo	Spoon worm
Urocyon littoralis santacruzae	Santa Cruz gray fox
Uromastix hardwicki	Indian spiny-tail lizard
Ursus americanus	Black bear
U. arctos	Alaskan brown bear
U. arctos middendorffi	Kodiak bear
Uta stansburiana	Side-blotched lizard, or ground uta
Varanus gouldii	Gould's monitor lizard
V. griseus	Desert monitor lizard
Vespa crabro	North American wasp
Vespula germanica	Wasp
Vipera aspis	Asp viper
Vulpes vulpes	Red fox
Vultur gryphus	Andean condor
Wallabia eugenii	Brush wallaby, or pademelon
Xantusia vigilis	Yucca night lizard
Xenodon merremii	South American colubrid
Xenopus laevis	Clawed frog
Xyleborus ferrugineus	Ambrosia beetle
Zalophus californianus	California sea lion
Zenaida asiatica	White-winged dove
Zenaidura macroura	Mourning dove
Zonotrichia albicollis	White-throated sparrow
Z. leucophrys	White-crowned sparrow
Zoogonus rubellus	Intestinal fluke of fish
Zootermopsis angusticollis	Pacific coast rotten-wood termite

continued

Appendix I. SCIENTIFIC NAMES AND CORRESPONDING COMMON NAMES

Part II. Plants

Scientific Name	Common Name	Scientific Name	Common Name
Acer pseudoplatanus	Sycamore maple, or plane-tree	H. rosa-sinensis	Chinese hibiscus
A. rubrum	Red maple	Hordeum vulgare	Barley
A. saccharum	Sugar maple		
Aesculus hippocastanum	Common horse chestnut	Ilex aquifolium	English holly
Allium cepa	Garden onion	Impatiens sp.	Impatiens
Ananas comosus	Pineapple	Ipomoea batatas	Sweet potato
Antirrhinum majus	Common snapdragon	Iris germanica	German iris
Asparagus albus	White asparagus		
A. officinalis	Garden asparagus		
Asplenium adiantum ni-grum	Black spleenwort	Juglans regia	Persian walnut
		Juniperus virginiana	Eastern red cedar
Avena sativa	Common oat		
		Lactuca sativa	Lettuce
Beta vulgaris	Common beet	Lathyrus odoratus	Sweet pea
Betula nana	Dwarf Arctic birch	Lespedeza stipulacea	Korean lespedeza
Bryonia dioica	Red berry bryony	Lilium bulbiferum	Bulbil lily
		L. longiflorum	Easter lily
		Linum usitatissimum	Common flax
Cannabis sativa	Hemp	Lycopersicon esculentum	Common tomato
Capsicum annuum	Green or mango pepper		
C. frutescens	Hot pepper	Malus pumila	Apple
Carica papaya	Papaya	Melilotus alba	White sweet clover
Castanea sp.	Chestnut		
Catalpa bignonioides	Southern catalpa		
Chenopodium album	Lamb's quarter	Nicotiana glauca	Tree tobacco
Chrysanthemum morifo-lium	Florist's chrysanthemum	N. langsdorffii	Tree tobacco
Citrullus vulgaris	Watermelon	N. tabacum	Common tobacco
Citrus limon	Lemon		
C. sinensis	Sweet orange	Oenothera biennis	Common evening primrose
Cocos nucifera	Coconut	Oryza sativa	Rice
Cucumis melo	Muskmelon		
C. sativus	Cucumber		
Cucurbita pepo	Pumpkin		
		Pastinaca sativa	Parsnip
		Persea americana	American avocado
Dahlia pinnata	Garden dahlia	Phaseolus vulgaris	Kidney bean
Daucus carota	Carrot	Phleum pratense	Timothy
		Phoenix dactylifera	Date
		Phyllitis scolopendrium	Hart's-tongue
Elodea canadensis	Canada waterweed	Picea abies	Norway spruce
Equisetum telmateia	Giant waterweed	Pinus densiflora	Japanese red pine
		P. pinea	Italian stone pine
		P. radiata	Monterey pine
Fagopyrum sagittatum	Buckwheat	Pisum sativum	Garden pea
Fagus sylvatica	European beech	Polypodium vulgare	Common polypody fern
Ficus glabrata	Fig	Populus deltoides	Eastern poplar
Fragaria sp.	Strawberry	P. nigra	Black poplar
Fraxinus excelsior	European ash	Prunus amygdalus	Almond
F. nigra	Black ash	P. domesticus	Garden plum
		P. laurocerasus	Common laurel cherry
		P. persica	Peach
Gladiolus gandavensis	Breeder's gladiolus	Pyrus communis	Pear
Glycine max	Soybean		
Gossypium hirsutum	Upland cotton		
G. roseum	Indian cotton	Quercus coccifera	Kermes oak
Helianthus annuus	Common sunflower	Ranunculus pseudofluitans	Floating water crowfoot
Hibiscus esculentus	Okra	Raphanus raphanistrum	Wild radish
		R. sativus	Garden radish

continued

Part II. Plants

Scientific Name	Common Name
Rheum rhaponticum	Garden rhubarb
Ribes nigrum	European black currant
R. rubrum	Northern red currant
Ricinus communis	Castor bean
Rosa sp.	Rose
Rumex crispus	Curly dock
R. pulcher	Fiddleleaf dock
Saccharum officinarum	Sugarcane
Salix glauca	Gray-leaf willow
S. herbacea	Pygmy willow
Secale cereale	Rye
Solanum tuberosum	Potato
Sorghum bicolor	Sorghum
Spinacia oleracea	Spinach
Syringa vulgaris	Common lilac
Taraxacum officinale	Dandelion

Scientific Name	Common Name
Taxus baccata	English yew
Tradescantia viridis	Wandering jew
Triticum aestivum	Wheat
Tropaeolum majus	Common nasturtium
Tulipa gesneriana	Common tulip
Ulmus glabra	Scotch elm
Vicia faba	Broad bean
Vigna sinensis	Common cowpea
Vitis vinifera	European grape
Yucca gloriosa	Mound lily yucca
Zea mays	Corn

Protozoa and nonvascular plants have not been included.

Part I. Animals

Common Name	Scientific Name	Common Name	Scientific Name
Abalone	*Haliotis rufescens*	Japanese	*Popillia japonica*
Agama	*Agama* sp.	predacious diving	*Dytiscus circumcinctus*
Albatross, black-footed	*Diomedea nigripes*	Bichir	*Polypterus senegalus*
Laysan	*D. immutabilis*	Bird shell	*Cardita floridana*
Alderfly, common	*Sialis lutaria*	Blackbird	*Turdus merula*
Alligator, American	*Alligator mississippiensis*	Blood worm	*Glycera dibranchiata*
Amphiuma	*Amphiuma means*	Bluegill, common	*Lepomis macrochirus*
three-toed	*A. tridactylum*	Boa constrictor	*Boa constrictor*
Anteater, spiny	*Tachyglossus aculeatus*	Bobwhite	*Colinus virginianus*
Aoudad, or North African	*Ammotragus lervia*	Bollworm, pink	*Pectinophora gossypiella*
wild sheep		Borer, European corn	*Ostrinia nubilalis*
Ape, Barbary	*Macaca sylvana*	Bowfin	*Amia calva*
Aphid, green peach	*Myzus persicae*	Brambling	*Fringilla montifringilla*
Ark shell	*Noetia ponderosa*	Brant	*Branta bernicla*
Armadillo, nine-banded	*Dasypus novemcinctus*	Brine shrimp	*Artemia salina*
Armyworm	*Pseudaletia unipuncta*	Bristletail or silverfish	*Petrobius maritimus*
southern	*Spodoptera eridania*	Budworm, spruce	*Choristoneura fumiferana*
Assassin bug	*Rhodnius prolixus*	Buffalo, Asiatic water	*Bubalus bubalis*
Auk	*Alca* sp.	Buffalo fish, black	*Ictiobus niger*
Axolotl, or Mexican sala-	*Ambystoma mexicanum*	Butterfish, gulf	*Peprilus burti*
mander		Butterfly, black swallow-	*Papilio polyxenes*
		tail	
		milkweed	*Danaus plexippus*
Baboon	*Papio leucophaeus*	swallowtail	*Papilio machaon*
	P. ursinus		
hamadryas or sacred	*P. hamadryas*		
olive	*P. anubis*	Cabbageworm, European	*Pieris brassicae*
	P. cynocephalus anubis	imported	*P. rapae*
yellow	*P. cynocephalus*	Caddisfly	*Limnephilus flavicornis*
Backswimmer	*Anisops pellucens*	European	*L. stigma*
	Notonecta glauca	Camel, Arabian, or drome-	*Camelus dromedarius*
Badger, American	*Taxidea taxus*	dary	
Bamboo worm	*Clymenella torquata*	Bactrian	*C. bactrianus*
Bandicoot	*Perameles gunnii*	Canary	*Serinus canarius*
short-nosed	*Isoodon obesulus*	Capuchin, brown or tufted	*Cebus apella*
Barracuda	*Sphyraena* sp.	white-fronted	*C. albifrons*
Bass, kelp	*Paralabrax clathratus*	Carp	*Cyprinus carpio*
largemouth	*Micropterus salmoides*	Cassowary, Australian	*Casuarius casuarius*
Bat, big brown	*Eptesicus fuscus*	Bennett's	*C. bennetti*
common brown	*Myotis myotis*	Cat	*Felis catus*
European brown	*Pipistrellus pipistrellus*	caracal	*F. caracal*
little brown	*Myotis lucifugus*	fishing	*F. viverrina*
long-eared	*Plecotus auritus*	flat-headed	*F. planiceps*
Mexican free-tail	*Tadarida brasiliensis mexi-*	Caterpillar, eastern tent	*Malacosoma americanum*
	cana	forest tent	*M. disstria*
Bear, Alaskan brown	*Ursus arctos*	red-humped	*Schizura concinna*
black	*U. americanus*	western tent	*Malacosoma pluviale*
Kodiak	*U. arctos middendorffi*	Catfish, blue	*Ictalurus furcatus*
Beaver, North American	*Castor canadensis*	brown bullhead	*I. nebulosus*
Old World	*C. fiber*	channel	*I. punctatus*
Bee, European bumble-	*Bombus agrorum*	flathead	*Pylodictis olivaris*
honey	*Apis mellifera*	gaff-topsail	*Bagre marinus*
Beetle, ambrosia	*Xyleborus ferrugineus*	sea	*Arius felis*
carab	*Carabus cancellatus*	walking	*Clarias batrachus*
	C. intricatus	white	*Ictalurus catus*
carrion	*Silpha carinata*	yellow	*I. natalis*
Colorado potato	*Leptinotarsa decemlineata*	Cattle	*Bos taurus*
diving	*Dytiscus marginalis*	Chicken	*Gallus gallus*
	Hydrophilus sp.	Chimpanzee	*Pan troglodytes*
European scarab	*Melolontha melolontha*	Chinchilla	*Chinchilla laniger*
ground	*Calosoma inquisitor*	Chipmunk, eastern	*Tamias striatus*

continued

Part I. Animals

Common Name	Scientific Name	Common Name	Scientific Name
least	*Eutamias minimus*	Cutlassfish, Atlantic	*Trichiurus lepturus*
Chiselmouth	*Acrocheilus alutaceus*	Cuttlefish	*Sepia officinalis*
Chiton	*Chiton tuberculatus*		
conspicuous	*Ischnochiton conspicuus*		
giant Pacific	*Amicula stelleri*	Damselfly	*Calopteryx virgo*
Civet, African palm	*Nandinia binotata*	Darner, green	*Anax junius*
Clam shrimp	*Cyzicus* cf. *heirosolymitanus*	Deer, fallow	*Dama dama*
Clam worm	*Nereis diversicolor*	Formosan sika	*Cervus nippon taiouanus*
Cobia	*Rachycentron canadum*	Japanese, or sika	*C. nippon*
Cobra, oriental common	*Naja naja*	large Malayan mouse	*Tragulus napu*
Cockroach	*Blaberus giganteus*	Père David's	*Elaphurus davidianus*
American	*Periplaneta americana*	white-tailed	*Odocoileus virginianus*
German	*Blattella germanica*	Dog	*Canis familiaris*
large tropical	*Blaberus discoidalis*	Dogfish, European spotted	*Scyliorhinus stellaris*
Madeira	*Leucophaea maderae*	Pacific spiny	*Squalus suckleyi*
oriental	*Blatta orientalis*	smooth	*Mustelus canis*
Cod, Atlantic	*Gadus morhua*	spiny	*Squalus acanthias*
Coelacanth	*Latimeria chalumnae*	Dolphin	*Delphinus delphis*
Colubrid, South American	*Philodryas* sp.	Pacific white-sided	*Lagenorhynchus obliquidens*
	Xenodon merremii	Donkey	*Equus asinus*
Condor, Andean	*Vultur gryphus*	Dormouse, common	*Muscardinus avellanarius*
Coot, American	*Fulica americana*	Douroucouli, three-	*Aotus trivirgatus*
Copepod, calanoid	*Acartia clausi*	banded	
	A. tonsa	Dove, Inca	*Scardafella inca*
	Calanus finmarchicus	mourning	*Zenaidura macroura*
	Diaptomus oregonensis	white-winged	*Zenaida asiatica*
Cottonmouth, eastern	*Agkistrodon piscivorus pisci-vorus*	Dragonfly, common skim-mer	*Libellula* sp.
Coyote	*Canis latrans*	European	*Aeshna grandis*
Crab, Atlantic fiddler	*Uca pugilator*	southern	*A. cyanea*
blue	*Callinectes sapidus*	Drum, banded	*Larimus fasciatus*
edible	*Cancer magister*	black	*Pogonias cromis*
fiddler	*Uca minax*	red	*Sciaenops ocellata*
	U. pugnax	Duck, mallard	*Anas platyrhynchos*
green	*Carcinus maenas*	muscovy	*Cairina moschata*
Guerin's freshwater	*Barytelphusa guerini*	North American wood	*Aix sponsa*
horseshoe or king	*Limulus polyphemus*		
Indo-Pacific king	*Tachypleus tridentatus*	Pekin or domestic	*Anas platyrhynchos domes-ticus*
marsh	*Sesarma reticulata*		
mitten	*Eriocheir sinensis*		
purple land	*Gecarcinus lateralis*		
purple shore	*Hemigrapsus nudus*	Earthworm	*Lumbricus terrestris*
rock	*Cancer irroratus*		*Pheretima posthuma*
serrate swimming	*Scylla serrata*	Earwig, European	*Forficula auricularia*
spider	*Libinia emarginata*	Earworm or bollworm, corn	*Heliothis zea*
striped rock	*Pachygrapsus crassipes*		
West Indies land	*Cardisoma guanhumi*	Echiuroid	*Arhynchite pugettensis*
Crane, demoiselle	*Anthropoides virgo*	Eel	*Anguilla anguilla*
sandhill	*Grus canadensis*	American	*A. rostrata*
Crappie, white	*Pomoxis annularis*	electric	*Electrophorus electricus*
Crayfish	*Astacus astacus*	Indo-Pacific worm	*Moringua linearis*
freshwater	*Orconectes immunis*	Japanese	*Anguilla japonica*
	O. virilis	mud, or siren	*Siren* sp.
Cricket, field	*Gryllus assimilis*	Elephant, African	*Loxodonta africana*
house	*Acheta domesticus*	Indian	*Elephas maximus*
mole	*Gryllotalpa gryllotalpa*		*E. maximus indicus*
Croaker, Atlantic	*Micropogon undulatus*	Elk, Roosevelt	*Cervus canadensis roosevelti*
Crocodile, common Ameri-can	*Crocodylus acutus*	Emu	*Dromiceius novaehollandiae*
		Ermine	*Mustela erminea*
Crossbill, red	*Loxia curvirostra sitkensis*	Eunicid worm	*Eunice biannulata*
Crow, hooded	*Corvus cornix*		
northwestern	*C. caurinus*		

continued

Common Name	Scientific Name
Falcon	*Falco sparverius*
peregrine	*F. peregrinus*
Fan worm, peacock	*Spirographis spallanzanii*
Finch, house	*Carpodacus mexicanus*
Firebug, European	*Pyrrhocoris apterus*
Flabelligerid	*Pharusa inflata*
Flounder, southern	*Paralichthys lethostigma*
yellowtail	*Limanda ferruginea*
Fluke, intestinal, of fish	*Zoogonus rubellus*
Fly, black blow	*Phormia regina*
bluebottle blow	*Calliphora vicina*
flesh	*Phaenicia cuprina*
	Sarcophaga bullata
fruit	*Drosophila euronotus*
	D. melanogaster
	D. pachea
horse bot	*Gasterophilus intestinalis*
house	*Musca domestica*
stable	*Stomoxys calcitrans*
vinegar	*Drosophila willistoni*
Fox, Arctic	*Alopex lagopus*
Santa Cruz gray	*Urocyon littoralis santa-cruzae*
red	*Vulpes vulpes*
Frog, Argentinian tree	*Phyllomedusa sauvagei*
bronze	*Rana clamitans*
bull-	*R. catesbeiana*
clawed	*Xenopus laevis*
common European	*Rana temporaria*
crawfish	*R. areolata*
European edible	*R. esculenta*
gray tree	*Hyla versicolor*
horned	*Ceratophrys ornata*
laughing or marsh	*Rana ridibunda*
leopard	*R. pipiens*
	R. pipiens pipiens
pig	*R. grylio*
South American leopard	*Leptodactylus ocellatus*
South American thread-toed	*L. typhonius*
wood	*Rana sylvatica*
Fulmar	*Fulmarus glacialis*
Galago	*Galago senegalensis*
thick-tailed	*G. crassicaudatus*
Gar, alligator	*Lepisosteus spatula*
longnose	*L. osseus*
Gazelle, Thomson's	*Gazella thomsoni*
Gecko, variegated ground	*Coleonyx variegatus*
Gemsbok	*Oryx gazella*
Gibbon, siamang	*Symphalangus syndactylus*
white-headed	*Hylobates lar*
Gila monster	*Heloderma suspectum*
Giraffe	*Giraffa camelopardalis*
Goat	*Capra hircus*
Goldfish	*Carassius auratus*
Goose, Andean, or huallata	*Chloephaga melanoptera*
blue	*Chen caerulescens*
greylag	*Anser anser*
Goosefish	*Lophius americanus*

Common Name	Scientific Name
Gopher, pocket	*Geomys bursarius*
Gorilla	*Gorilla gorilla*
Goshawk, gabar	*Melierax gabar*
Grasshopper, Carolina	*Dissosteira carolina*
differential	*Melanoplus differentialis*
red-legged	*M. femur-rubrum*
two-striped	*M. bivittatus*
Grebe	*Podiceps* sp.
western	*Aechmophorus occidentalis*
Grosbeak, evening	*Hesperiphona vespertina*
Guanaco	*Lama guanicoe*
Guinea pig	*Cavia porcellus*
Gull, glaucous	*Larus hyperboreus*
glaucous-winged	*L. glaucescens*
herring	*L. argentatus*
mew	*L. canus*
Haddock	*Melanogrammus aeglefinus*
Hagfish, Atlantic	*Myxine glutinosa*
Pacific	*Eptatretus stouti*
Hamster, golden or Syrian	*Mesocricetus auratus*
gray long-tailed	*Cricetulus griseus*
Hare, European	*Lepus europaeus*
Hartebeest, Jackson	*Alcelaphus buselaphus jacksoni*
Harvestfish, southern	*Peprilus alepidotus*
Hawk, Savannah	*Heterospizias meridionalis*
Hawkmoth, privet	*Sphinx ligustri*
spurge	*Hyles euphorbiae*
Hedgehog, European	*Erinaceus europaeus*
Heron, black-crowned night	*Nycticorax nycticorax*
great blue	*Ardea herodias*
Hippopotamus, Nile	*Hippopotamus amphibius*
Hornworm, tomato	*Manduca quinquemaculata*
Horse	*Equus caballus*
Hummingbird, black-chinned	*Archilochus alexandri*
ruby-throated	*A. colubris*
Hyena	*Hyaena* sp.
Ibis, wood, or wood stork	*Mycteria americana*
Ice fish	*Chaenocephalus aceratus*
Iguana, common	*Iguana iguana*
desert	*Dipsosaurus dorsalis*
spiny-tailed	*Ctenosaura acanthura*
Isopod, estuarine	*Cyathura polita*
Jackdaw, European	*Corvus monedula*
Jaguar	*Panthera onca*
Jararaca, or fer-de-lance	*Bothrops jararaca*
Jird, clawed	*Meriones unguiculatus*
Junco, slate-colored	*Junco hyemalis*
Kangaroo, great gray	*Macropus giganteus*
rat	*Potorous tridactylus*
red	*Macropus rufus*

continued

Part I. Animals

Common Name	Scientific Name	Common Name	Scientific Name
Katydid, European	*Tettigonia viridissima*	Lugworm	*Arenicola marina*
Kestrel	*Falco tinnunculus*	Lungfish, African	*Protopterus aethiopicus*
lesser	*F. naumanni*	Australian	*Neoceratodus forsteri*
Kinkajou	*Potos* sp.	South American	*Lepidosiren paradoxa*
Lacewing	*Osmylus fulvicephalus*	Macaque, bonnet	*Macaca radiata*
Lamprey, American brook	*Lampetra lamottei*	crab-eating	*M. fascicularis*
Pacific	*Entosphenus tridentatus*	Formosan rock	*M. cyclopis*
Pacific American	*Lampetra fluviatilis*	Japanese	*M. fuscata*
sea	*Petromyzon marinus*	moor	*M. maurus*
Langur, Hanuman	*Presbytis entellus*	pig-tailed	*M. nemestrina*
Leech	*Erpobdella testacea*	stump-tailed	*M. arctoides*
	Glossiphonia complanata		*M. speciosa*
	Helobdella stagnalis	Macaw, scarlet	*Ara macao*
	Piscicola geometra	Mackerel, Atlantic	*Scomber scombrus*
worm	*Erpobdella octoculata*	king	*Scomberomorus maculatus*
Lemming, varying	*Dicrostonyx groenlandicus rubricatus*	Man	*Homo sapiens*
		Mandrill	*Mandrillus sphinx*
Lemur, brown	*Lemur fulvus*	Mangabey, sooty	*Cercocebus torquatus atys*
ring-tailed	*L. catta*	Manatee	*Trichechus* sp.
Leopard	*Panthera pardus*	Mantid, European	*Mantis religiosa*
clouded	*P. nebulosa*	Manure worm, or brandling	*Eisenia foetida*
snow	*P. uncia*	Marine worm	*Sipunculus nudus*
Limpet, rough keyhole	*Diodora aspera*	Marmoset, or squirrel	*Saguinus geoffroyi*
slipper	*Crepidula fornicata*	monkey	
Lion	*Panthera leo*	cotton-top	*S. oedipus*
Lizard, Australian bearded	*Amphibolurus barbatus*	Marmot, Eurasian	*Marmota marmota*
chuckwalla	*Sauromalus obesus*	hoary	*M. caligata*
Colorado desert	*Uma notata notata*	yellow-bellied	*M. flaviventris*
fringe-toed		Mayfly	*Ephemera danica*
desert monitor	*Varanus griseus*	Mealworm, yellow	*Tenebrio molitor*
European fence	*Lacerta agilis*	Midge	*Chironomus thummi thummi*
fringe-toed	*Uma inornata*		
Gould's monitor	*Varanus gouldii*	Midshipman, Atlantic	*Porichthys porosissimus*
green anole	*Anolis carolinensis*	Milkweed bug, large	*Oncopeltus fasciatus*
green lacerta	*Lacerta viridis*	Mink	*Mustela vison*
Indian spiny-tail	*Uromastix hardwicki*	Mole	*Talpa europaea*
Mojave fringe-toed	*Uma scoparia*	eastern American	*Scalopus aquaticus*
ornate	*Amphibolurus ornatus*	Monkey, grivet	*Cercopithecus aethiops*
Pacific fence, or iguana	*Sceloporus occidentalis*	patas	*Erythrocebus patas*
		Philippine or crab-eating	*Macaca irus*
shingle-backed	*Trachydosaurus rugosus*	red howler	*Alouatta seniculus*
side-blotched, or ground uta	*Uta stansburiana*	rhesus	*Macaca mulatta*
South African armadillo	*Cordylus vittifer*	spider	*Ateles* sp.
		squirrel	*Saimiri sciureus*
southern alligator	*Gerrhonotus multicarinatus*	vervet	*Cercopithecus pygerythrus*
western whiptail	*Cnemidophorus tigris*	woolly	*Lagothrix lagotricha*
yucca night	*Xantusia vigilis*	Monkfish	*Lophius piscatorius*
Lizardfish, inshore	*Synodus foetens*	Mosquito, malaria	*Anopheles maculipennis*
Llama	*Lama glama*	northern house	*Culex pipiens*
Lobster, American	*Homarus americanus*	yellow-fever	*Aedes aegypti*
banded spiny	*Panulirus polyphagus*	Moth, cecropia	*Hyalophora cecropia*
European	*Homarus gammarus*	codling	*Carpocapsa pomonella*
Olivier's spiny	*Panulirus pencillatus*	cynthia	*Samia cynthia*
Pacific coast spiny	*P. interruptus*	giant silkworm	*Antheraea pernyi*
		greater wax	*Galleria mellonella*
Locust, African migratory	*Locusta migratoria migratorioides*	gypsy	*Porthetria dispar*
		Mediterranean flour	*Anagasta kuehniella*
desert	*Schistocerca gregaria*	polyphemus	*Antheraea polyphemus*
migratory	*Locusta migratoria*	silkworm	*Bombyx mori*

continued

Part I.   Animals

Common Name	Scientific Name	Common Name	Scientific Name
tobacco	*Ephestia elutella*	Perch, European	*Perca fluviatilis*
Mouflon	*Ovis musimon*	ocean, or red fish	*Sebastes marinus*
Mouse, California pocket	*Perognathus californicus*	Rio Grande	*Cichlasoma cyanoguttatum*
deer	*Peromyscus maniculatus*	white	*Morone americana*
house	*Mus musculus*	Periwinkle	*Littorina littorea*
meadow	*Microtus pennsylvanicus*	Petrel, giant	*Macronectes giganteus*
plains, or pale	*Perognathus hispidus*	Pheasant, ring-necked	*Phasianus colchicus*
pocket		Pickerel, grass	*Esox americanus vermicu-*
western harvest	*Reithrodontomys megalotis*		*latus*
Mud puppy	*Necturus maculosus*	Pigeon, street	*Columba livia*
Muksun	*Coregonus muksun*	wood	*C. palumbus*
Mullet, striped	*Mugil cephalus*	Pigfish	*Orthopristis chrysopterus*
white	*M. curema*	Pike, northern	*Esox lucius*
Mummichog	*Fundulus heteroclitus*	Pinfish	*Lagodon rhomboides*
Muskrat	*Ondatra zibethicus*	Plaice, European	*Pleuronectes platessa*
Mussel, edible	*Mytilus edulis*	Planarian, Alpine	*Crenobia alpina*
swan	*Anodonta cygnea*	freshwater	*Polycelis felina*
		marine	*Procerodes ulvae*
		Platypus	*Ornithorhynchus anatinus*
Native cat, eastern	*Dasyurus viverrinus*	Polecat	*Mustela putorius*
Nephtyid worm	*Nephtys caecoides*	Pompano, Florida	*Trachinotus carolinus*
	N. ciliata	Porcupine, North American	*Erethizon dorsatum*
Newt, California	*Taricha torosa*	Porpoise, Atlantic bottle-	*Tursiops truncatus*
European	*Triturus cristatus*	nosed	
red-bellied	*Taricha rivularis*	Dall's	*Phocoenoides dalli*
rough-skinned	*T. granulosa*	harbor	*Phocoena phocoena*
smooth	*Triturus vulgaris*	Possum, brush-tail	*Trichosurus vulpecula*
Nightjar, spotted	*Eurostopodus guttatus*	dormouse	*Cercaertus nanus*
Notothenid	*Notothenia gibberifrons*	Prawn, common	*Palaemonetes vulgaris*
	N. neglecta	Puffin, common	*Fratercula arctica*
		Puma	*Felis concolor*
		Python, Burmese or East	*Python molurus bivittatus*
Octopus	*Octopus cyanea*	Indian	
	O. dofleini	reticulated	*P. reticulatus*
Oligochaete, tubificid	*Tubifex tubifex*		
Opheliid	*Travisia pupa*		
Opossum, Colombian	*Caluromys derbianus*	Quahog, northern	*Mercenaria mercenaria*
common	*Didelphis marsupialis vir-*	Quail, California	*Lophortyx californicus*
	giana	European	*Coturnix coturnix*
Opossum-shrimp	*Metamysidopsis elongata*	Gambel's	*Lophortyx gambelii*
Orangutan	*Pongo pygmaeus*	Japanese	*Coturnix coturnix japonica*
Ostrich	*Struthio camelus australis*		
African	*S. camelus*		
Owl, barred	*Strix varia*	Rabbit, eastern cottontail	*Sylvilagus floridanus*
great horned	*Bubo virginianus*	European	*Oryctolagus cuniculus*
tawny	*Strix aluco*	Raccoon	*Procyon lotor*
Oyster, Virginia	*Crassostrea virginica*	crab-eating	*P. cancrivorus*
		Rail, Guam	*Rallus owstoni*
		Rat, black	*Rattus rattus*
Paddlefish	*Polyodon spathula*	cotton	*Sigmodon hispidus*
Parrotlet, green-runt	*Forpus passerinus spengeli*	Merriam's kangaroo	*Dipodomys merriami*
Pea-mouth	*Mylocheilus caurinus*	Norway	*Rattus norvegicus*
Peanut worm	*Phoscolopsis gouldii*	rice	*Oryzomys palustris*
	Phascolosoma agassizii	Ratfish	*Hydrolagus colliei*
	Siphonosoma ingens	Rattler, canebrake	*Crotalus horridus atricauda-*
	Themiste pyroides		*tus*
Peeper, spring	*Hyla crucifer*	Raven, common	*Corvus corex*
Pelican, brown	*Pelecanus occidentalis*	Rhea, common	*Rhea americana*
Pen shell	*Pinna nobilis*	Robin	*Turdus migratorius*
Penguin, Adélie	*Pygoscelis adeliae*	Rockfish, rasphead	*Sebastes ruberrimus*
Gentoo	*P. papua*	Rockhopper	*Eudyptes crestatus*
macaroni	*Eudyptes chrysolophus*	Roundworm, large	*Ascaris lumbricoides*
		Roundworm of birds & fish	*Eustrongylides* sp.

continued

2056

Part I.   Animals

Common Name	Scientific Name
Roundworm of horse	*Parascaris equorum*
Runner, blue	*Caranx crysos*
Sable	*Martes zibellina*
Salamander, black-bellied	*Desmognathus quadramaculatus*
common fire	*Salamandra salamandra*
eastern tiger	*Ambystoma tigrinum tigrinum*
hellbender	*Cryptobranchus alleganiensis*
Pacific giant	*Dicamptodon ensatus*
red-backed	*Plethodon cinereus*
slimy	*P. glutinosus*
spotted	*Ambystoma maculatum*
tiger	*A. tigrinum*
Salmon, Atlantic	*Salmo salar*
chinook	*Oncorhynchus tshawytscha*
chum	*O. keta*
coho	*O. kisutch*
pink	*O. gorbuscha*
sockeye	*O. nerka*
Sawfly, conifer	*Neodiprion lecontei*
European spruce	*Diprion hercyniae*
pine	*Neodiprion pratti pratti*
Scorpion, whip	*Heterometrus fulvipes*
Scorpionfly	*Panorpa communis*
Scoter, white-winged	*Melanitta deglandi*
Scud	*Gammarus duebeni*
Sculpin, shorthorn	*Myoxocephalus scorpius*
Sea anemone	*Metridium senile*
Sea cucumber	*Cucumaria miniata*
	Parastichopus japonicus
Sea hare	*Aplysia fasciata*
	Fimbria fimbria
California	*Aplysia californica*
giant black	*A. vaccaria*
Mediterranean	*A. depilans*
Sea lion, California	*Zalophus californianus*
Sea urchin	*Eucidaris tribuloides*
	Strongylocentrotus droebachiensis
western purple	*S. purpuratus*
Seahorse, short-nosed	*Hippocampus brevirostris*
Seal, gray	*Halichoerus grypus*
harbor	*Phoca vitulina*
hooded or bladder-nose	*Cystophora cristata*
South American fur	*Arctocephalus australis*
Weddell	*Leptonychotes weddelli*
Shark, Atlantic bonnethead	*Sphyrna tiburo*
Atlantic sharpnose	*Rhizoprionodon terraenovae*
cat, or European spotted dogfish	*Scyliorhinus caniculus*
small Atlantic black-tip	*Carcharhinus limbatus*
smooth hammerhead	*Sphyrna zygaena*
Sheep	*Ovis aries*
Sheepshead	*Archosargus probatocephalus*
Shimmy worm	*Nephtys hombergii*
Shrew, masked	*Sorex cinereus*

Common Name	Scientific Name
short-tailed	*Blarina brevicauda*
white-toothed	*Crocidura russula*
Shrimp	*Crangon vulgaris*
	Palaemonetes varians
Skate	*Raja punctulata*
barndoor	*R. laevis*
big	*R. binoculata*
clearnose	*R. eglanteria*
little	*R. erinacea*
longnose	*R. rhina*
winter or big	*R. ocellata*
Skink, Australian blotched blue-tongued	*Tiliqua nigrolutea*
Australian shingle-back	*T. rugosus*
blue-tongued	*T. scincoides*
Great Plains	*Eumeces obsoletus*
little brown	*Lygosoma laterale*
Skua, Antarctic	*Catharacta skua*
Skunk, striped	*Mephitis mephitis*
Sloth, Hoffman's two-toed	*Choloepus hoffmani*
three-toed	*Bradypus griseus*
	B. tridactyla
two-toed	*Choloepus didactylus*
Slowworm	*Anguis fragilis*
Slug	*Limax flavus*
Smelt, rainbow	*Osmerus mordax*
Snail, common mud	*Ilyanassa obsoleta*
dented garden, or petit-gris	*Helix aspersa*
edible	*H. pomatia*
freshwater	*Lymnaea palustris*
marine	*Potamopyrgus jenkinsi*
North American freshwater	*Bithynia leachi*
Snake, black	*Coluber constrictor*
broadbanded blue sea, or erabu	*Laticauda semifasciata*
brown water	*Natrix taxispilota*
bull	*Pituophis catenifer*
	P. sayi
common European grass or ringed	*Natrix natrix*
common garter	*Thamnophis sirtalis*
gopher	*Pituophis melanoleucus*
hog-nosed	*Heterodon platyrhinos*
king	*Lampropeltis getulus*
North American water	*Natrix sipedon*
ribbon	*Thamnophis sauritus*
western diamondback rattle-	*Crotalus atrox*
western terrestrial garter	*Thamnophis elegans*
Sole, lined	*Achirus lineatus*
Souslik	*Spermophilus citellus*
Spadefish, Atlantic	*Chaetodipterus faber*
Sparrow, European tree	*Passer montanus*
house	*P. domesticus*
Savannah	*Passerculus sandwichensis beldingi*
song	*Melospiza melodia*

continued

Common Name	Scientific Name	Common Name	Scientific Name
white-crowned	*Zonotrichia leucophrys*	southern	*B. terrestris*
white-throated	*Z. albicollis*	Woodhouse's	*B. woodhousei*
Spoon worm	*Urechis caupo*	Toadfish	*Halophryne dussumieri*
Squid, common American or Atlantic	*Loligo pealei*	gulf	*Opsanus beta*
		oyster	*O. tau*
Squirrel, Arctic ground	*Spermophilus undulatus*	Tongue shell	*Lingula unguis*
Columbian ground	*S. columbianus*	Tonguefish, Indo-Pacific	*Cynoglossus brevis*
eastern gray	*Sciurus carolinensis*	Torpedo, Atlantic	*Torpedo nobiliana*
eastern red	*Tamiasciurus hudsoni-cus*	electric ray	*T. torpedo*
		Tortoise, European	*Testudo graeca*
European red	*Sciurus vulgaris*	gopher	*Gopherus polyphemus*
Franklin ground	*Spermophilus franklini*	South American	*Testudo denticulata*
golden-mantled ground	*S. lateralis*	Triggerfish, gray	*Balistes capriscus*
		Triton, Oregon	*Fusitriton oregonensis*
thirteen-lined ground	*S. tridecemlineatus*	Trout, brown	*Salmo trutta*
			S. trutta fario
Starfish	*Asterias rubens*	eastern brook	*Salvelinus fontinalis*
Starling, common	*Sturnus vulgaris*	lake	*S. namaycush*
Stick insect	*Carausius morosus*	rainbow	*Salmo gairdneri*
Stickleback, threespine	*Gasterosteus aculeatus*	sand sea	*Cynoscion arenarius*
Stingray, roughtail	*Dasyatis centroura*	spotted sea	*C. nebulosus*
Stonefly	*Acroneuria pacifica*	Tuatara	*Sphenodon* sp.
European	*Dinocras cephalotes*	Tuna, bluefin	*Thunnus thynnus*
Stork, white	*Ciconia ciconia*	Turkey	*Meleagris gallopavo*
Sturgeon, green	*Acipenser medirostris*	Turtle, Atlantic logger-head	*Caretta caretta*
Sucker, high-fin carp	*Carpiodes velifer*		
long-nosed	*Catostomus catostomus po-catello*	common snapping	*Chelydra serpentina*
			C. serpentina serpentina
Sunfish, green	*Lepomis cyanellus*	eastern box	*Terrapene carolina*
Swan, black	*Cygnus atratus*	European pond	*Emys orbicularis*
trumpeter	*Olor buccinator*	Florida softshell	*Trionyx ferox*
Swine	*Sus scrofa*	midland painted	*Chrysemys picta marginata*
		musk	*Sternotherus odoratus*
		ornate box	*Terrapene ornata ornata*
Tadpole shrimp	*Triops longicaudatus*	painted	*Chrysemys picta*
Tamarin, black and red	*Saguinus nigricollis*		*C. picta belli*
Tapir, Asiatic	*Tapirus indicus*	red-eared	*C. scripta*
Tasmanian devil	*Sarcophilus harrisii*		*C. scripta elegans*
Terebellid worm	*Eupolumnia crescentis*	South American red-eared	*C. dorbignyi*
Termite, drywood	*Cryptotermes havilandi*		
Pacific coast rotten-wood	*Zootermopsis angusticollis*	spotted	*Clemmys guttata*
Tern, common	*Sterna hirundo*		
Terrapin, Antilles	*Chrysemys terrapen*	Vicuña	*Lama vicugna*
Carolina diamond-back	*Malaclemys terrapin centrata*	Viper, asp	*Vipera aspis*
		Vole, common	*Microtus arvalis*
Texas diamond-back	*M. terrapin littoralis*	ruddy	*Clethrionomys rutilus*
		tundra	*Microtus oeconomus*
Threadfin, Atlantic	*Polydactylus octonemus*	water	*Arvicola terrestris*
Tiger	*Panthera tigris*	Vulture, griffon	*Gyps fulvus*
Bengal	*P. tigris tigris*		
Siberian	*P. tigris altaica*		
Tiger cat	*Dasyurus maculatus*	Walking stick, short-horned	*Romalea microptera*
Tit, great	*Parus major*	Wallaby, brush, or pade-melon	*Wallabia eugenii*
Toad, American	*Bufo americanus*		
Argentine	*B. arenarum*	Wallaroo or euro	*Macropus robustus*
common European	*B. bufo*	Wasp	*Vespula germanica*
eastern narrow-mouthed	*Gastrophryne carolinensis*	North American	*Vespa crabro*
		Waterflea	*Daphnia magna*
marine	*Bufo marinus*		*Moina macrocopa*
Mediterranean green	*B. viridis*	Weasel, long-tailed	*Mustela frenata*
rococo	*B. paracnemis*	Webworm, fall	*Hyphantria cunea*

continued

Appendix II. COMMON NAMES AND CORRESPONDING SCIENTIFIC NAMES

Part I. Animals

Common Name	Scientific Name
Weevil, boll	*Anthonomus grandis*
Whale, Beluga or white	*Delphinapterus leucas*
gray	*Eschrichtius gibbosus*
killer	*Orcinus orca*
sperm	*Physeter catodon*
Whitefish	*Coregonus lavaretus*
mountain	*Prosopium williamsoni*
Wisent, European	*Bison bonasus*
Wolf, gray or timber	*Canis lupus*

Common Name	Scientific Name
Wombat	*Lasiorhinus latifrons*
Woodchuck	*Marmota monax*
Wren, northern house	*Troglodytes aedon*
Yak	*Bos grunniens*
Zebra, Grevy's	*Equus grevyi*

Part II. Plants

Common Name	Scientific Name
Almond	*Prunus amygdalus*
Apple	*Malus pumila*
Ash, black	*Fraxinus nigra*
European	*F. excelsior*
Asparagus, garden	*Asparagus officinalis*
white	*A. albus*
Avocado, American	*Persea americana*
Barley	*Hordeum vulgare*
Bean, broad	*Vicia faba*
castor	*Ricinus communis*
kidney	*Phaseolus vulgaris*
Beech, European	*Fagus sylvatica*
Beet, common	*Beta vulgaris*
Birch, dwarf Arctic	*Betula nana*
Bryony, red berry	*Bryonia dioica*
Buckwheat	*Fagopyrum sagittatum*
Carrot	*Daucus carota*
Catalpa, southern	*Catalpa bignonioides*
Cedar, eastern red	*Juniperus virginiana*
Cherry, common laurel	*Prunus laurocerasus*
Chestnut	*Castanea* sp.
Chrysanthemum, florist's	*Chrysanthemum morifolium*
Clover, white sweet	*Melilotus alba*
Coconut	*Cocos nucifera*
Corn	*Zea mays*
Cotton, Indian	*Gossypium roseum*
upland	*G. hirsutum*
Cowpea, common	*Vigna sinensis*
Crowfoot, floating water	*Ranunculus pseudofluitans*
Cucumber	*Cucumis sativus*
Currant, European black	*Ribes nigrum*
northern red	*R. rubrum*
Dahlia, garden	*Dahlia pinnata*
Dandelion	*Taraxacum officinale*
Date	*Phoenix dactylifera*
Dock, curly	*Rumex crispus*
fiddleleaf	*R. pulcher*

Common Name	Scientific Name
Elm, Scotch	*Ulmus glabra*
Evening primrose, common	*Oenothera biennis*
Fern, common polypody	*Polypodium vulgare*
Fig	*Ficus glabrata*
Flax, common	*Linum usitatissimum*
Gladiolus, breeder's	*Gladiolus gandavensis*
Grape, European	*Vitis vinifera*
Hart's-tongue	*Phyllitis scolopendrium*
Hemp	*Cannabis sativa*
Hibiscus, Chinese	*Hibiscus rosa-sinensis*
Holly, English	*Ilex aquifolium*
Horse chestnut, common	*Aesculus hippocastanum*
Impatiens	*Impatiens* sp.
Iris, German	*Iris germanica*
Lamb's quarter	*Chenopodium album*
Lemon	*Citrus limon*
Lespedeza, Korean	*Lespedeza stipulacea*
Lettuce	*Lactuca sativa*
Lilac, common	*Syringa vulgaris*
Lily, bulbil	*Lilium bulbiferum*
Easter	*L. longiflorum*
Maple, red	*Acer rubrum*
sugar	*A. saccharum*
sycamore, or plane-tree	*A. pseudoplatanus*
Muskmelon	*Cucumis melo*
Nasturtium, common	*Tropaeolum majus*
Oak, kermes	*Quercus coccifera*

continued

Appendix II. COMMON NAMES AND CORRESPONDING SCIENTIFIC NAMES

Part II. Plants

Common Name	Scientific Name	Common Name	Scientific Name
Oat, common	*Avena sativa*	Snapdragon, common	*Antirrhinum majus*
Okra	*Hibiscus esculentus*	Sorghum	*Sorghum bicolor*
Onion, garden	*Allium cepa*	Soybean	*Glycine max*
Orange, sweet	*Citrus sinensis*	Spinach	*Spinacia oleracea*
		Spleenwort, black	*Asplenium adiantum nigrum*
		Spruce, Norway	*Picea abies*
Papaya	*Carica papaya*	Strawberry	*Fragaria* sp.
Parsnip	*Pastinaca sativa*	Sugarcane	*Saccharum officinarum*
Pea, garden	*Pisum sativum*	Sunflower, common	*Helianthus annuus*
sweet	*Lathyrus odoratus*	Sweet potato	*Ipomoea batatas*
Peach	*Prunus persica*		
Pear	*Pyrus communis*		
Pepper, green or mango	*Capsicum annuum*	Timothy	*Phleum pratense*
hot	*C. frutescens*	Tobacco, common	*Nicotiana tabacum*
Pine, Italian stone	*Pinus pinea*	tree	*N. glauca*
Japanese red	*P. densiflora*		*N. langsdorffii*
Monterey	*P. radiata*	Tomato, common	*Lycopersicon esculentum*
Pineapple	*Ananas comosus*	Tulip, common	*Tulipa gesneriana*
Plum, garden	*Prunus domesticus*		
Poplar, black	*Populus nigra*		
eastern	*P. deltoides*	Walnut, Persian	*Juglans regia*
Potato	*Solanum tuberosum*	Wandering jew	*Tradescantia viridis*
Pumpkin	*Cucurbita pepo*	Watermelon	*Citrullus vulgaris*
		Waterweed, Canada	*Elodea canadensis*
		giant	*Equisetum telmateia*
Radish, garden	*Raphanus sativus*	Wheat	*Triticum aestivum*
wild	*R. raphanistrum*	Willow, gray-leaf	*Salix glauca*
Rhubarb, garden	*Rheum rhaponticum*	pygmy	*S. herbacea*
Rice	*Oryza sativa*		
Rose	*Rosa* sp.		
Rye	*Secale cereale*	Yew, English	*Taxus baccata*
		Yucca, mound lily	*Yucca gloriosa*

INDEX

To facilitate identification, the index includes the taxonomic order for animals and the family for plants, unless otherwise specified. As a further aid, the index lists the animals and plants as they are presented in the tables. Entries for a particular organism may therefore be found under the common name, under the scientific name, or under both. Where information is available under both, cross-references (and Appendixes I and II if more than one genus is applicable to a common name) make the data easily accessible. In some tables, only the formula for a chemical compound appears. When this occurs, the formula is listed in the index, with a cross-reference to the chemical name.

*	indicates diagram or graph
fn	indicates footnote material
hn	indicates headnote material

Abdomen: skin blood flow, 1709
Abdominal vein(s), 1682-1683, 1727
Abdominal wall, 1682-1683, 1686
Acanthias (see *Squalus*)
Acartia clausi, CALANOIDA, 1634, 1639
A. tonsa, 1642
Acclimation
    altitude: man, 1891 fn-1892 fn, 1893-1897
    temperature: reptiles, 1620 fn
Acer pseudoplatanus, Aceraceae, 1666
A. rubrum, 1664
A. saccharum, 1660
Acetaldehyde, 1543*, 1547, 1549
Acetal thiamine diphosphate, 1551*
2-Acetamido-1-(β′-L-aspartamido)-1,2-dideoxy-β-D-glucose, 1500
Acetate
    amino acid metabolism, 1546
    blood O_2 dissociation, 1599
    citric acid cycle, 1554 hn
    enzyme action, 1480
    fatty acid metabolism, 1538*
    feces, 1489
    nutritional requirement, 1445 fn
    respiration rates: plants, 1655
Acetic acid, 1503, 1520, 1976
Acetoacetate, 1538*, 1548, 1550
Acetoacetic acid, 1503, 1963
Acetoacetyl coenzyme A, 1538*, 1541*, 1551*
Acetobacter suboxydans, Pseudomonadaceae, 1546
Acetogenins, 1562*
α-Aceto-α-hydroxybutyrate, 1547
α-Acetolactate, 1550
Acetone, 1963
Acetone bodies (*see* Ketone bodies)
N-Acetyl-4-aminoantipyrine, 1986 fn
Acetylcholine, 1480
Acetylcholinesterase, 1480
Acetyl coenzyme A
    amino acid metabolism, 1545-1546, 1548-1549
    carbohydrate metabolism, 1542, 1543*
    citric acid cycle, 1554, 1555*, 1556 fn
    energy metabolism: muscle, 1557*
    fatty acid metabolism, 1538*
    metabolic interrelationships, 1551*
    natural products biosynthesis, 1562*

    nucleoprotein metabolism, 1553*
    sterol metabolism, 1541*
Acetylglucosamine, 1819
N-Acetyl-β-glucosaminidase (*see* Chitobiase)
Acetylkynurenine, 1499, 1520
Acetylneuraminyl sugars, 1497
Acetylphloroglucinols, 1562*
Acheta assimilis (see *Gryllus assimilis*)
A. domesticus, ORTHOPTERA, 1907, 1912
Achirus lineatus, PLEURONECTIFORMES, 1859
Achlya sp., Saprolegniaceae, 1650
Achromobacter, Achromobacteraceae, 1569 fn
Acid-base balance, 1493 hn (*see also* Blood: acid-base balance)
Acidemia, 1585, 1728-1729
Acidosis, 1594 hn, 1836*
Acid phosphatase: blood, 1946, 1972-1973
    lymph, 1946, 1972-1973
    tears, 2039
    urine, 1502, 1519
Acipenser, ACIPENSERIFORMES, 1678
A. medirostris, 1803
cis-Aconitate, 1445 fn, 1555*
Aconitate hydratase, 1555*
Aconitic acid, 1502, 1520
Acrocheilus alutaceus, CYPRINIFORMES, 1803
Acroneuria pacifica, PLECOPTERA, 1640
ACTH (*see* Adrenocorticotropin)
Actinium, 1531*, 1532
Actinomycins, 1563*
Action potential: cardiac tissue, 1730-1734
Actomyosin, 1557*
Acylase, monoglyceride, 1488
Acyl coenzyme A, 1551* (*see also* Fatty acyl coenzyme A)
Acyl dihydroxyacetone phosphate, 1539*
Acyl phosphate, 1558
Acyl proteins, 1551*
Adenine
    biosynthesis, 1565*, 1567*
    blood, 1805
    lymph, 1969
    nucleoprotein catabolism, 1553*, 1554 fn
    nutritional requirement, 1439
    urine, 1500
Adenine deaminase, 1552, 1553*, 1554 fn

† Class

† Class

† Class

---

† Class

Forficula auricularia, DERMAPTERA, 1915, 1918
Formaldehydrogenic steroids, 1515
5-Formamido-4-imidazolecarboxamide ribonucleotide, 1567*
Formate, 1489, 1547, 1550
Formic acid, 1498
Formiminoglutamic acid, 1499
Formulas, 1834 hn, 1836 hn (see also Equations)
N-Formylglycinamidine ribonucleotide, 1567*
10-Formyl-tetrahydrofolic acid coenzyme, 1567*
Forpus passerinus spengeli, PSITTACIFORMES, 1795
Fowl, 1818 (see also Chicken; Gallus)
Fragaria sp., Rosaceae, 1667, 1671
France: nutritional standards, 1450
Francium, 1531*, 1532
Fratercula arctica, CHARADRIIFORMES, 1795
Fraxinus excelsior, Oleaceae, 1667
F. nigra, 1664
Freezing point depression
      cerebrospinal fluid, 1976, 1978
      hemolymph, 1912-1913
      sweat, 1493
      tears, 2033
      urine, 1512, 1514, 1516
Freshwater
      oxygen consumption: fishes, 1624 hn, 1625-1629
                    invertebrates, 1643-1644
      respiratory medium, 1580
Fringilla montifringilla, PASSERIFORMES, 1617, 1693
Frog (see also specific genus)
      blood: chemical constituents, 1802, 1818
      cardiac tissue: electrical properties, 1733
      heart rate: hypothermia, 1749
Frond: respiration rates, 1666, 1668
Frontal lobes: nerve terminals, 1586
β-Fructofuranosidase, 1480, 1483
Fructokinase, 1542, 1543*
Fructose
      blood: man, 1819
             other mammals, 1821, 1824, 1963
      cerebrospinal fluid, 1976
      digestion, 1486*
      enzyme action, 1480
      hemolymph, 1936, 1938-1939
      lymph, 1963
      metabolism, 1543*
      urine, 1497
Fructose 1,6-diphosphate, 1543*, 1558, 1559*
Fructosediphosphate aldolase
      carbohydrate metabolism, 1542, 1543*
      photosynthesis, 1559*
      urine, 1512, 1518
Fructose-1-phosphate, 1543*, 1543 fn
Fructose-6-phosphate, 1543*, 1558, 1559*, 1561*
Frullania tamarisci, Frullaniaceae, 1658
FSH (see Follicle-stimulating hormone)
Fucopeptides, 1500
Fucoproteins, 1500
Fucose
      blood, 1819, 1963
      lymph, 1963
      urine, 1497
Fucosterol, 1435 fn, 1492

Fucus sp., Fucaceae, 1656
F. serratus, 1656
F. vesiculosus, 1656
Fulica americana, GRUIFORMES, 1795
Fulmarus glacialis, PROCELLARIIFORMES, 1606
Fumarate
      amino acid metabolism, 1545, 1550
      citric acid cycle, 1555*
      feces, 1490
      metabolic interrelationships, 1551*
      nutritional requirement, 1445 fn
      purine biosynthesis, 1567*
Fumarate hydratase, 1555*
Fumaric acid, 1503, 1520, 1554 fn
Fundulus heteroclitus, ATHERINIFORMES, 1626, 1803, 1827
Fungi (see also specific genus)
      amino acid metabolism, 1548
      nitrogen cycle in nature, 1569*
      nutrient requirements, 1433, 1435-1445
Furanose ring, 1561
Fusarium graminearum, Tuberculariaceae, 1653
F. lini, 1653
F. solani phaseoli, 1653
Fusiformocytes, 1913 hn
Fusitriton oregonensis, MESOGASTROPODA, 1631

GABA (see γ-Aminobutyric acid)
Gadolinium, 1531*, 1532
Gadus sp., GADIFORMES, 1610, 2021, 2032 (see also Cod)
G. callarias (see G. morhua)
G. morhua
      blood pressure, 1724
      erythrocytes & hemoglobin, 1852
      heart rate, 1694
      oxygen consumption, 1626
Galactokinase, 1542, 1543*
Galactose
      blood, 1819
      digestion, 1486*
      enzyme action, 1480
      metabolism, 1543*
      urine, 1497
Galactose-1-phosphate, 1543*
β-Galactosidase, 1480, 1483, 1519
Galactosyl-δ-hydroxylysine, 1500
Galago crassicaudatus, PRIMATES, 1755
G. senegalensis, 1604
Galeichthys felis (see Arius felis)
Galeus canis (see Mustelus canis)
Gallate, 1562*
Gallbladder lymphatics, 1964
Galleria mellonella, LEPIDOPTERA
      hemocytes, 1914
      hemolymph: chemical constituents, 1922, 1931, 1939
             physical properties, 1907, 1910-1912
Gallium, 1433, 1531*, 1532
Gallus domesticus (see G. gallus)

β-Glucosides, 1480
α-1,4-Glucosyl, 1561*
Glucosylgalactosyllysine, 1500
N-D-Glucosylglycine ester, 1445
Glucuronic acid, 1497, 1819, 1823-1824
β-Glucuronidase, 1502, 1519, 1972-1973
Glutamate
    amino acid metabolism, 1544 hn, 1545-1547, 1549
    aqueous humor, 2015-2017
    blood, 2015-2017, 2027-2029
    citric acid cycle, 1555*, 1556 fn
    photosynthesis, 1560*
    respiration rate: *Allomyces,* 1650
    vitreous humor, 2027-2029
Glutamate dehydrogenase
    amino acid metabolism, 1544 hn
    citric acid cycle, 1555*
    photosynthesis, 1560*
    urine, 1519
Glutamic acid
    aqueous humor, 2010
    blood: man, 1806
        other mammals, 1809-1810, 1966, 1969
        other vertebrates, 1811-1814
    cerebrospinal fluid, 1976
    citric acid cycle, 1556 fn
    enzyme action, 1481
    genetic code, 1566*
    hemolymph, 1919-1927, 1919 fn, 1928-1929
    lymph, 1966, 1969
    metabolic interrelationships, 1551*
    metabolism, 1546
    natural products biosynthesis, 1562*
    nutritional requirement, 1437, 1473
    polynucleotide biosynthesis, 1566 hn, 1567*-1568*
    sweat, 1494
    urine: man, 1498
        other mammals, 1513, 1515, 1517, 1519
    vitreous humor, 2023
Glutamic semialdehyde, 1549
Glutamine
    aqueous humor, 2010
    blood: man, 1805-1806
        other mammals, 1809, 1966, 2028
    cerebrospinal fluid, 1976
    genetic code, 1566*
    hemolymph: insects, 1919-1922, 1919 fn, 1925-1926, 1925 fn
        other invertebrates, 1928 fn-1929 fn, 1929
    lymph, 1966
    metabolism, 1545-1547
    nutritional requirement, 1444-1445
    polynucleotide biosynthesis, 1566 hn, 1567*-1568*
    urine, 1498, 1516
    vitreous humor, 2023, 2028
Glutamine-ketoacid aminotransferase, 1546
γ-Glutamyl transpeptidase, 1502
Glutathione
    amino acid metabolism, 1546

    blood, 1805-1806, 1808-1811, 1814
    nutritional requirement, 1445
    respiration rate: *Torula,* 1653
Glycera dibranchiata, POLYCHAETA†, 1631
D-Glyceraldehyde, 1543*
Glyceraldehyde 3-phosphate
    amino acid metabolism, 1549
    carbohydrate metabolism, 1543*
    photosynthesis, 1558, 1559*
Glyceraldehydephosphate dehydrogenase, 1542, 1543*, 1559*
D-Glycerate, 1549
Glycerides, 1958
Glycerol
    carbohydrate metabolism, 1543*
    digestion, 1488*
    enzyme action, 1479
    glycerolipid metabolism, 1539*
    hemolymph, 1938
    metabolic interrelationships, 1551*
    respiration rates: algae, 1655
    urine, 1497
Glycerolipid metabolism, 1539*
Glycerol kinase, 1542, 1543*
Glycerolphosphate dehydrogenase, 1542, 1543*
L-α-Glycerophosphate, 1488, 1539*, 1543*
Glycerophosphoryl base, 1539*
α-Glycerophosphorylcholine, 1436 fn
Glycerylphosphorylcholine, 1479
Glycinamide ribonucleotide, 1567*
Glycine
    aqueous humor, 2010, 2015-2017
    blood: man, 1805-1806
        other mammals, 1809-1811, 1966, 1969, 2015-2017, 2027-2029
        other vertebrates, 1811-1814
    cerebrospinal fluid, 1976
    citric acid cycle, 1556 fn
    genetic code, 1566*
    hemolymph, 1919, 1919 fn, 1920-1929
    lymph, 1966, 1969
    metabolic interrelationships, 1551*
    metabolism, 1547, 1549
    natural products biosynthesis, 1562*
    nutritional requirement, 1437, 1437 fn, 1474-1475
    purine biosynthesis, 1567*
    sweat, 1494
    urine: man, 1498
        other mammals, 1512-1513, 1515-1516, 1519
    vitreous humor, 2023, 2027-2029
Glycine amino nitrogen, 1933-1934
Glycine aminopeptidase, 1502
Glycine max, Fabaceae, 1661, 1663
G. soja (see *G. max*)
Glycogen
    blood, 1819
    digestion, 1486*
    enzyme action, 1480
    metabolism, 1542, 1543*, 1543 fn, 1557*
    respiration rate: *Saccharomyces,* 1651
    sweat, 1493 hn

---

† Class

† Class

† Class

---

† Class
†† Phylum

† Class

_____
■ Order

■ Order

—————

†† Phylum

---

† Class

---

†† Phylum

---

† Class